Eastern Europe
on a shoestring

David Stanley

W9-BJL-437

Eastern Europe on a shoestring
  1st edition

Published by
  Lonely Planet Publications
  Head Office: PO Box 617, Hawthorn, Victoria 3122, Australia
  US Office: PO Box 2001A, Berkeley, CA 94702, USA

Printed by
  Colorcraft, Hong Kong

Cover Illustration by
  Joanne Ryan

Published
  April 1989

Although the author and publisher have tried to make the information as
accurate as possible, they accept no responsibility for any loss, injury or
inconvenience sustained by any person using this book.

National Library of Australia Cataloguing in Publication Data

Stanley, David
  Eastern Europe on a shoestring.

  1st ed.
  Includes index.
  ISBN 0 86442 008 0.

  1. Europe, Eastern – Description and travel – Guide-books.
  I. Title.

914.7'04

About the Author

A quarter of a century ago David Stanley's right thumb carried him out of Toronto, Canada, and onto a journey which has so far wound through 123 countries. His travel guidebooks for the South Pacific and Micronesia opened those areas to budget travellers for the first time.

While working as a tour guide in Cuba between 1975 and 1980, Stanley got a taste of socialist tourism. Since then he's visited all the countries covered in this book many times. He claims he never intended to write about Eastern Europe, but was drawn into it by circumstance. An opportunity to ride the Trans-Mongolian Railway brought him back from China to finish a project he'd almost dropped.

Thousands of printouts later, all Stanley's personal possessions still fit in a medium-sized backpack. This book was written on a rented computer in borrowed apartments in West Berlin and Amsterdam. Although Stanley took voluminous notes quite openly during his many forays behind the 'Iron Curtain' the only interest he aroused was from motorists in Poznan and Budapest who demanded he explain why he was issuing parking tickets.

Lonely Planet Credits

Editors	Maureen Wheeler
	Tony Wheeler
Maps	Todd Pierce
	Fiona Boyes
	Ralph Roob
	Peter Flavelle
Cover Design	Graham Imeson
Design	Vicki Beale
Typesetting	Ann Jeffree

Thanks also to David Crawford, Richard Nebesky, Renate and Stefan Loose, Herbert Seul and Gisela E. Walther for text comments, to Greg Herriman and Chris Lee-Ack for map corrections and to Trudi Canavan for additional paste-up and the title page illustration.

A Warning & a Request

Things change – prices go up, schedules change, good places go bad and bad places go bankrupt – nothing stays the same. So if you find things better or worse, recently opened or long since closed, please write and tell us and help make the next edition better! All information is greatly appreciated and the best letters will receive a free copy of the next edition, or any other Lonely Planet book of your choice.

Extracts from the best letters are also included in the *Lonely Planet Update*. The *Update* helps us make useful information available to you as soon as possible – it's like reading an up-to-date noticeboard or postcards from a friend. Each edition contains hundreds of useful tips, and advice from the best possible source of information – other travellers. The *Lonely Planet Update* is published quarterly in paperback and is available from bookshops and by subscription. Turn to the back pages of this book for more details.

Contents

Introduction

Many people are intimidated by the thought of a trip to Eastern Europe. Their image of the region is based on western news stories of economic problems, dissidents and secret police. This coverage parallels reports in the Communist press of strikes, the homeless and police violence in capitalist states. The misinformation has led to absurd misconceptions on both sides. Some visitors are even convinced they'll be followed around by informers and have their hotel rooms 'bugged.'

Certainly, a visit to Eastern Europe involves considerable paperwork and advance planning but even the red tape teaches you something about the countries. It also helps stem the western tourist tide. In many ways Eastern Europe is the 'last frontier' of tourism in Europe. Because you'll be one of the few, instead of another of the many, you'll often be received with great courtesy and interest.

Although shortages of consumer goods do exist most of the things you'll need will be readily available. The only things you sometimes have to line up for are tickets and reservations. Eastern Europe has just as many museums, churches and castles as Western Europe, though they're less publicised, less crowded and more accessible. And you won't be discouraged by the admission fees.

There are many positive aspects to Eastern Europe. The vast forests, rugged mountains, quiet lakes and mighty rivers equal those of Western Europe in every

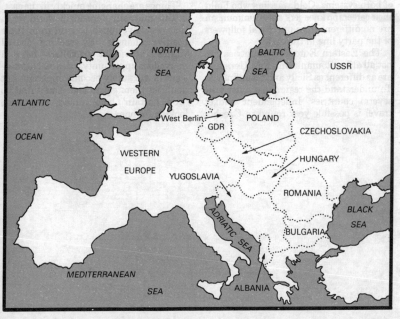

respect. Theatres and concert halls are much more accessible to budget travellers. Prices in general are lower and the people friendlier. Many locals are honoured to meet a visitor from 'the west.' Violent crime against visitors is almost unknown.

Apart from having an interesting holiday you'll get to see another social system in action. Socialism has brought with it the dignity of guaranteed employment, free education and medical care, accident, illness and old age pensions, subsidised housing and public transportation, plus many other benefits. When western politicians talk of 'human rights' one wonders how many of these very basic human rights they're interested in obtaining for their own people.

Too often we westerners put the rights of the individual above the welfare of the group. Thus guns, drugs and pornography are tolerated. In the east the opposite applies. By visiting Eastern Europe you'll gain a better understanding of the merits of both systems. Cold warriors who build their careers on knee-jerk anti-Communism are no different than uncritical followers of the party line in the east.

The Eastern European countries are not all alike. Romania and East Germany are as different as Sicily and Scandinavia. To understand the region you must visit several countries. Independent budget travel is possible year round in Czecho-slovakia, Hungary, Poland and Yugoslavia. During the summer camping season you can also travel cheaply in Bulgaria, Romania and the GDR. Only Albania and the USSR still make you come on a rigid package tour. You'll be amazed at the ease and convenience of travel. Food, entertainment, services and transport are universally cheap.

In this book I've tried not only to show you how to travel the way the locals do but also to see things through their eyes. Some of the comments in this book may surprise you but the intention is not to convince the reader that I'm a 'pinko-liberal' or 'dupe.' By challenging some of the negative preconceptions we westerners too often have about life in Eastern Europe I'm hoping you will be in a better position to decide for yourself where the truth lies. Although you probably won't be converted, I think you'll come to see that we don't have as many enemies as you have heard.

Things are changing quickly in the east. In this mutually dependent world we in the west have much to gain from these positive changes. By seeking shared values individual travellers have a marvellous opportunity to learn. Negative aspects will surely become apparent, but don't let them get to you. You'll find no 'iron curtain' here, unless you come looking for one.

country	area (square km)	country population	capital	capital population
West Berlin	480	2,000,000	West Berlin	2,000,000
GDR	108,179	16,700,000	East Berlin	1,100,000
Poland	312,677	37,100,000	Warsaw	1,700,000
Czechoslovakia	127,889	15,500,000	Prague	1,200,000
Hungary	93,030	10,700,000	Budapest	2,100,000
Romania	237,500	22,800,000	Bucharest	2,090,000
Bulgaria	110,912	8,950,000	Sofia	1,057,000
Yugoslavia	255,804	22,500,000	Belgrade	1,580,000
Albania	28,748	3,000,000	Tirane	202,000
USSR	22,400,000	278,000,000	Moscow	8,203,000

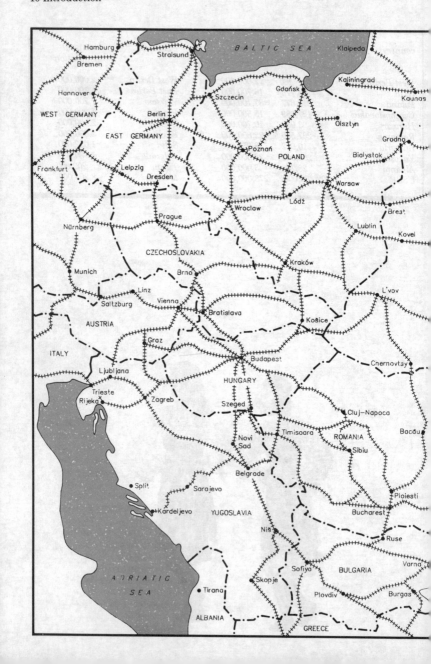

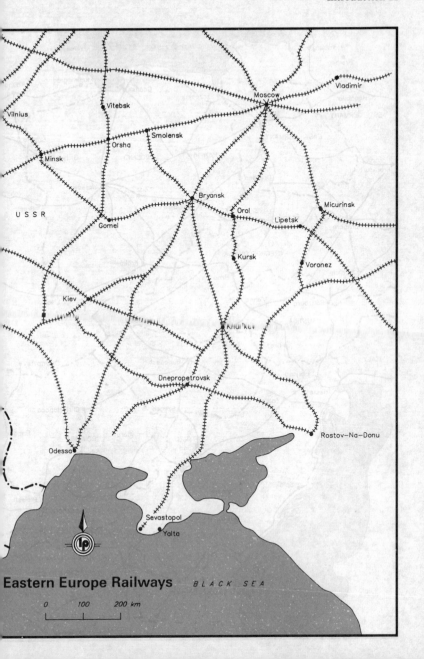

Vladimir

Moscow

Vitebsk

Vilnius

Orsha   Smolensk

Minsk

U S S R   Bryansk   Orol   Micurinsk

Gomel   Lipetsk

Kursk   Voronez

Kiev

Khar'kov

Dnepropetrovsk

Rostov–Na–Donu

Odessa

Sevastopol

Yalta

Eastern Europe Railways   *BLACK SEA*

0   100   200 km

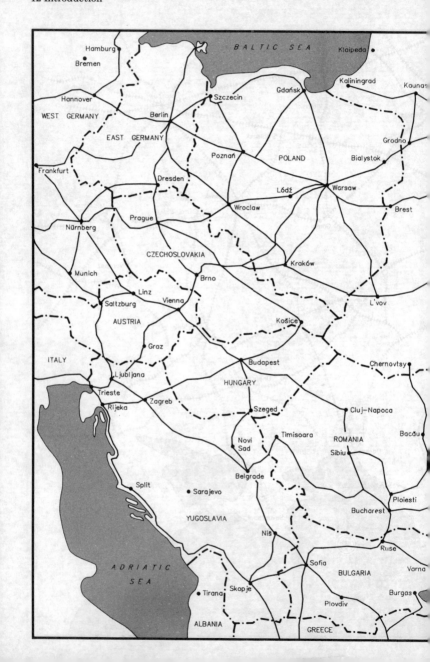

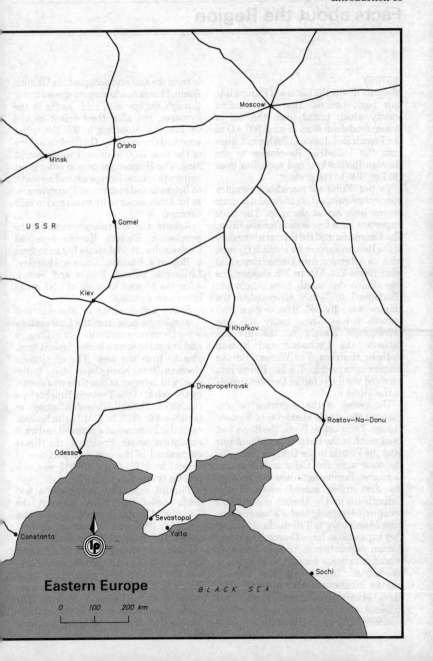

Eastern Europe

BLACK SEA

0   100   200 km

Facts about the Region

HISTORY

Marxists divide the history of Europe into four basic periods: the slave holding society which lasted until the fall of Rome; feudalism from around 500 AD to the French Revolution (1789); capitalism from the Industrial Revolution to the Russian Revolution; and socialism from 1917 or 1945 to the present.

To put Europe's incredibly complex history into perspective it's useful to draw several lines across the map. The most important such line is the Danube River. The Danube formed the northern boundary of the Roman Empire for about 500 years, with an extension into Dacia (Romania) from 106 to 271 AD. In 395 another line was drawn due south from Aquincum (Budapest) to North Africa when the empire was divided into eastern and western halves. Even today this line corresponds closely to the division between the Orthodox and Roman Catholic churches. The Western Roman Empire collapsed in 476 but Byzantium survived until the fall of Constantinople to the Turks in 1453.

The period of the migrating peoples changed the ethnic character of Eastern Europe. Long before Rome the Slavs had lived north of the Carpathian Mountains from the Vistula to the Dnieper rivers. To the west were the Celts and later the Germans. Beginning in the 6th century the Slav tribes moved south of the Carpathians and by the 9th century had occupied everything east of a line running from Magdeburg to Trieste. In the south they expanded as far as Greece. The Daco-Roman population of present Romania proved numerous enough to absorb the newcomers. In Albania the original Illyrian inhabitants also survived. The Slavs became peaceful farmers who lived in democratically governed communities.

In 896 the Magyars (Hungarians) swept in from the east and occupied the Danube Basin. Hungarian horsemen spread terror through Europe with raids as far as the Pyrenees, but after their defeat by the Germans at Augsburg in 955 the tribes accepted Christianity. On Christmas Day of the year 1000 Stephen I was crowned king. The Hungarians carved out a great empire in central Europe extending south to Belgrade and east across Transylvania. In 1018 they annexed Slovakia and in 1102 Croatia.

Around the millennium most of the peoples of Eastern Europe accepted Christianity. Feudal states began to form in Bohemia, Bulgaria, Croatia, Hungary, Lithuania, Poland, Russia and Serbia. After the Mongol invasion of 1241 many cities were fortified.

Saxon communities in Slovakia and Transylvania date from the 13th century when Germans were invited into Hungary and Poland to form a buffer against fresh attacks from the east. The continuous German *Drang nach Osten* (drive to the east) which began at this time was slowed by the defeat of the Teutonic Knights by a combined Polish-Lithuanian army at Grunwald in 1410. In 1701 Berlin became capital of Prussia and a renewed eastward expansion under Frederick the Great culminated in the complete partition of Poland by 1795. Only in 1945 was this process reversed.

Turkish expansion into Europe was made easier by rivalry between the Catholic (Austria, Hungary, Venice) and Orthodox (Bulgaria, Byzantium, Serbia) states. The defeat of Serbia at the Battle of Kosovo in 1389 opened the floodgates of the Balkans. The Hungarians managed to halt the Turkish advance temporarily at Belgrade in 1456, but in 1526 they were defeated at the Battle of Mohacs. The Turks spread as far north as the southern foothills of the Carpathians, drawing another line across the map of Europe. In 1529 they unsuccessfully laid siege to Vienna. Hungary remained under Ottoman rule until the defeat of the 2nd Turkish siege of Vienna in 1683. A combined Christian army liberated Buda in 1686 and by 1699 the Turks had been driven from all of Hungary.

In 1517 Martin Luther nailed his 95 theses to the door of the church of Wittenberg Castle launching the Protestant reformation. This soon took hold in northern Germany and the Thirty Years War between Protestants and Catholics devastated much of northern Europe from 1618 to 1648. A dispute between Poland and Sweden in the mid-17th century added to the destruction in central Europe. Plague columns still recall the pestilence and war which halved the populations of some countries.

The rise of the Austrian Hapsburg dynasty accompanied these wars. After the fall of Hungary to the Turks the Hapsburgs assumed the thrones of Hungary, Bohemia and Croatia. In 1620 the Catholic Hapsburgs tightened their grip on Bohemia, then expanded into Hungary and the Balkans in the wake of the declining Ottoman Empire. From 1703 to 1711 Hungarians led by the Transylvanian prince Ferenc Rakoczi II fought an unsuccessful war of independence against the Hapsburgs. During the 18th and 19th centuries the Hapsburgs controlled a vast empire from Prague to Belgrade and east into Transylvania. In 1867 Austria and Hungary agreed to share control of the region through a dual Austro-Hungarian monarchy.

Poland was wiped off the map of Europe by the partitions of 1722, 1793 and 1795. Prussia and Russia took most of Poland for themselves, with Austria receiving a small slice in the south. It's not hard to understand why the Poles sided with Napoleon, whose entry into Eastern Europe in 1806 marked a beginning of the transition from feudal autocracy to modern, bourgeois capitalism. Napoleon's final defeat in 1815 allowed the Prussians and Hapsburgs to re-impose their rule. In 1848 there were unsuccessful bourgeois-democratic revolutions throughout central Europe against the prevailing absolutism.

In the Balkans the uprisings and wars against Ottoman oppression continued into the 20th century. In 1876 the Bulgarians rose against the Turks leading to the Russo-Turkish War of 1877 and Bulgarian autonomy in 1878. Bulgarian independence followed in 1908. Romania and Serbia declared complete independence from the Turks in 1878. The Hapsburgs occupied Bosnia-Hercegovina in 1878 and annexed it outright in 1908. Macedonia and Albania remained under Turkey until the First Balkan War (1912). After the Second Balkan War (1913) Serbia and Greece divided Macedonia between themselves. Bulgarian dissatisfaction with this result led to further fighting during both world wars.

From 1240 to 1480 Russia was a vassal to the Mongol Golden Horde. Ivan IV the Terrible was crowned tsar in 1547 and during the 17th century Russians and Ukrainians colonised Siberia and the steppes to the Black Sea. Peter the Great was proclaimed emperor in 1721 and by the 19th century Russia had become a great power stretching from Warsaw to the Pacific.

Internally, however, Russia remained a backward, agricultural autocracy while Britain, Germany and other western countries developed into strong industrial states. In 1914 Hapsburg and Tsarist imperial ambitions clashed in the Balkans and all Europe was ˙drawn into a catastrophic war. Without significant industries Russia was unable to sustain this conflict indefinitely and in March 1917, a popular uprising led to the abdication of Tsar Nicholas II.

The bourgeois government which took over from the tsar was closely tied to western capitalist interests and attempted to keep Russia in the war alongside the British and French. This led to the Great

October Socialist Revolution which brought the Bolsheviks to power. By November 1918, war weariness led to the collapse of the autocracies in Austro-Hungary, Bulgaria and Germany as sailors mutinied and troops abandoned the fronts. In 1919 there were socialist revolutions in Germany and Hungary, but these were put down by right wing militarists. Had they succeeded humanity might have been spared the Nazi-fascist holocaust.

The end of WW I saw the restoration of Poland and the creation of Czechoslovakia and Yugoslavia. Although the new borders were supposed to follow ethnic boundaries, northern and western Bohemia went to Czechoslovakia despite the largely German population. Similarly the Hungarians of Slovakia, Transylvania and Vojvodina, the Albanians of Kosovo and the Ukrainians of south-east Poland all became homogeneous majorities in foreign countries adjacent to their motherlands. This situation and the socio-economic conditions in Germany were largely responsible for the rise of Hitler and the outbreak of WW II.

The history of Eastern Europe after 1933 is one of constant Nazi aggression backed by threats and violence. In September, 1938, Britain and France sold out Czechoslovakia at the Munich Conference, ending the possibility of any effective military resistance to the Nazis in the east. Bulgaria, Hungary and Romania soon fell in line behind Germany. Uncertain of western backing after Munich, the Soviet Union signed a non-aggression pact with Germany on 23 August 1939 to buy time. When Poland resisted Hitler's demands it was promptly invaded, touching off WW II. Yugoslavia and the USSR shared this fate in 1941.

Hitler's programme of military expansion led to the destruction of Germany. In February 1943, the German 6th Army capitulated at Stalingrad and by May 1945, the Soviet Army had captured Berlin. At the February 1945, Yalta Conference Churchill, Roosevelt and Stalin agreed on 'spheres of influence' in Europe. The Potsdam Conference of August 1945, divided Germany and Berlin into four occupation zones. The borders of Poland and the USSR moved west and those Germans who had not already fled East Prussia, Pomerania and Silesia were deported. The American, British, French and Soviet armies which fought their way into Germany in 1945 are still there today.

The world revolutionary process which began with the 1917 October Revolution developed into the world socialist system after 1945. In Bulgaria, East Germany, Hungary and Romania post war Communist-led governments took over from Nazi or monarcho-fascist regimes with the arrival of Soviet troops. Communist partisans took control in Yugoslavia and Albania. Czechoslovakia continued as a democratic coalition until the Communist Party took full control during a political crisis in March 1948.

The events in Czechoslovakia set off a chain reaction as the frustrated western Allies decided it was time to consolidate the areas under their control against further Communist advances. In June 1948, a new currency linked to the US dollar was introduced into the three western sectors of Berlin, allegedly to facilitate post-war reconstruction.

This created a tremendous problem for Soviet officials in East Germany where nationalisation of the economy was not yet complete. Rather than face an uncontrollable black market which would have bled them white, the Soviet Army closed the surface transit routes from West Germany to West Berlin a few days later. The air routes remained open and for 11 months the 'Berlin Airlift' supplied the western zones of the city. This crisis may be seen as the beginning of the 'Cold War.'

The lines were drawn even more clearly in 1949 when NATO formed in April. The Federal Republic of Germany was created in September, the German Democratic

Republic in October. The Council for Mutual Economic Aid, still the dominant economic planning body in Eastern Europe, also dates back to 1949. The Warsaw Pact was not signed until May 1955, when West Germany was admitted to NATO.

A second Berlin crisis occurred in August 1961 when the GDR built a Wall around West Berlin to stem the flow of refugees. The 1971 Quadripartite Agreement on Berlin, signed by the USA, USSR, UK and France, normalised the de facto situation in the city. Since the 1975 Helsinki Conference on Security & Cooperation at which 35 governments accepted the status quo in Europe, tensions have relaxed considerably.

By choice or circumstance Eastern Europe has taken the socialist road since 1945. Although all the countries have emphasised heavy industry, central planning and social justice, there have been wide variations in approach. The push and pull between reformers and conservatives has led to upheavals in East Germany (1953), Hungary (1956), Czechoslovakia (1968) and Poland (1956, 1970, 1976, 1981). Ironically, many of the demands made by 'revisionists' of those years are being voiced in the Kremlin today.

PEOPLE
The Slavs are by far the most numerous ethnic group in Eastern Europe. There are three distinct groups of Slavs: the West Slavs (Czechs, Poles, Slovaks and Sorbs), the South Slavs (Bulgarians, Croats, Macedonians, Montenegrins, Serbs and Slovenes) and the East Slavs (Belorussians, Russians and Ukrainians). The Albanians, Germans, Hungarians, Romanians, gypsies and the Baltic peoples are non-Slavic groups. The people of Latvia and Lithuania speak Indo-Germanic languages, while the Estonians are related to the Finns.

ECONOMY
The Eastern European equivalent of the EEC is the Council for Mutual Economic Assistance (CMEA or Comecon), founded in 1949. This body coordinates the economic activities of the world socialist community (Cuba, Mongolia and Vietnam are also members). Long term contracts make economic planning easier. Trade within the group was originally conducted in accounting roubles. This proved unworkable and today nearly all CMEA trade is done on a barter basis. The introduction of a convertible currency on the Hungarian model is envisioned by the CMEA planners. Together the CMEA countries account for more than a third of the world's industrial output.

The concept is that each country will specialise in producing whatever suits it best. In practice the Soviet Union provides Eastern Europe with raw materials such as oil, natural gas, iron ore, cotton, timber and mineral ores, receiving manufactured goods like machinery, textiles and footwear in return. In the past poor quality goods have been sent to the CMEA partners, the best products being sold in the west for hard currency. All of the Eastern European countries have fairly balanced trade, except Yugoslavia (not a CMEA member) which imports twice as much as it exports. The USSR has a substantial trading surplus.

Czechoslovakia and the GDR have the highest per capita incomes in Eastern Europe; Albania, Romania and Yugoslavia have the lowest. The emphasis on heavy industry and large defence budgets have led to shortages of consumer goods throughout the region. This very problem is now being tackled by Gorbachev's economic reforms which feature incentives and some decentralisation. Environmental issues such as acid rain and the risks that go with nuclear power generation call for urgent attention. Agriculture is collectivised in all of the countries except Poland and Yugoslavia. These two also stand out for their huge hard currency debts, inflation and related labour unrest.

GEOGRAPHY

The pivotal mountain range of central Europe is the Carpathians, which swings round from Romania into Czechoslovakia. There is excellent hiking in this range, especially at Sibiu (Romania), Stary Smokovec (Czechoslovakia) and Zakopane (Poland). The Balkan Range is shared by Albania, Bulgaria, Greece and Yugoslavia. Musala Peak (2925 metres) in Bulgaria's Rila Massif, is the highest in Eastern Europe. North-west of Ljubljana, Yugoslavia, are the Julian Alps.

One of the scenic highlights of Eastern Europe is the Dalmatian Coast of Yugoslavia. Here the mountains dip into the Adriatic to form a broken coastline with countless islands of Grecian beauty. The best beaches in the region are those along the Black Sea in Bulgaria and Romania. The Baltic coast at Rostock and Gdansk has a beauty of its own. The most popular lake in Eastern Europe is Hungary's Balaton.

Another great geographical feature of Eastern Europe is the Danube River. Napoleon called the Danube the 'king of the rivers of Europe.' The 2850-km-long Danube flows through eight countries past three capitals, 1075 km of it in Romania. To see the Danube at its best tour the Danube Bend in Hungary or Romania's delta. The greatest river north of the Carpathians is Poland's Vistula, which passes Cracow, Warsaw and Torun. Other famous rivers are the Elbe (at Dresden) and the Moldau (at Prague).

RELIGION

Protestants predominate in the GDR, Latvia and Estonia, with Protestant minorities in Hungary and Romania. Catholicism is the main religion in Czechoslovakia, Hungary, Lithuania, Poland and northern Yugoslavia. There are atheist majorities in Albania, Bulgaria and the USSR. Only Albania has officially outlawed religion.

In 1054 the Pope excommunicated the Church of Constantinople and all Orthodox churches which refused to accept Papal infallibility. Today the Orthodox faith is prevalent in the USSR, Bulgaria, Romania and eastern Yugoslavia with Patriarchates at Belgrade, Bucharest, Moscow, Sofia and Tbilisi, and Metropolias at Prague and Warsaw. There have been many attempts to re-unify the Orthodox and Roman Catholic churches. Some Orthodox churches have accepted Papal supremacy while retaining the Orthodox Eastern rite. These are known as Uniates or Greek Catholics.

LANGUAGE

German is probably the best international language to know in Eastern Europe, although Russian has been taught in the schools since 1945. German is widely understood by the older people in Czechoslovakia, Hungary and Transylvania (Romania). It's also helpful along the Adriatic and Black Sea coasts where German tourists prevail, in Poland and, of course, the GDR. If you know French, Italian or Spanish you won't understand spoken Romanian, but you'll pick up isolated words and the meaning of simple texts. There's always someone at major hotels and travel agencies who knows English. Many students and young professionals speak good English and are usually happy to have the chance to talk to western visitors.

It's always easier to make yourself understood if you write your message down using numbers instead of words. When buying tickets write down the time of the train, bus or performance according to the 24-hour clock, the date using a Roman numeral for the month, and the name of your destination. If you want to know about reservations write down a large capital R with a question mark. To ascertain a price repeat the name of the local currency in a questioning way (roubles? forint? etc), offering a pen and paper on which your informant can write the answer. A surprising amount of information can be communicated in this way, if you're imaginative.

Excluding the USSR, 12 major languages are spoken in the countries covered in this book. Eight of these (Bulgarian, Czech, Macedonian, Polish, Serbo-Croatian, Slovak, Slovene and Sorbian) are Slavic languages. Slavic languages spoken in the USSR include Belorussian (White Russian), Russian and Ukrainian (Ruthenian). These languages are closely related in grammar and vocabulary. If you pick up a few words of one you'll be surprised how the corresponding phrases in the others are almost identical. The other major languages you'll encounter are Albanian, German, Hungarian and Romanian.

In 863 the missionaries Sts Cyril and Methodius created the Slavonic alphabet used in Bulgaria, the USSR and parts of Yugoslavia. It only takes a few hours to learn this alphabet, so make the effort if you'll be visiting these countries. The Cyrillic script was used in Romania until the mid-19th century.

Almost all the Eastern European languages employ accents over the vowels. Since these are generally meaningless to English speakers none are used in this book. Be aware of them, however, as they're always used locally. The only place you really *must* remember them is when consulting indexes on local maps. If the name you're seeking doesn't appear at first glance check the same spelling further down the column where an accent appears over the first vowel.

Some German words and phrases follow:

Greetings & Civilities

hello	*hello*
goodbye	*auf Wiedersehen*
good morning	*guten Morgen*
good evening	*guten Abend*
please	*bitte*

thank you	*danke*
You are very kind.	*Das ist sehr nett von Ihnen*
yes	*ja*
no	*nein*

Small Talk

Do you speak English?	*Sprechen Sie Englisch?*
I don't understand.	*Ich verstehe nicht*
Where do you live?	*Wo wohnen Sie?*
What work do you do?	*Welchen Beruf haben Sie?*
I am a student.	*Ich bin Student*
I am very happy.	*Ich bin sehr glücklich*

Accommodation

youth hostel	*Jugendherberge*
campground	*Zeltplatz*
private room	*Privatzimmer*
Where is there a cheaper hotel?	*Wo gibt es ein preiswerteres Hotel?*
Should I make a reservation?	*Ist eine Reservierung notwendig?*
single room	*Einzelzimmer*
double room	*Doppelzimmer*
It is very noisy.	*Es ist sehr laut*
Where is the toilet?	*Wo ist die Toilette?*

Getting Around

What time does it leave?	*Wann fährt es ab?*
When is the first bus?	*Wann fährt der erste Bus?*
When is the last bus?	*Wann fährt der letzte Bus?*
When is the next bus?	*Wann fährt der nächste Bus?*
That's too soon.	*Das ist zu kurzfristig*
When is the next one after that?	*Wann fährt der übernächste?*
How long does the trip take?	*Wie lange dauert die Fahrt?*
timetable	*Fahrplan*
Where is the bus stop?	*Wo ist die Bushaltestelle?*

Where is the railway station?	*Wo ist der Bahnhof?*
Where is the taxi stand?	*Wo ist der nächste Taxistand?*
Where is the left-luggage room?	*Wo ist die Gepäckauf-bewahrung?*

Around Town

Where is .... ?	*Wo ist .... ?*
museum	*Museum*
palace	*Palast*
castle	*Burg*
concert hall	*Konzerthalle*
opera house	*Opernhaus*
musical theater	*Musiktheater*
tourist information office	*Fremden-verkehrsamt*
Where are you going?	*Wohin gehen Sie?*
I am going to	*Ich gehe nach ....*
Where is it?	*Wo ist es?*
I can't find it.	*Ich kann es nicht finden*
Is it far?	*Ist es weit?*
left	*links*
right	*rechts*
I want	*Ich möchte ....*
Do I need permission?	*Benötige ich eine Genehmigung?*

Entertainment

Where can I hear live music?	*Wo wird live-Musik gespielt?*
Where can I buy a ticket?	*Wo kann ich eine Karte kaufen?*
I'm looking for a ticket.	*Ich möchte eine Karte haben*
I want to refund this ticket.	*Ich möchte diese Karte zurücker-stattet haben*
Is this a good seat?	*Ist das ein guter Platz?*
at the front	*vorne*

Food

I am hungry.	*Ich bin hungrig*
I do not eat meat.	*Ich esse kein Fleisch*

self-service cafetaria	*Cafeteria mit Selbstbedienung*
grocery store	*Lebensmittelladen*
fish	*Fisch*
soup	*Suppe*
salad	*Salat*
fresh vegetables	*frisches Gemüse*
bread	*Brot*
ice cream	*Eiscreme*
hot coffee	*heisser Kaffee*
mineral water	*Mineralwasser*
beer	*Bier*
wine	*Wein*

Shopping

Where can I buy one?	*Wo kann ich das kaufen?*
How much does it cost?	*Wieviel kostet das?*
Is that the price per person?	*Ist das der Preis pro Person?*
Is that the total price?	*Ist das der Gesamtpreis?*
Are there any extra charges?	*Kommen da noch Kosten hinzu?*
That's (much) too expensive.	*Das ist (viel) zu teuer*
Is there a cheaper one?	*Gibt es noch etwas preiswerteres?*
Can I pay with local currency?	*Kann ich in Landeswährung zahlen?*

Time & Dates

today	*heute*
tonight	*heute abend*
tomorrow	*morgen*
the day after tomorrow	*übermorgen*
Monday	*Montag*
Tuesday	*Dienstag*
Wednesday	*Mittwoch*
Thursday	*Donnerstag*
Friday	*Freitag*
Saturday	*Samstag*
Sunday	*Sonntag*
What time does it open?	*Wann wird geöffnet?*
What time does it close?	*Wann wird geschlossen?*

| At what time? | *Um wieviel Uhr?* |
| when? | *wann?* |

Numbers

1	*eins*
2	*zwei*
3	*drei*
4	*vier*
5	*fünf*
6	*sechs*
7	*sieben*
8	*acht*
9	*neun*
10	*zehn*
11	*elf*
12	*zwölf*
13	*dreizehn*
14	*vierzehn*

15	*fünfzehn*
16	*sechzehn*
17	*siebzehn*
18	*achtzehn*
19	*neunzehn*
20	*zwanzig*
21	*einundzwanzig*
22	*zweiundzwanzig*
23	*dreiundzwanzig*
30	*dreissig*
40	*vierzig*
50	*fünfzig*
60	*sechzig*
70	*siebzig*
80	*achtzig*
90	*neunzig*
100	*einhundert*

The Cyrillic Alphabet

Аа	Бб	Вв	Гг	Дд	Ее	Ёё	Жж	Зз
a	b	v	g	d	e,je	o,jo	ž	z

Ии	Йй	Кк	Лл	Мм	Нн	Оо	Пп
ji,i	j	k	l	m	n	o	p

Рр	Сс	Тт	Уу	Фф	Хх	Цц	Чч
r	s	t	u	f	ch	c	č

Шш	Щщ	Ъъ	ыЫ	Ьь	Ээ	Юю	Яя
š	šč	–	y	–	e	u,ju	a,ja

Facts for the Visitor

VISAS

All of the Eastern European countries require a passport and visa. The passport must be valid six months beyond your departure from the region. Visas can be obtained at consulates in advance, except in the case of East Germany where transit visas are issued at the border only. Unless you're a Third World national you probably won't need a visa for West Berlin.

Romania and Yugoslavia grant tourist visas to visitors arriving at their borders and Hungary will also do so if you arrive by road, river or air. Still, it pays to get these visas at a consulate in advance as the fee charged at the border is invariably higher and you may have to wait in line. Bulgarian and East German tourist visas are available at the border if you have a voucher verifying prepayment of accommodation. Albanian, Czechoslovak, Polish and Soviet visas are *never* available at the border.

The Czechoslovak, Hungarian, Polish, Romanian and Yugoslav visas are usually issued immediately by consulates in neighbouring countries. Depending on political conditions there can be delays in getting a Polish visa, so don't leave it too late. Some Polish consulates levy a considerable surcharge for faster service. You'll get a Bulgarian tourist visa after a waiting period of a week to 10 days. East Germany and the USSR only grant tourist visas to those who have pre-paid accommodation for their entire stay. Albania can only be entered on a group visa obtained by a tour operator.

Consulates are generally open weekday mornings and visa fees (US$5 to US$25 per entry) must be paid in cash in hard currency (no travellers' cheques). Most countries will issue double entry visas upon request. Decide in advance if it's a tourist or transit visa you want. Transit visas are often cheaper and issued sooner, but it's usually not possible to extend a transit visa or change it to a tourist visa. In the case of Hungary *always* ask for a tourist visa even if you only intend to transit. The price is the same and you'll have the freedom to change your mind.

Have a good supply of passport photos with you. Make sure you actually look like your photo. If you've grown a beard since your passport photo was taken, for example, you could be required to shave the beard to convince border officials that it's actually you! They're very strict about this.

Don't list a sensitive occupation such as journalist, minister of religion, policeman or soldier on the visa application. If you are one of *those* put down teacher, truck driver, sales clerk, or something similar. They never check. Israeli stamps in your passport could cause problems on entry into some Eastern European countries.

Most visas may be used anytime within three to six months from the date of issue but Albanian, East German and Soviet visas are for specific dates. You're usually allowed to spend a month in a country. There are compulsory currency exchange regulations in Czechoslovakia, Poland and Romania. You may stay for the number of days for which you've changed money (US$10 to US$25 a day). Poland gives students a discount on the compulsory exchange rate, but this must be established at the time you apply for the visa.

The visa form may instruct you to report to police within 48 hours of arrival. If you're staying at a hotel or other official accommodation (campground, youth hostel, private room arranged by a travel agency, etc) this will be taken care of for you by the travel agency or the hotel or campground reception. An exception is East Germany where you must personally go to the police unless you're staying at an

Interhotel. The hotel or campground will stamp the back of your visa form to prove that you were registered and immigration will look at the stamps as you're leaving the country. If too many nights are unaccounted for you could have some explaining to do. Trying to alter the dates on the form to make them 'right' isn't a good idea.

If you're staying with friends or in a private room arranged on the street you're supposed to register with the police. Again, if it's only for a couple of nights during a two-week stay immigration probably won't make a fuss about the missing stamps, although technically you're breaking the law. No such stamps are necessary in Poland, Romania or Yugoslavia. Staying in private homes is forbidden in Romania.

You're required to have your passport with you at all times (this also applies in West Berlin). You'll have to show it when checking into hotels, changing money, etc. Very occasionally the police will ask to see your passport, usually on trains. If for some reason you don't wish to be controlled, travel by bus. If you stay 30 days or less in a country you don't need to apply for an exit permit. If you're staying for a longer period ask about this at a tourist office. If you lose your passport or visa and are issued a replacement then you *do* have to apply to the police for an exit permit before you will be permitted to leave the country.

If you were born in an Eastern European country be sure to check with their embassy in your present country of residence about any special regulations which might apply to you. You may still be considered a citizen of your country of birth and could have difficulty leaving once inside. You might have to serve in the local army for a year or two! This could even be the case if your parents emigrated when you were an infant or if you married an Eastern European. If you do find yourself in such a situation there's not much the embassy of your adopted land

will be able to do to rescue you. On the positive side, Poland and Romania offer a reduction in the compulsory exchange rate to those of Polish or Romanian ancestry. This must be arranged in advance at a consulate.

If you want a visa extension go to the official government travel agency (Balkantourist, Cedok, Ibusz, ONT, Orbis, Reiseburo der DDR, etc) and ask them how to go about it. You'll probably have to report to the police in person. Any required compulsory exchange must be completed first. Office hours are short and the lines long, so don't leave it till the last minute. Try to avoid this inconvenience by asking for enough time when you collect your visa in the first place.

If you want to live in a socialist country for a longer period enquire at the country's tourist office or embassy in your home country about language courses. Russian courses are the best way to get to know the USSR and are not terribly expensive. Some previous knowledge of Russian may be required. In Bulgaria there are courses in Esperanto.

The many rules and regulations described above, below and throughout this book aren't really as complicated as they may at first appear. In practice you'll easily be able to comply with them and the experience will become part of your visit. Keep in mind that the requirements can change overnight and the trend seems to be toward making things easier. You may be pleasantly surprised.

MONEY

The best currencies to have with you are US dollars or West German marks (DM). Take a mixture of cash and travellers' cheques. Have plenty of small denomination cheques and banknotes as it's often impossible to make change. *Failure to pay attention to this small detail can lead to tremendous problems once inside Eastern Europe.* If you have only large bills you may be forced to take change in local currency at a bad rate. If you ask an

Eastern European bank to convert your travellers' cheques into cash they'll only give you half the face value in dollars, the rest in local currency, if they will do it at all.

You can change your own currency or travellers' cheques into DM in West Berlin but the banks often charge high commissions (up to 10 DM) and give lousy rates. It's worth having a few travellers' cheques denominated in DM. American Express offices in Western Europe will break large American Express travellers' cheques down into smaller denominations at no charge. It's impossible to do this in Eastern Europe or to receive cash advances on credit cards. Credit cards themselves are of very limited use there.

One dollar bills make excellent tips, while US$5 and US$10 notes are seldom refused when offered as gifts! International railway tickets must be paid in hard currency (except in Yugoslavia where dinars are acceptable). Other places where you'll need western cash is at consulates, duty free shops and hard currency bars in hotels. Occasionally hotel bills and sightseeing tours must be paid for directly in hard currency.

Some countries such as Albania, East Germany, Poland and the USSR ask you to fill out a currency declaration listing all western currency in your possession upon arrival. Don't lose the form or all your money could be subject to confiscation! If you listed considerable amounts of cash they may ask to see it again upon departure, to verify that you didn't change it on the black market. It's OK to leave with less money than you declared but not more.

In Czechoslovakia, Poland and Romania you must change a fixed amount for every day you'll be there. This is sometimes done at the border, other times at a travel agency inside the country. You'll get a receipt which you must show when paying hotel bills. The amount spent will be deducted from the back of the receipt and once all your 'credit' is used up you'll have to change more money to pay such bills. Don't lose the receipt as you won't be able to spend the money at hotels without it and may even have to complete compulsory exchange all over again. In East Germany you must change DM 25 daily if you have a one-day or camping visa, but nothing if you pre-paid hotel or youth hostel accommodation in western currency. Those on package tours or with accommodation vouchers are always exempt from compulsory exchange. There's no compulsory exchange in Bulgaria, Hungary or Yugoslavia, although Bulgarian officials sometimes insist that you buy a three-day voucher at about US$50 a day.

You usually change money at travel agencies, almost never at a bank. Most of the countries have a standard official rate you receive wherever you change and travel agencies are faster and more efficient than banks. In Bulgaria travel agencies actually give a *higher* rate than banks. Weekends and evenings you can usually change money at the luxury hotels for the same rate but a small commission is sometimes charged. Hungary and Yugoslavia are the only countries in Eastern Europe where local banks give you anything close to the market value of your western currency.

When you change money officially you'll receive local currency with a purchasing power similar to money in Western Europe. All of the countries also have black markets offering up to six times the official rate on the street. This is illegal everywhere and you also run the risk of being ripped off. Hang onto your cash until you have the offered money in your hand, then count it one more time before putting it in your pocket. *If during an exchange the marketeer takes the local currency back from you after you've counted it, break off contact immediately as a rip-off is definitely intended.* In that circumstance the money you have counted will disappear in a sleight of hand trick and you'll end up with a much smaller amount. Know what the local currency looks like and don't be in a hurry.

Never change with two men together. If a second man appears while you're negotiating, split. Don't be pressured into changing more than you originally intended. Thieves will always insist that you change a large amount, one way of recognising them.

If you meet someone reliable and are able to do the act in private change enough to cover your entire remaining stay, to avoid having to take this serious risk a second time. Campgrounds and taxi cabs are often good places to change since you know with whom you're dealing. Although you can buy East German marks and Soviet roubles at a big discount at West Berlin banks, it's a serious offence to attempt to take this money into the GDR or the USSR.

You should also exercise considerable care. If the police apprehend you all the money involved will be confiscated and you could be fined, deported and even jailed. The consequences for your local contacts will be far worse (unless they happen to be plainclothes police, as is usually the case in East Berlin). We're not encouraging you to use the black market, so don't blame us if you get caught.

It's unfortunate that arbitrary official pricing, compulsory exchange at unrealistic rates and mandatory vouchers or package tours have created a situation where it's sometimes necessary to resort to these methods to bring average costs in line with travel expenses elsewhere in the world. Too often the 'cheapness' of a country depends on whether one uses the black market and honest visitors are penalised. In some countries prices are meaningless with some things wildly expensive and others ridiculously cheap. You'll soon learn where the bargains lie and what to avoid. Prices are fairly stable in Eastern Europe, but they can go up with a bang.

The import and export of all Eastern European currencies is prohibited, although small change is no problem. Excess local currency may be deposited at the border against a receipt allowing you to pick up the money again next visit. The socialist currencies are almost worthless outside the region. It's usually *impossible* to reconvert soft currency into hard currency, even if you change more than the minimum daily requirement or leave early. Only change what you need and go on a spending spree on your last few days if there's anything left.

CONDUCT

Meaningful foreign travel involves mental adjustments. This is especially true in Eastern Europe where your dress and manners will mark you as a visitor from the west. Don't play the rich uncle. Treat clerks and attendants normally without arrogance. But don't go to the other extreme. No one is out to get you.

It's best to avoid political discussions, unless someone else brings the subject up. Even then try not to mention Eastern European leaders by name. It's revealing to hear what is and what is not said but consider, you may be overheard by someone who only understands a small part of the conversation. Crowded bars are the worst places to talk politics. You won't be doing your local friends a favour by inspiring the police to ask for identification.

This does vary from country to country. You'll hear people openly criticising the system in Poland and Yugoslavia, while in Czechoslovakia, the GDR and Romania the opposite applies. Keep in mind that the locals understand their system far better than you do, so avoid the temptation to lecture. A low profile is appreciated by everyone. Many Eastern Europeans tend to think in economic rather than political terms. Western material possessions interest them far more than ideological freedoms. They often have a rosy picture of life in the west, not realising that many of their problems are universal.

Avoid sitting at the same table with uniformed soldiers or police as this can have unpleasant consequences for them and you. People who befriend you on the street may end up asking for gifts or favours, such as requests for you to make purchases at hard currency shops. This is often the case with young men who wish to 'practise their English.' Such contacts are seldom rewarding.

Officials in Eastern Europe are far less willing to 'bend' the rules to suit individual situations than officials in the west. Sometimes they will simply look the other way if they feel it's not worth the bother, but when confronted directly (if you create a scene, for example) they will enforce the regulations rigorously.

In embarrassing situations (such as being caught changing money on the black market, smuggling or camping in prohibited areas) it's better to plead ignorance and show remorse rather than argue or threaten. If you do get into serious trouble with the authorities assume an attitude of respectful dignity and wait to speak to someone who understands English. Persons in higher positions are better able to resolve problems quickly and fairly, so long as you remain cool. Don't expect much help from your embassy.

CLIMATE

Spring (April to mid-June) is the best time to come as the days are long and the touristic masses still haven't arrived.

Summer (mid-June to early September) is the time for hiking and camping, the peak season for budget travellers and everyone else. September is a good month along the Adriatic coast, but in October the campgrounds close down and the days become shorter. October to March can be rather cold and dark, but this is the peak theatre and concert season in the cities. The infrastructure is well developed so the climate need not be a problem for travellers.

BOOKS

If you're the sort of person who travels with two guidebooks *Frommer's Eastern Europe on $25 a Day* (Prentice Hall, New York) will balance your load nicely. Frommer provides detailed descriptions of medium to top end restaurants and hotels throughout the area – useful if you've got a lot of black money to unload. Bottom end places to stay and eat are treated as curiosities, while hiking and camping are not covered. Another drawback is the mass of trivia inserted to give the impression that the authors had actually dined or slept in every establishment listed in the book. The condescending tone is a little hard to stomach at times.

Only the most incorrigible snob would wish to use *A Guide to Central Europe* by Richard Bassett (Penguin Books, London, 1988) as a guidebook. The few practical tips are buried in a narrative confusing to navigate by armchair or foot. Bassett claims that his book is the first since 1915 to describe the cities of the former Hapsburg empire. It's a curious piece of nostalgia with a distaste for the present, a good book to thumb through and put back on the shelf.

If you read German *Osteuropa* by Norbert Ropers (Anders Reisen, Rowohit Taschenbuch Verlag GmbH, Hamburg) contains worthwhile background information on recent trends, although it really isn't a practical guidebook.

The only series of guidebooks in English with a weighty tome for each of the individual Eastern European countries (except Albania) is Nagel's Encyclopaedia-Guides, published in Switzerland. The Encyclopaedia-Guides to Romania and Bulgaria are the *only* serious guides to these countries in English. Although they provide a fair number of maps, good history and description, there's little practical information. Other drawbacks are size and price: the Bulgaria volume has 527 pages and costs US$30. Nagel's is highly recommended if you'll be spending a long time in one country.

Schedules for all the main Eastern European railway and ferry routes are given in the monthly *Thomas Cook Continental Timetable*. Thomas Cook travel agencies often sell single copies. If you can't procure one anywhere consider photocopying the Eastern Europe pages in someone else's copy. You'll find yourself referring to them constantly.

Volume One of the *International Youth Hostel Handbook* lists IYHF youth hostels in six Eastern European countries. The Bartholomew *World Travel Map, Eastern Europe* (1:2,500,000) is also very useful. *Let's Go: Europe* by Harvard Student Agencies (St Martin's Press, New York) is absolutely essential for budget travellers passing through Western Europe.

East Central Europe in the 19th & 20th Centuries by Ivan T Berend and Gyorgy Ranki (Akademiai Kiado, Budapest, 1977) provides a wealth of facts and figures on the period 1848 to 1945. *Eastern Approaches* by Fitzroy Maclean (The Reprint Society, London) is an inside account of British intrigue in Eastern Europe during WW II. The section on Yugoslavia is definitive.

Eastern Europe Since Stalin edited by Jonathan Steele (David & Charles, Newton Abbot, 1974) is a readable survey of the formative period 1953 to 1973. The texts of newspaper and magazine articles published in the east, plus landmark speeches by socialist leaders, are reprinted between blocks of even-handed editorial comment. This book not only covers the power shifts within the various Communist parties, but gives a feel for the perplexing problems Eastern European reformers face.

FILM & PHOTOGRAPHY

In all socialist countries it's prohibited to take pictures of anything that might be considered of strategic value, such as bridges, tunnels, harbours, docks, reservoirs, dams, railway stations, airports, government buildings, radio or TV stations, power plants, factories, laboratories, mines, border crossings, military installations, local soldiers or police.

This also applies in West Berlin where the American Forces Network broadcasts daily exhortations to listeners to contact the military police if they see anyone taking pictures from parked cars or 'of anything they're not supposed to.' It's forbidden to take photos out the window of an aircraft. Aside from this you may photograph anything you like. Ask permission before taking close-up photos of people.

Serious photographers should bring enough film with them as Kodak film is almost impossible to obtain. Some Eastern European colour films cannot be developed outside the originating country due to the different technological processes involved.

HEALTH

If you get mildly sick go to a pharmacy (chemist). Locally-produced drugs and medicines are ridiculously cheap and there's often someone there who understands a little English, German or at least sign language. Drug stores also sell multivitamins (ask for the 'forte' variety), bottled medicinal water and even herbal tea. One off-beat medicine to watch for is Vietnamese 'aromatic balm,' the Tiger Balm of the east, a good remedy for common colds. For diarrhoea get carbon tablets (Carbo activatus in Hungarian). Western brand names are unknown,

unavailable or prohibitively expensive in the east, so bring along any medicines you cannot do without. Prescriptions must be expressed in generic terminology.

Ask your embassy or a tourist information office for a referral to an English-speaking doctor or dentist. You'll get much better service if you call ahead to make an appointment. Private practice is far less common in the socialist countries than it is in the west. In some cases you may have to attend a government clinic, about which the local tourist office should know. In emergencies you can resort to the casualty ward of any large hospital.

Some European countries such as Britain have mutual agreements allowing free medical treatment for each others nationals. Sometimes they require an official form or document proving that the individual is insured in his/her home country. If you're one of the lucky ones get this before you leave home. Otherwise you'll have to pay for medical care in some socialist countries, while in others it's free for everyone. Hospital bed charges are levied everywhere. If you do get into this situation you'll find the rates are much lower than in capitalist countries. Sometimes you can arrange special medical attention for direct payment in hard currency, officially or unofficially.

Health resorts and spas are common in Bulgaria, Czechoslovakia, Hungary, Romania and Yugoslavia offering complete programmes with room and board against payment in hard currency. Of course the charges are much lower than those of similar establishments in Austria or West Germany. Tourist offices will have information about the spas, although they sometimes must be booked from abroad. Hungary is especially famous for its hot springs, which are accessible to everyone for very nominal amounts. Massage and other health services are available at these.

POST

If you wish to receive mail you're best to

have it sent care of your embassy. Get a current list of the addresses of your country's diplomatic missions from a passport office or public library before you leave home.

To send a parcel you must take it unwrapped to a main post office. Have the paper, string and tape ready. They'll sometimes ask to see your passport and note the number on the form. If you don't have a return address within the country just put your name care of any large tourist hotel. Air mail isn't that much more expensive than sea mail, so be sure to use it. In Romania you must pay duty in hard currency on souvenirs mailed from the country.

Once a parcel is accepted it will probably reach its destination. As in all other countries, if you put favourable comments on the back of postcards they won't be 'lost.' This applies even more if you're writing to acquaintances inside Eastern Europe.

TIME

Most of the places covered in this book are on Central European Time (Greenwich Mean Time plus one hour). Romania and Bulgaria are on East European Time (GMT plus two hours). The USSR spans 11 time zones, but all of the European portion is on Moscow Time (GMT plus three hours). If it's 6 pm in Berlin and Madrid it will be 7 pm in Bucharest and Sofia, 8 pm in Moscow, 5 pm in London, 12 noon in New York, 9 am in California and 3 am the next morning in Melbourne, Australia. Daylight Saving Time runs from the end of March to the end of September.

INFORMATION

Each of the Eastern European countries has an official government travel agency organising tourism within the country. These are the Reiseburo der DDR (German Democratic Republic), Orbis (Poland), Cedok (Czechoslovakia), Ibusz (Hungary), the Oficiul National de Turism (Romania), Balkantourist (Bulgaria), Albturist (Albania) and Intourist (USSR). In Hungary there are many other travel agencies (Cooptourist, Volantourist, Dunatours, etc) in addition to Ibusz. In Yugoslavia tourism is also decentralised.

These agencies have branches in nearly every city and town within their own country and foreign offices around the world. The addresses of overseas offices are listed in the various chapter introductions. These offices are primarily travel agencies which reserve hotel rooms, sell transportation tickets, sightseeing tours, etc. In most cases they also provide general tourist information.

Each country also has a student travel bureau which you should patronise if you have an IUS or ISIC student card or an IYHF youth hostel card. They are the Reiseburo der FDJ 'Jugendtourist' (German Democratic Republic), Almatur (Poland), the CKM (Czechoslovakia), Express (Hungary), the BTT (Romania), Orbita (Bulgaria), Ferijalni savez Jugoslavije (Yugoslavia) and Sputnik (USSR). Their primary task is to organise excursions for youth groups within their own country, but often they assist foreign youth as well.

Large cities often maintain municipal information offices which are excellent sources of information on local attractions, theatres, events, etc, but do not make travel arrangements. The national railway companies usually have a central ticket office in each major city within their respective country. Go to these for tickets and reservations rather than struggle with the throng at the station. These offices and some of the travel agencies are packed around mid-afternoon, so check the hours and go early or late. Students from Third World countries are an information source not to be overlooked. Most speak English or French and are quite friendly.

We've tried to list the most effective information offices throughout the book. The service at these offices varies, improving if you're both courteous and persistent. If it becomes obvious that an office is no more interested in helping you than you are in paying top dollar, leave quietly and make your own arrangements. Each chapter explains how this can be done.

ACCOMMODATION
Hotels
If you want to stay at a standard high-rise tourist hotel you'll find one in every city. In this book we've concentrated on the older, 2nd class hotels. There are still quite a few 'grand hotels' around, overflowing with Victorian elegance. The cheapest rooms begin around US$15 single, US$25 double. Often the price difference between a single and a double isn't that great. The cheapest hotels have only rooms with shared bath, which means you'll have to go down the corridor to use the toilet or shower. In Poland and Romania you may as well use up your compulsory exchange 'credit' at these hotels.

Hungarian and Yugoslav hotels are a lot more expensive than camping and private rooms, so you probably won't use them often. Czechoslovak and East German hotels can be quite affordable. In Bulgaria hotel bills must be paid directly in hard currency. If you do find a good inexpensive hotel be sure to book a room for your entire stay upon arrival. Otherwise you could find it's been reserved by someone else when you try to extend your stay.

In all of the Eastern European countries except Hungary there's a two or three-price system at hotels. Nationals of the country get the lowest rate, followed by visitors from other socialist countries. Persons from non-socialist countries pay the highest price of all, often in foreign currency. This explains why all those really expensive hotels are full. This is justified in a way because hotel prices, like currency exchange rates, are strictly artificial and wages in the west are much higher than those in the east. The idea is to make prices comparable to Western Europe. If everyone paid the same in local currency it would be ridiculously cheap for us.

In Albania and the USSR travel agencies will decide where you stay. The image of the cartoon capitalist in his black coat and top hat, a money bag in each hand, is still cherished by some Eastern European tourism planners. They've put hotel prices up so high only very affluent visitors can afford them. You may be a poor student or an overburdened worker on a short break, but the hard currency in your pocket says you're rich. For most Eastern Europeans foreign travel is an unheard-of privilege, thus western visitors are expected to pay luxury level prices.

Private Rooms
In Bulgaria, Czechoslovakia, Hungary, Poland and Yugoslavia some travel agencies will place you in a private home. There's often a 50% surcharge if you stay less than three or four nights but these rooms can be excellent value and are almost always cheaper than a hotel. Prices vary from US$5 to US$20 per person. Always ask for them first in the countries mentioned above. Sometimes

you'll be offered a private room *(sobe)* by a proprietor on the street. The price will be cheaper than what the agencies charge, but their quality control will be lacking. In Yugoslavia this is a common practice entailing no risk at all. In Poland while it's done, it's not kosher.

Camping

An even cheaper roof over your head is available at campgrounds where small bungalows are often available for just a little more than the camping fee (US$2 to US$5 per person). In the most popular resorts they'll all be full in July and August, but ask. There are numerous campgrounds in all of the countries which allow individual travel. Campgrounds may be open from April to October, May to September, or perhaps only June to August, depending on the category of the facility and demand. Quality varies from abysmal in Romania, to unreliable in Bulgaria, to crowded in Hungary, to good in East Germany, to variable in Poland.

You can't always go by what a tourist office tells you about campgrounds because they may not know or would rather see you staying at a hotel. Camping is the *only* cheap way to visit East Germany, Romania and Bulgaria, so try to be in those countries during the season and bring a tent. Freelance camping is usually prohibited, so before you pitch your tent on a beach or in an open field observe what others are doing. If in doubt, hide well.

Youth Hostels

The International Youth Hostel Federation (IYHF) handbook lists hostels in Bulgaria, Czechoslovakia, East Germany, Hungary, Poland and Yugoslavia. The hostels in Poland and Yugoslavia are fairly standard and easily used. Polish hostels are extremely basic but inexpensive (US$2) and friendly. Yugoslav hostels are crowded and overpriced (US$8). In East Germany advance hostel reservations are mandatory *before* you enter East Germany. Consult

that chapter for the procedure. The hostels in Bulgaria do exist but they're difficult to use as the wardens are unaccustomed to receiving western members. Reservations should be made at a 'Pirin' Travel Bureau in any Bulgarian city before going to the hostel.

In Czechoslovakia and Hungary the hostels are actually fairly luxurious 'youth' hotels with double rooms. In Hungary private rooms are cheaper than the hostels, while in Czechoslovakia the CKM Junior hotels are usually full. If you do manage to get into one you'll find it's excellent value at about US$5 per person.

Many Czechoslovak and Hungarian cities have dormitories known as 'tourist hostels' which are not connected with the International Youth Hostel Federation and have no rules (mixed dorms, no curfew, smoking and drinking in the room, etc). These are intended for visitors from other socialist countries and you'll have to be persistent to use them. They cost US$1 to US$2 per person. Ask the local tourist office for a referral.

Mountain 'Huts'

In the mountain areas of Bulgaria, Czechoslovakia, Poland, Romania and Yugoslavia there are mountain 'huts' or chalets offering dormitory accommodation at under US$10 per person and basic meals to hikers. It's usually not possible to reserve a bed at a hut, although in Bulgaria the huts and the IYHF youth hostels are the same thing. Weather conditions will probably limit your use of the huts to summer, although some are open year round. Huts near roads or cable cars fill up fast, as do those in popular areas such as the Tatra Mountains. The huts are excellent places to meet Eastern European students.

Waiting Rooms & Trains

Another place to stay in a pinch are railway station waiting rooms. So long as you have a ticket and know of a train leaving around 4.30 am this is no problem. In midsummer the floors at Budapest's railway stations are lined with sleeping bags and there's even a rude 'wake up' service at 5.30 am. In Romania waiting rooms are virtually the only cheap place to stay outside the camping season. It's even possible to sleep in the train station in Moscow. Always put your luggage in a coin locker or cloakroom before dozing off.

Also compare the price of a couchette or sleeper (US$3 to US$6) on an overnight train to a hotel room. The transportation is thrown in as a bonus. Couchettes are very practical in Bulgaria, Czechoslovakia, Poland, Romania and Yugoslavia, so use your creativity to figure something out. The catch is that's it's often hard to get a couchette or sleeper reservation, so don't leave it too late.

FOOD & DRINK

There are cheap self-service cafeterias (buffet express) in almost every Eastern European town. You usually pay at the end of the line, but sometimes (especially in Poland) you pay at the beginning of the line and get a ticket. Cashiers tend to be indulgent with tourists who can't speak their language, so just point at something acceptable someone else is eating. Otherwise ask the person in line behind you what a certain dish is called. You can usually get a beer with the meal (but never in Poland).

Some self-services offer genuine local dishes at ridiculously low prices. Three which come to mind are *Pod Arkadami Milk Bar*, ulica Rozana 1, Torun (Poland), *Mliecne Specialty*, Rybarska brana 9, Bratislava (Czechoslovakia), and *Tej Bistro*, Jokai ter 11, Pecs (Hungary). Self-services tend to close around 7 pm weekdays, at 1 pm on Saturday and all day Sunday. For busy sightseers they're just the place for breakfast or lunch. An even cheaper and faster place for a snack are sidewalk kiosks selling hot dogs or ice cream. These are common and impossible to list in a book.

Better restaurants stay open longer hours than the self-services. Hotel restaurants keep the longest hours and are usually receptive to foreign tourists, so try there if everything else is closed. In East Germany and the USSR the best restaurants insist on advance reservations. Have your hotel make these for you by phone or drop by in the morning. Throughout Eastern Europe restaurant menus are translated into German but only occasionally into English. Not everything on the menu will be available. As you enter the restaurant observe what others are eating and just point when the waiter comes.

Two sure signs of a good restaurant are a price list posted outside and a crowd of local people eating inside. Try the folklore restaurants where regional cuisine is offered. These are known as *csardas* in Hungary or *mexanas* in Bulgaria. In Czechoslovakia and Hungary there are excellent wine restaurants *(vinarna* or *sorozo)* and beer halls *(pivnice* or *borozo)*. Czech beer and Hungarian wine are among the best in the world. Budapest and Bohemia are famous for their pastries served at cafes *(kavarna)*.

There's no such thing as a private table in most Eastern European restaurants. You must share with whoever shows up, which can be a problem if you're a non-smoker. Men dressed in shorts are not admitted to better restaurants. After Western Europe you'll find food is cheap in Eastern Europe – there is no double pricing as there is at the hotels. A little extra money goes a long way here, so splash out now and then. It's customary to round up the bill.

ENTERTAINMENT

If you enjoy music and theatre you can see first rate performances at extremely low prices in Eastern Europe. One of the most appealing sides of socialism is its support for sports and the performing arts. Every large city has an opera house and a separate theatre for operettas and musicals. There will be a concert hall (filharmonia) plus dramatic, satirical and puppet theatres, and sometimes a regular circus. Jazz clubs are found in Czechoslovakia, Hungary and Poland. Jazz is also very popular in Leningrad and the Soviet Baltic republics.

Apart from the capitals many provincial towns such as Brno, Dresden, Gyor, Pecs and Wroclaw are important musical centres. Municipal information offices are your best source of information about cultural events. All performances are listed in the daily papers and although you may not know the language enough information will be comprehensible in the listings to enable you to locate the theatre and try for tickets.

There are theatrical ticket offices in Prague and Budapest, but you'll get better seats by going directly to the theatre box office (kassa) itself. If this fails try for a ticket at the door half an hour before showtime. If the box office still doesn't have any, make a little sign with the words 'I'm looking for a ticket' in the local language and stand outside holding it. Often people have extra tickets they got free from their place of employment and will be only to happy to sell them to you at the face value printed on the ticket. Except in Prague you probably won't have to go to this bother and will get tickets directly from the box office. In places where tickets are in high demand by both tourists and locals (such as in Dresden, Prague and Moscow) government travel agencies will be able to obtain a ticket for you against payment in hard currency. This jacks up the price considerably, but for performances at the Semperoper and Bolshoi it's still worth it.

Most theatres close for a six-week vacation during the summer. Instead look for performances by visiting companies at open air theatres or on public squares. Folklore programmes are often offered and there are summer festivals. Most Eastern European towns have a Cultural Centre which publishes a monthly list of regular events. Cinemas are cheap and usually show movies in the original language. Latecomers are not admitted and it's rude to walk out in the middle of a film. Smoking is not allowed in cinemas. Discos and night clubs stay open late everywhere except in Romania and are good places to make local contacts.

THINGS TO BUY

Many Eastern European countries are critically short of consumer goods. When something especially good comes on the market it sells out fast. Thus it's important to buy things when you see them! Books and records are good value, as are musical and scientific instruments. High quality art books are produced in Czechoslovakia, East Germany, Hungary and the USSR. Footwear and clothing are cheap in Czechoslovakia. Eyeglasses are inexpensive everywhere, so get an extra pair if you know your prescription.

Hard currency shops in all the countries sell imported goods and top quality local products. These shops are often located in luxury hotels and the prices are fairly reasonable. The company names to watch for are Beriozka or Kashtan (USSR), Comturist (Romania), Corecom (Bulgaria), Intershop (GDR), Intourist shop (Hungary), Pewex (Poland) and Tuzex (Czechoslovakia). Always save the receipts for purchases made with western currency. This will allow you to take the items out of the country without paying an export tax.

Goods purchased with local currency over a certain value are subject to tax. Customs officials get strict about this if it looks like you're trying to make a business of it by exporting too many of the same item. Duty is charged on valuable things like fur or leather coats, gold jewellery and antique watches, unless you have receipts to prove that you paid hard currency. If you have such things with you on arrival in Eastern Europe be sure to declare them.

Some of the export restrictions are listed in the various chapters of this book.

WHAT TO BRING

Bring western currency in small denominations. Have a good mixture of cash and travellers' cheques. If you'll be visiting West Berlin some of the cheques should be expressed in German marks. Carry a photocopy of your passport, travellers' cheques purchase receipts and other important documents in a secure place separate from the originals. Twenty or 30 passport size photos will be required for obtaining visas. An IYHF membership card could save you money in several Eastern European countries. If you're a student bring along a current International Student Identity Card (ISIC) and purchase an International Union of Students (IUS) card first chance you get.

Bring photos of your home, family, place of employment, etc, as conversation pieces. Take a bottle of wine, chocolate bars and some canned food to Romania and the USSR. Shaving cream is poor quality or unavailable in Eastern Europe. For maximum savings bring a tent and sleeping bag.

Personal notebooks are often checked and even confiscated by customs. Encode the names and addresses of local friends in your notebook (by putting a West German city and postal code after an East German street address, for example). Carry local addresses and letters on your person or bury them deep in your luggage.

The following items are prohibited entry into all socialist countries: video tapes, photos and printed materials of a pornographic or hostile nature (including horror films), weapons of offence (firearms, ammunition, spring-operated knives, batons, tear gas sprays, etc), walkie-talkies, radar detectors, gaming and slot machines, pure alcohol and the currency of any other socialist country. Books printed in the local language outside the country (including phrasebooks for tourists) are also sometimes banned. Some countries also prohibit western newspapers and magazines. Portable short wave radios, video and music cassettes cause problems occasionally.

While there's no problem bringing in the type of personal effects most people travel with, you can't bring things which are obviously intended for sale (such as five pair of Levis with the factory labels attached). Don't bring gold jewellery or gems as these are heavily scrutinised and must be declared in writing. If the declared items are subsequently stolen you could have problems on departure. Philatelic stamps, crystal glass, precious metals (gold, silver, platinum), gem stones, securities, lottery tickets, books printed before 1945, antiques and valuable works of art will also arouse keen interest from customs and could be confiscated. If in doubt ask about customs regulations when you apply for your visa.

Getting There

FROM NORTH AMERICA OR AUSTRALASIA
Surprisingly, airfares to Eastern Europe are expensive. If you're coming from North America, Australia or New Zealand your best bet is to buy the cheapest ticket to Western Europe and proceed from there. Get a discount one way from wherever you are to London, Amsterdam or Athens. Catch a bus to West Berlin or Sofia and cross the continent on Eastern European trains. At the other end you'll be able to pick up a plane ticket home from one of these three gateways, probably for less than you paid to come over. London and Athens are also good places to collect Eastern European visas.

From South-East Asia the very cheapest fares to Western Europe are offered by the Eastern European carriers. Ironically, these fares usually don't apply if you wish to terminate in Eastern Europe itself. The Aeroflot route from Singapore or Bangkok via Moscow is particularly popular. The fare from Singapore to London or other western European capitals via Moscow is S$780 (US$390) but through agents you can knock it down to a bit less than S$750 (US$375).

A variety of stopover options are available from as little as one day in Moscow to longer visits to a number of cities. A four day/three night Moscow package costs S$580 (US$290) with a single room or S$420 (US$210) each with a double room. That's the October to March low season stopover cost, it jumps about 30% in the high season. Visas take about a week to issue in Singapore and the cost depends on your nationality. For British passport holders they're S$10 (US$5) while for Americans or Australians they're S$28 (US$14).

On flights with Balkan-Bulgarian Airlines, Czechoslovak Airlines (CSA), LOT-Polish Airlines, Tarom-Romanian Air Transport and Yugoslav Airlines (JAT) you'll transit an Eastern European capital. Ask if you're allowed a free stopover, then check to see if you need a tourist visa. If you're told they're available at the airport, pick one up in advance anyway to be safe. Interflug flights from Singapore to East Berlin are no problem, but you must transit immediately to West Berlin by bus.

From the US Icelandair offers regular one-way fares to Luxembourg at competitive rates. Service is available from New York, Boston, Chicago and a number of other American cities with free onward bus connections in Luxembourg to Amsterdam, Frankfurt am Main, Wuppertal and Stuttgart. Ask Icelandair if motorcoach reservations are required. The cheapest Icelandair fares apply from November to mid-December, mid-January to February, and May to mid-June, although their 'last minute' tariff (available anytime but booked no more than seven days in advance) is similar. Call toll-free 800 223-5500 from anywhere in the US for information.

It's possible to get even cheaper one-way fares to Europe from 'bucket shops' in New York City. These agencies purchase blocks of 'empty' seats from airlines at a fraction of their value and pass the savings on to you. For example, TFI Tours (tel (212) 736-1140 or (800) 223-6363), 34 West 32nd St, 12th floor, New York, NY 10001, promises 'daily departures with guaranteed reservations on scheduled airlines.' The Sunday travel section of the *New York Times* carries ads from many such companies.

No cheap plane tickets are sold in Eastern Europe. A possible exception is West Berlin where Interflug tickets are reasonable. One-way fares out of East Berlin's Schonefeld Airport run DM 372 to Tunis, DM 574 to Cairo, DM 725 to

Singapore and DM 825 to Beijing, China. From Hong Kong and Singapore onward one-way fares are available to everywhere, a round-the-world connection. Any travel agent in Western Europe can book Interflug flights.

FROM WESTERN EUROPE
From Britain

The cheapest way from London is to take a bus to West Berlin. You may have to change buses in Amsterdam but there are immediate connections and a through ticket is sold at London's Victoria Coach Terminal (tel 730-0202). To go as a paying passenger in a private car contact the mitfahnzentrale (tel 654-3210), 56 Grant Place, London.

If you're bound for Yugoslavia, Romania or Bulgaria take a chance on a 'magic' bus to Belgrade, as advertised in the weekly entertainment papers *Time Out* and *LAM*. Most of the buses bound for Greece will drop you in Yugoslavia. A through train ticket from Britain to any Eastern European capital costs many times more than you'd pay for these buses. There are also direct flights from London but no bargains.

From Western Europe

Numerous railway lines link the two Europes but buses are often cheaper than trains. For example Budget Bus (tel 27-5151), Rokin 10, Amsterdam, has a bus to West Berlin twice a week for 90 Dutch guilders one way or to Zagreb, Yugoslavia once a week for 150 Dutch guilders one way. There's a reduction for those under 26 or over 60 years. For information on ride services *(mitfahrzentrale)* see the West Berlin chapter of this book.

There are ferries to Swinoujscie and Gdansk, Poland, from Travemunde (near Lubeck, West Germany). Other ferries to Poland depart Copenhagen (Denmark), Ystad (Sweden), Nynashamn (Sweden) and Helsinki (Finland). Ferries also connect Denmark and Sweden to the GDR.

For Czechoslovakia take a train from

Linz to Cesky Budejovice, a bus from Vienna to Brno or Bratislava, or a train from Vienna to Bratislava. For Hungary there are buses from Vienna to Sopron and Budapest, also trains. An alternative rail route is Graz, Austria, to Szombathely, Hungary. In summer the Danube hydrofoil glides from Vienna to Budapest.

There are many ways to reach Yugoslavia. Several railway lines converge on Ljubljana from Austria and Italy. The main line from Munich to Athens runs via Ljubljana and Belgrade. There are several trains a day between Thessaloniki and Skopje. If you have plenty of time and want to save a few dollars there's a secondary line from Florina, Greece, to Bitola, Yugoslavia. There are ferries from Corfu to Dubrovnik, also numerous lines across the Adriatic from Italy.

From Greece to Bulgaria a bus will be half the price of the train. Check out the budget travel agencies around Omonia Square, Athens, for deals. The main railway line from Europe to Istanbul passes through Sofia. There are cheap buses from Istanbul to Bucharest.

Eurail Connections

In 1989 Hungary became the first Eastern European country to accept the Eurail pass. Rail passengers must still obtain a Hungarian visa beforehand, but with this development Budapest has become even more of a gateway to the region. If you're bound for West Berlin you may use your pass as far as Helmstedt, West Germany. The separate ticket from Helmstedt to West Berlin (DM 43 one way) can be purchased at any railway station in West Germany.

Czechoslovakia bound, your Eurail pass will take you to Schirnding (West Germany) near Cheb. Vienna is a convenient gateway to Czechoslovakia and Hungary with frequent bus, boat and rail connections. If you begin or end your Eurail pass in that city you won't have to count the days spent touring the Austrian capital. Trieste, Italy, is the best gateway to Yugoslavia with 15 buses a day to nearby Koper and a boat to Istria.

International Train Tickets

There are three levels of railway fares in Eastern Europe. By far the most expensive are tickets between Western and Eastern Europe. Only buy these as far as your first possible stop within the region. Tickets between socialist countries are much less expensive. Cheaper still are domestic tickets within a single socialist country.

Fares between the seven Warsaw Pact countries are based on 'accounting roubles.' The rouble fare is converted into the local currency (zloty, crowns, forint, etc) and you pay the equivalent in whichever western currency you please. MAV Hungarian Railways gives foreigners a 50% discount on these already low fares if they pay in hard currency. At this rate you can go from Budapest to Berlin for US$10 1st class with US$6 extra for a sleeper! Pick up all your international tickets for travel within Eastern Europe in Budapest.

Peculiarities in pricing are illustrated in West Berlin where you can pay three times as much for a ticket to anywhere in Eastern Europe as you'd pay for exactly the same ticket in East Berlin. Another striking example is the price of a train ticket from China to Hungary, which is 10 times more expensive if purchased in the US or Japan than it would be in China or Hungary. (For information on the Trans-Siberian route to Europe see the Hungary and USSR chapters.)

Tickets between socialist countries are valid for two months outbound or four months for a round trip and you may stop over as often as you wish. The Inter-Rail pass (sold to persons aged 26 and under for unlimited railway travel in Western Europe) is valid in Hungary, Yugoslavia and Romania. The Eurail pass is accepted in Hungary.

In all the Eastern European countries international train tickets should be purchased at a travel agency, not in the railway station. If you're a student you're eligible for a 25% discount on international railway tickets between socialist countries. Pick up the required IUS student card at a student travel office in Eastern Europe or at Artu in West Berlin. Addresses and additional local money saving tips are interspersed throughout the book.

Package Tours

A package tour is the only way you'll get into Albania. Unless you're transiting or rich, you'll probably visit the USSR with a group. Any travel agent will know about these tours; check the relevant chapters of this book. A package tour to Bulgaria may also be worth looking into as package tourists don't need a visa and avoid a lot of other uncertain restrictions. Packages from Athens to Sofia by bus are relatively cheap if purchased locally.

By Canoe or Kayak

Every summer since 1956 several hundred people have paddled themselves down the Danube from Ingoldstadt, West Germany, to Silistra, Bulgaria, under the banner of the TID (Tour International Danubien). This is not a race! The 2000-km trip takes two months in daily laps of 40 to 60 km. Participants sleep in camps beside the river and combine sightseeing with travel.

Getting Around

AIR

Considering the cheapness of trains and buses within Eastern Europe, air travel is a real luxury. Aside from the speed, however, a plane trip can save you a bit of money on transit visas. In this category would be Warsaw to Belgrade (US$130 one way) and East Berlin to Sofia (DM 300 one way). If you like flying for fun domestic fares within Poland, Bulgaria and Yugoslavia are reasonable, although still much more than the train. In Romania domestic plane tickets must be paid in hard currency, which puts them out of range. In Czechoslovakia they're simply expensive. Only Yugoslavia has an airport tax, which is only a couple of dollars. All the other airports are free.

TRAIN

You'll do most of your travelling within Eastern Europe by train. All of the countries have well developed railway networks similar to those of Western Europe. You'll have a choice of local trains which stop at every station and expresses. Both have advantages. The local trains are only half the cost of the expresses but they never have reserved seats. Once you find a place to sit it's yours for the trip and since passengers are constantly coming and going you eventually get a place even on a full train. First class travel by local train costs about the same as 2nd class on an express and is quite comfortable, so long as you're in no hurry. First class compartments have six seats, 2nd class eight seats.

If you choose an express be sure to get an express ticket and ask if there are compulsory seat reservations. It's sometimes a hassle getting these tickets, so don't leave it too late. Expresses are often marked in red on posted timetables, local trains in black. The symbol R with a box around it means reservations are mandatory, while an R without a box may mean reservations are possible but not compulsory. The boards listing departures are usually yellow, those for arrivals are white.

Tickets for expresses are best purchased at the central railway ticket office a day before. On overnight trains always try for a couchette a few days in advance. Make sure your ticketing is all in order before you board the train. If you have to arrange a reservation, buy a ticket or upgrade a local ticket to express on a moving train you'll pay a healthy supplement.

Luggage

Almost every railway station in Eastern Europe has a baggage room where you can deposit your luggage as soon as you arrive. Many railway stations have complicated coin lockers. You compose a four-digit number on the inside of the door, insert a coin and close the locker. To open it again you arrange the same number on the outside and hopefully the door will open. Don't forget the number or the location of your locker!

BUS

Buses are slightly more expensive than trains. In most Eastern European countries buses complement the railways rather than duplicate their routes, but in Czechoslovakia and Hungary you have a choice of either. In this case you're better off taking buses for short trips and express trains for really long journeys.

The ticketing system varies in each country. To be safe always try to buy a ticket in advance at the station. If this is not possible you'll be told. In Czechoslovakia the CSAD bus system is computerised. Hungary and Yugoslavia also have good inexpensive bus services. Occasionally you'll be charged extra for baggage.

BOAT

A number of interesting boat trips are possible. One of the most unforgettable is the journey on the big Jadrolinija car ferry down the Dalmatian Coast of Yugoslavia from Split to Dubrovnik. The best river trips are through the Danube Delta from Braila to Sulina and up the Elbe River from Dresden to Bad Schandau. A hydrofoil along Bulgaria's Black Sea coast or up the Danube from Budapest to Vienna can be memorable. Other classic trips include the slow boats from Budapest to Esztergom or across Balaton Lake. In Poland each city on the Vistula offers a river trip in its vicinity and the Weisse Flotte is active around Berlin. Most services operate from April to October only, sometimes less.

LOCAL TRANSPORT

Public transport in Eastern Europe is incredibly cheap. The low price has no effect whatever on the service which is generally first rate. As one example, the U-Bahn (an underground Metro service)

is 11 times more expensive in West than East Berlin!

For all forms of public transport you must buy tickets in advance at a kiosk or from a machine. Information windows in bus and railway stations sometimes have tickets for local transport. Once aboard you validate your own ticket by using a type of punch positioned near the door. Watch how the locals do it. Different tickets are sometimes required for buses, trolley buses, streetcars and Metro (subway or underground), other times they're all the same. If all the kiosks selling tickets are closed ask another passenger to sell you a ticket. There are no conductors and tickets are seldom checked, but you'll be fined if an inspector catches you without a valid ticket.

In most cities buses and trams begin moving at 5 am or earlier and continue until around 10.30 or 11.30 pm. There are Metro lines in Berlin, Prague, Budapest, Bucharest, Moscow, Leningrad, Kiev and several other Soviet cities.

West Berlin

West Berlin's the sort of city that does things to you. Just getting there is an adventure as you're sucked through one of the tightest borders in history. The 162-km-long Wall around West Berlin defends East Germany from the power of the German mark. Conflicting impressions fly at you from every side and the prices will shock you. Yet it's surprising but true that the best things in West Berlin are free.

West Berlin's like a reckless adolescent looking for his/her place in the world. The arts, entertainment, festivals, politics, everything throbs with youthful energy. East Berlin, the capital of the German Democratic Republic, got over that when the Wall went up in 1961. Many of the two million West Berliners have found safe roles as consumers but there's a large counterculture community nurtured by young West Germans who come to the city to escape military service.

Whipped into a frenzy by the Nazis, then bombed and pillaged by the Allies, used as a pawn in the Cold War and cut in half by the Wall, it's not hard to understand why Berlin is full of contradictions. The west side of the Wall is deliberately left ugly and even the art and graffiti cannot lighten the sombre mood.

The United States treasures West Berlin as an embarrassment to the 'Communists' and, with the Soviets, enjoys seeing the Germans faced off. Like Hong Kong, West Berlin seems to serve the purposes of both sides and only young radicals want to rock the boat. Yet Berlin fulfils a valuable role in promoting contacts between the two Germanys. Here east meets west as nowhere else.

There's so much happening in West Berlin and so much to see that you'll only scratch the surface. The list of museums, monuments, memorials, art galleries and

exhibitions is endless. Keep in mind that this city is more appealing on the inside than on the outside. To really understand what it's all about takes time. A lot of people come to Berlin thinking of it only as a gateway to Eastern Europe, which of course it is. A few of them never get past the door.

Facts about the City

HISTORY

The first recorded settlement on the site was a place named Colln (1237) on Museum Island in what is now East Berlin. Medieval Berlin developed on the opposite bank of the Spree River near present St Nicholas Church and spread north-east to Alexander Platz. In 1432 these Hanseatic trading centres on the route from Magdeburg to Poznan were merged.

In 1442 and 1448 elector Friedrich II of Brandenburg conquered the previously independent city and established the rule of the Hohenzollern dynasty, which lasted until 1918. Berlin's importance increased in 1470 when the elector established his residence here and built a palace where the Palace of the Republic (in East Berlin) is today. Courtiers replaced merchants as the dominant social class. In 1539 the Protestant Reformation took hold. During the devastating Thirty Years War (1618-1648) Berlin lost half its population, but this was partly made up by thousands of Huguenot refugees fleeing religious persecution in France. Strong fortifications were built between 1658 and 1683.

Throughout the 17th and 18th centuries Prussia expanded eastward at the expense of Poland. In 1701 Frederick I made Berlin capital of the kingdom. Between 1648 and 1800 the population jumped from 6000 to 150,000. By 1734 the city had grown so large that the city walls had to be razed. The imposing restored palaces along Unter den Linden (in present East Berlin) went up in the 18th century as Frederick II (The Great) embellished Berlin.

The 19th century began badly with a French occupation from 1806 to 1813. In 1848 a democratic revolution was suppressed, stifling political development. Capitalism flourished under the reactionary regime which followed and Berlin grew into the 'largest tenement city in the world.' From 1850 to 1870 the population doubled as the Industrial Revolution took hold. In 1871 Bismarck united Germany into the Second Reich under Kaiser Wilhelm I making Berlin an Imperial city and the population continued to soar. By 1890 the population was 1,600,000, passing two million in 1905. The masses of immigrant workers lived under the worst conditions imaginable.

The years leading up to WW I saw Berlin become an industrial giant, but power was concentrated in the hands of an autocracy which blundered into WW I. The senseless wartime violence and the example of the Russian Revolution led to revolt throughout Germany. On 9 November 1918 Philipp Scheidemann, leader of the Social Democrats, proclaimed the German republic from a balcony of the Reichstag. A few hours later Karl Liebknecht proclaimed a Free Socialist Republic from a balcony of the Berlin City Palace. In January 1919 the Berlin Spartacists Karl Liebknecht and Rosa Luxemburg were murdered by remnants of the old Imperial army which entered the city and drowned the revolution in blood. Yet all through the golden years of the 1920s, while the bourgeois politicians debated at Weimar, Berlin remained the avant-garde cultural focus of Germany.

On the eve of the Nazi takeover the Communist Party under Ernst Thalmann was the strongest single party in 'Red Berlin,' polling 31% of the votes in 1932. Although Munich spawned the Nazi movement Hitler made Berlin its political centre. Beginning in February 1933 the opposition was crushed by brute force. All freely elected bodies were dissolved in 1934. Unable to turn back Germany marched toward disaster.

The results of Hitler's vicious plans for enslaving Europe came home to Berlin in the form of Anglo-American bombings. During the 'Battle of Berlin' from November 1943 to March 1944 British bombers made 35 major attacks on the city. Most of the pre-war buildings one sees today in downtown East Berlin, including almost all of Unter den Linden, had to be reconstructed from empty shells. A valiant attempt by German officers to overthrow the dictatorship on 20 July 1944 failed and between 180 and 200 of those involved were executed by the Nazis, 89 of them at the Plotzensee prison in Berlin. The 18,500 Soviet soldiers buried in Berlin remind us of the last terrible battle which raged in the city until 2 May 1945 when the Soviet Army took Berlin by storm, bringing the fascist madness and WW II abruptly to an end.

In August 1945, the Potsdam Conference sealed the fate of the city by agreeing that each power would occupy a separate zone. In June 1948 the city was split in two when the three Allies introduced West German currency and established a separate administration in the western sectors. The Soviets blockaded West Berlin because of this, but an airlift kept the city in the American camp as a 'bridgehead' for the destabilisation of Eastern Europe.

In October 1949 East Berlin became capital of the German Democratic Republic, an integral part of East Germany. Construction of the Wall in August 1961 was almost inevitable as East Germany could no longer support the drain of skilled labour lured west by higher wages. Between 1945 and 1961 some three million East Germans left.

The Wall is largely a result of West German refusal to recognise the German Democratic Republic as a sovereign state. As it is, any East German who 'escapes' through the Wall is given a West German passport the next day and never has to repay his/her education nor any of the other benefits of socialism. Since 1985 about 10,000 East Germans a year have been allowed to legally immigrate to the west. Women over 60 and men over 65 may freely leave for visits. Upon arrival in West Berlin they collect DM 100 'welcome money,' are given pensions and free public transportation. The Federal Republic is happy to pay this price to maintain the pretence that there is only one Germany.

The 1971 Quadripartite Agreement, a product of detente, institutionalised the status quo in Berlin, especially the normal functioning of the transit routes. The agreement also conceded that West Berlin was not part of the Federal Republic of Germany and that the West German parliament would no longer meet in the city.

Since both sides will only agree to the reunification of city and country on their own terms, the division no one wanted seems to have become permanent. Yet the Basic Law of the Federal Republic of Germany declares that Germany is one, preventing West German politicians from coming to grips with reality. During the 1970s most western governments recognised the GDR and opened embassies in East

Berlin. Without a constitutional amendment the Federal Republic is unable to do this, although they have a permanent representation office in East Berlin.

GOVERNMENT

West Berlin is still officially under occupation law and not a part of West Germany. Signs you see proclaiming American, British and French zones are not just there for the tourists. The three western Allies can overrule court decisions, remove elected officials and declare martial law as they please. Each May the three Allies stage a military parade on Strasse des 17 Juni as a show of strength. It's forbidden to demonstrate against this parade. Only West Berlin's status as an occupied territory guarantees access to the city from West Germany. If the three Allies were to turn West Berlin over to the Federal Republic the GDR could make formal recognition the price of continued access.

The West German representatives at Bundeshaus, Bundesallee 216-218 (U-Bahn – Spichern Strasse), have no executive power in West Berlin. Yet the city is incorporated into the legal, financial and economic systems of the Federal Republic and West Berliners carry West German passports. West Berliners cannot use a West German passport issued in West Berlin to travel in Eastern Europe, however. Their *Berliner Ausweis* is required. The ambiguity is part of the tightrope Germany has had to walk since 1945. West Berlin has deputies with limited voting rights in the West German parliament.

A local government exists by the grace of the three Allies. There's a popularly elected parliament (Abgeordnetenhaus) which in turn appoints a mayor and 16 senators who act as government ministers. Parliament and the senate meet at Rathaus Schoneberg. There are four main political parties: the Christian Democratic Union (conservatives), the Social Democratic Party (moderate socialists), the

Alternative List (environmentalists) and the Free Democratic Party (liberals). Until 1981 the SPD was the dominant party but the CDU has since overtaken it. The FDP usually joins the governing party in a coalition. Federal Republic subsidies account for half the Berlin budget. West Berlin is also divided into 12 independently-run boroughs. Any Berlin government which seriously displeased the three Allies could be removed by them at will.

An Allied Control Council of the four Allies (including the Soviets) meets in the former Prussian Supreme Court (1913), Potsdamer Strasse 186 (U-Bahn – Kleist Park). Only 30 of the 486 rooms in this huge building are actually in use. Around the corner at Pallas Strasse 30 is a gigantic Nazi bunker, one of 67 in West Berlin. In 1988 this was restored as an air raid shelter by the West Berlin government at a cost of DM 10 million. Considering that the only immediate function of the Control Council is the maintenance of air security over Berlin it's rather unfortunate that they should be the best protected.

PEOPLE

Berlin is the largest city in Germany. West Berlin with two million inhabitants occupies 480 square km, while 1.1 million people live in East Berlin (403 square km). A fifth of the people in West Berlin are pensioners. Prior to the building of the Wall some 60,000 East Berlin workers held jobs in West Berlin and crossed daily. Once the border was closed their places were taken by immigrants. There are a quarter million non-German residents of West Berlin, about half of them Turkish. The others are mostly Yugoslavs, Poles, Greeks and Italians. More than a quarter of the population of Kreuzberg is foreign. In addition 6000 American, 3000 British and 3000 French troops and dependants are present.

ECONOMY

West Berlin's importance as a contact point between east and west is paralleled by its role in European trade and commerce. Congresses, conventions, fairs and similar gatherings are constantly taking place here. West Berlin is the largest industrial centre between Paris and Moscow, especially in electronics, food processing, machinery and chemicals. High tech industries such as data processing, communications, research and environmental engineering are growing quickly.

The exceptional political and geographical situation of West Berlin has been both a disadvantage and a strength. Since most of West Berlin's trade is with West Germany the Federal Republic pays the GDR some DM 525 million a year for use of the transit routes. Only 2% of West Berlin's exports and 7% of imports flow to and from the German Democratic Republic. The local economy is heavily subsidised by West Germany but the cost of living remains high. To compensate for this everyone in West Berlin gets a tax-exempt 8% cash supplement to their gross income courtesy of the Federal Republic.

GEOGRAPHY

West Berlin, in the centre of Europe halfway between Amsterdam and Warsaw, is a 38-by-45-km capitalist island in a socialist sea. The 1945 partition sliced through the centre of the city placing the entire old town in the eastern sector. While much of East Berlin was rebuilt in concrete after the war the old residential neighbourhoods of West Berlin still have a turn of the century air. Crowded Kreuzberg is a counterculture/Turkish ghetto, while the spacious suburbs out toward the Grunewald Forest are strictly upper class.

The area presently comprising East and West Berlin only amalgamated in 1920 when eight towns, 59 villages and 27 landed estates were joined to form a single municipality. Towns like Tegel, Spandau, Kladow, Wannsee, Kopenick and Friedrichshagen maintain their separate identities until today.

Situated on the great plain of the northern German lowlands, roughly a third of West Berlin is made up of parks, forests, lakes and rivers. Berlin has more trees than Paris and more bridges than Venice. Much of this natural beauty of rolling hills and quiet shorelines is in the western half of West Berlin. Most of the people live in the half closest to East Berlin, as one would expect in a city cut in two.

The Spree River crosses West Berlin from the Reichstag to Spandau, where it joins the Havel River. North and south of Spandau the Havel widens into a series of lakes from Tegel to Potsdam. The lakes were gouged out by glaciers during the last Ice Age, the surrounding hills being formed from the debris as terminal moraines. From Potsdam the Havel flows on into the Elbe and past Hamburg before reaching the North Sea.

A dense network of canals links the other waterways. The Westhafen between the Tiergarten and Tegel Airport was once a much busier port than it is today. There are beautiful walks along some of the canals, such as the Landwehrkanal in Kreuzberg (U-Bahn – Hallesches Tor).

RELIGION

Sixty percent of West Berliners are Lutherans, 12.5% Catholics. The Catholic bishop in East Berlin includes West Berlin in his diocese. The Lutheran churches in the two Berlins are separated into Eastern and Western regions sharing a common church charter. Most Turkish Berliners are Muslim and some 17% of West Berliners profess no religion.

In 1933 there were 160,000 Jews in Berlin. Some 6500 live in West Berlin today. The Jewish Community Centre on Fasanen Strasse occupies the site of a synagogue burned in 1938.

FESTIVALS & HOLIDAYS

Aside from all the regular entertainment

West Berlin organises festivals with a vengeance. In February or March there's the International Film Festival, followed by the Theatre Meet in May. Then there's the Berlin Festival Weeks in September and the Jazz Fest in October or November. Tickets to these events sell out fast so write the Berliner Festspiele GmbH (tel 030-254890), Budapester Strasse 50, 1000 Berlin 30, a couple of months in advance if it's important to you to attend. If you're in Berlin in March don't miss the International Tourism Exchange at the Fairgrounds where you can learn about worldwide travel possibilities. Summertime borough street fairs and festivals are announced in the fortnightly entertainment magazines *Tip* and *Zitty*.

Public holidays in West Berlin include New Years Day (1 January), Easter Friday and Monday (around April, variable), May Day (1 May), Ascension Day (around May, variable), Pentecost (around June, variable), Memorial Day (17 June), Cemetery Day (3rd Wednesday in November) and Christmas (25 and 26 December).

LANGUAGE

Berlin is so well organised that once you understand the system it's possible to get around without saying anything to anyone. When you do need help there's almost always someone nearby who knows a little English. Hostel, theatre, travel agency and ride service staff invariably speak English, as do many persons working in shops, restaurants, bars, etc. Most young Berliners speak good English. Even a few words of broken German makes contact easier however.

In reading signs and consulting indexes be aware of the German umlaut accents ä (ae), ö (oe) and ü (ue), as well as a capital B with a tail used in the middle or at the end of a word to represent 'ss'. These accents are not used in this book but they do appear in all printed materials in German.

To assist English speakers in recognising long German place names quickly we've separated the words *strasse* and *platz* from the names of streets and squares. The commonly abbreviated *str* has been spelled out. While German books and signs would always read Kurfurstenstr and Alexanderplatz, we put Kurfursten Strasse and Alexander Platz.

Facts for the Visitor

VISAS

Theoretically the entry requirements are the same as those of West Germany. Unless you're a citizen of a Third World country you probably don't require a visa for a stay of up to three months. In practice you don't pass any West German customs and immigration controls as you enter West Berlin by mass transit. Perhaps the West German government feels the GDR does such a good job checking that anything more would be superfluous. Potential immigrants from the Middle East, Africa and Asia often take advantage of the situation to use West Berlin as a stepping stone to West Germany. All non-Germans require a passport to pass through East Germany. Transit visas (DM 5) are issued at the border. Remember that West Berlin is under occupation law and you're required to carry your passport at all times.

MONEY

US$1 = DM 1.85 (Deutsche Mark)

no compulsory exchange

The West German mark (DM) is the currency, divided into 100 pfennig (Pf). Credit cards are not widely used in West Berlin. Cash is the preferred means of payment. There are no restrictions on the import or export of cash or travellers' cheques.

A commission of DM 3 to DM 10 (ask first!) is charged every time you change foreign currency into German marks. If you know for sure you'll be visiting West Berlin buy some travellers' cheques expressed in German marks before you leave home. No commission is charged to cash a DM travellers' cheque and you don't have to worry about currency fluctuations.

If you'll be going on into Eastern Europe from West Berlin you'll need a supply of cash dollars or marks in small bills to cover petty expenditures which must be paid in western currency. A couple of hundred marks in 10s and 20s should suffice. Don't neglect to take care of this as travellers' cheques are usually not accepted to pay for visas, international railway tickets, duty free goods, etc.

Currencies of the socialist countries may be purchased at banks and exchange offices in West Berlin at considerable discounts but it's strictly forbidden to take this money into East Germany.

BOOKS & BOOKSHOPS

There's a Baedeker guide to Berlin in English. If you'll be spending some time in Berlin and read German the *Merian reisefuhrer, Berlin* (Deutscher Taschenbuch Verlag, Munich) is both comprehensive and selective. *Berlin ein Handbuch* by Loose, Mlyneck and Ramp (Michael Muller Verlag, Erlangen, 1988) is more oriented to the alternative scene. The best map of West Berlin is the indexed *Falkplan Berlin*.

The *Berlin Art Guide* by Irene Blumenfeld (Art Guide Publications, London, 1986) will lead you through the world of private art galleries in West Berlin. Unfortunately East Berlin only rates a six-page list of museums and theatres tacked on at the end.

Zoo Station, Adventures in East & West Berlin by Ian Walker (Atlantic Monthly Press, New York, 1987) is the account of a young man's odyssey through two Berlins. Walker explores West

Berlin's hip demimonde and East Berlin's dissident mood in the company of friends from both sides of the Wall. A fascinating glimpse of the counterculture scene.

For paperbacks in English try the Marga Schoeller Bucherstube, Knesebeck Strasse 33-34. They carry mostly fiction. There are two travel bookstores in West Berlin: Kiepert, Knesebeck Strasse 2 at Hardenberg Strasse (U-Bahn – Ernst Reuter Platz), and Schropp, Potsdamer Strasse 100 (U-Bahn – Kurfursten Strasse). They have maps and German guidebooks to almost everywhere.

NEWSPAPERS & MEDIA

In 1928 there were 147 political newspapers published in Berlin, more than any other city in the world. By 1939 the Nazis had reduced this to 29. There are now six daily German language newspapers in Berlin, the most independent of which are the *Tagesspiegel* and *Die Tageszeitung* (the 'taz'). Of special interest to visitors are the fortnightly magazines *Tip* and *Zitty* which cover virtually everything that's happening on the entertainment scene, both alternative and mainstream, in the two Berlins. The magazines come out on alternate weeks so one or the other should suffice for your stay. Although in German they're easy to follow. Surprisingly, no English newspaper or magazine is published in West Berlin.

FILM & PHOTOGRAPHY

Stock up on film in West Berlin, especially if you have any special needs. Kodak film is almost unobtainable in Eastern Europe, so buy it here. It's also relatively cheap to have your film processed in West Berlin.

There aren't many restrictions concerning photography in West Berlin. The Wall, the world's biggest outdoor art show, is a favourite subject and it's also fun to snap shots of East German border guards from wooden observation towers placed safely on the West Berlin side. For more excitement take the U-Bahn to

Oskar-Helene-Heim and train your camera on United States Headquarters, Clayallee 170. Unless you've got a Soviet passport the worst that can happen is that you'll lose your film and the experience will deepen your understanding of West Berlin.

GENERAL INFORMATION
Post

The West German post office is very fast and reliable, and very expensive. Aerogrammes take DM 1.40 to anywhere but you have to buy them in stationery shops. You can save by mailing all your postcards from East Berlin where postage is much cheaper. If you'd like to receive mail in West Berlin have it sent c/o your consulate or Poste Restante, Postamt Bahnhof Zoo, D-1000 Berlin 12, Germany. Such mail can be picked up at counter nine in the Zoo Station post office, but you'll have to show your passport. Public telephones in West Berlin take 20 pfennig and work well. To call East Berlin from West Berlin (20 pfennig) add the prefix 0372 to the number. From East Berlin to West Berlin the prefix is 849.

Electricity

220 volts AC.

Time

West Berlin is on Central European Time (Greenwich Mean Time plus one hour), the same time used from Madrid to Warsaw. Daylight Saving Time comes into effect at the end of March when clocks are turned one hour forward. At the end of September they're turned an hour back again.

Business Hours

Banking hours are weekdays 9 am to 1 pm. Most banks also open two afternoons a week but the days and times vary from bank to bank. Post offices are open weekdays 8 am to 6 pm, Saturday 8 am to 12 noon. Shops are generally open from 9 am to 6.30 pm weekdays and 9 am to 2 pm

Saturday, although most stay open until 6 pm the first Saturday of each month.

INFORMATION

For advance tourist information on West Berlin and/or hotel reservations write: Verkehrsamt Berlin, Europa Centre, D-1000 Berlin 30. Information on the political status of Berlin is available from: Informationszentrum Berlin, D-1000 Berlin 12, Hardenberg Strasse 20. For festival tickets write: Berliner Festspiele GmbH, D-1000 Berlin 30, Budapester Strasse 48. For information on exhibitions, trade fairs and congresses write: Ausstellungs Messe Kongress Gmbh, D-1000 Berlin 19, Messedamm 22.

ACCOMMODATION

Although you can always find a place to stay in West Berlin it won't necessarily be cheap. Hotel prices begin at DM 35 single, DM 60 double, and soon rise to DM 75 single, DM 145 double. Instead of the few huge luxury hotels one finds in East Berlin, West Berlin is characterised by a large number of smaller establishments. The least expensive are the 'hotel pensionen' and 'pensionen' which usually have only about 25 beds. The tourist offices in the railway station or Europa Centre will find you a hotel room, or just pick up a list and start calling. Some include a light breakfast of tea or coffee, bread, butter and jam in the rate.

An alternative to staying at a hotel is a youth hostel which will cost around DM 20 for bed and breakfast. Priority is given to those under age 27, although the hostels are open to anyone. You have to be an IYHF member or pay DM 20 for a guest card. The hostels fill up fast in summer and until early July they're often full up with noisy school groups. Make advance reservations or telephone before going out to the hostel. If you have a tent there are several campgrounds where you'll pay only DM 6.40 per person plus DM 5 per tent. They're far from the centre and may also be full, so call first.

It's possible but not cheaper to stay at a hotel in East Berlin instead of West Berlin. Prices begin at DM 48 single and soon jump into the luxury category. The easiest way to arrange this is go to the Interflug office below Bahnsteig B in Friedrich Strasse Railway Station. This office is on the West Berlin side of the passport controls and you can get there on the West Berlin transit system. The Service Buro at Interflug (open weekdays 8 am to 9 pm, weekends 9 am to 5 pm, closed for lunch from 12 noon to 1 pm daily) will call around until they find you a room, be it in East Berlin, Potsdam or anywhere else in the GDR. You then pay West German marks for a hotel voucher which will allow you to enter East Germany on a tourist visa without any additional formalities. In summer this office can grant you a camping visa for East Berlin or elsewhere at DM 25 a day. Having made such arrangements you are exempt from compulsory currency exchange in East Germany.

FOOD & DRINK

There's a restaurant for every cuisine under the sun in West Berlin, some 6000 of them. Most restaurants post their menu outside and daily specials are listed on a blackboard. A cooked lunch or dinner at an unpretentious West Berlin restaurant will run DM 15 if you order carefully. The price includes tax and service. Tipping is not obligatory although you can round your bill up to the next higher mark. Do this as you pay rather than leave money on the table. Lunch is the main meal of the day in Germany.

At those prices it's unlikely you'll wish to sit down to a meal more than once a day. Substantial snacks are available at the many *schnell imbiss* stands around the city. In addition to German standbys like *rostbratwurst* and *currywurst* most *imbiss* also have *doner kebab*, a filling Turkish sandwich of veal cut from a rotating gyro and stuffed into a big piece of pita bread with lots of salad. One of these with a can of beer shouldn't cost over five marks. Many *imbiss* also offer half barbecued chickens (DM 5).

The most famous traditional Berlin dish is *Eisbein mit Sauerkraut*, a huge, fatty knuckle of pork with pickled cabbage. *Boulette*, a big meatball containing breadcrumbs which you literally drown in mustard, was introduced by Huguenot immigrants in the 17th century. Or try Berlin liver cooked with onions and apple.

Breakfast cafes are a Berlin institution catering to the city's late risers. As they serve breakfast till 2 pm they're also good for lunch. Foreign restaurants are more common than German and the choice is endless. Among the best are the many unpretentious Greek restaurants which serve good food at reasonable prices. Yugoslavian establishments are fewer but similar.

German beer is famous and a German specialty is *weizenbier* which is made with wheat instead of hops and served in a tall half litre glass with a slice of lemon. *Berliner Weisse* or 'white beer' is a foaming low alcohol wheat beer with red or green fruit juice syrup added.

One Berlin treat to get acquainted with right away is a hot cup of 70 pfennig coffee dispensed by a coin-operated machine at many *Eduscho* and *Tchibo* outlets around West Berlin. You have to drink standing up and this deal isn't offered evenings or weekends (even though the shop itself may be open), but the throngs of local people tell you you're onto something good. Cookies, cakes and rolls are also sold. You'll soon learn to recognise the Eduscho and Tchibo trademarks from afar, but not all outlets offer this service.

Getting There & Away

TRAIN
There are direct trains to West Berlin from Hamburg (via Buchen), Hannover (via Helmstedt), Frankfurt am Main (via Bebra) and Munich (via Hof or Probstzella). Some trains on the Helmstedt-Berlin line are travelling between points as far apart as Paris, Oostende, Hoek van Holland, Warsaw and Moscow. Westbound all of these trains either begin at or pass through Friedrich Strasse Railway Station in East Berlin. There's also a boat train to Copenhagen (via Warnemunde) which originates at Zoo Station.

Eurail and Inter-Rail passes are not valid for the two-hour train trip from West Germany to West Berlin. Your pass will take you as far as Helmstedt, West Germany, where a separate ticket is required. You can purchase this in advance for DM 43 at any railway ticket office in West Germany.

Trains between Poland and Western Europe pass through West Berlin so you can get on or off at Zoo Station. Trains to Berlin from Czechoslovakia and Hungary, however, terminate at Lichtenberg Railway Station in East Berlin. From Berlin-Lichtenberg take the S-Bahn to Berlin-Friedrich Strasse where you enter West Berlin. Railway fares to Berlin are much cheaper from Eastern European cities than from Western Europe.

Train tickets to Berlin are valid for all railway stations in the city *(Stadtbahn)* which means that on arrival you may use the S-Bahn (but not the U-Bahn) network on both sides of the border to proceed to your destination on the same ticket.

BUS
Buses to West Berlin from Western Europe are a lot cheaper than trains. In Hannover contact Cebu-Reise-Centre (tel 0511-321777), Bahnhof Strasse 1. In Frankfurt am Main the bus to West Berlin leaves in the morning three times a week from bay seven in the bus station at the main railway station. In Munich bus tickets to West Berlin (DM 108, daily) are available from Bayern Express (tel 089-224457), Maximilians Platz 18.

There's a bus (90 Dutch guilders) twice a week between Amsterdam and West Berlin. This bus connects in Amsterdam with buses to and from London. In Amsterdam contact Budget Bus (tel 275151), Rokin 10. In London enquire at the Victoria Coach Station.

RIDE SERVICES

Aside from hitching the cheapest way to get to West Berlin from Western Europe is as a paying passenger in a private car. Such rides are arranged by *mitfahrzentrale* in all West German cities. You pay a reservation fee to the agency and your share of petrol to the driver. The local tourist information office will be able to direct you to a couple of such offices.

Eurostop operates a chain of 70 lift centres in seven different countries, including Amsterdam (Nieuwezijds Voorburgwal 256, tel 020-224342), Brussels (Marche-aux-Herbes 27, tel 02-5121015), London (Grant Place 56, tel 00441-6543210), Paris (84 Passage Brady, tel 1-42460066 or 47704670), Zurich (Fierzgasse 16, tel 01-422300), Vienna (Daungasse 1a, tel 0222-4370092), Montreal (4317, Rue St Denis, tel 514-2820121) and Milan (Via Col di Lana 14, tel 02-8320543), among others.

West Berlin

The city of West Berlin is contiguous with the political entity of West Berlin as described in this chapter.

Orientation

At some point you're sure to pass through Bahnhof Zoologischer Garten (Zoo Station) in central West Berlin. This main line station contains coin lockers (DM 2), a post office open 24 hours a day and a tourist information office which makes hotel reservations. The currency exchange office of the Deutsche Verkehrs-Kredit Bank (open until 9 pm Monday to Saturday, 6 pm Sunday) is just outside.

The ruin of Kaiser Wilhelm Memorial Church on Breitscheid Platz, a block away from Zoo Station, is your best central reference point. The tourist office and hundreds of shops are in the Europa Centre at the end of the square farthest away from the station. Kurfurstendamm (Ku'damm), West Berlin's most fashionable avenue, runs south-west from Breitscheid Platz.

North-east between Breitscheid Platz and East Berlin is the Tiergarten, a vast city park which was once a royal hunting domain. The Berlin Wall cuts south through the city from the Reichstag to the desolation of Potsdamer Platz where it swings east past Checkpoint Charlie to Kreuzberg, a counterculture centre.

Other important names to learn are Schoneberg, Dahlem, Charlottenburg, Tegel, Spandau and Wannsee, places you may visit at one time or another. While in West Berlin keep in mind that the street numbers usually (but not always) go up one side of the street and down the other. Also, there's sometimes more than one street with the same name. In such cases assume that the one referred to in this book is in Charlottenburg, the city centre. Be aware too that a continuous street may change names several times as it goes along. And watch out for speeding cycles on bike routes down the sidewalk!

Information

Tourist Information The Berlin Tourist Information Office (Verkehrsamt Berlin), Budapester Strasse 45 by the Europa Centre, is open daily from 7.30 am to 10.30 pm. In addition to supplying brochures and answering questions they'll find you a hotel room (although not the cheapest) for a DM 3 commission. Ask for a copy of their brochure *Tips fur Jugendliche Berlin-Besucher* which lists most budget accommodation.

The Informationszentrum, 2nd floor, Hardenberg Strasse 20 behind the

Deutsche Bundesbahn ticket office (weekdays 8 am to 7 pm, Saturday 8 am to 4 pm), is less oriented toward consumer tourism. They supply two excellent free booklets in English: *Berlin for Young People* and *Berlin - Outlook*. Although stimulating the booklets only tell half the story, presenting the official, bureaucratic viewpoint. The attendants at this office are especially good at answering questions about the political status of West Berlin, so don't be shy.

If you want to make contact with West Berlin's political counterculture try the cafe (closed Saturday) in the rear courtyard at Mehringhof, Gneisenau Strasse 2 (U-Bahn - Mehringdamm). Many alternative groups meet in this building. A green board on the main gate lists the times.

Banks American Express on Breitscheid Platz cash their own travellers' cheques without charging commission, but they give a lousy rate. If you're changing over US$20 you'll probably do better going to a bank and paying the standard DM 3 to DM 10 commission.

If you're embarking on a major trip through Eastern Europe you'll need lots of small denomination travellers' cheques. American Express in West Berlin will break their US$100 or US$50 travellers' cheques down into US$20s at no additional charge, the *only* place in the region where this can be done.

The Europa Centre Wechselstube, by the fountain on the opposite side of Breitscheid Platz from American Express, buys and sells banknotes of all countries without any commission charge. They give a better rate than the bank at Zoo Station.

Travel Agencies Travel agencies offering cheap flights advertise in the *Reisen* classified section of *Zitty*. The best of these is Alternativ Tours (tel 8812089), Wilmersdorfer Strasse 94 (U-Bahn - Adenauer Platz). They specialise in

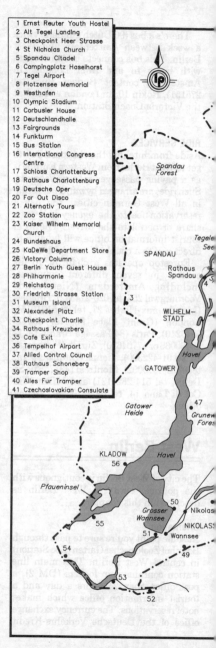

1 Ernst Reuter Youth Hostel
2 Alt Tegel Landing
3 Checkpoint Heer Strasse
4 St Nicholas Church
5 Spandau Citadel
6 Campingplatz Haselhorst
7 Tegel Airport
8 Plotzensee Memorial
9 Westhafen
10 Olympic Stadium
11 Corbusier House
12 Deutschlandhalle
13 Fairgrounds
14 Funkturm
15 Bus Station
16 International Congress Centre
17 Schloss Charlottenburg
18 Rathaus Charlottenburg
19 Deutsche Oper
20 Far Out Disco
21 Alternativ Tours
22 Zoo Station
23 Kaiser Wilhelm Memorial Church
24 Bundeshaus
25 KaDeWe Department Store
26 Victory Column
27 Berlin Youth Guest House
28 Philharmonie
29 Reichstag
30 Friedrich Strasse Station
31 Museum Island
32 Alexander Platz
33 Checkpoint Charlie
34 Rathaus Kreuzberg
35 Cafe Exit
36 Tempelhof Airport
37 Allied Control Council
38 Rathaus Schoneberg
39 Tramper Shop
40 Alles Fur Tramper
41 Czechoslovakian Consulate

West Berlin

0   2.5   5 km

42 Botanical Gardens
43 Dahlem Museum
44 Polish Consulate
45 Grunewald Hunting Lodge
46 United States Headquarters
47 Grunewald Tower
48 Hungarian Consulate
49 Checkpoint Dreilinden
50 Wannsee Youth Guest House
51 Wannsee Landing
52 Campingplatz Dreilinden
53 Campingplatz Kohlhasenbruck
54 Glienicker Brucke
55 Pfaueninsel Landing
56 Kladow Landing

unpublished, discounted tickets to anywhere in the world. Many of their flights leave from Amsterdam and you may do better waiting to buy your ticket there, although not always.

The main office of Interflug, the East German carrier, is upstairs below Bahnsteig B in Friedrich Strasse Railway Station (on the West Berlin side of the passport controls). They offer bargain fares out of Schonefeld Airport, such as DM 372 one way to Tunis, DM 574 one way to Cairo, DM 725 one way to Singapore and DM 825 one way to Beijing, China. Any travel agent in West Berlin can also book these flights.

ARTU, Hardenberg Strasse 9 near Zoo Station, offers flights at student (age 35 or less) or youth (age 25 or less) fares. They also sell the IUS student card (DM 7 and one photo) which will save you money in Eastern Europe. Transalpino, Budapester Strasse 46 on Breitscheid Platz, sells discount railway tickets to those under 26 plus cheap flights.

The Deutsches Reiseburo (DER), Kurfurstendamm 17, sells an Ameripass for unlimited Greyhound bus travel in North America, the only place in Berlin you can get them. This pass is much cheaper when purchased in Europe.

Tour Companies West Berlin is one of the best places to book package tours to the Soviet Union, available year round. Fares are relatively low because the groups fly out of East Berlin on Aeroflot and Interflug flights. Your Intourist guide will speak only German, but the tours are open to everyone. You must book at least three weeks in advance. Companies organising the trips include Intratours (tel 249079), Bayreuther Strasse 7-8, Intourist Reisen (tel 880077), Olivaer Platz 8, Olympia Reisen (tel 884282), Schluter Strasse 44, and Hansa Tourist (tel 882051), Kurfurstendamm 67. Intratours is especially recommended.

Western Consulates The Canadian Consulate is on the 12th floor of the Europa Centre (weekdays 9 am to 12 noon). The British Consulate-General, Uhland Strasse 7-8, opens weekdays 9 am to 12 noon and 2 to 4 pm. The US Consulate (tel 8195523, weekdays 8.30 am to 1 pm) was recently at Tempelhof Airport but may be relocated as security is tightened up, so call first.

Eastern Consulates Trying to pick up visas in West Berlin for the socialist countries is bad news. The consulates are inconveniently located in the posh suburbs south-west of downtown, far from one another. It's cheaper, faster and easier to collect these visas in East Berlin.

Definitely avoid the Polish Consulate, Richard Strauss Strasse 11 (bus No 19 from the Ku'damm, open Monday, Tuesday, Thursday and Friday 9 am to 1 pm). Huge crowds press into this tiny basement office (tourist visas DM 38 with a two-week wait). Polen Reisedienst nearby at Lassen Strasse 9 offers better service, but for arranging a standard tourist visa they want DM 60 if you can wait two weeks, DM 92 with a one-week wait. They require you to prepay a voucher for every day of your stay in Poland at DM 36 a day.

The Czech Consulate, Podbielskiallee 54 (U-Bahn – Podbielskiallee, weekdays 8.30 to 11 am), issues visas on the spot for DM 34 to DM 72, the price varying according to nationality. The Hungarian Consulate, Reiftragerweg 27-28 near Wannsee (S-Bahn – Schlachtensee, weekdays 9 am to 12 noon), also issues visas straight away for DM 35.

Things to See

City Centre The stark ruins of neo-Romanesque **Kaiser Wilhelm Memorial Church** (1895) in Breitscheid Platz, engulfed in the roaring commercialism all round, marks the heart of rebuilt West Berlin. The British bombing attack of 22 November 1943 left standing only the broken west tower. The former entry hall below the tower and the modern church (1961) may be visited.

By the Globe Fountain next to the tower assorted street artists and musicians play to the crowd. Just beyond rises the gleaming **Europa Centre** with a rotating Mercedes symbol on top. You can pay DM 2.50 to stand on the 20th floor observation deck but you can get a view almost as good for free from the 18th floor. North-east of the Europa Centre on Budapester Strasse is the elephant gate to West Berlin's **aquarium and zoo**, but it's a stiff DM 10.50 to see both (open daily).

Tiergarten Cultural Centre Some real architectural treats await you east of downtown on the way to the Wall. From the zoo continue east on Budapester Strasse to the Inter-Continental Hotel, then follow the Landwehrkanal to the **Museum for Design**, Klingelhofer Strasse 13-14 (closed Tuesday, admission DM 3, free Monday). This museum dedicated to the Bauhaus movement (1919-1933), which laid the basis for much contemporary architecture, is housed in a building designed by its founder, Walter Gropius.

Further east along the canal is the Bewag building (1932). Nearby is the **New National Gallery**, Potsdamer Strasse 50 (closed Monday, permanent collection free, special exhibitions DM 6), with 19th and 20th century paintings. This sleek ultramodern gallery (1968) is a creation of the famous architect Mies van der Rohe. The new **State Library** (closed Sunday) across the street, the largest library in Germany, contains reading, periodical and exhibition rooms.

The striking **Philharmonie** (1963) by Hans Scharoun is unique in that the orchestra is completely surrounded by rows of seats. Beside it is a matching Chamber Music Hall. The **Musical Instruments Museum**, Tiergarten Strasse 1 beside the Philharmonie (closed Monday, free), has a rich collection beautifully displayed. The **Museum of Arts & Crafts** (1985), Tiergarten Strasse 6 on the opposite side of the Philharmonie (closed Monday, free), houses precious objects from the Middle Ages to Art Deco. Red brick **St Matthew Church** (1846) stands amid the above buildings.

Along the Wall No one leaves Berlin without having a look at the notorious Wall. To see a relatively untouristed stretch of Wall take the U-Bahn to Schlesisches Tor and walk south-east to the end of Schlesische Strasse. The elevated U-Bahn line is actually cut here by the Wall as it crosses the Spree River. If you take Kopenicker Strasse north-west from the station you'll again bump into the Wall, which can be followed west to **Checkpoint Charlie**. Wooden observation platforms and graffiti along the way will keep you entertained.

Most tourists take the U-Bahn to Koch Strasse, the pedestrian crossing into East Berlin for foreign nationals. Trust free enterprise to come up with a Wall museum and the **Haus am Checkpoint Charlie** does brisk business (admission DM 3.50). Content yourself with the bizarre window display and save your money. The open fenced-off area opposite the Wall just west of Checkpoint Charlie is the site of the former SS/Gestapo headquarters, unpleasant reminders which the city saw fit to demolish. The **Martin Gropius Bau** (1881) next to this desolation is the venue of major exhibitions related to some aspect of life in Berlin (closed Monday, admission DM 8).

Continue along the Wall until you see the tour buses and souvenir stands. Here you can join the throng on a platform to stare into the no man's land behind the Wall which was **Potsdamer Platz**, once Berlin's busiest crossroads. It's said that Hitler shot himself in his bunker somewhere out there on 30 April 1945 as the Soviet Army closed in.

A km north along the Wall is the **Brandenburg Gate** (1791), a symbol of Berlin. From the platform here you get a peek down Unter den Linden into East

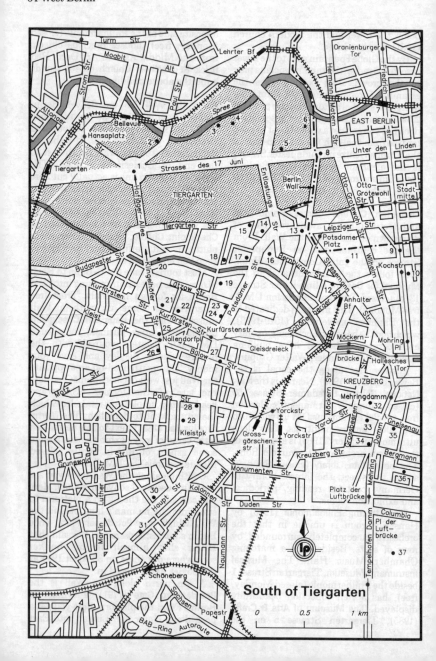

South of Tiergarten

1	Victory Column
2	Schloss Bellevue
3	Reederei Heinz Riedel
4	Kongresshalle
5	Soviet War Memorial
6	Reichstag
7	Friedrich Strasse Station
8	Brandenburg Gate
9	Checkpoint Charlie
10	Unemployment Office
11	Martin Gropius Bau
12	Jugendhotel International
13	Potsdamer Platz
14	Philharmonie
15	Museum of Arts & Crafts
16	State Library
17	New National Gallery
18	Bewag
19	Berlin Youth Guest House
20	Museum for Design
21	Zum Ambrosius Restaurant
22	Spatz Steakhouse
23	Schropp Bookstore
24	Made in Berlin Clothing
25	Flea Market
26	Metropol Disco
27	Turkish Bazar
28	Pallas Bunker
29	Allied Control Council
30	Empire International Disco
31	Odeon Theatre
32	Rathaus Kreuzberg
33	Riehmers Hofgarten Hotel
34	Mitwohnzentrale Kreuzberg
35	Mehringhof
36	Chamisso Platz
37	Tempelhof Airport

Berlin. The statue atop the gate was taken to Paris by Napoleon as a spoil of war, only to be returned to Berlin a few years later by the victorious Prussians. On the avenue near the gate is the **Soviet War Memorial** (1945), flanked by the first Russian tanks to enter Berlin. West Berlin police prevent visitors from approaching the memorial.

Up against the wall between the Brandenburg Gate and Spree River is the

Reichstag (1894). This imposing building served as the German parliament until it was burned by the Nazis on the night of 27-28 February 1933 as a pretext for rounding up their opponents. The restored Reichstag contains an excellent exhibition covering German history from 1800 to the present (closed Monday, admission free). Take a welcome rest in the projection room and watch free films (in German) on the Nazi period.

Tiergarten West Berlin's huge inner-city park, the Tiergarten, stretches west from the Wall toward Zoo Station. Once a private hunting ground of the prince electors, it became a park in the 18th century, in 1833-1838 it was landscaped with streams and lakes.

The **Kongresshalle** (1957) by the Spree River on the north side of the park is nicknamed the 'pregnant oyster' for its shape. The arched roof collapsed in 1980 but has since been rebuilt. Further east along the river is **Schloss Bellevue** (1785), built for Prince Ferdinand, brother of Frederick the Great and now an official residence of the President of West Germany. The **Victory Column** (1873), topped by a gilded statue of Victoria visible from much of the Tiergarten, commemorates 19th century Prussian military adventures. You may climb the 285 steps inside the column for a sweeping view (daily April to October, DM 1.20).

Charlottenburg Schloss Charlottenburg (1699), an exquisite Baroque palace on Spandauer Damm three km north-west of Zoo Station, was built as a country estate for Queen Sophie Charlotte (U-Bahn – Richard Wagner Platz or Sophie Charlotte Platz). Before the entrance is a Baroque equestrian statue of Sophie's husband, Frederick I (1700). Along the River Spree behind the palace are extensive French and English gardens (free admission), while inside the many buildings are an important group of museums. As most of the other palaces of the former kings of

Prussia are in Potsdam only Schloss Charlottenburg is easy to visit.

In the central building below the dome are the living quarters of Sophie and Frederick, which may only be seen with a German-speaking guide. The winter chambers of Frederick Wilhelm II, upstairs in the New Wing (1746) to the east, may be visited individually on the same ticket (closed Monday, admission DM 5.50). The **Romantic Art Collection** of the National Gallery is housed downstairs in this wing (closed Monday, free).

The combined palace ticket includes three buildings in the gardens. The **Schinkel Pavilion** (1825) was the summer house of Friedrick Wilhelm III. Further back by the river is the **Belvedere** (1790), a Rococo tea-house which now houses a collection of Berlin porcelain. The **Mausoleum** (1810) on the other side of the gardens contains the tombs of several kings and queens (closed in winter).

In addition to the above, three branches of the State Museum at Charlottenburg should not be missed (all closed Friday and free admission). The **Museum of Prehistory** occupies the west wing of the palace. Across the street at the beginning of Schloss Strasse are the Egyptian and Antiquities museums. The **Egyptian Museum** has a superb collection, including the 14th century BC bust of Queen Nefertiti from Tell el-Amarna. The **Museum of Antiquities** has objects from ancient Greece and Rome on four floors.

Huge crowds are often waiting for the guided tour of Charlottenburg Palace and it may be difficult to get a ticket. This being so content yourself with the facades, gardens and free museums. There's more than enough to see without paying.

West of the Centre Four km west of Zoo Station at a major crossroads is the **International Congress Centre** on Messedamm (U-Bahn – Kaiserdamm). This striking complex nicknamed *Das Superding* (The Super Thing) cost a billion German marks to erect in 1979. In the fairgrounds across the road from the ICC is the **Funkturm** (1926), a 138-metre-high tower you may ascend for DM 4. Only the police and taxi radios still use this tower.

Three stops west along the U-Bahn line is the **Olympic Stadium** (U-Bahn – Olympia-Stadion) where Hitler watched black American Jesse Owens steal the show at the 1936 Olympic Games. Not far away is **Corbusier House** (1957), Reichssportfeld Strasse 16, built to plans of the famous French architect.

Dahlem Museum One Berlin museum worth all the others combined is the **Dahlem Museum**, Lans Strasse 8 (U-Bahn – Dahlem-Dorf, closed Monday, admission free). Here is kept the better part of the former Prussian art collections amassed by Frederick the Great, evacuated from Museum Island during WW II and never returned to East Berlin. This fantastic museum full of old master paintings, sculpture, ethnography, Indian, Oriental and Islamic art will knock you over. Arrive early in the morning and plan to spend the day there. There's a cafeteria downstairs in the museum or have a picnic lunch on the grass outside.

A couple of blocks away is the **Botanical Garden**, Konigin Luise Strasse 6-8 (daily, DM 2.50 admission). The **Botanical Museum** (closed Monday, free) is just outside the garden.

Dark Memories The sombre lines of **Tempelhof Airport** (U-Bahn – Platz der Luftbrucke), now a US Air Force base and Police Headquarters, constitute the largest surviving architectural monument from the Nazi period. Seldom used today, before WW II this was the largest airport in Germany. The sinister grey buildings emblazoned with white stone eagles overpower the square, symbolising vividly the Nazi destruction of humanism. Not even the soaring **Airlift Monument** in the park subdues the sense of evil. But more striking than Hitler's creation is the Nazi eagle's head (1940) set up on a pedestal in front of the base by the US Air Force in 1985. The lack of sensitivity displayed by this act is truly amazing.

Along the Havel The eastern half of West Berlin may be crowded with roads, office buildings and apartments but the western portion is surprisingly green with forests, rivers and lakes. From April to October tourist boats cruise the waterways calling at picturesque villages, parks and castles. One ferry across the Havel from Kladow to Wannsee operates year round making possible a scenic circle trip.

Begin by taking the U-Bahn in the direction of Rathaus Spandau to Zitadelle. There's no charge to enter the grounds of **Spandau Citadel** (1594), main fortress of the Prussian kaisers, which once guarded the junction of the Havel and Spree rivers, still important trade routes. Tickets (DM 4) are required to visit the museum (closed Monday) from the gatehouse and climb the 154 steps of Julius Tower (1160).

Cross the Havel just west of the citadel and explore **Spandau village** which manages to retain a medieval air despite the trendy shops and department stores. **St Nicholas Church**, where elector Joachim II consented to the first Lutheran communion in 1539, is just north of Markt square. Lindenufer/Spandau landing below the bridge over the Havel, three blocks south-east of Markt, is an important departure point for tour boats to Tegel, Pfaueninsel and Wannsee.

From Rathaus Spandau at the south-west end of the village take bus No 34 south to Kladow. Halfway down you pass **Helle Berge** on the right, a good hiking area. Get off a few stops beyond the British airbase (ask the bus driver for the BVG-Personenschiffahrt). The Kladow ferry landing is at the bottom of the hill below the old church (ask).

The passenger ferry to Wannsee leaves hourly year round and the fare is a regular BVG transit ticket with transfers possible

(24 Hour Ticket not valid). The 15-minute trip across the **Havel** is quite beautiful with small sailboats all around. You pass a large bathing establishment by the shore. **Wannsee** is West Berlin's smartest summer resort.

Take double-decker bus No 6 due west from Wannsee to Glienicker Brucke and the East German border. Here you can peer across the ironically named **Brucke der Einheit** (Bridge of Unity) into Potsdam. The two Germanys exchange captured spies here. Overlooking the bridge is **Schloss Glienicke** (closed Monday), the summer residence of Prince Carl von Preussen from 1824 until his death in 1883 and the finest artistic ensemble of Berlin classicism and romanticism in West Berlin. Admission is charged to the palace but the enchanting wooded park is free.

There's a lovely walk along the Havel from the bridge to **Pfaueninsel** and beyond. Opportunities to lose yourself in the wooded hills here are many. All bus lines in this area run to Bahnhof Wannsee where you can catch the S-Bahn back to central West Berlin.

Lake Boats From Tegel to Potsdam the Havel River widens between the forests into a picturesque series of lakes. Most of the large tour boats are based at Wannsee (S-Bahn – Wannsee) and Tegel (U-Bahn – Tegel), although it's also possible to board at Kladow and Spandau.

The Stern und Kreisschiffahrt (tel 810004-0) operates three lines several times daily all summer. Line one runs from Wannsee to Glienicker Brucke via Pfaueninsel from mid-April to October (DM 5 one way, one hour). Line two operates from mid-May to September from Spandau to Kohlhasenbruck via Wannsee (DM 7 one way, two hours). Line three is a grand tour between Tegel and Wannsee taking anywhere from two to four hours depending on the route followed (mid-April to September, DM 7 to 10 one way). A Linien-Tageskarte

(DM 14.50) allows unlimited travel on the three lines for one day.

Other companies such as Reederverband (tel 3315017), Reederei Bruno Winkler (tel 3917010) and Reederei Triebler (tel 3315414) also operate on these routes and their schedules and prices are sometimes more convenient so check.

Canal & River Boats Companies based in kiosks along the riverside behind the Kongresshalle in Tiergarten (S-Bahn – Bellevue) offer cruises along narrow waterways which penetrate the heart of the city. 'Spreefahrt' (tel 3944954) runs a four-hour morning cruise (DM 10) down the **Spree River** to Spandau, returning along the Hohenzollernkanal past Tegel airport. A two-hour afternoon trip (DM 6) visits Westhafen and Schloss Charlottenburg. A commentary is provided in German.

One of the most popular trips is offered by Reederei Heinz Riedel (tel 6934646) whose kiosk is just downstream from the Kongresshalle. From April to October their boat travels two or three times daily (DM 7.50, three hours) down the Spree to the **Landwehrkanal**, then east through a lock and 'under the bridges' to the East German border at Kreuzberg. You can also catch this boat near Kottbusser Damm U-Bahn station around 11 am or 3 pm and travel only one way for DM 6. Both companies also operate in winter provided there's demand and not too much ice.

Friedrich Strasse Station It's possible to visit an East Berlin railway station without passing East German customs by taking the West Berlin transit system to Friedrich Strasse. Between Zoo Station and Friedrich Strasse the S-Bahn runs right along the Wall near the Reichstag allowing great inside views. If you arrive on one of the other two lines coming from West Berlin you'll pass eerie sealed stations almost underneath the Wall itself. S-Bahn trains from Frohnau in the north follow the Wall for several km between Schonholz and Gesundbrunnen stations, a fascinating ride not to be missed.

Friedrich Strasse Station, well inside East Berlin, is freely open to anyone and you're welcome to wander around and peruse the shops where West Berliners come to buy duty free cigarettes, liquor, coffee, chocolate, etc for DM. Lots of elderly East Germans also pass through this station, entering West Berlin in the morning and returning to East Berlin in the afternoon. East German soldiers patrol the station in threes.

It's actually a large complex of underground passageways as three lines cross the mainline from West Germany to Poland here. The S-Bahn line from Wannsee and Zoo Station mentioned above arrives upstairs at Bahnsteig B where the through trains also stop. Below this, past the entrance to customs, is the north/south S-Bahn line. You reach the U-Bahn line from Tegel to Alt-Mariendorf (via Koch Strasse or Checkpoint Charlie) from one end of the north/south line platform. The way to GDR customs is indicated by signs reading 'Zur Grenzubergangsstelle.'

Just below Bahnsteig B is an Interflug office open daily which sells air tickets. The Service Buro counter in this same office arranges camping visas, can reserve hotel rooms anywhere in the GDR, and sells tickets to theatres in East Berlin. All services are payable in West German currency only.

For full information on entry to East Berlin through Friedrich Strasse Station see East Berlin.

Places to Stay

Youth Hostels There are three IYHF youth hostels in West Berlin. The hostels do fill up on weekends and all summer so call before going out. To reserve a bed at a hostel write Deutsches Jugend-Herbergswerk, Tempelhofer Damm 32, 1000 Berlin 61. State precisely which nights you'll be there and enclose an International Postal Reply Coupon (available at any post office) so they can send back confirmation.

If you aren't already a YHA member you'll have to buy an International Guest Card for a one-time payment of DM 20. The cards are sold at the hostels. None of the hostels offer cooking facilities but breakfast is included in the overnight charge. Other meals are available for DM 5.30 each. The hostels stay open all day, year round.

The only hostel within walking distance of the city centre is the *Berlin Youth Guest House* (tel 2611097), Kluck Strasse 3, which charges DM 18.50 per person. The closest U-Bahn station to this long grey and white building by the Landwehr-kanal is Kurfursten Strasse. If you're coming from Tegel Airport take bus No 9 to the Inter-Continental then follow the canal east.

The ultramodern *Wannsee Youth Guest House* (tel 8032034), Badeweg 1 corner Kronprinzessinenweg, is in a pleasant lake-front location on Grosse Wannsee near the beach. Although 15 km south-west of the centre this hostel is only a five-minute walk from Nikolassee S-Bahn Station with fast commuter trains to Zoo Station and Friedrich Strasse. The easy access and good facilities are reflected in the higher price, DM 19.20 a bed.

Ernst Reuter Youth Hostel (tel 4041610), Hermsdorfer Damm 48, is in the far north of West Berlin. Take the U-Bahn to Tegel, then bus No 15 right to the door. The relaxed atmosphere reflects the remote location. Try here first if you're arriving at a busy time without a reservation.

Other Hostels Halfway between the Kluck Strasse Youth Hostel and Checkpoint Charlie you'll find the *Jugendhotel International* (tel 2623081), Bernburger Strasse 27. Rooms are DM 35 single, DM 64 double including breakfast. When things are busy you could have to share a three, four or five-bedded room at DM 32 per person. Beware, although this place is open to everyone it's often used by noisy school groups.

The *Studenthotel Berlin* (tel 7846720), Meininger Strasse 10 near Rathaus Schoneberg (U-Bahn), operates like a youth hostel but you don't need a card. Bed and breakfast is DM 27 per person in a double, DM 25 per person in a quad.

The *Jugendgastehaus am Zoo* (tel 3129410), Hardenberg Strasse 9a near Zoo Station, is DM 30 single, DM 50 double, DM 20 dormitory, DM 6 extra for breakfast. It's limited to persons under 27.

If everything else fails there's always the *Bahnhofsmission* at Zoo Station which provides dorm beds for DM 15 (no breakfast). The office is on Jebens Strasse below the train tracks just outside the station. They're there mostly to help down-and-outers.

Camping All three campgrounds in West Berlin charge DM 6.40 per person plus DM 5 per tent. The only one convenient to public transportation is *Campingplatz Kohlhasenbruck* (open April to September, tel 8051737) on Stubenrauch Strasse in a peaceful location overlooking the Grieb-nitzsee in the far south-west corner of West Berlin. Bus No 18 from Wannsee S-Bahn Station runs directly there.

If Kohlhasenbruck is closed or full you'll have to walk two km east along the Teltowkanal to *Campingplatz Dreilinden* (tel 8051201) at Albrechts-Teerofen.

Campingplatz Haselhorst (tel 3345955) is near Spandau two km north-west of Haselhorst U-Bahn Station. Walk north on Daum Strasse to Pulvermuhlenweg then west to the canal. Crowded with caravans and none too attractive, this campground has the advantage of being reliably open year round.

Cheaper Hotels There *are* inexpensive *hotel pensionen* in West Berlin. Listed below are some of the cheapest places in the streets off the Ku'damm west of Zoo Station. They're all small, plain and

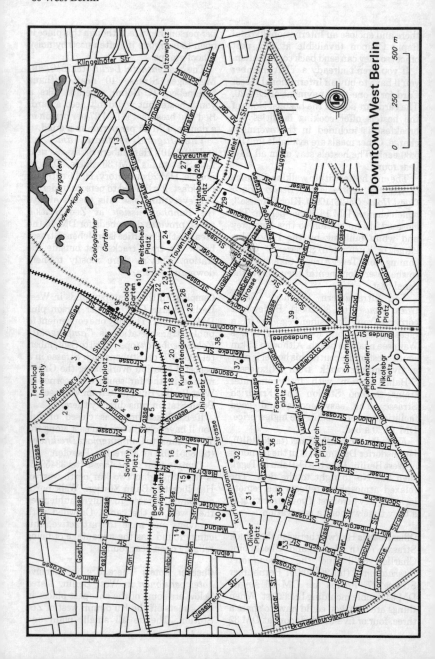

Downtown West Berlin

1	Kiepert Bookstore
2	ARTU Student Travel
3	School of Art Concert Hall
4	Dicke Wirtin Pub
5	Schwarzes Cafe
6	British Consulate
7	Informationszentrum
8	Theater des Westens/Quasimodo
9	Zoo Station
10	Filmzentrum Zoo Palast
11	Berliner Festspiele
12	Zoo & Aquarium
13	Inter-Continental Hotel
14	Salsa Pub
15	Go in Pub
16	Cafe Bleibtreu
17	Marge Schoeller Bucherstube
18	Zille Hof
19	Hotel Bristol Kempinski
20	Jewish Community Centre
21	Deutsches Reiseburo
22	American Express
23	Kaiser Wilhelm Memorial Church
24	Europa Centre
25	Ku'damm Eck
26	Wertheim Department Store
27	Jimsalat Cafe
28	Intratours
29	KaDeWe Department Store
30	Beiz Restaurant
31	Olympia Reisen
32	Big Eden Disco
33	Schalander Cafe
34	Intourist
35	Madow Pub
36	Loretta's Biergarten
37	Meineke Hotel
38	Ku'dorf
39	Bundeshaus

uncommercial, so expect no luxury and try calling first. You'll pay around DM 35 single, DM 60 double for a room with shared bath. Breakfast is usually DM 5 to DM 7 extra, although it's sometimes included in the price.

There are five budget places west of Zoo Station and north of the Ku'damm: *Hotelpension Elfert* (tel 3121236, 40 beds), Knesebeck Strasse 13/14; *Pension Am Savigny Platz* (tel 3138392, 10 beds),

Grolman Strasse 52; *Pension Centrum* (tel 316153, 11 beds), Kant Strasse 31; *Pension Niebuhr* (tel 3249595, 15 beds), Niebuhr Strasse 74; and *Pension Bachmann* (tel 3244488, 9 beds), Mommsen Strasse 27. The *Hotel Charlottenburger Hof* (tel 3244819, 61 beds), Stuttgarter Platz 14 outside Charlottenburg S-Bahn Station, is larger and farther away and thus more likely to have space.

Three similar hotels south of the Ku'damm are: *Hotelpension Pariser Eck* (tel 8812145, 38 beds), Pariser Strasse 19; *Pension Elton* (tel 8836155, 11 beds), Pariser Strasse 9; and *Pension Terminus* (tel 8814909), Fasanen Strasse 48.

Two good places just south of Breitscheid Platz are *Pension Riga* (tel 2111223, 32 beds), Ranke Strasse 23, and *Hotelpension Nurnberger Eck* (tel 245371, 18 beds), Nurnberger Strasse 24a.

If you'd rather stay out in Kreuzberg (U-Bahn – Mehringdamm) try *Hotelpension Sudwest* (tel 7858033, 14 beds), Yorck Strasse 80, or *Pension Kreuzberg* (tel 2511362, 23 beds), Grossbeeren Strasse 64.

Expensive Hotels A step down in price and up in local colour from the luxury places is the *Meineke Hotel* (tel 882811, 150 beds), Meineke Strasse 10, an old German-style inn a block off the Ku'damm. Rooms begin at DM 65 single, DM 105 double including breakfast – good value for West Berlin. A better choice if you don't mind being away from the centre is *Riehmers Hofgarten* (tel 781011, 50 beds), Yorck Strasse 83 in Kreuzberg. Bus No 19 from the Ku'damm passes the door. Rooms in this 1892 eclectic edifice are DM 84 single, DM 129 double, big breakfast included.

West Berlin's most exclusive hotel is the *Bristol Kempinski* (tel 881091, 640 beds), Kurfurstendamm 27, at DM 210 single, DM 240 double for a room without breakfast. Farther from the action, the *Berlin Inter-Continental* (tel 26020, 1150 beds), Budapester Strasse 2, begins at DM 230 single or double without breakfast. Stay at one of these if someone else is paying.

Long Term Rentals If you'd like to spend some time in Berlin look for someone willing to sub-let their apartment. Many Berliners take off for extended holidays and are only too happy to have the bills paid while they're gone. Check the *wohnungen* classified section in *Zitty* or advertise your own needs in *Die Tageszeitung* (tel 030-46090) or *Zitty* (tel 884296-0).

There are agencies called *mitwohnzentrale* which arrange private sub-rentals for periods as short as a day, week or month. They charge 10% of the monthly rental rate or DM 3 per person per day for short stays. Many advertise in the *wohnungen* section in *Zitty*. If you're staying under a month you'll end up sharing a flat with others, a good way to meet people as well as find a place to stay.

There's one *mitwohnzentrale* (tel 8826694) on the 2nd floor of the shopping arcade at Kurfurstendamm 227 (Ku'damm-Eck). They have fairly luxurious apartments for DM 50 single, DM 70 double per day, plus longer term, cheaper rooms. *Mitwohnzentrale Charlottenburg* (tel 3249977), Sybel Strasse 53 (U-Bahn – Adenauer Platz), has rooms for DM 20 to DM 25 a day per person or DM 400 a month. *Mitwohnzentrale Kreuzberg* (tel 7862003), Mehringdamm 72, has rooms for DM 15 to DM 25 daily per person. The monthly rate for a room in a shared flat is DM 200 to DM 400 per person. Whole flats are harder to locate (to DM 500 plus 10%). In Wilmersdorf try *Mitwohnzentrale Bundesallee* (tel 2134466).

Places to Eat
Substantial, inexpensive meals are consumed in the food halls of the large department stores, KaDeWe and Wertheim. At *KaDeWe* (U-Bahn – Wittenberg Platz) the top floor is the 'gourmet floor.'

Wertheim, Kurfurstendamm 232 near the Ku'damm-Eck, is less pretentious. In the basement at *Wertheim* you can have a great lunch for a lower than average price. There's also a supermarket down there.

Breakfast cafes are peculiar to Berlin. In addition to canned music in a genteel setting you can get a filling brunch of yoghurt, eggs, meat, cheese, bread, butter and jam for around DM 8.50 (coffee extra). Typical of the genre are *Cafe Bleibtreu*, Bleibtreu Strasse 45 (breakfast from 9.30 am to 2 pm), and *Schalander*, Olivaer Platz 4 (breakfast until 3 pm).

More expensive, bizarre and open round the clock is *Schwarzes Cafe*, Kant Strasse 148 (breakfast anytime). This is one place to get off the street if you happen to roll into West Berlin in the middle of the night (closed Monday night only). You'll never forget your first impression!

West Berlin's only salad bar is found at *Simsalat*, Ansbacher Strasse 11 just off Wittenberg Platz. You pay by weight: DM 1.80 per 100 grammes. A bottomless cup of coffee is DM 2.50, another Simsalat first. They're open from 8.30 am to midnight but closed Sunday.

German Food Since most West Berlin restaurants offer exotic cuisine finding authentic German fare takes a little doing. *Beiz*, Schluter Strasse 38 off the Ku'damm (open daily 6 pm to 2 am), is rather expensive. *Dicke Wirtin*, Carmer Strasse 9 off Savigny Platz, is an old German pub offering soup and stew. In summer make for *Loretta's Biergarten*, Lietzenburger Strasse 89 behind the ferris wheel. Stein of pils in hand at a long wooden table out back you'd swear you were in Bavaria.

More out of the way but full of atmosphere is *Zum Ambrosius*, Einem Strasse 14 (U-Bahn – Nollendorf Platz). The specials are marked on blackboards outside this rustic pub/restaurant. If Zum Ambrosius fails to please try *Spatz*, a block away at Kurfursten Strasse 56, a basement pub and steakhouse (opens at 6.30 pm daily except Sunday).

Subsidised Meals If everything listed above is too expensive, try for a hot subsidised meal (DM 4 to DM 8) in a government cafeteria. They're open weekdays only and you clear your own table. The *kantine* downstairs in Rathaus Charlottenburg, Otto-Suhr-Allee 100 close to Schloss Charlottenburg (U-Bahn – Richard Wagner Platz), serves non-employees at 2 pm. It's in the basement inside the building, not the expensive Ratskeller outside.

The *Rathaus Casino* on the 10th floor of Rathaus Kreuzberg, Yorck Strasse 4-11 (weekdays 7.30 am to 3 pm, U-Bahn – Mehringdamm), offers cheap lunch specials and great views. Everyone is welcome. Also good is the 5th floor *kantine* in the unemployment office *(arbeitsamt)* at Charlotten Strasse 90 near Checkpoint Charlie (weekdays 9 am to 1 pm).

The cafeteria in the *State Library* (closed Sunday) opposite the Philharmonie offers soup, salad and sandwiches, plus hot specials. You have to check your bag (free) to get in.

Kreuzberg Enjoy great salads (DM 6), omelettes (DM 6), baguettes, flutes, pizza and sundaes (DM 6) at *Cafe Exit* in one wing of the large church outside Sudstern U-Bahn Station. Daily specials such as chile con carne are posted on the wall. The cafe (open Monday, Tuesday, Thursday, Friday and Saturday 4 pm to midnight, Sunday 1 to 6 pm) is run by Born Again Christians and the evening activities inside the church itself offer a chance to meet people. Sudstern is one of the counterculture centres of Berlin and it seems half the population crowds into the *Wunderbar* right next to the U-Bahn station every evening.

Entertainment

West Berlin has a reputation for its nightlife and things don't start moving until 10 pm. That's the time to stroll down the Ku'damm amid all the glitter. A disco tout will hand you an invitation to *Big Eden*. Before you get sucked into any of the tourist joints along the strip take a look up Bleibtreu Strasse and around Savigny Platz where the locals go.

There are around 5000 pubs or *kneipen* in West Berlin and in the absence of licensing hours they're open day and night (usually 7 pm to 4 am). Many pubs offer live music and food. A cover charge of DM 2 to DM 8 may be asked if there's live music, although some places only charge admission on Friday and Saturday nights.

The music scene in West Berlin is constantly changing and for up-to-date information it's best to check the fortnightly magazines *Zitty* and *Tip* which carry complete listings of what's happening. The monthly *Berlin programme* (DM 2.50) lists mainstream cultural events.

Pubs *Quasimodo*, Kant Strasse 12a near Zoo Station (open from 8 pm, music from 10 pm), is a jazzkeller with live music every night. For folk music try *Go In*, Bleibtreu Strasse 17 (daily from 8 pm). *Salsa*, Wieland Strasse 13, features Latin American and Caribbean music. They open at 8 pm, have live music from 10 pm and offer free admission Sunday to Thursday. *Madow*, Pariser Strasse 23-24 (Wednesday to Sunday from 10 pm), features music from the 1970s. Prices are lower here on Wednesday, Thursday and Sunday nights.

Discos West Berlin discos are wild, you have to put a big effort into keeping up with the scene. The favourite tourist disco is *Big Eden*, Kurfurstendamm 202 (open daily from 7 pm). Outside of Friday and Saturday nights there's no cover, but they make up for it in the price of the drinks. If you'd rather dance with Berliners it's *Far Out*, Kurfurstendamm 156 beneath the bowling alley (open from 10 pm, closed Monday). *Society*, Budapester Strasse 42 opposite the Europa Centre, is similar.

For a slightly off beat trip try the *Metropol*, Nollendorf Platz 5 (U-Bahn – Nollendorf Platz), popular with gays and straights. Friday and Saturday nights here are wild. Rock concerts unroll at the Metropol (tel 2164122), but they're often sold out.

One disco with live music is *Empire International*, Haupt Strasse 30 (U-Bahn – Eisenacher Strasse). They open at 10 pm and are closed Sunday and Monday. Every Tuesday is Reggae Night at Empire with no cover charge.

Sex Lietzenburger Strasse west from Uhland Strasse is lined with clubs offering sex shows. West Berlin's lowlife red light area is along Potsdammer Strasse south of the Turkish Bazaar. The best hookers are picked up on the Ku'damm late at night. Gays patronise the cafes on Nollendorf Platz opposite the Metropol or lurk in the shadows at the Victory Column (Siegessaule) and adjacent Tiergarten. Since the AIDS scare things are a lot quieter than they were.

Films If you want to see a movie go on Wednesday *(kinotag)* when tickets are half price (DM 6). Check *Zitty* for complete listings. The *Filmzentrum Zoo Palast*, Hardenberg Strasse 29a near Zoo Station, contains nine cinemas (the film festival is held here). There are many other movie houses along Kurfurstendamm. Foreign films are dubbed into German.

See movies in the original English at the *Odeon Theatre* (tel 7815667), Haupt Strasse 116 (U-Bahn – Innsbrucker Platz or S-Bahn – Schoneberg). Show times are 6 pm, 8.30 pm and 10.45 pm, with an additional 3.30 pm show on Saturday and Sunday.

Theatres Theatre and concert tickets begin at DM 10 and rise to over DM 100. You'll do better for less going directly to the theatre box office rather than a ticket agency. If they're all sold out try again an hour before show time or look for scalpers on the street outside. Many people get free tickets from the West Berlin government which they sell to make a quick mark. Tickets to special events are available from the Festspielgalerie, Budapester Strasse 48 across from the Kaiser Wilhelm Memorial Church (daily 10 am to 7 pm). Most of the theatres close for summer holidays. West Berlin's not stuffy so you can attend theatre and cultural events dressed as you please.

Prior to the Nazi destruction of German culture, Berlin had 70 active theatres. Today there are 19 in West Berlin. The *Deutsche Oper* (1961), Bismarck Strasse 35 (U-Bahn – Deutsche Oper), is all glass and steel. Their box office opens weekdays 2 to 8 pm, weekends 10 am to 2 pm. The back rows are really back.

See operettas and musicals at the *Theater des Westens*, Kant Strasse 12 near Zoo Station (box office open 10 am to 7 pm, Sunday 3 to 7 pm). This beautiful old theatre (1896) has style but it's hard to see from the cheap seats.

This is no problem at the *Philharmonie*, Matthaikirch Strasse 1 (U-Bahn – Kurfursten Strasse, then bus No 48), where *all* seats are excellent. Do try to hear at least one concert at the Philharmonie. Other musical programmes are offered at the *School of Art Concert Hall*, Hardenberg Strasse 33 (tickets 3 to 6.30 pm weekdays, 11 am to 2 pm weekends).

The *Schiller Theater*, Bismarck Strasse 110 (U-Bahn – Ernst Reuter Platz, box office open 10 am to 7 pm daily), is West Berlin's premier venue for traditional German drama.

Things to Buy

Tauentzien Strasse is the main shopping street for affluent West Berlin consumers. At the Wittenberg Platz end of this street is KaDeWe (Kaufhaus des Westens), an amazing six-storey turn of the century department store which sells just about everything you can name. Wertheim, Kurfurstendamm 232, West Berlin's second department store, is less pretentious and less expensive. Shops selling discount cameras are along Augsburger Strasse near the Ku'damm.

Good inexpensive secondhand clothes of all descriptions may be had at Made in Berlin, Potsdamer Strasse 106 (U-Bahn – Kurfursten Strasse). You can find some pretty funky attire there!

The largest camping goods store in West Berlin with a good selection of top quality tents and backpacks is Alles fur Tramper, Bundesallee 88 (U-Bahn – Walther Schreiber Platz). Two stations away at U-Bahn Bundes Platz are the Tramper Shop, Detmolder Strasse 3, and Bergsport, Detmolder Strasse 10. They're not cheap but keep in mind that this kind of gear is unobtainable in Eastern Europe.

Where else in Berlin to pick up a genuine Iron Cross or a 1926 postcard than the flea market (Flohmarkt) above Nollendorf Platz U-Bahn station? The market, housed in an elevated station of a U-Bahn line cut by the Wall, is as much fun for sightseers as shoppers. You'll find real Berlin kitsch in the antique shops filling 16 genuine 1920 U-Bahn carriages. There's also an old fashioned pub. The flea market is open daily except Tuesday from 11 am to 7 pm.

The Nollendorf Platz flea market is strictly for tourists. There's a genuine open-air flea market every Saturday and Sunday morning on Strasse des 17 Juni at Tiergarten S-Bahn Station. Or visit Zille Hof, a junkyard at Fasanen Strasse 14 below the S-Bahn. Very exclusive antique shops line Fasanen Strasse between Lietzenburger Strasse and the Ku'damm.

Getting There & Away

Air Due to West Berlin's bizarre political status only American, British and French carriers such as Pan Am, British Airways and Air France may fly to the city. Their regular flights to Western Europe are much more expensive than the train or bus and are heavily booked. For information on cheap flights to far places see the listings of travel agencies under Orientation above.

Train Berlin-Zoologischer Garten on Hardenberg Platz is the main railway station in West Berlin, although some international trains also stop at Berlin-Wannsee or Berlin-Spandau. For train information call 3121042.

Train tickets from West Berlin to Western Europe are extremely expensive: DM 60 to Hannover, DM 107 to Frankfurt am Main, DM 136 to Munich, DM 135 to Amsterdam, DM 252 to London. Those under 26 years of age qualify for a Transalpino ticket at a considerable discount (Frankfurt am Main DM 83, Amsterdam DM 73, London DM 131). If you can afford the price of a train ticket be sure to also get a seat reservation (DM 3.50 extra) as some trains come in from East Berlin full of Third World immigrants bound for West Germany.

Tickets to the socialist countries are cheaper when purchased in East rather than West Berlin. For example, Berlin to Budapest costs DM 273 1st class plus an additional DM 80 for a sleeper when purchased at a travel agency in West Berlin but only DM 145 for both ticket and sleeper (1st class) from the Reiseburo der DDR, Alexander Platz 5, East Berlin. See the East Berlin section of this book for details. Train tickets to China cannot be purchased in East Berlin. They refer you to Intourist in West Berlin.

Bus The Funkturm Bus Station (U-Bahn – Kaiserdamm) is open from 5.30 am to 10 pm. Buses between West Berlin and Western Europe tend to be cheaper than the train. For example, the one way fare from West Berlin to Hannover is DM 49, to Frankfurt am Main DM 90, to Munich DM 108, to Amsterdam DM 90 (twice a week),to London DM 165. Checked

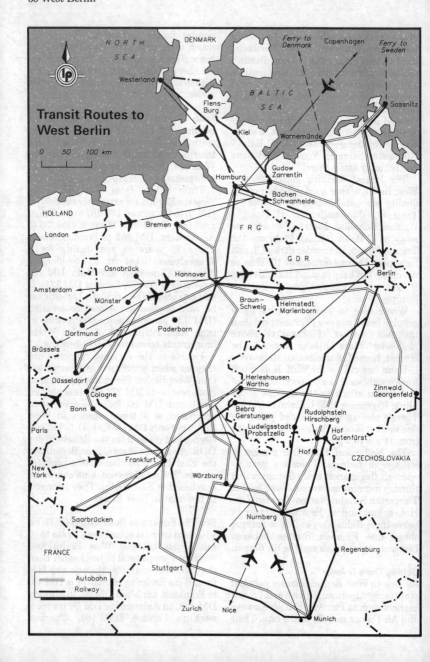

Transit Routes to West Berlin

0 50 100 km

NORTH SEA

DENMARK

Ferry to Denmark

Copenhagen

Ferry to Sweden

BALTIC SEA

Westerland

Flens-Burg

Kiel

Warnemünde

Sassnitz

Gudow Zarrentin

Hamburg

Büchen Schwanheide

HOLLAND

London

Bremen

FRG

GDR

Berlin

Osnabrück

Amsterdam

Hannover

Münster

Braun-Schweig

Helmstedt Marienborn

Dortmund

Paderborn

Brüssels

Düsseldorf

Herleshausen Wartha

Zinnwald Georgenfeld

Cologne

Bonn

Paris

Bebra Gerstungen

Rudolphstein Hirschberg

Ludwigsstadt Probstzella

Hof Gutenfürst

New York

Frankfurt

Hof

CZECHOSLOVAKIA

Würzburg

Nurnberg

Regensburg

Saarbrücken

FRANCE

Stuttgart

Zurich

Nice

Munich

Autobahn
Railway

baggage is DM 2 extra per piece. Those under 27 and over 60 get a 50% discount on trips within Germany, 20% on trips to Holland and London. Seats can be reserved a month in advance. For information on schedules and fares call 3018028.

Ride Services Next to hitching the cheapest way to get out of West Berlin is as a paying passenger in a private car. There are numerous agencies *(mitfahrzentrale)* in West Berlin arranging such rides. As a passenger you pay a DM 10 to DM 15 commission to the agency, plus petrol money to the driver.

One office is on the platform of the U1 U-Bahn line direction Schlesisches Tor at Zoologischer Garten underground station (tel 310331, open Monday to Saturday 8 am to 8 pm, Sunday 10 am to 4 pm). Another (tel 8827606, open daily 8 am to 8 pm, Sunday 10 am to 4 pm) is on the 2nd floor shopping arcade at Kurfurstendamm 227 (Ku'damm-Eck). Other *mitfahrzentrales* are listed in the 'Mitfahrer' classified section of *Zitty*. The people answering the phone in these offices always speak good English, so don't hesitate to call around. If you arrange a ride a few days in advance be sure to call the driver back the night before and again on departure morning to make sure he/she is still going.

Autostop You can hitch to Hannover, Munich and beyond from Checkpoint Dreilinden at Wannsee, entrance to the main highway corridor between West Berlin and West Germany. Take the S-Bahn to Wannsee, then walk less than a km up Potsdamer Chausee and follow the signs to Raststatte Dreilinden. There's always a bunch of hitchhikers here but everyone gets a ride eventually. Bring a small sign stating your destination and consider waiting until you find a car going right where you want to go.

Unless you're a German national you must pay DM 5 for a GDR transit visa.

Keep in mind that it's forbidden to leave the transit route while passing through East Germany, although it's all right to stop for a meal at an Intertank restaurant where you pay in West German currency.

Getting Around

Airport Transport Flughafen Tegel, six km north-west of Zoo Station, is the city's main commercial airport. The airport information number is 41012306. Regular BVG transit buses run to the terminal, bus No 8 from Kurt Schumacher Platz U-Bahn station, bus No 9 from the Inter-Continental Hotel via Zoo Station. No airport departure tax is charged on flights to West Germany, DM 11 on flights to other countries.

Aside from Tegel there's Tempelhof Airport, but it's used mostly for charters and American military flights. Flugplatz Gatow west of the Havel River is a British air force base.

Interflug, Aeroflot and most of the other Eastern European carriers fly from Schonefeld Airport, just outside the city limits of East Berlin. There are buses direct to Schonefeld from West Berlin's Funkturm Bus Station every half hour (DM 7). This bus crosses into the GDR at Checkpoint Waltersdorfer Strasse in Rudow, only a few minutes drive from Schonefeld. There's no departure tax but a DM 5 transit visa must be purchased at the border both coming and going. Male passengers are subjected to a hands-on body search for weapons after checking in at Schonefeld.

Public Transport The Berliner Verkehrs-Betriebe (BVG) operates an efficient, expensive suburban railway (S-Bahn), underground (U-Bahn), ferry and bus system which reaches every corner of West Berlin, plus Friedrich Strasse station in East Berlin. System maps are posted in all West Berlin stations. For transit information call 2165088.

Prior to WW II the S-Bahn was the most popular way of getting around Berlin. In

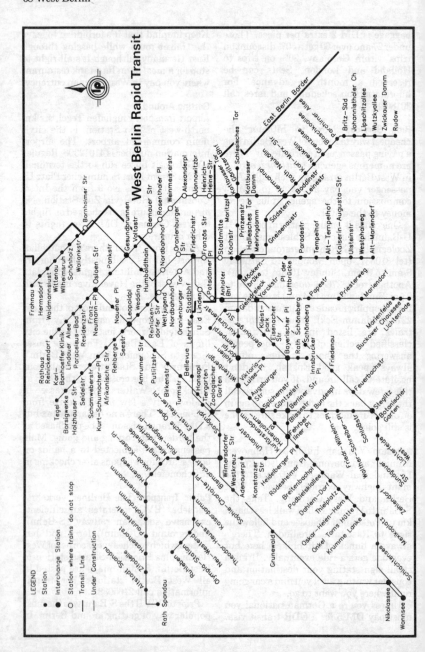

West Berlin Rapid Transit

LEGEND

- • Station
- ● Interchange Station
- ○ Station where trains do not stop
- — Transit Line
- ⸗ Under Construction

1943 it carried a never surpassed 737 million passengers. After the war the trains continued to be operated by the East German railway company, Deutsche Reichsbahn (DR). In August 1961 as the Wall went up Mayor Willy Brandt called on West Berliners to boycott the S-Bahn and the system went into decline, its place taken by the U-Bahn and double-decker buses. In 1984 the BVG took over running the S-Bahn from the DR and integrated it into its network. (The DR still controls the mainline railway in West Berlin and runs Zoo Station.) Today the combined S-Bahn and U-Bahn total 178 km of track with 153 stations, the longest subway in Germany. You'll find both systems easy to use.

Apart from the trains there are double-decker buses which offer great views from the upstairs front seats. The BVG ferry from Kladow to Wansee operates hourly year round with regular tickets and transfers accepted. There's also the new M-Bahn, an automated magnetic monorail which runs from Gleisdreieck U-Bahn station to the Philharmonie at Kemper Platz. Before the war streetcars were a popular form of transportation in Berlin. The only one left in West Berlin shuttles tourists along an abandoned elevated U-Bahn line from the Flea Market to the Turkish Bazaar.

A single DM 2.30 ticket allows unlimited transfers on all forms of public transport within two hours provided you continue travelling in one direction. (In East Berlin the fare is only 20 pfennig!) Round trips are not permitted. Multiple tickets with five rides for DM 10.50 are slightly cheaper. You validate your own ticket in a red automat at the entrances to the S and U-Bahn stations. There is no ticket control but if you're caught aboard a train without a valid ticket there's a DM 40 fine.

The S and U-Bahn lines close down between 1 and 4 am, but night bus lines run every 30 minutes all night from Zoo Station to key points such as Rathaus Spandau, Alt Tegel, Hermann Platz, Rathaus Steglitz, Mexiko Platz, etc. Regular fares apply.

Special Tickets The best transportation deal in West Berlin is the 24-Hour-Ticket (DM 8) which allows you to use most of the BVG network (but not the ferry across the Havel nor the bus to Pfaueninsel). Since the ticket is good for 24 hours it will overlap the morning or evening of another day allowing an extra ride. A slight variation on this is the two day (DM 16) or four day (DM 32) Touristenkarte which entitles you to use the whole network including the ferry but not the bus to Pfaueninsel. The Tourist Tickets are for consecutive calendar days. Bus drivers sell single tickets but multiple, 24-Hour and tourist tickets should be purchased in advance.

German Democratic Republic

Most people think of Germany as the familiar Federal Republic, as if the German Democratic Republic didn't exist. Berlin figures prominently on the tourist maps, but everything beyond East Berlin is unknown territory. Yet this quiet land of Bach, Brecht, Cranach, Goethe, Handel, Hegel, Humboldt, Schiller and Schumann is probably the most German portion of Germany. While West Germany has become Americanised, there's been no comparable Russianisation of East Germany. Small towns like Bautzen, Meissen, Naumburg, Quedlinburg, Stralsund and Wernigerode have a timeless medieval air.

The transplanted Soviet system has helped preserve as much as it replaced. This first German workers' and peasants' state is definite heir to Prussian puritanism and discipline. Here we find Berlin and Potsdam, the monumental cities of Frederick the Great. There's also the softer Saxon heritage of Augustus the Strong in Dresden and both the pilgrimage places associated with Martin Luther, Wittenberg (where he launched the Reformation) and Eisenach (where he took refuge and translated the Bible).

The German Democratic Republic is one of Eastern Europe's biggest surprises. At once doctrinaire, conservative, efficient, prosperous and advanced, it's been called the only Western European country in Eastern Europe. The present Communist regime is almost traditional: Saxony and Thuringia had long been socialist strongholds; Prussia and Russia fought side by side against Napoleon. Advance planning is essential to visit the GDR cheaply, but even the inevitable paperwork is an introduction to East German life. It's a rare opportunity, well worth taking.

Facts about the Country

HISTORY

Never part of the Roman Empire, the territory of the GDR was occupied by the West Slavs around the end of the 6th century. German merchants settled among them. In the 10th century the Saxons began pushing east and by the millennium the border between Germany and Poland was along the Oder River, about where it is today. The subjugated Slavic tribes intermingled with their conquerors and the Slavic language disappeared, except in tiny Sorbian pockets between Bautzen and Cottbus.

Market towns like Berlin, Erfurt, Magdeburg and Leipzig developed between the 10th and 13th centuries. Trade was first by river and sea, then by road. Wars with Poland continued through the Middle Ages as the Germans expanded east along the Baltic coast. In the 13th century the German knightly orders gained control of East Prussia, Latvia and Estonia.

In the 14th and 15th centuries the Hanseatic League developed a remarkable trading network from the Baltic to the

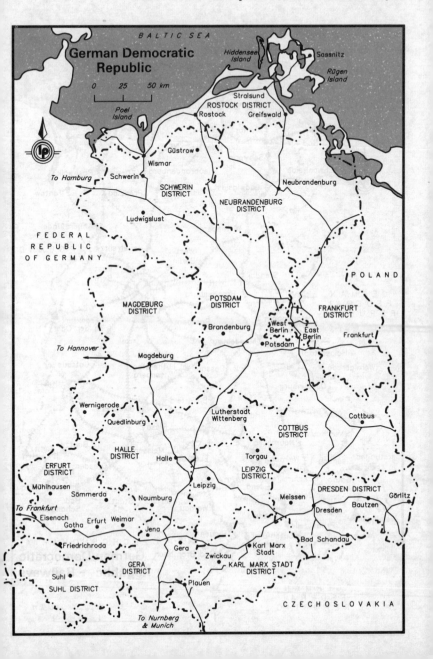

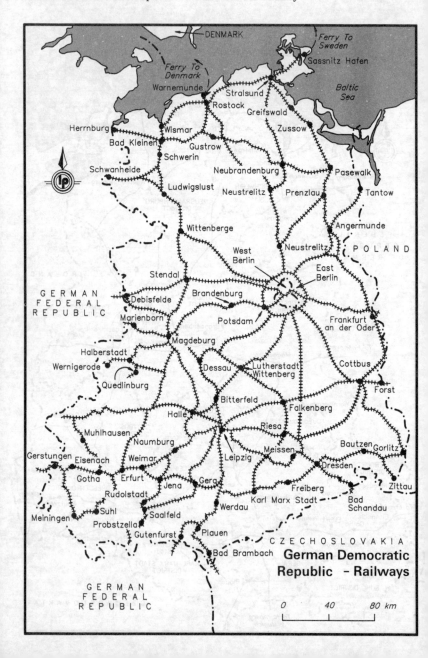

DENMARK

Ferry To Sweden

Sassnitz Hafen

Baltic Sea

Ferry To Denmark

Warnemunde

Stralsund

Rostock

Greifswald

Zussow

Herrnburg

Wismar

Bad Kleinen

Gustrow

Schwerin

Neubrandenburg

Pasewalk

Schwanheide

Ludwigslust

Neustrelitz

Prenzlau

Tantow

Wittenberge

Angermunde

West Berlin

Neustrelitz

P O L A N D

Stendal

East Berlin

Debisfelde

Brandenburg

G E R M A N
F E D E R A L
R E P U B L I C

Marienborn

Potsdam

Frankfurt an der Oder

Magdeburg

Halberstadt

Wernigerode

Dessau

Lutherstadt Wittenberg

Cottbus

Quedlinburg

Bitterfeld

Falkenberg

Forst

Halle

Riesa

Muhlhausen

Naumburg

Meissen

Bautzen

Gorlitz

Gerstungen

Eisenach

Weimar

Leipzig

Dresden

Gotha

Erfurt

Gera

Freiberg

Zittau

Rudolstadt

Jena

Karl Marx Stadt

Bad Schandau

Meiningen

Suhl

Saalfeld

Werdau

Probstzella

Gutenfurst

Plauen

C Z E C H O S L O V A K I A

Bad Brambach

**German Democratic
Republic – Railways**

G E R M A N
F E D E R A L
R E P U B L I C

0   40   80 km

North Sea. Independent city states such as Reval (Estonia), Riga (Latvia), Danzig (Gdansk), Stralsund, Rostock, Wismar, Lubeck, Hamburg, Bremen, Bergen (Norway) and Brugge (Belgium) flourished. Much of the medieval architecture we now admire in those ports went up at that time.

The interior towns were in a perpetual state of feud with the landed gentry. In 1412 Frederick of Nuremburg from the house of the Hohenzollern acquired the Mark Brandenburg. He subdued the gentry, then conquered the previously independent towns. In 1470 the elector of Brandenburg established his residence at Berlin.

In the early 16th century the Protestant reformation took hold in the nascent feudal states of North Germany – Brandenburg, Mecklenburg, Pomerania and Saxony. The Thirty Years' War (1618-1648) between the Protestant North Germans and the Hapsburg-Spanish Catholic forces led to unparalleled destruction. From a half to two-thirds of the population died in this part of Germany.

In 1660 Frederick William (the 'Great Elector') obtained East Prussian independence from Polish suzerainty. Elector Frederick I had himself crowned king of Prussia in 1701 and his son, Frederick William I, built Prussia into one of the strongest military forces in Europe with an efficient bureaucracy. The next king, Frederick II (the Great), took Silesia from Austria in 1742 and annexed West Prussia in 1772. By 1795 three partitions had wiped Poland off the map.

Prussia itself was defeated by Napoleon in 1806 and occupied by French troops. Heavy taxes were extorted from the occupied lands but a few democratic reforms were also introduced, such as the emancipation of the serfs in 1807 and the founding of Humboldt University in 1809. Napoleonic control sparked an upsurge of nationalism throughout Europe and the Prussian army was transformed from a mercenary force into a modern national army. In 1813 the combined armies of Austria, Prussia, Russia and Sweden defeated Napoleon at Leipzig.

After this War of Independence against French domination the development of industry led to the creation of an urban working class. After a strike in 1844 the Prussian semi-absolutist regime prohibited further strikes and in 1847 a 'potato revolt' in Berlin was suppressed. About the same time the 'United Assembly' denied funds to the king unless he produced a constitution and allowed representative government. When this was not forthcoming an unsuccessful bourgeois-democratic revolution broke out in 1848. In Berlin workers and students battled at over 200 barricades against disciplined Prussian troops.

Chancellor Otto von Bismarck consolidated Prussia's position as head of the confederation of North German states and the Franco-Prussian War of 1870 resulted from French fears of a powerful, unified Germany. After the Prussian victory the Prussian king, Wilhelm I, was proclaimed German emperor *(kaiser)* in the Hall of Mirrors at Versailles on 18 January 1871. The military despotism promoted the rapid development of a capitalist economy. The transition from capitalism to imperialism took place at the turn of the century but the aggressive expansion of German monopolies eventually provoked a conflict with British imperialism leading to war.

In January 1918 a strike by munition workers in Berlin was thwarted. The example of the October 1917 Revolution in Russia inspired a similar rebellion against the German kaiser in November 1918. The seamen's uprising in Kiel on 3 November 1918 marked the beginning of the November Revolution in Germany. On 9 November all workers in Berlin went on strike, the kaiser abdicated and the war was over.

A power struggle then developed between the right wing Social Democrats

Rosa Luxemburg

and the left wing Spartakus League, forerunner of the Communist Party. On 15 January 1919 the Spartakus leaders Karl Liebknecht and Rosa Luxemburg fell into the hands of counter-revolutionary soldiers and were murdered. Then in March 1919 thousands of workers were killed or imprisoned by the military on orders of the Social Democratic government. The enduring strength of the Berlin workers' movement is illustrated by the shift of the Reichstag to Weimar by the bourgeois Social Democratic regime.

The world economic crisis of 1929 led to massive unemployment, strikes and demonstrations. The German Communist Party under Ernst Thalmann gained strength. The monopolies and financial capital saw a way out of the crisis in the establishment of an open, terroristic dictatorship. Flick, Krupp, Thyssen, the IG-Farbenindustrie, the Siemens and the AEG trusts were among the main supporters of Hitler. Later these companies made huge profits from armaments orders, the murderous exploitation of the German working class and the use of slave labour from the concentration camps and occupied countries. A united anti-fascist front was not formed in Germany largely due to the anti-Communist paranoia of the leading Social Democrats.

On 30 January 1933 President Hindenburg appointed Hitler chancellor. The Reichstag fire of 27 February 1933 was the signal for a brutal wave of repression. All opposition to the Nazis was crushed and Hitler's vicious programme then proceeded with deadly efficiency. In October 1933 the fascists withdrew from the League of Nations and in March 1935 military service was re-introduced. In 1936 and 1937 anti-Communist pacts were signed with Japan and Italy, the demilitarised Rhineland was re-occupied in March 1936 and Fascist troops were sent to Spain from 1936 to 1939. Austria was annexed in March 1938, in October 1938 it was Czechoslovakia's turn and finally, in September 1939, Hitler invaded Poland leading to war with Britain and France.

Karl Liebknecht

Throughout the Nazi period underground groups of the German Communist Party maintained a heroic resistance which cost many of them their lives. A National Committee for a Free Germany was set up in the USSR in 1943 by emigrants and German prisoners of war while the German officers who attempted to assassinate Hitler in 1944 preserved the honour of their nation. On 23 April 1945 advance detachments of the 5th Soviet Guards made contact with the US 1st Army at Torgau on the Elbe River, 50 km north-east of Leipzig and on 8 May 1945 the German High Command surrendered.

After the war Germany suffered the fate of many of its recent victims. Pomerania, Silesia and East Prussia were annexed by Poland and the USSR and about 6,500,000 Germans were returned to Germany from Czechoslovakia, Hungary and Poland. The Oder-Neisse Line became the new eastern border. Germany was divided into four zones and Berlin was occupied by the four victorious powers pending the reunification of Germany.

In April 1946 the Communist and Social Democratic parties in the Soviet zone merged to form the Socialist Unity Party (SED), which won the elections later that year. They demanded the nationalisation of industry and by 1948 61% of production in the Soviet zone came from the public sector. A two-year development plan was drawn up in 1948, followed by a five year plan in 1951. In the other three zones the western allies favoured big business.

On 20 June 1948 a new currency linked to the dollar was introduced in the western sectors of Berlin, setting the stage for the permanent division of Germany. Four days later the USSR interrupted land traffic between the west zones and West Berlin. The western allies countered this with a military airlift operation which supplied West Berlin by plane. Late in 1948 all trusts, banks and insurance companies in East Berlin were expropriated and with these reforms in place the Soviet

Union lifted the blockade in May 1949. In September 1949 the Federal Republic of Germany was created out of the three western zones and in response the German Democratic Republic was founded in the Soviet zone on 7 October 1949 with Berlin as capital.

In March 1952 Washington and Bonn rejected an offer from Stalin of a united Germany on the basis of strict political and military neutrality. That such an option was indeed possible is proved by the implementation of the Austrian State Treaty of May 1955 which terminated the occupation of Austria through neutrality. The US preferred a separate West German state which could be part of military pacts aimed at the Soviet Union. After this rejection reunification was no longer considered possible by anyone in the east.

From 1945 to 1955 West Germany received US$4 billion in Marshall Plan aid from the US, while East Germany had to pay US$10 billion in war reparations to the Soviet Union. Whole factories and railway lines were dismantled and sent east. East Germany had to shoulder the full burden of responsibility for the wartime misdeeds of both Germanies. The strain on the GDR's economy reached breaking point on 17 June 1953, three months after Stalin's death, when East German workers went on strike over increased work norms. After the disturbances were put down by GDR police and Soviet troops the work load was reduced and on 1 January 1954 the USSR cancelled all outstanding reparations and debts.

A fifth of the population (3,500,000 people) left East Germany before 1961, most of them for economic reasons, but it was, however, a time of migration throughout Europe: 1,200,000 persons left Britain from 1953 to 1961. While causing economic havoc in the east, the influx of skilled manpower was a windfall worth billions to West Germany. Until May 1952 the GDR border with West Germany was fairly open. Then a five-km restricted area was created and border controls tightened. Potential refugees switched to defecting while on legal 'holiday' trips to the west. In 1956 travel authorisations became much more difficult to obtain and the tide of migration shifted to Berlin. There anyone could enter West Berlin simply by boarding the U-Bahn or crossing the street. In 1960 a reckless 'economic main programme' of rapid industrialisation and collectivisation in East Germany turned the flow of refugees into a flood.

On 13 August 1961 thousands of East German troops, police and workers militia suddenly appeared in East Berlin, took up positions at all major intersections and strung barbed wire along the border with West Berlin. Passengers arriving in the city by train were put back on board and told to go home. The temporary barrier was soon replaced by a high stone Wall. The building of the Berlin Wall must be seen against the background of the Bay of Pigs invasion of Cuba on 17 April 1961. International tensions were at breaking point and West Berlin was as much a thorn in the side of the GDR and USSR as Cuba appeared to be in the side of the US. The real seriousness of the situation is illustrated by a promise from Khruschev to take West Berlin if the US invaded Cuba.

Construction of the Wall allowed the GDR to proceed with its development without further interference from the west. The Wall served its purpose well and the subsequent economic revival of the GDR would have been impossible without it. While blackening the GDR's image in western eyes, the Wall brought stability. Only in 1964 did the GDR's economy begin to blossom. By the beginning of the 1960s the transition from capitalism to socialism was complete.

West Germany had been unwilling to accept the establishment of the GDR as an established fact, desiring reunification on its own terms and even the return of territories annexed by Poland and the USSR in 1945. Until the early 1970s the Federal Republic was able to prevent the Democratic Republic from being recognised in the west. The far-sighted *Ostpolitik* of Willy Brandt changed this. In 1970 West Germany signed a treaty with the USSR recognising the territorial integrity of all the states of Europe within their existing boundaries.

In 1971, with detente in full swing, a Quadripartite Agreement was signed by the Soviet Union, the US, Britain and France normalising the status quo in Berlin. With this agreement in place many western countries recognised the GDR and established diplomatic relations. In 1972 the FRG and the GDR agreed on a Basic Law to govern their bilateral affairs, although full recognition continues to be prevented by the West German constitution. In 1973 the GDR was admitted to the United Nations.

GOVERNMENT

The People's Chamber *(Volkskammer)* is the parliamentary body which formulates government policy through laws and resolutions. The Chamber elects the Council of Ministers and Council of State. The 500 elected members of the Chamber are from five political parties, the trade unions, the women's federation, youth and cultural groups. The Chamber meets in the Palace of the Republic on East Berlin's Marx Engels Platz.

The Council of Ministers *(Ministerrat)*, a body of the People's Chamber, is the effective government of the GDR running the day-to-day affairs of state. The national economy is planned and managed here. The Council of Ministers building is on Juden Strasse near Alexander Platz.

The Council of State *(Staatsrat)*, on the south side of Marx Engels Platz, acts as a collective head of state, controlling the Supreme Court, Prosecutor General, foreign policy and national security. The Chairman of the Council of State and the General Secretary of the Socialist Unity

Party Central Committee are usually the same person.

The Socialist Unity Party (SED) is the leading force in the GDR. The Communist Party of Germany was formed on 31 December 1918 from the Spartakus League led by Karl Liebknecht. Ernst Thalmann, the party leader before the Nazi take-over, was arrested at the beginning of March 1933. The Nazis never dared to face Thalmann in a courtroom and he was secretly murdered at Buchenwald on 18 August 1944. In 1946 the Communist and Social Democratic parties merged to become the Socialist Unity Party (SED). There are several other parties under the leadership of the SED in a National Front.

PEOPLE

There are 16,700,000 people in the GDR, compared to 61,300,000 in the Federal Republic. Of these 50,000 are foreign students, compared to 4,400,000 foreign residents of the Federal Republic. Prussians and Saxons form a majority of the population, with a small Slavic minority, the Sorbs and Wends, in the south-east corner of the country. Protestants make up 80% of the population, Catholics 8%. The southern half of the GDR is much more densely populated and industrialised than the north. In all 75% of the population live in urban areas.

ECONOMY

The GDR's only abundant natural resource is soft brown coal (lignite), used to generate electricity. The coal is obtained from open-pit mines in the Cottbus area. The GDR also has the most important reserves of uranium in Europe outside the USSR. Potash is mined around Stassfurt. In general, however, the GDR has far fewer natural resources and less industry than West Germany. The Ruhr always produced 90% of Germany's hard coal and steel.

While the West German 'economic miracle' received wide publicity in the 1960s, East Germany's recovery has been even more remarkable considering the wartime destruction, post-war reparations, loss of skilled manpower and isolation from western markets. Before the war, industry in what was then central Germany was light to medium industry dependent on raw materials (hard coal, coke, steel, etc) and semi-finished products from the west. The GDR had to start from scratch. Careful economic planning built the GDR into the largest industrial and trading nation in Eastern Europe and one of the world's top 10 industrial nations. After the war metallurgy, electric power, chemicals and general and electrical engineering developed. The major products are synthetic rubber and gas, plastics, fertilisers, ships, machinery, textiles, radios, TVs, household appliances, precision instruments, optical equipment, cameras and film. Industry accounts for 48% of the gross national product, services 41% and agriculture only 11%.

East Berlin is the largest industrial centre in the GDR, especially in electronics, machinery, textiles and chemicals. Industry is also concentrated around Halle, Leipzig and Karl Marx Stadt. Synthetic oil is produced from lignite by hydrogenation at Leuna between Halle and Leipzig. There's a modern steel mill at Eisenhuttenstadt near Frankfurt/Oder using Soviet ore and Polish or GDR coke. The southern hills of Saxony and Thuringia feature skilled industries developed from traditional handicrafts. The Carl Zeiss Works at Jena, which produces cameras and optical equipment, is a good example. Rostock is the major port.

Along with the other socialist countries the GDR is a member of the Council for Mutual Economic Assistance (CMEA). The USSR is the largest trading partner and exports of machinery, electrical products, transportation equipment and furniture go to the Soviet Union, Czechoslovakia, Poland and Hungary. Oil is imported from the USSR on the

Friendship Pipeline across Poland to the refinery at Schwedt on the Oder River.

Before the war much of Prussia was divided into 3000 huge landed estates. The land reform of 1945 divided all farms larger than 100 hectares among 544,000 farm workers, smallholders and refugees. In the 1950s there was a migration away from the farm to jobs in industry in the cities and in the early 1960s agriculture was collectivised. This rationalised and increased production through the use of modern equipment and fertilisers, while providing better security for the individual farmer. The main crops are wheat, rye, potatoes and sugar beets, with cattle and pigs the common livestock.

Living standards in the GDR are the highest in Eastern Europe. The per capita national income is double that of Poland, Hungary or Bulgaria, three times that of Romania and Yugoslavia, but only half that of heavily-industrialised West Germany. Public facilities such as transport, medical care and education are excellent and there's a lot of new low rental housing. The products in the stores are good and affordable. There's full employment and job security.

GEOGRAPHY

The GDR is a rectangle 500 km long and 350 km wide in north-east Germany, comprised of the traditional regions Brandenburg, Mecklenburg-Schwerin, Saxony and Thuringia. It extends over two geographical zones, the Central European Plain in the north and the mountain chain of the Mittelgebirge in the south. It covers 108,179 square km (compared to 248,687 square km in the Federal Republic). Including the capital, East Berlin, there are 15 districts (bezirks).

There's a great deal of variety in a small area. The tideless Baltic coast features fine sandy beaches, wooded surroundings and a favourable climate. Behind this are the many lakes of Mecklenburg. The Harz around Wernigerode is an area known for its old traditions and scenic beauty. Picturesque Thuringia, the 'Green Heart of Germany,' with its soft, rolling hills and valleys is a magnificent hiking area. The Rennsteig, a ridge path through the Thuringian forest, stretches 168 km with youth hostels spaced out along the way (Tabarz, Tambach-Dietharz, Oberhof); the 'Hohe Sonne' restaurant near Eisenach is the trailhead. In the Saxon Switzerland between Dresden and Bad Schandau along the River Elbe are picturesque rocks (steine) and gorges, sandstone cliffs and bizarre landforms.

FESTIVALS & HOLIDAYS

The GDR is a music lovers' paradise. Aside from the regular concerts there are music festivals of international repute throughout the year. They include the Berlin Music Biennial in February; the Thuringian Bach Festival, second half of March; the Vogtland Festival of Music in May; the Dresden Music Festival, the last week in May and first week in June; the Dresden International Dixieland Jazz Festival also in May; the Handel Festival in Halle in June; the Sanssouci Park Festival in Potsdam in June; the International Music Seminar in Weimar in July; the Berlin Festival of Music and Drama, the last week in September and first two weeks in October; and the Gewandhaus Festival in Leipzig in October. West German tour companies organise package tours taking in these events, the easiest way to be sure of tickets, accommodation, etc.

Since the 1920s on a Sunday in mid-January Berliners have taken part in a procession to the Socialists' Memorial at Friedrichsfelde Cemetery near the Berlin-Lichtenberg Railway Station where Rosa Luxemburg, Karl Liebknecht, Ernst Thalmann, Walter Ulbricht and many other leading revolutionaries are buried. On a Sunday in March the 'Sommergewinn' festival in Eisenach celebrates the driving out of winter with a km-long procession. For this event, which dates back to 1286, the town is decorated with the traditional symbols of a pretzel, a hen and an egg. The Leipzig Fair in March and September is one of Eastern Europe's main trade fairs. There's a large Christmas Fair off Alexander Platz in East Berlin the last week in November and first three weeks of December (daily 1 to 8 pm).

Public holidays include 1 January (New Year's Day), Good Friday, 1 May (Labour Day), Whit Monday, 7 October (Republic Day) and 25 and 26 December (Christmas).

Facts for the Visitor

VISAS

The information below may not apply to West German nationals, who are subject to special regulations. No photos are required for visas, of which the GDR issues four kinds: transit, tourist, visitor's and day visas. Tourist and visitor's visas cost DM 15 and are stamped into your passport, while day and transit visas cost only DM 5 and are separate pieces of paper. Rail and bus passengers between West Germany and West Berlin don't have to pay the DM 5, while those in cars do. Your passport will be stamped if you get a tourist, visitor's or transit visa, but not with a day visa. Those 16 and under get their visas free.

Transit visas are available at the border and do not allow any stopovers in the GDR, except perhaps a visit to a roadside restaurant if you're driving. You're expected to proceed directly to your destination without changing the means of transport. It's OK to change trains, if necessary, but you can't enter by car and leave by train or vice versa. If you arrive by air you may leave by bus, however. To be allowed to transit you must have a visa for your next destination, if necessary. The other types of visas do not require an onward visa.

To get a tourist visa you must have a

voucher from a travel agency specifying that you've prepaid accommodation for your entire period of stay. This could be in the form of actual hotel reservations or (from May to September) a camping permit. You have to set out an itinerary specifying which district you will be in each night. Once you have a voucher the tourist visa can then be issued by a GDR consulate or at the border itself. Since you've already paid for the voucher in hard currency you're exempt from compulsory exchange.

It's also possible to get a visitor's visa to stay with friends or relatives in the GDR, but you must apply a month in advance. You'll need a written invitation and will be liable to the DM 25 daily compulsory exchange. Your friends or relatives can also make application for you to visit from within the GDR itself, saving you the trouble.

Transit Visa

Deutsche Demokratische Republik
Ministerium für Auswärtige Angelegenheiten

Transitvisum

zur einmaligen Reise durch das Hoheitsgebiet der Deutschen Demokratischen Republik über die für den Transitverkehr zugelassenen Grenzübergangsstellen auf den vorgeschriebenen Verkehrswegen und der kürzesten Fahrtstrecke

M 5,- Verwaltungsgebühr

i. A.

Während des Transits ist ein Wechsel des Transportmittels nur mit Zustimmung der zuständigen Organe der DDR gestattet. In der Binnenschiffahrt berechtigt das Transitvisum zum Landgang an den dafür zugelassenen Orten.

A 19 8

Once inside the GDR on a tourist or visitor's visa it's obligatory to register with the police for every night you spend in the country. If you're staying at an Interhotel this formality will probably be taken care of for you, but if you're staying at a cheaper place you must report to the police in person within 24 hours of arrival. The campground attendant or hotel receptionist will tell you where to go. If you're lucky, you'll get a stamp valid for your entire period of stay in the GDR, making further visits to police stations unnecessary. The registration is valid only for the districts *(bezirks)* where you have reserved accommodation and these are listed in your passport. No registration is required for those with transit or day visas.

Day visas *(tagesvisum)* to visit East Berlin from West Berlin are readily available at the border. All you need is your passport and DM 5 for the visa, plus DM 25 to cover compulsory exchange. The entry points for day trippers are described under 'East Berlin' below. You may enter East Berlin any time after midnight and must leave by midnight the following night through the same border crossing you used to enter. You're not allowed to go beyond East Berlin city limits with this type of visa.

MONEY

DM 1 = 1 M (official)
(US$1 = 1.85 DM)

DM 25 daily compulsory exchange

One mark consists of 100 pfennigs. There are banknotes of 5 M, 10 M, 20 M, 50 M and 100 M. Everyone visiting the GDR must exchange DM 25 for each day they spend in the country at the official one to one rate. The days of arrival and departure count as two days. If you've prepaid an accommodation voucher this requirement will be deemed fulfilled. Transit passengers are also exempt. Men over 65 years of age and women over 60 get a reduced rate of DM 15 daily. Juveniles aged 14 need only change DM 7.50 and children under 14 are free. This money cannot be changed back into hard currency nor taken out of the GDR. If you change more than the minimum exchange requirement be sure to keep your receipts in order to be able to change back leftover East marks upon departure.

All western currency in your possession must be listed on a currency declaration upon entry. The import and export of East marks or the currency of any other socialist country is prohibited. Although banks in West Berlin will sell you East marks at the rate of six to one, it's illegal to take them to East Berlin and you face a stiff fine if caught.

Upon departure any East German currency left in your possession must be deposited at a bank against a receipt which allows you to pick up the money again next visit anytime within a year. If the amount you wish to deposit is over DM 25 you'll be asked to prove that you obtained it through official exchange. It's easier to simply spend all your East marks before you leave.

Changing money with private individuals within the GDR is against the law. This regulation is *strictly* enforced. Be especially wary of anyone asking to change money on the street as you'll probably spend the rest of your visit in a police station if you take the bait.

CLIMATE

The GDR lies in a transition zone between the temperate maritime climate of Western Europe and the rougher continental climate of East Europe. Continental and Atlantic air masses meet here. The mean annual temperature at Berlin is 11.1°C, the average range of temperatures varying from -0.7°C in January to 18°C in July. The average annual precipitation is 585 mm but there is no special rainy season. The camping season is May to September.

BOOKS & BOOKSHOPS

Most travel guidebooks to the GDR exist only in German. The best are *Kunstfuhrer durch die DDR* by Georg Piltz (Urania Verlag, Leipzig, 1969), *Reisebuch DDR* (VEB Tourist Verlag, Leipzig, 1985) and *Tourist-Fuhrer Museen* by Bernd Wurlitzer (VEB Tourist Verlag, Leipzig, 1983). A good West German guide to the GDR is *DuMont Kunst-Reisefuhrer DDR* (DuMont Buchverlag, Koln). *The Other Germany* by John Dornberg (Doubleday, New York, 1968) is a readable examination of life in the GDR during the period following construction of the Wall in 1961.

NEWSPAPERS & MEDIA

Neues Deutschland is the official organ of the SED. *Berliner Zeitung* is an independent daily paper.

FILM & PHOTOGRAPHY

Take enough film with you from the west. You can photograph anything you like *except* military installations, soldiers, border crossings and the Wall, bridges, harbours, railway stations, airports, factories, etc. If you want your picture taken with East German soldiers go to the Neue Wache on East Berlin's Unter den Linden where it's allowed.

GENERAL INFORMATION

Post

Compared to West Germany, postal rates are extremely low. Letters up to 20 grams are 35 pfennig, postcards 25 pfennig.

Electricity

220 volts AC, 50 Hz.

Time

The GDR is on Central European Time (Greenwich Mean Time +1). At the end of March the GDR goes on summer time and clocks are turned an hour forward. At the end of September they're turned an hour back.

Business Hours

The best days to visit East Berlin on a day visa are Wednesday and Thursday when virtually everything is open. In Berlin shops are generally open from 10 am to 7 pm (till 8 pm Thursday). Outside Berlin shopping hours are 9 am to 6 pm. On Saturday mornings only department stores and large shops are open. Banking hours are 8 am to 11.30 am weekdays, with afternoon openings on Tuesday and Thursday.

Museums may open as early as 9 am and close at 6 pm, although 10 am to 4 pm is more common. Most museums, monuments and theatres close on Mondays, although this varies. Admission to museums ranges anywhere from 50 pfennig to 2 M, although most charge 1 M. Students get a 50% discount with an IUS card.

The main restaurants are open from 10 am to midnight with varying closing days. The cheaper restaurants are closed on Saturday afternoon and Sundays, although places in the railway stations open daily. Night bars are open from 9 pm to 4 am.

INFORMATION

Information of all kinds is readily available in the GDR. All the cities have municipal information offices where you can purchase maps and guidebooks and ask questions. They're especially know-ledgeable about local events. Excellent indexed maps are also available at bookstores and newspaper kiosks.

Apart from the regular information office, each city has a branch of the Reiseburo der DDR, the government travel agency. They're more in the business of selling services such as theatre and transportation tickets, accommodation, tours, etc, but will answer simple questions if they can. Receptionists at large hotels are also helpful when they're not too busy. A more down to earth information source about food and entertainment is students from Third World countries.

Overseas information centres for the GDR include:

Britain
    Berolina Travel Ltd (tel 629-1664), 22 Conduit St, London W1R 9TB
Holland
    Kontakt International (tel 020-234771), Prins Hendrikkade 104, 1011 AJ Amsterdam
Japan
    Reiseburo der DDR (tel 405-1981), Aoyama Dai-ichi Mansion 303, 8-4-14 Akasaka, Minato-ku, Tokyo 107

ACCOMMODATION
Youth Hostels
The only really cheap ways of visiting the GDR are staying at youth hostels or by camping. The Reiseburo der FDJ 'Jugendtourist,' Alexander Platz 5, 1026 Berlin, GDR, controls East Germany's 44 youth hostels. They don't handle personal enquiries however, so if you want to reserve a bed at a hostel you must write them six weeks in advance stating which hostels you wish to use on which nights. Be specific. They will then reserve places for you at the hostels of your choice and send you a bill for the overnight fees (DM 12 a night for bed and breakfast in youth hostels, DM 15 a night in youth tourist hotels, payment in western currency). Pay this and they'll issue a voucher which will enable you to get a tourist visa at the border.

Only larger city hostels listed in the *International Youth Hostel Handbook* are described in this book. There are many others and a complete list is available from Jugendtourist. Priority is given to groups and although there's no maximum age limit, the hostels are mainly intended for young people. You must be a member of the International Youth Hostel Federation (IYHF) to use them.

Camping
Camping vouchers are easily obtained at any Reiseburo der DDR from May to September. You exchange DM 25 for each day you wish to stay and they give you a voucher which will get you a tourist visa at the border. The voucher is traded for East German currency at the Reiseburo der DDR office at the border. It's not possible to do this on the train, so rail passengers should arrange their camping visa in Berlin. You pay your camping fees directly, out of the compulsory exchange money.

You must specify exactly which campgrounds you wish to use on which days, so advance planning is essential. The Reiseburo der DDR publishes a list of approved Intercampings. Excepting those in Dresden and Leipzig, all are remote. There are many other campgrounds in the GDR, but foreign tourists are only permitted to stay at the Intercampings. Your camping voucher should be stamped by each campground to prove that you really did follow your itinerary. If you decide to spend the night at a hotel or hostel instead of camping you're in an uncertain position. Many campgrounds rent small bungalows for around 35 M, convenient if it's raining. However to get a camping visa you *must* have a tent and be prepared to use it.

A typical two-week camping trip around the GDR beginning in Berlin might go as follows: Potsdam (Werder/Havel) two nights, Dresden (Moritzburg) three nights, Leipzig (Leipzig-Nord) one night, Halle (Seeburg) or Naumburg (Bad Bibra) two nights, Weimar (Weissensee) two or three nights, Schwerin (Seehof) two nights, Wismar (Zierow) or Stralsund (Reinberg) two nights. The names of the nearest Intercampings are in brackets. You could tack a few nights at Berlin-Schmockwitz on to the end.

Hotels
East Germany's high profile accommodation is the Interhotels of Dresden, East Berlin, Erfurt, Gera, Halle, Karl Marx Stadt, Leipzig, Magdeburg, Oberhof, Potsdam, Rostock, Suhl and Weimar.

They charge DM 80 single and up, usually including breakfast. Reservations for these can be made without difficulty at any Reiseburo der DDR in Eastern Europe or at travel agencies worldwide. Room charges must be paid in advance in western currency in cash (travellers' cheques are sometimes not accepted).

There's no shortage of budget hotels, the officials just don't like you to use them. Many of the cheaper places listed in this book (charging 35 to 45 M and up) can be booked at the Reiseburo der DDR against pre-payment in western currency, but they don't like to do it and may just insist that you stay at an Interhotel. The Reiseburo der DDR, Alexander Platz 5, East Berlin, would probably be the best place to try. Alternatively, enter the GDR on a camping visa and try to book yourself into the cheaper hotels. Some of these hotels only accept guests with reservations, but many will take you if there's a vacancy. Most only have rooms without shower or bath.

Another way to evade the Interhotels is to stay in small towns where there isn't one. When you're booking your itinerary ask for Meissen instead of Dresden, Lutherstadt Wittenberg or Naumburg instead of Halle, Gotha or Eisenach instead of Erfurt, Wernigerode instead of Magdeburg, Brandenburg instead of Potsdam, Wismar or Stralsund instead of Rostock, etc. Train service within the GDR is good and the necessity to commute is more than compensated for by the chance to side-step the beaten tourist track. You're allowed to go anywhere inside the district (bezirk) in which you're staying.

Tours

The Reiseburo der DDR offers a variety of 'guaranteed tours' and one-week 'inclusive holidays' which work out cheaper and easier than individual hotel reservations. The five different 'guaranteed tours' begin on fixed dates throughout the year. You join the group at an East Berlin hotel

where you spend your first night, then tour the country by coach. The tours include transportation, sightseeing, most meals and evening entertainment according to the itinerary, but not travel to and from the GDR. They last anywhere from three to six nights and cost US$250 to US$450 per person with a single room supplement of US$100 to US$120. Some are 'music tours' which include opera or concert tickets.

The seven-day 'holidays' usually begin on a Saturday and cost US$175 to US$400 per person for room and board plus US$60 to US$120 single room supplement per week. A nominal visitor's tax is collected upon arrival at the resort. You have the choice of staying on the Baltic coast or in the mountains of the south. The three southern 'holidays' at Wernigerode, Friedrichroda and Bad Schandau are perfect for those who want to combine a little hiking with visits to picturesque small towns, while enjoying the security of a hotel.

In Eastern Europe book these trips directly with the Reiseburo der DDR. In Western Europe and elsewhere you should work through a travel agent. In Britain contact Berolina Travel (tel 01 629-1664), 22 Conduit St, London W1R 9TD. They will need to know your name, address, date of birth, nationality and passport number. You must book and pay three to six weeks in advance. With the tour voucher you'll be issued a tourist visa at the border.

FOOD & DRINK

As in the rest of Eastern Europe, food is relatively cheap in the GDR. Good quality beer, alcoholic drinks and coffee are available everywhere and there are no peculiar licensing regulations. If you find you're having trouble getting something to eat, try a hotel as these stay open late and are usually receptive to foreign tourists. The restaurants are almost always full and reservations are essential for groups although couples and individuals can usually squeeze in by spending a little time in line. Avoid the peak periods of 12 noon to 1 pm and 5 to 7 pm. The most exclusive restaurants in the GDR insist on advance reservations and won't admit chance arrivals, even if the place is empty. Tipping is not necessary although you can 'round up' the bill.

Some local specialities include *eisbein* (pickled knuckle of pork) with Sauerkraut found in Berlin, *rippenspeer* (spare ribs) in Kasseler, *bockwurst* (sausage), *kartoffelpuffer* (potato fritter), *rotwurst* (black pudding) and *rostbratl* (grilled meat) in Thuringer and *wurstchen* (sausage) in Halberstadter.

THINGS TO BUY

The easiest things to buy are books and maps. Relatively cheap travel guidebooks to other socialist countries are available if you shop around. Art reproductions, books, posters, catalogues and magazines are sold in museums and special shops. Simple musical instruments, sheet music and classical records are good buys, as are notebooks, albums, stationery and postcards. Handicrafts are sometimes available at public markets.

You're allowed to export up to 100 M worth of goods if you stay over four days, or up to a value of 20 M daily if you stay less. To take out gifts and purchases over these limits an export licence is required. Items you cannot take out include food, children's clothing, Meissen porcelain and East German currency. Items purchased at an Intershop for hard currency may be freely exported, provided receipts are held.

WHAT NOT TO TAKE

Don't take anything you don't need. Your possessions will be scrutinised by East German customs and the less you have the better. If you'll only be visiting East Berlin for the day leave most of your cash and valuables in West Berlin. It's prohibited to import East German currency, certain newspapers and magazines, weapons, two-way radios, etc, but it's OK to take a camera.

Getting There & Away

Entry by bicycle or moped is not allowed.

TRAIN

West Berlin is the most common gateway to the GDR and there are daily trains to West Berlin from Hamburg, Cologne/ Hannover, Frankfurt am Main and Nurnberg/Munich. These routes are described in the West Berlin chapter of this book. There are four main railway lines into East Germany from the socialist countries: Gdansk/Szczecin to Berlin, Moscow/Warsaw to Berlin, Warsaw/ Wroclaw to Dresden/Leipzig and Budapest/ Prague to Dresden/Berlin. Trains from Czechoslovakia terminate at East Berlin's Lichtenberg station, while trains from Poland go on to West Berlin's Zoo station and through to West Germany.

Train tickets to Berlin from the socialist countries are valid for all railway stations in East and West Berlin *(stadtbahn)*. This means that if you have a ticket to Berlin from Czechoslovakia you can take the S-Bahn from Berlin-Lichtenberg to Friedrich Strasse, clear customs, and continue on to Zoo Station in West Berlin on the same ticket. In the opposite direction, take the S-Bahn from West Berlin to Friedrich Strasse, get a transit visa and board the East Berlin S-Bahn to Berlin-Lichtenberg and your train. You cannot use the West Berlin U-Bahn in this way, however. If you have an international ticket to Poland purchased in East Berlin or elsewhere, you may board the train in West Berlin. Tickets to the socialist countries are cheaper at the Reiseburo der DDR in East Berlin than at West Berlin travel agencies, yet function the same. Holders of International Union of Students (IUS) cards receive a 33%

discount on journeys to other socialist countries.

BOAT

There are five large car ferries in each direction daily year round between Trelleborg, Sweden, and Sassnitz Hafen near Stralsund (DM 23 one way, four hours). Trelleborg is just south of Malmo, Sweden, near Copenhagen in Denmark. In June, July and August ferries also run between the Danish island of Bornholm and Sassnitz Hafen (DM 44 one way, four hours). Car ferry service is also good from Gedser, Denmark, to Warnemunde near Rostock (two hours, year round). For information in West Berlin contact the Schwedisches Reiseburo, Joachimstaler Strasse 10, 1000 Berlin 15.

Getting Around

TRAIN

Railway travel in the GDR is efficient, inexpensive and less crowded than in most other European countries. Fares are 8 pfennig per km in 2nd class, 11.6 pfennig per km in 1st class. Supplements for travel on express trains vary between 1.50 M and 5 M per journey in 2nd class, 3 M and 10 M in 1st class. Make sure you have the right ticket, otherwise you'll pay an additional supplement to the conductor. Arrivals *(Ankunft)* and departures *(Abfahrt)* are posted on boards in the stations. Always try to use the trains shown in red as these are expresses, but watch for the symbol R which indicates that you must make a computerised seat reservation.

Journey times from Berlin are one hour to Potsdam, about 2½ hours to Dresden, Halle, Leipzig and Schwerin, 3½ hours to Rostock and four hours to Erfurt. Most railway stations have cloakrooms where you can store luggage for only 40 pfennig a piece. All the cities described in this book are connected by fast trains.

There are several main railway routes worth knowing about. An important line is from Berlin-Lichtenberg or Berlin-Schoneweide to Halle, Weimar, Erfurt and (sometimes) Eisenach. This operates almost hourly and all of the Berlin trains call at Schonefeld Airport, a good place to pick them up. Schonefeld is also a good place to catch trains to Potsdam, Magdeburg, Leipzig and Dresden. Berlin to Dresden or Leipzig, and Dresden to Leipzig, are frequent. Two other main routes are Berlin-Lichtenberg to Stralsund or Rostock. Also very useful is the main line down the west side of the GDR from Rostock to Schwerin, Magdeburg, Halle and Leipzig with a through train every couple of hours. One of these services goes to Erfurt instead of Leipzig. Across the bottom of the GDR there are through trains running Dresden/Karl Marx Stadt/Gera/Jena/Weimar/Erfurt.

BUS

Bus routes complement but rarely duplicate the railway services. Schedules are usually posted in the railway stations. All city buses and trams require tickets purchased at kiosks. You validate your own ticket once aboard. Validate two such tickets if you have much luggage. Fares are low, generally about 20 pfennig a ride or a 10th the fare charged in West Berlin.

BOAT

From April to October Weisse Flotte excursion boats ply the lakes, rivers and coastline of the GDR, an excellent inexpensive way of seeing the country as you get around. In the north many of the trips are sold out a few days ahead, but the big paddlewheel steamers operating out of Dresden are eminently accessible. Use them to tour the Elbe and see much of Dresden District. The Weisse Flotte is also very active at Potsdam and East Berlin.

LOCAL TRANSPORT

Most taxis in the GDR don't have meters, so it's best to ask the price in advance. The price should be around 1 M per km, with an increase at night. Taxis are hard to find but there's usually a stand at the main railway stations. Join the queue. To get a cab elsewhere you telephone the taxi dispatcher and have one sent to you. You must pay for the taxi's round trip and trips out of town are double fare.

East Berlin

When Berlin was carved up in 1945 the old city centre with its bombed-out churches, palaces and museums fell into the eastern sector. Potsdam, summer residence of the Prussian royal family, was also included in the Soviet zone. Most of the buildings in West Berlin were less than a century old.

Since then the two Berlins have gone their own ways, a course made strikingly permanent in 1961 by the building of the Wall. East Berlin has grown into an impressive modern city, a showplace of Eastern Europe. For visitors its an unparalleled chance to compare the workings of capitalism and socialism side by side. Access is surprisingly easy. Since your initial forays into the east will probably be day trips you'll be constantly bouncing back and forth between conflicting impressions. For this reason it's better to cope with the bureaucracy and arrange to spend a few nights in East Berlin at a hotel or the Intercamping. That will give you a much better feel for the place.

You'll be following in the footsteps of Marx, Engels and Lenin, all of whom visited Berlin many times. The philosopher Hegel taught at the University of Berlin from 1818 to 1831, only one of the remarkable individuals who helped make this great city what it is today. Frederick II 'the Great' (reigned 1740-1786) commissioned many of the massive Baroque-Rococo buildings along Unter den Linden to symbolise his growing power. His most famous architect was Georg Wenzeslaus von Knobelsdorff who designed the Opera House and Humboldt University in Berlin, and the Sanssouci Palace in Potsdam. Even more striking is the adapted Greek architecture of the neo-Classical architect Karl Friedrich Schinkel who built the Schauspielhaus, Neue Wache and Altes Museum in Berlin, plus the Nikolaikirche and Charlottenhof Palace in Potsdam. These sights will keep you busy.

Remember that as a day visitor you're not allowed to go beyond the limits of the 11 boroughs of the city of East Berlin. A map on the back of your day visa clearly defines the area. All of the places mentioned in this section (except Schonefeld Airport) are within the permitted zone. Potsdam is beyond the fringe.

Orientation

The tourists' East Berlin revolves around Unter den Linden, the fashionable avenue of autocratic Berlin. Together with its continuation, Karl Liebknecht Strasse, they extend east from the Brandenburg Gate to Alexander Platz, the heart of today's socialist Germany. Between these two are East Berlin's finest museums, on an island in the Spree River. Most of the city's outlying sights are south-east, on or near this river which winds across the city for over 30 km.

You'll arrive at one end or the other of Friedrich Strasse, which runs due north from 'Checkpoint Charlie' to Friedrich Strasse Railway Station, both entry points into the GDR. If you arrived on foot over 'Checkpoint Charlie' walk up Friedrich Strasse three blocks to Stadmitte U-Bahn station, where you can catch a train directly to Alexander Platz (fifth stop). Put 20 pfennig (East or West) into the box at the station entrance and take a ticket. If you arrived at Friedrich Strasse Railway Station on the S or U-Bahn from

West Berlin, buy a strip of East Berlin S-Bahn tickets at the ticket window (1 M for five) and get back on the S-Bahn two stops to Alexander Platz. The 'Alex' is the best place to begin a visit to the German Democratic Republic.

Warning Don't cross against a red light in East Berlin. These are often frustratingly slow and timed in such a way that you only get half way across, then have to wait on the safety island for the next green. You may feel foolish waiting for the light to change just to cross a single lane with no cars in sight. Do wait, however, as policemen are on the watch for tourist jaywalkers and you'll definitely pay a fine if caught.

Information

The Berlin-Information tourist office below the TV tower near Alexander Platz Railway Station is open Monday 1 to 6 pm, Tuesday to Friday 8 am to 6 pm, Saturday and Sunday 10 am to 6 pm. They'll sell you a detailed map and can answer questions. The scale model of East Berlin in this office will help you find your bearings.

The Reiseburo der DDR, Alexander Platz 5, is a large travel agency (open daily) offering a variety of services. Downstairs you can book local sightseeing tours at Counter No 1, buy theatre and Weisse Flotte tickets (not for the same day) at Counter No 2, make train reservations at Counter No 5 and buy international railway tickets at Counter No 6. Upstairs Counter No 11 is a bank, Counter No 12 is the Foreigners Registration Office and Counter No 13 makes hotel reservations and sells camping vouchers. Counters No 1 and No 2 take East marks, counters No 6 and No 13 want hard currency. If you're in East Berlin on a package tour and want to visit West Berlin as a day trip (a switch!), a re-entry visa (DM 15) can be arranged at Counter No 12. If you have questions go to Counter

No 13 where they speak English. The Interflug office is adjacent.

The Reiseburo der DDR, Charlotten Strasse 45 off Unter den Linden, also sells international train tickets. This is the office which organises family visits if you have friends or relatives in the GDR. For information on youth hostels in the GDR try the Reiseburo der FDJ 'Jugend-tourist,' Friedrich Strasse 79a (weekdays 8 am to 6 pm).

Other Tourist Offices Tourist information on the other Eastern European countries is available from Orbis (Poland), Warschauer Strasse 5 (U-Bahn – Frankfurter Tor); Cedok (Czechoslovakia), Strausberger Platz 8 (U-Bahn – Strausberger Platz); Ibusz (Hungary), Karl Liebknecht Strasse 9; Intourist (USSR), Unter den Linden 51 and Balkantourist (Bulgaria), Unter den Linden 40.

Consulates Visas for the other socialist countries are more easily obtained in East Berlin than West Berlin. The Soviet Consulate is at Unter den Linden 65 (Monday, Wednesday and Friday 8 am to 12 noon). The Polish Consulate is at Unter den Linden 72 (Monday, Wednesday, Thursday and Friday 8.30 am to 1 pm). The Hungarian Consulate is at Otto Grotewohl Strasse 6 (Monday, Wednesday and Friday 9 am to 1 pm). The Czechoslovakian Consulate is at Otto Grotewohl Strasse 21 (Monday, Wednesday, Thursday and Friday 10 am to 11.30 am and 1 pm to 2.30 pm). All four of these are near the Brandenburg Gate. Visa fees must be paid in western currency and up to four passport photos are required for each. You can usually pick up Polish, Czechoslovakian and Hungarian tourist or transit visas on the spot.

Embassies The American Embassy, Neustadtische Kirch Strasse 4-5, and the British Embassy, Unter den Linden 32-34, are both near Friedrich Strasse Railway Station. The permanent representation

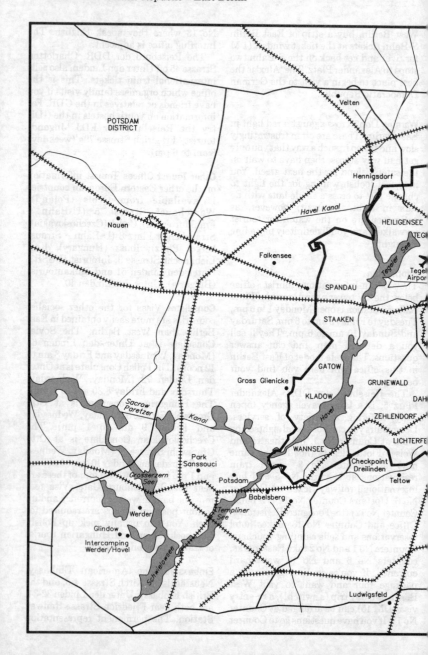

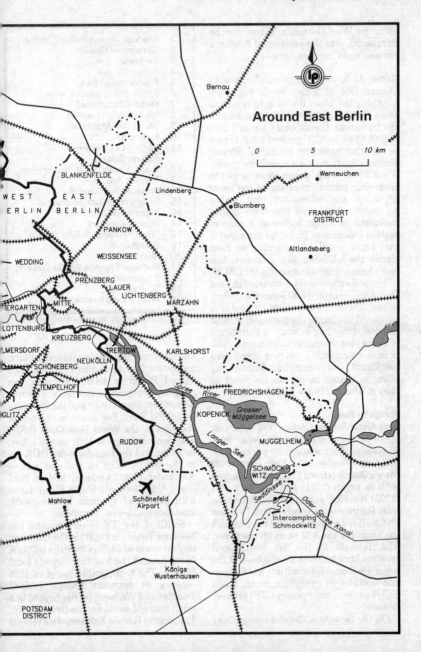

Around East Berlin

0   5   10 km

office for West Germany, Hannoversche Strasse 30, is at the junction of Friedrich Strasse and Chaussee Strasse.

Banks As a day visitor you'll have to change DM 25 officially. If you have anything left when it's time to return to West Berlin deposit it at the Staatsbank der DDR near 'Checkpoint Charlie' (open daily 6.45 am to 12.30 pm and 1 to 8.45 pm) or at the bank in Friedrich Strasse Railway Station (open round the clock). They'll give you a receipt allowing you to pick your marks up again at the same office on any subsequent visit within 12 months. You could also leave money overnight in a coin locker at a railway station (Alexander Platz, for example) if you know you'll be returning to East Berlin the following day. Actually, you won't have any trouble spending the DM 25.

Virtually any shop or restaurant in East Berlin will accept West German currency at the official one to one rate, but you're supposed to change the money at a bank or hotel. Only pay in western currency if it's for a visa or international train ticket, or in an emergency if you over-spend (at a restaurant, for example). Refuse any offers to change money on the street as they're almost always police set-ups.

Things to See
Near Alexander Platz Before WW II the vast open square that extends west from Alexander Platz was solidly packed with buildings. Today only 13th century **St Mary's Church** (closed Friday and Sunday) with its organ (1721) and marble pulpit (1703) remains, strangely isolated below East Berlin's soaring 365-metre **TV tower** (1969). If it's a clear day and the line isn't too long, pay the 3 M to go up the tower. The Telecafe at the 207 metre level revolves once an hour. At the base of the tower are tourist information, a cafe/disco and upstairs an exhibition centre (open daily) where contemporary GDR art may be seen.

On the far side of the elevated railway

1	Friedrich Strasse Railway Station
2	'Checkpoint Charlie'
3	TV Tower
4	Puppentheater
5	Friedrichshain Park
6	Sports & Recreation Centre
7	Berlin – Ostbahnhof
8	Weisse Flotte Landing
9	Soviet War Memorial
10	Kulturpark
11	Berlin – Lichtenberg Railway Station
12	'Egon Schultz' Youth Tourist Hotel
13	Tierpark Zoo
14	Soviet Army Museum
15	Karlshorst S-Bahn Station
16	Kopenick S-Bahn Station
17	Schloss Kopenick
18	Friedrichshagen S-Bahn Station
19	Spreetunnel
20	Muggel Tower
21	Rudower Chausee Border Crossing
22	Schonefeld Airport
23	Schmockwitz
24	Krossin Lake Intercamping

station from the tower is Alexander Platz, named for Tsar Alexander I of Russia who visited Berlin in 1805. This area was completely rebuilt in the 1960s. **Centrum Department Store** (1970) and the 39-storey Interhotel Stadt Berlin are on one side of the square, the **World Time Clock** (1969) and domed Congress Hall on the other. Interflug and the Reiseburo der DDR are in the tall building on the east side of Alexander Platz. Orderly, lifeless Karl Marx Allee (formerly Stalin Allee), faced with glass and concrete in the 1950s, stretches south-east from here.

South of the TV tower opposite the Neptune Fountain (1891) is the red-brick central tower of **Berlin City Hall** (1870). A frieze around the building depicts local history. The twin Gothic spires of 13th century **St Nicholas Church** (closed Tuesday and Wednesday) rise beyond a small restored section of medieval Berlin. The nearby Rococo **Ephraimpalais** (closed

Thursday and Friday) on Muhlendamm has paintings and old prints of Berlin, and a nice cafe.

Museum Island West of the TV tower, across the Spree River, is the great neo-Renaissance dome of **Berlin Cathedral** (1904) and the sleek contemporary lines of the **Palace of the Republic** (1976), which occupies the site of the Baroque City Palace demolished in 1950. A portal from the old palace has been incorporated into the facade of the **Council of State** building on the south side of the square. The Palace of the Republic (open daily 10 am to midnight) has something for everyone including wine restaurants, cafes, pubs, youth disco, theatres, art exhibitions, souvenir shops, a post office, bowling alley and soft lounge chairs, in addition to the GDR parliament.

Cathedral and Palace share an island in the Spree with a host of splendid museums. The imposing neo-Classical edifice (1829) beside the cathedral is Schinkel's **Altes Museum** (closed Monday and Tuesday), the oldest public museum in Berlin, where changing art exhibitions are presented. Behind this is the Neues Museum (1855) which is still being rebuilt, but you can visit the adjacent **National Gallery** (closed Monday and Tuesday) with 19th and 20th century paintings.

The **Pergamon Museum** (closed Monday and Tuesday) is a feast of antiquity, especially classical Greek, Babylonian, Roman, Islamic and Oriental. The Ishtar Gate from Babylon (580 BC), Pergamon Altar from Asia Minor (160 BC) and Market Gate from Miletus, Greece (2nd century AD) are world-renowned monuments. The **Bode Museum** (closed Monday, open till 8 pm on Thursday) houses sculpture, paintings, coins and Egyptian art, although not all sections are open every day. There's a good cafe upstairs in this museum.

Along Unter den Linden A stroll down

Unter den Linden from Museum Island to the **Brandenburg Gate** (1791) takes in the greatest surviving monuments of the former Prussian capital. All the captions may be in German at the **Museum of German History** (closed Friday) in the former Armoury (1706) opposite the Unter den Linden Palace (1732), but the extensive collection of objects, maps and photos is fascinating. Be sure to see the building's interior courtyard for its 22 heads of dying warriors by Andreas Schluter.

Next to this museum is Schinkel's Neue Wache (1818), now the **Memorial to the Victims of Fascism & Militarism** where you can see a ceremonial changing of the guard every Wednesday at 2.30 pm. **Humboldt University** (1753), the next building west, was originally a palace of the brother of Frederick II, converted to a university in 1810. Beside this is the massive **State Library** (1914). An equestrian statue of Frederick II stands in the middle of the avenue in front of the university.

Across the street from the university, beside the Old Library (1780) with its curving Baroque facade, is Knobelsdorff's **German State Opera** (1743). On Bebel Platz, the square between these buildings, the Nazis staged a notorious book burning on 10 May 1933. A decade later in scores of concentration camps they fulfilled Heinrich Heine's terrible prophecy: 'Where books are burned people too are burned in the end.' Behind this site is **St Hedwigs Cathedral** (1773), modelled on the Parthenon in Athens.

Detour south-west two blocks to Platz der Akademie to see the twin French and German cathedrals in perfect neo-Classical harmony. The cathedrals are copies of similar buildings on Piazza del Popolo in Rome. Today the French Cathedral (1780) is the **Huguenot Museum** (closed Monday and Friday). Some 20,000 French Huguenots settled in Berlin-Brandenburg after 1685. Between the cathedrals is the **Concert Hall** (Schauspielhaus), built by Schinkel in

1821 and reopened in 1986 after being completely reconstructed in the original style. A block west at Friedrich Strasse 176-179 is the **House of Soviet Culture** (closed Sunday) with art and photography exhibitions, a Russian bookstore (open weekdays) and soft lounge chairs for a break.

North of Friedrich Strasse The house at Chaussee Strasse 125, where the famous playwright **Bertolt Brecht** lived from 1953 until his death in 1956, can be visited Tuesday to Friday from 10 to 11.30 am, Thursday from 5 to 6.30 pm and Saturday from 9.30 am to 1 pm in groups of eight persons maximum with a German-speaking guide (admission free). Go into the rear courtyard and up the stairs to the right. The entrance is upstairs.

Next to Brecht House is **Dorotheenstadt Cemetery** with tombs of the illustrious, such as the architect Schinkel, the philosopher Hegel and Brecht himself. The **Natural History Museum** nearby at Invaliden Strasse 43 (closed Monday) has a good collection of dinosaurs and minerals, plus an interesting exhibit on Charles Darwin.

Retrace your steps and follow Oranienburger Strasse east to the gutted **synagogue** (1866) not far from the Bode Museum. On Kristallnacht, 9 to 10 November 1938, the Nazis used the assassination of a German diplomat in Paris as a pretext to pillage synagogues and loot Jewish businesses throughout the Reich. Half a century later the padlocked synagogue reminds us of this dark era. The working class neighbourhood behind the synagogue, especially Grosse Hamburger Strasse and Sophien Strasse, is worth a wander to capture a little of the flavour of bygone Berlin.

By U-Bahn Three interesting sights are accessible on East Berlin's two U-Bahn lines, which intersect at Alexander Platz. Take a train to Markisches Museum station. The collection of the **Markisches Museum** (closed Monday and Tuesday) is intended to illustrate the history of Berlin. Special features include a scale model of Berlin in 1750 and drawings by Heinrich Zille. Bears housed in a pit in the park behind the museum are official mascots of the city. **Otto Nagel Haus** (closed Friday and Saturday) on the Spree Canal nearby presents changing art shows.

Reboard the U-Bahn as far as Dimitroff Strasse Station, where the U-Bahn runs up onto an elevated section. (If everyone gets off at Alexander Platz it means you have to change platforms, although some trains run straight through from Otto Grotewohl Strasse to Pankow.) Disembark and walk west on Eberswalder Strasse past the stadium to the **Berlin Wall**. You've probably already seen the Wall from West Berlin. From East Berlin it looks quite different – no graffiti, concrete obstacles on the access roads and border guards watching you approach. There's even a tourist tower on the West Berlin side with a few indolents gawking in at you. It's quite a sight but you probably won't feel like hanging around long. Photography is forbidden.

Get back on the U-Bahn to Alexander Platz where you change for Tierpark. East Berlin's extensive **zoo** adjoins this station and admission is only one mark (compared to DM 8 at the West Berlin zoo). Schloss Friedrichsfelde (1690) within the zoo compound offers tours daily except Monday at 3 pm, weekends at 11 am and 1 pm also.

Karlshorst to Kopenick Take any southbound streetcar from the zoo entrance to Karlshorst S-Bahn station to visit East Berlin's most striking museum, housed in a building where the German High Command signed the unconditional surrender on 8 May 1945. The **Soviet Army Museum** (open Tuesday to Friday 9 am to 1 pm and 3 to 6 pm, Saturday 9 am to 4 pm, Sunday 9 am to 2 pm – free) is at the end of Fritz Schmenkel Strasse, about 700 metres from the station. The captions are all in Russian, although German labels are sometimes tacked on below. Gruesome photos of executed Nazi war criminals culminate this amazingly explicit exhibition.

Reboard the S-Bahn at Karlshorst and ride two stops east to Kopenick. Take tram No 86 south to reach the **Applied Arts Museum** or Kunstgewerbemuseum (closed Monday and Tuesday), housed in a Baroque palace (Schloss) built by the Dutch architect Rutger von Langerfeld between 1678 and 1688. This attractive museum near the junction of the Spree and Dahme rivers features a silver buffet service of 1698 from the Knights' Hall of the former City Palace. There's a huge park around **Great Muggel Lake** a couple of km east of here (bus No 27).

River Cruises The **Spree River** crosses Berlin from east to west connecting with an extensive network of lakes and canals. From April to October daily at 11 am and 3 pm the Weisse Flotte offers a scenic three-hour non-stop river cruise from Treptow Hafen, six km south-east of Alexander Platz, to Great Muggel Lake and back (the 'Muggelseefahrt'). Take the S-Bahn direction Konigs-Wusterhausen or Schonefeld to Treptower Park station which is directly opposite the terminus.

Prices are low but tickets are in high demand and weekends and holidays are always fully booked. To increase your chances of getting a seat go early, as soon as you enter East Berlin. Same day tickets are sold at the wooden ticket office labelled 'Tageskasse' or 'Kasse II' on the wharf (offerings are listed on a board). The regular ticket windows sell advance tickets only. Advance tickets are also available from Counter No 2 at the Reiseburo der DDR on Alexander Platz and are a good idea if you know you'll be returning to East Berlin a few days later. Cold lunches are served aboard.

While you're in the area visit the **Soviet War Memorial** (1949) nearby in Treptower Park. Five thousand Soviet soldiers are buried around this huge monument, built from the stones of Hitler's chancellery. The **Kulturpark**, East Berlin's amusement park (open mid-April to October from 1 to 7 pm daily except Monday and Friday), is beyond.

Places to Stay

Most people visit East Berlin from West Berlin on a day visa. If you want to stay longer you'll have to make an advance booking for a hotel room or camping place at the Reiseburo der DDR. With the voucher you receive from the Reiseburo you'll get a regular tourist visa (DM 15) valid for the number of nights for which you've prepaid accommodation in hard currency. These arrangements can be made at the Interflug office in Friedrich Strasse Railway Station (on the West Berlin side of customs) or at Counter No 13 in the Reiseburo head office, Alexander Platz 5.

Hostels The *'Egon Schultz' Youth Tourist Hotel* (open year round) is opposite the zoo at Franz-Mett-Strasse 7 (U-Bahn to Tierpark). Advance reservations from 'Jugendtourist' are essential (see the chapter introduction).

Camping The *Intercamping* (open May to September) is on Krossin Lake at Schmockwitz in the far south-east corner of East Berlin. Take tram No 86 from Kopenick or Grunau S-Bahn stations to the end of the line, then catch an infrequent bus or walk two km.

Cheaper Hotels The *Christliches Hospiz*, August Strasse 82, has rooms priced from DM 23 to DM 52. You can also request the *Hospiz am Bahnhof Friedrich Strasse*, Albrecht Strasse 8, or the *Hotel Newa*, Invaliden Strasse 115, but these are often full. At 70 M per person the *Adria Hotel*, Friedrich Strasse 134, is significantly more expensive.

Expensive Hotels East Berlin is full of luxury Interhotels. The *Metropol Hotel, Hotel Unter den Linden* and *Grandhotel* are all conveniently near Friedrich Strasse Railway Station. The *Hotel Stadt Berlin* is at Alexander Platz, while the *Palast Hotel* overlooks Marx Engels Forum. Prices at the Unter den Linden and Stadt Berlin begin at DM 130 single, DM 170 double, breakfast included, rising to DM 220 single, DM 280 double at the Grandhotel.

Places to Eat

Bottom End Weekdays you can get breakfast at the *Kleine Konditorei am Metropol Theater* opposite the exit from Friedrich Strasse Railway Station. *Quick*, a self-service in the Palast Hotel near Berlin Cathedral, is also convenient (daily 10 am to 8 pm). A grill and expensive cafe are adjacent.

There are lots of places to eat near Alexander Platz. Adjacent to the tourist office below the TV tower is a basic cafeteria (open daily 6 am to 6 pm). In the arcade at the east end of the Rathauspassage near the railway station is a cheap *Wurst Bar*, bockwurst is less than a mark.

Substantial, inexpensive meals with quick table service in spacious surroundings can be had at *Gaststatte Alextreff* (daily 10 am to 4 pm), upstairs between the elevated tracks and the Rathauspassage. Also good is the large modern cafeteria with the yellow sign (daily 10 am to 8 pm) in the *Hotel Stadt Berlin*, on the opposite side of Alexander Platz Railway Station from the TV tower. The *Zille Stube* upstairs is a tasteful restaurant.

Top End You can avoid long lines at the restaurants by dining at odd hours (such as 3 to 5 pm). One of the easiest places to experience a typical German meal is the *Ratskeller* below Berlin City Hall *(Rathaus)* just south of the TV tower. There are two separate sections to this restaurant with entrances at opposite ends of the building, so check the other if the line is too long at the first. Prices are moderate but the service tends to be slow. There's an even better *Ratskeller* below Kopenick Town Hall, not far from Schloss Kopenick.

For Czech food try *Morava*, upstairs in the Rathauspassage near Alexander Platz Railway Station. The *Gastmahl des Meeres*, Spandauer Strasse and Karl Liebknecht Strasse, specialises in seafood such as whole trout (charged by weight) and eel.

A hearty recommendation goes out to *Zur letzten Instanz*, Waisen Strasse 14-16 (closed weekends). This typical Berlin tavern (built in 1525) is a little hidden on a back street behind the Council of Ministers building south-east of Alexander Platz, but any Berliner could direct you. It's often crowded but the staff is receptive to foreign visitors. The place got it's present name 150 years ago when a newly divorced couple came in from the nearby courthouse with their witnesses for a few drinks. By the time they were ready to leave they'd made up and decided to remarry the next day, at which one of those present exclaimed, 'This is the court of last resort!'

An excellent late evening place to go is *Cafe 'Arkade,'* Franzosische Strasse 25 near Platz der Akademie, which stays open until midnight daily. Here you can enjoy excellent Viennese coffee, ice cream, drinks or whole meals in a pleasant relaxed atmosphere – a great place to spend your last East marks.

Entertainment

East Berlin beats West Berlin hands down as far as straight theatre goes. The productions are lavish with huge casts and the best seats cost the same as the cheapest tickets in West Berlin (about 15 M). Theatre box offices generally open from 12 noon to 6 pm. Good seats for performances on the same evening are hard to come by, although you can often obtain them for a show a few nights later if you know you'll be returning. Unclaimed tickets are generally made available at the

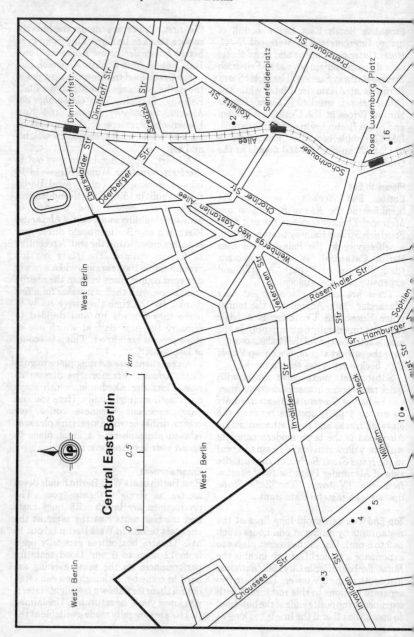

Central East Berlin

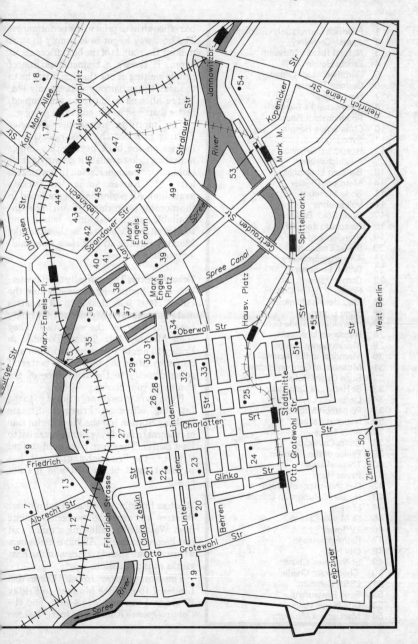

1	Friedrich Ludwig Jahn Stadium
2	Jewish Cemetery
3	Natural History Museum
4	Brecht House
5	Dorotheenstadt Cemetery
6	German Theatre
7	Nazi Bunker
8	Barenschenke Bierbar
9	Friedrichstadt Palast
10	Christliches Hospiz
11	Synagogue
12	Hospiz am Bahnhof Friedrichstrasse
13	Berlinen Ensemble
14	Metropol Theater
15	Bode Museum
16	Volksbúhne
17	Hotel Stadt Berlin
18	Reiseburo der DDR
19	Brandenburg Gate
20	Soviet Embassy
21	American Embassy
22	British Embassy
23	Comic Opera
24	House of Soviet Culture
25	Platz der Akademie
26	State Library
27	International Trade Centre
28	Humboldt University
29	Maxim Gorky Theater
30	Memorial to the Victims
31	Museum of German History
32	State Opera House
33	St Hedwig's Cathedral
34	Unter den Linden Palace
35	Pergamon Museum
36	National Gallery
37	Altes Museum
38	Berlin Cathedral
39	Palace of the Republic
40	Theaterkassen
41	Palast Hotel
42	Das Internationale Buch
43	House of Hungarian Culture
44	Market
45	St Mary's Church
46	TV Tower
47	Rathauspassage
48	City Hall
49	St Nicholas' Church
50	'Checkpoint Charlie'
51	CSSR Centrum
52	Sofia Restaurant
53	Otto Nagel Haus
54	Markisches Museum

box office an hour prior to the performance. The best way to get in is simply to start making the rounds of the box offices about 6 pm. If there's a tremendous line of people waiting at one theatre, hurry on to the next. Upper balcony seats are only 3 M. You're allowed to move to unoccupied, better seats just as the curtain is going up.

The morning newspaper *Berliner Zeitung* provides the evenings' theatre listings on the back page with symbols indicating ticket availability: * ausverkauft (sold out); ** einige Karten (a few tickets left); *** Karten vorhanden (tickets available). All performances are listed in the monthly programme *Wohin in Berlin*, available at newsstands, hotels and tourist offices. Many of the theatres take Monday evening off and close from mid-July to late August.

Ticket Agencies Theoretically the Theaterkassen on Spandauer Strasse beside the Palast Hotel sells tickets to all theatres and some concerts. In practice they rarely have anything for the same day. They open Monday 1 to 7 pm, Tuesday to Friday 10 am to 1 pm and 2 to 7 pm and Saturday 10 am to 1 pm. You're better off going directly to the box office of the theatre of your choice.

If you want to be sure of a ticket go to the Interflug office in Friedrich Strasse Railway Station (on the West Berlin side of customs) a few days prior to your visit to East Berlin. They even have hard-to-find tickets to the Friedrichstadt Palast, but payment must be in DM and it's not cheap.

Theatres Luckily all of East Berlin's best theatres are near the two entry points from West Berlin, allowing a quick exit just before midnight. All have snack bars where you can spend your remaining East marks at intermission.

The *State Opera House*, Unter den Linden 7 (box office Monday to Friday 10 am to 1 pm and 2 to 4 pm), and the *Comic Opera* (Komische Oper), Behren

Strasse at Glinka Strasse (box office Tuesday to Saturday 12 noon to 6 pm), offer operas and musicals. Berlin's wonderfully restored *Concert Hall* (Schauspielhaus) is on Platz der Akademie (box office Monday to Saturday 1 to 6 pm). Vaudeville musical revues are presented at the new *Friedrichstadt Palast* (1984), Friedrich Strasse 107, but they're permanently sold out. Check to see what's doing at the *Metropol Theater* opposite Friedrich Strasse Railway Station (box office Tuesday to Saturday 12 noon to 6 pm). Often it's music and tickets are much easier to come by at the Metropol than at the overrated Comic Opera.

If you understand German you can see drama at the *German Theatre*, Schumann Strasse 13a, the adjacent *Kammerspiele* (box offices of both open Tuesday to Saturday 12 noon to 5 pm), the *Maxim Gorky Theater* behind the Memorial to the Victims on Unter den Linden (box office weekdays 12 noon to 6 pm), and the *Volksbuhne*, Rosa Luxemburg Platz (box office Tuesday to Saturday 12 noon to 6pm). Even if your German is non-existent Bertolt Brecht's original theatre, the *Berliner Ensemble*, near Friedrich Strasse Railway Station (box office Monday 11 am to 5 pm, Tuesday to Friday 11 am to 6 pm), is worth attending for both the architecture and classic Brecht plays. *Mother Courage*, a chronicle from the Thirty Years' War which Brecht wrote in 1938 in anticipation of things to come, is often performed here. Tickets are usually obtainable.

Share the joys and fantasies of childhood at the *Puppentheater*, Greifswalder Strasse 81-84 just outside Ernst Thalmann Park S-Bahn station. Performances are often weekdays at 10 am and 2 pm, but check. Tickets are usually available at the door for foreign visitors.

Others You'll have to do your dancing in West Berlin. There's one disco below the TV tower and another in the Palace of the Republic but the required entry tickets are sold out weeks ahead. There's no trouble getting in the *Barenschenke Bierbar*, Friedrich Strasse 124 a couple of blocks north of Friedrich Strasse Railway Station, an unpretentious local pub with great atmosphere. It's easy to make friends at the bar.

The *Haus der Jungen Talente*, Kloster Strasse 68/70 south-east of Alexander Platz, is a cultural centre for youth with various clubs and dance workshops (open 3 to 10 pm Monday to Saturday). There's often live music in one of the rooms. This is more a place to meet people than to be entertained. The restaurant inside is good (open weekdays).

There's trotting at *Karlshorst Race Track* near Karlshorst S-Bahn Station after 3 pm Wednesday, Saturday or Sunday afternoons throughout the year (admission 2 M). All races are listed in *Wohin in Berlin*. Even if you're not a regular horse racing fan this is a wonderfully informal place to see ordinary local people enjoying themselves. Buy the programme at the gate if you intend to wager. There are stands dispensing really cheap sausage and beer (1 M deposit on the glass).

Things to Buy

Das Internationale Buch, Spandauer Strasse 4 (closes at 7 pm weekdays, 1 pm Saturday), has glossy art books, travel guidebooks and some maps, but they don't have much in English. Das Gute Buch beyond the World Time Clock on Alexander Platz is the best general bookstore in the city. High quality Soviet art books are available at Das Sowjetische Buch, Unter den Linden 17. The Kunstsalon, Unter den Linden 41, has East German art books, reproductions, sheet music, records and cassettes. The Galerie Unter den Linden, Unter den Linden 68 near the Brandenburg Gate (closed Sunday), sells excellent posters for around 3 M.

Souvenir shops in East Berlin sell miniature Captain of Kopenick dolls. This traditional character originated in

1906 when shoemaker Wilhelm Voigt dressed in a captain's uniform borrowed from a used clothing shop and ordered a few soldiers to accompany him to Kopenick town hall. There Voigt arrested the mayor and had the treasurer turn over his cash holdings. The incident ended in failure for Voigt as he was unable to find the passport forms and official stamp these authorities had previously refused him on grounds that he was not eligible to work in Prussia.

Products of Other Socialist Countries East Berlin is a good place to get an idea of the sort of things available in the other Eastern European countries. Several have cultural centres (open weekdays) in the city which sell their own books and maps, records, national handicrafts and souvenirs. The House of Hungarian Culture, Karl Liebknecht Strasse 9, and the Polish Cultural Centre, Karl Liebknecht Strasse 7, are opposite St Mary's Church near Alexander Platz. The Bulgarian Cultural Centre is at Unter den Linden 10, while the Czechoslovakian Cultural Centre (CSSR Centrum), Leipziger Strasse 60, is on the way to 'Checkpoint Charlie.'

Getting There & Away

From West Berlin The easiest way to get to East Berlin is to take the West Berlin S-Bahn or U-Bahn to Friedrich Strasse Railway Station, an entry point into the GDR. Signs reading *Zur Grenzubergangsstelle* indicate the way to East German immigration. You'll come out inside the East Berlin station itself with a room of coin lockers to the right. To return to West Berlin enter the new pavilion marked *Ausreise* beyond the taxi stand beside the main station.

Foreign visitors may also enter East Berlin on foot at 'Checkpoint Charlie' near West Berlin's Koch Strasse U-Bahn station. Nationals of West Germany may use the Prinzen Strasse/Heinrich Heine Strasse (U-Bahn – Moritz Platz) or

Bornholmer Strasse (U and S-Bahns – Gesundbrunnen) border crossings. Friedrich Strasse is usually simpler and is open to everyone. Checkpoint Charlie is open 24 hours a day while Friedrich Strasse only functions when the West Berlin transit system is operating. The customs check is stricter at Checkpoint Charlie than Friedrich Strasse. Day visitors must leave before midnight by the same border crossing they used to enter.

Train Railway tickets to Poland, Czechoslovakia and Hungary are cheaper in East Berlin than the same tickets purchased in West Berlin. You may use a ticket purchased in East Berlin to board a Poland-bound train at the Zoo Station in West Berlin (Stadtbahn). For the train to Prague get a transit visa at the Friedrich Strasse Railway Station border crossing as usual, then take the S-Bahn to Berlin-Lichtenberg. Your through ticket covers this ride.

International tickets are valid two months from the date of issue and may be purchased at Counter No 6 at the Reiseburo der DDR on Alexander Platz. A ticket to Budapest costs DM 90 1st class, DM 60 2nd class. Sleepers to Budapest are DM 54 (1st class), DM 35 (2nd class), or DM 10 for a couchette. To Poznan it's DM 31 1st class, DM 21 2nd class. If you're on a low budget only buy a ticket to Rzepin, the first major junction in Poland (DM 10). There you could get off and buy an onward ticket to Szczecin, Poznan or Wroclaw for zloty. It would also be cheaper to pay the Polish conductor the difference.

Railway Stations Bahnhof Berlin-Lichtenberg is the main railway station in East Berlin, with trains to all parts of the GDR. This station is easily reached by S-Bahn or on the Tiergarten U-Bahn line. Many trains to Dresden, Leipzig, Halle, Karl Marx Stadt, Gera, Erfurt and Magdeburg also leave from Bahnhof Berlin-Schoneweide. All trains to the south and west of the GDR stop at Flughafen Berlin-

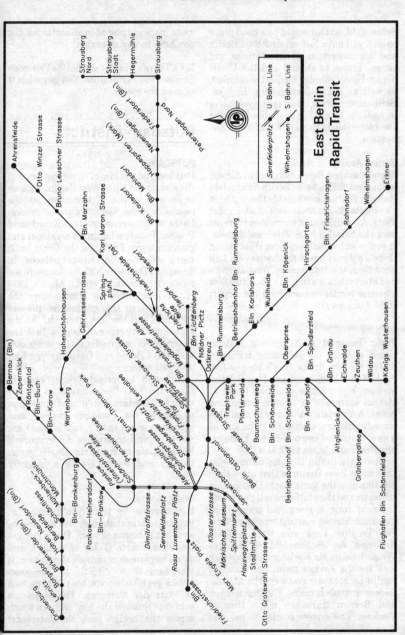

East Berlin Rapid Transit

U Bahn Line
S Bahn Line

Senefelderplatz
Wilhelmshagen

Strausberg Nord
Strausberg Stadt
Hegermühle
Strausberg
Petershagen Nord
Fredersdorf (Bln)
Neuenhagen (Mark)
Hoppegarten (Bln)
Bln Mahlsdorf
Bln Kaulsdorf
Bln Marzahn
Bln Karl Maron Strasse
Biesdorf
Springpfuhl
Friedrichsfelde Ost
Bln Lichtenberg
Nöldner Pltz
Ostkreuz
Rummelsburg
Betriebsbahnhof Bln Rummelsburg
Bln Karlshorst
Wuhlheide
Hirschgarten
Bln Köpenick
Friedrichshagen
Rahnsdorf
Wilhelmshagen
Erkner

Ahrensfelde
Otto Winzer Strasse
Bruno Leuschner Strasse
Hohenschönhausen
Gehrenseestrasse
Landsberger Allee
Frankfurter Allee
Storkower Strasse
Eln Rummelsburg
Eln Karlshorst
Oberspree
Bln Grünau
Eichwalde
Zeuthen
Wildau
Königs Wusterhausen

Bernau (Bln)
Zepernick
Röntgental
Bln-Buch
Bln-Karow
Wartenberg
Ernst-Thälmann Park
Greifswalder Strasse
Treptower Park
Plänterwald
Baumschulenweg
Bln Schöneweide
Bln Schöneweide
Bln Adlershof
Altglienicke
Grünbergallee
Flughafen Bln Schönefeld

Blankenburg
Schönholz
Pankow-Heinersdorf
Bln-Blankenburg
Bln-Pankow
Pankow (Vinetastrasse)
Schönhauser Allee
Prenzlauer Allee
Eberswalder Strasse
Dimitroffstrasse
Senefelderplatz
Rosa Luxemburg Platz
Alexanderplatz
Schillingstrasse
Strausberger Platz
Weberwiese
Frankfurter Tor
Magdalenenstrasse
Friedrichsfelde
Tierpark

Mühlenbeck
Mühlenbeck-Mönchmühle
Schildow (Bln)
Bergfelde
Birkenwerder (Bln)
Hohen Neuendorf (Bln)
Borgsdorf
Lehnitz
Oranienburg

Marx Engels Platz
Klosterstrasse
Märkisches Museum
Spittelmarkt
Hausvogteiplatz
Stadtmitte
Otto Grotewohl Strasse
Bln Friedrichstrasse
Janowitzbrücke
Berlin Ostbahnhof
Warschauer Strasse
Betriebsbahnhof

Schonefeld, so this would be a good place to go if you have just entered East Berlin and are uncertain about stations and times. Trains to Poland and the USSR depart Hauptbahnhof Berlin-Ostbahnhof, as well as Berlin-Lichtenberg. In West Berlin information on all railway services in Eastern Europe is available from the Deutsche Reichsbahn (DR) office at Zoo Station.

Getting Around

Airport Transport Berlin-Schonefeld Airport is adjacent to Flughafen Berlin-Schonefeld Railway Station just outside the southern city limits, 25 km south-east of Alexander Platz. All southbound trains stop there, as does the S-Bahn from Friedrich Strasse. It you're in transit to or from West Berlin there's a direct bus connection every half hour from the terminal to West Berlin's Funkturm bus station via the Rudower Chausee border crossing near the airport (DM 7 one way).

Public Transport A 20 pfennig S-Bahn ticket is valid on all public transport within the city limits. Buy a strip of five for 1 M at a kiosk or at any U or S-Bahn station. You validate your own ticket at station entrances or aboard trams and buses. A *Touristenfahrkarte* is available for unlimited travel on the S-Bahn for 1 M a day, unlimited use of S-Bahn, U-Bahn, streetcars and buses for 2 M a day.

The East Berlin S-Bahn differs from the one in West Berlin in that more than one line uses the same track. Destination indicators on the platforms tell you where the next train is going. All trains from Friedrich Strasse run to Alexander Platz. For Treptow Park you want a train destined for Schonefeld or Konigs Wusterhausen. For Karlshorst or Kopenick look for the Erkner train. For Bahnhof Berlin-Lichtenberg you want the Ahrensfelde or Strausberg trains. The Oranienburg and Bernau trains go north through Pankow. The system is easy to use and route maps are posted in all carriages, but you have to pay attention.

Taxis There's a taxi stand beside Friedrich Strasse Railway Station. You pay what it says on the meter.

Potsdam District

POTSDAM

Potsdam, on the Havel River just beyond the south-west tip of West Berlin, became important in the 17th century as the residence of the Elector of Brandenburg. Later, with the creation of the Kingdom of Prussia, Potsdam became a royal seat and garrison town. Frederick the Great built many of the marvellous palaces in Sanssouci Park which visitors come to see today. At Potsdam on 21 March 1933 Hitler proclaimed to Hindenburg 'the union between the symbols of the old greatness and the new strength.' At the Potsdam Conference of August 1945 the victorious Allies agreed upon the temporary division of Berlin and Germany into four occupation zones.

Although temptingly close, keep in mind that East Berlin day visas are not valid for Potsdam. You'll need more than a day to see Potsdam anyway and accommodation (and a tourist visa) are not that hard to arrange. Give yourself enough time to enjoy the lovely parks, palaces and waterways in a leisurely way.

Orientation

If you come by train you'll arrive at Potsdam-Hauptbahnhof, five km south-west of the centre of town. Buy a strip of tram/bus tickets (1 M) at a kiosk and catch any streetcar outside the station. If you want to go directly to Sanssouci Palace get off when you see the huge arch at Platz der Nationen. The streetcars continue through the city and run south across the bridge past the Interhotel

Potsdam. For the Bassin Platz bus station leave the streetcar at Platz der Einheit. For the tourist office get out a stop later near Nikolaikirche. The closest S-Bahn stations to Sanssouci are Bahnhof Potsdam-West and Bahnhof Wildpark.

Information

Potsdam-Information, Friedrich Ebert Strasse 5 next to the Nikolaikirche, has maps and brochures. If they're closed try the reception of the nearby Interhotel Potsdam. Reiseburo der DDR is at Friedrich Ebert Strasse 115 and Jugendtourist is at Allee nach Sanssouci 2.

Things to See

Sanssouci Park Begin your visit at Knobelsdorff's **Schloss Sanssouci** (1747), a famous Rococo palace with glorious interiors. Tickets are sold at a small window behind the palace and since visitors are only admitted in groups at periodic intervals with a German-speaking guide, it's important to arrive early if you want a ticket for that day (open daily year round). Don't miss the room with the golden spiders' web motif on the ceiling.

While you're waiting for your assigned tour to begin, visit the Bildergalerie (daily May to October) on the east side of Sanssouci or the small picture gallery at the west end of the palace. The **Orangerie** (1862) just west of Sanssouci Palace is also worth seeing, both for the copies of 47 Raphael frescoes inside and the view of all Potsdam from the tower (daily May to October). The **Chinese Teahouse** (1757) is just south of here.

The late Baroque **Neues Palais** (1769), summer residence of the royal family, is by far the largest and most imposing building in the park, the one to see if your time is limited. Visitors are admitted individually as they arrive, so you shouldn't have trouble getting in (open daily year round). Avoid coming from 12.45 to 1.30 pm when the ticket seller takes off for lunch.

Schinkel's **Schloss Charlottenhof** (1826) must also be visited on a German-language tour, but don't wait around too long if the crowds are immense. The exterior of this Italian-style mansion is more interesting than the interior (open May to October).

Downtown Potsdam The Baroque **Brandenburg Gate** on Platz der Nationen bears the date 1770. From this square a pleasant pedestrian street, Klement Gottwald Strasse, runs directly east to **Sts Peter & Paul Church** (1868). The Bassin Platz bus station is adjacent to this church. From here Friedrich Ebert Strasse runs north to **Nauener Tor** (1755), another monumental arch. The red brick buildings on the left (east) side of Friedrich Ebert Strasse look as if they were lifted straight out of Holland. Follow Friedrich Ebert Strasse south and you'll come to the great neo-Classical dome of Schinkel's **Nikolaikirche** (1849), the **Film Museum** (closed Monday), the Interhotel Potsdam (1969) and the Weisse Flotte.

Neuer Garten This winding park along the west side of Heiliger Lake is one place to relax after all the high art in Park Sanssouci. The **Military Museum** (closed Monday) in the Marble Palace (1792) right on the lake contains photos, uniforms and weapons relating to German military history from 1525 to the present day.

Further north is **Cecilienhof Palace**, an English-style country manor built in 1913-1916 for Princess Cecilie, a daughter of Kaiser Wilhelm II. It's quite a contrast to the Rococo palaces and pavilions in Sanssouci Park. Cecilienhof is remembered as the site of the 1945 Potsdam Conference and large photos of the participants Stalin, Truman and Churchill are inside (open daily year round). Part of the building has been made into a luxury hotel.

Excursion Boats Weisse Flotte excursion boats operate on the lakes around

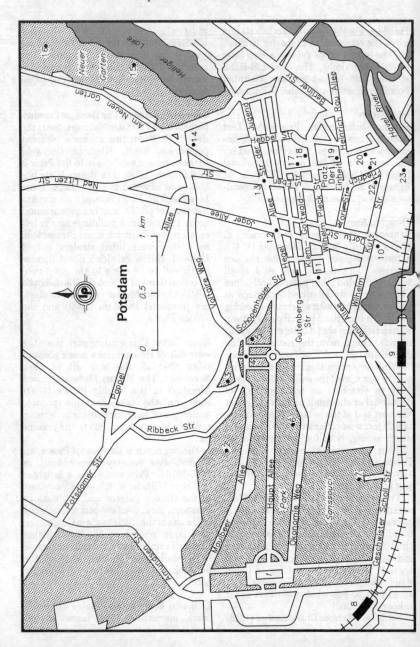

1	Neues Palais
2	Orangerie
3	Broiler Beer Garden
4	Schloss Sanssouci
5	Bildergalerie
6	Chinese Teahouse
7	Schloss Charlottenhof
8	Bahnhof Wildpark
9	Bahnhof Potsdam-West
10	Potsdam Museum
11	Platz der Nationen
12	Jägertor
13	Nauener Tor
14	Youth Hostel
15	Military Museum
16	Cecilienhof Palace
17	St Peter & Paul Church
18	Bassin Platz Bus Station
19	Post Office
20	Nikolaikirche
21	Potsdam-Information
22	Film Museum
23	Interhotel Potsdam/Weisse Flotte

Potsdam, departing from the dock below the shiny Interhotel Potsdam. There are boats to Werder, but none to East Berlin (West Berlin is in the way). Monday, Wednesday and Saturday at 8 am there's a boat down the Havel all the way to Brandenburg (12.50 M single or return, four hours). From Brandenburg it would be easy to return to Potsdam or Berlin by train. Shorter local cruises leave regularly between 8.30 am and 5 pm from 28 April to 21 September. Buy your ticket a day ahead if you can.

Places to Stay

Hostels To stay at Potsdam's youth hostels you must obtain written reservations from 'Jugendtourist' a month ahead (see the chapter introduction). There are two hostels. The older one at Eisenhard Strasse 5, between central Potsdam and the Neuer Garten, is by far the more convenient. The *Werder Youth Tourist Hotel*, Am Schwielochsee 110, is in a new building by Schwielow Lake not far from

the Intercamping listed below (same bus to get there).

Camping If you're on a budget you'll probably end up at *Intercamping Werder/Havel*, Riegelspitze, eight km south-west of Potsdam. They charge 6 M per tent and 5 M per person a night to camp (own tent). There are also small bungalows which go for 29 M single, 34 M double, but they're booked solid in July and August. Officially, the campground office is open 9 am to 12 noon and 3 to 6 pm, but there's often someone around later. The snack bar near the middle of the campground has a pleasant terrace overlooking the lake (open Wednesday to Friday 12 noon to 8 pm, weekends 11 am to 2 pm and 3 to 8 pm). Enquire there if the campground office is closed when you arrive. A small grocery store is opposite the snack bar. The Glindowsee almost surrounds the campground and in summer you can swim.

Bus D-31 Werder from platform No 2 at Potsdam's Bassin Platz bus station passes within a five-minute walk of the campground every couple of hours. One bus departs Bassin Platz daily at 6 pm. The bus goes down Lenin Allee within a few hundred metres of Potsdam Hauptbahnhof but doesn't stop right in front of the station, so make certain you're waiting at the right bus stop.

Hotels The flashy five-star *Interhotel Potsdam*, Lange Brucke, is the place to stay if you have money (125 M single, 206 M double). The *Hotel Jagertor*, Hegel Allee 11, is 75 M single, 120 M double. You could also try booking a room in advance at one of the four small hotels in Brandenburg and commute to Potsdam.

Places to Eat

There are lots of fancy restaurants just behind the triumphal arch on Platz der Nationen and along Klement Gottwald Strasse. Notice the *Am Stadttor* and *Gastmahl des Meeres* near the arch. The

Nationalitatengaststatte 'Bolgar,' Klement Gottwald Strasse 35-36, offers Bulgarian food (closed Monday). The restaurant in the *Interhotel Potsdam* has a good, inexpensive breakfast buffet – you pay for what you take.

Getting something to eat while touring Sanssouci Park can be problematic, so consider taking a picnic lunch. Otherwise try the large beer garden directly behind and to the north-west of Sanssouci Palace. You can't see it from the palace and there's only one tiny sign reading 'Zum Broiler,' so look around or just follow the crowd, which is the main drawback as the lines can be unending. There are different counters selling beer, cakes, ice cream, chicken and other hot meals, but you'd spend the whole afternoon waiting to get all that. You'll probably have to settle for coffee and cakes, where the lines are manageable.

Getting There & Away

The S-Bahn runs from Berlin-Karlshorst Station to Potsdam every hour, calling at Flughafen Berlin-Schonefeld on the way. All fast trains between Berlin and Magdeburg also call at Potsdam. The S-Bahn costs less than a mark. If you want to take a fast train be sure to get an express ticket, otherwise the conductor will charge you a supplement of 6.60 M. A couple of trains a day call at Potsdam between Rostock and Leipzig, but the timing is difficult. It's simpler to change at Berlin-Schonefeld for Potsdam. There's a cloakroom for luggage storage in Potsdam Hauptbahnhof (open 24 hours).

Bus D-1 runs from Schonefeld airport to Potsdam's Bassin Platz bus station twice an hour. There are no luggage storage facilities at the bus station, only toilets and a few cheap places to get a snack.

Magdeburg District

MAGDEBURG

Magdeburg, by the Elbe River midway on the autobahn from Berlin to Hannover, was severely damaged by wartime bombing. Today it's rebuilt in steel and concrete and only merits a brief visit. Magdeburg is seen as a bulwark against Western Europe and large numbers of Soviet soldiers and civilians are present. Most signs in the railway station are in Russian and German.

Information

Magdeburg-Information is at Alter Markt 9. Reiseburo der DDR is at Wilhelm Pieck Allee 14. Jugendtourist is at Luneburger Strasse 16.

Things to See

Most of the things to see are centred around the soaring 13th century Gothic **Dom** with its fine sculptures and the **Rathaus** on Alter Markt just to the north. Between these is the 12th century Romanesque convent **Unser Lieben Frauen**, now a museum (closed Monday). The **Historical Museum** (closed Monday) is on Otto von Guericke Strasse at the corner of Danz Strasse, just west of the Dom.

Places to Stay

There's no Intercamping in Magdeburg District so to stay the night you may have to book a room at a hotel. They'll want to give you the four-star *Interhotel International* (95 M single, 168 M double) opposite the railway station, but the *Gruner Baum Hotel* beside the station at Wilhelm Pieck Allee 40 is cheaper and more relaxed.

The two-star *Hotel Gewerkschaftshaus*, Julius Bremer Strasse 1, is just off Alter Markt. There's also a very luxurious *youth tourist hotel* at Leiter Strasse 10 adjacent to the Interhotel. Best of all, ask the Reiseburo der DDR to book you a room at the *Weisser Hirsch* or *Zur Post* hotels (both 45 M single, 84 M double) in Wernigerode, a picturesque town in the Harz Mountains south-west of Magdeburg and still within the district. You'll be able to visit the city en route without actually having to stay in it.

Getting There & Away

Although many trains between West Germany and West Berlin pass this way, most don't stop. There is one train a day from Cologne and Hamburg. Trains from East Berlin leave from a variety of stations but all pass Schonefeld Airport and Potsdam, carrying on to Halberstadt. Magdeburg is on the mainline route of trains from Rostock and Schwerin to Leipzig or Erfurt. Trains from Leipzig to Magdeburg run via either Halle or Dessau.

Dresden District

DRESDEN

During the 18th century the Saxon capital Dresden became famous as the German Florence. During the reigns of Augustus the Strong (born 1670, ruled 1694-1733) and his son Augustus III (ruled 1733-1763) artists, musicians, actors and master craftsmen flocked to the Dresden court from Italy, particularly from Venice. Canaletto depicted the rich architecture of the time in many paintings which now hang in Dresden's Alte Meister Gallery alongside countless masterpieces purchased for Augustus III. The great Baroque palaces with their priceless art treasures and the brilliant musical traditions survive today, despite devastation in 1945.

The Elbe River cuts a curving course between the low rolling hills and in spite of modern rebuilding in concrete and steel Dresden holds our affection. There are numerous museums and with the many palaces and outstanding excursions, there is ample reason to spend more time in the area. Fortunately the facilities are good and three nights are the bare minimum required to do Dresden justice.

Orientation

There are two main railway stations, Dresden-Hauptbahnhof on the south side of town and Dresden-Neustadt on the north. Both stations have all facilities, but the Hauptbahnhof is more convenient. Take tram No 11 (under the tracks beside the station) to get to Post Platz near the Zwinger. Or walk to town along Prager Strasse, the pedestrian mall directly in front of the station.

Information

The tourist information office at Prager Strasse 10, on the east side of the mall in front of the Hauptbahnhof, sells maps and theatre tickets and there's an accommodation service. Change money here or at the nearby luxury hotels. Reiseburo der DDR is at Ernst Thalmann Strasse 22. Jugendtourist is at Salvador Allende Platz 1.

Books Dresden's best bookstore by far is Das Internationale Buch, Kreuz Strasse 4 behind the Rathaus. They feature an excellent selection of hard-to-find guidebooks to Eastern Europe, plus maps.

Museum Tickets A season ticket to most Dresden museums is available at the museums themselves for 5 M (3 M for students). It may not save you much money, but it will help you avoid the long ticket queues. The museums which accept it are listed on the back.

Police Registration Unless you've done so elsewhere or are staying at an Interhotel, you *must* register your passport at the efficient Auslander Service on Rampische Strasse in the ultramodern building behind the Frauenkirche ruins. There are two sides to this office. You want the small room on the right, not the door on the left

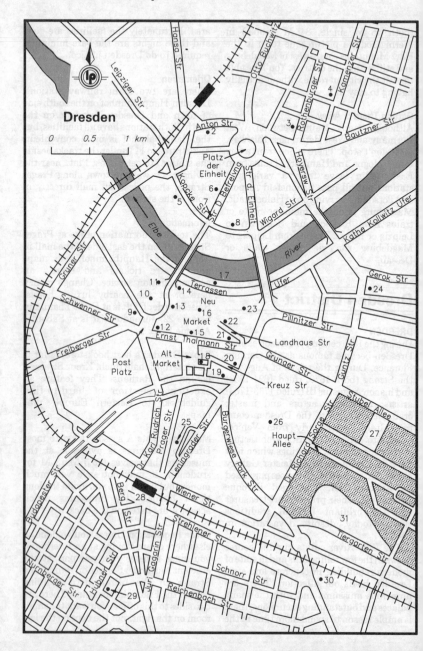

Dresden

0   0.5   1 km

1
Anton Str
2
3
4
Platz der Einheit
6
5
7
8
Str d Betreiung
Str d Einheit
Kopcke Str
Hoyersw Str
Wigard Str
Bautzner Str
Rothenburger Str
Kamenzer Str
Otto Buchwitz
Hansa Str
Leipziger Str
Elbe
River
Kathe Kollwitz Ufer
Gerok Str
24
Terrassen
Ufer
17
11
14
10
13
Neu
16
Market
23
22
9
12
15
21
20
18
19
Gruner Str
Schwenner Str
Freiberger Str
Ernst Thalmann Str
Landhaus Str
Pillnitzer Str
Guntz Str
Kreuz Str
Post Platz
Alt Market
25
26
Haupt Allee
Stubel Allee
27
Dr Karl Rudrich Str
Prager Str
Leningrader Str
Burgerwiese Park Str
Dr Richard Sorge Str
28
Wiener Str
Berg Str
Budapester Str
Strehlener Str
Tiergarten Str
31
Nürnberger Str
Hubner Str
Juri Gagarin Str
Schnorr Str
29
Reichenbach Str
30

1	Dresden-Neustadt
2	Alt Dresden Winzer Stube
3	Hotel Rothenburger Hof
4	Hotel Stadt Rendsburg
5	Japanisches Palais
6	Romantic Museum
7	Goldener Reiter
8	Museum für Volkskunst
9	Staatsschauspiel
10	Zwinger
11	Semperoper
12	Restaurant Am Zwinger
13	Palace Ruins
14	Catholic Hofkirche
15	Palace of Culture
16	Transportation Museum
17	Weisse Flotte
18	Kreuzkirche
19	Neues Rathaus
20	Hotel Gewandhaus
21	City Historical Museum
22	Auslander Service
23	Albertinum
24	Kupferstichkabinett
25	Tourist Office
26	Hygienemuseum
27	Botanical Gardens
28	Dresden-Hauptbahnhof
29	'Rudi Arndt' Youth Hostel
30	Hotel Astoria
31	Zoo

with the long line of locals waiting to enter.

Things to See

Dresden Altstadt Dresden's main art treasures are concentrated in two large buildings, the Baroque **Zwinger** (1728) and the Albertinum. There are five museums in the Zwinger. The most important are the **Alte Meister Gallery** (with old master paintings including Raphael's Sistine Madonna – closed Monday) and the **Historisches Museum** (with a fantastic collection of ceremonial weapons – closed Wednesday). There's also the Mathematics Saloon (with old instruments and time pieces – closed Thursday), the Museum fur Tierkunde

(natural history – closed Thursday and Friday), and the Porcelain Collection (closed Friday), all housed in opposite corners of the complex with separate entrances.

The **Albertinum** (all museums closed Thursday) on a terrace overlooking the river contains a group of museums no less illustrious, especially the **Neue Meister Gallery** (with renowned 19th and 20th century paintings) and the **Grunes Gewolbe** or 'Green Vault' (one of the finest collections of jewel-studded precious objects in the world).

Between these two near the end of Georgij Dimitroff Bridge is the Catholic **Hofkirche** (1755) with the ruins of the Renaissance Royal Palace directly behind. These are slowly being restored as part of a long term programme. Between Hofkirche and Zwinger is Theater Platz with Dresden's glorious opera house, the neo-Renaissance **Semperoper**. The first opera house on the site opened in 1841 but burned down in 1800. Rebuilt in 1878, it was again destroyed in 1945 and only re-opened in 1985. The Dresden opera has a tradition going back 350 years. Many works by Richard Strauss, Carl Maria von Weber and Richard Wagner premiered here.

From the east side of the Hofkirche follow Augustus Strasse, with its 102-metre long Procession of Princes on the outer wall of the old royal stables, to Neumarkt. Here stand the massive ruins of the **Frauenkirche** (1738), once the greatest Protestant church in Germany, a reminder of the 1945 Anglo-American bombings. Some 35,000 people died in this atrocity which happened at a time when the city was jammed with refugees and the war almost over. The figure of Martin Luther keeps watch. On this same square is the interesting **Transportation Museum** (closed Monday) and, nearby south-east down Landhaus Strasse, the **City Historical Museum** (closed Friday), well worth a look if only for the building erected in 1776.

South across Ernst Thalmann Strasse

toward the Hauptbahnhof are the **Neues Rathaus** (1912) and **Kreuzkirche** (1792) in the Alt Markt area, the historic hub of Dresden until 1945. The Kreuzkirche is famous for its boys' choir.

Dresden Neustadt The Goldener Reiter statue (1736) of Augustus the Strong at the north end of Georgij Dimitroff Bridge beckons you to visit Neustadt, the section of Dresden least effected by the wartime bombing. The Strasse der Befreiung is a pleasant pedestrian mall with the **Romantic Museum** (closed Monday and Tuesday) at No 13. In Platz der Einheit at its north end there's an evocative marble monument to the poet Schiller. Other museums in the vicinity of the Goldener Reiter include the **Museum fur Volkskunst** (closed Monday), a folk art collection at Kopcke Strasse 1, and the **Japanisches Palais** (1737), Karl Marx Platz, with Dresden's famous ethnological museum.

Farther Afield The **Army Museum** (closed Monday), Dr Kurt Fischer Platz 3, is on the northern side of Neustadt. Dresden's most surprising attraction is the **Indianer Museum** founded by adventure writer Karl May (closed Monday), Holderlin Strasse 15, at Radebeul eight km northwest of Dresden-Neustadt (trams No 4 or 5). Here you'll see a huge collection of authentic North American Indian clothing and artefacts kept in an oversized log cabin!

Afternoon Sidetrip East From 1765 to 1918 **Pillnitz Palace** on the Elbe east of Dresden was the summer residence of the kings and queens of Saxony. The most romantic way to get there is by Weisse Flotte excursion boat from near Dresden's Georgij Dimitroff Bridge. If time is short take tram No 14 from Ernst Thalmann Strasse or tram No 9 from in front of the Hauptbahnhof east to the end of the line, then walk down to the riverside and cross the Elbe on a small ferry operating year round. The museum at Pillnitz closes at 4 pm and every Monday but the gardens and palace exterior with its oriental motifs are far more interesting than anything inside (which must be visited on a boring German-language tour). So don't worry if you arrive too late to get in. In summer the Dresden Philharmonic Orchestra sometimes holds concerts here.

After enjoying the gardens (which stay open till 8 pm) take a bus from the loop at the west end of the park back along the right bank of the Elbe to Loschwitz near the north end of the Elbe Bridge just east of Dresden. Here you'll find an extremely interesting **funicular railway** or 'Bergbahn' (the entrance is hidden – ask) which climbs to the Luisenhof Restaurant, an exclusive cafe on an enclosed terrace with a fantastic view of the Elbe and Dresden. From the cafe follow Plattleite north a few blocks through Weisser Hirsch to the streetcar line (tram No 11), which you will take west back to Dresden.

On the Elbe From mid-April to mid-October the Weisse Flotte (White Fleet) runs daily paddlewheel steamers upriver from Dresden to Schmilka in the Sachsische Schweiz near the Czech border. Shorter trips terminate at Pirna and Bad Schandau. Between Pirna and Bad Schandau the scenery climaxes at medieval **Konigstein Castle** on a hilltop to the west. From mid-May to September there are daily excursions downriver to Meissen and Riesa.

Fares are low and the scenery beautiful, but don't count on getting anything to eat aboard as food service is erratic. The boats are big and departures frequent, so you shouldn't have any difficulty getting a ticket even in mid-summer.

Places to Stay

Hostels & Camping 'Rudi Arndt' Youth Hostel, Hubner Strasse 11, is a nine-minute walk from the south exit of the Hauptbahnhof.

There are two Intercampings near

Dresden. The closest is *Dresden-Mockritz Camping* just south of the city. Take bus No 76 direction Mockritz directly there from behind Dresden Hauptbahnhof (frequent). There are bungalows (34 M) but they're often full and in summer this campground can be very crowded.

A more appealing and distant possibility is *Moritzburg Camping* on Mittel Teich, a 10-minute walk beyond Schloss Moritzburg (take the Moritzburg bus from Dresden Hauptbahnhof bus station). The campground is spacious, there's a restaurant and even small caravans (camping trailers) for 20 M (often full). The lake is too murky for swimming but rowboats are available. The nearby park offers hours of restful walks. Recommended.

Cheaper Hotels If you're going to have a travel agency book you a room in Dresden before you arrive, consider requesting the *Goldener Lowe Hotel* (30 M per person) in Meissen or the *Hotel Lubin* (86 M single, 110 M double) in Bautzen. You'll not only save money but will experience small town life. Commuting to Dresden is easy.

The *Astoria Hotel* on Ernst Thalmann Platz near the zoo is the least pretentious Interhotel in Dresden, but it's out of the way and hardly a bargain (from 80 M single, 126 M double). *Hotel Gewandhaus*, Ring Strasse 1 beside the Rathaus, only looks expensive (57 M single, 80 M double). For character and location you can't beat it.

Two inexpensive hotels within walking distance of Bahnhof Dresden-Neustadt are the *Hotel Rothenburger Hof*, Rothenburger Strasse 17, and the *Hotel Stadt Rendsburg*, Kamenzer Strasse 1.

There's a cluster of cheap hotels at Weisser Hirsch, a suburb east of Dresden and north of the Elbe, but you'll have a hard time getting into any of them. Most have *besetzt* (full) notices on the door and the others don't answer. If you'd like to try anyway, take tram No 11 from beside Dresden-Hauptbahnhof or in front of Bahnhof-Neustadt as far as the *Park Hotel*, Bautzner Land Strasse 7. Try the pensions nearby at Plattleit 43, 45 and 49, the *Hotel Felsenburg*, Rissweg 68, and *Fremdenheim Goldschmidt*, Hietzig Strasse 8. The *Park Hotel* itself is an excellent place to stay (35 M double), although noise from the downstairs disco late at night and streetcars in the very early morning can be a problem. The hotel restaurant is unpretentious and colourful (hot meals after 4 pm only).

Expensive Hotels Three gleaming high-rise tourist hotels, the *Interhotel Newa* (125 M single, 170 M double), the *Konigstein*, and the *Lilienstein*, stand on Prager Strasse near the Hauptbahnhof. But the absolute pinnacle of bourgeois decadence is the five-star *Interhotel Bellevue* (168 M single, 240 M double) across the river on Kopcke Strasse near the Goldener Reiter. Avoid all four of these if you can.

Places to Eat
A quick, easy place to snatch a bite between museums is the modern *Restaurant Am Zwinger* on Post Platz, the large square on the south side of the Zwinger. The big cafeteria at street level is open daily till 8 pm and there are more exclusive restaurants upstairs.

Good inexpensive meals with full service are available at *Gaststatte Am Gewandhaus* in a separate building behind the hotel of the same name near the Rathaus. No smoking is allowed (!) and they're open till 10 pm.

For something special dine at the *Kugelgen Haus Restaurant*, Strasse der Befreiung 13 below the Romantic Museum in Neustadt (open 11 am to midnight). There's a beer cellar in the cellar.

Entertainment
Dresden's two largest theatres, the *Semperoper* and *Staatsschauspiel*, stand on opposite sides of the Zwinger. The *Staatsoperette*, Pirnaer Land Strasse 131, is in the far east suburbs of the city

(trams No 6, 9, 12, 14). Tickets for all three theatres may be had at the Zentrale Vorverkaufskasse in the Altstadler Wache, the stone building on Theater Platz opposite the Semperoper between the equestrian statue and the palace ruins (closed Wednesday, Saturday and Sunday). All theatres close for holidays from mid-July to the end of August.

If you get a chance for tickets to the Semperoper grab them with profuse thanks for the performances are brilliant and the opera house is Dresden's architectural highlight. If you want to be sure of a ticket to the Semperoper try for one at the Reiseburo der DDR in East Berlin. Every seat will be full, mostly with West Germans bused in for the performances. Note that the opera restaurant is rather hidden in the basement below the cloakrooms.

The *Tonne Jazz Club* on Schiessegasse behind the Albertinum often offers live jazz Thursday and Friday at 8 pm. The *Alt Dresden Winzer Stube* on the square in front of Bahnhof Dresden-Neustadt is a local hangout (Tuesday to Saturday 5 pm to midnight).

Getting There & Away
Dresden is just over two hours south of East Berlin's Lichtenberg railway station by fast train. The Leipzig, Riesa, Dresden service (1½ hours) is very frequent. Trains from Erfurt run via Karl Marx Stadt and Gera. There are direct trains to and from Wroclaw, Prague and Munich.

Getting Around
Buy a 1-M strip of six bus/tram tickets at a kiosk as soon as you arrive. Remember that baggage costs another fare. One of the most useful streetcars is tram No 11 which runs between the two railway stations via Post Platz and on to Weisser Hirsch in the far north-eastern suburbs.

MEISSEN
Meissen is a perfectly preserved old German town, the site of Europe's most northerly vineyards. It's easily accessible as a half day trip from Dresden by train or riverboat (May to September).

Albrechtsburg, the medieval quarter, crowns a ridge high above the Elbe. The towering 13th century Gothic cathedral (fine sculpture) and Renaissance palace (1471), now a major museum (open daily), are visible from afar. Below, Meissen stretches out like a Lucas Cranach painting, the old buildings completely unmarred by the block concrete edifices which now dominate Dresden.

Pick up a map at the tourist office, Willy Anker Strasse 32 in the lower town, and explore. Nearby at Rathenauplatz 3 is the **Town Museum** (closed Friday) and also close by, on Markt Platz, the **Frauenkirche** and **Rathaus** (1472).

Since 1710 Meissen has been famous around the world for its porcelain. The crossed blue swords insignia of its 'White Gold' chinaware is unmistakable. You can visit the factory at Lenin Strasse 9, a km south-west of town. There are often impossibly long lines for the factory tours, but you should be able to get into the museum without difficulty (open April to October, closed Monday).

Places to Stay
Although you can daytrip here from Dresden it would be worth staying if you could manage to book a room at the *Hotel Goldener Lowe*, Rathenauplatz 6 (60 M double). *Intercamping Scharfenberg* at Rehbocktal is three km south-east of Meissen on the main road to Dresden.

Getting There & Away
Direct buses run from Meissen to Moritzburg. The stop for this bus is on Bahnhof Strasse back toward the bridge not at the bus station, so ask. The hours are posted in the railway station and nearby bus terminal. Meissen is on the railway line from Dresden to Leipzig via Dobeln.

MORITZBURG

Moritzburg Palace (1733) rises impressively from its lake like a French Renaissance chateau. Try to come during visiting hours (closed December and January, closed Tuesday in November and February, closed Monday year round) as the interior is impressive. Behind the palace a huge park stretches out and a walk through the woods is just the thing to clear a travel-weary head. Get a map from the information office (summer only) near the palace entrance and hike to **Fasanen-schlosschen** (1782), a former hunting villa now a natural history museum (open daily mid-March to October). Then backtrack through the forest to the *campground* on Mittel Teich where you can rent a rowboat to tour the lake.

Getting There & Away

Bus service between Dresden and Moritzburg (14 km) is fairly good. Ask at the bus station beside Dresden Hauptbahnhof.

Leipzig District

LEIPZIG

Leipzig, the GDR's second city, is right in the middle of the southern half of the country. This, together with the musical traditions and the city's role as host to East Germany's most important trade fairs, puts Leipzig on most GDR itineraries. Aside from its business-oriented present, Leipzig is a city with a past. Here Bach worked from 1723 until his death in 1750, Napoleon met defeat in 1813 and Georgi Dimitroff stood up against the Nazis in 1933. Leipzig was always a major publishing and library centre, hosting today Eastern Europe's most important annual book design exhibition. The Intercamping is convenient and a full day can be spent doing the round of museums.

Leipzig Fair The Leipzig Fair, a major vehicle of east-west trade, is the only medieval fair to survive into our times. The tradition goes back to medieval

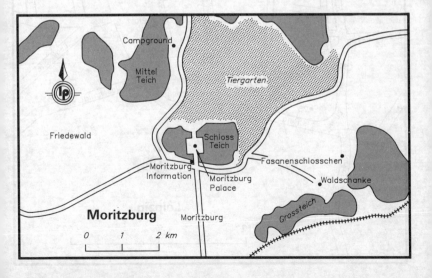

Moritzburg

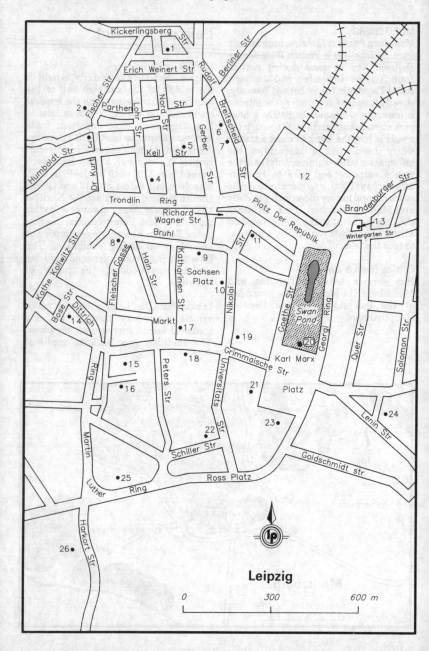

Leipzig

0   300   600 m

1	Haus Ingeborg
2	Zoo/Kongresshalle
3	Pension Am Zoo
4	Hotel Norddeutscher
5	Interhotel Merkur
6	Cafe Vis a Vis
7	Hotel Vier Jahreszeiten
8	Hotel Burgerhof
9	Leipzig-Information
10	Orion Night Club
11	Park Hotel
12	Leipzig-Hauptbahnhof
13	Hotel Bayrisher Hof
14	Schauspielhaus
15	St Thomas Church
16	Bach's House
17	Old Town Hall (Altes Rathaus)
18	Auerbachs Keller
19	St Nikolai Church
20	Opera House
21	University
22	Egyptian Museum
23	Concert Hall
24	Grassimuseum
25	New Town Hall (Neues Rathaus)
26	Georgi Dimitroff Museum

markets at the crossing of the Via Regia from Western Europe to Poland and the Via Imperii from the Baltic to Nuremberg. In the 16th century spices, wines and metal goods from the south traded for wool, canvas and hides from the north. Chartered in 1165, the original fair was held on the market square in front of the Rathaus.

Today the spring trade fair in mid-March features engineering, electrical engineering, electronics and instrumentation, while the autumn trade fair in early September emphasises chemicals, motor vehicles, textile machinery, printing and paper-making equipment. Consumer goods are shown at both fairs, with a book fair accompanying the spring fair and sporting equipment displayed at the fall fair. For more information write the Leipzig Fair Agency, Queensgate Centre, Orsett Rd, Grays, Essex RMI7 5DJ, England. The Fair Card costs £16 and

should be ordered from this agency two months in advance. At fairtime, when all Leipzig and vicinity hotels are fully booked, private rooms materialise at the Reiseburo der DDR.

Orientation

Leipzig-Hauptbahnhof (1915), with 26 platforms the largest terminal station in Europe, is adjacent to the downtown area. To get to the centre of the city use the underpass in front of the station to cross wide Platz der Republik. Most of Leipzig's streetcar lines stop in the centre of this square. Historic Markt square with the Old Town Hall is a couple of blocks south-west. Here you'll find museums and churches, inviting restaurants and cafes.

Giant Karl Marx Platz, three blocks due east of Markt, is socialist Leipzig, the Space Age lines of the university (1975) and concert hall (1981) juxtaposed against the leaden Stalinist mass of the opera house (1960). Leipzig's famous International Fairgrounds are about three km south-east along Lenin Strasse. The massive Battle of Nations Monument looms just beyond.

Information

Leipzig-Information (closed weekends) is at Saschsenplatz 1 between the Hauptbahnhof and Old Town Hall. Bear just after going through the underpass. Reiseburo der DDR, 'Alte Waage', Katharinen Strasse 1-3. Jugendtourist, Karl Tauchnitz Strasse 3.

Things to See

Old Leipzig The Renaissance **Old Town Hall** (1556) on Markt is one of the largest in Germany. Today it houses the City History Museum (closed Monday). Behind the Old Town Hall is the **Alte Borse** (1687) with a monument to Goethe (1903) in front. Goethe called Leipzig 'a little Paris.' **St Nikolai Church** (1165) between Markt and Karl Marx Platz has a remarkable interior. Just west of Markt is

St Thomas' Church (1212) with the tomb of composer Johann Sebastian Bach in front of the altar. The Thomas Choir which Bach led is still going strong. Beside the church at Thomaskirchhof 16 is **Bach's house**, now a museum (open daily).

Follow the streetcar line that passes St Thomas due south a few blocks to reach the **Georgi Dimitroff Museum** (closes at 2 pm weekends and every Monday), housed in the former Supreme Court of the Reich (1888). This important museum has an excellent collection of old master paintings downstairs, but don't miss the **Reichstag Fire Museum** upstairs (the entrance is obscure, so ask). Here you'll see the original courtroom where Dimitroff made a fool of Hermann Goering in 1933 and listen to a recording in English describing the proceedings.

Other Sights Leipzig has many other museums but more impressive is the **Battle of Nations Monument** on Lenin Strasse, beyond the fairgrounds about five km south-east of the railway station (trams No 15 or 20). To get there from the Dimitroff Museum catch tram No 21 beside the Neues Rathaus. This tremendous structure was erected in 1913 to commemorate a victory by combined Prussian, Austrian, Swedish and Russian armies during the Napoleonic wars. After his defeat at Leipzig Napoleon abdicated and was exiled to Elba. Climb up on top of the monument for the view (open daily until 4 pm).

An afternoon visit to Leipzig's **zoo** is a good way to top off a busy day. The zoo is renowned for its breeding of lions and tigers. The entrance is off Kurt Fischer Strasse beside the Kongresshalle, a short walk north-west from the station or old town. In summer the zoo stays open till 7 pm.

Places to Stay

Hostels & Camping *Intercamping Leipzig-Nord*, Am Auensee, is in a pleasant wooded location near the city (take trams No 10, 11 or 28 to Wahren, then walk eight minutes). Bungalows and A-frame huts are sometimes available for 19 M per person. The *'George Schumann' Youth Hostel* at Kathe Kollwitz Strasse 64-66 is in the western section of the city.

Cheaper Hotels The *Haus Ingeborg Hotel*, Nord Strasse 58 a couple of blocks north of the Interhotel Merkur, has simple rooms with shared bath at 49 M double. You may have to look for the manager up on the 3rd floor. *Pension Am Zoo*, Dr Kurt Fischer Strasse 23, is also worth a try.

There are many medium-priced hotels within walking distance of the railway station, including the *Park Hotel*, Richard Wagner Strasse 7, the *Hotel Bayrischer Hof*, Wintergarten Strasse 13, the *Hotel Vier Jahreszeiten*, Rudolf Breitscheid Strasse 23, the *Hotel Norddeutscher Hof*, Lohr Strasse 4, and the *Hotel Burgerhof*, Grosse Fleischergasse 4.

Expensive Hotels As a major trade fair city Leipzig has no less than six Interhotels. The soaring five-star *Interhotel Merkur* near the station is top of the line at 124 M single, 172 M double with breakfast. The overpriced *Astoria* (140 M single, 210 M double) is right beside the station and the four-star *Stadt Leipzig* opposite. The *Am Ring* on Karl Marx Platz, the *Zum Lowen* behind the Astoria, and the three-star *International* (85 M per person) on Trondlin Ring all face noisy streetcar lines.

Places to Eat

Auerbachs Keller, downstairs in the Madler-Passage just south of the Rathaus (look for the statues with scenes from Goethes' *Faust*), is large and unpretentious. You shouldn't have any trouble getting in. They serve full meals at moderate prices. (After carousing with students at Auerbach's Keller, Mephistopheles and Faust left riding on a barrel.) The *Naschmarkt Buffet*, nearby at Grimmaische Strasse 10, is a cheap cafeteria, but they close early at 6 pm. The *Burgkeller* across the street is between these two in price.

Entertainment

Ask at Leipzig-Information about performances and tickets to the *Opernhaus* and ultra-modern *Gewandhaus Concert Hall* (1983), both on Karl Marx Platz. The composer Mendelssohn was once conductor of the Gewandhaus Orchestra, Europe's oldest (established 1743). The *Schauspielhaus*, Bose Strasse 1, is a few blocks west of Markt. There's also the *Theater der Jungen Welt* on Kurt Fischer Strasse in the Kongresshalle by the zoo. All theatres close for holidays in July and August.

For late evening entertainment try the *Orion Night Club*, Nikolai Strasse 39-45 north of St Nikolai Church, which opens 9 pm to 4 am Tuesday to Saturday. *Cafe Vis a Vis*, Rudolf Breitscheid Strasse 33 a block north of the west exit from the Hauptbahnhof, is a great little bar/cafe with a friendly young clientele (closed Sunday and Monday).

Getting There & Away

Fast trains connect Leipzig to Berlin-Lichtenberg (two hours). The Berlin train passes through Lutherstadt Wittenberg, home of Martin Luther. Service between Leipzig and Dresden via Riesa is frequent. Other trains run to Karl Marx Stadt, Gera, Weimar and Halle. An overnight train with sleepers is available to Rostock. International trains from Leipzig run direct to Frankfurt am Main, Cologne and Warsaw.

The main baggage room at Leipzig Hauptbahnhof won't accept backpacks and the coin lockers are often full. Instead take your pack to the oversized baggage room just inside the far west exit from the station, beside the stairs down.

Getting Around

Leipzig's city transportation system is based on streetcars so buy a strip of tickets at a kiosk as soon as you arrive. You validate your own ticket once aboard.

Halle District

LUTHERSTADT WITTENBERG

Wittenberg is famous as the home of Martin Luther, but the painter Lucas Cranach the Elder also lived here (from 1504 to 1547). Wittenberg was capital of Electoral Saxony until 1547, when the elector moved to Weimar. It was here at Wittenberg Castle that Luther launched the Reformation, an act of the greatest cultural importance to all of Europe. Today the unspoiled town centre contains many artistic monuments and museums connected with those events.

Orientation

The railway station is a pleasant 10-minute walk from the centre of town. Walk a few hundred metres south-east and take the road under the tracks, then straight up on the street that cuts across the park into Collegien Strasse. This will bring you to the Lutherhalle, then keep straight to Markt Platz and Schloss Platz beyond.

Martin Luther

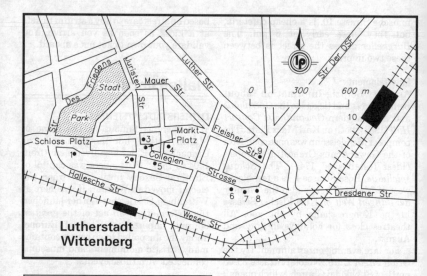

Lutherstadt Wittenberg

1 Wittenberg Castle
2 Lucas Cranach's House
3 Old Town Hall
4 St Mary's Church
5 Hotel Goldener Adler
6 Melanchthon Museum
7 Hotel Wittenberg Hof
8 Lutherhalle
9 Post Office
10 Railway Station

Information

Wittenberg-Information is at Markt 4. Reiseburo der DDR is at Strasse des Friedens 4.

Things to See

The **Lutherhalle**, Collegien Strasse 54, contains the original room furnished by Luther in 1535. Luther moved into this monastic building in 1508 when he came to teach at Wittenberg University. After dissolution of the monastery in 1522 the building was considered Luther's property and remained so until his death in 1546. Since 1883 it has been a Luther Museum. The home of Luther's friend, the humanist Philip Melanchthon (1497-1560), nearby at Collegien Strasse 60, is also a museum.

In Gothic **St Mary's Church** where Luther preached is a large altarpiece (1547) by Lucas Cranach the Elder. This masterpiece contains portraits of Luther, his confessor, his son, Melanchthon and many other townspeople, plus a self-portrait of Cranach himself. The baptismal font and marble tombstones in this church are also remarkable. Imposing monuments to Luther and Melanchthon stand in front of the impressive **Old Town Hall** (1535) nearby. Over the Town Hall's Renaissance portico (1570) is Justitia with sword and scales. From the portico balcony sentences were passed and executions carried out.

At the west end of town is **Wittenberg Castle** (1525) with its huge rebuilt Gothic church. It was here that Luther launched the Reformation on 31 October 1517 by nailing his 95 theses to the door. In 1858 a bronze door replaced the wooden door of Luther's time. His tomb may be viewed below the pulpit. Melanchthon's tomb is opposite. There are two museums in the castle: a natural history downstairs and a city museum upstairs. All of Wittenberg's museums are closed on Mondays.

Places to Stay

There are two attractive, inexpensive hotels: the *Hotel Wittenberger Hof* (49 M single, 84 M double), Collegien Strasse 56 beside the Lutherhalle, and the *Hotel Goldener Adler* (66 M single, 96 M double), Markt 7 just off Markt Platz. The Goldener Adler is the better and serves a good breakfast. The *'Otto Plattner' Youth Hostel* is housed in the castle.

Getting There & Away

Less than two hours south from Berlin-Lichtenberg by fast train, Wittenberg is on the main line to Leipzig and Halle. All the Berlin trains stop at Schonefeld Airport. There's a restaurant and baggage room at Wittenberg station.

HALLE

Halle, a bustling industrial city 40 km north-east of Leipzig, is the chemical capital of the GDR. Despite this a few churches and museums in the old town justify a brief visit. Many new apartments are being built in the historic centre of Halle near the Handel Museum and the tasteful way this is being done demonstrates how far the science of city planning has come since Berlin and Dresden were rebuilt. Many Halle residents live in Halle Neustadt, a dormitory community on the west side of the Saale River.

Orientation

Streetcars in Halle follow a roundabout route so to get to the centre from the Hauptbahnhof walk through the underpass and straight down the shopping mall, Klement Gottwald Strasse, past 15th century Leipziger Turm to Markt.

Information

Halle-Information at Kleinschmieden 6 on the corner of Grosse Stein Strasse, a block north of Markt, can supply a poor map and answer questions. Reiseburo der DDR is at Klement Gottwald Strasse 6. Jugendtourist is at Klement Gottwald Strasse 27.

Things to See

In the centre of Markt, Halle's central square, is a statue of the great composer George Frederick Handel. You can't miss **Markt Kirche** (1529) with its four tall towers which dominate the square. Go inside to see the exquisitely decorated Gothic interior. Friedmann Bach, eldest son of Johann Sebastian Bach, served as organist here for 20 years. Also on Markt is the **Roter Turm** (1506), a great red tower now an art gallery. Just south of Markt at Grosse Marker Strasse 10 is the **City Historical Museum** (closed Friday).

Handel was born in Halle in 1685 and his home at Grosse Nikolai Strasse 5 has been converted into a major museum (closed Monday). Handel left Halle in 1703 and, after stays in Hamburg, Italy and Hannover, spent the years 1712 to 1759 in London where he achieved great fame. Mementos of the period make the museum worth visiting and it offers the added attraction of a pleasant coffee shop.

Places to Stay

Camping The closest Intercamping is at Seeburg on the northern shore of the Susser See, 20 km west of Halle (last bus from Halle at 8.30 pm). The Seeburg bus departs the bus station near Moritzkirche in the centre of Halle, not the Hauptbahnhof. It's an additional 15-minute walk from the bus stop to the campground. A good alternative is the Intercamping at Bad Bibra (see Naumburg below).

Hotels You're better off staying at Lutherstadt Wittenberg and seeing Halle in transit. If you must stay, the four-star *Interhotel Stadt Halle* on Thalmann Platz near the Haupbahnhof has everything you could ask for (120 M single, 200 M double). The medium-priced *Hotel 'Rotes*

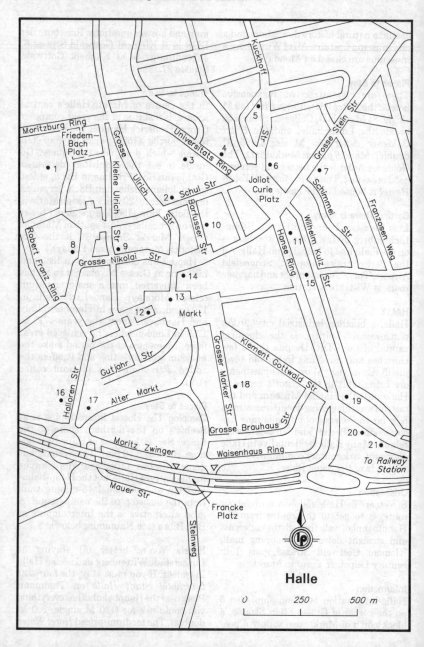

Halle

0   250   500 m

1	Moritzburg Art Museum
2	Neues Theater
3	Martin Luther University
4	Theater des Friedens
5	Marthahaus Christliches Hospiz
6	Gaststätte Martha-Klause
7	Hotel Weltfrieden
8	Dom (old cathedral)
9	Händel Museum
10	Hotel Pilsner Urquell
11	Post Office
12	Markt Kirche
13	Roter Turm
14	Halle-Information
15	Red Flag Monument
16	Bus Station
17	Moritzkirche
18	City Historical Museum
19	Leipziger Turm
20	Theaterkasse
21	Hotel 'Rotes Ross'

Ross' at Klement Gottwald Strasse 76 between the station and centre of town is a better bet price-wise, location-wise and atmosphere-wise.

Halle is short on budget accommodation, but you could try *Hotel Pilsner Urquell*, Barfusser Strasse 20, *Hotel Weltfrieden*, Grosse Stein Strasse 64-65, and *Marthahaus Christliches Hospiz*, Adam Kuckhoff Strasse 5-8.

Entertainment

Find out what's happening at the Theaterkasse, Klement Gottwald Strasse 82. The *Theater des Friedens* on Joliot Curie Platz is Halle's main stage, but there's also the *Neues Theater* at Grossen Ulrich Strasse 51. The best little bar in town is *Gaststatte Martha-Klause*, Martha Strasse 28 near Theater des Friedens (Monday to Friday 3 to 11 pm). It's the perfect place to go after the show.

Getting There & Away

Halle is on the route of fast trains from Rostock and Magdeburg to Leipzig or

Erfurt, also from Berlin-Lichtenberg or Berlin-Schoneweide to Erfurt and Eisenach. Coming from Dresden, you may have to change at Leipzig. Between Lutherstadt Wittenberg and Halle you may have to take a local train (one hour).

NAUMBURG

Naumburg is one of those pretty little medieval towns Germany is famous for. It's strategically located between Halle/Leipzig and Weimar with frequent trains. There are two youth hostels in the area and an Intercamping at Bad Bibra, all of which makes it well worth including in a GDR itinerary.

Orientation

The railway station is two km north-west of the old town, but there are frequent buses (drop coins in the box by the front doors). If you'd rather walk follow the disused streetcar tracks up to Stephan Platz on the north edge of the old town.

Information

Naumburg Information is at Lindenring 38. Reiseburo der DDR is at Wilhelm Pieck Platz 6.

Things to See

Naumburg is picturesque, its old town hall (1528) and Gothic church (1218-1523) rising above the central marketplace. The **City Historical Museum** (closed Monday) is beyond the polyclinic on the east side of Naumburg at Grochlitzer Strasse 49-51.

In the ancient western quarter of the town stands the magnificent Romanesque **Dom of Sts Peter & Paul** with the famous 13th century statues of Uta and Ekkehard in the west choir. The cloister, crypt, sculpture and four tall towers of this great medieval complex are unique.

Places to Stay

Accommodation in Naumburg is limited. The *Hotel Goldener Lowe*, Salz Strasse 15-16 near the centre, is usually full. The only other place to stay is the *'Werner Lamberz' Youth Tourist Hotel* at Am Tennis Platz 9, four km on the opposite side of Naumburg from the train station.

There's an *Intercamping* at Bad Bibra, Am Waldschwimmbad, 19 km north-west of Naumburg (last bus from Naumburg railway station at 7.30 pm). The closest railway station to Bad Bibra is Laucha, five km east of the campground.

Getting There & Away

There are fast trains to Naumburg from Halle, Leipzig, Jena and Weimar, and a local line to Sommerda.

FREYBURG

Freyburg, eight km north-west of Naumburg and easily accessible by train or bus, is also picturesquely situated in the Unstrut Valley with a large medieval castle on the wooded hilltop directly above. The castle will be closed for restoration for many years to come, but the adjacent tower (closed Monday) may be visited for its splendid view.

There's one small hotel in Freyburg, the *Zur Neuenburg* at Wasser Strasse 27, but the *'Friedrich Ludwig Jahn' Youth Hostel* on the road up to the castle is a better bet. The bus to Bad Bibra Intercamping passes Freyburg.

Erfurt District

WEIMAR

Not a monumental city nor a medieval one, Weimar appeals to more refined tastes. As a repository of German humanistic traditions it's unrivalled, but these can be difficult to assimilate by a foreign visitor in a rush. The parks and small museums are meant to be savoured, not downed in one gulp.

Many famous men lived and worked here, including Lucas Cranach the Elder (in 1552-1553), Johann Sebastian Bach (1708-1717), Christoph Martin Wieland (after 1772), Friedrich Schiller (1799-1805), Johann Gottfried Herder (1776), Johann Wolfgang von Goethe (1775-1832), Franz Liszt (in 1848 and 1869-1886), Walter Gropius, Lyonel Feininger, Vassili Kadinsky and Paul Klee. The State Bauhaus, which laid the foundations of all contemporary architecture, functioned in the city from 1919 to 1925.

Weimar is best known abroad as capital of the republic which paved the way for fascism, but you won't see any reference to it here. The horrors of Buchenwald are well remembered, however.

Orientation

The centre of town is a 20-minute walk south of the railway station. Buses run

1	Weimarhalle
2	City Historical Museum
3	Jacobskirchhof
4	Post Office
5	Students' Club 'Kasselturm'
6	Parish Church
7	Herder Museum
8	Goethe-Schiller Archive
9	Bus Loop
10	German National Theatre
11	Kunsthalle
12	Wittums Palace
13	Weimar-Information
14	Schlossmuseum
15	Schiller Haus
16	Museum Ticket Office
17	Rathaus
18	Lucas Cranach's House
19	Interhotel Elephant
20	Franz Liszt Music School
21	Library of German Classics
22	Goethe Museum
23	Christliches Hospiz
24	'15 August' Youth Hostel
25	Museum of Prehistory
26	Liszt House
27	Goethe's Cottage
28	Goethe-Schiller Mausoleum
29	Marzgefallenen Monument
30	Romisches Haus

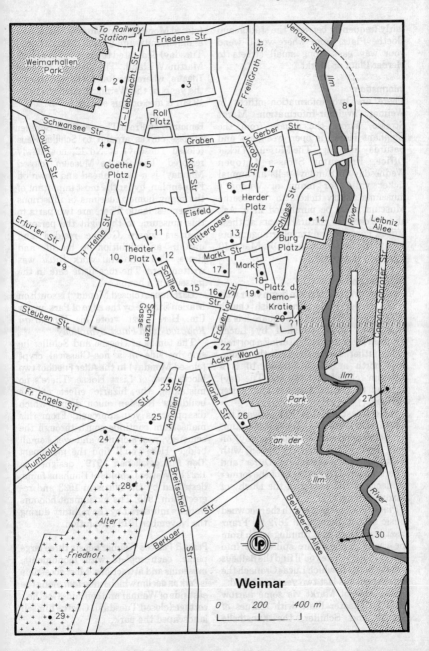

Weimar

0   200   400 m

fairly frequently between the station and Goethe Platz, from where you'll wend your way east along small streets to Herder Platz or Markt.

Information

There are two information offices in Weimar. Weimar-Information, Markt Strasse, across the square from the Elephant Hotel, is open weekdays and Saturday mornings. The Museum Ticket Office, Frauentor Strasse 4 (open Wednesday to Sunday) sells an annual ticket valid for many of Weimar's museums. Entry tickets to the Goethe Museum *must* be purchased here. Ask about tickets to cultural events at these offices. For practical travel arrangements turn to the Reiseburo der DDR, Markt 10 (closed Wednesday).

Things to See

City Centre A good place to begin your visit is at Herder Platz. The **parish church** (1500) in the centre of the square has an altarpiece (1555) finished by Lucas Cranach the Younger, featuring a portrait of his father, Lucas Cranach the Elder. Just north at Jakob Strasse 10 is a museum (closed Monday and Tuesday) devoted to the philosopher and writer Herder.

A block east of Herder Platz toward the Ilm River is Weimar's major art museum, the **Schlossmuseum** (closed Monday) on Burg Platz. This large collection, with masterpieces by Cranach, Durer and others, occupies three floors of the former residence of the elector of the Duchy of Saxony-Weimar.

Platz der Demokratie with the renowned music school founded in 1872 by Franz Liszt is up the street running south from the castle. This square spills over into Markt Platz, where you'll find the **Rathaus** and the house in which Lucas Cranach the Elder spent his last two years and died.

Due west of Markt via some narrow lanes is Theater Platz with statues of Goethe and Schiller, the **Kunsthalle**

(closed Monday) and **Wittums Palace**, now a major museum (closed Monday and Tuesday) dedicated to the poet Christoph Martin Wieland. The **German National Theatre**, where the Reichstag met during the years of the Weimar Republic (1919-1933), is also on this square.

Famous Men From Theater Platz Schiller Strasse curves around to **Schiller Haus** (closed Tuesday) at No 12, now newly restored. The **Goethe Museum** (closed Monday) is a block ahead and down on Frauenplan, by far the most important of the many home museums of illustrious former residents. There are two parts to this museum, to the right the personal quarters where Goethe resided and upstairs an exhibition on his life and times. The immortal work *Faust* was written here. The nice little cafe in the museum is a bonus.

Liszt House (closed Monday) is south on Marien Strasse by the edge of Park an der Ilm. Here Liszt wrote his *Hungarian Rhapsody* and *Faust Symphony*.

The tombs of Goethe and Schiller lie side by side in a neo-Classical crypt (closed Monday) in the **Alter Friedhof** two blocks west of Liszt House. There's no mistaking the bizarre effect of the buildings' Russian onion domes which disappear as you approach! From this mausoleum continue south through the cemetery, past a church and over a small bridge. Here you'll find the monument **'Den Marzgefallenen 1919'**, designed in 1922 by Walter Gropius of Bauhaus fame, destroyed by the Nazis in 1933 and re-erected in 1945. The monument honours workers murdered by the military during the November 1918 Revolution.

Parks & Palaces Weimar boasts three large parks, each replete with monuments, museums and attractions. Most accessible is **Park an der Ilm** which runs right along the east side of Weimar and contains Goethe's cottage (closed Tuesday). Goethe himself landscaped the park.

A km or two further south is **Belvedere Park** with a Baroque palace (open May to September, Wednesday to Sunday), Orangerie, viewpoints, etc. **Tiefurt Park**, a few km east of the railway station, is similar but smaller (palace closed on Monday). Duchess Anne Amalia organised famous intellectual 'Round-Table Gatherings' here in the late 18th century. Get there on bus No 3 from Goethe Platz hourly.

Buchenwald The Buchenwald museum and memorial are on Ettersberg Hill, beyond a large Soviet military base 10 km north-west of Weimar. You first pass the memorial (open at any time) with mass graves of some of the 56,500 victims from 18 nations. The concentration camp and museum (closed Monday and after 4 pm other days) are a km beyond. German anti-fascists, Soviet and Polish prisoners of war and many others, were held at Buchenwald for slave labour purposes in nearby underground armaments factories. On 11 April 1945, as American troops approached, the prisoners rose in armed rebellion, overcame the SS guards and liberated themselves. Many prominent German Communists and social democrats, Ernst Thalmann and Rudolf Breitscheid among them, were murdered here so Buchenwald has a special place in today's socialist Germany.

Buses run to Buchenwald from Weimar Hauptbahnhof (bus platform 31) every hour or so. It's also possible to catch a bus to Buchenwald from the bus loop behind the German National Theatre. Enquire about times at Weimar-Information.

Places to Stay

Hostels & Camping Weimar has three youth hostels, all in the southern section of the city a couple of km away from the railway station. The closest is the '15 August' Youth Hostel at Humboldt Strasse 16 near the Alter Friedhof. A couple of blocks south-west is the 'Ernst Thalmann' Youth Hostel, Windmuhlen

Ernst Thälmann

Strasse 16. The 'Maxim Gorki' Youth Tourist Hotel is on the opposite side of the cemetery at Zum Wilden Graben 12.

The closest Intercamping in Erfurt District is at Weissensee, Am Terrassebad, seven km north-west of Sommerda. Take a direct bus to Sommerda from stop No 25 in front of Weimar station or a train from Erfurt to Sommerda, then another bus to Weissensee, then walk 20 minutes.

Hotels Weimar's best hotel is the three-star Interhotel Elephant (80 M single, 130 M double) on Markt Platz. Actually, it's a characterful old building quite appropriate for Weimar, fine if you can afford it. Not far away is the budget Christliches Hospiz, Amalien Strasse 2 near Goethehaus.

There are two medium-priced hotels on the square in front of the railway station, the Einheit-Weimar (50 M single, 90 M double) and the *International* (55 M single, 100 M double), both all right although the taps in the Einheit give off a terrible screech.

Places to Eat

For a city with the literary traditions of Weimar there are remarkably few cafes. Restaurants are also few and far between, so don't wait too late to eat. The restaurant in Weimarhalle back by the park off Karl Liebknecht Strasse is OK, but they're closed by 8.30 pm. The hotel restaurants in the Einheit-Weimar and International hotels in front of the station are unpretentious, accessible, inexpensive and good. They're open till 9.30 pm.

Entertainment

The *German National Theatre* on Theater Platz is the city's main theatre and the box office is just inside. Weekends there's sometimes a disco in the *Students' Club 'Kasselturm'* in the round tower on Goethe Platz.

Getting There & Away

There are direct trains to Weimar from Berlin-Lichtenberg, Leipzig, Magdaberg (via Halle), Eisenach (via Erfurt) and Frankfurt am Main. Trains from Dresden arrive via Karl Marx Stadt and Jena. There's frequent service from Erfurt to Weimar, a 15-minute trip.

ERFURT

This trading and university centre founded by St Boniface in 742 is the main city of the Thuringian region. Undamaged during the war, Erfurt is a town of towers and flowers with colourful patrician mansions gracing the well-preserved medieval quarter near the station. Industry has kept to the modern suburbs. Each summer the International Horticultural Exhibition (IGA) takes place in the western section of Erfurt.

Orientation

As you come out of the railway station turn left, then right and walk straight up Bahnhof Strasse. In a few minutes you'll reach the Anger, a large square at the city's heart. Keep straight ahead and follow the streetcar tracks along Hermann Jahn Strasse past the Rathaus till you come to Dom Platz, Erfurt's most impressive sight.

Information

Erfurt-Information is at the corner of Bahnhof Strasse and Juri Gagarin Ring, halfway between the station and the Anger. The Reiseburo der DDR is at Anger 62. Jugendtourist is at Fischmarkt 6.

Things to See

The 13th century Gothic **Dom** and adjacent **Severikirche** crown a hilltop just west of the old town. The woodcarvings in the choir and figures on the portals make the Dom a 'must see' (open until 5 pm Monday to Saturday, 4 pm Sunday). Cross Dom Platz and take Markt Strasse east to Fischmarkt, the medieval city centre. Historical buildings such as the **Rathaus** (1871), **Haus Zum Breiten Herd** (1584) and the **House of the Red Ox** (1562) surround this square.

The eastbound street beside the Rathaus leads to the medieval **Kramerbrucke** (1325), now completely restored and lined on each side with timber-framed shops. This is the only such bridge north of the Alps! Continue east on Futter Strasse a block till it terminates at Lenin Strasse with the **City Historical Museum** (closed Friday and Saturday) around the corner at number 169. Behind this museum at Juri Gagarin Ring 140 is a large **Ethnographic Museum** (closed Monday and Tuesday) with a fascinating collection of Thuringian folk artefacts. Go south on Juri Gagarin Ring and turn west at the Interhotel Kosmos to return to the Anger. The **Anger Museum** (closed Monday and Tuesday) is on the corner of Bahnhof Strasse, where your city tour began.

Places to Stay

Erfurt is not the place to look for budget accommodation. If the Reiseburo der DDR is booking your room you'll do better staying in Gotha or Eisenach. The *'Karl Reimann' Youth Hostel*, Hochheimen Strasse 12, is on the western side of the city (tram No 5 southbound to the terminus).

The huge four-star *Interhotel Erfurter Hof* in front of the train station has great atmosphere, but you pay for it (115 M single, 190 M double). Atmosphere is sadly lacking in the out-of-place three-star *Interhotel Kosmos* a few blocks away. Its soaring silhouette is reflected in its prices (100 M single, 160 M double). The only two cheaper possibilities are the *Hotel Burgerhof*, Bahnhof Strasse 35/36 beside Erfurt Information, and the smaller *Hotel Gaedke*, Garten Strasse 74 two blocks away.

Getting There & Away

Erfurt is well connected by train to Eisenach, Suhl, Sommerda, Weimar, Dresden (via Jena) and most other cities in the GDR. The mainline from Berlin-Lichtenberg reaches Erfurt via Halle. To and from the Baltic coast you may have to change at Magdeburg although some trains run straight through. The railway station is almost a city in itself. The restaurant is upstairs at track level.

EISENACH

Eisenach is a picturesque medieval town in the south-west corner of the GDR on the edge of the Thuringian forest. From Romanesque Wartburg Castle overlooking Eisenach the landgraves ruled medieval Thuringia. Richard Wagner based his opera *Tannhauser* on a minstrel's contest in Wartburg Castle in 1206-1207. Martin Luther was kept in protective custody here by the elector under the assumed name 'Squire Jorg' after being excommunicated and put under the ban of the Empire by the Pope.

More recently the first country-wide proletarian party, the Social Democratic Workers' Party, was founded here by August Bebel and Wilhelm Liebknecht in 1869. Another first was the first automobile produced in Eisenach in 1898. Today the sturdy little Wartburg cars assembled in the local factory are seen all over Eastern Europe.

Orientation

Eisenach is the westernmost town in Eastern Europe. The railway station and medieval Wartburg are on opposite sides of town. If time is short take a bus or taxi to the Wartburg and walk back through the forest. To walk to the castle from the station follow Bahnhof Strasse west under the arch, cross the square and continue west on Karl Strasse to Markt. Two blocks west of Markt is Schlossberg with the Predigerkirche Museum (closed Monday) on the corner. Follow Schlossberg directly south-west and you'll come to Wartburg.

Information

Eisenach-Information, Bahnhof Strasse 5 near the station, can supply maps and brochures (closed Saturday afternoons and Sundays). Ask for the current address of their Konzertburo, which has tickets to most local events.

Things to See

Most tourists come to Eisenach to see the old fortress of **Wartburg** on a hilltop overlooking the Thuringian forests and hills. Martin Luther translated the New Testament from Greek into German while in hiding here in 1521-1522, thus making an immense contribution to the development of a uniform written German language. In summer huge crowds line up for tours of Wartburg's palace (open daily) and its Romanesque great hall, so count on waiting a while unless you arrive early. The view from Wartburg's tower (no line) alone is worth the trip.

In town the **Thuringian Museum** (closed Monday) in the former town palace (1751), Markt 24, has a collection of

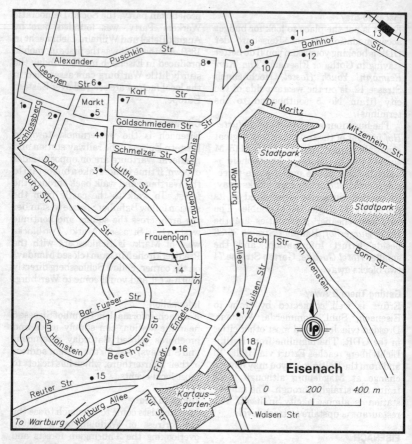

Eisenach

0   200   400 m

To Wartburg

ceramics and paintings of local interest. On the corner beyond the Georgenkirche is **Lutherhaus** (open daily), the future reformer's home from 1498 to 1501. The late Gothic architecture is far more interesting than the exhibits. Don't miss **Bachhaus** (open daily) on Frauenplan, where the composer was born in 1685. After a look around the museum go down into a room where recordings of Bach's best music are played.

The composer Wagner is not much in favour these days and he only rates a small display in the **Reuter-Wagner Museum** (closed Saturdays) on the back way up to Wartburg. If you visit it ask directions to the **Gedenkstatte Parteitag 1869** (closed Monday) nearby at Friedrich Engels Strasse 57, which has a fascinating exhibit on the 19th century workers' movements in Germany. The adjacent Kartausgarten with its 1825 tea house is a relaxing contrast to it all.

Places to Stay

Eisenach has long been a tourist centre of note, so accommodation is not lacking. The *Bahnhofshotel* and *Park Hotel* (60 M

1	Predigerkirche Museum
2	Post Office
3	Lutherhaus
4	Residenzhaus
5	Georgenkirche
6	Thuringian Museum
7	Rathaus
8	Thüringer Hof Hotel
9	Nikolaikirche
10	Park Hotel
11	Eisenach-Information
12	Bahnhofshotel
13	Railway Station
14	Bachhaus
15	Reuter-Wagner Museum
16	Gedenkstätte Parteitag 1869
17	Automotive Museum
18	Stadt Eisenach Hotel

single, 110 M double) are both near the station and the more expensive *Thuringer Hof Hotel* nearby, just beyond the old gate behind the statue of Martin Luther.

A step up in class and elevation is the *Stadt Eisenach Hotel* (60 M single, 110 M double) overlooking the Kartausgarten, or stay at the *Hotel Auf der Wartburg* (72 M single, 120 M double) up beside the castle, a place for romantics and lesser tourists. The *'Artur Becker' Youth Hostel* is at Marienta 124, in the valley below Wartburg.

Getting There & Away
Train connections to Erfurt are good and through trains running between Frankfurt am Main and Berlin-Lichtenberg also call here.

Schwerin District

SCHWERIN
Almost surrounded by lakes, Schwerin is perhaps the most picturesque town in the GDR. This former seat of the Grand Duchy of Mecklenburg is an interesting mix of medieval and 19th century architecture. It's small enough to get around and packed with attractions, an OK place to stop on the way north to the Baltic coast.

Orientation
As you come out of the railway station you'll see a large hotel on your right. Go toward it, then down the hill to Pfaffen Teich, a lake where you turn right again. The city centre is beyond the south end of this lake, focusing on Markt. Further south, around Schlossinsel on the Schweriner See, are the museums, parks and tour boats which will keep you entertained.

Information
Schwerin-Information, Am Markt 11, opens daily, but only mornings on weekends. Reiseburo der DDR is at Grosser Moor 9. Jugendtourist is at Dr W Kulz Strasse 3.

Things to See
Above Markt rises the tall Gothic **Dom**, a superb example of North German red brick architecture; climb the tower for the view. The winding medieval streets of the old town complement well the verdant parks and gardens along the lakes. Schwerin's neo-Gothic **Schloss** (closed Monday) is on an island connected to the lakeside promenades by causeways. At the end of the causeway on the city side is the **State Museum** (closed Monday) with an excellent collection of old Dutch masters including Franz Halls, Rembrandt, Rubens and Bruegel. The other causeway leads to the 18th century **Schlossgarten**. Schwerin's **zoo** is three km south-east of here.

On the Lakes From May to September Weisse Flotte excursion boats operate on the **Schweriner See** from Schlossbucht, the landing beside the museum opposite the castle. The cruises are often sold out a few days in advance. It's much easier to get a ticket for the ferry trip south from the

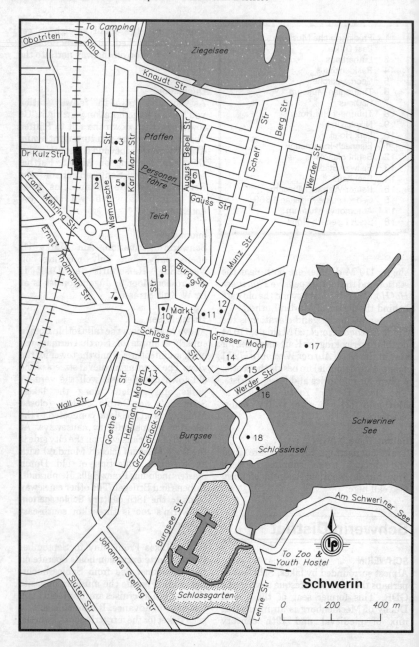

Schwerin

1	Railway Station
2	Hotel Stadt Schwerin
3	Hotel Polonia
4	Bahnhofshotel
5	Niederlandischer Hof Hotel
6	Hospiz am Pfaffenteich
7	Hotel Wendenhof
8	Post Office
9	Dom
10	Schweriner Cafe
11	Schwerin-Information
12	Alt Schweriner Schantstuben
13	Bus Station
14	Staatstheater
15	State Museum
16	Weisse Flotte
17	Marstall
18	Schloss

same landing to Zippendorf, a lakeside resort near the zoo. Departure times are posted.

Places to Stay

Hostels & Camping Schwerin's *'Kurt Burger' Youth Hostel* is on Waldschulenweg just opposite the entrance to the zoo, about four km south of the city centre (bus No 15 from the bus station on Hermann Matern Strasse).

Seehof Intercamping, 10 km north of Schwerin on the west shore of the Schweriner See, is easily accessible on bus No 8 from the bus station, or take any northbound streetcar from the railway station to the end of the line at KGW (Klement Gottwald Werk) and catch bus No 8 there. Buses run hourly as late as 10.30 pm daily. There aren't any bungalows and in summer it's crowded, but there's a snack bar open till 9 pm and of course the lake for swimming and rowboating.

Hotels In summer all of Schwerin's hotels are full. The *Polonia* and *Bahnhofshotel* are opposite the railway station. The expensive *Hotel Stadt Schwerin* (81 M single, 126 M double) looms to one side.

Others worth a look are the *Hotel Wendenhof*, Wismarsche Strasse 104 a couple of blocks south of the station, and the *Hospiz am Pfaffen Teich*, Gauss Strasse 19 near the far landing of the small ferry which crosses Pfaffen Teich from near the station. Best of all, try for a room at the *Niederlandischer Hof Hotel*, Karl Marx Strasse 12 right on Pfaffen Teich, a block down from the Hotel Stadt Schwerin. This is unquestionably the most tasteful of Schwerin's hotels but you'll probably have to book ahead to get in.

Places to Eat

The *Alt Schweriner Schantstuben* on the Schlachtermarkt behind Schwerin-Information in the old town serves meals till 10 pm and wine till midnight. The *Schweriner Cafe*, Busch Strasse 7 just off Markt, is a great place to get a coffee during the day and a drink at night.

Getting There & Away

Fast trains arrive regularly from Rostock, Magdeburg, Halle, Leipzig and Berlin-Lichtenberg. From Weimar and Erfurt you may have to change at Magdeburg. From Wismar it's often faster to change trains in Bad Kleinen than to wait for a through service.

Rostock District

WISMAR

Westernmost and smallest of the Baltic resorts, Wismar is about halfway between Rostock and Lubeck. It became a Hanseatic trading city in the 13th century. It's a pretty little town, slightly off the beaten track, a welcome change from overcrowded Rostock and Stralsund. Because Wismar is on the way to the West German border security tends to be a little tighter than elsewhere in the GDR. Many Soviet soldiers are stationed here.

Orientation

The railway station is adjacent to the old quarter of this small Baltic port. To reach Markt and the Rathaus walk four blocks south on Bahnhof Strasse to a major intersection where you turn right along Lubsche Strasse. Markt is two blocks down on the left.

Information

Wismar Service at Lubsche Strasse 44 behind the Rathaus has maps, brochures, decals, etc. Next door is a shop selling political posters and badges, including huge photos of various socialist personalities. The Reiseburo der DDR is at An der Hegede 1.

Things to See

Like many other German cities Wismar was a target for Anglo-American bombers just a few weeks prior to the end of the war. Of the three great red brick churches that once rose above the rooftops only **St Nikolai** is still intact. Its 37-metre tower is the highest in the country. The massive red shell of **St George's** has been left as a reminder of the April 1945 raids. Cars now park where 13th century **St Mary's** once stood, although the great brick steeple still towers above. Apart from this it's hard to believe that Wismar's gabled houses were seriously bombed. Nearby in a corner of Markt are the graceful old **Waterworks** (1602) and the **Rathaus** (1817-19). The **City Historical Museum** (closed Monday) at Schweinsbrucke 8 near St Nikolai has many interesting exhibits.

To get out onto the Baltic, board a Weisse Flotte excursion boat to Timmendorf or Kirchdorf on **Poel Island**, very popular summer bathing resorts for Germans. The trips operate from May to September (2 M same day round trip). You can also get to Poel by bus several times a day.

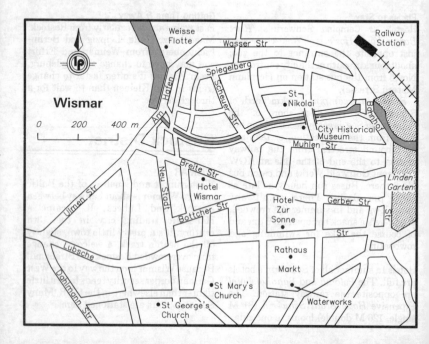

Wismar

0   200   400 m

Places to Stay

The best place to stay is the picturesque *Hotel Wismar* at Breite Strasse 10. The hotel has a good restaurant which stays open till 10 pm. The *Hotel Zur Sonne*, Lubsche Strasse 51 opposite Wismar Service, is cheaper but run down.

If these are full you'll have to pitch your tent at *Zierow Intercamping*, on the coast eight km north-west of Wismar. Bus service to Zierow terminates at 5 pm, after which you'll either have to take a taxi (just under 20 M) or a highway bus to Gagelow from where it's a four km walk downhill to Zierow. There's a store at Zierow but no bungalows. At night old American movies dubbed into German are run in a large tent beside the campground.

Getting There & Away

Trains arrive from Rostock every couple of hours and from Berlin-Lichtenberg twice a day. Between Schwerin and Wismar it's often quicker to change trains at Bad Kleinen than to wait for a through service.

ROSTOCK

Rostock, the largest city in the northern half of the GDR, is also a teeming tourist centre. Warnemunde, Rostock's beach town 12 km north, is absolutely packed in summer as half the population of the GDR heads north to the sea. In the 14th and 15th centuries Rostock was an important Hanseatic city trading with Riga, Bergen and Brugge. The university founded in 1419 was the first in Northern Europe. The salty city centre along Kropeliner Strasse retains the flavour of this period well. Today Rostock is a major Baltic port and shipbuilder. The giant Warnow shipyards were built from scratch after 1957.

Information

Rostock-Information, Lange Strasse 5, is quite a distance from the train station. To get there take any streetcar outside the station and get off at the next stop after the Rathaus and St Mary's Church in the centre of town. The Reiseburo der DDR is at Hermann Duncker Platz 2. Jugendtourist is at Kropeliner Strasse 10.

Things to See

Rostock's greatest sight is 13th century **St Mary's Church** which survived the war unscathed. This great medieval brick edifice contains a Gothic bronze baptismal font (1290), a functioning astronomical clock (1472), a Renaissance pulpit (1574) and a Baroque organ (1770), all artistic treasures. Climb the church tower for the view.

Kropeliner Strasse, a broad pedestrian mall lined with 15th and 16th century burger houses, runs west from the Rathaus on Ernst Thalmann Platz to **Kropeliner Tor** (closed Thursday) on the city walls. Halfway along, off the south-west corner of Universitats Platz, is the **Kloster 'Zum heiligen Kreuz' Museum** (closed Monday) in an old convent (1270).

Rostock also has a good **Maritime Museum** (closed Friday) on the south side of Karl Marx Platz, opposite the tower at the entrance to town from the railway station. If you've got a little spare time Rostock's **zoo** (tram No 11) is pleasant and there's a large beer garden opposite the entrance.

Warnemunde

It's easy to get to Warnemunde on the double-decker S-Bahn. Trains depart frequently from Rostock station. The 25-minute trip takes you past row after row of modern apartment blocks to the Baltic coast.

From the station turn left and cross the small bridge over **Alter Strom**, the old harbour. This picturesque inlet is still lined with quaint fishermen's cottages, one of which has been converted into a **museum** (open daily in July and August, Wednesday and Sunday the rest of the year). It's straight ahead from the bridge, a block back from Alter Strom.

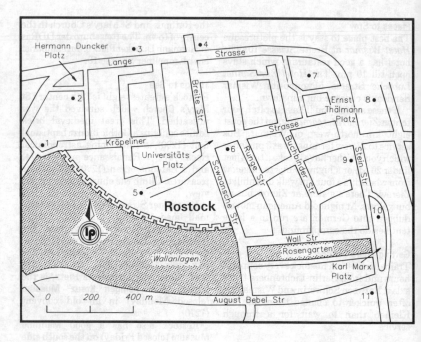

1 Kröpeliner Tor
2 Interhotel Warnow
3 Rostock-Information
4 Ostseegaststatte
5 'Zum Heiligen Kreuz' Museum
6 University Library
7 St Mary's Church
8 Rathaus
9 Hotel Nordland
10 Steintor
11 Maritime Museum

After a brief visit return to Alter Strom and follow the crowded promenade north to the sea where German tourists congregate. From May to October Weisse Flotte boats depart from near the mouth of Alter Strom on harbour cruises (2 to 4 M), but they're usually fully booked a few days in advance. Warnemunde's beach stretches west from the lighthouse, chock-a-block with bathers.

Places to Stay

In summer reserve a room in advance using western currency or pray hard. The closest Intercampings are at Wismar and Stralsund, and even the youth hostel is inconvenient. The *Hotel am Bahnhof* (60 M single, 100 M double) opposite Rostock Hauptbahnhof doesn't have much going for it other than location, but give it a try. If they're full ask if they can get you a room at the old *Hotel Nordland*, Stein Strasse 7 near the Rathaus. The four-star *Interhotel Warnow*, Hermann Duncker Platz 4, is deluxe (130 M single, 210 M double).

The only other hotels are on the beach at Warnemunde. The *Strand Hotel* and *Promenade Hotel* are not cheap but have an excellent seaside atmosphere – recommended. There's also the high-rise *Neptun Hotel* (129 M single, 192 M double) for those with five-star wallets and Sheraton tastes. The *'Traditionsschiff' Youth Hostel* is in a converted freighter on the harbour between Rostock and Warnemunde (S-Bahn to Lutten Klein station, then walk 25 minutes).

Places to Eat
The *Ostseegaststatte*, Lange Strasse 9 near Rostock-Information, has an English menu complete with the calorie count of each dish in the upstairs dining room. They specialise in seafood and there's a pizzeria downstairs. The service is good.

Getting There & Away
There are direct trains to Rostock from Berlin-Lichtenberg, Schwerin, Magdeburg, Erfurt and Leipzig (via Potsdam or Halle). Trains run Stralsund, Rostock, Wismar, Schwerin every couple of hours. Overnight trains with sleepers are available to and from Leipzig.

Rostock is one of the easiest cities in the GDR to reach from West Berlin as there are two through car-ferry trains a day between Berlin-Zoo Station and Copenhagen via Rostock. Due to the expense of buying a ticket in West Berlin it's probably better to use this train to go from Rostock *to* West Berlin, however. These trains connect with the international ferry service from Warnemunde to Gedser, Denmark.

STRALSUND
Stralsund, an enjoyable city on the Baltic due north of Berlin, is nearly surrounded by lakes and the sea, which once contributed to its defence. A Hanseatic city in the Middle Ages, Stralsund later formed part of the Duchy of Pommern-Wolgast. From 1648 to 1815 Stralsund was under Swedish control. Today it's an attractive old town with fine museums and buildings, pleasant walks and a restful, uncluttered waterfront.

Orientation
From the railway station cross the causeway to the right and you're in the old town. Continue up Tribseer Strasse to Lenin Platz and you'll have St Mary's Church on the right and the museums of Monch Strasse on the left.

Information
The Reiseburo der DDR is at Alter Markt 10

Things to See
First visit 15th century **St Mary's**, a massive red brick edifice typical of North German Gothic church architecture. Climb the 345 steps of the tower for a sweeping view of all of Stralsund. Nearby on Monch Strasse are two excellent museums. The **Historical Museum** (closed Friday and Saturday in winter) has a large collection housed in the cloister of an old convent. Stralsund's highlight is the adjoining convent church, now a fantastic **Oceanographic Museum & Aquarium** (closed Monday and Tuesday in winter). Both temperate and tropical seas are represented with admirable precision and the only sour note is sounded by an unfortunate display on the 'benefits' of commercial whaling.

From these museums make your way north through the old city to Alter Markt with the medieval **Rathaus**, itself a delightful sight, and **St Nikolai Church** (1350), impressive but closed for long-term restorations. There are many gabled Baltic houses on the small streets just north of Alter Markt. The old harbour is close by. You'll want to stroll out along the sea wall, then walk west along the waterfront park for a great view of Stralsund's skyline.

Year round (ice permitting) Weisse Flotte ships depart the old harbour for **Hiddensee Island** (4 M same day round trip). Harbour cruises (1 M an hour) are offered from May to September. If you're short on time or have difficulty getting tickets just take the regular ferry across to Altefahr on **Rugen Island**. It operates eight

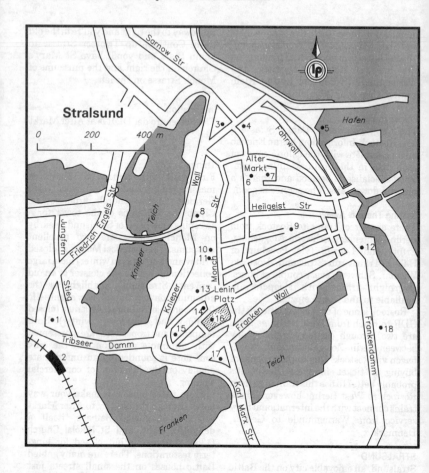

Stralsund

0   200   400 m

Sarnow Str

Hafen

Alter Markt

Fahrwall

Heilgeist Str

Wall Str

Mönch Str

Jungfern Stieg

Friedrich Engels Str

Knieper Teich

Knieper

Lenin Platz

Tribseer Damm

Franken Wall

Franken Teich

Karl Marx Str

Frankendamm

Franken

times a day from May to early October (25 pfennig one way).

Places to Stay

The functional old *Hotel Am Bahnhof* is right opposite the train station. Cheaper yet is the *Nordland Hotel* on Platz der Solidaritat just across the causeway. You're better off, however, at the *Hotel Schweriner Hof* in a good location on Lenin Platz beside St Mary's Church. The hotel restaurant is recommended.

Stralsund doesn't have an Interhotel (fortunately?) so the best they have to offer is the depressing *Hotel Baltic* (65 M single, 120 M double), a monolithic Stalin-era building at Frankendamm 17 in an ugly neighbourhood south of the harbour.

Stralsund's *'Grete Walter' Youth Hostel* on the other hand is great, in the old waterworks (1690) at Am Kutertor 1 near the Oceanographic Museum. There's a very good cafe/bar attached to the hostel

1   Hotel Am Bahnhof
2   Railway Station
3   Theatre
4   Kniepertor
5   Weisse Flotte
6   Rathaus
7   St Nikolai's Church
8   'Grete Walter' Youth Hostel
9   St Jacob's Church
10 Oceanographic Museum &
    Aquarium
11 Historical Museum
12 Heilgeistkirche
13 Post Office
14 Hotel Schweriner Hof
15 Nordland Hotel
16 St Mary's Church
17 Bus Station
18 Hotel Baltic

so make a point of taking a break there after touring the museums.

The closest *Intercamping* is at Stahlbrode on the coast, about 19 km south-east of Stralsund and four km from Reinberg off the main road to Berlin.

Getting There & Away

Express trains arrive from Rostock, Magdeberg, Leipzig and Berlin-Lichtenberg. Some of the Berlin trains run straight through from Leipzig to Stralsund. International trains between Berlin Zoo and Stockholm or Oslo use the car ferry between Sassnitz Hafen and Trelleborg, Sweden. You can travel on this train direct from Stralsund to West Berlin. In the other direction ticketing problems and inconvenient schedules make it inadvisable.

Poland

Aside from the USSR, Poland is by far the largest country in Eastern Europe. Caught between the pincers of Germany and Russia, Poland has had a tumultuous past. The weight of history is on Cracow, a 16th century royal city, Gdansk (Danzig), the Hanseatic trading town where WW II began, Auschwitz, a reminder of the depths to which humanity can descend, and rebuilt Warsaw, symbol of the resilient Polish spirit. Fervently Catholic, reluctantly socialist, the Poles love to talk politics. Freedom of speech is tolerated in Poland, although there's press censorship.

Aside from the historical and cultural sides to this subtle land of Chopin and Copernicus, there's the gentle beauty of Baltic beaches, quiet lakes and majestic mountains, all requiring time to appreciate. Each of the separate regions of Poland has its own character: Mazovia (around Warsaw), Little Poland (in the south-east), Silesia (in the south-west), Great Poland (in the west) and Pomerania (in the north). Palpable differences remain between the areas once controlled by Austria, Germany and Russia.

Despite the prevailing impression, Poland is a peaceful, safe place to visit. Once you're through the paperwork there are relatively few hassles. Even the dead weight bureaucracy has the advantage of keeping down the number of visitors. You'll find the Poles eager to meet you and you'll share the minor frustrations of their everyday life. It's an experience you won't easily forget.

Facts about the Country

HISTORY

In the 6th and 7th centuries AD the West Slavs pushed north and west and occupied most of what is now Poland.

Mieszko I adopted Christianity in 966, a date considered to mark the formation of the first Polish state. In the year 1000 the Gniezno Archbishopric was founded and in 1025 Boleslav the Brave took the title king. His successor, Boleslav the Bold, consolidated the power of the Piast dynasty over a territory very similar to the Poland of today.

There was constant pressure from the west as the Germans pushed into Pomerania (in the north along the Baltic Sea) and Silesia (in the south along the Odra River). In the mid-12th century the country was divided into four principalities. A weakened Poland soon fell prey to invaders. In 1226 the Teutonic Knights, a Germanic military and religious order, was invited to come to Poland to subdue the restive Prussians. Once the knights had subjugated the Baltic tribes they turned their attention to the Poles. The order set up a state in the lower Vistula area east of Gdansk/Torun, ruled from their castle at Malbork. Mongol invasions devastated Southern Poland in 1241 and 1259.

Poland was reunified in 1320 but the knights held onto Pomerania and Prussia. From the 14th to 17th centuries Poland was a great power. It's said that the 14th century king Casimir III the Great, last of the Piast dynasty, 'found a Poland made of wood and left one made of masonry.' His administrative reforms increased the significance of towns like Cracow, Lublin and Poznan. In 1385 Princess Jadwiga married the Duke of Lithuania, uniting the two countries under the Jagiello dynasty. In 1410 the combined Polish, Lithuanian and Ruthenian (Ukrainian) forces defeated the Teutonic Knights at Grunwald south of Olsztyn. After the Thirteen Years' War (1454-1466) the Teutonic Order was broken up and Prussia became a fiefdom of the Polish Crown.

In 1490 King Casimir IV of Poland assumed the Hungarian throne. The early 16th century monarch Sigismund I the Old brought the Renaissance to Poland. In 1543 Copernicus published his immortal treatise *De Revolutionibus Orbium Coelestium*. Poland and Lithuania were formally united as one country in 1569 to oppose Russian expansion. After the death of Sigismund Augustus in 1572 the Jagiello dynasty became extinct and the power of the feudal nobility increased. In the early 17th century Sigismund III, a king from the Swedish Vasa line, moved the capital from Cracow to Warsaw. For a time Poland was successful in wars against Sweden and Moscow, but in 1655 a Swedish invasion ('the deluge') destroyed the Polish towns. King Jan III Sobieski, builder of Warsaw's Wilanow Palace, led a crusade against the Turks which resulted in their removal from Hungary after 1683.

Weak leadership, constant wars and the domination of the gentry over the middle class led to the decline of Poland in the 18th century. In the first partition of Poland in 1772 Russia, Prussia and Austria took 29% of the national territory. After a second partition in 1793 Tadeusz Kosciuszko led a war of independence but was defeated in 1795. A subsequent third partition that year wiped Poland right off the map of Europe until 1918. The

oppressed Poles supported Napoleon who set up a Duchy of Warsaw in 1807 and led his Grand Army to Moscow from there in 1812. After 1815 Poland again came under Tsarist Russia. There were unsuccessful uprisings against this in 1831, 1848 and 1864 with Poland's position worsening after each one.

Poland was completely overrun by the Germans during WW I, but in 1919 a Polish state was again established by the Treaty of Versailles. The reactionary Polish government took advantage of Soviet weakness to annex part of the Ukraine in 1922. Poland also participated in the Nazi dismemberment of Czechoslovakia in 1938, but soon fell victim to Hitler.

WW II began in Gdansk (at that time the Free City of Danzig) where 189 Poles at Westerplatte held out for a week against the battleship *Schleswig Holstein*, Stuka dive bombers and thousands of German troops. To the west the Polish Pomorska Brigade of mounted cavalry met General Guderian's tanks, medieval lances against modern armour, in a final suicidal charge. As these events took place the Soviet Union reoccupied the areas taken from them in 1922, to prevent their falling into German hands.

Poland was the only country in Europe which never produced any quislings (collaborators). The Nazi Governor General Hans Frank ruled those areas not directly incorporated into the Reich. There were two resistance groups: the London-directed Armia Krajowa (Home Army) and the Communist Gwardia Ludow (People's Guard), later the People's Army. In June 1944 the Red Army liberated Lublin and set up a Communist-led provisional government.

Six million people died in Poland during the Nazi terror, half of them Jews, a fifth of the population. The Warsaw Ghetto Uprising of 1943 is a heroic chapter in human resistance to fascism and war. The Warsaw Uprising was begun on 1 August 1944 by the Home Army as Soviet

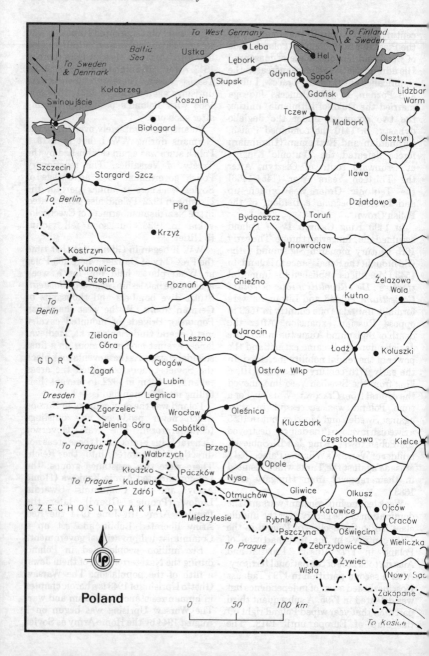

Poland

forces approached the right bank of the Vistula River. The intention was to evict the retreating Germans from Warsaw and have a non-Communist force in place to greet the Soviet Army but the uprising was premature. The Nazis brought up reserves to halt the Red Army in Praga across the river, then engaged the 50,000 Polish irregulars in house to house combat. By 5 October, when the remaining partisans surrendered with honour, some 250,000 Poles had died, many of them civilians slaughtered *en masse* by SS troops.

All the remaining inhabitants were then expelled from the city and German demolition teams levelled Warsaw street by street. The Soviet armies which entered the city three months later encountered only desolation. Accusations were made at the time that the Soviets had called on the Poles to rise up, then stood by while they were slaughtered. These claims have never been proved. No one denies that London ordered the uprising for political reasons. Looking across the Vistula today one wonders how many of *us* would have the courage to try to cross the river in the face of withering fire from dug-in Nazi positions. Ironically the Germans set the stage for a post-war Communist Poland by physically eliminating the bulk of the non-Communist resistance within the country.

After the war Silesia and everything east of the Odra and Nysa rivers returned to Poland after centuries of German control. In 1948 the road to socialism was marked by the formation of the Polish United Workers' Party. The creation of the Warsaw Pact in 1955 guaranteed Poland's postwar borders. Poland's unique history has led to a love/hate relationship with its giant neighbour, the USSR. Few peoples prize their independence more passionately than the Poles. It's significant that Poland today hosts only two Soviet army divisions, while there are four in Hungary, five in Czechoslovakia and 20 in the GDR.

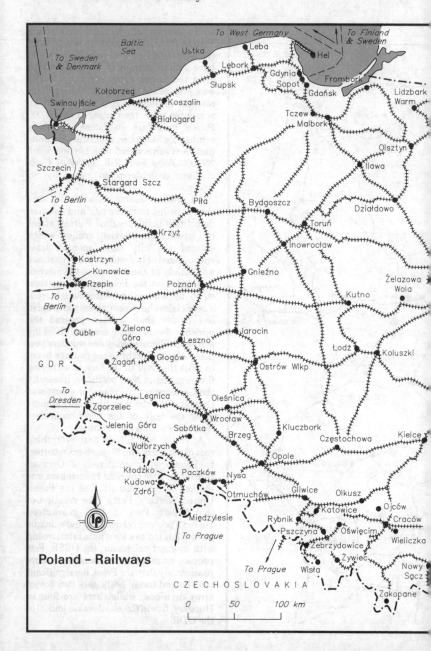

Poland – Railways

To Sweden & Denmark

Baltic Sea

To West Germany

To Finland & Sweden

Ustka
Leba
Hel
Lebork
Frombork
Słupsk
Gdynia
Sopot
Kołobrzeg
Gdańsk
Lidzbark Warm
Koszalin
Swinoujście
Tczew
Malbork
Olsztyn
Białogard
Szczecin
Ilawa
Stargard Szcz
Działdowo
To Berlin
Piła
Bydgoszcz
Toruń
Inowrocław
Krzyż
Kostrzyn
Kunowice
Gniezno
Żelazowa Wola
Rzepin
Poznań
To Berlin
Kutno
Zielona Góra
Jarocin
Gubin
Leszno
Łódź
Koluszki
Żagań
Głogów
Ostrów Wlkp
GDR
To Dresden
Legnica
Oleśnica
Zgorzelec
Wrocław
Kielce
Jelenia Góra
Sobótka
Kluczbork
Brzeg
Częstochowa
Wałbrzych
Opole
Kłodzko
Paczków
Nysa
Gliwice
Olkusz
Kudowa Zdrój
Otmuchów
Katowice
Ojców
Międzylesie
Rybnik
Cracków
Pszczyna
Oświęcim
Wieliczka
To Prague
Zebrzydowice
Żywiec
To Prague
Wisła
Nowy Sącz
CZECHOSLOVAKIA
Zakopane

0   50   100 km

Kętrzyn
Gizycko
Suwałki
Elk
To Leningrad
Mikolajki
Kuźnica Białostocka
Białystok
USSR
To Moscow
Warsaw
Siedlce
Terespol
Łuków
To Kiev
Dęblin
łdom
Lublin
Kazimierz Din
Zamość
Sandomierz
Rozwadów
Przeworsk
Rzeszów
To Lvov
Tarnów
Jarosław
Przemyśl
Medyka
Krynica
Zagórz
Ustrzyki Dolne
To Budapest

Recent History

In December 1970 workers throughout Poland went on strike over food price increases and 300 were shot down during demonstrations. Then Edward Gierek replaced Wladyslaw Gomulka as party leader and persuaded the strikers to return to work.

Gierek launched Poland on a reckless programme of industrial expansion to produce exports which could be sold on world markets. Money to finance this was supplied by western banks and by 1981 the country had run up a hard currency debt of US$27 billion. Many of the ill-founded heavy industry schemes ended in failure as a recession in the west shrank the markets for Polish exports at the end of the 1970s.

This decade of mismanagement left Poland bankrupt. Living standards fell sharply as Poland was forced to divert goods to export from domestic consumption, to earn hard currency with which to service the debt. This led to widespread labour unrest. In 1980 a wave of strikes forced Gierek out and marked the emergence of Lech Walesa's 'Solidarity' movement. Previous popular upheavals of this kind had occurred in 1956, 1970 and 1976. 'Solidarity' claimed all it wanted was self-management of the factories by workers' councils instead of central planning. At first the Polish government was conciliatory, recognising 'Solidarity' in August 1980, and conceding to a five-day work week. In September 1981, many of 'Solidarity's' demands for reduced central planning and greater worker control over enterprises were met.

Things soon got out of hand as union militants challenged government authority. Strikes and obstruction threatened Poland with economic collapse and a Soviet military intervention which might have led to civil war. Martial law was declared on 13 December 1981 and 'Solidarity' was formally dissolved by the Seym (Parliament) in October 1982. By July 1983 martial law could be lifted.

Defeated by its own excesses, 'Solidarity' had 10 million members (a million of them also Communist Party members) in its heyday. Western countries such as the US encouraged 'Solidarity,' but failed to provide Poland with the economic aid necessary to make reform possible. This contradiction didn't prevent the Reagan administration from using martial law as an excuse for imposing economic sanctions against Poland in 1982.

A year after the imposition of martial law General Wojciech Jaruzelski introduced economic reforms of his own based on greater autonomy for state corporations. In April 1986, the government set in motion 'second stage' reforms providing for decentralisation, worker control of companies, greater competition, incentives, a market economy and some political pluralism. But Poland's problems are far from solved. In 1988 inflationary strikes followed government attempts to remove uneconomic food subsidies. Quick solutions remain as evasive as ever.

PEOPLE

With 37 million inhabitants, 312,677-square-km Poland is the seventh largest country in Europe, almost as big as East Germany, Czechoslovakia and Hungary combined. The country is divided into 49 voivodships (regions). The south-west is the most densely populated part, especially the area around Lodz and Katowice, while the north-east is the least populated. Over half the population lives in towns and cities, the six largest of which are Warsaw, Lodz, Cracow, Wroclaw, Poznan and Gdansk. There's a housing shortage forcing many young families to live with in-laws.

At the end of WW II millions of Germans were evicted from East Prussia and western Poland, their places taken by further millions of Poles from the Lvov region of the Ukraine. Half a million Ukrainians, Belorussians and Lithuanians were resettled in the USSR. These forced migrations created a homogeneous population. Before the war minorities accounted for 30% of the population of Poland. Today only 1.5% are minorities, mostly Ukrainians and Belorussians. Tragically few of the 3.5 million Polish Jews survived the war. Ten million Poles live abroad in North America, the Soviet Union, France and Brazil. Poles refer to the overseas Polish community as 'Polonia.'

ECONOMY

After WW II Poland was a patchwork of small farmers with 38% of the economy in ruins. In the rebuilding process the emphasis was placed on heavy industry leading to serious shortages of consumer goods. Industry, services and agriculture each contribute about a third to the gross national product. Heavy industries include steel mills (at Warsaw, Cracow and Katowice), shipbuilding (at Gdansk), mining machinery and chemicals, while among the light industries are textiles (at Lodz), food products, paper, timber and glass. Poland is the fourth largest producer of hard bituminous coal in the world, most of it from Silesia. Brown coal is burned for electricity. Sulphur and copper are extracted in southern Poland. These activities have created tremendous environmental problems.

A quarter of the population lives from agriculture. Poland is the world's second largest producer of rye. Sugar beets, wheat, oats and barley are also important. Poland is unique in Eastern Europe in that 83% of agricultural land is privately farmed by small holders, while 15% is owned by the state and only 2% by cooperatives.

Poland has hard currency debts of over US$30 billion. Exports of machinery, coal, transportation equipment and chemicals are sent to the CMEA countries. The USSR is Poland's main trading partner supplying raw materials such as metals and phosphates for industry, plus 80% of Poland's crude oil. It's only through the favourable terms of this trade that Poland can cope. Meat and gasoline are rationed.

GEOGRAPHY

Poland stretches 650 km from north to south 650 km and 690 km from east to west. It's a low country with all of the mountains in the south. The Sudeten Mountains south of Jelenia Gora in Silesia are 280 km long and 50 km wide, with a medium height of 1200 metres culminating in Sniezka (1605 metres). The Beskydy and Pieniny mountains in the Western Carpathians run along the Slovak border north of the Tatras. The Bieszczady Mountains in the Eastern Carpathians are open grassy peaks which reach 1346 metres at Tarnica.

Poland's highest mountains are the rocky Tatras, a section of the Carpathian Range Poland shares with Slovakia. The Polish Tatras (150 square km) are 50 km long and rise to Rysy (2499 metres), while the Slovak Tatras (600 square km) culminate in Gerlach (2654 metres).

Lowland predominates in central Poland, a land of great rivers such as the Vistula, Odra, Warta and Bug. The entire drainage area of the Vistula, the mother river of Poland, lies within its boundaries. Poland has more post-glacial lakes than any country in Europe except Finland. West of the Vistula is the Pomeranian lake district, east are the picturesque Mazurian Lakes. The coastal plain along the broad sandy 524-km-long Baltic coast is spotted with sand dunes, bays and lakes, separated from the sea by narrow sandbars. Forests cover 27% of the country.

RELIGION

Freedom of religion is guaranteed in the Polish Constitution and 94% of the Poles are nominal Catholics. Fifty-one Catholic newspapers and magazines are published with a total print run of one million. The Catholic University in Lublin and the Academy of Catholic Theology in Warsaw are church-controlled institutions. There are 20,000 priests (compared to 11,000 in 1937). On Sundays every church is full to overflowing. Czestochowa with its Black Madonna is a major pilgrimage centre. The narrow line between church and state is hard to define in Poland. Catholic support for 'Solidarity' is fairly open, something of a balance to the atheism of scientific Communism. Both sides recognise the advantage of getting along.

FESTIVALS & HOLIDAYS

Two Warsaw events not to miss are the Jazz Jamboree the last 10 days of October and the Golden Washboard (traditional jazz) in January. Wroclaw's Jazz on the Odra festival in early March is equally good. In May there are the student festivals, Juvenalia in Cracow and Neptunalia in Gdansk. June is a month of folk festivals in Kazimierz, Olsztyn, Ostroleka and Zywiec.

Summer events on the Baltic coast include the Fama Student Artistic Festival in Swinoujscie (July), Sopot's International Song Festival (August) and Gdansk's Dominican Fair (August). The Festival of Highland Folklore in Zakopane, Warsaw's Festival of Contemporary Music and the Torun International Old Music Festival are leading September events. As many as eight trade fairs a year are held in Poznan, the largest of which are the International Technical Fair in June and the Consumer Goods Fair in September.

Public holidays in Poland include 1 January (New Years), Easter Monday, 1 May (Labour Day), Corpus Christi (early June), 22 July (National Day), 1 November (All Souls' Day), 25 and 26 December (Christmas).

LANGUAGE

German is widely understood in Poland, English sometimes. The first words a visitor to Poland should learn are *prosze* (please, pronounced 'pro say') and *dzigkuje!* (thank you, pronounced 'jin kuya'). Another Polish word you'll learn quickly is *remont* which means something like 'under repair.' You'll see this word posted frequently on museums, hotels and restaurants which close for extended renovations. Another common word is *nie ma* which means something like 'nothing' or 'not available.' Also be aware of *tak* (yes), *nie* (no), *dzien dobry* (good morning), *do widzenia* (goodbye) and *nieczynne* (closed).

Beginning with Monday the days of the week in Polish are *poniedzialek, wrotek, sroda, czwartek, piatek, sobota, niedziela*. While trying to make yourself understood in Poland you'll greatly increase comprehension by writing the message or word down on a piece of paper.

Facts for the Visitor

VISAS

To enter Poland you must have a passport and visa (two photos). Visas are *not* issued at the border. Your passport must be valid six months beyond the validity of the visa. Citizens of Austria, Finland and Sweden do not require visas. There's a compulsory exchange requirement which says you must change 36 West German marks (DM) or the equivalent in any other hard currency for each day you spend in Poland, so it's important to estimate accurately just how long you really do wish to stay before going in to get the visa. Since you must personally register with police if you stay over a month, it's best to limit your stay to 30 days maximum.

The first and last days of your stay in Poland are not counted against the duration of stay noted on the visa, nor is there any compulsory exchange for these 'free' days. Students (with an IUS or ISIC card), persons under 21 years of age and those of Polish descent are only required to change DM 16 daily. If you're eligible for the reduced rate, ask for it when applying for the visa as it will be noted in

your passport. All those with pre-paid hotel reservations or in transit for less than 24 hours are exempt from compulsory exchange.

The compulsory exchange of hard currency into zloty is sometimes done at the border, sometimes not. If it's not done on arrival you should go to a bank or travel agency in the first Polish city you reach and change enough money there to meet the exchange requirement for your entire stay. The exchange will be noted in your passport and checked upon departure. Don't lose the receipt! In many western countries you have to buy a voucher or exchange order to cover compulsory exchange from an Orbis office abroad *before* you can apply for a Polish visa.

The price you pay for a Polish tourist visa and the length of time you must wait to get it varies considerably. Berlin is a bad place to pick up a Polish visa as they'll either charge you the earth (DM 70) or make you wait a couple of weeks, or both. It's easier to get the visa in East Berlin than West Berlin. In London and Budapest Polish visas are granted immediately, while in Belgrade they'll tell you to come back in two weeks. In North America it takes consulates three weeks to issue the visa! This considered, it's best to get your Polish visa well in advance, allowing yourself the opportunity to try somewhere else if they make things too difficult.

Polish visas may be used anytime within three months from the date of issue. A cheaper 24-hour transit visa is also available (onward visa required). The visa form says that you must register with the police within 48 hours of crossing the border. This regulation is primarily aimed at visitors who stay with Polish friends or relatives. If you're staying in any type of official accommodation (hotel, youth hostel, campground, etc) this formality will be taken care of for you. If you have to extend your visa within Poland Orbis can be of assistance, so enquire there first.

MONEY

US$1 = over 500 zloty (official)

DM 36 daily compulsory exchange (DM 16 for students)

Like Yugoslavia, Poland is caught in the grip of inflation. In 1981 one US dollar was worth 34 zloty (zl), in 1986 160 zloty and in early 1988 300 zloty. For this reason most prices in this chapter are given in US dollars. Bear in mind that these are only approximations arrived at by converting zloty into dollars at the *official* rate. In Poland you pay for everything except visas, duty free goods and international transportation tickets directly in Polish zloty. Only when paying hotel bills do you have to show an exchange receipt.

There are two exchange rates in Poland. The official rate is used in all official transactions such as changing money at a bank, buying a ticket at a travel agency or paying hotel bills. There's also a black market rate which is four times higher but strictly against the law. Tourists in Warsaw are often asked to change money on the street. Although it's almost routine to do this, keep in mind that if you're caught the money involved will be confiscated, you may have to pay a considerable additional fine and could even be deported. That's only fair because at the black market rate restaurant meals, domestic transportation, admissions and local goods are ridiculously cheap.

Upon arrival in Poland make sure your finances are in order as the customs officer will ask you to fill out a currency declaration specifying precisely how much money you have with you. Each different currency must be listed, with cash and travellers' cheques separated on different lines. Gold jewellery must also be declared on the form. Customs may actually ask to see the money and have you count it out in front of them before stamping the form. Upon departure from Poland you'll have to give the form back to the customs officer and you won't be allowed to take out more foreign currency than is listed on it. Customs is most interested in large amounts of western currency in cash. If you declared such an amount on entry customs may ask to see it again upon departure, to verify that you still have most of it with you and didn't change it on the black market. If you under-declared your money in order to have something to change on the black market it can be confiscated if found upon departure.

The import and export of Polish

currency is prohibited. Zloty banknotes printed before 1975 are worthless. It's impossible to reconvert zloty into hard currency.

CLIMATE

Poland has a moderate continental climate with considerable maritime influence along the Baltic coast. Spring is a time of warm days and chilly nights, while summer (June to August) can be hot. Autumn (September to November) brings some rain and there can be snow from December to March. In the mountains the snow lingers until mid-April. July is the hottest month, February the coolest. The sea coast is the sunniest part of the country in summer; the Carpathian Mountains are sunnier in winter. Conditions are changeable from year to year.

BOOKS & BOOKSHOPS

Bookstores in Poland sell excellent city and regional maps, often complete with indexes. Tram and bus routes are shown on the maps, which is handy. Usually a particular bookshop will only have two or three different maps available, so to get a complete collection for all the cities on your itinerary you'll have to keep trying as you go along.

A good local travel guide is *A Polish American's Guide to Poland* by Tadeusz Wojnowski (Interpress, Warsaw, 1984), formerly titled *Poland, A Guide for Young Tourists*. This humorous book is extremely hard to find, so grab one if you spot it in a bookstore. As a practical guide for the independent traveller it's unique in Eastern Europe.

Polish for Travellers by Berlitz is a useful language guide you should pick up before leaving home. *Poland, Phoenix in the East* by William Woods (Penguin Books, England, 1972) takes an objective look at the history of Poland from 1939 to 1971. Anyone curious about the Warsaw Uprising, re-incorporation of Silesia into Poland, etc, should read Woods. In the US

write Hippocrene Books, 171 Madison Ave, New York, NY 10016 for their free catalogue of 'Polish Interest Books from Hippocrene.'

NEWSPAPERS & MEDIA

Trybuna Ludu is the official daily paper and there are several others, all government owned. A section near the back of this and other dailies carries announcements of concerts, plays, etc, plus cinema times and even museum hours. It doesn't take any knowledge of Polish to understand these listings as Handel is Handel and Schubert Schubert in any language. The name and address of the theatre are usually given and a quick stop there to check the information and pick up tickets clinches the matter. When checking theatre listings it's important to check *both* local papers, as the list in one may be incomplete.

HEALTH

Most foreigners have to pay for medical treatment. Citizens of Great Britain receive free treatment if they can prove coverage back home. In Warsaw call your embassy for the name of a private doctor experienced in treating foreigners. Elsewhere ask tourist information for advice.

GENERAL INFORMATION
Post & Telephone

You're better off receiving mail care of your embassy in Warsaw rather than poste restante which is unreliable. Most mail boxes are red. In large cities there are green mail boxes for local mail, red boxes for long distance mail and steel-blue boxes for airmail. Always use airmail, even for parcels.

Trying to make international telephone calls from Poland is almost hopeless. You'll wait around for hours and hours without success. A far better idea is to send a telegram to your party with a time and telephone number where you can be reached since incoming calls go right through. The price of telephone calls placed from hotels is deducted from your foreign currency exchange receipt.

Electricity
220 volts AC, 50 Hz.

Time
Greenwich Mean Time plus one hour. Poland goes on summer time at the end of March when clocks are turned an hour forward. At the end of September they're turned an hour back.

Business Hours
Shops are generally open weekdays from 10 am to 5 pm, although this can vary an hour or two either way. Grocery stores open earlier. Most businesses post their hours on the door. Milk bars tend to open between 6 and 8 am and close between 5 and 7 pm. Restaurants stay open later, but only first class restaurants are open as late as 10 pm. Most milk bars and some restaurants are closed Saturday afternoon and Sunday, although enough stay open to make finding something to eat no problem.

Museums usually open at 9 or 10 am and close anywhere from 3 to 6 pm, with slightly shorter hours in winter. Most museums close on Mondays, although a few maverick institutions close on Tuesdays and occasionally both days. Most are also closed on days following public holidays. Most live theatres are closed on Mondays and all summer.

INFORMATION
Orbis is the government travel agency organising tourism in Poland with 180 offices around the country. Like western travel agencies, their main function is to make reservations, sell transportation tickets and book rooms at luxury hotels. They will also give information if they're not too busy. Orbis offices abroad (listed below) tend to be a lot more cooperative than those within Poland.

Most cities also have local tourist offices, such as Syrena in Warsaw and Wawel Tourist in Cracow, usually identified by the letters IT *(informacja turystyczna)* on the door. These are better sources of information but have fewer tickets. Sometimes they offer private room accommodation. Gromada, Juventur, Sports Tourist and Turysta are tourism cooperatives catering exclusively to the domestic market. They don't usually arrange accommodation, sell train tickets or speak English.

The Polish Tourists & Country-Lovers' Association (PTTK) has offices in resort areas which often sell hiking maps, know about accommodation in city dormitories, campgrounds and mountain huts, and even have information on hitchhiking (autostop). Have a look inside whenever you see the letters PTTK.

Almatur is the Travel & Tourism Bureau of the Socialist Union of Polish students. Their offices issue the International Union of Students (IUS) card (US$1), valid for student discounts on museum admissions and train or ferry tickets. They are also excellent sources of general information.

Orbis offices abroad include:

Austria
Orbis (tel 63-0810), Schweden Platz 5, 1010 Vienna

Britain
    Polorbis (637-4971), 82 Mortimer St, London W1N 7DE
Finland
    Orbis (tel 44-5448), Fredrikinkatu 81 B 12, 00100 Helsinki
France
    Orbis (tel 4742-0742), 49 Avenue de l'Opera, 75002 Paris
Holland
    Orbis (tel 25-3570), Leidsestraat 64, 1017 PD Amsterdam
Italy
    Orbis (tel 475-1060), Via Veneto 54a, Rome
Sweden
    Orbis (tel 23-5348), Birger Jarlsgatan 71, 114-35 Stockholm
USA
    Orbis (tel 236-9013), 333 North Michigan Ave, Chicago, Illinois 60601
    Orbis (tel 391-0844), 500 Fifth Ave, New York, NY 10036
West Germany
    Polorbis (tel 52-0025), Hohenzollernring 99-101, 5000 Cologne 1
    Polorbis (tel 33-7686), Glockengiesserwall 3, 2000 Hamburg 1

ACCOMMODATION

Every time you pay an accommodation bill the amount paid will be deducted from the back of the exchange receipt you received when you completed the compulsory exchange to cover your period of stay in Poland. If the back of the paper fills up with stamps and figures this is no problem since the hotel reception will simply glue another piece of paper onto the bottom of the original form and continue deducting. You have credit until the total amount you changed has been used up, at which time you'll have to change more money to pay your accommodation bills. It's highly unlikely that anyone who has changed DM 36 a day, stays in middle to bottom end accommodation and takes an overnight train now and then will ever use up all of his/her credit. In fact, you'll probably leave Poland with thousands of zloty credit to spare.

Except in Warsaw, you should always be able to find a hotel costing less than your daily exchange requirement. It's interesting to note that tourists from socialist countries get a 40% discount on hotel rates and Poles pay about half that, or 30% of what tourists from capitalist countries (KK) pay. This explains why all those expensive hotels were full.

Hotel prices are lower in the off season. The high season could be 1 June to 30 September, or 1 April to 31 October. Rates are usually posted on a board at hotel reception desks (look for the column marked 'KK'). Compare the price of a room with private bath to one with shared bath. Sometimes it's only a few hundred zloty difference, other times it's a couple of thousand. In all tourist hotels a US$1 per person fiscal registration fee is charged the first night. On arrival day hotel rooms cannot be occupied until after 2 pm or 4 pm, so leave your things at the station.

Foreign tourists are allowed to stay in any hotel in Poland, except holiday homes owned by factories, trade unions, etc. Orbis hotels are all in the expensive, 1st class category. Municipal hotels are usually cheaper and the PTTK has a chain of 'Dom Turysty' and 'Dom Wycieczkowy' with hotel rooms and rather expensive dorm beds. If in doubt about the quality ask to see a room before checking in, in which case it's unlikely they'll try to give you their worst room.

Youth Hostels

Poland is the only country in Eastern Europe with youth hostels similar to those of Western Europe. Overnight fees are only US$1.50 for students and members, US$2 for others. Although there's no maximum age limit, persons under 26 have priority. Children under age 10 cannot use the hostels. Groups larger than five persons must book a month in advance and Polish school groups crowd the hostels from mid-May to mid-June.

The hostels are closed from 10 am to 5 pm. You must arrive before 9 pm.

All 1200 IYHF hostels in Poland are run by the Polskie Towarzystwo Schronisk Mlodziezowych (PTSM) and have a green triangle over the entrance. The word for youth hostel is *schroniska mlodziezowych* – important to know when asking directions. In cities where there's more than one youth hostel, if the first you visit is full they may be willing to call around to the others to find you a bed.

International Student Hotels

In July and August the Polish student travel agency, Almatur, arranges accommodation in vacant student dormitories in 19 university towns. The addresses of these hotels change annually so you'll have to visit an Almatur office for the current list. Orbis offices abroad sometimes have the list. You share a room of two to four beds and there are usually cheap cafeterias and even disco clubs on the premises.

Almatur sells open vouchers for these hotels at US$7 per night for full time students, US$10 per night for young people under 35. Persons over 35 are not accommodated. With such a voucher you're guaranteed bed and breakfast without reservations, provided you arrive by 2 pm. If you buy nine vouchers the 10th is free. Without a voucher these hotels are slightly more expensive. Ask about Almatur 'Student Travel Vouchers' (STV) or 'Youth Travel Vouchers' (YTV) at Orbis offices abroad before applying for your Polish visa. By purchasing the vouchers there your compulsory exchange requirements (DM 16 or DM 36) may be covered at the same time. Unused vouchers are refunded in Polish currency.

Almatur also organises excellent weekly horse-back riding and sailing holidays which foreign students may join. In July and August there are Almatur International Camps of Labour in which participants work 46 hours a week as construction, agricultural, or forest labourers. After work there are excursions, sporting and cultural events, etc. Details from Orbis offices abroad.

Camping & Private Rooms

There are 400 campgrounds in Poland, many offering small timber bungalows which are excellent value. IFCC card holders get a 10% discount on camping fees. Theoretically most campgrounds are open May to September, but they tend to close early if things are slow. The opening and closing dates listed in official brochures (and this book) are only approximate.

It's also possible to stay in private rooms in Poland, although they're far less common than in Hungary or Yugoslavia. A few municipal tourist offices *(Biuro Zakawaterowan)* arrange private rooms but their prices are high, almost what you'd pay for a budget hotel. During busy periods all their rooms could be full.

Sometimes you're offered a private room by an individual on the street outside a tourist office or private room agency. Not only are their prices lower and open to bargaining but the amount isn't deducted from your exchange receipt. The trouble is, it's not strictly legal as you're supposed to register with the authorities in each new place you visit. As long as you stay in official accommodation this is done for you. But if you accept an unlicensed private room the householder will not register you nor will he/she be happy to learn that you went in to the police and registered yourself, thereby providing clear evidence of their untaxed moonlighting. However in some cities like crowded Cracow and Gdansk these 'black' rooms are the best places to stay, so it's up to you to decide whether it's worth the small risk of being caught unregistered. Beware of rooms far from the centre of town.

FOOD & DRINK

Polish Specialties

Poland is a land of hearty soups such as

botwinka (beet greens soup), *kapusniak* (sauerkraut soup), *zacierka* (noodle soup) and *zur* (sour cream soup). Many traditional Polish dishes originated farther east, including Russian borsch or *barszcz* (red beet soup), Lithuanian *chlodnik* (cold cream soup), *kolduny* (turnovers with meat) and *kulebiak* (cabbage and mushroom loaf). Two world famous Polish dishes are *bigos* (sauerkraut and meat) and *pierogi* (dumplings served with potatoes and cheese or sauerkraut and mushrooms).

A few special Polish dishes to watch for on restaurant menus are roast duck *(kaczka)* or goose *(ges)* with apples, pound steak *(zraz)* in cream sauce, breaded pork cutlet *(kotlet schabowy)*, pea puree with pig's leg *(golonka)* and sauerkraut, tripe *(flaki)* Polish style and sauerkraut with sausage and potatoes. Beef-steak tartar is raw minced meat with a raw egg, sardine, chopped onions and seasoning. Only sample this at a first class establishment where you can be sure of the quality.

Mushrooms *(grzyby)* have always been great favourites in Poland, either boiled, pan-fried, stewed, sautéed, pickled or marinated. Potatoes are made into dumplings *(pyzy)*, patties or pancakes *(placki ziemniaczane)*. Cucumbers are served fresh sliced, seasoned with pepper, honey or cream as a salad *mizeria*. *Cwikla* is a salad of red beetroot with horseradish. A traditional desert is *mazurek* (shortcake). In early summer you can get fresh strawberries, raspberries or blueberries with cream.

Drink

Like the USSR, Poland has been tightening up on alcoholism and the situation can be confusing. Some restaurants have special hours when they serve beer and these appear to be purely arbitrary. You may just be finishing a dry meal when the waitress suddenly brings you a bottle. Other times you're refused service while the people at the next table

are drinking. Despite these frustrations it's forbidden to bring your own drinks with you into the restaurant. Many restaurants have certain rooms in which alcoholic drinks are not served at all (beware of signs reading *Sala bezalkoholowa*). It's always difficult to get a beer after 10 pm but in some places beer is readily available at 8 am!

Even first class restaurants are subject to the above. Beer is usually served warm and it can be hard to get one with a meal. When ordering beer at expensive restaurants always ask for Polish beer, unless the price of imported beer is clearly indicated on the menu. Otherwise you could end up paying seven times more for German Beck beer than you would for an acceptable Polish equivalent such as Zywiec or Okocim. All wine is imported so pay attention to the price which may be for a glass, not a bottle. Polish vodka (served chilled) is available at government liquor stores. Red and black currant juices are popular non-alcoholic drinks.

Milk Bars

In Poland the word 'bar' is almost always used in the sense of snack bar or refreshment bar, and 'cocktail' means fruit cocktail or something similar. The cheapest and best places to eat in Poland are milk bars *(bar mleczny)*. These are also the best places to try local dishes not available at expensive restaurants. They're ideal for vegetarians as meat is never served. Nor is alcohol. Most milk bars close Saturday afternoons and all day Sunday.

Milk bars are self service. You either pay at the end of the line cafeteria-style or, more often, you pay first and get a receipt which you hand to the woman dispensing the food. This can be confusing if you don't know the Polish name of whatever it is you want, but the cashiers are usually patient and will try to understand if you point to something someone else is eating. Sometimes you'll order the wrong thing, which adds to the excitement. Milk bar lines usually move quickly, so don't be put off.

Restaurants

Restaurants and coffee shops at the luxury Orbis hotels are open to non-guests. Invariably they have the widest selection of dishes and the best service, although the atmosphere can be pretentious and even dull. Unlike hotel rooms which cost foreigners four times more than Poles pay, meals at hotel restaurants are the same price for everyone which makes them relatively cheap. Amounts paid at restaurants in zloty are not deducted from your exchange receipt. These are the *only* places in Poland where you can get a good English breakfast of bacon and eggs with juice (about US$3).

Before trying to decipher a Polish menu ask what's actually available as very few restaurants offer everything listed. In Polish restaurants it's customary to occupy any vacant seat, which can be a problem if you don't smoke. It's also customary to round restaurant bills up to the next higher unit (but only in places with table service, not milk bars). Lunch is the main meal of the day. A *kawiarnia* is a cafe, a *winiaria* a wine bar. If you're invited to dinner at a Polish home be sure to take flowers for the lady of the house.

THINGS TO BUY

Cepelia shops belonging to the Folk Art & Crafts Cooperatives Union sell authentic local handicrafts such as tapestries, rugs, embroidery, lace, hand-painted silks, sculptures in wood, pottery, paper cutouts, folk toys, wrought iron objects, silver jewellery and amber necklaces. Jubiler stores sell jewellery and excellent Soviet watches. Works by living professional artists are sold at Desa shops. Imported goods and export quality Polish products are sold in Pewex and Baltona hard currency shops. Western alcohol and cigarettes are cheaper at Pewex than they are in the west.

While some items may seem terribly

cheap, you should remember that they're intended for personal use or as souvenirs only. Upon departure from Poland if it seems to the customs officer that you're trying to make a business of it (by having too many of the same item, for example) you could be required to pay export duty. Desa shops have complete information on complicated and changeable Polish export regulations, so check before making large purchases. The export of crystal goods and antiques is restricted. Items purchased with hard currency may usually be freely exported provided you have official sales receipts.

Getting There & Away

FROM BERLIN

Most trains between Western Europe and Warsaw call at West Berlin's Zoo station. Cheap railway tickets to Poland purchased in East Berlin are valid on this line and you may board the train in West Berlin. If you really want to save money only get a ticket from Berlin to Rzepin (DM 10 if purchased in East Berlin), the first major junction inside Poland. There you could buy a cheap onward ticket with zloty and connect for Szczecin, Poznan, Wroclaw or Cracow. For more information see the Berlin section of this book. There's a nightly train with sleepers from East Berlin's Lichtenberg station to Gdansk via Szczecin. Another line goes from Leipzig to Wroclaw via Dresden.

FROM CZECHOSLOVAKIA

There are overnight trains between Prague and Warsaw (via Wroclaw). A more important line runs from Prague and Vienna to Warsaw via Katowice. From Budapest trains run to Warsaw via Hatvan, Zilina and Katowice. Change at Katowice for Cracow. There's a direct line from Budapest to Cracow via Kosice.

FROM ROMANIA

There's a daily train between Bucharest and Warsaw which avoids Czechoslovakia and Hungary by transiting the USSR. Sleepers are available to and from Warsaw or Cracow. Check with a Soviet consulate to determine whether a transit visa is required.

TRAIN

It's important to keep in mind that there are three price levels for tickets on Polish trains. The most expensive are tickets to Poland from Western Europe. Avoid these by breaking your journey in Berlin, Czechoslovakia or Hungary, from where you pay the much cheaper rate for travel between socialist countries. Cheaper still are domestic fares within Poland itself. You can easily take advantage of these by breaking your journey at the first city inside Poland (Szczecin, Poznan, Wroclaw, Katowice, Cracow, etc).

BOAT

Polferries offers regular service year round to Swinoujscie from Copenhagen, Denmark (240 Danish crowns one way), and Ystad, Sweden (200 Swedish crowns one way). The Ystad service is daily; from Copenhagen it's four times a week. There are longer, less frequent ferry trips to Gdansk from Nynashamn, Sweden (360 Swedish crowns one way), and Helsinki, Finland (300 FIM one way). From June to September the same company also has ferries twice a week from Travemunde, West Germany, to both Swinoujscie (DM 100 one way) and Gdansk (DM 160 one way). Round-trip fares are proportionately cheaper. Holders of IUS or ISIC student cards get a 10% discount on ferry tickets.

Getting Around

TRAIN

As in other European countries, train departures (*odjazdy*) are usually listed on a yellow board while arrivals (*przyjazdy*) are on a white board. Express trains are in red, local trains in black. Watch for the symbol R enclosed in a box which indicates a fully reserved train. Departure boards also indicate whether a train offers both 1st and 2nd class accommodation, plus the train number and departure track (*peron*).

Express trains (*expresowy*) with seat reservations are the best way to travel. Direct trains (*pospieszne*) are also fast and don't usually require reservations, but are much more crowded. Local trains (*osobowe* or *normalne*) are OK for short trips and never require reservations. Train reservations can be made up to two months in advance at Orbis offices but on departure day only at the railway station.

Tickets for express trains are more expensive than tickets for local stopping trains, so make sure you've got the correct ticket for your train (by writing your destination and the departure time on a piece of paper to show the cashier, for example). Otherwise the conductor will charge you a supplement. Tickets *are* checked on Polish trains. In large stations tickets for different trains are sold at different windows. Check the train number over the window to make sure you're in the right line. First class is 50% more than 2nd class. Holders of the IUS students card (available from Almatur) get a 25% discount on train tickets for travel within socialist countries. Polish railways goes on their summer timetable (with extra services) around the first of June.

Overnight trains are a good way of saving money in Poland while getting to your destination. A 1st class ticket and sleeper are always less than the price of the cheapest hotel and the amount isn't deducted from your exchange receipt. A sleeper puts you in the next city early in the morning, saving a lot of time. Second class couchettes (US$1.50) contain six beds to the compartment, three to a side. First class sleepers have only two beds. There's a third type called 'special' 2nd class which has three beds to the compartment (US$3). The attendant in the sleeping car sells soft drinks and coffee and express trains often carry good stand-up dining cars. You can't beat a breakfast of *flaki* (tripe) and coffee (US$2.50).

Sleepers and couchettes must be booked at Orbis, the Polish travel agency, not at railway stations. Booking a couchette or sleeper usually involves waiting in line at Orbis for an hour or more and since Orbis is usually closed on weekends, advance planning is required. You often don't know if anything's available till you get to the head of the line. Orbis is less crowded in the off season.

Railway Stations

Railway stations in Poland have good facilities: left luggage rooms open round the clock, cafeterias, waiting rooms, newsstands, posted timetables, etc. When you check baggage at railway cloakrooms you must declare the value of the object in zloty. The amount you're charged is then relative to the value declared. There are public toilets in all railway stations (and in many other places) and you're expected to pay around US$0.10 to use them.

OTHER TRANSPORT

Long distances in Poland are more commonly covered by train (PKP) than by bus (PKS). Buses are used mostly in mountainous areas, such as around Zakopane. Seats on long distance buses can and should be booked ahead.

Hitchhiking is legal and commonly practised in Poland. There's even an official 'autostop' card complete with coupons for drivers available from PTTK offices! While Polish motorists aren't likely to insist that foreign riders show such a card they may accept some small payment.

LOCAL TRANSPORT
Public Transport

Local buses and streetcars cost about US$0.05 a ride, but tickets must be purchased in advance at kiosks or Ruch newsstands. Drivers don't sell tickets. Tickets purchased in one Polish city may be used in another. You punch the ticket yourself as you board. Public transport operates from 5.30 am to 11 pm. Night buses after 11 pm are double fare, express buses *(pospieszny)* triple fare. Luggage is an extra fare.

Taxis

Taxi meters have difficulty keeping up with inflation. At last report taxis charged twice the meter fare. This could change as the meters are adjusted, so check by asking any Polish acquaintance. It doesn't hurt to round the fare up. Outside city limits and after 11 pm taxis charge double. Luggage and the number of passengers doesn't affect the fare.

Taxis are usually found at regular taxi stands where you join the line waiting. Flagging down a taxi on the street is pot luck. There are always taxi stands in front of train stations and considering how inexpensive taxis are, it's foolish not to use them. A short trip around town may cost US$1, while an hour-long search for a youth hostel including a 10-km drive out of town may reach US$6, tip included. If a driver is especially helpful in finding a cheap place to stay tip him generously. Beware of taxis waiting in front of the tourist hotels which will try to overcharge. Always insist that the meter be turned on and carry proper change. If there's no meter agree on the price before. Beware of unmarked, unmetered 'pirate' taxis.

Warsaw

In a way Warsaw reborn from wartime destruction epitomises the Polish nation. The Vistula River cuts a curving course

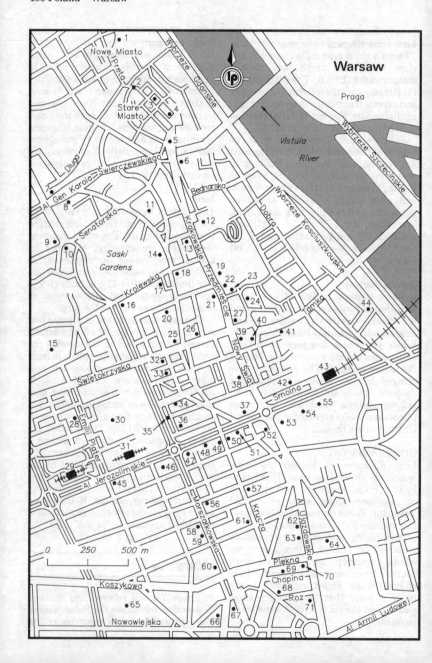

1	New Town Square	37	Orbis (train tickets)
2	Barbican	38	Familijny Milk Bar
3	Old Town Square	39	Wagon-lits Tourisme
4	St John's Cathedral	40	Almatur
5	Plac Zamkowy	41	Chopin Museum
6	St Anne's Church	42	Smolna Youth Hostel
7	Gruba Kaska Cafeteria	43	Powisle Station
8	Jewish Museum	44	Dom Nauczyciela ZNP Hotel
9	Museum of Revolutionary Politics	45	Automobile Club
10	Saski Hotel	46	Metropol Hotel/Orbis
11	Grand Opera House	47	Forum Hotel
12	Council of Ministers	48	Kasy Teatralne
13	Hotel Europejski	49	Intourist
14	Tomb of the Unknown Soldier	50	Reiseburo Interflug
15	Synagogue	51	Praga Bar
16	Orbis	52	Rybka Restaurant
17	Zacheta Art Gallery	53	Party House
18	Hotel Victoria	54	National Museum
19	University of Warsaw	55	Armed Forces Museum
20	Ethnographic Museum	56	Hungarian Cultural Centre
21	Church of the Holy Cross	57	Grand Hotel
22	Universytecki Milk Bar	58	Balkantourist
23	PTTK	59	Czecholslovakian Cultural Centre
24	Teatr Polski	60	Zlota Kurka Milk Bar
25	German Bookstore	61	Syrena
26	Srodmiescie Self-Service Bar	62	Bulgarian Consulate
27	Academy of Sciences	63	American Embassy
28	Akwarium Club	64	Canadian Embassy
29	Central Station	65	Politechnical University
30	Palace of Culture	66	LOT Polish Airlines
31	Srodmiescie Station	67	MDM Hotel
32	Main post office	68	Czechoslovakian Consulate
33	Filharmonia	69	Romanian Consulate
34	Bar Hybrydy	70	Hungarian &
35	Department stores		Yugoslavian Consulates
36	Zodiak Bar	71	British Embassy

across Poland, from the Carpathian Mountains in the south to the Baltic in the north. Halfway down sits Warsaw, off centre now that both the country's borders have moved west. Fortified in the 14th century and capital since 1596, Warsaw has long resisted foreign domination: by the Swedes in the 17th century, Tsarist Russia in the 19th century and Nazi Germany and the Soviet Union in the 20th century.

Today this turbulent history is experienced better nowhere else. The masterful rebuilding of old Warsaw and its harmonious union with the new symbolise the determination of the Polish people to develop and build without sacrificing an identity which has always been their greatest strength. You'll witness that identity in the museums and churches, but more directly in the surprisingly candid people. Warsaw is a fascinating layer cake you'll need several days to digest.

Orientation

If you're coming by train you'll probably arrive at Central Station beside the Palace of Culture & Science near the corner of Aleje Jerozolimskie and Marszalkowska. Dump your things in the baggage room and start hotel hunting using the listings below. If you arrived by plane the airport transportation possibilities are described under Getting Away.

Warsaw has many focal points but you'll soon become acquainted with Plac Zamkowy, gateway to old Warsaw, and the Royal Way which runs 10 km southeast from this square to Wilanow Palace with changing names: Krakowskie Przedmiescie, Nowy Swiat, Aleje Ujazdowskie, Belwederska, Jana Sobieskiego and Aleje Wilanowska. Plan your sightseeing around this corridor.

Information

Tourist Offices Just opposite Central Station is the Polski Zwiazek Motorowy (Polish Automobile Association), Aleje Jerozolimskie 63, where you should be able to buy a good indexed map of Warsaw.

Standard tourist information is theoretically available from Syrena, ulica Krucza 16/22, just down from the Grand Hotel about six blocks from the station, but don't make a special trip. The information counter at Orbis, ulica Bracka 16, corner Aleje Jerozolimskie, is more receptive, but this is a travel agency not a tourist office and they're usually very busy. Other Orbis offices are at Marszalkowska 142, corner of Krolewska, and upstairs in the Metropol Hotel, Marszalkowska 99a. There's also an information cum souvenir shop marked 'IT' at Plac Zamkowy 1 in the old town.

Other Information Offices Student travel is handled by Almatur, ulica Kopernika 23, and they're generally helpful. They'll be able to tell you about the International Student Hotels (US$7 to US$10 a night) which are open in July and August only.

Use these if you can and try to make bookings for other Polish cities. Also ask about one-week Almatur sailing and horseback riding trips.

If you don't have the International Youth Hostel Handbook, a booklet listing all Polish youth hostels is available from PTSM (Polskie Towarzstwo Schronisk Mlodziezowych), ulica Chocimska 28, 4th floor, suite 423 (weekdays 8 am to 3 pm). The Biuro Autostop, ulica Narbutta 27a (entrance at rear, around the block) sells the 'autostop' card and supplies information on hitching around Poland. When you join (US$1.50) you're given bonus coupons for motorists, hitchhiking maps and a booklet explaining the whole programme.

Books & Maps Poland's best bookstore is PDK Universus, corner of Gagarina and Belwederska just south of Lazienki Park (open weekdays 11 am to 7 pm). Foreign books are to the right as you enter.

Excellent East German books, travel guides and maps can be obtained at the German bookstore at ulica Swietokrzyska 18 – highly recommended if you'll be visiting the GDR.

The Czechoslovakian Cultural Centre, Marszalkowska 81, provides tourist information and there's a Czech bookstore adjacent for maps and guides. Balkantourist, Marszalkowska 83, has information on Bulgaria. The Hungarian Cultural Centre, Marszalkowska 76/80, dispenses Hungarian travel information, books and records, and there's a Hungarian travel office (Ibusz) around the corner.

Embassies Most of the embassies you'll want to visit to pick up visas or mail are located along Aleje Ujazdowskie between Party House and Lazienki Park. The largest and most ostentatious is the American Embassy, Aleje Ujazdowskie 29/31. The Canadian Embassy is just down the street opposite at ulica Matejki 1/5. The British Embassy (which New Zealanders should also use) is two blocks south of these, at the corner of Aleje

Ujazdowskie and Aleje Roz. The Australian Embassy, however, is at ulica Estonska 3/5 south of the stadium on the far side of the Vistula (take a taxi).

Visas for Socialist Countries The Eastern European embassies are all in the vicinity of the US Embassy. The Bulgarian Consulate, Aleje Ujazdowskie 33/35 (open Monday, Wednesday and Friday 10 am to 12 noon), offers tourist visas valid three months from the date of issue for US$14 and one photo. First, however, you must purchase Bulgarian travel vouchers worth US$17.25 for each day you wish to spend in Bulgaria from Orbis, Marszalkowska 142.

Visas for the other Socialist countries are more easily obtained. The Yugoslavian and Hungarian consulates are side by side on Aleje Ujazdowskie, a block south of the US Embassy, and both are open Monday, Wednesday and Friday from 9 am to 12 noon. Hungarian visas cost US$9 and two photos for each entry and are issued at once. Be sure to get a tourist and not a transit visa. The Romanian Consulate is around the corner at ulica Chopina 10. Nearby at ulica Koszykowa 8, corner of Aleje Roz, is the Czechoslovakian Consulate (Monday to Friday 8 am to 12 noon). They'll give you a visa right away upon payment of US$6 and two photos for each entry. Transit and tourist visas cost the same but in transit there is no compulsory exchange.

GDR & Soviet Visas To visit East Germany one must first go to the Reiseburo Interflug, ulica Krucza 46, where they take your western currency and issue a voucher. You then take the voucher to the GDR Consulate, Aleje 1 Armii Wojska Polskiego 2/4 a block west of Lazienki Park, where they issue your visa immediately for DM 15. The hitch is you must tell the Reiseburo exactly which days you'll be staying in the GDR and where – which cities, which days. From May to September you can get a camping

visa for DM 25 a day but in winter you must stay at an Interhotel which can cost upwards of US$70 a night. If you only wish to transit East Germany on the way to West Berlin or beyond the transit visa is issued on the train for DM 5 and there's no need to visit either of the above offices.

Intourist, ulica Krucza 45 across the street from the Reiseburo, will book hotels rooms in Moscow and elsewhere for around 60 roubles a night double, but they have no tours to the USSR out of Warsaw for westerners. For Trans-Siberian travel they'll refer you to Orbis, Marszalkowska 142. All travel to the USSR takes a minimum of one month to arrange.

Things to See

The Old Town From Plac Zamkowy you enter the old city along ulica Swietojanska. You'll soon come to the Gothic **St John's Cathedral** then Rynek Starego Miasta, the old town square. If you're there at 10 am be sure to catch the film at the **City Historical Museum**, Rynek Starego Miasta 28 (closed Monday), which unforgettably depicts the wartime destruction of the city. It's hard to believe that all the 17th and 18th century buildings around this square have been completely rebuilt from their foundations. Stroll around, visiting the shops, galleries and restaurants.

Continue north a block on ulica Nowomiejska to the 15th century **Barbican Gate**, part of the medieval walled circuit around Warsaw. Walk toward the river inside the walls a bit to find the city's symbol, the **Warsaw Mermaid**. (Once upon a time a mermaid rose from the river and told a fisherman named Warsz that a great city would arise here.) Everything north of this wall is New Town (Nowe Miasto). Straight ahead on Freta, beyond several historic churches, is Rynek Nowego Miasta with more churches. The delightful streets and buildings in both Old and New towns are best explored casually on your own without a guidebook.

The Royal Way On a tall pillar (1644) in the

centre of Plac Zamkowy is a statue of King Sigismund III Vasa, who transferred Poland's capital from Cracow to Warsaw. The **Royal Castle** (1619) on the east side of the square developed over the centuries as successive Polish kings added wings and redecorated the interior. In 1945 all that remained was a heap of rubble but from 1971 to 1974 the castle was carefully rebuilt. The interior is still closed to visitors. On the south side of Plac Zamkowy is **St Anne's Church** (1454), one of the most beautiful in the city.

Continue south on Krakowskie Przedmiescie noting the many aristocratic residences, especially the **Radziwill Palace** (1643) now the Council of Ministers, on the left beside a church. The Warsaw Pact was signed in this building on 14 May 1955. **Warsaw University**, a complex of 17th and 18th century royal residences, is a block beyond on the same side. The large church on the other side of the street and a little further down is the 17th century **Church of the Holy Cross**. The heart of Frederic Chopin is preserved in the second pillar on the left hand side of the main nave of this church.

In front of the 19th century **Academy of Sciences** (Staszic Palace) nearby stands the famous statue (1830) of Polish astronomer Nicolaus Copernicus by the Danish sculptor Bertel Thorvaldsen. Below the Academy toward the river is the **Chopin Museum**, ulica Tamka 41 (open weekdays 10 am to 2 pm), which has memorabilia such as Chopin's last piano. They'll play recordings of his music if you ask.

Good Museums To add depth to your knowledge of the city centre return to the Church of the Holy Cross and take ulica Traugutta, the first street north, west a block to the **Ethnographic Museum** (closed Monday), ulica Kredytowa 1. This large museum has collections of tribal art from Africa, Oceania and Latin America, as well as Polish folklore. North a block beyond the circular church is the **Zacheta**

1	Citadel
2	Gdanska Station
3	Laundromat
4	Warsaw Ghetto Monument
5	Grand Opera House
6	Old Town Square (Rynek)
7	Zoo
8	Nowa Praga Hotel
9	Stadion Bus Station
10	Stadium
11	Syrena Hotel
12	Karolkowa Youth Hostel
13	Central Bus Station
14	Zachodnia Station
15	'Druh' Hotel
16	Camping OST 'Gromada'
17	Central Station
18	Palace of Culture
19	National Museum
20	MDM Hotel
21	Remont Students Club
22	GDR Consulate
23	Youth Hostel Office
24	Biuro Autostop
25	Belvedere Palace
26	Chopin Monument
27	Gallery of Sculpture
28	Lazienki Palace
29	PDK Universus Bookstore

Art Gallery (closed Monday) which often stages great shows. In Saski Gardens just beyond this gallery is the **Tomb of the Unknown Soldier** with a permanent honour guard. North again is the massive **Wielki Opera House** (1965) with the Warsaw Nike monument in front.

Now go west on ulica Senatorska to a major intersection. Across the square is the Municipal Building with the **Museum of Revolutionary Politics** (closed Monday) in the corner closest to the Saski Hotel. A block north of here and around behind the unfinished and abandoned skyscraper is the **Museum of the Jewish Historical Institute**, entrance from the west side of the building at Aleje Swierczewskiego 79 (open Monday to Friday 10 am to 3 pm). Before WW II a third of the population of Warsaw was Jewish.

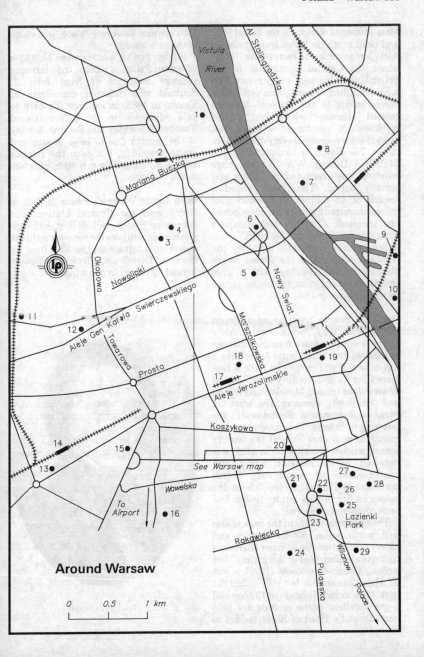

Around Warsaw

0   0.5   1 km

More Museums Return to the Royal Way and head south on Nowy Swiat crossing Aleje Jerozolimskie to **Party House** (1951), where the Central Committee of the Polish United Workers' Party meets. The large building beside this on Aleje Jerozolimskie is the **National Museum** (closed Monday) which has a fine collection of paintings, although not everything is accessible every day. Be sure to see *The Battle of Grunwald* by Jan Matejko. During WW II this huge painting was evacuated to Lublin and secretly buried. The Nazis offered a reward of 10 million Reichsmarks for information leading to its discovery but no one accepted. After the war Matejko's work was uncovered and restored.

Toward the riverside next to the National Museum is the **Armed Forces Museum** (closed Tuesday) with a large assortment of old guns, tanks and planes on the terrace outside.

The Royal Palaces Southbound again on the Royal Way, walk down Aleje Ujazdowskie past many foreign embassies to **Lazienki Park** (it's a little far so take a bus or taxi if you can). The park is best known for its 18th century neo-Classical **Water Palace** (closed Monday and during bad weather), summer residence of Stanislaus Augustus Poniatowski, the last king of Poland. This reform-minded monarch, who gave Poland the world's second written constitution in 1791, was deposed by a Russian army and confederation of reactionary Polish magnates in 1792. The Nazi SS set the palace on fire in 1944 but by 1965 it had been completely restored.

The **Orangerie** (1788) in the park is also well worth seeing for its theatre and gallery of sculpture. On summer afternoons concerts are often held in this gallery. The striking **Chopin Monument** (1926) is just off Aleje Ujazdowskie but still within the park. On summer Sundays at 12 noon and 5 pm excellent piano recitals are held here. Poland's Head of State resides in

18th century **Belvedere Palace**, just south of the monument.

Six km further south on bus No 193 is **Wilanow Palace** (1696), the Baroque summer residence of King John III Sobieski who defeated the Turks at Vienna in 1683. In summer it's hard to gain admission to the palace (closed Tuesday, Thursday and the first Sunday of the month) due to large groups and limited capacity, but even the exterior and 18th century French style park are worth the trip.

Other Sights Warsaw's **Palace of Culture** (1955) near the Central Station is a depressing Stalin-era building, although you may care to take the elevator up to the observation terrace on the 30th floor for the view. There's also a **Technical Museum** (closed Monday) in one wing.

Fryderyk Chopin

Most of the **Citadel** (1834) on the north side of the city is still occupied by the military, however part of it may be visited through the Brana Stracen, the large gate near the middle of the Citadel wall on the river side. This large fortress was built by the Russians after a Polish uprising in 1830. There's a museum (open Tuesday to Saturday 9 am to 4 pm) and plaques recalling the Poles executed here by the Tsarist forces a century or more ago. Buses No 118 and 185 stop near the Citadel entrance. Other than perhaps the **Zoological Gardens** there is little of interest for visitors on the east side of the Vistula.

Places to Stay

Hostels & Camping The *Youth Hostel* (tel 27-89-52) at ulica Smolna 30 is on the top floor of a large concrete building a few minutes' walk from Warsaw Powisle Railway Station in the centre of the city. Go in the entrance with the green triangle and up to the top of the stairs.

The ulica Karolkowa 53a *Hostel* (tel 32-88-29), just off Aleje Gen Karola Swierczewskiego, is less convenient. To get there catch a westbound tram No 1, 13, 20, 24, 26, 27 or 34 from outside the tunnel below Plac Zamkowy. Get off at 'Centrum-Wola' department store, then walk back on the right and look for a three-storey building among the trees.

From May to September the best place to stay in Warsaw is *Camping OST 'Gromada'* (tel 25-43-91), ulica Zwirki i Wigury 32, south-east of town on the road in from the airport. Tent space is US$1.50 per person and bungalows (if you get one!) are US$7 per person. There's a large restaurant on the grounds and the atmosphere is informal and welcoming.

The *'Druh' Young People's Hotel* (tel 22-67-69), ulica Niemcewicza 17 about a km from Warsaw Zachodnia Railway Station, has four-bed rooms for US$26 – OK if you're a small group. Singles pay for the whole room.

Cheaper Hotels & Private Rooms The Syrena Travel Office (tel 25-72-01), ulica Krucza 17 across the street from the Syrena Tourist Office, arranges accommodation in private homes at US$14 single, US$20 double. Although the office stays open till 8 pm you should try to get there before 4 pm. Even then there may be nothing available. You cannot occupy the room until 6 pm so leave your luggage at the station.

One of the best places to stay in Warsaw is *Dom Nauczyciela ZNP* (tel 27-92-11), Wybrzeze Kosciuszkowskie 31/33, on the Vistula Embankment – take a taxi to get there. This modern hotel is actually a school teachers' hostel but visitors are accommodated when rooms are available at US$14.50 single, US$21 double (shared bath).

The *Hotel Saski* (tel 20-46-11), Plac Dzierzynskiego 1, has rooms without bath at US$20 single, US$30 double. Showers are extra. This small 141-bed hotel has real character and a fine location, but unfortunately it's usually full.

The *Hotel Syrena* (tel 32-12-57), ulica Syreny 23 off Gorczewska, is similar to the Saski in price but much larger, so you have a better chance of a room. A drawback is it's location on the far west side of Warsaw, although there's frequent bus service.

In a pinch you could also consider the *Nowa Praga Hotel* (tel 19-50-01), in a poor location east of the zoo on the far east side of the river. Prices are about the same as at the Saski and Syrena but it doesn't have much going for it.

If all else fails try the *PTTK Dom Turysty Hotel* (tel 26-30-11), Krakowskie Przedmiescie 4/6 opposite the Academy of Sciences, where double rooms with dirty public toilets are US$37 – poor value. If you're alone they may permit you to share a double with a stranger for US$18 each and there are rumours of six-bed dormitories for a few zloty less. Getting in takes persistence.

Expensive Hotels All of Warsaw's other hotels are in the luxury tourist bracket. The *Polonia* and *Metropol* are right opposite the Palace of Culture a block from Central station, good for anyone absolutely exhausted and with a pocket full of money. The 751-room *Forum Hotel* nearby is exactly the same as any high-rise Hilton.

The sterile *Warszawa, Dom Chlopa, Victoria-Inter-Continental* and *Grand* hotels are not far from the Forum, but the *Europejski Hotel* (tel 26-50-51), Krakowskie Przedmiescie 13, is your best bet for location, facilities and atmosphere. Erected in 1859 in the neo-Renaissance style, this was Warsaw's first modern hotel. Be prepared for off-season room rates beginning at US$50 single, US$75 double with bath. The *Bristol Hotel* (1901) across the street has been closed for many years. It would be an excellent second choice if and when it were ever reopened.

Less known is the *MDM Hotel* (tel 21-62-11), Plac Konstytucji 1 directly south down Marszalkowska from the Forum. Rooms begin at US$24 single without bath, US$45 with bath. It's a little out of the way but transport from here is good. Plac Konstytucji is Warsaw's best example of an overpowering Stalinist square which makes the MDM fun, fun, fun.

Places to Eat

In The Old Town Warsaw's finest restaurants are on Rynek Starego Miasta, the old town square. Most famous is the *Bazyliszek Restaurant*, Rynek Starego Miasta 7/9 (upstairs). Sloppy dressers are not welcome. The *Kamienne Schodki Restaurant*, Rynek Starego Miasta 26, specialises in roast duck with apples.

The *Rycerska Restaurant*, ulica Szeroki Dunaj 11 just a block and a half from the old town square, has no beer but there's a nice terrace out back where you can sit and write postcards. Meals are inexpensive. *Pod Barbakanen*, corner of Freta and Mostowa just north of the old town gate (Barbikan), is a cheap milk bar with blue chequered tablecloths!

Along the Royal Way There are many places to eat along this busy corridor. *Universytecki Milk Bar*, Krakowskie Przedmiescie 20, and *Familijny Milk Bar*, Nowy Swiat 39, are cheap. The *Staropolska Restaurant*, Krakowskie Przedmiescie 8 beside Dom Turysty, offers table service. The *Srodmiescie Cafeteria*, ulica Swietokrzyska 14 a block west of the Academy of Sciences, is easy because you pay at the end of the line.

Farther south near the National Museum are *Szwajcarski Milk Bar*, Nowy Swiat 5, and the adjacent *Zlota Rybka Restaurant*, Nowy Swiat 5/7, which specialises in fish dishes.

In the City Centre Two large cafeterias in the centre of town are the *Praga Bar*, in the middle of the block at Aleje Jerozolimskie 11/19, and the *Zodiak Bar*, behind Wars Centrum Department Store.

Bambino Milk Bar, Krucza 21 beside Air France diagonally opposite the Grand Hotel, offers typical Polish food at low prices. *Zlota Kurka Milk Bar*, Marszalkowska 55/57, is near Plac Konstytucji.

Gruba Kaska Cafeteria, corner of Marcelego Nowotki and Aleje Swierczewskiego near the Jewish Historical Institute, is large and modern with a good selection.

Entertainment

Check for theatre, concert and cinema offerings in the daily newspapers. For theatre tickets try Kasy Teatralne, Aleje Jerozolimskie 25. They have tickets for many events. The Filharmonia booking office is at ulica Sienkiewicza 12. Warsaw's *National Philharmonic Orchestra* is Poland's finest. For some concerts you enter by the ulica Moniuszki entrance on the other side of the building. Tickets for the *Wielki Opera House*, Plac

Teatralny, and the *Warsaw Operetta*, ulica Nowogrodzka 49 near Central Station, are sold at the theatres. The *Teatr Polski*, ulica Karasia 2 near Dom Turysty, stages classical drama.

The *Akwarium Club*, Emilii Plater 49 just across from the Palace of Culture and north of Central Station, is the place for hot jazz and local action. Friday and Saturday there's a student disco at *Bar Hybrydy*, ulica Kniewskiego 7/9 (downstairs) behind the department stores a block east of the Palace of Culture.

Winiarnia Fukier, Rynek Starego Miasta 27, is an old wine shop with great atmosphere and good company. The *U Hopfera Wine Shop*, Krakowskie Przedmiescie 53 near Plac Zamkowy, is similar to Fukier.

Things to Buy

The best places to shop for souvenirs, amber jewellery, clothing, etc, are the boutiques in the ulica Krucza 23/31 block, directly across from the Grand Hotel. The high prices are justified by the quality.

For contemporary art try Desa, Nowy Swiat 23, a gallery which displays current trends in painting. There are other shopping possibilities along Nowy Swiat in this vicinity.

The department stores on the east side of the Palace of Culture are more public curiosities than places to shop. The shop at ulica Nowomiejska 17 beside the Barbican Gate in the old town sells a great variety of Polish postcards.

Getting There & Away

Air The LOT Polish Airlines office is at ulica Warynskiego 9 near Plac Konstytucji. Yugoslav Airlines, Nowogrodzka 31 near the Forum Hotel, books direct flights from Warsaw to Belgrade for US$130 one way. There's no airport tax in Poland.

Train International trains depart Warsaw Central Station for Berlin Zoo, Cologne, Paris, Frankfurt am Main, Leipzig, Prague, Vienna, Budapest, Moscow and Leningrad. There's a daily train between Warsaw and Bucharest which avoids Czechoslovakia and Hungary by transiting the USSR. Check to see if you need a Soviet transit visa. Domestic expresses run to every part of Poland. All these trains require mandatory seat reservations.

Train Tickets Virtually all express trains leaving Warsaw carry mandatory seat reservations. These seats can be reserved at Central Station or Orbis. Sleepers or couchettes cannot be booked at the railway station however. All bookings must pass through the narrow funnel at Orbis, ulica Bracka 16, where you'll wait an hour or two (closes at 4 pm). Couchettes are very cheap at US$1.50 on the slow trains, US$3 on the fast trains, but Orbis could do with computers for their reservations staff! Each booking must be made individually by telephone from the agency to the central booking office, then each ticket is written out by hand. Painfully slow. It's somewhat easier to purchase international railway tickets between socialist countries at this office but payment must be made in western currency. Prices are reasonable.

Both domestic and international railway tickets can also be purchased at the smaller Orbis office in the Metropol Hotel, Marszalkowska 99a, but you won't find it any faster and the international window closes at 2 pm. Wagon-lits Tourisme, Nowy Swiat 64, sells train and air tickets to points outside Eastern Europe.

Bus Syrena, Krucza 16/22, sells advance bus tickets to places all over Poland – essential! The Central Bus Station serving western and southern Poland is on the west side of the city near Warsaw Zachodnia Railway Station.

The Stadion Bus Station serving northeast Poland, including the Lake District, is on the east side of the Vistula. The easiest way to get there is to take a commuter train from Warsaw Srodmiescie

Railway Station in front of the Palace of Culture east to Warsaw Stadion Railway Station which adjoins the bus terminal.

Getting Around
Airport Transport Bus No 175 goes to the Okecie International Airport (10 km), bus No 114 to the Domestic Airport. To get between them (about three km) take either bus up ulica Zwirki i Wigury a few stops, cross the street and take the other bus back (or just grab a cab).

Buses & Trams In Warsaw trams and buses of the 100, 200, 300 series cost US$0.10 a ride, while trams (trolleys) and buses numbered in the 400s and 500s are US$0.20, as are night buses numbered 600. Buses of the 700 and 800 series are US$0.30, and baggage is US$0.10 extra on all services. You're liable for a US$8 fine if caught without a valid ticket during a spot check. You must purchase a ticket at a newsstand (Ruch) before boarding the service, then validate it once aboard by punching it in a device near the door. Drivers don't sell tickets.

Taxis As everywhere else in Poland all taxis have meters and, at last report, you paid double the amount shown. Watch for taxi stands, the only places you can be reasonably certain of eventually getting a cab. There are several taxi stands at Central station so check the others if the first one you see has a long line of waiting passengers.

City Tours The Orbis office at ulica Swietokrzyska 20 opposite the main post office books Orbis city sightseeing tours, but this is more easily done at the reception desks of the Forum, Grand, Victoria or Europejski hotels. The tours cost anywhere from US$7 to US$11 per person. The Sunday trip to Chopin's home at Zelazowa Wola is especially recommended. A tour to Wilanow Palace would ensure that you actually get inside. No tourist excursion boats operate on the

Warsaw reach of the Vistula River at the moment.

South-East Poland

Much of south-eastern Poland still bears a gentle bucolic air. Here in 'Little Poland' (Malopolska) you'll see people working the fields as they have for centuries and long wooden horse carts along the roads. Until 1918 the region was divided into two parts. Everything north of the Vistula and a line drawn east from Sandomierz (including Lublin and Zamosc) came under Russian control in 1815. South of this was 'Galicia' under the Hapsburgs of Austria. Cracow remained semi-independent until 1846 when it was annexed by Austria. After an abortive uprising in 1863-64 Tsarist Russia suppressed Polish culture in the territory they occupied, while the southern areas enjoyed considerable autonomy under the Austro-Hungarian Empire. In 1915 Germany evicted the Russians and in 1918 the whole area once again became Polish. The impact of this chequered history can still be seen.

While nearby industrial cities like Katowice and Lodz have little to offer the average visitor, nearly every foreign tourist makes it to Cracow, one of the great art centres of Europe. Some also join the hordes of Polish excursionists on their way to the mountains around Zakopane. There's much more to south-eastern Poland, however, from the holy sanctuary of Jasna Gora at Czestochowa, to perfectly preserved Renaissance Zamosc, to the superb Baroque palace at Lancut, to the horrors of Auschwitz, Birkenau and Majdanek. It's easy to lose the crowds in the unspoiled mountains along the southern border of Poland. Here is Poland to be savoured.

LUBLIN
Long a crossroads of trade, Lublin was an

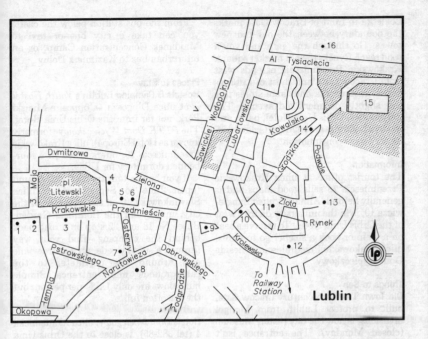

Lublin

1	Tourist Office
2	Hotel Lublinianka
3	Post Office
4	Karczma Lubelska Restaurant
5	Dom Wycieczkowy
6	Orbis (train tickets)
7	J Osterina Theatre
8	Brigittine Church
9	Polonia Restaurant
10	Cracow Gate
11	Old Tribunal
12	Cathedral
13	Dominican Church
14	Town Gate
15	Lublin Castle
16	Bus Station

creating the largest European state of the time. Beginning in the 17th century Lublin saw repeated foreign invasions by Swedes, Austrians, Russians and Germans, culminating in the Nazi death camp at Majdanek. For a time in 1944 Lublin was capital of liberated Poland.

Somehow the compact old town (Stare Miasto) retains the flavour of this turbulent past with its narrow crumbling streets, defensive towers and ominously isolated castle, long a prison. During the 19th century the city expanded west to Plac Litewski and today spectacular growth mushrooms in all directions. Many foreign students study at the Lublin Catholic University, Poland's only private university.

Orientation

The railway station is several km south of the city centre so catch a bus or taxi. Plac

important point of contact between Poland and Lithuania. In 1569 a political union of these kingdoms was signed here

Lokietka in front of Cracow Gate marks the boundary between the old and new towns. Go through the gate and you'll soon reach Rynek, the old market square. Krakowskie Przedmiescie extends west from Cracow Gate and most of Lublin's hotels, restaurants and large stores line this slightly decadent old avenue. The universities, Orbis Unia Hotel, parks and modern buildings are on Aleje Raclawickie, its westward continuation.

Information

The tourist office at ulica Krakowskie Przedmiescie 78 sells good maps and is generally helpful. Almatur, ulica Langiewicza 10, is in the university district west of the Orbis Unia Hotel. To reserve a seat on a train or book a sleeper go to Orbis, ulica Krakowskie Przedmiescie 29 beside Dom Wycieczkowy.

Things to See

Old Town The 14th century **Cracow Gate**, built to protect Lublin from Mongol invasions, is now the **City History Museum** (closed Monday). The entrance isn't obvious so look for it. You get a good view of Lublin from the top floor. Rather than enter the old town straight away go south-east a block on ulica Krolewska to reach the Baroque **cathedral**. Beside the cathedral is another tower (also a museum) and a passage into the old city. Walk straight ahead to Market Square (Rynek) with the 16th century **Tribunal** in the centre and many old town houses around. East of here at the end of ulica Zlota is the beautiful **Dominican Church**, rebuilt after the fire of 1575. In the first chapel to the right of the entrance is a large historical painting *The Lublin Fire of 1719*.

As you leave the church turn right and continue north down the slope and through the Town Gate to **Lublin Castle** which originated in the 13th century but assumed its present form in 1826. During the war it was a Gestapo jail. There's a good view from in front of the castle and a large museum inside (closed Monday).

From the bus station below the castle you can take a city bus or taxi to Majdanek Concentration Camp, or an interurban bus to Kazimierz Dolny.

Places to Stay

Hostels & Camping Lublin's *Youth Hostel* is at ulica Dlugosza 4a opposite Miejski Park, not far from the Orbis Unia Hotel. The *PTTK Dom Wycieczkowy* (formerly known as Hotel Europa), ulica Krakowskie Przedmiescie 29, offers a bed in a four-bedded dormitory for US$9.

If you have a tent try the campground (open June to September) at ulica Slawinkowska 46 on the west side of the city, up beyond the Botanical Garden. Buses No 18 and 32 stop on a road back behind the camping: find your way through a small woods, up a narrow lane and around the perimeter to the campgrounds' main entrance. Simple bungalows are only US$4 per person, but they're often full.

Hotels *Dom Noclegowy*, ulica Akademicka 4 (tel 382-85), is close to the Orbis Unia Hotel, beside the university (US$16 single, US$26 double). The *Hotel Lublinianka*, ulica Krakowskie Przedmiescie 56, is about the cheapest regular hotel (US$20 single, US$26 double).

Places to Eat

There's a pizzeria at ulica Krakowskie Przedmiescie 61 next to the park. The *Ogrodowy Milk Bar* at ulica Krakowskie Przedmiescie 57 is nearby. *Turystyczny Milk Bar*, ulica Krakowskie Przedmiescie 29, is also cheap. Another in this vein is the *Staromiejski Milk Bar*, ulica Trybunalska 1 just inside the Cracow Gate in the old town.

The restaurant in the *Orbis Unia Hotel* is the best in Lublin and the only place in town where you can be sure of a cold beer. Their menu is in English and French. Less expensive is the *Polonia Restaurant* at ulica Krakowskie Przedmiescie 6 near the Cracow Gate. The *Karczma Lubelska*

Restaurant, Plac Litewski 2, is a local hangout in the evening, sometimes with live music.

Entertainment

For Filharmonia tickets check the ticket office at ulica Osterwy 7. Just around the corner opposite the Brigittine Church is the ticket office of the *J Osterina Theatre*. The *Teatr Muzyczny* is in the 'Garnizonowy Klub Oficerski' near the Orbis Unia Hotel. The ticket office is just inside the front door. There's also an excellent restaurant here where you're welcome to have lunch with the local military brass. Look in the daily paper *Sztandar Ludu* which lists performances at all these theatres.

Getting There & Away

Express trains connect Lublin to Warsaw. Local trains run to Przemysl (via Rozwadow) and Zamosc. There's an overnight train with couchettes to and from Cracow. Buses run west to Kazimierz Dolny and Lodz, south-west to Cracow and Zakopane, and south-east to Zamosc.

AROUND LUBLIN
Majdanek

Majdanek Concentration Camp, just south-east of Lublin (buses No 23, 28, 153 and 156 pass the site), was the second largest Nazi death camp in Europe. Here, where 360,000 human beings were coldly eliminated, barbed wire and watchtowers, rows of wooden barracks and the crematoria have been left as a memorial to the dead and a warning to the living. An even more gripping memorial is the immense concrete dome covering the ashes of the victims. Poles often bring bunches of flowers to leave here.

As you arrive you'll see a massive stone monument by the highway. There's a sweeping view of the camp from there. The museum (open 8 am to 3 pm daily except Monday) is in the barracks to the right, outside the barbed wire fence on the west. Among the more gripping exhibits are two large buildings holding hundreds of thousands of pairs of shoes. The huge camp you see today is only a fraction of the facility the Nazis intended as part of their extermination programme. The Soviet Army cut short their work.

Kazimierz Dolny

This charming old Polish town on the banks of the Vistula River is best done as a day trip from Lublin, 40 km east. Accommodation in Kazimierz is tight and everything can be seen in a couple of hours. Buses leave fairly often from platform No 3 at Lublin's bus station and take 1½ hours. Departure times are posted on the platform but buy your ticket inside the station. Before WW II the population of Kazimierz was predominantly Jewish, mostly peasant farmers, but all were killed.

Everything in Kazimierz is within walking distance of the burgher houses on Rynek. The engaging interior of the Renaissance parochial church above the square shelters one of the oldest organs in Poland (1620). From the nearby ruins of the 14th century **castle** built by Casimir the Great one gets a panoramic view of town, river and vicinity. There's a **museum** (closed Monday) on ulica Senatorska, but chances are you'll prefer a bottle of the local Warka beer at the beer garden below the church. Lots of Polish tourists visit Kazimierz in summer.

ZAMOSC

Zamosc hasn't changed much since the 16th century when its chessboard street pattern was laid down by the Italian architect Bernardo Morando. The intact town square has an almost Latin American flavour with its long arcades and pastel shades.

Jan Zamoyski, chancellor and commander-in-chief of Poland, founded Zamosc in 1580 as an ideal Renaissance urban settlement and impregnable barrier against Cossack and Mongol raids from the east. Its position on a busy trade route

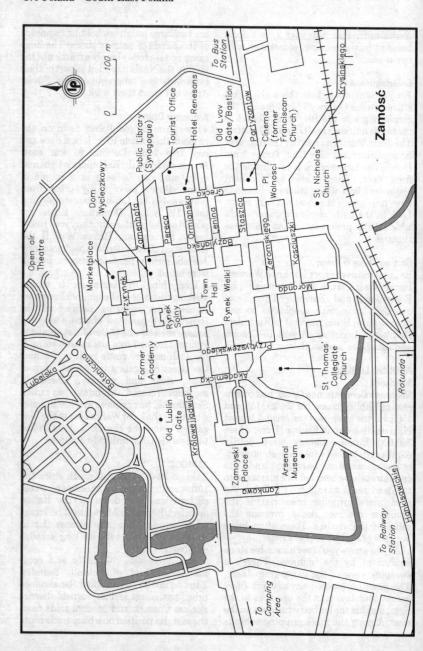

Zamość

0 100 m

To Bus Station

Krysinskiego

Tourist Office

Public Library (Synagogue)

Hotel Renesans

Old Lvov Gate/Bastion

Partyzantow

Cinema (former Franciscan Church)

Pl. Wolnosci

St Nicholas' Church

Open air Theatre

Dom Wycieczkowy

Marketplace

Zamenhofa

Pereca

Ormianska

Grecka

Lenina

Staszica

Zeromskiego

Kosciuszki

Bazylianska

Przyrynek

Rynek Solny

Town Hall

Rynek Wielki

Przybyszewskiego

Morandd

Former Academy

Akademicka

St Thomas' Collegiate Church

Lubelska

Botaniczna

Old Lublin Gate

Krolowejjadwigi

Zamoyski Palace

Arsenal Museum

Zamkowa

Rotunda

Hankiewwickiej

To Railway Station

To Camping Area

midway between Lublin and Lvov prompted merchants of many nationalities to settle here. Zamosc's fortifications withstood Cossack and Swedish attacks in 1648 and 1656 but by the 18th century its military value had dwindled. Later it was used as a military prison.

The Nazis renamed Zamosc, Himmlerstadt and expelled the Polish inhabitants from 292 nearby villages. Their places were taken by German colonists to create an eastern bulwark for the Third Reich. Surrounded by parks and totally unspoiled today, Zamosc is unique in Eastern Europe.

Orientation

The bus and train stations are on opposite sides of Zamosc, each about two km from the centre. The present marketplace is on the north edge of the old town along ulica Przyrynek. The Hotel Renesans is three blocks from there with the tourist office right behind.

Information

The tourist office (tel 710-06) is behind Hotel Renesans and they may know of private rooms. They open weekdays 7 am to 4 pm, Saturdays 9 am to 12 noon.

Things to See

You'll want to begin on Rynek Wielki, surrounded by Italian-style arcaded dwelling houses once owned by wealthy Greek and Armenian traders. The curving exterior stairway was added to the 16th century **town hall** in 1768. Just off the south-west corner of this square at ulica Staszica 37 the famous German revolutionary, Rosa Luxemburg, was born in 1870.

Continue west a bit to **St Thomas' Collegiate Church** (1598), a three-aisled Mannerist basilica. South-west of this church is the old **Arsenal** (1583), now a museum. The **Zamoyski Palace** (1585) nearby lost much of its character when it was converted into a military hospital in 1831. North again on ulica Akademicka is

the former **Academy** (1648). The fortifications opposite this building have been beautifully landscaped and made into a park extending east along the north side of Zamosc to the **open air theatre**.

Re-enter the town south from the theatre to see the old **synagogue** (1620) at the corner of Zamenhofa and Bazylianska, now a public library. Do go inside. East on Zamenhofa you come again to the bastions of Zamosc. Turn right and walk south toward **Lvov Gate** (1820) where you'll find a 16th century bastion with endless passageways you may enter.

Return to Rynek Wielki and follow ulica Moranda due south from the square. Cross the park and go under the train tracks and over a bridge till you get to the **Rotunda** (1831), a circular gun emplacement where the Nazis liquidated their victims. Today it's something of a Polish national shrine.

Places to Stay

In July and August there's a *Youth Hostel* (tel 44-71) at ulica Partyzantow 14 between the bus station and town. The *PTTK Dom Wycieczkowy* (tel 26-39), beside the old synagogue on ulica Zamenhofa, is only US$10 per person but perennially full. Other alternatives are the *PTTK Camping* (tel 24-99) on ulica Krolowej Jadwigi, a km west of town, and the *Sports Hotel* (tel 60-11) behind the stadium between the campground and town.

The tourist office may know of private rooms, otherwise the best place to stay is the modern *Hotel Renesans* (tel 20-01), ulica Grecka in the old city. A pleasant room with private bath will run US$20 single, US$30 double. They're often full so call ahead for reservations. The *Hotel Jubilat* near the bus station is more expensive, less convenient and not as attractive.

Places to Eat

Zamosc's best is the *Hetmanska Restaurant*, ulica Staszica 1, which specialises in *zur* (sour soup) and pork chop *a la Zamoyski*.

Getting There & Away

There are trains and buses between Lublin and Zamosc. Buses also run south to Jaroslaw, Lancut and Rzeszow. To or from Przemysl you change at Jaroslaw. Jaroslaw's bus and train stations are adjacent.

PRZEMYSL

Przemysl, on the Soviet border 80 km south-east of Rzeszow, has long been the boundary between Poland and the lands to the east. The River San curves between the wooded foothills of the Carpathians and on the slopes of the main town loom six huge churches and their towers. The Austrians fortified Przemysl in 1873 and fought bitterly against Tsarist forces here in 1914-1915. Today a direct railway link from Romania via the USSR makes Przemysl a potential gateway to Poland. Off the beaten track, Przemysl is also a jumping off point for the Bieszczady Mountains further south.

Orientation

From Przemysl Glowny Railway Station go up the slope to ulica Mickiewicza, then right and straight ahead all the way into town. The bus station is on the opposite side of the railway tracks but to get between the two stations you have to go the long way around.

Information

Try the Hotel Dworcowy at ulica Dworskiego 4 opposite the railway station.

Things to See

Przemysl is a city of churches and parks with Rynek at its heart. In the south-east corner of Rynek stands the Baroque

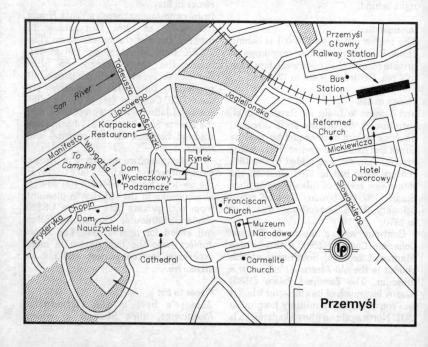

Przemyśl

Franciscan Church (1778), extraordinarily rich in paintings and decorative details. Just above this church is the **Muzeum Narodowe** (closed Monday) with a good collection of Ukrainian folk costumes and icons. The **Carmelite Church** behind and above the museum is beautifully decorated and has a pulpit in the form of a fully-rigged sailing ship. Przemysl's **cathedral** (1571) with its massive detached tower is to the west of here. There's a small **castle** on the wooded hilltop above the cathedral.

The Bieszczady Mountains
The enormous mountain pastures of this sparsely populated region in the south-east corner of Poland offer hiking in summer and cross-country skiing in winter. Heavy fighting took place here in 1945-1947 between Ukrainian nationalists and Polish soldiers. Some of the many youth hostels in this area are listed in the IYHF handbook, but most only open in July and August. Other tourist hostels and campgrounds exist; look for the 1:75,000 *Bieszczady Mapa Turystyczna* which lays out the possibilities.

Get there by taking a train to Ustrzyki Dolne, then a bus from there to Ustrzyki Gorne village right in the heart of the mountains near the Czech and Soviet borders. The train trip between Przemysl and Ustrzyki Dolne is interesting because you pass through Soviet territory most of the way and guards come aboard the train to make sure all the windows are closed, etc.

Places to Stay & Eat
Hotel Dworcowy, ulica Dworskiego 4 opposite the railway station, is often full. *Dom Wycieczkowy 'Sportowy,'* Mickiewicza 30, a seven-minute walk from the station to the left, has rooms at about the same price as the Dworcowy: US$13 single, US$20 double. The 'Sportowy' is large and clean, but you use the toilet down the hall.

Less convenient to the station but just on the edge of the old town is *Dom Nauczyciela* (tel 27-68), 2nd floor, ulica Chopina 1 (tel 27-68), where rooms begin at US$6.50 single. The *PTTK Dom Wycieczkowy 'Podzamcze'*, nearby at ulica Waygarta 5, could be tried if Dom Nauczyciela is full. Finally, *Camping 'Zamek,'* a km upriver from the bridge, on the opposite side of Przemysl from the stations, has 15 bungalows and, of course, camping space.

For meals the *Karpacka Restaurant*, ulica Kosciuszki 5 near the bridge, stays open till midnight every day but Sunday.

Getting There & Away
Three main railway lines converge on Przemysl, two from Warsaw via Lublin or Radom, another from Szczecin via Poznan, Wroclaw, Katowice, Cracow and Rzeszow. Couchettes are available to Wroclaw and Szczecin. The Cracow-Przemysl service is frequent and trains run continually between Rzeszow and Przemysl. For Zamosc change to a bus at Jaroslav. International trains to Lvov (USSR), Bucharest, Sofia and Varna also pass through Przemysl.

RZESZOW
Rzeszow's attractions don't really warrant a special visit although the city could be useful as a stopping place. The impressive 17th century palace at Lancut is only 17 km east. The massive housing projects *(osiedle)* encircling Rzeszow have all been created since 1945, a dramatic example of what socialism has done for a previously depressed area.

Orientation
The bus and train stations are adjacent to one another on the north side of the old town. Plac Farny is Rzeszow's hub with Rynek, the main square, and ulica 3 Maja, the main street, nearby.

Information
Informacja Turystyczna is at ulica Asnyka 10 near the stations. Orbis is at

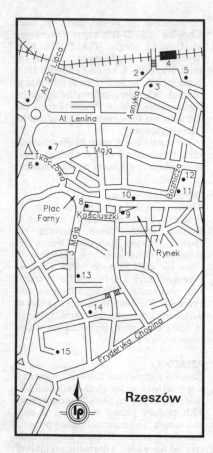

1	Hotel Rzeszow
2	Bus Station
3	Hotel Polonia
4	Railway Station
5	Dom Wycieczkowy
6	Theatre
7	Bernadine Church
8	Parish Church
9	Old Town Hall
10	Youth Hostel
11	Old Town Synagogue
12	New Town Synagogue (Arts Centre)
13	Museum
14	Lubomirskich Palace
15	Castle (former jail)

Places to Stay

Rzeszow is not outstanding for accommodation. The *PTTK Dom Wycieczkowy*, Plac Kilinskiego 6 right in front of the stations, has simple rooms with shared bath for US$15 single, US$20 double. Nearby is *Hotel Polonia*, ulica Grottgera 16, a little more expensive.

The *Youth Hostel* is at Rynek 25, right in the heart of the old town. There are no camping facilities in Rzeszow.

Places to Eat

The *Rzeszowska Restaurant*, ulica Kosciuszki 9, serves local specialties such as roast goose. There's a milk bar downstairs at *Dom Wycieczkowy*, but the entrance is around the corner.

Getting There & Away

Rzeszow is on the main railway lines from Przemysl to Warsaw and Cracow. For Lublin and Zamosc take a bus.

LANCUT

Near Rzeszow, the magnificent Renaissance palace at Lancut was built in 1629 by the feudal magnate Stanislaw Lubomirski. Originally surrounded by powerful fortifications, these were dismantled in the 18th century. Toward the end of the 19th century the Potocki family rebuilt

ulica 3 Maja 9. Almatur is at ulica Akademicka 2.

Things to See

From the **Parish Church** on Plac Farny follow ulica 3 Maja south to the **museum** (closed Monday) in the 17th century Piarist Monastery at No 19. There's an old Austrian jail near the end of the street. Two old **synagogues** are on ulica Boznicza just north of Rynek, one of which is now an Arts Centre.

the palace in French Baroque style. The palace is today a **Museum of Interior Decoration** containing numerous furnished rooms, each unique. On the far side of the park is a pavilion where the antique **carriage collection** is kept.

Tickets to both museums must be purchased in a separate building outside the compound. Ask for the *kasa*. The palace closes at 2 pm some days and all day Monday, but the park is open daily till sunset.

Places to Stay & Eat
One wing of the palace is now the *Hotel 'Zamkowy'* (tel 26-71) with rooms for US$26 single, US$33 double – a great place to splurge those surplus zloty. There's also a good restaurant in there.

Getting There & Away
Buses arrive frequently from Rzeszow. The bus station adjoins the park but the railway station is about two km away (take a taxi).

CRACOW
Over a millennium ago Prince Krak founded a settlement on Wawel Hill, above a bend of the legendary Vistula River. Boleslav the Brave built a cathedral on this hill in 1020 and transferred the capital here from Poznan in 1039. The kings of Poland ruled from Wawel Castle until 1596 and even later Polish royalty continued to be crowned and buried in Wawel Cathedral.

At this crossing of trade routes from Western Europe to Byzantium and Southern Europe to the Baltic a large medieval city developed. Miraculously spared destruction in WW II, Stare Miasto, the old town, harbours world class museums and towering churches. Kazimierz, the now-silent Jewish quarter, tells of a sadder recent history and Auschwitz is close by.

Cracow was a medieval student's town. Jagiellonian University, established at Cracow in 1364, is Poland's oldest.

Copernicus studied here. It's still the second largest university in Poland (after Warsaw) and 10% of the present population are higher education students. During Juvenalia, the student's festival in mid-May, the town really comes to life.

Cracow (population 800,000) is the third largest city in Poland. Just east of Cracow is the socialist community of Nowa Huta with its Lenin Steel Works. Yet it's the older, royal Cracow which draws us back again and again. This is the one Polish city you simply cannot miss.

Orientation
The bus and train stations are adjacent to one another just outside the north-east corner of the old town. Ulica Pawia, with the tourist office and several hotels, flanks the stations to the west. To walk into town follow the crowds into the underpass at the corner of Pawia and Lubicz, then bear slightly right and lose yourself in the old streets until you come out on Rynek Glowny, Cracow's glorious Market Square.

Information
There's an excellent tourist information office at ulica Pawia 8, a few minutes' walk from the stations. They'll give you maps and brochures, and direct you to the accommodation service next door. They're open Sundays and holidays until 2 pm.

Almatur, Rynek Glowny 7, and the US Consulate, ulica Stolarska 9, are both in the old town. Dom Ksiazki, ulica Podwale 5/6, sells books in English, German and other foreign languages.

Things to See
Around Market Square You'll probably want to begin your visit on Rynek Glowny, Cracow's wonderful Market Square, the largest medieval town square in Europe. The Renaissance **Cloth Hall** (Sukiennice) dominates the square and there's a large craft market under the arches. Upstairs is a museum (closed Tuesday) of 19th century paintings, including several well-known historical works by Jan Matejko.

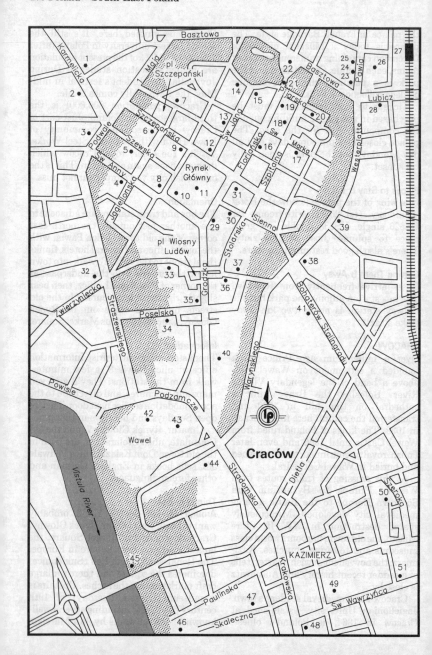

1	Carmelite Church
2	Bar Kapitanski
3	Dom Ksiazki/Akademjcki Milk Bar
4	Collegium Mauis
5	Pizzeria
6	Teatr Stary
7	Mysliwska Restaurant
8	Cultural Centre
9	City Historical Museum
10	Town Hall Tower
11	Cloth Hall (Sukiennice)
12	Orbis (train tickets)
13	Cartoon Gallery
14	Hotel Francuski
15	Czartoryski Art Museum
16	Zywiec Restaurant
17	Orbis (bus tickets)
18	Hotel Pod Zlota Koturca
19	Restauracja Pod Baszta
20	Teatr Im J Slowackiego
21	St Florian's Gate
22	Barbican
23	Hotel Polonia
24	Hotel Warszawski
25	Tourist Office
26	Bus Station
27	Krakow Glowny Station
28	Hotel Europejski
29	Almatur/Teatr 38
30	Pioneer Milk Bar
31	Church of Our Lady
32	Filharmonia
33	Franciscan Church
34	Archaeological Museum
35	Balaton Restaurant
36	Grodzka Restaurant
37	Dominican Church
38	Post Office
39	PTTK Dom Turysty
40	St Peter & Paul Church
41	Museum Historii Fotografii
42	Wawel Cathedral
43	Wawel Castle
44	Bernadine Church
45	Excursion Boats
46	Pauline Church
47	St Catherine's Church
48	Ethnographic Museum
49	Corpus Christii Church
50	Jewish Cemetery
51	Jewish Museum

The 14th century **Church of Our Lady** fills the north-east corner of Rynek Glowny. The huge main altarpiece (1489) by Wit Stwosz is the finest sculptural work in Poland. The altar's wings are opened daily at 12 noon. A trumpet call sounded hourly from one of the church towers recalls a 13th century trumpeter cut short by a Mongol arrow.

On the opposite side of the Cloth Hall is the 14th century **Town Hall Tower**, complete with a cafe serving honey wine (mead) in the cellar. The Town Hall itself was demolished in 1820. Take sw Anny (the street running west from the corner of the square closest to the tower) a block to the Collegium Maius, oldest surviving part of **Jagiellonian University**. Enter the Gothic courtyard. Also visit the **City Historical Museum** at Rynek Glowny 35.

Go north from the Cloth Hall to the **art gallery** at ulica sw Jana 14 which specialises in pornographic comic books. Further up at sw Jana 17 is the **Czartoryski Art Museum** (closed Wednesday) with Leonardo da Vinci's *Lady with an Ermine* among other illustrious works. Raphael's *Portrait of a Young Man*, stolen from this museum during WW II, has never been recovered.

The Royal Way Around the corner from the Czartoryski Museum on ulica Pijarska is a remaining stretch of the medieval city walls which once surrounded Cracow, where the greenbelt is today. Go through **St Florian's Gate** (1307) to the **Barbican**, a defensive bastion built in 1498. Cracow's **Royal Way** runs south from St Florian's Gate to Wawel Castle.

Re-enter the city and follow ulica Florianska south to Rynek Glowny, then south again on ulica Grodzka. At Plac Wiosny Ludow where the streetcar tracks cut across Grodzka are two large 13th century **monastic churches**, Dominican on the east and Franciscan on the west. John Paul II resided in the Episcopal Palace across the street from the Franciscan Church for a dozen years until he was elected pope in 1978. A block south again on Grodzka is ulica Poselska with the **Archaeological Museum** to the right at number 3. Farther south on Grodzka is the 17th century **Sts Peter & Paul Church**.

Continue south another block, then take the lane on the right which leads to the ramp up to Wawel Castle. **Wawel Cathedral** (1364) will be on your left as you enter. Before going inside buy a ticket to climb the tower and visit the crypt at the small office opposite (closed Sunday morning). For four centuries this church served as the coronation and burial place of Polish royalty and 100 kings and queens are interred in the crypt. The Sigismund Chapel (1539), the one on the south side with the gold dome, is considered to be the finest Renaissance construction in Poland.

The 16th century **main palace** (closed Monday) is behind the cathedral. The ticket you buy at the gate will admit you to the different museum departments arrayed around the great Renaissance courtyard. Wawel is famous for its 16th century Flemish tapestry collection, but there is much else of interest including the crown jewels and armoury. The castle's greatest treasure is the 12th century Piast coronation sword, the 'Szczerbiec.' Many of the exhibits were evacuated to Canada in 1939 where they survived the war. During WW II Hans Frank, the Nazi governor general of Poland (later condemned to death at Nuremberg), resided in the castle.

In summer excursion boats operate on the **Vistula River** from below Wawel Castle, making scenic 1½ hour trips upriver to Bielany (US$1).

Kazimierz Founded in the 14th century by Casimir the Great, Kazimierz was settled by Jews a century later. To get there from the castle walk south along the riverside and under the bridge to the 18th century **Pauline Church**, which you enter from the east side. Visit the crypt and then go east on ulica Skaleczna past **St Catherine's Church** to ulica Krakowska where you again meet the streetcar tracks. Follow these south a block to the **Ethnographic Museum** (closed Tuesday). East on ulica sw Wawrzynca is Gothic **Corpus Christi Church**.

Continue east on this street till it terminates at a 15th century synagogue, now the **Jewish Museum** (closed Monday). The old **Jewish cemetery** at ulica Szeroka 40 is just north of here. East of the cemetery you'll encounter another streetcar route which will take you back to the city centre (trams No 3 or 13). On the way you'll pass the **Muzeum Historii Fotografii**, ulica Bohaterow Stalingradu 13. The nude photography shows attract big crowds.

The Salt Mines
The **underground cathedral** at Wieliczka, 13 km south-east of Cracow, can be reached by bus or train. You enter the 1000-year-old mines down an elevator shaft, then follow a guide through the many theme chambers carved from solid salt. It's all a bit artificial but certainly a change of pace from museums and churches. Try to arrive by 2 pm to be sure of getting on a tour; they open early every day.

Back to Nature
Ojcow National Park, 22 km north-west of Cracow, is set in a picturesque forested valley sprinkled with cliffs and caves. Hiking trails fan out from the Ojcow bus stop. There's a museum in the large Renaissance courtyard at **Pieskowa Skala Castle**, nine km beyond Ojcow, but only a small part of the castle may actually be visited.

Huge tour groups are waiting to enter when the doors open at 10 am (closed Monday). Both park and castle are easily accessible from Cracow on the Olkusz bus and the bus ticket is usually purchased on the bus itself, although try getting one in the station. There's no way to carry on from Olkusz directly to Auschwitz, so make it a day trip.

Places to Stay

Youth Hostels There are three *Youth Hostels*, all west of the old town. The closest to the centre is in the functional concrete building at ulica Oleandry 4 beyond Hotel Cracovia. Although this is the largest hostel in Poland it's often full in summer. There's a second hostel behind the large Augustine Church at Tadeusza Kosciuszki 88 just west of the city (trams No 1, 2, 6 or 21 to the terminus). Members stay in a one time convent overlooking the Vistula River. During July and August only there's a summer youth hostel in the concrete dormitory at the end of ulica Zlotej Kielni on the far west side of Cracow (trams No 4, 8 or 12).

Camping From June to September *Camping 'Krak,'* ulica Radzikowskiego by the traffic circle in the far north-west corner of Cracow, offers good camping facilities at US$3 per person (own tent). The adjacent four-star motel is super expensive but the motel bar is handy. Buses No 118, 173, 208, 218 and 228 all pass 'Krak' (ask for bus No 208 at Cracow station).

Cheaper Hotels & Private Rooms The easiest hotel accommodation is at the big, crowded *PTTK Dom Turysty*, ulica Westerplatte 15/17, an eight-minute walk from the stations. The rooms are overpriced at US$22 single, US$33 double, and the only real reason to come here is if you're interested in a bed in one of the eight-bed dormitories which go for US$7.50 each. If not, consider this place as a last resort only. There's a large restaurant downstairs.

During July and August visit Almatur, Rynek Glowny 7 (in the arcade), to find out about the International Student Hotels both here and in other cities, which are the best places to stay. Those over age 35 cannot use these hotels.

At ulica Pawia 8 near the stations is an office arranging stays in private homes for around US$13 single, US$20 double. The rooms are often far from the city centre, so ask first. This office or the one next door can also help you find a hotel.

You may also be offered a private room by someone on the street outside. The price will be similar to those charged by the office but you won't receive a stamp on your currency exchange paper, so it's not really kosher. It should be alright if you're only staying a few nights, but decide for yourself.

The *Hotel Warszawski*, ulica Pawia 6, is right next to this office, about US$20 single, US$26 double. The *Hotel Polonia*, ulica Basztowa 23 just around the corner from the Warszawski, charges about the same. Also very near the bus and train stations is the *Hotel Europejski*, ulica Lubicz 5, similarly priced to the Warszawski and Polonia. Streetcar noise can be a problem at these hotels. The *Hotel Pod Zlota Koturca*, ulica Szpitalna 30 in the old city, is US$19 single, US$29 double – quieter and good value.

Expensive Hotels Of the three Orbis hotels the *Francuski*, ulica Pijarska 13, is the most elegant, convenient and least expensive. Rooms at this 57-room hotel erected in 1912 are US$30 single, US$50 double.

By far the most unusual place to stay in Cracow is the *Hotel Pod Kopcem*, Aleje Waszyngtona (tel 220-55), located in a 19th century Austrian fortress on a hilltop overlooking the city. There's a cool forest surrounding the hotel, plus coffee shop and restaurant. Room rates begin at US$33 without bath. If you wanted to splurge once in Poland, this is it! Bus No 100 terminates in front of the hotel. Ask the tourist office to call ahead to make sure there's room but even if you're not staying, the Hotel Pod Kopcem merits a visit.

Places to Eat

Around Market Square The *Pioneer Milk Bar*, ulica Sienna 1 just off Market

Square, is a great cheap place for breakfast. It's a little hidden in the red brick building half way up the block. The *Zywiec Restaurant*, ulica Florianska 19, is colourful yet inexpensive. At *Restauracja Pod Baszta*, ulica Florianska 55, you can sometimes get beer with your meal!

West of Market Square The pizzeria at ulica Szewska 14 is quick and easy. Other cheap places to eat in this vicinity include the *Ludowa Restaurant*, ulica sw Anny 7, the *Mysliwska Restaurant*, Plac Szczepanski 7, and *Akademjcki Milk Bar*, ulica Podwale 5. *Bar Kapitanski* at ulica Karmelicka 14 farther west, dishes out huge pieces of fried fish to those in the line at the counter.

South of Market Square The *Grodzka Restaurant*, Plac Dominikanski 6, offers table-service meals in unpretentious surroundings. For better Hungarian food than you'll get in Hungary try the highly recommended *Balaton Restaurant*, ulica Grodzka 37.

Entertainment
Look at the listings in the daily papers. One of the first things to do in Cracow is visit the *Filharmonia* booking office (open weekdays 10 am to 12 noon and 5 to 7 pm), ulica Zwierzyniecka 1, for tickets to any concerts which happen to coincide with your stay. Don't be fooled by the low price of the ticket, this orchestra ranks with the best in the world.

The *Teatr Im J Slowackiego*, ulica Szpitalna, offers classical theatre, opera and ballet. The *Teatr Miniatura* is just behind and shares the same box office.

In the evening there's sometimes jazz at the *Pod Jaszczurami Student Club*, Rynek Glowny 8. Films and other events happen at the *Cultural Centre*, Rynek Glowny 27. The *'Rotunda' Students' Cultural Centre*, ulica Oleandry 1, has a good Saturday night disco.

Getting There & Away
Train Cracow is on the main railway line between Przemysl and Szczecin via Katowice, Opole, Wroclaw and Poznan. Another important line through the city is Warsaw to Zakopane. There are direct trains from Budapest via Kosice and Muszyna. Coming from Prague or Vienna you usually change at Katowice, although in summer there's a daily train direct from Vienna.

Tickets Train tickets, reservations and couchettes are available from Orbis on the north side of Market Square. The Orbis office at ulica sw Marka 25 sells long distance bus tickets for the next or subsequent days. Expect long lines at both these offices.

Getting Around
Streetcars and city buses use the same US$0.10 tickets, so buy a bunch as soon as you arrive.

The Orbis office in the Hotel Cracova, Aleje Puszkina 1, offers city sightseeing tours (US$5) plus day trips to the salt mines and Auschwitz (US$8) several times a week from mid-May to September.

THE TATRA MOUNTAINS
Poland is a flat open land of lakes and rivers but in the south the Sudeten and Carpathian mountain ranges break through the plains. The Tatra Mountains 100 km south of Cracow are the highest knot of these ranges with elevations averaging 2000 metres. Here folded granite and limestone were shaped by glaciation to create a true Alpine environment.

The Czechoslovak border runs along the ridges of these jagged Carpathian peaks. The entire Polish portion of the range is included in Tatra National Park (217 square km). Zakopane is a busy resort year round. For visitors it's a chance to do some hiking and meet the Poles in an unstructured environment. Many students come here on holidays and your conversations with them will be as memorable as the rugged landscape itself.

Orientation

Zakopane, at an altitude of 800 to 1000 metres, will be your base. The bus and railway stations are adjacent to one another on the north-east edge of town. From the railway station cross the street and take ulica Kosciuszki past the bus station straight into town. You'll pass the tourist office on the left then Hotel Giewont before reaching the post office, your reference point in Zakopane. The cable car to Mt Kasprowy Wierch is at Kuznice, four km south of the stations.

Information

The tourist information office is at ulica Kosciuszki 7 on the way in from the stations. The helpful Orbis office beside the post office can book couchettes to Warsaw or Wroclaw, bus tickets to Cracow and Morskie Uno Lake, cable car tickets to Mt Kasprowy Wierch (US$2 round trip), and tours to Chocholowska (US$1.50). Most of the trips go several times a day. These tickets are often sold out days ahead, so make your bookings as soon as you arrive at Zakopane.

The Biuro Obslugi Ruchu Turystycznego (PTTK), Krupowki 37 next to the Europejska Cafe just up from Orbis, will have information on mountain 'huts' (hostels). They open weekdays 7 am to 8 pm, Saturdays 8 am to 12 noon. Count on all the tourist offices being closed Saturday afternoon and all day Sunday.

Things to See & Do

In Zakopane The **Tatra Museum**, hidden among the trees behind Dom Turysty just down from the post office, is worth a brief visit. Walk down ulica Krupowki from here and turn left on ulica Koscieliska to reach an old wooden church with a pioneer cemetery behind.

Return to the corner of ulica Krupowki and proceed west under the overpass to the **funicular railway** up Mt Gubalowka (1136 metres). The last return trip is at 8 pm (US$0.50 round trip). There's a great view from the top.

Mountain Climbing The best thing to do in Zakopane is to climb **Mt Giewont** (1909 metres). Walk or take a taxi a couple of km up ulica Strazyska to the trailhead, then follow a broad track up through the forest to some huts where there's a small tea shop. Here one goes right and circles around climbing steeply to the shoulder of the mountain (red trail). From the cross atop Giewont one gets a sweeping view of Zakopane and the Tatras, a truly magnificent spectacle on a clear day.

Return to Zakopane along the blue trail down the Kondratowa Valley (easier going), finishing at the cable car terminus at Kuznice. Refreshments are sold at the *Hala Kondratowa Hostel*. The whole circle trip can be done in about six hours without too much difficulty.

Cable Car Every Polish tourist tries to make the cable car trip to the summit of **Mt Kasprowy Wierch** (1985 metres). Unless you've booked an advance ticket with Orbis get there early, preferably by 8 am. There's a restaurant on top but they don't open till 9.30 am. Many people return to Zakopane on foot down the Gasienicowa Valley and the more intrepid walk the ridges all the way across to Morskie Ono Lake via Piec Stawow, a very strenuous hike taking a full day.

Morskie Ono One of the highlights of a visit to Zakopane is the bus trip to Morskie Ono Lake. It's best to book return tickets a few days in advance at Orbis, although tickets are often available on the bus itself. A couple of hours at the lake is enough. The bus terminates at Wlosienica from where it's a 20-minute walk uphill to the lake. There's a large tea shop serving *bigos* (boiled cabbage) at the lakeside.

A stone path runs right around this mountain-girdled glacial lake, a lovely 40-

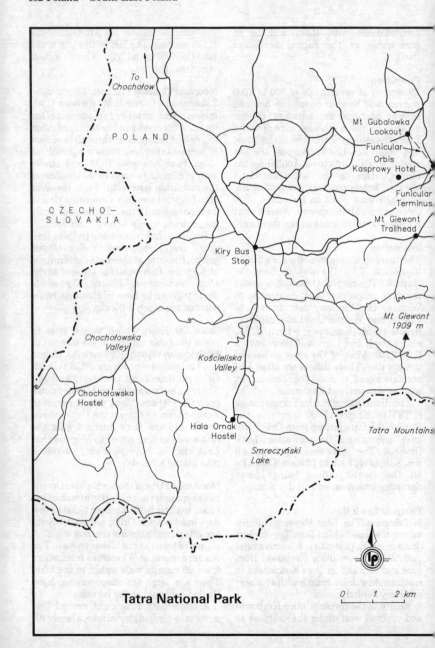

Tatra National Park

To Chochołów

POLAND

CZECHO-
SLOVAKIA

Mt Gubalowka
Lookout

Funicular

Orbis
Kasprowy Hotel

Funicular
Terminus

Mt Giewont
Trailhead

Kiry Bus
Stop

Mt Giewont
1909 m

Chochołowska
Valley

Kościeliska
Valley

Chochołowska
Hostel

Hala Ornak
Hostel

Tatra Mountains

Smreczyński
Lake

0   1   2 km

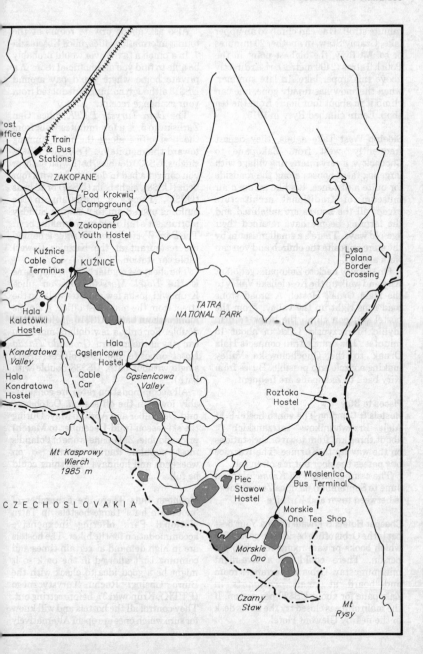

minute stroll. One can climb to an upper lake, Czarny Staw, in another 20 minutes or so. **Mt Rysy**, the highest point in the Polish Tatras (2499 metres), rises directly above this upper lake. In late summer, when the snow has finally gone, one can climb it in about four hours from the tea shop. Lenin climbed Rysy in 1913.

Sidetrip West Take a bus, they depart frequently, west from Zakopane to **Chocholow**, a very interesting village with large log farm houses along the roadside for quite a distance. It's like an open-air museum of traditional architecture except all the houses are inhabited and the farming people have retained their age-old ways. There's a small museum by the store opposite the church and you can walk around.

On the way back to Zakopane get off at Kiry and walk up the Koscieliska Valley to the Hala Ornak Hostel. A broad stone road runs right up the valley. From the hostel you can climb the black trail to idyllic Smreczynski Lake in about 15 minutes. The orange trail connects Hala Ornak to the Chocholowska Valley making a circle trip possible. Buses from Kiry back to Zakopane are frequent.

Places to Stay
Hostels & Camping The youth hostel is at Aleje Przewodnikow Tatrzanskich 3, about three km from town or the stations on the way up to Kuznice. The Kuznice bus passes the door but it's often full.

The campground *'Pod Krokwiq'* (open June to September) on ulica Zeromskiego is between town and Kuznice.

Cheaper Hotels & Private Rooms Your best bet is the Orbis office beside the post office which books private rooms for US$5 per person. There could be a five-night minimum stay. Orbis also arranges room and board at small *pensjonats* in Zakopane for about US$20 per person. If the main office is closed try the Orbis desk in the nearby Giewont Hotel.

Also ask about private rooms at the tourist information office, ulica Kosciuszki 7. In a pinch a taxi driver would probably be able to find you an unofficial room in a private home where you'd pay around US$13 although nothing is deducted from your exchange receipt.

The *Dom Turysty PTTK*, ulica Gen Zaruskiego 5, is a few minutes walk from the post office along the road running toward the mountains. There are US$22 singles, US$30 doubles, both with bath, or you can get a bed in dormitories with four beds (US$8), eight beds (US$7) or 28 beds (US$5). There's a restaurant in the building open 8 am to 9.30 pm; Sunday mornings it's full of old men drinking beer. The *Dom Wycieczkowy Kuznice* is behind the restaurant at the Kuznice (lower) cable car station.

The cheapest regular hotel in Zakopane is the *Hotel Morskie Ono* on ulica Krupowki, just a few minutes walk up the street from the main post office. A simple room without bath is US$16 single, US$26 double. For only a few dollars more you can stay at the modern *'Gromada' Gazda Hotel* opposite the post office (US$21 single without bath, US$38 double with bath).

All accommodation rates are considerably lower in the off season, October to mid-December and April to May. During the ski season (mid-December to March) prices double. Zakopane is one of Poland's most popular tourist centres so on weekends and holidays everything could be full.

Mountain Huts There are a number of 'mountain huts' (large hostels) in Tatra National Park offering inexpensive accommodation for the hiker. The hostels are in high demand at certain times and camping isn't allowed in the park so it might be a good idea to check with the Biuro Obslugi Ruchu Turystycznego (PTTK), Krupowki 37, before setting out. They control all the hostels and will know for sure which ones are open. Alternatively you could just take pot luck there'll be a bed for you (don't arrive too late in this case).

The easiest 'hut' to get to from Zakopane is the giant *Hala Kalatowki Hostel* (84 beds), a 30-minute walk from the Kuznice cable car station (accessible by local bus). Half an hour beyond Kalatowki on the trail to Giewont is the *Hala Kondratowa Hostel* (20 beds). For location and atmosphere it's great but note the small size.

Hikers wishing to traverse the park could begin at the *Roztoka Hostel* (96 beds), accessible via the Morskie Ono bus. An early start from Zakopane, however, would allow one to visit Morskie Ono in the morning and continue through to the *Piec Stawow Hostel* (70 beds), a couple of hours walk on the blue trail over a high pass from Morskie Ono. Piec Stawow (Five Lakes) is by far the most scenically-located hostel in the Polish Tatras.

A good days' walk west of Piec Stawow is the *Hala Gaslenlcowu Hostel* (100 beds), from which one can return to Zakopane. In the western part of the park are the *Ornak* (75 beds) and *Chocholowska* (161 beds) hostels, connected by trail.

Places to Eat

The best restaurant in Zakopane is the one in the *Hotel 'Orbis-Giewont'* diagonally across from the post office. Their menu is in English and German and they even have cold beer. Try a dish with *bryndza* (sheep cheese). Their cafe serves a good breakfast for around US$3. The restaurant in the *'Gromada' Gazda Hotel* nearby is also good (but the beer's warm).

Getting There & Away

The Tatry Express (reservation required) takes just over six hours to cover the 467 km from Warsaw to Zakopane. From Cracow to Zakopane it's faster to take a bus than the train, but try to book advance tickets. Overnight trains arrive from Wroclaw and Warsaw. Book your couchette well ahead.

There's a direct Volanbus from Budapest to Zakopane (US$8, nine hours), an excellent way to get from Hungary to Poland (Czech transit visa required).

Pedestrians with onward visas may use the Lysa Polana highway border crossing off the road to Morskie Ono. From Lysa Polana there's a road around to Tatranska Lomnica via Zdiar (30 km). In perfect weather rugged backpackers with an early start could hike from the border over mountain passes well above 2000 metres to the Zbojnicka or Teryho chalets in Slovakia. For many reasons this route is probably more practical northbound than southbound, however. See The High Tatras in the Czechoslovakia chapter of this book for details.

OSWIECIM

Auschwitz (Oswiecim) and Birkenau (Brzezinka), two deadly Nazi concentration camps 54 km west of Cracow, have been preserved as memorials to the four million people of 08 nationalities who perished here. From all Europe the fascists brought Jews and others for slave labour purposes in the nearby armaments factories. Aside from the main camps there were 40 sub-camps scattered throughout the area. As one group of starving victims became too weak to continue they were led into the gas chambers, their places taken by fresh arrivals off the trains.

It's difficult to conceive of the minds that could invent such a system. Children (especially twins) were held in the camps for medical experimentation. Father Maximilian Kolbe, who voluntarily took the place of another inmate sentenced to death in 1941, was declared a saint by Pope John Paul II in 1983. For us a visit to these haunting memorials reveals the unimaginable brutality of war and warns of the danger in putting politics above people. These lessons more than justify the trip.

Orientation

Today the main Auschwitz camp contains

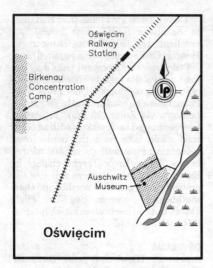

Oświęcim

a museum (closed Monday, admission free), cinema, restaurant and hotel, while the Birkenau camp has been left more or less as it was found. Oswiecim Railway Station is about a km north of the Auschwitz Museum. Birkenau is three km north-west of Auschwitz or two km south-west of the train station.

There are no buses to Birkenau, so it's best to take a taxi from Oswiecim Railway Station to Birkenau first. Ask to be driven around to the monument at the back of the camp. Have the taxi wait so you'll have a ride on to Auschwitz. There's frequent bus service from the Auschwitz Museum back to the railway station.

Birkenau

The museum and film at Auschwitz tell the terrible tale eloquently, but to really grasp the full magnitude of the crime Birkenau simply *must* be seen. Birkenau surprises by its vast size. At the back of the camp is a monument flanked on each side by the sinister ruins of a gas chamber/ crematorium, blown up by the retreating Nazis. Each gas chamber accommodated

2000 and there were electric lifts to raise the bodies to the ovens. From the monument you'll have a view of the railway lines which brought victims to the wooden barracks stretching out on each side, almost as far as you can see. The camp could hold 200,000 inmates at a time.

Auschwitz

Established in May 1940, Auschwitz was the original extermination camp. The museum is in the various prison blocks, with different blocks dedicated to victims from different countries. You won't forget the thousands of individual ID photos of the dead. Finally there's a gas chamber and crematorium. Pick up the guidebook which contains maps of the sites, plus penetrating information and photos. The cinema shows a Soviet film taken just after the 1945 liberation. Ask when they'll be showing the English version to a group. If you buy 15 tickets they'll schedule an English showing just for you, although the film's message is clear in any language. Near the museum entrance is a flower shop if you'd like to leave a token. Children under 13 are not admitted.

Near Oswiecim

The Baroque palace at **Pszczyna**, 25 km west of Oswiecim, is now a museum (closed Monday). The palace, about a km from the station, is situated in a large park at one corner of the picturesque town square (several restaurants here). Get to Pszczyna by direct train from Katowice, or from Oswiecim with a change of trains at Czechowice.

Places to Stay

The *hotel* (tel 232-17) at Auschwitz is located directly above the museum entrance. Comfortable rooms with a sink inside but shared bath are US$7 single, US$11 double. There's a large cafeteria alongside (closes early).

Getting There & Away

Auschwitz is fairly easy to reach. Local trains run almost hourly to Oswiecim from Cracow and Katowice. There are also direct buses from Cracow to the Auschwitz camp gate.

CZESTOCHOWA

Czestochowa is the spiritual heart of Poland. Pilgrims from every corner of the country come to Jasna Gora Monastery to worship the image of the Black Madonna, Poland's holiest icon. The best time to arrive is dawn when the churches are overflowing with nuns in silent prayer. This could be the most sacred place you'll ever visit.

History

Czestochowa was first mentioned in 1220. In 1382 Wladyslaw Duke of Opole invited the Paulites of Hungary to establish Jasna Gora Monastery. The famous icon of the Black Madonna was brought from the east in 1384. The story goes that it had been painted at Jerusalem long before. In 1430 the image was cut by invading Protestant Hussites. During restoration a scar from the sword blow was left on the Madonna's face as a reminder.

Early in the 17th century the monastery was fortified and subsequent Swedish (1655) and Russian (1770) sieges were resisted. Rebuilding took place after a fire in 1690 and centuries of patronage increased the richness of Jasna Gora. Industry developed at the end of the 19th century with the building of the railway from Warsaw to Vienna. Today Czestochowa has a steel works with 30,000 employees, plus clothing, chemical and paper industries.

Orientation

From the railway station walk north a block to Aleje Najswietszej Marii Panny, locally known as Aleje NMP. Jasna Gora is on a low hill at the end of this important avenue, a km due west. If you're arriving in the early morning darkness you'll see a bright light high above the monastery.

Information

PTTK tourist office is at Aleje NMP 39. Orbis is at Aleje NMP 40. Almatur is at ulica Zawadzkiego 27, a northward continuation of Aleje Tadeusza Kosciuszki.

Things to See

Today **Jasna Gora Monastery** retains the appearance of a fortress, a vibrant symbol of Catholicism tossed in a secular sea. Inside the compound are two churches. On the high altar of the smaller, less ornate church is the image of the Black Madonna. It's hidden behind a silver curtain (1673) and only exposed during the frequent religious services. This makes it difficult to have a close look. The adjacent Baroque church is beautifully decorated.

The Black Madonna. The scars on the face are from a sword blow inflicted during a Protestant incursion into the Sanctuary in 1430.

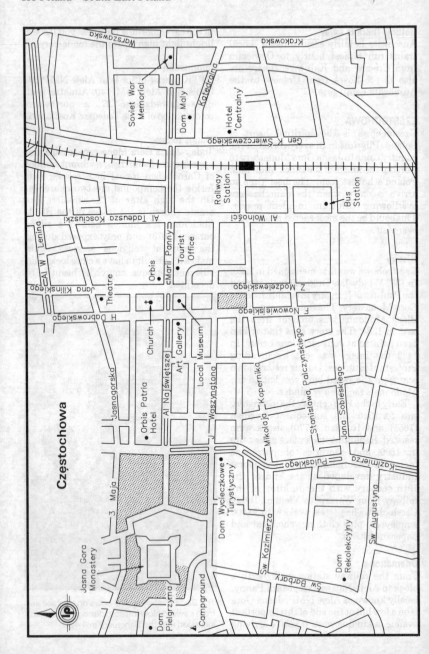

Częstochowa

- Jasna Gora Monastery
- Dom Pielgrzyma
- Campground
- 3 Maja
- Jasnogorska
- Theatre
- Jana Kilińskiego
- Al W Lenina
- H Dąbrowskiego
- Orbis Patria Hotel
- Al Najświętszej
- Church
- Art Gallery
- Local Museum
- Waszyngtona
- Orbis
- Marii Panny
- Tourist Office
- Z Modzelewskiego
- F Nowowiejskiego
- Al Tadeusza Kościuszki
- Al Wolności
- Railway Station
- Bus Station
- Gen K Świerczewskiego
- Soviet War Memorial
- Dom Mały
- Hotel 'Centralny'
- Katedralna
- Warszawska
- Krakowska
- Dom Wycieczkowe 'Turystyczny'
- Mikołaja Kopernika
- Stanisława Palczynskiego
- Jana Sobieskiego
- Pułaskiego
- Kazimierz
- Sw Kazimierza
- Sw Barbary
- Sw Augustyna
- Dom Rekolekcyjny

There are also three museums to visit within the monastery's defensive walls. You can't miss the **Arsenal**. The **600 Year Museum**, containing Lech Walesa's 1983 Nobel Prize, is just beyond. The **Treasury** *(Skarbiec)* is rather hidden. It's above and behind the two churches and you enter from an outside terrace.

Places to Stay

Due to the crowds of pilgrims accommodation is always tight. On weekends and religious holidays it's nearly hopeless. Czestochowa is within day trip range of Cracow. Otherwise visit while in transit from Warsaw to Cracow or Cracow to Opole. It only takes a few hours to see Jasna Gora.

Near the Train Station The old *Hotel 'Centralny'*, opposite the east exit from the railway station, is poor value at US$26 double (no singles). Reservations for the slightly cheaper *Dom Maly* (US$17.50 single, US$21 double), nearby at ulica Katedralna 18, are handled by the 'Centralny' reception. Unless you offer a backhander to the desk clerk it's unlikely there'll be room.

The Biuro Zakwaterowan, in an office right above Dom Maly's reception desk, arranges private rooms when they have any. The *Youth Hostel*, ulica Waclawy Marek 12, is inconvenient since it's located on the opposite side of town from the monastery. To get there follow ulica Krakowska south a km and keep watching on the right.

Near the Monastery The accommodation around Jasna Gora Monastery is better. *Dom Pielgrzyma*, the large building on the north side of the parking lot behind the monastery, has beds for pilgrims and wayfarers at US$5 (check-in from 3 to 8 pm, doors close at 10 pm). On the other side of the parking lot is a pleasant new campground (open June to September, US$3 per person) with a few bungalows (US$21 single, US$32 double). There's a snack bar. The *Dom Rekolekcyjny*, ulica sw Barbary 43 a couple of blocks south of Jasna Gora, also shelters pilgrims.

The *Dom Wycieczkowe 'Turystyczny,'* ulica Pulaskiego 4/6 on the top floor of a sports centre near Jasna Gora, is the same price as Dom Maly and reservations must also be made at the Hotel 'Centralny' reception (see above). The four-star *Orbis Patria Hotel*, also near Jasna Gora, is too expensive to consider (US$46 single, US$73 double), but you can be sure of a good meal in their restaurant or a drink at their bar.

Getting There & Away

There are direct trains to Czestochowa from Warsaw, Opole, Katowice and Cracow. Warsaw-bound trains from Budapest, Vienna and Prague stop here.

Silesia

Silesia (Slask) in south-western Poland is the industrial heart of the country. Although Silesia accounts for only 6% of Poland's area, it provides a fifth of its wealth, including half its steel and 90% of its coal (8% of the world supply). The Upper Silesian Basin around Katowice, source of both the Vistula and Odra rivers, is densely developed and populated. Lower Silesia stretches north-west along the Odra past Wroclaw. The Opole area between Katowice and Wroclaw is known as Green Silesia for its fertile fields.

Silesia was originally inhabited by Slavic tribes, the largest of which, the Slenzanie, gave their name to the region. Medieval Silesia was autonomous under Piast princes. In the 14th century Silesia was annexed to Bohemia and from 1526-1742 it was under the Hapsburgs of Austria. Frederick the Great took Silesia for Prussia in 1742. Throughout the German period the large Polish minority was subjected to 'Germanisation.' After WW I there were unsuccessful Polish nationalist uprisings but Silesia remained part of Germany until 1945. That year the German population was expelled and Silesia became Polish after a lapse of six centuries.

While tourists may not be attracted to the industrial wonders of Katowice and vicinity, Wroclaw is a lovely historic city with an intense cultural life. Opole and Brzeg are convenient stops off the beaten track, while the Sudeten Mountains west of Klodzko (the 'Gory Stolowe') and south of Jelenia Gora (Karkonoski Park Narodowy) lure hikers.

OPOLE

Opole (Oppeln), a pleasant small town on the Odra River, gets so few tourists you'll be an object of curiosity if you stop there. It's a good place to wander around without being distracted by too many sights. The location midway between Cracow, Czestochowa and Wroclaw couldn't be

better. The town's only real claim to fame is the Festival of Polish Song, held in the Open-air Theatre on Pasieka Island in June.

Orientation

The main railway station (Opole Glowne) and bus station are adjacent on the south side of town. March straight up ulica Krakowska to Rynek, the central square. A few trains stop at Opole Wschodnie Station, just north-east of town along ulica Oleska.

Information

The tourist information office is at ulica Krakowska 15/17 near the centre of town. Orbis, ulica Krakowska 31, reserves couchettes. Almatur is at Plac Armii Czerwonej 1.

Things to See

The Italianate **town hall** (1936) in the

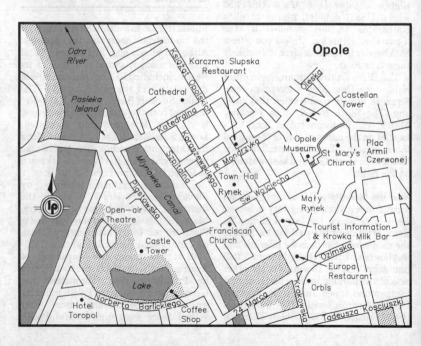

centre of Rynek is surrounded by rebuilt 18th century burgher houses. From the east corner of the square follow ulica sw Wojciecha two blocks to the **Opole Museum** (closed Monday) with a pictorial collection of local interest. **St Mary's Church** is just above. Retrace your steps to the south corner of Rynek and the 14th century **Franciscan Church**. The tombs of the Opole Piasts are in a chapel to one side. Opole **Cathedral** is north-west of Rynek.

Follow ulica Katedralna west to the Mlynowka Canal and cross the bridge to Pasieka Island. A little south is a small lake in a very pleasant park with a good coffee shop to one side. The single **tower** overlooking the park is all that remains of the 14th century Piast castle. There's considerable river traffic on the **Odra River**, mostly coal barges. You see it all on a stroll down the west side of Pasieka Island to the pedestrian bridge at the island's south end. Opole's **zoo** is in the large park over the bridge.

Places to Stay

The *Opole Hotel* in front of the railway station is expensive at US$26 single, US$39 double and up. Better value is the *Hotel Toropol* (tel 366-91), upstairs in the sports centre at ulica Norberta Barlickiego 13 on Pasieka Island. It's just beyond the artificial lake, a seven-minute walk from downtown – US$10 per person. The people in the travel agency below the hotel are helpful.

There are two places to stay south of Opole Glowne Station, across the bridge over the railway tracks. The youth hostel is in the large apartment building at ulica Struga 16, right at the end of the bridge (open July and August only). *Hotel 'Sportowy,'* ulica Kowalska 2, is behind the large athletic centre a couple of blocks farther south. Opole is without camping facilities.

Places to Eat

The *Krowka Milk Bar*, ulica Krakowska 13 a block from the main square, is cheap. Two better restaurants near the centre are the *Karczma Slupska*, ulica Ksiazat Opolskich 6, and the *Europa*, across the street from the Orbis office.

Getting There & Away

Opole is on the main railway line from Przemysl to Szczecin via Cracow, Katowice, Brzeg, Wroclaw and Poznan. There are also direct trains from Czestochowa, Nysa and Rzepin.

BRZEG

Brzeg on the Odra River can be seen as a stopover between Opole and Wroclaw. Brzeg 'castle' is on the opposite side of town from the station, so take a taxi. It's a magnificent Renaissance **palace** (1560) with a fine sculptured portal and courtyard, now a museum. Right in front of the palace is an imposing Baroque **Jesuit church**.

On your way back to the station visit 13th century **St Nicholas Church**, a towering red-brick Gothic edifice, and the Renaissance **town hall**, both in the middle of town. Get something to eat in the milk bar at 41 Armii Czerwonej. Brzeg has only one hotel, the *Piast* at ulica Piastowska 14.

WROCLAW

Wroclaw, historic capital of Lower Silesia, was German Breslau until 1945. After the war the Germans were deported to Germany and the city resettled by Poles from Lvov in the Ukraine. Today it's greatly underrated by tourists for this enjoyable big city by the Odra has everything a visitor could ask for: first class museums, historic buildings, concert halls, theatres, parks and over 120 canals, plus a picturesque central square and a memorable cluster of churches by the river.

Wroclaw is a lively cultural centre with music and drama second to none. It's also a students' city and the clubs are packed if anything's happening. In addition it's all conveniently located so you can do most of

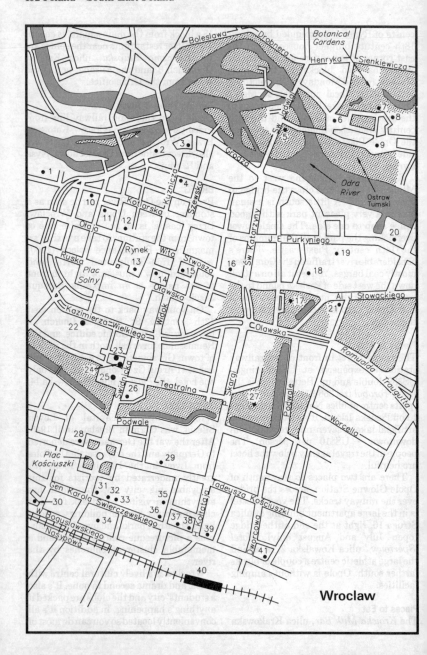

Wroclaw

1	Arsenal
2	Collegium Maximum
3	Jesuit Church
4	Kalambur Theatre
5	Church of the Virgin Mary on the Sands
6	Church of the Holy Cross
7	Botanical Gardens
8	Archdiocesan Museum
9	Cathedral
10	Rura Jazz Club
11	St Elizabeth's Church
12	Bookstore
13	Ratusz (Town Hall)
14	Feniks Department Store
15	Church of St Mary Magdalene
16	Art Gallery
17	Orbis Panorama Hotel
18	Museum of Architecture
19	Panorama Raclawicka
20	National Museum
21	Post Office
22	Archaeological Museum
23	St Dorothy's Church
24	Monopol Hotel
25	Opera House
26	Corpus Christi Church
27	Bastion
28	KDM Resraurant
29	Palacyk Student Club
30	Polski Theatre
31	Orbis
32	Tempo Cafeteria
33	Hotel Polonia
34	Operetka Theatre
35	Odra Hotel
36	Wzorcowy Milk Bar
37	Europejski Hotel
38	Tourist Office
39	Grand Hotel
40	Railway Station
41	Bus Station

your sightseeing on foot. Accommodation is plentiful in every category, transport easy and even the shopping is good. It's just the place to begin a Polish sojourn and could end up being that favourite city you return to just before you leave.

Orientation

Wroclaw Glowny Railway Station is the most convenient in Poland for location and the excellent facilities. Most of the hotels are nearby. To walk to Rynek, the old market square, turn left on ulica Swierczewskiego and walk three blocks to ulica Swidnicka. Turn right and continue straight into town.

Information

The 'Odra' tourist information office, ulica Swierczewskiego 98, is below Hotel Piast diagonally opposite the railway station. Orbis, ulica Swierczewskiego 62, is where you go to buy international train tickets, reserve couchettes, etc. Almatur, ulica Kosciuszki 34, will know about International Student Hotels in summer.

Things to See

The Old Town As you walk along ulica Swidnicka into town you'll pass **Corpus Christi Church** on the right and the neo-classical **Opera House** on the left. Next to the Monopol Hotel is **St Dorothy's Church.** When you reach the pedestrian underpass turn left a block to the Ethnographic and Archaeological **museums** (both closed Monday). They have separate entrances but are in the same complex at ulica Kazimierza Wielkiego 34.

Continue west again in the same direction and turn right across the street first chance you get, then straight around into Plac Solny which spills into Rynek, the medieval market place with its Renaissance and Baroque burgher houses. Wroclaw's Gothic **Ratusz** (town hall) is one of the most intricate in Poland and now contains a museum (closed Monday and Tuesday) in the arched interior. At the north-west corner of Rynek is **St Elizabeth's Church.** The two small houses on the corner connected by a gate are known as Hansel and Gretel.

Walk east from this church along the north side of Rynek and continue due east on ulica Wita Stwosza with a digression to visit the **Church of St Mary Magdalene** on the right. Note the Romanesque portal on the far side of the church.

Museums & Churches Keep straight on ulica Wita Stwosza till you reach the Orbis Panorama Hotel. The **Museum of Architecture** (closed Monday) is in the 15th century convent across the street from the hotel. Around behind this museum (ask directions) is the **Panorama Raclawicka**, a huge 360° painting of a battle in 1794 in which the national hero, Tadeusz Kosciuszko, led the Poles against Russian forces intent on partitioning Poland. Ask for headphones with an English translation of the commentary. You may have difficulty getting tickets as visitors are only admitted in groups every 20 minutes. If you can't get in right away buy a ticket for a later showing.

Just east beside the park is the **National Museum** (closed Monday) with a large collection of masterpieces of medieval Silesian art. Cross the bridge over the Odra beside the museum, taking a glance upstream at the **Most Grunwaldzki** (1910), the most graceful of Wroclaw's 85 bridges.

On the north side of the river turn left when the streetcar tracks bend right and walk west into Ostrow Tumski, an old quarter inhabited since the 9th Century. The chapels at the rear of the Gothic **Cathedral of St John the Baptist** deserve special attention. The **Archdiocesan Museum** (closed Monday) is at ulica Kanonia 12 between the cathedral and the **Botanical Gardens**. West again from the cathedral is the two-storey Gothic **Church of the Holy Cross**. Keep straight and cross the small bridge to the 14th century **Church of the Virgin Mary on the Sands** which has a stunning Gothic interior.

Southbound now, follow the streetcar tracks across another small bridge then turn right and follow the riverbank. A block or two down you'll reach a large **Jesuit Church** (1755) with the **Collegium Maximum** (1741) just beyond. Inside this ornate Baroque building is the magnificent Aula Leopoldina, now used for formal university functions. After completing the above tour it may surprise you to hear that Wroclaw was 70% destroyed during the war. This marvellous reconstruction success is something to be shared by us all.

Parks & Zoo Take a taxi or trams No 2, 4, 10, or 12 east to Wroclaw's enjoyable **zoo**. In summer **excursion boats** operate on a branch of the Odra several times a day from the landing beside the zoo. Across the street from the zoo is a famous early work of modern architecture, **Centenary Hall** (1913) by Max Berg. Try to get inside to appreciate this great enclosed space (tip the watchman). The steel needle beside the hall was the symbol of the 1948 Exhibition of the Regained Territories. In the park beyond is an attractive **Japanese garden**, among other things.

Places to Stay

Camping & Hostels Wroclaw's best campground is near the Olympic Stadium north of the zoo on the east side of the city (trams No 9, 16, 17 and 32 pass the entrance). English and German are spoken. Camping space is US$1 per person and there's a row of simple, clean bungalows which go for US$8.50 single or double, US$12 triple. From 15 May to 30 September foreigners wishing to pitch a tent are *never* turned away.

Less inviting is *Camping 'Sleza,'* ulica Na Grobli 16/18 east of downtown and not too convenient to anything. They charge US$2 single, US$3 double to camp (own tent) and also have bungalows at US$6.50 per person, but they're usually full although they are available year round.

Just a few hundred metres further along at ulica Na Grobli 30/32 is Wroclaw's *Youth Hostel* in what looks like a converted warehouse.

Cheaper Hotels A whole row of relatively inexpensive hotels line ulica Swierczew-skiego, to the left as you come out of the railway station. The *Grand Hotel*, ulica Swierczewskiego 102 right across from the station, is US$21 single, US$30 double

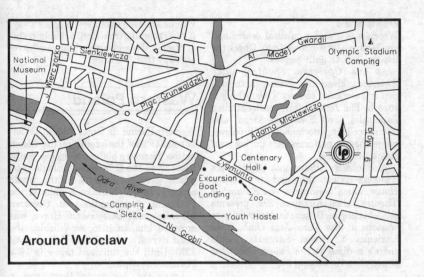

Around Wroclaw

without bath. *Hotel Piast*, just west on the next corner, is cheaper but often occupied by groups.

At US$25 single or US$36 double for a room with bath the *Hotel Europejski*, ulica Swierczewskiego 94/96, is overpriced. Better value is the friendly *Odra Hotel* around the corner at ulica Stawowa 13 (US$17 single with bath). *Hotel Polonia*, ulica Swierczewskiego 66, is priced about the same as the Grand.

Expensive Hotels Of the four Orbis hotels the charming *Monopol Hotel* (erected in 1890) beside the Opera is the most colourful (from US$40 single, US$55 double), although the ultramodern *Panorama Hotel* is also convenient. Avoid the *Orbis-Novotel* and the *Orbis-Wroclaw*, both way off in the southern suburbs.

Places to Eat
Near the Train Station The *Wzorcowy Milk Bar*, ulica Swierczewskiego 86 a block from the station, is cheap. The tiny *pizzeria* at ulica Swierczewskiego 81 serves good inexpensive chunks of pizza.

Tempo Cafeteria, ulica Swierczewskiego 64, is large and stays open till 9 pm. Full meals or just coffee and pudding are available here. The *KDM Restaurant* on Plac Kosciuszki is more exclusive.

There's a wicked little bar downstairs in the *Odra Hotel* specialising in hot sausages and vodka straight, to the accompaniment of breaking glass and shouts from the proprietress. It closes at 9 pm.

In the Old Town *Bar Ratuszowy*, Rynek Ratusz 27a corner of Sukiennice behind the old town hall, has a cheap little cafeteria upstairs. The *Ratuszowa Restaurant* in the basement of the old town hall has no beer and the menu is only in Polish, but there's atmosphere. They close at 7 pm. Try the *golonka* soup!

Winiarnia Bachus, Rynek 16, is a wine cellar open in the evening (cover charge). If you want to be sure of a good meal try the restaurant or coffee shop in the *Panorama Hotel*.

Entertainment

Wroclaw is a major cultural centre and you'll have a lot to choose from. Check the listings in both daily papers.

At the *Operetka Theatre*, ulica Swierczewskiego 67, actors, actresses, costumes, music, scenery – everything is superb. The *Teatr Polski*, nearby at ulica Zapolskiej 3 off Swierczewskiego, also offers excellent performances. If Wroclaw's *mime theatre* performs here during your stay don't miss it.

Also check *Filharmonia Hall*, ulica Swierczewskiego 17, and the *Opera House*, ulica Swidnicka 35. *Kalambur Theatre*, ulica Kuznicza 29a, presents student theatre. Be sure to attend any jam sessions at the *Rura Jazz Club*, ulica Lazienna 4. Great! Saturday nights there's a disco at the *Palacyk Student Club*, ulica Kosciuszki 34.

Things to Buy

Wroclaw's shopping is concentrated around Plac Kosciuszki and along ulica Swidnicka to Rynek. The best department store is Feniks, Rynek 31/32 opposite the old town hall. Be sure to have a look around. There's an excellent Russian bookstore at Rynek 14, many of the books are in English or German. Other foreign books including East German art books are available from the bookstore at Rynek 59.

Getting There & Away

Mainlines from Szczecin to Przemysl (via Poznan and Cracow) and Warsaw to Jelenia Gora (via Lodz) cross at Wroclaw. Other direct trains come from Gdynia/Gdansk (via Poznan). There's service from Poznan and Katowice every couple of hours.

Several trains a day arrive from Frankfurt am Main and Hannover/Cologne in West Germany (via Dresden and Leipzig). Both daily trains from Prague arrive in the middle of the night. The one which leaves Prague at 11 pm carries sleeping cars only but does not run from December to March. Dresden and Prague are each about seven hours away. If you're coming from Berlin change trains at Rzepin. Poland couldn't have a better gateway than Wroclaw.

Western Poland

Western Poland or Great Poland (Wielkopolska) was the cradle of the Polish nation. Here on a plateau along the Warta River lived the Polanians, a Slavic tribe which gave their name to the whole country. In 966 Mieszko I, duke of the Polanians, was baptised at Gniezno. Mieszko's son, Boleslav the Brave, was crowned king in 1025, establishing the Piast dynasty which ruled Poland until 1370. Until the shift to Cracow in 1039 Poznan was capital.

From the beginning there was a constant threat from the Germans. Western Poland was annexed to Prussia in 1793. After Bismarck set up the German Empire in 1871 Germanisation and German colonisation became intense. Returned to Poland in 1918, the area was seized by the Nazis in 1939 and devastated during the liberation battles of 1945.

Today the rebuilt regional capital Poznan is a great industrial, commercial and historical city, well worth a stop on the way to or from Berlin. Szczecin is the western gateway to the Baltic coast, while Swinoujscie is the terminus of ferries from West Germany, Denmark and Sweden.

POZNAN

Poznan (Posen), on the main east-west trade route halfway between Berlin and Warsaw, has long been a focal point of Polish history. A fortified castle stood on Ostrow Tumski (Cathedral Island) in the 9th century and from 968 to 1039 Poznan was capital of Poland. In 1253 Stare Miasto (Old Town) was founded on the left bank of the Warta River and it continued to play a major role in the life of the country.

A 1956 strike for higher wages by workers at the huge Cegielski Engineering Works was one of the first of its kind in Poland. Today Poznan is the site of Poland's largest international trade fairs, although the good restaurants, historic places and varied museums draw visitors year round.

Orientation

Poznan Glowny Railway Station is a 20-minute walk from the centre of the city. From the main exit between platforms one and four walk north to the second street, ulica Czerwonej Armii, which you follow east. Turn left with the streetcar tracks at Aleje Marcinkowskiego, then right at the Bazar Hotel and straight ahead to Stary Rynek, the old town square.

Information

The tourist office at Stary Rynek 77 is extremely helpful and sells maps. Book international train tickets and couchettes at Orbis, ulica Czerwonej Armii 33. Almatur, ulica Aleksandra Fredry 7 behind the Palace of Culture, will have information on International Student Hotels (open July and August). Many other student-oriented offices are in the same building. The US Consulate is at ulica Chopina 4.

Things to See

Museums There are half a dozen museums in the historic buildings on or near Stary Rynek. Begin with the one in the Renaissance **old town hall** (closed Saturday) which envelops you in Poznan's medieval past. The coffered ceiling in the vestibule dates from 1555. Daily at 12 noon a bugle sounds and butting heraldic goats appear above the clock on the town hall facade opposite Proserpina's fountain. The **Musical Instruments Museum** (closed Monday), Stary Rynek 45, is one of the best of its kind in Europe.

Nearby at the south-east corner of the square is the **Archaeological Museum** in a 16th century Renaissance palace. Make a side trip to the end of ulica Swietoslawska from beside this museum to visit the Baroque **parish church**, originally a Jesuit church. There's a peculiar **Military Museum** (closed Monday) full of little lead soldiers in one of the modern buildings in the very centre of Stary Rynek itself. Notice the art gallery opposite. There are two more museums, one political (Stary Rynek 3) and the other literary (Stary Rynek 84), on the west side of the square near the tourist office.

Go up ulica Franciszkanska near the tourist office to the beautiful 17th century **Franciscan Church**. In the Castle of Przemysl on the hill opposite is the **Decorative Arts Museum** (closed Monday and Tuesday). Go around the church and west on ulica Paderewskiego to the *Bazar Hotel*. The **National Museum** (closed Monday) with Poland's best collection of Dutch and Spanish paintings, is in the large building across the street on the hotel's north side. By now your head will be spinning, so adjourn to the cafe or restaurant in the hotel for refreshments.

Other Sights The historic centre of Poznan has a lot more to offer than just museums, things you'll be able to discover for yourself without a guidebook. However a few sights just outside the centre should be brought to your attention. Walk north from the Bazar Hotel to the end of Aleje Marcinkowskiego, then turn right, then left on the first street. You'll pass two old churches before reaching the striking **Polish war memorial**. Pass it and continue north on Aleje Stalingradzka to the **Citadel**. There's much to see here, including a couple of war museums (closed Monday) and monuments to the Soviet liberators. The **Commonwealth War Cemetery** here is a moving sight for English-speaking visitors.

Poznan's towering red brick Gothic **cathedral** is at Ostrow Tumski on the east

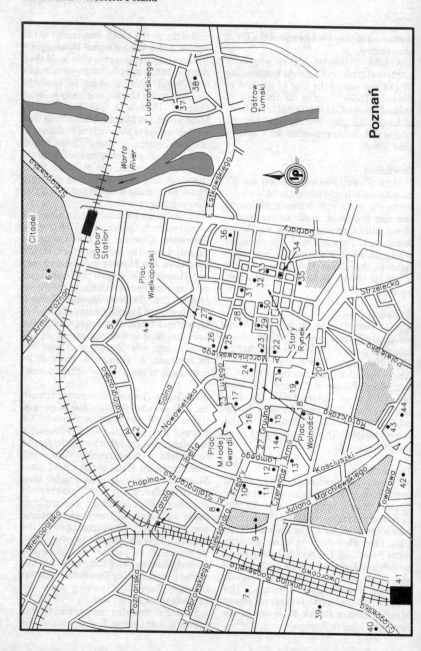

Poznań

1	Krekucha Restaurant
2	Stalingradzka Youth Hostel
3	Orbis Polonez Hotel
4	Carmelite Church
5	Polish War Memorial
6	Commonwealth War Cemetery
7	Orbis Mercury Hotel
8	Opera House
9	Solidarity Monument
10	Almatur
11	Palace of Culture
12	Lech Hotel
13	Wielkopolska Hotel
14	Moulin Rouge Night Club
15	Smakosz Restaurant
16	Polski Theatre 'Narod Sobie'
17	Pod Arkadami Milk Bar
18	Orbis (train tickets)
19	Przyneta Restaurant
20	St Martin's Church
21	Poznanski Hotel
22	Orbis Bazar Hotel
23	National Museum
24	As Cafeteria
25	Post Office
26	Astoria Restaurant
27	Vegetable Market
28	Decorative Arts Museum
29	Franciscan Church
30	Tourist Office
31	Dom Turysty PTTK
32	Old Town Hall
33	Musical Instruments Museum
34	Archaeological Museum
35	Parish Church
36	Dominican Church
37	Archdiocesan Museum
38	Cathedral
39	International Fairgrounds
40	Biuro Zakwaterowania
41	Poznan Glowny Railway Station
42	Bus Station
43	Musical Theatre
44	Orbis Poznan Hotel

side of the Warta River. Any eastbound streetcar from the north side of town will take you there. Pay US$0.15 to light up the Byzantine-style Golden Chapel (1841), mausoleum of Mieszko I and Boleslav the Brave, behind the main altar. The **Archdiocesan Museum** (open

daily) at the north end of ulica Lubranskiego near the cathedral is surprisingly rich.

Poznan's most compelling sight is a large bronze monument in the park beside the Palace of Culture, which you'll probably have seen on your way in from the railway station. The two huge crosses bound together symbolise the struggle of Polish workers for 'bread and freedom' and the dates recall events which led to the 'Solidarity' trade union: 1956 (Poznan), 1970 (Gdansk), 1976 (Radom), 1980 (Gdansk). The very existence of this monument illustrates vividly what an amazing country Poland is!

Kornik & Rogalin

Each of these small towns 20 km south of Poznan boasts a large magnate palace in expansive parks. The two are similar so unless you've got plenty of time one might be representative of the other (both closed Monday). The 19th century English-style country manor at **Kornik** is the easiest to reach with frequent bus service from Poznan. Buses between Kornik and Rogalin are only a couple of times a day, but maybe you'll be lucky!

There's a bus from Rogalin directly back to Poznan every couple of hours. If you do get to **Rogalin** don't miss the small art gallery hidden behind the 18th century Rococo palace. Its collection of 19th century German and Polish paintings is quite good. Some of the oak trees in the surrounding park are almost nine metres around and 1000 years old.

Places to Stay

Hostels Of Poznan's four *Youth Hostels* the closest to Poznan Glowny Railway Station is at ulica Berwinskiego 2/3 (tel 63680), the tall yellow building opposite Kasprzaka Park. To get there leave the station by the west exit and go left along ulica Glogowska till you come to the park (five minutes).

Closer to the old town but a 20-minute walk from the train station is the *Youth Hostel* at Aleje Stalingradzka 32/40 (tel

56706). If your train happens to stop at Poznan Garbary Railway Station it's closer. The hostel is hidden down a corridor up on the top floor of this huge institutional building.

Poznan has two more hostels which you could try in a pinch. The *Youth Hostel* (tel 321-412) at ulica Jesionowa 127 is near Poznan Debiec Railway Station, south of the city. Like the Stalingradzka facility it's in a large concrete school building.

The *Youth Hostel* at ulica Gluszyna 127 is 10 km south-east of Poznan but it's smaller, with a friendly management. There's no phone so you'll just have to take a chance going out there: take bus No 58 from Poznan Staroleka Railway Station (accessible by local train or tram).

All four youth hostels are supposed to be open year round, but seldom are. Considering how expensive the hotels are you might be wise to make the rounds by taxi (after 5 pm when they're open) until you find a bed.

Camping *Poznan-Strzeszynek Camping*, ulica Koszalinska 15, is on the far north-west edge of Poznan (bus No 106). It's open June to September. *Dom Turysty PTTK*, Stary Rynek 91, has beds in eight-bed dormitories for US$7 per person.

Cheaper Hotels & Private Rooms The *Lech* and *Wielkopolska* hotels on ulica Czerwonej Armii between the railway station and town are outrageously overpriced at US$28 single, US$50 double with bath. Only marginally better is the *Poznanski Hotel*, Aleje Marcinkowskiego 22, at US$32 single, US$39 double for the cheapest room (including breakfast).

Far better value than any of these is the historic *Orbis Bazar Hotel*, Aleje Marcinkowskiego 10 opposite the Poznanski, just off Plac Wolnosci. The Bazar (opened 1842) was a centre of Polish nationalism during the late 19th and early 20th centuries, as a display in the lobby proclaims. Simple clean rooms with wash

basin but shared bath begin at US$25 single, US$32 double.

The Biuro Zakwaterowania, ulica Glogowska 16 at the end of the long white building across from the west exit from the railway station, is supposed to arrange accommodation in private homes but they're unreliable and may just tell you to go to a hotel.

Expensive Hotels There are a number of high-rise luxury hotels in Poznan. They all have about the same to offer, so choose by location alone. The *Orbis Mercury* is closest to the international fairgrounds and railway station, while the *Orbis Polonez* is quieter, cheaper and nearer the sightseeing attractions. The *Orbis Poznan* is in a poor location near the bus station, while the *Orbis Novotel* is out on the highway east of Poznan and convenient to nothing but your car. During the main trade fair in early June all accommodation will be fully booked.

Places to Eat
Old Town The *U Dylla Restaurant*, Stary Rynek 37 in front of the old town hall, is the best place to eat on Market Square. The *Ratuszowa Wine Cellar*, Stary Rynek 55, is for real: you go down into the cellar to get wine.

West of the Old Town There are many good places to eat in the streets and squares west of the old town, beginning with the *Bazar Hotel* which boasts one of the best hotel restaurants in Poland. Try the Polish dishes like boiled knuckle, tripe, *kolduny* (meat turnovers) and veal *zraziki* (scallops). Hopefully they'll have some Czech beer left. The atmosphere is great!

Just two blocks west of here is the *Smakosz Restaurant*, ulica 27 Grudnia 9, which is open till 10 pm and serves good food. The *Mewa Milk Bar*, Plac Wolnosci 1 below Hotel Poznanski, is good for breakfast. *As Cafeteria*, Plac Wolnosci 18 beside Raczynskich Library, serves meals and there's a beer garden attached which sometimes has that good Poznanski Pils.

The *Astoria Restaurant*, ulica 23 Lutego 29 opposite the main post office, is a good local restaurant with table service. The *Pod Arkadami Milk Bar*, Plac Mlodej Gwardi 10, is great for a snack.

The *Przyneta Restaurant*, ulica Czerwonej Armii 34, specialises in fish dishes (with syrupy warm Czarna Perla beer to wash it all down), while the *Dieletyczna Restaurant* next door is cheaper but also good. The *Gwarny Milk Bar*, ulica Lampego 10 up the street beside the Lech Hotel, is even cheaper.

The *Krekucha Restaurant*, ulica Karola Libelta 37 north of the Opera House, specialises in game dishes such as wild duck or venison and is open till 10 pm.

A Splurge If you're looking for a place to take that special someone choose the *Plrucku Reotaurant* in Solacki Park just west of the city (tram No 9 from in front of the Bazar Hotel). They're open till 9 pm or later and there's sometimes live music. It's not cheap, but there's a terrace overlooking the lake where you could while away an afternoon or evening.

Entertainment

Poznan doesn't excel in theatre and music but try the *Polski Theatre 'Narod Sobie,'* ulica 27 Grudnia, which sometimes has good programmes. There's also the *Opera House* at ulica Aleksandra Fredry 9 in the park behind the 'Solidarity' monument. Check for performances by the Poznan Boys' & Mens' Philharmonic Choir.

The *Moulin Rouge Night Club*, ulica Kantaka 8/9, offers more basic entertainment in the form of a midnight floor show which includes striptease! There's a cover charge and minimum consumption.

Things to Buy

On opposite sides of the street at the corner of Lampego and 27 Grudnia near the Lech Hotel are an excellent bookstore

(maps on the top floor) and record shop. There's an Antykwariat (second hand) bookstore at Stary Rynek 54. Keep in mind that books printed before 1945 cannot be exported from Poland. Visit the large flower and vegetable market in Plac Wielkopolski in the old town.

Getting There & Away

Direct trains arrive at Poznan from Paris, Hoek van Holland, Copenhagen, Berlin Zoo, Szczecin, Gdynia/Gdansk, Olsztyn, Elk, Torun, Warsaw, Moscow, Kiev, Cracow and Wroclaw. As you see, it's quite a crossroads! If you're arriving in Poland from Western Europe via Berlin, stop here instead of going straight through to Warsaw!

GNIEZNO

In the year 1000 Boleslav the Brave and the German emperor Otto III had an historic meeting at Gniezno. Today there are two things to draw you to this small town 50 km east of Poznan. The **Museum of the Origin of the Polish State** (10 am to 5 pm daily except Mondays) by Jelonek Lake on the west side of town is actually a unique multimedia presentation of the early history of Poland. Unless you want to see the programme in Polish drop by the museum soon after you arrive in Gniezno and book an English showing. Then visit the 14th century Gothic **cathedral** in the centre of town. The life story of St Adalbert appears on the cathedral's famous Romanesque bronze doors (1170), inside below the tower. The silver sarcophagus of this saint is on the cathedral's main altar.

Places to Stay & Eat

If you'd like to spend the night in Gniezno the *Hotel Centralny*, ulica Chrobrego 32 beside the theatre, is US$18 single, US$29 double. Otherwise it's the *Youth Hostel* at ulica Pocztowa 11. Both these are near the adjacent bus and train stations.

The *'Mokka' Cafe*, ulica Chrobrego 7

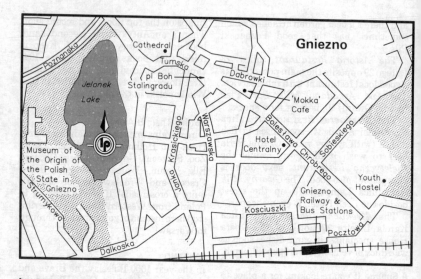

between stations and cathedral, is good for a morning snack.

SZCZECIN

Szczecin (Stettin), one-time capital of West Pomerania, was captured by the Swedes in 1630. They sold it to Prussia in 1720 and until 1945 it was part of Germany. After the first partition of Poland in 1772 this town near the mouth of the Odra River became the main port of Berlin. Destroyed in WW II, Szczecin wasn't rebuilt as carefully as were Gdansk, Warsaw, Poznan and Wroclaw.

Today this thoroughly Polish city near the GDR border is more of a gateway to Poland or the Baltic coast than a destination in itself. There are ferries to and from Scandinavia from nearby Swinoujscie, a daily train to and from East Berlin, and good railway connections to the rest of Poland. Half a day is enough to see the scattered red brick remnants of Gothic and neo-Gothic Szczecin.

Orientation

You'll probably arrive at Szczecin Glowny Railway Station near the river on the south edge of downtown. The bus station is just north. From it follow the streetcar tracks north-west to the Harbour Gate at the east end of Plac Zwyciestwa, a five-minute walk.

Information

The Pomerania Biuro Turystyki (tourist office), Aleje Jednosci Narodowej 50, is of little help. Orbis on Plac Zwyciestwa sells international train tickets and books couchettes. For information on ferries to West Germany, Denmark and Sweden go to Polferries, ulica Wielka 28.

Things to See

In 1725 the Prussians erected the **Harbour Gate** (off Plac Zwyciestwa) to mark the purchase of this area from the Swedes for two million thalers. Today the gate houses a shop with a good selection of Polish handicrafts. The old city was between here and the river. Walk north on Aleje Niepodleglosci two blocks and turn right onto Plac Zolnierza Polskiego to the **National Museum** (closed Monday). This museum and its annex across the street have a collection of paintings and artefacts of local interest.

Continue east toward the river to the 14th century **Castle of the Dukes of Pomerania**, a fine Renaissance building with a lookout tower you can climb, cafe, art gallery and theatre. Musical events are often held here during the day, so check early enough to have time to come back. The **City Museum** (closed Monday) in the 15th century town hall, near the Orbis Arkona Hotel between castle and river, has many interesting old maps and paintings. These show vividly how much of the old quarter around the now isolated old town hall was lost. On your way back into town you'll pass the late Gothic **St James Church** – impressive with its soaring interior, now fully restored.

Excursion Boats North-east along the riverside from here, beyond the ugly concrete overpass, is **Dworzec Morski**, a landing for harbour tour boats (last departure at 1 pm, US$3) and hydrofoils to Swinoujscie (US$4 one way), operating from April to November. The commuter ferry to Plaza Mielenska, a nearby beach, also allows a fair glimpse of the harbour.

On Waly Chrobrego, the high embankment above Dworzec Morski, stand monumental buildings erected just after WW I. The middle one at the top of the stairs is a museum and theatre. There's an excellent view of the river and port from here.

Places to Stay

Hostels The *Youth Hostel*, ulica Unislawy 26, is up Aleje Wyzwolenia north of the centre, on the top floor of a large school just off Plac J Kilinskiego (trams No 2 and 3). Look for the green triangles over the door and go up to the top of the stairs (registration 5 to 8 pm only). In July and August there's a summer *Youth Hostel* at ulica Grodzka 22 in the old town.

Camping The *PTTK Camping* (tel 613-264) at Dabie, a few km east of Szczecin, is easily accessible on public transport. Take tram No 2, 7 or 8 to the end of the line, then bus No 56, 62 or 72 till you see the sign on the left. Szczecin Dabie Railway Station is closer to the campground than the main station. Camping (own tent) is US$2 per person or rent a bungalow for US$13 single or double, US$15 triple. It's open May till September and English is spoken.

Hotels Closest to the stations is the *Dom Turysty PTTK*, Plac S Batorego 2, which charges US$18 single, US$25 double for a plain room without sink or toilet. It's often crowded with noisy adolescents. The *Pomorski* and *Piast* hotels on bustling Plac Zwyciestwa are around US$21 single, US$27 double. Of the two the Piast may be preferable.

Similarly priced but more pleasant than any of these is the *Gryf Hotel*, Aleje Wojska Polskiego 49. The additional distance from the stations is compensated for by breakfast and private bath included in the price of the attractively decorated rooms.

Places to Eat

Milk Bar Extra, Aleje Niepodleglosci 5 diagonally opposite the main post office, serves cheap cafeteria-style meals (closed Sundays). The *Balaton Restaurant* on Plac Lotnikow offers Hungarian food. The *Chief Restaurant* on Plac Grunwaldzki is excellent, you can have Baltic *shashlik*, a shish kebab of fish and meat served with rice and fried mushrooms.

Getting There & Away

A main line runs from Szczecin to Przemysl in south-eastern Poland via Poznan, Wroclaw, Opole and Cracow. Other trains to Wroclaw go via Rzepin. Trains from Warsaw arrive via Poznan. One through train a day calls at Szczecin between Gdynia and Berlin-Lichtenberg. Local service from Gdynia or Poznan to Szczecin is frequent. Local trains operate between Swinoujscie and Szczecin Glowny

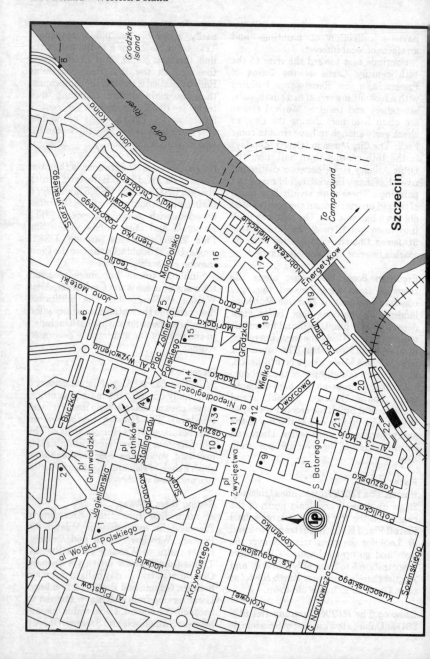

Szczecin

1	Gryf Hotel
2	Chief Restaurant
3	Balaton Restaurant
4	Pomeraina Biuro Turystyki
5	Gate of Prussian Homage
6	Orbis Neptun Hotel
7	Museum
8	Dworzec Morski Hydrofoil Landing
9	Piast Hotel
10	Orbis
11	Pomorski Hotel
12	Harbour Gate
13	Post Office
14	Milk Bar Extra
15	National Museum
16	Castle of the Dukes of Pomerania
17	City Museum
18	St James' Church
19	St John's Church
20	Bus Station
21	Dom Turysty PTTK
22	Szczecin Glowny Railway Station

via Szczecin Dabie. Couchettes are available from Szczecin to Gdynia, Warsaw, Wroclaw, Cracow and Przemysl.

SWINOUJSCIE

This fishing port at the mouth of the Swina River, is a popular Baltic beach resort. Walk west along the broad beach to the East German border. Large car ferries arrive here from Travemunde (West Germany), Copenhagen (Denmark) and Ystad (Sweden). The train and bus stations and international ferry terminal are on the east side of the river. A car ferry (free for pedestrians) crosses frequently to the town and campground (ulica Slowackiego 5) on the west bank, where the hydrofoil from Szczecin (64 km) calls.

Northern Poland

Baltic beach resorts such as Kolobrzeg, Ustka, Leba, Hel and Krynica Morska combine with historic cities like Gdansk and Torun, museum towns like Malbork, Frombork and Lidzbark Warminski, and the picturesque lake districts around Olsztyn, Gizycko and Suwalki to make northern Poland one of the most attractive and varied touring regions in the country.

Two areas of special interest to naturalists are the Mazurian Lakes (described below) and Slovincian National Park, west of Leba. Here a shifting bar of white pine-covered sand dunes separates Lake Lebsko from the Baltic. Leba is only 94 km north-west of Gdynia by train or bus and there are three campgrounds in the town.

History

Northern Poland has been shaped by outside events. The area became a battleground between Poles and Germans in the year 1226, when the Teutonic Knights were invited here to help subdue the restive Prussian tribes. From their castles at Malbork (Marienburg) and Torun (Thorn) the knights defied the king of Poland until their defeat in the 15th century by combined Polish/Lithuanian forces. Although the Duchy of Prussia was a vassal of Poland in the 16th century, wars with Sweden and internal dissent weakened Poland's position in the 17th century.

In 1772 the first partition of Poland brought everything south to Torun under Prussian control (Torun itself wasn't annexed by Prussia until 1793). After the Congress of Vienna in 1815 Poland southeast of Torun came under Tsarist Russia, a situation that persisted until WW I. In 1919 the Treaty of Versailles granted Poland a narrow corridor to the sea, separating East Prussia from the rest of Germany. Since the Free City of Danzig (Gdansk) was populated mostly by Germans, the Polish government built Gdynia from scratch after 1922.

In 1939 Hitler's demand for a German-controlled road and rail route across Polish territory to East Prussia and the incorporation of Danzig into the Third Reich sparked WW II. In 1945 the German inhabitants were expelled from East Prussia. Poland got Olsztyn (Allenstein) and the lake district, while the Soviet Union took Kaliningrad (Konigsberg). Today there's no tourism to that corner of the Russian Federation, while northern Poland is open to view.

TORUN

Torun, halfway between Warsaw and Gdansk, was founded by the Teutonic Knights in 1233. Its position on the Vistula River at a crossing of trade routes made it an important member of the Hanseatic League. The wealth this brought is reflected in Torun's three towering Gothic churches. Two are near Rynek Staromiejski, the old town square in the merchant's quarter, while the third adjoins Rynek Nowomiejski, the new town square in the craftsmen's quarter. The ruins of the knight's castle can still be seen by the river between these two districts. Fortunately medieval Torun, enclosed in surviving sections of the city walls, was not seriously damaged in WW II. It offers a chance to step briefly back in history without a lot of other tourists on your heals. Torun is slightly off the beaten track.

Orientation

There are several railway stations in Torun. Although Torun Miasto is closer to the centre of town, most trains stop at Torun Glowny, the main station on the south side of the river. Catch a bus in front of the station and get off at the first stop across the bridge. Walk east from the stop and within minutes you'll be on Rynek Staromiejski, the old town square. The bus station is near the northern edge of town, an easy walk.

Information

Orbis is at ulica Zeglarska 31 on Rynek Staromiejski. Almatur, at ulica Gagarina

1	Ethnographical Museum
2	Ethnographic Park
3	Bus Station
4	Copernicus University
5	Municipal Theatre
6	Polonia Hotel
7	St Mary's Church
8	Pizzeria
9	Pod Arkadami Milk Bar
10	Old Town Hall
11	Orbis (train tickets)
12	Oriental Art Museum
13	Pod Golebiem Restaurant
14	Staromiejska Restaurant
15	Bar Express
16	Copernicus Museum
17	St John's Church
18	Pod Orlem Hotel
19	Archaeological Museum
20	Crooked Tower
21	Monastery Gate
22	Sailor's Gate
23	Bridge Gate
24	Youth Hostel
25	Castle Ruins
26	Excursion Boat Landing
27	St James' Church

21, is in the university district north-east of the centre.

Things to See

The Old Town A placard in front of the old town hall on Rynek Staromiejski lists the opening hours of Torun's six museums. Begin with the **historical museum** (closed Monday) in the old town hall itself. This 14th century building is one of the largest of its kind in the Baltic states. The statue of Copernicus beside the town hall was erected in 1853. Don't miss the nearby **oriental art museum** in 15th century Pod Gwiazda house at Rynek Staromiejski 35, featuring a hanging wooden staircase dated 1697. Just off the north-west corner of the square is 14th century **St Mary's Church**, a typical Gothic hall church with all naves of equal height.

Gothic **St John's Church**, on ulica Zeglarska south of Rynek Staromiejski, is

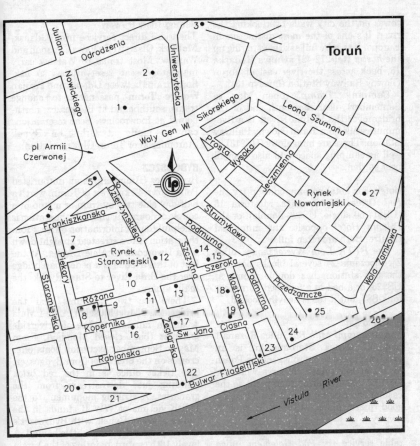

Toruń

remarkable for its soaring white interior and the richness of its altars. West at ulica Kopernika 17 from this church is the birthplace (in 1473) of astronomer **Nicolaus Copernicus**, now a museum dedicated to the man who moved the earth and stopped the sun (closed Monday). Copernicus stayed in Torun until his 17th birthday when he left to study in Cracow.

Go around the corner beyond the museum and walk straight down to the riverside. Here you'll see the medieval **walls and gates** which once defended Torun. Walk east along the river past the castle ruins. To reach the ruins turn left, then left again on ulica Przedzamcze. The **Castle of the Teutonic Knights** was destroyed in 1454 but its massive foundations are visible. Early 14th century **St James Church** is off Rynek Nowomiejski in the north-east section of the old town. The flying buttresses on this church are rare in Poland.

Places to Stay
Hostels & Camping Torun's *Youth Hostel*, ulica Podmurna 4, is in an ancient brick

tower on the city walls overlooking the river. It's one of the most distinctive in Europe! If they're full ask them to ring up the *hostel* (tel 272-42) at ulica Rudacka 15, back across the river east of Torun Glowny Railway Station (bus No 13).

Camping 'Tramp' (open May to September), near the south end of the bridge over the Vistula River, is a five-minute walk from Torun Glowny Railway Station. There are bungalows (US$13) as well as camping space and also a small beer garden.

Hotels For hotel accommodation try the *Pod Orlem Hotel*, ulica Mostowa 15 (US$17.50 single, US$26 double), or the *Polonia Hotel* opposite the municipal theatre. Both are often full.

The *PTTK Dom Wycieczkowy*, ulica Zjednoczenia 24 several blocks north of the bus station, has double rooms at US$26, or a bed in a four-bed dormitory for US$7, but it too is heavily booked.

Places to Eat
Pod Arkadami Milk Bar, ulica Rozana 1 just off Rynek Staromiejski, is an excellent place to sample genuine Polish dishes at low prices. Observe what the local people are eating then point so the cashier can ring up your order. There's a good pizza place at ulica Rozana 5 nearby.

For more sedate dining with proper table service try *Pod Golebiem*, ulica Szeroka 37. *Bar Express*, ulica Szeroka 24, is a self-service cafeteria where you pay for what you choose. The *Staromiejska Restaurant*, ulica Szczytna 2 around the corner from Express, is a popular full-service restaurant (beer!) open till 10 pm.

Entertainment
The *Municipal Theatre* is on Plac Armii Czerwonej at the north entrance to the old town. Every second Friday at 7 pm there's a concert in the old town hall. Check the local paper for events.

Getting There & Away
There are direct services from Gdansk, Malbork, Olsztyn (via Ilawa), Poznan and Warsaw. Most trains to Warsaw carry mandatory seat reservations, so ask. Some trains between Gdansk and Poznan require Torun passengers to change trains, southbound at Bydgoszcz, northbound at Inowroclaw. Seat reservations can be made at Orbis on Rynek Staromiejski or Torun Glowny station.

BYDGOSZCZ

Bydgoszcz (Bromberg) is an untouristed Polish town 47 km west of Torun, worth a half-day side trip by train or a stop of a couple of hours. Just outside the station is a helpful tourist information office. From the station take a streetcar straight down ulica Dworcowa to Aleje 1 Maja. At the foot of this avenue is a pedestrian bridge over the Brda River to Stary Rynek, the main square.

There are two museums near the bridge: the **District Museum**, Aleje 1 Maja 4, and a museum in the old riverside **granaries** (both closed Monday). From May to September excursion boats offer cruises on the **Brda River** from Bydgoszcz. The ticket office is in the red brick building just downstream from the granaries. A striking monument to the Polish victims of WW II stands in the centre of Stary Rynek, with Bydgoszcz's Gothic **parochial church** a little behind. A lovely 16th century painting of the Virgin with a rose graces the high altar of this church. The Galeria Sztuki Wspolczesnej in a corner of Stary Rynek sells contemporary Polish artworks.

Places to Stay & Eat
The *Orbis Pod Orlem Hotel*, Aleje 1 Maja 14, was built in 1898. *Ratuszowy Milk Bar*, ulica Dluga 28 just up from Stary Rynek, offers basic meals.

GDANSK
The Tri-City conurbation, Gdansk-Sopot-Gdynia, stretching along the west side of

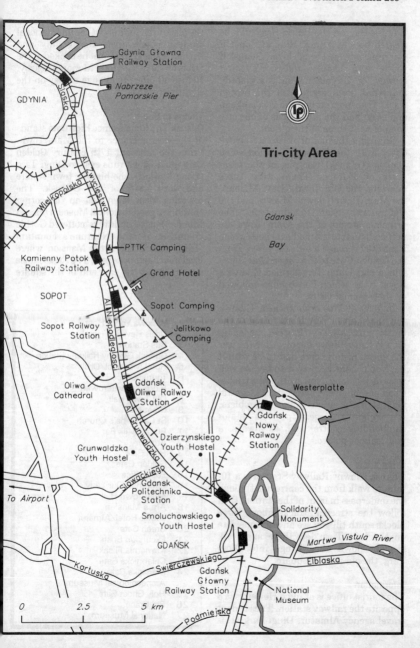

Gdansk Bay on the Baltic Sea, may be treated here as a unit. Stay at Sopot if you're a confirmed beach lover, Gdansk if you're into history and don't mind crowds, or Gdynia if you enjoy seedy industrial ports slightly off the beaten track. Transport around the area is cheap and easy, and the attractions of one city complement those of the others.

Gdansk's beautiful historic centre dates from the Hanseatic period when Danzig (Gdansk) was one of the main ports of Europe. There were three quarters: the Old Town (Stare Miasto), the Main Town (Glowne Miasto) and the Old Suburb (Stare Przedmiescie). The principle streets of the Main Town are perpendicular to the medieval port, which is reached through a series of gates. From the Golden Gate to the Green Gate, ulica Dluga and Dlugi Targ formed Gdansk's Royal Road which Polish kings followed on their annual visits.

In 1939 at Westerplatte near Gdansk the first shots of WW II were fired as the battleship *Schleswig-Holstein* opened up on a Polish military depot. After the war the entire historic core had to be rebuilt but you'd hardly know it today, so well was the job done. Now, with industrialisation and billowing smokestacks, central Gdansk has a serious pollution problem. It's Poland's largest port, a major shipbuilding centre, and, as always, a political hot potato.

Orientation

Gdansk Glowny Railway Station is a 10-minute walk from the centre. Go through the underpass in front of the station, then follow the streetcar tracks about three blocks south till you see an old stone gate on the left. Turn left there and walk straight down ulica Dluga into Dlugi Targ, the old market square.

Information

The tourist office is at ulica Heweliusza 8 opposite the railway station. The student travel agency Almatur, Dlugi Targ 11, is the place to enquire about the international student hotels open during July and August. Couchettes must be booked at the Orbis office in the Hotel Monopol nearby. Refuse all offers to change money on the street in Gdansk.

Things to See

Gdansk The Renaissance **High Gate** stands at the west entrance to the Main Town. From the adjacent 17th century **Golden Gate** ulica Dluga runs east to Dlugi Targ (Long Market), the historic town square and very heart of old Gdansk. The towering **Main Town Hall** on the corner contains a good **Historical Museum** (closed Monday) in the buildings' coffered Gothic chambers. Behind Neptune's Fountain (1613) stands the **Artus Mansion** where local merchants once met. The Renaissance **Green Gate** at the east end of the square

1	Walowa Youth Hostel
2	Orbis Hevelius Hotel
3	Bus Station
4	Gdansk Glowny Railway Station
5	Hotel Monopol/Orbis
6	Tourist Office
7	Biuro Zakwaterowan
8	Old Town Hall
9	Great Mill
10	St Catherine's Church
11	Ruczaj Milk Bar
12	Armoury
13	High Gate
14	Golden Gate
15	Post Office
16	Church of Our Lady
17	Main Town Hall
18	Artus Mansion
19	Jantar Hotel/Almatur
20	Green Gate
21	Excursion Boats
22	Kawiarnia Flisak
23	Chlebnicka Gate
24	Mariacka Gate/ Archaeological Museum
25	Holy Ghost Gate
26	Big Crane
27	National Museum

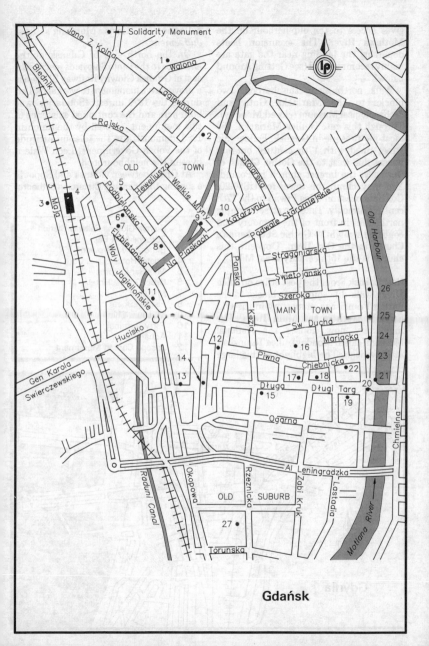

Gdańsk

gives access to the old harbour on the Motlawa River. The excursion boats departing the landing near the gate are highly recommended (see Getting Around below).

Walk north along the harbour two blocks to the Mariacka Gate and **Archaeological Museum** (closed Monday). Through this gate is ulica Mariacka, the most picturesque in Gdansk. Follow this street lined with 17th century burgher houses due west to the Gothic **Church of Our Lady**, the largest church in Poland. You may climb the tower for US$0.20. Continue west on ulica Piwna to the 17th century **Armoury**. Take the street running north from in front of the Armoury and continue straight to Gothic **St Catherine's Church** in the Old Town. Opposite this church is the 15th century **Great Mill**.

Near Gdansk From the post office on ulica Dluga walk due south four blocks to the former Franciscan monastery in the Old Suburb, south of the Main Town. The monastery now houses the **National Museum** (closed Monday), ulica Torunska 1 at Rzeznicka. The highlight of this large

collection is Hans Memling's *Last Judgement*.

On the north side of Gdansk at the entrance to the **Lenin Shipyards** just north-east of Gdansk Glowny Railway Station is a provocative **monument** to workers killed during the 1970 unrest. 'Solidarity' was born here and the continued existence of this monument, erected by the union in 1980, demonstrates the tolerant attitude of the Polish Government. Lech Walesa lives in the neighbourhood.

At Oliwa between Gdansk and Sopot is a soaring 13th century **Cistercian cathedral**

1	Gdynia-Glowna Railway Station
2	Zdrowie Milk Bar
3	Biuro Zakwaterowan
4	Bristol Hotel
5	Milk Bar Ekspres
6	Orbis Gdynia Hotel
7	Museum
8	Fishing Boats
9	Museum Ship
10	Ferry Terminal
11	Aquarium
12	Joseph Conrad Monument

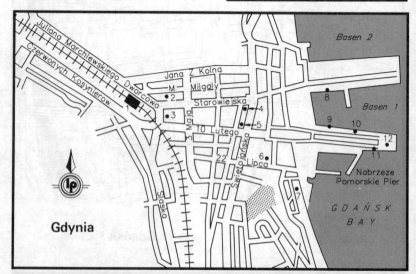

Gdynia

in a park, with a museum (closed Monday) in the adjacent monastery. The cathedral's 18th century Rococo organ is one of the best in Europe. Get there on trams No 8, 12 and 15, or by electric train to Gdansk Oliwa Station.

Sopot, north again by electric train, is a fashionable beach resort with Poland's longest pier jutting out into the Baltic.

Gdynia Gdynia's broad main pier, Nabrzeze Pomorskie, points out into Gdansk Bay. Down its centre runs an attractive pedestrian walkway past museum ships, ferry terminals, an aquarium and finally a monument to the writer Joseph Conrad. For food and accommodation at Gdynia and Sopot see below.

Excursion Boats From April to October excursion boats to Westerplatte (US$1) depart several times daily from the landing near Gdansk's Green Gate. This is one of the best trips of its kind in Poland, allowing a fine cross-section view of Gdansk's harbour. The first shots of WW II were directed at the Polish naval garrison at **Westerplatte** and a towering monument (1968) with sweeping views commemorates their heroic resistance. Bus No 106 also connects Gdansk to Westerplatte.

From mid-May to September there are boats across the Baltic from Gdansk to the unpolluted beaches of **Hel** on the Hel Peninsula (US$1.50 one way). June to August boats go to Gdynia. Alternatively, take a boat from Gdansk to Hel, then a second from Hel to Gdynia or Sopot. Be sure to get out on the water if you're in the area in season.

Places to Stay

Hostels There are four hostels in the Gdansk area, open year round. Most convenient is the *Youth Hostel* at ulica Walowa 21, a large red brick building set back from the road, only a five-minute walk from Gdansk Glowny Railway Station. There are no showers, however.

The other three hostels are between Gdansk and Sopot, too far to walk. First is the *hostel* at ulica Smoluchowskiego 11 (trams No 2, 6, 8, 12, 13 and 14 pass nearby).

For the *hostel* in the large red school building at ulica Dzierzynskiego 11 take trams No 2, 4, 7, 8, or 14 which stop outside.

The friendly *Aleje Grunwaldzka 238/ 240 Hostel* is in a small sports complex near Oliwa. Trams No 8, 12 and 15 pass nearby, but you'll miss it unless you ask someone who knows the way.

Camping The Tri-City's best camping is at the *Jelitkowo Campground* (tel 53-27-31) near the beach between Gdansk and Sopot, a seven-minute walk from the terminus of trams No 2, 4 and 15. The charge to camp (own tent) is US$2 single, US$3.50 double, and there are 27 bungalows available at US$4.50 single or double, US$6.50 triple – great if you get one. They open from May to September.

There's another campground, *Sopot Camping*, open June to August at ulica Bitwy Pod Plowcami 79, about a km north of Jelitkowo on the main highway, which doesn't have any bungalows but is closer to the beach.

The *PTTK Camping* is a convenient five-minute walk from Sopot-Kamienny Potok Railway Station. Only tent space is available (no bungalows), the facilities are basic and it can get crowded in the summer (open June to September).

Hotels & Private Rooms – Gdansk Private rooms (US$12 single, US$17 double) are arranged by the Biuro Zakwaterowan at the beginning of ulica Elzbietanska near the Gdansk Glowny Railway Station (open daily 7 am to 7 pm in summer). Freelancers on the sidewalk outside this office may have an unofficial private room to offer you. Decide for yourself if the savings are worth the small risk of staying unregistered in unlicensed accommodation.

About the only medium-range hotel in

Gdansk is the *Jantar Hotel*, Dlugi Targ 19, with rooms at US$19 single, US$26 double. You couldn't ask for a more central location – if you get in there you're lucky.

Hotels & Private Rooms – Sopot Several expensive resort hotels line the sandy shores stretching wide and white north from Jelitkowo to well beyond Sopot. Behind the PTTK Camping near Sopot-Kamienny Potok Railway Station is the *PTTK Dom Turysty*, but it's no bargain at US$26 single. It's usually full of groups which get a discount rate. The nearby *Maryla Hotel* at ulica Sepia 2 costs less, but is usually full.

The *Dworcowy Hotel* near the Sopot Railway Station is also cheaper but nearly impossible to get into. A better bet is the Biuro Zakwaterowan beside the Dworcowy which arranges stays in private rooms. If they can't help, hang around outside the office looking lost, baggage in hand, and wait until someone approaches you.

If the price is no concern of yours, the four-star *Orbis Grand Hotel* by the pier right on Sopot Beach should be your choice. This 118-room resort hotel built in 1926 is easy walking distance from Sopot Railway Station, the perfect escape after sightseeing. At US$67 single, US$95 double with bath (high season) it's a *bargain*.

Hotels & Private Rooms – Gdynia There's a Biuro Zakwaterowan at ulica Dworcowa 7 near Gdynia Glowna Railway Station which arranges accommodation in private homes for US$13 single, US$20 double. The *Bristol Hotel*, ulica Starowiejska 1, doesn't usually take foreigners, but ask.

Places to Eat
Gdansk *Palowa Coffee House* in the basement of the Main Town Hall on Dlugi Targ is a good place to sit and read, or eat cakes and ice cream. The *Neptun Milk Bar*, ulica Dluga 32-34, serves hearty cheap meals cafeteria-style. *Staro-Gdanski*

Milk Bar, ulica Dluga 18/19, is similar. The *Gedania Restaurant*, just opposite the Staro-Gdanski, has table service, beer (!) and live music after 8 pm. The restaurant downstairs in the *Jantar Hotel*, Dlugi Targ 19, serves unpretentious, filling meals.

There's a great *pizzeria* (spaghetti available!) at ulica Piwna 51, just up the street from the Church of Our Lady. The *Ruczaj Milk Bar*, ulica Waly Jagiellonskie 8 not far from the train station, is a good place for breakfast. The dumplings and mushrooms are good – watch what the locals take.

Sopot The *Zdrojowy Milk Bar* on Plac Konstytucji 3 Maja not far from the Sopot Railway Station has cheap cafeteria meals. The expensive restaurant in the *Orbis Grand Hotel* by the pier offers grilled salmon, smoked eel and tenderloin *zrazy* (pound steak) in a loaf of bread.

Gdynia The restaurant at the *Bristol Hotel*, ulica Starowiejska 1, serves good meals and there's a bar attached. Nearby at ulica Swietojanska 16 between the Bristol and the pier is *Milk Bar Ekspres* which offers cheap cafeteria food. The *Zdrowie Milk Bar*, ulica Starowiejska 56 near Gdynia Glowna Railway Station, is also a cheap cafeteria.

Entertainment
Check the local papers and ask tourist information about events. The *Wybrzeza Theatre*, ulica sw Ducha 2, is behind the armoury in the Main Town. The *State Baltic Opera and Concert Hall*, Aleje Zwyciestwa 15, is near Gdansk Politechnika Railway Station. In Gdynia there's the *Musical Theatre*, Plac Grunwaldzki 1 near the Orbis Gdynia Hotel. Summer activities include organ concerts at Oliwa Cathedral and performances at the *open-air opera* in the park just west of Sopot Railway Station.

Kawiarnia Flisak, ulica Chlebnicka 10/11, Gdansk, offers reasonable drink prices and friendly locals (open daily 2 pm to 2 am). The cocktail bar at the flashy *Orbis Hevelius Hotel* in Gdansk is also a good place to mix.

Getting There & Away

Direct trains arrive at Gdynia/Gdansk from Berlin-Lichtenberg (via Szczecin), Szczecin, Poznan, Wroclaw, Warsaw (via Malbork) and Olsztyn (also via Malbork). Couchettes are available to Prague, Warsaw, Szczecin and Berlin. Car ferries arrive at Gdansk from Travemunde (West Germany), Nynashamn (Sweden) and Helsinki (Finland).

Getting Around

Streetcar lines carry you north from Gdansk to Oliwa and Jelitkowo. To Westerplatte you can go by bus or boat. Cheap commuter trains run constantly between Gdansk-Sopot-Gdynia. Tickets are obtained from automatic machines.

MALDONK

From 1309 to 1457 Malbork (Marienburg) was the capital of the Teutonic Knights and one of the largest medieval fortified castles in Europe. The **castle** overlooking the Nogat River, a branch of the Vistula, was badly damaged during the war but has now been largely restored. It consists of the service facilities of the Lower Castle (between the railway line and the main gate), the 14th century Middle Castle where the Grand Master lived and the 13th century High Castle.

The first courtyard features an outstanding museum of Polish amber. Three floors of exhibits are to be seen in the rooms around the second courtyard (High Castle). One hall contains a superb collection of inlaid antique weapons. In the far corner a passageway leads to the Gdanisko Tower. Yes, the gaping hole in the floor was the toilet! At least four hours are required to explore this imposing monument (open 8.30 am to 5 pm May to September, 9 am to 2.30 pm October to April, closed Mondays).

Places to Stay

If you'd like to spend the night there's a campground (open June to August) on ulica Portowa about two km beyond the castle, away from the station. The *Hotel Sportovy* (open year round) behind the campground has rooms at US$14 single, US$32 double.

Getting There & Away

Malbork can be seen as a stopover between Gdansk and points south or east, or visit it as a day trip from Gdansk (58 km). The castle is a 15-minute walk from the train station.

OLSZTYN

From 1466 to 1772 Olsztyn belonged to the Kingdom of Poland and from 1516 to 1521 none other than Nicolaus Copernicus, administrator of Warmia, commanded Olsztyn Castle. Here he made astronomical observations and began writing *On the Revolutions of Celestial Bodies*. With the first partition Olsztyn became Prussian Allenstein and remained so until 1945. For us Olsztyn is more important as a jumping-off point for the lake district farther east than as a destination in itself. You can see the city's historic sites in a couple of hours.

Orientation

Olsztyn Glowny Railway Station and the bus station are adjacent on the north-east side of town, a 15-minute walk from the centre. Walk south-west on ulica Partyzantow past Plac Gen Bema to Aleje Dabrowszczakow on the left. When this street terminates in the downtown area cross the street and look for ulica 22 Lipca which will take you to High Gate and the old town. Olsztyn Zachodni Railway Station is just a short walk west of the castle.

Information

The tourist office in the PTTK complex beside the High Gate is helpful in providing maps of the Mazurian Lakes

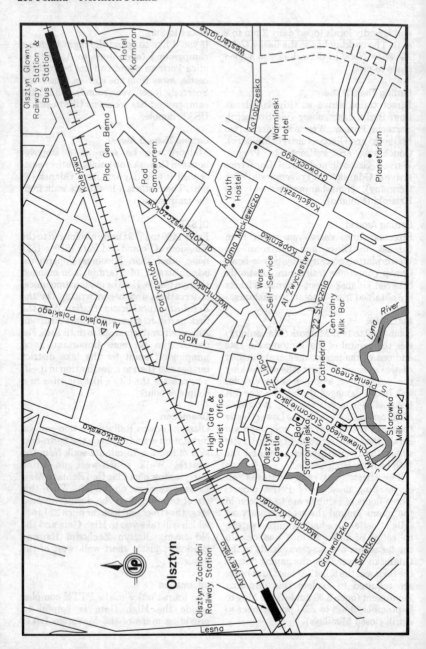

Olsztyn Glowny Railway Station & Bus Station

Hotel Kormoran

Westerplatte

Kolobrzeska

Warminski Hotel

Glowackiego

Planetarium

Kolejowa

Plac Gen Bema

Pod Samowarem

al Dabrowszczakow

Youth Hostel

Adama Mickiewicza

Kosciuszki

Kopernika

Wars Self-Service

Al Zwyciestwa

Warminska

Partyzantów

Al Wojska Polskiego

1 Maja

22 Stycznia

Centralny Milk Bar

Lyna River

22 Lipca

S Pieniéżnego

Cathedral

High Gate & Tourist Office

Staromiejska

Staromiejska

Bar

Olsztyn Castle

Mickiewicza

Starowka Milk Bar

Marcina Kromera

Grunwaldzka

Smetka

Olsztyn Zachodni Railway Station

Artyleryjska

Lesna

Olsztyn

and advice. It's open weekdays 9 am to 6 pm, Saturday 10 am to 2 pm.

Things to See

High Gate is all that remains of the 14th century city walls. Just west, **Olsztyn Castle** contains a good museum (closed Monday) with some explanations posted in English including much on Copernicus. The old market square nearby is surrounded by gabled burgher houses. Red brick **St James Cathedral** just south-east dates from the 16th century.

The Copernicus Trail

Frequent buses run 46 km north from Olsztyn to **Lidzbark Warminski**, site of a 14th century castle now a museum (closed Monday). This was the seat of the Warmia bishops and Copernicus also stayed here for a time.

The famous astronomer later spent 30 years in **Frombork** on the Vistula Lagoon between Lidzbark Warminski and Gdansk. He's buried in Frombork's 14th century cathedral and there's a Copernicus museum (closed Monday). From Frombork you can get a ferry across to Krynica Morska on the Amber Coast in summer.

Places to Stay

Olsztyn's *Youth Hostel* is at ulica Kopernika 45 between the stations and town, an eight-minute walk from either.

The cheapest hotel is the *PTTK Dom Wycieczkowy* in the High Gate, ulica Staromiejska 1 (US$8 single, US$14 double). The *Warminski Hotel*, ulica Glowackiego 8 about a 10-minute walk from the stations, is US$22 single for a room with shared bath.

The *PTTK Camping* on ulica Sielska above Lake Krzwe (Ukiel) is about five km west of town. Bus No 7 from the railway station passes the gate.

Places to Eat

Wars Self-Service, Aleje Zwyciestwa 218 at the city end of Aleje Dabrowszczakow, is cheap and has a place attached to get cakes and coffee. The *Centralny Milk Bar*, ulica Pienieznego 18 just around the corner from the PTTK, is also good. In the middle of the old town *Starowka Milk Bar*, ulica Marchlewskiego 3-4 offers cheap cafeteria food.

For a beer with the boys try *Pod Samowarem*, Aleje Dabrowszczakow 26 between the stations and town. Light snacks are also served, but they close at 8 pm. The *Bar Staromiejska* in the old town serves wine till 10 pm.

Getting There & Away

There are direct trains from Gdynia/Gdansk (via Malbork), Poznan (via Torun) and Warsaw (via Dzialdowo). If the timing doesn't allow you to use the Gdansk train you may have to change trains twice to travel between Malbork and Olsztyn (no direct buses). For the Mazurian Lakes look for a train to Elk and get off at Mikolajki or Ruciane-Nida.

THE MAZURIAN LAKES

Gizycko, 105 km east of Olsztyn by bus, is the tourist centre of the Mazurian lake district. There are literally thousands of post-glacial lakes to the north and south of Gizycko. Hitler's wartime headquarters, the 'Wolf's Lair' at Gierloz, is near Ketrzyn, two km west of Parcz Railway Station on the line to Wegorzewo, 30 km west of Gizycko. Only cracked concrete bunkers remain but the place is significant as the site of the 20 July 1944 assassination attempt. Tragically, a heavy wooden table saved the dictator and as many people died and as much property was destroyed in the last year of war as in the first five combined.

In summer the best gateway to the lakes for hikers and campers is **Mikolajki**, 86 km east of Olsztyn on the railway line to Elk. *Camping 'Wagabunda'* is at ulica Lesna 2. Mikolajki is just north of the **Mazurian Landscape Park** and Lake Sniardwy (110 square km), the largest lake in Poland. Europe's largest surviving community of wild swans is at nearby Lake Luknajno.

Hiking trails lead south from Mikolajki through the densely forested park past many lakeside campsites to **Ruciane-Nida** (23 km). Ruciane-Nida, in the heart of the Piska Forest between picturesque Beldany and Nidzkie lakes, has a *PTTK*

campground a 15-minute walk from the station, where you'll find trains back to Olsztyn. Pick up the 1:60,000 *Jezioro Sniardwy* map or the 1:120,000 *Wielkie jeziora mazurskie* map at a bookstore before you come.

Czechoslovakia

Czechoslovakia, a medium-sized country in the heart of Europe, is rich in history and natural beauty. The rugged Tatras of Slovakia and historic towns of Bohemia are unsurpassed. The medieval cores of some 40 towns have been preserved and about 4000 fairytale castles, chateaux, manors and ruins are scattered about the countryside. In the towns and cities are concentrated a total of 500 museums and 40,000 artistic monuments. Complementing this heritage are the achievements of socialism in housing, education and industry. There's so much to see that you could make repeated visits to this appealing land.

Czechoslovakia is doubly inviting for its cultured, friendly people and excellent facilities. The hotels, restaurants and transportation network are equalled only in the GDR, but in Czechoslovakia there are far fewer restrictions. Ninety percent of English-speaking visitors limit themselves to Prague. Those clever few who escape the hordes in the capital soon experience how people go out of their way to be helpful. For everything outside Prague is still off the beaten track.

Facts about the Country

HISTORY

In antiquity this area was inhabited by the Celts and never part of the classical Roman Empire. Germanic tribes conquered the Celts in the 4th century AD and between the 5th and 10th centuries the West Slavs settled here. From 830 to 907 the Slavonic tribes united into the Great Moravian Empire and adopted Christianity.

Toward the end of the 9th century the Czechs seceded from the Great Moravian

Empire and formed an independent state. In 995 the Czech lands were united under the native Przemyslid dynasty as the principality of Bohemia. The Czech state became a kingdom in the 12th century and reached its peak under Pzremysl Otakar II from 1253 to 1278. Many towns were founded at this time.

In 1310 John of Luxembourg gained the Bohemian throne through marriage and annexed the kingdom to the German Empire. His son, Charles IV, became King of the Germans in 1346 and Holy Roman Emperor in 1355. Inclusion in this medieval empire led to a blossoming of trade and culture. The capital, Prague, was made an Archbishopric in 1344 and in 1348 Charles University was founded. These kings were able to keep the feudal nobility in check, but under Wenceslas IV (1378-1419) the strength of the monarchy declined. The church became the largest land owner.

In 1415 the religious reformer John Huss, rector of Charles University, was burnt at the stake at Constance. His ideas inspired the Hussite revolutionary movement which swept Bohemia from 1419 to 1434. After the defeat of the Hussites the Jagiello dynasty occupied the Bohemian throne. Vladislav Jagiello

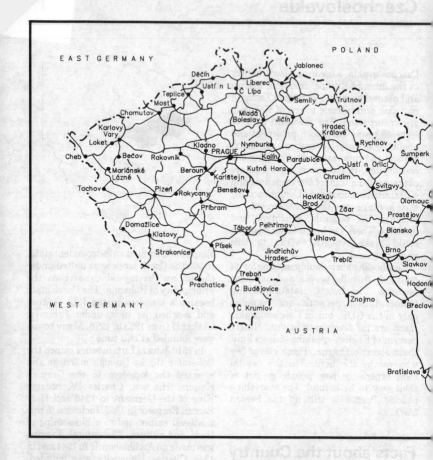

merged the Bohemian and Hungarian states in 1490.

Slovakia had a somewhat different history from Bohemia. In the first half of the 10th century the Magyars invaded Slovakia and in 1018 annexed it to Hungary. Slovakia remained part of Hungary until 1918. When the Turks overran Hungary in the 16th century the Hungarian capital moved from Buda to Bratislava.

With the death of Ludovic Jagiello at the Battle of Mohacs in 1526 the Austrian

Hapsburg dynasty ascended to the thrones of Bohemia and Hungary. After the defeat of the uprising of the Czech Estates in 1620 a long period of forced re-Catholicisation, Germanisation and oppression began. During the early 19th century a National Revival Movement rediscovered the linguistic and cultural roots of the Czechs and Slovaks. Despite the defeat of the bourgeois-democratic revolution of 1848, the industrial revolution took firm hold in the Czech lands.

In 1914 Austro-Hungarian expansionism

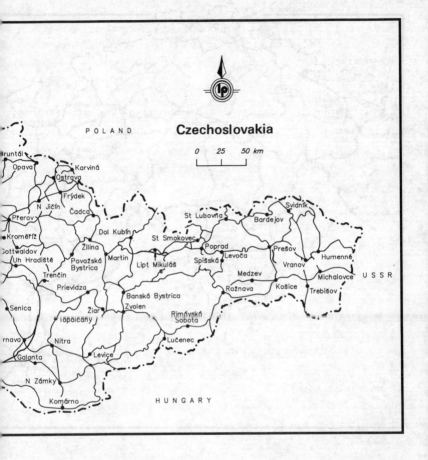

Czechoslovakia

0   25   50 km

POLAND

USSR

HUNGARY

Bruntál, Opava, Karviná, Ostrava, Frýdek, N Jičín, Čadca, Přerov, Kroměříž, Dol Kubín, St Lubovňa, Svidník, Bardejov, Gottwaldov, Uh Hradiště, Žilina, St Smokovec, Poprad, Prešov, Humenné, Považská Bystrica, Martin, Lipt Mikuláš, Spišská, Levoča, Vranov, Trenčín, Medzev, Michalovce, Prievidza, Rožnava, Košice, Trebišov, Senica, Banská Bystrica, Žiar, Zvolen, Rimavská Sobota, Topoľčany, Lučenec, Trnava, Nitra, Levice, Galanta, N Zámky, Komárno

in the Balkans led to war but no fighting took place in the area that is now Czechoslovakia. On 29 October 1918 the Czechoslovak Republic, a common state of the Czechs and Slovaks, was proclaimed. The first president was T G Masaryk, followed in 1935 by Eduard Benes who later headed a government-in-exile in London. Three-quarters of the industrial potential of the former Austro-Hungarian Monarchy fell within Czechoslovakia, as did three million Germans.

After annexing Austria in the Anschluss of March 1938 Hitler turned his attention to Czechoslovakia. By the infamous Munich Dictate of 30 September 1938 Britain and France surrendered the border regions of the republic to Nazi Germany. In March 1939 the Germans occupied the rest of the country. The Czech lands were converted into the so-called Protectorate of Bohemia and Moravia while a clero-fascist puppet state was set up in Slovakia.

On 29 May 1942 the acting Nazi Reichs-Protector, Reinhard 'Hangman' Heydrich,

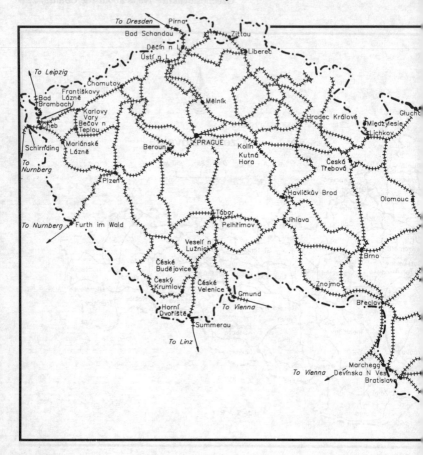

was assassinated by two Czechs who had been parachuted in from London for the purpose. As a reprisal the Nazis surrounded the peaceful village of Lidice, 25 km north-west of Prague, shot all the males and deported all the females to concentration camps. The anti-fascist resistance culminated in the Slovak National Uprising (SNP) in the autumn of 1944. Soviet troops occupied the country after the German surrender in May, 1945. Unlike Germany and Poland which were devastated during WW II, Czechoslovakia was largely undamaged.

After liberation a National Front was set up from the parties which had taken part in the anti-fascist struggle. In April 1945, even before the rest of the country had been freed, a meeting of the Front at Kosice laid down a programme for national and democratic revolution. A power struggle developed between the socialists and those who favoured capitalism. Resentment against the west after the Munich sell-out was rife and the

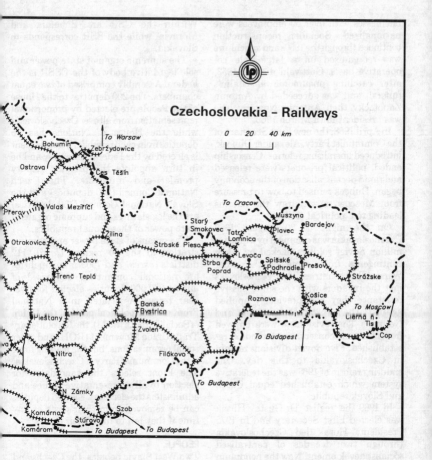

Czechoslovakia – Railways

0   20   40 km

To Warsaw

Bohumín
Zebrzydowice
Ostrava
Čes Těšín
Přerov
Valaš Meziříčí
To Cracow
Otrokovice
Žilina
Starý Smokovec
Muszyna
Bardejov
Tatr Lomnica
Plavec
Štrbské Pleso
Púchov
Levoča
Spišské Podhradie
Prešov
Trenč Teplá
Štrba
Poprad
Strážske
Banská Bystrica
Roznava
Košice
Piešťany
Zvolen
To Moscow
Čierna n. Tis
Nitra
Fiľakovo
Čop
N Zámky
To Budapest
Komárno
Štúrovo
Szob
Komárom
To Budapest   To Budapest

strength of the Communist Party grew. In the Constituent National Assembly elections of May 1946 the Communists won 38% of the votes and the social democrats 15.6%, forming a National Front majority. Communist Party chairman Klement Gottwald became the Prime Minister.

In February 1948 the social democrats withdrew from the coalition in an attempt to overthrow Gottwald. Demonstrations and a general strike convinced President Benes to accept the resignations of the 12 government ministers involved and appoint Communist replacements. The new government then prepared a revised constitution and in fresh elections in May 86% of voters supported the National Front. Benes resigned in June (and died in August) and in July Klement Gottwald became President. These events took place at a time when there were no Soviet troops in the country.

In March 1948 the new government approved a land reform bill limiting property ownership to 50 hectares. All businesses with over 50 employees were nationalised. Socialist reconstruction continued through the 1950s and agriculture was reorganised on a large-scale cooperative basis. Gottwald died in 1953, after catching pneumonia at Stalin's funeral, and was succeeded by Antonin Zapotocky then Antonin Novotny who was president until March 1968.

In April 1968, the new First Secretary of the Communist Party, Alexander Dubcek, introduced liberalising reforms. Censorship ended, political prisoners were released and rapid decentralisation of the economy began. Dubcek refused to bow to pressure from Moscow to withdraw the reforms leading to a political crisis.

On the night of 20 August 1968 Czechoslovakia was occupied by a quarter million Soviet soldiers backed by token contingents from some of the other Warsaw Pact countries. The Czechoslovaks met the invaders with the same passive resistance they had previously applied against the Austro-Hungarians and Germans. The 'revisionists' were removed from office and conservative orthodoxy reestablished. Five Soviet divisions remain in Czechoslovakia to this day. One enduring reform of 1968 was the federative system which established equal Czech and Slovak republics.

In 1969 the 'realist' Dr Gustav Husak was elected First Secretary and in 1975 President. Husak led Czechoslovakia through two decades of centralised socialist development. Now the pendulum is moving the other way as Soviet reformers urge restructuring on the reluctant Czechoslovak leadership. The irony is that many of the reforms of the Gorbachev revolution are similar to those of the 'Prague Spring' of 1968.

GOVERNMENT

Czechoslovakia is one state, two nations and three historic lands. The Czechoslovak Socialist Republic (CSSR) is a federation of the Czech Socialist Republic (CSR) and the Slovak Socialist Republic (SSR).

Within the CSR are Bohemia and Moravia, while the SSR corresponds to Slovakia.

The supreme organ of state power and sole legislative body of the CSSR is the Federal Assembly comprised of two equal chambers. The 200 deputies to the House of the People are elected by proportional representation from all over Czechoslovakia while the House of Nations has 75 deputies from each republic. The president is elected by the Federal Assembly and he in turn appoints the premier, deputy premier and ministers. The Czech National Council (200 deputies) and the Slovak National Council (150 deputies) are the legislatures and supreme organs of state power of these equal republics.

The organs of state power and administration in the 10 regions (kraj), 112 districts (okres) and 7503 municipalities are national committees composed of almost 200,000 deputies elected for five-year terms. Associated in a National Front are five political parties, the Union of Socialist Youth (SSM), the Revolutionary Trade Union Movement (ROH) and other social organisations, but the leading force is the Communist Party of Czechoslovakia. The Front selects the candidates for election to all representative bodies and administers the elections. Elected deputies can be removed from their posts at any time if they fail to fulfil their duties.

PEOPLE

Two West Slavic peoples, the Czechs and the Slovaks, inhabit the country. Czechs account for 64% of the population, Slovaks 30%. After WW II most of the German inhabitants were evicted although about 60,000 remain. In addition there are Hungarians (4%), Poles (0.4%), Ukrainians (0.3%) and other minorities including gypsies. Nominally 55% of the people are Catholic, 10% Protestant. The ancient folk traditions are best preserved in East Slovakia.

Czechoslovakia has 15,500,000 inhabitants. The major cities are Prague

(1,200,000), Bratislava (380,000), Brno (372,000), Ostrava (325,500), Kosice (203,000) and Plzen (170,000).

ECONOMY

Czechoslovakia has a centrally planned economy with industry producing 70% of the national income. This industry, once concentrated in the Czech lands, is now more evenly spread throughout the country. The famous Skoda Works at Plzen are balanced by the chemical industry at Bratislava, cement works at Banska Bystrica and an iron mill at Kosice. There's a major industrial area around Ostrava with coal mining, chemicals, a steel mill and auto production. Bratislava and Prague are also important industrial centres. The Czechoslovak economy is so highly developed that there's even a labour shortage filled by Vietnamese guest workers!

Engineering is the most important industry. Every fourth engineering project is for export. Electrical engineering, metallurgy, chemicals and rubber are also important. Czechoslovakia has abundant sources of power. Over 120 million tons of coal are extracted annually and there are several nuclear generating stations. The most important fields of consumer production are textiles, leather, glass, porcelain and ceramics. Bata shoes originated at Gottwaldov east of Brno. Good quality, inexpensive consumer goods are readily available inside the country.

The collectivisation of agriculture has made possible the use of modern farm machinery to increase production, even though the work force has declined to a third its pre-war size. Cooperatives account for about three-quarters of agricultural land, state farms the rest.

Economic development is co-ordinated by the Council of Mutual Economic Assistance (CMEA) which handles 70% of Czechoslovakia's foreign trade. Leading exports are machinery, industrial and transportation equipment, electrical goods, iron and steel, power plants, complete factories and refineries, most of it going to the CMEA countries. Oil, natural gas and raw materials comprise half of imports. Machinery and equipment are also imported.

GEOGRAPHY

Czechoslovakia is a land-locked country of 127,889 square km, 78,864 square km of it in the CSR, 49,025 square km in the SSR. About 55% of the land is used for agriculture, the rest is largely mountain and forest. Forests cover a third of the country. In Bohemia the forests have been decimated by acid rain resulting from the burning of coal. As yet the Slovakian forests are less affected. Approximately 33% of Czechoslovakia lies above 500 metres and 3% over 1000 metres.

Bohemia nestles between the Sumava Mountains along the West German border, the Ore Mountains (Krusne Hory) along the East German border and the Giant Mountains (Krkonose) along the Polish border east of Liberec. There are thousands of small fish ponds in South Bohemia, many of them dating from the Middles Ages.

The most popular hiking area is the Carpathian Range, only the Tatras of Slovakia exceed 2000 metres. Zilina is caught between the Beskydy of Moravia and the Little Fatra (Mala Fatra) of Slovakia while to the east are the High Tatras (Vysoke Tatry). Gerlach (2655 metres) is the highest of the mighty peaks in this spectacular alpine range which Czechoslovakia shares with Poland. The Low Tatras (Nizke Tatry) are between Poprad and Banska Bystrica.

The plains of East Slovakia are a transition to the steppes of the Ukraine. Southern Slovakia is a fertile lowland stretching down to the Danube.

The Morava River flows out of Moravia and enters the Danube just west of Bratislava. The Vah River of Slovakia joins the Danube at Komarno. The Danube itself forms the border with

Hungary from Bratislava to Sturovo/ Esztergom. The most famous river of Bohemia is the Moldau (Vltava) which originates near the Austrian border and flows north through Cesky Krumlov, Ceske Budejovice and Prague. It eventually joins the Labe, which becomes the Elbe in East Germany. The Moldau and Labe drain 40% of the country into the North Sea, while the Danube and tributaries drain another 54% into the Black Sea. The Baltic-bound Odra River originates in Czechoslovakia near Ostrava but soon enters Poland.

The opportunities for hiking are almost endless. There are four national parks: Krkonose (east of Liberec), Nizke Tatry (between Banska Bystrica and Poprad), Vysoke Tatry and Pieniny (both north of Poprad). The 120 square-km Moravian Karst north of Brno features limestone caves, subterranean lakes and the Macocha Abyss, 128 metres deep.

FESTIVALS & HOLIDAYS

The Prague Spring Music Festival happens in May. Also in May is the festival of dance songs in Bratislava. The Bratislava Lyre in May or June features rock concerts. In August the Frederic Chopin Music Festival occurs in Marianske Lazne. Karlovy Vary comes back with the Dvorak Autumn Music Festival in September. The 'Bratislava Jazz Days' are in September and Prague's International Jazz Festival is in October. Both Brno and Bratislava have music festivals in October. The Bohemian Beer Festival, the Czech answer to Munich's Oktoberfest, bursts upon Plzen in October.

The International Trade Fair of consumer goods unfolds in Brno in April or May. In August or September there's the 'Bread-Winning Motherland' Agricultural Exhibition in Ceske Budejovice.

Public holidays include 1 January (New Year's Day), Easter Monday, 1 May (Labour Day), 9 May (Liberation Day), 25 and 26 December (Christmas).

LANGUAGE

Czech and Slovak are two closely related, mutually comprehensible Slav languages which evolved from the same mother tongue during the 1000 year separation of these peoples. Take for example the similarity of the names of the days of the week. In Czech they're *pondeli, utery, streda, ctvrtek, patek, sobota, nedele* and in Slovak *pondelok, utorok, streda, sturtok, piatok, sobota, nedela*. In Czech yes and no are *jo* and *ne*, while in Slovak they're *ano* and *nie*. One word you'll soon learn wherever you are is *vyprodano* (sold out). German is widely understood, especially in western Czechoslovakia. Everybody learns Russian at school but English is less known.

Facts for the Visitor

VISAS

A passport and visa are required to enter Czechoslovakia. The visa is *not* available at the border. If you don't have a visa you will be refused entry. Czechoslovak tourist and transit visas are readily available at consulates throughout Europe at a cost of US$5 to US$30 and two photos per entry (maximum two entries per visa). Visas may be used any time within three months of the date of issue. Complete the application clearly and completely using block letters. Any irregularity, even changing pens halfway through, will mean you'll have to fill out another form and line up again. Long hair and beards could cause problems.

A transit visa is just that and cannot be changed to a tourist visa upon arrival. There is no compulsory exchange for transit passengers leaving within 24 hours. To use a transit visa you must have a visa for the next country on your route beyond Czechoslovakia and the GDR. There have been cases of Third World nationals trying to enter West Germany without proper visas, then being dumped back into the unwilling arms of the Czechoslovak authorities. You may have to explain that you don't require a visa for West Germany. If you *are* a citizen of an Arab or African country you won't be allowed to transit Czechoslovakia without a West German visa.

When you apply for a tourist visa you will be asked how many days you wish to stay in Czechoslovakia, to a maximum of 30 days. This number will be written on the visa and you will have to change DM 30 for each of those days, either at the border itself or sometime during your stay. Children aged 15 and under only have to change DM 15 daily. There is no daily exchange for infants five and under, nor for those on prepaid package tours. Thus it's important to calculate accurately the number of days you really do wish to spend in the country *before* you apply for a tourist visa. When you leave Czechoslovakia the immigration officer will check the visa for a stamp verifying that you did change the required amount of money. If you don't have this stamp you will have to pay the money directly to him against a receipt allowing you to pick up the equivalent in Czechoslovak crowns next visit. Don't lose your visa form or exchange receipts as these and their attendant stamps are valuable documents in Czechoslovakia.

If you aren't sure how long you wish to stay, sign up for the longest period you *might* wish to spend in the country. Once inside change money officially as you go along for the time you're actually there. If you get a 15-day visa but leave after 10 days the customs officer will probably let you depart if you have exchange receipts for DM 300. A problem could arise if you're required to change the whole amount at the border upon arrival as there are no refunds.

The alternative is to get a shorter visa and extend your stay at a police station once inside Czechoslovakia. Extensions cost 60 Kcs to 120 Kcs and you must complete the official exchange for the additional days. If you wish to stay longer than 30 days you will have to extend at least once. Bratislava is a good place to do it and Cedok offices can advise on the procedure. Offices handling these matters open for short hours and have long lines, so don't leave it till the last day!

Entry stamps into Czechoslovakia give the hour as well as the date of entry. For example, a stamp reading 23 10 9 – 2 indicates that you entered on 23 October 1989 at 2 am. The length of stay is calculated in multiples of 24 beginning with this hour, in other words the first and last days count as one day. To allow for transit time you are permitted to leave six hours after the completion of the last 24 hour period. So, if you entered at 23 10 9 – 2 with a 25-day tourist visa you would have to depart by 8 am on 17 November 1989 (17 11 9 – 8).

Your visa form will be stamped by hotels, hostels, room finding services and campgrounds every day. Theoretically you should have a stamp to account for each night spent in the country. The visa form bears a notice advising you to report to police within 48 hours of arrival, but this is aimed mostly at those who stay with relatives or friends. If you get an official stamp from the place where you're staying you don't have to bother registering. If you do stay with the locals they probably won't wish you to register your presence in their home with the police. If you're travelling around and have a lot of other stamps from hotels the missing nights probably won't be noticed, but you are breaking the law.

The above may seem like a lot of red tape but it's actually quite straightforward. You may enter the country at any time within three months of the date of issue of the visa, go wherever you want without further formalities (so long as you stay in official lodgings) and depart across any border you choose. You're even allowed to walk or ride a bicycle across highway border points, and DM 30 a day isn't too much to expect to have to spend.

MONEY

US$1 = 9 crowns (Kcs) (official)

DM 30 daily compulsory exchange

There are banknotes of 10, 20, 50, 100, 500 and 1000 Kcs. As noted above you must change DM 30 or the equivalent in any hard currency for each day of your stay in Czechoslovakia. Sometimes they ask you to do this at the border. If not, go to a Cedok office in the first town you reach and make the exchange there. They'll stamp your visa form and give you Czechoslovak crowns (Kcs) at the official rate. Hang onto your exchange receipt as additional proof that you completed the compulsory exchange. Package tourists receive a special 36% 'bonus' exchange rate for non-refundable vouchers purchased abroad. This rate is never applied to compulsory exchange transactions.

There's a thriving black market in Prague which offers 2½ times the official rate and up for cash on the street. Be aware that this is illegal and although many visitors succumb to the temptation, special care should be taken. Beware of receiving worthless banknotes issued before the currency reform of 1953. Don't hand over your money until you have a firm grasp on theirs. After a few days in Prague you may conclude that everyone's on the take, but if you are caught all the money involved will be confiscated, you'll have some heavy explaining to do and no one to blame but yourself.

However you change, once you have Czechoslovak money you'll have to spend it as it's almost impossible to change back into hard currency. The import or export of Czechoslovak crowns is illegal but you can deposit excess crowns with customs upon departure to be picked up next visit within three years. Simply spending the money is more fun.

CLIMATE

The climate is midway between maritime and continental. Czechoslovakia enjoys warm summers and mild winters with clearly defined spring and fall. The eastern part of the country is cooler and drier than the west.

BOOKS & BOOKSHOPS

Guide to Czechoslovakia by Simon Hayman (Bradt Publications, England, 1987) is a practical guidebook aimed at the independent budget traveller. There is much information on hiking – a rarity in guides to Europe! It's distributed in the US by Hippocrene Books, 171 Madison Ave, New York, NY 10016.

Czechoslovakia by Ctibor Rybar (Olympia, Prague, 1982) is a handy little guidebook with alphabetical listings. It's available at Czechoslovak bookstores.

NEWSPAPERS & MEDIA

Over 100 newspapers and magazines are published in Czechoslovakia. *Rude Pravo* is the official daily paper with editions in Czech and Slovak. *Vecerni Praha* is an afternoon Prague paper. *Welcome to Czechoslovakia* is a quarterly tourist review. The only foreign publications available in Czechoslovakia are Communist newspapers like the *Morning Star*.

HEALTH

All health care is free to citizens of Czechoslovakia. First aid is provided free to visitors in case of an accident. Otherwise a fee must be paid by foreigners, sometimes in hard currency. British nationals receive free medical attention.

There are 900 curative mineral springs and 57 health spas in Czechoslovakia using mineral waters, mud or peat. Most famous are the spas of West Bohemia (Frantiskovy Lazne, Karlovy Vary and Marianske Lazne). Although these resorts are pleasant to visit and anyone can join in the 'drinking cure' by imbibing liberal quantities of warm spring water, to receive medical treatment at a spa you must book in advance through Balnea in Prague or Slovakoterma in Bratislava. The recommended stay is 21 days. Daily prices begin at DM 56 single, DM 88 double in the cheapest category in the winter season and rise to DM 135 single, DM 232 double in the top category during the main summer season. Accompanying persons not taking spa treatment get about a third off. From October to April prices are reduced. The price includes medical examination and care, spa curative treatment, room and board, and the spa tax. The clientele tends to be elderly. Cedok offices abroad will have full information about spa treatments.

GENERAL INFORMATION

Post

In Prague it's best to have your mail sent care of your embassy where it will be held longer and more reliably. Elsewhere if you want to use poste restante include the words 'Posta 1' in the address. Always use airmail. It's generally OK to send letters from Czechoslovakia but wait to mail your parcels from Hungary if possible.

Electricity

220 volts AC, 50 Hz.

Time

Greenwich Mean Time plus one hour. At the end of March Czechoslovakia goes on summer time and clocks are turned an hour forward. At the end of September they're turned an hour back.

Business Hours

Weekdays stores open around 9 am and close at 6 pm. Some stay open until 7 pm on Thursdays. Many small stores close for a long lunch, re-opening by 3 pm at the latest. Other stores are closed Monday mornings. Almost everything closes around 1 pm Saturday and all day Sunday. Hotel restaurants are open every day.

Most museums are closed on Mondays and the day following a public holiday. Many gardens, castles and historic sites in Czechoslovakia are closed from November to March and open weekends only in April and October. In spring and fall you may have to wait around for a group to form before being allowed in, so again it's better to go on weekends. In winter before making a long trip out to some attraction in the countryside be sure to check to see if it's open. Some isolated sights take an hour off for lunch and ticket offices often close at 4 pm, even if the building itself is open later. The main town museums stay open year round. Students usually get 50% off the admission price at museums, galleries, theatres, cinemas, fairs, etc. Many churches in Czechoslovakia remain closed except for services.

INFORMATION

Cedok is the official government travel agency organising tourism in Czechoslovakia. They have 165 branch offices around the country and should be consulted first if you have questions, wish to change money, or want accommodation, travel or sightseeing arrangements made. They're oriented toward the top end of the market. Buy international railway tickets from them.

Czechoslovakia's youth travel bureau is CKM Student Travel (Cestovna Kancelaria Mladeze) with offices in most cities. They're a better source of information on money-saving arrangements than Cedok and sell the IUS student card. Two organisations which arrange accommodation and treatment at health spas and mineral springs are Balnea in the Czech Socialist Republic and Slovakoterma in the Slovak Socialist Republic. There are municipal information offices in Prague and Bratislava. They're very knowledgeable about sightseeing, food and entertainment but don't make reservations or sell tickets.

Austria
    Cedok (tel 52-0199), Parkring 12, Vienna 1
Belgium
    Cedok (tel 511-6870), Rue d'Assaut 19, 1000 Brussels
Britain
    Cedok (tel 629-6058), 17-18 Old Bond St, London W1X 3DA
Denmark
    Cedok (tel 12-0121), Vester Farigagsgade 6, 1605 Copenhagen V
France
    Cedok (tel 742-8773), 32 Avenue de l'Opera, Paris 2e
Holland
    Cedok (tel 22-0101), Leidsestraat 4, Amsterdam C
Italy
    Cedok (tel 46-2998), Via Bissolati 33, 00187 Rome
Sweden
    Cedok (tel 20-7290), Sveavagen 9-11, 111 57 Stockholm
Switzerland
    Cedok (tel 211-4245), Urania Strasse 34/2, 8001 Zurich
USA
    Cedok (tel 689-9720), 10 East 40th St, New York, NY 10016
West Germany
    Cedok (tel 23-2975), Kaiser Strasse 54, Frankfurt am Main

ACCOMMODATION

Czechoslovakia has a good network of hotels covering the entire country. The further you get off the beaten track the easier it will be to find a room. You may pay for hotel rooms directly in Czechoslovak currency and unlike Poland and Romania these expenditures are not deducted from any official currency exchange receipt, except at luxury hotels where you may be required to prove that you changed enough money legally to cover the bill. Prices are reasonable by European standards. If you have a room with shared bath you may have to pay extra to use the public shower. Almost all of the hotels (excluding holiday homes owned by unions and factories) will accept foreign guests.

There are five categories of hotels: A* deluxe (five stars), A* (four stars), B* (three stars), B (two stars) and C (one star). In this book we feature B-category hotels which usually offer reasonable comfort for under 200 Kcs single, 300 Kcs double. Prices outside Prague are lower and Czechoslovaks pay 50% less. In small towns and villages there are sometimes also C-category hotels, but renovations have upgraded most of them to B-category in the cities. Cedok will find you a room in a tourist hotel, but you'll often do better looking around on your own. Unlike Hungary, private rooms are not readily available to western tourists. They do exist however, so always ask for them first at Cedok offices. Most carry a four-night minimum stay.

Camping

Camping is popular in Czechoslovakia. There are campgrounds in all the tourist spots, usually open from May to September. The campgrounds are primarily intended for motorists so you're often surrounded by noisy caravans and car campers. The campgrounds are open to everyone and often accessible on public transport. There's usually no hot water. Most have a small snack bar selling beer and they're good places to meet people. Many have small bungalows for rent which are slightly cheaper than a hotel room. Pitching your own tent in these campgrounds is definitely the least expensive way to go. Freelance camping is prohibited.

Youth Hostels

Czechoslovakia doesn't have any permanent IYHF youth hostels with dormitory beds. Many of the places listed in the IYHF handbook are actually rather luxurious 'youth' hotels with single and double rooms, and most are permanently full. In summer student dormitories are converted into temporary youth hostels. Hostelling is controlled by CKM Student Travel with offices in all cities. A valid IYHF membership card is required to stay at CKM youth hostels.

To get into a hostel it's best to go first to the CKM office and ask them to make a reservation for you. These offices open for very short business hours, sometimes only weekday afternoons. If you go directly to the hostel itself, your chances range from 'no hope' in Prague to 'maybe if you're lucky' elsewhere. Occasionally CKM offices will agree to make advance bookings for you over the phone at hostels in other cities. You'll have to pay the telephone charges. Booked from abroad the price of the hostels rockets to that of a B-category hotel, although the money paid counts against compulsory exchange. Officially the CKM Junior hotels are meant for persons under 30 years of age, although this is not applied to foreigners with youth hostel cards. The people in CKM offices are usually very friendly and good sources of general information.

There's another category of hostel not connected with the CKM. Tourist hostels (turisticke ubytovny) are intended for visitors from other socialist countries and provide very basic dormitory accommodation without the standards and controls associated with IYHF hostels (men and women mixed, smoking in the room, no curfew, etc). They're very cheap but you'll have to be persuasive and persistent to stay in them. Ask about tourist hostels at Cedok offices and watch for the letters TU on accommodation lists in languages other than English.

FOOD & DRINK

The food in Czechoslovakia is good. You'll rarely have trouble getting something to eat but if you do try the dining room of any large hotel. There the service is standard, they stay open later and don't close on weekends. You can usually get a good cooked breakfast at a hotel. Don't expect to be served if you arrive within half an hour of closing time. A service charge is included in the bill so tipping is optional.

The cheapest places to eat are the self-services (samoobsluha) which you'll find everywhere. Sometimes they have something really tasty like barbecued chicken or hot German sausage. In Bohemia make frequent visits to the great little pastry shops (kavarny or cukrarny) which offer cakes, puddings and coffee as good as anything you'll find in neighbouring Austria.

Local Specialties

Prazska sunka (smoked Prague ham) is taken as an hors-d'oeuvre with Znojmo gherkins, followed by a thick soup such as bramborova (potato soup) and zeleninova (vegetable soup). The Czechs serve meat dishes with knedliky (dumplings) or sauerkraut while the Slovaks favour paprika and a pasta called halusky. Carp (kapr) from the Bohemian fish ponds can be breaded and fried or baked. Vegetarian dishes include smazeny syr (fried cheese) and knedliky s vejci (scrambled eggs with dumplings). Czech fruit dumplings (ovocne knedliky) come with melted butter or curd cheese and a whole fruit inside.

Drink

Bohemian beer (pivo) is about the best in the world and readily available at restaurants. The most famous brands are Budvar (the original Budweiser) and Plzensky Prazdroj (the original pilsener). Czech beer halls (pivnice) put Munich to shame and most also serve full meals. South Moravia and Slovakia south of Bratislava are famous for their wine. You can be sure of a good feed at a vinarna (wine restaurant). Special things to try include Becherovka, an exquisite bitter-

sweet Czech liqueur made at Karlovy Vary, zubrovka (vodka with herb extracts) and slivovice (plum brandy). Connoisseurs should visit the wine museum in Bratislava and beer museum in Plzen, both outstanding.

THINGS TO BUY

You're allowed to export goods worth up to a total value of 1000 Kcs. Shoes and clothing are fairly cheap, but check the quality carefully. Records and musical instruments are worth pricing. Outside Prague the largest department store chain is Prior.

Tuzex hard currency shops sell imported goods, china, Bohemian crystal, Jablonec costume jewellery, garnets (a red gemstone), fancy leather goods, special textiles, lace, antiques and souvenirs. Be sure to keep the receipts for anything purchased here as you may be required to prove you paid hard currency to export the goods duty free from Czechoslovakia. Crystal not purchased at Tuzex is subject to 100% duty.

In most shops and supermarkets the number of persons inside is controlled by shopping carts or baskets. You cannot enter without one, so pick one up at the door or stand in line and wait for someone to leave. You must even pick up a shopping basket when you enter a bookstore!

Getting There & Away

TRAIN

The easiest way to get there is by train. Prague is on the main line used by all direct trains from Berlin to both Vienna and Budapest, so access from any of those cities is easy. All the Budapest trains pass through Bratislava. From West Germany you'll probably transit Nuremberg and Cheb. Trains from Munich go via Plzen. Connections with Warsaw will be through either Wroclaw or Katowice.

Two lesser-known routes between East Germany and Czechoslovakia are Leipzig to Karlovy Vary and Zittau to Liberec. Vienna (Sudbahnhof) to Bratislava is only a short 64 Km hop done twice a day. Alternatively there are trains from Vienna (Nordbahnhof) to Breclav. Twice a day there's service between Linz, Austria, and Ceske Budejovice with a change of trains at Summerau.

Some trains between Poland and Hungary pass through Slovakia, an interesting backdoor entry. The Polonia Express from Warsaw to Budapest stops at Zilina, while the Cracovia Express from Cracow to Budapest runs through Kosice, the major gateway to eastern Czechoslovakia. Both daily trains from Moscow pass through Kosice.

Railway Fares

Keep in mind that railway fares within Czechoslovakia are much cheaper than tickets to Austria or West Germany. Between Western and Eastern Europe pay as little of the Czech portion in hard currency as you can. Try using border towns such as Cheb, Plzen and Bratislava as entry/exit points. In other words buy tickets which terminate or begin in them. When leaving you can buy a ticket as far as the border using Czechoslovak crowns, then pay the German or Austrian conductor on the other side.

Fares to neighbouring socialist countries (Berlin, Poland, USSR, Hungary) are cheap enough that you needn't worry about this. All international tickets must be paid in hard currency and are valid for two months with unlimited stopovers. Students with an IUS card get a 25% discount on international train tickets to other socialist countries.

BUS

Bus service to and from Austria is cheaper but less frequent than the train. There's a bus twice a day from Vienna (Mitte Busbahnhof) to Brno (129 kms, three hours) and Bratislava (64 kms, two hours). There are several bus lines from Hungary to Czechoslovakia, but none from Poland. Try to buy your ticket the day before.

Getting Around

TRAIN

As far as reservations and ticketing go, the Czechoslovakian State Railways (CSD) are still back in the 19th century. Timetables are hard to understand and the clerks at the information counters *never* speak English, not even in major stations. Some trains require seat reservation but it's hard to determine exactly which ones do and even more problematic to make them if you need them.

Many trains operate only on certain days, but the footnotes on the timetables are incomprehensible. On posted timetables *prijezdy* is arrivals and *odjezdy* is departures. The letter R inside a box or circle means reservations are mandatory while an R alone usually means reservations are only recommended. To get a departure time from information write down your destination and the date you wish to travel, then point to your watch. If this doesn't work ask at a Cedok office which will be accustomed to dealing with foreigners. They may also be able to sell you the ticket and make any necessary reservations.

If you plan to travel on an express train *(rychlik)* make sure you get an express train ticket, otherwise the conductor will levy a 10 Kcs fine. Ordinary trains are called *osobni*. Ticket counters will happily sell you an invalid ticket and you'll have no recourse. Express trains are usually marked in red on posted timetables and fast train tickets often have a red strip across the middle. If you have to purchase a ticket or pay a supplement on the train for any reason (even if the station ticket office was closed) you'll have to pay 10 Kcs or more in extra charges to the conductor. First class is 50% more than 2nd class.

One way to save on hotel bills while getting around is by using overnight trains. Cheap couchettes are available from Kosice to Bratislava, Brno, Decin, Karlovy Vary, Liberec, Prague and vice versa. Book these as far in advance as possible at a Cedok office.

BUS

Within Czechoslovakia CSAD express buses are faster and more convenient than the train. Buses are a little more expensive than trains, but by European standards both are absurdly cheap. More buses leave in the morning so get an early start. Since bus ticketing is computerised at main stations you can book a seat ahead and be sure of a comfortable trip. At large stations make sure you're in the right ticket line.

Reservations can only be made in the originating station of the bus. Way stations are rarely computerised and at peak periods you may have to stand part of the way if you don't have a reservation. Tickets for local buses and some express buses can be purchased directly from the driver. There's sometimes a small additional charge for baggage.

All over Czechoslovakia, if you want to find a bus station or bus stop write the letters CSAD on a piece of paper and show it to someone. If you want to find a railway station write CSD on the paper.

Most bus and railway stations have a baggage room (uschovna). Some left luggage offices had a 15 kg maximum weight limit but if yours is heavier you can offer to put your own pack up on the shelf. If this doesn't work a US$1 banknote will. If you loose the receipt you'll have to pay a 25 Kcs fine to recover your luggage.

LOCAL TRANSPORT

Buses and trams within cities operate from 4.30 am to 11.30 pm daily. In Prague some main bus routes operate every 40 minutes all night. Tickets (1 Kcs) sold at newsstands must be cancelled once aboard. There are no conductors. Tickets are hard to find at night, on weekends and out in residential areas, so carry a good supply. One crown coins are used to enter the Prague Metro. A new ticket is required each time you change vehicles.

Prague

Prague is like a history lesson come true. As you walk among the long stone palaces or across the Karluv Most, with Smetana's Moldau flowing below and pointed towers all around, you'll feel as if history had stopped somewhere back in the 18th century. Goethe called Prague the prettiest gem in the stone crown of the world. A millennium earlier in 965 the Arab-Jewish merchant Ibrahim Ibn Jacob had described Prague as a town of 'stone and lime.'

This storybook city in the centre of Bohemia experienced two architectural golden ages, a Gothic period under Holy Roman Emperor Charles IV and a Baroque period during the Hapsburg Counter Reformation. During the 18th century Czech culture was suppressed so it's not surprising that Prague's two greatest Baroque architects, Christopher and Kilian Dienzenhofer, were Germans.

Today Prague is the seat of the governments of the CSR and CSSR, both houses of the Federal Assembly and the leading centre of much of the country's intellectual and cultural life. Unlike Warsaw, Budapest and Berlin which were major battlefields during WW II, Prague escaped almost unscathed. Since the war careful planning and preservation have prevented haphazard modern development.

Prague has so much to offer in the way of historic buildings and museums that you won't finish seeing it. Don't attempt to. Get close to the city and leave it. While everyone will want to spend a few days in this great European art centre, it's only in the little towns of Bohemia or the mountains of Slovakia that you'll learn what this country is really all about. You'll find later that your most treasured memories are of places the folks back home never heard of.

Orientation

Prague nestles in a picturesque valley, its high hills topped by castles, its river spanned by 17 bridges. This river, the Moldau (Vltava), swings like a question mark through the centre of the city separating Mala Strana (Little Quarter), with the Baroque homes of the nobility, from Stare Mesto (Old Town), the early Gothic city centre. Above Mala Strana is Hradcany, the medieval castle district where royalty resided, while Nove Mesto (New Town) is a late Gothic extension of Stare Mesto to the south, almost as far as the old citadel, Vysehrad. Only in 1784 did these four royal towns unite within a single system of fortifications.

Unforgettable features include Prague Castle, which is visible from almost everywhere in the city, and Vaclavske namesti (Wenceslaus Square), Prague's Champs Elysees, which points north-west to Staromestske namesti, the old town square. Between these two squares is Na prikope, a busy pedestrian street where most of the information offices are found.

Information

Tourist Information The best place to pick up brochures and ask questions is at the Prague Information Service, Na prikope 20. Their courteous, helpful staff are a relief, but they cannot find you a room nor sell you any tickets. The CKM Student Travel Centre, Jindrisska 28, is also helpful with information, but they cannot make reservations at hotels or youth hostels.

Cedok, Na prikope 18, sells international train tickets (payment in Western currency). This office is also the easiest place to change money to cover your DM 30 daily requirement. Balnea, Parizska 11, can arrange accommodation and treatment at Czech spas for US$30 a night and up, all inclusive (food, lodging, medical attention).

The travel office of the International Union of Students, Parizska 25, sells the IUS student identity card for 15 Kcs. These are very handy for discounts in museums, etc. The card also gains you a 25% discount on international train tickets in Eastern Europe, so be sure to get one if you're eligible.

Bookstores The Knihkupectvi Bookstore, Staromestske namesti 16, has a good selection of maps. Nadas, Hybernska 5 beside the Lenin Museum, sells railway timetables and city maps.

Embassies Most of the foreign embassies are below the castle in Mala Strana, including the British Embassy, Thunovska 14, the Romanian Consulate, Nerudova 5 (open Monday, Wednesday and Friday 10 am to 12 noon, visas US$24), the American Embassy, Trziste 15, and the West German Consulate, Vlasska 19. The Hungarian Consulate, I V Micurina 1 (Monday, Tuesday, Wednesday, Friday 10 am to 1 pm), and Canadian Embassy, Mickiewiczova 6, are near Hradcanska Metro station.

On the other side of town near Muzeum Metro station are the Polish Consulate, Vaclavske namesti 49 (weekdays 8.30 am to 12 noon), and the Bulgarian Consulate, Krakovska 6. If you want an East German tourist visa enquire at Reiseburo der DDR, Parizska 7. GDR transit visas are issued at the border, not in advance.

Things to See

Hradcany Prague's finest churches and museums are found in Hradcany, the wonderful castle district stretching along a hilltop west of the river. The easiest way to organise a visit is to take the Metro to Malostranska, then tram No 22 up the hill around to the back of Hradcany as far as

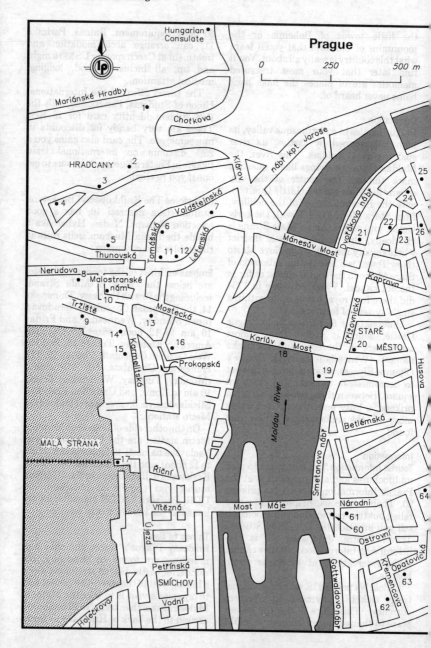

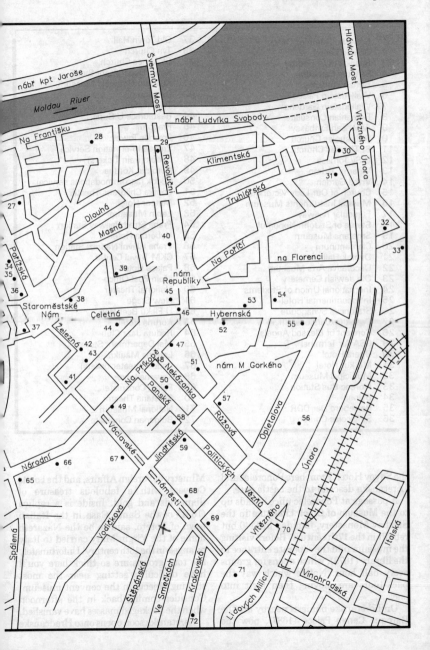

1	Belveder Summer Palace	37	Old Town Hall
2	Golden Lane	38	Tyn Church
3	Basilica of St George	39	St James Church
4	St Vitus Cathedral	40	Kotva Department Store
5	British Embassy	41	Klement Gottwald Museum
6	Wallenstein Palace	42	Carolinum
7	Wallenstein Gardens	43	Tyl Theater
8	Romanian Consulate	44	Restaurace U Supa
9	American Embassy	45	Pragotur
10	St Nicholas Church	46	Powder Tower
11	St Thomas Church	47	Prague Information Service
12	U Sv Tomase	48	Cedok (train Tickets)
13	Vinarna Jadran	49	Automat Koruna
14	Vrtba Garden	50	Cedok (accommodations service)
15	Church of Our Lady Victorious	51	Loutka Childrens Theater
16	Musical Instruments Museum	52	Meteor Hotel
17	Funicular Railway	53	Lenin Museum
18	Statue of St John Nepomuk	54	Praha Stred Railway Station
19	Smetana Museum	55	Hybernia Hotel
20	Clementinum	56	Praha Hlavni Nadrazi Station
21	Dvorak Hall	57	CKM Travel Center
22	Decorative Arts Museum	58	Palace Hotel
23	Old Jewish Cemetery	59	Main Post Office
24	Inernational Union of Students	60	National Theater
25	Intercontinental Hotel	61	New Stage
26	Staronova Synagogue	62	U Fleku Beer Hall
27	Cedok (excursions office)	63	Koruna Hotel
28	Convent of Blessed Angels	64	Reduta Jazz Club
29	CSA Air Terminal	65	Maj Department Store
30	Opera Hotel	66	Laterna Magika
31	Merkur Hotel	67	Cedok (theater tickets)
32	Municipal Museum	68	Kavarna Luxor
33	Florenc Bus Station	69	Polish Consulate
34	Balnea	70	Smetana Theatre
35	Reiseburo Der DDR	71	National Museum
36	St Nicolas Church	72	Bulgarian Consulate

the Savoy Hotel. From here Pohorelec and Loretanska descend to the castle gate.

A passage at Pohorelec ulice 8 leads up to the **Museum of Czech Literature** in the Strahov Monastery, founded in 1140 but rebuilt in the 17th century. Before visiting the museum find the separate entrance to the library (1679), which opens for groups every half hour. Notice which way the pack-tours are moving then melt into one.

On Loretanske namesti nearby are the Baroque **Cernin Palace** (1687), now the Ministry of Foreign Affairs, and the **Loreta Convent** with a fabulous treasure of diamonds and gold. Inside is a replica (1631) of the Santa Casa in the Italian town of Loreto, said to be the Nazareth home of the Virgin Mary carried to Italy by angels in the 13th century! Unfortunately the tour groups are so thick here you'll have difficulty getting near the most striking objects in the convent museum. Consider coming back in the afternoon when the packaged masses have vanished.

Loretanska soon opens onto Hradcanske

namesti, with the main gate to Prague Castle at its east end. At Hradcanske namesti 2 is the **Military Historical Museum** (closed Monday), housed in the Renaissance Schwarzenberg-Lobkowitz Palace (1563).

Just across the square at number 15 is the 18th century Sternbersky Palace containing the **National Gallery**. This has the main collection of European paintings in the country with whole rooms of Cranachs and Picassos. Fortunately the groups never have time to visit so you can see it in relative peace. (This and the many other branches of the National Gallery around Prague open Tuesday to Sunday from 10 am to 6 pm.)

Prague Castle Prague Castle was founded in the 9th century, then rebuilt and extended many times. Always the centre of political power, it's still the official residence of the president. As you enter the castle compound under an arch dated 1614 you'll see the cathedral **treasury** in a chapel directly in front. On the north side of this courtyard is the **Castle Picture Gallery** with a good collection of Baroque paintings in what was once a stable.

The second courtyard is dominated by **St Vitus Cathedral**, a glorious Gothic structure begun in 1344 by order of Emperor Charles IV and only completed

in 1929. The stained glass windows, frescoes and tombstones (including that of the founder) merit careful attention. From the cathedral's Wenceslas Chapel (1366) an entrance leads to a chamber containing the Bohemian crown jewels.

Adjacent to the clock tower on the south side of the cathedral is the entrance to the **Old Royal Palace** with its huge Vladislav Hall (1486-1502). A ramp to one side allowed mounted horsemen to ride into the hall and conduct jousts indoors. On 23 May 1618 two Catholic councillors were thrown from the window of an adjacent chamber by irate Protestant nobles, an act which touched off the Thirty Years War which devastated Europe from 1618 to 1648.

As you leave the palace the **Basilica of St George** (1142), a remarkable Romanesque building, will be directly in front of you. In the Benedictine convent next to the church is the National Gallery's collection of Czech art from medieval to 18th century (closed Monday). There's a small bar in the museum where you can get a much needed cup of coffee and a piece of cake.

Behind this gallery follow the crowd into **Golden Lane** (zlata ulicka), a 16th century tradesman's quarter of tiny houses built into the castle walls. From

Prague Castle

PRAŽSKÝ HRAD

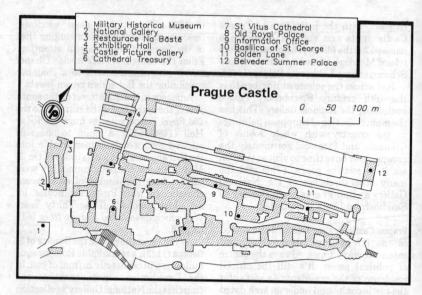

1 Military Historical Museum
2 National Gallery
3 Restaurace Na Baště
4 Exhibition Hall
5 Castle Picture Gallery
6 Cathedral Treasury
7 St Vitus Cathedral
8 Old Royal Palace
9 Information Office
10 Basilica of St George
11 Golden Lane
12 Belveder Summer Palace

Prague Castle

the east end of the castle a stairway leads back down toward Malostranska Metro station.

Mala Strana From Malostranska Metro station follow Valdstejnska around to Valdstejnske namesti past many impressive palaces, especially the **Wallenstein Palace** (1630) which fills the entire east side of the square. A famous figure in the Thirty Years War, General Albrecht Wallenstein started out on the Protestant side then went over to the Catholics and built this palace with the expropriated wealth of his former colleagues. In 1634 the Hapsburg emperor learned that Wallenstein was about to switch sides once again and had him assassinated at Cheb. The palace gardens are accessible May to September through a gate at Letenska ulice 10, a block over.

Continue south on Tomasska and round the corner on to Letenska to reach **St Thomas Church** (1731), a splendid Baroque edifice. Behind Malostranske namesti nearby is formerly Jesuit St **Nicholas Church** (1755), the greatest

Baroque building in Prague, its dome visible from afar. Mala Strana was built up in the 17th and 18th centuries below the protective walls of Prague Castle by the victorious Catholic clerics and noblemen on the foundations of the Renaissance palaces of their Protestant predecessors.

After a wander around the square follow the tram tracks south along Karmelitska. At the back of the courtyard at Karmelitska 25 is the **Vrtba Garden** (1720) with interesting statuary. Just beyond at Karmelitska 13 is the **Church of Our Lady Victorious** (1613) with the venerated wax Holy Infant of Prague (1628). Originally erected by Lutherans, this church was taken over by the Carmelite order after the Catholic victory at the Battle of White Mountain (1620) depicted in a painting in the church choir.

Backtrack a little and take narrow Prokopska ulice toward the river. You'll soon reach a beautiful square surrounded by fine Baroque palaces. Keep straight left on Lazenska toward the massive stone towers of the **Church of Our Lady Below the**

Chain. On the right as you approach the church is the **Museum of Musical Instruments** (closed Monday), Lazenska 2, in the one time Palace of the Grand Order of the Maltese Falcon.

To the left of the church Lazenska leads out to Mostecka with **Karluv Most** (1357) to the right. This enchanting bridge graced by 30 18th century statues was the only bridge in Prague until 1841. Take a leisurely stroll across it, but first climb the tower on the Mala Strana side for a great bird's eye view. At the middle of the bridge is a bronze statue (1683) of St John Nepomuk who was thrown to his death in the river in 1383 when he refused to tell King Wenceslas IV what the queen had confided to him at confession.

Across on the Stare Mesto side of the bridge is the 17th century **Clementinum**, once a Jesuit college but now the State Library with over three million volumes. After Prague Castle this is the largest historic building in the city. To the right and around at the end of Novotneho lavka is the **Smetana Museum** (closed Tuesday), in a former waterworks building beside the river. Ask to hear a recording of the composers' music.

Stare Mesto Beside the Clementinum narrow Karlova ulice leads east toward Staromestske namesti, Prague's old town square and still the heart of the city. At its centre is a monument to the religious reformer John Huss, erected in 1915 on the anniversary of his death by fire at the stake in 1415. Below the clock tower of the **Old Town Hall** is a Gothic horologe (1410) which entertains the throng with apostles, Christ, a skeleton and the cock every hour on the hour. Immediately after the show a tour of the building, including the 15th century council chamber, begins inside.

In another corner of the square is Baroque **St Nicholas Church**, designed by Kilian Dienzenhofer. More striking is the Gothic **Tyn Church** (1365) with its twin steeples. The tomb of the 16th century Danish astronomer Tycho de Brahe is beside the main altar and the church is extremely rich in artworks. Unfortunately the Tyn Church keeps capricious hours. If the main entrance is shut check to see if they forgot to lock the side door at Celetna 5.

From a corner of Staromestske namesti near the horologe take Zelezna ulice south-east to the **Carolinum**, Zelezna 9, the oldest remaining part of Prague University, founded by Charles IV in 1348. Next to this at Zelezna 11 is the neo-Classical **Tyl Theatre** (1783) where the premier of Mozart's *Don Giovanni* took place in 1787 with the composer himself conducting.

Around the corner at Rytirska 29 is the **Klement Gottwald Museum** (closed Monday), an ornate neo-Renaissance palace (1894) with an exhaustive photo display on the recent political history of the country. From one corner of this building Na mustku leads into Vaclavske namesti or Wenceslas Square, Prague's fashionable boulevard where 'revisionist' demonstrators gathered in 1968 (Metro – Mustek).

Don't walk up the square just now but go round the corner to the left into Na prikope, a crowded pedestrian mall which leads to the **Powder Tower** (1474) on namesti Republiky. Gunpowder was stored here in the 18th century and the tower only received its neo-Gothic appearance in 1886. On summer weekends you may climb the tower.

Hybernska ulice runs due east from here to Praha stred Railway Station (Metro – namesti Republiky). The **Lenin Museum**, Hybernska 7, is dedicated to the history of socialism. In 1912 Lenin chaired the illegal 6th conference of the Russian Social Democratic Workers Party in this building.

Other Museums One of Prague's finest yet lesser known museums is the 13th century **Convent of Blessed Angels**, Na Frantisku, by the river in Josefov. Here is kept the National Gallery's collection of 19th century Czech art, with many paintings depicting historical scenes of special interest to visitors. There's a good restaurant in this museum so visit around lunch time.

If you're into music there's the **Mozart Museum** in Villa Bertranska, Mozartova 169 (Metro – Moskevska). Mozart wrote *Don Giovanni* here in 1787. Similarly there's the **Antonin Dvorak Museum**, Ke Karlovu 20 (Metro – I P Pavlova), in the Baroque summer residence (1720) of a noble family.

Vysehrad Take the Metro to Gottwaldova where the new **Palace of Culture** (1981) and Forum Hotel rise above a deep ravine crossed by the Klement Gottwald bridge. From here the twin towers of neo-Gothic **Peter & Paul Church** are visible to the west. Walk toward them through the gates of 17th century **Vysehrad Citadel**, seat of the 11th century Przemyslid princes of Bohemia. You pass the Romanesque **Rotunda of St Martin** before reaching **Slavin Cemetery** behind Peter & Paul Church. Many distinguished people are buried here, including the composers Smetana (1824-1884) and Dvorak (1841-1904). The view of the Moldau Valley from the citadel battlements along the south side of the Vysehrad ridge is superb.

Monday Specials In Prague on a Monday? Most museums and galleries will be closed, but the National Museum (closed Tuesday) and Jewish Ghetto (closed Saturday) stay open. Looming above the south-east end of Vaclavske namesti is the neo-Renaissance **National Museum** (1890) with ho-hum collections on theatrical and natural history (Metro – Muzeum). In front of the museum is an equestrian statue of the 10th century king Vaclav I or St Wenceslas, patron saint of Bohemia.

The **Prague Ghetto**, Parizska 19 (Metro – Staromestska), includes a fascinating variety of monuments, now part of the State Jewish Museum. The early Gothic Staronova Synagogue (1270) is one of the oldest in Europe. All-inclusive tickets are sold in the museum across the lane from the synagogue, beside which is the pink Jewish Town Hall with its picturesque clock tower (16th century). Follow the crowd down U Stareho Hrbitova to the Klausen Synagogue (1694) and another section of the museum.

The collections of the State Jewish Museum have a remarkable origin. In 1942 the Nazis brought the objects here from 153 Jewish Communities in Bohemia and Moravia for a planned 'museum of an extinct people' to be opened once their extermination programme was complete! The interior of one of the buildings bears the names of 77,297 Czech Jews with the names of the camps where they perished.

Behind the Klausen Synagogue is the **Old Jewish Cemetery** with 12,000 tombstones, an evocative sight. The oldest grave is dated 1439 and by 1787, when the cemetery ceased to be used, the area had became so crowded that burials were carried out one on top of the other as many as 12 layers deep!

Also open on Monday is Prague's large **zoo**, on a wooded hillside north-east of the city. Get there on bus No 112 from Fucikova Metro station. Next to the zoo is the early Baroque **Troya Chateau** (1685).

One Last Museum On your last afternoon in Prague set aside a little time for the **Municipal Museum** (closed Monday), the large white neo-Renaissance building above Sokolovska Metro station. Here you'll see maps and photos of the numerous monuments you've visited around town, plus interesting artefacts to put them in perspective. But the museum's crowning glory is a huge scale model of Prague created in 1834. Don't miss it!

Karlstejn It's an easy daytrip to **Karlstejn Castle**, 28 km south-west of Prague, erected by King Charles IV in the mid-14th century. Trains leave about once an hour from Praha-Smichov Railway Station (a 40-minute journey). The towering castle crowns a ridge above the village, a 20-minute walk from the station (open till

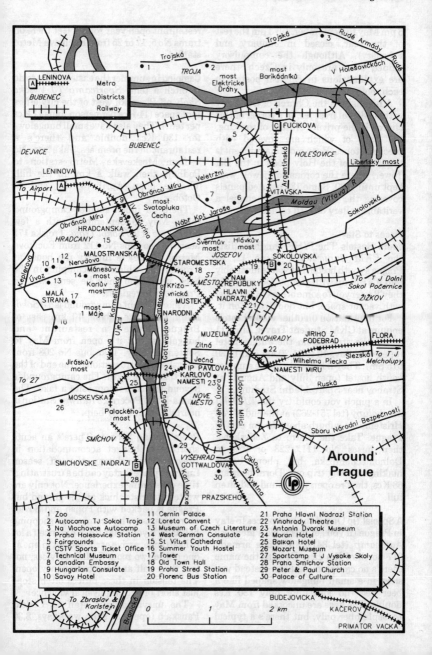

Around Prague

1 Zoo
2 Autocamp TJ Sokol Troja
3 Na Vlachovce Autocamp
4 Praha Holesovice Station
5 Fairgrounds
6 CSTV Sports Ticket Office
7 Technical Museum
8 Canadian Embassy
9 Hungarian Consulate
10 Savoy Hotel

11 Cernin Palace
12 Loreta Convent
13 Museum of Czech Literature
14 West German Consulate
15 St Vitus Cathedral
16 Summer Youth Hostel
17 Tower
18 Old Town Hall
19 Praha Stred Station
20 Florenc Bus Station

21 Praha Hlavni Nadrazi Station
22 Vinohrady Theatre
23 Antonin Dvorak Museum
24 Moran Hotel
25 Balkan Hotel
26 Mozart Museum
27 Sportcamp T J Vysoke Skoly
28 Praha Smichov Station
29 Peter & Paul Church
30 Palace of Culture

0   1   2 km

5 pm May to September, till 3 pm the rest of the year, closed in January and February). Although the compulsory guided tours are only in Czech, there are explanations in English posted in each room.

A highlight is the Church of Our Lady with medieval frescoes. In a corner of this church is the private oratory of the king, the walls of which are covered with precious stones. Even more magnificent is the Chapel of the Holy Rood in the Big Tower, where the coronation jewels were kept until 1420. Some 128 painted panels covering the walls make this chapel a veritable gallery of 14th century art.

Places to Stay

Youth Hostels The IYHF handbook lists the *CKM Juniorhotel*, Zitna 12, as Prague's youth hostel, but you're invariably told it's full up with groups. Occasionally they'll refer you to some other CKM hostel with vacant space, but don't count on it.

For information on other youth hostels enquire at CKM Student Travel, Zitna 11 across the street from the Junior hotel (open weekdays 10 to 11.30 am and 12.30 to 5 pm). They'll know about the summer youth hostel (open July and August) at Strahov near Spartakiadni Stadium.

In a pinch you could try the *TJ Dolni Mecholupy* (tel 751-262) at the end of Pod Hristem in a suburb about 10 km east of Prague. Take the Metro to Zelivskeho, then buses No 111, 228 or 229 to Dolnomecholupska, but phone before making the long trip out. Dorm beds are 68 Kcs, they're open year round and often full.

A Special Tip One of the best places to stay in Prague (if you get in!) is *Na Vlachovce Autocamp* (tel 841-290), Rude armady 217 north of the city. Despite the name there's no campground here. Instead you sleep in a small bungalow shaped like a beer keg (no joke!) for only 130 Kcs double. The kegs are uncorked from May to September only, but there's a typical restaurant open year round. Get there on trams No 5, 17 or 25 from Fucikova Metro station.

Camping In summer the easiest thing to do is pitch a tent. *Sportcamp TJ Vysoke Skoly* off Plzenska west of the city offers tent space (11 Kcs per person, plus 11 Kcs per tent). They also have small bungalows for 130 Kcs double and there's a restaurant on the premises. Take tram No 7 from Moskevska Metro station to Podhaji, then walk a km up the hill. They're open April to the end of October.

There's a much smaller campground (open May to September) with a few bungalows at *TJ Sokol Troja*, Trojska 171 near the zoo (bus No 112 from Fucikova Metro). If they're full try the house at Trojska 157 which has camping in the back yard. You may be sent back to Pragotour to register.

A more distant campground is *TJ Sokol Dolni Pocernice*, about 10 km east of Prague. There's a restaurant and bungalows, but it's open from May to September only. Take bus No 208 from Zelivskeho Metro station to the end of the line, then walk a km. The campground is beyond the church opposite a lake. The Praha-Dolni Pocernice Railway Station is nearby, if that's any help.

Room Finding Services There's an acute shortage of budget accommodation in Prague. Even during the off season finding a place to stay can be a frustrating, time consuming experience. Not only are western tourists thick on the ground but Prague is packed with Polish and Soviet tour groups who come on shopping holidays. If you'd like to save yourself a lot of heartache, arrive early and get in line at one of the two room finding services, not less than half an hour before they open. The tension in these offices often stops just short of actual physical violence.

The unsympathetic staff at Cedok, Panska 5 (opens at 9 am weekdays, 8.30

am weekends), will try to force you into an expensive hotel. A combination of persistence, pleas and tears *may* motivate them to help you find something suitable.

If not, make a dash for Pragotour, U Obecniho domu 2 near the Powder Tower. The accommodation window at Pragotour usually opens at 10 am, but check. They're not so stingy with the less expensive hotels (from 179 Kcs single, 280 Kcs double) and also arrange private rooms (108 Kcs single, three night minimum stay).

Once you have something suitable book for your entire stay in Prague, otherwise you risk having to go through this again. All private rooms are far from the city centre and no advance reservations for a return trip later on are accepted. By 11 am everything but the luxury hotels may be booked.

You may be offered a private room by an individual on the street outside Pragotour or Cedok. The terms will be infinitely better than anything available inside but these arrangements are illegal unless you register with the police, which your host probably won't want you to do. Still, it beats sleeping in the railway station.

Hotels If you go directly to the hotels yourself you're almost always turned down, *unless* you offer the desk clerk a small tip in western currency. This should inspire them to go over their books again and 'discover' a room for you. A couple of dollars is enough.

Here's a list of B-category hotels in geographical sequence across the city: *Opera Hotel*, Tesnov 13 (Metro – Sokolovska); *Merkur Hotel*, Tesnov 9; *Atlantic Hotel*, Na porici 9; *Hybernia Hotel*, Hybernska 24; *Meteor Hotel*, Hybernska 6 (Metro – namesti Republiky); *Palace Hotel*, Panska 12; *Adria Hotel*, Vaclavske namesti 26 (Metro – Mustek); *Koruna Hotel*, Opatovicka 16; *Moran Hotel*, Na Morani 15 (Metro – Karlovo namesti); *Balkan Hotel*, Svornosti 28

(Metro – Moskevska); and *Savoy Hotel*, Keplerova 6 (tram No 22).

Rooms in these begin at 168 Kcs single, 252 Kcs double with shared bath. One expensive hotel to know about is the *Pariz*, an eclectic fin-de-siecle edifice across the street from Pragotour. If you're going to let them sock it to you, you may as well go down in style. If you still don't have a room check out the floor at Hlavni nadrazi Railway Station.

Places to Eat

Stare Mesto Filling your stomach in Prague is much easier than finding a bed. A good cheap restaurant near Staromestske namesti is *Vegetarka*, upstairs at Celetna 3 beside Tyn Church. As the name implies they specialise in vegetarian dishes. Further up this street at Celetna 22 is *Restaurace u Supa*, a good place for a beer and a meal. Also try *U Prince*, Staromestske namesti 28 near the old town hall.

Mala Strana About the only place in Mala Strana to get a snack is *Vinarna Jadran*, Mostecka 21. *U Sv Tomase*, Letenska 12 (Metro – Malostranska), is a beer cellar which also serves meals (daily 11 am to 11 pm).

Hradcany The *Restaurace Na Baste*, just inside the Prague Castle to the left, is an unpretentious place to get a decent meal. The *Obcerstveni Bufet* in a corner of Golden Lane is the only place in Hradcany to get a fast beer and sausages.

Self-service About the cheapest and quickest place to eat in Prague is *Automat Koruna*, at the corner of Vaclavske namesti and Na prikope above the Mustek Metro station. There are lines for everything but they move quickly. You eat standing up. In one corner of Automat Koruna beside the coffee stand is a deluxe grill where you can get shish kebab and steaks.

Others *Kavarna Luxor*, upstairs at Vaclavske namesti 41, offers coffee and cakes in unpretentious elegance. *U Kalicha Restaurant*, Na bojisti 12 (Metro – I P Pavlova), serves excellent Czech meals and big mugs of beer (open daily 11 am to 3 pm and 5 to 11 pm).

Entertainment

Don't come to Prague for the music! To get opera tickets you almost have to be a Party member in good standing as 60% of the seats are reserved for trade unionists and most of the rest go to tour groups from the USSR. The same goes for *Laterna Magika* performances and all the best concerts. Even the smallest theatres are fully booked weeks ahead! Look for the *vyprodano* (sold out) notices before trying to figure out what's on.

You may be told to try for a ticket at the door half an hour before curtain time, but your chances of getting in this way are not good. One way to cut through the red tape is by offering a backhander of a couple of dollars to the ticket clerk. Another ploy is to stand outside the *National Theatre* just before show time waving a five dollar bill and hope someone's greed is stronger than his/her love of culture. Less dramatically, your hotel desk clerk might be able to come up with tickets for a little hard cash.

The bourgeois pretensions of socialist Prague are reflected in a notice at the ticket windows reminding the public to attend opera and ballet performances in 'social attire.' Try going in naked.

Theatres Opera and ballet are performed at the neo-Renaissance *National Theatre* (1883), Narodni 2, while the ultramodern *New Stage*, Narodni 4, specialises in serious theatre. Opera and ballet are also presented at the *Smetana Theatre* on Vitezneho unora (Metro – Muzeum).

For operettas and musicals it's the *Karlin Theatre of Music*, Krizikova 10 near Florenc Bus Station (Metro – Sokolovska). Prague's main concert venue is neo-Renaissance *Dvorak Hall*, namesti Krasnoarmejcu (Metro – Staromestska), where the Prague Spring Music Festival is held in May. The *Vinohrady Theatre*, namesti Miru 7 (Metro – namesti Miru), presents Czech drama.

Lighter Fare For jazz try *Reduta*, Narodni 20 (special show at 9.30 pm). The *Laterna Magika*, Narodni 40 (Metro – Narodni), offers a unique combination of theatre, dance and film. *U Fleku*, Kremencova 11, is a genuine German-style beer hall which brews its own dark ale. There's a cabaret show here at 9.30 pm (25 Kcs cover charge) but beware of overcharging. Also check out the *Loutka Children's Theatre*, namesti Maxima Gorkeho 28.

Ticket Agencies Cedok, Vaclavske namesti 24, sometimes has tickets for the National Theatre, so ask there first. Nearby in the Alfa Cinema Arcade is Sluna, Vaclavske namesti 28, which sells tickets for concerts and many other events advertised on posters in the office. There's a second Sluna office in the arcade at Panska 4 opposite Cedok's accommodation service. Tickets to sports events are available from CSTV, Dukelskych hrdinu 13, but you must go at least one day before.

Things to Buy

The KOTVA Department Store on namesti Republiky is the largest in the country. There's also MAJ Department Store, Narodni and Spalena.

Getting There & Away

Train Trains run between Berlin-Lichtenberg and Prague (via Dresden) every three or four hours. Several of the trains arriving from Berlin carry on to Vienna. There's service twice a day from Nuremberg (via Cheb) and daily from Linz (via Horni Dvoriste). Many trains arrive from Budapest (via Brno and Bratislava). From Poland you have the choice of arriving via Wroclaw or Katowice. There are overnight trains with sleepers to and from Kosice.

Railway Stations Prague has four main railway stations. International trains between Berlin and Budapest often stop at Praha-Holesovice station (Metro – Fucikova) on the north side of the city. Other important trains terminate at Praha hlavni nadrazi (Metro – Hlavni nadrazi) or Praha stred (Metro – namesti Republiky), both of which are close to the city centre. Some local trains to the south-west depart Praha-Smichov station (Metro – Smichovske nadrazi) to the south.

Bus Buses to Karlovy Vary, Brno and most other towns in the western half of the country and as far away as Bratislava depart the Praha-Florenc Bus Station, Krizikova 4 (Metro – Sokolovska).

Bus Tickets Reservations at P Florenc Bus Station are computerised! To obtain a ticket determine the departure time *(odjezdy)* of your bus by looking on a posted timetable or asking at Information. Then get in line at any of the ticket counters. Check to make sure your bus isn't on the 'sold out' *(vyprodano)* list on the television screens here. If it is, pick another bus. The further ahead you book the better your chances of getting the bus you want. Your bus ticket indicates the platform number *(stani)* and seat number *(sed)*. You may be charged 3 Kcs extra for baggage. The coaches are quite comfortable (no standing) and fares low.

Getting Around

Airport Transport Ruzyne Airport is 17 km west of the city centre. Every half hour an airport bus (6 Kcs) departs the CSA Czechoslovak Airlines office, Revolucni 25 (Metro – namesti Republiky). You can

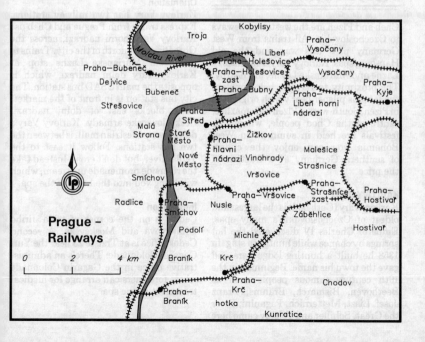

also get there on city bus No 119 from Leninova Metro station.

Public Transport All public transport in Prague costs 1 Kcs a ride. Buy a good supply of tickets at newsstands and kiosks, then validate your own ticket as you enter the vehicle or Metro. The three lines of the Metro connect all bus and railway stations, as well as many tourist attractions. Using the Metro is easy.

Sightseeing Tours The Cedok office at Bilkova 6 near the Inter-Continental Hotel arranges bus excursions to historic sites in the environs, including castles and spas. Departures are only during the high season (15 May to 15 October) and prices run 190 Kcs to 260 Kcs. You meet the bus at the Inter-Continental Hotel.

West Bohemia

Cheb and Plzen are the western gateways to Czechoslovakia. All trains from West Germany pass this way and the old Hapsburg spas, Karlovy Vary, Frantiskovy Lazne and Marianske Lazne, are nearby. The proximity to Bavaria helps explain the famous pilsner beer which originated in Plzen. South-west of Plzen is Domazlice, centre of the Chod people, where folk festivals are held in summer. In West Bohemia you can enjoy the charm of southern Germany at a fraction of the price.

KARLOVY VARY
Karlovy Vary (Carlsbad) is the largest and oldest of Czechoslovakia's many spas. Emperor Charles IV discovered the hot springs by chance while hunting a stag. In 1358 he built a hunting lodge here and gave the town his name. Beginning in the 19th century famous people such as Beethoven, Bismarck, Brahms, Franz Josef, Liszt, Metternich, Paganini, Peter the Great, Schiller and Tolstoy came here

to take the waters and busts of a few of them grace the promenades.

There are 12 hot springs containing 40 chemical elements used in medical treatment of diseases of the digestive tract and metabolic disorders. If you have diarrhoea or constipation this is the place to come. Mineral deposits from the springs form stone encrustations which are sold as souvenirs. Karlovy Vary's herbal Becherovka liqueur is known as the 13th spring.

Karlovy Vary still bears a definite Victorian air. The elegant colonnades and boulevards go well with the many peaceful walks in the surrounding forest park. The picturesque river valley winds between wooded hills, yet the spa offers all the facilities of a medium sized town without the bother. After hustling around Prague this is just the place to relax. It's hard not to like Karlovy Vary.

Orientation
Karlovy Vary has two railway stations. Express trains from Prague and Cheb use Karlovy Vary horni nadrazi, across the Ohre River just north of the city. Trains to and from Marianske Lazne stop at Karlovy Vary dolni nadrazi, which is opposite the main CSAD bus station. The city bus station is in front of the market, three blocks east of dolni nadrazi. Ceskoslovenske armady, Karlovy Vary's downtown pedestrian mall, is between the two bus stations. Follow it east to the Tepla River, but don't cross. Instead take the riverside promenade upstream, which will bring you into the heart of the spa.

Information
Cedok is on the corner of trida Jiriho Dimitrvova and Moskevska. A second Cedok office is at Trziste 23 near the Yuri Gagarin Colonnade. There's an administrative office in the Gagarin Colonnade where foreigners can arrange for medical treatment at the spa.

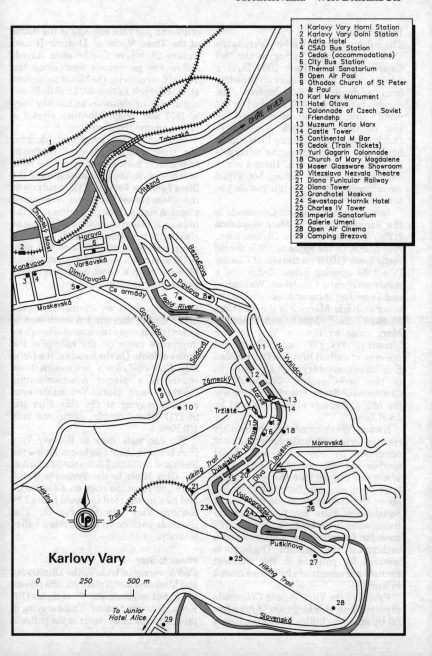

1 Karlovy Vary Horni Station
2 Karlovy Vary Dolni Station
3 Adria Hotel
4 CSAD Bus Station
5 Cedok (accommodations)
6 City Bus Station
7 Thermal Sanatorium
8 Open Air Pool
9 Othodox Church of St Peter
   & Paul
10 Karl Marx Monument
11 Hotel Otava
12 Colonnade of Czech Soviet
   Friendshp
13 Muzeum Karla Marx
14 Castle Tower
15 Continental M Bar
16 Cedok (Train Tickets)
17 Yuri Gagarin Colonnade
18 Church of Mary Magdalene
19 Moser Glassware Showroom
20 Vitezslava Nezvala Theatre
21 Diana Funicular Railway
22 Diana Tower
23 Grandhotel Moskva
24 Sevastopol Hornik Hotel
25 Charles IV Tower
26 Imperial Sanatorium
27 Galerie Umeni
28 Open Air Cinema
29 Camping Brezova

Karlovy Vary

0   250   500 m

To Junior
Hotel Alice

Things to See

The pulsing heart of Karlovy Vary is the Vridlo or Sprundel Spring in the **Yuri Gagarin Colonnade**. Here 2000 litres a minute of 72.2°C water shoot up 12 metres from a depth of 2500 metres. The colonnade (built in 1975) is named for the world's first astronaut, who visited the spa in 1961 and 1966. Throngs of Czechoslovak tourists, funny little cups in hand, pace up and down the colonnade taking the 'drinking cure.' Bring a cup of your own for some piping hot liquid refreshment and maybe it'll just do you some good!

Just above the Gagarin Colonnade is the Baroque **Church of Mary Magdalene** (1736) designed by Kilian Dienzenhofer. Also nearby on the opposite hill is the **old castle tower** (1608) on the site of Charles IV's 1358 hunting lodge. Today it's a restaurant open till 1 am (closed Wednesday and Thursday). Almost directly below the tower at Karla Marxe 3 is the **Karl Marx Museum** (closed Monday and Tuesday). Marx came to Karlovy Vary to cure himself in 1874, 1875 and 1876. Ask the museum attendant to put on the recorded English commentary. Just a little north is the neo-Classical **Colonnade of Czechoslovak-Soviet Friendship**, formerly the Mill Colonnade (1881), designed by Josef Zitek.

Karlovy Vary's numerous sanatoria are reserved for patients undergoing treatment prescribed by physicians and casual tourists are not admitted. One place where you *can* get into the water is the large open air pool *(bazen)* on the hill above the tastelessly modern Thermal Sanatorium. Here you bathe in warm spring water to the beat of rock music. It's great fun but no diving is allowed and a bathing cap must be worn. The *bazen* is reserved for patients in the morning; tourists are admitted afternoons from 2 to 9 pm.

Return to the Yuri Gagarin Colonnade to pursue your 'drinking cure.' After a free fill-up cross the bridge beside the Cedok office and pay your respects at the **House of the Three Moors** or Dagmar House, Trziste 25, where Goethe once stayed. Follow the promenade west along the Tepla River noticing the Moser Salesroom at Dukelskych hrdinu 40. Ludvik Moser began making glassware at Karlovy Vary in 1857 and today Bohemian crystal is prized around the world.

Just before the Grandhotel Moskva, one time meeting place of European aristocracy, notice an alley on the right which leads to the bottom station of the **Diana Funicular Railway**. Take a ride up to the **Diana Tower** for great views and pleasant walks through the forest. If the railway is closed a network of footpaths also begins near this station. If instead of going up you continue along the river you'll soon reach the **Galerie Umeni** (closed Monday) with a select collection of fine Bohemian porcelain and crystal.

Loket If you have an afternoon to spare take a CSAD bus eight km south-west to Loket (about every two hours). There's an impressive **castle** on the hilltop in the centre of town. On the facade of the *Hotel Bily Kun* on Loket's picturesque town square is a plaque commemorating Goethe's seven visits. You might even consider staying at the *Bily Kun* (tel 94-171) where double rooms are only 150 Kcs.

You can walk back to Karlovy Vary from Loket in about two hours. Follow the black and white trail down the left bank of the Ohre River to the **Svatosske Rocks**. Here you cross the river on a footbridge and pick up the road to Doubi (served by Karlovy Vary city bus No 6). This riverside path down the forested valley is lovely.

Places to Stay

Cedok, corner of trida Jiriho Dimitrvova and Moskevska, will place you in a private home, but you must stay three nights (100 Kcs a night per person). Those staying in private rooms must report to the police in an alley near the *Grandhotel Moskva* (no problem). If you're only staying one night your best bet is the *Adria Hotel*, Konevova 1 opposite the CSAD bus station. Other hotels closer to the spa include the *Sevastopol-Hornik*, Volgogradska 27 (140 Kcs single, 180 Kcs double), and the higher class *Otava Hotel*, I P Pavlova 4 (218 Kcs single, 328 Kcs double).

For youth hostellers the cheapest place to stay is the *Juniorhotel Alice* (tel 4379) about four km south of town (bus No 7 direction Brezova). Beware of a hefty surcharge to take a shower! In summer the hostel will be full. Not far away is the *Motel Brezova* (260 Kcs double) which has a campground (53 Kcs double) open April to October.

Places to Eat

The best place for breakfast is *Continental M-Bar*, Trziste 27 near the Yuri Gagarin Colonnade. There's a great little ice cream parlour inside the M-Bar and just up the hill at Trziste 31 is a grill with tasty barbecued chicken and cold beer. More beer is available at *Budvar* beside Hotel Otava, also meals. The cheapest place to eat is *Bufet Patria* next to Budvar. Don't tell your high society friends you go there.

Entertainment

Karlovy Vary's main theatre is the *Divadlo Vitezslava Nezvala* on Leninovo namesti not far from the Yuri Gagarin Colonnade. Notice the theatres' tiny ticket counter in the colonnade itself. From mid-April to mid-September there are concerts in the colonnade daily except Monday. Among the many cultural festivals are jazz (March), singing (June), magic (July), international films (every other July), music (August and September) and touristic films (September). Ask about these and other events at the Kulturni Sluzby (cultural offices) in Thermal Sanatorium. There's a disco in the *Grandhotel Moskva*.

Getting There & Away

There's a direct train from Berlin-Lichtenberg to Karlovy Vary via Leipzig and Frantiskovy Lazne (reservation required). Cheb and Marianske Lazne are connected to Karlovy Vary by local trains. There are direct trains to Prague, but it's faster and easier to come by bus (eight daily). Bus is the only way to go directly to Plzen. Seats on express buses can be reserved in advance by computer at the CSAD bus station. An international bus links the spa to Vienna. Couchettes are available to and from Kosice.

Getting Around

Before boarding a city bus buy some tickets at a kiosk. A good service to know about is city bus No 11 which runs from Horni nadrazi Railway Station to the city bus station, then on over the hills to Leninovo namesti and the Yuri Gagarin Colonnade.

CHEB

This old medieval town on the Ohre River near the western tip of Czechoslovakia is an easy daytrip by train from Karlovy Vary or Marianske Lazne. Only a few km north of the West German border, Cheb (formerly Eger) retains a strong German flavour.

Information

Cedok is at trida Ceskoslovensko-Sovetskeho Pratelstvi and trida 1 maje. If you're arriving fresh from West Germany you can complete compulsory money exchange in this office. If they're closed try the Hotel Hvezda nearby.

Things to See

The area around the railway station is ugly, but only a few minutes away up trida Ceskoslovensko-Sovetskeho Pratelstvi is the picturesque town square, all the burgher houses with sloping red tile roofs. In the middle of this square is **Spalicek**, a cluster of 13th century Gothic houses which were once shops. Behind these is

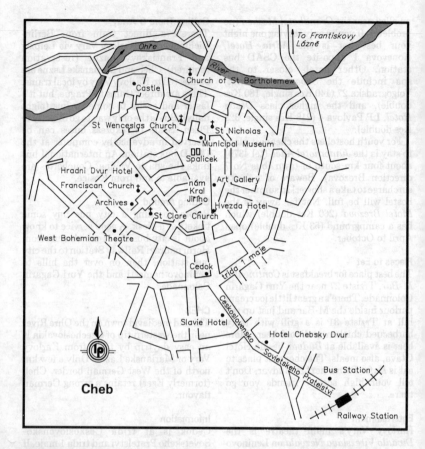

Cheb

the **Municipal Museum** (closed Monday) with an excellent historical exhibition. The Thirty Years War military commander Albrecht Wallenstein was murdered here in 1634 and the museum devotes a room to him. Also on the square is the Baroque New Town Hall (1728), now the **city art gallery**.

Back behind the Municipal Museum is **St Nicholas Church**, a splendid Gothic structure with a soaring sculpture-filled interior. Notice the excellent portal (1270) and the Romanesque features such as the twin towers. A few blocks away is **Cheb**

Castle (open April to October, closed Monday) erected in the 12th century by Friedrich I Barbarossa, leader of the Eastern Crusades. The Black Tower dates from 1222 but the exterior fortifications are 17th century.

Places to Stay

There are a number of small hotels in Cheb (see the map). The cheapest is the *Hotel Chebsky Dvur*, trida Ceskoslovensko-Sovetskeho Pratelstvi 43 near the station, but it's usually full. The next cheapest are the *Slavie* and *Hradni Dvur*. More hotels (such as the *Slovan*, Narodni trida 5) are to be found at Frantiskovy Lazne (Franzensbad), an old spa from the Austro-Hungarian Empire only five km north of Cheb.

The nearest campgrounds are at Drenice on Jesenice Lake, five km east of Cheb, and Amerika, two km south-east of Frantiskovy Lazne.

Getting There & Away

Most trains arriving in Czechoslovakia from Nuremberg call here. The train from Berlin-Lichtenberg and Leipzig calls at nearby Frantiskovy Lazne. There are trains from Prague via Chomutov and Karlovy Vary or via Plzen and Marianske Lazne. Local trains run to Frantiskovy Lazne but beware of express trains on this route which levy a huge surcharge. Buses to Frantiskovy Lazne are cheaper and more frequent.

MARIANSKE LAZNE

Marianske Lazne (Marienbad) is Czechoslovakia's most famous spa, but in many ways it ranks second to Karlovy Vary. The resort developed quickly during the second half of the 19th century, but famous guests began arriving before then. The elderly Goethe wrote his *Marienbader Elegie* for young Ulrika von Levetzow here. The 628-metre elevation gives the spa a brisk climate which goes well with the pine-clad Bohemian hills to the north.

Marianske Lazne boasts 140 mineral springs, 39 of which are used for treating diseases of the kidneys, urinary and respiratory tracts. The hillsides and open spaces around the massive Victorian bathhouses and hotels have been landscaped into parks. Maps of the many possible walks are posted at the Maxim Gorky Colonnade. This is definitely the way to go as the area around the spa centre itself is disappointing.

Orientation

The adjacent bus and train stations are three km south of the centre of town. Follow Ceskoslovenske armady, which becomes Odboraru, due north.

Information

Cedok is at Odboraru 46.

Things to See

The **Maxim Gorky Colonnade** (1889) is the centre of Marianske Lazne. Throngs of the faithful promenade back and forth here, each with a teapot of hot mineral water in his/her hand as a sign of devotion to the 'drinking cure.' At one end of the colonnade is the **Pavilion of the Cross Spring** (1826), while at the other is a new musical fountain which puts on free shows for the crowd at intervals. The canned music is sometimes a little off key, but that's Marienbad.

Above the colonnade is the **Municipal Museum** (open Tuesday and Thursday only) on Gottwaldovo namesti, where Goethe stayed in 1823. In front of this is the circular Catholic church (1848), while below are **Rudolph's Pavilion**, the former casino (now a social club) and the **New Baths** (1895).

In a park just north-west of the centre is the **Pavilion of the Forest Spring** (1869) with bronze statues of Goethe and Ulrika nearby. Down toward the railway station are **Ferdinand's Spring** and **Rudolph's Spring** (1823).

Places to Stay

There is plenty of accommodation in Marianske Lazne but in mid-summer everything will be taken. On Plzenska beside the stadium, only a five-minute walk from the stations, is the *Start Motel* (182 Kcs double), a good place to start. Camping at the motel is 10 Kcs per person plus 21 Kcs per tent. It's noisy and cramped. Larger and quieter, *Autocamp Luxor* is four km south-west of the railway station by a roundabout route (take a taxi if you can). The *CKM 'Krakonos' Youth Hostel* (tel 2624) is at the top of a toboggan

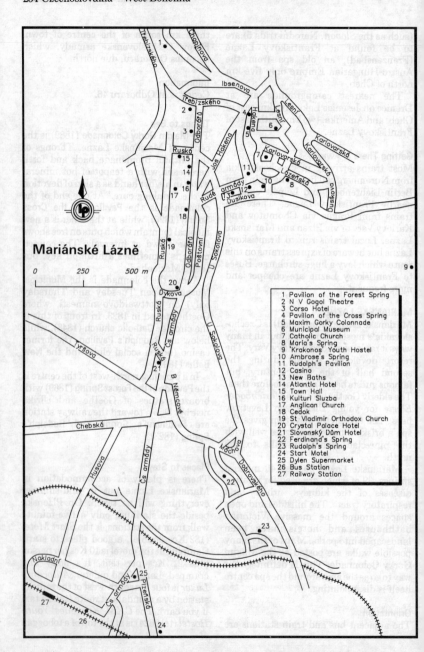

Mariánské Lázně

0   250   500 m

1 Pavilion of the Forest Spring
2 N V Gogol Theatre
3 Corso Hotel
4 Pavilion of the Cross Spring
5 Maxim Gorky Colonnade
6 Municipal Museum
7 Catholic Church
8 Maria's Spring
9 'Krakonos' Youth Hostel
10 Ambrose's Spring
11 Rudolph's Pavilion
12 Casino
13 New Baths
14 Atlantic Hotel
15 Town Hall
16 Kulturi Sluzba
17 Anglican Church
18 Cedok
19 St Vladimir Orthodox Church
20 Crystal Palace Hotel
21 Slovanský Dům Hotel
22 Ferdinand's Spring
23 Rudolph's Spring
24 Start Motel
25 Dylen Supermarket
26 Bus Station
27 Railway Station

run six km from the stations (bus No 12 to the door).

Hotels on the way into town from the stations include the *Slovansky Dum*, Ceskoslovenske armady 22; the *Crystal Palace Hotel*, Ceskoslovenske armady 2; the *Atlantic Hotel*, Odboraru 26; and the *Corso Hotel*, Odboraru 16. If all these are full see what you can come up with at Cedok, Odboraru 46.

Entertainment

For information on events ask at the Kulturni Sluzba, Odboraru 38. Also check the *N V Gogol Theatre* (1868). There's a disco in the *Corso Hotel*, Odboraru 16.

Getting There & Away

There are no direct buses between Marianske Lazne and Karlovy Vary, so you're forced to take a local train (two hours). If you'd like to stop off somewhere between the spas choose Becov nad Teplou, where you'll find a castle in a wooded valley. Train service to Cheb and Plzen is better. Most international expresses between Nuremberg and Prague call at Marianske Lazne.

PLZEN

The city of Plzen, midway between Prague and Nuremberg, is capital of West Bohemia. This town at the confluence of four rivers was an active medieval trading centre. In 1859 an iron works was founded at Plzen, which Emil Skoda purchased 10 years later. The Skoda Engineering Works became a producer of high quality armaments which attracted heavy bombing at the end of WW II. The rebuilt Skoda now produces machinery, automobiles and locomotives.

The beer has been brewing at Plzen for 700 years and the town is famous as the original home of pilsner. The only genuine pilsner trade mark is Plzensky Prazdroj, or Pilsner Urquell in its export variety. Although the emphasis is on industry, Plzen has sights enough to keep you busy

for a day. Devoted beer drinkers will not regret the pilgrimage.

Orientation

Plzen has six bus stations, none of them near the two railway stations. The largest is the Central Autobus nadrazi, Leninova ulice opposite the Skoda Works due west of J K Tyla Theatre, with direct buses to Karlovy Vary, Marianske Lazne, Prague and Ceske Budejovice. The main railway station, Gottwaldovo nadrazi, is on the east side of town. Between these is the old town centred around namesti Republiky.

Information

Cedok is at Sedlackova 12, just off namesti Republiky.

Things to See

The most convenient place to begin sightseeing is on namesti Republiky, the old town square. Gothic **St Bartholomew Church** in the middle of the square has the *was closed* highest tower in Bohemia (100 metres). Inside the soaring 13th century structure are fine stained glass windows and a Gothic Madonna (1390) on the high altar. Outstanding among the many gabled buildings around the square is the Renaissance **Town Hall** (1559).

An old town house on the east side of the square contains the extensive **Ethnographical**

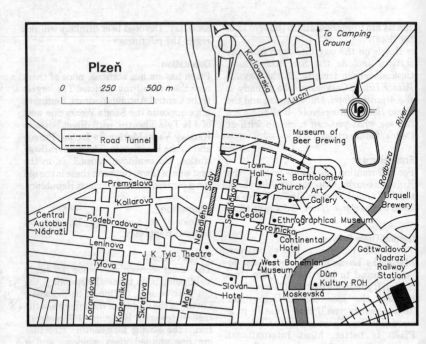

Museum. Just south on Frantiskanska is the 14th century **Franciscan Church**. The **West Bohemian Museum** (natural history, paintings) is behind this church, around the block.

Beer Lovers Only Plzen's most interesting sight by far is the **Museum of Beer Brewing** (closed Monday), Veleslavinova ulice 6, north-east of namesti Republiky. Located in an authentic medieval malt house, the museum displays a fascinating collection of artefacts related to brewing. Ask for the typewritten explanatory text in English or German.

Just around the corner at Perlova 6 is an entrance to one section of the nine km of medieval **underground corridors** below Plzen. These were originally built as refuges during sieges, hence the numerous wells. Later some were used to store kegs of beer. To enter you must wait for a group of at least five persons to gather, then follow them through on a boring Czech tour (closed Monday and Tuesday).

The famous **Urquell Brewery** is only a 10-minute walk from here, a little north of Gottwaldovo nadrazi Railway Station. Only groups organised by travel agencies are admitted to the brewery, but the twin-arched gate dated 1842-1892, which appears on every genuine pilsner label, is visible from the street. Right beside the gate is the Restaurace Prazdroj, just the place for a mug of that 12-proof brew.

Places to Stay & Eat
Two fine old B-category hotels near the centre of town are the *Slovan*, Smetanovy sady 1 (140 Kcs single, 217 Kcs double, shared bath), and the more expensive *Continental*, Zbrojnicka 8. The two campgrounds are at Bila Hora, five km north of the city (bus No. 20).

Art museum in old meat market has drawings + lithographs by Delacroix, Gericault & Goya.

The cheapest place to eat is *Bufet Slavie* in the Cas Cinema Arcade on namesti Republiky. Pilsner Urquell is on tap.

Entertainment

For entertainment check out the *JK Tyla Theatre* (1902) or the ultramodern *Dum kultury ROH* beside the river.

Getting There & Away

All international trains from Munich (via Furth im Wald) and Nuremberg (via Cheb) call at Plzen. There are fast trains to Ceske Budejovice, Cheb and Prague. Train service to Marianske Lazne is also good, but for Karlovy Vary take a bus.

South Bohemia

South Bohemia is the most German-looking part of Czechoslovakia. The many quaint little towns have a Bavarian or Austrian flavour, enhanced by some 5000 medieval carp ponds in the surrounding countryside. On the Sumava ridge south-west of Prachatice is Mt Boubin (1362 metres) with its primeval forest of spruce, pine and beech. The Moldau (Vltava) River originates on this plateau.

After WW I South Bohemia was given to Czechoslovakia on historical grounds, although over half its population was German. Hitler's claims to the area nearly touched off war in 1938. After WW II the Germans left and the region became Czech. Germanic influences linger in the hearty food and drink. Well off the beaten track, South Bohemia is overflowing with history.

CESKE BUDEJOVICE

Ceske Budejovice, the regional capital of South Bohemia, is a charming medieval city midway between Plzen and Vienna. Here the Moldau (Vltava) River meets the Malse and flows due north to Prague. In 1832 the first horse-drawn railway on the continent arrived here from Linz, Austria, directly south. High quality Kohi-Noor pencils are made in Ceske Budejovice, but the city is more famous as the original home of Budweiser beer (Budvar to the Czechs). It's a perfect base for day trips to dozens of nearby attractions, so settle in for a couple of days. Quaint little Bohemian towns within easy commuting distance include Cesky Krumlov, Jindrichuv Hradec, Pisek, Prachatice, Tabor and Trebon.

Orientation

It's a 10-minute walk west down trida Marsala Malinovskeho from the adjacent bus and train stations to namesti Jana Zizky, the centre of town.

Information

Cedok is at Norberta Fryda 31. CKM Student Travel is at Osvobozeni 14.

Things to See

Namesti Jana Zizky, a great square surrounded by 18th century arches, is one of the largest of its kind in Europe. At its centre is **Samson's Fountain** (1727) and to one side stands the Baroque **town hall** (1731). The allegorical figures on the town hall balustrade (Justice, Wisdom, Courage and Prudence) are matched by four bronze dragon gargoyles. Hanging 72 metres above the opposite side of the square is the **Black Tower** (1553), with great views from the gallery if you're lucky enough to get in. Beside this tower is **St Nicholas Cathedral**.

The back streets of Ceske Budejovice, especially Ceska ulice, are lined with old burgher houses. West near the river is the former **Dominican Monastery** (1265) with another tall tower. Beside the church is an old salt warehouse. Stroll along the riverside behind here, south past remaining sections of the 16th century walls. The **Museum of South Bohemia** (closed Monday) and the **Museum of the Revolutionary Movement** are on opposite sides of the river just south of the old town.

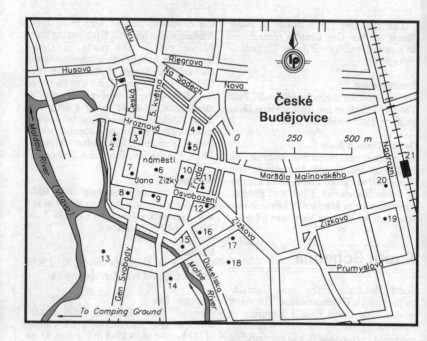

Ceské
Budějovice

1	Rabenstein Tower
2	Dominican Monastery
3	Masne Kramy Beer Cellar
4	Cedok
5	St Nicholas Cathedral
6	Samson Fountain
7	Town Hall
8	Bishop's Palace
9	Slunce Hotel
10	Zvon Hotel
11	St Anne's Church
12	CKM Student Travel
13	Open Air Theatre
14	Museum of the Revolutionary Movement
15	Mestsky Dum Kultury
16	Museum of South Bohemia
17	Dum Kultury ROH
18	Jiroceste Theatre
19	Bus Station
20	Malse Hotel
21	Railway Station

Hluboka nad Vltavou One sidetrip not to miss takes in the neo-Gothic Tudor palace at Hluboka nad Vltavou, 10 km north, easily accessible by bus. There had been a castle here since the 13th century, but in the years 1841-1871 the landowning Schwarzenberg family rebuilt the edifice on a grand scale and laid out the extensive park. The palace's 144 rooms were inhabited right up to WW II.

The romantic palace interiors with their original furnishings are closed from November to March and every Monday, but the park is open any time. Also available year round is the **Alsova Jihoceska Galerie**, a truly exceptional collection of Gothic painting and sculpture (and Dutch painting) in the former palace riding school.

Places to Stay / *small, simple rooms. Clean*

The *Malse Hotel* (143 Kcs double) is opposite the railway station. For a longer

120 cr for single w/ sink, no bath

stay try the *Zvon Hotel*, namesti Jana Zizky 28 (104 Kcs single), or the *Slunce Hotel*, namesti Jana Zizky 37, both on the central square. Cedok, Norberta Fryda 31, doesn't know of any private rooms. Ask at CKM, Osvobozeni 14, for summer youth hostels.

If it's summer consider camping at Dlouhe Louce, a 20-minute walk south-west of town (bus No 6). Tent space is available May to September, bungalows (260 Kcs triple) year round. The *Stromovka Autocamp* is just beyond *Dlouhe Louce Autocamp*.

Places to Eat   *great atmosphere*

About the best place in town for a colourful meal is the '*Masne Kramy*' beer hall in the old meat market (1560) at the corner of Hroznova and 5 kvetna. There's another good beer hall on the ground floor inside at the back of the *Zvon Hotel*. Upstairs is a more sedate restaurant.

Entertainment

Ceske Budejovice has two cultural centres, both near the Museum of South Bohemia. The *Mestsky Dum Kultury* is by the river while the *Dum Kultury ROH* is across from the statue of Lenin. Make sure the 'event' you choose to attend isn't a political lecture in Czech! The *Jihoceske Divadlo* behind Dum Kultury ROH is your best bet for opera, ballet, or serious theatre.

Getting There & Away

Twice a day there's a train to and from Summerau on the Austrian border, with connections to and from Linz. Connections with trains from Prague to Vienna are made at Veseli nad Luznici, 41 km north-east. There are fast trains to Plzen, Prague and Jihlava. For shorter distances you're better off travelling by bus.

CESKY KRUMLOV

This small medieval town 25 km south of Ceske Budejovice is one of the most picturesque in Europe, its appearance almost unchanged since the 18th century. Built on an S-shaped bend of the Moldau (Vltava) River, the castle occupies a ridge along the left bank. The old town centre sits on the high tongue of land on the right bank. The 13th century Gothic border castle, rebuilt into a huge Renaissance chateau by 16th century Italian architects, is second only to Prague Castle as a fortified Bohemian palace/citadel. It's a little out of the way but well worth the effort to visit.

Information

Cedok is at namesti Klementa Gottwalda 15.

Things to See

Get off the bus at Cesky Krumlov Spicak, the first stop in town. Just above this stop is the **Budejovicka Gate** (1598) which leads directly into the old town. On the right two blocks south is the **castle** entrance. The oldest part of the castle is the lower section with its distinctive round tower, but it's the massive upper castle which contains the great palace halls open to visitors. It's said the castle is haunted by a White Lady who appears from time to time to forecast doom.

Just across the high bridge beyond the palace is the unique Baroque **chateau theatre**. Behind this a road to the right leads up to the former **riding school**, now a cultural centre. Cherubs above the door offer the head and boots of a vanquished Turk. The road straight ahead on the left from the theatre climbs to the Italian-style castle **gardens**. The **'Bellarie' summer pavilion** and a modern revolving open air theatre are features of these gardens. The castle interiors are open from April to October only, but you can walk through the courtyards and gardens almost anytime.

On namesti Klementa Gottwalda across the river in the old town are the Gothic **town hall** and a Baroque plague column (1716). Just above the square is **St Vitus Church** (1439), a striking Gothic hall

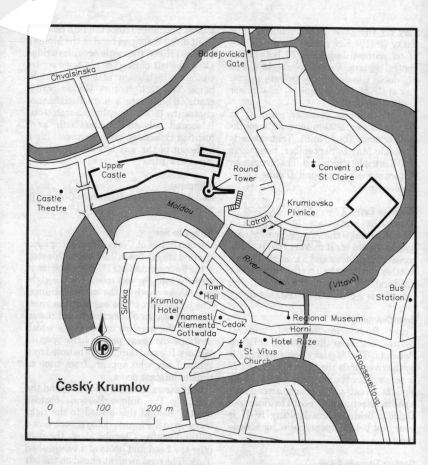

Český Krumlov

0   100   200 m

church. Nearby is the Regional Museum (closed Monday) with a surprisingly good collection housed in the old Jesuit seminary (1652). The scale model of Cesky Krumlov in 1800 is a highlight. Continue a few blocks in the same direction keeping left (ask directions) and you'll soon find the Autobusove nadrazi and a bus back to Ceske Budejovice. There's a great view of town from near this bus station.

museum has basic English guide if ask for it.

Places to Stay & Eat

Although Cesky Krumlov is an easy daytrip from Ceske Budejovice, there are several hotels if you'd like to linger. The *Krumlov Hotel* on namesti Klementa Gottwalda has atmosphere, as does the *Hotel Ruze* opposite the Regional museum. The *Vysehrad Hotel* is a modern building north of the town on the way to the train station. All are B* category. For lunch try the 'Petra Voka' goulash at *Krumlovska Pivnice*, Latran 13 below the castle.

Getting There & Away

8 cr. from C. Budejovice

The best way to come is by bus. Service from Ceske Budejovice is quite frequent. Trains run at greater intervals and the station is several km north of town.

TABOR

In 1420 God's warriors, the Hussites, founded Tabor as a military bastion in their defiance of Catholic Europe. The town was organised according to the biblical precept 'nothing is mine and nothing is yours, because the community is owned equally by everyone.' This extreme non-conformism helped give the word Bohemian the meaning we associate with it today. Planned as a bulwark against Catholic reactionaries in Ceske Budejovice and further south, Tabor is a mass of narrow broken streets with protruding houses which were intended to weaken and shatter an enemy attack. Below ground catacombs totalling 15 km provided a refuge for the defenders. A visit to this friendly old town, 100 km south of Prague, explains something about Czechoslovakia today.

Information

Cedok is at trida 9 kvetna 658.

Things to See

A statue of the Hussite commander, Jan Zizka, graces Zizkovo namesti, Tabor's main square. Around the square are the homes of rich burghers, spanning the period from late Gothic to Baroque. On the north side is the Gothic **Church of the Transfiguration of Our Lord on Mt Tabor** (1440-1512) with Renaissance gables and a Baroque tower (1677).

The other imposing building on Zizkovo namesti is the early Renaissance town hall (1521), now the **Museum of the Hussite Movement**, with the entrance to a visitable 800-metre stretch of the underground passages. The museum has been closed for restoration for several years, so you might enquire before coming.

At the south-west entrance to the old town is the **Bechyne Gate**, near a round tower remaining from a 14th century castle.

Places to Stay

There are four hotels in Tabor. Your best bet is the *Slavia Hotel* opposite the adjacent bus and train stations. The other three hotels are on 9 kvetna between the stations and downtown. You first come to the old *Slovan Hotel*, next the modern *Palcat Hotel*, and finally the undesirable *Jordan Hotel*.

Getting There & Away

Tabor is on the main railway line between Prague and Vienna. The line from Ceske Budejovice to Prague also passes here. Local trains run to Pelhrimov. To go to Ceske Budejovice, Jihlava, or Plzen you're better off taking a bus.

PELHRIMOV

All buses between Tabor and Jihlava call at Pelhrimov, an attractive old town despite the tasteless modern suburbs which have enveloped it. Bus service between Pelhrimov and Jihlava is frequent enough to make feasible a stopover of a couple of hours. Two monumental 15th century **city gates** remain and on the main square are many old houses, one of which is now the local **museum**. Behind this museum are a 16th century **chateau** and the huge **parish church**. The *Hotel Slavie* is also on the main square.

Moravia

Moravia, the third historic land of the CSSR, is often overlooked by tourists visiting Bohemia and Slovakia. This an attraction in itself, but Moravia has its own history and natural beauties such as the karst area north of Brno. The theatres and art shows of Brno, the capital, await discovery. Moravian folk art traditions culminate in late June at the Straznice Folk Festival (between Brno and Bratislava). Heavy industry is concentrated in North Moravia adjacent to Polish Silesia, while fertile South Moravia produces excellent wines. Well placed in the geographical centre of the country, Moravia is worth a stop.

JIHLAVA

During the 14th century Jihlava grew rich as a silver mining centre. The Royal Mint was originally here. Dating from this time are three large Gothic churches and the huge town square. Mining subsequently declined to be replaced by cloth-spinning, a tradition maintained in the textile factories of today.

Orientation

Jihlava has two railway stations, both on the north side of town. Jihlava-Mesto Railway Station is fairly close to the

CSAD Bus Station and the centre, but only trains on the line to Ceske Budejovice and Tabor call here. Trains from Prague and Brno stop at Jihlava-Hlavni nadrazi Railway Station, two km north. To walk to the centre of Jihlava from either station ask directions to the expensive Hotel Jihlava. Once there ask for the Grandhotel which is only a block from namesti Miru, the main square.

Information

Cedok is at namesti Miru 50. CKM Student Travel is at 9 kvetna 46.

Things to See

Namesti Miru, Jihlava's vast central square, takes up three city blocks in the very core of the city. Two fountains and a Baroque plague column (1690) grace the square, while on the north-east side are the 14th century **town hall** (enter to see the Gothic vaulting) and the Jesuit **Church of**

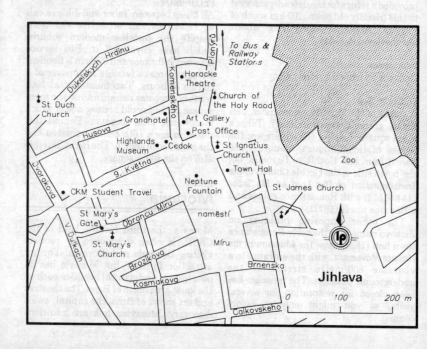

St Ignatius. In the north-west corner is the **Museum of the Bohemian-Moravian Highlands** (closed Monday) with a large collection of minerals, coins, stuffed animals and local historical artefacts housed in a large 16th century guild house. Unfortunately namesti Miru is somewhat spoiled by the modern department store senselessly plopped down in the middle of the square, a rare example of unplanned development in a country so protective of historical environments.

The streets off namesti Miru lead to small treasures. At Komenskeho 10 is the **city art gallery** with its painted Gothic vault. Obrancu miru leads to **St Mary's Minorite Church** (1250) and a Renaissance **town gate**. East of the square is 14th century **St James Parish Church**, its huge Gothic structure overlooking the city walls and a deep wooded valley. Inside the church is a splendid wrought iron baptismal font made by J Hirt of Nuremberg (1599) and Gothic statuary but the building is usually shut. A path behind the church leads down to the **city zoo**.

Places to Stay

There are two B-category hotels, the *Beseda Hotel* and the *Grandhotel*, both near the centre of town. The *Pavov Autocamp* is far to the north (take bus No 1 or 2).

Entertainment

The best theatre is the *Horacke Divadlo* at Komenskeho 24 near the *Grandhotel*.

Getting There & Away

Some trains between Praha stred, the main railway station in Prague, and Brno call at Jihlava. Havlickuv Brod, 27 km north, is a junction where most expresses between Prague and Budapest stop. There are occasional express trains to Ceske Budejovice, but buses are more practical for most travel to and from Jihlava.

ZNOJMO

High towers rise above this town 89 km north of Vienna, the deep valley of the Dyje River winding below. In the 11th century Prince Bretislav I built a castle to control the busy trade route which passed here. Early in the 19th century promenades took the place of demolished city walls. Today Znojmo is known for its gherkins (small pickles) and wines.

Orientation

The bus and train stations are adjacent just south-east of the old town. Follow Klementa Gottwalda north to namesti Vitezstvi, then left on Leninova to namesti Miru.

Information

Cedok is at Obrokova 1.

Things to See

The pointed **town hall steeple** (1448) rises above one end of namesti Miru, **Wolf's Tower** above the other. Between these is the **art gallery**, namesti Miru 11. Proceed north-west across two squares to the **Museum of South Moravia** in the former Minorite Monastery. Opposite the museum is a brewery which blocks the way to **Znojmo Castle** and the 11th century **Rotunda of St Catherine** where remarkable Romanesque wall paintings (1134) are said to exist. The brewery totally encloses these monuments and you can't even get near (ask anyway, visiting conditions could change).

Visible to the south of the museum is the Gothic **Church of St Nicholas**. From the two-storied **Chapel of St Wenceslas** (1521) beside this church you get an excellent view of the scenic valley and the dam on the River Dyje. Trails along the ravine allow you to explore this quaint corner of old Znojmo.

Places to Stay

The cheapest hotel is the *Cerny Medved*, namesti Miru 7, but the *Znojmo Hotel* at Leninova 1 on the traffic circle near the

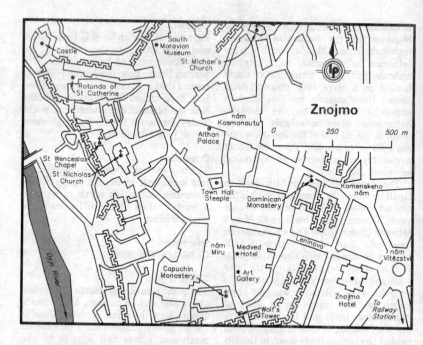

stations is larger and more convenient. The campground is at Suchodrdly u Znojma, three km north-east of the railway station.

Getting There & Away

There are local trains between Znojmo and Brno every couple of hours. Train service to Jihlava is less frequent and bus travel is much quicker. For Bratislava change trains at Breclav. To and from Vienna you must also go via Breclav, although there's said to be a direct bus.

BRNO

Halfway between Budapest and Prague, Brno (Brunn) is the third largest city in Czechoslovakia. The country's most important international trade fairs take place in the city (in February, April and September). Botanist Gregor Mendel, who formulated the modern theory of heredity, worked in Brno. The compact centre of this surprisingly untouristed city holds a variety of fascinating sights and the cultural life is rich. Although you can 'do' Brno in a very busy day, stay longer and delve deeper. This is the sort of place you want to return to.

Orientation

Brno's main railway station is at the south edge of the old town core. The new Autobusove nadrazi (bus station) is another 800 metres south, beyond Prior Department Store. To get to the bus station go through the pedestrian tunnel under the train tracks, then follow the crowd along the elevated walkway. Opposite the railway station is the beginning of trida Vitezstvi, a main thoroughfare which streetcars and pedestrians follow into triangular namesti Svobody, the centre of town.

Information

Cedok is at Divadelni 3. CKM Student Travel is at Ceska 11.

Things to See

As you enter the city on trida Vitezstvi keep sharp left into Kapucinske namesti to reach the **Capuchin Monastery** (1651). In the ventilated crypt (closed Monday) below the church are the intact mummies of monks and local aristocrats deposited here before 1784. At the west end of Kapucinske namesti is the Dietrichstein Palace (1760), with the numismatic and natural history sections of the **South Moravian Museum** (closed Monday). The rest of this museum is undergoing long-term restoration so check the nearby palaces to see if other sections have reopened.

The street in front of the monastery soon leads into namesti 25 unora and its colourful **open-air market**. Carp used to be sold from the waters of the Parnassus Fountain (1695) at Christmas time. Locate the **Reduta Theatre**, namesti 25 unora 4, where Mozart performed in 1767. The operettas presently presented at the Reduta are excellent.

On ulice Radnicka just off the north side of the square is Brno's 13th century **Old Town Hall** with a splendid Gothic portal (1511) below the tower. Inside the passage behind the portal are a stuffed crocodile (or 'dragon') and a wheel, traditional symbols of the city. Legend tells how the 'dragon' once terrorised wayfarers approaching the nearby Svratka River while the wheel was made by a cartwright in league with the devil.

Continue north and sharp left, which will bring you to **St Michael's Church** (1679) and the former Dominican Convent. At ulice Dominikanska 9 beside the church is the Renaissance **House of the Squires of Kunstat** (closed Monday), where special art exhibitions are held. Facing the square on the opposite side of the church is the 16th century **New Town Hall** with impressive courtyard, stairways and

frescoes. Around the corner at ulice Husova 14 is the **Moravian Gallery of Applied Art** (closed Monday).

In the large park on the hill above this gallery is the sinister silhouette of **Spilberk Castle**, founded in the 13th century and converted into a citadel and prison during the 17th century. Until 1857 opponents of the Hapsburgs were held here, including the Italian poet Silvio Pellico and other members of the *carbonieri*. Later the Nazis tortured their victims in dungeons below Spilberk. Sections of the castle and the castle museum will be closed for restoration until 1994, but you should be able to get into the Gestapo casemates. The view from the ramparts is fine.

On Petrov Hill opposite Spilberk is the neo-Gothic **Cathedral of Sts Peter & Paul**, rebuilt in the late 19th century on the site of an older basilica. The Renaissance **Bishop's Palace** adjoins. In 1645 a Swedish general besieging Brno declared he would leave if his troops hadn't captured the city by 12 noon. At 11 am the Swedes were about to scale the walls when the cathedral bell-keeper suddenly rang noon. True to his word General Torstensson broke off the attack and since that day the cathedral bells have rung 12 noon at 11 am.

From Petrov Hill descend into namesti 25 unora and keep straight on ulice Orli to the **Technological Museum**, another Brno curiosity. Buy a ticket for the Panorama, a rare apparatus installed here in 1890 which offers continuous showings of the wonders of the world in 3-D. The programme is changed every couple of weeks so there are lots of regular visitors. Nearby on ulice Minoritska is **St John's Church** (rebuilt 1733) with fine altarpieces, organ and painted ceilings.

On nearby namesti Svobody is a striking plague column (1680). At ulice Gagarinova 1 in a corner of the square is the **Ethnological Museum** (closed Monday) with Moravian folk costumes and implements. Just north is the 13th century parish church, **St James**, with a soaring nave in the purest Gothic style.

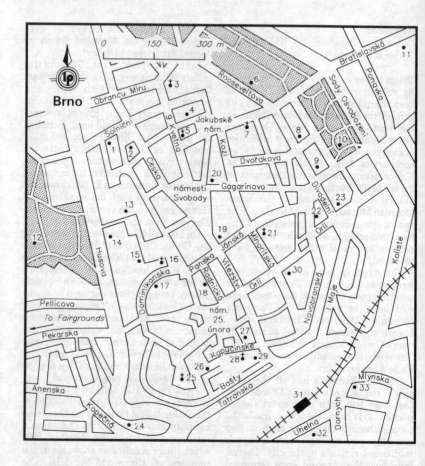

This is Brno's most powerful church. **St Thomas Church** and the former **Augustinian Monastery** (now a museum of socialism) are just north again.

Also worth seeing is the **City Art Gallery** (Dum Umeni), Malinovskeho namesti 2 beside the theatre. Excellent art exhibitions are sometimes staged in this gallery. **Villa Tugendhat** (1932), a classic work of modern architecture designed by Ludwig Mies van den Rohe, is at Cernopolni 45 above Luzanky Park, a km north-east of St Thomas Church.

Slavkov u Brna On 2 December 1805 the famous 'Battle of the Three Emperors' (Austerlitz) took place in the open, rolling countryside between Brno and Slavkov u Brna. Here Napoleon Bonaparte, a product of emerging bourgeois capitalism, defeated the combined armies of Austria and Russia, defenders of the aristocratic, feudal past. The battle was decided at Pracky Kopec, a hill 12 km west of Slavkov u Brna where a monument was erected in 1912. After the battle Napoleon spent four days concluding an armistice

1	Slavia Hotel
2	CKM Student Hotel
3	St Thomas Church
4	Hotel U Jakuba
5	St James Church
6	Janacek Theatre
7	Jesuit Church
8	Theatre Ticket Office
9	Mahenovo Theatre
10	City Art Gallery
11	Radost Puppet Theatre
12	Spilberk Castle
13	International Hotel
14	Moravian Gallery
15	New Town Hall
16	St Michael's Church
17	House of Kustat
18	Old Town Hall
19	Europa Hotel
20	Ethnographical Museum
21	St John's Church
22	Morava Hotel
23	Cedok
24	Korso Hotel
25	Cathedral of Saints Peter & Paul
26	South Moravian Theatre
27	Reduta Theatre
28	Capuchin Monastery
29	Bufet
30	Technological Museum
31	Main Railway Station
32	Prior Department Store
33	Metropol Hotel

at the Baroque **chateau** (1705) in Slavkov u Brna.

Slavkov u Brna (Austerlitz) is 21 km east of Brno and easily accessible by bus from Brno's Autobusove nadrazi (ask about times and platform numbers at the information window). The chateau historical exhibit on Napoleon's life is open Tuesday to Sunday from April to November. The decorated palace rooms and the gallery wing (separate ticket) are open daily April to October. Unfortunately Pracky Kopec hill is difficult to reach by public transport.

Scenic Caves The Moravian Karst area (Moravsky Kras), 20 km north of Brno, is formed by the underground Punkva River. There are a number of caves, chasms, canyons, lakes and the 138-metre deep **Macocha Abyss**. At Punkevni (connected to Macocha) small boats carry tourists on the river into the deepest caves to see stalactites and stalagmites. Other caves to be visited include Katerinska, Balcarka and Sloupsko-Sosuvske. Traces of prehistoric humans have been found in the caves.

To get there take a bus or train to Blansko, then walk eight km east through the wooded countryside. Alternatively take a bus to Jedovnice, four km southeast of Punkevni. From 20 May to 23 September Cedok, Divadelni 3, Brno, organises bus tours to the caves (80 Kcs including lunch). A cave tour for locals (and stray foreigners) departs Blansko Bus Station early summer mornings. Cave admissions are included in the price. The caves are open to the public year round but try to get there in the morning as the guides start to knock off around 2 pm. In summer there will be queues to get in.

Places to Stay

Brno has four B-category hotels. The *Korso*, Kopecna 10, and *Metropol*, Dornych 5, are both near the railway station. In the centre of town are the *Morava*, Novobranska 3, and the *Europa*, Janska 1/3. A step up in price is the *Hotel U Jakuba*, Jakubske namesti 6 (202 Kcs single). If these are all full try the *Slovan Hotel*, Lidicka 23 (181 Kcs single, 368 Kcs double), north across the park from St Thomas Church. Beware of streetcar noise at all the hotels.

Cedok, Divadelni 3, arranges rooms in private homes for 100 Kcs a night (fournight minimum stay). CKM Student Travel, Ceska 11, knows of accommodation for youth hostellers and students in disused student dormitories, but only during July and August.

Autocamp Bobrava is at Modrice,

12 km south of the city. Take trams No 2, 14 or 17 to the end of the line, then walk two km. Otherwise take a train to Popovice Railway Station, 500 metres from the campground.

Places to Eat

The cheapest and easiest place to eat is the stand-up *bufet* at the corner of ulice Basty and trida Votezstvi, just opposite the railway station. *Pipi Grill*, namesti Svobody 11, offers roast chicken and beer, which you also consume standing up.

Entertainment

Opera and ballet are performed at the modern *Janacek Theatre* (1965), Sady osvobozeni, while the nearby neo-Baroque *Mahenovo Theatre* (1882) presents serious drama. Try to see an operetta at the *Reduta Theatre* (1760) on namesti 25 unora. The singing and dancing are excellent and programmes enjoyable even if you can't understand Czech.

For tickets to the Janacek, Mahenovo and Reduta go to Statniho divadla u Brno, Dvorakova 11, a small booking office behind the Mahenovo Theatre (open weekdays 12.30 to 5 pm, Saturday 9 am to 12 noon). They're usually helpful to foreign visitors.

Brno's satirical theatre is the *Vecerni Brno*, Jakubske namesti 5 beside St James Church. If you're around on Sunday don't miss the *Radost Puppet Theatre*, Bratislavska 32, which puts on shows at 10 am and 2.30 pm (Sunday only). It's kids' stuff but great fun if you haven't enjoyed puppets for a while. Evenings there's dancing at the *Europa Hotel*, Janska 1/3 (closed Sunday).

Getting There & Away

There are two buses a day between Vienna (Mitte Bahnhof) and Brno. All trains between Budapest and Berlin call at Brno. To and from Vienna change trains at Breclav. To and from Kosice change trains at Prerov. Direct trains from Bratislava and Prague are frequent. For shorter trips buses are faster and more efficient than the trains. To and from South Bohemia a bus is best.

1	Slavin War Memorial
2	Lenin Museum
3	Archbishop's Palace
4	Klement Gottwald Monument
5	Hungarian Consulate
6	Grassalkovich Palace
7	Palace Hotel
8	Church of The Holy Trinity
9	Michael Tower
10	Mirbach Palace
11	Franciscan Church
12	Clarissine Monastery
13	Palace of the Royal Chamber
14	Old Town Hall
15	Wine Museum
16	Primatial Palace
17	Hummel Music Museum
18	BIPS Information Bureau
19	Mliecne Specialty
20	National Theatre
21	Theatre Ticket Office
22	PO Hviezdoslava Theatre
23	Cedok (train tickets)
24	Slovenska Restaurant
25	Cedok (currency Exchange)
26	Krym Hotel
27	Slovak National Museum
28	Hydrofoil Terminal
29	Reduta Air Terminal
30	Slovenska Filharmonia
31	Carlton Hotel
32	Slovak National Gallery
33	CKM Student Travel
34	St Martin's Cathedral
35	Decorative Arts Museum
36	Bratislava Castle
37	Bus 29 To Devon Castle
38	Danube Bridge

Bratislava

Bratislava, in wine-growing country on the banks of the Danube, is capital of the Slovak Socialist Republic and the second largest city in Czechoslovakia. The

Bratislava

0   250   500 m

Austrian border is almost within sight of the city and Hungary is just 16 km away. Founded in 907 AD, Bratislava (called Pozsony in Hungarian, Pressburg in German) became the capital of Hungary in 1541 after the Turks forced the Hungarians to withdraw from Buda, their previous capital. It remained Hungary's capital for nearly three centuries. Between 1563 and 1830 11 Hungarian kings and seven queens were crowned in St Martins Cathedral. A university, the Academia Istropolitana, was founded at Bratislava by the king of Hungary in 1467. Bratislava flourished during the reign of Maria Teresa of Austria (1740-1780) and some imposing Baroque palaces were built. In 1918 the city was included in the newly formed Republic of Czechoslovakia. Many beautiful monuments survive in the old town to tell of this glorious past and Bratislava's numerous museums are surprisingly rich.

Orientation

Bratislava's main railway station, Hlavna

stanica, is several km north of town, so catch a streetcar. Hviezdoslavovo namesti is a convenient reference point with the old town to the north, the Danube to the south, Bratislava Castle to the west and Sturova ulice to the east. The main bus station (Autobusova Stanica) is in a convenient modern building on Mlynske nivy a little over a km east of Sturova ulice.

Information
General information about the city is supplied by BIPS (Bratislava Information & Publicity Service), Rybarska at Leningradska off Hviezdoslavovo namesti (weekdays 8 am to 4 pm, Saturday 8 am to 1 pm). CKM Student Travel is at Hviezdoslavovo namesti 16.

For currency exchange go to Cedok, Sturova 13. The Cedok office at Jesenskeho 5 sells international railway tickets. Slovakoterma, Radlinskeho 13, arranges stays at health spas throughout Slovakia.

Consulates Bratislava is an alternative to Prague for collecting visas. The Hungarian Consulate General is at Palisady 54-60 off Mierove namesti. Nearby are the consulates general of the GDR, Palisady 47, Bulgaria, Kuzmanyho 1/a, and the USSR, Godrova 4. The Romanian Consulate General is at Frana Krala 11 behind the Lenin Museum. The consulates of Yugoslavia, Holubyho 9, and Poland, Hummelova 4, are in the residential area north-west of the castle.

Things to See
Begin your visit with the **Slovak National Museum** (1928) opposite the hydrofoil terminal on the river. The museum features anthropology, archaeology, natural history and geology – notice the large relief map of Slovakia. A little up the riverfront is the ultramodern **Slovak National Gallery**, Bratislava's major art collection with a good Gothic section. The gallery building itself is interesting for the daring incorporation of an 18th century palace into the design.

Backtrack a wee bit and take Mostova north to the neo-Baroque **Slovak National Theatre** (1886) with Ganymede's Fountain (1833) in front. Crowded, narrow Rybarska brana penetrates the old town to namesti 4 aprila with Roland's Fountain (1572) in the centre of the square. To one side is the Old Town Hall(1421), now the **Municipal Museum** with an extensive collection housed in finely decorated rooms and torture chambers in the casemates. Entry is from the picturesque inner courtyard.

Leave the courtyard through the east gate and you'll be on a square before the **Primatial Palace** (1781). Enter to see the Hall of Mirrors where Napoleon and the Austrian emperor Franz I signed a peace treaty in 1805. In the municipal gallery on the 2nd floor are rare English tapestries (1632). St George's Fountain stands in the courtyard. Saturdays the palace is crowded with couples being married, but is still open to visitors. Just beyond this palace is the **Hummel Music Museum**, Klobucnicka 2, in the one-time home of composer Johann Hummel (1778-1837).

Return through the Old Town Hall courtyard and turn left to the **Museum of Wine Production**, Radnicna 1 (closed Tuesday), in the Apponyi Palace (1762). Next head north on Dibrovovo namesti to the **Franciscan Church** (1297) with a two-storey chapel and crypt (open Saturday only). The sexagonal church tower is visible from behind the building. Opposite this church is the **Mirbach Palace**, Dibrovovo namesti 11, a beautiful Baroque building housing a fine art collection.

From the palace continue around on narrow Zamocnicka ulice to the **Michael Tower**, which houses a collection of antique arms. The view from the tower is great. Go north through the tower arch into the old Barbican with the extensive **Pharmaceutical Museum** on the right. Out the north gate and across the street is the

Church of the Holy Trinity (1725), an oval edifice with fine frescoes.

Return below the Michael Tower and stroll down Michalska to the **Palace of the Royal Chamber** (1756) at Michalska 1. Now the university library, this building was once the Hungarian Parliament. In 1848 serfdom was abolished here, marking the end of feudalism in Hungary.

Take the passage west through the palace to the Gothic **Church of the Clarissine Order** with a unique pentagonal tower (1360) supported on buttresses. Continue west on Farska, then left and straight ahead to the coronation church, **St Martin's Cathedral** (15th century). Inside notice the bronze statue (1734) of St Martin cutting off half his robe for the beggar.

Castles on the Danube The busy motorway in front of St Martin's follows the moat of the former city walls. Construction of this

route and the adjacent bridge were rather controversial as several historic structures had to be pulled down and vibrations from the traffic have structurally weakened the cathedral. Find the passage under the highway and head up toward **Bratislava Castle**, built above the Danube on the southernmost spur of the Little Carpathian Range. At the foot of the hill you'll pass the Decorative Arts Museum (closed Tuesday).

Since the 9th century Bratislava Castle has been rebuilt several times and served as the seat of Hungarian royalty until it was finally burned out in 1811. Reconstructed from 1953 to 1962, the castle now houses a large historical museum with a heavy political orientation. If you're museumed-out you can safely give this one a miss, but do climb up to the castle for the view. The present Slovak National Council meets inside the castle.

As you return from the castle take a

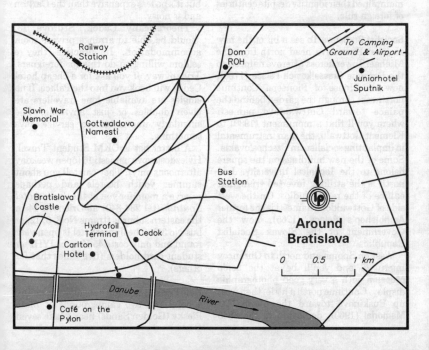

stroll on one of the pedestrian walkways across the sweeping new **SNP Bridge** (1972) over the Danube. At the far side you can take an elevator (3 Kcs) up one of the pylons to a cafe 80 metres above the river. Even the toilets have a view!

Below the Bratislava end of SNP Bridge is a city bus terminal where you can catch city bus No 29 west along the Danube to the Gothic ruins of **Devin Castle**, on a hill where the Morava and Danube rivers meet. The castle withstood the Turks but was burned in 1809. Stay on the bus to the end of the line and follow the signs back to the castle. Austria is just across the rivers from Devin so you could be questioned by border guards if you stray off the approved route.

From the 1st to 5th centuries Devin and Bratislava castles were frontier posts of the Roman Empire, manned by the 14th Legion. Today they're regarded as symbols of the Slavic peoples who maintained their identity despite centuries of foreign rule.

Socialist Bratislava To see a bit of the new socialist Bratislava head north from the Michael Tower across Mierove namesti to the Baroque **Grassalkovich Palace** (1760), now the House of Pioneers. Continue north-east through the garden behind the palace toward Gottwaldovo namesti where you'll find a monument (1980) to Klement Gottwald, the man instrumental in implanting socialism in Czechoslovakia. Some of the new buildings on the square belong to the **Technical University**. Just north is the striking inverted triangular edifice of the radio studios. On the west side of Gottwaldovo namesti is the former **Archbishop's Palace** (1765), now the Government of the Slovak Socialist Republic.

West on Spojna and north to Obrancov mieru 25 and you'll be at the **Lenin Museum** with a very good photographic display. Continue north a little, then west up Puskinova toward the **Slavin War Memorial** (1960), dedicated to the 6845 Soviet soldiers who died in the battle for Bratislava in 1945. There's a good view of modern Bratislava from here.

Unless otherwise noted, all of the above galleries and museums are closed on Mondays.

Places to Stay

There's a shortage of budget hotels in Bratislava. The cheapest is the unappealing B-category *Palace Hotel*, Postova 1, at 161 Kcs single, 248 Kcs double. Noisy streetcars rattle below the windows.

If you're alone and all the Palace's singles are full, you'll do better for less at the higher class *Carlton Hotel*, Hvierdoslavovo namesti 2. This huge hotel has 124 B-category single bedded rooms without bath for 207 Kcs single, 305 Kcs double, but you have to specifically request them or they'll put you in an A-category suite. The only other moderately priced hotel is the *Krym Hotel*, Safarikovo namesti 7, but it's no less expensive than the Carlton and is noisy.

Theoretically Cedok, Sturova 13, should be able to arrange private room accommodation. In practice they're seldom willing to do this for foreigners. Try anyway. If you ask for a cheap hotel Cedok will book you into the Palace. If no singles are available lone travellers are given doubles or just anything. The singularly unimaginative service says something.

A better bet is CKM Student Travel, Hviezdoslavovo namesti 16 (open weekday afternoons only). They can tell you about summer youth hostels and perhaps reserve a room for you at the *Juniorhotel Sputnik* (tel 234-340) at Drienova 14 in the eastern suburbs (trams No 8, 9, 12, or bus No 38). The Juniorhotel is open year round and only costs 45 Kcs for IYHF or student card holders (five times that for others).

Zlate Piesky There are bungalows, a motel, a hotel and two campgrounds at Zlate Piesky (Golden Sands) near a lake seven km north-east of Bratislava. Take trams No 2, 4 or 10 to the end of the line, then buses No 32 or 35 direct to Zlate Piesky.

The motel campground is open May to September only, but the motel reception (tel 65-170 or 60-578) rents out the campground bungalows year round for 174 Kcs double (no singles). Nearby is *Hotel Flora* with double rooms for 273 Kcs (no singles). There's a restaurant in the hotel. Near the hotel is the reception of a second campground.

Places to Eat

Local dishes are available at the *Slovenska Restaurant* in the arcade at Sturova 3. There's a good bar upstairs. Faster and cheaper Slovakian food is dished out at stand-up *Mliecne Speciality*, Rybarska brana 9 near the National Theatre.

A wine restaurant worth trying is *Velki Frantiskani Vinaren*, in the old monastery at Dibrovovo namesti 10. Other typical smoky wine-cellars known as *pod viechou* are found in Bastova and Zamocnicka alleys near the Michael Tower. If all else fails the upstairs restaurant in the *Palace Hotel* is quite good and open to 11 pm.

Entertainment

Opera and ballet are presented at the *National Theatre* (1836), Hviezdoslavovo namesti. For serious drama it's the *Divadlo P O Hviezdoslava*, Leningradska 20. Tickets to these theatres are sold in an office (open weekdays 12 noon to 8 pm) at the corner of Jesenskeho ulice and Komenskeho namesti behind the National Theatre, but they're often sold out a few days in advance. The Slovenska Filharmonia is based in the neo-Rococo *Reduta Palace* (1914) on Palackeho at Mostova across the park from the National Theatre. Ask inside about concerts.

There's always something happening at the white marble *Dom ROH* (Trade Union House) on namesti Frantiska Zupku (trams No 2, 4, 6, 8, 9, 10, 12 and 14). This major cultural centre includes a cinema, restaurant, bar and two theatres, plus exhibition areas. Tickets to major events at Dom ROH go on sale at the box office at 3 pm. Ask the people at BIPS to explain what's on at Dom ROH, a good place to experience the type of entertainment average Czechoslovaks appreciate.

Getting There & Away

All express trains between Budapest and Prague call at Bratislava. There are several local trains a day between Vienna (Sudbahnhof) and Bratislava. One bus a day connects Vienna (Mitte Busbahnhof) to Bratislava (74 Austrian shillings). Train service from Kosice to Bratislava (via Poprad and Zilina) is fairly frequent and couchettes are available on the night train. To and from Banska Bystrica or Nitra and Bratislava take a bus. From May to September there are Raketa hydrofoils to and from Budapest, Komarno and Vienna. The Vienna service is often fully booked by groups.

Hitching to Hungary or Austria If you don't want to bother getting a Hungarian visa and an international train ticket take a local train or bus to Komarno and walk across the bridge to Komarom, Hungary. You could also take city bus No 116 to Cunovo from the city bus terminal below the Bratislava end of SNP Bridge and try to walk or hitch into Hungary. Hungarian visas are available at highway border crossings.

Vienna is only 64 km west of Bratislava. The Austrian border is about two km across SNP Bridge and along Viedenska cesta, walking distance from Bratislava. Hitching into Austria is much easier than into Hungary and you won't stand out as much at the border.

Getting Around

Airport Transport The CSA Reduta Air Terminal, Mostova 1-3, is just around the corner from the Carlton Hotel. Airport buses leave from here and there's a very convenient left luggage service if you need it. You can also get to Ivanka Airport on city bus No 24 from the railway station (eight km).

Slovakia

Slovakia is the least touristed part of Czechoslovakia. Bratislava is on the beaten track between Budapest and Prague, but few visitors make the long detour out to see the magnificent High Tatras or the unspoiled medieval towns of East Slovakia. The Carpathian Mountains take up much of the SSR, while south of Nitra is the fertile Danube Plain. Two-thirds of Czechoslovakia's vineyards are on the south and east slopes of the Little Carpathians.

The rural Slovaks are a people apart from the urbane Czechs. The peasant background is evident in the folk costumes seen in remote Slovak villages on Sundays, the traditional meal of roast goose with potato pancakes and the colourful handicrafts. During the first week of July folk dancers from all over Slovakia meet at the Vychodna Folklore Festival, 32 km west of Poprad.

For 1000 years Slovakia was Hungarian and many ethnic Magyars still reside in the republic. There are 180 picturesque castles and castle ruins in Slovakia, the largest of which are Spissky hrad, east of Levoca, Orava Castle above Oravsky Podzamok village, 81 km north of Banska Bystrica, and Trencin Castle in West Slovakia. Slovakia east of Bratislava has more to offer the adventurous budget traveller than any other part of Czechoslovakia.

NITRA
Nitra is embraced by a bend of the River Nitra where the mountains meet the plains. The early-feudal Great Moravian Empire established a seat here in the 9th century and in 827 prince Pribina ordered the first church in Slovakia to be built. In the 11th century Nitra became a bishopric and an Episcopal Palace and Romanesque rotunda were erected, followed by a stone castle in the 13th century. Then began repeated invasions and wars which devastated the area, so much of what we see today dates back no further than the Baroque. Today Nitra is an important marketplace and educational centre. Only 81 km east of Bratislava and connected by frequent bus, Nitra may be worth a brief halt or a one-night stop.

Orientation
The adjacent bus and train stations are just west of Leninova trieda, a main thoroughfare which runs north into the city centre. The old town and castle are north again on a low hill overlooking the surrounding countryside.

Information
Cedok is at Leninova trieda 74.

Things to See
Everything worth seeing is near the medieval **castle**, which was completely rebuilt in the 17th century. Inside the castle walls are the **cathedral** and **Bishop's Palace** (1739). Just outside the castle gate is a splendid Baroque plague column. Below the castle on ulice Samova are the **Regional Museum** and the **Agricultural Museum**, as well as the **Franciscan Church**. The **Studeneho Art Gallery** is in the former District Administration Building at the bottom of the hill. All the museums are closed Monday.

Places to Stay & Eat
If you'd like to spend the night in Nitra you can choose between the modern three-star *Zobor Hotel*, Leninova 7 (156 Kcs single, 328 Kcs double), or the cheaper *Slovan Hotel*, Saratovska 14. The nearest campground (with bungalows) is on a small wooded lake at Jelenec, 20 km north-east.

There are two popular restaurants on ulice Gorazdova. *Furmanska Vinaren*,

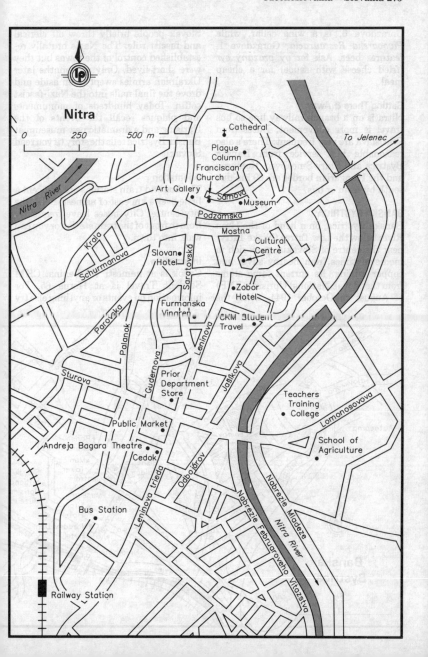

Nitra

0   250   500 m

To Jelenec

Cathedral

Plague
Column

Franciscan
Church

Art Gallery

Samova

Museum

Podzamska

Mostna

Cultural
Centre

Krala

Schurmanova

Slovan
Hotel

Saratovské

Zobor
Hotel

Nitra River

Furmanska
Vinaren

CKM Student
Travel

Paroyska

Leninova

Jašiková

Palanok

Prior
Department
Store

Sturova

Gudernova

Teachers
Training
College

Lomonosovova

Public Market

School of
Agriculture

Andreja Bagara Theatre

Cedok

Leninova trieda

Odbojárov

Nabrezie Mladeze

Nitra River

Bus Station

Nabrezie Februaroveho Vitazstva

Railway Station

Gorazdova 6, is a wine cellar, while *Pivovarska Restauracia*, Gorazdova 1, features beer. Ask for *vy prazany syr* (fried cheese with sauce) for a cheap meal.

Getting There & Away

Nitra is on a branch railway line so bus travel is more convenient. Buses from Bratislava are very frequent. There's also reasonable bus service from Banska Bystrica and Stary Smokovec. Komarno and the Hungarian border are 69 km due south by train or bus.

BANSKA BYSTRICA

Banska Bystrica, on a bend of the Hron River below the Low Tatras (Nizke Tatry) near the centre of Slovakia, grew rich in medieval times from nearby silver and copper mining. Its current fame stems from the Slovak National Uprising (SNP) of August to October 1944, when the Slovak people briefly threw off clerical and fascist rule. The Nazis brutally re-established control of the towns but they were short-lived. Only six months later Ukrainian armies swept them aside and drove the final nails into the Nazi-fascist coffin. Today hundreds of monuments and plaques recall the events of the Uprising and a dramatic new museum at Banska Bystrica tells the story (if you read Slovak).

Orientation

The bus and train stations are adjacent a little over a km east of namesti SNP, the city centre. City buses leave frequently from in front of the train station or you can walk into town.

Information

Cedok is at namesti V I Lenina. CKM Student Travel is at Horna 65. For information on events or anything else try

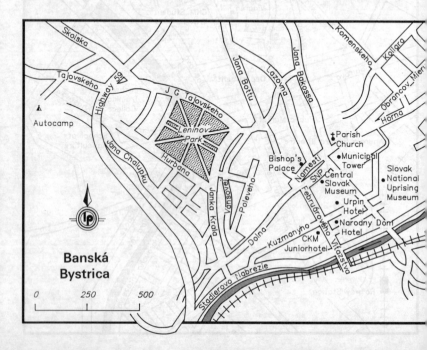

Banská Bystrica

0   250   500

the Cultural Information office in the Barbican of the old city gate near the Parish Church.

Things to See

Begin with the **Slovak National Uprising Museum** (closed Monday), the town's main sight. The museum's twin concrete pods are poised spectacularly on a ridge above the *Lux Hotel*, with towers remaining from the old city walls on each side. Inside groups are shown a film on the uprising (they arrive fairly frequently so you should be lucky).

From this museum find your way west to namesti SNP, the central square. On this square are the **Central Slovak Museum**, namesti SNP 4, an art gallery, namesti SNP 16, the **Bishop's Palace**, namesti SNP 19, the **Municipal Tower** (1567), namesti SNP 24, and the **Jesuit Church**.

Just north-east you'll see a cluster of churches and towers, site of the original

13th century mining settlement. The first tower belongs to the Barbican of an **old city gate**. Beyond is another art gallery in the Renaissance **town hall** (1565) with arcades. The Gothic **Parish Church** is behind this and just beyond near the entrance to the cemetery is king **Matthias Corvinas' House** (1479) and the **Church of the Holy Cross** (1452). Enter the cemetery to see the remaining walls and towers of the **castle** (1510).

Zvolen Only 20 km south of Banska Bystrica and connected by frequent bus is the intact medieval **castle** of Zvolen, built in the years 1370-1382 as a summer residence for King Louis the Great of Hungary. In the 15th century Zvolen was held by the Hussites and in 1548 it was rebuilt in the Renaissance style as a bulwark against the Turks. In the 18th century the Esterhazys decorated the ceiling of a hall in the castle's western wing with the portraits of 78 Roman emperors. Today exhibitions of the Slovak National Gallery are held at Zvolen Castle.

Places to Stay

The cheapest place to stay is the *CKM Juniorhotel*, Februaroveho vitazstva 12, but it's usually full. Nearby are two three-star hotels, the *Narodny Dom* and the *Urpin*. The *J G Tajovskeho Theatre* is next to the Narody Dom Hotel.

Your most expensive choice would be the appropriately named *Lux Hotel*, a high-rise monster satisfying bourgeois tastes. The campground (with bungalows) is near the *Hotel Turist* beyond Leninov Park, walking distance west of town.

Getting There & Away

An overnight train with couchettes arrives from Prague and the Polonia Express from Warsaw to Sofia calls here (reservations required). There are direct trains to Banska Bystrica from Kosice, but within Slovakia you're usually better off travelling by bus. Buses from Bratislava

Nitra and Zvolen. There's no direct railway line between the High Tatras and Banska Bystrica making bus travel mandatory. Bus departure times are posted at the station, a few minutes walk from the main railway station.

THE HIGH TATRAS

The High Tatras (Vysoke Tatry) are the only truly alpine mountains in Czechoslovakia. This 27-km-long granite massif covers 260 square km, the northernmost portion of the Carpathian Range. The narrow rocky crests soar above wide glacial valleys with precipitous walls. At 2655 metres Gerlachovsky Stit is the highest mountain in the country. Several dozen other peaks exceed 2500 metres. Enhancing the natural beauty packed into this relatively small area are 30 valleys, bubbling streams and almost 100 glacial lakes. From 1500 to 1800 metres elevation there's a belt of brushwood and knee-pines, while above this is alpine flora and bare peaks. The lower reaches are covered by dense coniferous forests.

Since 1949 most of the Slovak portion of this jagged range has been included in Tatras National Park (TANAP), which complements a similar park in Poland. A network of 350 km of hiking trails reaches all the alpine valleys and many peaks. The famous red-marked Magistrala Trail follows the south crest of the High Tatras for 65 km through a striking variety of landscapes. The routes are clearly colour-coded and easy to follow. Park regulations require you to keep to the marked trails and refrain from picking flowers.

Orientation

The best centre for visitors is Stary Smokovec, a turn-of-the-century resort well connected to the rest of the country by road and rail. Streetcar-style electric trains run frequently between the three main tourist centres in the park, Strbske Pleso, Stary Smokovec and Tatranska Lomnica. At Poprad the trains link up with the national railway system. Buses

also run very frequently between the resorts. Cable cars, chairlifts and a funicular railway carry you up the slopes to hiking trails, which soon lead you away from the throng. During winter skiers flock to the area and there are excellent facilities for them.

Information

Cedok is just above the railway station at Stary Smokovec. Our map is intended only for initial orientation. Start asking for the *Vysoke Tatry 21* map at bookstores as soon as you arrive in Czechoslovakia. Good maps are *sometimes* available at hotels or newsstands inside the park.

Climate When planning your trip keep in mind the elevation. At 750 metres the campgrounds will be too cold for a tent from October to mid-May. In November there's snow. Avalanches are a danger from November to June and the higher trails will be closed. Beware of sudden thunderstorms, especially in the alpine areas where there's no protection. Avoid getting lost if clouds set in. The assistance of the Mountain Rescue Service is not free.

Things to See

Above Stary Smokovec From Stary Smokovec (1025 metres) a funicular railway carries you up to Hrebienok (1280 metres), a ski resort with a view of the Velka Studena Valley. If the funicular isn't running it takes less than an hour to walk up to Hrebienok (green trail). The *Bilikova Chalet* is a five-minute walk from Hrebienok.

For great scenery follow the blue trail from Hrebienok to *Zbojnicka Chalet* in the Velka Studena Valley (three hours). Beyond Zbojnicka the blue trail climbs over a 2428 metre pass and descends to the Polish border.

The green trail leads north from Hrebienok to *Teryho Chalet* in the Mala Studena Valley (three hours). The *Nalepkova Chalet* is only an hour from

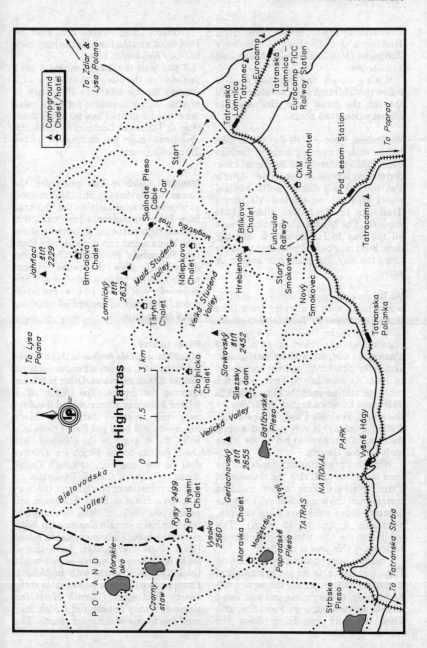

The High Tatras

To Zdiar & Lysa Polana

To Lysa Polana

To Poprad

To Poland

POLAND

Marskie-oko

Czarny-staw

Bielovodska Valley

Rysy 2499

Pod Rysmi Chalet

Vysoka 2560

Gerlachovsky stit 2655

Moravka Chalet

Popradske Pleso

Batizovske Pleso

Strbske Pleso

To Tatranska Strba

Velicka Valley

Slavkovsky stit 2452

Zbojnicka Chalet

Sliezsky dom

TATRAS NATIONAL PARK

Vysne Hagy

Magistrala Trail

To Tatranska Strba

0   1.5   3 km

Jahnaci stit 2229

Brnčalova Chalet

Lomnicky stit 2632

Teryho Chalet

Malá Studená Valley

Veľká Studená Valley

Ndlepkova Chalet

Skalnate Pleso Cable Car   Start

Magistrala Trail

Bilikova Chalet

Hrebienok

Starý Smokovec

Nový Smokovec

Funicular Railway

Tatranska Polianka

Tatranské Lomnica Tatranec

Tatranské Lomnica – Eurocamp FICC Railway Station

Eurocamp

Tatranské Lomnica

CKM Juniorhotel

Pod Lesom Station

Tatracamp

▲ Campground
♠ Chalet/hotel

Hrebienok up this same way. A round trip Hrebienok / Nalepkova / Teryho / Zbojnicka / Hrebienok would take around eight hours.

If it's a cloudy day you may want to follow the 'Tatranska magistrala' red trail through the forest from Hrebienok to Sliezsky dom (two hours).

Via Strbske Pleso An all-day circle hike begins with a morning train to Strbske Pleso (1355 metres) and its glacial lake. Swimming is possible in summer. After a look around this flashy health and ski resort take the red-marked Magistrala Trail up to Popradske Pleso (1494 metres). The Magistrala continues east all the way to Hrebienok via Sliezsky dom. Food may be available at the chalets along the way, but pack your own to be sure.

Via Tatranska Lomnica A shorter round trip would begin with a morning train from Stary Smokovec to Tatranska Lomnica (898 metres). In 1937 a cable car was opened from the resort up to Skalnate Pleso (1751 metres), with an extension to Lomnicky Stit (2632 metres) completed in 1941. As soon as you arrive visit the cable car station near the Grandhotel in Tatranska Lomnica to pick up tickets for the ride to Skalnate Pleso. The cable car (closed Tuesday) is very popular among tourists, so you have to get to the office early to book the trip.

While you're waiting for your departure time to roll around, visit the museum of Tatras National Park a few hundred metres from the bus station at Tatranska Lomnica (open weekdays 8 am to 5 pm, weekends 8 am to 12 noon). The exhibition on the natural and human histories of this area is excellent.

There's a large observatory at Skalnate Pleso and the cable car to the summit of Lomnicky Stit. Hopefully the service will be running, the sky clear and you won't have to wait too long to go. From Skalnate Pleso it's only two hours down the

'Tatranska magistrala' red trail to Hrebienok and the funicular railway back to Stary Smokovec.

If you visit the Tatras during a peak period the place is overflowing with tourists do the Skalnate Pleso trip in reverse. It's a lot easier to get in the cable car at the Skalnate Pleso for a ride down than at Tatranska Lomnica for a ride up. Hundreds may be waiting to go at Tatranska Lomnica.

Mountain Climbing You can reach the summit of Slavkovsky Stit (2452 metres) in nine hours round trip on the blue trail from Stary Smokovec. Rysy Peak (2499 metres) right on the Polish border is about nine hours round trip from Strbske Pleso (via Popradske Pleso and *Chalet Pod Rysmi*). To scale the peaks without marked hiking trails (Gerlachovsky Stit included) you must hire a mountain guide. Members of recognised climbing clubs are exempt.

Places to Stay
Many of the hotels you see in this area are owned by the trade unions and are only for the use of their members. Other hotels are reserved for groups. The Cedok office (closed Saturday afternoon and Sunday) near the railway station at Stary Smokovec will help you find a room in a hotel, but it won't be the cheapest. Ask about private rooms which are a better deal in the long run, although Cedok doesn't like giving them to foreigners.

If the price doesn't bother you, the four-star *Grandhotel* at Stary Smokovec will satisfy you. Built in 1905, this majestic building has a certain elegance the high-rise hotels lack. Since many of the rooms (both single and double) have shared bath, it's not as expensive as you might think (205 Kcs single with breakfast). Cheaper double rooms are available at the nearby B-category *Udernik Hotel* (no singles). If they're both full Cedok may send you to one of the other resorts. The only C-category hotel is the *Bystrina* at Novy Smokovec.

The best place to stay if you have a youth hostel card is the *CKM Juniorhotel Vysoke Tatry* at Horny Smokovec. The charge will be around 45 Kcs and the hotel is open year round, but it's 'always' full so make reservations at a CKM Student Travel office as far in advance as possible.

Camping There's no camping within Tatras National Park. The nearest commercial campground to Stary Smokovec is the *Tatracamp* near Pod lesom Railway Station, three km down the road to Poprad (bungalows available). There's also a campground at Tatranska Strba below Strbske Pleso and two campgrounds a couple of km from Tatranska Lomnica (near Tatranska Lomnica-Eurocamp Railway Station on the line to Studeny Potok).

The largest of these two is the *Eurocamp FICC* (open year round) with restaurants, bars, supermarket, stores, swimming pool, luxury bungalows, hot water and row upon row of parked caravans. The smaller and more personal *Tatranec Campground* (bungalows available) is halfway between the Eurocamp and Tatranska Lomnica.

Chalets Up on the hiking trails are about eight mountain chalets *(chata)*. Cedok would rather have you spending money at a hotel and may just say they're all closed or full. Slovakotour in the MS 70 Hotel at Novy Smokovec will have better information or just set out and try to book yourself into a chalet on the spot. Given the limited capacity and popularity of this area, the chalets could well be full. Signs at the trail heads usually inform you whether the chalets are open. Although food is available at the chalets you should carry in some of your own.

The chalets basically come in three varieties. The *Moravku Chalet* on Popradske Pleso (1500 metres, 82 dorm beds) and

Sliezsky dom (1670 metres, 79 dorm beds) are large mountain hotels with both dormitories and private rooms. *Bilikova* (1255 metres, 68 beds), *Nalepkova* (1475 metres, 20 beds) and *Brncalova* (1551 metres, 52 beds) are rustic wooden buildings on the Magistrala Trail. *Pod Rysmi* (2250 metres, 13 beds), *Zbojnicka* (1960 metres, 18 beds) and *Teryho* (2015 metres, 21 beds) are high mountain chalets built of stone. These three make perfect bases for alpine exploration, but make sure they're open and available before setting out.

Getting There & Away

There are regular express buses from Bratislava to Tatranska Lomnica via Nitra, Banska Bystrica and Stary Smokovec. Bus service to and from Presov is fairly frequent. By train take one of the expresses running between Prague or Bratislava and Kosice and change at Poprad-Tatry (couchettes available). Narrow gauge electric train service between Poprad-Tatry and Stary Smokovec is very frequent. Alternatively get off the express at Tatranska Strba and take the cog-wheel railway up to Strbske Pleso (over 20 services daily).

To & from Poland There's a highway border crossing between Czechoslovakia and Poland at Lysa Polana near Javorina, 30 km from Tatranska Lomnica via Zdiar by bus. No visas are issued on either side of this border, so come prepared. There's a bank on the Polish side where you can complete Polish compulsory exchange, but no Czechoslovak bank at Lysa Polana. If you're unable to change money on either side of the border the bus driver will probably take your smallest banknote in hard currency to cover the fare into town. The buses are less crowded on the Czechoslovak side. See The Tatra Mountains in the Poland chapter of this book for information on conditions on the Polish side.

In perfect weather it would be possible

to hike north to Lysa Polana from the *Teryho Chalet* in half a day. This green trail crosses a 2372-metre pass, so it's only for experienced hikers with light packs. There's also a blue trail from Zbojnicka to Lysa Polana, but it runs right along the border itself. To avoid being turned back by border guards take the green trail. If you're really young, strong and foolish you could hike right across from Stary Smokovec to Lysa Polana in a day.

LEVOCA

In the 13th century the king of Hungary invited Saxon Germans to colonise the eastern borderlands of his kingdom as a protection against Mongol incursions. One of the towns founded at this time was Levoca (Leutschau), 26 km east of Poprad-Tatry. Granted urban privileges in 1271, the Levoca merchants grew rich in the 14th century. To this day the medieval walls, street plan and central square of Levoca have survived, unspoiled by modern developments. The town is an easy stop on the way from Poprad-Tatry to Presov or Kosice.

Information

Cedok is at Mierove namesti 46.

Things to See

Bastions and 15th century walls greet the traveller who arrives by bus at namesti Slobody. The old town begins just through **Kosice Gate** with the **New Minorite Church** (1750) on the left. Levoca's central square, Mierove namesti, is full of things to see. In 15th century **St James Church** is a gigantic Gothic high altar (1517) by Master Pavol, one of the largest and finest of its kind in Europe. Adjacent to St James is the Gothic **Town Hall** enlivened by Renaissance arcades, today the **Museum of the Spis Region**.

There's an **Art Museum** in the 15th

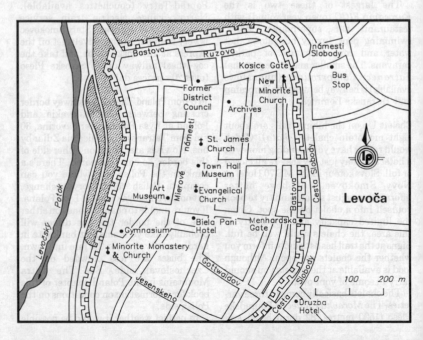

Levoča

century house at Mierova namesti 40. Have a peek in the courtyard of Mierove namesti 43. The former district council (1826), Mierove namesti 59, is in the Empire style, as is the **Evangelical Church** (1837), which once served the German community. Thurzov dom (1532), Mierove namesti 7, now the **State Archives**, is another fine building.

Places to Stay
Levoca has two hotels, the *Biela Pani Hotel* (C-category), Mierove namesti 36, and the larger *Druzba Hotel* (B-category), Cesta Slobody 22 just outside the walls. The restaurant in the Druzba is good. *Levocska Dolina Autocamp* (with bungalows) is three km north of namesti Slobody.

Getting There & Away
Levoca is connected by local train to Spisska Nova Ves, a station on the Prague-Kosice mainline 13 km south. Bus travel is more practical with frequent service to Poprad-Tatry, Spisske Podhradie and Presov.

SPISSKY HRAD
Spissky hrad, 10 km east of Levoca, is the largest castle in Czechoslovakia. The castle occupies a long ridge 180 metres above the town of Spisske Podhradie. Founded in 1209 and reconstructed in the 15th century, Spissky hrad repulsed the Mongols in 1241. The castle burned in 1780 but the ruins and site are spectacular.

Presumably you'll want to visit in transit, so drop your pack at left luggage in Spisske Podhradie Railway Station. Cross the level crossing over the tracks near the station and follow the yellow markers straight up to the castle (closed November to April and every Monday). If the first gate is locked try the second one higher up. Even if both are closed the exterior still justifies a stop. The highest castle enclosure contains a round Gothic tower, a cistern, a chapel and a rectangular Romanesque palace perched over the abyss.

Getting There & Away
Trains run to Spisske Podhradie from Kosice (with a change at Spisske Vlachy) every couple of hours. Buses from Presov, Levoca and Poprad-Tatry are quite frequent.

PRESOV
This old town 36 km north of Kosice is a busy market centre. Presov received a royal charter in 1374 and, like Bardejov to the north and Kosice to the south, was an eastern bulwark of the Kingdom of Hungary. In June 1919 a Slovak Council Republic was proclaimed at Presov, part of a larger socialist revolution in Hungary. This was quickly suppressed by the big landowners whose holdings were threatened and in 1920 the region was incorporated into Czechoslovakia. Presov is the centre of the Slovak Ukraine, the breadbasket of Czechoslovakia. It's a more central base for exploring the region than Kosice, although the cultural offerings are less.

Orientation
Slovenskej republiky rad, Presov's central square, is a 15-minute north walk up Leninova from the adjacent bus and train stations.

Information
Cedok is at Slovenskej republiky rad.

Things to See
The most imposing structure in the city is 14th century **St Nicholas Church** with its Gothic structure and Baroque organ and altars. Behind this is the **Evangelical Church** (1642). To one side is the **Museum of the Slovak Council Republic** (closed weekend afternoons and every Monday), housed in Rakoczi House, Slovenska republiky rad 86. In addition to the archaeology, history and natural history displays, there's a large fire-fighting exhibit.

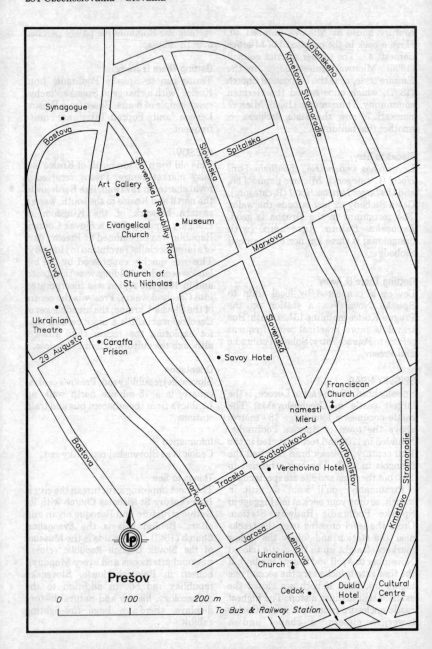

Synagogue

Bastova

Art Gallery

Slovenskej Republiky Rad

Evangelical Church

Museum

Spitalska

Slovenska

Marxova

Valjanskeho

Kmetovo Stromoradie

Church of St. Nicholas

Jarkova

Ukrainian Theatre

29 Augusta

Caraffa Prison

Savoy Hotel

Slovenská

Franciscan Church

namesti Mieru

Bastova

Jarkova

Svatoplukova

Hurbanistov

Verchovina Hotel

Tracska

Jarosa

Leninova

Ukrainian Church

Cedok

Kmetovo Stromoradie

Dukla Hotel

Cultural Centre

Prešov

0   100   200 m

To Bus & Railway Station

Places to Stay

Of the three hotels the *Dukla*, Slovenskej republiky rad 2, is the newest, and the *Verchovina*, Slovenskej republiky rad 26, the oldest, but the best place to stay is the *Savoy Hotel*, Slovenskej republiky rad 50 on the square.

Entertainment

The new *Cultural Centre* is opposite the Dukla Hotel, but the best drama is seen at the *Divadlo Jonasa Zaborskeho* behind the Savoy Hotel. Also check the *Ukrainian National Theatre*, Jarkova 77.

Getting There & Away

The daily Cracovia Express between Cracow and Budapest calls at Presov. Another route to Poland involves a local train to Plavec on the Polish border, then a connecting train to Muszyna in Poland itself. Trains north to Bardejov and south to Kosice are frequent enough, but bus travel is faster on these routes. To Spisske Podhradie, Levoca and the High Tatras you'll want to go by bus.

BARDEJOV

Bardejov received municipal privileges in 1320 and became a free royal town in 1376. Trade between Poland and Russia passed through the town and in the 15th century the Bardejov merchants grew rich. After an abortive 17th century revolt against the Hapsburgs the town's fortunes declined, but medieval Bardejov survived. Since 1954 the town plan and Gothic-Renaissance houses of wealthy merchants lining the sloping central square have been carefully preserved. Much of the town walls, including moat, towers and bastions, remains intact today.

Orientation

The new combined bus/train station at Bardejov is a five-minute walk from namesti Osloboditelov, the main square.

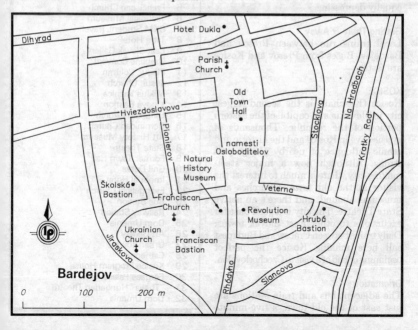

Bardejov

0   100   200 m

Things to See

The 14th century **Parish Church of St Egidius** is one of the most remarkable buildings in the country, complete with no less than 11 tall Gothic altarpieces (1460-1510), all with their original paintings and sculptures! The 15th century bronze baptismal font is also worth noting, as is the structural purity of the church itself.

Near this church is the **Old Town Hall** (1509), the first Renaissance building in Slovakia. Two **museums** (closed Sunday and Monday) face one another on ulice Rhodyho at the south end of the square. One has an excellent natural history collection.

Places to Stay

Bardejov is easily seen as a daytrip from Presov or Kosice, which is best as the B-category *Dukla Hotel* near the Parish Church is large but uninspiring. The C-category *Topla Hotel*, Fucikova 25, is equally depressing.

Getting There & Away

Local trains run between Presov and Bardejov. Buses from Presov and Kosice are faster.

KOSICE

Kosice (Kaschau) is the second largest city in Slovakia and capital of the eastern portion of the republic. Thousands of gypsies live in Kosice and the historic and ethnic influence of nearby Hungary is strong. Although now a major steel-making city, there is much to interest the visitor in the old town. Churches and museums abound, and there's an active State Theatre. The city is a good base for excursions to other East Slovak towns. Daily trains between Cracow and Budapest call here making Kosice the perfect beginning or end of a visit to Czechoslovakia.

Orientation

The adjacent bus and train stations are just east of the old town, a five-minute walk along ulice generala Petrova. This street will bring you into namesti Slobody which becomes Leninova both north and south of the square. Much of your time in Kosice will be spent on this colourful street.

Information

Cedok is in the Slovan Hotel, Rooseveltova 1. CKM Student Travel is at Leninova 82. There's no Hungarian or Polish consulate in Kosice, so be sure to get your onward visa beforehand in Prague or Bratislava.

Things to See

Begin with the **Cathedral of St Elizabeth** (finished 1508), a magnificent late Gothic

1	Hutnik Hotel
2	Dom Kultury ROH
3	East Slovak Museum
4	Prior
5	Franciscan Church
6	Technical Museum
7	CKM Student Travel
8	Tatra Hotel
9	East Slovak Gallery
10	Ursuline Convent
11	Plague Column
12	Jesuit Church
13	Miklus Vaznica
14	Katova Bastion
15	Ukranian Church
16	Dominican Church
17	Art History Museum
18	State Theatre
19	Former Town Hall
20	Grill Detva
21	Imperial Hotel
22	Evangelical Church
23	Bus Station
24	Railway Station
25	Dom Umenia
26	Art Gallery
27	Urban Tower
28	Cathedral
29	Kosice Program House
30	Forgacs Palace
31	"Thalia" Hungarian Theatre
32	Dom Umenia

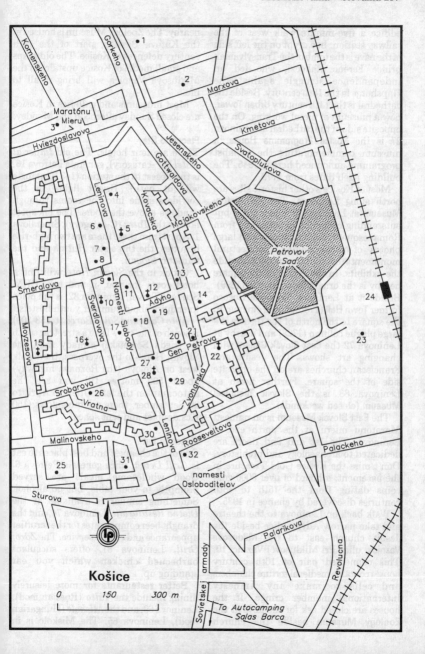

Košice

0   150   300 m

To Autocamping
Salas Barca

edifice a five-minute walk west of the railway station. In a crypt on the left side of the nave is the tomb of the Transylvanian prince Ferenc Rakoczi, who led an independence struggle against the Hapsburgs in the 18th century. Beside the cathedral is the 14th century **Urban Tower**, now a museum of metal working. On the opposite side of the cathedral at Leninova 27 is the **Kosice Programme House**, a museum commemorating the socialist programme announced here in 1945. The building itself dates from 1779.

Most of Kosice's other historic sites are north along Leninova. The **Art History Museum** at Leninova 40 has a small but outstanding collection of art works from Romanesque to contemporary with large photos of corresponding architectural monuments tastefully mounted alongside the exhibits. In the centre of the square nearby is the ornate **State Theatre** (1899). Beside it at Leninova 59 is the Rococo former **Town Hall** (1780), now a cinema. In the square to the north of the theatre is a large plague column (1723) and nearby at Leninova 72 the **East Slovak Gallery** with changing art shows. The Jesuit and Franciscan churches are on the opposite side of the square. Further north at Leninova 88 is the **Slovak Technical Museum** (closed weekends).

The **East Slovak Museum** is on namesti Maratonu mieru at the north end of Leninova. The 1st and 2nd floors are dedicated to archaeology and prehistory. Don't miss the Kosice Gold Treasure in the basement, a hoard of over 3000 gold coins dating from the 15th to 18th centuries discovered by chance in 1935.

Walk back on Leninova to the theatre and take narrow Adyho ulice beside the Jesuit church east to the **Miklusova Vaznica**, ulice Pri Miklusovej Vaznici 10. This connected pair of 16th century houses contains medieval torture chambers and cells to make any Amnesty International member cringe. If the houses are closed ask for the keys at the **Zoology Museum** beside the church

nearby. The Zoology Museum is housed in the Katova Bastion, part of the 15th century defences of Kosice. The old maps and small model of Kosice upstairs in the Miklusova Vaznica will bring it all to life.

Most museums and galleries in Kosice are closed Sunday afternoon and Monday.

Places to Stay

There are four hotels. The old *Imperial Hotel* (B*-category), generala Petrova 16, is the closest to the station (143 Kcs single without bath). Bright lights in the corridors shine into the rooms through windows above the doors. The cheapest hotel is the *Tatra* (C-category), Smeralova 1. Apart from these there are two high-rise beauties, the three-star *Hutnik* and the four-star *Slovan*.

Cedok in the *Slovan Hotel* will find a hotel room for you, if you ask. CKM Student Travel, Leninova 82, is the place to enquire about summer youth hostels.

Auto Camping Salas Barca (tel 58-309) is south of the city. Take a streetcar south on trieda Sovietskej armady from the Slovan Hotel to the overpass, then walk west on Alejova (the Roznava highway) about 500 metres till you see the autocamp on the left. Open 15 April to 30 September, there are bungalows (150 Kcs double) and tent space.

Places to Eat

One of the cheapest and best places to eat is *Grill Detva*, ulice generala Petrova 6. Good wholesome meals are served promptly to your table, but no alcohol. Something similar is available at the *Dietna Restaurant*, Leninova 74, and the draught beer compensates for the scruffier appearance and erratic service. The *Zdroj Grill*, Leninova 81, offers succulent barbecued chicken which you eat standing up.

Better restaurants for more leisurely dining include the *Yalta* (Russian food), Leninova 69, and the *Miskolc* (Hungarian food), Leninova 65. The Miskolc is in

Levoca House, a 16th century warehouse reconditioned into restaurant, cafe and nightclub. There are several *vinaren* (wine bars) on Leninova, north of the theatre. On Sunday all but the Dietna and hotel restaurants may be shut.

Entertainment

Your best bet for a musical evening is the *State Theatre*. Tickets are sold in an office on the east side of the building. The *'Thalia' Hungarian Theatre* and the *State Philharmonic 'Dom Umeria'* are both in the south-west corner of the old town, but performances are only once or twice a week. For special events check out *Dom Kultury ROH* near the Hutnik Hotel and the Cultural Information Office, generala Petrova 21.

Getting There & Away

Daily express trains between Budapest and Cracow roll through Kosice, making access to Hungary and Poland easy. If the timing is inconvenient look for a local train to Hidasnemeti on the Hungarian border, where you can connect to Miskolc, Hungary. Kosice receives all trains between Prague and Moscow.

Overnight sleepers are available to and from Kosice and Prague, Brno, Bratislava, Decin and Karlovy Vary. Day trains connect Kosice to Prague (via Poprad-Tatry), Bratislava (via Banska Bystrica) and Presov. Book international tickets and sleepers with Cedok. For shorter trips to Presov, Bardejov and Spisske Podhradie you're better off taking a bus.

Hungary

Without question, Hungary is the most accessible Eastern European country. Only a short hop from Vienna, this romantic land of Franz Liszt, Bela Bartok, gypsy music and the blue Danube welcomes visitors. You'll be enchanted by Budapest, once a great imperial city, and Pecs, the warm heart of the south. The fine wines, fiery paprika, sweet violins, good theatre and colourful folklore will conspire to extend your stay. The friendly Magyars are as inviting as goulash soup.

The best thing about Hungary is the price. Here's one country where the government doesn't discriminate against western tourists with double pricing, compulsory exchange and artificially low official exchange rates. There's no obligation to make advance hotel reservations, buy vouchers or join a rigid package tour. In fact, you're almost encouraged to stay with local families as a paying guest. You're free to go anywhere in the country, how and when you like. All of this works to your advantage. If you've been duped by the distorted image of 'Communism' in fashion in the western news media, Hungary is the place to get your feet on the ground. It's the ideal place to kick off an Eastern European trip.

Facts about the Country

HISTORY

The Celts occupied Hungary in the final centuries BC but were themselves conquered by the Romans in 10 AD. From the 1st to the 5th centuries all of Hungary west and south of the Danube (the area today known as Transdanubia) was included in the Roman province of Pannonia. The Roman legion stationed at Aquincum (Budapest) guarded the north-eastern frontier of the Empire. In 408 the West Goths invaded the area, followed in 451 by Attila's Huns, then the Lombards and Avars. From 795 Pannonia was part of the Carolingian Empire.

In 896 seven Magyar tribes under chief Arpad swept in from beyond the Volga River and occupied the Danube Basin. They terrorised Europe with raids as far as France and Italy until their conversion to Roman Catholicism in the late 10th century. Hungary's first king and patron saint, Stephen I, was crowned on Christmas Day in the year 1000, marking the foundation of the Hungarian state. After the Mongols sacked Hungary in 1241 many cities were fortified.

Feudal Hungary was a large and powerful state which included Transylvania (in present Romania) and Croatia (in present Yugoslavia). The medieval capital shifted from Szekesfehervar to Esztergom, Buda and Visegrad. Universities were founded in Pecs (1367) and Buda (1389).

In 1456 at Nandorfehervar (present Belgrade) Hungarians under Janos Hunyadi stopped a Turkish advance north. Hungary experienced a brief flowering of the Renaissance during the Golden Age under Hunyadi's son, Matthias Corvinus, who ruled from 1458 to 1490. In 1514 a peasant army assembled for a crusade against the Turks turned on the landowners. The serfs were eventually suppressed and their leader Gyorgy Dozsa executed, but Hungary was seriously weakened. Then, in 1526, the Hungarian army was defeated by the Turks at Mohacs and in 1541 the Turks occupied Buda.

The Kingdom of Hungary was reduced to a Hapsburg-dominated buffer strip between Balaton Lake and Vienna with its seat at Pozsony (Bratislava). Continued Hungarian resistance to the Turks resulted in heroic battles at Koszeg (1532), Eger (1552) and Szigetvar (1566). Though a vassal, the Principality of Transylvania was never fully integrated into the Ottoman Empire. When the Turks were finally evicted in 1686 through the combined efforts of the Christian armies of Europe, Hungary was subjected to Hapsburg domination.

From 1703 to 1711 Ferenc Rakoczi II, Prince of Transylvania, led a War of Independence against the Austrians, which was eventually overcome through force of numbers. At this time the Hapsburgs demolished any medieval fortifications which had survived the Turkish period to deny their use to Hungarian rebels. Aside from destruction, all the Turks left behind were a few bath houses in Buda and a couple of mosques in Pecs.

Hungary never fully recovered from these disasters. Most of the country's medieval monuments had been destroyed and beginning in the 18th century Hungary had to be rebuilt almost from scratch.

The bourgeois-democratic revolution of 1848 led by Lajos Kossuth and the poet Sandor Petofi against the Hapsburgs demanded freedom for the serfs and independence. Although defeated in 1849 the uprising shook the oligarchy. In 1867 there was a compromise between the Austrian capitalists and Hungarian landowners and the Austro-Hungarian Monarchy was formed. Although this partnership stimulated industrial development it proved unfortunate in the long run as Hungary came to be viewed by its neighbours as a tool of Hapsburg oppression. After WW I Hungary became independent from Austria but lost two-thirds of its territory and 60% of its population to Czechoslovakia, Romania and Yugoslavia. The loss of Transylvania fuels resentment against neighbouring Romania to this day.

A brief 133-day socialist government led by Bela Kun was overthrown by counter-revolutionary elements in August 1919, and thousands were killed, imprisoned or forced to flee the country. In March 1920, Admiral Miklos Horthy established a reactionary regime which lasted a quarter century. In 1941 the Hungarian desire to recover the lost territories drew the country into war alongside the Nazis. Nearly half a million Jewish Hungarians were murdered during this senseless conflict. When Horthy tried to make a separate peace with the Allies in October 1944, the occupying Germans put the fascist Arrow Cross Party in power. By 4 April 1945 all of Hungary had been liberated by the Soviet Army.

After the fighting died down the large estates were divided among the peasantry and the means of production nationalised. In 1948 the Communist and Social Democratic parties merged to become the Hungarian Workers' Party. During the early 1950s Hungary followed the Stalinist line of collectivised agriculture and heavy industry. In February 1956 Nikita Khrushchev denounced Stalin at a closed session of the 20th Party Congress in Moscow. In July the conservative party leader Matyas Rakosi was forced to resign, raising expectations of widesweeping reform and democratisation.

On 23 October 1956 Soviet troops participated in the suppression of student demonstrations in Budapest, leading to a general rebellion. That evening the reformer Imre Nagy was made prime minister. The disorders spread and on 1

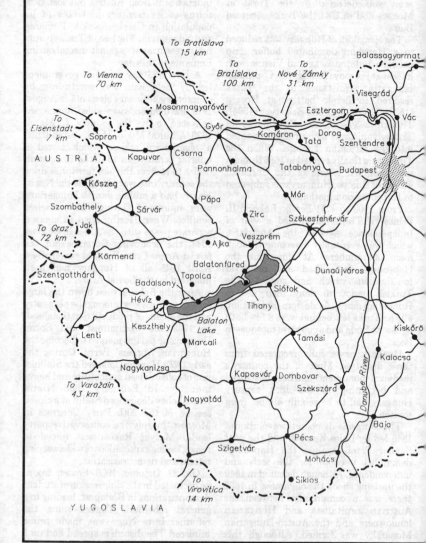

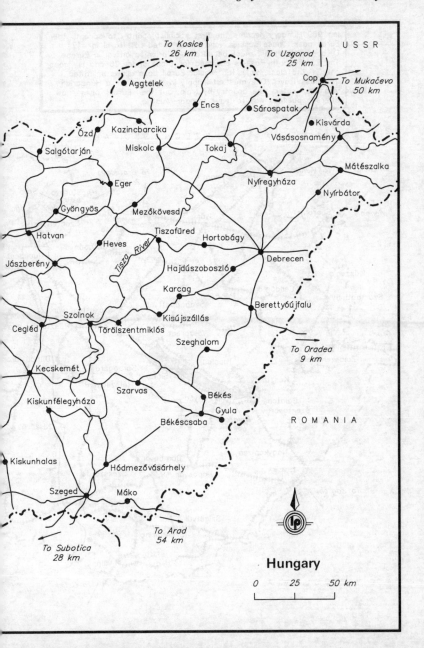

In 1989 Hungary became the first socialist country to accept the Eurail pass. These passes, valid for unlimited rail travel in 17 European countries, must be purchased prior to arrival in Europe. The Eurail Youth Pass is designed for those under 26 and is good only in 2nd class, while the regular Eurail pass allows unlimited 1st class travel. One must still apply in advance for a Hungarian visa to enter the country by train, but the Eurail pass now offers a painless way to leave through Austria.

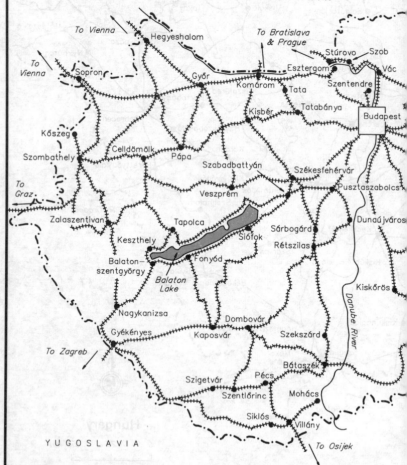

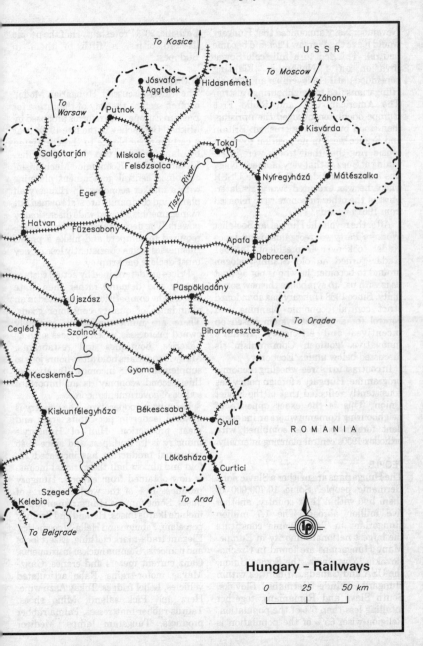

Hungary – Railways

0   25   50 km

November Nagy announced that Hungary would leave the Warsaw Pact and become neutral. This led to a full-scale Soviet invasion on 4 November. Fighting continued until 11 November and 200,000 Hungarians fled to neighbouring Austria. The American CIA and Radio Free Europe openly encouraged the uprising, then stood by as it was crushed. Britain and France were in no position to object considering that their troops were intervening at Suez at that very moment. Nagy was arrested and deported to the USSR where he was executed two years later. Most of the other prisoners were released from 1961 onwards.

After the revolt the Hungarian Socialist Workers' Party was reorganised and Janos Kadar took over as president. In 1961 Kadar turned an old Stalinist slogan around to become, 'he who is not against us is with us,' to symbolise the new social unity. Since 1968 Hungary has abandoned strict central economic planning and control for a market system based on incentives and efficiency. Kadar's innovative 'goulash Communism' is discussed below under 'Economy.'

In contrast to its free-wheeling economic programme, Hungary's foreign policy has consistently reflected that of the Soviet Union. This is the exact opposite of neighbouring Romania where an independent foreign policy is combined with orthodox 1950s central planning internally.

PEOPLE

The Hungarians are neither a Slavic nor a Germanic people. Some 10,700,000 of them live within their country, another five million abroad. The 1.7 million Hungarians in Transylvania constitute the largest national minority in Europe. Many Hungarians are found in Czechoslovakia, Yugoslavia, the Soviet Union, the USA and Canada. Minorities within Hungary include Germans, Slovaks, South Slavs and Romanians, together totalling less than 5% of the population. Religion-wise, 65% of the population is Catholic, 20% Protestant. Half the people live in cities, a fifth of them in Budapest.

ECONOMY

The widely discussed 'Hungarian Model' is often seen as the way of the future for Eastern Europe. The reforms proposed by Mikhail Gorbachev in the late 1980s bear a certain resemblance to those initiated by Janos Kadar two decades earlier. Kadar's 'New Economic Mechanism' combined central government planning with a market economy. In Hungary all plants and companies are state owned but management is allowed wide discretionary powers. The decentralised enterprises are required to compete and make a profit. Businesses which consistently lose money must declare bankruptcy.

Prices are determined by actual costs or supply and demand rather than state edicts. The competition has resulted in an abundance of quality consumer goods. There are numerous small, privately owned businesses, often services such as bakeries, boutiques and restaurants. Many Hungarians hold after-hours jobs to supplement their incomes. Taxation of this 'second economy' is an important source of government income.

Farming is cooperative. The country is a world leader in per capita grain and meat production. Half of Hungary's industry is in Budapest and since 1945 industrial production has increased 12-fold and almost half the national income is now obtained from exports. Hungary produces 10% of the worlds' exports of buses. Some famous Hungarian products include Ikarus buses, Herend and Zsolnay porcelain, Fabulon and Helia-D cosmetics, Elegant trade-mark clothing, Elzett locks and padlocks, Gamma nuclear instruments, Ganz current meters and cranes, Ganz-Mavag motor-trains, Raba articulated vehicles, Lehel fridges, Tokay Aszu wine, Herz and Pick salami, Mino shoes, Taurus rubber mattresses, Palma rubber products, Tungsram lamps, Medicor medical instruments and Videoton electronic devices. The economy is not all sunshine, however. Problems for Hungary include shrinking foreign markets for the country's goods, double-digit inflation and a US$7.7 billion hard currency debt to western creditors.

Since the war half the population has moved into modern new homes and there is free medical care and many other benefits despite the economic problems. Hungarians are allowed to make tourist trips to the west and, significantly, nearly all of them choose to return to Hungary.

GEOGRAPHY

Hungary is a people's republic divided into 19 counties. Budapest is further divided into 22 districts. Hungary occupies the Carpathian Basin in the very centre of Eastern Europe. The 417-km Hungarian reach of the Danube River cuts through a southern extension of the Carpathian Range at the majestic Danube Bend north of Budapest. The Danube divides Hungary's 93,030 square km in two: to the east is the Great Plain, to the west Transdanubia. The 579 km of the Tisza River in Hungary crosses the Great Plain about 100 km east of the Danube.

Two-thirds of Hungary is below 200 metres. The almost treeless Hungarian *puszta* between the Danube and Romania is a harbinger of the steppes of the Ukraine. Balaton Lake (598 square km) between the Danube and Austria reaches only 11.5 metres at its deepest point. The lake's average depth is three to four metres and the waters warm quickly in summer. The 'mountains' of Hungary are actually hills as they seldom reach 1000 metres (mountains in Czechoslovakia and Romania pass 2000 metres). The highest peak is Kekes (1015 metres) in the Matra Mountains north-east of Budapest.

CULTURE

Hungary is a paradise for culture vultures. In Budapest there are several musical events to choose from each evening and the best opera tickets never go over US$5. Culture is heavily subsidised by the state. Unlike Prague, tickets *are* available and the friendly Hungarians usually go out of their way to help foreign visitors get seats. Aside from the traditional opera, operetta and concerts, there are rock and jazz concerts, folk dancing, pantomime, planetarium performances, literary evenings, movies, floorshows and circuses to keep you smiling.

Excellent performances are also seen in provincial towns such as Gyor, Szombathely, Pecs, Szeged, Eger and Debrecen, all of which have fine modern theatres. Information about events is readily available at tourist offices or in the *Daily News*. Budget an extra week in Hungary just to take full advantage of this wonderful opportunity.

FESTIVALS & HOLIDAYS

Among Hungary's most outstanding events are the Budapest Spring Festival (last third of March), Budapest Country Music Meeting (June), Hortobagy International Horse Show (June), Sopron Festival Weeks (mid-June to mid-July), Gyor Summer Music Festival (July), Pecs Summer Theatre Festival (June and July), Eger 'Agria' Events (end of June to mid-August), Szentendre Summer Festival (July), Szeged Open-air Festival (mid-July to mid-August), Szombathely Savaria Days (August) and Budapest Art and Music Weeks (September and October). The Budapest International Fair in the second half of May features industrial products, in the middle of September it focuses on consumer goods. The first Sunday in June there's a Folk Art Fair in Gyor.

The public holidays are New Year's Day (1 January), Liberation Day (4 April), Easter Monday, Labour Day (1 May), Constitution Day (20 August), Revolution Day (7 November) and Christmas (25 and 26 December). Constitution Day is celebrated with sporting events, parades and fireworks. That day there's a Flower

Festival in Debrecen and a Bridge Fair in nearby Hortobagy.

LANGUAGE

The Hungarians speak a language only they understand. Of the languages of Europe only Finnish and Estonian are related. Many Hungarians understand German, however. Those with a knowledge of English are less common. As usual, if you have trouble making yourself understood, try writing it out. Be aware of Hungarian accents which are not used in this book.

Some words to know include *koszonom* thank you, *igen* yes, *nem* no, *viszontlatasra* goodbye, *szinhaz* theatre, *penztar* ticket office, *elkelt* sold out, *keptar* art gallery, *nyitva* open, *zarva* closed, *szoba* room, *allomas* station, *naponta* daily, *hetkoznap* workdays, *erkezik* arrivals, *indul* departures, *utca* street, *korut* boulevard, *ut* road, *ter* square, *utja* avenue, *setany* promenade. The days of the week are: *hetfo, kedd, szerda, csutortok, pentek, szombat, vasarnap.* Surnames are put before given names.

Facts for the Visitor

VISAS

Everyone entering Hungary must have a passport valid at least nine months ahead and a visa. Visas are issued on the spot at Hungarian consulates upon receipt of a US$10 to US$15 fee and two photos. A double entry tourist visa is US$25 to US$30 and four photos. Be sure to get a tourist rather than a transit visa. A tourist visa allows a stay of up to 30 days and can be used anytime within three or six months. A transit visa is only good for a stay of 48 hours, cannot be extended and costs the same price. On a transit visa you must enter and leave through different border crossings and must have a visa for your next country.

If you'll be arriving by road, hydrofoil or air you can get the visa at the border or airport (you still need the two photos) but it's better to get the visa in advance at a diplomatic office. If you're travelling by train you *must* obtain the visa in advance. Rail passengers arriving without visas are either refused entry or obliged to leave the train and go to a highway entry point for the visa, *provided one happens to be nearby!* Nationals of Austria, Finland and Sweden do not require visas to visit Hungary.

A notice on the visa form instructs you to report to police within 48 hours of arrival. If you're staying in a private room arranged by a Hungarian travel agency, or at a hotel or campground, this formality will be taken care of for you. The agency or hotel will stamp your visa form and write in the nights you stayed with them. If you're staying with friends you're supposed to report to the police in person. Upon departure from Hungary the Immigration officer will scrutinise the stamps. If too many nights are unaccounted for you'll have some explaining to do. Your visa serves as an exit permit and you can leave Hungary anytime within the 30 day validity.

MONEY

US$1 = 45 forint (Ft) (official)

no compulsory exchange

The Hungarian forint is divided into 100 fillers. There are banknotes of 10, 20, 50, 100, 500 and 1000 forint. A commission of 1% is charged on exchanges. Main post offices are often good places to change money. It's very difficult to change excess forints back into hard currency. You may be successful at a main branch of the National Bank but you'll only be allowed to re-exchange half the amount you changed originally, verified by receipts. It's simpler just to spend all your Hungarian money before leaving.

You're only allowed to import or export

100 forint. If you declare a larger amount upon departure Customs will take the money and give you a receipt allowing you to pick up your forints at a savings bank next visit, less 3% service charge. It's a good idea to bring the permitted 100 forint with you as the lines at exchange counters in Budapest railway stations are horrendous. Also they don't open until 8 am so if you arrive earlier you won't even be able to leave your pack at left luggage or use the toilets without a few coins! Western banks or Hungarian tourists you meet elsewhere may be able to sell you a small bill. There's no great advantage to bringing over 100 forint with you and Customs will confiscate larger amounts if they find them. The import or export of 500 or 1000 forint notes is strictly prohibited.

If you have trouble changing money at a Budapest railway station risk riding the Metro without a ticket to Deak ter, then walk a few blocks to the 24-hour-a-day Ibusz office at Petofi ter 3. There you'll be able to change money without difficulty. If you want to book accommodation at Ibusz or another agency do it first, before changing money. They accept travellers' cheques and give change in forint.

Hungarians routinely tip doctors, dentists, waiters, hairdressers and taxi drivers about 10%. Hungary is beginning to feel the inflationary pressures which have gripped Yugoslavia. Food prices are going up fast, accommodation more slowly, while transport costs are fairly steady. Hungary is still reasonable because it doesn't discriminate against western tourists with a two or three price system, as is the case in all other Eastern European countries. What you pay for a hotel room will be about the same as a Hungarian would pay.

The black market in Hungary is not a hot proposition because banks and travel agencies give you a rate very close to the real market value of the forint. Of course a black market does exist, as Ibusz offices in Budapest tacitly admit by requiring that you pay for your accommodation in hard currency. Those Arab students hanging around Keleti Railway Station aren't there for nothing. Take care, however. Many of the persons offering to change money on the street in Budapest are thieves who have no intention of actually giving you the high rate they quote. They'll attempt to switch the money for paper or small bills at the last minute and

will rush off exclaiming that the police are coming if you object. If you're offered more than 50% above the official rate a rip-off is definitely intended.

As everywhere in Eastern Europe, unofficial exchanges are illegal and the law is strictly enforced. The black market is seldom used by tourists and you'll soon see that even at the official rate Hungary is still one of the cheapest countries in Europe, so why push it?

CLIMATE

Hungary's climate is temperate continental with Mediterranean and Atlantic influences. Of 2054 hours of sunshine a year at Budapest, 1526 occur in the period April to September. July is the hottest month, January the coldest. The mean annual temperature is 10°C. May, June and November are the rainiest months, although more rain falls in the west than in the east.

BOOKS & BOOKSHOPS

Books are good value in Hungary and many titles are available in English. *Hungary, A Comprehensive Guide* (Corvina, Budapest, 1981) is strong on maps and background information. It's all you need for a long stay. An American edition of the same book is published by Hippocrene Books, 171 Madison Ave, New York, NY 10016. While visiting Budapest be sure to pick up an inexpensive indexed city map at a bookstore.

NEWSPAPERS & MEDIA

The *Daily News/Neueste Nachrichten* is available at newsstands from Tuesday to Saturday in English and German (7 Ft). You'll be impressed by the frank reporting. The *News* has a section listing upcoming events around the country. More such listings are found in the monthly *Programme in Hungary* (in English and German), free from tourist offices. Two English-language magazines are the *Hungarian Digest* and *The New Hungarian Quarterly*. The *Budapester Rundschau*

is a German-language weekly paper. Hungary's economic weekly, *Heti Vilaggazdasag* (HVG), is one of the most provocative news magazines in Eastern Europe (published in Hungarian only). Western magazines are sold at the luxury hotels.

HEALTH

There are hundreds of thermal baths in Hungary, most of them open to the public. Tourists receive free first aid treatment at clinics and hospitals. Hospital emergency and out-patient attention, free for Hungarians, is available to visitors at reasonable rates. Prescription drugs and all medicines are very cheap.

In Budapest call your embassy for the name of a doctor or dentist accustomed to treating foreigners. If your own embassy won't refer you, phone any other which speaks your language and assume the role of a visitor from that country. Telephone the doctor or dentist to make an appointment before going in for treatment.

GENERAL INFORMATION
Post

Postage is low and the service comparatively reliable, if slow. Letters take 20 days to go from Western Europe to Budapest, 10 days to go from Budapest to Western Europe.

Electricity

220 volts, AC.

Time

Greenwich Mean Time plus one hour. The clock is put an hour forward at the end of March, an hour back at the end of September.

Business Hours

Grocery stores open weekdays from 7 am to 6 pm, department stores from 10 am to 6 pm. Most shops stay open until 8 pm Thursday. Saturday they close at 12 noon. Post offices open weekdays from 8 am to 6 pm, Saturday from 8 am to 2 pm. Most museums are closed on Monday and free on Saturday. Museum admissions are rarely over 15 Ft. Students get into all museums free and pay half price for many cultural events.

INFORMATION

Every Hungarian town has a travel agency which doubles as an accommodation service and tourist information centre. The largest travel agency is Ibusz with 120 offices in Hungary plus representatives overseas (see the list below). Other national travel agencies with offices around the country include Cooptourist and Volantourist. Regional travel agencies in provincial centres (Dunatours, Siotour, Mecsek Tourist, etc) are often more familiar with their own local area. There's almost always someone in the office who speaks either English or German and you'll find them very helpful. The addresses of all these agencies are listed in the relevant sections of this book.

Australia
 Ibusz, 8/321 Edgecliff Rd, Woollahra, Sydney, NSW 2025
Austria
 Ibusz (tel 51-555), Karntner Strasse 26, 1010 Vienna 1
Belgium
 Ibusz (tel 511-6484), Rue du Luxembourg 6, 1040 Brussels

Britain
 Ibusz (tel 493-0263), 6 Conduit St, London W1R 9TG
Finland
 Ibusz (tel 65-3969), Sepankatu 3-5 C, 00150 Helsinki
France
 Ibusz (tel 4742-5025), 27 Rue de Quatre-Septembre, 75002 Paris
Holland
 Ibusz (tel 649-851), Strawinskylaan 1425, 1077 XX Amsterdam
Italy
 Ibusz (tel 483-441), Via V E Orlando 75, 00185 Rome
Japan
 Ibusz (tel 404-8089), No 13, Togensha Building, 3rd floor, 12-10, Roppongi 4-chome Minato-ku, Tokyo 106
Spain
 Ibusz (tel 241-2544), Juan Alvarez Mendizabal 136, 28008 Madrid
Sweden
 Ibusz (tel 23-2030), Beridarebanan 1, Stockholm
USA
 Ibusz (tel 582-7412), Rockefeller Center, Suite 520, 630 Fifth Ave, New York, NY 10111
West Germany
 Ibusz (tel 2191-0204), Mauritiussteinweg 114-116, 5000 Cologne 1
 Ibusz (tel 25-2018), Baseler Strasse 46/48, Frankfurt am Main
 Ibusz (tel 37-3078), Grosser Burstah 53, 2000 Hamburg 11
 Ibusz (tel 55-7217), Dachauer Strasse 5, 8000 Munich 2
 Ibusz (tel 29-6233), Kronprinz Strasse 6, 7000 Stuttgart

ACCOMMODATION
Private Rooms

There are beds for 100,000 people in private rooms in Hungary, costing 80-500 Ft single, 120-700 Ft double depending on whether the room is 1st, 2nd or 3rd class. Private rooms at Balaton Lake are slightly more expensive. Single rooms are sometimes hard to come by, but even at the double room rate it's inexpensive. There's a linen supplement if you stay only one or two nights. In Budapest you may have to take a room far from the centre of town, but public transport is good and very cheap.

This is your best accommodation bet by far. You share a house or flat with an Hungarian family. The toilet facilities are usually communal but otherwise you can close your door and enjoy as much privacy as you please. All 1st and some 2nd and 3rd class rooms have shared kitchen facilities.

The rooms are assigned by travel agencies which take your money and give you a voucher bearing the address. The offices close at 4 pm weekdays and 1 pm Saturday, so you must arrive in a town early. Longer hours are common in summer. If the first room they offer seems too expensive, ask if they have a cheaper one. There are usually several agencies offering private rooms, so ask around if the price is higher than usual or the location inconvenient. The rooms only become available after 5 pm.

Youth Hostels

Hungary is one of the few countries in the world where, aside from camping, the hostels listed in the IYHF handbook are *not* the cheapest places to stay (private rooms are cheaper). Many of the places listed in the IYHF handbook are not youth hostels at all but medium-priced hotels. Most give a discount if you show a youth hostel card, bringing the price down to the usual international hostel rate (about US$7). Some hostels give an additional 25% discount if you show a student card. There's no age limit at the hostels, they remain open all day and they're often good places to meet Eastern European young people.

Express is the Hungarian travel agency officially responsible for youth hostels, so check with them first. In summer they may know of temporary youth hostels set up in student dormitories. Although the IYHF handbook insists that you must visit the Express office before going to the hostel, this is not the case with the hotel hostels which will admit you without the mediation of Express.

Tourist Hostels

There's another class of accommodation which is similar to western youth hostels but not included in the IYHF handbook. A tourist hostel *(turistaszallo)* offers beds in separate dormitories for men and women. There are no rules (no curfew, smoking and drinking allowed in the room, etc) and a youth hostel card is not required. Tourist hostels are found in many cities and most stay open year round. The overnight fee will be under US$2 but they're not accustomed to receiving western visitors. You may have to ask the local tourist office or Express to call ahead in order to gain admission.

Camping

Hungary has 140 to 150 campgrounds and these are the cheapest places to stay. They're often in attractive locations and offer the opportunity to meet local people. Prices vary from 10 to 50 Ft per person, plus 40 to 150 Ft per tent for one, two and three-star camping sites. An additional 30 Ft per person 'resort tax' is levied in some areas. Most are open from mid-May to mid-September and rent small bungalows (from US$4) to visitors without tents. In mid-summer the bungalows may all be gone so it pays to check with the local tourist office before making the trip. Members of the International Camping & Caravanning Club (FICC) usually get a 10% discount, student card holders a 50% discount. Freelance camping is prohibited.

Hotels

Hungarian hotels are significantly more expensive than private rooms, but cheap by international standards (from US$10 single or double). A hotel may be the answer if you're only staying one night or arrive too late to get a private room. Most of the cheaper hotels are included in this book.

If you want to be sure of a place to stay in

another Hungarian city have a travel agency (Ibusz, Express, Cooptourist, Dunatours, Volantourist, etc) reserve a hotel room for you. They'll need a couple of days notice and in addition to the regular room rate you must pay the telex charges and a 10% commission. Still, in the busy summer season it may be worth it.

A 15% turnover tax is added to all accommodation charges in Hungary. The prices listed in this book do not include this tax which is additional.

FOOD & DRINK

Hungary has a tasty national cuisine all its own. Many dishes are seasoned with paprika, a red spice which appears on restaurant tables beside the salt and pepper. Hungarian goulash (gulyas) is a thick beef soup cooked with onions and potatoes. Porkolt is meat stewed in lard with onions and paprika. If sour cream is added to porkolt it becomes paprikas. Cabbage is an important vegetable in Hungary, either stuffed in the Turkish fashion (toltott kaposzta) or made into a thick cabbage soup (kaposzta leves) popular among late diners. Other delicacies include goose liver sandwiches and paprika chicken (paprikas csirke) served with tiny dumplings.

Fisherman's soup (halaszle) is a rich mixture of several kinds of boiled fish, tomatoes, green peppers and paprika. Balaton Lake pike perch (sullo) is generally served breaded and grilled.

Noodles with cottage cheese and tiny cubes of crisp fried bacon (turos csusza) goes well with the fish dishes. Hungarian cream cheese (korozott) is a mixture of sheep cheese, paprika and caraway seeds. Strudel (retes) is a typical layered pastry filled with apple, cherry, cabbage, curd or cheese.

Drinks

Hungarian wines match the cuisine admirably. The best wines have a Hungarian flag around the top of the bottle. The finest are those produced in the volcanic soils of Badacsony, Eger, Sopron and Tokaj. Southern Hungary (Pecs, Villany and Szekszard) is also noted. One of the best Hungarian red wines is Egri Bikaver, while Tokaji aszu is a very sweet golden-white wine of an almost liqueur consistency. Louis XIV of France called Tokaji aszu 'the king of wines and wine of kings.' Medoc Noir is a strong, sweet red dessert wine. Others to watch for are Tihany Cabernet, Villany Pinot Noir, Soproni Kekfrankos, Badacsony Keknyelu, Csopak Reisling and Mori Ezerjo (white). Pick up a bottle of any of these at a local supermarket. Also try the apricot, cherry or plum brandy (palinka). Mecseki and Hubertus are two exquisite Hungarian liqueurs.

Restaurants

Hungarian restaurants (etterem or vendeglo) are relatively cheap. Meal prices average US$2 at a self-service, US$3 in a local restaurant and US$5 in a tourist restaurant. Lunch is the main meal of the day. Most restaurants offer a set lunch (menu) weekdays and this is always good value. It usually consists of soup, side salad, main course and

occasionally dessert. Printed menus are often translated into German, and occasionally, into English.

Language difficulties can cause misunderstandings so it's worth checking your bill carefully. If no service charge was been added you might follow the Hungarian practice of giving a 10% tip directly as you pay (don't wait to leave money on the table). Waiters sometimes overcharge foreigners slightly making this unnecessary, although you can still 'round up' the bill. Gypsy musicians are also accustomed to receiving tips. Give them a small bill and they'll move on to the next table. At better restaurants it's obligatory to check your coat (2 Ft). If you're on a strict budget have a soft drink with your meal as most restaurants stock only the more expensive brands of beer and wine. Coffee after the meal is always cheap.

A *csarda* is a traditional inn offering spicy fare and fiery wine. *Borozo* denotes a wine restaurant, *sorozo* a pub offering draft beer with the meal. A *bisztro* is an inexpensive restaurant, often self-service *(onkiszolgalo)*. *Bufes* are the cheapest places, although you may have to eat standing at a counter. Pastries, cakes and coffee are served at a *cukraszda*, while an *eszpresszo* is a cafe. A *bar* is a night club with music and dancing. In Hungary the ice cream is worth lining up for.

THINGS TO BUY

Stores in Hungary are well stocked. Prices are low for almost everything a tourist would wish to buy and the quality of the products high. Food, alcohol, folk music records and books are exceptionally cheap and the selection excellent. On the other hand, clothing and footwear are better value in Czechoslovakia. Traditional products include folk art embroidery and ceramics, bone lace, dolls and Herend, Kalocsa or Zsolnay porcelain. Visitors are allowed to export 3000 Ft worth of goods without receipts, although not in commercial quantities.

Getting There & Away

Budapest is connected to all surrounding countries by road, rail, river and air. There's bus service from Vienna (Austria) and Zakopane (Poland). Trains arrive from every neighbouring capital. In summer there's a hydrofoil service between Vienna and Budapest. Details of all of these services are given in the Budapest section of this book.

TRAIN

International trains to Budapest enter Hungary from Cracow and Kosice via Miskolc, from Warsaw via Zilina, from Berlin and Prague via Komarom and Sturovo. From Vienna you can catch a train to Budapest via Hegyeshalom, or Vienna-Sopron direct. There's also service from Graz (Austria) to Szombathely. From Yugoslavia the possibilities are Zagreb to Budapest via Kaposvar or Belgrade to Budapest via Subotica. A local train runs from Osijek to Pecs. From Romania you have a choice of entering via Oradea or Arad. All of these services are daily or several times daily.

Train Tickets

Railway tickets between socialist countries are very cheap, especially when purchased in Hungary. For example, Budapest to Berlin is only US$10 1st class, US$6 extra for a sleeper. Budapest-Prague is US$6 1st class. The reason is that MAV Hungarian Railways gives a 50% discount to tourists who pay in western currency and the fares are low to begin with. You don't get the reduction on tickets to Yugoslavia, however. Budapest-Belgrade will cost US$14 2nd class, although it's a lot closer than Berlin. A ticket to Sofia is twice as expensive via Belgrade as it would be via Bucharest, although the Romanian visa fee (US$21) cancels out this saving.

Tickets to Western Europe cost the same in Hungary as they would in the west, about five times as much as comparable tickets in Eastern Europe. Persons under 26 years of age can get a 35 to 50% reduction on all railway tickets, domestic or international, by showing a student or youth hostel card issued by the IUS, ISTC or IYHF. All student card holders regardless of age are eligible for a 25% discount on tickets to other socialist countries. International train tickets are valid for two months, a return portion for four months, and stopovers are allowed.

Trains to Moscow & China

Ibusz, Tanaks korut 3/c, Budapest, sells train tickets from Budapest to China for only US$90 one way in 1st class with a sleeper. Problem is, it takes a month for the reservations to come through and you can't get a Soviet transit visa without a booking. Ask about cancellations, you may be lucky. This same office will also reserve hotel rooms in Moscow (from US$80 a night, payable in advance) but it takes a month to do so. Book your return train ticket to Moscow (US$50 1st class) at the same time.

Getting Around

TRAIN

Most railway lines converge on Budapest. Trains are comfortable, reliable and not overcrowded. If you'll be using them extensively you can buy a complete timetable with an explanation of the symbols in English for only 60 Ft. In Hungarian railway stations the yellow board indicates departures *(indul)*, the white board arrivals *(erkezik)*. Express trains are indicated in red, local trains in black. All railway stations have left luggage offices, most of which stay open 24 hours a day. A few large bus stations also have luggage rooms, but they generally close by 7 pm.

Express trains are twice as expensive as local trains. When purchasing your ticket

make sure it has a red strip across the middle to indicate that it's for the express. If you buy a ticket on the train (rather than in the station) there's a 100 Ft surcharge. Some express trains are fully reserved. Seat reservations for these cost 12 Ft in the station or 40 Ft from the conductor. Inter-Rail passes (available only to those under 26) are accepted in Hungary, but not Eurail passes.

BUS

Hungary's bright yellow Volanbuses are a good alternative to the trains and only a little more expensive. They are essential for crossing the bottom of the country, for example to go Szombathely / Keszthely / Kaposvar / Pecs / Szeged / Gyula. For short trips in the Danube Bend or Balaton Lake areas buses are recommended. Timetables are clearly posted at stations and stops. If you have a front seat you'll see more from the bus than you would on the train, while being a little cramped. Tickets are usually available from the driver, but ask in the station to be sure. There are sometimes lines for inter-city buses so it's wise to arrive at the stop early.

BOAT

In summer there are regular passenger boats on Balaton Lake and the Danube (Budapest to Esztergom). Full details on these are given in the relevant sections below.

Budapest

Budapest straddles a curve of the Danube where Transdanubia meets the Great Plain, exactly halfway between Sofia and Berlin. One Hungarian in five lives here and Miskolc, the next largest Hungarian city, is only a 10th the size. More romantic than Belgrade, more easy-going than Prague, Budapest is the Paris of Eastern Europe. The Romans built the town of

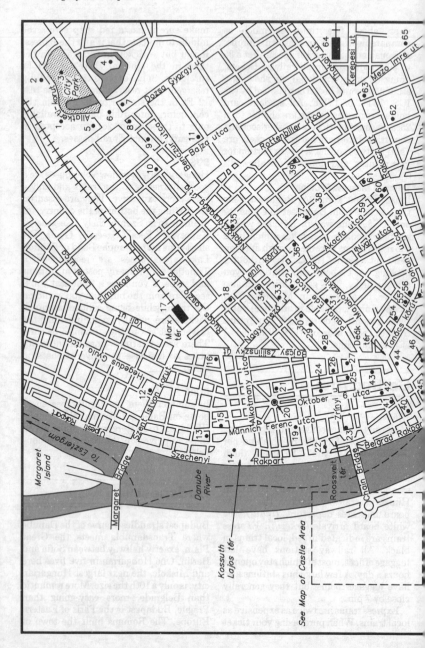

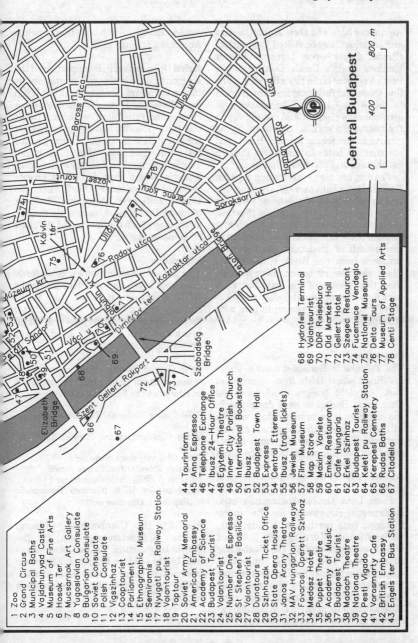

Central Budapest

0   400   800 m

1 Zoo
2 Grand Circus
3 Municipal Baths
4 Vajdahunyad Castle
5 Museum of Fine Arts
6 Hosok Ter
7 Mucsarnok Art Gallery
8 Yugoslavian Consulate
9 Bulgarian Consulate
10 Soviet Consulate
11 Polish Consulate
12 Vigszinhaz
13 Cooptourist
14 Parliament
15 Ethnographic Museum
16 Semiramis
17 Nyugati pu Railway Station
18 Volantourist
19 Toptour
20 Soviet Army Memorial
21 American Embassy
22 Academy of Science
23 Budapest Tourist
24 Volantourist
25 Number One Espresso
26 St Stephen's Basilica
27 Volantourist
28 Dunatours
29 Szinhazak Ticket Office
30 State Opera House
31 Janos Arany Theatre
32 MAV Hungarian Railways
33 Fovarosi Operett Szinhaz
34 Medosz Hotel
35 Puppet Theatre
36 Academy of Music
37 Budapest Tourist
38 Madach Theatre
39 National Theatre
40 Pesti Vigado
41 Vorosmarty Cafe
42 British Embassy
43 Engels ter Bus Station
44 Tourinform
45 Anna Espresso
46 Telephone Exchange
47 Ibusz 24-Hour Office
48 Egytemi Theatre
49 Inner City Parish Church
50 International Bookstore
51 Ibusz
52 Budapest Town Hall
53 Express
54 Central Etterem
55 Ibusz (train tickets)
56 Jewish Museum
57 Film Museum
58 Map Store
59 Maxim Variete
60 Emke Restaurant
61 Cafe Hungaria
62 Erkel Szinhaz
63 Budapest Tourist
64 Keleti pu Railway Station
65 Kerepesi Cemetery
66 Rudas Baths
67 Citadella
68 Hydrofoil Terminal
69 Volantourist
70 DDR Reiseburo
71 Old Market Hall
72 Gellert Hotel
73 Szegec Restaurant
74 Fucemuce Vendeglo
75 National Museum
76 Delta Tours
77 Museum of Applied Arts
78 Centi Stage

Aquincum here and their amphitheatres and aqueduct may be visited just north of Obuda. Layer upon layer of history blankets Buda's Castle District, while Pest's Vaci utca is the city's Bond St for its fine shops and fashionable clientele. Add to this a big City Park brimming with attractions, a chairlift and cog railway in the nearby Buda Hills, riverboats plying upriver to the scenic Danube Bend, and hot thermal baths in authentic Turkish bathhouses and you have Budapest.

The city has many fascinating aspects. Eastern Europeans come for the shopping and to get a taste of the west, while we westerners revel in the nightlife, theatres, museums, restaurants and cafes, all at a fraction of the cost back home. It's hard to get enough of Budapest. As the river descends from the Black Forest to the Black Sea few cities are more striking than this 'Queen of the Danube.' Kick back for a week or two, and when you leave there'll be one more person in love with Budapest.

Orientation

The Danube is Budapest's main street dividing historic Buda from commercial Pest. All eight bridges which cross the Danube at Budapest were destroyed in the war and later rebuilt. Most visitors will arrive at one of the three main railway stations, Keleti (east), Nyugati (west) and Deli (south), all on the Metro lines which converge at Deak ter on the northern edge of the downtown shopping area.

From Deak ter Nepkoztarsasag utja, Budapest's Broadway for its many theatres, runs north-east to City Park, while Tanacs, Muzeum and Tolbuhin koruts swing around to the Szabadsag Bridge and Gellert Hill. Important crossroads in the city are Baross ter before Keleti station, Blaha Lujza ter where Rakoczi ut meets Lenin korut, and Moszkva ter just north of Deli station and Castle Hill. Obuda is at the west end of the

Arpad Bridge north of Buda, while Aquincum is north of that.

Arrival Upon arrival in Budapest avoid the staggering lines in the railway stations by taking the Metro direct to Deak ter. If you don't have any Hungarian money take a chance and ride 'black' without a ticket this time. You can leave your luggage at the bus station on Deak ter (you pay the fee later when you collect the bags). Tourist information is nearby at Suto utca 2 and although they don't rent private rooms or change money they'll direct you to nearby offices which do both. The Ibusz office at Petofi ter 3, only a short walk away, offers both services round the clock (they never close).

Information

Your best information source is Tourinform, Suto utca 2 (the narrow street beside the NDK Centrum at Deak ter Metro station), open daily 8 am to 8 pm. Ibusz, Felszabadulas ter 5, supplies free travel brochures and is very good about answering questions.

Other Tourist Offices Information on the other Eastern European countries is available at the following offices:

Balkantourist (Bulgaria), Nepkoztarsasag utja 14/16
Cedok (Czechoslovakia), Kossuth Lajos ter 18
Orbis (Poland), Vorosmarty ter 6
Yugoslav Travel Office, Parizsi utca 9
Intourist (USSR), Felszabadulas ter 1
Reiseburo der DDR (German Democratic Republic), Dimitrov ter 2/3

Also try the Czechoslovak Cultural Centre, Nepkoztarsasag utja 21, the Polish Information Centre, Nagy-mezo utca 15, the German Democratic Republic Information Centre, Deak ter 3, and the Soviet House of Culture, Semmelweis utca 1-3.

Post & Telephone The main post office with poste restante is at Petofi Sandor utca 13 near Deak ter. The best place in Eastern Europe to make international telephone calls is upstairs at Petofi Sandor utca 17 (open weekdays 7 am to 9 pm, Saturday 7 am to 8 pm, Sunday 7 am to 1 pm). Ask the clerks on duty for the area code, then use the coin telephones against the wall. Calls within Europe go through immediately and are fairly cheap. For North America and Australia have plenty of coins ready.

Bookstores The International Bookstore, Vaci utca 32, has travel guides and maps, plus Hungarian and foreign art books. In the arcade at Petofi Sandor utca 2 is a bookstore which stocks maps of cities all across Europe. The newsstand at Petofi Sandor utca 17 has lots of reading material in English. The NDK Centrum at the entrance to the Metro on Deak ter contains an excellent German bookstore with East German maps and travel guides. There's a self-service map store at Nyar utca 1 (Metro – Blaha Lujza ter).

Western Embassies The British Embassy (which also serves Australians and New Zealanders, tel 182-888) is very conveniently located at Harmincad utca 6 just off Vorosmarty ter. The American Embassy (tel 119-629 or 124-224) is a few blocks north at Szabadsag ter 12. The Canadian Embassy (tel 365-728 or 365-738), Budakeszi ut 30 (bus No 22 from Moszkva ter Metro station), is below the Buda Hills. The West German Consulate (weekdays 9 am to 12 noon, tel 224-204 or 225-277) is at Nogradi utca 8 in the Buda Hills (bus No 21 from Moszkva ter Metro station to Orban ter, then ask).

Eastern European Consulates Budapest is a good place to pick up visas for other Eastern European countries. The consulates are in two clusters, one along Nepkoztarsasag utja, the other near Nepstadion ut south-east of City Park.

Included in the first group are the Yugoslavian Consulate on Hosok ter opposite the Mucsarnok Art Gallery (open Monday to Friday 10 to 11.30 am, visas 260 Ft per entry), and the Bulgarian Consulate, Nepkoztarsasag utja 115 (open Monday, Tuesday, Thursday, Friday 9 am to 1 pm). You must wait a week to get a Bulgarian visa (US$14).

The Soviet Consulate, Nepkoztarsasag utja 104 (open Monday, Wednesday, Friday 10 am to 1 pm), also needs a week or more to issue visas (US$10). You must have confirmed transportation reservations right through the USSR plus accommodation vouchers for each night to be spent in a Soviet city. The Polish Consulate, Bajza utca 15 (open Monday, Tuesday, Thursday, Friday 10 am to 2 pm) and the Chinese Embassy, Benczur utca 17 corner of Bajza utca (hours unknown), are nearby.

Included in the second group are the Romanian Consulate, Thokoly ut 72 (Monday, Wednesday, Friday 9 am to 12 noon) and the Czechoslovakian Consulate, Nepstadion ut 22 (weekdays 8.30 am to 1 pm, visas US$6). Beware of arriving here to find over a hundred Turks or Arabs off trans-European buses ahead of you in line for Czech transit visas to West Germany. It's also extremely crowded on Mondays with everyone who has been waiting all weekend to apply for a visa.

For East German tourist visas consult the DDR Reiseburo, Dimitrov ter 2/3. The GDR Consulate, Nepstadion ut 101 (Monday, Wednesday and Friday 9 am to 12 noon), will only give you a tourist visa if you already have a voucher from them. East German transit visas are obtained at the border, not in advance. The Mongolian Embassy is inconveniently located at Istenhegyi ut 59-61 in the Buda Hills (bus No 21 from Moszkva ter Metro station). At last report they opened Monday from 1 to 3 pm, Wednesday and Friday from 9 am to 11 am and 1 to 3 pm.

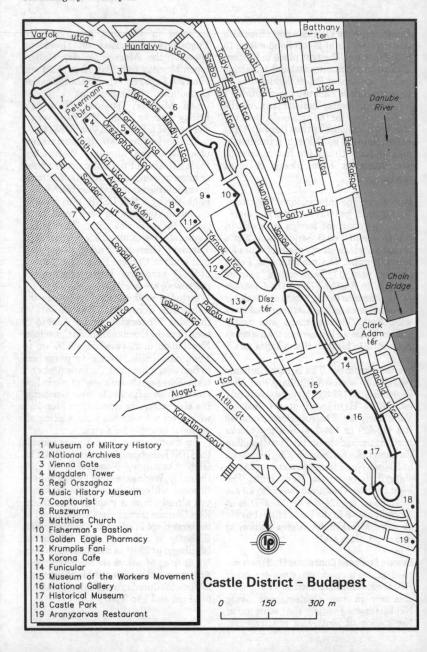

Castle District – Budapest

0   150   300 m

1 Museum of Military History
2 National Archives
3 Vienna Gate
4 Magdalen Tower
5 Regi Orszaghaz
6 Music History Museum
7 Cooptourist
8 Ruszwurm
9 Matthias Church
10 Fisherman's Bastion
11 Golden Eagle Pharmacy
12 Krumplis Fani
13 Korona Cafe
14 Funicular
15 Museum of the Workers Movement
16 National Gallery
17 Historical Museum
18 Castle Park
19 Aranyzarvas Restaurant

Things to See
Buda Most of Budapest's medieval
vestiges are in Varhegy, the Castle
District of Buda. The easiest way to get
there is to take the Metro to Moszkva ter,
cross the bridge above the square, and
continue straight up Varfok utca to
Varhegy's **Vienna Gate**. Bus No 16 follows
this same route from the bridge. Through
the gate, keep sharp left on Petermann
biro utca past the National Archives to
Kapisztran ter. The **Magdalen Tower** is all
that's left of a Gothic church destroyed in
the last war. The yellow neo-Classical
building facing the square is the **Museum
of Military History**, which you enter from
the ramparts side.

Walk south-east along Toth Arpad
setany, the ramparts promenade, enjoying
the views of the Buda Hills. The long
black and white building below you is
Budapest's Deli Railway Station. Halfway
along the ramparts you'll catch a glimpse
of the neo-Gothic tower of **Matthias Church**
up Szentharomsag utca. The church,
once the royal coronation church (rebuilt
1896), has a colourful tile roof outside,
colourful murals inside and a museum
which you enter through the crypt. Ask
about organ concerts in the church.
Behind Matthias Church is an equestrian
statue of St Stephen (977-1038), Hungary's
first king. Alongside the statue is the
Fisherman's Bastion, a late 19th century
structure which offers great views of
Parliament and the Danube.

From the plague column (1713) in front
of Matthias Church Tarnok utca runs
south-east to the gate of the **Palace of Buda
Castle**. The palace enjoyed its greatest
splendour under King Matthias in the
second half of the 15th century. Since
then it has been destroyed and rebuilt
three times, the last after WW II. Today
the palace contains three important
museums. The **National Gallery** has a huge
collection of Hungarian works of art from
Gothic to contemporary. The **Historical
Museum** shelters objects discovered
during the recent reconstruction of the

palace, plus a good overall display on
Budapest through the ages. The **Museum
of the Workers Movement** offers photographic insights into the socialist side of
Hungarian political history.

Varhegy rewards the wanderer and a
leisurely stroll up and down its main
streets, Tancsics Mihaly utca, Fortuna
utca, Orszaghaz utca and Uri utca, will be
punctuated with all sorts of discoveries.
Notice the little Gothic seats in the
gateways to the houses and the old
fashioned streetlights which give the area
an air of romance in the evening.

When you've had enough return to the
Fisherman's Bastion and make your way
down the steps toward the river. Turn
right along the river to the **Chain Bridge**
(1849), the first to be built across the
Hungarian section of the Danube. At the
Buda end of the bridge is a vehicular
tunnel under Castle Hill, a funicular
railway back up to the palace and the Zero
Kilometre Marker for all highway distances
in Hungary.

From the Chain Bridge take any tram
headed south along the right bank of the
Danube. Get off at Moricz Zsigmond
korter, the second stop beyond the Gellert
Hotel. Walk back a little and board bus No
27 at Villanyi ut 5. This bus will take you
right up to the **Citadella**. You can also walk
up to the Citadella from beside the Gellert
Hotel. This commanding fortress was
built by the Austrians in 1854 to control
the rebellious Hungarians. The Statue of
Liberty at the south end of the Citadella
recalls the Soviet soldiers who died to
liberate Hungary in 1945. The bronze
soldier statue was pulled down during the
1956 uprising but replaced a year later.
Now it's guarded day and night. You'll get
your most memorable views of Budapest
and the Danube from this hill. Walk back
down to the river through the park.

Pest Industrialisation allowed Budapest
to develop rapidly during the late 19th
century and one of the nicest places to get
a feeling for this period is **City Park**, north-

east of the centre. Take the Metro to Szechenyi Furdo. This line, the oldest underground railway on the continent, opened in 1896. You'll come out of the station right in the middle of the park beside the **Municipal Baths** (1913), behind which are an **amusement park**, the **Grand Circus** and the **zoo** (closed Wednesday).

Cross the busy boulevard to the south-east and you'll come to **Vajdahunyad Castle** (1896), a fascinating hodge-podge of replicas of actual buildings, many in what is now Romania. The **Agricultural Museum** is housed in the castle (snackbar inside). Upstairs in the Petofi Centre, also in the park, is the **Museum of Flight & Space Travel** (closed in winter). The prize exhibit is a Junkers F-13, the world's first metal passenger plane. (The world's first hijacking involved a Junkers F-13. In 1921 the Hungarian crown prince hired an excursion plane in Switzerland and ordered it to be flown to Hungary in an abortive putsch!) Budapest's **Transportation Museum** is near the Flight Museum.

City Park's dominant feature is **Hosok ter** with a great monument erected for the millennium of the Magyar conquest of Hungary in 896. The Tomb of the Unknown Soldier is also here. On the south-east side of the square is the **Mucsarnok Art Gallery**, the most prestigious in the city, where important contemporary art shows are held. On the other side of the square is the **Museum of Fine Arts** (1895), one of the richest of its kind in Europe. Here you'll see Hungary's major collection of foreign art with prints and ancient sculpture on the ground floor, European paintings on the 1st floor, and European sculpture on the 2nd floor. It's best to begin with the Spanish paintings to the left at the top of the stairs, then see the 2nd floor. These tend to close temporarily as the guards go to lunch, etc, and you can always come back later.

From Hosok ter stately Nepkoztarsasag utja runs straight into the heart of Pest. To save yourself a long walk take the Metro to Opera. The **State Opera House** was built in the Italian neo-Renaissance style in 1884. Many of the other great buildings along this section of Nepkoztarsasag utja also date from this time. Proceed south-west on this fashionable avenue and round the corner onto Bajcsy Zsilinszky ut. The 96-metre-high neo-Renaissance dome of **St Stephen's Basilica** (1905) will loom before you. Go inside. The right hand of King Saint Stephen, founder of the Hungarian state, is kept in the chapel at the rear of the church behind the altar.

Cross the square in front of the basilica and keep straight a block on Zrinyi utca, then right on Oktober 6 utca. At Oktober 6 utca 15 you can get a great ice-cream cone. Proceed straight ahead onto Szabadsag ter with the National Bank (1905) to the right and the Television Company (also 1905) to the left. At the end of the square in front of the American Embassy is the **Soviet Army Memorial** (1945).

As you look up Vecsey utca from the memorial you'll see the great neo-Gothic silhouette of **Parliament** (1904) on Kossuth Lajos ter. The National Assembly meets here and the Council of Ministers is also housed in the building. The exterior is impressive but individual tourists are not allowed inside. The **Ethnographic Museum** (1896) also faces Kossuth Lajos ter.

There's a Metro station on the south side of Kossuth Lajos ter. For a good long view of Parliament take the Metro one stop to Batthyany ter, where you'll also find a large public market hall and some old churches. Note the very deep tunnel as the line dives under the Danube at this point.

Obuda/Aquincum In 1872 three towns – Buda, Pest and Obuda – united to form Budapest. Obuda is most easily reached by taking the HEV suburban railway from Batthyany ter Metro station to Arpad hid mh. Follow Korvin Otto ter from Arpad hid into Fo ter, the beautifully restored centre of old Obuda. **Obuda Town Hall** is at Fo ter 3, but the most interesting building is the Baroque **Zichy Mansion** (1748), Fo ter 1. Orchestral concerts are often held in the mansion courtyard in summer. At the back of the courtyard is an art gallery and the unique **Kassak Museum**, a tiny three-room exhibition housing some real gems of early 20th century avant-garde art.

Return to the HEV and take a train a few stops further north to Aquincum vm. Aquincum was the key military garrison of the Roman province of Pannonia. A **Roman aqueduct** passed this way from a spring in the nearby park and remains have been preserved in the median of the modern highway alongside the HEV railway line. The 2nd century civilian **amphitheatre** is right beside the station. A few hundred metres away is a large excavated area and the **Aquincum Museum** (open May to October, closed Monday). Don't miss the ancient musical organ with bronze pipes.

From Aquincum you have a choice of returning to Budapest or taking the HEV on to Szentendre (see below). As far as Aquincum regular yellow Metro tickets can be used on the HEV, but to go to Szentendre you must buy a special ticket which is checked by a conductor.

Other Museums Three museums on the south side of Pest are worthy of special attention. The twin-towered synagogue (1859) on Dohany utca, the largest functioning synagogue in Europe, contains the **Jewish Museum** (open weekdays from mid-April to mid-October). The former Jewish Ghetto extends back behind this synagogue.

The **National Museum**, Muzeum korut 14-16 (Metro - Kalvin ter), houses Hungary's main collection of historical relics in a large neo-Classical building (1847). Begin with the section on the ground floor behind the cloakroom which covers the period up to the Magyar conquest. Upstairs is a continuation of Hungarian history and, in a place of honour before the entrance, the coronation regalia. In the opposite wing is a large

natural history exhibit with dioramas to show the fauna in natural settings.

Only four blocks away is the **Museum of Applied Arts**, Ulloi ut 35-37 (Metro - Ferenc krt). The Art Nouveau exterior suggests what is to be seen inside.

A final museum to conclude your tour of Budapest would be the **Kiscelli Museum** on a hill above Obuda (bus No 60 from Batthyany ter Metro station). Housed in the former monastery of the Trinitarian order (1760), the fine collection of drawings and paintings of Budapest a century or more ago make the trip worthwhile (Tuesday to Sunday 10 am to 4 pm).

Almost all Budapest museums are closed on Monday and free on Saturday.

The Buda Hills If you have children with you the Buda Hills are the place to take them. The variety of transportation opportunities makes visiting fun. Begin with a ride on the **cog railway**, which has wound up through pleasant wooded suburbs into the Buda Hills since the 1870s. The lower terminus of the cog railway is on Szilagyi Erzsebet fasor opposite Hotel Budapest and walking distance from Moszkva ter Metro station. The fare is only one blue bus ticket (daily, year round).

Near the upper terminus of the cog railway is Szechenyi-hegy Station of the **Pioneer Railway**, a 12-km scenic route (no service on Monday). Excepting the engineer, this line is completely staffed by children to interest them in transportation careers. Catch a train to Janos-hegy Station and walk up through the forest to the lookout tower on Janos-hegy (529 metres) with its 360° view. The **Janos-hegy Chairlift** (daily year round from 10 am to 4 pm, 15 Ft) will take you down to Zugligeti ut where you can catch bus No 158 back to Moszkva ter Metro station.

If instead of getting out at Janos-hegy you had stayed on the Pioneer Railway to Huvosvolgy Station, the northern terminus, you could have caught tram No 56 back to Moszkva ter.

Margaret Island When your head begins to spin from all the sights take a walk from one end to the other of Margaret Island. Bus No 26 from beside Nyugati Railway Station covers the island or get there on trams No 4 or 6, which stop halfway across the unusual three-way bridge leading to Margaret. As you stroll among the trees and statues you'll encounter the ruins of two medieval monasteries, a small zoo, a rose garden, an open air theatre, swimming pools, cafes and a pseudo Japanese garden (beside Hotel Thermal). The island is such a relaxing, restful place you'll seem ages away from the busy city.

Something Different Budapest's most offbeat sight is **Kerepesi Cemetery** on Mezo Imre ut near Keleti Railway Station. Today the cemetery is used mainly for political purposes but a century ago it was the final resting place of Hungary's most wealthy and prominent. The evocative sculptured monuments scattered among the trees give Kerepesi a unique, almost classical air which will enchant the wanderer. The most notable personages built themselves huge mausoleums which go well with recent memorials to the socialist victims of the revolutions of 1919 and 1956. Half the streets in Hungary are named after people buried here.

Places to Stay

Private Rooms The best value for accommodation in Budapest is private rooms assigned by local travel agencies. They generally cost 200 Ft single, 300 Ft double plus US$1 to US$2 tax, with a 10% supplement if you stay less than four nights. To get a single or a room in the centre of town you may have to try several offices. There are lots of rooms available and even in July and August you'll be able to find something.

Below we list a variety of agencies beginning with those closest to the transportation terminals. Most are open only during normal business hours. If you arrive late or on a weekend try the nonstop Ibusz accommodation centre at Petofi ter 3 (Metro – Deak ter) which never closes.

Near Keleti Station The Ibusz office in Keleti Railway Station has private rooms but in summer they go quickly. Budapest Tourist at Baross ter 3, just beyond the overpass on the opposite side of the square from Keleti station, also has private rooms (and changes money). The lines are much shorter here. Another branch of Budapest Tourist, a 10-minute walk away at Lenin korut 41, is open from 8 am to 8 pm Monday to Saturday. Ibusz, Lenin korut 55, also has private rooms.

Near Nyugati Station Ibusz at Nyugati Railway Station does not arrange private rooms. Instead try Cooptourist in the underground concourse at the entrance to the Metro below Nyugati station. They have no singles. Volantourist, Lenin korut 96 quite near Nyugati, is open till 8 pm weekdays, 4 pm Saturday. In the opposite direction is Cooptourist, Kossuth Lajos ter 13 near Parliament.

Near Engels ter Bus Station Volantourist, Bajcsy-Zsilinszky ut 16 (closed Saturday), is very near the station. Also nearby are Dunatours and Cooptourist, side by side at Bajcsy-Zsilinszky ut 17 behind St Stephen's Basilica. Another Volantourist office with private rooms is at Oktober 6 utca 13. Toptour, Munnich Ferenc utca 26, is a little further along in the same direction. One of the largest offices in the city offering private rooms is Budapest Tourist, Roosevelt ter 5 (open Saturday and Sunday mornings and until 7 pm weekdays).

Near Deli Station At Deli Railway Station private rooms are arranged by Ibusz at the entrance to the Metro or Budapest Tourist in the mall in front of the station. Also try

Cooptourist, Attila ut 107, directly across the park in front of Deli station.

Near the Hydrofoil Terminal Volantourist, Belgrad rakpart 6, is near the landing of the boats from Esztergom and Vienna. There are two Volantourist offices here, so note the address carefully. Also in this vicinity are Delta Tours, Kalvin ter 7, and Ibusz, Felszabadulas ter 5.

Youth Hostels Budapest doesn't have a regular year round dormitory-style youth hostel. The *Hotel Ifjusag* (tel 353-331) listed in the IYHF handbook is instantly booked solid weeks ahead if you ask for the YHA rate (US$15). In summer from 2 July to 31 August nine student dormitories (200 Ft) are thrown open to YHA members. To get into one you should go to the main Express office at Semmelweis utca 4 (Metro – Astoria), which is open business hours. Ask here about the *Hotel Express* (tel 753-082), Beethoven utca 7/9 (800 Ft double). There's also an Express office at Keleti Railway Station, but chances are they'll be too busy changing money for tourists to bother about youth hostels. Try asking anyway if there's no line.

Camping Budapest's largest campground, with a capacity for 1300 guests, is *Romaifurdo* in a large park north of the city. Take the HEV suburban railway from Batthyany ter Metro station to Romaifurdo vm station, which is within sight of the campground. The facility is open year round so it's up to you to decide if it's warm enough for camping. There's a large swimming pool opposite the campground with lots of green grass on which to stretch out and a disco nearby. In summer (May to September) there's a ferry service on the Danube from Romai part (embankment) near the campground to Margaret Island.

A somewhat better campground up in the Buda Hills is *Harshegyi Camping* (open May to mid-October). Take bus No 22 from Moszkva ter Metro station and watch for the signs on the right. Both campgrounds are operated by Budapest Tourist, Roosevelt ter 5, so that would be the place to ask about on-site bungalows, etc. There's also Zugligeti Camping at the bottom station of the Buda Hills chairlift (bus No 158 from Moszkva ter Metro station).

Hotels A hotel room will cost considerably more than a private room but they don't mind if you stay only one night. The only hotel in the city centre which even approaches being cheap is the *Medosz Hotel* (tel 531-700), Jokai ter 9 (1500 Ft double including breakfast). There's no sign outside so look for the modern building marked 'haza' beside the 'Babszinhaz' (Metro – November 7 ter).

If you'd like to stay in a castle above the Danube try for a room at the *Citadella Hotel* (tel 665-794) in the Citadella itself. The 11 rooms go for only 600 Ft double but they're often full. There's also a cheap dormitory *(turistaszallas)* at the Citadella, usually booked by youth groups.

North of the city near Romaifurdo is the *Sporthotel Lido* (tel 886-865), Nanasi ut 67, with rooms year round for 320 Ft per person. The bungalows beside the hotel are cheaper but only available in summer.

There are two large budget hotels on the Metro line east of Keleti station. The *Hotel Saturnus* (tel 634-353), Pillango utca 10 (Metro – Pillango utca) is 420 Ft for a double without bath. The *Epitok Hotel* (tel 840-677), Nagy Lajos kiraly utja 15 (Metro – Ors Vezer ter) is 420 Ft single, 720 Ft double with breakfast.

Where to stay if the price isn't important? Perhaps the five-star *Hotel Thermal* (tel 321-100) on Margaret Island (4120 Ft single, 5870 Ft double). It's quiet and you have all the facilities of a luxury spa right there on the premises. The recently renovated *Ramada Grand Hotel* beside Hotel Thermal is similarly priced.

1 Romaifurdo Campground
2 Lido Sporthotel
3 Civilian Amphitheatre
4 Aquincum Museum
5 Huvosvolgy Station
6 Janos-hegy Station
7 Janos-hegy
8 Harshegy Camping
9 Chairlift
10 Canadian Embassy
11 Palvolgyi Cave
12 Kiscelli Museum
13 Fo ter, Obuda
14 Szemlohegyi Cave
15 Military Amphitheatre
16 Bus Stop for Caves
17 Hotel Thermal
18 Casino
19 Lucas Baths
20 Szechenyi-hegy Station
21 Cog Railway Upper Terminus
22 West German Consulate
23 Cog Railway Lower Terminus
24 Kiraly Baths
25 Parliament
26 Nyugati pu Railway Station
27 Deli pu Railway Station
28 Matthias Church
29 Budapest Castle
30 Racz Baths
31 Citadella
32 Petofi Centre
33 Transportation Museum
34 GDR Consulate
35 Romanian Consulate
36 Czechoslovakian Consulate
37 Keleti pu Railway Station
38 Trotting Track
39 People's Stadium
40 Budapest Sports Hall
41 Nepstadion Bus Station
42 Hotel Saturnus
43 Epitok Hotel
44 Hungarexpo
45 Planetarium
46 Buda Park Theatre

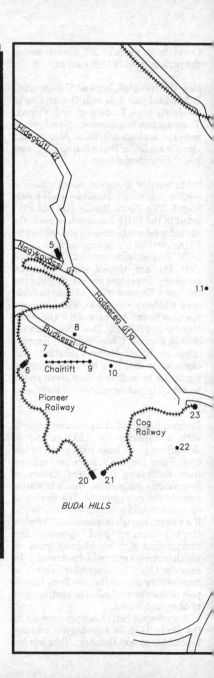

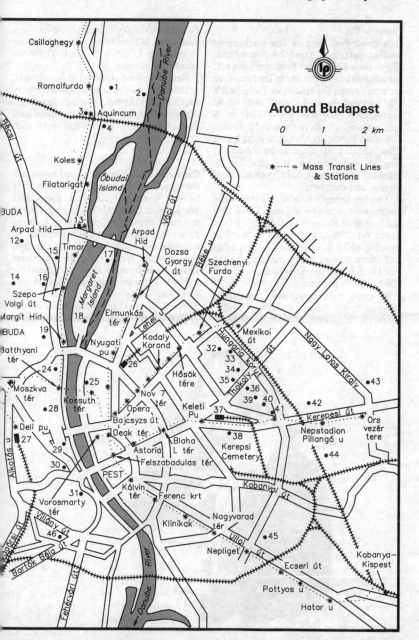

Around Budapest

0   1   2 km

* ····· = Mass Transit Lines & Stations

Csillaghegy

Romaifurdo   • 1

    • 2   Danube River

    3 • Aquincum
    • 4

Koles

Filatorigat   Óbudai Island

BUDA
Arpad Hid   13
12 •   Vaci út

15   Timar   17   Arpad Hid

    Dozsa Gyorgy út   Béke u   Szechenyi Furdo

14   16
Szepo   Volgi út
Margit Hid
BUDA   18   Elmunkás tér   Lehel u   Mexikoi út

    19   Nyugati pu   Kodaly Korond   Hungaria Korut
Batthyani tér
    26   32
    24 •   Hősök tére   33
Moszkva tér   • 25   34   Thakaly út
    Nov 7 tér   35   36   • 43
    28 •   Kossuth tér   Opera   Keleti   39   40
Deli pu   Bajcsyzs út   Pu   41   • 42
    27   Deak tér   37   Kerepesi út
    29   Blaha   Ors vezér tere
    30   Astoria   L tér   • 38   Nepstadion
    Felszabadulas tér   Kerepsi   Pillangó u
    PEST   Cemetery   • 44
    31 •   Kálvin tér   Ferenc krt   Kobanyoi út
Vorosmarty tér
    46 •   Villany út   Klinikak   Nagyvarad tér   Kobanya-Kispest
    Nepliget   • 45   Ullol út
    Ecseri út
    Bartok Bela út   Fehervari út   Danube River   Pottyos u
    Hatar u

Places to Eat

Downtown Pest Despite the overbearing waiters and prices, *Apostolok Restaurant*, Kigyo utca 4-6 just off Felszabadulas ter, is included in every guide to Budapest, so we won't break the tradition. Perhaps it's the central location and old world atmosphere that draw the tourists in. A less pretentious choice would be *Pepita Oroszlan Vendeglo*, Vaci utca 40 at Iranyi utca, which posts their menu outside in English and German. It's good for its pleasant open atmosphere, pork and beef dishes, and cold beer.

Another touristy selection is the *Emke Restaurant*, upstairs at Lenin korut 2 on the corner of Rakoczi ut (Metro – Blaha Lujza ter). Its saving grace is the folk dancing which is presented most evenings at 7.30 pm to diners who pay only for the meal and drinks (no cover charge). Figure 250 to 300 Ft per person.

A good neighbourhood restaurant offering gypsy music, a German menu, large servings and moderate prices is *Fucemuce Vendeglo*, Kofarago utca 5 on a backstreet behind the National Museum (open daily 11 am to 11 pm). There are lunchtime specials.

Real Arab food is served at *Semiramis*, Alkotmany utca 20 near Nyugati Railway Station (additional seating upstairs). *Number One Espresso*, Guszev utca 9 off Engels ter, is a good local pub with draught beer (no food).

Cafeterias The cheapest places to eat are the big self-service cafeterias. The tourists haven't managed to spoil these yet! Watch what the locals are having. One of the most convenient of these is *Central Etterem*, Tanacs korut 7 near Deak ter. In summer they move some tables out onto the sidewalk. Watch the price of the beer which could be more than your meal!

Near Nyugati Railway Station it's *Non-Stop Etterem*, Marx ter 5. The *Emke Bufe* on Akacfa utca on the corner of Rakoczi ut (Metro – Blaha Lujza ter) is

Franz Liszt, pianist

a cheap stand-up self-service offering barbecued chicken and beer.

Onkiszolgalo Etterem, Alkotas utca 7/B beside Deli Railway Station, is a cheap cafeteria with big egg omelettes in the morning and grilled chicken all day.

Cafes Like Vienna, Budapest is famous for its cafes and the most famous of the famous is the *Vorosmarty Confectionery* on the west side of Vorosmarty ter, long a fashionable meeting place of the city's elite. *Anna Espresso*, nearby at Vaci utca 7, is slightly less formal. Their large green sign beckons.

The *Cafe Hungaria*, Lenin korut 9-11 (Metro - Blaha Lujza ter), has been a Budapest institution since 1895. The elegant, turn-of-the-century decor goes well with the literary world which still meets there. There's a good cafe at Nepkoztarsasag utja 70 opposite the puppet theatre.

Castle District Expensive restaurants popular among tourists abound in the Castle District. One worth mentioning is the *Regi Orszaghaz*, Orszaghaz utca 17, which combines wine with the medieval atmosphere. *Krumplis Fani*, Disz ter 8, is one of the few places to get an inexpensive meal up here.

The perfect place for coffee and cakes is the crowded *Ruszwurm Cafe*, Szentharomsag utca 7 near Matthias Church (closed Wednesday). The Castle District's most illustrious cafe is *Korona*, Disz ter 16 opposite the palace gate. Try the pastries and Viennese coffee. Literary evenings (in Hungarian) are held here certain weekdays at 7 pm (tickets 60 Ft). There's a good little wine cellar at Tancsics utca 10 opposite the Music History Museum.

Below Castle Hill The *Aranyszarvas Restaurant*, Szarvas ter below Castle Hill, offers game food such as wild pig, pheasant and venison daily until midnight (expensive yet unpretentious). The *Szeged Restaurant*, Bartok Bela ut 3 beside the Gellert Hotel, specialises in fish dishes.

A Special Tip There are a number of good restaurants around Fo ter, Obuda (HEV suburban railway from Batthyany ter Metro to Arpad Hid mh). The *Postakocsi Restaurant*, Fo ter 2, is one. Although tourist-oriented they don't get nearly as many foreigners as the places on Castle Hill, which makes them a lot more appealing. If you're looking to impress someone, Obuda won't let you down. Menus are posted outside.

Markets The old Pest market hall (closed Sunday) is on Dimitrov ter (Metro - Kalvin ter). There's a large supermarket (open Monday, Tuesday, Thursday and Friday 6 am to 8 pm, Wednesday and Saturday 7 am to 4.30 pm, Sunday 7 am to 1 pm) in the old market hall on the south side of Batthyany ter near the Metro station. Stock up.

Entertainment

Music At least one visit should be paid to the *State Opera House* (1884), Nepkoztarsasag utja 22 (Metro - Opera), to see the frescoes and incredibly rich gilded decoration in the Italian Renaissance style. The box office is on the left side of the building (closed Monday). Budapest has a second opera house, the *Erkel Szinhaz* at Koztarsasag ter 30 near Keleti station. Tickets are sold just inside the main doors.

Operettas are presented at the *Fovarosi Operett Szinhaz*, Nagy-mezo utca 17 a block from the State Opera House. Try for tickets inside although they're often sold out. The *National Theatre* on Hevesi Sandor ter four blocks from Keleti also offers musical programmes, including rock operas such as *Stephen, the King*. The musical *Cats* has been at the *Madach Theatre*, Lenin korut 31/33, for years.

Budapest's main concert hall is the *Pesti Vigado*, Vigado ter 2 (Metro - Vorosmarty ter). Other concerts are held at the *Academy of Music*, Majakovszki-jutca 64 at Liszt Ferenc ter (Metro – November 7 ter).

In addition to the above, musicals are put on at the *Janos Arany Theatre*, Paulay Ede utca 35 (Metro – Opera), and jazz concerts often happen at the *Egytemi Theatre*, Marcius 15 ter (Metro – Felszabadulas ter).

Summertime In July and August most of the theatres are closed for holidays. The cabarets remain open and folk dancing can be seen at several locations. From mid-April to mid-October the Folklor Centrum offers traditional Hungarian dancing to gypsy band music at the *Arany Janos Theatre*, Paulay Ede utca 35 (Metro – Opera). Similar programmes are presented by the Art Union at Orszaghaz utca 28 in the Castle District on Thursday, Friday and Saturday from June to mid-September. There's also an evening variety show at the *Casino Etterem*, an open-air restaurant on Margaret Island. Tourinform on Suto utca will have up-to-date information on programmes and times.

Visual Theatre Pantomime programmes occur several nights a week at 7.30 pm at the *Centi Szinpad*, Ulloi ut 45 (Metro – Ferenc korut). It's something of an underground theatre. Yes, it's on the 3rd floor of that old apartment building (no signs). Take the lift up. If you arrive early you should be able to get a ticket at the door.

The *Puppet Theatre*, Nepkoztarsasag utja 69 (Metro – Vorosmarty utca), presents afternoon shows designed for children, evening programmes for adults. There's a special adult performance on Monday evenings. Showtime is generally 3 pm weekdays, 11 am and 4 pm Saturday and Sunday. They'll usually make room for foreign tourists.

Spectacles The *Grand Circus*, Allatkerti korut 7 (Metro – Szechenyi Furdo),

appears Wednesday to Sunday with afternoon performances at 3.30 pm Thursday to Sunday, evening performances at 7.30 pm Wednesday to Saturday. There are also morning shows Saturday and Sunday. Although the matinees are occasionally booked out by school groups, there's almost always space in the evening. Advance tickets are sold at the circus itself. If they don't have good seats for the performance you wish to attend, ask at the circus administrative office, Nepkoztarsasag utja 61.

Other Events Budapest's *Planetarium* (Metro – Nepliget) features exciting laser light shows to the accompaniment of rock music. There are usually shows Thursday to Monday at 6 and 7.30 pm. Tickets (100 Ft) may be purchased at the door or from any Budapest ticket agency.

The *Film Museum*, Tanacs korut 3 (Metro – Astoria), offers classic films in the original language with as many as seven showings daily. It's sometimes hard to figure out what's on as the female ticket sellers speak only Hungarian and are not overly cooperative, so be persistent.

Saturday afternoon there are races at the *trotting track*, Kerepesi ut 9 near Keleti station (bus No 95).

Ticket Agencies The busiest theatrical ticket agency is the Szinhazak Jegyirodaja, Nepkoztarsasag utja 18 (Metro – Opera). They have tickets to numerous theatres and events, although the best are gone a couple of days in advance.

For concert tickets try Orszagos Filharmonia, Vorosmarty ter 1.

As you pursue your quest for tickets you're sometimes told everything is sold out. You often get better seats by going directly to the theatre box office than you would by dealing with a ticket agency. Theatre tickets cost anywhere from 50 to 200 Ft.

Teens & Twenties The youth scene revolves around the *Petofi Centre* in City Park

(Metro – Szechenyi furdo) where rock concerts are held several nights a week. There's also a restaurant and cinema in the complex. Ask at the information counter about English language clubs. This is a good place to meet local young people.

Nightlife Budapest has an active nightlife with numerous discos and cabarets. Perhaps the swankiest nightclub is *Maxim Variete* in the Emke Hotel, Akacfa utca 3 (Metro – Blaha Lujza ter). Their chorus line consists of 14 scantily dressed Maxim girls and there are magicians, acrobats, singers and dancers in a Las Vegas style extravaganza. Showtimes are 8 and 11 pm daily except Sunday (reservations recommended weekends and holidays). Admission is 200 Ft and there's an additional 350 Ft minimum consumption. More of the same at the *Moulin Rouge Night Club* beside the Operetta Theatre (Metro – Opera).

Thermal Baths Budapest is a major spa with numerous bathing establishments open to the public. There are 140 thermal springs in Budapest gushing forth over 40 million litres of warm mineral water daily. Begin your bathhouse tour with the Gellert Baths (entry through the side entrance of the eclectic hotel of the same name below Gellert Hill). The thermal pools here maintain a constant 44°C and a large outdoor pool is open in summer.

There are two famous bathing establishments near the Buda end of Elizabeth Bridge. The Rudas Baths beside the river were built by the Turks in 1566 and retain a strong Islamic flavour. Rudas is open daily for men, but women should make for the Rac Baths at the foot of the hill on the opposite side of the bridge approaches. Rac is reserved for women on Monday, Wednesday and Friday; on Tuesday, Thursday and Saturday men are admitted.

Everyone passing this way should seek out the well room (closed Sunday) below the bridge within sight of the Rudas Baths. Here you can indulge in the 'drinking cure' for only a forint. Give the coin to the cashier who will give you a ticket which entitles you to a big mug of hot radioactive water.

The Kiraly Baths, Fo utca 84 (Metro – Batthyany ter), are genuine Turkish baths erected in 1566. Like Rac there are alternate days for males (Monday, Wednesday and Friday) and females (Tuesday, Thursday and Saturday). During the 19th century Budapest's favourite spa was the Lucas Baths, Frankel Leout 25. This large complex remains a good place to go to sample everything from the 'drinking cure' to the big thermal pool.

If you'd rather bathe in ultramodern surroundings there's the *Hotel Thermal* on Margaret Island.

The easiest way to get to the baths is to take the Metro to Batthyany ter, then a streetcar south for Rac, Rudas and Gellert, or walk north to Kiraly and Lucas. For Hotel Thermal take bus No 26 from Nyugati Railway Station. All of the above establishments offer massage and similar services. It's all part of the Budapest experience, so give it a try. Admission is rarely over US$1.

Getting There & Away

Railway Stations Budapest has three main railway stations, all connected by Metro. Of the two on the Pest side of the Danube Keleti Railway Station receives trains from Vienna Westbahnhof, Bratislava (via Komarom), Prague (via Sturovo), Warsaw (via Zilina), Cracow (via Kosice), Moscow, Bucharest (via Arad), Belgrade and Zagreb (via Kaposvar). Services from Prague (via Sturovo) and Bucharest (via Oradea) arrive at Nyugati. There are exceptions to the above, however, so be sure to check carefully which station you'll be using. Trains from western Hungary and Graz, Austria, generally use Deli station on the Buda side of the city.

If you'll be arriving in Budapest on a special summer train that continues on through to another destination (Berlin to Bulgaria, for example) beware of missing the stop as they often don't go in to a main station.

Station Facilities Nyugati Railway Station is an historic iron structure built in 1877 by Eiffel of Paris. When Keleti Station opened in 1884 it was the most modern in central Europe. Keleti has somewhat better facilities than Nyugati, but there can be a long line at the baggage storage area (6 Ft a piece). Coin lockers are only 4 Ft but they're confusing to operate and often full. In a pinch you could ask the woman at the restaurant cloakroom in Keleti station to watch your pack for about 20 Ft. In Nyugati station the left luggage office is on track 10 beside Ibusz, through a poorly marked door with a yellow sign reading *poggyaszmegorzo gepackaufbewarung*.

There are often very long lines to change money at both Express and Ibusz in Keleti station. In Nyugati station the Ibusz office for currency exchange is beside track 10. None of these offices open until 8 am. If the lines to change money are impossibly long in Keleti try the Orszagos Takarekpenztar (National Savings Bank), Rakoczi ut 84 a block from the station (open weekdays 8 am to 1 pm).

There's generally no problem about stretching out a sleeping bag in either station but check your pack in the baggage room first. The police will wake you around 5.30 am.

Train Tickets MAV Hungarian Railways office, Nepkoztarsasag utja 35 (Metro – Opera), is the place to purchase international train tickets or make advance seat reservations for Hungarian express trains. Ibusz, Tanacs korut 3/c, also sells these tickets. Payment in western currency is required. The Ibusz

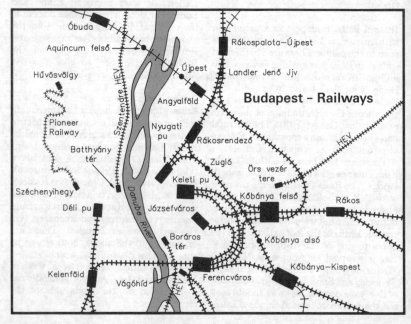

office in Keleti station will sell you a ticket to Arad or Oradea, Romania, for about US$3.

Buses There are two important bus stations in Budapest. For buses to Esztergom (frequent) and most other points west of the Danube try the Engels ter bus station (Metro – Deak ter). Some buses for places east of the Danube depart the Nepstadion bus station (Metro – Nepstadion). There's a left-luggage office at Engels ter bus station, open till 6 pm.

International Buses There are two buses daily between Budapest's Engels ter bus station and the Autobusbahnhof Mitte, Vienna. Tickets (700 Ft one way) are available at the station. There are departures at 7 am and 5 pm from each end daily. In Budapest inquire at the Engels ter bus station; in Vienna at Blaguss Reisen (tel 651681), Wiedner Hauptstrasse 15. If you decide to come to Budapest from Vienna on the spur of the moment take a bus because you can get a Hungarian visa at the border.

Twice a week (on Wednesday and Saturday) there's a bus from the Engels ter bus station to Zakopane, Poland (359 Ft one way), a nine-hour trip. You'll need a Czech transit visa and a Polish visa to take this one.

Vienna Hydrofoils Hydrofoil service on the Danube from Budapest to Vienna operates from 31 March to 24 October on Monday, Wednesday and Friday. From 28 April to 14 September there is daily service and from 30 June to 31 August it's twice daily. Off season departures from Vienna are on Tuesday, Thursday and Saturday. Fares are ATS 550 one way, ATS 900 round trip. The hydrofoil takes five hours to cover the 282 km between the two cities. In Vienna tickets are available from Ibusz (tel 532686), Karntner Strasse 26, or DDSG (tel 266536), Handelskai 265.

Boats to the Danube Bend Mahart riverboats operate on the Danube daily from 1 May to 28 September between Budapest and Esztergom. Some boats go via Szentendre, others via Vac, making it possible to do a round trip on different arms of the Danube. The Szentendre route is the more scenic. All services stop at Visegrad, Nagymaros and Domos. The boats begin at Vigado ter (Metro – Vorosmarty ter) on the left bank. They all make a first stop at Bem Jozsef ter on the right bank near Margit hid HEV station, a 10-minute walk upriver from Batthyany ter Metro station. This five-hour scenic cruise is highly recommended for a running view of Budapest and the river. There's an open deck upstairs where you can sit. The fare is about US$1 for the full one way trip.

Getting Around

Airport Transport There are two terminals several km apart at Budapest Ferihegy Airport, 16 km south-east of the centre. Malev Hungarian Airlines flights use the new Ferihegy 2 terminal, while all other airlines fly out of the older Ferihegy 1 terminal. Airport buses depart the Engels ter bus station every hour from 5 am to 9 pm (ticket from the driver). You can also get to Ferihegy by taking the Metro to Kobanya-Kispest, then bus No 93 (red number) which calls at both terminals. Bus No 93 (black number) calls at Ferihegy 1 only.

Public Transport Budapest has three underground Metro lines, all intersecting at Deak ter. The HEV suburban railway, which runs north from Batthyany ter Metro station, is in effect a fourth Metro line. There's also a very extensive network of streetcar, trolley and bus services.

To use public transport you must buy tickets at a kiosk, newsstand, or Metro entrance. Tickets for Metro, streetcars, trolleys and HEV (as far as the city limits) are yellow and cost 2 Ft each. Bus tickets are blue and 3 Ft each. You validate your ticket once aboard. Every time you change vehicles you must cancel a new ticket. The Metro operates from 4.30 am till just after 11 pm. Certain tram and bus lines operate throughout the night.

A day ticket for public transportation is available, 16 Ft for all trams, trolleys, HEV and Metro, 24 Ft buses as well. You must specify the day you wish to use the pass when purchasing it. If you'll be spending over a week in Budapest consider getting a monthly pass valid on all trams, trolleys, Metro and HEV within the city (valid up to the fifth day of the following month). The price is only 75 Ft, but you must supply one passport size photo. This pass is sold at all Metro stations.

Local Ferries From May to September passenger ferries run every 15 minutes from 7 am to 7 pm between Boraros ter beside Petofi Bridge and Park 9 Majus on Obudai-sziget with seven stops along the way. Buy two 10 Ft tickets at the kiosk for a full round trip and validate each once aboard. The ferry stop closest to the Castle District is Batthyany ter, while Marcius 15 ter is not far from Vorosmarty ter, a convenient place to pick up the boat on the Pest side. Beer and soft drinks (but no food) are sold aboard. The views of Budapest are great.

At 3 and 5.30 pm daily from May to October there's a 1½ hour cruise on the Danube from the yellow ticket office at Vigado ter below the Duna Inter-Continental Hotel (40 Ft). There are also evening cruises from the same office at 8 pm daily. The night lights of the city rising to the castle, Parliament and citadel make this trip far more attractive than the afternoon cruises and the timing doesn't conflict with other sightseeing. Ask too about summertime evening disco and folklore boats.

The Danube Bend

North of Budapest the Danube breaks through the Pilis and Borzsony mountains in a sharp S-bend. Here medieval kings once ruled Hungary from majestic palaces overlooking the river at Esztergom and Visegrad. East of Visegrad the river divides into two branches with Szentendre and Vac facing different arms. Today the historic monuments, easy access, good facilities and forest trails combine to put the area at the top of any visitors' list. This is the perfect place to come on a Danube River cruise.

SZENTENDRE

A trip to Szentendre, 20 km north of Budapest on an arm of the Danube, should not be missed. In the 17th century Serbian merchants fleeing the Turks settled here, bringing with them the flavour of the Balkans. Although most returned home in the 19th century, the Serbian appearance remained. In the

1	Preobrazenska Church
2	Ferry to Szentendre Island
3	Barczy Fogado
4	Belgrade Church
5	Serbian Art Collection
6	Czobel Bela Museum
7	Catholic Parish Church
8	Amos-Anna Museum
9	Dunatours
10	Greek Church
11	Gorog Kancso Vendeglo
12	Kovaks Margit Museum
13	Szentendre Picture Gallery
14	Kmetty Museum
15	Rab-Raby Vendeglo
16	Peter & Paul Church
17	Barcsay Collection
18	Pozarevacka Church
19	Roman Sculpture Garden
20	Post Office
21	HEV Railway & Bus Station

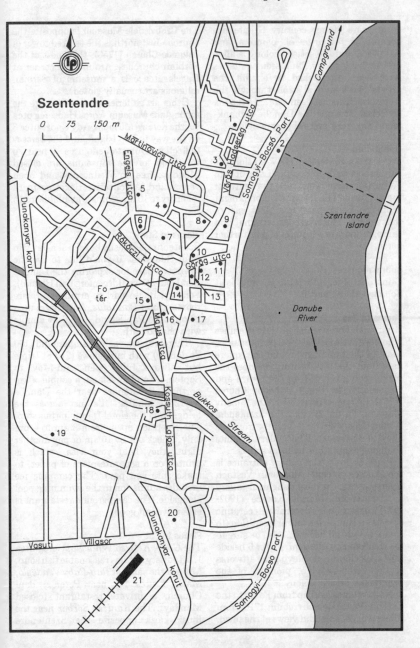

Szentendre

0   75   150 m

early years of our century Szentendre became a favourite of painters and sculptors, and the artists' colony is alive and thriving today. Numerous galleries have been established to exhibit the artists' work and a stroll through the winding streets between exotic Orthodox churches, or along the Danube embankment, is a most enjoyable experience.

Orientation

From the Szentendre HEV station it's only a short walk up Kossuth Lajos utca to Fo ter (formerly Marx ter), the centre of the old town. The Danube Embankment (Somogyi-Bacso part) is a block east of this square. The riverboat terminal and campground are a couple of km further north.

Information

Dunatours (Idegenforgalmi Hivatal) is at Somogyi-Bacso part 6

Things to See

Begin with Fo ter which on July evenings becomes a stage for theatrical performances. Most of the buildings around the square date from the 18th century, as does the plague column (1763) in the centre and **Blagovesztenska Greek Orthodox Church** (1752) in one corner. Visit the **Kmetty Museum**, Fo ter 21, and the **Szentendre Picture Gallery**, Fo ter 2-5 (entry from the alley at the rear). The gallery mounts changing exhibitions by local artists.

Right opposite the gallery entrance is the **Kovacs Margit Museum**, Vastagh Gyorgy utca1, the most delightful gallery in Szentendre. Margit Kovacs (1902-1977) based her decorative ceramic objects on Hungarian folk art traditions to create a style all her own. Also be sure to see the **Ferenczy Museum**, Fo ter 6 beside the Greek Church, displaying the artworks of the Ferenczy clan, pioneers of the Szentendre artists' colony.

Narrow lanes lead up from Fo ter to the Catholic **Parish Church** (rebuilt 1710) from where you get splendid views of the town.

The **Czobel Bela Museum** is opposite the church. Just north is the tall red tower of **Belgrade Church** (1756), the finest of the Serbian churches. Around the corner at Engels utca 5 is a museum of Serbian religious art (usually closed).

Other art galleries worth seeing are the **Amos-Anna Museum**, Voros Hadsereg utca 10, the **Kerenyi Museum**, Ady Endre utca 6 on the way to Pap Island, and the **Barcsay Collection**, Dumsta Jeno utca 10 near Fo ter. Most of the museums are closed Monday, free on Wednesday and open year round. A collective ticket/postcard for entry to 10 museums is available for 15 Ft.

Places to Stay

Szentendre can easily be seen as a day trip from Budapest. If you'd like to use the town as a base for exploring the Danube Bend Dunatours (Idegenforgalmi Hivatal), Somogyi-Bacso part 6, arranges private rooms. *Hotel Danubius*, Ady Endre utca 28 opposite Pap Island, is 700 Ft double with shared bath.

There's an expensive campground (190 Ft double) with bungalows (210 Ft triple but always full) open mid-May to September on Pap Island, a couple of km north of Szentendre near the Danube riverboat landing. It's just across the bridge from the Hotel Danubius bus stop. The reception opens from 8 am to 4 pm only. Check out by 10 am or pay another night (they hold your visa, which is printed on a separate piece of paper, to make sure you pay). The camping fee includes admission to the swimming pool alongside. The campground restaurant is expensive but good.

Places to Eat

The *Gorog Kancso Vendeglo*, Gorog utca 1, is touristy but has reasonable fish soup. More of the same at *Rab-Raby Vendeglo*, Majus 1 utca 1/A near Peter & Paul Church, a private restaurant (closed Monday). The *Kanizsa Sorbar* near the Ibusz kiosk opposite the Szentendre

Island ferry wharf is good for a cheap meal. The most colourful place in town to eat is *Barczy Fogado*, an old inn at Voros Hadsereg utca 30 – well worth the extra money.

Getting There & Away

Access couldn't be easier. Take the HEV suburban railway from Budapest's Batthyany ter Metro station to the end of the line. There are several trains an hour. Buses from Budapest's Engels ter bus station also run to Szentendre frequently. From May to September Danube riverboats between Budapest and Esztergom call at Szentendre a couple of times daily. The landing is near Pap Island, a km north of the centre.

VAC

Vac, on the left bank of the Danube 34 km north of Budapest, is far less touristed than the places on the right bank. Medieval Vac was destroyed by the Turks and much had to be rebuilt by the Catholic bishops in the 18th century. There are several beautiful churches and squares, but Vac's chief attraction is a chance to see a little more of the romantic Danube and Hungarian small town life.

Information

Dunatours is at Szechenyi utca 14

Things to See

As you leave the railway station proceed straight ahead on Szechenyi utca and you'll soon reach Marcius 15 ter which contains some of Vac's most beautiful buildings. Notice especially the Baroque City Hall (1731) at No 11 and the Gothic palace at No 6 opposite, now the Institute for the Deaf & Dumb. A few blocks north of this square beside the prison on Koztarsasag ut is Hungary's only triumphal arch, erected in 1764 for Queen Maria Teresa.

Return to Marcius 15 ter and visit the lovely Dominican Church (1699) on the south side. The interior decoration of this Rococo building is breathtaking. At the back of the courtyard at Marcius 15 ter 19 near this church is an art gallery in a former church (1792). The market behind the Dominican Church is also worth a visit.

Follow Koztarsasag ut south past the public swimming pool and Baroque Statue of the Trinity (1750) to Konstantin ter, which is dominated by the massive neo-Classical cathedral (1762). This building with its huge Corinthian columns outside and extensive frescoes inside is one of the best of its kind in Hungary. On Muzeum utca, which begins near the Bishop's Palace (1768) at the west end of the square, is the Vak Bottyan Museum (closed Monday) with a small but select local history exhibit and a lapidarium in the basement.

Continue on Muzeum utca till you see the Franciscan Church (1721) before you. The Baroque pulpit, altars and organ in this building are splendid. A lane beside the church leads down to the Danube embankment which you should follow north. Beyond the ferry terminal is a 15th century round tower remaining from the old city walls. If you have time take the ferry across the river to Szentendre Island for the views.

Places to Stay & Eat

Dunatours, Szechenyi utca 14, can find you a private room. There are two small private pensions at Liszt Ferenc setany 13 near the ferry terminal, both offering rooms for about 300 Ft double. The *Pokol Csarda* (closed Tuesday) just across the river on Szentendre Island serves fish soup. A good unpretentious place to enjoy a substantial meal is the *Szechenyi Etelbar* on the corner of Szechenyi utca and Sallai Imre utca near the train station.

Getting There & Away

Access is easy on hourly trains from Budapest's Nyugati station. The first railway line built out of Budapest reached Vac in 1846. It's possible to cross the

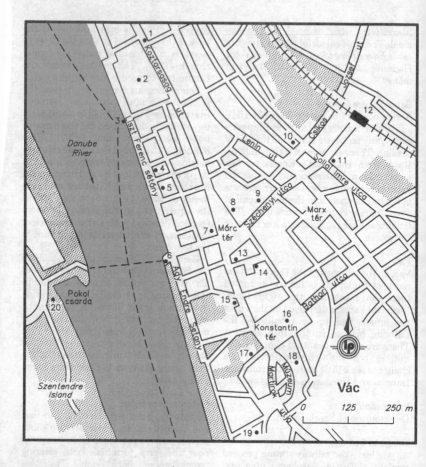

Danube by local ferry and return to Budapest via Tahitotfalu and Szentendre. For Visegrad catch a train west to Nagymaros.

VISEGRAD

Visegrad is superbly situated on a horseshoe bend of the Danube between the Pilis and Borzsony mountains. For hundreds of years the river was the border of the Roman Empire. After Mongol invasions in the 13th century the Hungarian kings built a mighty citadel on a hilltop with a wall running down to a lower castle near the river. In the 14th century a royal palace was built on the flood plain at the foot of the hills and the Angevin court moved here in 1323. For nearly two centuries Hungarian kings and queens alternated between Visegrad and Buda. The reign of the Renaissance monarch King Matthias in the 15th century was the period of greatest glory for Visegrad.

The destruction of Visegrad came with the Turks and later in 1702 the Hapsburgs

1	Triumphal Arch
2	Prison
3	Riverboat Terminal
4	Private Pensions
5	Round Tower
6	Ferry Terminal
7	City Hall
8	Institute for the Deaf & Dumb
9	Dunatours
10	Bus Station
11	Szechenyi Etelbar
12	Railway Station
13	Dominican Church
14	Market
15	Statue of the Trinity
16	Cathedral
17	Bishop's Palace
18	Vak Bottyan Museum
19	Franciscan Church
20	Pokol Csarda

blew up the citadel to prevent Hungarian independence fighters from using it as a base. All trace of the palace was lost until 1934 when archaeologists following descriptions in literary sources uncovered the ruins we visit today. Unfortunately current development around Visegrad, including a barrage across the river, is casting a veil of uncertainty over the area.

Information
The Dunatours office at Fo utca 3/a often gives misleading advice, so check.

Things to See
The **palace ruins** at Fo utca 27 may be visited daily except Monday year round from 9 am to 4 pm. Highlights are a red marble well bearing the coat of arms of King Matthias in the Gothic courtyard and, on an upper terrace, a copy of the lion fountain. The original well and fountain are kept in the museum at **Solomon's Tower**, which should be visited next. The tower is on a low hill above the Danube a few hundred metres from the palace ruins. This was part of a lower castle intended to

control river traffic. The 13th century walls are up to eight metres thick! The tower museum is open from May to September daily except Monday, but the exterior can be enjoyed anytime.

Visegrad citadel (1259) is on a high hill directly above Solomon's Tower, accessible on hiking trails (signposted 'Fellegvar'). From June to August a local bus (10 Ft) runs up to the citadel from the side street in front of the King Matthias statue near the Danube riverboat wharf. Restoration work on the three defensive levels of the citadel will continue for many years but the view of the Danube Bend from the walls is absolutely stunning, one of the most scenic spots in Europe. On another hill nearby is the **Nagy-Villam Lookout Tower** which offers a different fabulous view.

There are numerous opportunities for hiking in the mountainous forest behind Visegrad. One trail marked with blue strips leads 11.6 km from Nagy-Villam to Pilisszentlaszlo via Papret. If markers stop appearing you're off the track. Hikers should buy the 1:40,000 *A Pilis* topographical map of the area at a tourist office or bookstore. New roads which cut across the trails at several points are not marked on this map!

Near Visegrad
There's a warm water swimming pool at Lepence beside the road halfway between Visegrad and Domos. An excellent half day hike from Domos climbs to Dobogoko village via the Ram-szakadek Gorge (about three hours). There are sweeping views of river and mountains through openings in the forest along the way. From Dobogoko there are buses to Esztergom or Pomaz va HEV suburban railway station, but it's an easy downhill walk back to Domos via Kortvelyes or Lukacs-arok for a circle trip. These trails through the **Pilis Nature Reserve** are clearly marked and there are raspberries in early summer.

Alternatively one can take a small ferry across the Danube from Domos to Domosi

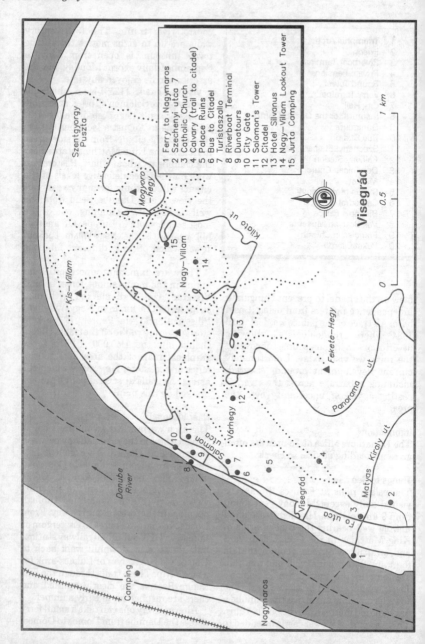

Visegrád

1 Ferry to Nagymaros
2 Szechenyi utca 7
3 Catholic Church
4 Calvary (trail to citadel)
5 Palace Ruins
6 Bus to Citadel
7 Turistaszollo
8 Riverboat Terminal
9 Dunatours
10 City Gate
11 Solomon's Tower
12 Citadel
13 Hotel Silvanus
14 Nagy–Villam Lookout Tower
15 Jurta Camping

atkeles, then climb to caves visible on the hillside and back into the hills behind Nagymaros.

Places to Stay

Dunatours, Fo utca 3/a on the main highway opposite the riverboat terminal, arranges private rooms (500 Ft double) or *turistaszallo* (hostel) accommodation. One *turistaszallo* is nearby at Salamontorony utca 5, another at Szechenyi utca 7, both closed in winter. From June to August the Szechenyi utca 7 hostel (by the small stream back behind the church with the green tower) is a good place to try since they also have bungalows and allow camping.

Jurta Camping (open from mid-May to September) is high up on a hillside north of the Nagy-Villam Tower (bus service from June to August only, otherwise a stiff 40-minute uphill hike). They rent four-person tents (280 Ft for the tent), bungalows and have a small, expensive restaurant. The nearest grocery store is back down in Visegrad. It's quiet but crowded with cars and mobile homes.

A third campground is at Nagymaros, across the Danube by ferry. The campsite is near the river up the busy highway beyond the petrol station, two km north of the ferry. Open May to September this one has the advantage of hot showers and direct trains to Budapest. Camping is 124 Ft double, bungalows 324 Ft double (highway and railway noise free). There's a restaurant on the premises.

Perhaps the best camping at the Danube Bend is at Domos, six km west of Visegrad. It's behind a meadow with a lovely view of the river only a few minutes walk from the riverboat landing and bus stop. Open June to mid-September, the charge is 156 Ft for two persons to camp or 300 Ft for a two-bed cabin (often full). It can get crowded in mid-summer but the facilities are excellent: clean washrooms, hot water, burners for cooking and a small bar. There's a grocery store and a large restaurant in the village a 10-minute walk

away. Best of all, the hills behind Domos are one of the best hiking areas in Hungary and the monuments of Visegrad and Esztergom only a short hop away by bus or boat.

Places to Eat

Maros Vendeglo, near the Nagymaros ferry wharf across the Danube, is just enough off the beaten tourist track to remain unspoiled. In summer you dine on a terrace overlooking the river. The food is good, prices moderate. Check the ferry times carefully if you want to return late to Visegrad.

Getting There & Away

Buses between Budapest's Engels ter bus station and Esztergom sometimes go via Visegrad. Bus service is more frequent from stand 1 or 2 at the Szentendre HEV suburban railway station. Some buses from the HEV continue all the way up to Nagy-Villam, so ask.

Hourly ferries (3 Ft) cross the Danube to Nagymaros. Don't panic if the large car ferry closes down early for the night. A smaller passenger launch usually takes its place. Trains between Budapest-Nyugati and Szob run along the left (north) bank of the Danube about every hour with stops at Vac, Nagymaros, Zebegeny, etc. Nagymaros station is just inland from the ferry wharf across the river from Visegrad. From May to September Danube riverboats between Budapest and Esztergom call at Visegrad.

ESZTERGOM

Esztergom, opposite Sturovo, Czechoslovakia, at the west entrance to the Danube Bend, is one of Hungary's most famous historic cities. Stephen I, founder of the Hungarian state, was born and crowned at Esztergom which remained capital of Hungary from the 10th to 13th centuries. After the Mongol invasion the king and court moved to Buda but Esztergom remained the ecclesiastical centre, as it is today. Originally the clerics

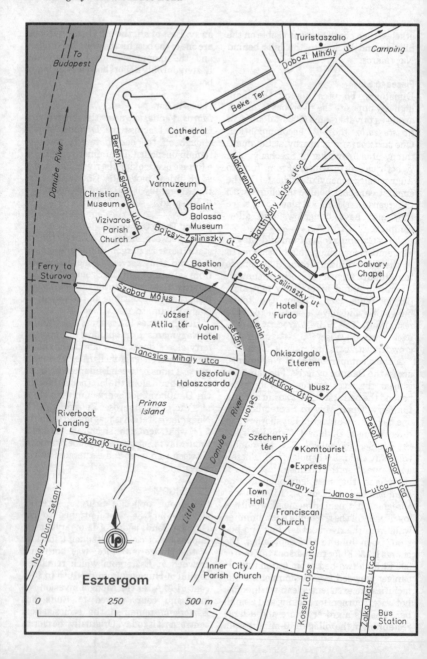

To Budapest

Turistaszalio

Camping

Dobozi Mihály út

Danube River

Beke Ter

Cathedral

Berény, Zsigmond utca

Makarenko út

Christian Museum

Varmuzeum

Balint Balassa Museum

Vizivaros Parish Church

Bajcsy–Zsilinszky út

Batthyány Lajos utca

Ferry to Sturovo

Bastion

Szabad Május 1

Bajcsy–Zsilinszky út

Calvary Chapel

József Attila tér

Volan Hotel

sétány

Lenin

Hotel Furdo

Tancsics Mihaly utca

Onkiszalgalo Etterem

Uszofalu Halaszcsarda

Mártirok útja

Danube River

Sétány

Ibusz

Primas Island

Riverboat Landing

Gőzhajó utca

Petofi Sandor utca

Széchenyi tér

Komtourist

Express

Nagy–Duna Setany

Arany

Janos

utca

Town Hall

Franciscan Church

Esztergom

Little Danube

Inner City Parish Church

Kossuth Lajos utca

Zalka Mate utca

Bus Station

0   250   500 m

lived by the riverbank and royalty on the hilltop above. When the king finally left the archbishop moved up and occupied the palace, maintaining Esztergom's prominence.

The Turks ravaged the town and much had to be rebuilt in the 18th and 19th centuries. An ill-conceived building programme continues in the centre today.

Information

Komtourist is at Szechenyi ter 13. Express is at Szechenyi ter 7.

Things to See

The bus station is a couple of blocks southeast of Szechenyi ter, the medieval market place, where the **town hall** (1773) is today. A block south is the **Inner City Parish Church** (1757) near a branch of the Danube. Cross on the footbridge to Primas Island and follow Gozhajo utca directly across to the riverboat landing on the main Danube channel. Continue north along the river and cross the bridge to **Vizivaros Parish Church** (1738). Esztergom's famous **Christian Museum** is in the adjacent **Primate's Palace** (closed Monday) at Berenyi utca 2. This is one of the best art collections in Hungary so don't miss it. Nearby at Bajcsy Zsilinszky ut 63 is the **Balint Balassa Museum** with objects of local interest.

You can't help noticing **Esztergom cathedral** on a high hill above the Danube, the largest church in Hungary. The building was rebuilt in neo-Classical style in the 19th century but the red marble Rakocz chapel (1510) on the south side was moved here from an earlier church. Below the cathedral is a large crypt, but most interesting is the treasury at the front of the church behind the altar. Many priceless medieval objects are kept here, including the 13th century Hungarian coronation cross. Crypt and treasury both open daily except Monday from 10 am to 3 pm. Beside the cathedral at the south end of the hill is the **Varmuzeum** (closed

Monday) with remnants of the medieval royal palace (1215). Parts of the complex in early French Gothic style have been masterfully reconstructed. The views from this hill are great.

Places to Stay

Private rooms are assigned by Komtourist, Szechenyi ter 13, and Ibusz, Martirok utja 1. Two inexpensive hotels in the centre of town are the stately *Hotel Furdo*, Bajcsy Zsilinszky ut 14 (800 Ft double with breakfast), and the modern *Volan Hotel*, Jozsef Attila ter 2 (320 Ft single, 400 Ft double with breakfast). There's a public swimming pool behind Hotel Furdo.

The *turistaszallo* at Dolozi Mihaly ut 8 near the cathedral offers cheap dormitory accommodation. Ask Komtourist to refer you. *Vadvirag Camping* (open May to September) is a couple of km east of Esztergom on the road to Visegrad and they have bungalows.

Places to Eat

A recommended restaurant is the *Uszofalu Halaszcsarda*, Szabad Majus 1 setany 4 on Primas Island (closed Tuesday). Try the fish soup. The restaurant in *Hotel Furdo* is also good. If you only want to fill your stomach *Onkiszolgalo Etterem*, upstairs at the back of the ugly shopping centre behind Bastya Department Store on Bajcsy Zsilinszky ut, is cheaper and faster. There's an excellent map store beside this restaurant.

Getting There & Away

The railway station is at the south edge of town and the trains are painfully slow, so you're better to come by bus or boat. Bus service is frequent from Budapest's Engels ter bus station. To go to Western Hungary look for a bus or train to Komarom. There are Mahart riverboats to and from Budapest several times a day from May to September. A ferry crosses the Danube to Sturovo, Czechoslovakia, 10 times a day from May to September. This border crossing may only be used by citizens of Czechoslovakia and Hungary, however.

Western Hungary

Beyond the Bakony Mountains northwest of Balaton Lake lies the Kisalfold or 'Little Plain' bounded by the Danube and the Alps. Conquered by the Romans but never occupied by the Turks, this enchanting corner of Transdanubia is surrounded by a string of picturesque small towns with a decidedly European air. The old quarters of Sopron and Gyor are brimming with the residences of prosperous burghers and clerics, while Koszeg offers an intact medieval castle and Fertod a magnificent Rococo palace. Sopron, only 69 km south of Vienna (bus service), is a convenient gateway to Eastern Europe.

TATA

In summer it might be worth stopping at Tata, a pleasant town on a lake between Budapest and Gyor. Tata Railway Station is a couple of km from town, so take a city bus to the main bus station (Autobuszallomas) near **Oregvar Castle**. This moated Gothic castle sits right on the edge of Oreg-to (Old Lake). The original structure was destroyed in wars long ago and during the 19th century part of the castle was rebuilt in neo-Gothic. This now houses the **Kuny Domokos Museum** (Tuesday to Sunday 10 am to 2 pm). Nearby is a former country estate of the Esterhazy family (1765), now a hospital.

Lake Cseke is a smaller lake at Tata with a pleasant walkway around.

Places to Stay

Two inexpensive hotels in the centre of town are the *Hotel Kristaly*, Ady Endreut 22 (500 Ft double), and the *Hotel Malom* nearby (420 Ft double). For private rooms try Cooptourist, Topart setany 18, a block from these hotels.

Tata has two campgrounds both with bungalows. The *Fenyesfurdo Camping* at the hot springs north of Tata is about a km from Tata Railway Station. The *Oreg-to Camping*, on Vertesszolosi ut near the lake, is closer to Tovaroskert Railway Station if you're arriving by local train. Oreg-to tends to open earlier in the season than Fenyesfurdo.

Getting There & Away

Tata is on the main railway line between Budapest and Gyor/Sopron. Trains are more frequent than buses and most expresses stop here.

GYOR

Gyor (Raab) is an historic city on a branch of the Danube midway between Budapest and Vienna. Stephen I established a bishopric at Gyor in the 11th century. In the mid-16th century a strong fortress was

1	Thermal Baths
2	Bishop's Palace
3	Cathedral
4	Borsos Miklos Collection
5	Arc of the Covenant Monument
6	Margit Kovacs Collection
7	Halasz Csarda
8	Xantus Janos Museum
9	Former Charity Hospital
10	Casemates Museum
11	Vaskakas Taverna
12	Napoleon House
13	Carmelite Church
14	Korzo Restaurant
15	Pharmacy Museum
16	St Ignatius Church
17	Szechenyi Cultural Centre
18	Orszagos Philharmonia
19	Kisfaludy Theatre
20	Express
21	Volantourist
22	Magyar Bufe
23	Ciklamen Tourist
24	Ibusz
25	City Hall
26	Railway Station
27	Bus Station

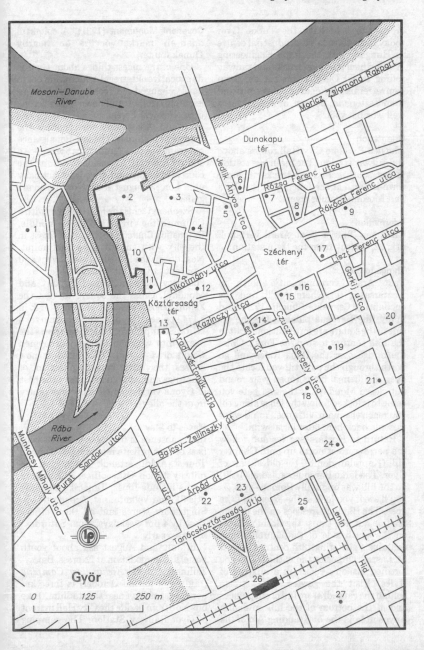

Mosoni–Danube River

Dunakapu tér

Móricz Zsigmond Rakpart

Jedlik Ányos utca

6

Rózsa Ferenc utca

Rákóczi Ferenc utca

7

8

9

2

3

5

4

1

17

Liszt Ferenc utca

Széchenyi tér

10

Alkotmány utca

Gorkij utca

11

16

15

12

Köztársaság tér

Kazinczy utca

Czuczor Gergely utca

20

13

Kazinczy utca

14

Aradi vértanúk útja

Lenin út

19

21

18

Rába River

Munkácsy Mihály utca

Fürst Sándor utca

Bajcsy-Zsilinszky út

24

Jókai utca

Árpád út

23

22

25

Lenin

26

27

Tanácsköztársaság útja

Híd

Győr

0   125   250 m

erected to hold back the Turks. Gyor today is the third largest industrial centre in Hungary with the Raba Engineering Works which produces trucks and railway rolling stock. Despite this the old town centre retains its charm. Less touristed than Esztergom, Sopron, or Eger, Gyor is well worth a visit.

Orientation

The neo-Baroque City Hall towers above the railway station. The main bus station is just south across the tracks. The old town is north at the junction of the Raba and Mosoni-Danube rivers.

Information

Ciklamen Tourist is at Aradi vertanuk utja 22, a block from the train station

Things to See

Take Aradi vertanuk utja north to Koztarsasag ter where you'll find the enchanting **Carmelite Church** (1725) and many fine Baroque palaces. On the far side of the square are fortifications built in the 16th century to stop the Turks. Cross the bridge over the Raba River and go north through the park till you locate the open air **thermal baths** (open year round but closed Monday). If the first gate you come to is locked follow the fence along till you reach the main entrance. You'll want to come back here later for a swim!

Return to Koztarsasag ter and follow the narrow street north up onto Chapter Hill (Kaptalan-domb), the oldest part of Gyor. The large Baroque **cathedral** (1639) on the hill was originally Romanesque, as you'll see if you look at the exterior of the apse. The Baroque frescoes on the ceiling are fine but don't miss the Gothic chapel on the south side of the church which contains a glittering 13th century bust of St Laszlo. Opposite the cathedral is the fortified **Bishop's Palace** in a mixture of styles. Visit the garden. The streets behind the cathedral are full of old palaces and at the bottom of the hill on Jedlik Anyos utca is the outstanding **Arc of the Covenant Monument** (1731). A colourful open-air market occurs on nearby Dunakapu ter.

One of the nicest things about Gyor is its evocative old streets, which seem not to have changed in centuries. Take a leisurely stroll up and down Rozsa Ferenc utca, Rakoczi Ferenc utca, Liszt Ferenc utca and Alkotmany utca noting the many fine buildings. The late Renaissance palace at Rakoczi Ferenc utca 6 was once a charity hospital. Go inside to admire the courtyards. Napoleon stayed at Alkotmany utca 4 on 13 August 1809. Now it's an art gallery.

Szechenyi ter is the heart of Gyor with a Column of the Virgin (1686) in the middle. **St Ignatius Church** (1641) is the finest in the city with superb pews and pulpit. Next door is the Benedictine Convent and adjacent to it at Szechenyiter 9 a **Pharmacy Museum** (closed Sunday and Monday). Cross the square to visit the **Xantus Janos Museum**, Szechenyi ter 5, in a 1743 palace. Beside it at Szechenyi ter 4 is Iron Stump House which still sports the beam into which itinerant journeymen would drive a nail. This building now houses the Imre Patko Collection of paintings and African art, one of the best of Gyor's various small museums (entry from the alley).

Places to Stay

In the absence of inexpensive hotels your best bet is a private room from Ciklamen Tourist, Aradi vertanuk utja 22 near the railway station. Other offices with private rooms include Ibusz, Tanacskoztarsasag utja 31, and Volantourist, Arpad ut 51/b. Singles are scarce and all these offices close by 4 pm weekdays, 1 pm Saturday, so arrive early.

In July and August ask about youth hostel accommodation at Express, Bajcsy-Zsilinszky ut 41. *Kiskut-liget Camping* (mid-April to mid-October) is three km north-east of Gyor near the stadium. Take bus No 8 from beside the City Hall in front of Gyor Railway Station. The camping has bungalows and a motel (420 Ft double).

Places to Eat

If you want class the *Vaskakas Taverna* at Koztarsasag ter 3 in the casemates below the castle offers gypsy music but is a little expensive. Cheaper but still atmospheric is *Halasz Csarda*, Rosza Ferenc utca 4, with fish dishes. The *Magyar Bufe*, Arpad ut 18, is a good neighbourhood wine cellar serving Hungarian fish soup and Balaton wine (closed Sunday).

The cheapest meals in Gyor are consumed at the *Korzo Restaurant*, Lenin ut 13, with juicy barbecued chicken. It's self-service, but there are tables to sit down at.

Entertainment

Gyor has one of the most striking new theatres in Hungary, the *Kisfaludy Theatre* on Czuczor Gergely utca. You can't miss the Vasarely mosaics covering the exterior walls! The box office is just inside. Gyor's ballet company is internationally recognised. Nearby at Czuczor Gergely utca 28 is the Orszagos Filharmonia where you can enquire about concerts. Also check the *Szechenyi Cultural Centre*, Szechenyi ter 7.

Getting There & Away

Gyor is well connected by express train to Budapest's Deli Station and Sopron. There's also a secondary line with local trains south to Veszprem via Pannonhalma. To and from Vienna Westbahnhof you may have to change at Hegyeshalom since crack trains like the Wiener-Walzer and Orient Express don't stop at Gyor. A better route to Vienna is through Sopron. To and from Czechoslovakia change at Komarom.

PANNONHALMA

Pannonhalma Abbey, a functioning Benedictine monastery 18 km south of Gyor, stands on a hilltop 300 metres above the Transdanubian plain. Admission to the abbey (closed Monday) is only with a group; you wait at the entrance for one to form.

Founded in 996, Pannonhalma has been restored and extended numerous times, so today you see quite a patchwork of styles. The rather rushed tour takes you through the Gothic cloister (1486), into the Romanesque basilica (1225) and down to the 11th century crypt. The 55 metre tower was erected in 1830 and the impressive Empire-style library (also on the tour) dates from the same period. The visit concludes with a look in the one-room 'picture gallery.'

The view of the surrounding area from this hill is excellent and Pannonhalma is a good excuse to get out of the city and see an attractive slice of Hungarian country life. There are several restaurants in the village below the abbey and from mid-May to mid-September a campground.

Getting There & Away

Local trains between Gyor and Veszprem call at Pannonhalma every couple of hours. An easy day trip from Gyor, Pannonhalma is best approached by bus, however, as the train station is a couple of km south-west of the abbey.

SOPRON

Sopron, on the Austrian border 217 km west of Budapest, is surrounded by the green eastern ridges of the Alps. Sopron (the ancient Scarbantia) has been an important centre since Roman times. The Mongols and Turks never got this far so numerous medieval structures have come down to us intact. In the old quarter, still partially enclosed by medieval walls built on Roman foundations, almost every building is historic. This is Sopron's principle charm and a wanderer among the Gothic and Baroque houses is rewarded at every turn. Some of the buildings are now museums and you can peek into the courtyards of many others.

Sopron

500 m

250

0

Köszeg út

Harkai út

Köszegi út

Sarudi utca

Löver Campground

Vas Gereben utca

Felsöbüki Nagy Pál utca

Lokomotiv Hotel

Torna-Gazdasàg körút

József Attila utca

Szabadsàg körút

Városligeti út

Walking Trails

Ciklamen út

Vàrisi út

Szabadsàg körút

Löver Hotel

Karoly Lookout

Orientation

From the main railway station walk north on Matyas kiraly utca, which becomes Lenin korut after a few blocks. Lenin Korut and Ogabona ter form a loop right around the old town following the line of the former city walls. Sopron's Fire Tower is between the north end of Lenin korut and Fo ter, the old town square. The bus station is on Lackner Kristof utca off Ogabona ter.

Information

Ciklamen Tourist is at Ogabona ter 8 on the corner of Lackner Kristof utca. Express is at Matyas kiraly utca 7.

Things to See

The 61 metre high **Fire Tower** above Sopron's north gate, erected after the fire of 1676, is the symbol of the city. You can climb up to the Renaissance loggia for a marvellous view (closed Monday) and see the excavated remains of the original Roman gate below.

Fo ter, just beyond the tower, is the heart of the old town. In the centre of the square is the Holy Trinity Column (1701) and beyond this the Benedictine **Goat Church** (1300), built by a goatherd with gold uncovered by his beasts! In the adjoining building is the Gothic Chapter House, now a museum (closed Monday).

Across the street from the Goat Church is the Esterhazy City Palace, now a most interesting **Mining Museum** (closed Wednesday). There are several other museums on Fo ter. **Fabricus House** at No 6 is a comprehensive historical museum with impressive Roman sculpture in the Gothic cellar. **Storno House** at No 8 is a famous Renaissance palace, now an art gallery/museum (both houses closed Monday).

Sopron's most unique museum is housed in the 14th century **synagogue** (closed Tuesday) at Uj utca 22. Jews were an important part of the community until their expulsion in 1526.

1	Bus Station
2	Volantourist
3	Ciklamen Tourist
4	Rejpal House
5	Poncichter Wine Cellar
6	Church of the Holy Spirit
7	St Michael's Church
8	Ibusz
9	Fire Tower
10	Storno House
11	Fabricus House
12	Mining Museum
13	Goat Church
14	Tourist Hostel
15	St George's Church
16	City Walls
17	PM Sorozo/Borozo
18	Evangelical Church
19	Synagogue
20	Arcaded House
21	Orsolya Church
22	Cesar-Pince Wine Cellar
23	Hotel Pannonia
24	Bisztro
25	Toptour
26	Dominican Church
27	Liszt Cultural Centre
28	Onkiszolgalo Etterem
29	Express

Outside the Centre The **Liszt Ferenc Museum** is in a villa at the corner of Majus 1 ter and Muzeum utca (closed Monday).

To see some of Sopron's surroundings take bus No 10 to **Kertvaros** and climb the Baroque stairway to the Hill Church. Better yet take bus No 1 or 2 to the Lover Hotel and hike up through the forest to the **Karoly Lookout** for the view.

An hourly bus from the main bus station runs 10 km north to **Fertorakos** where the mammoth halls and corridors of the old stone quarry are an impressive sight (open daily year round, 10 Ft). In summer concerts and operas are performed in the theatre situated in the largest chamber.

Places to Stay

The *Hotel Pannonia*, Lenin korut 73, is

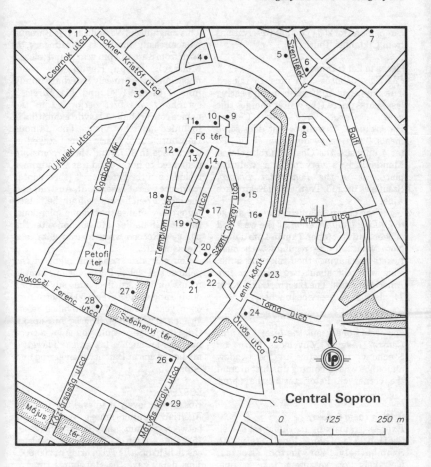

Central Sopron

0   125   250 m

1160 Ft double, or 300 Ft per person if you show a youth hostel card. *Hotel Lokomotiv*, Szabadsag korut 1 south of the railway station (bus No 2), is 500 Ft double. The reception is upstairs on the 3rd floor.

There are two tourist hostels *(turistas-zallo)* offering dormitory accommodation, one at Uj utca 8 in the old town, the other at Ferenczi Janos utca 4, the street beginning near the bus station. Reservations for these are made at Ciklamen Tourist, Ogabona ter 8, which also has private rooms. Other private rooms can be

arranged at Volantourist, Lackner Kristof utca 1; Ibusz, Lenin korut 41 and Toptour, Otvos utca 9.

The *Lover Campground* is three km south of the station up Koszegi ut. Take bus No 12 direction 'Loverek fele' from either the bus or train stations right to the campground, or buses No 1 or 2 to the *Lover Hotel* then walk a km through the forest. Tenting is possible mid-April to mid-October and in summer there are small bungalows for 100 Ft. In winter heated rooms are available at the campground for 250 Ft double (reservations from Ciklamen Tourist).

Places to Eat & Drink

PM Sorozo/Borozo, Uj utca 13 (closed Tuesday), has an English menu bearing last years' prices (the waiter charges this years'). *Cesar-Pince Wine Cellar*, Hatsokapu 2, is touristy but does serve meals. The *Gyogygodor Wine Cellar*, Fo ter 4 opposite the Goat Church (closed Monday), is a very popular watering place, as is the *Poncichter Borozo*, Szentlelek utca 13. Try the local Kekfrankos wine.

For the cheapest lunch you ever ate go to *Onkiszolgalo Etterem* at the west end of Szechenyi ter (open 7 am to 4 pm daily). Note what all the regulars with meal tickets are having, then take the same. This will cost about two forint or five American cents! The *Bisztro*, Lenin korut 74, also has self-service lunches.

Entertainment

For events check out the *Liszt Cultural Centre* (Magyar Muvelodes Haza) on Szechenyi ter. Posters in the window announce what's coming up. Just around the corner on Petofi ter is the *Petofi Theatre*.

Getting There & Away

Express trains run to Budapest's Deli Station via Gyor, local trains to Szombathely. For Fertod, Koszeg, Keszthely, or Veszprem take a bus. There's a bus to Vienna Monday to Saturday (246 Ft one way). Tickets are sold by Ibusz. There are also several trains every day to and from Vienna's Sudbahnhof with a change at Wiener Neustadt or Ebenfurth. When boarding at Sopron be in the station an hour early to clear Customs.

FERTOD

Don't miss the 126-room Esterhazy Palace (1766) at Fertod, 28 km east of Sopron and readily accessible by bus.

This magnificent Versailles-style Baroque palace, easily the finest in Hungary, is open from 8 am to 4 pm year round (closed Monday). Joseph Haydn was court musician to the princely Esterhazy family from 1761 to 1790 and his *Farewell* symphony was first performed in the palace concert hall. A Haydn exhibition is included in the visit. The famous Hapsburg queen Maria Teresa stayed in the palace in 1773 and three rooms are dedicated to her. Fertod was the summer residence of the Esterhazy's (their winter residence was at Eisenstadt, Austria) and the large French Park behind the palace helps one visualise the bygone splendour. In the Grenadier House opposite the palace's Rococo wrought-iron gate is a pleasant cafe.

You can also spend the night in the palace (tel 99/45-971). Clean, simple rooms on the 3rd floor are only 250 Ft double and there's even a 50 Ft dormitory open year round. Make advance reservations at Ciklamen Tourist in Sopron. Only in Hungary could you enjoy a treat like this for such a low price! There's a medicinal spa at Balf between Fertod and Sopron.

KOSZEG

Koszeg is a lovely medieval town on the Austrian frontier among verdant hills between Sopron and Szombathely. In 1532 the garrison of Koszeg's 13th century castle held off a Turkish army of 200,000. This delay gave the Hapsburgs time to mount a successful defence of Vienna, ensuring Koszeg's place in European history. The houses along the street in front of the castle were erected in a saw-toothed manner to give defenders a better shot at an enemy. Jurisich ter, Koszeg's main square, hasn't changed since the 18th century.

Information

Savaria Tourist is at Varkor 59.

Kőszeg

```
0        250        500 m
```

1 Calvary Chapel
2 Jurisich Chapel
3 St James Church
4 Apothecary Museum
5 City Gate
6 Savaria Tourist
7 Church of the Sacred Heart
8 Kulacs Restaurant
9 Bus Station
10 Park Hotel
11 Railway Station

Things to See

The **City Gate** (1932) bears exterior reliefs depicting the 1532 siege. Inside is a branch of the Miklos Jurisich Museum (closed Monday). The gate leads into Jurisich ter where a Statue of the Virgin (1739) and the town well (1766) adjoin two fine churches. The **Church of St Emerich** (1615) is closer to the gate. Behind it is **St James Church** (1403), a splendid Gothic building with medieval frescoes. Be sure to visit the Baroque **Apothecary** at Jurisich ter 11.

The other highlight of Koszeg is **Jurisich**

Castle (1263), now an historical museum (closed Monday). The courtyard and towers of this Gothic bastion have an almost fairytale air.

Other sights include the neo-Gothic **Church of the Sacred Heart** on Varkor (you can't miss it) and the Baroque chapel on **Calvary Hill**, a 25-minute hike.

Places to Stay & Eat

Although Koszeg can easily be seen as a stopover between Sopron and Szombathely, there are plenty of places to stay. Savaria

Tourist, Varkor 59, arranges private rooms. The Express office next door can book you a room at the *Hotel Park* on Felszabadulas Park just west of Koszeg (540 Ft double, a dollar off if you show a youth hostel card). If Express is closed go directly to the hotel. In summer there's also the *Express Hotel Panorama* on Szabo-hegy Hill (bus No 2 from the railway station), but no singles.

The cheapest accommodation is the dorm beds at the *turistaszallo* in Jurisich Castle (open April to mid-October). A good restaurant at Koszeg is the *Kulacs*, Beke ut 12.

Getting There & Away
There are frequent trains and buses from Szombathely. The most interesting way to get there is on the morning bus from Sopron. At one point the bus takes a shortcut through no-man's-land between the barbed wire barriers on the Austrian border and you see soldiers on patrol, watchtowers, etc.

SZOMBATHELY
Szombathely, the seat of Vas County and a major crossroads in western Hungary, was founded as Savaria by the Roman Emperor Claudius in 43 AD. It soon became capital of Upper Pannonia and an important stage on the Amber Road from Italy to the Baltic. Destroyed by an earthquake in 455 and pillaged by the Mongols, Turks and Hapsburgs, Szombathely only regained its former stature when a bishopric was established here in 1777.

In 1945, just a month before the end of the war, American bombers levelled the town and it's a credit to Hungary that so much has been restored. Although off the beaten tourist track Szombathely has all the facilities you could ask for, making it an ideal stop on your way around the country.

Orientation
The railway station is five blocks east of Martirok tere along Savaria ut. The bus station is on Petofi Sandor utca behind the cathedral. Szombathely's busiest square is Koztarsasag ter, a long block south of Martirok tere.

Information
Savaria Tourist is at Martirok tere 1.

Things to See
Begin with the rebuilt neo-Classical **cathedral** (1791) on Berzsenyi Daniel ter. Between the cathedral and the bus station are the excavated 4th century **remains of Roman Savaria**, including mosaics, roads and a medieval castle. On the other side of the cathedral is the Baroque **Bishop's Palace** (1783) and beyond this on Hollan Erno utca, the **Schmidt Museum** (closed Monday), a fascinating assortment of small treasures collected by a local doctor prior to his death in 1975.

Follow your map down to Rakoczi Ferenc utca to see the reconstructed 2nd century **temple of the Egyptian goddess Isis**. A festival is held here in August. The **Szombathely Gallery** overlooking the temple is the best modern art gallery in Hungary (closed Monday). Also worth visiting is the **Savaria Museum** (closed Monday) on Savaria ut, which is especially strong on archaeology and natural history. There's a large Roman lapidarium (collection of architectural fragments) in the basement.

On the west side of Szombathely is a major open-air **ethnographic museum** or Skansen (open 10 am to 4 pm, closed Monday) with 50 reconstructed folk buildings. It's on a lake near the campground (bus No 7 to the terminus).

Places to Stay
Private rooms are assigned by Savaria Tourist, Martirok tere 1, and Ibusz, Savaria ut 3. In summer Express, Bajcsy-Zsilinszky utca 12, may know of youth hostels. If these offices (all adjacent to one another) are closed, make straight for the *Tourist Hotel* in Jokai Park west of

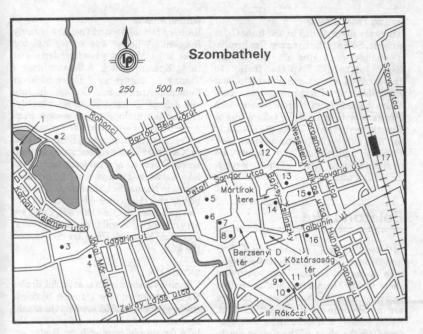

1	Skansen
2	Camping
3	Liberation Memorial
4	Tourist Hotel
5	Bus Station
6	Roman Ruins
7	Cathedral
8	Schmidt Museum
9	Temple of Isis
10	Szombathely Gallery
11	Bartok Hall
12	Arts & Sports Hall
13	Ibusz
14	Savaria Tourist
15	Savaria Museum
16	Franciscan Church
17	Railway Station

downtown. They have rooms for 400 Ft double, or beds in an eight-bed dormitory for 62 Ft per person.

From May to September there's a campground with bungalows on Kondics Istvan utca by a lake west of town (bus No 7 to the terminus). Check out the swimming pool nearby.

Places to Eat
Szombathely's most elegant restaurant is in the *Savaria Hotel* on Martirok tere. They don't sully their menu with prices. For a less pretentious meal try the *Gyongyos Etterem*, Savaria ut 8 nearby. They have a cheap 'menu' at lunchtime, but the food and service are always good here (closed Monday).

Entertainment
Hopefully something will be happening in *Bartok Hall*, a former synagogue (1881) opposite the Szombathely Gallery on Rakoczi Ferenc utca, now used as a concert hall. Also check the *Arts & Sports Hall*. The friendly people at Savaria Tourist may also know of events.

Getting There & Away

There are direct trains to and from Graz, Austria. Some of the Graz services involve a change of trains at the border (Szentgotthard). Express trains to Budapest (Deli) go via Veszprem and Szekesfehervar. There are frequent local trains to Koszeg and Sopron. For southern Hungary or Balaton Lake take a bus to Keszthely via Hevis. There are also early morning express trains to and from Pecs. Railway information and tickets are available from MAV Tours, Bajcsy-Zsilinszky utca 10/a.

Balaton Lake

In the very heart of Transdanubia, 77-km-long Balaton Lake is the largest freshwater lake in central Europe. The south-east shore of this 'Hungarian sea' is shallow and in summer the warm sandy beaches are a favourite family vacation spot. Better scenery and more historic sites are found on the shore of the deeper north-west end of the lake. The Benedictine crypt of Tihany Abbey is the oldest extant church in Hungary. During the Turkish period the border between the Ottoman and Hapsburg empires ran down the middle of the lake. North of the lake are the Bakony Hills and the extinct volcanoes of the Tapolca Basin.

The many towns and villages along both shores have an organic connection to this ancient lake. This is wine-making country. To avoid pollution the use of private motorboats is prohibited, making Balaton a favourite yachting centre. Scenic railway lines run along both shores and there are no less than 39 campgrounds around the lake. If you want to spend some time in the area get hold of the *A Balaton* 1:40,000 topographical map available at Budapest bookstores which illustrates the many hiking possibilities.

Getting Around

Railway service around the lake is fairly frequent. A better way to see Balaton Lake is by Mahart passenger ferry and these operate Siofok / Balatonfured / Tihany / Tihanyi-rev / Balatonfoldvar from mid-April to mid-October. In July and August the service is almost hourly. During the main summer season from June to mid-September ferries ply the entire length of the lake from Balatonkenese to Keszthely with frequent stops on both shores. There are also car ferries across the lake between Tihanyi-rev / Szantodrev (April to November), Revfulop / Balatonboglar and Badacsony / Fonyod (the last two mid-April to mid-October). Fares are very cheap: US$1 will take you anywhere. Of course in winter there are no boats on the lake.

SIOFOK

The milky green Sio River at Siofok drains Balaton Lake into the Danube. Siofok is the largest and busiest town on the south-east shore and the main gateway to the lake for people coming from Budapest. There are six huge campgrounds, plus workers hostels, holiday cottages and expensive hotels. On summer weekends this Hungarian Riviera can get extremely crowded.

Orientation

Siofok stretches for several km along the east shore of Balaton Lake. The train, bus and lake boat terminals are clustered near the Sio River. Many travel agencies and large stores are near Fo ter between the bus station and the river. Dimitrov Park between the train tracks and lake is surrounded by tree-lined streets of old mansions, while east along the lakeside is a high-rise strip of pricey tourist hotels.

Information

Siotour is at Szabadsag ter 6

Things to See

A **lock** at the mouth of the river controls

the flow of water from Balaton Lake. Almost 2000 years ago the Romans dredged the riverbed here to lower the level of the lake. There's a fairly interesting **museum** presenting the history of the Balaton area at Sio utca 2 near the highway bridge over the river. Summaries in English and German are posted.

Places to Stay

For private rooms try Siotour, Szabadsag ter 6, a few minutes' walk from the stations. If this office is closed when you arrive there's a second Siotour office with longer hours on Petofi setany near *Hotel Hungaria*. The Ibusz office in Siofok doesn't have private rooms.

None of the campgrounds are near the centre. If you're coming from Budapest by train get off at Balatonszabadi vm station, only 200 metres from the gate of *Strand Camping*. Strand Camping is recommended for its excellent location on a good bathing beach, ample shade and casual atmosphere. A large grocery store and snack bars are nearby. Strand is also open longer than the other Siofok campgrounds (mid-May to September) and there's usually lots of space. Also near Batatonszabadi vm station is a Siotour office offering private rooms, currency exchange, etc. Bus No 2 runs the four km from Strand to Siofok bus station or you can walk along the lakeshore most of the way. The only drawback are the washing facilities which are cramped for such a big place.

Places to Eat

Two fairly expensive restaurants are *Fogas Etterem*, Fo utca 184 opposite the train station, and *Matroz Etterem*, Martirok utca 13 beside the lake boat terminal. A better bet is a whole grilled chicken *(grill csirke)* from the snack bar on the corner diagonally opposite the museum, eaten picnic style on a riverside bench.

Entertainment

On summer Wednesday evenings at 9 pm folklore programmes are presented at the *open air theatre* in Dimitrov Park or in the *Cultural Centre*, Fo ter 2. Ask Ibusz, Fo utca 174, about this.

Getting There & Away

Trains between Budapest's Deli Station and Nagykanizsa call at Siofok every couple of hours. For Veszprem change at Lepseny, for Keszthely change at Balaton-szentgyorgy. Some trains go straight through to Keszthely from Siofok. A branch line runs south from Siofok to Kaposvar. There are Mahart ferries to Balatonfured and Tihany from mid-April to mid-October. From June to mid-September the ferries continue as far as Badacsony.

BALATONFURED

Balatonfured, an elegant spa with the easy-going grace Siofok lacks, is called the 'Mecca of cardiacs' for its curative waters. Situated on the north shore of Balaton Lake between Tihany and Veszprem, it's been *the* fashionable bathing resort on the lake since 1772 when a medicinal bathing establishment was set up here. During the 19th century it became an important meeting place for Hungarian intellectuals. The town still bears an aristocratic air, although the formerly private sanatoriums are now public and the clientele more likely to be trade unionists than affluent bourgeois.

Orientation

The bus and train stations are adjacent a km north-west of the spa centre. Some buses stop near the ferry landing below the Round Church on Jokai Mor utca. From in front of the church Blaha Lujza utca runs directly into Gyogy ter where our visit begins.

Information

Balatontourist Nord is at Blaha Lujza utca 5.

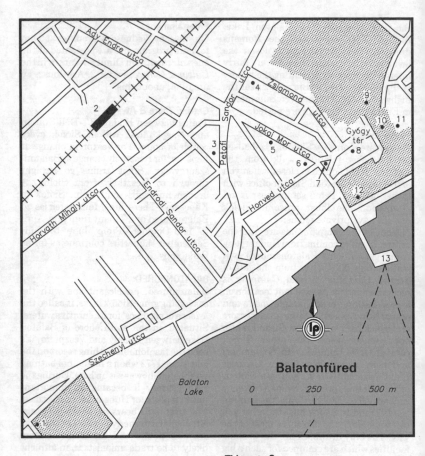

Balatonfüred

Balaton Lake

0   250   500 m

1	FICC Rally Camping
2	Railway Station
3	Ibusz
4	Aranycsillag Hotel
5	Cooptourist
6	Jokai Museum
7	Round Church
8	Balatontourist
9	Balaton Pantheon
10	Kossuth Well
11	State Hospital
12	Tagore Statue
13	Ferry Wharf

Things to See

The heart of the spa is Gyogy ter with its **well house** where budget travellers may fill their canteens with radioactive mineral water. The park along the nearby lakeshore is worth a promenade. Near the wharf notice the statue of the Hindi poet **Rabindranath Tagore** before a lime tree he planted in 1926 to mark his recovery from illness here. The poem Tagore wrote for the occasion is reproduced on a plaque in English. Inland a little, diagonally opposite the **Round Church** (1841), is the house/museum of novelist Mor Jokai.

Places to Stay

MAV Tours has an office in the railway station which may be able to find you a private room. Other offices with private rooms are Ibusz, Petofi utca 4/a, Cooptourist, Jokai Mor utca 23, and Balatontourist Nord, Blaha Lujza utca 5. The *Aranycsillag Hotel*, Zsigmond utca 1, is 350 Ft single, 470 Ft double including breakfast.

There's only one campground at Balatonfured but it has a capacity for 3000 persons. The *FICC Rally Camping* (open mid-April to mid-October) is beside *Hotel Marina* on the lake three km from the railway station.

Getting There & Away

Balatonfured is two hours from Budapest (Deli) by express train, three hours by local train. The line continues to Tapolca via Badacsony. Bus service to Tihany and Veszprem is frequent. There are Mahart ferries to Siofok from mid-April to mid-October.

TIHANY

The Tihany Peninsula almost bisects the north end of Balaton Lake. The consensus is that this is the most beautiful place around and in summer Tihany gets more than its share of tourists. After a visit to the famous abbey you can easily leave the hordes behind on a hike past the hilly peninsula's inner lake, Belso Lake, with its rare flora, fish and birdlife. Kulso Lake has almost dried up.

Orientation

Tihany Abbey sits on a ridge above the Tihany ferry landing on the east side of the peninsula's high plateau. Tihany village is perched above Belso Lake just below the abbey. Lake boats also call at Tihanyi-rev, the car ferry landing at the south end of the peninsula.

Things to See

The magnificent twin-towered **abbey church** (1719) is outstanding for its Baroque altars, pulpit and organ, but pride of place goes to the 11th century crypt at the front of the church. Here is found the tomb (1060) of the abbey's founder, King Andrew I. The earliest written relic of the Hungarian language (dating from 1085) was found here. The monastery beside the church has been converted into the **Tihany Museum** (open 9 am to 5 pm year round, closed Monday). There's an extensive lapidarium in the museum basement. In summer there are organ concerts in the church.

A promenade, Pisky setany, runs along the ridge north from the church to the Echo Restaurant passing a cluster of folk houses, now an open air museum (closed November to April and every Monday). From the restaurant you can descend to the harbour or continue up on green and red-marked hiking trails which pass this way. The red trail crosses the peninsula between the two lakes to **Csucs Hill**, from where there are fine views (two hours).

Places to Stay & Eat

The Balatontourist Nord office below Rege Presso arranges private rooms in summer only. There's a campground at Tihanyi-rev. The Rege Presso beside the abbey offers a marvellous panoramic view from its terrace but to eat you'll do better at Kecskekorom Csarda, Kossuth Lajos utca 19 a few hundred metres north-west of the main road.

Getting There & Away

Buses cover the 11 km from Balatonfured Railway Station regularly. The bus stops at both ferry landings before climbing to Tihany village just below the abbey. The Balaton Lake ferries call at Tihany from mid-April to mid-October. Catch them at the harbour below the abbey or at Tihanyi-rev, the car ferry terminal at the south end of the peninsula. From April to November the car ferry crosses the narrow neck of Lake Balaton from Tihanyi-rev to Szantodrev frequently.

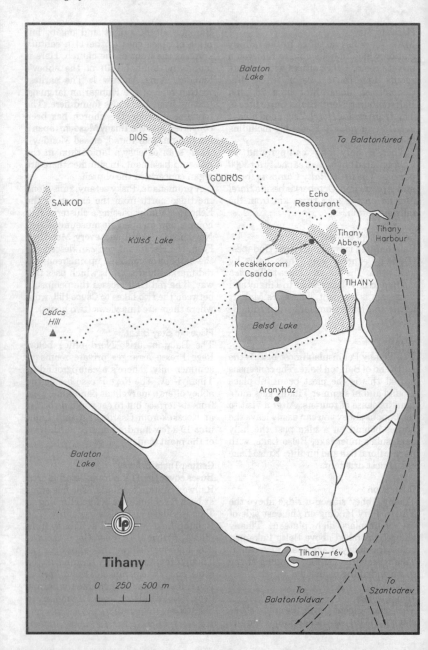

Balaton Lake

To Balatonfured

DIÓS

GÖDRÖS

Echo Restaurant

SAJKOD

Külső Lake

Tihany Abbey

Tihany Harbour

Kecskekorom Csarda

TIHANY

Csúcs Hill

Belső Lake

Aranyház

Balaton Lake

Tihany-rév

Tihany

0   250   500 m

To Balatonfoldvar

To Szantodrev

VESZPREM

Veszprem in the Bakony Hills 20 km north of Balaton Lake is built on five hills. The old town stands on an abrupt headland overlooking a gorge. At the end of the 10th century Prince Geza founded the first Hungarian bishopric here. A century later Veszprem belonged to Hungary's queen. Much was destroyed during fighting between Turks, Hungarians and Hapsburgs and in 1702 the castle was demolished. In the 18th century much had to be rebuilt by the feudal land-owning bishops. Off the beaten track, the picturesque buildings and scenery make Veszprem worth a visit anytime.

Orientation

The train station is on the far north side of town so take a city bus to the bus station (which also has a left luggage service), conveniently near Kossuth Lajos utca. Travel agencies, supermarkets and department stores are all on Kossuth Lajos utca, a modern shopping mall behind flashy Hotel Veszprem. From the crossroads at the lower end of this mall turn left to reach the Bakony Museum, right for Voros Hadsereg ter at the entrance to historic Veszprem.

Information

Balatontourist Nord (Idegenforgalmi Hivatal) is on the mall behind Hotel Veszprem

Things to See

The Baroque **Fire Tower** (1815) rises above Voros Hadsereg ter at the south end of the old town. Only one street, Tolbuhin utca, runs the length of this easily defendable hill. Medieval Veszprem was ravaged by the Turks and Hapsburgs, so many of the imposing palaces seen today are Baroque. As you go up Tolbuhin utca you'll pass under the **city gate**, reconstructed in 1936 and containing a small museum. There are other museums at Nos 3, 14, 29 and 35 Tolbuhin utca but all are closed from November to April.

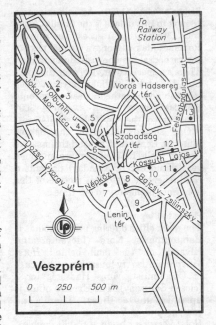

Veszprém

0   250   500 m

1	Benedek Hill
2	Cathedral
3	Bishop's Palace
4	Fire Tower
5	City Gate Museum
6	Cooptourist
7	Petofi Theatre
8	County Hall
9	Bakony Museum
10	Ibusz/Express
11	Hotel Veszprem
12	Balatontourist Nord
13	Bus Station

Veszprem **cathedral** dominates a square near the end of Tolbuhin utca behind the Baroque Holy Trinity Column (1750). The cathedral was completely rebuilt in neo-Romanesque style in 1910 but the original Gothic crypt remains. The other massive building on the square is the

Bishop's Palace (1776). At Tolbuhin utca 18 next to this palace is the **Gizella Chapel** with 13th century frescoes. The ruins of Romanesque St George's Chapel next to the cathedral may be visited in summer. There's a spectacular view over the gorge from the end of Tolbuhin utca. A steep lane behind the cathedral leads down onto **Benedek Hill** where a sweeping 360° panorama of the Sed Valley awaits you.

One should also visit the **Bakony Museum**, Lenin ter 5 beyond the massive County Hall (1887). The museum (open year round except Monday) presents a comprehensive historical picture of this area from prehistory to our times.

Places to Stay

The main office offering private rooms is Balatontourist Nord (Idegenforgalmi Hivatal) on the mall behind *Hotel Veszprem*. Also try Ibusz, Kossuth utca 6, or Cooptourist, Voros Hadsereg ter 2 (closed Saturday). The Express office is upstairs above Ibusz. There's no campground at Veszprem and rooms at *Hotel Veszprem* begin at 650 Ft double.

Getting There & Away

Veszprem is on the railway line between Budapest (Deli) and Szombathely. There are also direct trains from Gyor via Pannonhalma. Balatonfured and Veszprem are connected by frequent bus service (40 minutes). Other useful buses run to Pecs (via Siofok) and Keszthely.

BADACSONY

Badacsony between Balatonfured and Keszthely lies in a picturesque region of basalt peaks among some of the best hiking country in Hungary. Vineyards hug the sides of Badacsony's extinct volcanic cone (elevation 437 metres). The benign climate and rich volcanic soils make this an idea winemaking area and in summer Austrian devotees of Bacchus congregate. If you like your wine Badacsony is for you.

Information

Balatontourist Nord is at Park utca 10 behind the railway station.

Things to See

An **art gallery** (open daily from May to October except Monday) near the railway station displays the works of local painter Jozsef Egry (1883-1951), who lived here from 1918 onwards. Egry skilfully captured the beauty of Balaton at different times of day.

The beaten tourist track at Badacsony extends up through the vineyards to the **Boraszati Wine Museum** (open mid-May to mid-October, closed Monday). You'll pass some very touristy wine restaurants on the way, including one labelled 'Bormuzeum.' The museum isn't much (captions in Hungarian, German and Russian only) but the views of mountain and lake are good.

The flat-topped forested massif overlooking the lake is just the place to escape the tipsy herd. If you'd like a running start on climbing catch the 'Badacsony Taxi,' a topless jeep which departs Badacsony post office from 9 am to 7 pm mid-May to mid-September (16 Ft a seat). The jeep will drop you at the Kisfaludy House Restaurant where a large map outlining the well marked trails is posted by the parking lot. There are numerous outlooks and a tall wooden tower offering splendid views to the hiker.

Places to Stay

For private rooms look for the Balatontourist Nord office on Park utca back behind the railway station. The closest campground (mid-June to mid-September) is by the lake just under a km west of the station. It's casual but bring mosquito repellent. Hotplates are available for cooking.

The *Egry Jozsef Fogado*, Kisfaludy utca 2 in nearby Badacsonytomaj village, has rooms from 300 Ft (open mid-April to mid-October).

Places to Eat

There's a cheap self-service restaurant, the *Onkiszolgalo Etterem*, to the right as you leave the wharf. The 'Csemege' grocery store is to the left (open weekends in summer). In summer many shoddy snack bars near the railway station dispense wine to rowdy Austrians. Second-class sausage and fish are available at first class prices.

A better place to eat is the *Hableany Etterem*, a modern restaurant facing the park behind the railway station. If you don't mind Austrian-level prices, the *Halaszkert Etterem* (Fisherman's Hut) nearby is Badacsony's best. A good local dry white wine is Badacsony Keknyelu.

Getting There & Away

The ferry wharf is near Badacsony vm Station on the railway line from Budapest (Deli) to Tapolca. A boat ride to Badacsony from Siofok or Balatonfured is the best way to get the feel of Balaton Lake (operating June to mid-September). There are also ferries to Keszthely at this time.

If you want to swim in the lake take a ferry across to Fonyod. Ferries between Badacsony and Fonyod are fairly frequent (mid-April to mid-October). In Fonyod you can connect for southern Hungary by taking a train direct to Kaposvar, then a bus on to Pecs from there.

KESZTHELY

Keszthely at the west end of Balaton Lake is a fairly large and not especially attractive town you'll pass through on your way from western to southern Hungary. The town does have a few attractions, good facilities and boat service on the lake from June to mid-September. It might be worth a night.

Orientation

The bus and train stations are fairly close to the ferry terminal on the lake. From the stations follow Martirok utja up the hill, then right on Kossuth Lajos utca into town. Helikon Palace is at the north end of this street.

Information

Zalatour is at Kossuth Lajos utca 32.

Things to See

Keszthely's finest sight is **Helikon Palace**, the former residence of the land-owning Festetics family, built in 1745 and greatly extended in 1887. The palace, now a museum, is open from 9 am to 5 pm year round except Mondays. A highlight of the 101-room palace is the library, but the entire complex is richly appointed and well worth seeing.

In 1797 Count Festetics founded Europe's first agricultural institute here and even today Keszthely is noted for its large Agricultural University. Part of the original school, the **Georgikon Manor**, Bercsenyi Miklos utca 67, is now a museum (open April to October, closed Monday) with antique farming equipment, etc. It's only a couple of blocks from the palace. The **Balaton Museum** (closed Monday) is on Kossuth Lajos utca toward the railway station.

Places to Stay

The 18th century *Amazon Hotel*, Georgikon utca 1 near the palace, is 435 Ft single, 500 Ft double, no breakfast. From April to mid-October the *Helikon Turistaszallo*, Honved utca 22, offers dorm beds.

As usual, a private room is your best bet. Try Ibusz, Szechenyi utca 1-3, Zalatour, Kossuth Lajos utca 32, or Volantourist, Kossuth Lajos utca 43, all near one another in the centre. Cooptourist, Tanacskoztarsasag utja 26, is closer to the train station. In summer Express, Kossuth Lajos utca 22, knows about private rooms and youth hostels.

There are several campgrounds near the lake, all with bungalows. As you leave the train station head south across the tracks and you'll soon reach *Camping II* which is hemmed between the tracks and a road. Unless you're completely beat

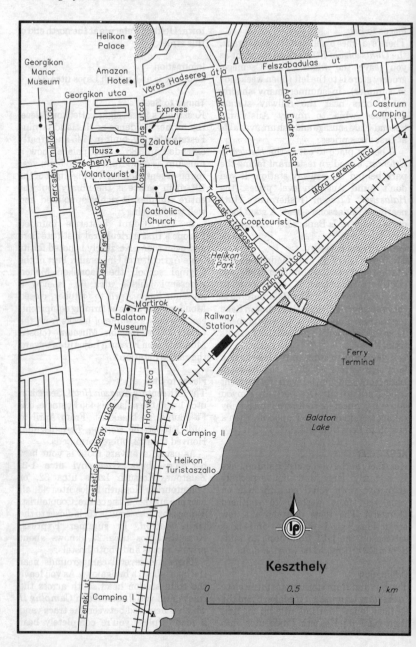

Keszthely

0   0.5   1 km

avoid staying here and keep walking south along the lakeshore another 10 minutes to *Camping I* (open May to September) which is in a more attractive location. Better facilities are offered by *Castrum Camping*, Mora Ferenc utca 48 (open April to October), a 15-minute walk north of the train station.

Getting There & Away
Keszthely is on a branch line between Tapolca and Balaton-szentgyorgy, so railway service is poor. Occasional fast trains arrive from Budapest (Deli) via Siofok. For Pecs take a train to Kaposvar, then change to a bus. A bus station with services to most of western Hungary adjoins the railway station. Some buses for southern Hungary leave from opposite the Catholic church in the centre of town, however, so check carefully. Volantourist, Kossuth Lajos utca 43, has information on buses. There are ferries to Badacsony from June to mid-September. In July and August these boats continue on to Siofok.

HEVIZ
In a country with 1500 thermal baths there just had to be a real thermal *lake*. Gyogy Lake, the largest warm-water lake in Europe, averages 30°C at the surface and red Indian water lilies blossom in summer. Eighty million litres of thermal water gush daily from a depth of one km at a rate of 1000 litres (one cubic metre) a second, flushing the lake completely every two days. Radioactive mud from the lake bed is effective in the treatment of locomotor disorders. In winter the steaming waters, which never fall below 24°C, seem almost surreal. Wooden catwalks have been built over the lake allowing you to swim in comfort. In winter thermal baths adjacent to the lake provide service from 7 am to 4 pm daily. There's a beach on the north shore.

Only six km west of Keszthely, Heviz is easy commuting distance by bus or get a private room right at the spa. Cooptourist

and Zalatour, both on Rakoczi utca, or Volantourist, Somogyi Bela utca 2/b, can help you find one. All these offices are near the bus station, as is the lake itself. There are *zimmer frei* signs near the Piroska Restaurant, Kossuth Lajos utca 10.

Southern Hungary

Southern Transdanubia close to Yugoslavia is characterised by rolling hills and an almost Mediterranean climate. Near Mohacs on the Danube in 1526 the Hungarian armies under King Louis II were routed by a greatly superior Ottoman force. As a result the gracious southern city Pecs still bears the imprint of a century and a half of Turkish rule. The good facilities in Pecs make it a perfect base for day trips to the castles of Szigetvar and Siklos, the spas at Harkany and Sikonda, and hiking trails through the Meksek Hills. It's also an excellent gateway to Osijek, Yugoslavia.

KAPOSVAR
Kaposvar, a large town between Balaton Lake and Pecs, probably doesn't warrant a visit on its own but is a convenient stepping stone between western and southern Hungary, or a place to pick up the train to Zagreb, Yugoslavia.

Orientation
The bus and railway stations are a block apart on the south side of downtown Kaposvar. Majus 1 utca is a pleasant pedestrian mall with most of the museums, hotels and tourist offices.

Information
Siotour is at Majus 1 utca 1.

Things to See
There are two museums: an **art gallery** at the corner of Iranyi Daniel utca and Majus 1 utca, and the **Rippl-Ronai Museum**, Majus 1 utca 10, in the neo-

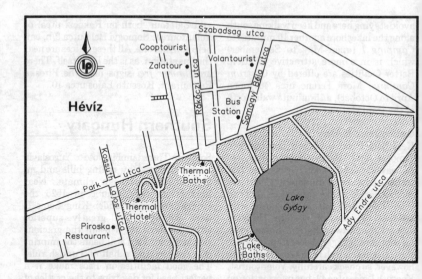

Classical **County Hall** (1828). Both are open from 10 am to 6 pm daily except Monday. The **Kaposvari Galeria**, Rakoczi ter 4 (closed Monday), is near the train station.

Places to Stay

There's no campground at Kaposvar. The cheapest hotel is the *Csonkonai Fogado*, Majus 1 utca 1 (from 270 Ft single, 420 Ft double). The Siotour office, also at Majus 1 utca 1, can arrange private rooms, or try Ibusz, Tanacshaz utca 3.

Places to Eat

The *Bisztro*, Rakoczi ter 2 near the train station, is a cheap cafeteria. An inexpensive restaurant offering large portions is *Ipar Vendeglo*, Tanacshaz utca 8 (closed Sunday).

Entertainment

Kaposvar's best theatre is the *Csiky Gergely Szinhaz* in the centre of Rakoczi ter opposite the railway station. The Szinhaz Jegypenztar, Majus 1 utca 8, has tickets for theatres and all cultural events.

Getting There & Away

Bus service between Kaposvar and Pecs is fairly frequent. There are local trains north to Fonyod and Siofok, and occasional buses to Keszthely. The daily afternoon Maestral Express train from Budapest (Keleti) to Zagreb calls at Kaposvar. Reservations are not required but buy your ticket in advance at MAV Tours, Csokonai vm utca (through the passage from Majus 1 utca 21), or Ibusz, Tanacshaz utca 3. You can also get to Yugoslavia by taking a local train to Gyekenyes, the border station, where you change for Koprivnica.

PECS

Pecs, a large historical city in southern Hungary between the Danube and Drava rivers, is the seat of Baranya County. The fine position on the southern slopes of the Mecsek Hills gives Pecs a relatively mild climate and the red tile roofs of the houses accentuate the Mediterranean flavour. Zsolnay porcelain and Pannonia champagne are made here.

For 400 years Sopianae (Pecs) was capital of the Roman province of

Pannonia. Early Christianity flourished here in the 4th century. In the 11th century Stephen I, Hungary's first king, made Pecs a bishopric. The first Hungarian university was founded here in 1367 and the city's humanistic traditions climaxed with the Latin poet Janus Pannonius. City walls were erected after the Mongol invasion of 1241 but in 1543 a century and a half of Turkish rule began. The Turks left their greatest monuments in Pecs and these, combined with imposing churches and synagogue, over a dozen museums, possibilities for hiking through the Mecsek Hills, and varied excursions, make Pecs the perfect place to spend a couple of days. If you only have time for two Hungarian cities make them Budapest and Pecs.

Orientation

The bus and train stations are about three blocks apart on the south side of downtown. Use the maps provided here to find your way north to Szechenyi ter where 12 streets meet. Numerous city buses also run up this way (ask). The left luggage office in the main railway station is in an obscure building at the far west end of track one. Left luggage at the bus station closes at 7 pm; at the railway station it's open around the clock.

Information

Mecsek Tourist is at Szechenyi ter 9. The main post office is at Jokai Mor utca 10. International telephone calls are made from there.

Things to See

Szechenyi ter is the bustling heart of Pecs, dominated on the north by the former **Mosque of Gazi Kassim Pasha**, the largest Turkish building in Hungary. Now a Catholic church, Islamic elements such as the mihrab, a prayer niche on the south-east side, are easy to distinguish. Behind the mosque/church is the **Archaeological Museum** with materials from prehistory up to the Magyar conquest. Informative

summaries in English and German are posted in each room.

From this museum follow Janus Pannonius utca a block west to Dom ter, a virtual treasure-trove of monuments. Let yourself be drawn up through the park to the tremendous four-towered **cathedral**. The oldest part of the building is the 11th century crypt, but the entire complex was heavily rebuilt in neo-Romanesque style in 1881. Behind the **Bishop's Palace** (1770) beside the cathedral is a 15th century barbican remaining from the old city walls.

Kaptalan utca which climbs east from the top of Dom ter is lined with museums. The most famous is the **Vasarely Museum**, Kaptalan utca 3, with 150 original examples of op-art. Across the street is the **Zsolnay Porcelain Museum**, Kaptalan utca 2, mostly Art Nouveau (captions in German). A room downstairs in the same building contains sculptures by Amerigo Tot.

Return to Dom ter and visit the **Csontvary Museum**, Janus Pannonius utca 11, dedicated to the early 20th century painter-philosopher Tivadar Csontvary. His painting of the ruins of Baalbek, Lebanon (1905), is a masterpiece. On the corner opposite this museum is a good little wine cellar in front of the men's WC – it's probably time for a shot.

In the centre of the southern portion of Dom ter is an excavated 4th century Roman Christian **mausoleum** with striking frescoes of Adam and Eve, and Daniel in the lion's den, certainly a remarkable sight unique in central Europe. Nearby at Geisler Eta utca 14 are the ruins of a 4th century Early Christian chapel. It's only open in summer but you can enter the courtyard and peek in through the windows anytime.

Follow your map south-west a few blocks from Dom ter to the 16th century **Jakovali Haszan Djami**, Rakoczi ut 2 (closed Wednesday), the best preserved Turkish monument in Hungary. Also known as the 'Little Mosque,' the

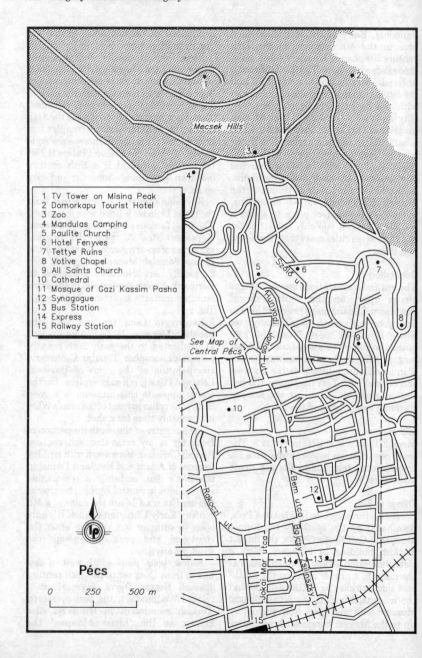

1 TV Tower on Misina Peak
2 Domorkapu Tourist Hotel
3 Zoo
4 Mandulas Camping
5 Paulite Church
6 Hotel Fenyves
7 Tettye Ruins
8 Votive Chapel
9 All Saints Church
10 Cathedral
11 Mosque of Gazi Kassim Pasha
12 Synagogue
13 Bus Station
14 Express
15 Railway Station

Mecsek Hills

See Map of
Central Pécs

Pécs

0   250   500 m

building and minaret are perfectly preserved, now part of a museum of Turkish culture.

After seeing the Little Mosque follow Pec's most enjoyable pedestrian malls, Sallai utca and Kossuth Lajos utca, due east across the city. You'll pass three beautiful old churches and the ornate National Theatre (check for performances). Just beyond **St Stephen** (1741), the third church, turn right to Felsomalom utca 9 where you'll find an excellent **Historical Museum** which will sum up all you've seen. Visitors to the synagogue (1869) on Kossuth ter are offered an informative text on the Jewish faith in their own language (open May to October, closed Saturday). All of Pecs' museums except the Little Mosque and synagogue are closed on Mondays.

Head for the Hills

Every visitor should take a trip up into the **Mecsek Hills.** Bus No 35 from stand 2 in front of the railway station climbs to the 194-metre-high TV tower on Misina Peak (534 metres). You can also pick up bus No 35 from the Kossuth statue on Kossuth ter in the centre of town. There's a restaurant below the viewing balcony high up in the **TV tower** (open Tuesday to Sunday 11 am to 6 pm) offering panoramic views. If you order something there check the prices on the menu beforehand or you could end up paying double. The observation platform (20 Ft) offers an unobstructed view (no glass). Bus No 35 also passes Pecs' delightful **zoo** (open daily year round 9 am to 6 pm).

There are numerous, well-marked hiking trails fanning out from the TV Tower. Pick up the 1:40,000 *A Mecsek* topographical map which shows them all. Armed with this map you could also take a bus from Pecs Bus Station to Orfu or Abaliget and hike back over the hills.

Places to Stay

Mecsek Tourist and Ibusz, the two offices arranging private rooms, face one another at the south end of Szechenyi ter. The cheapest hotel in town is the *Minaret Hotel*, Sallai utca 35 (150 Ft per person), in the old Franciscan monastery. To get in it may be necessary to show a youth hostel card and you may have to register at either *Hotel Pannonia* around the corner or at Express, Bajcsy-Zsilinszky utca 6 near the bus station, but it's often full.

The other budget places to stay are all up in the Mecsek Hills. The *Domorkapu Tourist Hostel* (150 Ft per person, tel 72/15-987) is below Vidam Park (bus No 35) but it's closed in winter. The *Hotel Fenyves*, Szolo utca 65 (240 Ft double, tel 72/15-996), has a great view of the city. Take bus No 34 or 35 to Szot Udulo Szallo, then walk down to the hotel.

Mandulas Camping (open mid-April to mid-October) near the zoo has bungalows (500 Ft double) as well as tent space. Take bus No 34 right to the door or bus No 35 to the zoo then walk five minutes.

Places to Eat

An inexpensive place to try real Hungarian country food is the *Tej Bistro*, Jokai ter 11, a self-service, stand-up operation. If you'd rather sit down and spend more there's the *Elephant Sorozo* across the square. Good hotel restaurants are to be found in the *Minaret Hotel*, Sallai utca 35, and the *Nador Hotel*, Szechenyi ter 15, a gourmet's delight. Both these have cheap *menu* meals at lunchtime.

Entertainment

Pecs has famous opera and ballet companies. If you're told the *National Theatre* on Kossuth Lajos utca is sold out try for a cancellation at the box office an hour before showtime. Concert tickets are easier to come by at the Filharmonia office beside the National Theatre. In summer there are occasional organ concerts in the cathedral.

Getting There & Away

Express trains run regularly to Budapest

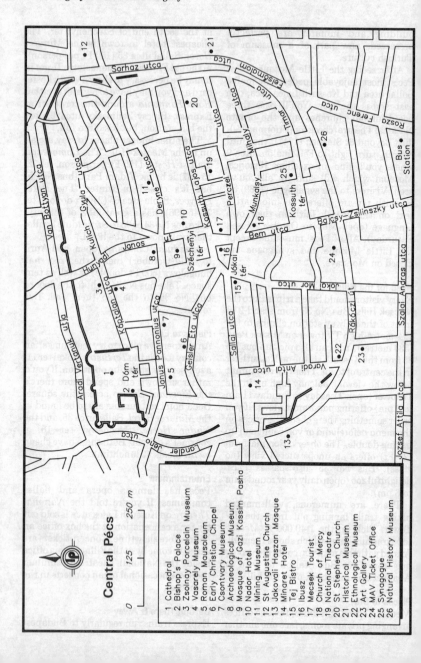

Central Pécs

0   125   250 m

1   Cathedral
2   Bishop's Palace
3   Zsolnay Porcelain Museum
4   Vasarely Museum
5   Roman Mausoleum
6   Early Christian Chapel
7   Csontvary Museum
8   Archaeological Museum
9   Mosque of Gazi Kassim Pasha
10 Nador Hotel
11 Mining Museum
12 St Augustine Church
13 Jakovali Haszan Mosque
14 Minaret Hotel
15 Tej Bistro
16 Ibusz
17 Mecsek Tourist
18 Church of Mercy
19 National Theatre
20 St Stephen Church
21 Historical Museum
22 Ethnological Museum
23 Art Gallery
24 MAV Ticket Office
25 Synagogue
26 Natural History Museum

(Deli) and one early morning express goes to Szombathely (via Gyekenyes). Some trains to Budapest carry compulsory seat reservations. There are two local trains a day between Pecs and Osijek, Yugoslavia. The office in the train station selling tickets for this service is only open weekdays 8 am to 6 pm, Saturdays 8 am to 12 noon (US$1.50 in hard currency plus 66 Ft one way). Train reservations and tickets are more easily available at MAV, Rakoczi ut 39/c. There are also buses to Osijek. To go to Szeged, Siklos, Kaposvar or Veszprem take a bus.

SZIGETVAR

Szigetvar, 33 km west of Pecs and easily accessible by train, is famous in Hungarian history as the place where 2482 Hungarians held off 207,000 Turks for 33 days in 1566. When the fort was about to fall the remaining defenders under Miklos Zrinyi sallied out and met their end in bloody hand-to-hand combat. The **fortress** (1420) with its four corner bastions is still there and contains a museum which focuses on the battle (open year round 10 am to 3 pm, closed Monday).

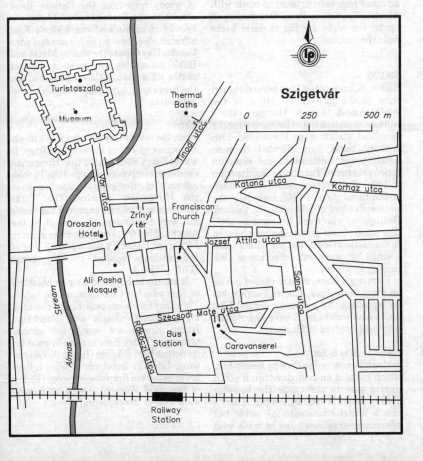

Included in the museum is a mosque built soon after the fall of Szigetvar. Of the minaret only the base remains. A second mosque, the **Ali Pasa Mosque** (1589), now a church, is in the centre of town.

Places to Stay

A scowling lion on Zrinyi ter faces the modern *Oroszlan Hotel*, where rooms are 430 Ft single, 780 Ft double with breakfast. Mecsek Tourist in the hotel can find you a room in a private home. From April to mid-November there's a *turistaszallo* (dormitory) in the fort but advance reservations must be made with Mecsek Tourist in Pecs. One reason to spend the night are the thermal baths near the fortress.

SIKLOS

Siklos, 32 km south of Pecs beyond the red wine producing Villany Hills, is the southernmost town in Hungary. On a hilltop overlooking the surrounding farmland stands a well-preserved 15th century **castle**, now divided between hotel, hostel, restaurant and museum (open year round Tuesday to Sunday 9 am to 4 pm). Part of the museum is dedicated to the Revolution of 1848, especially the progressive lord of Siklos Castle, Casimir Batthyany, who freed his serfs in 1847. The tomb of this gentleman may be seen in the castle's Gothic chapel. There's also a small but excellent collection of 19th century costumes.

Harkany village, six km east of Siklos on the road to Pecs, has well-known **hot spring baths** and a good campground. The medicinal waters here have the richest sulphuric content in Hungary.

Places to Stay & Eat

Siklos is connected to Pecs by hourly bus, which make it an easy day trip. If you'd like to stay in the castle the two-star *Tenkes Hotel* is 1000 Ft double. There's also a hostel *(turistaszallo)* inside but advance reservations must be made with

Mecsek Tourist in Pecs (45 Ft per person). The restaurant in the castle casemates is often reserved for groups, in which case repair to the *Kozponti Etterem*, Kossuth ter 5, in town below the castle.

Northern Hungary

Northern Hungary is the most mountainous part of the country. The southern ranges of the Carpathians stretch east along the Czech border in a 1000-metre-high chain of woody hills from the Danube Bend almost to the Soviet border. Miskolc is heavily industrialised but historic Eger offers an ideal base for sightseers and wine tasters. Day trips to the nearby Matra and Bukk mountains are possible. Farther north, right beside Czechoslovakia, are the caves near Aggtelek, Hungary's most extensive.

EGER

Eger, the seat of Heves County, is a lovely Baroque city full of historic buildings. It was at Eger Castle in 1552 that Hungarian defenders temporarily stopped the Turkish advance into Europe and helped preserve the Hungarian identity. The Turks returned in 1596 and captured the castle but were themselves thrown out by the Austrians in 1687. Later Eger was a centre for Ferenc Rakoczi's unsuccessful War of Independence against the Hapsburgs (1703-1711).

It was the bishops and later archbishops of Eger who built the town we see today. The many handsome palaces and churches along Kossuth Lajos and Szechenyi Istvan streets are worthy of special attention. Today Eger is more famous for its potent Egri Bikaver (Bull's Blood) red wine. Literally hundreds of wine cellars are to be seen in Szepasszonyvolgy (Valley of Beautiful Women), just a 20-minute walk west of the cathedral.

Information

Eger Tourist is at Bajcsy-Zsilinszky utca 9.

Things to See

The first thing you see as you come into Eger from the bus or train stations is the huge neo-Classical **cathedral** (1836) on Szabadsag ter. Opposite this is the Rococo college (1785). Buy a ticket just inside the college door to see the frescoed library in room 48 on the 1st floor and the **Museum of Astronomy** (Tuesday to Sunday 10 am to 1 pm) on the 6th floor of the tower at the back of the building. On the 9th floor of the tower is the periscope (same ticket), a unique apparatus which allows you to spy on all of Eger unobserved. Along Kossuth Lajos utca is the Baroque **County Hall** at number 9 with elegant wrought iron gates and an old prison in the courtyard.

At the east end of Kossuth Lajos utca across Dozsa Gyorgy ter is **Eger Castle**, erected after the Mongol invasion of 1242. Inside this great fortress are the foundations of St John's Cathedral, destroyed by the Turks. Models and drawings in the castle's **Dobo Istvan Museum** (closed Monday) give a clear idea of how the cathedral once looked. This museum, housed in the Gothic Bishop's Palace (1470), is named for the hero who led the resistance to the Turks in 1552. Below the castle are underground chambers hewn from solid rock which may be toured with a guide (150 Ft).

The Baroque **Minorite Church** (1771) on Dobo Istvan ter was designed by the famous Prague architect Dientzenhofer. In front of the church is a statue of Dobo Istvan and reliefs showing a battle against the Turks. In the shadow of the castle in the old town is a 35-metre-high **Turkish minaret**, the northernmost Turkish monument in Europe.

After so much history clear your head in **Nepkert Park**, once the private reserve of bishops. The **thermal baths** beside the park date from the Turkish period (open 12 noon to 6 pm, men on Tuesday, Thursday and Saturday, women on Monday, Wednesday and Friday). There are also open air baths here – enjoy them!

Places to Stay

On summer weekends accommodation is tight so arrive early. For private rooms visit Eger Tourist, Bajcsy-Zsilinszky utca 9 in the centre of town (closed Sunday). Ibusz, in the alley behind Eger Tourist, also has private rooms. If these offices are closed the *Tourist Motel*, Mekcsey Istvan utca 2, may be able to find a private room for you. Rooms at the motel are 270 Ft double.

Express, Szechenyi Istvan utca 28 (open weekdays 8 am to 3.30 pm), has information about summer youth hostels. *Buttler-Haz*, Kossuth Lajos utca 26, is a real youth hostel with beds in eight-bed dormitories for 62 Ft (no curfew, no rules). Ask Eger Tourist or Express to refer you. The place is full of smoking, snoring Poles who come and go at all hours of the night but are very friendly. The modern *Hotel Unicornis* across the street is only 520 Ft double should Buttler-Haz prove more than you can handle.

The centrally-located *Mini Motel*, Lenin ut 11, is 270 Ft double. The campground is at Rakoczni utca 79, several km north of Eger (bus No 10, 11, 12, or 13 from the train station). Open May to September, there are bungalows (280 Ft double).

Places to Eat

The best place to eat is the *Kazamata Etterem* on Szabadsag ter below the cathedral steps. You can get a cheap stand-up lunch at *Tej Milk Bar*, SzechenyiIstvan utca 2. There are many wine restaurants among the wine cellars of Szepasszonyvolgy. The best is *Kodmon Csarda*. To get there locate the Gardonyi Theatre on Lenin ter near the cathedral, then walk west on Telekesy Istvan and Bacso Bela streets. When you come to a fork go left down the incline.

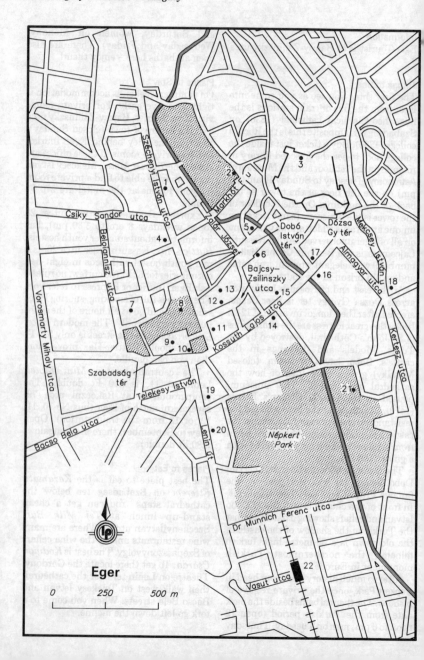

Eger

0   250   500 m

1	Express
2	Turkish Minaret
3	Dobo Istvan Museum (castle)
4	Former Jesuit Church
5	Cooptourist
6	Minorite Church
7	Bus Station
8	Archbishop's Palace
9	Cathedral
10	Kazamata Etterem
11	College
12	Eger Tourist
13	Ibusz
14	Franciscan Church
15	County Hall
16	Buttler-Haz
17	Hotel Unicornis
18	Tourist Motel
19	Gardonyi Theatre
20	Mini Hotel
21	Thermal Baths
22	Railway Station

Getting There & Away

Eger is connected to Budapest's Keleti station by express train. It's sometimes quicker to take a local train to Fuzesabony, where you can connect with an express to Budapest or a local train to Debrecen. There are also buses to Budapest from Eger's bus station.

AGGTELEK

Hungary's largest and most famous scenic caves are the **Baradla Caves** due north of Eger/Miskolc on the Czech border. The caves stretch 22 km underground, 18 km of which is in Hungary and seven km in Czechoslovakia. The easiest way to get there is to take the morning Volan bus from Eger to Aggtelek (three hours). The same bus returns to Eger in the afternoon, allowing plenty of time for a short tour of the caves.

Alternatively spend the night at Aggtelek and take one of the longer tours. The short tour (one hour) includes recorded music in the 'concert hall.' At the underground lake boat trips are offered when the water is high enough. Beautiful

karst formations are seen. There's another entrance to Baradla at Josvafo, six km east of Aggtelek, and different short tours are offered there. Two-hour trips begin at Vorosto between Aggtelek and Josvafo, and in summer there's even an epic six-hour cave tour during which visitors must carry lamps. All tours are led by guides who only set out when five tickets have been sold (you may have to buy the extra tickets when things are slow). Next to the Aggtelek entrance to Baradla is a small museum on the flora and fauna of the area, featuring the skeleton of a prehistoric bear found in the cave.

Places to Stay

The bus from Eger stops in front of the modern *Cseppko Hotel* at Aggtelek, where rooms are 370 Ft double including breakfast. The hotel has a good restaurant. There's also a campground with bungalows at the Aggtelek entrance (open mid-April to September) and a youth hostel above the museum (40 Ft per person in four-bunk dorms).

Eastern Hungary

Eastern Hungary, the Great Plain, is a wide expanse of level *puszta* drained by the Tisza River. Foreign visitors to the region are introduced to the lore of the Hungarian cowboy and his long-horned, grey cattle or the nomadic shepherds and their tiny sheep-dogs. Kecskemet, Szeged and Debrecen are centres of the west, south and east *puszta*.

DEBRECEN

Debrecen, Hungary's third city, sits on a flat plain at the centre of a rich agricultural area 230 km east of Budapest. In 1540 the inhabitants converted to Calvinism and Debrecen is still the most Protestant city in Hungary. In the 17th century Debrecen was right on the border

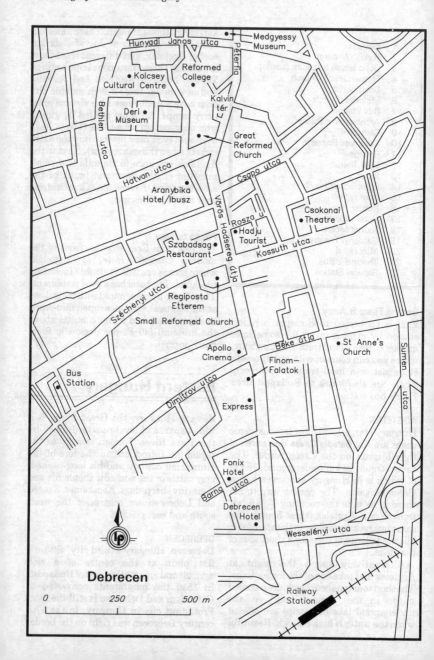

Debrecen

0   250   500 m

of territories controlled by the Turks, Hapsburgs and Princes of Transylvania. By paying tribute to all three it gained a measure of independence and became a great trading centre. Plundered by the Catholic Hapsburgs more than once, revolutionary governments challenging autocratic regimes in Vienna and Budapest were established in Debrecen in 1849 and 1944. Since the war this city has enjoyed peace and prosperity under socialism.

All trains between Moscow and Budapest call here and Debrecen would be just the place to terminate a trans-Siberian odyssey and ease into Hungarian life without the tourists in line in Budapest. Friendly Debrecen is well off the beaten track.

Orientation
Debrecen has only one streetcar line and this runs due north up Voros Hadsereg utja from the railway station to Kalvin ter, the centre of town, continuing north again into Nagyerdo Forest Park where the camping and recreation facilities are found.

Information
Hajdu Tourist is at Voros Hadsereg utja 20.

Things to See
You can't miss the **Great Reformed Church** (1823) on Kalvin ter, heart of the city. This huge neo-Classical building is the largest Protestant church in Hungary. Behind the church is the **Reformed College** (1816) which contains an historical museum (closed Monday) and the largest church-operated library in Hungary. The library (worth seeing) and oratory are upstairs.

A block away is the **Deri Museum** (closed Monday) with a diverse collection, the highlight of which is Mihaly Munkacsys' *Ecce Homo* painting which fills an entire wall. The folklore section is also good. The four recumbent statues in front of the museum are by Ferenc Medgyessy, a Debrecen sculptor who merits a museum of his own a couple of blocks away at Peterfia utca 28.

Places to Stay
The *Hotel Debrecen* opposite the train station is 700 Ft double (no singles). A better choice would be the *Hotel Fonix*, Barna utca 17 just two blocks away (210 Ft single, 550 Ft double). Try showing your youth hostel card here for a discount. In July and August ask about student dormitory accommodation at Express, Voros Hadsereg utja 77 (weekdays 8.30 am to 3 pm). For private rooms it's Hajdu Tourist, Voros Hadsereg utja 20, or Ibusz, across the street in the *Aranybika Hotel*. If these offices are closed try the *Apartman Hotel*, Voros Hadsereg utja 22.

From May to September campers are well taken care of at the campground in *Nagyerdo Forest Park*, about five km north of the station. Take the streetcar as far as the *Thermal Hotel* (550 Ft single, 700 Ft double), then ask directions to the campground. There are bungalows at the campsite. And don't forget to check out the thermal baths in the above mentioned hotel!

Places to Eat
One of the best restaurants, yet still quite reasonable, is the *Regiposta Etterem*, Szechenyi utca 6, in the oldest house in Debrecen (menu in German). The Swedish king Charles XII spent a night here on his way home from Turkey in 1714. Also fairly good is the *Szabadsag Restaurant*, Voros Hadsereg utja 29. Most people walk straight through the downstairs dining room and head for the self-service section upstairs which is very cheap. An even cheaper place is *Finom-Falatok*, Voros Hadsereg utja 69, a meat market offering stand-up meals to colourful regulars. Peek in the pots and point. The bar attached sells wine by the glass.

Entertainment

For such a backwater Debrecen has a rich cultural life. Check out the *Csokonai Theatre* (1861) on Kossuth Lajos utca where operas and operettas are performed. The ticket office (weekdays 1 pm to 7.30 pm) is just inside. Also ask at Orszagos Filharmonia in the City Hall, Voros Hadsereg utja 20. Concerts only happen every couple of weeks and the tickets are sold out. Make yourself known to the friendly staff of the Filharmonia office and they'll sell you a rush seat at the door just before the performance. These usually take place at the new *Kolcsey Cultural Centre* behind the Deri Museum. The centre also has a mini cinema. From June to August there are organ concerts in the Great Reformed Church.

Getting There & Away

All trains between Budapest/Belgrade and Moscow call here. The service from Debrecen to Budapest (Keleti or Nyugati) via Szolnok is more frequent. For Eger you change trains at Fuzesabony. There are also direct buses between Debrecen and Eger. For Oradea, Romania, you change trains at Puspokladany. For Arad, Romania, take a bus to Bekescsaba where you can catch a train. For Kosice, Czechoslovakia, take a bus to Miskolc and

catch a train from there. Railway tickets and information are available from MAV Tours, Rozsa utca 4.

HORTOBAGY

Between Debrecen and Eger the railway crosses the famous Hungarian *puszta*, a vast flat plain of damp grasslands. The area was depopulated during the Turkish period and in the 18th century used for breeding horses, cattle and sheep. The centre of the *puszta* is Hortobagy.

A km from the train station is the Nine-Arched Bridge (1833), the longest stone bridge in Hungary. Adjacent to the bridge are the Hortobagy Csarda, a typical restaurant and the Herdsman Museum (open Tuesday to Sunday 9 am to 5 pm year round). The museum is housed in an old wagon shed (1780) and contains shepherds' clothing, tools and folk art. A circular thatched building alongside displays the flora and fauna of Hortobagy National Park.

Hortobagy is best visited in summer when fairs and horse shows are held near the bridge. The colourful five-in-hand driving of Debrecen is sometimes seen, as are real Hungarian cowboys! There's a large campground (May to September) beside the museum.

Romania

Romania, a little known Balkan country straddling the Carpathian Range, offers surprising variety from alpine peaks and Black Sea beaches to the mighty Danube River. The towns of Transylvania are straight out of medieval Hungary or Germany, while the exotic Orthodox monasteries of Moldavia and Bukovina suggest Byzantium. Constanta is heavily Roman and Turkish, and Bucharest has a Franco-Romanian cityscape all its own. Fine museums and churches are scattered throughout – few countries in Eastern Europe feature such a kaleidoscope of cultures as Romania.

There's another side to Romania, however, one of economic hardship and political stagnation. Here independent travellers share the everyday problems of the people as nowhere else. Tourist facilities exist everywhere, but they're geared to the big spender. For shoestring travellers Romania can be the adventure of a lifetime, but only in summer when it's possible to camp. Even the food is better then! In the cold, dark Romanian winter (October to April) add about US$20 to your daily budget and shorten your stay. Romania chastises the unwary and rewards the intrepid. By avoiding hotels and living rough you can capture the essence of this colourful, perplexing land.

Facts about the Country

HISTORY

Ancient Romania was inhabited by Thracian tribes. The Greeks called them the Getae, the Romans knew them as Dacians, but actually they were a single Daco-Getae people. Beginning in the 7th century BC the Greeks established trading colonies along the Black Sea at Callatis (Mangalia), Tomis (Constanta) and Histria.

In the 1st century BC a Dacian state was established to meet the Roman threat. The last king, Decebalus, consolidated this state but was unable to prevent the Roman conquest in 105-106 AD.

The Romans recorded their expansion north of the Danube on two famous monuments, Trajan's Column in Rome and the 'Tropaeum Trajani' on the site of their victory at Adamclisi in Dobrogea. Most of present Romania, including the Transylvanian plateau, came under their rule. The slave-owning Romans brought with them a superior civilisation and mixed with the conquered tribes to form a Daco-Roman people speaking a Latin tongue. A noted visitor during the Roman period was the Latin poet Ovid, exiled to the Black Sea by Emperor Octavian Augustus.

In the face of Goth attacks in 271 the Emperor Aurelian decided to withdraw the Roman legions and administration south of the Danube, but the Romanised Vlach peasants remained in Dacia. Waves of migrating peoples, the Goths, Huns, Avars, Slavs, Bulgars and Hungarians, swept across this territory from the 4th to 10th centuries. The Romanians survived in village communities and gradually assimilated the Slavs and other peoples

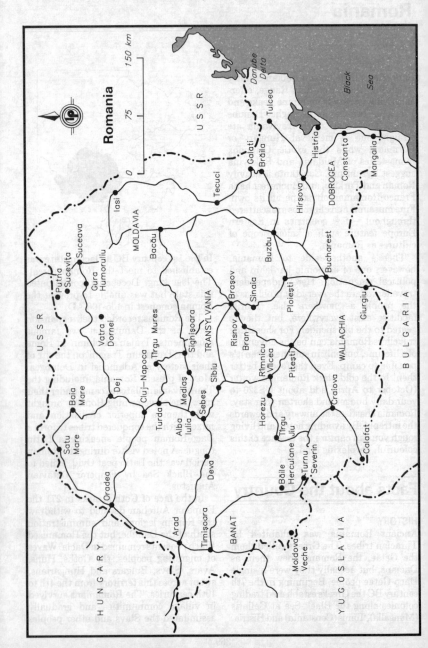

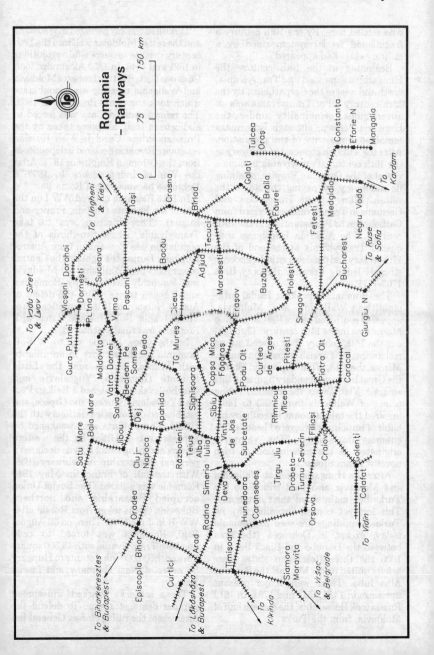

Romania
– Railways

0   75   150 km

who settled here. By the 10th century a fragmented feudal system ruled by a military class had appeared.

Beginning in the 10th century the Hungarians expanded into Transylvania, north and west of the Carpathians. By the 13th century all of Transylvania was an autonomous principality under the Hungarian crown, although Romanians remained a majority of the population. After the Turkish conquest of Hungary in the 16th century Transylvania became a vassal of the Ottoman Empire, retaining its autonomy by paying tribute to the sultan. Many of the Hungarians and Germans in Transylvania converted from Catholicism to Protestantism in the 16th century. The Austrian Hapsburgs conquered Transylvania at the end of the 17th century and put down an independence struggle led by Francisc Rakoczy II in 1703-1711.

The Romanian-speaking feudal principalities, Wallachia and Moldavia, appeared south and east of the Carpathian Mountains in the 14th century. Throughout the 15th century they offered strong resistance to Turkish expansion north. Mircea the Old, Vlad Tepes and Stefan the Great became legendary figures in this struggle. Vlad Tepes 'the Impaler,' ruling prince of Wallachia from 1456 to 1462, inspired the tale of Count Dracula by his habit of impaling the severed heads of his enemies on stakes. (The vampires originated in the imagination of Irish novelist Bram Stoker.)

After the Hungarian defeat Wallachia and Moldavia also paid tribute to the Turks but maintained their autonomy. This indirect control explains why no Turkish buildings are seen in Romania today, except in Dobrogea (the area between the Danube and Black Sea). In 1600 the three Romanian states were briefly united under Michael the Brave at Alba Iulia. There were major peasant uprisings in 1437, 1514 and 1784. In 1812 Russia took Bessarabia, the eastern half of Moldavia, from the Turks.

Turkish suzerainty persisted in Wallachia and the rest of Moldavia well into the 19th century despite unsuccessful revolutions in 1821 and 1848. In 1859 Alexandru Ioan Cuza was elected to the thrones of Moldavia and Wallachia creating a national state which took the name Romania in 1862. The reform minded Cuza was forced to abdicate in 1866, his place taken by the Prussian Prince Carol I. With Russian assistance Romania declared independence from the Ottoman Empire in 1877. After the War of Independence in 1877-78 Dobrogea became part of Romania.

In 1916 Romania entered WW I on the side of the Entente (Britain, France and Russia). The objective was to take Transylvania, where two-thirds of the population was Romanian, from Austro-Hungary. During the fighting the Central powers occupied Wallachia but Moldavia was staunchly defended by Romanian and Russian troops. With the defeat of Austro-Hungary in 1918 the unification of Transylvania, Bukovina and Banat with Romania was finally achieved.

In the years leading up to WW II Romania sought security in an alliance with France, Britain and the Little Entente (Romania, Yugoslavia and Czechoslovakia). It signed a Balkan Pact with Yugoslavia, Turkey and Greece, and established diplomatic relations with the USSR. These efforts were weakened by appeasement of Hitler by the western powers and King Carol II, who declared a personal dictatorship in February 1938. With the fall of France in May 1940 Romania was isolated. The Soviet Union occupied Bessarabia and northern Bukovina (areas taken from Russia after WW I) in June 1940. Then, on 30 August 1940, Romania was forced to cede northern Transylvania with 43,500 square km and 2,600,000 inhabitants to Hungary by order of Nazi Germany and fascist Italy.

These setbacks sparked widespread popular demonstrations. To defend the interests of the ruling classes General Ion

Antonescu forced Carol II to abdicate in favour of his son Michael and imposed a fascist dictatorship. German troops were allowed to enter Romania in October 1940. In June 1941 Antonescu joined Hitler's criminal anti-Soviet war. Deep-seated anti-Nazi resentment smouldered among the Romanian soldiers and people. As the war went badly and the Soviet Army approached Romania's borders, a rare national consensus was achieved. On 23 August 1944 Romania suddenly changed sides, captured 53,159 German soldiers present in Romania at the time, and declared war on Nazi Germany. By this dramatic act Romania salvaged its independence and shortened the war. By 25 October the Romanian and Soviet armies had driven the Hungarian and German forces from Transylvania. The Romanian army went on to fight in Hungary and Czechoslovakia. Half a million Romanian soldiers died while their country was on the Axis side, another 170,000 after it joined the Allies, appalling losses.

After national liberation the government of Dr Petru Groza launched Romania's social liberation. Parliamentary elections in November 1946 were won by the progressive parties. A year later the monarchy was abolished and a Romanian People's Republic proclaimed. The Communist and Social Democratic parties united as the Romanian Workers' Party in 1948, the name being changed back to Romanian Communist Party in 1965. In June 1948 the means of production were nationalised and a planned economy instituted. Emphasis was placed on industrialisation, agricultural co-operativisation, education and culture.

Romania today is unique in Eastern Europe for its independent foreign policy based on disarmament, detente and peaceful coexistence with all countries based on equality, respect for national sovereignty, mutual advantage and non-interference. While a member of the Warsaw Pact Romania does not participate in Pact military manoeuvres and no foreign troops are stationed in the country. Although Romania never broke with the Soviet Union as Tito's Yugoslavia and Mao's China did, Romania refused to assist in the intervention in Czechoslovakia in 1968.

GOVERNMENT

Romania is a socialist republic led by the president of the State Council who is also secretary general of the Romanian Communist Party. The Grand National Assembly is comprised of deputies elected for five-year terms. The Council of Ministers is the supreme body of the state administration. Romania is divided into 40 counties *(judet)* plus the municipality of Bucharest. Elected people's councils function at the county, municipality, town and commune levels. Executive committees of the people's councils run the local administration. The Romanian Communist Party with over two million members is the leading force in Romanian society. Council and assembly members need not be party members.

PEOPLE

The population is 22,800,000 of which 43% live in towns and cities. Bucharest (2,090,000) is by far the largest city, followed by Cluj, Timisoara, Iasi, Brasov, Galati, Craiova and Constanta in that order. The largest minorities are Hungarians (8%) and Germans (2%). Many of the quarter million gypsies in Romania before WW II were murdered by the Nazis. Romania is the only Romance-language country without a Roman Catholic background. Seventy percent of the population is Romanian Orthodox, 10% Greek Orthodox and 14% Catholic.

The position of the 1.7 million Hungarian minority in Romania continues to sour relations with neighbouring Hungary. In 1987 Bucharest denounced publication of a three-volume *History of Transylvania* in Hungary, while Budapest protested the closing of all Hungarian-language newspapers and magazines in Romania. Feelings ran strong at an unofficial June 1988 demonstration by 50,000 people in Budapest, protesting plans to relocate 7000 Romanian villages, many of them in Transylvania. Romania responded by closing the Hungarian consulate in Cluj. The Soviet Union has attempted to mediate between the parties.

ECONOMY

The 1965 Romanian Constitution declares that agricultural land and the means of production, finance and transport are social property. The economy is run on the basis of democratic centralism or central planning. Agriculture accounts for 31% of the gross national product, industry 55% and services 14%. Romania exports crude oil, minerals, machinery, food products and chemicals to both Germanies, the USSR and Italy. Self-sufficiency is a goal and since 1980 Romania's foreign debt has been reduced from $11 billion to $5.8 billion.

Investment priorities for Romania are heavy industry and infrastructure projects such as the Danube Canal (from Agigea to Cernavoda) and the Bucharest Metro. The huge Iron Gates Hydro-power Project at Turnu Severin on the Danube was made possible by the close friendship between Yugoslavia's Marshall Tito and Romania's Nicolae Ceausescu. The Ploiesti oilfields north of Bucharest have been pumping for over a century, but the giant iron and steel works at Galati has risen since WW II.

Romania is still a developing country. The emphasis on heavy industry is in line with Romania's long-range goal of self-reliance but it's led to shortages of food and consumer goods. The lines are long at stores and petrol pumps. Cars are often parked for a km along the highway waiting to fill up and gasoline is rationed to 30 litres a month.

GEOGRAPHY

With 237,500 square km Romania is larger than Hungary and Bulgaria combined. The Danube River completes its 2900-km course through eight countries here in Romania's Danube Delta. South of the delta is the Black Sea coast and west from it, along the Bulgarian border, stretch the Danube lowlands. Most of central and northern Romania is taken up by the U-shaped Carpathian Mountains.

The highest point in the Romanian Carpathians is Moldoveanu (2544 metres) in the Fagaras Mountains south-east of Sibiu. The Transylvanian plateau occupies the centre of the U, while the Moldavian plateau is to the east.

The Carpathians account for about a third of the country's area with alpine pastures above and thick forests below. Another third of Romania is hills and tablelands covered with orchards and vineyards. The final third is a fertile plain of cereals, vegetables, herbs and other crops.

FESTIVALS & HOLIDAYS

In June there's the Hercules Festival at Baile Herculane. Many folklore festivals unfold along the coast in summer, including one in Tulcea in August and another in Braila in September. Fall sees musical festivals in Transylvania, such as Sibiu's Cibinium in September and Cluj's Musical Autumn in October. In December there are the Days of Bihor Culture in Oradea. The Bucharest International Fair in October is Romania's main trade fair.

The public holidays in Romania are 1 and 2 January (New Years), 1 and 2 May (Labour Days), and 23 and 24 August (Liberation Days).

LANGUAGE

Romanian is much closer to classical Latin than the other Romance languages. The grammatical structure and basic word stock of the mother tongue are well preserved. Some Slavic words were incorporated in the 7th to 10th centuries, as the Romanian language took definite shape. Until the mid-19th century Romanian was written in the Cyrillic script. Today English and French are the first foreign languages taught in Romanian schools. German is useful in Transylvania.

Some Romanian words to know are *da* yes, *nu* no, *va rog* please, *mult cumesc* thank you, *cit costa?* how much, *gara* station, *autogara* bus station, *statia de autobuze* bus stop, *buna dimineata* good morning, *buna sera* good evening and *unde este* where is. The days of the week are *Luni, Marti, Miercuri, Joi, Vineri, Simbata, Duminica*.

Facts for the Visitor

VISAS

Romanian visas are the most easily obtained in Eastern Europe and the most expensive. You can get the visa right on the train upon arrival or in advance at a Romanian consulate. Either way the price will be about US$25 regardless of how long you intend to stay. The best way to compensate for this high admission fee is to spend longer in the country.

Nationals of Austria, Denmark, Finland, Iceland, Norway, Portugal, Sweden and some Third World countries do not require visas. Americans are supposed to get 24-hour Romanian transit visas free of charge upon arrival. If you're forced to pay make an official complaint at the next US embassy you visit.

As you're getting the visa you'll have to specify exactly how many days you wish to remain in Romania. You will then be required to change US$10 for each of those days, the exchange being made with customs right on the train. There's no refund if later you decide to shorten your stay. Your last day in Romania does not count for compulsory exchange (no exchange that day). Children under 14 and those who have prepaid hotel accommodation are exempt from compulsory exchange. Although those transiting Romania within 24 hours are also supposed to be exempt, customs officials have been known to insist that they pay too. Theoretically persons of Romanian origin are also exempt, but you better verify this in advance at a Romanian consulate. Upon paying the US$10 per diem you'll get a receipt enabling you to spend the money at hotels. Don't lose it!

Once inside Romania you can extend your stay by officially exchanging US$10 for each additional day you wish to stay and then reporting to police. Any ONT tourist office will be able to advise you on the procedure but you're better off estimating your period of stay accurately in the first place.

MONEY

US$1 = 9 lei (official)

US$10 daily compulsory exchange

At the official rate Romanian currency is over valued and most prices are based on the official rate. A basic hotel room will cost 200 lei single, a cafeteria meal will be 40 lei. Romanians earn about 2500 lei a month, so it's expensive for them too. One lei consists of 100 bani. To control the black market the largest banknote is 100 lei, the equivalent of US$11 at the official rate.

When you change money at a tourist office or at the border you're given a receipt which allows you to use the money to pay hotel bills. Without the receipt your lei are worthless at hotels and campgrounds. International train tickets, domestic airline tickets, ONT sightseeing tours and luxury goods purchased at hotel 'shops' must be paid directly in hard currency. Be sure to have plenty of US$1 or DM 5 notes to cover these small expenditures, otherwise you'll be forced to accept change in lei. Everything else (domestic bus and train tickets, taxis, restaurant meals, theatre and museum admissions and local goods) may be paid in lei without any receipts.

There's a 1% commission charged on official exchanges. It's impossible to change Romanian lei back into hard currency, even though the exchange receipt assures you that it can be done. It's forbidden to import or export Romanian currency but excess lei may be deposited with customs upon departure, to be picked up again next visit.

There's a black market in Romania which offers five times the official rate for cash dollars or DM. Using it is much more dangerous than similar transactions in Czechoslovakia and Poland for two reasons. First it's strictly illegal and the law *is* enforced. Even worse, many of the individuals who offer to change money on the street do not intend to pay you at all but simply to trick you out of your cash. They flash a thick wad of 100 lei notes, count out the agreed price for your dollars or marks, roll the money up into a tight little roll, then switch rolls at the last instant. Later when you take the money out to count it again you discover a roll of newsprint with a 100 lei note plastered on top. These operators will insist that you change at least US$50 or DM 100 (even in

lei, US$10 doesn't make much of a roll), so that's one sure way to recognise them. Gangs of Arab students in Bucharest earn pocket money doing this, but you must be on guard everywhere in Romania.

If you're set on cutting your costs by 500% (and we're not suggesting you do it) deal with people you meet in campgrounds rather than on the street. Tourists from Czechoslovakia and Poland often make good intermediaries. Don't be in a hurry. Wait till you meet the right person then change enough to cover your entire remaining stay, avoiding the need to take this serious risk a second time. Don't blame us if you're cheated or reported to the police. Beware of theft in Romania.

CLIMATE

Romania has a variable continental climate. It can be cold in the mountains, even in mid-summer. The annual average temperature is 11°C in the south and on the coast, but only 2°C in the mountains. Romanian winters can be extremely cold. In summer there's usually hot sunny weather on the Black Sea coast. Annual rainfall is 600-700 mm, much of it in spring. The mountains get the most rain, the Danube delta the least.

BOOKS & BOOKSHOPS

Romanian Invitation by William Forwood (Garnstone Press, London, 1968) contains much useful background information on every part of the country. Even if you don't read German *Rumanien Touristen Fuhrer* (Editura Sport-Turism, Bucharest, 1985) contains enough maps and important addresses to make it worth purchasing. Romanian bookstores sometimes carry it. A recommended West German guide to the country is *DuMont Kunst-Reisefuhrer Rumanien* by Evi Melas (DuMont Buchverlag, Koln).

NEWSPAPERS & MEDIA

The main daily papers are *Scinteia*, organ of the Central Committee of the Communist Party, *Romania Libera*, organ of the National Council of the Socialist Unity Front, and *Scinteia Tineretului*, organ of the Central Committee of the Union of Communist Youth. *Holidays in Romania* is a monthly magazine published in English, French and German by the Ministry of Tourism. *Romania Today* is a monthly magazine which paints a pretty official picture of the country.

In Bucharest current American newspapers are displayed in a showcase on the sidewalk in front of the American Library on Strada Alexandru Sahia, around behind the National Theatre. The police allow you to approach and read.

FILM & PHOTOGRAPHY

Take all the film you'll need with you.

HEALTH

Foreigners must pay for medical treatment in Romania. Diarrhoea can be a problem so take extra care of what you eat and drink, and bring a remedy just in case.

One third of all European sources of mineral or thermal waters are concentrated in Romania. There are 160 spas. The mud baths on Lake Techirghiol at Eforie Nord go well with the salty lake water and nearby Black Sea. Other important spas are Baile Felix (near Oradea), Baile Herculane (known since Roman times), Sovata (east of Tirgu Mures) and Vatra Dornei. Ask for the brochure *Health Sources & Original Treatments in Romania* at ONT offices abroad.

Some of the spas offer special treatments using the unique Romanian products Gerovital H3, Aslavital, Pell-amar, Covalitin, Boicil Forte and Ulcosilvanil. Gerovital H3 and Aslavital are drugs used against ageing effects, Pell-amar (extracted from sapropel mud) treats rheumatism, Covalitin dissolves kidney stones, Boicil Forte (extracted from medicinal herbs) relieves ankyloses and rheumatic pains, and Ulcosilvanil is for the treatment of gastro-duodenal ulcers.

GENERAL INFORMATION

Post

Main post offices are open daily until 8 pm, Sunday until 12 noon. Mail boxes are yellow and labelled *Posta*. When mailing purchases home from Romania you may be asked to pay an export duty of 20% of the value in hard currency, calculated at the official rate. The Romanian postal service is slow and unreliable: mail your things elsewhere. If you simply *must* receive mail here have it sent care of your embassy, not to poste restante.

Electricity

220 volts AC, 50 Hz.

Time

Greenwich Mean Time plus two hours. Romania goes on summer time at the end of March when clocks are turned an hour forward. At the end of September they're turned an hour back. To save electricity the streets are dimly lit in Romania which is another good reason to visit in summer, when it stays light later.

Business Hours

Some stores close for a mid-afternoon siesta. After all, this is a Latin country! Set both your clocks back when you come to Romania, the one on your wrist and the one that tells you when to have a good time. By law all bars and restaurants in Romania are closed by 10 pm, even in the Black Sea resorts at the height of the tourist season. Although erratic, beer service tends to terminate a little before 8 pm. Theatrical performances and concerts usually begin at 7 pm, except Mondays when most are closed. Sporting events are usually on Wednesday, Saturday and Sunday.

INFORMATION

The 'Carpati-Bucuresti' National Tourist Office (ONT) is the government agency controlling tourism in Romania. Everything they arrange, from accommodation to railway tickets or sightseeing tours, must be paid in western currency. Visit their offices for free travel brochures, but don't expect them to help you save money as their function is exactly the opposite. It's usually better to go directly to hotels, rather than have ONT make accommodation bookings for you. County tourist offices (*Oficiul Judetean de Turism*) are usually a lot more helpful than ONT, but you'll often have to fend for yourself in this country. Romania's student travel organisation, the BTT, has little to offer individual foreign students.

The main ONT information office addresses abroad are:

Austria
ONT (tel 34-3157), Wahringer Strasse 6-8, 1090 Vienna

Belgium
ONT (tel 218-0079), Place de Brouckere 46, Brussels 1000

Britain
ONT (tel 584-8090), 29 Thurloe Place, London SW7 2HP

Denmark
ONT (tel 24-6219), Vesterbrogade 55-A, 1620 Copenhagen

France
ONT (tel 742-2714), 38 Avenue de l'Opera, Paris 75002

Holland
ONT (tel 23-9044), 165 Weteringschans, 1017 XD Amsterdam C

Israel
ONT (tel 66-3536), 1 Ben-Yehuda, Tel Aviv

Italy
ONT (tel 474-2983), 100 Via Torino, 00184 Rome

Spain
ONT (tel 458-7895), Avenida Alfonso XIII 157, Madrid 16

Sweden
ONT (tel 21-0253), Vasahuset, Gamla Brogatan 33, 11120 Stockholm

Switzerland
ONT (tel 211-1730), Schweizergasse 10, 8001 Zurich

USA
ONT (tel 697-6971), 573 Third Ave, New York, NY 10016

West Germany
ONT (tel 371-047), Cornelius Strasse 16, 4000 Dusseldorf
ONT (tel 236-941), Neue Mainzer Strasse 1, 6000 Frankfurt am Main

ACCOMMODATION

Romanians are not allowed to accommodate foreigners in their homes nor give them a place to camp. Aside from this, there's no bureaucratic requirement to register with the police, get hotel stamps on a visa form, or account for every night spent in the country. This is a considerable advantage, not to be overlooked by budget travellers.

The big crunch in visiting Romania is financial. At an exchange rate of nine lei to the US dollar hotels are expensive and in winter you don't have many alternatives beyond sleeping in railway waiting rooms or on overnight trains. You're lucky if you find a room for under 150 lei single, 250 lei double, even in the most run-down places. A good modern hotel will only be about a hundred lei more than a flea bag, so this is one country where the cheapest isn't always the best value. Many Romanian hotels have been reclassified as 1st class simply to increase the prices, thus a 1st class hotel in no way insures a 1st class room. To boot, the lowest category of hotel is 2nd class, so all 3rd and 4th class hotels are listed as 2nd class automatically. Some of the cheapest 2nd class hotels have instructions not to admit foreign tourists.

On the positive side, Romanian hotel keepers will go out of their way to find you a room, even in hotels with large 'no vacancy' *(nu avem locuri)* notices on the door. This is partly because western tourists must pay four times more than Romanians for the same rooms. Still, it's comforting to know that you'll almost always be able to find something. Breakfast is usually included in the price.

Hotel bills may be paid in lei, but you must present the receipt you got when you paid your US$10 daily exchange requirement. The amount spent is deducted from the back of the receipt and you can go on using the same receipt until all your credit is used up, at which time you'll have to change more hard currency to pay for accommodation. Only if you camp or sleep in a railway waiting room every second night will you be able to avoid doing this.

Camping

As there are no youth hostels or private rooms in Romania, camping is the *only*

way to see the country on a low budget. Of course you'll need a tent and will have to come in summer. Of the 154 campgrounds on the official *Popasuri Turistice* map/list we mention those most convenient to attractions and public transport. There are dozens of official campgrounds along the Black Sea coast, the perfect place to relax for a few days and meet young Eastern Europeans. A campground with bungalows is called *popas turisticas*. Most campgrounds only open from June to mid-September.

Freelance camping is prohibited in cities and along the Black Sea coast, but not necessarily elsewhere. If you see local tourists camping in an open field there's nothing to prevent your joining them. If you're camping alone try to keep out of sight of the road. If anyone hints that there could be a problem about camping somewhere, *believe them* and go elsewhere. Don't ask a Romanian for permission to camp somewhere as they're forbidden to give it. You could get someone in serious trouble without even being aware. Wherever you camp take care of your gear. Don't go off and leave valuable objects unattended. There are lots of stories about rip-offs.

Cabane

Although you can pitch a tent anywhere you like in the mountains you may find it too cold to do so. In most mountain areas there's a network of cabins or chalets with restaurants and dormitories where hikers can put up for the night. The official *Cabane Turistice* map lists 148 *cabane*. Prices are much lower than hotels and no reservations are required but arrive early if the *cabana* is in a popular location (such as adjacent to a cable car terminus, etc). Expect to encounter good comradeship rather than cleanliness or comfort at these hostels.

Students' Hostels

If you're under 30 and in Romania in July and August try asking about BTT students' hostels *(caminul de studenti)* at tourist offices. Theoretically they're available in many cities at 100 lei single, 130 lei double (breakfast not included). Trouble is, the locations change annually and even if you manage to find such a hostel you may very well be told it's only for groups. You'll be something of a curiosity so an exception may be made or perhaps a male foreign student will invite you to stay with him (Romanian students cannot do so). If a tourist office recognises the existence of the students' hostels have them call to make a reservation before going out.

FOOD & DRINK

In the busiest Romanian restaurants diners are served in shifts rather than individually. Here's how it works. Once the restaurant is full of people eating the waiters disappear until almost everyone is finished. Then they come back to clear the tables and collect the bills. The next service does not begin in earnest until most of the old group has left and the tables are filling up with hungry new clients. Then all the orders are taken in one swoop and as the food is being prepared they bring everyone their bread, wine, cutlery, etc. Like magic everyone's food comes out in quick succession. Many restaurants are short of staff and this is the only way they can cope with the high demand, but it does involve some waiting. Aggressively demanding service will not win you any friends, nor perhaps even be successful. Thus, if you don't have time for a leisurely meal patronise the self-service cafeterias.

One important way to make things easier for everyone in restaurants is to only order things you see on other tables. Just get the waiters' attention and point. Not only will this eliminate language problems and unwelcome surprises, but the waiter will appreciate the time saved trying to decipher the menu and will probably reciprocate by bringing you your meal sooner. Many things on the menu won't be available anyway.

The price difference between first and third class restaurants is not great, so splash out now and then. When ordering wine at a restaurant compare the price of a glass and a bottle, as it's usually much better value to order the whole bottle. At restaurants the service charge is included in the bill and there's no need to tip extra. You can round the bill up a little if you want.

Romanian Specialties

Romanian favourites include *ciorba de perisoare* (a spicy soup of meat balls and vegetables), *ghiveciu* (vegetable stew), *tocana* (onion and meat stew), *ardei umpluti* (stuffed peppers), *mititei* (highly seasoned grilled meatballs), *sarmale* (cabbage or vine leaves stuffed with spiced meat and rice) and *pastrama* (smoked goat meat). *Mamaliga* is a maize porridge that goes well with everything. Typical desserts are *placinte* (turnovers) and *cozonac* (a brioche). Turkish sweets such as *baclava*, *cataif* and *halva* are common.

Among the best Romanian wines are Cotnari, Murfatlar, Odobesti, Tirnave and Valea Calugareasca. Red wines are *negru*. *Must* is a fresh, unfermented wine available during the wine harvest. *Tuica* (plum brandy) is taken at the beginning of a meal. Romanians drink Russian-style tea but Turkish coffee.

THINGS TO BUY

Due to the scarcity of nearly all consumer goods it may be better to do your shopping with western currency in hotel or Comturist 'shops'. Wine purchased at hotel 'shops' is better quality and considerably cheaper than bottles you can buy with lei. The 'shops' also carry plum brandy, Gerovital H3 and Pell-amar cosmetics, embroidered blouses and Romanian handicrafts. At hard currency 'shops' you'll be assured top quality at reasonable prices and will have no problem taking the items out of Romania. Be sure to get an itemised receipt to show customs, otherwise you could be charged export duty if the total value is over 1000 lei. 'Muzica' stores sell Romanian records. Considering how strict Romanian customs can be, you're best to limit yourself to a few small souvenirs and do your heavy shopping elsewhere. Don't try to export any sort of food or drink as it's subject to 100% duty.

'Shops' in luxury hotels often sell coffee and western cigarettes not available in local stores. Arab and African students make profits by purchasing these items for hard currency, then re-selling them to Romanians at inflated prices in lei. You'll sometimes be asked if you have anything of this nature to sell.

WHAT TO BRING

Romanian customs regulations are complicated but not always enforced. Upon arrival valuables such as cameras, binoculars, portable radios or TVs, cassette recorders, musical instruments, portable typewriters, works of art and precious jewellery *may* be listed on a customs declaration form. Whether you care to get into this or not is up to you but having made such a declaration you'll be able to re-export the articles without question. If customs suggests you put down a cash deposit politely refuse and insist on filling out a declaration. The problem is, if the items listed are subsequently lost or stolen you face a fine for having 'sold' them, unless you can persuade the local police to give you a stamped statement verifying the theft. Considering that the Romanian officials really *aren't* out to get you, forget the declaration if the customs officers themselves don't bring it up and your possessions obviously belong to you. Gifts worth up to a total of 2000 lei may be imported duty free.

If coming from Hungary bring some food with you, especially chocolate bars. Kent is the number one favourite cigarette in Romania, so bring a few packs for gifts. Packs of Kent are almost a second currency in Romania, performing the same function as a folded $20 bill back home. While working wonders with service industry personnel, such things should *not* be offered to officials. Duty free allowances are four litres of wine, one litre of spirits, 200 cigarettes and 200 grams each of coffee and cocoa, but only for personal use (not re-sale). Uncanned meats and dairy products are prohibited entry.

Getting There & Away

TRAIN

Most budget travellers arrive in Romania by train. Fares to and from Hungary and Bulgaria are cheap. A one way ticket Arad/Oradea-Budapest is only US$6, while Bucharest-Ruse is US$4, and only half that if you're coming in instead of going out! You can save a little money by going across the country on a domestic ticket purchased for lei, although Bucharest-Budapest is only US$15 one way, Bucharest-Sofia US$11, still cheap. If you're Yugoslavia-bound there's a daily express from Timisoara to Belgrade.

A more unusual route is Poland to Romania direct via the Soviet Union. There are through trains between Warsaw and Bulgaria, but only get Przemysl-Suceava if you want the cheapest ticket. Check with a Soviet Consulate to find out if you need a transit visa. Northbound you'll need a Polish visa.

International railway tickets must be purchased at a CFR ticket agency or ONT tourist office for western currency. Some offices are obliging and will give you change in cash dollars when you buy a ticket with a large denomination travellers' cheque.

BOAT

Two Romanian cruise ships, the *Carpati* and *Oltenita*, ply the Danube regularly between Vienna and Romania with stops at Budapest, Belgrade and Giurgiu. In summer companies such as Rotours

Individualtouristik GmbH, 6000 Frankfurt am Main 1, West Germany, arrange fortnightly package tours using these ships. Prices range from DM 1264 to DM 2408, including a round trip by train from Frankfurt to Vienna, one way by riverboat (six or seven nights), the other way by air, a week at a Black Sea hotel and all meals. There's a DM 180 reduction if you don't require the train ticket from Frankfurt. Any travel agent in Western Europe could book this trip.

Getting Around

TRAIN

The Romanian State Railways (CFR) runs two types of trains, local (*personal* or *cursa*) and express (*accelerat* or *rapide*). The express trains charge a supplement (15-30 lei) and carry only reserved seats. Tickets with automatic seat reservations for express trains should be purchased the day before at the downtown CFR ticket agency. Advance tickets are not available at railway stations. If you have to buy a ticket for a same-day express you must buy it at the station beginning about an hour before the departure, but you're not guaranteed a seat or even a ticket if the line is too long. Tickets for local trains are usually purchased at the station the same day. Make sure you're in the right ticket line and never get on a train without a ticket as you'll be fined and put off at the next station. On posted timetables *sosire* is arrivals, *plecare* departures.

If you have an international through ticket you're allowed to make stops along the route but must pay another reservation fee each time you re-board. If the international ticket was issued in Romania you must also pay the express train supplement each time. Inter-Rail passes (sold to those under 26) are accepted in Romania, but not Eurail. Even with such a pass you must pay the express train reservation fee. No fees or supplements

are payable on local trains. The Romanian State Railways has been known to sell a reservation for the same seat several times, so try to take it in stride if you're a victim.

Since the local trains have no reservations you don't have to worry about being kicked out of your seat if you find one. Local trains take twice as long, but often they're less crowded than the expresses. Since people are constantly getting on and off you eventually get a seat. The passengers on local trains are invariably more interesting, real Romanian country folk. First class travel on local trains is quite comfortable and costs about the same as 2nd class on an express. Bring along a good book and enjoy a leisurely trip. Only express trains carry restaurant cars, however, so fill your canteen before boarding.

Sleepers are available from Bucharest to Arad, Cluj, Timisoara, Tulcea and other points – a good way to cut hotel expenses. Book these in well in advance at a CFR downtown ticket agency.

BUS

Romanian buses (ITA) are less reliable and more crowded than the trains. On rural routes only one or two jam-packed buses may run a day. You usually have to purchase your ticket before boarding. If you haven't pre-purchased a ticket at a bus station (*autogara*) you could have problems with the driver. If the bus is the only way to get there try to reserve a seat by buying a ticket the day before. Arrive early at the stop.

OTHER TRANSPORT

All domestic Tarom flights must be paid in dollars. Navrom offers passenger boat service on the Danube from Braila and Galati to Tulcea and on into the Danube Delta. Hitchhiking in Romania is very difficult as the few cars are usually full. Also, due to petrol rationing of 30 litres a month, motorists won't be going far. If desperate for a ride try waving a pack of Kent cigarettes.

TOURS
ONT sightseeing tours are sometimes useful to get to out of the way attractions, but they generally operate only in summer and must be paid in hard currency. Book ONT tours at any ONT office or at the reception of a luxury hotel. Foreigners are not permitted to join sightseeing tours intended for Romanians (which are paid in lei).

LOCAL TRANSPORT
Public transport costs one lei for trams and Metro, 1.50 lei for trolley buses and 1.75 lei for regular city buses. Tickets must be purchased at kiosks and tobacconists then validated once aboard. Service is usually from 5 am to 11 pm daily. Taxis in Romania have meters and you pay what it says.

Bucharest

Bucharest (Bucuresti), on the plains between the Carpathian foothills and the Danube, became capital of Wallachia in 1459 during the reign of Vlad Tepes. Now a city of over two million the size of Budapest and West Berlin, Bucharest is the metropolis of Romania and its capital since 1862. The broad tree-lined boulevards, park-girdled lakes, pompous public buildings and imposing monuments have a smooth Parisian flavour. Aside from the usual complement of museums the city has a gentle Latin air which goes well with the mysticism of the Orthodox churches. In summer the parks are relaxing, but more interesting are colourful downtown streets such as Calea Victoriei and Strada 30 Decembrie. If you've travelled in Portugal or Italy you'll see much that's familiar, all with a funny Romanian twist which will make you like the place. Do your business in Bucharest, collect visas,

buy a train ticket and gather information, then get out to see the country itself. Two full days is enough for this city.

Orientation
Bucharest's main railway station, Gara de Nord, is a couple of km north-west of central Bucharest. Leave your luggage at the special foreigners-only cloakroom beside track No 14. The other baggage rooms with tremendous lines are not allowed to serve you, thank God. Left from the station is Calea Grivitei which you follow east to Calea Victoriei, then south to Piata Gheorghe Gheorghiu-Dej and the Ateneul Roman.

Use the Ateneul Roman (which appears on the back of the 100 lei banknote) as an orientation point in the city centre. Across the square in front of it is the Palace of the Republic, while two blocks behind on Bulevardul Magheru is the ONT tourist information office. Other focal points in the city include the market-place, Piata Unirii, to the south of downtown, then Piata Universitatii a few blocks north with the Municipal Museum, National Theatre and Inter-Continental Hotel.

Piata Victoriei is the northern focal point, from which Soseaua Kiseleff leads north along Herastrau Park to the airports at Baneasa (eight km) and Otopeni (19 km) and the campground.

Information
The ONT tourist office, Bulevardul Magheru 7 (open Monday to Saturday 7.30 am to 8.30 pm, Sunday 8 am to 7 pm) supplies travel brochures, changes money, books sightseeing tours and answers questions. The service here varies from friendly to unbelievably rude, depending on whom you talk to. There's a branch ONT office in Gara de Nord railway station at the end of track one (daily 7.30 am to 10 pm, Sunday 8 am to 3 pm) which makes hotel reservations. You can buy an excellent indexed map of Bucharest in *Budapest* bookstores but it's not available in Romania.

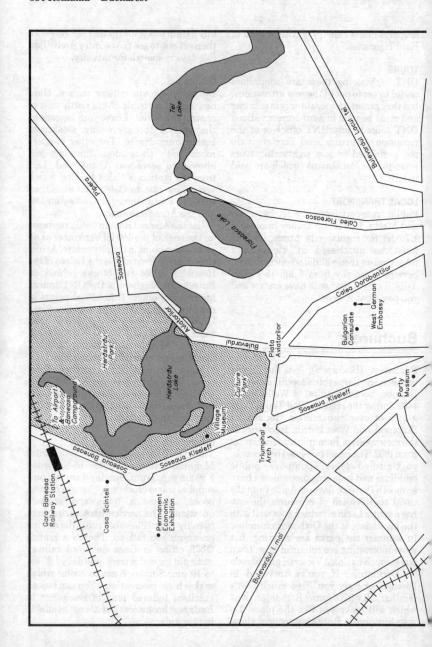

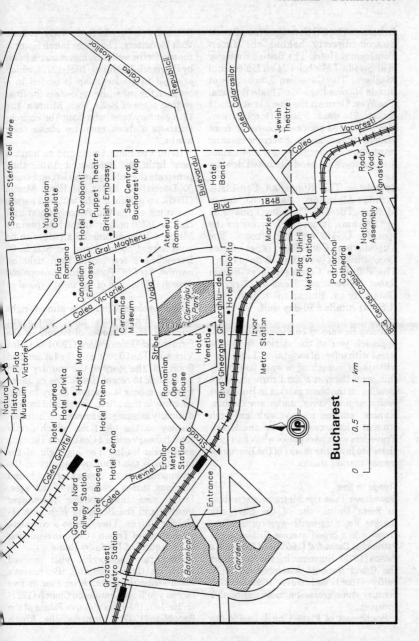

Bucharest

Embassies The US Consulate is on Strada Snagov directly behind the Inter-Continental Hotel. The British Embassy is at Strada J Michelet 24 off Bulevardul Magheru. The Canadian Embassy is at Strada Nicolae Iorga 36 off Piata Romana. The West German Embassy is at Strada Rabat 21 near Piata Dorobantilor. Heavily armed police are posted in front of all foreign embassies. Everyone entering must show his/her passport, and names and numbers are carefully noted down.

Consulates The Hungarian Consulate, Strada Alexandru Sahia 63 (open Monday, Tuesday, Thursday, Friday 9.30 to 11.30 am), issues tourist visas on the spot for US$14 and two photos. The Yugoslavian Consulate is at Calea Dorobantilor 34 (weekdays 10 am to 1 pm). The Bulgarian Consulate is at Strada Rabat 5 (weekdays 9 am to 12 noon). Obtaining a Bulgarian tourist visa (US$14) entails a 10-day wait.

Warning Beware of confidence men who approach you at the station or on the street with offers of assistance. Later they will ask for something or want you to buy things for them at a hard currency shop. Dealing on the black market in Bucharest is *dangerous*. Never, under any circumstances, change money with an Arab student who accosts you on the street. Travellers with backpacks who can't give chase are favourite marks of the Bucharest money market sharks.

Things to See

Downtown Take the Metro or a streetcar to Piata Unirii, site of the busy city market. From the south-west corner of the crossroads a broad avenue climbs to the **Patriarchal Cathedral** (1658) and **Patriarch's Palace** (1875). Surrounding the church are the **Grand National Assembly** (1907), a belfry (1698) and three 16th to 17th century stone crosses, a most impressive complex.

South-east of Piata Unirii, beside the Seminary on Strada Radu Voda, is **Radu Voda Monastery**. The large church is worth the trip for the wall paintings commissioned by Patriarch Justinian (1901-1977), which are still fresh. Justinian is buried in a tomb on the left while opposite is the final resting place of Radu Voda Mihnca, the 17th century ruler who built the church. Portraits of both men are above their tombs.

Return to Piata Unirii and go north a very little on Bulevardul 1848, then penetrate the old city to the left on Strada 30 Decembrie. Enter the **Hanul Manuc** (1808), an old inn on the left, and peruse the ruins of the **Old Princely Court** and church (1559) nearby. In the 16th century Mircea Ciobanul ordered a palace to be built here. Continue west on Strada 30 Decembrie a few blocks then right on narrow Strada Postei to **Stavropoleos Church** (1730), one of the most typical in the city.

Stavropoleos Church is almost right behind Bucharest's most important museum, the **Museum of History** in the former Post Office Palace (1900) on Calea Victoriei. The 50 rooms on the 1st and 2nd floors tell the story of the country from prehistoric to recent times. The entrance to these rooms is obscure, so try to find your way in there first. You should have no difficulty locating the intriguing 'homage' display on the top floor, which firmly establishes President Ceausescu's stature as a world leader. The highlight of the museum is the fabulous treasury in the basement, full of objects of gold and precious stones created over the ages. Don't miss the neolithic *Hamangia thinker* and the *Brooding Hen with its Golden Chicks*. There's also a complete plaster cast of Trajan's Column depicting the conquest of Dacia by Rome.

After this memorable visit proceed north on Calea Victoriei, Bucharest's main shopping street. After four or five blocks you'll see **Cretulescu Church** (1722) on the left, then the massive **Palace of the Republic** (1937), formerly the king's palace and presently seat of the State Council. The only part of the palace open to the public is the **Fine Arts Museum**, entered from Strada Stirbei Voda (10 am to 6 pm, closed Monday, 10 lei). This extensive collection houses European and Romanian art on four floors. Across Piata Gheorghe Gheorghiu-Dej from the palace is the neo-Classical **Ateneul Roman** (1888), the city's main concert hall.

Uptown North on Calea Victoriei is Piata Victoriei, on the far side of which is the **Natural History Museum**, and beside it, the **Museum of the Romanian Communist Party** (daily 9 am to 5 pm, Saturday 9 am to 2 pm, closed Monday). The entrance to the Party Museum is around back, beyond the dramatic mural.

If you don't mind walking a km or so Soseaua Kiseleff will carry you north to the **Triumphal Arch**, erected in the middle of the traffic circle in 1936 to commemorate Romania's victory in WW I. Beyond this is **Herastrau Park** and the **Village Museum** (closed Monday) with 297 rural Romanian buildings assembled here in a rich mixture of styles. This is one of Bucharest's most appealing attractions.

North again on Soseaua Kiseleff is the Stalinist mass of **Casa Scinteii** (1956) facing Piata Scinteii, a statue of Lenin appropriately in front. Much of Romania's publishing industry is housed in this building. From here plenty of buses run back toward town.

Gardens If you still have time to spare rent a row boat in **Cismigiu Park**, an enjoyable 19th century garden just west of downtown. Walk west on Bulevardul Gheorghe Gheorghiu-Dej past the opera to the **Botanical Garden** on Soseaua Cotroceni in the eastern section of the city (Metro – Eroilor). The gardens open from 7 am to 8 pm in summer, 8 am to 5 pm in winter, but the Botanical Museum and greenhouse may be visited only on Tuesday, Friday and Sunday from 9 am to 1 pm.

Around Bucharest
Snagov, 34 km north of Bucharest, is a favourite picnic spot with a 16th century church on an island in the lake. Vlad Tepes, the notorious Count Dracula, is buried on the island. There are two campgrounds and an oak forest here. Three trains a day run between Bucharest's Gara Baneasa and Snagov. On Sunday there's a train from Gara de Nord. ONT offers a half day coach excursion to Snagov (US$11.50).

Places to Stay
Camping *Camping Baneasa*, in the forest beyond Baneasa Airport north of the city, usually has plenty of space for tent campers (47 lei) and there are also bungalows. The facilities are good and Bucharest's zoo adjoins the site. From Gara de Nord take bus No 105 to Piata Scinteii (the end of the line), then bus No 148 right to the camping. The last bus runs around 10.30 pm Monday to Saturday, 8.30 pm Sundays.

Hotels There are lots of old 2nd class hotels in Bucharest and it's usually no problem finding a room, even in mid-summer. Prices average 219 lei single, 350 lei double, sometimes including breakfast (shared bath). Rates are slightly lower from November to mid-December. The ONT office at Gara de Nord will book a bed for you at one of the hotels listed below, or just set out on your own. Avoid accepting a room facing onto a busy thoroughfare where the traffic could wake you at 5 am. Ask if breakfast is included. If you're not completely satisfied compare prices and appearances at the next hotel before deciding. They all want to have you because the official price you pay is many times higher than what locals pay for the same room. There are two clusters of inexpensive hotels, one around the train station and another downtown.

Hotels Near Gara de Nord The closest hotels to the railway station are the *Bucegi* and

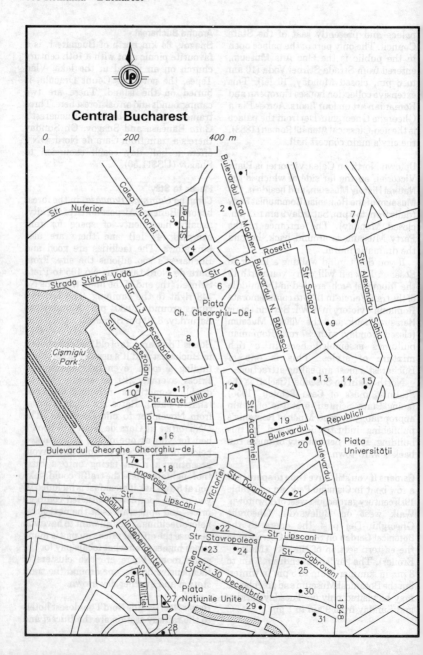

Central Bucharest

0   200   400 m

1	Nottara Theatre
2	Tourist Office
3	'Shop'
4	Ateneul Roman
5	Fine Arts Museum
6	Theodor Aman Museum
7	Hungarian Consulate
8	Cretulescu Church
9	American Consulate
10	Hotel Opera
11	Hotel Carpati
12	Hotel Muntenia
13	Intercontinental Hotel
14	National Theatre
15	American Library
16	Hotel Cismigiu
17	Hotel Central
18	CFR/Tarom Ticket Agency
19	University
20	Municipal Museum
21	Russian Church
22	Carul cu Bere
23	Museum of History
24	Stavropoleos Church
25	Hotel Universal
26	Hotel Tranzit
27	Operetta Theatre
28	Bucur Restaurant
29	Hotel Rahova
30	Old Princely Court
31	Hanul Manuc Inn

the *Cerna*, to your right as you come out the main entrance. To your left at Bulevardul G Duca 2 is the cheap, noisy and full *Hotel Dunarea*. Turn right on Calea Grivitei and you'll pass the *Grivita* and *Oltena* hotels at numbers 130 and 90 respectively. Around the corner to the left from the Oltena is *Hotel Marna*, Strada Buzesti 3, one of the best of the lot. Get a room on the back side to escape the streetcar noise. The Marna price includes breakfast in the good little milk bar downstairs.

Hotels Downtown There are quite a few places to stay near Cismigiu Park. The noisy *Hotel Venetia*, Piata Mihail Kogalniceanu 2, and *Hotel Dimbovita*, Bulevardul Schitu Magureanu 6, are south-west of the park.

East of the park are *Hotel Cismigiu*, Bulevardul Gheorghe Gheorghiu-Dej 18, *Hotel Opera*, Strada Brezoianu 37, *Hotel Carpati*, Strada Matei Millo 16, and *Hotel Muntenia*, Strada Academiei 21. The Carpati charges 25 lei extra to use the communal shower! *Hotel Banat*, Piata Rosetti 5, is on Bulevardul Republicii east of the *Inter-Continental Hotel*.

South in the oldest part of the city are the *Hotel Rahova*, Calea Rahovei 2, and *Hotel Universal*, Strada Gabroveni 12. Finally, there's the slightly less expensive *Hotel Tranzit*, Strada Militiei 4 a block back behind the Operetta Theatre.

One 1st class hotel deserves a mention, the *Hanul Manuc* (tel 131415), Strada 30 Decembrie 62 in the old city. This traditional inn has great character, if you don't mind paying 675 lei for a double (no singles). There are only 32 rooms so have ONT call ahead.

Places to Eat
Self service There are self-service cafeterias in the *Central* and *Inter-Continental* hotels, both downtown. The one in the Inter-Continental (downstairs, entrance outside the hotel) is especially good. Also try the self-service in the *Dorobanti Hotel*, a little north on Strada M Eminescu.

Restaurants The restaurant in Gara de Nord is always packed or closed, so if you want a meal while waiting for a train cross the street to the *Bucegi Hotel* (to the right as you stand in front of the station). The service is good there.

Two typical Romanian restaurants in the southern section of old Bucharest are the *Bucur Restaurant*, Strada Poenaru Bordea near the Operetta Theatre, or the *Hanul Manuc*, an historic old inn at Strada 30 Decembrie 62 near Piata Unirii. Both restaurants have pleasant beer gardens in summer, elegant indoor restaurants in winter. If you can't afford Hanul Manuc check out *Lacto Rahova*, nearby at Strada 30 Decembrie and Calea

Rahovie. They serve simple Romanian meals at low prices. The *Carul cu Bere* on Strada Stavropoleos near the History Museum has a large beer cellar with *mititei* and other tasty treats.

Entertainment

Theatres Bucharest has many theatres, so try to see a show one of the nights you're there. Check the daily papers for listings. Tickets are available at Casa Aria, Calea Victoriei 68-70. If at all possible attend a performance at the Ateneul Roman, the main concert hall in Bucharest. Tickets are sold in the office around the north side of the building.

A couple of blocks away is the shiny new *National Theatre*, Bulevardul N Balcescu 2 opposite the Inter-Continental Hotel. The *Teatrul de Marionete si Papusi 'Tandarica,'* just off Piata Cosmonautilor near the Dorobanti Hotel, presents innovative, amusing puppet shows, sometimes in the afternoon. The *Teatrul Evreiesc de Stat* (State Jewish Theatre), Strada Iuliu Baras 15, is a few blocks east of Piata Unirii.

Two blocks south of the National Historical Museum is the *Operetta Theatre*, Piata Natiunile Unite. The *Romanian Opera House*, Bulevardul Gheorghe Gheorghiu-Dej 70-72, is west of Cismigiu Park, a little out of the way (Metro – Eroilor).

Things to Buy

All of the luxury hotels have hard currency 'shops' where you'll find imported goods and high quality Romanian products not available in Romanian stores. The Comturist Magazin upstairs in the Hotel Dorobanti is one of the largest. A shabby nameless building at Strada Gabriel Peri 9 near the Ateneul is Romania's 'Diplomatic Shop.' Both it and another 'shop' on the same street at number 3 are usually closed for 'inventory' or some other unknown reason, but try them just for laughs. Muzica, Calea Victoriei 41-43, has the city's best selection of records and musical instruments. To see what the average Romanian has to choose from visit the Hala Unirii market hall on Piata Unirii.

Getting There & Away

Train You'll probably arrive by train from Bulgaria or Transylvania at Bucharest's Gara de Nord Station. Service to Sofia via Ruse is a couple of times a day. There are also several expresses daily to Budapest with two routes diverging at Brasov. The northern route is through Cluj and Oradea, while the southern line runs through Sibiu and Arad. To Belgrade you'll pass through Turnu Severin and Timisoara. For the Black Sea beaches catch a train to Mangalia, for the Danube Delta you can choose between Braila and Tulcea, for Bukovina it's Suceava. To get off the beaten track take a train to Iasi, capital of Moldavia. Most trains use the Gara de Nord although a few to Tulcea use Bucharest-Obor Railway Station east of the centre.

Train Tickets The CFR railway ticket agency (downstairs) and the Tarom airline office (upstairs) share the same building on Strada Domnita Anastasia back behind the Central Hotel off Bulevardul Gheorghe Gheorghiu-Dej (open Monday to Saturday 7 am to 8 pm, Sunday 7 am to 1 pm). Come here to purchase international railway tickets or any plane tickets (both payable in western currency). Railway fares are around US$4 to Ruse, US$11 to Sofia, US$15 to Budapest. The staff is generally helpful and will reserve a seat for you for an extra 8 lei. You can also make reservations on domestic express trains here (at least a day ahead). Visit the CFR office early or late in the day as it's jammed mid-afternoon.

Getting Around

Airport Transport Twelve times a day (seven times on Sundays) a bus departs the CFR/Tarom downtown ticket agency for Baneasa Domestic Airport (4 lei) and

Otopeni International Airport (8 lei). Pay the driver.

Public Transport Bucharest has two flashy new Metro lines offering rides for a one lei coin a trip. The first line cuts across the lower section of the city from north-west to south-east with a key station at Piata Unirii about halfway along. The second line runs north from here to Piata Romana and beyond.

Tickets for other forms of public transport should be purchased at a kiosk. Each ticket is valid for two trips and you validate it once aboard: 2 lei for streetcars, 3 lei for trolley buses and 3.5 lei for regular buses. All can be extremely crowded so hang onto your wallet. After 11 pm when public transport has shut down and the street lights gone out (to conserve energy) you'll have to take a cab.

The Black Sea Coast

Dobrogea (Dobrudja), the flat neck of land between the Danube and the Black Sea, was joined to Romania in 1878 when a combined Russo-Romanian army drove the Turks from Bulgaria. This relatively recent accession accounts for the many Islamic buildings in the area. In antiquity the region was colonised first by Greeks then Romans, who left behind a great deal for us to admire. From 46 AD Dobrogea was the Roman province of Moesia Inferior. At Adamclisi (Tropaeum Traiani) the Romans scored a decisive victory over the Geto-Dacian tribes which made possible their expansion north of the Danube. Later Dobrogea fell under Byzantium and in 1418 it was conquered by the Turks.

The train from Bucharest crosses the Danube at Cernavoda on a great iron bridge erected in 1895. It then follows the new Danube Canal for almost its entire 65-km length. The canal, opened by President Ceausescu in 1984, shortens the sea trip from Constanta to Cernavoda by

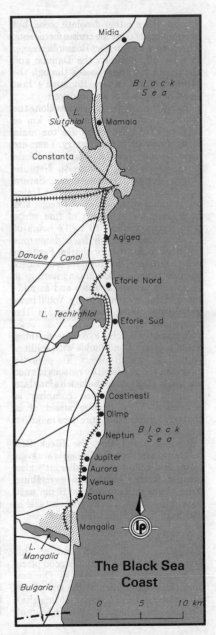

The Black Sea Coast

400 km. It's a rather desolate scene, but believe it or not there are cruises for tourists. This is a prestige project Romania is eager to show off. Between the Danube and Constanta the train passes through the Murfatlar area where Romania's best sweet dessert wines are produced.

Today the soft sandy beaches along the southern half of Romania's 245 km of tideless Black Sea coast are the main focus of tourism in the country. There are nine modern resorts: Mamaia, Eforie Nord, Eforie Sud, Costinesti, Neptun-Olimp, Jupiter, Venus-Aurora, Saturn and Mangalia. Each summer the trains are jammed with hordes of Czechs and East Germans in search of fine white sand, warm waters, 10 to 12 hours of sunshine and freedom from dangerous undersea rocks, fish, or sharks. Far from being a nuisance, the crowds of vacationers have motivated the Romanian government to provide proper facilities and in mid-summer things become lively. You'll have interesting young neighbours in the campgrounds.

At times the beaches look like something out of a James Bond movie with soldiers patrolling, watch-towers at periodic intervals, etc. For security reasons it's not allowed to stroll along the beach alone late at night and freelance camping is prohibited. What they're afraid of is anybody's guess but it sure does make for a memorable holiday.

Keep in mind that the Black Sea beaches of neighbouring Bulgaria are even better and the crowds smaller. It's also cheaper further south and everything doesn't bang shut promptly at 10 pm, as it does in Romania. The biggest obstacle is that hard-to-get Bulgarian tourist visa.

MANGALIA

Mangalia at the south end of the Romanian Black Sea strip is a good place to go for starters. Founded by Dorians from Heraclea Pontica at the end of the 6th century BC, Callatis (Mangalia) offers several archaeological sites. More of

a draw are the workers' resorts along the Romanian Riviera to the north: Saturn, Venus, Aurora, Jupiter, Neptun and Olimp. Costinesti is one gigantic students' playground, a real carnival if you're looking for action. Beach hopping's the thing to do on a hot summers' day and it really becomes a zoo.

Information

There are ONT tourist offices in Restaurant Central and the Mangalia Hotel. CFR railway ticket office, Strada Stefan cel Mare 16.

Things to See

The city of Mangalia doesn't have a lot to offer, yet it's worth a couple of hours. There are two Casas de Cultura: a new white one near the train station and an older Casa with a large mural on the facade a few hundred metres away in the centre of town. Cultural events occur in the older Casa most summer evenings and foreign tourists are welcome. Near the post office, not far from the old Casa, is an intact **Turkish mosque** (1460) open 9 am to 12 noon and 2 to 7 pm in summer.

Back near the new Casa is the **Callatis Archaeological Museum** (open 9 am to 8 pm in summer) with a good collection of Roman sculpture, etc. A 4th century necropolis was recently destroyed to make way for the high-rise building adjacent to the museum. Down on the beach beside the Hotel Mangalia are the ruins of a 6th century **paleo-Christian basilica**, beside which is a small folk art museum.

Places to Stay

Camping The best place to stay is *Saturn Camping*, less than a km from Mangalia Railway Station (you can see the tents from the train window as you're coming in). Get there from the station on foot or take buses No 14, 15, or 20 two stops north, right to the campground entrance. They almost always have space for tenters (47 lei per person). This campground is recommended for its good facilities including occasional warm showers, shady trees, snack and beer bars, plus easy access to coastal buses and the beach. Alternatively, there are similar campgrounds in the string of tourist resorts to the north – Venus, Jupiter, Neptun and Olimp – all accessible by frequent bus.

Hotels There are countless luxury tourist hotels along the strip, for example, the *Hotel Adriana* at the entrance to Venus near *Venus Camping*. One of the few budget hotels in the area is the *Hotel Central* on Mangalia's main square opposite the old Casa de Cultura. They charge 143 lei per person, but are usually full. There's an ONT tourist office in the adjacent Restaurant Central which may be able to find you a room elsewhere, but be prepared to pay top dollar. Prices are highest in the full season (July and August).

If you're aged 14 to 30, have a student card and are very persistent you *might* be able to stay at the *Costinesti BTT youth tourism resort*, 17 km north of Mangalia. To avoid disappointment try to have ONT reserve one of the 5330 beds there for you in advance.

Getting There & Away
The end of the line on the Black Sea route, Mangalia is easily accessible from Bucharest by fast train (six hours). Buses No 12 and 20 operate between Mangalia and Constanta. Bus No 12 goes along the main highway, while bus No 20 calls at all the beach resorts as far north as Olimp, terminating at Constanta Railway Station.

Getting Around
In summer open-sided jeep buggies haul wagon loads of tourists back and forth between Mangalia and Olimp for 4 lei a ride or 12 lei for a complete trip, a fun way to orient yourself on what the area has to offer. The buggies stop at all the beaches.

ONT offers various bus excursions from the beach resorts, for example to the Roman ruins at Adamclisi (US$10) or Histria (US$9). There are also cruises on the Danube Canal (US$12), sometimes with wine tasting and dinner at Murfatlar included (US$21). Information should be available at any hotel or campground reception, otherwise ask at the Mangalia Hotel.

EFORIE NORD
Eforie Nord, 17 km from Constanta, is the first resort south of the city (commuting distance). Stay here if you'd like to combine urban sightseeing with beach life. *Camping Singai*, a few hundred metres west of Eforie Railway Station, is right on Techirghiol Lake but rather far from the Black Sea beaches. The shortest route to the campground is to walk west to the far end of the railway platform, cross the tracks and follow a path to a breach in the wall. Unfortunately Singai is noisy and only recommended if you're arriving late from Bucharest and need a quick place to crash. Techirghiol Lake, which adjoins the campground, is famous for its black mud baths effective against rheumatism. The cold mud baths are the only place in Romania where mud-covered nudism is allowed. The lake's waters are four times as salty as the sea, in fact the lake is two metres below sea level.

Better camping is available at *Camping Meduza* near *Hotel Prahova* on the north side of Eforie Nord. It's closer to the beach but much farther from the train station. For a hotel room ask at the information desk in the *Cristal Hotel* near the bus stop in the centre of town.

Getting There & Away
All trains between Bucharest/Constanta and Mangalia stop at Eforie Nord. Buses to Eforie Nord from Constanta Railway Station include No 10, 11, 12 and 20.

CONSTANTA
Constanta, midway between Istanbul and

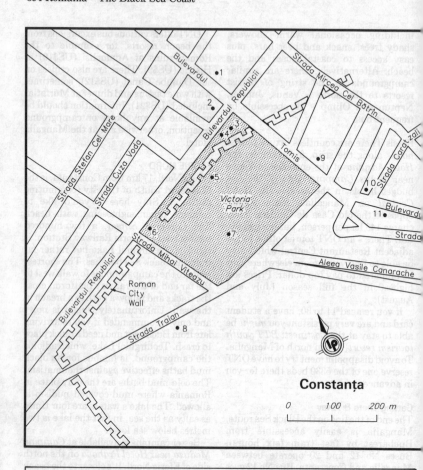

Constanța

0   100   200 m

1 Art Museum	15 Roman Mosaic
2 Hotel Continental	16 Mosque
3 Hotel Victoria	17 Casa Cu Lei
4 Old City Wall	18 Roman Baths
5 Archaeological Museum	19 Catholic Church
6 Fantasio Theatre	20 Basilica Ruins
7 Victory Monument	21 Ion Jalea Sculpture Museum
8 Naval History Museum	22 Orthodox Cathedral
9 Hotel Constanta	23 Archaeological Site
10 Folk Art Museum	24 Hotel Palace
11 Mosque	25 Genoese Lighthouse
12 Synagogue	26 Aquarium
13 Statue of Ovid	27 Casino
14 Archaeological Museum	

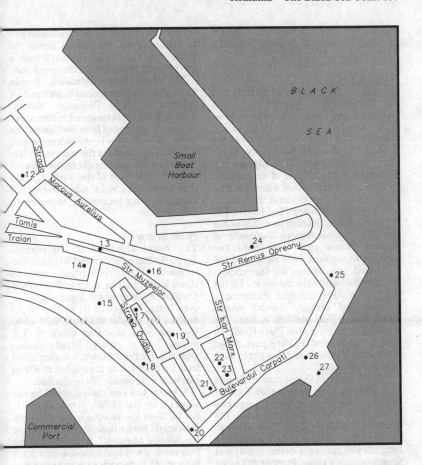

Orientation

Constanta Railway Station is about two km west of the old town. Most of the trolley buses in front of the station go in that direction. Check the transit route map on the wall of the kiosk in front of the trolley stop where you buy your ticket. The city beach is at the end of Bulevardul Republicii. From Hotel Continental Bulevardul Tomis runs south-east to Piata Ovidiu, heart of old Constanta.

Odessa, is Romania's largest port. In Roman times Tomis (Constanta) was also the main port in these parts and much remains from every period of Constanta's colourful history. Despite ugly industry to the north and west the picturesque old town has a charming Mediterranean air. The excellent museums are within reach of excellent but crowded beaches. It's almost a world apart.

Information

The ONT tourist information desk is inside Hotel Continental, Bulevardul

Tomis 69. The CFR railway ticket office is at Aleea Vasile Canarache 4 near the Archaeological Museum.

Things to See

Constanta's most renowned attraction is the **Archaeological Museum** on Piata Ovidiu with exhibits on three floors. Most of the cases bear captions in English and German. The most unusual objects are kept in the treasury downstairs. Don't miss the 2nd century AD sculpture of a serpent with the muzzle of an antelope and eyes, ears and hair of a human. Also outstanding is the Goddess Fortuna, a horn of plenty in her arms and Pontos, god of the Black Sea, leaning on a ship at her feet. The archaeological fragments of Roman Tomis spill over onto the surrounding square. Be sure to read the translated inscriptions on the ancient tombstones beside the museum. Facing these is another museum sheltering a gigantic 3rd century **Roman mosaic** discovered in 1959 and left *in situ*. The statue of Ovid, erected on Piata Ovidiu in 1887, brings to mind the Latin poet, exiled to Constanta in 8 AD and thought to have been buried there.

A block south of this square on Strada Muzeelor is a large **mosque** (1910) with a 140-step minaret you may climb, then two blocks farther down the same street, the **Orthodox Cathedral** (1885). Turn left onto the waterfront promenade and continue a little till you reach the **casino** (1904) and **aquarium**, face to face. Further the same way is the **Genoese lighthouse** (1860), then the pier with a fine view of old Constanta.

The other worthwhile sights can be covered by returning to Piata Ovidiu and Bulevardul Tomis, which you follow north-west to the Continental Hotel. Halfway up Bulevardul Tomis you pass another mosque and the **Folk Art Museum** in an ornate building on the right. When you reach the hotel turn left and explore Victoria Park, which has remains of the 3rd century **Roman city wall**, pieces of Roman sculpture and a modern monument to victory. From the terrace across the street from the monument you'll have a good view of the modern commercial port.

The **Naval History Museum**, Strada Traian 53, offers exceptionally informative exhibits on early Romanian history. Although the captions are all in Romanian much can be garnered from the illustrations alone. As in all other Romanian museums, no mention is made of the war years 1941-1944 when Romania fought on the German side. The last year of the conflict, when they were on the 'right' side, receives full attention – an interesting approach to history.

Places to Stay

The *Hotel Continental*, Bulevardul Tomis 69, has rooms for 289 lei single, 388 lei double. The *Hotel Victoria* across the street is only half as much and the *Hotel Constanta*, Bulevardul Tomis 46, is an even better bet at 139 lei single, 200 lei double, but they're suddenly 'full' when they see your capitalist passport. Try anyway. *Hotel Palace*, Strada Remus Opreanu 5 in the old town, has a beautiful location overlooking the sea but at 500 lei single, 550 lei double it's overpriced.

A better top end choice would be the *Casa Cu Lei* (tel 18050), Strada Dianei 1, not far from the mosque in the old town (you might notice their sign while visiting the Mosaic Museum). They've only got four nicely decorated rooms, so you don't have much hope without a reservation.

Places to Eat

There are many restaurants in every category but deluxe along Bulevardul Tomis between Hotel Continental and the Archaeological Museum. Take your pick. *Lacto-Vegetarian*, Bulevardul Tomis 78, is good and cheap. If the occasion calls for something better try the *Casa Cu Lei* mentioned above. Even if you're not eating, their bar is a pleasant oasis.

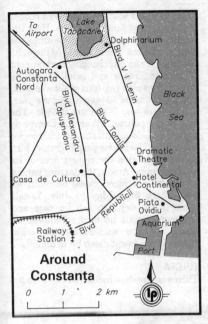

Around Constanța

```
0      1      2 km
```

northern Romania take a Bucharest-bound train west to Fetesti and change for Faurei or Buzau.

HISTRIA

The Graeco-Roman ruins at **Cetatea Histria**, the oldest ancient settlement in Romania, are on the coast about 70 km north of Constanta. Founded in 657 BC by Greek merchants from Miletus, Histria was protected by the Dacians and absorbed by the Romans. Beyond the **museum** (closed Monday) is a city wall complete with towers and gates, built at the end of the 3rd century AD with materials from buildings destroyed during the Gothic invasion of 248 and the foundations of basilicas, residences and temples. By the end of the 7th century AD Histria had been abandoned.

Histria is difficult to reach unless you take the ONT sightseeing tour (US$9). A crowded local bus runs a couple of times a day between Autogara Constanta Nord (tram No 100 from the train station) and Mihai Viteazu (on the railway line to Tulcea), but it will drop you 11 km from the site. There's a basic campground at Histria if you get stuck.

Entertainment

The *Fantasio Musical Theatre*, Bulevardul Republicii 11, offers good programmes. The *Dramatic Theatre*, Strada Mircea del Batrin 97, is in the park opposite the post office.

Things to Buy

Magazin Plafar, Strada Mircea Cel Batrin 3 just off Piata Ovidiu, sells excellent, cheap herbal remedies for stomach problems, etc. Marketers on Piata Ovidiu sell money. There are Comturist hard currency shops in the Continental and Palace hotels.

Getting There & Away

Constanta is well connected to Bucharest by fast train and there are through connections to Transylvania in summer. Local trains run north to Tulcea (via Medgidia) and south to Mangalia. For

MAMAIA

Mamaia (not Miami!), just to the north of Constanta, is Romania's old established beach resort catering to international and other 'high class' tourists, while the string of newer beach resorts south of the city are intended for the East Block masses. Budget travellers will probably be more at home in the latter, but Mamaia is also fun. Romania's only gambling casino is here.

Ovidiu Island

An excursion boat (10 lei) ferries tourists across Lake Mamaia from the wharf near Mamaia Casino to Ovidiu Island every hour or two during the summer season. Try the local seafood in the thatch-roofed restaurant on the island if you've got time.

Places to Stay

The campground at Mamaia is at the north end of the six-km strip, 200 metres beyond the terminus of trolleys No 41 and 50, but it's small and usually chock-a-block in summer. If it's full they'll refer you to the *Hanul Piratilor campground* a km north (bus No 23) which should be able to accommodate you. For information on hotel rooms ask at the tourist office in the *Perla Hotel* at the south end of the strip.

Getting There & Away

Getting between Constanta and Mamaia by trolley bus is easy. Catch No 41 from Constanta Railway Station, or No 50 from the city centre.

The Danube Delta

The 4340-square-km Danube Delta on the

Black Sea just south of the Soviet border is the youngest land in Europe. Here the mighty Danube splits into three arms, the Chilia, Sulina and Sfintu Gheorghe channels. It's an everchanging environment of marshes, reeds and sandbars as the river carries over two tons of silt a second, making Romania 40 metres longer a year.

The flora and fauna are unique. The only large pelican colony in Europe is found here, along with another 250 species of birdlife. The converging migratory bird routes make this the richest area of its kind in Europe. Among the dazzling variety of insects are mosquitoes, encountered everywhere from May to July. Locals come to the delta to fish for carp and sturgeon. Small boats are required to really see the wildlife as the main channels are swept clean by hydrofoils.

TULCEA

Tulcea is a modern industrial city without

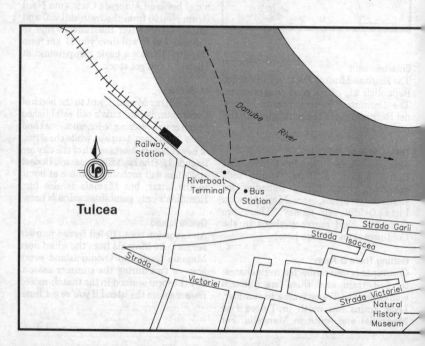

much to detain you more than a couple of hours. If you can avoid Tulcea and its aluminium smelter entirely then do so. Its position on the Danube at a crossing of transportation routes makes this difficult, but try to arrive before noon so you can catch an onward ferry the same day. On your return connect immediately with the ferry to Braila, an alternative and much nicer gateway to the Danube Delta.

Orientation

Tulcea's bus, train and Navrom ferry terminals are adjacent by the Danube. There's a promenade along the riverside from here to the Delta Hotel. Inland a block from the hotel is Piata Civica, the modern centre of rebuilt Tulcea.

Information

Try the desk of the Delta Hotel, Strada Isaccea 2, although they're not usually helpful unless you're on a package tour.

Book a sleeper out of Tulcea at the CFR Travel Agency at Strada Progresului 28 near the Natural History Museum.

Things to See

As you stroll along the river you'll see the **Independence Monument** (1904) on Citadel Hill at the far eastern end of town. This is reached by following Strada Gloriei from behind the Egreta Hotel to its end. There's a fairly good **historical museum** just below the monument and the view is worth the trip. On your way back watch for the minaret of the Turkish **Azizie Mosque** (1863) down Strada Independentei. The **Natural History Museum and Aquarium**, Strada Progresului 32 behind Patria Cinema west of Piata Civica, should be visited if you have time. The collection of Danube fish is good.

Places to Stay

Try to arrive in Tulcea before noon as the

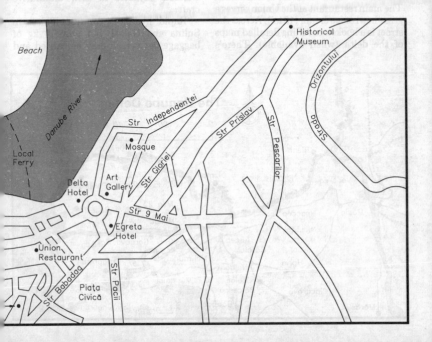

hotels are expensive and there's no campground in the city. Of the two high-rise hotels the *Egreta* is the cheaper, but at 250 lei single, 400 lei double for a room with shared bath it's no bargain. All rooms at the *Delta Hotel* are 462 lei double (no singles).

A 'no camping' regulation within Tulcea city limits is strictly enforced by police. In a pinch take the hourly passenger ferry across the Danube and follow the path downstream a little. There are places to pitch a tent along the riverside there. The closest official campground is near Murighiol (Independenta), 40 km southeast of Tulcea by bus, then three km on foot. The facilities here are abysmal and the only return bus to Tulcea departs Murighiol at 5 am!

Places to Eat

The easiest place to eat is the autoservice cafeteria at the *Union Restaurant*, Strada 23 August near the Delta Hotel. The main restaurant at the Union serves a great bowl of ice cream (18 lei). Across the street is a bookstore selling detailed maps of the delta (when available). There's another good cafeteria on the back side of the *Egreta Hotel*.

Getting There & Away

There are local trains from Constanta via Medgidia (four hours). The daily express train from Bucharest (five hours) just misses all of that days' ferries, forcing you to spend the night in troublesome Tulcea. A better bet is the overnight train to and from Bucharest's Obor Railway Station. Buses arrive in Tulcea from Constanta, Braila and Galati.

ON THE DANUBE

The only part of the delta readily accessible to foreigners is the middle arm of the Danube, which cuts directly across from Tulcea to Sulina (71 km). Much river traffic uses the Sulina arm which was straightened for this purpose in the 19th century. You pass huge ocean going ships rising out of the water and East German kayakers in their diminutive craft.

'Rapid' hydrofoils run from Tulcea to Sulina and Galati, but only 10 kg of baggage per person may be carried and

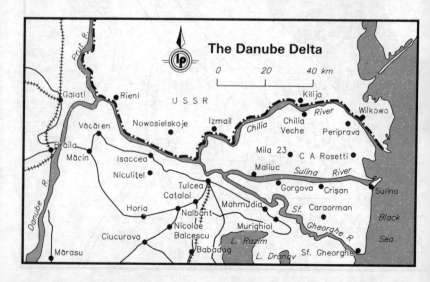

departures are often cancelled without notice.

A better choice are the 'classic' ferryboats to Braila, Galati and Sulina, departing daily just after 12 noon year round (up to 30 kg baggage allowed). Ferry tickets go on sale at the terminals about an hour before departure. In summer the queues are long, so get in the correct line early.

The ferry's first stop is at the *Salcia Hotel* at Maliuc, 27 km from Tulcea. There's a campground near the hotel. The ferry then continues to Crisan, from whence sidetrips are possible on smaller ferries to Mila 23 and Caraorman. The 1st class *Lebada Hotel* is on the opposite side of the Danube from the Crisan ferry landing and a km upstream. Once again, you may camp in the vicinity of the hotel. Rowboats are sometimes available at Crisan and Maliuc.

There are also Navrom ferries to Periprava (103 km) and Sfintu Gheorghe (113 km) on the north and south arms of the Danube, but foreign tourists aren't allowed on those services.

Tours There are expensive ONT tours through the delta, payable in western currency (US$40 and up). Sign up at the friendly Delta Hotel in Tulcea. The delta wildlife generally moves off quickly when it hears these noisy tourist boats coming.

SULINA

Sulina is the highlight of the ferry trip from Tulcea and you get a great view of it as the ship sails through the middle of town on its way to the landing. You pass derelict old dredges and ships. The riverfront promenade is most evocative at sunset, as the pink fireball drops behind the Danube.

The only specific attractions at Sulina are the old lighthouse you pass between the landing and the hotel, and an overgrown 19th century British cemetery on the way to the beach. Carry on a km to this beach where you'll see how Danube silt has created a channel far out into the Black Sea. You'll also see a long line of Romanian radar installations among the dunes, pointed at the Soviet Union. This broad beach continues 30 km south, all the way to Sfintu Gheorghe.

There's an expensive new hotel at Sulina, or you can camp free in the cow pasture opposite. There's a surprisingly good bookstore on the riverfront, but nowhere decent to eat. Sulina is not connected to the European road network so there are few vehicles.

Getting There & Away

It's possible to go straight through from Braila to Sulina or vice versa on Navrom 'classical' ferries which connect at Tulcea, an eight-hour trip. Through tickets are sold, saving you the major inconvenience of having to line up again in Tulcea. You change boats at Tulcea and may have a few hours to look around.

UPRIVER FROM TULCEA

The ferry trip between Tulcea and Galati is especially interesting since the Danube here marks the boundary between Romania and the USSR. You'll sail along the electric fence which encloses this vast, enigmatic country. You get a fine continuous view of Rieni, the second most important Soviet Danube port (Izmail is on the northern arm of the Danube), perhaps the best free peek possible into the Soviet Union.

Galati is a large industrial city with docks and shipyards stretching for kms along the riverside. Galati's massive housing complexes, which fill the city and cover entire hillsides, are best appreciated from aboard ship. It's strongly recommended that you continue to Braila, the ferry's next port of call (you may have to change boats in Galati).

BRAILA

Braila is a sleepy 19th century Danube town full of charming turn-of-the-century mansions, tree-lined boulevards and restful parks. Piata Lenin, a lovely central square at the heart of the city, is complete with statues, fountain, tower, church and people sitting on benches under the trees. It's a perfect gateway to the delta or a good place to end your trip. There are onward connections to Bucharest and northern Romania by train.

Orientation

From the Navrom ferry terminal walk straight up Strada Imparatul Traian to Piata Lenin, the central square. To reach Braila Railway Station, about two kms north-west at the end of Strada Victoriei, catch a city bus from in front of the CFR Agentie de Voiaj on this square.

Information

The tourist office is at Strada Republicii 58. The CFR railway ticket office is at Piata Lenin 11.

Things to See

In the middle of **Piata Lenin** is a 17th century mosque converted into a Romanian Orthodox church in 1835 and a bust of Emperor Trajan (1906). The **Historical Museum** (closed Monday) is on the north side of Piata Lenin. Check for performances at the Dramatic Theatre on the west side of the square. On the east side of Piata Lenin like Grandma's last tooth stands high-rise Hotel Traian. Behind this odd monstrosity, in a mansion on Strada Belvedere, is the local **art gallery** (closed Monday).

Walk north on Strada Belvedere two blocks, then turn left on Strada Gradina Publica to reach a large **public park** with a view of the Danube. South of Piata Lenin on the street beside Hotel Danubiu is a huge **Greek Orthodox church** (1872).

Places to Stay

There are three wonderful old 2nd class hotels in Braila, all offering spacious rooms with shared bath for 162 lei single, 275 lei double with breakfast. The nicest is the *Hotel Danubiu* on Piata Lenin, brimming with old world flavour. Nearby are the *Hotel Pescarus*, Strada Republicii 17, and *Hotel Delta*, Strada Republicii 56. *Hotel Traian* wants 335 lei single.

There's a basic campground at Sarat Lake, seven km south-west of Braila.

Places to Eat

There's a self-service restaurant in *Hotel Traian*. Also try *Restaurant Lacto Vegetarian* opposite Central Cinema, up Calea Galati from beside the museum.

Getting There & Away

The times of all trains departing Braila are posted in the window of the CFR Agentie de Voiaj in front of Hotel

Braila

1 Hotel Delta
2 Hotel Pescarus
3 Historical Museum
4 Hotel Traian
5 Art Gallery
6 Public Park
7 Hotel Danubiu
8 Orthodox Church
9 Ferry Terminal

Danubiu. Tickets can be purchased inside. There are direct trains to Bucharest (book a seat on a fast train for the next day), but northbound to Iasi or Suceava you change at Galati. There are morning Navrom ferries downriver on the Danube from Braila to Tulcea and Sulina. Get a through ticket to Maliuc, Crisan or Sulina and avoid Tulcea where you must change boats.

Moldavia

Moldavia, one of the three original principalities of Romania, is a land of excellent horses and rich folklore. Some of Romania's best vineyards are at Cotnari between Iasi and Suceava. The centre of medieval Moldavia was Bukovina in the easily defended Carpathian foothills. From Suceava Stefan cel Mare (Stefan the Great), called the 'athlete of Christ' by Pope Pius VI, led the resistance to the Turks for nearly half a century (1457-1504). This prince and his son, Petru Rares, erected fortified monasteries throughout Bukovina. On the exteriors were stunning frescoes intended to educate the illiterate masses. Only with Petru Rares' defeat by the Turks in 1538 did Moldavia's golden age wane.

Later the emphasis shifted to the Moldavian plateau, an inclined plain stretching from Galati to Putna. Romanian Moldavia is only the western half of the medieval principality. Bessarabia, the portion east of the Prut River, was taken by Russia in 1812, at a time when Moldavia was still a vassal of the Ottoman Empire. Although recovered by Romania during the chaotic inter-war period, Bessarabia is now a union republic of the USSR. Bukovina in northern Moldavia was controlled by the Hapsburgs of Austria from 1775 to 1918. Although Bukovina gets lots of tour groups, the rest of the region (Iasi included) is well off the beaten track.

IASI

Iasi (Jassy) became capital of Moldavia in 1565. When the principalities of Moldavia and Wallachia united in 1859, Iasi served as the national capital until replaced by Bucharest in 1862. This illustrious history accounts for the great monasteries, churches, public buildings and museums which surprise visitors who had never heard of the place. Always a leading intellectual centre, Romania's first university was founded here in 1860. You'll need a full day at least to see Iasi.

Orientation

To reach Piata Unirii, the city's heart, from the railway station walk north-east two blocks on Strada 30 Decembrie, then right on Soseaua Arcu. From Piata Unirii, Strada Stefan cel Mare runs south-east past the Metropolitan Cathedral to the massive Palace of Culture, one of Romania's finest buildings. Calea 23 August runs north-west from above the square to the university and Copou Park.

Information

The tourist office is in the alley beside Hotel Unirea off Piata Unirii. The CFR railway ticket office is on Piata Unirii across from Hotel Traian. Casa Cartii on Strada Stefan cel Mare is one of the best bookstores in Romania. There are even books in English and German!

Things to See

Golia Monastery (1660), overlooking Tirgu Cucu, is a few blocks east of Piata Unirii along Strada Cuza Voda. Its walls and tower shelter a 17th century church with twin domes, frescoes, intricate carved doorways and iconostasis.

Take a streetcar from Tirgu Cucu up to **Copou Park** (monuments, gardens, literary museum), then walk back down Calea 23 August. You'll pass the huge neo-Classical **university** (1897). Just before the statue in the middle of the street, turn left to the 1858 mansion housing the **Casa Pogor Literary Museum**, Strada I C Frimu

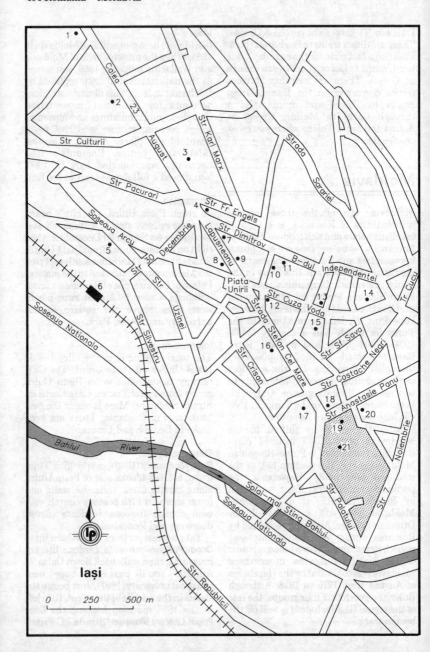

Iaşi

0   250   500 m

1	Copou Park
2	University
3	Casa Pogor Literary Museum
4	Restaurant Expres
5	Bus Station
6	Railway Station
7	Museum of the Union
8	Hotel Traian
9	Hotel Unirea
10	Theatrical Museum
11	Natural History Museum
12	Hotel Continental
13	Filharmonia
14	Golia Monastery
15	National Theatre
16	Metropolitan Cathedral
17	Church of the Three Hierarchs
18	Party House
19	Dosoftei House
20	Hotel Moldova
21	Palace of Culture

4. In the garden in front of the museum is a Soviet war cemetery.

Downhill again and across Piata Tineretului proceed to the **Museum of the Union**, Strada Lapusneanu 14, in a large Empire building (1806) which was the residence of Prince Alexander Ioan Cuza (1820-1873). On Piata Unirii at the foot of this street is a statue (1912) of the man. Prince Alexander Ioan Cuza was the founder of modern Romania, who achieved the union of Wallachia and Moldavia in 1859.

Continue east on Strada Cuza Voda a block to Strada V Alecsandri, where you turn left and walk half a block to the **Theatrical Museum** on the right. Up around the corner on the right at Bulevardul Independentei 16 is the **Natural History Museum**. A visit to these minor museums gives you the chance to enter two old Moldavian buildings.

Backtrack to Piata Unirii and follow Strada Stefan cel Mare directly south-east toward the monumental Palace of Culture. Along the way you'll pass two magnificent churches on the right, first the **Moldavian Metropolitan Cathedral**

(1886) with four towers and a cavernous interior, then the fabulous **Church of the Three Hierarchs** (1639), the exterior of which is completely covered with intricate decorative patterns carved from stone. Inside is the tomb of the church's founder, Prince Vasile Lupu, and the aforementioned Prince Alexander Ioan Cuza.

The giant neo-Gothic **Palace of Culture** (1906-1925), formerly the Administrative Palace, contains four museums: historical, fine arts, ethnological and technical. In addition there are special exhibitions. Separate tickets are sold for each – you could end up with six or seven if you visit everything. As with most of Iasi's other museums they're all closed on Mondays. You'd probably have to be a specialist to appreciate the neolithic Cucuteni pottery in the Historical Museum, but it's worth noting for its importance to European prehistory.

On the square in front of the Palace of Culture is an old stone building in which metropolitan Dosoftei printed the first major work in verse to appear in the Romanian language (1673). Behind this is the swank new headquarters of the local Communist Party. Also on the square is **St Nicolae Domnesc Church** (1492), Iasi's oldest building, and an equestrian statue of Stefan the Great (1883).

Places to Stay

There are four hotels in Iasi, all graded 1st class. The imposing but expensive old *Hotel Traian* is on Piata Unirii (330 lei single, 610 lei double). The modern 13-storey high-rise *Hotel Unirea* on the same square is cheaper at US$28 single, US$38 double. Arab and African students congregate here. A block away at Strada Cuza Voda 4 is the *Hotel Continental* where rooms begin at US$18 single, US$28 double. They'll claim all the cheaper rooms are full. Both the Traian and Continental suffer from streetcar noise in the very early morning.

There's a pleasant campground in the forest at Lake Ciric near Iasi airport, about six km north of town. The easiest way to get there is by taxi (50 lei), or take a streetcar to Tirgu Cucu then wait for the hourly bus. On the lake near the campground is a restaurant specialising in Romanian cuisine.

Places to Eat

The easiest place in Iasi to eat is *Restaurant Expres* on Piata Tineretului, up Strada Lapusneanu from Piata Unirii.

Entertainment

On the east side of Strada Stefan cel Mare nearly opposite the Metropolitan Cathedral is the neo-Baroque *National Theatre* (1896). Tickets for events here and at the nearby *Filharmonia* are available from the Agentia Teatrala on Strada Stefan cel Mare near the Metropolitan Cathedral.

Getting There & Away

Iasi is on the main line between Bucharest and Kiev via Kishinev, capital of Bessarabia. Expresses to Bucharest and Suceava leave several times a day. For Braila you may have to change trains at Birlad and Galati.

Bukovina

The painted churches of Bukovina are among the greatest artistic monuments of Europe. Erected at a time when northern Moldavia was threatened by Turkish invaders, the monasteries were surrounded by strong defensive walls. Great popular armies would mass inside these walls, waiting to do battle. To educate, entertain and arouse the illiterate soldiers and peasants unable to enter the church or understand the Slavonic liturgy, well-known Biblical stories were portrayed in cartoon-style registers, a unique mass media. The exterior of the church at Sucevita Monastery is almost completely covered with these magnificent 16th century frescoes.

What catches our attention is the realistic manner of painting human figures in vast compositions against a backdrop not unlike the local landscape of the forested Carpathian foothills. Over the centuries the colours have preserved their freshness, from the greens of Sucevita to the blues of Voronet and the reds of Humor. The church domes are a peculiar combination of Moorish crossed arches and Byzantine pendentives with larger than life paintings of Christ or the Virgin peering down from inside.

If your time is limited Voronet and Moldovita monasteries, both quite accessible by bus and train, will give you a good cross-section of what Bukovina has to offer. To do a complete Suceava, Putna, Radauti, Sucevita, Moldovita, Humor, Voronet circuit on your own will require at least three days of hard going and is not recommended outside the camping season. The tourist office in Suceava doesn't organise tours to the monasteries. You must join an ONT tour in Bucharest (US$89 for two days) or try to ingratiate yourself with the foreign tour escort (*not* the Romanian guide) of any group you happen to meet along the way.

SUCEAVA

Suceava was capital of Moldavia from 1388 to 1565. Today it's a gateway to the painted churches of Bukovina. There are a few churches and an historic fortress to see, but four hours are enough here. If your time is short head straight for Gura Humorului and skip Suceava.

Orientation

There are two railway stations, Gara Suceava Burdujeni and Gara de Nord, both a couple of km north of Piata 23 August, the centre of town (take a bus).

Information

The tourist office, Strada N Balcescu 2, is beside Hotel Suceava on Piata 23 August. The CFR railway ticket agency, Strada N

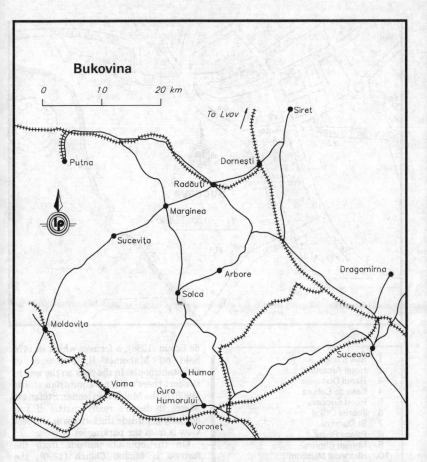

Bukovina

0   10   20 km

To Lvov

Siret

Putna

Dornești

Rădăuți

Marginea

Sucevița

Arbore

Dragomirna

Solca

Moldovița

Suceava

Humor

Vama

Gura
Humorului

Voroneț

Balcescu 8, is beside the post office nearby.

Things to See
The foundations of the 15th century **princely palace** are near the bus stop at Piata 23 August. The large church beyond is **St Dumitru** (1535) and opposite is the main Suceava vegetable market. Just west of Piata 23 August at Strada Ciprian Porumbescu 5 is the **Hanul Domnesc**, a 16th century princely guest house now the Ethnographical Museum (closed Monday).

The collection of folk costumes and photos is quite good. Return to Piata 23 August and follow Strada Stefan cel Mare south past the park to the surprisingly informative **District Historical Museum**, Strada Stefan cel Mare 33.

Backtrack a little to the park and take Strada V I Lenin south-east to the **Monastery of Sfintu Ioan cel Nou** (1522) or St George. The paintings on the outside of the church are badly faded but they give you an idea of the painted churches Bukovina is famous for.

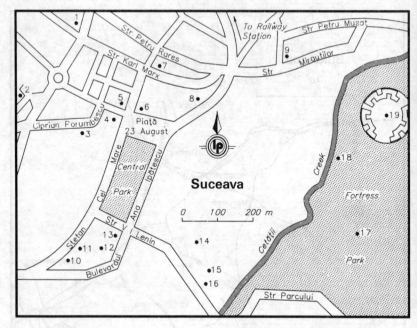

Suceava

0   100   200 m

1	Bus Station
2	Hotel Arcasul
3	Hanul Domnesc
4	Casa de Cultura
5	Hotel Suceava
6	Tourist Office
7	St Dumitru
8	Palace Ruins
9	Mirauti Church
10	Historical Museum
11	Self-service Restaurant
12	Hotel Bukovina
13	Hotel Parc
14	Sf Ioan Cel Nou
15	Casa Tineretului
16	Hotel Balada
17	Cemetery
18	Statue of Stefan Cel Mare
19	Cetatea de Scaun

Continue on Strada V I Lenin till you see signs pointing the way to the **Cetatea de Scaun** (1388), a fortress which in 1476 held off Mahomet II, conqueror of Constantinople. In the park on the way to the fort there's a huge equestrian statue (1966) of the Moldavian leader, Stefan cel Mare. It doesn't really matter if you actually get inside the fortress as the best view is from the parking lot.

On the opposite hillside from the fortress is **Mirauti Church** (1390), the original coronation church rebuilt in the 17th century. Get there by taking the path down through the park on the left (west) side of the fortress. Mirauti is only a short walk from your starting point.

Places to Stay

A double room in the 2nd class *Hotel Parc*, Bulevardul Ana Ipatescu 6, is 265 lei. The only other less expensive hotel is the *Casa Tineretului* behind *Hotel Balada* on Strada V I Lenin, but it's often full with groups. All Suceava's other hotels are expensive tourist facilities with little to distinguish between them. The campground is on Strada Ilie Pintilie between Gara de Nord and Suceava.

Places to Eat

There's a rather poor self-service restaurant beside Tineretului Cinema on Strada Stefan cel Mare, not far from the Historical Museum, and another self-service across the street from Gara Suceava Burdujeni.

Getting There & Away

Express trains to Bucharest, Iasi and Cluj-Napoca are fairly regular. Local trains of interest to visitors run west to Vatra Dornei via Gura Humorului and north-west to Putna via Radauti.

PUTNA

Putna Monastery, founded in 1466, is still a very active religious community. Groups of monks chant mass just before sunset. The role this and similar institutions play in socialist Romania is perhaps explained by a text posted just inside Putna's church: 'The monastery of Putna, the first foundation of Stefan the Great, princely necropole and a real centre of Romanian culture through the centuries, represents a living testimony of the cultural and artistic traditions of the Romanian people and by that a remarkable school of patriotism.' Stefan the Great himself is buried in the church.

The large building behind the church contains a rich museum of medieval manuscripts and rare 15th century textiles. Place of honour goes to the *Tetraevanghel* of 1473 with a portrait of the prince offering the book to the virgin.

Places to Stay

Accommodation at Putna is good. Just outside the monastery gate is a large tourist complex with a hotel (190 lei single, 250 lei double), open year round. Adequate meals are served in the hotel restaurant. Beside the hotel are many small bungalows and a campground (18 lei per person). These open May to mid-September.

Some people camp freelance in the field opposite the rock-hewn hermits' cave at Chilia near the train station. To get there follow the river upstream to a wooden bridge which you cross, then keep straight. The spiritually inclined could ask special permission to stay in the monastery.

Getting There & Away

Trains run to Putna from Suceava (via Radauti) every couple of hours, making Putna Monastery one of the most accessible in Bukovina. The large monastic enclosure is at the end of the road, just under two km from the station.

RADAUTI

This is an uninteresting market town with several buses a day to Sucevita Monastery. If you don't coincide with a convenient departure, take a bus to Marginea and walk or hitch the last nine km to the monastery. The bus station is two blocks from Radauti Railway Station. The *Hotel Bukovina* on Piata Republicii has rooms from 109 lei single, 164 lei double, but it's often full. There's a **folk art museum** opposite the hotel with local pottery and embroidered coats.

SUCEVITA

The church inside the fortified monastic enclosure at Sucevita (1586) is almost completely frescoed inside and out. As you enter you first see the *Virtuous Ladder* fresco covering most of the north exterior wall, which shows the 30 steps from Hell to Paradise. On the south outside wall is a tree symbolising the continuity of the Old and New testaments. The tree grows from the reclining figure of Jesse, who is flanked by a row of ancient philosophers. To the left is the Virgin as a Byzantine princess, angels holding a red veil over her head. Aside from the church, there's a small museum to visit at Sucevita Monastery.

If you've time climb the hill opposite the monastery for the view. Freelance camping is possible in the field at the foot of this hill, across the stream from the monastery. There's also the Hanul Sucevita, a restaurant about a km back toward Radauti, which rents expensive rooms (350 lei) and inexpensive bungalows (56 lei per person).

Sucevita is by far the most difficult monastery to reach on public transport. Service from Radauti is infrequent and only one bus a day (early morning) runs the 36 km from Sucevita to Moldovita. Hitching is not easy (wave a pack of Kent cigarettes). The westbound highway winds up and over a high mountain pass, through forests which enclose both Sucevita and Moldovita monasteries.

MOLDOVITA

As at Sucevita, Moldovita Monastery (1532) consists of a strong fortified enclosure complete with towers and gates, the magnificent painted church at its centre. Both monasteries are in the care of pious nuns and have undergone careful restoration in recent years.

Several of the paintings at Moldovita are unique. For example, on the south exterior wall of the church is a depiction of the defence of Constantinople in 626 against Persians dressed as Turks, and on the porch a representation of the Last Judgement. Inside the sanctuary on a wall facing the original carved iconostasis is a portrait of Prince Petru Rares (the founder) and his family offering the church to Christ. All these works date from 1537. In the small museum at Moldovita Monastery is Petru Rares' original throne.

There's a campground (Popas Turistic) with bungalows between the station and the monastery, and a satisfactory restaurant in the Complex Commercial nearby on the road to Vama.

Getting There & Away

Moldovita Monastery is much easier to reach than Sucevita since it's right above Vatra Moldovitei Railway Station, on a 14-km branch line from Vama off the Suceava-Cluj mainline. There are three trains a day in each direction.

GURA HUMORULUI

This small town 36 km west of Suceava on the main railway line to Cluj-Napoca is an ideal centre for visiting the monasteries. Most trains stop here. The adjacent railway and bus stations are a seven-minute walk from the centre of town. There are nine buses a day to the painted churches of Humor and Voronet, each about six km from Gura Humorului. On Sunday, however, bus service is greatly reduced. The walk back to town from Voronet is enjoyable, passing many large farm houses. In summer both churches stay open till 8 pm.

Humor

At Humor (1530) the best paintings are on the south exterior wall. There's a badly faded depiction of the siege of Constantinople, with the legend of the Return of the Prodigal Son beside it to the right. Notice the feast scene and five dancers. Above this is the devil as a woman (the figure with wings but no halo). On the porch is a Last Judgement. In the first chamber inside the church are scenes of martyrdom. In the middle chamber is the tomb of Toader Bubuiog. Just above and to the left is his portrait, offering the church to Christ.

Voronet

The Last Judgement, which fills the entire west wall at Voronet, is perhaps the most marvellous, unified composition of any of the frescoes on the Bukovina churches. At the top angels roll up the signs of the zodiac to indicate the end of time. The middle register shows humanity being brought to judgement. On the left St Paul escorts the believers, while on the right Moses brings forward the unbelievers. These latter are from left to right, Jews,

Turks, Tartars, Armenians and negroes – a graphic representation of the prejudices of the time. Below is the resurrection. Even the wild animals give back pieces of bodies to complete those rising from the graves. The sea also gives forth its victims.

At the top of the north wall is Genesis, from Adam and Eve on the left to Cain and Abel on the right. The south wall features another *Tree of Jesse* with the genealogy of Biblical personalities. In the vertical register to the left of this is the story of the martyrdom of St John of Suceava (this saint is buried in the Monastery of Sfintu Ioan cel Nou in Suceava). Inside facing the iconostasis is the famous portrait of Stefan the Great offering Voronet church to Christ. This prince ordered Voronet erected in 1470, although the paintings date from 1547.

Places to Stay & Eat

The *Hotel Carpati* up the street beside the post office in Gura Humorului is 210 lei. Otherwise try the *Motel Arinis* just outside town which also has small bungalows, or camp free in the field beside the river between Gura Humorului and Voronet. There's a self-service restaurant opposite the post office.

VATRA DORNEI

This health resort high up in the Carpathians is easily accessible as all trains between Suceava and Cluj-Napoca stop here. It's a good place to know about if you need somewhere to stop for the night, not a town you'd go out of your way to see. There are two railway stations about a km apart. You want Vatra Dornei Bai Railway Station, which is right opposite the thermal baths.

A large park full of pine trees stretches up from the picturesque old spa. On Strada 7 Noiembrie near Vatra Dornei Bai station are the Ethnographic Museum and a large synagogue farther along. A chairlift on a hill opposite will take you up into the mountains.

Information

The tourist office is at Strada Republicii 5. The CFR railway ticket office is at Strada 7 Noiembrie 28.

Places to Stay

There are two expensive hotels, the *Caliman* and the *Bradul*, adjacent to the park. Cheaper hotels are the *Hotel Dorna*, Strada 7 Noiembrie 15, and *Hotel Bistrita*, Strada 7 Noiembrie 29, both often full. Up the steps above the church at the end of Strada 7 Noiembrie is the *Cabana Runc*, with small bungalows *(popas)* and a large camping area on a hilltop overlooking Vatra Dornei.

Transylvania

To most people the name Transylvania conjures up haunted castles, werewolves and vampires. Certainly the 14th century castles of Bran and Hunedoara appear ready-made for a Count Dracula movie, but Vlad Tepes was a real prince who led

Vlad Tepes

Romanian resistance to Ottoman expansion in the 15th century. His habit of impaling the heads of slain Turkish foes on stakes may seem extreme but Transylvania has had a tumultuous past.

For 1000 years right up to WW I Transylvania was part of Hungary. In the 10th century a Magyar tribe, the Szeklers, settled here, followed in the 12th century by Saxon merchant/knights. The seven towns they founded, Bistrita (Bistritz), Brasov (Kronstadt), Cluj (Klausenburg), Medias (Mediasch), Sebes (Muhlbach), Sibiu (Hermannstadt) and Sighisoara (Schassburg), gave Transylvania its German name, Siebenburgen. Although Romanians have always constituted a majority, Hungarians still number 1,700,000 in Transylvania and half a million Germans are present.

The princes of Transylvania enjoyed substantial autonomy. Two of them became Hungarian national heroes: Iancu of Hunedoara, who defeated the Turks at Belgrade in 1456, and Francisc Rakoczy II, who fought for Hungarian independence from Austria from 1703 to 1711. In 1600 Michael the Brave joined Transylvania to Wallachia and Moldavia, a union which endured until he was assassinated a year later.

Although easily accessible from Hungary (daily trains, visas issued at the border), the Transylvanian plateau is one of the last travel frontiers of Europe. Facilities such as hotels, campgrounds, restaurants, trains and buses exist but unless you're on a tour you won't get much help from officialdom in using them. Aside from the enchanting old towns there are rugged mountains to climb all round. For lovers of medieval art and history it's an unparalleled chance to escape the hordes in Budapest and Vienna and have an untamed corner of the old Austro-Hungarian Empire all to themselves.

SINAIA

This well-known winter resort snuggles at an altitude of 800 to 930 metres in a narrow valley sliced between the mountains. Sinaia and nearby Busteni are perfect starting points for summer hikes into the Bucegi Carpathians. Cable cars carry you up to the crest without effort from points on the main railway line between Bucharest and Brasov. Until 1920 the Hungarian-Romanian border ran along Predeal Pass just north. For convenience we've included Sinaia with Transylvania when it actually belongs with Wallachia.

Information

The tourist office is just up the hill from the train station at Bulevardul Carpati 19 opposite Hotel Sinaia. They're usually very helpful.

Things to See

Above the park and the Palace Hotel is **Sinaia Monastery**, named for Mt Sinai. The large Orthodox church you see as you enter dates from 1846, but an older church (1695) with its original frescoes is in the compound to the left. Beside the newer church is a museum.

Peles Castle (1883), former royal summer residence and once a museum, is now a retreat for high officials and closed to the public. Peles was built to resemble a German hunting lodge for the Prussian princeling Carol I, King of Romania. The castle access roads are also closed, so the only glimpse you can get of it is from the cable car.

The Short Hike

Summertime swarms of Romanian day trippers take the cable car from Sinaia up to *Cabana Miorita* (2000 metres) in the Bucegi Mountains. From Miorita they walk north to *Cabana Piatra Arsa* (1.5 hours) and on to *Cabana Babele* (another hour) where they catch a second cable car back down to the railway at Busteni. The walk from Miorita to Babele is not difficult, involving a 50-metre drop to Piatra Arsa (1950 metres) then a climb back up to Babele (2206 metres). This explains the routes' tremendous popularity.

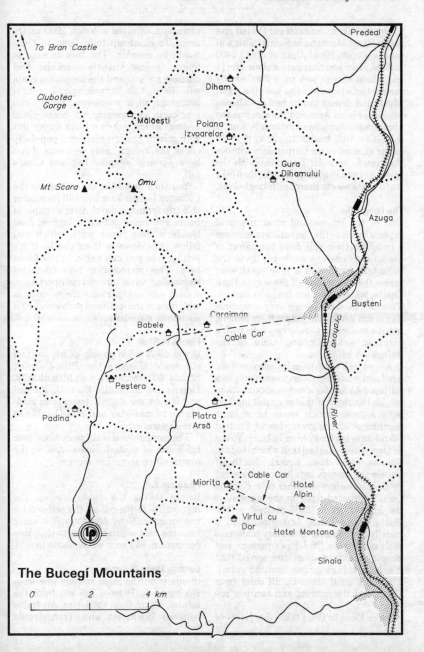

To Bran Castle

Clubotea
Gorge

Diham

Mălăeşti

Poiana
Izvoarelor

Gura
Dihamului

Mt Scara   Omu

Azuga

Bușteni

Caraiman

Babele   Cable Car

Peştera

Prahova River

Padina

Piatra
Arsă

Mioriţa   Cable Car

Hotel
Alpin

Virful cu
Dor

Hotel Montana

Sinaia

The Bucegí Mountains

0   2   4 km

You catch the first cable car (11 lei) just above Hotel Montana in Sinaia. This will take you up to Hotel Alpin at about 1400 metres. Here you change to a chair lift (11 lei) which carries you up a further 557 metres to Cabana Miorita near the crest. Meals and drinks can be had at cabanas Miorita, Piatra Arsa and Babele, but the accommodation offered in these is usually full. It's a well beaten track, so if you'd rather experience the Carpathians without the crowds consider beginning with the cable car from Busteni to Babele, then hike north all the way to Bran Castle (see below).

The Long Hike

One of the easiest and most practical expeditions into the Carpathians involves a two-hour train ride from Bucharest to Sinaia or Busteni, a cable car up to the mountain crest, and a hike north-west across the mountains all the way to Bran Castle, where there are buses to Brasov. This can be done in one very strenuous day if you get an early start from Babele, but it's preferable to take two days with a night at either *Cabana Omu* or the 'refuge' on Mt Scara.

As you look north from Babele you'll see a red and white television transmitter on a hilltop, looking like a rocket about to take off. To the right of this is a trail marked with a cross which leads to a large monument with a great view of Busteni (45 minutes each way from Babele). To the left is a yellow-marked trail which leads to Cabana Omu (two hours). North of Babele the scenery gets better with great drops into valleys on either side. Cabana Omu is situated right on the summit at the highest point (2505 metres) in the Bucegi Carpathians. Accommodation is usually available on dormitory platforms with mattresses (28 lei per person) and simple meals are sometimes served (but it's best to bring your own food and water). There are good views on all sides from Omu, and the sunsets and sunrises are great.

From Omu to Bran takes five hours or more and involves a tough 2000 metre drop. To climb up from Bran to Omu would be murder. The trail is easy to follow (yellow triangle markers) and chances are you and the mountain goats will have this surprisingly beautiful landscape all to yourselves. From Omu you begin by crossing Mt Scara (2422 metres) where there's a plain empty hut with a hard wooden platform, popularly called the 'refuge.' Stay here only if you have a warm sleeping bag and Omu's full.

You then begin the descent down the Ciubotea Gorge. Your legs will remember this trip for many days! After a couple of hours you come out on a logging road beside a river (wash up!), which you follow right down to Bran Castle. If it's getting late you can camp in the forest here. This invigorating hike combines sightseeing, adventure and transportation, a great way to experience the mountains with none of the logistical problems you'll encounter elsewhere.

Places to Stay

If you don't mind paying dearly for real old world elegance the *Palace Hotel*, Strada 30 Decembrie 4, may fill both bills. Hotel rates at Sinaia, Busteni, Predeal and Brasov are slightly lower from mid-March to mid-May and mid-October to mid-December.

The campground is at Izvory Rece, four km south of central Sinaia. Ask at the tourist office about bus service.

Places to Eat

Before taking the cable car up the mountainside pig out at the self-service restaurant in *Hotel Montana*. You enter from the road which leads up to the cable car station. Fill your water bottle here.

Getting There & Away

Sinaia is on the main railway line from Bucharest to Brasov, 126 km from the former, 45 km from the latter. All trains between Bucharest and Transylvania stop here. Local trains to Busteni, Predeal and Brasov are quite frequent.

RISNOV & BRAN

Both Risnov and Bran, in the foothills south-west of Brasov on the main road to Pitesti, are well known for their castles. Bran Castle (1378) is heavily promoted as a tourist attraction. It's hard to visit Romania without seeing it in travel brochures or on postcards. The tour buses rarely visit Risnov Castle, which is larger but less accessible than Bran.

Risnov

A short 15-km train ride on the Zarnesti line from Brasov, Risnov has the double attraction of castle and a convenient campground. From the railway station you'll see the large 14th century castle on a distant hilltop. Reach it (open Tuesday to Sunday 10 am to 4 pm) up the stairs behind the Casa de Cultura on Piata 23 August, about a km from the station.

The campground is in the forest just below the castle, near a restaurant and public swimming pool. There are bungalows (125 lei) in the campground, or you may camp for 32 lei. It's a little crowded, but at last report the washroom facilities were OK. There are hiking trails in the vicinity for those not interested in downing big mugs of beer on the restaurant terrace above the pool.

Bran

Over-promoted Bran Castle originated as a toll station erected by the German merchants of Brasov to regulate trade between Transylvania and Wallachia. Although impressive in itself, Bran is *not* Count Dracula's castle as some travel guides infer (see Curtea de Arges below). Beside the castle entrance is a collection of Transylvanian farm buildings in a park. You may visit these on the same admission ticket.

Bran Castle (9 am to 4 pm) is easily accessible by bus from Risnov train station. The buses usually connect with local trains to and from Brasov. Buy your bus ticket at the kiosk beside the bus stop at Risnov station. In Bran pick up your return bus ticket at the Cofetarie on the corner near the castle. Bus times are posted. Avoid Bran on Sunday (fewer buses) and Monday (castle closed).

BRASOV

Brasov is a pleasant medieval town flanked by verdant hills on either side. The original German mercantile colony was protected by the walls of old Kronstadt (Brasov). The Romanians lived at Scheii, just outside the walls to the south-west. Strategically situated at the meeting point of three principalities, Brasov was a major medieval trading centre. Today the city's tractor, truck and textile factories are more important than commerce and endless rows of concrete apartment blocks have risen to house the proletariat. Fortunately they're far enough away not to spoil the charm of Brasov's quaint old town.

Orientation

The train station is far north-east of the centre of town, so take trolley bus No 4 (ticket at the kiosk) to Parcul Central (if you're looking for a hotel) or the Black Church (if you're sightseeing). Strada Republicii, Brasov's pedestrian promenade, is crowded with shops and cafes from Parcul Central to Piata 23 August.

Information

The tourist information office is at the back of the lobby of the Carpati Hotel, Bulevardul Gheorghe Gheorghiu-Dej 25 on Parcul Central. The CFR railway ticket office is at Strada Republicii 53 opposite Hotel Postavarul.

Things to See

In the middle of Piata 23 August is the town hall (1420), now the **Historical Museum** (closed Monday). The 58-metre high Trumpeter's Tower above the building dates from 1582. The Gothic

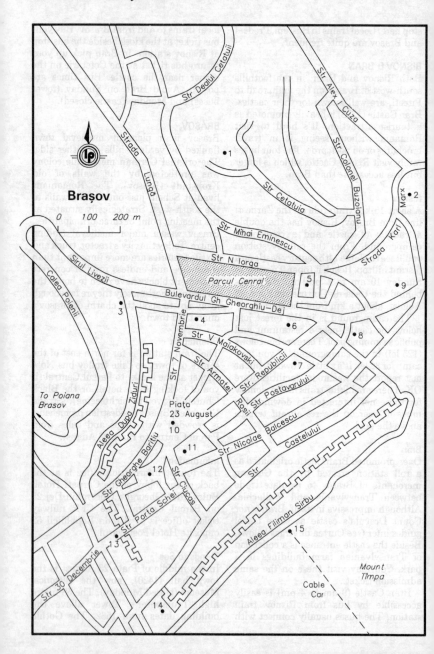

Brașov

0   100   200 m

To Poiana
Brasov

Str Dealul Cetatii

Str Alex I Cuza

Str Colonel Buzoianu

Str Cetatuia

Str Karl Marx

Strada Lungă

Strada Karl Marx

Str Mihai Eminescu

Str N Iorga

Parcul Central

Bulevardul Gh Gheorghiu-Dej

Sirul Livezii

Calea Poienii

Str 7 Noiembrie

Str V Maiakovski

Str Armatei Rosii

Str Republicii

Str Postavarului

Str Nicolae Balcescu

Castelului

Aleea Dupa Ziduri

Str Gheorghe Baritiu

Str Porta Schei

Str Cucas

Str 30 Decembrie

Piata
23 August

Aleea Filiman Sirbu

Mount
Timpa

Cable
Car

1	Citadel
2	Hotel Turist
3	County Library
4	Hotel Carpati
5	Municipal Council
6	Folklore Museum & Art Gallery
7	Hotel Postavarul
8	District Council
9	Dramatic Theatre
10	Historial Museum
11	Cerbul Carpatia
12	Black Church
13	Schei Gate
14	Weaver's Bastion
15	Timpa Cablecar

Black Church (1384-1477), still used by German Lutherans, looms just south of the square. As you walk around the building to the entrance notice the statues on the exterior of the apse. The originals are now inside at the back of the church and oriental 'rugs hang from every balcony. The church's name comes from its appearance after a fire in 1689. Recitals on the 1839 organ (5 lei) are given at 6 pm in summer.

Go south-west a little to the neo-Classical **Schei Gate** (1828), then walk up Strada 30 Decembrie to Piata Unirii. Here you'll find the black-spired Greek Orthodox Church of **St Nicolae din Scheii** (1595). Beside the church is the **First Romanian School Museum** with a collection of icons, paintings on glass, old manuscripts, etc. The clock tower (1751) was financed by the empress of Russia and there's a picturesque cemetery opposite.

Return as you came and turn right before Schei Gate to reach the 16th century **Weaver's Bastion**, a little hidden above the sports field. This corner fort on the old city walls contains a museum with a fascinating scale model of Brasov in the 17th century. The model itself was created in 1896. Above the bastion is a pleasant promenade through the forest overlooking the town. Halfway along you'll come to the **Timpa Cablecar** (open

year round), which rises from 640 metres to 960 metres for a stunning view of the entire area.

Places to Stay

The only medium-priced hotels are the *Sport Hotel*, Strada V Maiakovski 3 behind the Carpati Hotel (from 198 lei single, 308 lei double with shared bath) and the *Turist Hotel*, Strada Karl Marx 32 (from 185 lei single, 290 lei double). The most characterful of the 1st class hotels is the *Hotel Postavarul*, Strada Republicii 62 (from 363 lei single, 550 lei double).

For camping see Risnov above. Alternatively take bus No 20 from the Biblioteca Judeteana (County Library) at the west end of Parcul Central, 13 km to the winter ski resort of Poiana Brasov, where you could camp freelance in the forest. From Poiana Brasov there are cable cars up to cabanas *Cristianul Mare* (1704 metres) and *Postavarul* (1602 metres).

Places to Eat

The easiest place to eat is *Autoservire Pioana* beside Hotel Capital, Bulevardul Gheorghe Gheorghiu-Dej 19. *Bufetul Postavarul* on Strada Republicii opposite Hotel Postavarul offers large servings of real Romanian food.

There's also the straightforward *Lacto-Vegetarian Restaurant* on Piata 23 August on the corner with Strada 7 Noiembrie. Brasov's most famous restaurant is the *Cerbul Carpatin* in Hirscher House (1545) on Piata 23 August. There's a wine cellar here open 5 to 10 pm, while the restaurant upstairs serves from 10 am to 10 pm.

Entertainment

For concerts and theatre ask at the Theatrical Ticket Agency, Strada Republicii 4 just off Piata 23 August.

Getting There & Away

Brasov is well connected to Bucharest, Sibiu and Cluj by fast trains. Local trains along the line from Brasov to Sibiu drop hikers headed for the Fagaras Mountains. If you're bound for Bran Castle take a Zarnesti train as far as Risnov.

SIGHISOARA

Sighisoara, birthplace of Vlad Tepes, is a perfectly preserved medieval town in beautiful hilly countryside. No less than 11 towers remain on Sighisoara's intact city walls, inside which are sloping cobbled streets lined with 16th century burgher houses and untouched churches. All trains between Bucharest and Budapest (via Oradea) pass here, so watch for it out the window if you're foolish enough not to get off.

Orientation

Follow Strada Garii south from the train station to a Soviet war cemetery, where you turn left to the large Orthodox church. Cross the Tirnava Mare River on the footbridge here and take Strada Morii to the left, then keep right all the way up to Piata Lenin and the old town. Many of the facilities you'll want to use are found along a short stretch of Strada Gheorghe Gheorghiu-Dej to the left off Strada Morii.

Information

The tourist office is at Strada Gheorghe Gheorghiu-Dej 10, beside the Steaua Hotel. The CFR railway ticket office is at Strada Gheorghe Gheorghiu-Dej 2.

Things to See

The first tower you reach above Piata Lenin is the massive **Clock Tower** on Piata Muzleuli. The 1648 clock stopped long ago and the 14th century tower is now a **museum** (Tuesday to Sunday 9 am to 3.30 pm) with a very good collection of local artefacts, a scale model of the town and a superb view from the walkway on top. Next to the tower is the **monastery church** (1515) with a collection of Oriental rugs hanging on each side of the nave (usually closed). Nearby on Piata Muzeului is the house in which **Vlad Dracul** lived from 1431 to 1435,

now a restaurant upstairs and wine cellar downstairs.

Piata Cetatii, complete with benches and fine old houses, is the heart of old Sighisoara. Continue up Strada Scolii from the square to the 172 steps of the **Covered Stairway** (1642). This leads to the Gothic **Bergkirche** (1345) with its frescoes of knights in armour rescuing damsels in distress. The old German tombstones in the church and adjacent **cemetery** are fascinating. The church opens daily from 12 noon to 1 pm. Leave a donation if the caretaker opens for you at other times.

Places to Stay

The *Steaua Hotel*, Strada Gheorghe Gheorghiu-Dej 12 (from 200 lei single, 325 lei double), is the only hotel.

You can camp on a hilltop above the town, but it's a stiff half hour hike up from the railway station. Walk east along the train tracks to a bridge, then cross the tracks and turn left to a road leading up. At the end of this road is the *Dealul Garii Restaurant*, where you can rent a bungalow for 144 lei or pay 21 lei to camp. The bungalows are good, but facilities for tenters are poor to non-existent, so you might consider camping freelance in the surrounding forest (keep out of sight of the road).

There's a better campground at Hula Danes, but it's four km out of town on the road to Medias and bus service from the *autogara* beside the train station is lousy.

Getting There & Away

All trains between Brasov and Cluj-Napoca stop at Sighisoara. For Sibiu you'll probably have to change trains at Medias or Copsa Mica.

SIBIU

Founded in the 12th century on the site of the Romanian village of Cibinium, Sibiu (Hermannstadt) has always been one of the leading cities of Transylvania. Destroyed by the Mongols in 1241, the

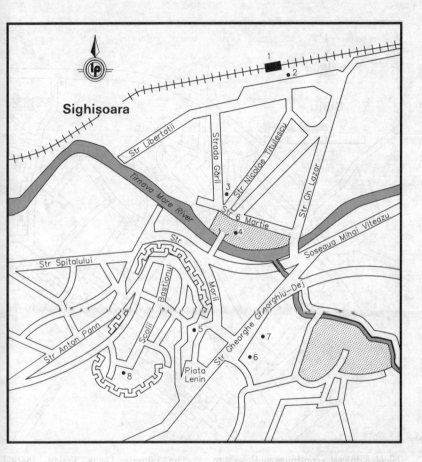

Sighişoara

1	Railway Station
2	Bus Station
3	Soviet War Cemetery
4	Orthodox Church
5	Clock Tower
6	Tourist Office
7	Steaua Hotel
8	Bergkirche

town was later surrounded by strong walls. Much remains from this colourful history and Sibiu is also a gateway to the

Fagaras Mountains, Romania's best hiking area. The camping facilities are good and Sibiu is just far enough off the beaten track to be spared the tourist tide that occasionally engulfs Brasov. If you only visit one Romanian city make it Sibiu.

Orientation

The bus and train stations are adjacent near the centre of town. Stroll up Strada General Magheru four blocks to Piata Republicii, the historic centre. From the opposite corner of the square Strada

Sibiu

Nicolae Balcescu continues south-west to Piata Unirii, another focal point.

Information
The ONT tourist office is at Strada Nicolae Balcescu 53 on Piata Unirii. Ask here about cabana accommodation if you intend to hike in the Fagaras Mountains. If you're a student visit the BTT Youth Travel Office, Strada Kornhauser 4 beside Hotel Bulevard. The CFR railway ticket agency is at Strada Nicolae Balcescu 6 next to the Imparatul Romanilor Hotel.

The Libreria Dacia Traian, Piata Republicii 7, often stocks useful Romanian maps and guidebooks. If you're staying at the Dumbrava campground check out the hotel reception of the nearby Hanul Dumbrava, which sells good maps and brochures.

Things to See
There's no better place to begin your sightseeing than at the top of the Council Tower (1588) on Piata Republicii, now the **City Historical Museum**. The old maps and photos go well with the view of red roofs,

1	Hat Shop
2	Ursulines Church
3	Franciscan Church
4	Pharmaceutical Museum
5	Casa Artelor
6	Evangelical Church
7	Primaria Veche Museum
8	Council Tower
9	Catholic Cathedral
10	Brukenthal Museum
11	Hotel Imparatul Romanilor
12	CFR Railway Ticket Agency
13	Natural History Museum
14	Orthodox Cathedral
15	Soldisch Bastion
16	BTT Student Travel
17	Tourist Office
18	Hotel Bulevard

the Fagaras Mountains beckoning to the south. After this visual treat walk along the square past the Baroque **Catholic Cathedral** (1728) to the **Brukenthal Museum** (closed Monday), the oldest and finest art gallery in Romania. Founded in 1817 by Baron Samuel Brukenthal, governor of Transylvania, the museum is housed in his aristocratic Baroque palace (1785). Aside from the paintings, there are excellent archaeological and folk art collections housed in the same building. Note especially the folk paintings on glass!

Just west along Strada Octombrie Rosu is the **Primaria Veche** (1470), now a Historical Museum. Nearby on Piata Grivita is another of Sibiu's many highlights, the Gothic **Evangelical Church** (1300-1520). As you enter you see four magnificent Baroque funerary monuments on the upper nave, then the organ of 6002 pipes (1772). In summer organ concerts are given Wednesdays at 6 pm. Take a long look at the fresco of the Crucifixion (1445) up in the sanctuary, a splendid work. There's a large collection of old tombstones in the closed-off section behind the organ but you have to ask to be

let in. The church itself opens Monday to Saturday from 9 am to 1 pm.

From here you have the choice of going down the 13th century **Staircase Passage** into the lower town, thick with local characters and popular scenes, or continuing south-west along Strada 1 Mai to the **Orthodox Cathedral** (1906), a monumental building styled after Hagia Sofia in Istanbul. Strada Tribunei around the corner on the left will carry you into Piata Unirii, where you'll find the beginning of a pleasant walk north-east along a section of the 16th century **city walls**.

If you've got an extra afternoon it's well worth taking in the **Museum of Popular Techniques** (open May to October, Tuesday to Sunday 10 am to 6 pm) in **Dumbrava Park** (trolley No 1 from the station). A great number of authentic old Transylvanian rural buildings and houses have been re-assembled around several lakes in the park to create an **open air ethnographical museum**. The zoo here adds to the interest.

Places to Stay

Camping The only reliable inexpensive way to go is camping and there are two good campgrounds near Sibiu. The closest is beside the *Hanul Dumbrava Restaurant*, four km south-west of town (trolley bus No 1 from the train station direct to the site). Camping costs 42 lei, while a small cabin is only about 100 lei more. For Romania the facilities are good and there's plenty of space.

Fourteen km north of Sibiu on the railway line to Copsa Mica is Ocna Sibiului with a large campground in the forest. The many natural pools and geological curiosities around Ocna Sibiului make it a popular bathing resort. The campground is very near the station and most trains stop here.

Hotels & Hostels The hotels are all expensive but the most colourful is the centrally-located *Imparatul Romanilor*,

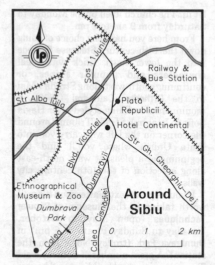

Around Sibiu

Strada Nicolae Balcescu 4 (from 261 lei single, 418 lei double). Personalities such as Franz Liszt and Johann Strauss once stayed here. Also good is the imposing *Hotel Bulevard*, Piata Unirii 10 (from 325 lei single, 446 lei double). Avoid the nearby *Hotel Continental*, Calea Dumbravii 2-4, which is of the concrete and glass high-rise variety. The *Hanul Dumbrava* (see above) is slightly cheaper than any of these.

For accommodation in student hostels during July and August inquire at the BTT Youth Travel Office, Strada Kornhauser 4 beside Hotel Bulevard.

Places to Eat

Autoservire Expres has two locations, Strada General Magheru 42 between the railway station and Piata Republicii, and Strada 1 Mai 7 not far from the Brukenthal Museum. Closer to the stations at Strada 9 Mai and Piata Garii you'll find the *Ospatarie*, where you can get local food and cheap beer.

Things to Buy

Perhaps the most distinctive souvenir of Romania you'll ever find may be purchased at the men's hat shop, Strada 9 Mai 50 a couple of blocks from the stations. Good luck trying to get the colourful ones through Customs!

Getting There & Away

Sibiu is on the railway line from Brasov to Arad. For Hunedoara Castle change at Simeria. Local trains bound for Brasov and Bucharest stop at the Fagaras trailheads. For Sighisoara or Cluj-Napoca you may have to change at Copsa Mica, although some trains go direct, so ask.

THE FAGARAS MOUNTAINS

In summer hordes of East German backpackers descend on the Fagaras Mountains, a section of the Carpathian Range in central Romania. Here they soon get lost in Alpine glory. It's hard not to join them, in fact, Fagaras is the most popular hiking area in the country. First get a good map at a bookstore, tourist office, or luxury hotel reception. Just keep looking until you find one.

The easiest access is from Sibiu, local trains on the Fagaras line to Brasov pass many starting points. One of the best places to get off is Gara Sebes Olt, from where you can hike to *Cabana Suru* (1450 metres, 60 beds) in about five hours via Sebesu de Sus (450 metres). *Cabana Negoiu* (1546 metres, 170 beds) is seven hours east of Suru across peaks up to 2306 metres high.

Alternatively ask about the daily morning bus from Sibiu direct to *Cabana Poiana Neamtului* (706 metres, 39 beds). From here it's a three hour climb to *Cabana Barcaciu* (1550 metres, 20 beds), then another two hours to Cabana Negoiu. From Porumbacu de Jos Railway Station you can hike up to Cabana Negoiu in about seven hours. Eight strenuous hours east of Cabana Negoiu is *Cabana Bilea Lac* (2034 metres, 170 beds), where there's a cable car down to *Cabana Bilea*

Cascada (1234 metres, 63 beds) and the road out. On this section you pass Mt Negoiu (2535 metres), second highest in Romania.

If you want to begin your trip at Bilea Cascada and use the cable car to avoid an 800 metre climb, take the afternoon bus from Sibiu to Cirtisoara, a 22-km walk from Bilea Cascada. Sundays there's a bus from Sibiu direct to Bilea Cascada. Another way to get to Bilea Cascada is to take a train to Halta Cirta station, which will add about an hour to your walk. The ruins of a fortified 13th century Cistercian monastery are about a km north of Cirta station. The cabanas near the cable car may well be full of tourists with cars, forcing you to camp.

A seven-hour walk east of Bilea Lac is *Cabana Podragu* (2136 metres, 100 beds) which you can use as a base to climb Mt Moldoveanu (2544 metres), Romania's highest peak. From Podragu you can descend to the railway at Arpasu de Jos (420 metres) or Ucea in a day or continue east along the ridge. Other ways to get into this area include the road due north from Curtea de Arges to Bilea Lac (no bus service beyond Capatineni) or a train north from Rimnicu Vilcea to Turnu Rosu or Gara Podu Olt near Gara Sebes Olt.

To hike Fagaras you must be in good physical shape and have warm clothing and sturdy boots. The trails are well marked but keep in mind the altitude and be prepared for cold and rain any time. From November to April these mountains are snow-covered, August and September are the best months. Basic food is available at the cabanas mentioned above, but carry a good supply of biscuits. Keep your water bottle full. You'll meet lots of other hikers eager to tell you of their adventures and with the help of a good map you'll soon know exactly where to go.

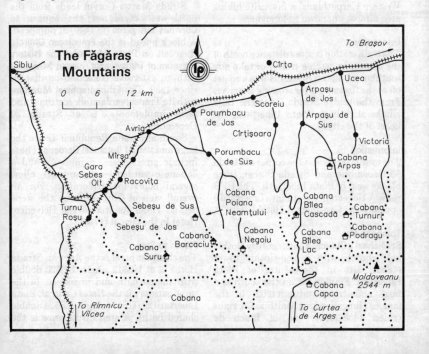

CLUJ-NAPOCA

Cut in two by the Somesul Mic River, Cluj is as Hungarian as it is Romanian. Its position near the middle of Transylvania made it a crossroads, which explains its present role as an educational and industrial centre. Known as Kolozsvar to the Hungarians and Klausenburg to the Germans, the old Roman name Napoca has been added to the city's official title to emphasise its Daco-Roman origin. The history of Cluj goes back to Dacian times. In 124 AD during the reign of Hadrian Napoca attained municipal status and was elevated to a colony by Emperor Marcus Aurelius. German merchants arrived in the 12th century and after the Mongol invasion of 1241 the medieval earthen walls of *castrenses de Clus* were rebuilt in stone. Today there are several good museums and a large botanical garden to see in Romania's second largest city. To the south-west are the Munti Apuseni or Western Carpathians, a favourite hiking area almost unknown to foreigners.

1	Belvedere Hotel/Citadel
2	Astoria Hotel
3	Hungarian State Theatre
4	History Museum of Transylvania
5	Birthplace of Matthias Corvinus
6	Franciscan Church
7	Pharmaceutical Museum
8	St Michael's Church
9	Banffy Palace
10	Agentie Teatrala
11	Orthodox Cathedral
12	National Theatre
13	Reformed Church
14	Continental Hotel
15	Ethnological Museum
16	Tourist Office

Orientation

The train station is some distance north of the centre, so catch a trolley or take any southbound bus on Strada Horea and get off at the first stop after crossing the river. From the bridge Strada Gheorghe Doja climbs slightly to Piata Libertatii, the heart of the city.

Information

The tourist office is at the corner of Strada 30 Decembrie and Strada Sincai, three blocks west of Piata Libertatii. The CFR railway ticket office is at Piata Libertatii 9 opposite the Continental Hotel.

Things to See

St Michael's Church, a 15th century Gothic hall church with a neo-Gothic tower (1859), sits in the centre of Piata Libertatii. Flanking it on the south is a huge equestrian statue (1902) of the famous Hungarian king Matthias Corvinus (ruled 1458-1490), son of Iancu de Hunedoara. On the east side of the square is the **Fine Arts Museum** in the Baroque Banffy Palace (1785). Diagonally across the street is a **Pharmaceutical Museum** on the site of Cluj's first apothecary (1573).

Strada Mattei Corvin leads from the north-west corner of the square to **Corvinus' birthplace** (in 1440) at number 6. A block ahead is the **Franciscan Church**, then left on Piata Muzeului the **History Museum of Transylvania** (closed Monday) with an extensive collection on display since 1859. The **Ethnographical Museum**, with its Transylvanian folk costumes and farm implements, is at Strada 30 Decembrie 21.

South at Strada Republicii 42 are the large and varied **Botanical Gardens**. These include greenhouses, a museum and a Japanese garden – in summer allow several hours for exploration. For an overall view of Cluj climb up the steps behind Hotel Astoria to the Belvedere Hotel in the **citadel** (1715).

Places to Stay

The cheapest hotel is the *Astoria*, Strada Horea 3, at US$12 single, US$20 double with shared bath and breakfast. In the same category is the *Hotel Central*, Piata Libertatii 29 (US$14 single, US$24 double shared bath). A step up in price is the

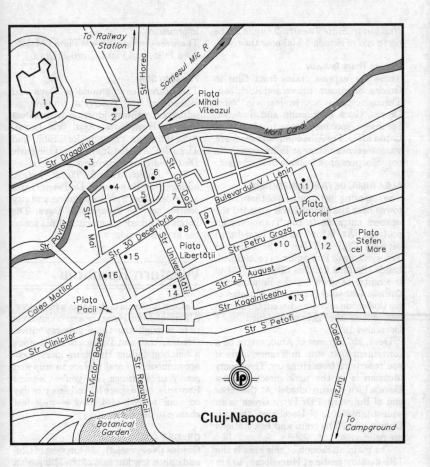

Cluj-Napoca

Hotel Continental on the south-west corner of Piata Libertatii (US$22 single, US$32 double with shared bath). The newer *Hotel Siesta* behind the tourist office is about the same price as the Continental. *Hotel Transilvania*, Strada Gheorghe Doja 20, does not admit foreign tourists.

There's a campground at Padurea Faget, seven km south of Cluj. Bus No 48 from Piata Mihai Viteazul 29 goes within three km of it. The *Cabana Faget Padure* (33 beds) is nearby.

Places to Eat

One of the best places to eat in Cluj is the *Lacto-Vegetarian Restaurant*, Piata Libertatii 12. For seafood try the *Restaurantul Pescarul* on Strada Universitatii next to Cinema Arta behind the Continental Hotel.

Entertainment

The Agentie Teatrala, Strada Dr Petru Groza 36, has tickets for most events. The neo-Baroque *National Theatre* (1906) is nearby on Piata Victoriei. There's also the

Hungarian State Theatre & Opera at the north end of Strada 1 Mai near the river.

Getting There & Away
There are express trains from Cluj to Oradea, Sighisoara, Brasov and Bucharest. Through trains run to Iasi via Vatra Dornei, Gura Humoruliu and Suceava. For Sibiu you may have to change at Copsa Mica. For Alba Iulia or Hunedoara you sometimes change at Teius, sometimes not. Sleepers are available to Bucharest.

ALBA IULIA, DEVA & HUNEDOARA
The imposing fortifications of these three towns near the Mures River guarded the western entrance to the Transylvanian plateau. At Alba Iulia (Karlsburg) between Cluj and Deva the union of Transylvania to Romania was proclaimed. Inside the **Alba Carolina Citadel** (1735) in the centre of town are the Romanesque **Catholic Cathedral** (1290), the **Museum of the Unification** and the adjacent **Unification Hall** where the act was signed on 1 December 1918.

Deva, 157 km east of Arad, might be a convenient first stop in Transylvania if you're arriving from Hungary. The **County Museum** is in the park directly below Deva's 13th century **citadel**. At the other end of Bulevardul Dr Petru Groza is an equestrian statue of Decebalus, the last Dacian king. The train and bus stations are nearby.

The main attraction of this area is the 14th century castle at Hunedoara, 13 km south of Deva. In the late 15th century **Hunedoara Castle** became the residence of the Corvin family, which ruled Hungary at the time. The castle well was hewn through 30 metres of solid rock by Turkish prisoners. This amazing fairytale castle with pointed towers, drawbridge, high battlements and Knights' Hall (1453) is easily Romania's finest Gothic structure, yet it's almost unknown outside the country! Hunedoara's grimy steel mill is a less appealing feature.

Information
There are tourist offices at Piata 1 Mai 22, Alba Iulia, and Piata Unirii 2, Deva.

Places to Stay
The nearest campground to Deva and Hunedoara is *P T Strei* at Simeria, an important railway junction with direct lines to Hunedoara, Arad (via Deva), Alba Iulia (via Vintu de Jos), Sibiu and Tirgu Jiu. At Alba Iulia there's the basic *Dintre Salcii campground*.

The *Bulevard* and *Turist* hotels, adjacent on Bulevardul Dr Petru Groza and close to both railway station and city centre, are the cheapest in Deva. The hotels in Hunedoara and Alba Iulia are on the expensive side.

Western Romania

Western Romania is Romania's front door. All trains from Hungary and Yugoslavia pass through the three gateway cities, Oradea, Arad and Timisoara. Each offers a touch of fading Hapsburg glory, easy accommodation and a place to stop and get your bearings. If you're leaving Romania, have spare lei and an extra day on your tourist visa, this is your last chance to use them.

ORADEA
Oradea (Nagyvarad), 153 km west of Cluj and only a few km east of the Hungarian border, is capital of Bihor County. Situated right on the edge of the Carpathian Mountains and Danube Basin, Oradea has an attractive downtown area but nothing in particular to warrant a special trip. It may be useful as a stopover if you're travelling to or from Budapest, however.

Orientation
The railway station is quite a distance south-east of town, so take a streetcar to Piata Victoriei (ask to make sure you're on the right one). Piata Republicii with the

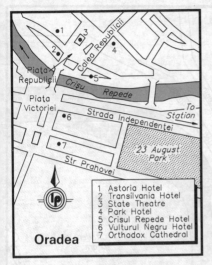

Oradea

1 Astoria Hotel
2 Transilvania Hotel
3 State Theatre
4 Park Hotel
5 Crisul Repede Hotel
6 Vulturul Negru Hotel
7 Orthodox Cathedral

tourist office, hotels and State Theatre is just across the bridge over the Crisu Repede River. Calea Republicii, the main pedestrian mall, runs north-east from beside the State Theatre.

Information

Oficiul Judetean de Turism is at Piata Republicii 4. The CFR railway ticket office is at Piata Republicii 2.

Things to See

There are a couple of impressive churches on Piata Victoriei, plus many big eclectic and art nouveau buildings on the two downtown squares. The largest museum is in the **Episcopal Palace** (1779), out toward the railway station far from downtown. This 100-room Baroque building with 365 windows was modelled after the Belvedere Palace in Vienna. The Catholic cathedral adjacent to the museum is the largest Baroque church in Romania.

Baile Felix, a famous year round health spa with an open-air swimming-pool of thermal water, is only eight km south-east of Oradea. There's even a thermal lake

covered by the rare Nymphea Lotus Thermalis.

Places to Stay

The cheapest hotels are the *Park*, Strada Republicii 5 (107 lei single), and the *Vulturul Negru*, Strada Independentei 1, both near the centre of town. The *Transilvania, Astoria* and *Crisul* hotels, all near Piata Republicii, are slightly more expensive but not bad. The nearest campground is at Baile 1 Mai, near Baile Felix nine km south-east of Oradea.

Getting There & Away

A daily train from Bucharest to Budapest (via Cluj) stops here in the morning. You can buy a ticket to Hungary at the CFR railway ticket agency on Piata Republicii. Otherwise just get a ticket to the border (Episcopia Bihor) and pay the Hungarian conductor on the other side in hard currency. Many other trains run north to Satu Mare, south to Arad, and east to Cluj.

ARAD

Arad sits in winemaking country on the Mures River which drains much of central Transylvania. The river loops around Arad's 18th century citadel before flowing due west to Szeged, Hungary. Parks also surround the fort, crowded with bathers in the river and pools. Only 20 km south of the Hungarian border by rail, Arad is a better entry point than Oradea. Hunedoara Castle, Sibiu and Sighisoara are on the main line east.

Orientation

The station is a couple of km north of the centre. Take a streetcar (buy a ticket at the stop) down Bulevardul Republicii into town.

Information

The local tourist office is at Bulevardul Republicii 72 opposite the impressive city hall (1865). There's also a special ONT tourist office offering a greater variety of services to foreigners in the flashy Hotel

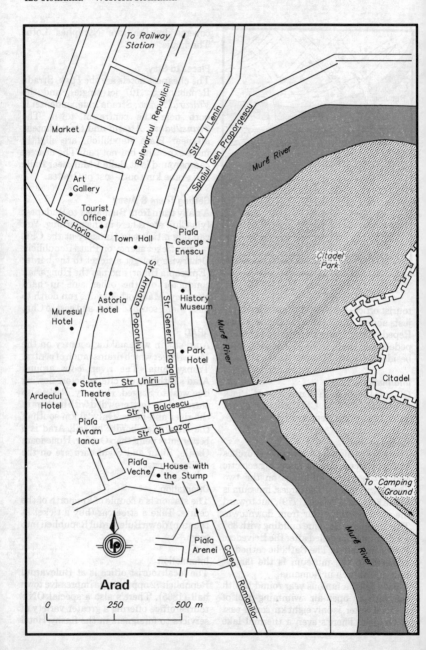

To Railway Station

Bulevardul Republicii

Str V I Lenin

Splaiul Gen Praporgescu

Mureß River

Market

Art Gallery

Tourist Office

Str Horia

Town Hall

Piaßa George Enescu

Citadel Park

Str Armata Poporului

History Museum

Str General Dragalina

Mureß River

Astoria Hotel

Muresul Hotel

Park Hotel

Citadel

State Theatre

Str Unirii

Ardealul Hotel

Str N Balcescu

Piaßa Avram Iancu

Str Gh Lazar

Piaßa Veche

House with the Stump

To Camping Ground

Mureß River

Piaßa Arenei

Calea Romanilor

Arad

0   250   500 m

Astoria nearby. The CFR railway ticket office is at Strada Unirii 1.

Things to See

On Piata George Enescu behind the town hall mentioned above is the **History Museum** (closed Monday) in the Palace of Culture (1913). The large display covers the entire history of the area, although the exhibits are difficult to see due to the low lighting. Walk south on attractive Bulevardul Republicii to the neo-Classical **State Theatre** (1874). On a corner at Piata Veche, two blocks beyond the theatre, is a stump where apprentice blacksmiths once hammered a nail to symbolise their acceptance into the guild. You'll notice it by the large padlock alongside.

Places to Stay

The *Hotel Ardealul* (265 lei double, no singles) beside the State Theatre is a fine old neo-Classical building (1841) with a music room where Brahms, Liszt and Strauss once gave concerts. *Hotel Muresul*, Bulevardul Republicii 88, is 165 lei single, 275 lei double. To reach the *Sub Cetate Campground* cross the bridge near the *Park Hotel*, turn right and follow the river downstream a km or so to 'Popas Turistic.'

Getting There & Away

Several trains a day call at Arad between Budapest and Bucharest (via Sighisoara). Change at Vintu de Jos for Sibiu. Local trains run north to Oradea and, more frequently, south to Timisoara. There's an overnight train with sleepers between Bucharest and Arad.

TIMISOARA

The Banat Plain around Timisoara (Temesvar), an eastward extension of Vojvodina in Yugoslavia, has a history similar to Transylvania. If you're coming from Yugoslavia you'll probably enter through Timisoara, the largest city in Western Romania. The Serbian influence is evident in a few of the churches and central Timisoara has a garden-like, Mediterranean air. The Bega Canal curving through the city leads into the Tisa River in Yugoslavia. There are all the usual sights to see, but Timisoara is more of a place to spend the night than a destination.

Orientation

Gara Timisoara-Nord Railway Station is just west of downtown. If you're walking keep straight east on Bulevardul Republicii to the opera house, then north a block to verdant Piata Libertatii. Piata Unirii, the old town square, is two blocks north again.

If you'd rather ride catch the streetcar with the black No 1 just outside the station, which does a great scenic loop through the centre of town. It doesn't matter if you're too enthralled to get off because they all come back the same way.

Information

The tourist office is at Strada Piatra Craiului 3 behind Hotel Banatul. The CFR railway ticket office is at Bulevardul 23 August 2.

Things to See

Piata Unirii is Timisoara's most picturesque square with a Baroque **Catholic Cathedral** (1774), fountain and palace, plus a **Serbian church** (1754). People come from afar to fill their water bottles at a spring which bubbles forth in front of the cathedral.

Take Strada V Alecsandri south from the Serbian church to Piata Libertatii and the **Old Town Hall** (1734). Keep straight on Strada K Marx to the 15th century **Huniades Palace**, housing the local history museum (closed Monday).

Go west a little to the opera house, which looks straight down Bulevardul 30 Decembrie to the exotic domed **Orthodox Cathedral** (1936). Between opera and cathedral is a column with the figures of Romulus and Remus, a gift from the city of Rome. The cathedral is in a park near

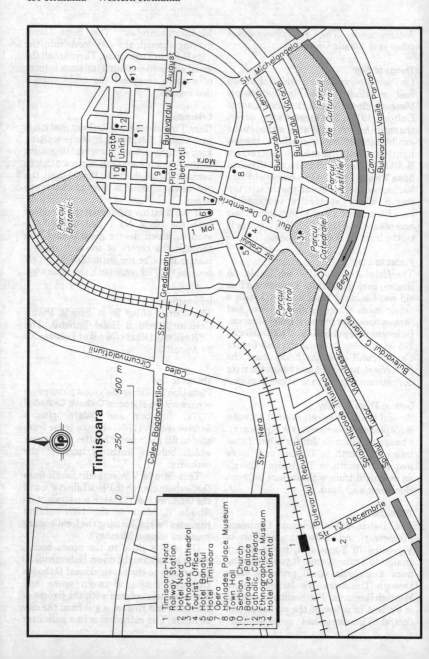

Timişoara

1 Timişoara-Nord
  Railway Station
2 Hotel Nord
3 Orthodox Cathedral
4 Tourist Office
5 Hotel Banatul
6 Hotel Timişoara
7 Opera
8 Huniades Palace Museum
9 Serbian Church
10 Town Hall
11 Baroque Palace
12 Catholic Cathedral
13 Ethnographical Museum
14 Hotel Continental

the Bega Canal. The parks along this canal are worth an extended stroll.

Places to Stay

The *Hotel Nord* around the corner from Timisoara Nord Station is overpriced and run down, but there if you need it. Better hotels near the city centre include the *Hotel Banatul*, Bulevardul Republicii 5, and the nearby *Hotel Timisoara*, Strada 1 Mai 2 adjacent to the opera. The high-rise *Hotel Continental* on Bulevardul 23 August is the most expensive hotel in Timisoara.

Camping The campground is in the Padurea Verde forest on the opposite side of town from Timisoara-Nord Railway Station. The streetcar with the black No 1 outside the station will take you directly there. Ask to be let off at the 'camping.' Timisoara-Est Railway Station is much closer to the campground, but few trains stop there. Tent space costs 32 lei or pay 200 lei for a small cabin. There's a restaurant on the premises (closes at 8 pm).

Getting There & Away

The daily express from Belgrade arrives around midnight and returns to Yugoslavia the next morning. Timisoara is 1½ hours south of Arad by local train. Service to Bucharest is fairly frequent via Baile Herculane, Orsova, Drobeta-Turnu Severin and Craiova. Sleepers are available to Bucharest.

Wallachia

Wallachia occupies the Danube plain north to the Carpathians' crest. Although the mighty Danube flows right along the southern edge of Wallachia the river is best seen between Moldova Veche and Drobeta-Turnu Severin in the west, where it breaks through the Carpathian Chain at the legendary Iron Gates. Calafat and Giurgiu are historic river ports connected with neighbouring Bulgaria. The Wallachian princes built their first capitals, Curtea de Arges, Cimpulung and Tirgoviste, close to the protective mountains. In the 15th century Bucharest gained the ascendancy, a role it maintains today.

THE IRON GATES

South of Baile Herculane the train runs along the north bank of the Danube through the famous Iron Gates. Between Orsova and Drobeta-Turnu Severin the line passes a concrete hydroelectric dam, on top of which is a road linking Romania to Yugoslavia. You get a good view of everything from the train window. The dam has tamed the whirling Danube 'cauldrons' west of Orsova, once a major navigational hazard as the river raced through a narrow defile. There are ferries on the Danube lake above the dam daily year round from Orsova Railway Station to Moldova Veche (99 km), departing Orsova in the afternoon around 2.30 pm.

DROBETA-TURNU SEVERIN

Drobeta-Turnu Severin Railway Station is in an ugly industrial area, but the 19th century town centre is only a 10-minute walk east. Follow Bulevardul Republicii above the station all the way to the **Muzeul Portilor de Fer** (closed Monday), a large museum with a fine exhibit on the natural history of the Danube River including an aquarium with Danube fish! Other sections of the same museum cover history and ethnography. There's much on the Roman period including a scale model of the bridge thrown across the Danube just below the museum in 103 AD. A statue of Apolodorus of Damascus, who built the bridge on orders of Emperor Trajan, is in front of the museum and alongside are the ruins of **Castrul Drobeta**, a 2nd to 3rd century Roman fort which protected it. Also to be seen are the foundations of a 14th century **basilica**.

There's not much else to detain you in Drobeta-Turnu Severin (no campground), so a four-hour stop is enough. Have lunch at the *Lacto Vegetarian Restaurant* on Piaţa 23 August beside the market in the city centre.

Getting There & Away
All trains between Bucharest and Timisoara call here. Local trains make shorter, more frequent trips in both directions.

TIRGU JIU
Oltenia, the area west of the Olt River, is associated with the famous Romanian sculptor Constantin Brancusi (1876-1957) whose unique work may be seen in his home town Tirgu Jiu and in the art museum at Craiova. In 1937-1938 Brancusi, then at the peak of his career, created in Tirgu Jiu a stunning memorial to those who fell in WW I. The Brancusi monuments are the only things to detain you in Tirgu Jiu, so make it a quick stop on the way to somewhere else.

Information
The tourist office is at Strada Tudor Vladimirescu 17. The CFR railway ticket office is at Strada Unirii, Block 2.

Things to See
The **Columna Infinita** (Endless Column), a towering brass-coated iron monument, is a few blocks north-east of the station. Calea Eroilor, the street with the Orthodox church in the middle, runs due west from the column. When you see the ornate Liceul (high school) just beyond the church, turn right and you'll soon reach the **County Museum** (closed Monday). Further along Calea Eroilor is a park with Brancusi's **Poarta Sarutului** (Kissing Gate) straight ahead. Beyond it is the **Masa Tacerii** (Table of Silence), surrounded by 12 round chairs.

Places to Stay
The arrangements are poor. Tirgu Jiu has

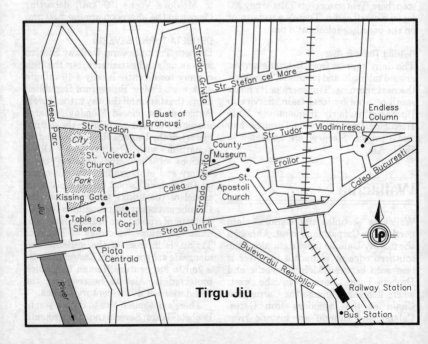

Tirgu Jiu

only one expensive hotel, the *Gorj*, a block from the Kissing Gate. Both campgrounds are far from town. The one at Dragoeni, 11 km east, has fairly frequent bus service from Piata Centrala but is officially for bungalow accommodation only. The *Castrul Roman Campground* is at Bumbesti-Jiu, 18 km north of Tirgu Jiu by bus or train.

Getting There & Away

The adjacent bus and train stations are walking distance from the centre of town. There are no direct buses to Tirgu Jiu from Drobeta-Turnu Severin. You have to come by train with a change at Filiasi. There are expresses to Bucharest via Craiova. For Deva and Hunedoara catch a train headed north to Simeria. For Curtea de Arges take an infrequent bus to Rimnicu Vilcea via Horezu, then another bus on to Curtea de Arges.

HOREZU

Horezu is a picturesque village with the impressive 17th century **Hurezi Monastery** three km north off the main road to Rimnicu Vilcea. A good alternative to the dismal accommodation in Tirgu Jiu and Curtea de Arges is Horezu's *Stejarii campground*, midway between the two. The campsite is beside the road right in Horezu itself and there are bungalows, the problem is in getting there. There are buses from Rimnicu Vilcea every couple of hours but from Tirgu Jiu it's only once or twice a day. Check the times carefully and try to purchase an advance ticket.

CURTEA DE ARGES

Once the capital of Wallachia, this small town has two outstanding churches which make a visit worthwhile. As the accommodation situation is poor plan your departure as soon as you arrive. Three or four hours here should be sufficient.

Information

Filiala de turism in the Hotel Posada, Bulevardul Republicii 27-29.

Things to See

Coming from the adjacent bus and train stations you first reach the **Prince's Church** (1352), every inch of its interior filled with striking 14th century frescoes. This church, adjacent to ruins of the medieval princely court, is the oldest well preserved feudal monument in Wallachia.

A little over a km further along the boulevard in the same direction is a famous monastery, with the dazzling **Bishop's Church** at the centre of its courtyard. The frescoes were repainted late in the 19th century and don't compare with those in the Prince's Church. The architecture and exterior, however, are a unique blend of pseudo-Islamic decoration superimposed on a great Orthodox plan. The tombs of the early 20th century royal family are just inside the door.

The Bishop's Church was built by Master Manole for Neagoe Basarab, prince of Wallachia, in 1512-1517. It's said that just as the finishing touches were being added the prince ordered the scaffolding removed, leaving the architect perched atop a tower. Neagoe's intention was to prevent Manole from building another church to rival this one in beauty. Manole made wings from the shingles and attempted to fly down. In the place where he crashlanded a spring gushed forth, the **Fintina Mesterului Manole**, which you'll find in the park across the street from the monastery. Another story claims that Manole buried his wife alive beneath the church to ensure that it would never crumble.

Places to Stay

There's no campground in Curtea de Arges and the *Hotel Posada* near the monastery is ultra expensive. North at Corbeni on the way to Capatineni (see below) is the *Dumbrava campground*.

Getting There & Away

There are direct trains from Bucharest to Curtea de Arges. Buses run every hour or two between Curtea de Arges and

Rimnicu Vilcea, where there are trains north to Sibiu.

Count Dracula's Castle

Twenty-three km north of Curtea de Arges near a large hydroelectric dam are the ruins of 14th century **Poienari Citadel**. The castle's round towers are attributed to Vlad Tepes, prince of Wallachia. It's about an hours' climb up from the village and only ruined walls remain, but the views are spectacular. Get there from Curtea de Arges on the Capatineni bus. Only one or two buses a day come this far.

North beyond the dam the highway clings to the side of Vidraru Lake and snakes up to *Cabana Bilea Lac* in the Fagaras Mountains. No buses go beyond Capatineni and it might take a pack or two of Kent cigarettes to get a ride from a motorist. *Cabana Cumpana* (920 metres, 138 beds) is on the west side of the lake about three hours walk from the castle.

Bulgaria

Bulgaria has an enigmatic reputation. Tales of intrigue seem to be confirmed by stamp-happy border guards determined to separate you and your money. Tourism officials add to the fun by stacking the rules in their favour. The various rates of exchange, complicated visa regulations, segregated hotels and assorted paperwork speak of a Byzantine heritage.

This image is only partly justified. Economically Bulgaria is better off than any of its neighbours and the people are far friendlier than the jaded Yugoslavs and Greeks. The Rila Mountains and Black Sea coast are natural attractions of European stature. Transport, food, museums, monuments, public services, climate – everything is good. And even the red tape is easy to comply with, if you manage to figure it all out.

The Cyrillic script and Turkish mosques are constant reminders that Bulgaria has one foot firmly in the east. Bulgaria has been liberated by Russia twice (in 1877 and 1944). This close historical relationship has made Bulgaria one of the Soviet Union's most dependable allies and no Soviet troops are stationed here. The only parallels are Cuba and Vietnam. Even the Bulgarian custom of shaking the head to show agreement and nodding to say no is unique. A visit to such a remarkable country can be a memorable experience!

Facts about the Country

HISTORY

In antiquity present Bulgaria, the land of Orpheus and Spartacus, belonged to the Kingdom of Macedonia and the inhabitants were Thracians. By 46 BC the Romans had conquered the whole peninsula, which they divided into Moesia Inferior north of the Stara Planina and Thrace to the

south. Slav tribes arrived in the mid-6th century and absorbed the Thraco-Illyrian population. The Slavs were peaceful farmers organised in democratic local communities.

In 679 the Bulgars, fierce Turkic horsemen ruled by khans (chiefs) and boyars (nobles), crossed the Danube from their homelands north of the Black Sea. In 681 Khan Asparoukh founded the First Bulgarian Kingdom (681-1018) at Pliska in Moesia. In 1981 the 1300th anniversary of this foundation was passionately celebrated. The kingdom expanded south at the expense of Byzantium and in the 9th century extended into Macedonia. The Bulgars were eventually assimilated by the more numerous Slavs, adopting their language and way of life.

In 865 Tsar Boris I was frightened into accepting Christianity by a picture of hell painted on the palace walls by a Byzantine monk. In 870 the Bulgarian church became independent with its own patriarch. The kingdom attained its greatest power under Tsar Simeon (893-927) who moved the capital to Preslav and extended his empire as far west as the Adriatic. Even the Serbs were brought under his rule.

Simeon's attempts to gain the Byzantine crown for himself weakened the country,

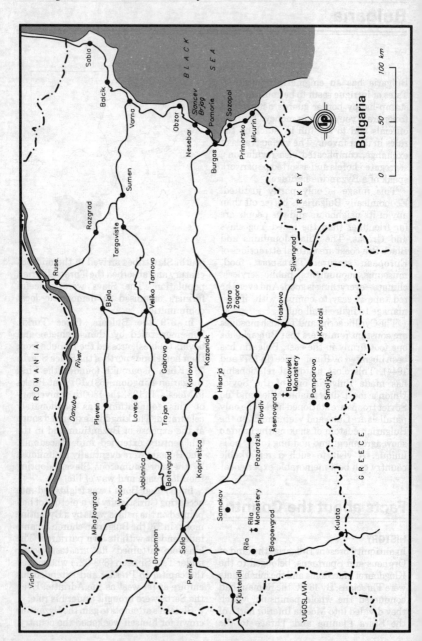

Bulgaria – Facts about the Country 437

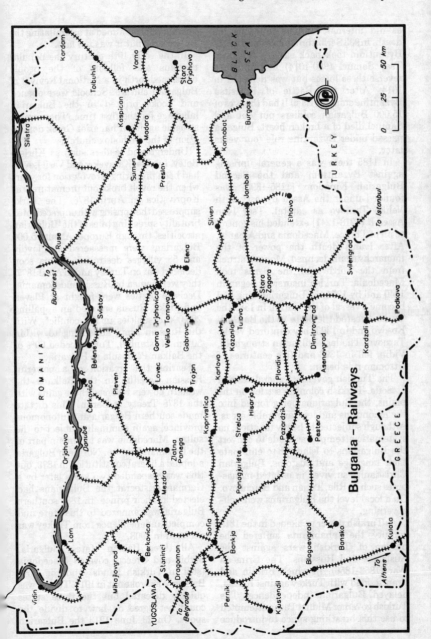

Bulgaria – Railways

as did internal conflicts following his death. In 933 Serbia broke away and in 972 Byzantium took back eastern Bulgaria. Tsar Samuel (980-1014) attempted to reverse these losses but was defeated in 1014. After the Battle of Belasitsa Byzantine emperor Basil II had the eyes of 15,000 Bulgarian soldiers put out and Samuel died of a broken heart. Bulgaria passed under Byzantine rule four years later.

In 1185 there was a general uprising against Byzantium and the Second Bulgarian Kingdom (1185-1396) was founded under the Assen dynasty with Veliko Tarnovo as capital. Tsar Ivan Assen II (1218-1241) extended his control to all of Thrace, Macedonia and Albania. After Ivan's death the power of the monarchy again declined. Mongols struck from the north and the Serbs took Macedonia. Turkish incursions began in 1340 and by 1371 the Bulgarian king had become a vassal of the sultan. In 1389 the Turks defeated the Serbs at the Battle of Kosovo and in 1393 they captured Veliko Tarnovo. The last Bulgarian stronghold, Vidin, fell in 1396 and five centuries of Ottoman rule began.

The Turkish governor general resided at Sofia. Turkish colonists settled on the plains, the Bulgarians being forced into the mountains and less favourable areas. Although subjected to heavy taxation, no systematic attempt was made to convert the Bulgarians to Islam or to eliminate their language and customs. Bulgarian Christianity survived in isolated monasteries such as Rila, Trojan and Batchkovo. On a local level the Bulgarians were self-governing.

As Turkish power weakened in the 18th century the inhabitants suffered the burden of Turkish wars against the Austrians and Russians. The Crimean War (1853-1856), in which Britain and France sided with Turkey against Russia, delayed Bulgarian independence. The Turkish governor Midhat Pasha attempted to use this breathing space to introduce belated reforms aimed at assimilating the Bulgarians, but it was too late.

In the early 19th century the popular customs and folklore of the people blossomed forth in a National Revival of Bulgarian culture. Schools were opened and books printed in the Bulgarian language for the first time. There was a struggle against Phanariot Greek domination of the Orthodox church.

Underground leaders such as Khristo Botev, Lyuben Karavelov and Vasil Levski had been preparing a revolution for years when the revolt broke out prematurely at Koprivstica in April 1876. The Turks suppressed the uprising with unprecedented brutality spreading tales of the 'Bulgarian atrocities' through Europe. About 15,000 Bulgarians were massacred at Plovdiv and 58 villages destroyed. Serbia soon declared war on Turkey and in April 1877, they were joined by Russia and Romania. Decisive battles were fought at Pleven and Sipka. Russia suffered an appalling 200,000 casualties in the conflict. With the Russian army advancing to within 50 km of Istanbul, Turkey ceded 60% of the Balkan Peninsula to Bulgaria.

Fearing the creation of a powerful Russian satellite in the Balkans the western powers reversed these gains with the 1878 Treaty of Berlin. This dictate made southern Bulgaria an 'autonomous province' again nominally subject to the sultan. Macedonia was to remain part of the Ottoman Empire. Northern Bulgaria adopted a liberal constitution in 1879, but this was suspended two years later by a German aristocrat the Bulgarians had elected as their prince. In 1885 southern Bulgaria was annexed to this state and complete independence from Turkey was declared in 1908.

All three Balkan states, Bulgaria, Serbia and Greece, coveted Macedonia (still in Turkish hands) and the First Balkan War broke out in 1912. Turkey was quickly defeated but the three states could not agree on how to divide the spoils. On 29 June 1913 the Bulgarian army suddenly attacked their Serbian and Greek allies, probably on orders from the king. The Second Balkan War soon resulted in Bulgaria's defeat by these countries and Romania. Macedonia was divided between Serbia and Greece while Romania took a fertile slice of Bulgarian land in the north.

Bulgarian disenchantment with the loss of Macedonia and the pro-German sympathies of the king led Bulgaria to side with the Central Powers against Serbia and Russia in WW I. There was widespread opposition to this policy within Bulgaria and in September 1918, a mutiny among the troops led to the abdication of King Ferdinand and an armistice. Bulgaria lost additional territory to Greece and Serbia.

Elections in 1920 brought the anti-war leader Aleksandr Stamboliski to office. His government passed an agrarian reform bill dividing the large estates. Serious problems were caused by Macedonian refugees in Bulgaria and continuing terrorist activities in Macedonia itself. Stamboliski was killed during a right wing coup in June 1923. In September 1923, an armed uprising by Agrarians and Communists was suppressed and thousands were killed in the reactionary terror which followed. The Communist leader Georgi Dimitrov narrowly escaped to Russia.

An amnesty in 1926 restored a degree of normality to the country and the League of Nations provided financial aid to resettle the Macedonian refugees. The world economic crisis of the 1930s led to an authoritarian trend in all of Eastern Europe and in 1935 King Boris III took personal control. On 24 January 1937 Bulgaria signed a treaty of 'inviolable peace and sincere and perpetual friendship' with Yugoslavia.

Bulgarian claims to Macedonia again led the country to side with Germany and in 1941 it joined in the Nazi invasion of Yugoslavia. Fearing a popular uprising King Boris rejected German demands to declare war on the USSR. In 1942 an underground Fatherland Front was formed to resist the pro-German government. King Boris died mysteriously in August 1943, and a Council of Regency was set up to govern until his six-year-old son, Prince Simeon, came of age. The Front planned an armed uprising for 2 September 1944.

In August 1944, with the Soviet Army advancing across Romania, Bulgaria declared itself neutral and disarmed the German troops present. The USSR insisted that Bulgaria declare war on Germany, whereupon Soviet soldiers entered Bulgaria unopposed. Fatherland Front partisans took Sofia on 9 September 1944 and the Bulgarian Army fought alongside the Soviet Union until the war's end.

After a referendum in 1946 Bulgaria was proclaimed a republic and Georgi Dimitrov was elected premier on 27 October 1946. Peace treaties were signed in 1947 and all Soviet troops left the country. In 1954 all outstanding disputes with Greece were settled and in 1955 Bulgaria was admitted to the UN. In the 1980s Bulgaria joined Greece in calls for a Balkan nuclear free zone but relations with Turkey remain strained.

Beginning in the late 1940s industrialisation and the collectivisation of agriculture were carried out. Under Todor Zhivkov, Bulgaria's leader for over four decades, the country became one of the most prosperous in Eastern Europe. Within the framework of central planning managers were allowed some flexibility and workers were given incentives to exceed their norms. Spare time private plot farming was allowed.

GOVERNMENT

The 400-member National Assembly is the sole legislative body. It elects the State Council, Council of Ministers, Supreme Court and Chief Public Prosecutor. The permanently functioning State Council holds executive powers while the Council of Ministers administers the economy and People's Councils run the local administrations. There are two political parties, the Bulgarian Communist Party and the Bulgarian Agrarian Party. Other mass organisations include the Fatherland Front, the Dimitrov Young Communist League and the Bulgarian Trade Unions. Bulgaria is divided into 28 districts *(okrugs)*, themselves divided into municipalities *(rayoni)* and villages *(obshtini)*.

PEOPLE

About nine million people live in Bulgaria, over a million of them in the capital Sofia. The other major cities are Plovdiv (367,195), Varna (295,038), Ruse (178,920), Burgas (178,239), Stara Zagora (141,722) and Pleven (135,899). Dimitrovgrad and Pernik are major industrial centres.

The Bulgarians, like the Serbs, are South Slavs. Many Bulgarians consider the Macedonians as Bulgarians, a subject which has involved Bulgaria in three wars this century. Religion is only practised by a minority (30% Orthodox, 5% Muslim and 1% Catholic).

The largest national minorities are Turks (5%) and gypsies (2.5%). The Turks live mostly in the north-east and in the eastern Rhodopi foothills. From 1949 to 1951 some 155,000 Turks were expelled from Bulgaria. The Bulgarian government says the remaining Turks are welcome to leave, but only if they *all* go. This they are unlikely to do willingly as the standard of living in Bulgaria is far higher than that of Turkey. Highly educated individual Bulgarians of Turkish ancestry are not permitted to immigrate. Now there's a programme to assimilate the Turkish minority. All of them have been required to take Bulgarian names.

ECONOMY

The Bulgarian constitution declares that the means of production and natural resources belong to the state. Five-year plans are prepared and implemented by the Council of Ministers. Half the national budget is devoted to economic development and industry has increased dramatically since the war, now contributing over half the gross national product.

There are iron and steel works at Pernik and Kremikovci, on opposite sides of Sofia. The chemical plant at Dimitrovgrad produces fertilisers and there's a large petrochemical plant at Burgas. Modern textile mills are found at Plovdiv, Sliven and Sofia. Other important industries are machine building, food processing and consumer goods production.

Brown coal found near Pernik is used by the iron industry while lignite from Dimitrovgrad is burned in thermoelectric plants. There are hydroelectric projects in the Rhodopi Mountains but Bulgaria is the country most dependent on nuclear power in Eastern Europe with 32% of its electricity so generated. The first nuclear power plant opened in 1974 at Kozloduj on the Danube. Some oil and gas is produced north-east of Varna and there are small oil refineries at Ruse and Burgas.

Prior to WW II agriculture suffered from the over division of the land but today the large co-operative and state farms have increased production by employing machinery, irrigation, fertilisers and agricultural specialists. Two-thirds of the land is devoted to cereals, including wheat, corn, barley, rye, oats and rice. Also important are industrial crops such as sunflowers, cotton, sugar beets and tobacco. Bulgarian fruits and vegetables are outstanding.

About 75% of Bulgaria's foreign trade is conducted with the CMEA countries, the USSR alone accounting for over half. Exports of machinery, transportation equipment, chemicals, vegetables and fruit are sold to the USSR, the GDR, Poland and Greece. Bulgaria is the world's second largest exporter of cigarettes.

Bulgaria is more prosperous than any of its four neighbours. There are adequate supplies of attractive consumer goods in the stores and food is readily available. The good quality cigarettes, coffee and beer are striking in comparison with Romania or Poland. The average wage is about 200 leva a month and Bulgaria allots about 30% of the national budget to social services, a substantial additional income for the people.

GEOGRAPHY

Bulgaria occupies the eastern half of the Balkan Peninsula at the crossroads of Europe and Asia. An amazing variety of landforms are jammed into this relatively small area (110,912 square km). From the high banks of the Danube a wind-swept plain slopes up to the rounded summits of the Stara Planina (Balkan Mountains). This east-west range runs right across the northern half of the country from the Black Sea to Yugoslavia. The Sredna Gora branch is separated from the main range by a fault followed by the railway from Sliven to Sofia. Some 70% of the world's rose oil (used in the manufacture of cosmetics and perfumes) comes from the Valley of Roses near Kazanlak in this fault.

Southern Bulgaria is even more mountainous. Musala Peak (2925 metres) in the Rila Massif south of Sofia is the highest mountain between the Alps and Trans-Caucasia, almost equalled by Vihren Peak (2915 metres) in the Pirin Massif further south. These sharply glaciated massifs with their bare rocky peaks, steep forested valleys and glacial lakes are the geographical core of the Balkans – a paradise for hikers.

The Rhodopi Range stretches west along the Greek border from Rila and Pirin, separating the Aegean from the Thracian Plain of central Bulgaria. This plain opens on to the Black Sea coast with great bays and coastal lakes at Burgas and Varna. The long sandy beaches north, south and between these cities are among the finest in Europe.

Railways follow the great rivers of Bulgaria from Sofia: the Iskar north-east toward the Danube, the Marica south-east into Turkey, and the Struma south into Greece. About a third of Bulgaria is forested with deciduous trees in the lowlands and conifers in the mountains.

FESTIVALS & HOLIDAYS

Bulgarians observe a number of traditional customs and folk feasts of interest. Trifon Zarezan on 14 February is the ancient festival of the winegrowers. Vines are pruned and sprinkled with wine for a bounteous harvest. On 1 March Bulgarians present one another with *martenitsi*, red and white tasselled threads worn for health and happiness at the coming of spring. Lazarouvane (1 April) is a folk ritual associated with spring and youth. At noon on 2 June sirens announce a moments' silence in tribute to those who fell for Bulgaria's freedom. Students' Day is 8 December. Koledouvane is the ritual singing of Christmas carols on 24 and 25 December.

The March Musical Days are held annually at Ruse, followed by the Sofia Music Weeks in late May and early June. The Festival of Roses with folk songs and dances takes place at Kazanlak and Karlovo at the beginning of June. Also in June are the Varna Summer Festival of Music and the Ballroom Dancing Competition at Burgas. In November there's the Katya Popova Laureate Season at Pleven. The Plovdiv International Trade Fair is dedicated to consumer goods in May, industrial products in September.

Public holidays include 1 January (New Years Day), 1 and 2 May (Labour Days), 24 May (Day of Bulgarian Culture), 9 and 10 September (Liberation Days) and 7 November (Revolution Day).

LANGUAGE

The Cyrillic alphabet used in Bulgaria, the USSR and parts of Yugoslavia dates back to the 9th century when Cyril and Methodius translated the Bible into Old Bulgarian. Since virtually everything in the country is written in Cyrillic it's essential to learn part of the alphabet. To assist in deciphering signs get hold of one of the Cyrillic maps of Bulgaria available for a pittance at newsstands and bookstores.

For most Bulgarians Russian is the second language. There's always someone who speaks English or German at the reception of large hotels and at Balkantourist offices, although their information can be misleading. Apart from this, only well educated Bulgarians understand English.

Some words to know are *ja* (yes), *ne* (no), *ima* (there is), *neema* (there isn't), *kolko sstruwa?* (how much?), *molya* (please), *blagodarja* (thank you), *dobro utro* (good morning), *dobar den* (good day), *otworeno* (open) and *satworeno* (closed). The days of the week are *ponedelnik, wtornik, ssrjada, tschetwartak, petak, ssabota, nedelja*. *Dobre* (good) is a useful response in many situations.

Facts for the Visitor

VISAS

Most visitors entering Bulgaria need a visa which must be obtained in advance at a Bulgarian consulate. Tourist visas aren't usually available at the border, although new regulations allow you to get one there if you have a voucher for at least three nights prepaid accommodation. Consulates require a week to 10 days to process tourist visa applications, so apply well in advance. The consulate doesn't keep your passport during this period, however, and you only pay the visa fee (US$14 to US$30) after your application has been approved. The waiting period is fairly routine and most visa applications are granted.

You must specify the number of days you wish to stay in Bulgaria, to a maximum of 90 days. As there's no compulsory exchange put down the longest possible period you *might* stay, to avoid the hassle of having to get an extension. Nationals of Austria and all Scandinavian countries do not require visas. Group tourists arriving on a package tour are also visa exempt.

A tourist visa may be used anytime within three months of the date of issue. Thirty-hour transit visas are cheaper and easier to get (often without any waiting), but an onward visa may be required. Transit visas cannot be changed to tourist visas upon arrival. If you're in transit you're not supposed to stay at a hotel and most won't accept you if they see a transit visa. Transit visas are *sometimes* also available at the border.

People entering Bulgaria on tourist visas may be asked to show a voucher for two or three nights prepaid food and accommodation (at about US$50 a night). If you don't have such a voucher upon arrival you could be asked to purchase one at the border. It's sometimes possible to get around this by agreeing to buy the voucher at the exchange counter, then 'forgetting' to do so. Bulgarian immigration can be rather hard-nosed at times, so don't argue this point too strongly or you could be refused entry.

Rubber Stamps

When you enter Bulgaria you're given a white 'Departure Card' by immigration. This card should remain in your passport. Hotels, hostels, campgrounds and tourist offices arranging accommodation will stamp the back of it each night and write in the days you spent with them. When you leave Bulgaria immigration will check the card to make sure you have a stamp for every night you spent in the country. If one or two nights are missing it's generally no problem, but if too many nights are unaccounted for they could levy an on-the-spot US$100-plus fine. If you take an overnight train hang onto the couchette receipts to prove it. Although tempting, it's probably not a good idea to try to alter the dates on your card.

With this in mind don't lose the card and check to make sure everyone stamps it as they should. The purpose of the card is not to control your movements, but simply to force you to stay in official accommodation where, hopefully, you'll spend a lot of money. If you camp in the mountains, stay with friends or in a private room arranged on the street you don't get a stamp and are liable for the fine. In some such cases you may be able to register with the police and get a stamp from them, although your host probably won't wish you to do so.

In some areas only the luxury hotels are authorised to accept you and stamp the card. If the campground or hostel where you intended to stay happens to be closed or forbidden to accommodate westerners, this system can put you in a very precarious position. Unless you have unlimited funds this annoying regulation limits your freedom of movement considerably. Take it as a good example of the petty bureaucratic controls Bulgarians have to live with all their lives.

Warning

Official policy on tourism in Bulgaria can be summed up in one word: unpredictable. They can (and have) brought in regulations overnight which reduced the exchange rate by 50%, tripled private room prices, required the purchase of luxury hotel vouchers and made it necessary to pay all

hotel bills directly in hard currency, all without notice before or after. What will come next is anybody's guess, but consider everything in this chapter only as a description of the way things may have been.

MONEY

US$1 = 1 lev (official)
US$1 = 1.30 lev (transit tourist rate)
US$1 = 1.80 lev (packaged tourist rate)

no compulsory exchange

Banknotes come in denominations of 1, 2, 5, 10 and 20 leva. One lev (plural – leva) is divided into 100 stotinki. No currency declaration is required upon entry and there's no minimum daily exchange requirement but there are several different rates of exchange. The official rate of US$1 = 1 lev is used for official purposes such as buying international railway tickets. Tourists with a voucher get an 80% premium on the official rate every time they change money, while those in transit or on business get only 30% premium. With or without a voucher exchange counters sometimes give 30%, sometimes 80%, so ask beforehand.

Inflation is fairly low and prices are reasonable.

It's usually quicker to change money at Balkantourist offices. Banks often don't give the tourist premiums. Hang on to the exchange receipt or 'Bordereau' as this may be required when paying camping fees, etc. Don't change too much money as all hotel bills and sightseeing tours must be paid directly in hard currency, not in leva. They calculate the bill using the 30% premium rate, the most disadvantageous to you. Bring western currency in cash in small banknotes or small denomination travellers' cheques to settle these bills without a lot of bother. If you don't have exact change you may be forced to accept change in leva. Campgrounds and hostels usually take leva, but you must present the pink exchange paper you got when you changed your money. The amount will be deducted from the back of the slip and you can go on using it until all your 'credit' is used up.

It's almost impossible to change leva back into hard currency, which is what the black market is all about. Bulgarians need western currency to buy imported goods in hard currency shops. Vietnamese and Ethiopian students sometimes have extra cash they want to take out of the country. Czech and Polish tourists, who get an artificially high rate of exchange for their national currencies, are often willing to sell you leva at a good rate. The main disadvantage to these transactions is their illegality. Dealing on the street is risky and the penalties heavy so, if you must, wait till you meet someone reliable then do the act in private. You'll get anywhere from three to five leva to the dollar, but beware of counterfeit leva or worthless banknotes issued before the 1962 monetary reform. Balkantourist often requires those booking private rooms or package tours to purchase meal vouchers to reduce the incentive to change money unofficially. The import and export of leva are prohibited.

CLIMATE

Bulgaria has a temperate continental climate. The Rhodopi Mountains form a barrier to the moderating Mediterranean influence of the Aegean, while the Danube Plains are open to the extremes of central Europe. The Black Sea moderates temperatures in the eastern part of the country. Rainfall is highest in the mountains.

BOOKS & BOOKSHOPS

Bulgaria, A Guide by Dimiter Michailow and Pantscho Smolenow (Sofia Press, Sofia, 1983) will come in handy for addresses and background information. *Sofia, A Guide* by the same authors (Sofia Press, Sofia, 1981) is also useful. Also watch for *Atlas fur Motor-Touristik Bulgariens* (Kartographie, Budapest, 1984), an indexed map-guide (in German). These books are very inexpensive and often available at local bookstores in Eastern Europe.

The most complete travel guidebook to Bulgaria in English is *Nagel's Encyclopaedia Guide*. An excellent West German guide to the country is the *DuMont Kunst-Reisefuhrer Bulgarien* by Gerhard Eckert (DuMont Buchverlag, Koln, 1984).

NEWSPAPERS & MEDIA

The daily paper *Rabotnichesko Delo* is the official organ of the Communist Party. *Narodna Mladezh* is the daily of the Young Communist League. The *Sofia News* is a weekly newspaper in English, French, German and Russian which carries theatre and concert listings in the back. The monthly magazine *Bulgaria* provides an official picture of the country while *Discover Bulgaria* is a monthly tourist-oriented magazine.

HEALTH

Visitors receive free medical attention in case of accident or emergency. Longer treatments must be paid for but the rates are reasonable. Prescribed medicines are cheap (unless imported from the west).

There are over 600 curative mineral hot springs at 190 locations in Bulgaria. Those of Bankya, Hissarja and Kjustendil have been known since antiquity. Other Bulgarian spas include Sandarski, Velingrad and Narecenski Bani.

GENERAL INFORMATION
Post
Only books printed in Bulgaria in Bulgarian may be mailed from Bulgaria. Keep this in mind if you see a coffee table Soviet art book you fancy. Once purchased you'll have to carry it out of the country in your luggage.

Electricity
220 volts AC, 50 Hz

Time
Greenwich Mean Time plus two hours. At the end of March Bulgaria goes on summer time and clocks are turned an hour forward. At the end of September they're turned an hour back.

Business Hours
Many stores close for lunch from 1 to 2 pm. Some offices are closed from 12 noon to 1 pm.

INFORMATION
Balkantourist is the official government travel agency organising tourism in Bulgaria. They arrange expensive accommodation, change money, book sightseeing tours, etc. Many of their offices are unprepared to deal with individual tourists and can give disastrously misleading advice, especially on facilities outside their immediate area.

Budget travellers are better received at Orbita, the youth travel agency, and 'Pirin,' the travel agency of the Bulgarian Tourist Union. 'Rila' railway ticket offices are found in the city centres. Balkantourist offices abroad include:

Austria
  Balkantourist (tel 57-7762), 13 Rechte Wienzeile, 1040 Vienna
Belgium
  Balkantourist (tel 513-9610), 62 Rue Ravenstein, 1000 Brussels
Britain
  Balkantourist (tel 499-6988), 18 Princess St, London W1R 7RE
Denmark
  Balkantourist (tel 12-0510), 0 Vester Farimagsgade, 1606 Copenhagen V
Finland
  Balkantourist (tel 64-6044), 9 Annankatu, 00120 Helsinki 12
France
  Balkantourist (tel 261-6968), 45 Avenue de l'Opera, 75002 Paris
Greece
  Balkantourist (tel 363-4675), 12 Akademias St, Athens
Holland
  Balkantourist (tel 24-8431), 43 Leidsestraat, 1017 NV Amsterdam
Italy
  Balkantourist (tel 85-6438), 14 Viale Gorizia, 00198 Rome
Spain
  Balkantourist (tel 242-0720), Calle Princesa 12, 28008 Madrid
Sweden
  Balkantourist (tel 11-5191), 30 Kungsgatan, 11135 Stockholm
Switzerland
  Balkantourist (tel 221-2777), Steinmuhle Platz 1, 8023 Zurich
Turkey
  Balkantourist (tel 145-2456), 8 Gumhuryet Cad, Taksim Gezisi, Istanbul

USA

  Balkantourist (tel 722-1110), 161 East 86th
  St, New York, NY 10028

West Germany

  Balkantourist (tel 882-7418), Kurfurstendamm 175, 1000 West Berlin 15

  Balkantourist (tel 295-2846), Stefan Strasse
  1-3, 6000 Frankfurt am Main 1

ACCOMMODATION

Hotels

Bulgaria would be a fairly inexpensive
country if it weren't for the price of the
hotels. While condemning discrimination
abroad Bulgaria has created a mini-
apartheid system at home, based on
national origin. Western tourists are
required to stay at the better Balkantourist
hotels. Cheaper local hotels, guesthouses
and dormitories are often reserved for
Bulgarians only. In Sofia they compromise
and let you stay at the 2nd class hotels
while paying 1st class prices.

Hotel rooms are about the same price
single, double or triple, so try to team up
with other western travellers. All hotel
bills must be settled directly in western
currency, which jacks the price up a little
more. You'll rarely find a hotel under
US$15 single, US$20 double (with shared
bath and usually breakfast). Hotels are
classified from one to five stars. The most
expensive hotels are called Interhotels
which can have anything from three to
five stars.

Private Rooms

Balkantourist claims to have available
146,000 beds in private houses and flats,
110,000 of them at the seaside. The
availability of private rooms is according
to the law of supply and demand. If any
hotel rooms are empty Balkantourist
won't be interested in helping you find
lodgings in a private home. But when all
the hotels are full (such as during the
Plovdiv fair or along the Black Sea coast
in mid-summer) they may even suggest
this alternative. In Sofia private rooms
are now as expensive as hotels. Singles

often have to pay for doubles. Always ask
Balkantourist about private rooms as
your first accommodation preference. You
may be lucky.

Student Hotels

If you have a student card the Orbita
Youth Travel Agency, Stambolijski
bulevard 45, Sofia, may be able to book
rooms for you in student hotels around the
country. You have to get through to the
right person upstairs in the Orbita
building; the woman in the currency
exchange office on the main street can't
help you. Once the reservations are made
you buy a voucher from Orbita to pay for
the rooms at about US$8 to US$10 a night.
If you know your itinerary and are able to
make reservations at Orbita, this service
could save you a lot of trouble.

There are Orbita hotels in Rila village
(about 22 km from the monastery), Batak
(in the mountains south of Plovdiv),
Lovec (between Troyan and Pleven),
Veliko Tarnovo, Sumen and Varna, plus
Kavarna and Primorsko resorts on the
Black Sea. Reservations can also be made
for similarly-priced hotels in Koprivstica
and Kotel. Some student hotels are open
only in summer. Unfortunately, the Orbita
Student Hotel in Sofia has been closed for
years with no reopening in sight.

Youth Hostels

The IYHF handbook lists 46 youth hostels
(hijas) in Bulgaria. Most of them do in
fact exist, but if you go directly to one and
try to check in you'll probably be told it's
full, closed, or under reconstruction.
Many wardens are unwilling to take the
responsibility of accepting you without an
advance reservation. Some of the hostels
are intended for groups and close down
when no group is present.

Reservations for youth hostels are
handled by 'Pirin,' the travel bureau of the
Bulgarian Tourist Union. 'Pirin' offices in
various cities around Bulgaria are listed in
the travelling section of this chapter. Go
to them *before* going to a hostel. A current

YHA membership card will be required. The main 'Pirin' office is at Stambolijski bulevard 30, Sofia. Bulgarian youth hostels are seldom used by western members, so set a good example.

Camping

The latest (1984) Balkantourist *Camping-platze* map lists 103 campgrounds in Bulgaria. Although the map claims many of them are open from May to October, they can only be safely relied upon from June to early September. *These are the months budget travellers should plan to visit Bulgaria.* The opening dates for campgrounds listed in this book are only approximations and not guaranteed by the author. It's no use asking Balkantourist about camping because they really don't know.

Camping fees average 5 leva a night. Most campgrounds rent small bungalows, but these are sometimes full so bring a tent if you're on a budget. Campgrounds along the coast tend to be very crowded, while those in the interior usually have bungalows available for just slightly more than the cost of camping. All of the Balkantourist campgrounds accept foreigners, but some of the others do not. Freelance camping is prohibited.

FOOD & DRINK

The food is good and plentiful in Bulgaria. The price difference between a good hotel restaurant and the cheapest self-service is only about two to one, so it's worth splashing out a little. By western standards prices are extremely low. Waiters at nice restaurants expect the bill to be 'rounded up' to the next round figure. In fact tips are an important part of their income. A folk style restaurant serving traditional Bulgarian dishes is known as a *mehana* or *mexana*, often located in a basement and offering live music. Lunch is the main meal of the day.

The wines come in both red (Cabernet, Gamza, Mavrud, Melnik, Merlot, Otel and Pamid) and white (Dimyat, Misket, Riesling, Rkatsitelli and Tamyanka) varieties. Pamid wine dates from the time of the ancient Thracians. Bulgarians swear by *slivova* (plum brandy). Bulgarian fruit juices (apricot, peach, plum) are exported all over Eastern Europe. Coffee and beer are readily available.

Bulgarian Specialties

A *Shopska Salad* is made of fresh diced tomatoes, cucumbers and peppers covered with grated white sheep's cheese *siren*. *Cheese a la Shoppe* is baked in an earthenware pot. Bulgarian yoghurt is famous and *tarator* is a refreshing cold soup of yoghurt, diced cucumber and ground walnuts. *Plakiya* and *gyuvech* are rich fish and meat stews.

Other popular Bulgarian dishes with a Turkish flavour include *kebabcheta* (grilled meat rolls), *kavarma* (meat and vegetable casserole), *drob sarma* (chopped lamb liver baked with rice and eggs), *surmi* (stuffed vine or cabbage leaves) and *kebab* (meat on a spit). *Banitsa* is a baked cheese, spinach or boiled milk pastry like Yugoslav *burek*, while *mekitsas* is a batter of eggs and yoghurt fried in oil.

THINGS TO BUY

Typical purchases include embroidered dresses and blouses, linen, carpets, Valley of Roses perfume, pottery, leather goods, dolls in national costume, silver filigree jewellery, recordings of folk music and wrought copper and iron. Eye glasses are very cheap and easily available in Bulgaria.

You're allowed to take out locally-purchased souvenirs and articles for personal use worth up to a total of 50 leva. Items purchased for hard currency at Corecom shops may be exported duty free if receipts are shown. Corecom outlets are often located in the luxury hotels. Some large Corecom shops selling consumer goods like colour TVs and vacuum cleaners are reserved for model workers with special bonus coupons.

Getting There & Away

TRAIN

The main railway routes into Bulgaria are from Edirne (Turkey), Thessaloniki (Greece), Nis (Yugoslavia) and Bucharest (Romania). All these lines are served several times a day with through trains from Istanbul, Athens, Munich, Berlin (via Belgrade or Bucharest), Warsaw and Moscow. The famous Orient Express line from Belgrade to Istanbul runs through Sofia and Plovdiv.

Train Tickets

Sample international railway fares from Sofia are 11 leva to Bucharest, 23.63 leva to Budapest via Romania, 58.90 leva to Budapest via Yugoslavia, 11.70 leva to Nis, Yugoslavia, 23.30 leva to Belgrade, Yugoslavia, 23.60 leva to Thessaloniki, Greece, and 32.90 leva to Istanbul, Turkey. All fares are payable in western currency converted into leva at the 'V-11' official rate at 'Rila' railway ticket offices. Theoretically IUS student card holders get a 30% discount on international train tickets between socialist countries. Ask about seat reservations when you buy the ticket.

Even though it's much further to go to Budapest via Romania than it is through Yugoslavia, it's less than half the price because the fare is calculated in 'accounting roubles.' Unfortunately the savings are wiped out by the Romanian transit visa fee (US$24) and an obligatory US$10 official exchange rip off.

It's cheaper to get tickets for the shortest possible distances across borders, then arrange an onward domestic ticket on the other side. Examples are Dimitrovgrad (Yugoslavia) to Sofia and Bucharest (Romania) to Ruse. Arriving from Greece or Turkey it's probably best to avoid undue attention from Bulgarian immigration by having a ticket through to Sofia or Plovdiv.

If you wish to leave in those directions, however, you'll save money by departing on foot. For Thessaloniki take a local train to Kulata. For eastern Greece or Turkey take a local train to Svilengrad. A daily morning train runs between Svilengrad and Kastanea (Greece). For Turkey if you can't get a train ticket for the 39-km Svilengrad-Edirne hop, take a bus, taxi or hitch from Svilengrad to the border post, Kapitan-Andreevo (14 km), and walk out. Moneychangers and Turkish buses to Edirne wait on the other side.

BUS

One of the best ways to arrive is on the regular bus service between Athens and Sofia (US$20 one way). A train ticket Athens-Sofia is twice as expensive and the customs check tends to be stricter on the train. Ask around at the budget travel agencies on Omonia Square, Athens, for tickets. Cheap package bus tours to Bulgaria are available from the same offices, eliminating the need to apply for a visa. In Sofia you'll find the Greek buses at the Novotel Europa near the Central Railway Station. Make arrangements with the Greek drivers in the morning for a seat that afternoon.

PACKAGE TOURS

There are numerous all inclusive tours to the Black Sea resorts. These are fairly cheap but you're tied to a hotel and outside the peak season (June to mid-September) facilities are limited. The tours do offer the convenience of fixed dates and an absence of red tape.

More imaginative (and three times as expensive) are the tours featuring a seven-day cruise along the Danube from Ruse to Vienna. Balkan Holidays (tel 01 493-8612), 19 Conduit St, London W1R 9TD, England, offers a two-week package from London for about £1000 per person (double occupancy). Included are the cruise, flights, taxes, hotels and all meals. Similar trips on Romanian ships are slightly longer and cheaper, but not as luxurious and more difficult to book.

Getting Around

AIR
Balkan Air has several daily flights from Sofia to Varna and Burgas (27 leva one way). You can pay with Bulgarian currency without receipts. Other flights operate from Sofia to Gorna Oryahovitsa, Ruse, Silistra and Vidin, if you're really in love with flying.

TRAIN
Bulgarian trains are classified as *ekspresen* (express), *brzi* (fast) or *putnichki* (slow). Trains from Sofia to Burgas go via either Karlovo or Plovdiv. Trains from Sofia to Varna go via either Karlovo or Gorna Orjahovica. All trains from Sofia to Ruse go via Pleven and Gorna Orjahovica. Service between Sofia and Plovdiv is fairly frequent. Sleepers and couchettes are available between Sofia and Burgas/Varna.

Gorna Uryahovitsa is a main railway junction in northern Bulgaria where trains from Sofia, Ruse, Varna and Stara Zagora meet. The branch line south from Gorna Oryahovitsa to Stara Zagora via Veliko Tarnovo is the only north-south line across the centre of the country. Another branch line runs from Ruse to Varna, although buses (via Sumen) are faster and more frequent on this route.

BUS
Long distance buses serve many points not directly connected by train. Take a bus to go from Sofia to Rila Monastery or Vidin, from Pleven to Trojan to Plovdiv, from Varna to Burgas, etc. Only as many tickets are sold as there are seats, so it's important to arrive at the station early to make sure you get one. You usually buy the ticket at an office rather than from the driver. Long distance buses generally leave in the very early morning.

BOAT
From May to September hydrofoils operate along the Black Sea coast between Varna, Nessebar, Pomorie, Burgas, Sosopol, Primorsko and Mitschurin. Fares are low (for example, Varna to Burgas is only 7.50 leva plus a small additional charge for luggage) but there are big crowds. Tickets go on sale an hour before the departure but you have to be there a little before that and even then there's no guarantee you'll get on. Have your passport ready.

From May to mid-September hydrofoils zip up the Danube daily from Ruse to Svistov and Vidin (8 leva one way, six hours), departing each end in the very early morning. The schedule can be interrupted by low water levels, so call Ruse (tel 2-27-91) for information. The ferry across the Danube from Vidin to Calafat (Romania) operates several times a day from May to December (2 leva).

LOCAL TRANSPORT
City Buses
The same blue 6 stotinki bus tickets can be used on city buses all over Bulgaria, except in Sofia where the tickets are pink. Buy city bus tickets at information counters in bus and train stations. Trams and trolley buses operate from 4 am to 1 am, buses until 12 midnight.

Taxis
Taxis are plentiful in Bulgaria and you can even flag them down on the street. They're most easily found in front of train stations. Taxis in Bulgaria charge what the meter says and are not expensive. They don't usually charge you for the return journey, even if it's out of town. Fares are 50% higher from 10 pm to 5 am. Always try to take a taxi with a meter that works.

Sofia

Sofia sits on a 550-metre-high plateau in western Bulgaria at the foot of Mt Vitosa. The position at the very centre of the

To Railway Station

Public Market

Slivnica

Cvjatko Radojnov

Volgograd

Georgi Dimitrov

G S Rakovski

Iskar

Marsal Birijuzov

Zdanov

Knjaz Dondukov

Janko Zabunov

Gen Zaimov

Largo

Pl. 9 Septemvri

Pl. Lenin

Stambolijski

Central Park

Ruski

Sipka

Pl Narodno Sabranie

Aksakov

Alabin

Vasil Levski

Rakovski

Septemvri

Ivan Vasov

Ruski

Vitosa

Stefan

Karadze

General Gurko

Marsal Tolbuhin

Balgaria

Neofit Rilski

Graf Ignatiev

Patriarch Evtimij

Marsal Tolbuhin

Dragan Cankov

Fritjof Nansen

Balgaria

Sofia

1	Edelweis Hotel	33	US Embassy
2	Shredna Gora Hotel	34	Art Gallery
3	Zdravec Hotel	35	Georgi Dimitrov Mausoleum
4	Synagogue	36	Concert Bureau
5	Banya Bashi Mosque	37	Sala Bulgaria
6	Central Baths	38	National Army Theatre
7	Iskar Hotel	39	Slavinska Beseda Hotel
8	St Petra Semerdjuska	40	Kpum Restaurant
9	Party House	41	Museum of the
10	Balkantourist		Revolutionary Movement
11	National Youth Theatre	42	Balkan Airlines
12	National Art Gallery	43	Monument to the Liberators
13	Natural History Museum	44	National Assembly
14	St Nicholas Russian Church	45	Soviet Army Monument
15	National Opera & Ballet	46	Ivan Vasov Museum
16	Church of St Sophia	47	'Ivan Vasov' National Theatre
17	Patriarch's Palace	48	'Rila' Railway Ticket Office
18	Alexander Nevski Church	49	Main Post Office
19	Foreign Art Gallery	50	Puppet Theatre
20	State Musical Theatre	51	Budapest Restaurant
21	Serdika Hotel	52	Satirical Theatre
22	Romanian Consulate	53	'Slavejkov' Concert Hall
23	National Library	54	Bookstore
24	Art Gallery	55	Sevastopol Hotel
25	University	56	Self-Service Restaurant
26	National Museum of History	57	Former Black Mosque
27	Interhotel Office	58	Turkish Embassy
28	Holy Sunday Cathedral	59	Vasil Levski Stadium
29	St George's Rotunda	60	Anniverary Monument
30	Theological Academy	61	Cultural Centre
31	Mexana Koprivshtitsa Restaurant	62	British Embassy
32	National Archaeological Museum	63	Hungarian Consulate

Balkan Peninsula, midway between the Adriatic and Black Seas, made Sofia a crossroads of trans-European routes. The present city centre is attractive with large traffic-free areas paved with yellow bricks. It's a remarkably clean, quiet city considering that much of Bulgaria's industry is concentrated here. If you can find reasonable accommodation Sofia repays an unhurried stay.

History

Under changing names Sofia has a history that goes back thousands of years. The Romans built strong walls around Serdica (Sofia), their capital of Inner Dacia. After the Hun invasion of 441 the town was rebuilt by the Byzantines. The Slavs gave Sredets (Sofia) a key role in the First Bulgarian Kingdom, then in 1018 the Byzantines re-took Triaditsa (Sofia). At the end of the 12th century the Bulgarians returned and Sredets became a major trading centre of the Second Bulgarian Kingdom. The Turks captured Sofia in 1382 and made it the centre of the Rumelian beylerbeyship. The city declined during the 19th century feudal unrest, but with the establishment of the Third Bulgarian Kingdom in 1879 Sofia again became capital.

Orientation

The central railway station is on the north side of downtown. From the station bulevard Georgi Dimitrov curves around and runs south through ploschtad Lenin. Beyond Holy Sunday Cathedral this thoroughfare becomes Vitosa bulevard, the fashionable avenue of modern Sofia. Many travel agencies and airline offices are found along Stambolijski bulevard, west from the cathedral.

Largo opens east from ploschtad Lenin and spills into ploschtad 9 Septemvri. The Georgi Dimitrov Mausoleum on ploschtad 9 Septemvri is the very heart of the city, its disciplined honour guard indicative of the new regime. Ruski bulevard continues south-east as far as the university, then runs on and out of the city as bulevard V I Lenin.

Information

Tourist Offices The main Balkantourist office handling individual tourists is at Knjaz Dondukov 37 in the centre of town (open 7 am to 10 pm). They reserve expensive accommodation, change money and book sightseeing tours. They may deign to answer questions about other matters if you're courteous and they're not too busy. The Interhotel office (open 8 am to 8 pm) at uliza Sveta Sofija 4 near Holy Sunday Cathedral also provides maps, brochures and advice. They're far less busy than the main Balkantourist office.

For information on hiking and hostelling go to 'Pirin' Travel Bureau, Stambolijski bulevard 30. The Orbita Youth Travel Agency, Stambolijski bulevard 45a, handles student travel. Try the bookstore at the corner of Vasil Levski and Graf Ignatiev for maps and guidebooks.

Socialist Tourist Offices Along Stambolijski bulevard west of Holy Sunday Cathedral are the tourist information offices of the USSR (at No 24), Hungary (No 26), Czechoslovakia (29), Poland (29) and East Germany (37).

Embassies The US Embassy, Stambolijski bulevard 1, is near the Georgi Dimitrov Mausoleum. The British Embassy, Tolbuhin bulevard 65 east of the Cultural Centre, serves all Commonwealth nationals.

Consulates The Romanian Consulate, Dimitar Poljanov 10, opens Monday, Wednesday and Friday 10.30 am to 12.30 pm, while the Yugoslavian Consulate, Sipka 7, works weekdays 9 am to 12 noon. The Hungarian Consulate, directly behind the British Embassy, opens Monday, Tuesday, Thursday and Friday 9 am to 11 am. You shouldn't need visas for Greece or Turkey.

Things to See

Sightseeing in Sofia is centred mostly around museums, although there are a number of old churches and mosques to visit. Begin with the largest, neo-Byzantine **Alexander Nevski Church** (1912), a memorial to the 200,000 Russian soldiers who died for the independence of Bulgaria. In the crypt is a museum of icons (closed Tuesday). The 6th century basilica across the square in front of Alexander Nevski is the **Church of St Sophia**, which gave its name to the city. The **Tomb of the Unknown Soldier** is by the church wall. The large building behind Alexander Nevski contains the **Foreign Art Gallery**, with an important collection of European paintings, plus African, Japanese and Indian art. Unfortunately all the labels are in Cyrillic only.

The street south from Alexander Nevski empties into ploschtad Narodno Sabranie (1884) with the **National Assembly** and an equestrian statue (1905) of Alexander II, the Russian tsar who freed Bulgaria from the Turks. Boulevard Ruski runs west into ploschtad 9 Septemvri, the heart of official Sofia. At bulevard Ruski 14 is the **Museum of the Revolutionary Movement** with an exciting audio-visual exhibit. Beyond the park is **St Nicholas Russian Church** (1913), then the **Natural Science Museum**, bulevard Ruski 1 (open Tuesday to Thursday), with flora and fauna on four floors.

You'll then reach ploschtad 9 Septemvri, dominated by the **Georgi Dimitrov Mausoleum** (open Wednesday, Friday, Sunday 2 to 5 pm). Handbags must be left

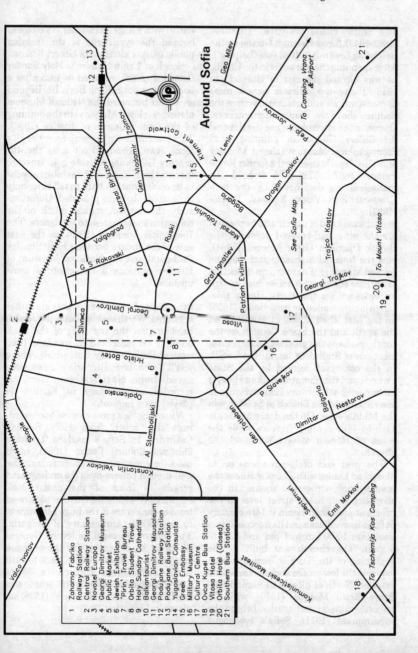

Around Sofia

To Camping Vrana & Airport

To Mount Vitoša

See Sofia Map

To Camping Kos Camping

To Tschernija Kos Camping

1 Zaharna Fabrika Railway Station
2 Central Railway Station
3 Novotel Europa
4 Georgi Dimitrov Museum
5 Public Market
6 Jewish Exhibition
7 'Pirin' Travel Bureau
8 Orbita Student Travel
9 Holy Sunday Cathedral
10 Balkantourist
11 Georgi Dimitrov Mausoleum
12 Podujane Railway Station
13 Podujane Bus Station
14 Yugoslavian Consulate
15 Greek Embassy
16 Military Museum
17 Cultural Centre
18 Ovca Kupel Bus Station
19 Vitoša Hotel
20 Orbita Hotel (Closed)
21 Southern Bus Station

at a nearby cloakroom (free). Dimitrov (1882-1949) faced Herman Goring at the Reichstag fire trail in 1933 (see 'Leipzig'). After spending the war years in the USSR, he was elected premier of Bulgaria in 1946. Today top officials review mass demonstrations and celebrations from the podium above the mausoleum entrance. Opposite the mausoleum are the **National Art Gallery** (Bulgarian painting) and **Ethnographical Museum** (closed Monday and Tuesday), housed in the former Royal Palace (1887). The park behind the mausoleum is dominated by the neo-Classical **Ivan Vasov National Theatre** (1907).

At the west end of ploschtad 9 Septemvri are the nine lead-covered domes of the Buyuk Djami or Great Mosque (1494), now the **National Archaeological Museum** (closed Monday). The excellent collection of antique sculpture is accessible through an entrance on the Party House side. Largo is surrounded by **Party House** (1955) on the east, the Council of Ministers on the north and the State Council on the south, perhaps the greatest architectural erections of Stalinism outside the USSR. In the courtyard formed by the State Council and the Sheraton Balkan Hotel is an imposing 4th century Roman Rotunda converted into the **Church of St George** in the Middle Ages. On the dome inside are 11th to 14th century frescoes while the ruins of Roman streets surround the church.

The west end of Largo opens on to ploschtad Lenin, with a huge statue of the man looking across the square. In the shopping mall below street level in the centre of ploschtad Lenin is 14th century **St Petra Semerdjuska** and its frescoes (open weekdays 10.30 am to 1 pm and 3.30 to 6 pm). The church was built at the beginning of the Turkish period, which explains the low profile and inconspicuous exterior. North of ploschtad Lenin is the **Banya Bashi Mosque** (1576) with its majestic minaret and nearby, behind the supermarket (1911), Sofia's **synagogue**

(1910) with a huge chandelier. Two blocks beyond the synagogue is the teeming public market along uliza Georgi Kirkov.

South of Lenin Square is **Holy Sunday Cathedral** (1863), restored in 1925 after a bomb attempt on King Boris III. Beyond on Vitosa bulevard the **National Museum of History** (closed Monday) in the building of the former Courts of Justice (1936). This huge museum takes up an entire city block (two floors). Don't miss the 4th century BC Panagyurishte gold treasure in room three. Some of the exhibits appear to be copies, but it's hard to tell since only Bulgarian labels are provided. Unfortunately this neglect makes much of the collection meaningless to foreigners. The **Theological Academy** (1905) on the east side of the square between Holy Sunday Cathedral and the National Museum of History contains a collection of icons upstairs.

Other Sights Sofia's other sights are rather scattered. Worth seeking out is the **Jewish Exhibition** on the top floor of the bank building on ploschtad Vazrazdane (due west of Holy Sunday Cathedral), where you'll learn how Bulgaria's Jews were saved from Nazi extermination. A recorded commentary in English is played upon request.

Vitosa, Sofia's most elegant boulevard, runs due south from Holy Sunday Cathedral to Sofia's modern **'Lyudmila Zhivkova' Cultural Centre** (1981), often used for concerts and conferences. The well-dressed passers-by in the underground arcade in front of the centre look surprisingly affluent. On the square in front of the centre is the huge Monument to the 1300th Anniversary of Bulgaria. The **Military Museum**, bulevard General Skobelev 23, is nearby. On the opposite side of the Cultural Centre back toward Alexander Nevski Church is **Saints Sedmotchislenitsi Church** in what was originally the 'Black Mosque' (1528) on uliza Graf Ignatiev.

Mt Vitosa Mt Vitosa (2290 metres), the rounded mountain which looms just eight km south of Sofia, is a popular ski resort in winter. In summer the chairlift operates for the benefit of sightseers. If you have a little extra time take a bus (80 stotinki) up Mt Vitosa to *Hija Aleko*, where there's a chairlift approaching the summit. There are a number of tourist hotels on the mountain, but they're geared for package tourism and have little to offer the individual visitor. Everything can be seen in a couple of hours and the best view of the city is obtained during the bus ride up. From this mountain you get a good view of the thick blanket of smog hanging over Sofia. The Vitosa bus departs from near the southern terminus of trams No 2 and 9.

Places to Stay

Youth Hostels If you have a current YHA membership card go to the 'Pirin' Travel Bureau, Stambolijski bulevard 30, which can make the necessary reservations for you. The 'Knyazhevo Youth Hostel,' listed in the IYHF handbook, is actually the *BTU Touristicheski Dom*, located on the far south-west side of Sofia. Take tram No 5 to the end of the line, then bus No 58 or 59 four stops, then walk one km up a steep hill. Don't go without first making a reservation at 'Pirin,' however, or all you may find is a padlocked gate.

There are also several hostels on Mt Vitosa listed in the IYHF handbook. *Hija Aleko* on Mt Vitosa is not listed but sometimes also available. You may hear of a hostel called 'Turisticheska Splany Zdravjets' near the train station, but it does not accept western visitors.

Camping *Camping Vrana* (open May to October) is nine km out on the Plovdiv highway. From the Central Railway Station take bus No 213 out onto bulevard V I Lenin, then change to bus No 5, 6, or 7 which pass the site. Alternatively, take streetcars 4 or 10 south-east to the end of the line, then catch bus No 5 or 6 which

begin there. Camping is 5 leva, bungalows 30 leva. There's a restaurant on the premises with waiters who regularly overcharge western tourists. Don't pitch your tent too close to this restaurant if you want to get any sleep.

Tschernija Kos Camping, 11 km south-west of Sofia on the main highway to Greece, offers tenting (5 leva) and bungalows (6.50 leva). From the city centre take tram No 5 to the end of the line, then buses No 58 or 59 till you see a huge white statue beside the road. Though farther from Sofia than Vrana, this site is friendlier and more attractive. It's convenient if you're travelling to or from Rila Monastery. Both these campgrounds have plenty of space for tenters.

Balkantourist Balkantourist, Knjaz Dondukov 37 (open 7 am to 10 pm), will make hotel or private room reservations for you, but only after 12 noon when the rooms become 'available.' If you're there around that time you might get a one-star (2nd class) hotel room with shared bath for about US$17 single, US$29 double, breakfast included.

Balkantourist also has private rooms for around US$24 double (no singles available) and you get a daily 'bonus refund' of 10 leva 'breakfast money.' If you arrive late in the day you may be told that even these overpriced alternatives are gone and only the really expensive hotels still have rooms.

Hotels The *Shredna Gora Hotel*, bulevard Georgi Dimitrov 60, and the *Edelweis Hotel*, bulevard Georgi Dimitrov 79, are on a noisy streetcar route between the train station and the centre of town. The *Iskar Hotel*, uliza Iskar 9, is also afflicted with streetcar noise, but it's in a better location only a block from Balkantourist. The best of the one-star hotels, the *Sevastopol*, uliza Rakovski 116 at Graf Ignatiev (tel 875941), is nearly always full. All four of these are about 22 leva single, 37 leva double with breakfast (shared bath).

A far better hotel is the two-star *Slavinska Beseda*, uliza Rakovski 127 not far from the Ivan Vasov National Theatre. It's quiet and convenient, but the rates are 41 leva single, 71 leva double.

Places to Eat

Bottom End There are three good places to fill your stomach on Vitosa bulevard opposite the National Museum of History, get to know them early in your stay. In the yellow building near Holy Sunday Cathedral at the beginning of the boulevard is a very popular self-service restaurant open 6.30 am to 10 pm daily. You pay as you leave.

A similar but slightly better establishment is through the narrow doorway at Vitosa bulevard 5/7. Between these two is the *Mexana Koprivshtitsa Restaurant*, downstairs from the arcade at Vitosa bulevard 1/3, which offers Bulgarian specialties in swank surroundings (certainly not 'bottom end'). There's another self-service restaurant at Graf Ignatiev 32/34.

Top End One of the nicest places in Sofia to eat is the *Kpum Restaurant*, uliza Dobrudza 2 near ploschtad Narodno Sabranie. In summer you dine in the courtyard surrounded by greenery and the waiters all speak English. Try the *kavarma* – delicious. With soup and beer your bill should be around 10 leva. For Hungarian food in an elegant setting it's the *Budapest Restaurant*, uliza Stefan Karadza 9 opposite the Satirical Theatre.

Entertainment

Sofia's finest is the *National Academic Theatre for Opera & Ballet* on uliza Janko Zabunov not far from Alexander Nevski Church. Tickets are sold inside and you should be able to get one (3 leva). For something lighter check out the *'S Makedonski' State Musical Theatre* on bulevard Volgograd behind Alexander Nevski. You'll enjoy the operettas put on here, even if they are in Bulgarian.

The *Puppet Theatre*, uliza Gurko 14, never fails to please. Nearby is the *Satirical Theatre*, uliza Stefan Karadza 26. You won't understand a word of it, but the acting is superb. The *'Ivan Vasov' National Academic Theatre*, uliza Vasil Levski 5, presents classical theatre.

For concert tickets visit the Concert Bureau beside Aeroflot near the Georgi Dimitrov Mausoleum. Many concerts take place in the *Sala Bulgaria*, just around the corner from the bureau at uliza Aksakov 3. Others are performed in the *Cultural Centre*. At all the theatres performances begin at 7 pm with matinees on weekends.

Things to Buy

The best shops for traditional handicrafts and Soviet fine art books are along bulevard Ruski near ploschtad Narodno Sabranie. The people shop at Central Department Store (ZUM) on ploschtad Lenin. Better stores for Bulgarian consumers are along Vitosa bulevard and in the arcade below the Cultural Centre.

Getting There & Away

Train All railway service in Bulgaria focuses on Sofia. There are international lines to Belgrade, Athens, Istanbul, Bucharest and points beyond. The Greek border at Kulata is 225 km due south by train. Important domestic expresses run to Ruse (via Pleven), to Varna (via Pleven or Karlovo) and to Burgas (via Karlovo or Plovdiv). For Veliko Tarnovo change at Stara Zagora, Tulovo or Gorna-Orjahovitza. Plovdiv is only two hours from Sofia by express. A local line east to Kazanlak serves Koprivstica, Karlovo (for Trojan) and Kazanlak (for Sipka). Sleepers and couchettes are available to Burgas and Varna.

Railway Station Sofia's Central Station can be a little confusing. In addition to the Cyrillic destination indicators, the tracks are haphazardly numbered in either Roman or Arabic numerals! Allow an extra 10 minutes to find your train, then ask several people to ensure that it really is the right one!

Domestic tickets are sold downstairs with different queues for different destinations, so again ask. International tickets should be purchased the day before at 'Rila' (see below).

There's a currency exchange cum tourist information office in the Central Railway Station, open 6.30 am to 10 pm. In the event this is closed try the massive white Novotel Europa Hotel, visible from in front of the station, which changes money on a similar schedule.

Train Tickets For all international railway tickets visit 'Rila,' uliza General Gurko 5 (open weekdays 8 am to 7 pm). They'll tell you the price of your ticket in leva. You must then go to the National Bank (open weekdays 9 am to 11.45 am and 2 pm to 5.45 pm) beside the Georgi Dimitrov Mausoleum on ploschtad 9 Septemvri and change that amount on form 'V-11' at the official rate. Make sure the bank clerk understands the purpose of the exchange so it all comes out straight. Then with the bank receipt 'Rila' will issue your ticket without delay. As soon as you have a ticket go to another window where you can make a seat reservation.

Domestic train tickets are available from the ticket office at bulevard Georgi Dimitrov 23. For couchettes go to the ticket office at bulevard Georgi Dimitrov 79.

Bus Places more easily reached by bus than by train include Rila Monastery, Troyan, Gabrovo and Vidin. Direct services to Rila Monastery depart the Ovca Kupel Bus Station (trams No 5 or 19), while Troyan and Gabrovo buses leave from the Podujane Bus Station near Podujane Railway Station north-east of the centre.

Bus Tickets For information on all long-distance buses leaving Sofia and advance tickets visit the ticket office in the arcade below the Cultural Centre at least one day

before. For information about buses to Thessaloniki and Athens, ask at the information desk in the Novotel Europa Hotel. The Athens bus departs this hotel around 12 noon and you pay your fare directly to the driver in hard currency.

Getting Around

Airport Transport Vrazdebna Airport, 12 km east of Sofia, is accessible on city buses No 84 and 284 from the stop opposite bulevard Tolbuhin 4 near the university. The main Balkan Airlines office is on ploschtad Narodno Sabranie off Ruski bulevard, with a branch in the arcade below the Cultural Centre.

Public Transport Sofia's public transport system is based on streetcars, supplemented by buses and trolley buses. Purchase tickets (6 stotinki) valid on all vehicles in advance at kiosks.

Western Bulgaria

BANKYA

A good place to escape the crowds is Bankya spa, only 17 km west of Sofia. Few foreign tourists ever visit the town, but it's popular among the Bulgarians filling the 40 sanatoria and promenading through the well-kept parks. When imbibed the spa's mineral waters stimulate the digestive system. The **mineral baths** are on the park, a few blocks west of the railway station. There are separate sections for men and women and admission is cheap.

If you'd like to stay in Bankya the 'Zimmernachweis' office opposite the open bathing pool near the station arranges private rooms. There's also a campground with bungalows about half a km back toward Sofia from Ivanyane Railway Station, the station before Bankya. Trains to the spa leave Sofia's Central Railway Station every half hour or so.

THE RILA MOUNTAINS

The majestic Rila Mountains south of Sofia are *the* place to go hiking. Every summer hundreds of East German backpackers inundate the area and they make good English-speaking companions on alpine expeditions. Mountain hostels *(hijas)* provide basic dormitory accommodation. Although many of the *hijas* serve meals, you had best bring food. For current information on trail conditions and the hostels be sure to enquire at the 'Pirin' Travel Bureau, Stambolijski bulevard 30, Sofia.

The classic trip is across the mountains from Complex Malyovitsa to Rila Monastery, which can be done in two days straight or three with a visit to the Seven Lakes. A longer route to Rila begins at the ski resort of Borovec and includes a climb to the top of Musala Peak (2925 metres), highest in the Balkan Peninsula. You could also do both and make it a round trip in a little over a week.

Via Malyovitsa

Although you can take a bus straight from Sofia to Rila Monastery, a more rewarding way to get there would be to hike across the mountains south-west from Samokov. Buses to Samokov (62 km from Sofia) leave frequently from the bus station below the overpass beyond Sofia's Park-Hotel Moskva (trams No 14 and 19). There's an onward bus from Samokov to Complex Malyovitsa approximately every two hours. At the Complex (elevation 1700 metres) is a hotel run by the 'Pirin' Travel Bureau (make reservations at their Sofia office) and the Central School of Alpinism.

About an hour's hike above Complex Malyovitsa is the *Hija Malyovitsa* (2000 metres), where a dorm bed and bowl of soup are usually available. From Hija Malyovitsa you can hike up to *Hija Sedemte ezera* (no meals served, bring food) in about six hours. This hija is right beside one of the legendary Seven Lakes on a mountain plateau at 2200 metres

elevation. A notorious sun worshipping cult was centred on these lakes before the war, but now of course it's banned. From Hija Sedemte ezera you can hike down to Rila Monastery (elevation 1147 metres) in five hours.

Via Borovec

Catch the bus to Samokov (as described above) where you'll find another bus to Borovec (elevation 1300 metres, 72 km from Sofia). This popular ski resort is upmarket, so arrive early enough to make the stiff four-hour hike up to *Hija Musala* (2389 metres) the same day. Check to see if the cable car to *Hija Jastrebec* is operating from Borovec, which would save you quite a climb.

Musala Peak is only two hours beyond Hija Musala. Carry on another five hours to *Hija Boris Hadzisotirov* (2185 metres) beside Granchar Lake. There's a restaurant here and a road south to Jakoruda. The next day it will be five hours to *Hija Ribni ezera* (2230 metres) between the Fish Lakes. The Smradlivo ezero (Stinking Lake), largest lake in the Rila Mountains, is only an hour from the hostel. Rila Monastery is a six-hour walk from Ribni ezera.

Rila Monastery

Rila, Bulgaria's largest and most famous monastery, blends into a narrow valley 119 km south of Sofia, three hours by bus. Rila was founded by Ivan Rilski in 927 as a colony of hermits. In 1335 the monastery moved three km to its present location. **Hrelyu's Tower** (the clock tower beside the church) is all that remains from this early period.

By the end of the 14th century Rila Monastery had become a powerful feudal force owning many villages. Plundered in the 15th century, Rila was restored in 1469 after the relics of Ivan Rilski were brought here from Veliko Tarnovo in a nation-wide patriotic procession. Under adverse conditions Rila Monastery helped keep Bulgarian culture alive during the long Dark Age of Turkish rule (15th to 19th

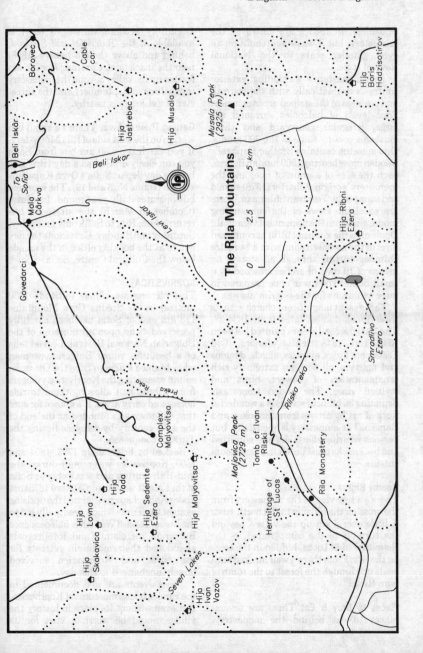

The Rila Mountains

Borovec

Cable car

Beli Iskar

To Sofia

Mala Cărkva

Govedarci

Hija Jastrebec

Hija Musala

Musala Peak
(2925 m)

Levi Iskar

Hija Boris Hadzisotirov

0   2.5   5 km

Hija Ribni Ezera

Smradlivo Ezero

Rilska reka

Preka reka

Complex Malyovitsa

Hija Vada

Hija Sedemte Ezera

Hija Malyovitsa

Malyovica Peak
(2729 m)

Tomb of Ivan Rilski

Hermitage of St Lucas

Rila Monastery

Hija Lovna

Hija Skakavica

Hija Ivan Vazov

Seven Lakes

centuries). In 1833 a fire destroyed the monastery, but it was soon rebuilt on an even grander scale in the National Revival style.

The monastery's forbidding exterior contrasts dramatically with the warmth and cosiness of the striped arcades inside. Four levels of balconies surround the large, irregular courtyard and three **museums** occupy some of the 300 rooms. One museum contains Brother Raphael's wooden cross bearing 1500 human figures, each the size of a grain of rice, and the monastery's original charter (1378) signed and stamped by Tsar Ivan Shishman. There are excellent views of the surrounding mountains from the uppermost verandah. Don't miss the kitchen (1816) at courtyard level of the northern wing with a 24 metre chimney cutting through all storeys by means of 10 rows of arches crowned by a small dome. Food was once prepared in huge cauldrons for the pilgrim masses.

The present magnificent **church** with its three great domes dates from 1834-37. The 1200 frescoed scenes painted between 1840 and 1848 depict donors, Old Testament kings, apostles, angels, demons and martyrs, all with an extremely rich ornamentation of flowers, birds and stylised vines. The gilded iconostasis depicting 36 biblical scenes is a wonderful work of art by artists from Samokov and Bansko. The monastery is open daily, but persons wearing shorts are not admitted and backpacks must be left in a cloakroom outside.

Nearby Sights

There's a fine view of the monastery from the cross on the hillside to the north-east. A little over a km up the valley, beyond the turn-off to the campground, is the **Hermitage of St Lucas**, hidden in the trees on the left. From there a well marked trail leads up through the forest to the tomb of Ivan Rilski.

Places to Stay & Eat There are several places to eat behind the monastery.

Dormitory accommodation (3 leva) is available at the *Touristicheski Spalnia*, behind and above the old bakery (1866) near the snack bars. *Camping Bor* is a km further up the valley beyond the monastery (open June to September) and the three-star *Hotel Rilets* is nearby.

Getting There & Away There's a small bus station on the west side of Rila Monastery. If you catch the 6.30 am bus from Sofia you can easily do Rila as a day trip. Two buses a day depart Sofia's Ovca Kupel bus station (trams No 5 and 19). The morning bus operates daily year round. In winter (October to March) the afternoon bus returns from Rila to Sofia only on Friday, Saturday and Sunday. Get tickets the day before at the booking office in the arcade below the Cultural Centre, Sofia.

KOPRIVSTICA

This picturesque village (altitude 1030 metres) in the Sredna Gora Mountains 113 km east of Sofia has been carefully preserved as an open air museum of the Bulgarian National Revival. Legend tells of a beautiful young Bulgarian woman who obtained a *firman* from the Ottoman sultan exempting the Koprivstica villagers from tribute and allowing them to ride horses and carry arms. It's known for sure that the town was founded at the end of the 14th century by refugees fleeing the Turkish conquerors.

Sacked by brigands in 1793, 1804 and 1809, Koprivstica was rebuilt during the mid-19th century and was as big as Sofia at the time. It was here on 20 April 1876 that Todor Kablechkov proclaimed the uprising against the Turks which eventually led to the Russo-Turkish War. After independence Bulgarian merchants and intellectuals abandoned their mountain retreats for the cities and Koprivstica survived largely unchanged to this day.

These events are well documented in the various house/museums of Koprivstica. But even without its place in history the village would be worth a visit for its

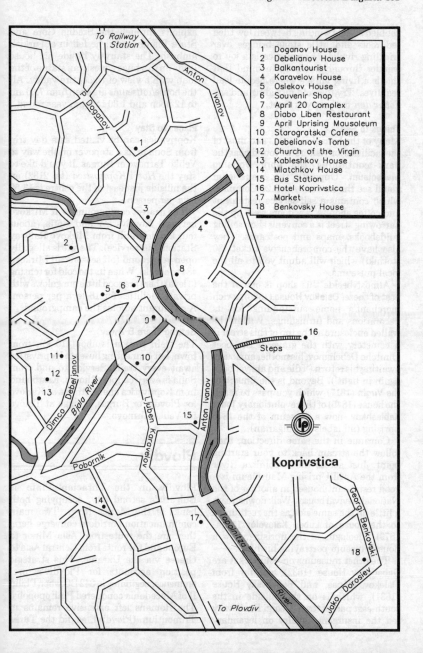

1 Doganov House
2 Debelianov House
3 Balkantourist
4 Karavelov House
5 Oslekov House
6 Souvenir Shop
7 April 20 Complex
8 Diabo Liben Restaurant
9 April Uprising Mausoleum
10 Starogratska Cafene
11 Debelianov's Tomb
12 Church of the Virgin
13 Kableshkov House
14 Mlatchkov House
15 Bus Station
16 Hotel Koprivstica
17 Market
18 Benkovsky House

To Railway Station

Anton Ivanov

Pl Doganov

Bjala River

Dimco Debeljanov

Ljuben Karavelov

Pobornik

Anton Ivanov

Steps

Georgi Benkovski

Jako Dorosiev

Topolnitza River

Koprivstica

To Plovdiv

cobbled streets winding between low tiled red roofs and little stone bridges over trickling rivulets. Koprivstica is a joy to wander through but keep in mind that this is a living village where people lead real lives. Try to avoid intruding and say *dobar den* to those you meet.

Things to See

Many of the house/museums and most of the facilities for visitors are found near the park containing the **April Uprising Mausoleum**. Opposite the mausoleum you'll see the modern April 20 Complex, which contains a self-service restaurant and coffee shop. A few doors west up the narrowing street is a souvenir shop selling guidebooks, maps and postcards. They also have the comprehensive ticket (30 stotinki) which will admit you to all the local museums.

Almost beside this shop is one of the best of these, **Oslekov House** (1856), a rich merchant's home outstanding for its decorations and furnishings. Within the walled enclosure at the top of this street is a cemetery with the grave of the poet Dimtcho Debelianov, his mother anxiously awaiting his return ('I die and am yet born again in light'). Beyond is the **Church of the Virgin** (1817) which you pass to reach the house (1845) of the revolutionary **Todor Kableshkov**, now a museum of the 1876 uprising (all labels in Bulgarian).

Continue in the same direction, then follow the stream back to your starting point. Just across the Topolnitza River from the April Uprising Mausoleum is a good restaurant housed in another of the National Revival houses. Walk downstream a little on the same side as the restaurant to the **house of Luben Karavelov** (1834-1879), ideologue of the uprising, now a house/museum portraying his life.

The other museums on your ticket are **Debelianov House** (1832), not far from Oslekov House, and **Benkovsky House** (1831), which is on the hillside in the south-east part of town. Georgi Benkovsky led the insurgent cavalry on legendary

exploits through the Sredna Gora and Stara Planina until he fell in a Turkish ambush. The stairway beside his house leads up to a huge equestrian statue of the man with a view of the entire valley. All the house/museums are open from 7.30 am to 12 noon and 1.30 to 5 pm year round.

Places to Stay

Koprivstica can be visited as a day trip from Sofia or as a stopover on the way to Veliko Tarnovo or Burgas. If you'd like to stay the *Hotel Koprivstica* (tel 2182) on the hillside just east of the centre is 13.50 leva per person.

The nearest campground is at Mirkovo between Koprivstica and Sofia, about four km downhill from Mirkovo Railway Station (bus service). The site is allegedly open year round (off season call Mirkovo 484 to check). When its too cold for tenting (3 leva) there are good little bungalows with private facilities for 18 leva per person. A restaurant adjoins the campground.

Getting There & Away

The train station is about 10 km from town, but connecting buses to Koprivstica await every train. Service to and from Sofia is every couple of hours. Eastbound from Koprivstica change trains at Karlovo for Plovdiv or Burgas, change at Tulovo for Veliko Tarnovo.

Plovdiv

Plovdiv on the Thracian Plain is Bulgaria's second city, occupying both banks of the Marica River. Two main communication corridors converge here, they are the route from Asia Minor to Europe and the route from Central Asia to Greece via the Ukraine. This strategic position accounts for Plovdiv's pre-eminence, beginning in 342 BC when Philip II of Macedonia conquered Philippopolis. The Romans left extensive remains in Trimontium (Plovdiv), as did the Turks who made the city one of their most important centres. But it was the Bulgarian National Revival which gave Plovdiv's Three Hills the picturesque aspect we appreciate today. There's a lot to see and Plovdiv shouldn't be missed, but accommodation is expensive. If you can arrange a morning arrival and an afternoon departure, so much the better. One day is enough to see Plovdiv.

Orientation

The railway station is south-west of the old town. Cross the square in front of the station and take uliza Ivan Vazov on the right straight ahead into Central Square, a five-minute walk. Uliza Vasil Kolarov, Plovdiv's pedestrian mall, runs due north from this square, with the old town reached by narrow streets to the right. The area north of the river is a grey modern suburb devoid of interest.

Information

The Balkantourist office, Moskva bulevard 34 (open daily 7 am to 9 pm), is near the Fairgrounds north of the river. Their information is questionable and they're of little help in finding a place to stay so it's not worth going out of your way to visit them. The 'Pirin' Travel Bureau, General Vladimir Zaimov 3, has information on hiking and hostelling in the Rhodopi Mountains. The 'Rila' railway ticket office is at uliza Vasil Kolarov 45.

Things to See

Begin your sightseeing with the excavated remains of the **Roman Forum** behind the modern post office on Central Square. Uliza Vasil Kolarov, a bustling pedestrian mall, runs north from this square to the 15th century Djoumaya or **Friday Mosque**, still used for Islamic religious services. Below ploschtad 19 Noemvri in front of the mosque is a section of the **Roman amphitheatre** (2nd century AD).

Continue straight ahead on the mall (now uliza Rajko Daskalov) and through an underpass to the **Imaret Mosque** (1445),

now a museum. Plovdiv's **Archaeological Museum** is nearby on ploschtad Suedinenie to the left. A copy of the 4th century BC gold treasure from Panagyurishte (now at the National Historical Museum in Sofia) is on display.

Return to the Djoumaya Mosque and go east on uliza Maxim Gorki, up into Trimonium, the old city. The **Ethnographical Museum**, in a mansion (1847) on uliza Doctor Tchomakov just beyond the end of Maxim Gorki, has a collection of folk costumes. Up the street from this museum is a hilltop with the **ruins of Eumolpias**, a 2nd millennium BC Thracian settlement now being excavated by Dr A Peykov. The view from here is good. The street beside the Ethnographical Museum leads down through **Hissar Kapi**, the eastern Roman city gate, to Georgiadi House (1846), the **National Revival Museum**.

To the south of this museum is a picturesque cobbled quarter, colourful 19th century houses crowding the winding streets, so do a little exploring. At uliza Knyaz Ceretelev 19 is the house in which the French poet Alphonse de Lamartine stayed in 1833 during his *Voyage en Orient*. Nearby to the west and directly above the south entrance to a big highway tunnel is the **Roman theatre** (2nd to 4th centuries), now restored and once again in use. Below the theatre on the downtown side is **St Marina Church** (1869) with a photogenic wooden tower and intricate iconostasis. From here it's only five minutes back to your starting point. Most of the museums are open 9 am to 12 noon and 2 pm to 5 pm Tuesday to Sunday.

Places to Stay

Western visitors to Plovdiv are only allowed to stay in 1st class hotels. Perfectly acceptable 2nd class hotels, such as the *Hotel Republica* in the centre of town, are forbidden to take you. The reason is largely financial. Local officials want to make as much money off you as they can and are prepared to apply socialist democracy to do it.

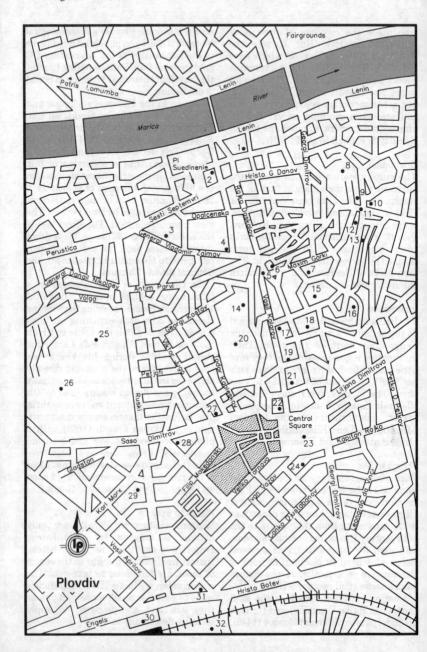

1	Archaeological Museum
2	Mosque Museum
3	Natural History Museum
4	Puppet Theatre
5	Roman Amphitheatre
6	Djoumaya Mosque
7	Church of the Holy Virgin
8	Eumolpia Ruins
9	Ethnographical Museum
10	National Revival Museum
11	Hissar Kapi
12	Church of Constantine & Jelena
13	A-La-Frangas Restaurant
14	Museum of the Revolution
15	Roman Theatre
16	Lamartine House
17	Art Gallery
18	St Marina Church
19	Hotel Bulgaria
20	Clock Tower
21	Railway Ticket Office
22	Bookstore
23	Post Office
24	Party House
25	Open Air Theatre
26	Monument to the Soviet Army
27	Art Gallery
28	Opera House
29	Leipzig Hotel
30	Railway Station
31	Bus Station
32	Rhdopi Bus Station

Camping *Camping Trakia* (open May to October) is at the *Gorski Kat Restaurant* about four km out on the Sofia highway, a continuation of Moskva bulevard west of Plovdiv. Take bus No 4 or 18 to the end of the line, then walk one km along the highway. There's a good restaurant and the site is uncrowded (US$5 cash to camp, US$12 for a bungalow, single).

Hotels The cheapest hotels open to westerners are the high-rise *Hotel Leipzig*, Ruski bulevard 70, four blocks from the railway station (US$24 single, US$35 double), and the drab concrete *Hotel Bulgaria* in the centre of town (US$23 single, US$32 double, breakfast included).

The *Novotel, Trimontium* and *Maritsa* hotels are much more expensive.

Private Rooms Balkantourist, Moskva bulevard 34, arranges private room accommodation for westerners *only* during the Plovdiv Fair (a couple of weeks in May and September). Even then you'll probably pay as much as you would for a hotel. Ask about youth hostels at the 'Pirin' Travel Bureau (tel 223958), General Vladimir Zaimov 3 although there isn't one in Plovdiv itself.

Places to Eat
The *A-La-Frangas Restaurant*, uliza Cyril Nectariev 17 near the National Revival Museum, offers excellent Bulgarian meals on the outside patio for about 9 leva with beer.

Entertainment
Opera tickets are available from offices on both sides of the cinema opposite Hotel Bulgaria. There's an office selling theatre tickets at uliza Vasil Kolarov 49.

Getting There & Away
All trains between Istanbul and Belgrade pass through Plovdiv. Sofia is only two hours away by frequent fast train. Plovdiv to Burgas is four hours with a few overnight services (couchettes Sofia-Burgas). For Veliko Tarnovo you must change trains at Stara Zagora.

Plovdiv has several bus stations. Buses to Troyan leave from the Northern Bus Station. Buses to Pazardzik and Asenovgrad depart the station near the main railway station. Buses to Pamporovo and Smoljan use the Rhodopi Bus Station across the train tracks from this station.

BATCHKOVO MONASTERY
Thirty km south of Plovdiv beside the highway up the Tschepelarska Valley is the Monastery of Batchkovo, founded in 1083 by the Bakouriani Brothers. This is the largest of its kind in Bulgaria after Rila. Sacked by the Turks in the 15th

century, major reconstruction began 200 years later.

Inside the high courtyard are two churches, the smaller 12th century **Archangel Church**, painted in 1841 by Zahari Zograph, and the large **Church of the Assumption of Our Lady** (1604). On the north side of the courtyard is a small **museum**, while one corner of the south side is occupied by the former **refectory** (1606) with a marvellous painting of the Genealogy of Jesus on the ceiling (painted 1623-1643). The refectory is usually locked, so give a leva or two donation to anyone who takes the trouble to let you in.

Through the gate by the refectory is **St Nicholas Chapel** with a superb Last Judgement painted in 1840 by Zahari Zograph on the porch. Note the condemned Turks on the right (no halos), and Zahari's self portrait in the upper left corner (no beard).

Just below the monastery is a restaurant, campground (4 leva) and bungalows (8 leva). To get there take a bus from Plovdiv to Assenovgrad, then another on to Batchkovo.

Further South

In case you're tempted to venture further up the valley into the Rhodopi Mountains you should know that Smoljan is a modern city devoid of charm and Pamprovo a sterile ski resort catering only to packaged tourists. To boot, the two campgrounds near Smoljan are forbidden to accept western visitors who are expected to stay at the expensive *Smoljan Hotel*. There are other, more welcoming places to visit than this.

The Black Sea Coast

Every summer Bulgaria's Black Sea beaches vie with those of neighbouring Romania to lure the vacationing masses of Czechoslovakia, Poland and East Germany. Burgas and Varna take on a carnival

atmosphere as campgrounds and hotels fill up, while small towns like Nessebar and Sozopol become literally jammed with tourists. Fortunately the hotel developments are concentrated in a few flashy resorts like Albena (38 hotels), Zlatni Pjasaci or Golden Sands (67 hotels), Cajka, Druzba (19 hotels) and Slantchev Briag (112 hotels), all absolutely packed with packaged Germans and Brits. The 'Georgi Dimitrov' International Youth Centre at Primorsko is a programmed students' hangout. But all along the 378-km-long coast it's fairly easy to escape the crowds and have a stretch of tideless golden beach to yourself.

The climate is warm and mild. In winter it rarely drops below 0°C. The average summer mean day temperature is a warm 23°C but sea breezes keep it cool. Summer is the best time to come. Everything will be open, the restaurants will have their tables out on the sidewalks, the water will be warm and hydrofoils will carry you along the coast in comfort. The resorts are quite accustomed to receiving large numbers of visitors and they'll find a place to squeeze you in somewhere. In the off season (mid-September to the end of May) even the big hotels slash staff and services drastically.

Best of all, it's cheap. This is one part of Bulgaria where you won't have to search far for a place to camp. If you don't have a tent, start campground hopping along the coast till you find one with a bungalow available. Or ask Balkantourist to assign you a private room. The Bulgarian coast is cheaper and less congested than that of Romania, with fewer guards, better food and later closing hours. To stay at one of the new resorts, however, you're better off coming on a package tour. Any way you do it you'll have an exciting time and make lots of new friends.

BURGAS

Some 250 years ago fishermen from Pomorie and Sozopol founded Burgas on a narrow spit between Burgasko Ezero and

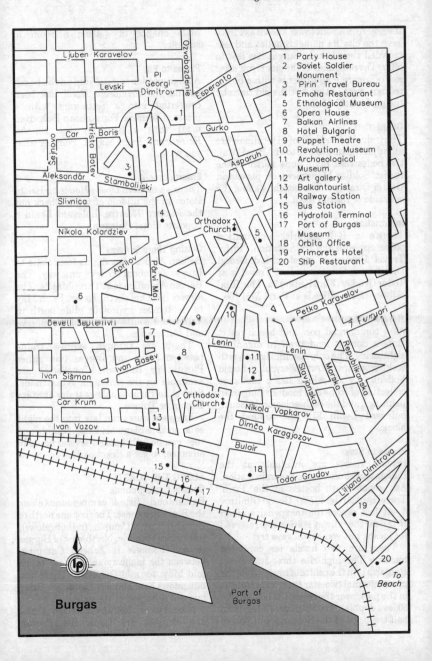

1 Party House
2 Soviet Soldier
Monument
3 'Pirin' Travel Bureau
4 Emoha Restaurant
5 Ethnological Museum
6 Opera House
7 Balkan Airlines
8 Hotel Bulgaria
9 Puppet Theatre
10 Revolution Museum
11 Archaeological
Museum
12 Art gallery
13 Balkantourist
14 Railway Station
15 Bus Station
16 Hydrofoil Terminal
17 Port of Burgas
Museum
18 Orbita Office
19 Primorets Hotel
20 Ship Restaurant

Ljuben Karavelov
Levski
Pl Georgi Dimitrov
Ozvobozdenie
Esperanto
Gurko
Asparuh
Car Boris
Hristo Botev
Sejnovo
Aleksandâr
Stambolijski
Slivnica
Nikola Kolardziev
Aprilov
Pârvi Maj
Orthodox Church
Develi Septemvri
Petko Karavelov
7 Furruari
Ivan Basev
Lenin
Lenin
Republikanska
Ivan Sisman
Slavjanska
Morsko
Car Krum
Orthodox Church
Nikola Vapkarov
Ivan Vazov
Dimčo Karagjozov
Bulair
Todor Grudov
Liljana Dimitrova
Port of Burgas
To Beach
Burgas

the sea. An ancient tower known as Pirgos gave the city its name. Smaller and less crowded than Varna, Burgas has less to offer. The north side of the city is row after row of concrete apartments with a big oil refinery west of that but the old town by the port is still nice.

Orientation
The train, bus and hydrofoil terminals are all adjacent in the old town. Parvi Maj, the pedestrian mall, runs north to the Soviet Soldier Monument on ploschtad Georgi Dimitrov. The beach is along the east side of the old town.

Information
There's a Balkantourist information office opposite the train station. 'Pirin' Travel Bureau is at ploschtad Georgi Dimitrov 5. Orbita Student Travel is at Todor Grudov (Filip Kutev) 2a. The 'Rila' railway ticket office is at Parvi Maj 106.

Things to See
As a commercial port and beach resort Burgas doesn't lend itself to organised sightseeing. The only specific sights worth seeking out are the **Art Gallery**, uliza Sterju Vodenicarov 22, which has a mediocre collection of icons and modern Bulgarian paintings, and the **Archaeological Museum**, bulevard Lenin 21, just around the block.

Places to Stay
Private rooms are available at the Balkantourist office near the train station. Ask about youth hostels at the 'Pirin' Travel Bureau (tel 42758), Georgi Dimitrov 5. At last report the inexpensive *Hotel Briz* near the railway station was reserved for locals, but you can always try.

There are two hotels for capitalist tourists. The high-rise three-star *Hotel Bulgaria* is in the centre of town, while the more informal two-star *Primorets Hotel* is in the park near the beach (31 leva single, 50 leva double). The Primorets is less than half the price of the Bulgaria, but you've little chance of getting a room in summer.

Places to Eat
A large wooden 'pirate' ship on the beach behind the *Primorets Hotel* has been converted into a restaurant with a pleasant terrace. For a cheap Bulgarian meal with a beer try the *Emoha Restaurant*, Parvi Maj 81. Point at what you want.

Entertainment
There's a modern *Opera House* on Hristo Botev in the middle of town. Check out the *Puppet Theatre*, bulevard Lenin 8 opposite Hotel Bulgaria.

Getting There & Away
Balkan Airlines has flights from Sofia to Burgas for about 27 leva one way. The Balkan Air office is at Parvi Maj 24. The airport is six km north of town. From May to September hydrofoils glide north to Varna and south to Sosopol, Primorsko and Mitschurin.

There are through express trains between Sofia and Burgas (via either Plovdiv or Karlovo). Couchettes are available on the overnight Sofia trains. For Veliko Tarnovo change trains at Stara Zagora or Tulovo.

Frequent buses run late into the night as far north as Slantchev Briag. Southbound they can be fully booked several hours in advance, so get a ticket early.

ALONG THE COAST
Coastal Campgrounds
Balkantourist lists 45 campgrounds along the Black Sea coast. The first one north of Burgas is Europa Camping (no bungalows), just before Pomorie. North-east of Burgas beyond Pomorie is Acheloi Camping, between the highway and the sea (open mid-May to mid-October). There are bungalows here and any Slantchev Briag bus will drop you at the gate.

Near Obsor, halfway between Varna and Burgas, are Luna and Prostor campgrounds, both with bungalows and both right beside the main highway less than a km apart (open June to September). All of the above are right on the main highway between Burgas and Varna.

Slantchev Briag

Slantchev Briag (also known as 'Sonnenstrand' or 'Sunny Beach') is a large tourist complex with a vast sandy beach 36 km north of Burgas. There are two campgrounds at the north end of the strip, the Slantchev Briag and, a few hundred metres beyond, the Emona. Both have bungalows (8 leva), but you'd be lucky to get one. Tenting is 6.50 leva. Both are open May to mid-October. For hotel accommodation visit the Balkantourist office on the main street. Watch your change in heavily touristed Slantchev Briag.

NESSEBAR

Nessebar, the Dorian Messambria, was developed by Byzantine exiles on a small rocky peninsula connected to the mainland by a narrow isthmus. Remnants of city walls rise above the bus stop, while along the winding cobbled streets are picturesque stone and timber houses with jutting 1st floors. Scattered through the town are over a dozen medieval churches, most of them in ruins.

Of special interest is 11th century **St Stefan** above the hydrofoil terminal, almost completely covered inside with 16th century frescoes. The small but select collection of the **Archaeological Museum** is housed in the 10th century church of St John. In summer tourists from the nearby resorts clog the narrow streets of Nessebar and you run a zigzag course to stay out of their way.

The Balkantourist office arranges private accommodation in Nessebar. Jam-packed buses run regularly between Nessebar and Slantchev Briag (10 km),

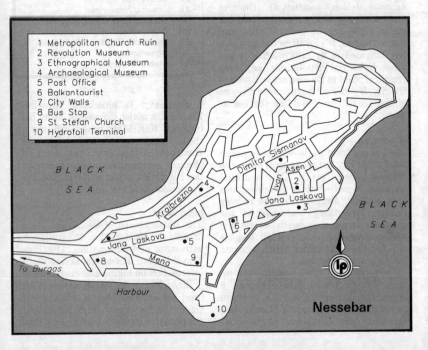

1 Metropolitan Church Ruin
2 Revolution Museum
3 Ethnographical Museum
4 Archaeological Museum
5 Post Office
6 Balkantourist
7 City Walls
8 Bus Stop
9 St Stefan Church
10 Hydrofoil Terminal

Nessebar

where you change buses for Burgas or Varna. There's also the more comfortable hydrofoil which connects Nessebar to points up and down the coast. Demand for seats usually outstrips supply, so get in line early.

VARNA

Varna, the largest Bulgarian port on the Black Sea, has become the 'summer capital of Bulgaria.' The city's history began in 570 BC when Miletian Greeks founded ancient Odessos. Varna flourished under the Romans who left extensive ruins. The Turks captured the town in 1393. In 1444 the Polish/Hungarian king Vladislav III Jagiello was killed in battle at Varna while leading a crusade against Ottoman expansion. Varna became a great trading centre after the Crimean War.

In recent years Varna has developed into an ideal resort with excellent beaches, parks, museums, historic sites, accommodation, restaurants, theatres and teeming pedestrian malls. Even the street signs are in both Cyrillic and Roman letters! It's an attractive city on a bay hemmed in by hills offering scenic views. Industrial installations like the big chemical plant at Devnya are well west of the city. If you don't have time to do more of the coast, come and see the sea at Varna.

Orientation

The bus and train stations are on opposite sides of the city but many local buses run between them (ask). The hydrofoil terminal is just south of the downtown area, walking distance from the railway station. Everything north-east of the hydrofoil terminal is beach, everything west commercial port. The left luggage office at the train station is in a separate building across the street.

From the train station walk north up uliza Avram Gacev into ploschtad 9 Septemvri, the centre of town. A broad pedestrian mall, bulevard V I Lenin, runs east from here. North-west of ploschtad

1	Puppet Theatre
2	Post Office
3	Bus to Albena
4	Museum of History & Art
5	Party House
6	Orbita Hotel
7	'Pirin' Travel Bureau
8	Bus to Panorama
9	Assumption Cathedral
10	Dramatic Theatre
11	Town Council
12	Opera House
13	Barbecued Chicken
14	Railway Ticket Office
15	Ethnographic Museum
16	Corecom Shop
17	Balkantourist
18	Railway Station
19	Balkan Airlines
20	Musala Hotel
21	Roman Thermae
22	Worker's Museum
23	Roman Baths
24	Hydrofoil Terminal
25	Sofia Press Agency
26	Tcherno More Hotel
27	National Revival Museum
28	Odessa Hotel
29	Palace of Culture
30	Aquarium
31	Marine Museum

9 Septemvri is ploschtad Varnenska Komuna, a major crossroads. From here bulevard Karl Marx runs north-west to the bus station and the airport. The great Asparouh Bridge over the navigable channel between Varnensko Ezero and the Black Sea is just south of ploschtad Varnenska Komuna.

Information

The Balkantourist office, Avram Gacev 33 near the train station, is very helpful with maps and information. The 'Pirin' Travel Bureau, Hristo Kabakciev 13, has information on hiking and hostelling.

Buy advance domestic railway tickets (and get information) at uliza Avram Gacev 10 just down from ploschtad 9 Septemvri. Couchette bookings are made

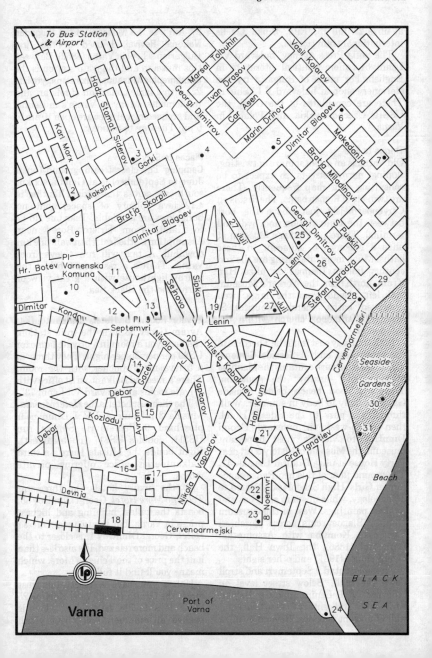

Varna

To Bus Station & Airport

BLACK SEA

Port of Varna

Beach

Seaside Gardens

at uliza 27 Juli 13. 'Rila,' Sipka 3, sells international train tickets.

The Sofia Press Agency, bulevard V I Lenin 51, offers political literature in English. For maps of Bulgaria try the stationery shop at bulevard V I Lenin 6. There are consulates of the GDR, the USSR, Czechoslovakia and Poland in Varna.

Things to See
Old Varna is an oriental maze of twisting, sloping, narrow streets, so expect to be consulting your map frequently. There are two sets of **Roman baths**. The first is on Cervenoarmejski just above the port between the train station and hydrofoil terminal. There's a **Worker's Museum** at uliza 8 Noemvri 5, adjacent to these baths. Much more interesting are the 2nd century **Roman Thermae** on uliza Han Krum, north from the Worker's Museum and left. Aside from the large, well preserved baths, there's beautiful **St Anastasius Orthodox church** within the compound.

Find your way east from the Thermae to the south-west end of **Seaside Gardens**. This attractive park contains the **Maritime Museum** and, nearby, the **Aquarium**. There's a good beach below Seaside Gardens, body to body in summer. Walk through the park to the Odessa Hotel, then north-west on bulevard Georgi Dimitrov to Varna's most important museum, the **Museum of History & Art** near Party House at uliza Dimitar Blagoev 41. The ground floor of this neo-Renaissance former Girls' High School is dedicated to archaeology, while upstairs are icons and modern paintings. West of this museum Dimitar Blagoev cuts across ploschtad Varnenska Komuna with Assumption Cathedral (1886), the Town Hall, the Opera House (1921) and other sights.

Cross ploschtad 9 Septemvri and stroll down the mall. Below street level on bulevard V I Lenin opposite Balkan Airlines is a 2nd century **Roman tower** and wall of ancient Odessos. Beyond at uliza

27 Juli 9 is the **Museum of the Bulgarian National Revival**, housed in the first Bulgarian school in Varna (1862). Between this museum and the train station is the **Ethnographic Museum**, uliza Panagyuriste 22, with a large collection of folk art and implements. Many of Varna's museums and archaeological sites are open 10 am to 5 pm Tuesday to Sunday.

Places to Stay
Camping The closest campground (open June to September) is at Galata, six km south-east across the bridge. Tenting is 4.12 leva (plenty of space), but no bungalows are available. Take bus No 17 to Galata from Hristo Botev near Assumption Cathedral, then walk one km downhill. A taxi will run 4 leva from Varna. There's a restaurant below the nearby lighthouse with a great view of Varna and the Black Sea.

Private Rooms & Hotels Balkantourist, Avram Gacev 33 near the train station, can book you a room in a private home for US$9 per person per night. They throw in a 5 leva meal voucher with the room. There's a second Balkantourist office with private rooms at bulevard V I Lenin 73.

The cheapest hotel is the *Hotel Musala*, Musala 3 off bulevard V I Lenin near ploschtad 9 Septemvri. Singles run US$11, doubles US$17 (no breakfast). Right beside the Musala there's a third Balkantourist office offering private rooms.

Of the luxury hotels the three-star *Tcherno More Hotel*, Georgi Dimitrov 35, boasts the tallest building and highest prices in Varna, but the two-star *Odessa Hotel*, Georgi Dimitrov 1, is closer to the beach and more relaxed. It's also less than half the price of the Tcherno More, which means you'll find it full.

Unless you have a reservation just forget the *Orbita Hotel*, Vasil Kolarov 25 (33.20 leva double, no singles), which is packed all summer. Ask about youth hostels at the 'Pirin' Travel Bureau (tel 222710), Hristo Kabakciev 13.

Places to Eat

Bulevard Georgi Dimitrov between the Tcherno More and Odessa hotels is solidly lined with restaurants serving meals to tourists at the sidewalk tables. Stroll along till you see someone eating a dish you fancy. There's a restaurant at the corner of ploschtad 9 Septemvri and bulevard V I Lenin serving half chickens and beer in unpretentious surroundings. You can get coffee across the street.

Entertainment

The *Opera House* and *Dramatic Theatre* are both located in ploschtad 9 Septemvri. Nearby at bulevard Karl Marx 5, behind the post office, is the *Puppet Theatre*. The *'Lyudmila Zhivkova' Festival Complex* on bulevard Georgi Dimitrov opposite the Odessa Hotel is used mainly for congresses.

Getting There & Away

Balkan Airlines has flights Sofia to Varna for about 27 leva one way. Bus No 15 connects Varna Airport to town. The Balkan Airlines office is on bulevard V I Lenin at uliza Sipka. From May to September hydrofoils run south to Nessebar, Pomorie, Burgas, Sosopol, Primorsko and Mitschurin.

There are express trains to Sofia (via Pleven or Karlovo). Couchettes are available to Sofia on the overnight service. For Veliko Tarnovo change trains at Gorna Orjahovitza. Two trains a day go direct to Ruse. In summer there are special trains from Varna to Berlin (via Ruse and Bucharest) and Warsaw (via Bucharest and the USSR).

Transportation is good to the beach resorts to the north of Varna, continuing late into the night. Southbound buses to Nessebar, etc, terminate around 6 pm. Varna to Burgas is three hours by bus.

Bus No 99 runs to Camping Panorama at Zlatni Pjasaci (Golden Sands), 17 km north-east of Varna, from beside

Assumption Cathedral until late evening. The bus to Albena (further north-east) leaves from the corner of Maksim Gorki and Hadzi Stamat Siderov (last bus around 8 pm). Purchase tickets in advance at a kiosk.

MADARA

If your train is going to put you into Varna too late to find a place to stay, consider stopping over at Madara, 18 km east of Sumen. Next morning there'll be several trains on to Varna (2½ hours). Madara is also a convenient stopover between Ruse and Varna. It makes a perfect base for exploring the nearby capitals of the First Bulgarian Kingdom, Preslav and Pliska. Under the cliffs at Madara are a cave and, high up on the rock face, the famous 8th century **relief** of a horseman spearing a lion.

From the train station a wide stairway leads two km up toward the cliffs. Here you'll find a good campground (open May to October) with bungalows (6.60 leva) and tent space (2.70 leva). A large restaurant is near the campground. There's a youth hostel at Madara, the *Hija 'Madarski Konnik.'* Advance reservations must be made at the 'Pirin' Travel Bureau, uliza Hristo Botev 15, Sumen. Also ask 'Pirin' about the *Hija 'Patleyna'* near Preslav. If you show up at 'Patleyna' without a booking you'll be turned away.

Northern Bulgaria

Ancient Moesia between the Stara Planina and the Danube was the cradle of the Bulgarian state. Some tourists make it to Veliko Tarnovo, capital of the Second Bulgarian Kingdom, but Pliska and Preslav, capitals of the First Bulgarian Kingdom, are well off the beaten track. The National Revival left famous monasteries at Preobrazhenski and Trojan. Then, during the Russo-Turkish War, the great battles of Pleven and Sipka decided the fate of modern Bulgaria. Coming or going from Romania, northern Bulgaria is the gateway to both countries. Most travellers cross the 'Friendship Bridge' at Ruse, but the Calafat-Vidin ferry is a viable alternative.

PLEVEN

Pleven, between Ruse and Sofia 35 km south of the Danube, is best known as the site of an 1877 battle between the Turks under Osman Pasha and a Russo-Romanian army. An entire Turkish army of 11 pashas, 2000 officers and 37,000 men was encircled and captured in this decisive engagement. Aside from sites related to the battle, there are parks and an inviting city centre to see. Pleven doesn't get a lot of western visitors, so you'll be assured a warm welcome.

Orientation

Pleven's bus and train stations are adjacent on the north side of town. Bulevard V I Lenin runs straight south toward the centre, passing many large stores. Ploschtad 9 Septemvri is the very heart of the city. Georgi Dimitrov, a pleasant pedestrian street, curves back toward the stations from this spacious square.

Information

Balkantourist is at San Stefano 3 near the District Museum. The 'Pirin' Travel Bureau, Tsvetan Spassov 21-23, has information on hiking and hostelling. For international railway tickets go to 'Rila,' Zamenhoff 2.

Things to See

Begin your visit with Pleven's most unique sight, the 1877 Panorama on a hilltop above the city. Bus No 1 runs directly there from the railway station via bulevard Lenin. Inside this large building (1977) is a fantastic 360° mural painting of the 3rd assault on Pleven (11 September 1877). Another huge painting shows the final Turkish attempt (10 December 1877) to break out of their encirclement. Buy the

1	Railway Station
2	Bus Station
3	Hotel Pleven
4	St Paraskeva Church
5	Mexana Restaurant
6	Bookstore
7	St Nicholas Church
8	Dramatic Theatre
9	Railway Ticket Office
10	National Revival Park
11	Hotel Rostov na Don
12	Monument to the Soviet Army
13	Puppet Theatre
14	Party House
15	Town Hall
16	City Art Gallery
17	The Common Grave
18	Concert Hall
19	Mausoleum
20	Balkantourist
21	District Museum
22	District Art Gallery
23	Freedom Monument
24	Panorama

brochure which explains the many details or request a guide who speaks a language you understand (no additional charge). Hand luggage must be left at a kiosk outside.

From the panorama walk down the broad path east through Skobelev Park, veering to the left at the end. You'll see period artillery pieces, an ossary and numerous monuments to the dead. In the centre of the monumental stairway leading back down to the city is a Freedom Monument. On the right at the bottom of the steps is an ultramodern Art Gallery (1978). The old military-style building across the street is the District Historical Museum. This truly impressive collection covers the entire history of Pleven and vicinity plus theatrical and natural history.

As you leave ask the museum attendants to direct you toward the Mausoleum of Russian & Romanian Soldiers (1907). This red and white striped building on

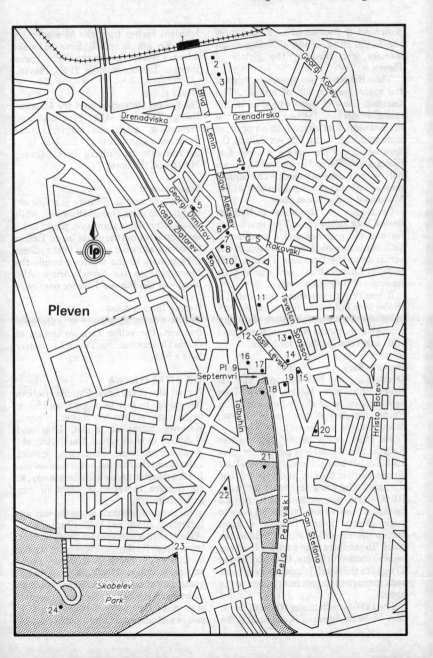

ploschtad 9 Septemvri commemorates the 31,000 Russian and 4500 Romanian soldiers who died in the Battle of Pleven.

The attractive open square in front of the mausoleum is full of interest. The **Common Grave** of those who died in the struggle against fascism is near the mausoleum. Just beyond, in an oriental style building, is the **City Art Gallery**. On another side of the square is a red flag flying above Party House and the town hall with a musical clock. The square merges into uliza Georgi Dimitrov at the **Monument to the Soviet Army**.

Continue down this street to **National Revival Park** on the right. This small park features old cannons and a museum of 19th century period rooms. Around the corner from the Dramatic Theatre is **St Nicholas Church** (1834), now a good little museum of Bulgarian icons.

If you've still got some time catch a trolley from bulevard Lenin to **Kailuka Park** at Mosta. This extensive park with very enjoyable footpaths between ponds and cliffs can keep you busy for hours.

Places to Stay

Overlooking the bus station is the 14-storey three-star *Pleven Hotel*. Less expensive is the 12-storey two-star *Hotel Rostev Na Don* in the centre of town (about 20 leva per person).

You may camp beside the two-star *Kailaka Hotel* (2.50 leva per person, plus 2.50 leva per tent) in lovely Kailaka Park six km south of the city. If things are slow they may offer you a deal on a hotel room (16.50 leva per person with private facilities). Get a room on the 3rd floor to avoid disco noise. There's a good restaurant out on the terrace behind the hotel. To get there take a trolley from the railway station to Mosta, then bus No 4 or 23 right to the hotel. It's only a 25-minute walk through the forest from Mosta to the hotel.

The IYHF youth hostel *'Touristicheski dom Tsvetan Spassov'* is on a hill a few hundred metres from the Mosta trolley stop. To get in you'll have to make advance reservations at the 'Pirin' Travel Bureau, Tsvetan Spassov 21-23, Pleven.

Places to Eat

For typical Bulgarian food try *Mexana*, Georgi Dimitrov 123. Pleven's most memorable meals are served at the *Peshterata Restaurant*, located in a natural cave in Kailaka Park between Mosta and the hotel.

Entertainment

Pleven's *Dramatic Theatre* is a fine old building on uliza Georgi Dimitrov, while the *Concert Hall* stands on ploschtad 9 Septemvri behind the mausoleum. Tickets for events at either are sold in the offices with posters in the windows beside the Monument to the Soviet Army. Also check out the *Puppet Theatre* nearby.

Getting There & Away

Trains to Sofia, Ruse and Varna are fairly frequent. For Veliko Tarnovo change at Gorna Orjahovitza. For Trojan Monastery take a bus.

THE STARA PLANINA

A good slice of the Stara Planina (Balkan Range) can be seen on a loop from Pleven to Veliko Tarnovo via Lovec, Trojan, Karlovo, Kazanlak, Sipka, Etar and Gabrovo, or vice versa. You'll visit old monasteries, war memorials, quaint villages and the forested peaks themselves. It's not possible to do all this in one day, so you'll have to spend a night or two somewhere.

All the campgrounds along the way are between Karlovo and Veliko Tarnovo, all of them with bungalows for those without tents. From Karlovo to Pleven you'll have a choice of youth hostels or fairly expensive hotels. If you have an IYHF youth hostel card visit a 'Pirin' office to learn about the various hostels in the area and make the required reservations. If you're a student an Orbita office may be able to reserve a bed for you at the *Orbita Youth Complex* at Lovec.

Trojan

Trojan town, 71 km south of Pleven and 124 km north of Plovdiv, is connected to both cities by several buses a day. Tickets should be purchased the day before. **Trojan Monastery** is 10 km east of Trojan town and an hourly bus from Trojan town runs right to the door. Before setting out on this side trip leave your pack at Trojan bus station and buy an onward bus ticket to Karlovo or Plovdiv. There's a good **Arts & Crafts Museum** on Trojan town's main square.

Trojan Monastery, founded in 1600, is famous in Bulgaria as a centre of the Bulgarian National Revival. The church was rebuilt in 1835 and covered with frescoes by Zacharie Zographe. Look for his self portrait, paint brush in hand, by one of the windows inside the church. The condemned in the *Last Judgement* on the church's exterior facade are Turks. Visit the small museum up on the monastery's 3rd floor. There's a guest house in the monastery, but it's only open to Bulgarians. Everyone's welcome to sample the local plum brandy, however.

The IYHF youth hostel *'Touristicheski dom Nikola Gaberski'* is on the hill just east of Trojan town's bus station. If you know you want to stay there stop to make reservations at 'Pirin' (tel 20135), uliza Stefan Karadzha 2, Lovec.

'Pirin' will also be able to tell you about the *Hija 'Zora'* (open July and August only) at Apriltsi, 19 km east of Trojan Monastery by bus. Apriltsi is the base for climbing Mt Botev (2376 metres), highest in the Stara Planina. *Hija 'Pleven'* is up near the summit.

Karlovo

Trains and buses from Karlovo to Kazanlak are frequent. The nearest official campground is at Bjala Reka (bungalows available) on the road to Kazanlak, about 15 km east of Karlovo.

The *Sevtopolis Campground* is on the same highway, closer to Kazanlak.

Kazanlak

Many trains from Sofia to Burgas or Varna call at Kazanlak, tucked between the Stara Planina and Sredna Gora mountains in the Valley of Roses. In Tjulbeto Park just north-east of the centre is a 4th century BC Thracian tomb with Hellenistic frescoes of battle scenes, a funeral feast and a chariot race. Tourists aren't allowed in the original tomb but a full-scale replica has been constructed nearby. The two-star *Zornitsa* and *Roza* hotels are in Kazanlak.

From in front of Kazanlak Railway Station take bus No 6 (frequent) to Sipka. This bus passes the *Kasanlaschka Rosa Campground* (open May to mid-October) between Sipka and Kazanlak. It's the highest category campground on this circuit and the most likely to have an (expensive) bungalow if you need it.

Sipka

Sipka is a quaint old town below the Balkan Range. Poking above the trees near the bus stop are the five golden onion-shaped domes of a huge **votive church** (1902) built after the Russo-Turkish War. Ask the woman selling bus tickets about the times of buses over the Sipka Pass to Gabrovo, then go have a look at the church. You'll get a great view of the Valley of Roses from up there. The roses bloom from late May to early June.

At the top of **Sipka Pass** (1200 metres) is a large monument (1934) commemorating the Russian troops and Bulgarian volunteers who fought back numerous attacks by vastly superior Turkish forces in August 1877. The *Stoletov Campground* (bungalows) is also up at the pass, but it gets cool at night.

The *Hija 'Buzludzha'* is near a huge circular memorial pavilion, 12 km east of the pass along a side road. To stay there an advance reservation must be made at a 'Pirin' office.

Etar

Northbound from Sipka, get off the Gabrovo bus at the *Ljubovo Campground* (open mid-May to September). Here you'll find nice little bungalows as well as tent space, but no restaurant. Ljubovo is only two km west of the **Etar Ethnographic Village Museum** (frequent bus service).

At Etar (open daily 8 am to 5 pm) you'll see Bulgarian craftsmen (shoemaker, baker, hatter, cart maker, jeweller, glass worker, potter, etc) practising their age old trades in typical 18th and 19th century Gabrovo houses reassembled here. You can purchase their work on the spot. At the far end of the village is a small taverna where you can sample the local brew or have lunch. From Etar you'll have no trouble finding a bus on to Gabrovo, then another bus to Veliko Tarnovo.

VELIKO TARNOVO

Veliko Tarnovo (Great Tarnovo) is laced with history. The Yantra River winds through a gorge in the centre of this 'city of Tsars,' picturesque houses clinging to the cliffs. Almost encircled by the river, the ruined citadel Tsarevets recalls the Second Bulgarian Kingdom (1186-1393) when Veliko Tarnovo was capital. North-west, across the abyss, is now overgrown Trapezica hill, residence of the nobles and courtiers, while below in the valley the artisans' and merchants' quarter is marked by medieval churches. Renowned monasteries stood on Sveta Gora Hill, where the university is today. The narrow streets of old Veliko Tarnovo bear the imprint of the Bulgarian National Revival, while the modern city spreads west. This is one town you won't want to miss.

Orientation

The railway station is down by the river, far below the centre of town (catch buses No 4, 12, or 13). On the way up you'll pass the bus station on uliza Hristo Botev. This street ends at a T-junction with uliza Vasil Levski and the modern city to the left, uliza Georgi Dimitrov and its continuation uliza Dimitar Blagoev to the right.

Information

The Balkantourist office is at Vasil Levski 1 nearly opposite the theatre. For information on hostels and hiking try the 'Pirin' Travel Bureau, Dimitar Blagoev 79. Check train times at the railway ticket office, Hristo Botev 12 opposite the Orbita Hotel.

Things to See

Opposite the Yantra Hotel on Dimitar Blagoev you'll see a stairway leading up into picturesque streets. Go up and bear left, then down stone-surfaced uliza G S Rakovski where Bulgarian craftsmen keep small shops. At number 17 is the **Ethnographic Museum** in the Hadji Nicoli Inn (1858), one of the best known National Revival buildings in Bulgaria. The street above G S Rakovski is lined with quaint old houses and terminates at a church.

Return to the Yantra Hotel and walk east keeping right (follow the bus route down) to the **Bulgarian National Revival Museum** (open 8 am to 12 noon and 1.30 to 5.30 pm Tuesday to Sunday). The museum is in old town hall (1872), the large blue building you see straight ahead. Notice the stone building with six arches beside this museum. The **Archaeological Museum** is in the basement, down the stairway between the two buildings (same hours).

Follow the bus route down once more (street on the left) to the entrance to **Tsarevets Hill**, sacked and burned by the Turks in 1393. This vast fortress offers great views from rebuilt **Ascension Patriarchal Church** at the top of the hill. Just below it to the north are the foundations of the extensive **Royal Palace** on three terraces. Twenty successive kings ruled Bulgaria from this palace. Continue north to a bluff directly above the large textile factory. This was **Execution Rock** where traitors were pushed into the Yantra River.

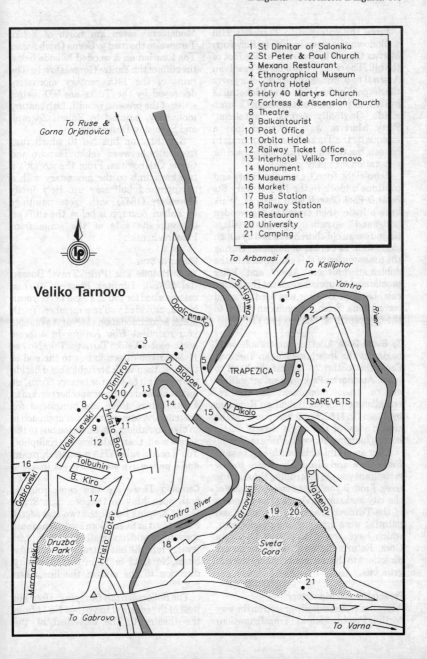

1 St Dimitar of Salonika
2 St Peter & Paul Church
3 Mexana Restaurant
4 Ethnographical Museum
5 Yantra Hotel
6 Holy 40 Martyrs Church
7 Fortress & Ascension Church
8 Theatre
9 Balkantourist
10 Post Office
11 Orbita Hotel
12 Railway Ticket Office
13 Interhotel Veliko Tarnovo
14 Monument
15 Museums
16 Market
17 Bus Station
18 Railway Station
19 Restaurant
20 University
21 Camping

Veliko Tarnovo

To Ruse &
Gorna Orjanovica

To Arbanasi

To Ksiliphor

Yantra River

Opalcena

I-5 Highway

TRAPEZICA

TSAREVETS

N Pikolo

D Blagoev

G Dimitrov

Vasil Levski

Hristo Botev

Tolbuhin

B. Kiro

Gabrovski

Marmarijska

Druzba
Park

Hristo Botev

Yantra River

D Naidenov

T Tarnovski

Sveta
Gora

To Gabrovo

To Varna

From the entrance to Tsarevets Hill walk down the steep incline to **Holy Forty Martyrs Church** by the river at the foot of the hill. The church was built by Tsar Ivan Assen II to commemorate his victory over the despot Teodor Komnin at Klokotnitsa in 1230, as recorded on the Assen Column inside. Originally a royal mausoleum, Forty Martyrs was converted into a mosque by the Turks. There are murals to be seen, but the church has been closed for restoration for many years.

Turn right (don't cross the river) and continue a block to the 14th century **Sts Peter & Paul Church** with frescoes. Walk back a little, then cross the big wooden bridge and keep right up through the village till you see an old church enclosed by a high stone wall, **St Dimitar of Salonika**. During the consecration of this church in 1185 the nobleman brothers Assen and Peter proclaimed an uprising against Byzantine rule. Later St Dimitar was used for royal coronations. From here you can return to the city centre on bus No 7 or 11.

To Sveta Gora Another memorable walk begins at the Interhotel Veliko Tarnovo. Cross the footbridge behind the hotel to reach **Assenovtsi Park** with an art gallery and a great monument to the re-establishment of the Bulgarian Kingdom by Assen I in 1186. From here you'll get the classic view of the city's tiers of rustic houses hanging above the Yantra Gorge.

After an eyeful walk south-east toward **Sveta Gora** and climb the stairs to the restaurant you see protruding through the trees. From it you'll get a sweeping view of the city and surroundings. The founders of the Turnovo schools of literature and painting were active in the monasteries, which have now disappeared, of Sveta Gora. Return the way you came or ask directions to the university, where you can get a bus.

Preobrazhenski Monastery

A recommended sidetrip or stop on the way north is Preobrazhenski (Transfiguration) Monastery, seven km north of Veliko Tarnovo on the road to Gorna Orjahovitza. The location on a wooded hillside below the cliffs of the Yantra Gorge is lovely. The ruins of the 14th century monastery destroyed by the Turks are 500 metres south of the present, rebuilt, 19th century monastery, painted by Zahari Zograph and Stanislav Dospevski.

Get there on bus No 10 which runs frequently between Veliko Tarnovo and Gorna Orjahovitza. From the stop it's a two km climb to the monastery with a *campground* half way up. **Holy Trinity Monastery** (1847) with more paintings by Zahari Zograph is below the cliffs on the opposite side of the gorge from Preobrazhenski.

Places to Stay

Youth Hostels The 'Pirin' Travel Bureau (tel 20373), Dimitar Blagoev 79, can reserve a bed for you at a local IYHF youth hostel, provided you're a member. Youth hostel accommodation (4 leva) is available year round at *Hija Ksilifor* in a forest north-east of Veliko Tarnovo. Take No 7 or 11 Mavrikov direction bus to the end of the line, then walk straight ahead beside the river a bit to a textile factory. Turn left up the hill and continue another two km to a cafe where there are bungalows for hostellers. A somewhat easier approach is to take an Arbannassi direction bus to the access road, then walk down to Ksiliphor. You'll need a valid YHA membership card and a persuasive attitude to get in.

Camping There are two campgrounds, both open May to October. The *Sveta Gora Camping* beside the two-star *Motel Sveta Gora* in Sveta Gora Park is the most convenient and has small bungalows (9.90 leva). From the bus or train stations take buses No 4, 12 or 13 in the University direction to the end of the line, then ask.

The *Boliarski Stan Camping* is four km west of the centre of town (bus No 11 from the theatre to the cloverleaf at the junction of the Varna and Sofia highways). Bungalows (4.90 leva) are available and there's lots of space to camp.

Private Rooms & Hotels Ask at Balkantourist, Vasil Levski 1, for private room accommodation. *Hotel Orbita*, Hristo Botev 15, is inexpensive but usually full. Try anyway, the reception is up at the top of the stairs. Two-star *Hotel Etar* (20 leva single, 25 leva double) is in the building directly behind the Orbita. There's also the three-star *Yantra Hotel*, Velchova Zavera 4 at Dimitar Blagoev. The flashy four-star *Interhotel Veliko Tarnovo* is double or triple the price of any of the above.

Places to Eat

There's a good market west on Vasil Levski at Dimitar Ivanov. Stock up on fresh vegetables and fruit here. For a typical Bulgarian meal try *Mexana*, hidden away on the small square with a monument dated 1883, off Georgi Dimitrov east of the post office. Shish kebab and salad with a couple of beers will run 8 leva.

Getting There & Away

To get a train to Pleven, Sofia, Ruse, or Varna, take a frequent bus No 10 to Gorna Orjahovitza Railway Station. Some local trains direct to Ruse call at Veliko Tarnovo Railway Station. To and from Burgas or Plovdiv change trains at Stara Zagora or Tulovo. Gabrovo and Etar are more easily reached by bus.

RUSE

Ruse, the largest Bulgarian Danube port, is a gateway to the country. Soviet and Bulgarian riverboats call here, as do twice daily trains from Bucharest. The double-decker highway/railway Friendship Bridge (1954), six km downstream, links Ruse to Giurgiu, Romania. Along the Bulgarian right bank of the Danube are parks and promenades full of mementos of the two liberations (1878 and 1944). This might be

a nice place to break your journey if it weren't so hard to find inexpensive accommodation outside the camping season.

History

A Roman fortress, Sexaginta Prista, was established here in 70 AD as part of the defensive 'Danubian Lines.' Although strengthened by Justinian in the 6th century, the fort was finally obliterated during the 'barbarian' invasions of the 7th century.

The Slavs forsook the site and in the 9th century built the town of Cerven 30 km south on an easily-defensible loop of the Cerni Lom River. Six churches, city walls and a citadel have been excavated at Cerven. The rock-cut cave churches of Ivanovo between Cerven and present Ruse are another reminder of this period. After the Ottoman conquest in 1388 Cerven was abandoned.

The Turks rebuilt and strongly fortified Rouschouk (Ruse). The Russians captured the city in 1773 and 1811, but were forced to withdraw due to the Napoleonic attack on Moscow. In 1864 under the reforming Turkish *vali* (district governor) Midhat Pasha, founder of the Young-Turk Movement, Rouschouk was modernised and became capital of the Danubian Vilayet (including everything west to Nis, Yugoslavia). In 1866 a railway from Ruse to Varna linked the Danube directly to the Black Sea.

Ruse was a centre of the underground struggle against Ottoman rule until its liberation by Russian troops in 1878. The eclectic architecture of the city centre dates from the building boom which followed. With the rapid expansion of industry a strong proletarian movement developed and from 1919 to 1921 Ruse was run as a Communist-led commune. The years 1923 to 1944 were ones of struggle against an increasingly brutal monarcho-fascist regime. Since the war the local economy has grown so dramatically that one week's present production equals that

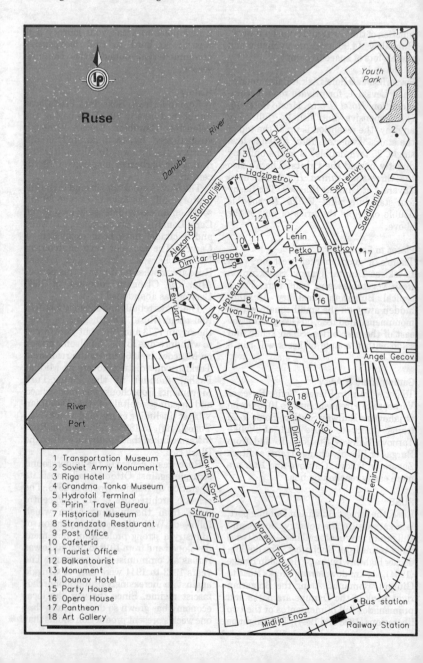

Ruse

1 Transportation Museum
2 Soviet Army Monument
3 Riga Hotel
4 Grandma Tonka Museum
5 Hydrofoil Terminal
6 "Pirin" Travel Bureau
7 Historical Museum
8 Strandzata Restaurant
9 Post Office
10 Cafeteria
11 Tourist Office
12 Balkantourist
13 Monument
14 Dounav Hotel
15 Party House
16 Opera House
17 Pantheon
18 Art Gallery

of all of 1948. The machine-building industry is centred here.

Orientation

The bus and train stations are adjacent on the south side of town. There's luggage storage in the bus station. From the stations walk or take a bus a km north up bulevard Georgi Dimitrov to ploschtad Lenin, the centre of town. Among the 18 streets which meet on this square is uliza 9 Septemvri, Ruse's pedestrian mall, which runs off in both directions. The hydrofoil terminal is straight down Dimitar Blagoev from ploschtad Lenin.

Information

Tourist information is on ploschtad Lenin at Dimitar Blagoev 45. There's a Balkantourist office on Rayko Daskalov just off ploschtad Lenin, but they'll probably refer you to the Balkantourist desks in the Riga and Dounav hotels for information and currency exchange. For hiking and hostelling information ask at the 'Pirin' Travel Bureau, Dimitar Blagoev 1. Orbita Student Travel is at uliza G Rakovski 13. For international railway tickets go to 'Rila,' Dimitar Blagoev 27-39.

Things to See

Most of Ruse's monuments and museums open from 9 am to 12 noon and 3 to 6 pm, daily except Mondays. The **City Art Gallery** is at bulevard Georgi Dimitrov 45 between the train station and ploschtad Lenin. The **Monument to Liberty** (1908) by the Italian sculptor Arnoldo Zocchi dominates ploschtad Lenin.

At the end of Pelko D Petkov, due east of the square, are the graves of Ruse's revolutionary heroes in a gold-domed **Pantheon** (1978). North-east of the Pantheon at the end of Saedinenie is the **Soviet Army Monument** (1949) with **Park na mladezta** (Youth Park) and the Danube beyond.

Railway buffs won't want to miss the **Transportation Museum**, by the Danube

below the park, in what was the first railway station in Bulgaria (1866). There's a large collection of old equipment including steam locomotive 148, the 'Sultanie,' Bulgaria's first.

Proceed upstream along the Danube to the Riga Hotel, where there's an attractive terrace and promenade. Overlooking the Danube near this hotel is the **'Grannie Tonka' Museum**, bulevard Aleksandar Stambolijski 6. Seven of Grannie Tonka's children participated in the 1876 uprising against the Turks. One of them, Bilyana Raicheva, resided in the museum building.

Places to Stay

Ask about private rooms at the information office at Dimitar Blagoev 45 on ploschtad Lenin. There's no guarantee they'll have anything for you but there are several cheaper hotels in Ruse, such as the *Splendid*, uliza 9 Septemvri 49. Unfortunately 'capitalist tourists' are required to stay at the low-rise two-storey *Dounav Hotel* on ploschtad Lenin or the 20-storey three-star *Riga Hotel* overlooking the river, both very expensive.

The *Ribarska Koliba Campground* (open May to mid-October) is six km out of Ruse on the road to Sofia (bus No 6 or 16). It's 4.20 leva to camp or 5 leva for a bungalow. There's a small bar by the gate.

A km beyond the campground is the IYHF youth hostel, the *Hija Prista* (tel 34167). It's unlikely they'll accept you without a reservation from the 'Pirin' Travel Bureau (tel 27869), Dimitar Blagoev 1, Ruse.

Places to Eat

There's a cheap self-service cafeteria in the building beside the post office on ploschtad Lenin. The *Strandzhata Mehana*, uliza Ivan Dimitrov 5, is one of the city's best restaurants.

Near the Danube, down the hill from the *Ribarska Koliba Campground*, is the *'Fisherman's Lodge'* restaurant where a full meal with beer will set you back about

10 leva. Live music and an outdoor terrace make this a pleasant place on a summers' evening. Take a sunset stroll along the riverside before dinner.

Getting There & Away

There are two trains a day to Bucharest and Moscow, plus one daily to Warsaw (via the USSR). Two trains a day go from Ruse to Varna with others on this line stopping short at Kaspican (near Madara). Other direct expresses run to Sofia via Pleven, including one overnight train. For Veliko Tarnovo change trains at Gorna Orjahovitza. Local trains from Ruse to Plackovci and Momcilgrad go direct to Veliko Tarnovo.

From May to mid-September hydrofoils ply the Danube between Vidin and Ruse (8 leva), departing each end in the very early morning. Off-on riverboats also connect Ruse to Svistov and Silistra but low water levels and technical problems often interrupt these services.

Balkan Airlines flights are available year round to Sofia and Plovdiv. The airline office is at Tsurkovna Nezavisimost 1. Express buses run to Silistra and Varna, each twice daily. The campground and youth hostel are in a perfect location if you want to hitch to Veliko Tarnovo, Pleven, or Sofia.

Yugoslavia

Yugoslavia, the land of the South Slavs, occupies much of the western half of the Balkan peninsula. It's a rich mosaic of mountains, rivers and seascapes, climates, cultures, customs, cuisines and peoples. Many disparate influences have shaped the Yugoslav Federal Republic: Venetian along the coast, Austrian in Slovenia, Hungarian in Vojvodina and Turkish in Bosnia-Hercegovina, Kosovo and Macedonia. Serbia and Croatia have always been jealous leading actors in this decentralised state.

Tourism is focused along the Adriatic coast where the combination of history, natural beauty, good climate, clear water and easy access are unsurpassed. There are numerous seaside resorts and the swimming is good. The atmosphere is relaxed – there are few rules about behaviour and few formalities. Since 1960 nudism has been promoted and Yugoslavia is now *the* place to go in Europe to practice naturism. But the resorts are impersonal, artificial environments, out of touch with real Yugoslav life. It's a world built around tourists: you'll have few personal encounters with the people. And yet, it's possible to enjoy yourself on a low budget. Yugoslavia's not the sort of country you fall in love with right away, but it would be hard to find another with as much to offer.

Facts about the Country

HISTORY

Yugoslavia's history is complex as it's actually the history of many countries. The original inhabitants were the Illyrians, followed by the Celts who arrived in the 4th century BC. In 229 BC the Romans began their conquest, establishing a colony at Salona (near Split) in Dalmatia. Under Augustus the empire extended to

Singidunum (Belgrade) on the Danube, including the provinces of Illyricum (Dalmatia), Moesia (Serbia) and Pannonia (Croatia). In 285 AD Emperor Diocletian decided to retire to his palace/fortress in Split, today the greatest Roman ruin in Eastern Europe. When the empire was divided in 395 what is now Croatia and Bosnia-Hercegovina stayed with the Latin Western Empire, while present Serbia and Macedonia went to Byzantium. Visigoth, Hun and Lombard invasions marked the fall of the Western Empire in the 5th century.

In the middle of the 6th century Slavic tribes (Serbs, Croats and Slovenes) crossed the Danube in the wake of the Great Migration of Nations and occupied most of what is now Yugoslavia. In the 9th century the Serbs were converted to the Orthodox Church by Cyril and Methodius. In 969 Serbia broke free from Byzantium and established an independent state. In the north the Croats picked up the legacy of Roman civilisation forming a kingdom under Tomislav in 925. Slovenia came under the Holy Roman Empire in the 10th century. Byzantium re-established its authority over the South Slavs in the 11th century, but in 1102 Romanised Croatia united with Hungary to defend itself against Orthodox Byzantium. In 1242 a Mongol invasion devastated Hungary and Croatia.

An independent Serbian Kingdom reappeared in 1217. Numerous frescoed Orthodox monasteries were erected during this 'Golden Age.' Then, at the Battle of Kosovo in 1389, the Serbian army was defeated by the Ottoman Turks, ushering in 500 years of Islamic rule. The Serbs were pushed north as the Turks advanced into Bosnia in the 15th century and the city state of Venice occupied the coast. In 1526 the Turks defeated Hungary at the Battle of Mohacs, adding territory north and west of the Danube to their realm. In 1527 Croatia turned to the Hapsburgs of Austria for protection and remained under their control until 1918. The Adriatic coast was threatened but never fully conquered by the Turks. After the

naval Battle of Lepanto in 1571 this threat was much reduced.

The first centuries of Turkish rule brought stability to the Balkans but as the power of the sultan declined local Turkish officials and soldiers began to oppress the Slavs. In the 16th and 17th centuries the Turks strengthened their hold on Bosnia-Hercegovina as an advance bulwark of their empire. After their defeat at Vienna in 1683, the Turks began a steady retreat. By 1699 they had been driven out of Hungary and many Serbs moved north into Vojvodina where they enjoyed Hapsburg protection.

After Venice was shattered by Napoleonic France in 1797, Austro-Hungary moved in to pick up the pieces along the coast. Napoleon's merger of Dalmatia, Istria and Slovenia into the 'Illyrian Provinces' in 1805 stimulated the concept of South Slav unity. In 1848 a bourgeois democratic

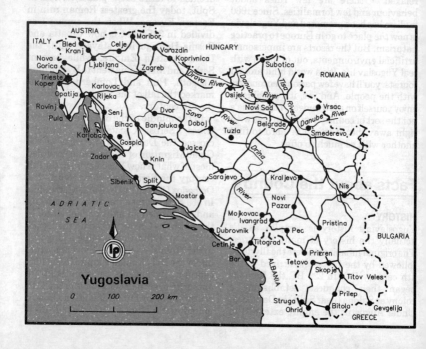

revolution against the old autocracy was suppressed, but serfdom was abolished. The brief Napoleonic experience and the national revival movements of the mid-19th century led to a reawakening among the South Slavs and there were uprisings against the Turks in Bosnia and Bulgaria in 1875-1876.

In 1878 Turkey suffered a crushing defeat by Russia in a war over Bulgaria. At this point Austria-Hungary occupied Bosnia-Hercegovina, annexing it completely in 1908. A revolt in 1815 had led to de facto Serbian independence in 1816. Serbia's autonomy was recognised in 1829, the last Turkish troops departed in 1867 and in 1878 complete independence was achieved. Montenegro also declared itself independent of Turkey in 1878.

Macedonia remained under Turkish rule right into the 20th century. In the First Balkan War (1912) Serbia, Greece and Bulgaria combined against Turkey for the liberation of Macedonia. The Second Balkan War (1913) saw Serbia and Greece join forces against Bulgaria, which had claimed all of Macedonia for itself. WW I was an extension of these conflicts as Austro-Hungary used the assassination of Archduke Ferdinand as an excuse to overrun Serbia. Russia and France came to Serbia's aid. In the winter of 1915-1916 a defeated Serbian army of 155,000 retreated across the mountains of Montenegro to the Adriatic where they were evacuated to Corfu. In 1918 these troops fought their way back up into Serbia from Thessaloniki, Greece.

A Kingdom of Serbs, Croats and Slovenes was proclaimed in 1918 under the king of Serbia. In 1929 the name was changed to Yugoslavia. The Vidovdan constitution of 1921 created a centralised government dominated by Serbia. This

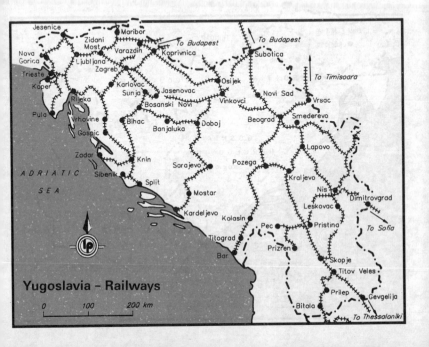

Yugoslavia – Railways

0   100   200 km

was strongly opposed by the Croats and other minorities, forcing King Alexander to end the political turmoil by declaring a personal dictatorship in 1929. The assassination of the king in 1934 led to a regency which continued the Serbian dictatorship. Corruption was rampant and the regent tilted toward friendship with Nazi Germany.

Under German pressure Yugoslavia joined the Tripartite Alliance, a fascist military pact, on 25 March 1941. This sparked mass protest demonstrations and a military coup which overthrew the pro-fascist regency. Peter II was installed as king and Yugoslavia abruptly withdrew from the alliance. Livid with rage, Hitler ordered an immediate invasion. The country was carved up between Germany, Italy, Hungary and Bulgaria. A fascist Ustase puppet government was set up in Croatia.

Almost immediately the Communist Party under Josip Broz Tito declared an armed uprising. There was also a monarchist resistance group, the Cetniks, but they proved far less effective than Tito's partisans. After 1943 the British gave full backing to the Communists. The partisans played a major role in WW II by tying down huge German armies, but Yugoslavia suffered terrible losses. Almost a tenth of the population died in the war. The resistance did guarantee Yugoslavia's post war independence.

In 1945 the Communist Party (which had been officially banned since 1920) became the only political party, as it is today. Tito broke with Stalin in 1948 and received US$2.5 billion in economic aid from the US and UK between 1950 and 1960. Since the break Yugoslavia has followed its own 'road to socialism' based on a federal system, self-management, personal freedom and non-alignment. The decentralisation begun in 1951 was to

Political Divisions

0   100   200 km

lead to the eventual 'withering away of the state' of classical Marxism. Since Tito's death in 1980 there has been a collective state presidency rotated annually among nine members. These nine are elected every four years by the national assembly and the regional parliaments of the six republics: Croatia, Bosnia-Hercegovina, Macedonia, Montenegro, Serbia and Slovenia. Yugoslavia has never been a member of the Warsaw Pact or NATO.

PEOPLE

Most of the 22.5 million people in Yugoslavia are South Slavs, including Croats (22%), Macedonians (6%), Montenegrins, Serbs (40%) and Slovenes (8%). Non-Slavic minorities include Albanians (6%), Hungarians (2%) and Turks. Half the population is Orthodox, 32% Catholic and 10% Muslim. There has always been a degree of rivalry between the largest groups, the Catholic, Romanised Croats and the Orthodox, Byzantine Serbs. The Macedonians and Montenegrins are also Orthodox, the Slovenes Roman Catholic. Bosnia-Hercegovina is a mixture of Catholic, Orthodox and Muslim.

ECONOMY

The Yugoslav economy functions on the basis of self-management. Elected workers' councils run the factories and businesses, with co-ordination from producers' councils on a regional level. State control is limited to the broadest economic planning. This system has led to inefficiencies and an expensive duplication of services without the full benefits of open competition. There are many privately-owned small businesses.

Exports of machinery, chemicals, electrical equipment and food products are sent to the USSR, Italy, West Germany and the US, but total imports are double total exports. Agriculture still accounts for 40% of the gross national product, services 34% and industry only 26%.

The importance of agriculture is indicative of a backwardness not immediately apparent to the casual tourist. After WW II Yugoslavia was a war-torn land of peasants. From 1948 to 1951 a concentrated attempt was made to form agricultural co-operatives, but this failed and 85% of the land is still worked privately by small farmers. In 1953 individual private holdings were reduced to 15 hectares maximum.

Yugoslavia today is one of the most indebted counties on earth with about US$21 billion in hard currency obligations. Borrowing from the west worked fine while Tito was alive, but the burden is now being felt. The state is attempting to maintain social services despite 15% unemployment and 170% inflation. There have been strikes against falling real wages and the closure of uneconomic enterprises. In the meantime Yugoslavia has been transformed into a nation of consumers. Inequalities are already evident: you don't have to look far to find the 'nouveau riche.' Some private business is allowed and Yugoslavia seems embarked on the road to capitalism. Whether the future will bring political or economic upheaval remains to be seen, as does the reaction of Yugoslav Communists.

GEOGRAPHY

It's said that Hernan Cortez described Mexico to the king of Spain by taking out a leaf of parchment, crinkling it up and dropping it onto a table with the words 'that, Your Majesty, is the map of Mexico.' Yugoslavia is no less a mass of mountains. Mountains and plateaux account for three quarters of this 255,804 square km country, the remainder being the Pannonian Plain on both sides of the Sava, Danube and Tisa rivers in the north-east. The mountains of Slovenia are part of the Alps, while most of the rest of Yugoslavia's mountains belong to the Balkan Range. The highest peak is Triglav (2863 metres) in the Julian Alps near Austria, but Titov vrh (2748 metres) in Macedonia's Sar Planina is only slightly lower.

Most of the rivers flow north into the Danube, which runs through Yugoslavia for 588 km. Its tributary, the Sava, is 940 km long. Many smaller rivers have cut deep canyons in the plateau creating memorable train rides. There are 300 lakes, but only five over 10 square km in size. The largest are lakes Shkodres (Skadar), Ohrid and Prespan in the south on the Albanian border. Forests cover 34% of the land.

The Adriatic Coast is only 628 km long as the crow flies, but it's so indented that the actual length is 2092 km. If the coastlines of the islands are added to the total the length becomes 6116 km. Most of the narrow coastal belt at the foot of the Dinaric Mountains belongs to Croatia. Only a small southern section of seashore close to Albania is part of Montenegro. The fantastic Bay of Kotor is the only real fjord in southern Europe. Most of the beaches along this jagged coast are rocky. The 12-km-long sandy strip at Ulcinj is an exception. Officially there are no private beaches in Yugoslavia, although you must pay to use 'managed' hotel beaches.

Yugoslavia's offshore islands are every bit as beautiful as those in Greece. There are 725 islands along this submerged Adriatic coastline, 66 of them inhabited. The largest islands are Krk, Rab and Losinj in the north, Brac, Hvar and Korcula in the south. Many are barren with high mountains that drop right into the sea. It would take several visits to see even a small part of what this country has to offer.

FESTIVALS & HOLIDAYS

In July and August there are summer festivals in Dubrovnik, Krk, Ljubljana, Ohrid and Split. The Balkan Festival of Original Folk Dances & Songs occurs in Ohrid in early July. That same month there's also an International Review of Original Folklore in Zagreb. Jazz festivals are held in Ljubljana (mid-June) and Zagreb (October). The Belgrade International Theatre Festival is in mid-September. Some noted international fairs include the Zagreb Spring (mid-April) and Autumn (mid-September) Grand Trade Fairs, and the Novi Sad Agricultural Fair (mid-May).

Public holidays throughout Yugoslavia include 1 and 2 January (New Years Days), 1 and 2 May (Labour Days), 4 July (Partisan Day), and 29 and 30 November (Republic Days). In addition, there are the following regional holidays: 7 July (Serbia), 13 July (Montenegro), 22 July and 1 November (Slovenia), 27 July (Croatia, Bosnia and Hercegovina) and 2 August and 11 October (Macedonia). If any of these should fall on a Sunday then the following Monday or Tuesday is a holiday.

LANGUAGE

Serbo-Croatian is the most common language, followed by Slovenian and Macedonian. Serbo-Croatian is an amalgam of the two main Slavic dialects. The language of Montenegro is Serbian.

German is the most common second language, both for historical and touristic reasons, and because of the number of returned 'guest workers' from West Germany. Italian is widely spoken along the coast.

Both the Latin and Cyrillic alphabets are in common use. Slovene and Croatian are written in the Latin alphabet, Serbian and Macedonian in Cyrillic.

Days of the week in Croatian are: *ponedjeljak, utorak, srijeda, cetvrtak, petak, subota, nedjelja.* Two words to know are *ima* (there is) and *nema* (there isn't).

Facts for the Visitor

VISAS

Entry into Yugoslavia is easy. You may enter by any means you like and leave when and where you choose. Although a visa may be required, it will be issued on the spot at any Yugoslav consulate. Some consulates give it free, others charge US$6 per entry. Visas are valid for one or two entries from three to six months from the date of issue for a stay of 90 days. If necessary, you can also get a 30-day 'Tourist Pass' at the border for a couple of dollars. Nationals of Austria, Belgium, Denmark, Finland, France, West Germany, Iceland, Ireland, Italy, Japan, Luxembourg, the Netherlands, Norway, Portugal, Spain, Sweden, Switzerland, the United Kingdom and many other nationalities do not require visas.

You're supposed to have your passport with you at all times. If you're staying at a hotel or campground they may keep your passport at the desk and give you a stamped card which serves the same purpose. Officially, if you stay somewhere other than organised accommodation (hotel, private room from an agency, campground, etc) you're supposed to report to the local authorities within 24 hours. It's unlikely you'll ever have to do such a thing, but the police can bring it up if you're caught camping freelance, staying in a private room arranged on the street or with friends. You don't need to get any stamps on a visa form to prove where you stayed (as you do in Hungary or Bulgaria).

MONEY

The dinar is currently suffering 170% annual inflation.

no compulsory exchange

All banks and tourist offices in Yugoslavia change hard currency into dinars at the standard official rate without commission. A passport is required to change travellers' cheques but not for cash. Yugoslav banks won't accept Greek 1000 drachma notes. There's no compulsory exchange of currency. The Yugoslavs compensate for this by making foreigners pay extra for accommodation, meals, admissions, etc, and by levying a daily tourist tax of about US$1.50 per person.

The black market in Yugoslavia is a joke, offering only about 5% more than the banks. Although the risks are also minimal, it's simply not worth wasting your time and precious cash in such penny ante dealings. Go to any bank, travel agency or hotel and change there. Only exchange what you're sure you'll need, however, as it's *impossible* to change Yugoslav dinars back into hard currency.

You're only allowed to import or export 50,000 dinars once a year in notes of 1000 or less. There's no reason to do either as

the bank rate within Yugoslavia is as good as anything you'll find abroad and most foreign banks won't accept Yugoslav currency. You might want to bring along a small quantity of dinars to ease your entry, however.

Since price controls were relaxed and market forces allowed to rule, Yugoslavia has been caught in the grip of roaring inflation. Of course the exchange rate is somewhat indexed to inflation, so each day you get more and more dinars for your hard currency. In this book it would be ridiculous to quote prices in dinars which would be totally off six months later. Instead, *we list all prices in US dollars*. Of course, these are only approximations and you pay for almost everything directly in dinars, but at least you'll have an idea of real costs.

The Yugoslav government itself bases all accommodation rates on dollars or German marks (DM), so you seldom profit from the nose-diving dinar. Transportation price increases sometimes fall behind, but the cost of almost everything else seems to go up faster than your dollars, pounds or marks. Since the dinar is devalued almost daily it's bad business to change over US$50 at a time. If you know you'll be near a bank or exchange office, you might even want to change small amounts like US$20 daily. During the summer tourist season the government plays the same game by holding the exchange rate of the dinar steady, forcing tourists to pay increasingly higher prices. In September they float the dinar down to its real inflation-adjusted level. Avoid dinar travellers' cheques which are dead losers to inflation.

Costs

Once the bargain basement of Europe, Yugoslavia has become considerably more expensive than its neighbours Greece and Hungary. It's now about the same as Italy, still cheaper than Austria or West Germany. As yet you don't need a wheelbarrow full of money to buy a loaf of bread, but lunch will set you back thousands of dinars, your hotel room tens of thousands.

Transportation, concert and theatre tickets are fairly cheap and food is average priced. Accommodation is increasingly expensive, partly because the rates are linked to hard currency, but more because of a two-price system in which foreigners pay several times more than locals for hotels, private rooms, campsites, etc. Transportation and theatre tickets are cheap because everyone pays the same price.

Average prices per person are US$5 to US$10 for a private room, US$3 for a meal at a self-service, US$0.50 to US$1 for a museum admission and US$2 to US$3 for an average intercity bus fare. If you're on a budget you can do it for US$20 a day if you eschew all luxuries, even less if you camp and eat only groceries. A student card will get you half-price admission at many museums and galleries. The east and far south of the country are cheaper than the north and west.

The cheapest entertainment in Yugoslavia is a movie. Admissions are always low and the sound-tracks in the original language. Low-grade American films are the standard fare, however. Check the time on your ticket carefully as admission is not allowed once the film has started. It doesn't cost anything at all to participate in the early evening *korzo*, a casual promenade enjoyed by great crowds in the town centres.

Cheating The official double pricing for accommodation has set a dangerous precedent. Waiters in restaurants now feel it's OK to abuse foreigners who may not understand the currency or prices, aren't regular customers and are unable to complain anyway. Check your bill in any establishment which caters mostly to tourists as they *habitually* overcharge. Be careful in a place which doesn't have a menu with prices clearly stated. Foreigners are often charged extra for bread, potatoes and side salads with their meals. When ordering an espresso coffee or cappuccino you may be served an oversized cup for double or triple price. Even ice cream sellers and bartenders will cheat you unless you check the price first. Your own hotel or campground restaurant is less likely to rip you off (you might complain at the reception), but *always* check the menu to clarify prices before ordering. It's too bad it's like this but you're made an even greater fool if you let yourself be taken advantage of without protesting. If you're arriving from Italy you'll be partly acclimatised.

CLIMATE

The climate varies from Mediterranean along the Adriatic coast to continental inland. The high coastal mountains help shield the coast from the cold northerly winds, making for an early spring and late fall. In spring and early summer a landward breeze called the *maestral* keeps the temperature down along the coast. Winter winds include the *bura* from the north and *siroko* from the south. The sunny coastal areas are enjoyable from April to October.

BOOKS & BOOKSHOPS

The Rough Guide to Yugoslavia (Routledge Kegan Paul, London, 1985) covers a lot more ground in far greater detail than can be included here. A good West German guide to the country is *DuMont Kunst-Reisefuhrer Jugoslawien* (DuMont Buchverlag, Koln). Rebecca Wests' *Black Lamb & Grey Falcon* is a classic portrait of pre-war Yugoslavia.

NEWSPAPERS & MEDIA

There are no local English language newspapers or magazines in Yugoslavia. *Newsweek* is sold at corner newsstands in Yugoslavia, a clear indicator of how liberal this 'Communist' country really is.

GENERAL INFORMATION

Post

To mail a parcel from Yugoslavia take it unwrapped to a post office where they will wrap and seal it. You then fill out six or seven forms, stand in line for a while and hopefully get it off. Not all post offices will do this, however. Allow several hours to complete the transaction.

Electricity

220 volts AC, 50 Hz.

Time

Greenwich Mean Time plus one. Yugoslavia goes on summer time at the end of March when clocks are turned an hour forward. At the end of September they're turned an hour back.

Business Hours

Most government offices are closed on Saturday. Shops stay open Saturdays until 3 pm. Weekdays many shops close for lunch from 12 noon to 4 pm but stay open until 8 pm. Department stores and self-services generally stay open throughout the day. Some self-services open Sunday mornings.

With such a high rate of inflation the money has to move fast so banks in Yugoslavia keep long hours, often 7 am to 7 pm weekdays, 7 am to 12 noon Saturday.

INFORMATION

Yugoslav tourist offices abroad include:

Austria
 Yugoslav National Tourist Office (tel 512-7174), Mahler Strasse 3, 1010 Vienna

Belgium
  Yugoslav National Tourist Office (tel 219-5828), Rue Royale 103c, 1000 Brussels
Denmark
  Yugoslav National Tourist Office (tel 11-6300), Trommesalen 2, 1614 Copenhagen V
France
  Yugoslav National Tourist Office (tel 4268-0707), 31 Bulevard des Italiens, 75002 Paris
Greece
  Yugoslav National Tourist Office (tel 360-4670), 4 Voukourestiou St, Athens
Holland
  Yugoslav National Tourist Office (tel 75-0646), Jan Luykenstraat 12, 1071 CM Amsterdam
Italy
  Yugoslav National Tourist Office (tel 46-1455), Via Veneto 10, 00187 Rome
  Yugoslav National Tourist Office (tel 86-7607), Via Pantano 2, 20122 Milan
Sweden
  Yugoslav National Tourist Office (tel 10-1993), Slojdgatan 10, 10386 Stockholm 40
Switzerland
  Yugoslav National Tourist Office (tel 252-1270), Limmatquai 70, 8001 Zurich
UK
  Yugoslav National Tourist Office (tel 734-5243), 143 Regent St, London W1
USA
  Yugoslav National Tourist Office (tel 757-2801), Rockefeller Center, Suite 210, 630 Fifth Ave, New York, NY 10020
West Germany
  Yugoslav National Tourist Office (tel 16-1704), Graf Adolf Strasse 64, 4 Dusseldorf
  Yugoslav National Tourist Office (tel 20-798), Goethe Platz 7, 6 Frankfurt am Main
  Yugoslav National Tourist Office (tel 59-5545), Sonnen Strasse 14, 8 Munich 2

ACCOMMODATION

Tourism in Yugoslavia is built around groups who arrive on cheap package holidays for a week or two at the beach. Motorists are also catered for, but independent budget travel is becoming more of a challenge. The cost of private rooms has been jacked up to hotel levels and minimum stays of four nights imposed to discourage transients. If you stay less than four nights there's a 50% surcharge. The amount you pay for accommodation in dinars is calculated according to that day's exchange rate, an inflation-proof system which ensures that foreign tourists always pay top dollar.

Most of the prices are listed in official hotel, private room and camping directories, but they're not always accurate. Add US$1 to US$2 per person per night 'residence tax' to all official accommodation rates. Hotel and private room rates on the coast are reduced in the off season. Yugoslavs get a 65% discount, which explains why all those expensive hotels were full. Most hotels include breakfast in the room price. This consists of one cup of tea from the pot, two miserable pieces of bread and a bit of butter and jam.

Private Rooms

As in Hungary, the best accommodation in Yugoslavia is private rooms in local homes. These can be arranged by travel agencies, but it's cheaper to deal directly with proprietors you meet on the street offering *zimmer* or *sobe*. This way you avoid the residence tax and four-night minimum stay, but forego the agency's quality control. The householder gets off without paying a commission to the agency and tax on the income. Hang around bus stations and ferry terminals, luggage in hand, looking lost, and someone will approach you.

You can also go directly to houses with *sobe* signs. If the price asked is too high, bargain. You might get a lower rate by offering to pay in cash dollars or DM. Be sure to clarify whether the agreed upon price is per person or for the room. Although finding a room this way is common practice along the Adriatic coast, be discreet as technically you're breaking the law by not registering with the police. Don't brag to travel agencies about the low rate you got, for example.

In the interior you'll probably have to work through a travel agency. The rooms are classified according to categories I, II or III. Private apartments are also available. Singles are expensive and hard to find. Some rooms are excellent, other times the landlord is coming in every half hour with only a brief knock on the door. Generally, what you pay for a private room won't be much more than camping or youth hostel charges. Also, in a country where people are often indifferent to foreigners, staying in a private room is a way of meeting a local family.

Youth Hostels

The Ferijalni savez Jugoslavije operates a couple of dozen IYHF youth hostels around the country. They're sometimes referred to as the 'mladost' or 'omladinski' hotel. Some are overpriced, others close during the winter and most are inconveniently located. There's usually a midnight curfew. Overnight charges range from US$4 to US$10. Although they're open to anyone, persons under age 27 get priority. In mid summer they can all be full. A Youth Hostel Association membership card is not necessary, although it does get you a lower rate.

The most convenient hostels are those in Bled, Sarajevo, Skopje and Zagreb, all of which are open year-round. Useful summer hostels include those in Dubrovnik, Ohrid and Zadar. The Belgrade hostel is far from the centre, overcrowded and overpriced, but there if you need it. Some hostels have double rooms as well as the usual dormitories. None are luxurious.

In July and August you can often rent vacant rooms in student dormitories. Check with tourist information about this, although they're sometimes as expensive as hotels.

Camping There are about 150 campgrounds in Yugoslavia, half of them along the coast. Tourist information offices can supply a complete list. Most operate from May to September only, although a few are open in April and October. In early May and late September check carefully to make sure the campground really is

open before beginning the long trek out. Don't go by the opening and closing dates you read in travel brochures or this book, as these are only approximate. Even local tourist offices can be wrong.

Many campgrounds are expensive for backpackers because the prices are set in dollars or DM per person with no extra charge per tent, caravan, car, electric hook-up, etc. This is fine for people with mobile homes who occupy a large area, but rough on those who have only a small tent and are forced to subsidise their overloaded neighbours. If you don't have a vehicle you're better off at campgrounds which have a much smaller fee per person and charge extra per tent, automobile, caravan, electric hook-up, etc. These prices are given in the official 'Camping' brochure.

The campgrounds give you a chance to meet normal, friendly Yugoslav people unaffected by the tourist glut. West Germans are the largest users of Yugoslavian campgrounds. Unfortunately many are gigantic 'autocamps' with restaurants, shops and row after row of caravans. Nudist campgrounds (marked FKK) are among the best because their secluded locations ensure peace and quiet. Freelance camping is officially prohibited everywhere, so keep well out of sight of the road and don't build a fire.

FOOD & DRINK

Self-service cafeterias are quick, easy and inexpensive. The quality of the food varies. If the samples behind glass look dried out, ask them to dish out a fresh plate for you. Better restaurants aren't that much more expensive if you choose carefully. A service charge is included so you only need to round up the bill.

The cheapest breakfast is *burek*, a greasy layered pie made with cheese (*sir*) or meat (*mes*) available everywhere (US$0.75). Ice cream cones are priced by the scoop. A load of fruit and vegetables from the local market can go to make a healthy, cheap picnic lunch. There are plenty of supermarkets in Yugoslavia. Dairy products (especially butter) are expensive, while beer and liquor purchased at supermarkets are very cheap.

Yugoslavia's turbulent history is reflected in the regional cuisines, from Austrian strudel in Slovenia, Italian pizza and pasta in Istria and Dalmatia, Hungarian goulash in northern Serbia and Turkish kebab in Bosnia and Macedonia. Some national dishes include *cevapcici* (small patties of spiced, minced meat, grilled), *raznjici* (a shish kebab of chunks of pork or veal with onions and peppers on a skewer, grilled), *sarma* (chopped meat and rice in sauerkraut or vine leaves), *punjena tikvica* (zucchini stuffed with minced meat and rice), stuffed peppers (peppers stuffed with minced meat, rice and spices, cooked in tomato sauce), *duvec* (mixed vegetables and meat roasted in an oven with grated cheese), *musaka* (eggplant and potato baked in layers with minced meat), Macedonian *gravce na tavce* (beans in a skillet) and *bosanski lonac* (Bosnian stew of cabbage and meat). A Serbian salad consists of raw peppers, onions and tomatoes, seasoned with oil, vinegar and chilli. Also watch for *kajmak* (cream from boiled milk, salted and turned into cheese). Yugoslavia is also famous for its red and white wines, plum brandies *(sljivovica)*, cognacs and liqueurs.

THINGS TO BUY

Among the traditional handicraft products of Yugoslavia are fine lace from the Dalmatian islands, hand-made embroidery, woodcarvings, woollen and leather items, carpets, filigree jewellery, ceramics, national costumes and tapestries.

Getting There & Away

TRAIN

There are countless ways to come to Yugoslavia. International trains between Munich and Belgrade (via Villach) are frequent, often continuing to Istanbul (via Sofia) or Athens. Vienna trains enter via Maribor. Trains from Paris to Belgrade go via Venice and Trieste. The mainline between Budapest and Belgrade is through Subotica. There's also a route from Budapest to Zagreb and local trains between Pecs and Osijek. From Romania an overnight train runs Bucharest to Belgrade (via Timisoara). Express service from Sofia to Belgrade (via Nis) is several times a day. The southern mainline between Belgrade and Athens is through Skopje and Thessaloniki. There's also a local line which takes all afternoon to cover the 39 km between Bitola and Florina (Greece).

Only buy a ticket as far as your first stop in Yugoslavia as domestic fares are much cheaper than international fares. Consider breaking your journey in Maribor or Ljubljana for this purpose alone. The same applies if you're going north through Hungary to a point beyond Budapest (to Berlin, Prague or Warsaw, for example). It's much cheaper to buy a ticket only as far as Budapest, then another there. An IUS student card will get you a reduction on railway fares from Yugoslavia to other socialist countries. Railway fares in Italy are also cheap, so if you can get that far it won't cost much to take a train to Trieste.

BUS

From Britain the cheapest way to Yugoslavia is on one of the transcontinental buses headed for Greece, as advertised in the weekly London entertainment magazines. These buses aren't supposed to accept passengers bound only for Yugoslavia. Of course they all will, but you could end up being dumped at a way station far from prying eyes in the town centres.

From West Germany the buses of the Deutsche Touring GmbH are much cheaper than the train. For example, Munich to Rijeka is DM 55 by bus, DM 80 by train (2nd class). Cologne-Belgrade is DM 145 by bus, DM 235 by train (2nd class). Other West German buses bound for Yugoslavia (with sample one way fares) depart Dortmund (DM 133), Cologne (DM 115), West Berlin (DM 115), Frankfurt am Main (DM 92), Mannheim (DM 89), Stuttgart (DM 75) and Nurnberg (DM 60). Baggage is DM 2 extra per piece. Service is usually only once or twice a week, but they operate year-round. Information is available at bus stations in the above cities.

BOAT

One of the nicest ways to come is on the motor ship *Dionea*, the last of the Lloyd passenger boats. Fares are low because Rome subsidises the service as a way of showing the flag up and down the formerly Italian Istrian coast. The *Dionea* departs a wharf in downtown Trieste for Koper, Piran, Porec, Rovinj and Pula at 8 am daily except Wednesday in summer. There are two sailings weekly in March, October and November, four weekly in May and June and six a week from July to mid-September.

Fares from Trieste on the *Dionea* run US$8 to Porec or Rovinj, US$10 to Pula. If you're going from Yugoslavia toward Trieste it's less. In Yugoslavia you buy your ticket once aboard, except in Pula where there's an office. In Trieste the agents are Adriatica di Navigazione, Piazza Duca degli Abruzzi, 1/A. This service cannot be used for travel between two Yugoslavian ports, only from Istria to Trieste or vice versa. Check exact departure times at local tourist offices.

Adriatica Line car ferries cross the sea year-round between most large Italian ports (Trieste, Venice, Rimini, Ancona, Pescara, Bari) and Zadar, Split and Dubrovnik. Any travel agent will have times, frequencies and tickets. Fares range from US$38 to US$47 one way, deck with a 50% surcharge in July and August. Bicycles are carried free. Jadrolinija car ferries also service Ancona from mid-June to September.

From April to mid-October the Jadro-linija car ferry between Rijeka and Bar continues on to Corfu and Igoumenitsa (Greece) a couple of times a week. Corfu to Dubrovnik is US$42 deck one way. Ferry tickets from Yugoslavia to Italy or Greece must be paid in foreign currency.

Getting Around

AIR

Domestic airfares within Yugoslavia are low and when you combine this with the rugged terrain and long distances a flight or two on Jugoslav Airlines (JAT) might be worth considering. For example, you can fly Pula/Zadar for US$16, Belgrade/Dubrovnik for US$22, Split/Skopje for US$27, or Ohrid/Ljubljana for US$33. A student card could get you a 10% discount. Some flights only operate once or twice a week, so check well in advance. In summer all flights are heavily booked. If you decide not to go at least 24 hours before a flight you can present your unused ticket at any JAT office for a prompt refund in full. JAT runs inexpensive buses to the airports from city centres and the domestic airport tax is only US$1. Fifteen kg of checked baggage is allowed on domestic flights. There are efficient, computerised JAT offices in all the large cities.

Adria Airways also operates many routes within Yugoslavia, including such unusual runs as Belgrade/Portoroz and Zagreb/Mali Losinj. Especially useful are their direct flights between the Adriatic coast and Macedonia, which is badly covered by road and rail. Examples are Ohrid/Dubrovnik, Skopje/Split, Skopje/Pula, Skopje/Sarajevo, Skopje/Titograd and Skopje/Dubrovnik. Adria also has many flights to and from main resort cities such as Split (to Sarajevo, Belgrade, Ljubljana and Osijek) and Dubrovnik (to Belgrade, Osijek and Ljubljana). Some flights only operate during the peak summer season, however. Since JAT and

Adria compete on many routes check both to determine which is more convenient before booking.

TRAIN

Railway service along the interior mainline Ljubljana / Zagreb / Belgrade / Skopje is adequate and there are branch lines down to the coast at Split (from Zagreb), Kardeljevo (via Sarajevo) and Bar (from Belgrade). Some of the routes through the mountains are highly scenic, especially Jesenice to Nova Gorica, Sarajevo to Kardeljevo and Mojkovac to Bar. There are four classes of trains: *ekspresni* (express), *poslovni* (rapid), *brzi* (fast) and *putnicki* (slow). Make sure you have the right sort of ticket for your train. Some of the new trains carry only 1st class seats. Inter-Rail passes are valid in Yugoslavia, but not Eurail.

One of the best travel bargains in Yugoslavia are 2nd class couchettes, costing only about US$4. Nearly all overnight trains to Belgrade carry couchettes. You arrive in the early morning, have the day to look around, before taking another couchette on to somewhere else. Another useful run is Ljubljana to Bitola via Skopje. Couchettes are surprisingly easy to book in the originating city of the train. It's usually done at a specific travel agency rather than in the station itself. The information counter in the station will tell you where to go. Travel agencies all over Yugoslavia can book couchettes between other cities in advance over the phone. Their commission is only about US$1 per booking, so keep this excellent service in mind. Buying a couchette on the train itself is problematic as the attendants may claim everything's full until you offer a gratuity. Remember that even with a couchette or sleeper ticket you must also buy an actual train ticket in the station where you board.

On posted timetables the word for departures is *odlazak* or *polazak*; for arrivals it's *dolazak*. All railway stations (except in Kosovo) have left luggage offices where you can dump your bag for about US$0.40. These are cheaper, more co-operative and open longer hours than cloakrooms in bus stations, so use the railway facility if the bus and train stations are adjacent.

BUS

Fast express buses go everywhere in Yugoslavia, often many times a day. Along the Adriatic coast they are the main means of transport. They'll stop to pick up passengers at designated stops anywhere along their route. Fares within Yugoslavia are low; buses charge about US$1 for each hour of travel. Expect to cover about 40 km in that time. Checked luggage is extra, around US$0.50 a piece. If your bag is small try carrying it onto the bus to avoid paying.

Bus tickets must be purchased at the office, not from drivers. Try to book ahead to be sure of a seat. Lists of departures over the various windows at the bus stations tell you which one has tickets for your bus. Your ticket will only be valid on buses of the issuing company and only for the departure specified on the ticket. You might be able to use it on an earlier bus of that company if there's room, but if you miss your bus it's unlikely you'll get a refund. Without an advance ticket you'll only be allowed on if there happen to be vacant seats.

In some places like Dubrovnik where supply doesn't always meet demand, trying to catch a bus can be quite an experience! Always check for overnight buses which get you where you're going for what you'd have to pay for a room anyway. Don't expect to get much sleep, however, as the inside lights will be on and music blasting the whole night. The front seats on buses are often reserved for invalids. Beware of buses leaving 10 minutes early.

BOAT

From April to mid-October Jadrolinija car ferries operate almost daily along the coastal route Rijeka / Rab / Zadar / Sibenik / Split / Hvar / Korcula / Dubrovnik / Bar, with some continuing on to Greece. They're a lot more comfortable than the buses, if several times more expensive. With a through ticket you can stop over at any port for up to a week, provided you notify the purser beforehand and have your ticket validated. This is much cheaper than buying individual tickets. Fares are slightly higher from mid-June to September. Kvarner Express are agents for these ferries, so enquire about departure times and prices at any of their offices throughout Yugoslavia. The most scenic section is Split to Dubrovnik, which all of the ferries cover during the day. Rijeka to Split (US$19 deck) is usually an overnight trip in either direction. Bring some food and drink aboard with you.

A ferry connection between Pula and Zadar via Mali Losinj operates six times a week from mid-June to mid-September, weekly the rest of the year, except February when there's no service. Local ferries connect the main offshore islands to the mainland. The most important of these are Brestova to Porozine on Cres Island (year-round), Baska on Krk Island to Lopar on Rab Island (June to September), Jablanac to Misnjak on Rab Island (year-round), Zadar to Preko (year-round), Split to Supetar on Brac Island (year-round), Split to Stari Grad or Vira on Hvar Island (year-round), Drvenik to Sucuraj on Hvar Island (year-round), Kardeljevo to Trpanj (year-round) and Orebic to Korcula Island (year-round). In the off season service is greatly reduced, so check.

LOCAL TRANSPORT

Public transport strip tickets or tokens are available from newsstands. If you pay a city bus or streetcar driver directly it will be about double fare.

Car rentals in Yugoslavia are very expensive. Taxi fares are average, but make sure that the meter is turned on.

The hitching in Yugoslavia is lousy. There are lots of little cars but they're usually full and local motorists are not noted for their courtesy. Tourists never stop.

Croatia

Croatia (Hrvatska) extends in an arc from the Danube to Istria and south along the Adriatic coast to Dubrovnik. Roman Catholic since the 7th century and under Hungary since 1102, Croatia only united with Orthodox Serbia in 1918. Croatia's centuries of resistance to Hungarian and Austrian domination continue today in its jealously guarded position within the Yugoslav federal system.

The republic has a near monopoly on tourism to Yugoslavia. The strikingly beautiful Mediterranean landscapes so close to central Europe draw nearly 10 million visitors a year, although the crowds are smaller in late spring and early autumn. The Croatian capital, Zagreb, is the cultural centre of Yugoslavia.

OSIJEK

Osijek, on the right bank of the Drava River near its confluence with the Danube, is a useful exit/entry point for those travelling between Yugoslavia and Hungary. Vinkovci, on the main railway line from Belgrade to Zagreb, is only 40 km south of Osijek.

Places to Stay

Accommodation is much cheaper in Hungary than Yugoslavia, so try to go on to Pecs the same day. If you get stuck Hotel Turist opposite Osijek Railway Station is US$30 single, US$45 double. For private rooms try the tourist office at A Cesarca 2 in the centre of town. You may camp near the Copacabana Restaurant just across the river from downtown.

Getting There & Away

There are two Hungarian trains a day

between Osijek and Pecs, Hungary, a pleasant two-hour trip. Tickets for this journey (US$3) can be purchased at the Croatia Express office in Osijek Railway Station, which also changes money.

If you don't already have a Hungarian visa you'll have to take one of the three daily buses between Osijek and Pecs (US$2.50) and get your visa at the border since visas are not available on the train. In Osijek the bus and train stations are adjacent.

There are also flights to Osijek from Belgrade (US$17), Dubrovnik (US$23), Split (US$25) and Pula (US$24).

KOPRIVNICA

The daily Maestral Express between Budapest and Zagreb crosses the border between Gyekenyes, Hungary, and Koprivnica, Yugoslavia.

Information

Walk straight out of the railway station past the bus station on Ulica Mose Pijade, toward Croatia Express and General-turist which can answer questions. The Ljubljanska Banka is adjacent. All these offices stay open until 7 pm weekdays.

Places to Stay & Eat

The agencies don't rent private rooms and the one hotel in Koprivnica is very expensive. There's a basic campground at Soderica Lake, 16 km north-east of Koprivnica (bus service from the bus station or take a train to Botovo between Koprivnica and Gyekenyes). The local hangout in Koprivnica is the *Kralus Cellar*, a pub in the centre of town.

Getting There & Away

If you take the Maestral Express between Kaposvar and Koprivnica (US$5) you'll arrive in Yugoslavia at 6 pm. There are also three local trains a day between Gyekenyes and Koprivnica.

ZAGREB

Zagreb, the second largest city in Yugoslavia and capital of Croatia, is a far more attractive, enjoyable city than Belgrade. Spread out toward the Sava River, Zagreb sits on the southern slopes of Medvednica, the Zagreb uplands. Medieval Zagreb developed from the 11th to 13th centuries in the twin towns of Kaptol and Gradec; Kaptol with St Stephen's Cathedral and Gradec centred on St Mark's Church. The clerics established themselves in Kaptol while Gradec was the craftsmen's quarter. Much of medieval Zagreb remains today, although the stately 19th century city between it and the railway station is the present commercial centre. There are many fine parks and museums in both upper and lower towns. Zagreb is also Yugoslavia's main centre for primitive or naive art.

Orientation

As you come out of the railway station you'll see a series of parks and pavilions directly in front of you. Many banks and travel agencies are along the street up the left side of these parks. Just up Praska from the north end of the parks is the tourist office on Trg Republike, the main city square. The bus station is one km east of the railway station. Tram No 6 runs from the bus station to the railway station and on up to Trg Republike.

Information

The tourist office, Trg Republike 11, opens weekdays 8 am to 9 pm, weekends 9 am to 6 pm. The quality of service varies, so try another clerk if the first one you get isn't amenable.

There's an information office for Plitvice National Park at Trg Tomislava 19 where you can buy a park map and hear the bad news about increasing accommodation rates. Poste restante is held in the post office on the east side of the railway station. There's a 24-hour exchange office in the railway station.

Consulates There's no Hungarian consulate

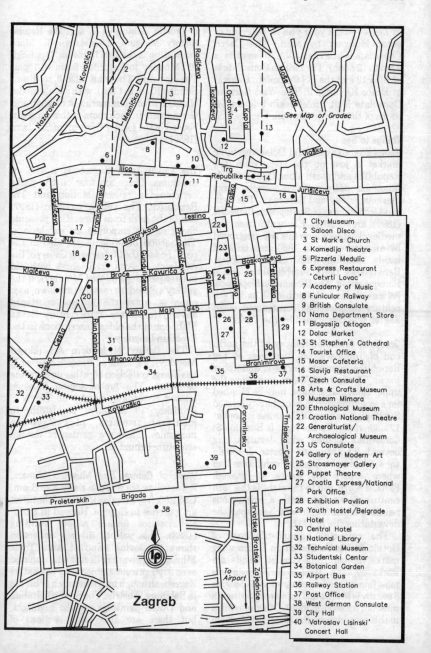

1 City Museum
2 Saloon Disco
3 St Mark's Church
4 Komedija Theatre
5 Pizzeria Medulic
6 Express Restaurant 'Cetvrti Lovac'
7 Academy of Music
8 Funicular Railway
9 British Consulate
10 Nama Department Store
11 Blagasija Oktogon
12 Dolac Market
13 St Stephen's Cathedral
14 Tourist Office
15 Mosor Cafeteria
16 Slavija Restaurant
17 Czech Consulate
18 Arts & Crafts Museum
19 Museum Mimara
20 Ethnological Museum
21 Croation National Theatre
22 Generalturist/ Archaeological Museum
23 US Consulate
24 Gallery of Modern Art
25 Strossmayer Gallery
26 Puppet Theatre
27 Croatia Express/National Park Office
28 Exhibition Pavilion
29 Youth Hostel/Belgrade Hotel
30 Central Hotel
31 National Library
32 Technical Museum
33 Studentski Centar
34 Botanical Garden
35 Airport Bus
36 Railway Station
37 Post Office
38 West German Consulate
39 City Hall
40 'Vatroslav Lisinski' Concert Hall

Zagreb

See Map of Gradec

To Airport

in Zagreb so get your visa in Belgrade or enter Hungary by road. The Czech Consulate is at Prilaz JNA 10 (weekdays 9 am to 12 noon). The British Consulate is at Ilica 12 and the US Consulate General at Brace Kavurica 2. The West German Consulate is at Proleterskih brigada 64, south of the railway station.

Things to See

Kaptol Zagreb's colourful Dolac vegetable market is just up the steps from Trg Republike and north along Opatovina. It functions daily with especially large markets Friday and Saturday. The twin neo-Gothic spires of **St Stephen's Cathedral** (1899) are nearby. Elements from the medieval cathedral on this site, destroyed by an earthquake in 1880, can be seen inside, including 13th century frescoes, Renaissance pews, marble altars and a Baroque pulpit. The Baroque **Archiepiscopal Palace** surrounds the cathedral, as do 16th century fortifications constructed when Zagreb was threatened by the Turks.

Gradec A funicular railway at the north end of Tomiceva, off Ilica west of Trg Republike, connects the lower and upper towns. The **Lotrscak Tower**, just above the upper funicular station, may be climbed for a sweeping 360° view of the city (closed Sunday). A cannon in the tower is fired at 12 noon daily. To the right is Baroque **St Catherine's Church** with Jezuitski trg beyond. The **Muzejski prostor**, Jezuitski trg 4, is Zagreb's premier exhibition hall where superb art shows are staged. Farther north and to the right is the 13th century **Stone Gate** with a miraculous painting of the Virgin which escaped the devastating fire of 1731.

The colourful painted-tile roof of Gothic **St Mark's Church** on Radicev trg marks the centre of Gradec. Inside are works by Ivan Mestrovic, Yugoslavia's most famous modern sculptor. At Mletacka 8 nearby is **Mestrovics' former studio**, now a museum (closed Monday). Other museums in this area include the **Historical Museum**

of Croatia, Matoseva 9, and the **Natural History Museum**, Demetrova 1. More interesting is the **City Museum**, Opaticka 20 (Monday to Saturday 9 am to 1 pm, Tuesday and Thursday also 5 to 8 pm, Sunday 10 am to 1 pm), with a scale model of old Gradec. Summaries in English and German are in each room of this museum housed in the former Convent of St Claire (1650).

The Lower Town Zagreb is a city of museums. There are four on the parks between the railway station and Trg Republike. The yellow pavilion (1897) across the park from the station presents changing contemporary art exhibitions. The second building north, also in the park, houses the **Strossmayer Gallery** of the Academy of Arts & Sciences with old master paintings (closed Monday). If the gallery's closed for reasons unknown, as it often is, enter the interior courtyard anyway to see the 11th century Baska Slab, one of the oldest inscriptions in the Croatian language.

The **Gallery of Modern Art** (closed Monday), adjacent at Brace Kavurica 1, has a large collection of rather uninspiring paintings. The **Archaeological Museum** (closed Saturday), nearby at Trg N S Zrinjskog 19, displays prehistoric to medieval artefacts, plus Egyptian mummies. There's a garden of Roman sculpture behind.

West of Centre The **Museum Mimara**, Rooseveltov trg 5 (open daily 3 to 8 pm, US$1.50, free Monday), is one of the finest art galleries in Europe. Housed in a neo-Renaissance former school building (1883), this select, diverse collection shows the loving hand of Ante Topic Mimara, a private collector who donated over 3750 priceless objects to his native Zagreb, although he spent much of his life in Salzburg, Austria. The Spanish, Italian and Dutch paintings are the highlight, but there are also large sections of

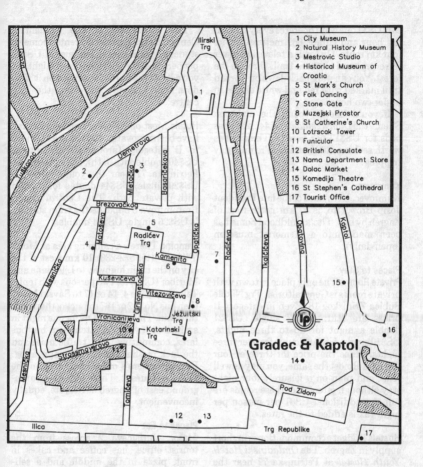

1 City Museum
2 Natural History Museum
3 Mestrovic Studio
4 Historical Museum of Croatia
5 St Mark's Church
6 Folk Dancing
7 Stone Gate
8 Muzejski Prostor
9 St Catherine's Church
10 Lotrscak Tower
11 Funicular
12 British Consulate
13 Nama Department Store
14 Dolac Market
15 Komedija Theatre
16 St Stephen's Cathedral
17 Tourist Office

Gradec & Kaptol

glassware, sculpture and Oriental art. Don't miss it.

Nearby on Trg Marsala Tita is the neo-Baroque **Croatian National Theatre** (1895) with Ivan Mestrovic's Fountain of Life (1905) in front. The **Ethnographic Museum**, Trg Mazuranicev 14 (Tuesday, Wednesday, Thursday 9 am to 1 pm and 5 to 7 pm, Friday, Saturday, Sunday 9 am to 1 pm) has a large collection of Croatian folk costumes with English explanations. South of here is the art nouveau **National Library** (1907). The **Botanical Garden** on

Ulica Mihanoviceva (open April to October, closed Monday, free) is attractive for the plants and landscaping as well as its restful corners.

Sljeme A cable car *(zicara)* runs up Sljeme, the forested mountain (1035 metres) behind Zagreb (also known as Mt Medvednica). To get there take tram No 14 to Mihaljevac (the end of the line), then tram No 15 to its terminus at Dolje. Go through a tunnel and follow a footpath 10 minutes to the lower terminal. The cable car (US$1 one way) operates every hour on the hour and climbs 669 metres over its four km route. On top is a television tower (no entry) and pleasant trails through the forest. You can walk back down on a broad trail marked with red and white circles in under two hours.

If you'd like to spend the night on Sljeme the *Dom 'Izvidae'* (tel 445-226) has beds for US$12 per person. Their bar is worth seeking out even if you're only day tripping.

Kumrovec

Kumrovec, birthplace of the late President Josip Broz Tito, is 57 km north-west of Zagreb by bus. Tito's childhood home has been made into a memorial museum (open daily).

Places to Stay

Private Rooms The only place in town with private rooms is Generalturist, Trg Nikole Subica Zrinjskog 18. Even in category II prices are stiff: US$13 single, US$21 double a night for up to three nights, US$10 single, US$16 double for over three nights. Since the price for three or four nights is almost the same, you may as well relax and plan on a leisurely four-night stay although often all of these rooms are full. An additional US$1 per person per night tax is added to the rates.

Hostels Budget accommodation is in short supply in Zagreb. The *Omladinski Hotel/ Youth Hostel* at Petrinjska 77 near the railway station is open year-round. Its prices are higher: US$4 for those under age 27, US$7 for those over 27, both in the dormitory. The few double rooms cost US$23, but they're usually booked solid by Yugoslavs who pay a lot less. You don't have to be a YHA member to stay in the hostel, so it's a good last resort if nothing else turns up. Ask about accommodation in other youth hostels and at *Dom 'Izvidae'* on Mt Sljeme at the Youth Tourist Centre, Petrinjska 73 beside the hostel.

The Turist-biro at the Studentski Centar, Savska cesta 25, rents rooms in student dormitories in summer at US$22 per person. A valid student card might net you a lower rate, but don't count on it. The dorms are usually far from the city centre.

Hotels Most of the older hotels in Zagreb have been renovated and the prices raised to B category (around US$30 single, US$40 double with bath). *Hotel Belgrade*, Petrinjska 71 near the youth hostel, is US$29 single, US$44 double for a room with private bath. The *Central Hotel*, Branimirova 3 opposite the train station, is US$26 single, US$44 double.

Camping There's a camping area at *Motel 'Plitvice'* (tel 522-230) 10 km west of the city on the main highway to Ljubljana and Maribor (US$9 for two persons with tent). Take trams No 4, 14 or 17 to Savski Most, then bus No 112 or 167 to Lucko, then walk three km. This may be OK for one night in a pinch or if you're a hitchhiker, but bus fares, commuting time, traffic noise and the lack of shade make it unappealing. Evenings there's often live music in the motel restaurant. There's another campground east of Zagreb at Sesvete, equally inconvenient.

Places to Eat

Mosor, Jurisiceva 2 across from the tourist office, has coffee and cakes in front, pizza in the middle and a self-service cafeteria at the back. Soup and salad with bread makes a cheap lunch. The *Slavija Restaurant*, Jurisiceva 18, has an informal US$3 lunchtime counter 'menu' including soup, salad, hot main plate and dessert.

In summer the *Express Restaurant 'Cetvrti Lovac,'* Dezmanova 2, moves its tables out onto the street and dispenses real pizza at reasonable prices in a friendly atmosphere. *Pizzeria Medulic*, Meduliceva 2 at Ilica, serves vegetarian food in the back dining room and the menu is in English. Their pizza is also good.

Restaurant 'Jana' Samoposluga, Petrinjska 79, a self-service cafeteria near the youth hostel. There's a super cheap dining hall at the *Studentski Centar*, Savska cesta 25, but student ID is checked at the door.

Entertainment

Zagreb is much more a happening city than Belgrade. Its theatres and concert halls present a great variety of programmes throughout the year. Many (but not all) are listed in the monthly brochure *Zagreb events & performances*, usually available from the tourist office. The daily paper *Vecernji list* carries cinema, concert, exhibition and museum listings. Even if you don't read Serbo-Croatian the information isn't hard to decipher. It's also worth making the rounds of the theatres in person to check the calendars. Tickets are usually available, even for the best shows. A small office (look for the posters) in the Blagasija Oktogon, a passage connecting Trg bratstva i jedinstva to Ilica near Trg Republike, also sells theatre tickets. Many free outdoor performances are offered during the International Folklore Festival the second half of July.

The majestic *Croatian National Theatre*, Trg Marsala Tita 15, presents opera and ballet performances (box office Monday to Saturday 9 am to 1 pm and 5 to 7 pm, tickets US$5). The *Komedija Theatre*, Kaptol 9 near the cathedral, stages operettas and musicals. The ticket office of the *'Vatroslav Lisinski' Concert Hall*, just south of the railway station, is open weekdays 10 am to 1 pm, 5.30 to 7.30 pm, Saturday 10 am to 1 pm. Concerts also happen at the *Academy of Music*, Gunduliceva 6a near Trg Republike. There are performances at the *Puppet Theatre*, Ulica 8 maja 35, Sundays at 10 am and 12 noon. In summer Wednesdays at 6 pm there's folk dancing in the courtyard at Kamenita 15 near St Mark's Church.

Zagreb's most popular disco is *Saloon*, Tuskanac 1a (open after 9 pm daily). Weekends it's packed. In the evening the cafes along Tkalciceva north off Trg Republike buzz with activity as overflow crowds spill out onto the street, drinks in hand. Farther up on Kozarska ulica the city youth clusters shoulder to shoulder. Trg bratstva i jedinstva also has more interesting streetlife than Trg Republike. A late stroll through these areas will demonstrate that Zagreb isn't as staid as you thought!

Things to Buy

Ilica is Zagreb's main shopping street. Get in touch with Yugoslav consumerism at Nama Department Store on Ilica near Trg Republike. The shops and grocery stores in the passage under the tracks beside the railway station stay open long hours.

Getting There & Away

Train The *Maestral Express* departs Zagreb for Budapest every morning. Alternatively take a train to Koprivnica and a local train into Hungary from there. You must *already* have a visa to enter Hungary by train. If you don't have a visa take a train to Osijek from where there are buses to Pecs, Hungary. Visas are available at highway border crossings.

Zagreb is on the Munich / Ljubljana / Belgrade and Vienna / Maribor / Belgrade mainlines. There are other direct trains from Zagreb to Kardeljevo (11 hours), Osijek (four hours), Rijeka (four hours), Sarajevo (seven hours), Split (seven hours) and Zadar (seven hours). Some trains out of Zagreb carry only reserved 1st class seats, so check.

Croatia Express, Trg Tomislava 17 near the train station, books couchettes (about US$3) to points throughout Yugoslavia – a perfect way to beat Zagreb's high hotel prices. Couchettes are available to Belgrade, Bitola, Kardeljevo, Pula, Sarajevo, Sibenik, Skopje, Split and Zadar.

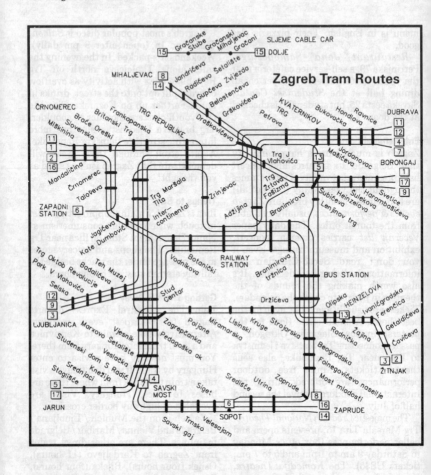

Zagreb Tram Routes

Bus Buses depart Zagreb's bustling big bus station for most of northern Yugoslavia and points beyond. Buy an advance ticket at the station if you'll be travelling far. There are 20 buses a day between Zagreb and the Plitvice Lakes (130 km, US$3), many continuing on to Zadar. Nine daily buses run to Tito's birthplace village, Kumrovec. Some international services worth knowing about are Zagreb to Vienna (daily, US$18), Munich (daily, US$53), Paris (Wednesday and Saturday,

US$55), Berlin (Saturday, US$70) and Istanbul (Wednesday and Saturday, US$25). There's no bus to Hungary.

Getting Around

Public transport is based on an efficient network of streetcars, although the city centre is compact enough to make them unnecessary. The tourist office sells a day pass valid on all trams and buses for US$2. Enter trams through the rear doors to pay your fare. Airport buses (US$1.25)

leave frequently from beside the Esplanade Hotel across the square from the railway station.

PLITVICE LAKES

The 16 pristine Plitvice Lakes lie in a forested valley almost midway between Zagreb and Zadar. Numerous waterfalls and cascades connect the lakes, arrayed in a series of terraces stepping down to the Korana River Gorge. The falls sometimes pour from subterranean passages in the karst landscape and the dissolved lime they deposit on the lake beds gives the water its unique blue/green colour. Countless trout are seen swimming in the crystal clear waters.

All this is great, but overcharging by the park authorities and overcrowding by huge flocks of tourists make a visit something of a sacrifice and occasionally an ordeal. Although the area is definitely worth seeing, it rates second to the Julian Alps in both beauty and variety, despite what the glossy brochures or Unesco would have you believe.

Orientation

There are two entrances: Ulaz 2 adjacent to the Upper Lakes and Ulaz 1 near the Lower Lakes. There are parking lots, restaurants, ticket counters and turist biros at both, but Ulaz 2 has a more reliable bus stop and all of the park hotels. You can leave luggage at Restaurant Poljana at Ulaz 2 for US$0.50.

Information

There are Turist Biros at both park entrances. Get hold of the useful 1:50,000 'tourist map' of the park (US$0.50).

Entry Fee

Admission to Plitvice National Park is US$12 for foreign tourists, US$7 for foreign students and US$2 for Yugoslavs. The price includes use of the park shuttle buses and one ride along the length of Kozjak Lake on the park tourist boat. If you want to spend a second day in the park have your hotel, campground, or private room agency stamp the ticket to avoid having to pay again. Only official National Park accommodation (including everything listed below) can do this.

Some travellers have managed to visit Plitvice without buying a ticket as the only place they're punched is on the tourist boat along the length of the lake (from A to Z). Tickets are not always strictly controlled on the shuttle buses which carry you into the park. Other ways to get around the exorbitant admission price are to share a single ticket between several people, taking turns visiting, or to ask someone at the campground to give you a used ticket they no longer require, then have it stamped at the reception for free entry the next day. It's also easy to simply walk in free on the road from Poljanak village to the top of the highest falls in the Lower Lakes area. Of course we're not suggesting you actually *do* any of the above. Plitvice National Park is quite justified in charging foreigners six times as much as locals!

Things to See

The beaten tourist track at Plitvice involves taking the shuttle bus from Ulaz 2 to Labudovac at the top of the Upper Lakes, then following the boardwalks down to Kozjak Lake where you board the park tourist boat from A to Z. After a quick look at some of the Lower Lakes tourists reboard the shuttle bus back to Ulaz 2 or return by boat. Many people end up seeing only the Upper Lakes.

Actually this is a big mistake as the Lower Lakes area is more beautiful, less crowded and the waterfalls much higher. All the pretty pictures you see in the park brochures were taken at the Lower Lakes. Best of all, the falls give into the fantastic Korana Gorge with many possibilities for swimming in the river. Officially swimming is allowed in Proscansko Lake and the west shore of Kozjak Lake only, so avoid attracting attention. There are large caves in the gorge walls which you may

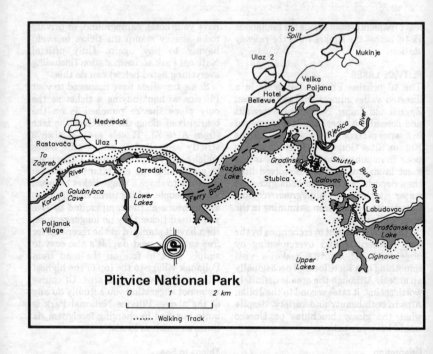

Plitvice National Park

0   1   2 km

······· Walking Track

visit free. Not many visitors get this far and if you come in the late afternoon you'll be all alone.

A boardwalk runs right down the Korana Gorge then climbs the cliff to a trail back to Ulaz 1. If you're staying at Autocamp Korana you could continue three km down the gorge to the village, then ask directions back to the camp. The overgrown trail begins on the hillside at the first switchback above the end of the boardwalk. Don't leave it too late to go down this way however, as the trail would be impossible to follow in the dark.

Places to Stay

Hotels Accommodation at Plitvice is not cheap. The easiest way to go is to stay in one of the park hotels at Ulaz 2. *Hotel Bellevue* is US$12 single, US$23 double for a room without bath, breakfast included. *Villa Poljana* nearby is only a dollar or so

more expensive. The reception at Hotel Plitvice, which is next to Hotel Bellevue, handles bookings for Villa Poljana. In both hotels you'll automatically be given a room with private bath for US$22 per person unless you specifically request a room with shared facilities.

Private Rooms Private rooms from the Turist Biro at Ulaz 2 are US$11 single, US$21 double, but breakfast is not included and they're situated from three to six km from the park. There's also a Turist Biro at Ulaz 1 and if you're sure it's a private room you're after you'd do better going directly there as the rooms will be closer. If you stay four nights or more there's a 20% discount. In winter you may simply be told there are no private rooms.

Camping It's much cheaper to camp but unfortunately both official campgrounds are far away. *Autocamp Korana* is eight km up the road to Zagreb and although the bus passes the gate the stop is a km away. Some drivers will drop you right there if you ask nicely. If you don't have a tent or it's raining you can rent a caravan at Korana for US$12 single, US$18 double, US$21 triple (no water or cooking facilities inside). Small bungalows cost the same but they're often reserved for noisy school groups. The restaurant at Korana is expensive but there's a good grocery store.

Fifteen km down the road to Zadar is *Borje Autocamp*, a similar operation. It's usually easy to get a bus from Borje as many of the long-distance services stop at the campground restaurant for a coffee break. At both campgrounds the fee is US$4 per person, US$3 per tent, and both are open mid-April to October. The altitude (650 metres) can mean occasionally cool camping. Officially there's no camping within the park itself but you'll find plenty of unofficial places to pitch a tent. Keep in mind this is against the rules and be discreet.

Places to Eat

The 'market' beside the Turist Biro at Ulaz 2 sells such basic necessities as liquor, candies and cheap souvenirs. They *don't* carry a great deal of food. You can get bread, milk and cheese to fill your stomach. Restaurant Poljana at Ulaz 2 has a reasonable self-service section.

Getting There & Away

It's easy to get to Plitvice by bus. There are 19 buses daily from Zagreb (three hours, US$3) and about nine from Zadar (four hours, US$4). The nearest train stations are Vrhovine (1½ hours, US$1.50) and Bihac (one hour, US$1), but bus service from these is less frequent. Catching a bus out of Plitvice in the late afternoon can be difficult at weekends when they whiz past full. Most buses do stop at Ulaz 2, however. Call out your destination as you board to

avoid taking the wrong bus. The Turist Biro at Ulaz 2 has a list of bus times.

Getting Around

The shuttle buses and boats operate every 30 to 40 minutes throughout the day. In winter all services (but not prices) are greatly reduced.

Slovenia

Slovenia is clearly a transitional zone between Eastern and Western Europe. The cities bear the imprint of the Italian Counter-Reformation, while up in the Julian Alps one feels the proximity of Austria. Slovenia was under Germanic rule throughout its history, first as part of the Holy Roman Empire, then under the Hapsburgs. Yet the Slovene inhabitants of this northernmost region have retained a Slavic culture all their own. Slovenia today has the highest standard of living in Yugoslavia. Mass tourism is exploited in resorts like Bled, Koper, Portoroz and Piran, and foreign motorists jam the highways. Yet, while commercialised attractions like the Postojna Caves have become a rip-off, the rugged Alps and vibrant Ljubljana retain their appeal.

LJUBLJANA

Foggy Ljubljana (Laibach), capital of Slovenia, is a pleasant small city a third the size of Zagreb, 135 km to the east. The most beautiful part is along the Ljubljanica River below the castle. Ljubljana began as the Roman Emona. The Italian influence continued after the Counter-Reformation when many churches were built. Despite the Austrian overtones the city has a Slavic air all its own. You can easily see the best of Ljubljana in a day and don't worry, the fog can clear up by mid-morning.

Orientation

The bus and train stations are adjacent on

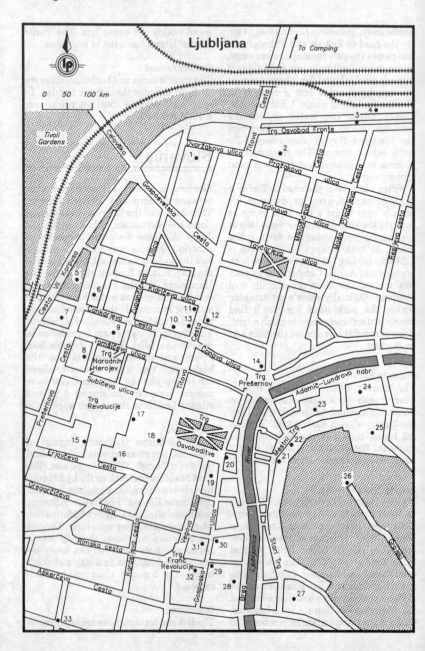

Ljubljana

To Camping

0   50   100 km

Tivoli
Gardens

Celovška

Cesta

Cesta

Trg Osvobod Fronte

Dvoržakova ulica

Titova

Cesta

Cesta

Cesta

Cesta

Gosposvetska

Prežakova
ulica

Cesta

Trdinova
ulica

Miklošičeva

cesta

Pražakova
ulica

Pražakova

Cesta

Resljeva

Cesta

Moše Pijade ulica

VII Korpusa

Župančičeva

Kidričeva ulica

Tavčarjeva
ulica

Cesta

Cesta

Cankarjeva

Cesta

Tomšičeva ulica

Trg
Narodnih
Herojev

Subičeva ulica

Titova

Copova ulica

Trg Prešernov

Adamič–Lundrovo nabr

Prešernova

Trg
Revolucije

Trg

Osvoboditve

Mestni Trg

Erjavčeva
Cesta

Gregorčičeva
Ulica

Vegova Ulica

River

Ljubljanica

Stari Trg

Grad

Rimska cesta

Kardeljeva cesta

Trg
Franc
Revolucije

Gosposka

Breg

Aškerčeva
Cesta

1	Slovene Alpine Association
2	Post Office
3	Bus Station
4	Railway Station
5	Serbian Orthodox Church
6	National Gallery
7	Modern Art Gallery
8	National Museum
9	Opera House
10	Daj-Dam
11	'Skyscraper'
12	Kompas
13	Tourist Information Centre
14	Franciscan Church
15	Cultural and Congress Centre
16	Pizzeria Parma
17	Maximarket
18	Ursuline Church
19	University
20	Filharmonia
21	Municipal Gallery
22	Town Hall
23	Cathedral
24	Vegetable Market
25	Puppet Theatre
26	Castle
27	St James Church
28	Pri Vitezu Restaurant
29	Town Museum
30	Academy of Sciences
31	National Library
32	Open Air Theatre
33	Roman City Wall

the north side of town. Walk west a block or two to Titova cesta, a broad avenue which leads south into the centre. The old town and castle are south-east, just across the river.

For an all-round view of central Ljubljana take the elevator up to the terrace bar atop the 'skyscraper' at the corner of Titova cesta and Kidriceva ulica (no admission fee, normal prices).

Information
The Tourist Information Centre is at Titova cesta 11. The bank at Copova 3 is open Saturday afternoon and Sunday morning. For information on hiking in the Julian Alps and excellent trail maps and guides visit the Slovene Alpine Association, Dvorzakova 9 (at the back of the yard).

Things to See
The most picturesque sights of old Ljubljana are found along the Ljubljana River, a tributary of the Sava, which curves around below imposing Castle Hill. From the Tourist Information Centre on Titova cesta follow Copova ulica down to Presernov trg with its inviting **Franciscan Church** (1660) and the famous 'three bridges' over the river. Cross one of these and veer left to **Ljubljana Cathedral** (1708) which contains impressive frescoes. The large open air **vegetable market** behind the cathedral is colourful.

Retrace your steps a little south-east to the **Town Hall** (1718), behind the fountain on Mestni trg. Enter the town hall to see the two courtyards then proceed to the **Municipal Gallery**, Mestni trg 5, where changing exhibits appear. Stari trg is to the south of this in the heart of the old town, full of atmosphere day and night. **Ljubljana Castle** on the hill above Stari trg has been closed for restoration for many years, but the tower may be climbed for the view. Several lanes off Stari trg lead up.

There's a second interesting area worth exploring on the east side of the Ljubljanica River. The **Town Museum**, Gosposka ulica 15 (Tuesday to Friday 10 am to 12 noon, 4 to 6 pm, Saturday and Sunday 10 am to 12 noon), is a good place to start. The museum has a well presented collection of Roman artefacts, plus a scale model of Emona (Ljubljana) to help it all make sense. Upstairs are period rooms. North on Gosposka ulica at Trg osvoboditve is the university building, formerly the Regional Parliament. The **Ursuline Church** (1726) is nearby. If you still have time go east on Subiceva ulica to the National Museum.

The **National Museum**, Trg herojev 1 (closed Monday, free on Saturday) includes mediocre prehistory, natural history and ethnography collections. The highlight is an ancient Celtic situla (pot) from the 6th century BC sporting an evocative relief. Unfortunately none of the captions are in English or German. The **National Gallery**, Cankarjeva 20 (closed Monday), offers 19th century portraits and landscapes, plus copies of medieval frescoes. You enter the upstairs rooms through a closed, unmarked door.

Diagonally across the street is the **Modern Art Gallery**, Cankarjeva 15 (closed Monday), with changing exhibitions. The Serbian Orthodox church between the two art galleries is open afternoons. Through the underpass from the Modern Art Gallery are the relaxing **Tivoli Gardens**.

Places to Stay

Private Rooms The Tourist Information Centre, Titova cesta 11, has private rooms for about US$6 single, US$11 double, but they may not be in the city centre. Kompas, across the street at Titova 12, also has private rooms but they're often full up. In summer ask at the Tourist Information Centre about accommodation in vacant student dormitories.

Hotels The cheapest hotel is the functional *Ilirija* (tel 551-173), Trg prekomorskih brigad 4 beside the Siska Cinema off Celovska cesta (US$11 single, US$18 double with shared bath). It's two km north-west of the city centre, so call before trekking out. On the way there you'll pass the *Bellevue Hotel* (tel 313-133), an old yellow building above the north end of Tivoli Gardens (US$15 single, US$22 double with shared bath). This elegant old hotel with its terrace overlooking the city should be your first choice if you don't mind paying a little extra for convenience and a touch of class.

Camping *Camping Jezica* is by the Sava River at the north end of Titova cesta (bus No 8 to the terminus), six km from the city centre. There's a large, shady camping area (US$6 per person) and new deluxe bungalows (US$20 single, US$30 double) for those without tents. This recommended site is open May to September.

Places to Eat

There's a self-service cafeteria in the basement at *Emona*, Titova cesta 9 beside the Tourist Information Centre, but it's neither cheap nor good. They do have green salads, however. Avoid the bottled drinks which are grossly overpriced. A world better (and maybe cheaper) is *Daj-Dam*, around the corner at Cankarjeva cesta 4, with a US$2 'menu' in the rear dining room.

Good, cheap pizza is served at *Pizzeria Parma*, downstairs in the mall off Erjavceva cesta beside the Cultural Centre. It's so good you may have to stand around waiting for a seat (come at odd hours). It's open 9 am to 9 pm, closed Sundays and has an English menu. The *Pri Vitezu Restaurant* at 20 Breg facing the river has a US$3 lunchtime 'menu.' In summer you can eat on the terrace outside.

Entertainment

Ljubljana enjoys a rich cultural life. The Tourist Information Centre puts out a monthly *Calendar of Events*. The ticket office of the neo-Rococo *Opera House*, Zupanciceva ulica 1, opens weekdays 10 am to 12 noon and an hour before the performance. Ljubljana's ultramodern *Cultural & Congress Centre 'Cankarjev dom'* includes four theatres. The symphony orchestra often appears in the Big Hall. For tickets and information look for their office downstairs in the adjacent shopping mall (weekdays 1 to 8 pm, Saturday 9 am to 12 noon, and an hour before performances).

Also check for concerts at the *Filharmonia* at Trg osvoboditve 9 (ticket office open 10 am to 12 noon). In summer things happen in the *Ljubljana Festival Open Air Theatre* on Trg francoske revolucije opposite the Town Museum. The *Puppet Theatre* is at Krekov trg 2 near the vegetable market. In the evening check out the bars and cafes on Presernov trg and in the old town. It can get pretty lively.

Things to Buy
The largest department store in town (with a supermarket in the basement) is Maximarket on Trg revolucije.

Getting There & Away
From Ljubljana to Koper the train is cheaper, faster and more comfortable than a bus. To Rijeka, Zagreb and Maribor you're also better off by train. But be sure to take a bus if you're headed from Bled or Bohinj in the Julian Alps. The train station there is far from the action.

There are through trains to Trieste and Venice, or take a local train to Villa Opicina and change there for Trieste. There's an international bus from Ljubljana to Munich (US$25), Ulm (US$35) and Stuttgart (US$40) on Thursday and Saturday. Details at the bus station.

Getting Around
Buy bus tokens in advance at a newsstand.

POSTOJNA
The much-touted **Postojna Caves** between Ljubljana and Rijeka are a bit of a rip-off. For US$12 a head hordes of tourists are taken on a miniature train ride between the colourfully-lit karst formations. You'll hear a predictably insipid commentary in your own language. If this sort of thing appeals to you the caves are walking distance from Postojna bus or railway stations (closer to the bus station). There are visits at 9.30 am and 1.30 pm daily year-round, with more frequent tours from April to October and on Sunday. Dress warmly as the cave is cool.

JULIAN ALPS
Yugoslavia shares the Julian Alps in the far north-west corner of Slovenia with Italy. Three-headed Mt Triglav (2864

metres), the country's highest peak, is scaled regularly by hundreds of summer weekend mountaineers, but there are countless less ambitious hikes. Lakes Bled and Bohinj make ideal starting points: Bled with its chic resort facilities, Bohinj right beneath the rocky crags themselves. Most of this spectacular area falls under Triglav National Park. A few possible routes are mentioned below.

BLED
Bled, a fashionable resort at 501 metres altitude, is set on an idyllic two-km-long emerald lake which you can walk right around in under two hours. Trout and carp proliferate in the crystal clear lake water which is surprisingly warm, a pleasure to swim in. The climate is also good: there's no fog at Bled during the summer. To the north-east the Karavanke Range forms a natural boundary with Austria. Bled was discovered by mass tourism long ago, but somehow you couldn't call it spoiled.

Orientation
The village is at the east end of the lake below Castle Hill. The bus station is also here, but Lesce-Bled Railway Station is about five km east. In addition there's Bled-Jezero, a branch line railway station above the west end of the lake, where the campground is also found.

Information
The tourist office is on Ljubljanska cesta across from the *Park Hotel*. Tourist information is also dispensed by the Turisticno Drustivo souvenir stand in the casino building. The Triglav National Park office is midway along the lake's north shore.

Things to See
The neo-Gothic **Parish Church** (1904) with frescoes done in 1937 is just above the bus station. Follow the road around north-west to the youth hostel where there's a trail up to the castle (grad). **Bled Castle**

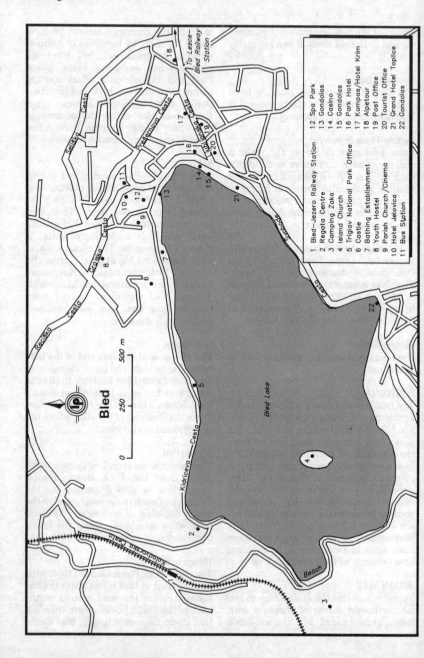

Bled

0   250   500 m

Bled Lake

To Lesce–
Bled Railway
Station

1 Bled–Jezero Railway Station
2 Regata Centre
3 Camping Zaka
4 Island Church
5 Triglav National Park Office
6 Castle
7 Bathing Establishment
8 Youth Hostel
9 Parish Church/Cinema
10 Hotel Jelovica
11 Bus Station
12 Spa Park
13 Gondolas
14 Casino
15 Gondolas
16 Park Hotel
17 Kompas/Hotel Krim
18 Alpetour
19 Post Office
20 Tourist Office
21 Grand Hotel Toplice
22 Gondolas

(open daily, US$1.25) was the seat of the bishops of Brixen (South Tyrol) for over 800 years. Set atop a steep cliff directly over the lake, it offers magnificent views in clear weather. The **Castle Museum** presents the history of the area and allows a peep into the 16th century chapel. By the altar is a fresco of the Holy Roman emperor Henry II presenting the church to Christ in 1004.

The other feature of Bled which immediately strikes the eye is a tiny island at the west end of the lake. From the massive red and white belfry rising above the dense vegetation the tolling 'bell of wishes' echoes across the lake. Below the present Baroque church are the foundations of a pre-Romanesque chapel, unique in Slovenia. Most tourists reach the island on one of the large hand-propelled gondolas, which let you off for a half hour visit (US$2.50 round trip, admission to church and belfry included). If there are two or three of you it would be cheaper to hire a rowboat from the bathing establishment below the castle (US$2.50 an hour for three persons, US$1 kayaks for individuals). Avoid the boat

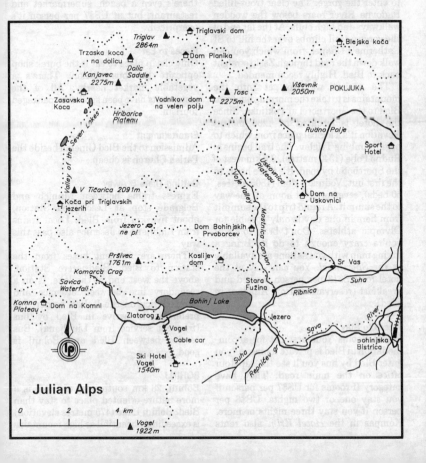

Julian Alps

0   2   4 km

rentals near the Park Hotel which are 50% more expensive. It's also quite feasible to swim across to the island from the beach at Zaka Camping, although you might not feel comfortable visiting the church in your bathing suit. In winter you can skate across the ice to the island.

An excellent half-day hike from Bled features a visit to the **Vintgar Gorge**. Begin by taking the Krnica bus from Bled to Zgornja-Gorje. From beside the 'Gostilna' opposite the church follow the signposted road through lovely alpine countryside to Vintgar (two km), where you pay US$0.50 to enter the gorge. The clear trout-filled Radovna River roars below the wooden walkways and high cliffs. At the far end of the gorge a trail climbs over the hill to St Catherine's Chapel, from which you can walk down the road through Zasip straight back to Bled. Highly recommended.

The easiest way to get into the mountains is to take the morning bus from Bled to the Sporthotel at Pokljuka. Since the hotel is situated at 1266 metres elevation it's a logical place from which to begin climbing Triglav. The trail begins at Rudno Polje (1340 metres), 2.5 km west of the Sporthotel by road. It's three hours to the first hut, Vodnikov dom (1805 metres, 50 beds), seven or eight hours all the way to the summit. A round trip to the summit from here in one day is only possible for Olympic athletes. Don't brag to us if you're crazy enough to do it! Bring a hiking map with you as none are available at the *Sporthotel*. You can stay at the hotel for US$13 per person for bed and breakfast (reservations from Alpetour in Bled).

Places to Stay
Private Rooms Your best bet for accommodation in Bled is private rooms. As you enter Bled by bus you'll see the Alpetour office on the main road. They have category II rooms for US$7 per person if you stay one or two nights, US$6 per person if you stay three nights or more. Kompas in the *Hotel Krim* also rents

private rooms for just a little more. Forget Bled's hotels which start at US$30 single.

Hostels The *Bled Youth Hostel*, Grajska cesta 17 (open year-round), is conveniently situated just up the hill from the bus station and the surroundings are nice, but it's hard to justify the US$8 overnight charge for bed and breakfast.

Camping *Camping Zaka* (open May to September) is in a quiet valley at the west end of Bled Lake about two km from Bled bus station. The location is good and there's even a beach, supermarket and restaurant, but at US$7 per person it's overpriced.

Places to Eat
Only cheap place to eat is the burek shop opposite the bus station. There's a vegetable market nearby. All of the restaurants have been spoiled by packaged tourism.

Entertainment
Admission to the Bled Cinema beside the Parish Church is cheap.

Getting There & Away
Express trains between Munich and Belgrade stop at Lesce-Bled Station, about five km from Bled. Local trains from Ljubljana to Jesenice also pass this way.

There are frequent buses from the station to Bled. Bled-jezero Station, above the west end of the lake, is on a secondary line between Jesenice and Nova Gorica on the Italian border. It's preferable to arrive in Bled by bus (frequent service from Ljubljana). Bus service between Bled and Bohinj is good.

BOHINJ
Bohinj, 28 km south-west of Bled, is a more nature-oriented place to stay than Bled. Bohinj Lake (475 metres elevation) is exceedingly beautiful as high mountains

rise directly from the basin-shaped valley. Secluded beaches for nude swimming are encountered off the trail along the north shore. There are many hiking possibilities out of Bohinj, including an ascent of Triglav. Bohinj often has a morning fog which clears before 12 noon.

Orientation

The area's main tourist centre is Jezero at the east end of the lake. A km north across the Sava River sits the old town, Stara Fuzina, at the mouth of the Mostnica Canyon. *Hotel Zlatorog* is at the west end of the lake near the campground and Vogel cable car.

Information

The Turist Biro is at Jezero.

Things to See

A footpath leads over the 'Devil's Bridge' and up the **Mostnica Canyon** into the Voje Valley just north of Stara Fuzina. The *Dom bohinjskih prvoborcev*, an hours' hike up this deep gorge from Stara Fuzina, is a beginning point for climbing Triglav. It costs US$5 per person to stay at the Dom.

The 'Zicnice Vogel' cable car, near the campground at the west end of Bohinj Lake, can carry you 1000 metres up into the mountains (US$3.50 one way, US$5 round trip, closed in November). From the *Ski Hotel* (1540 metres) on top you can scale **Mt Vogel** (1922 metres) in a couple of hours for a sweeping view of everything. Be careful in fog!

Places to Stay

Private Rooms The Turist Biro and Globtour, both at Jezero, have private rooms for US$6.50 per person for one or two nights, US$5 per person for three or more nights. Ask if there's anything cheaper if the first room they offer seems too expensive. Many houses here and in Stara Fuzina village bear *sobe* signs.

Camping Alternatively there's the *Zlatorog*

Campground (open May to September) at the west end of the lake. At US$7 per person it's expensive, but the location right on a lake beach is lovely and it's a good base for hiking.

Getting There & Away

Train The closest railway station is Bohinjska Bistrica on the Jesenice-Nova Gorica line, six km east of Jezero. This mountain railway is one of the most picturesque in Yugoslavia, but don't be in a hurry. To and from Italy you connect at Nova Goriza for Gorizia Centrale. To and from Austria you connect at Jesenice for Villach. The connections to Istria are bad.

Bus Istria and Ljubljana bound, you're better off taking a bus. Buses are fairly frequent between Bohinj and Ljubljana, covering the 83 km in two hours (US$2). These buses stop at Jezero then run right along the south shore of Bohinj Lake, terminating at the Hotel Zlatorog at the west end of the lake.

TREKKING TRIGLAV

The Julian Alps are one of the finest hiking areas in Eastern Europe. A mountain trip here is also an excellent way to meet young Yugoslavs, so take advantage of this opportunity if you're in the country in the hiking season. Mountain huts *(planinska koca)* are scattered throughout the range, normally less than five hours' walk apart. The huts in the higher regions are open from July to September, in the lower regions from June to October. No reservations are possible at the huts but the ones around Triglav become crowded on Friday and Saturday nights. A bed for the night shouldn't be over US$10 per person. Meals are also sold, so you don't need to carry a lot of gear. Leave most of your things below.

Warm clothes, sturdy boots and good physical condition are indispensable. Above 1500 metres you could encounter true winter weather conditions anytime. The best months to do it are August and

September. Keep to the trails well marked with red-white circles. Before you come pick up the *Bohinj Bled in Okolica* 1:50,000 excursion map or something similar at a bookstore. These maps are *sometimes* also available locally.

The circular three-day route described below is not the shortest nor the easiest way to climb Yugoslavia's highest mountain, but it is one of the most rewarding. Get hold of the booklet *How to Climb Triglav* or the brochure *An Alpine Guide* which provide infinitely more detail than can be included here.

The Route An hour's hike west of the Zlatorog Campground at Bohinj is the Savica Waterfall, source of the Sava River, which gushes from a limestone cave and falls 60 metres into a narrow gorge. From here a path zig-zags up the Komarca Crag. From the top of this cliff (1340 metres) there's an excellent view of the lake. Farther north, three hours from the falls, is the hut *Koca pri trigavskih jezerih* (1683 metres, 120 beds) at the south end of the fantastic Valley of the Seven Triglav Lakes. Spend the night here. If you're still keen and it's not too late you can climb nearby Mt Ticarica (2091 metres, one hour from the hut) for a sweeping valley view. The Komna Plateau to the south was a major WW I battlefield.

The next morning you hike up the valley past the largest glacial lakes, then north-east to the desert-like Hribarice Plateau (2358 metres). You descend to the Dolic saddle (2164 metres) where the hut *Trzaska koca na dolicu* (2120 metres, 60 beds, four hours from Koca pri trigavskih jezerih) offers a night's rest. You could well carry on to *Dom Planika* (2408 metres, 80 beds), 1½ hours beyond, although on weekends Dom Planika is packed. From this hut it's just over another hour to the summit of Triglav (2864 metres), a well-beaten path. If you decide to do the trip in reverse, Dom Planika is a seven-hour climb from Stara

Fuzina or about six hours from the Sporthotel, Pokljuka.

The way down passes the hut *Vodnikov dom na velem polju* (1805 metres, 50 beds), less than two hours from Dom Planika. There are two routes between Vodnikov dom and Stara Fuzina: down the Voje Valley or over the Uskovnica pasture. Uskovnika is a little longer but allows better views. The way to Rudno Polje and the Sporthotel, Pokljuka, branches off the Uskovnica route. Stara Fuzina (546 metres, four hours down from Vodnikov) is back near Bohinj Lake.

Istria

Istria, the wide peninsula just south of Trieste, Italy, has been a political basketball. Italy got Istria from Austria after WW I, then had to give it up to Yugoslavia after WW II. There's still a large Italian minority in Istria and their language is widely spoken. Marshall Tito also wanted Trieste as part of Yugoslavia, but in 1954 the Anglo-American occupiers returned the city to Italy so it wouldn't fall into the hands of the 'Communists.' Today the Koper-Piran strip belongs to Slovenia, the rest to Croatia.

The Istrian Riviera basks in the Mediterranean landscapes and climate for which the Yugoslav coast is famous. The long summer season from May to October attracts big crowds. This and the proximity to central Europe are its main drawbacks. Hordes of motorists from Italy, Yugoslavia, Austria, etc, vie with swarms of holiday-makers on cheap package tours from Britain. In midsummer all accommodation will be jammed and the police come down heavily on freelance campers. Industry and heavy shipping along the north side of Istria around Koper and Isola mean polluted waters. The farther south you go in Istria the quieter it gets with cleaner water, fewer cars, less industry and fewer

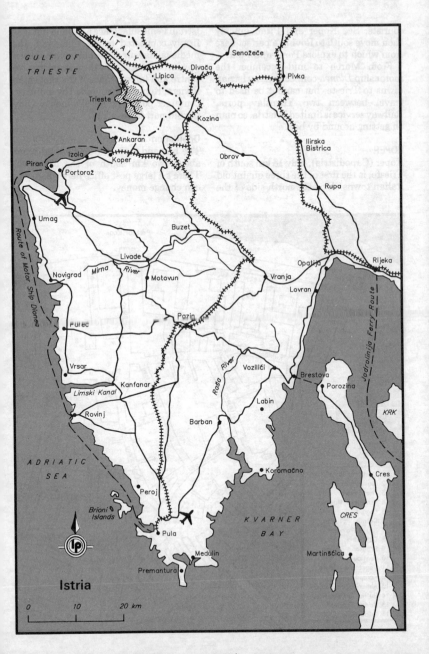

Istria

0   10   20 km

tourists. See Koper and Piran quickly then move south to Rovinj, a perfect base from which to explore Porec and Pula.

From March to mid-December the motor ship *Dionea* connects many Istrian towns to Trieste, but cannot be used to travel between two Yugoslav ports. Railway service is limited in Istria, so plan on getting around by bus.

KOPER

Koper (Capodistria), only 18 km south of Trieste, is the first of the three quaint old Italian towns along the north side of the Istrian Peninsula. Once an island but now firmly connected to the mainland, the medieval flavour of the old town has been preserved intact. Now the administrative centre and largest town of the Slovenian Riviera, Koper is surrounded by industry, container ports and developments. Only the old part is beautiful.

Orientation

The bus and train stations are adjacent about two km south of the old town. There's a large post office here where you can change money.

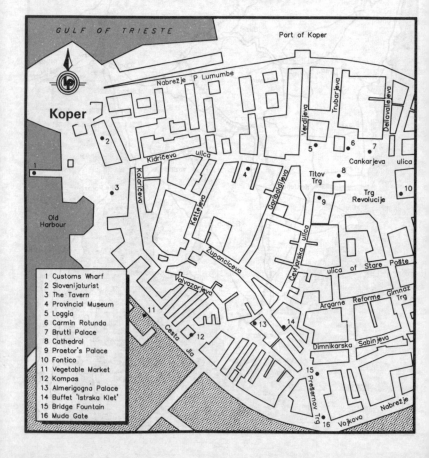

1 Customs Wharf
2 Slovenijaturist
3 The Tavern
4 Provincial Museum
5 Loggia
6 Carmin Rotunda
7 Brutti Palace
8 Cathedral
9 Praetor's Palace
10 Fontico
11 Vegetable Market
12 Kompas
13 Almerigogna Palace
14 Buffet 'Istrska Klet'
15 Bridge Fountain
16 Muda Gate

Information

Slovenijatourist is at Ukmarjev trg 7 opposite the small boat harbour.

Things to See

From the stations you enter Presernov trg through the **Muda Gate** (1516). Follow the crowd past the **Bridge Fountain** (1666) and up into Cevljarska ulica (Shoemakers' St), a narrow pedestrian street that opens onto Titov trg, Koper's historic central square.

Most of the things to see in Koper are clustered around the **Town Tower** (1480) on Titov trg, visible from afar. The 15th century **cathedral**, the **loggia** (1464) and the **Praetor's Palace** (1452) all belong to the Venetian Gothic style. The lower portion of the cathedral facade is Gothic, the upper part Renaissance. On the narrow lane beside the cathedral is an earlier building, the Romanesque **Carmin Rotunda** (1317). Trg Revolucije behind the cathedral contains several more old Venetian palaces.

The excellent **Provincial Museum** (Tuesday to Friday 9 am to 1 pm, Saturday 9 am to 12 noon) is in the Belgramoni-Tacco Palace on Kidriceva ulica between Titov trg and the small boat harbour. The museum features old maps and photos of the area, Italianate sculpture and copies of medieval frescoes.

Places to Stay

Slovenijatourist, Ukmarjev trg 7 opposite the small boat harbour, has private rooms at US$18 double. At these prices insist on something in the old town. The private rooms from Kompas, opposite the vegetable market, are even more expensive! Private rooms from the Slovenijatourist office in the railway station are far more expensive than those offered at the central office. There's no campground in Koper (see Izola below).

Places to Eat

The *Buffet 'Istrska klet,'* Zupanciceva ulica 39 just up from the Bridge Fountain, offers a filling US$3 set lunch weekdays (closed Saturday).

Getting There & Away

There are 15 daily buses from Trieste to Koper (US$1.25). To Ljubljana the train is more comfortable than the bus. There's an overnight train to Belgrade with couchettes available.

Getting Around

There's a bus about every half hour between Koper and Piran calling at Izola and Portoroz. This service terminates just outside the old harbour of Piran.

IZOLA

Izola between Koper and Piran is an active fishing town with its own cannery. The bus stops beside the old town which was once located on an island, hence the name.

Places to Stay

Autocamp Jadranka (open June to September) is conveniently located on the waterfront a km west of Izola (coming from Koper get off at the next stop after you see the tents). It costs US$5 per person. Unfortunately it's unbelievably noisy due to the adjacent highway. Unless it's very late you're better off going on to the campgrounds in Portoroz or Piran.

PORTOROZ

Portoroz (Port of Roses) is a bloated resort on a sandy bay five km south-east of Piran. Obala, the main drag, is a solid strip of hotels, restaurants, bars, travel agencies, shops, discos, parked cars, tourists and the occasional tree. There's even a casino for those with spare money to throw away.

Places to Stay

For private rooms try Generalturist, Obala 14, the Turist Biro, Obala 16, or Slovenijaturist, Obala 18. Kompas, Globtour and Kvarner Express are further west on Obala. Don't expect any bargains.

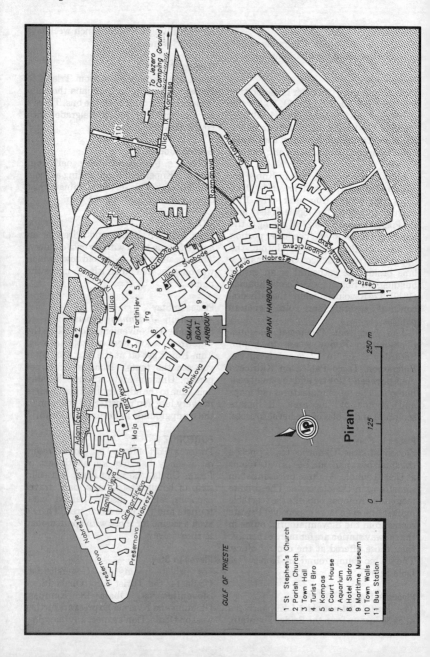

GULF OF TRIESTE

Piran

PIRAN HARBOUR

SMALL BOAT HARBOUR

Tartinijev Trg

To Jezero Camping Ground

0   125   250 m

1 St Stephen's Church
2 Parish Church
3 Town Hall
4 Turist Biro
5 Kompas
6 Court House
7 Aquarium
8 Hotel Sidro
9 Maritime Museum
10 Town Walls
11 Bus Station

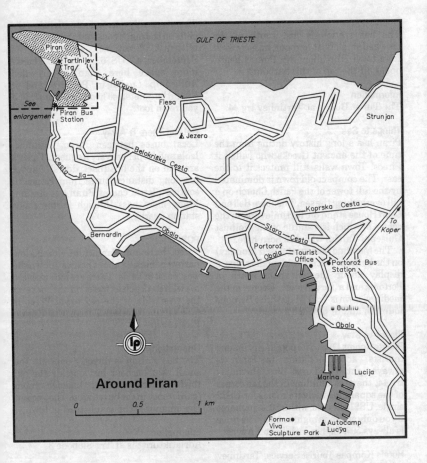

Around Piran

0   0.5   1 km

GULF OF TRIESTE

Piran
Tartinijev Trg
'X Korpusa
Fiesa
See enlargement
Piran Bus Station
Strunjan
Jezero
Belokriska Cesta
Jla
Cesta
Koprska Cesta
To Koper
Stara Cesta
Bernardin
Obala
Portorož
Obala
Tourist Office
Portorož Bus Station
Bushu
Obala
Marina
Lucija
Forma Viva Sculpture Park
Autocamp Lucija

From mid-May to mid-September there's *Autocamp Lucija*, beyond the marina at the south end of Portoroz. It's on the Seca Peninsula not far from the Forma Viva Sculpture Park (ask for the 'marina' bus stop). Not only is it extremely cramped but you can expect to pay US$12 per person to pitch a tent. In July and August it could be full.

Getting There & Away

The Portoroz bus station is in the middle of things just off the strip. In summer there's a hydrofoil service to Venice (US$35 one way).

PIRAN

Piran would be nice if it weren't for all the cars driving up and down looking for a parking place and the tourists consuming conspicuously at waterfront seafood restaurants. Set on a point at one extreme of the Istrian Peninsula, Piran has a distinct Italian air. If you can put up with a little bustle and noise, picturesque old Piran is still worth exploring.

Orientation

The bus station is just south of the crowded small boat harbour, an easy walk from town. Tartinijev trg, Piran's heart, opens off the top of this harbour.

Information

The Turist Biro is at Tartinijev trg 44.

Things to See

Piran has a long history dating from the time of the ancient Greeks who called it Pireos. Town walls still protect it to the east. The compact old town is dominated by the tall tower of the **Parish Church** on a hill overlooking the sea. The **Town Hall** and **Court House** stand on Tartinijev trg, in the centre of which is a statue of the violinist Guiseppi Tartini who was born here.

The **Maritime Museum** (closed Monday) on the harbour features old model ships, a display about the salt pans south of Portoroz and a Tartini room. Deeper in the medieval town is Trg 1 Maja with a Baroque fountain and **St Stephen's Church**.

Places to Stay

Private Rooms Due to its popularity among tourists, accommodation in Piran is always tight. The Turist Biro, Tartinijev trg 44, the pink building in the far corner of the square, has private rooms for US$9 single, US$13 double, with a 50% surcharge if you only stay one night or two. The price is always 50% higher in July and August.

Hotels Kompas Tourist Service, Tartinijev trg 10, has self-contained apartments for US$20 double, but they're fully booked all summer. The cheapest hotel is the *Sidro*, Tartinijev trg 14 (US$19 single, US$28 double with shower), overpriced but full anyway with Yugoslavs who pay a pittance. Remember that US$1.25 per person per night tax will be added to all accommodation charges in Piran/Portoroz.

Camping The only half way reasonable place to stay at Piran is *Camping Jezero* at Fiesa, a km or two east of the old town.

There's a really narrow footpath below the cliffs on the north coast or hike up over the hill (ask directions). Open May to September, it's US$6 per person. There's more space here than at crowded *Autocamp Lucija* in Portoroz and it should be quieter, so head for Jezero first if you're on foot.

Getting There & Away

Local buses between Piran, Portoroz, Izola and Koper are very frequent. Tickets are sold on the bus (back doors). Only a few long distance buses from Koper to southern Istria call at Piran bus station. Many more pass through Portoroz bus station nearby.

POREC

Porec, the Roman Parentium, sits on a low narrow peninsula about halfway down the west coast of Istria. There are many places to swim in the clear water off the rocks on the west side of the old town. Porec is quieter, more relaxed than the Koper/ Piran strip.

Orientation

The bus station is directly opposite the small boat harbour just outside the old town. There's a left luggage room *(garderoba)* in the bus station. The ancient Dekumanus is the main street of town.

Information

Adriatikturist is at Trg Slobode 3.

Things to See

There are many historic sites in the old town. The ruins of two **Roman temples** lie between Trg Marafor and the south end of the peninsula. Archaeology and history are featured in the four-floor **Regional Museum** in an old Baroque palace at Dekumanus 9 (captions in German and Italian).

The main reason to visit Porec however is to see the 6th century **Euphrasian Basilica** with its wonderfully preserved Byzantine mosaics. The capitals, sculpture and

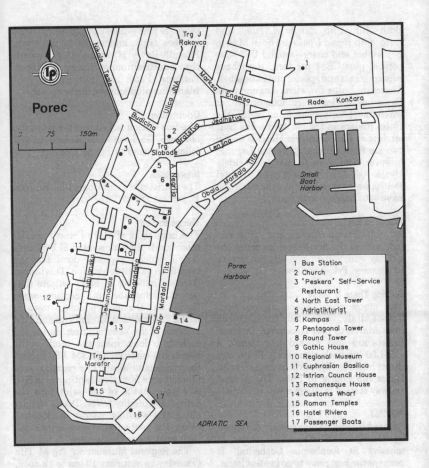

Porec

2   75   150m

Trg J Rakovca

Nikola Tesla

Marksa I Engelsa

Ulica JNA

Budicina

Hratstva I Jedinstva

Trg Slobode

V I Lenjina

A Negrija

Obala Maršala Tita

Rade Končara

Small Boat Harbor

Porec Harbour

Ljubljanska

Beogradska

Sekmunova

Obala Maršala Tita

Trg Marafor

ADRIATIC SEA

1 Bus Station
2 Church
3 'Peskera' Self–Service Restaurant
4 North East Tower
5 Adriatikturist
6 Kompas
7 Pentagonal Tower
8 Round Tower
9 Gothic House
10 Regional Museum
11 Euphrasian Basilica
12 Istrian Council House
13 Romanesque House
14 Customs Wharf
15 Roman Temples
16 Hotel Riviera
17 Passenger Boats

architecture are remarkable survivors of that distant period. Entry to the church is free and for a small fee you may visit the adjacent 4th century mosaic floor of an Early Christian basilica.

There are passenger boats every half hour to **Sveti Nikola**, the small island opposite Porec harbour, but it's crowded with expensive hotels and a bore.

Places to Stay

Accommodation in Porec is tight and the campgrounds far from the centre, so you might want only to stop off for the day on your way south.

Private Rooms Adriatikturist, Trg Slobode 3, rents private rooms for US$8 per person. If you only stay one to three nights there's a 30% surcharge. Kompas around the corner at A Negrija 4 has private rooms for similar prices. To all accommodation add US$1.50 per person per night 'residence tax.'

Camping There are two campgrounds at Zelena Laguna, six km south of Porec.

Both *Autocamp Zelena Laguna* and *Autocamp Bijela Uvala* are open May to September and charge around US$3 per person, plus US$4 per tent. Both have supermarkets and special nudist beaches. There are buses to Zelena Laguna from Porec bus station every hour or two, or catch the hourly boat from beside the Hotel Riviera in the old town. The boat landing at the Parentium Hotel is nearly two km from Autocamp Zelena Laguna, however, and even further from Bijela Uvala. Ask if the boat will go on to Hotel Delfin, which is closer. Take the bus if you have your luggage with you.

Places to Eat

At *Self-Service Restaurant 'Peskera,'* just outside the north-west corner of the old city wall, you dine on an open terrace in summer. Prices are low.

Getting There & Away

The motor ship *Dionea* arrives from Trieste, Italy, one to four times a week from March to mid-December. In Porec tickets are sold aboard but there's a US$1.50 embarkation tax. There are direct buses to Rijeka via Buzet or Pazin. Buses run hourly to Pula. The nearest railway station is 30 km away at Pazin.

ROVINJ

Relaxed Rovinj, its high peninsula topped by the great 57-metre-high tower of massive St Euphemia Cathedral, is perhaps the best place to go in all of Istria. Wooded hills punctuated with low-rise luxury hotels surround the town, while the 13 green offshore islands of the Rovinj archipelago make for varied views. The charming atmosphere of cobbled inclined streets in the old town is as picturesque as the others farther north, only the tourists are fewer and pedestrian precincts keep motorists under control. Still an active fishing port, you actually see local people leading normal lives! Private rooms are still expensive and the hotels prohibitive unless you're on a cheap package tour, but there are many quiet campgrounds on the beaches north and south of the town. Friendly Rovinj is just the place to escape the industrial/tourist frenzy of Koper, Portoroz, Porec and rest up for your island-hopping journey farther south.

Orientation

The bus station is just south-west of the old town. Go down to the waterfront and follow it around to Trg M Tita.

Information

The tourist office is at Obala Pino Budicin 12 just off Trg M Tita.

Things to See

The only sight of Rovinj worth special attention is the **Cathedral of St Euphemia** (1736), which completely dominates the town from its hilltop location. This largest Baroque building in Istria reflects that period during the 18th century when Rovinj was the most populous town in Istria, an important fishing centre and the bulwark of the Venetian fleet. Inside the cathedral don't miss the tomb of St Euphemia (martyred in 304 AD) behind the right-hand altar. The remains were brought here from Constantinople in 800. A copper statue of the saint tops the cathedrals' mighty tower. Take a wander along the winding narrow backstreets below the cathedral. Local artists sell their work along Grisia ulica.

The **Regional Museum** on Trg M Tita (Tuesday to Saturday 10 am to 12 noon, Sunday 7 to 9 pm, US$1 admission) contains an unexciting collection of paintings and a few Etruscan artefacts found in Istria. These might harbour some interest if the captions were in something more than Serbo-Croatian and Italian.

The **Franciscan Convent**, up the hill at E de Amicis 36, (weekdays 8 am to 10 am and 3 to 5 pm) also has a small museum. Better than either of these is the **Rovinj Aquarium** (established 1891), Obala Giordano Paliaga 5 (daily, US$1), which keeps a good collection of local marine life

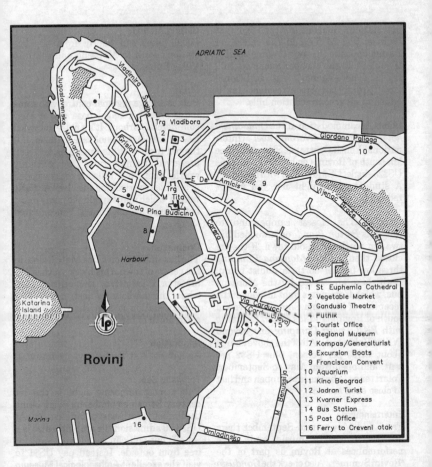

ADRIATIC SEA

Trg Vladibora

Giordano Paliaga

Jugoslavenske Mornarice

Vladimira Svalbe

Grisia

Trg M Tita

E De L'Amicis

Vijenac Brace Lorenzeto

Obala Pina Budicina

Harbour

Katarina Island

Rovinj

Via Carducci (Carducijevo)

M Benussija

Marina

Omladinska

1 St Euphemia Cathedral
2 Vegetable Market
3 Gandusio Theatre
4 Putnik
5 Tourist Office
6 Regional Museum
7 Kompas/Generalturist
8 Excursion Boats
9 Franciscan Convent
10 Aquarium
11 Kino Beograd
12 Jadran Turist
13 Kvarner Express
14 Bus Station
15 Post Office
16 Ferry to Crveni otak

from poisonous scorpion fish to colourful anemones.

When you've seen enough of town follow the waterfront south past the Park Hotel to **Punta Corrente Forest Park**. Here you can swim off the rocks, climb a cliff, or just sit and admire the offshore islands.

Excursion boats take tourists on half day scenic cruises to **Crveni otok** (US$4) or the **Lin Kanal** (US$7), with an hour ashore at the turn-around points. It's also possible to go to Crveni otok (Red Island) on the hourly ferry (US$2.50 round trip).

There's a frequent ferry to nearby **Katarina Island** (US$1.25 round trip).

Places to Stay

Private Rooms Many offices in Rovinj offer private rooms beginning at US$6 per person with a 30% surcharge for a stay of less than four nights. Pula and Porec are commuting distance from Rovinj so having to stay four nights may not be such a problem. Try Jadran Turist, Ulica Via Carducci 4 opposite the bus station, Kvarner Express on the harbour near the bus station, Generalturist and Kompas both on Trg M Tita in the centre, or Putnik opposite the tourist office nearby. If you're told the cheaper rooms are full, try another agency. An additional US$1.50 daily per person 'residence tax' is added to all accommodation bills.

Hotels Accommodation at the *Omladinski hotel 'Karavan – Naromtravel'* (International Youth Centre) at Skaraba, three km south of Rovinj (no bus service), runs US$25 single, US$40 double with breakfast. A student card might net you a 10% reduction.

Camping The closest campground to Rovinj is *Porton Biondi* on a wooded hill two km north of the old town. If they're closed there's *FKK Monsena Camping* three km farther north, a nudist camp. Both these are served by the Monsena bus, which terminates right in front of the reception of Monsena Camping. Five km south of Rovinj is *Villas Rubin Camping* with *FKK Polari Camping* just beyond (Villas Rubin bus). All of the above charge about US$3 per person, plus US$2 per tent, and open from May to September. Polari tends to be the first to open and last to close each season.

Entertainment
From mid-May to mid-September there are twice weekly music and stage performances at Rovinj as part of the 'Rovinj Summer.' Also check the *Gandusio Theatre* on Trg Valdibora or *Kino Beograd* on the harbour.

Getting There & Away
The motor ship *Dionea* shuttles between Rovinj and Trieste one to three times a week from March to mid-December. Fares are reasonable. The closest railway station is Kanfanar, 19 km away on the Pula-Divaca line. There's a bus from Rovinj to Pula every hour.

Getting Around
Local buses run hourly from the bus station, north to Monsena and south to Villas Rubin.

PULA
Pula is a large regional centre with some industry, a big naval base and a busy commercial harbour. It's a noisy, crowded city where you may not care to linger, but the old town with its museums and well preserved Roman ruins are certainly worth a visit. Near Pula are rocky wooded peninsulas overlooking the clear Adriatic waters, which may explain the many resort hotels and campgrounds concentrated there.

Orientation
The bus station is on Ulica Mate Balote in the centre of town. One block south is Trg bratstva i jedinstva, the central hub, while the harbour is just north. The railway station is near the water about a km north of town.

Information
Arenaturist is at Trg bratstva i jedinstva 4.

Things to See
Pula's most imposing sight is the 1st century **Roman amphitheatre** overlooking the harbour north-east of the old town. At US$2.50 admission the amphitheatre is a rip-off, but you can see all you want for free from outside. Instead pay US$1 to visit the excellent **Archaeological Museum** on the hill opposite the bus station (closed Sunday). All the captions are in Serbo-Croatian only but there's a lot to see. Behind the museum is the **Roman Theatre** while along the street facing the bus station are **Roman walls** which mark the east boundary of old Pula.

Follow these walls south and continue down Trg bratstva i jedinstva to the **Triumphal Arch of Sergius**. The street beyond the arch winds right around old Pula with several changes of names. Follow it to Trg Republike where you'll

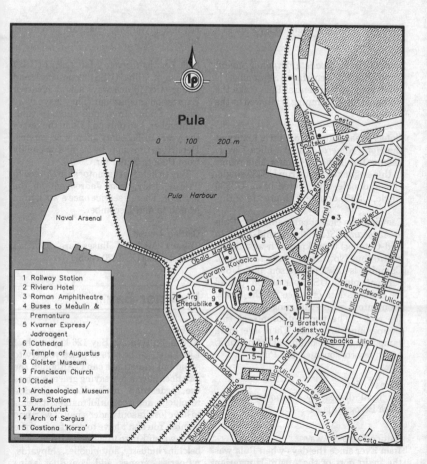

Pula

0   100   200 m

Pula Harbour

Naval Arsenal

1 Railway Station
2 Riviera Hotel
3 Roman Amphitheatre
4 Buses to Medulin &
   Premantura
5 Kvarner Express/
   Jadroagent
6 Cathedral
7 Temple of Augustus
8 Cloister Museum
9 Franciscan Church
10 Citadel
11 Archaeological Museum
12 Bus Station
13 Arenaturist
14 Arch of Sergius
15 Gostiona 'Korzo'

find the ancient **Temple of Augustus**. Above this square is the **Franciscan Church**. A museum (US$1) in the cloister of this church contains paintings, medieval frescoes, a Roman mosaic, etc.

Better value and not to be missed is the **National Revolution Museum** (US$0.30) in the 17th century Venetian citadel on a high hill in the centre of the old town. Aside from the exhibits, which deal mostly with the partisan struggle in WW II, the views of Pula from the citadel walls are unsurpassed.

Places to Stay

Private Rooms Arenaturist, Trg bratstva i jedinstva 4 a block from the bus station, has private rooms for US$8 per person with an additional 30% surcharge if you stay less than four nights. Other offices offering this service at similar rates are Slovenijaturist, Ulica Mate Balote 4, and Brioni Turist Biro, Ulica Jugoslavenske Narodne Armije 3, on opposite sides of the bus station, or Globtour, Trg bratstva i jedinstva 10. Actually, if you're going to stay four nights, you're better off getting a room in Rovinj and seeing busy Pula as a day trip.

Hostels The *Ljetovaliste Ferijalnog Saveza Youth Hostel* (open May to September) is three km south of central Pula (take the Verudela bus). Camping is allowed at the hostel.

Hotels Treat yourself to a little luxury at the *Hotel Riviera*, Splitska ulica 1 overlooking the harbour. Comfortable rooms in this elegant old hotel run US$27 single, US$36 double with shared bath, US$30 single, US$55 double with private bath.

Camping The closest campground to Pula is *Autocamp Stoja* (open mid-April to mid-October) three km south-west of the centre (bus No 1 Stoja to the terminus). Camping is US$3 per person, plus US$2 per tent, plus a US$1 per person 'police' fee. There's lots of space on the shady promontory with swimming possible off the rocks. The two restaurants at this campground are good. There are more campgrounds at Medulin and Premantura, beach resorts south-east of Pula.

Places to Eat
For local dishes try *Gostiona 'Korzo,'* Ulica Prvog maja 34.

Getting There & Away
Train Ever since the days when Pula was the main port of the Austro-Hungarian Empire the railway line in Istria has run north toward Italy and Austria instead of east toward what is now Yugoslavia. Most local trains terminate at Divaca near Trieste, where you connect for Ljubljana. Couchettes are available between Pula and Belgrade year-round, Pula and Zagreb in summer, saving you a night's accommodation.

Bus Buses to Rijeka are sometimes crowded, especially those continuing on to Zagreb, so reserve a seat a day in advance if you can. There are also direct buses to Split.

Boat For the ferry to Mali Losinj (US$7 one way), Silba (US$10 one way) and Zadar (US$13 one way) ask at Kvarner Express on the harbour. They leave daily except Friday from mid-June to mid-September, and only on Friday the rest of the year. In February there's no service. Departure time may be 5 am! You can fly from Pula to Zadar for US$16.

Buy tickets for the motor ship *Dionea* to Trieste, Italy, from Jadroagent on the harbour. There's service once a week from March to mid-December.

Getting Around
Tokens for city buses are sold at newsstands (US$0.20 each).

Kvarner Bay

RIJEKA
Rijeka, on Kvarner Bay 126 km south of Ljubljana, is the sort of place you try to avoid but sometimes can't. Although the city does have a few saving graces such as the pedestrian mall, Korzo narodne revolucije, and a colourful market, it seems to have lost its soul under a hail of wartime bombs. You don't have to dive far into the old town off Korzo to sense the decay. The belching industry, automobiles, shipyards, refineries, cranes and container ships jammed into the narrow coastal strip aren't beautiful. This largest of all Yugoslav ports does have a sort of crude energy, however, and if you like punishment Rijeka will give it to you.

Orientation
The bus station is on Trg Zabica below the Capuchin Church in the centre of town. The left luggage office in the bus station is often full up and they don't like backpacks anyway. If you get this story just take your bag to the larger *gardaroba*

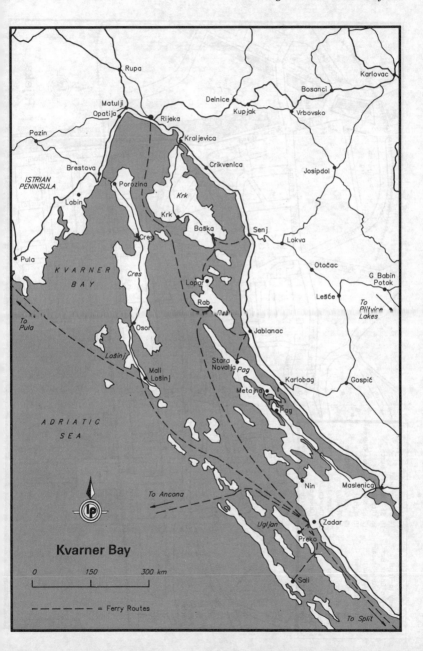

Kvarner Bay

0   150   300 km

– – – – = Ferry Routes

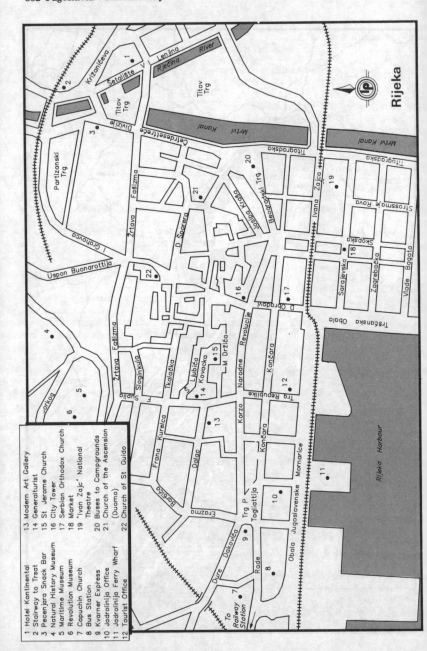

Rijeka

1 Hotel Kontinental
2 Stairway to Trsat
3 Pecenjara Snack Bar
4 Natural History Museum
5 Maritime Museum
6 Revolution Museum
7 Capuchin Church
8 Bus Station
9 Kvarner Express
10 Jadrolinija Office
11 Jadrolinija Ferry Wharf
12 Tourist Office
13 Modern Art Gallery
14 Generalturist
15 St Jerome Church
16 City Tower
17 Serbian Orthodox Church
18 Market
19 'Ivan Zajc' National Theatre
20 Buses to Campgrounds
21 Church of the Ascension (Duomo)
22 Church of St Guido

in the railway station, a seven-minute walk due west. The Jadrolinija ferry wharf (no left luggage) is just a few minutes east of the bus station. Korzo narodne revolucije runs east through the centre toward the filthy Rjecina River, once the border of Italy and Yugoslavia (the Italian name of the city, Fiume, means river).

Information

The tourist office is at Trg Republike 9 near the harbour.

Things to See

The **Modern Art Gallery**, Dolac 1 (closed Monday), is upstairs in the public library. The **Maritime Museum** and **National Revolution Museum** (both closed Sunday and Monday) are adjacent at Zrava fasizma 18 above the downtown. Bullet holes in the side of the Maritime Museum, the former governor's palace (1893), remind one of 1945.

If you have some time to kill **Trsat Castle**, on a high ridge overlooking Rijeka and the canyon of the River Rjecina, is your best bet. Get there on bus No 1 from town or climb the 559 steps up from the arch beside the Jugobanka Rijeka at the north end of Titov trg. In the Middle Ages the 13th century castle belonged to the Frankopan princes of Krk, but was completely remodelled by the Irish general Laval Nugent in the 19th century. Today it serves the Travel Industry. There's also a Franciscan Monastery (1453) at Trsat.

Places to Stay

Hotels & Private Rooms Rather than stay in depressing Rijeka you're better off catching an onward bus to Krk. If there's no choice the cheapest hotel is the old *Hotel Kontinental*, Setaliste V I Lenjina 1 (US$17 single, US$29 double for a room with shared bath). Kvarner Express, Trg P Togliattija 3, and Generalturist, F Supila 2, have private rooms for US$12 per person with a 30% discount if you can put up with Rijeka for four or more nights.

Add US$1 tax per person per night to all accommodation.

Camping There are two campgrounds outside Rijeka. *Preluk Camping* is beside the busy highway between Rijeka and Opatja (bus No 32). *Kostrena Camping* is 10 km east of the city on the road to Split, out near the oil refineries (bus No 10). Both suffer from traffic noise, charge US$3 per person, US$2 per tent plus tax and are unreliably open May to September. City buses to these campgrounds leave from Beogradski trg.

Places to Eat

Restoran Index, Ulica Borisa Kidrica 18 between the bus and railway stations, has a good self-service section *(samoposluzi)* with set 'menus' for breakfast, lunch and dinner (under US$2). It's cheap, clean and straightforward. A quick stand-up snack bar is *Pecenjara*, Titov trg 6 across the river from Hotel Kontinental.

Entertainment

Performances at the *'Ivan Zajc' National Theatre* (1885) are mostly drama in Serbo-Croatian, although opera and ballet are sometimes offered. The ticket office is open weekdays and Saturday morning.

Getting There & Away

Train Trains run from Rijeka to Ljubljana (via Postojna) with a change of trains at Pivka necessary on many services. Some trains to Zagreb have only 1st class seats. There's an overnight train to Belgrade with couchettes.

Bus There are 13 buses a day between Rijeka and Krk using the huge Tito Bridge. Buses to Pula, Koper, Ljubljana, Zagreb, Rab, Zadar and Split are also frequent.

Boat Jadrolinija, Obala jugoslovenske mornarice 16, sells tickets for the large coastal ferries between Rijeka and Dubrovnik from mid-April to mid-October. Fares run US$19 to Split, US$23 to Dubrovnik. Some of these ships go on to Corfu, Greece. This ship is also supposed to call at Rab (US$7), but if there's 'fog' (ie not enough passengers to drop off or pick up) they cancel the stop without notice and leave you holding your bags.

The southbound ferries leave Rijeka at 6 pm several times a week. Since the ships travel between Rijeka and Split at night you're better off boarding in Split and travelling south to Dubrovnik if you want to see anything. Or buy a through ticket from Rijeka to Dubrovnik or Corfu and have the purser validate your ticket for a stopover in Split.

KRK

Krk, Yugoslavia's largest island (409 square km), is barren and rocky with little vegetation. It's the first main Adriatic island you come to on the way south and it's *on* the beaten tourist track. Since completion of the Tito Bridge it has suffered too rapid development. Still, the main town Krk is rather picturesque and the camping facilities are good.

Orientation

The bus from Baska and Rijeka stops just outside the old walls of Krk town.

Information

There's a Turist Biro or Kvarner Express.

Things to See

The **Frankopan Castle** and lovely 12th century Romanesque **cathedral** are in the lower town near the harbour. In the upper part of Krk are three old monastic churches. The narrow streets are worth exploring if you can ignore the hordes from Stuttgart and Manchester.

Places to Stay

Private Rooms Kvarner Express on the harbour has private rooms for US$14 double plus a 50% surcharge for less than three nights. Similar rooms can be had from the Turist Biro in the unmarked white building a few hundred metres west on the waterfront.

Camping There are three campgrounds. The closest is *Camping Jezevac* on the coast a 10-minute walk south-west of town. The rocky soil makes it nearly impossible to use tent pegs, but there are lots of stones to anchor your lines. There's good shade and places to swim. *Camping Bor* is on a hill inland from Jezevac, while *Camping Politin FKK* is a naturist camp south-east of Krk.

Getting There & Away

Thirteen buses a day to and from Rijeka make Krk the perfect escape from that city. En route the bus crosses the massive Tito Bridge. Bus service from Krk to Baska (20 km, one hour) is also good.

BASKA

Baska, at the south end of Krk Island, is a popular resort with a long sandy beach set below a high ridge. Most of the buses from Rijeka to Krk go on to Baska and you might consider going all the way if swimming and scenery are your main interests. These are better at Baska than Krk.

Orientation

The bus from Krk stops at the edge of the old town between the beach and the harbour. To reach the Lopar ferry follow the street closest to the water through the old town south-east less than a km.

Places to Stay

Private Rooms The tourist office, Zvonimirova 114 just up the street from the bus stop, has private rooms for US$14 double (plus 30% if you stay less than four nights).

Camping There are two camping possibilities. *Camping Zablace* (open May to September) is on the beach visible southwest of the bus stop (look for the rows of caravans). In heavy rain you could get flooded here. A better bet is *FKK Camping*

Bunculuka (open May to September) over the hill east of the harbour (a 15-minute walk). It's quiet, shady and convenient to the ferries and town.

Getting There & Away
In summer (June to August) there are car ferries from Baska direct to Senj on the mainland between Rijeka and Zadar. The ferry from Baska to Lopar on Rab Island operates about three times a day from June to September (US$2). The rest of the year you could be forced to backtrack to Rijeka to get further south.

RAB
Rab Island, near the centre of the Kvarner Island Group, is one of the most enticing in the Adriatic. The north-east side of Rab is barren and rocky, the south-west side fairly green with pine forests. The high mountains protect Rab from the colder northern and eastern winds. Medieval Rab town is built on a narrow peninsula pointing south enclosing a sheltered harbour. The old stone buildings climb from the harbour to a cliff overlooking the sea.

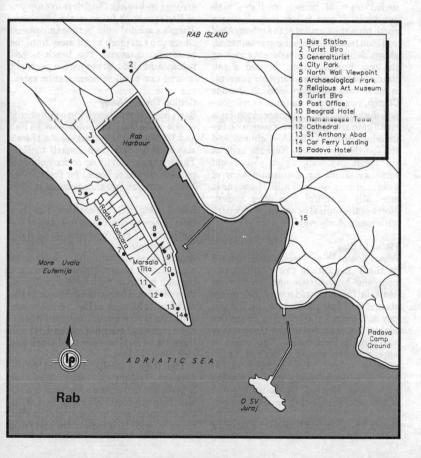

1 Bus Station
2 Turist Biro
3 Generalturist
4 City Park
5 North Wall Viewpoint
6 Archaeological Park
7 Religious Art Museum
8 Turist Biro
9 Post Office
10 Beograd Hotel
11 Namanasque Tenti
12 Cathedral
13 St Anthony Abad
14 Car Ferry Landing
15 Padova Hotel

RAB ISLAND

Rab Harbour

Rade Koncara

More Uvala Eufemija

Marsala Tita

Padova Camp Ground

ADRIATIC SEA

Rab

O SV Juraj

Orientation

The bus station is near the harbour, a five-minute walk from the old town. The large Jadrolinijna ferries tie up near the Beograd Hotel in the old town.

Information

The Turist Biro has two branches, one near the bus station (look carefully, it's badly marked but stays open all day) and another on Marsala Tita in the old town.

Things to See

Four tall church towers rise above the red-roofed mass of houses on Rab's high peninsula. If you follow Rade Koncara north from the **Convent of St Anthony Abad** you soon reach the Romanesque **cathedral**, alongside a pleasant belvedere overlooking the sea. Further along, beyond a tall Romanesque tower and another convent, is a second belvedere and **St Justine Church**, now a small museum of religious art. Just past the next chapel look for a small gate giving access to a park with the foundations of Rab's oldest church and the fourth tower. Rade Koncara ends at the north city wall, which you should certainly climb for a splendid view of town, harbour, sea and hill. The scene is especially beautiful just after sunset. North of the wall is the extensive city park with many shady ways.

Places to Stay

Private Rooms Private rooms are dispensed by the Turist Biro at two locations, one near the bus station and another on Marsala Tita in the old town. Their prices start at US$7 per person plus tax, but you pay 30% more if you only stay one or two nights. Generalturist on the harbour may also have private rooms. You could be approached by women at the bus station offering *sobes*. They've been rather spoiled by overspending tourists and the high rates charged by hotels, tourist offices, etc, so expect to have to bargain.

Hotels The cheapest hotel is the *Beograd*

on the harbour in the old town. The second-rate orchestra they have playing in the restaurant could keep you awake but the rooms are reasonable, US$14 single, US$23 double with breakfast in June and September, US$20 single and US$36 double in July and August (hotel closed other months). Full board at the Beograd is only about US$4 per person extra!

Camping If that's all too expensive stroll south along the waterfront about 25 minutes to *Autocamp Padova* (US$3 per person, US$2 per tent) at Banjol. If you're arriving by bus ask the driver to drop you at *Restaurant St Lucia* on the hill above. There's a wooded ridge by the campground where you can pitch a tent away from the noise and caravans. The beach is just below. Add US$1.20 per person per night 'tourist tax' to all accommodation rates.

Getting There & Away

Bus The most reliable way to come or go is on one of the two daily buses between Rab and Rijeka. In the tourist season there's also a direct bus from Zagreb to Rab. These services can fill up so book ahead if possible. If you're bound for the Plitvice Lakes from Rab you change buses at Senj.

Boat Getting to Rab is not easy. The ferry from Baska on Krk Island to Lopar at the north end of Rab operates thrice daily June to September only. From June to August there are ferries from Senj on the mainland to Lopar. Unless you're on a through bus to or from Rijeka or Zagreb the year-round ferry from Jablanac on the mainland to Misnjak on Rab is problematic. Jablanac is four km off the main Rijeka-Split highway (downhill all the way) and there are no local buses from Misnjak into Rab town (11 km).

The large Jadrolinija coastal ferries between Dubrovnik and Rijeka are supposed to call at Rab a few times a week and this would certainly be the best, if not the cheapest way to come, *except* that they arrive in the middle of the night and don't stop at all if the captain decides there aren't enough passengers waiting to make it worth his trouble (ie there's 'fog'). The ships' agents at Rab are Kvarner Express but their information about schedules can be way off, so take care.

LOPAR

The bus stop in Lopar is a few hundred metres up the road from the ferry landing. It's unmarked so ask. There's a bus every hour or two to Rab town. *Camping Rajska Plaza* (San Marino) is about four km south of the Lopar ferry landing, across the peninsula.

Dalmatia

Dalmatia occupies the central portion of the Yugoslav Adriatic coast from Zadar to Kardeljevo, offshore islands included. In ancient times' this was an important Roman province. In the 6th century Slavic tribes arrived and in the early 15th century Venice purchased it from the Croatian king Ladislas. Historical relics abound in towns like Zadar, Sibenik, Trogir, Split, Hvar and Korcula, framed by a striking natural beauty of barren slopes, green valleys and clear water. Although not unexplored, Dalmatia is less touristed than overcrowded Istria and Dubrovnik.

ZADAR

Zadar (Zara), the main city of northern Dalmatia, occupies a long peninsula between the harbour and the Zadar Channel. The city of Iader was laid out by the Romans, who left behind considerable ruins. Later the area fell under Byzantium which explains the centrally-planned Orthodox churches. In 1409 Venice took Zadar from Croatia and held it for four centuries. Dalmatia was included in the Austro-Hungarian Empire during most of the 19th century, with Italy exercising control from 1918 to 1943.

Badly damaged by Anglo-American bombing raids in 1943-1944, much of the city had to be rebuilt. Luckily the original street plan was respected and an effort made to harmonise the new with what remained of old Zadar. Although the scars of war are still painfully visible, the narrow traffic-free stone streets are full of life and Zadar can be a fascinating place to wander. Tremendous 16th century fortifications still shield the city on the landward side and high walls run along the harbour. None of the various museums are exceptional and the monuments show signs of wear, but Zadar is surprising for its variety of sights. It is also famous for its Maraska cherry liqueur.

Orientation

Narodni trg is the heart of Zadar. Long distance buses from places like Rijeka, Zagreb and Split stop at the central bus station between the walls of the old town and the harbour, very convenient to everything. The railway station is a km south-east of the harbour and old town. The local bus station, with services to nearby villages such as Nin, is adjacent to the railway station.

Information

Sunturist is on Narodni trg.

Things to See

The main things to see are near circular **St Donatus Church**, a 9th century Byzantine structure built over the Roman forum. The outstanding **Museum of Church Art** (closed Monday) in the Benedictine Monastery opposite offers a substantial display of reliquaries and religious paintings. The obscure lighting deliberately recreates the environment in which the objects were originally kept. The 13th century **Cathedral of St Anastasia** nearby never really recovered from wartime destruction. The **Franciscan Monastery** a few blocks away is more cheerful. A large Romanesque cross in the treasury behind the sacristy is worth seeing.

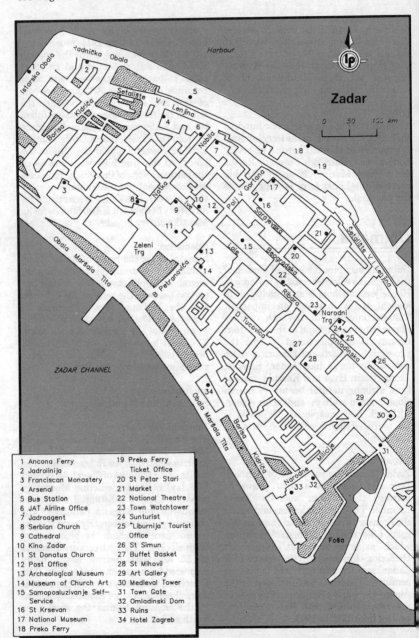

Zadar

0   50   100 km

1   Ancona Ferry
2   Jadrolinija
3   Franciscan Monastery
4   Arsenal
5   Bus Station
6   JAT Airline Office
7   Jadroagent
8   Serbian Church
9   Cathedral
10 Kino Zadar
11 St Donatus Church
12 Post Office
13 Archeological Museum
14 Museum of Church Art
15 Samoposluzivanje Self—
    Service
16 St Krsevan
17 National Museum
18 Preko Ferry
19 Preko Ferry
    Ticket Office
20 St Petar Stari
21 Market
22 National Theatre
23 Town Watchtower
24 Sunturist
25 "Liburnija" Tourist
    Office
26 St Simun
27 Buffet Basket
28 St Mihovil
29 Art Gallery
30 Medieval Tower
31 Town Gate
32 Omladinski Dom
33 Ruins
34 Hotel Zagreb

Other museums include the **Archaeological Museum** (closed Monday) across from St Donatus and the **Ethnological Museum** in the Town Watchtower (1562) on Narodni trg. More interesting is the **National Museum** on Poljana V Gortana just inside the Sea Gate. This excellent historical museum features scale models of Zadar from different periods and old paintings and engravings of many coastal cities. Upstairs there's a display on the activities of the partisans. The same admission ticket will get you into the local **Art Gallery**. Unfortunately the captions in all of Zadar's museums are in Serbo-Croatian only.

Any of the many travel agencies around town can supply information on the daily tourist cruise to the **Kornati Islands** (US$25 including lunch). As this is about the only way to see these beautiful islands it's worthwhile if you can spare the cash, but the trips are cancelled during bad weather and all winter.

Places to Stay

Private Rooms Finding a place to stay in Zadar is usually no problem. If you're arriving by bus you'll probably be offered a private room before your pack hits the pavement. If not head for Narodni trg and the Sunturist office or 'Liburnija' at Omladinska ulica 1 around the corner, both of which offer private rooms for US$7 per person plus a 30% surcharge if you stay less than four nights. Women offering private rooms on the street outside don't levy this surcharge and are willing to bargain.

Hostels The *Borik Youth Hostel* (open May to mid-October) is on the coast a few km north-west (ask for 'Ferjalni savez Hevatake').

Hotels *Hotel Zagreb* on the promenade is US$25 single, US$40 double for a room with private bath and breakfast.

Camping *Autocamp Borik* (open May to September, US$3 per person, US$2 per tent) is near a large hotel complex four km north-west of Zadar. There's even a beach! Buses No 5 and 8 pass both hostel and autocamp.

Autocamp Punta Bajlo is on a quiet shady headland overlooking the sea 2.5 km south-east of the old town (bus No 2). It's walking distance from the railway station: turn left toward the sea and ask directions after a block or two. Camping is US$3 per person, US$2 per tent (May to September).

Places to Eat

The cheapest and easiest place to eat is *Samoposluzivanje Self-Service* in the passage at Beogradska 9 (open daily). The restaurant in the train station is also good.

Entertainment

Zadar is not an outstanding cultural centre and the action on the streets is likely to be more lively than that on stages. At night the old town really comes to life! Small bars like *Buffet Basket*, Tucovica 4, buzz till midnight. You can always check the shabby *National Theatre* to see if there's anything doing and *Omladinski Dom*, where rock concerts sometimes occur. You'll probably have to settle for a movie at *Kino Zadar*, however.

Getting There & Away

Train & Bus Couchettes are available from Zadar to Zagreb and Belgrade. Otherwise train service out of Zadar is bad, usually involving an uncoordinated change of trains at Krin. Instead catch one of the frequent buses to Rijeka, Zagreb (via the Plitvice Lakes), or Split.

Boat Lots of ferries call at Zadar. From Zadar there are weekly ferries to Rimini (US$38), Ancona (US$38), Trieste (US$45) and Bari (US$47). These large Italian ships of the Adriatica Line are quite luxurious but in July and August fares are up to 50% higher. The Pula ferry leaves daily except Wednesday from mid-June to mid-September, then Wednesday only most of the rest of the year, with a stop at Mali Losinj. For information on services to Ancona (Italy) and Pula contact Jadroagent on Ulica Natka Nobila just inside the city walls.

Jadrolinija, Radnicka obala 7 on the harbour, sells tickets for the coastal ferry to Rijeka, Split, Dubrovnik, etc, operating mid-April to mid-October. This ship usually departs Zagreb just after midnight in both directions. Almost once an hour year-round there's a small car ferry from Pier 7, Zadar, to Preko on Ugljan Island (US$1 one way), a nice trip to put in the time. Tickets are sold at the kiosk opposite Pier 7. The shortest ferry route is the rowboat ride across the harbour from the bus station to the Maraska seawall (US$0.15).

TROGIR

Trogir, a lovely medieval town on the coast just 20 km west of Split, is well worth a day trip from Split or a stop if you're coming down from Zadar. The old town occupies a tiny island in the narrow channel between Ciovo Island and the mainland, just off the coastal highway. Many sights are seen on a 15-minute walk around the island which bears Trogir.

Orientation

The heart of the old town is a few minutes' walk from the bus station. After crossing the small bridge near the station go through the North Gate. Trogir's finest sights are around Narodni trg, slightly left and ahead.

Information

The Turist Biro opposite the cathedral sells a map of the area for US$0.15.

Things to See

The glory of the **cathedral** on Narodni trg is the Romanesque portal of Adam and Eve

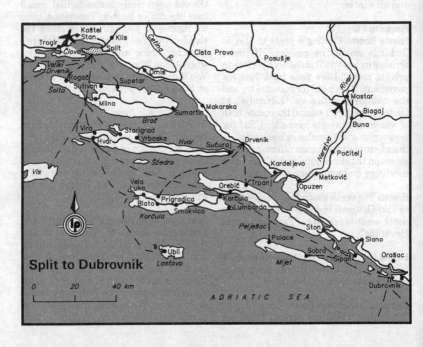

Split to Dubrovnik

0   20   40 km

ADRIATIC   SEA

(1240) by Master Radovan, which you can admire for free anytime. Enter the building through an obscure back door to see the perfect Renaissance Chapel of St Ivan, choir, pulpit, ciborium and treasury. You can even climb the cathedral tower for a delightful view. Also on Narodni trg are the **Town Hall** with an excellent Gothic staircase and the Renaissance loggia.

Places to Stay

Private Rooms If you'd like to stay at Trogir the Turist Biro opposite the cathedral has private rooms for US$10 single, US$14 double, less 30% if you stay longer than four nights.

Camping *Autocamp 'Soline'* is a few minutes walk from Trogir bus station. If it's too noisy there's *Camping Rozac* on Ciovo Island (connected to Trogir by a bridge), a half hour walk from Trogir bus station or take the Okrug bus. *Medena Camping* is just off the highway to Zadar about four km west of Trogir. All these charge US$3 per person, US$3 per tent.

Getting There & Away

Southbound buses from Zadar will drop you here; getting a bus north from Trogir can be more difficult as they often arrive full from Split. City bus No 37 runs between Trogir and Split every 20 minutes throughout the day, with a stop at Split airport en route.

SPLIT

Split (Spalato), the largest Yugoslav city on the Adriatic coast, is the heart of Dalmatia. The old town is built around the harbour on the south side of a high peninsula sheltered from the open sea by many islands. Ferries to these islands are constantly coming and going. The entire west end of the peninsula is a vast wooded mountain park while industry and the ugly commercial/military port are mercifully situated far enough away, inland and on the north side of the peninsula. The high coastal mountains set against the blue Adriatic provide a striking frame to the scene.

Split attained fame when the Roman emperor Diocletian (245-313), famous for his persecution of early Christians, had his retirement palace built here from 295 to 305 AD. After his death the great stone palace continued to be used as a retreat by Roman rulers. When the nearby colony Salona was abandoned in the 7th century many of the refugees barricaded themselves behind the high palace walls where their descendants live to this day.

First Byzantium then Croatia controlled the area, but from the 12th to 14th centuries medieval Split enjoyed a large measure of autonomy which favoured its development. The western portion of the old town around Narodni trg dates from this time and became the focus of municipal life while the area within the palace walls proper continued as the ecclesiastical centre.

In 1420 the Venetians conquered Split and this led to a slow decline. During the 17th century strong walls were built around the city as a defence against the Turks. In 1797 the Austrians arrived and with only a brief interruption during the Napoleonic wars they remained until 1918.

Since 1945 Split has grown into a major industrial city with large apartment-block housing areas. Much of old Split remains however and combined with the exuberant nature makes it one of the most fascinating cities in Europe.

Orientation

The bus, train and ferry terminals are adjacent to one another on the east side of the harbour, a short walk from the old town. Don't leave your pack in left luggage at the bus station where they charge foreigners double. Instead walk 100 metres toward town and patronise the railway station *gardaroba* which has fixed prices and is open non-stop. Titova obala, the waterfront promenade, is your best central reference point in Split.

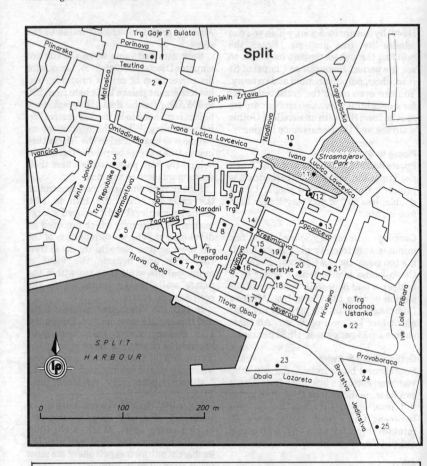

1	Croatian National Theatre	14	West Palace Gate
2	Bastion Self-Service Restaurant	15	Temple of Jupiter
3	Dalmacija Concert Hall	16	Slavija Hotel
4	Ero Restaurant	17	Basement Halls of Palace
5	Dalmacijaturist	18	Vestibule
6	JAT Office	19	Peristyle
7	Tourist Office	20	Cathedral
8	Central Hotel	21	East Palace Gate
9	Ethnological Museum	22	Market
10	National Revolution Museum	23	Airport Bus Stop
11	Statue of Gregorius of Nin	24	Adria Airlines
12	North Palace Gate	25	Bus & Train Stations
13	Town Museum		

Information

The tourist office is at Titova obala 12. The British Consulate is at Titova obala 10.

Things to See

There's much more to see than can be mentioned here so pick up a local guidebook if you're staying longer than a day or two. The old town is a vast open air museum made all the more interesting by the everyday life still going on throughout.

Diocletian's Palace facing the harbour is one of the most imposing extant Roman ruins anywhere. It was built as a strong rectangular fortress with walls 215 by 180 metres long and reinforced by towers. The imperial residence, temples and mausoleum were south of the main street connecting the east and west gates.

Enter through the central ground floor of the palace at Titova obala 22. On the left you'll see the excavated basement halls (US$0.50), empty but impressive. Continue through the passage to the **Peristyle**, a picturesque colonnaded square, the neo-Romanesque cathedral tower rising above. The **vestibule**, an open dome above the ground floor passageway at the south end of the Peristyle, is overpowering. On the east side of the Peristyle is the **cathedral**, originally Diocletian's mausoleum. The Romanesque wooden doors (1214) and stone pulpit are worth noting. You may climb the tower for a small fee. A lane off the Peristyle opposite the cathedral leads to the **Temple of Jupiter**, now a baptistry.

The west palace gate opens onto medieval Narodni trg, dominated by the 15th century Gothic former Town Hall, now the **Ethnological Museum** (closed Sunday). Trg Preporoda between Narodni trg and the harbour contains the surviving north tower of the 15th century Venetian garrison castle which once extended to the waters' edge. The east palace gate leads into the market area.

In the Middle Ages noblemen and rich merchants built residences within the old palace walls, one of which, the Papalic Palace, Papaliceva 5, is now the **Town Museum**. Through the northern palace gate is the powerful statue of 10th century Slavic religious leader Gregorius of Nin by Ivan Mestrovic (1929). The **National Revolution Museum**, housed in the nearby former City Hospital (1872) at I L Lavcevica 15, recalls wartime partisan activities through photos.

Split's least known yet most interesting museum is the **Naval Museum** (open 9 am to 12 noon, closed Monday, free) in Gripe Fortress (1657) on a hilltop east of the old town. The large exhibit of wartime maps, photos, artefacts and scale models is fascinating, but unfortunately all of the captions are in Serbo-Croatian. Also worth the walk is the **Archaeological Museum**, Zrinjsko-Frankopanska 25 north of town (open mornings only, closed Monday). The best of this valuable collection first assembled in 1820 is in the garden outside. The items in the showcases inside the museum building would be a lot more interesting if the captions were in something more than Serbo-Croatian.

The other Split museums are west of the old town. The **Museum of Croatia** on Setaliste Mose Pijade (closed Monday) looks impressive outside but inside the lack of captions legible to anyone other than Yugoslavs makes it hardly worth seeing. Some of the exhibits appear to be replicas but it doesn't really matter since you don't know what you're looking at anyway! A welcome contrast to this neglect is encountered at the **Mestrovic Gallery**, Setaliste Mose Pijade 46 (daily 9 am to 6 pm). Here you see a well arranged collection of works by Yugoslavia's premier modern sculptor, Ivan Mestrovic, who built the gallery as a personal residence in 1931-39. Bus No 12 passes the gate. There are beaches on the south side of the peninsula below the gallery.

From the Mestrovic Gallery it's possible to hike straight up **Marjan Hill**. Go up Kersovani ulica on the west side of the gallery and keep straight up the stairway and cement driveway to Put Meja ulica.

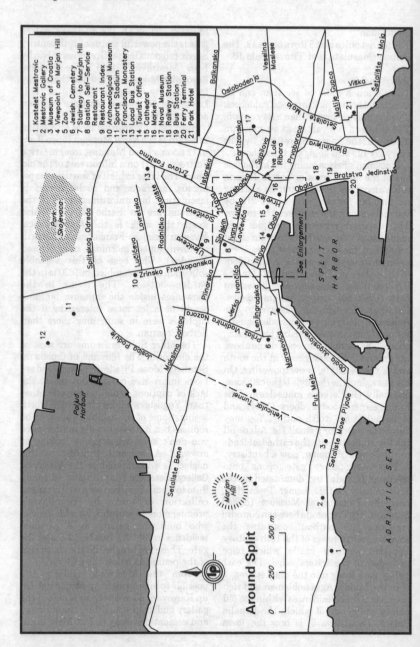

1 Kastelet Mestrovic
2 Mestrovic Gallery
3 Museum of Croatia
4 Viewpoint on Marjan Hill
5 Zoo
6 Jewish Cemetery
7 Stairway to Marjan Hill
8 Bastion Self–Service
9 Restaurant Index
10 Archaeological Museum
11 Sports Stadium
12 Franciscan Monastery
13 Local Bus Station
14 Tourist Office
15 Cathedral
16 Market
17 Naval Museum
18 Railway Station
19 Bus Station
20 Ferry Terminal
21 Park Hotel

Around Split

0   250   500 m

Turn left and walk west to Put Meja 76. The trail begins on the west side of this building. Marjan Hill offers trails through the forest, viewpoints, old chapels and the local zoo.

Places to Stay

Private Rooms Because it doesn't live only from tourism Split is somewhat cheaper than the other Adriatic resorts. The best budget accommodation is *zimmers* offered by women who look for clients around the bus and railway stations. Aside from the peak summer season you can bargain about the price, but rooms tend to be rather basic and outside the city centre. They typically cost around US$5 per person. Better, more convenient rooms are available from the tourist office, Titova obala 12, and Dalmacijaturist, Titova obala 5. Prices begin at US$10 single, US$15 double, less 30% if you stay four nights or more.

Hotels The cheapest hotels are the ageing *Central Hotel*, Narodni trg 1 opposite the Ethnographical Museum (US$23 single, US$31 double with shared bath), and the quieter *Slavija Hotel*, Buvinova 3 (US$27 single, US$37 double with shared bath, US$31 single, US$44 double with private bath). Both these are in the old town.

If you're willing to pay that, however, you're much better off at the *Park Hotel*, Setaliste 1 Maja 15 (US$39 single, US$47 double with private bath). This attractive resort hotel is a 10-minute walk from the old town, but more convenient to the bus/railway stations and the beach.

Camping The nearest campground is at Trstenik, five km east near the beach (buses No 7 or 17).

Places to Eat

The cheapest place in town is *Restaurant Index*, a self-service at Ujeviceva 10. Better fare for only a little more is available at *Bastion Self-Service*, Marmontova 9 (open daily). The *Ero Restaurant*, Marmontova 3, offers local specialties.

Entertainment

In summer you'll probably find the best evening entertainment in the small streets of the old town or along the waterfront promenade. In winter opera and ballet is presented at the *Croatian National Theatre* (1893), Trg Gaje Bulata. For concerts check the *Dalmacija Concert Hall*, Trg Republike 1 beside *Kino Marjan* (box office weekdays 10 am to 12 noon, 5 to 9 pm, Saturday 9 am to 12 noon).

Getting There & Away

Air The Adria Airlines office faces the waterfront near the railway station, while JAT Airlines is at Titova obala 9.

Train There are overnight trains from Split to Zagreb and Belgrade. Some of the day trains to Zagreb have only 1st class seats. For railway tickets and couchette reservations go to Croatia Express beside the train station. Couchettes are inexpensive.

Bus Advance bus tickets with seat reservations are recommended. There are through buses almost hourly to Titograd, Dubrovnik, Sarajevo, Zagreb and Rijeka.

Boat Two offices in the large Marine Terminal opposite the bus station sell tickets for all ferries. Jadrolinija handles year-round services to Supetar on Brac Island (US$2), with frequent daily departures. There are also daily ferries year-round to Hvar, Vira, or Stari Grad on Hvar Island (US$3), Rogac on Solta Island and Vela Luka on Korcula Island (US$4). Jadrolinija also runs the big coastal ferry from Rijeka to Dubrovnik calling at Rab, Hvar and Korcula (mid-April to mid-October). The southbound ferry trip to Dubrovnik (eight hours) is highly recommended, although several times more expensive than the bus. This ship usually leaves Split at 8 am southbound and 7 pm northbound, but it's not always daily so check the schedule at a travel agency beforehand. Some services go on to Greece.

Large Italian ferryboats of the Adriatica Line connect Split to Pescara (US$40), Ancona (US$40), Trieste (US$45), Venice (US$45) and Bari (US$45) weekly. Fares are up to 50% higher in July and August. Tickets for these are available from Jadroagent in the Marine Terminal.

Getting Around
Airport Transport The bus to Split Airport leaves from Obala Lazareta 3, a five-minute walk from the above mentioned terminals.

Public Transport Line up for city bus tickets at one of the very few kiosks around town which sells them. Newsstands don't have these tickets. For Trogir buy a zone 3 ticket. Solin and Trstenik are zone 1. Validate the ticket once aboard. You can

also pay the driver but that costs double. There's a US$10 fine if you're caught without a ticket.

SALONA
The ruins of the ancient city of Salona (Solin), among the vineyards at the foot of the mountains just north-east of Split, is about the most interesting archaeological site in Yugoslavia. They are easily accessible on city bus No 1 or 1A from opposite Dalmacijaturist, Titova obala 5 in Split. Surrounded by noisy highways and industry today, Salona was capital of the Roman province of Dalmatia from the time Julius Caesar elevated it to the status of colony. Salona held out against the barbarians and was only evacuated in 614 AD when the inhabitants fled to Split and neighbouring islands in the face of Avar and Slav attacks.

Get off the bus at the large parking lot near Snack Bar Salona. **Manastirine**, the

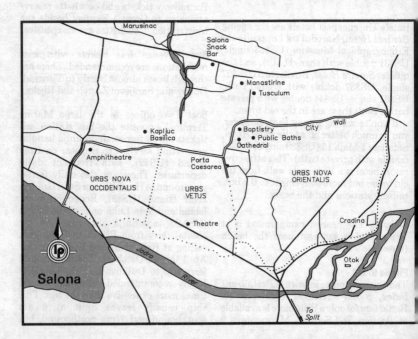

fenced area behind the parking lot, was a burial place for early Christian martyrs prior to the legalisation of Christianity. Excavated remains of the subsequent cemetery and the 5th century basilica are highlights, although this area was outside the ancient city itself. Overlooking Manastirine is 'Tusculum,' the custodians' residence, with interesting sculpture embedded in the walls.

A path bordered by cypresses leads south to the northern **city wall** of Salona. Notice the covered aqueduct along the inside base of the wall. The ruins you see in front of you as you stand on the wall were the Early Christian cult centre, including the three-aisled 5th century **cathedral** and small **baptistry** with inner columns. **Public baths** adjoin the cathedral on the east.

South-west is the 1st century east city gate, **Porta Caesaria**, later engulfed in the growth of Salona in all directions. Grooves in the stone road left by ancient chariots can still be seen at this gate.

Walk west along the city wall quite a distance to the **Kapljuc basilica** on the right, another martyrs' burial place. At the west end of Salona is the huge 2nd century **amphitheatre**, only destroyed in the 17th century by the Venetians to prevent it from being used as a refuge for Turkish raiders. From the amphitheatre walk east along the busy highway to the 1st century **Roman theatre**. The centre of ancient Salona north of this theatre has never been properly excavated. Continue east along the highway to an intersection where you'll find a bus back to Split.

HVAR

Hvar town on Hvar Island cherishes its reputation as one of the most exclusive, chic resorts on the Dalmatian Coast. The fashionable crowd sets the prices for meals and accommodation, which are high for Yugoslavia, low for Europe. Between the steep pine-covered slopes and azure Adriatic lies medieval Hvar, its Gothic palaces hidden among the narrow back-

streets below the 13th century city walls. Beaches are scarce here so everyone ends up taking a launch (US$1 one way) to the nudist island of Jerolim, just offshore.

Orientation

The big Jadrolinija ferries will drop you right in the centre of old Hvar. The barge from Split calls at Vira, four km north across the ridge (bus service), while other ferries service less expensive Stari Grad, 20 km east.

Information

The Turist Biro is beside the Jadrolinija landing.

Things to See

The full flavour of medieval Hvar is best savoured gently on the back streets of the old town. At each end of town is a monastery with a prominent tower. The **Dominican Monastery** at the head of the bay was destroyed by the Turks in the 10th century. The local Archaeological Museum is now housed among the ruins. At the south-east end of Hvar is the Renaissance **Franciscan Monastery** with a fine collection of Venetian painting in the church and adjacent museum.

Smack in the middle of Hvar is the imposing Gothic **arsenal**, its great arch visible from afar. Upstairs off the arsenal terrace is Hvar's prize, the first municipal theatre in Europe (1612), rebuilt in the 19th century. Try to get into the theatre (not the lacklustre cinema downstairs!) to appreciate its delightful human proportions. On the hilltop high above Hvar town is a **Venetian fortress** (1551), well worth the climb for the sweeping panoramic views.

Places to Stay

Private Rooms The Turist Biro in town beside the Jadrolinija landing will find you a private room for US$10 single, US$16 double in the cheapest category. More private rooms at the same rates are available at Dalmacijaturist on the

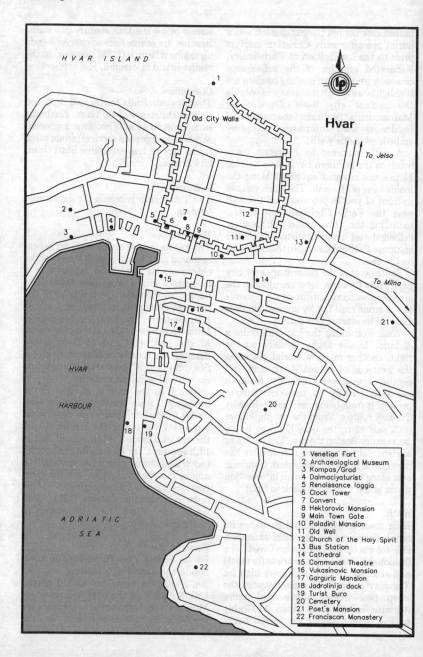

HVAR ISLAND

Old City Walls

Hvar

To Jelsa

To Milna

HVAR HARBOUR

ADRIATIC SEA

1 Venetian Fort
2 Archaeological Museum
3 Kompas/Grad
4 Dalmaciyaturist
5 Renaissance loggia
6 Clock Tower
7 Convent
8 Hektorovic Mansion
9 Main Town Gate
10 Paladini Mansion
11 Old Well
12 Church of the Holy Spirit
13 Bus Station
14 Cathedral
15 Communal Theatre
16 Vukasinovic Mansion
17 Garguric Mansion
18 Jadrolinija dock
19 Turist Buro
20 Cemetery
21 Poet's Mansion
22 Franciscan Monastery

waterfront beyond the small boat harbour, at Kompas/Grad near the Duty Free Shop a little further along, and at an office in the bus station. You can bargain for a lower rate with proprietresses who approach you at the ferry landing.

Hotels The cheapest hotel is the *Galeb* (open April to October, US$21 single, US$39 double), around the bay beyond the Franciscan Monastery.

Camping In mid-summer every room in Hvar could be full, forcing you to take a bus 20 km across the island to less crowded and less expensive Stari Grad. *Camping Vira* is just above the port where the smaller car ferry from Split ties up, four km from Hvar town.

Getting There & Away
From mid-April to mid-October Jadrolinija ferries between Rijeka and Bar call at Hvar almost daily, by far the best if not the cheapest way to come. Northbound they leave around 4 pm, southbound at 10 am. The Turist Biro beside the Jadrolinija landing sells ferry tickets.

There's a daily local ferry from Hvar town direct to Split, leaving Hvar at the crack of dawn and returning in the afternoon. The barges from Vira and Stari Grad to Split operate several times daily year-round at more convenient times. Ask at the bus station about connecting buses to Vira. There are also buses to Stari Grad.

KORCULA
Korcula hugs a small hilly peninsula jutting into the Adriatic Sea. With its round defensive towers and compact cluster of red-roofed houses, Korcula is a typical medieval Dalmatian town. In contrast to Turkish cities like Mostar and Sarajevo, Korcula was controlled by Venice from the 14th to 18th centuries. Venetian rule left its mark, especially on Cathedral Square which could have dropped out of Italy. The best beaches on the island are at Lumbarda, eight km east of town (bus service).

Orientation
If you arrive on the big Jadrolinija car ferry, no problem – they'll drop you below the walls of the old town of Korcula on Korcula Island. The passenger launch from Orebic is also convenient, terminating at the old harbour, but the barge from Orebic goes to Bon Repos in Dominice, several km from the centre.

Information
Putnik Marko Polo Turist Biro is near the old town.

Things to See
Other than following the circuit of the former city walls or walking along the shore, sightseeing in Korcula centres on Cathedral Square. The Gothic **Cathedral of St Mark** features two paintings by Tintoretto (the Three Saints on the altar and the Annunciation to one side).

The **Treasury** in the 14th century Abbey Palace next to the cathedral is worth a look, and even better is the **Town Museum** in the

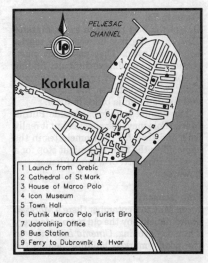

1 Launch from Orebic
2 Cathedral of St Mark
3 House of Marco Polo
4 Icon Museum
5 Town Hall
6 Putnik Marco Polo Turist Biro
7 Jadrolinija Office
8 Bus Station
9 Ferry to Dubrovnik & Hvar

15th century Gabriellis Palace opposite. It's said Marco Polo was born in Korcula in 1254 and you climb the tower of his alleged house for a fee. There's also an **Icon Museum** in the old town. It isn't much of a museum but visitors are let into the beautiful old Church of All Saints as a bonus.

Places to Stay

Private Rooms Putnik Marko Polo Turist Biro arranges private rooms in Korcula (US$12 single, US$16 double), but you'll do better with private operators you meet on the wharf. There are numerous *sobe* and *zimmer* signs around town.

Hostels The *Letovaliste FSH Youth Hostel* (open June to mid-September only) is near the junction of the Trajekt, Lumbarda and Korcula roads (one km from the Orebic car ferry, two km from Korcula).

Camping Near the hostel, 300 metres up the Lumbarda road, is *Solitudo Autocamp*. A better campground is *Autocamp 'Kalak'* behind *Hotel Bon Repos*, not far from the Orebic car ferry. No bungalows, but tenting is around US$4 and the beach is close by.

Places to Eat

One of the best places to eat is *Pizzeria Timun* on the bay between the tourist hotels and town. They post their menu outside, but you'll have difficulty finding a table. Alternatively try the *Restaurant Grill Planjak* between the supermarket and the Jadrolinija office in town.

The nameless milk bar beside Putnik Marko Polo may look cheaper but it really isn't and they fry their omelettes in the same oil as the fish. You might stop for a bowl of spaghetti or a cup of lemon tea, however.

Entertainment

From May to September there's *Moreska* sword dancing by the old town gate every Thursday evening. *Cinema Liburna* is in the poorly marked building behind the

Liburna Restaurant near the bus station. What's on is posted outside the milk bar mentioned above, not at the cinema.

Getting There & Away

Getting to Korcula is easy since all the big Jadrolinija coastal ferries between Split and Dubrovnik tie up at the landing adjacent to the old town. If you didn't plan a stop here, your glimpse of Korcula from the railing will make you regret it. Ferry tickets may be purchased at the Jadrolinija office or Putnik Marko Polo (same prices).

Coming from Belgrade, Sarajevo or Mostar, take the train to Kardeljevo, then a ferry to Trapanj on the Peljesac Peninsula. A waiting bus will carry you across Peljesac to Orebic, from where ferries to Korcula are frequent. There's also a twice daily bus service from Dubrovnik to Orebic and Korcula. Instead of the barge-type car ferry between Orebic and Korcula which lands at Bon Repos a couple of km from town, look for the passenger launch which will drop you at the Hotel Korcula right below the old town's towers. There's a tourist office at the landing in Orebic where you can check times or rent a private room for the night if it's getting late.

A third approach is on the daily ferry from Split to Vela Luka at the west end of Korcula Island. A dozen daily buses link Vela Luka to Korcula town.

Dubrovnik

After Venice, Dubrovnik (Ragusa) was the most important medieval city state on the Adriatic. Until the Napoleonic invasion of 1806 it remained an independent republic. Like Venice, Dubrovnik now lives mostly from tourism. Conspicuous consumption by hordes of affluent visitors has converted the city into something of a tourist trap and at peak periods it's a bit of a circus. Yet Stari Grad, the perfectly

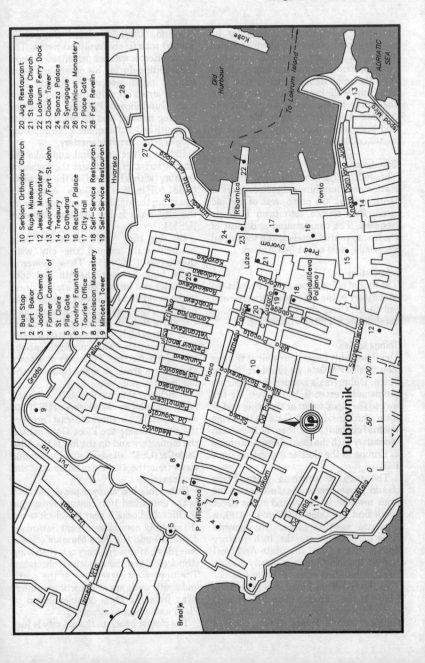

1 Bus Stop
2 Fort Bokar
3 Jadran Cinema
4 Former Convent of
   St Claire
5 Pile Gate
6 Onofrio Fountain
7 Tourist Office
8 Franciscan Monastery
9 Minceta Tower
10 Serbian Orthodox Church
11 Rupe Museum
12 Jesuit Monastery
13 Aquarium/Fort St John
14 Treasury
15 Cathedral
16 Rector's Palace
17 City Hall
18 Self-Service Restaurant
19 Self-Service Restaurant
20 Jug Restaurant
21 St Blaise Church
22 Lokrum Ferry Dock
23 Clock Tower
24 Sponza Palace
25 Synagogue
26 Dominican Monastery
27 Ploce Gate
28 Fort Revelin

Dubrovnik

0   50   100 m

preserved old town, is unique for its marble-paved squares, steep cobbled streets, tall houses, convents, churches, palaces, fountains and museums, all cut from the same light coloured stone. The intact city walls keep motorists at bay and the southerly position between Split and Albania makes for an agreeable climate and lush vegetation. Ferry, bus and air routes converge on the city.

Orientation
The Jadrolinija ferry terminal and bus station are a few hundred metres apart at Gruz, several km north-west of the old town. Bus service into town is fairly frequent. The campground and most of the luxury tourist hotels are on the Lapad Peninsula, west of the bus station.

Information
The tourist office opposite the Franciscan Monastery in the old town is brusque and unhelpful. Cross-check their information carefully as it's often misleading.

Things to See
You'll probably begin your visit at the bus stop outside Pile Gate. As you enter the city Placa, Dubrovnik's wonderful pedestrian promenade, extends before you all the way to the clock tower at the other end of town. Just inside Pile Gate is the huge Onofrio Fountain (1438), then the Franciscan Monastery with the third oldest pharmacy in Europe in the cloister (operating since 1391).

The urge to continue down Placa should prove irresistible. In front of the clock tower at the other end of the street you'll find the Orlando Column (1418), a favourite meeting place. On opposite sides of Orlando are the 16th century Sponza Palace (now the State Archives) and St Blaise's Church, a lovely Italian Baroque building you may enter free.

At the end of the broad street beside St Blaise is the Baroque cathedral (closed) and, between the two churches, the Gothic Rector's Palace (1441), now a museum (US$1.50, closed Sunday in winter) with finely furnished rooms. The elected Rector was not permitted to leave the building during his one-month term without permission of the Senate. The narrow street opposite this palace opens onto Gunduliceva Poljana, a bustling morning market, and up the stairway at the south end of the square is the imposing 18th century Jesuit Monastery.

Return to the cathedral and take the narrow street in front past the Cathedral Treasury (with a Raphael) to the Aquarium (US$1.50) in Fort St John. Above the aquarium through an obscure entrance off the city walls is the Maritime Museum (US$1).

By this time you'll be ready for a leisurely walk around the city walls themselves (US$0.75). These powerful walls, built between the 8th and 16th centuries and intact today, are the finest in the world and Dubrovnik's main claim to fame. They enclose the entire city in a curtain of stone over two km long and up to 25 metres high, with two round towers, 14 square towers, two corner fortifications and a large fortress. The views over town and sea are great, so make this walk the highpoint of your visit.

Whichever way you go you'll notice the large Dominican Monastery (US$1.50, closed Sunday) in the north-east corner of the city. Outside the Ploce Gate behind the monastery and up the hill is the Atlas Cable Car (US$3.50) which offers panoramic views from the 412-metre summit of Srd Mountain.

Dubrovnik has many other sights such as the unmarked 16th century synagogue at Ulica Zudioska 5 near the clock tower (10 am to 12 noon daily except Saturday, donation) and the Rupe Museum (closed Saturday), a former granary now sheltering ethnological and archaeological collections. The uppermost streets below the north and south walls are also worth a wander, away from the crass commercialism of Placa and adjacent streets.

The closest beach to the old city is just

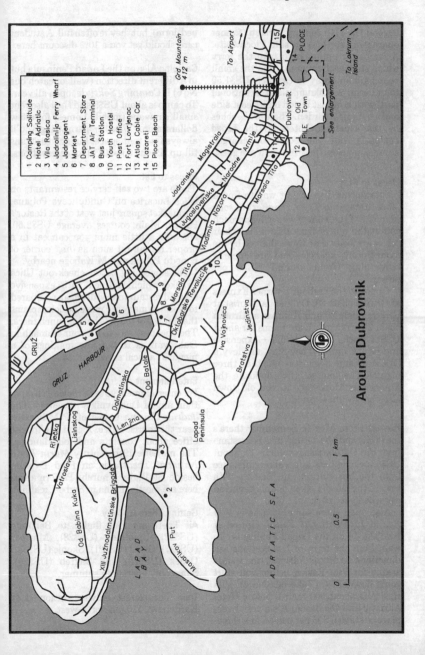

1 Camping Solitude
2 Hotel Adriatic
3 Vila Rasica
4 Jadrolinija Ferry Wharf
5 Jadroagent
6 Market
7 Department Store
8 JAT Air Terminal
9 Bus Station
10 Youth Hostel
11 Post Office
12 Fort Lovrjenac
13 Atlas Cable Car
14 Lazareti
15 Ploce Beach

Around Dubrovnik

beyond the 17th century **Lazareti** (former quarantine station) outside Ploce Gate. A far better option is to take the ferry which shuttles frequently from the small boat harbour (May to October, US$1.50 round trip) to **Lokrum Island**, a national park with a nudist beach on its east side and a botanical garden. There are beaches by the expensive hotels on the **Lapad Peninsula**, but you could be charged admission unless they think you're a guest.

Places to Stay

Private Rooms The easiest way to find a place to stay is to accept the offer of a *sobe* from one of the women who will approach you at the bus or ferry terminals. Their prices are lower than those charged by the room-finding agencies and are open to bargaining (from around US$6 per person).

Opposite the harbour Kvarner Express at Gruska obala 29, Dalmacija-Tourist at Gruska obala 30 and Kompas at Gruska obala 26 arrange private rooms for about US$14 single, US$20 double – expensive and best avoided. They may also levy a 30% surcharge if you stay less than three nights! The tourist office opposite the Franciscan Monastery in the old town also charges these prices.

Hostels From May to September there's the IYHF *youth hostel* up Vinka Sagrestana from Put Oktobarske revolucije 17, about US$5 for members. It's walking distance from the bus station, up Marsala Tita toward the old city, then double back and ask when you reach the cliffs.

· Also open these same months is *Vila Rasica International Youth Centre* at Ivanjska 14 on the Lapad Peninsula. To walk from the ferry or bus stations ask directions to Hotel Adriatic, then start asking for Vila Rasica before you start going downhill (or take bus No 4). Vila Rasica is about 500 metres before Hotel Adriatic and the beach. It's a very lively place to stay (US$8 per person in a three-bed dorm), but they're often full. A student card should get you a 10% discount here.

Camping Also on the Lapad Peninsula but in a different direction (walk or catch bus No 6) is *Camping Solitude*, open all year. To camp is about US$5 and they also rent small caravans (mobile homes) for a few dollars more. Weather permitting you'll always find tent space, but the caravans fill up. Phone 050-20770 for reservations.

Places to Eat

There are two self-service restaurants on Ulica Lucarica off Gunduliceva Poljana, the market square just west of the Rector's Palace. Main courses average US$2.50. For only a little more you can eat in a proper restaurant such as *Jug*, corner of Izmedu Polaca and M Kaboge nearby.

For something better check out Ulica Prijeko which is lined with expensive seafood restaurants, still cheap compared to West Germany or France, which explains the throngs of tourists having lunch there. The cheapest way to fill your stomach in Dubrovnik is to buy the makings of a picnic at a local supermarket.

Entertainment

For entertainment go see a movie – cheaper than any of Dubrovnik's museums. The *Jadran Cinema* is just off P Milicevica near the tourist office. Ask at the tourist office about concerts and folk dancing. The majestic 19th century *Marin Drzic National Theatre* is on Pred Dvorom beside St Blaise Church. Performances here are mostly drama in Serbo-Croatian.

Getting There & Away

Air There are JAT flights to Belgrade (US$22), Ljubljana (US$28), Maribor (US$27), Ohrid (US$21), Skopje (US$33), Osijek (US$23) and Zagreb (US$25). Some only operate in summer.

Train The closest railway station is at Kardeljevo, 110 km north-west.

Bus During the busy summer season and on weekends buses out of Dubrovnik can be crowded, so it's important to get in line for a ticket well before the scheduled departure time. Southbound buses to Kotor and Bar arrive from the north, so seats cannot be reserved in advance. If you're in line an hour before the departure you should get on.

Boat The Jadrolinija coastal ferry north to Korcula, Hvar and Split (mid-April to mid-October) is far more comfortable than the bus, if several times more expensive. Still, it's well worth the extra. The ferry to Korcula, Hvar and Split leaves at 10 am several times a week, to Bar and Greece at 5 pm once or twice a week. Sample ferry prices from Dubrovnik are: to Korcula US$8, to Hvar US$10, to Split US$12, to Corfu US$29, to Igoumenitsa US$30.

A local ferry leaves Dubrovnik for Mljet Island (US$4) at 1 pm daily except Sunday year-round. Tickets for these lines can be bought from travel agencies or Jadrolinija opposite the port.

There are weekly Adriatica Line car ferries year-round from Dubrovnik to Bari (US$40), Rimini (US$45), Ancona (US$45), Trieste (US$47) and Venice (US$47). In July and August fares are up to 50% higher. Tickets for international ferries are sold by Jadroagent, Gruska obala 26 at the port.

Getting Around

Airport Transport Cilipi International Airport is 24 km south-east of Dubrovnik. The airport bus (US$1.50) leaves from the JAT Air Terminal near the bus station 90 minutes prior to all JAT flights.

Public Transport Buy tickets for city buses at a kiosk.

Montenegro

The Socialist Republic of Montenegro (Crna Gora) fills a corner of south-central Yugoslavia directly above Albania. The republic's Adriatic coastline attracts masses of visitors, but there are also the spectacular Moraca and Tara canyons in the interior. Between Titograd and Kolasin a scenic railway runs right up the Moraca Canyon with fantastic views between the countless tunnels. West of Mojkovac, the next station after Kolasin, is the 60-km-long Tara Canyon, second largest in the world. Durmitor National Park near Tara Canyon is far enough off the beaten track to be attractive to intrepid hikers. Both canyon and park are accessible twice a day on the Zabljak bus from Mojkovac.

Other dominant features of this compact republic are the winding Bay of Kotor and Shkodres (Skadar) Lake, largest in the Balkans and shared with Albania.

History

Only tiny Montenegro kept above the Turkish tide which engulfed the Balkans for over four centuries. Medieval Montenegro was part of Serbia. After the Serbian defeat in 1389 the inhabitants of this mountainous region continued to resist the Turks. In 1482 Ivan Crnojevic established an independent principality at Cetinje ruled by elected *vladike* (bishops). After 1697 the succession was limited to the Petrovich Njegosh family.

The strangest *vladike* was the monk Stephen the Small who claimed to be the murdered Russian emperor Peter III, husband of Catherine the Great. The trusting Montenegrins accepted this and followed Stephen on raids against Turks and Venetians alike. In 1769 Catherine herself sent an ambassador to Montenegro to denounce the little monk and remove him from office. Stephen so impressed the emissary, however, that he was given a Russian staff uniform and promises of support against the Turks. Later an explosion during road-building work blinded the monk. He retired to a monastery where in 1773 he was murdered by a Turkish spy.

The wars with the Turks and Albanians continued until 1878, when the European portion of the Ottoman Empire largely collapsed and Montenegrin independence was recognised by the Congress of Berlin. In 1916 the Austrians evicted the bishop-king and after WW I Montenegro was incorporated into Yugoslavia. In 1946 the administration shifted to Titograd, a modern city with little to interest the visitor.

KOTOR

The Bay of Kotor, south-east of Dubrovnik halfway to Bar, is a great Norwegian-style fjord gripped by steep slopes. The best place to stop is the town of Kotor, which has good onward bus service south. The bus station is convenient to the old town, shaken badly by the 1979 earthquake and only now being rebuilt. Your wanders through the walled quarter should take you to the cathedral, Orthodox church and **Naval Museum** (US$1), all fairly obvious. The city walls zigzag up the mountainside behind Kotor offering splendid views of the fjord for the adventuresome climber.

Places to Stay

To spend the night in Kotor contact Putnik in the red booth near the main town gate or Montenegro Express in the plush *Hotel Fjord* at the head of the bay, a few hundred metres from the bus station. Both have private rooms for around US$8 per person.

CETINJE

Cetinje, plop atop a high plateau between the Bay of Kotor and Shkodres (Skadar) Lake, is the old capital of Montenegro, subject of song and epic poem. The barren easily defended slopes help explain

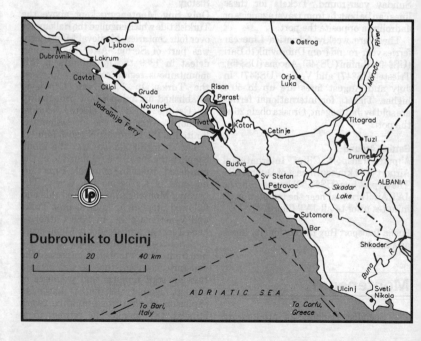

Dubrovnik to Ulcinj

0   20   40 km

Montenegro's independence and much remains of old Cetinje from museums, to palaces, to monasteries. Unfortunately the numerous tour buses which arrive around midday throw cold water on the romance.

Things to See

The most imposing building in Cetinje is the **State Museum**, the former palace (1871) of Nicola I Petrovic, the last king. Looted during WW II, only a portion of the original furnishings remain but the many portraits and period weapons give a representative picture of the times. Nearly opposite this is the older 1838 residence of the prince bishop Petar II Petrovic Njegos, who ruled from 1830 to 1851. This building, now a museum, is also known as **'Biljarda Hall'** for a billiard table installed in 1840, the first in Yugoslavia.

Around the side of Biljarda Hall is a large glass-enclosed pavilion containing a fascinating relief map of Montenegro created by the Austrians in 1917 for tactical planning purposes. Ask one of the Njegos Museum attendants to let you in. Beyond the map is **Cetinje Monastery**, founded in 1484 but rebuilt in 1785. Not far away is Vladin Dom, the former Government House (1910), now the **National Gallery**. A collective ticket to all the museums is available for US$3.50.

Back toward the bus station is 15th century **Vlach Church** (rebuilt 1864), surrounded by a fence formed from the barrels of 2000 captured Turkish rifles.

Twenty km away on top of **Mt Lovcen** (1574 metres) is the mausoleum of Njegos, who was a revered poet as well as ruler. There are no buses up and taxis want US$20 round trip, but the building is visible in the distance from Cetinje. From the parking lot one must climb 461 steps to the mausoleum.

Places to Stay

If you're looking for a private room try Intours near the State Museum (US$7 per person).

Getting There & Away

Some buses between Dubrovnik and Titograd pass through Cetinje. There's also bus service to Kotor and Budva.

BUDVA

Budva is another easy place to break your journey south. The beach begins near the bus station and the old walled town is only a few minutes' walk away. Unfortunately old Budva was devastated by the 1979 quake and has been closed off for several years as reconstruction proceeds. Only a few km south-east of Budva is the former village of Sveti Stefan of picture postcard fame, now entirely part of a tourist resort.

Places to Stay

There are many fancy hotels around Budva catering to package holiday-makers from Britain, but you're better off in a private room (US$11 per person) arranged by an agency such as Montenegro Express, Kompas, Putnik or Turist Biro, all on Marsala Tita close to the bus station.

BAR

Bar is an uninteresting port city, terminus of the railway from Belgrade and ferry lines from Rijeka, Bari (Italy) and Corfu (Greece).

Orientation

The ferry terminal in Bar is only a few hundred metres from the bus station, but it's over two km to the railway station.

Places to Stay

Unless your ferry comes in too late, catch a bus to Ulcinj right away, a far better place to stay. In Bar Montenegro Express, near the new department store not far from the harbour, arranges private rooms. North of Bar there's a good beach at Sutomore and a campground on the way.

Getting There & Away

Train & Bus There are four trains a day to Belgrade (two with couchettes) and buses to Dubrovnik and Ulcinj.

Boat The Jadrolinija car ferries run north from Bar to Rijeka almost daily from mid-April to mid-October. A couple of times a week during these months there's service south to Corfu and Igoumenitsa in Greece. The ferries tend to call at Bar at very inconvenient hours. Northbound they leave around 5 am and southbound they arrive/depart at 9 pm. The ferry from Bar to Bari (Italy) is US$33 one way (US$45 in July and August), but there is no service in January and February.

ULCINJ

A broad military highway tunnels through hills between the olive groves for 25 km from Bar to Ulcinj near the Albanian border, the only Muslim town on the Yugoslav coast. The Turks held Bar and Ulcinj for over 300 years and today most of the inhabitants are ethnic Albanians.

Orientation

You'll arrive at Ulcinj bus station about two km from Mala Plaza, the small beach below the old town. It's an interesting walk to Mala Plaza and you'll pass several buildings with *sobe* and *zimmer* signs where you can rent a room.

Information

'Neptune' Montenegroturist is on Mala Plaza.

Things to See

The ancient ramparts of Ulcinj overlook the sea, but most of the buildings inside were shattered by the 1979 earthquake and reconstruction has been slow. The **museum** by the upper gate is now open and you can walk among the ruins and along the wall.

Places to Stay

Private Rooms The 'Neptune' Montenegroturist office, right on the beach at Mala Plaza, will place you in a private room for a reasonable charge.

Hostels Very near the bus station is the

IYHF *'Bratstvo-Jedinstvo' Youth Hostel* in a large white school building. It's only open during the summer when the students are on holidays.

Camping Alternatively catch a bus to Velika Plaza (Great Beach), Ulcinj's famous 15-km stretch of unbroken sand, which begins about five km south-east of town. There are two campgrounds here, *Milena* and *Neptun*. *Camping Bojana* is a little farther along, closer to Albania.

On Ada Island, just across the Bojana River from Albania, is a nudist colony most easily accessible by boat from Mala Plaza (US$3 round trip).

Places to Eat

There are numerous inexpensive restaurants opposite Robna Kuca Ulcinj between the bus station and Mala Plaza.

Getting There & Away

Buses from Bar are fairly frequent. In Bar connect with the train to Belgrade, a bus to Dubrovnik or a ferry to Greece.

Bosnia-Hercegovina

Bosnia-Hercegovina is a mountainous region in the very middle of Yugoslavia, cut off from the sea by Croatia. Most of the rivers of the republic flow north into the Sava. Only the Neretva cuts south from Mostar through the Dinaric chain to Kardeljevo on the Adriatic. There are over 30 peaks from 1700 to 2386 metres high.

The Romans settled by the mineral springs at Ilidza near Sarajevo. Later the Turks made Sarajevo capital of Bosnia. Hercegovina is named for Herceg (Duke) Stjepan Vukcic who ruled from his mountain top castle at Blagaj near Mostar until the arrival of the Turks in 1468. During the 400 year Turkish period Bosnia-Hercegovina was completely assimilated and became the border of the

Islamic and Christian worlds. A third of the local Serbian population is still Muslim. Aside from Mostar and Sarajevo described below, Travnik and Jajce are historic towns with an authentic oriental air.

In 1878 it was decided at the Berlin Congress that Bosnia-Hercegovina would be occupied by Austro-Hungary. The population, which desired autonomy, had to be brought under Hapsburg rule by force. Resentment that one foreign occupation had replaced another became more intense when Austria annexed Bosnia outright in 1908. The assassination of the Hapsburg heir, Archduke Ferdinand, at Sarajevo in 1914 led Austria to declare war on Serbia. When Russia supported Serbia and Germany came to the aid of Austria, the world was soon at war. During WW II this rugged area was a partisan stronghold.

MOSTAR

Mostar, a medium-sized city among vine-yards between Dubrovnik and Sarajevo, is the main centre of Hercegovina. Founded by the Turks in the 15th century at a strategic river crossing, Kujundziluk, the old quarter, has all the carefully groomed attractions needed to satisfy the thousands of daily visitors. The postcard-perfect Turkish bridge (1566) arches 20 metres above the green water in the Neretva River gorge, a guard tower at each end, mosques on all sides, and a nearby strip to service the packs of tourists. You can join them and see the sights in a stopover of three hours or less.

Orientation

As you leave the adjacent bus and train stations head west toward the new bridge, but don't cross. Turn left onto Ulica Mladena Balorde which, with contin-uations, will take you south into Kujundziluk.

Information

Hetmos Turist is below the Neretva Hotel on Trg Republike.

Things to See

Before reaching the **Turkish Bridge** you'll pass two mosques of note. The **Karadoz Bey Mosque** (1557) opposite Ulica Brace Fejica 54 is the larger, but the **Koski Mehmed Pasha Mosque** (1619) offers the bonus of a chance to climb the minaret for a stunning view of everything for your ticket.

After 'doing' the bridge look for the **City Museum**, which is right beside the eastern guard tower but entered off Marsala Tita, the main road above. This museum has two parts, a signposted revolutionary

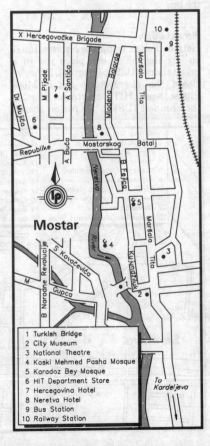

1 Turkish Bridge
2 City Museum
3 National Theatre
4 Koski Mehmed Pasha Mosque
5 Karadoz Bey Mosque
6 HIT Department Store
7 Hercegovina Hotel
8 Neretva Hotel
9 Bus Station
10 Railway Station

museum and an archaeological section in the old mosque alongside. Be sure to ask the attendant to open the mosque if it's closed. The scale model of Mostar inside is a highlight. The **New Orthodox Church** (1873) on the hillside above the museum is the largest in the republic.

Pocitelj South of Mostar by the highway to Metkovic are the castle and mosque of the old Turkish village of Pocitelj, now completely dedicated to tourism and its art. It's not worth a special trip, but do try to get a glimpse of it as you go by on the bus.

Places to Stay
Hetmos Turist, below the Neretva Hotel on Trg Republike, can place you in a private home (US$7 per person). If they're closed the *Hercegovina Hotel*, Mose Pijade 18 near HIT Department Store, is the cheapest (US$11 per person shared

bath). The nearest campground is at Buna, 12 km south near the main road.

Entertainment
Mostar's theatre is at Marsala Tita 119.

Getting There & Away
There are trains to Kardeljevo, Sarajevo, Zagreb and Belgrade. Train service to and from Sarajevo is frequent enough, but carefully check the times of buses to Split (179 km) or Dubrovnik (139 km) and try for an advance ticket. In case of difficulty take a train to Kardeljevo and look for a bus there. For Korcula connect with the year-round ferry to Trpanj at Kardeljevo.

It's a wonderfully picturesque train ride north from Mostar. The line runs along the Neretva Valley between high cliffs, loops up around a lake, and snakes through the mountains to Sarajevo.

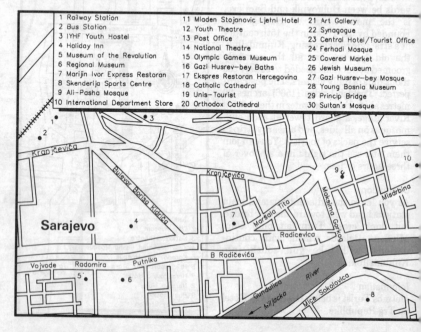

1 Railway Station	11 Mladen Stojanovic Ljetni Hotel	21 Art Gallery
2 Bus Station	12 Youth Theatre	22 Synagogue
3 IYHF Youth Hostel	13 Post Office	23 Central Hotel/Tourist Office
4 Holiday Inn	14 National Theatre	24 Ferhadi Mosque
5 Museum of the Revolution	15 Olympic Games Museum	25 Covered Market
6 Regional Museum	16 Gazi Husrev-bey Baths	26 Jewish Museum
7 Marijin Ivor Express Restoran	17 Ekspres Restoran Hercegovina	27 Gazi Husrev-bey Mosque
8 Skenderija Sports Centre	18 Catholic Cathedral	28 Young Bosnia Museum
9 Ali-Pasha Mosque	19 Unis-Tourist	29 Princip Bridge
10 International Department Store	20 Orthodox Cathedral	30 Sultan's Mosque

Sarajevo

SARAJEVO

Sarajevo, near the geographical centre of Yugoslavia, is capital of the Republic of Bosnia-Hercegovina. Set in hilly, broken countryside by the Miljacka River, Sarajevo's 73 mosques give it the strongest Turkish flavour of any city in the Balkans. From the mid-15th century till 1878 Turkish governors ruled Bosnia from Sarajevo. The name comes from *saraj*, Turkish for 'palace'. When the Turks finally withdrew a half century of Austro-Hungarian domination began, culminating in the assassination of Archduke Franz Ferdinand and his wife by conspirators who desired a South Slav republic.

The essence of this rich history is well preserved in Bascarsija, the picturesque old Turkish bazaar, full of mosques, markets and local colour, and along a riverfront largely unchanged since that fateful day in 1914. Sarajevo is perhaps the most evocative city in Yugoslavia.

Orientation

The bus and train stations are adjacent, a couple of km west of the old town. Tram No 1 loops east by the river directly into town. Buy a ticket at the kiosk and punch it once aboard.

Information

The tourist office at Jugoslovenske narodne armije (JNA) 50, provides maps and brochures.

Things to See

Begin your visit at **Bascarsija**, the old Turkish marketplace. This medieval square still pulses with life as craftsmen ply their trades, *cevapcici* sizzles on the grills and believers hurry to any of the ubiquitous mosques for prayer. The **Brusa Bezistan** (1551), a former silk market, now caters to tourism, but you'll see more locals than visitors in Bascarsija – it's for real, not show.

51 Mt Trebevic Cable Car
52 City Museum
53 St Michael the Archangel
54 Marica Han
55 Starigrad Hotel
56 Cekrecki Mosque
57 Brusa Brezistan
58 Bascarsija Mosque
59 Old Town Hall

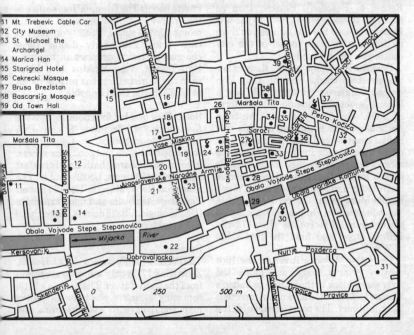

Stroll along Ulica Saraci which soon becomes Ulica Vase Miskina, Sarajevo's throbbing pedestrian corridor. At Saraci 77 is the **Marica Han**, a 17th century caravanserai where traders once rested. A little farther along you'll reach the **Gazi Husrev-bey Mosque** (1531), Yugoslavia's largest, which you may enter outside of prayer times for a fee. Notice the fountain in the courtyard and the **Kursumli Medresa** (1537), a former Islamic school across the street. At the start of Ulica Vase Miskina is the 16th century **Covered Market** on the left.

Continue along to the **Catholic Cathedral**. Behind this on Marsala Tita are the **Gazi Husrev-bey Baths**, now a nightclub. Walk east to the **Jewish Museum** (closed Monday), Marsala Tita 98, which is housed in the old Sephardic Synagogue erected in the 16th century by refugees from Spain. At Marsala Tita 87 is **St Michael the Archangel Serbian Orthodox Church**, rebuilt in 1730 after a fire. There's an icon museum in the adjacent building. Return to Bascarsija Square, then go north up Remzije Omanovica to the **City Museum** (closed Sunday) where you'll see an informative scale model of the city centre you just perused.

Back to Bascarsija again, then follow the streetcar tracks east till they loop around Sarajevo's **old town hall** (now a library), erected in pseudo-Moorish form in 1895. On 28 June 1914 Austrian Archduke Franz Ferdinand and his wife paid a courtesy call here, then rode west along the riverside in an open car to the second bridge where they met assassin's bullets. Retrace their route where streetcars rattle today and see the story in the **Young Bosnia Museum** on the corner at Obala Vojvode Stepe 36. On the sidewalk beside the museum are footprints where Gavrilo Princip stood and fired the first shots of WW I.

Cross the Miljacka River on the 18th century Princip Bridge and follow the river east a block to the Careva or **Sultan's Mosque** (1566), which adjoins an important Islamic library. The court *(seraglio)* of the Bosnian governors was once here. Continue east by the river to the market opposite the old town hall. Signs point the way south a few hundred metres to the cable car up *Mt Trebevic* (US$1.50 round trip), departing every hour on the hour. Don't miss it. The bobsled course from the 1984 Winter Olympics is just below the upper station.

After (or before!) your ride up Trebevic, jump on any streetcar and get out at the first stop after the Holiday Inn. The large building across the road is the **Regional Museum** (closed Monday) with extensive archaeology, ethnography and natural history collections, plus a compact botanical garden and some unusual funerary monuments in the courtyard. The modern building alongside is the **Museum of the Revolution** (closed Friday). Both museums close around 5 pm, so don't leave it too late.

Places to Stay

Private Rooms The Olimpik Tours office in the railway station arranges private rooms (US$14 single, US$20 double), but their prices are nearly double those charged by travel agencies in the city. Unis-Tourist, Vase Miskina 16 a block from the tourist office, has private rooms at US$7 single, US$12 double.

Hotels Your best bet for a hotel room is the *Central Hotel*, Zrinjskog 8 and JNA beside the tourist office. The Central has a convenient location and good atmosphere. A room with shared bath and breakfast will run US$16 single, US$25 double. The *Starigrad Hotel*, Marsala Tita 126 just off Bascarsija, is noisier and more expensive (US$18 single, US$28 double, shared bath and breakfast).

Hostels

The IYHF *'Dom Firijalaca' Youth Hostel*, Zadrugina 17, is only a short walk uphill from the train station. The route is a little confusing so unless you have a detailed map you'll have to ask directions and watch for signs pointing the way to the 'Omladinski Hotel.' Registration begins at 2 pm, doors shut at 11 pm, US$5 for members.

Up on Mt Trebevic a 20-minute walk from the upper cable car station is the *Dom Odmora Mladost* (tel 535-921) with rooms for US$8. Bus No 38 from Princip Bridge goes close to this hostel. Do call before going up, as it fills.

In July and August young travellers may find a bed at one of the student dormitories. Try the *Mladen Stojanovic Ljetni Hotel*, Ulica Radiceva 4d near the centre, or the larger *Bratstvo Jedinstvo Studentski Centar*, aleja Branka Bujica 2 at Nedzarici among the block apartments between Sarajevo and Ilidza (trams No 5 or 7 west to the loop).

Camping Tent campers may stay at *Autocamp Ilidza* (tel 621-432), 10 km west of Sarajevo, for US$3 per person (open May to September). Bungalows here are US$20 double, US$27 triple. Take tram No 3 west to the terminus, then walk along Dzemala Bijedica to the bridge. The information office at the end of this bridge will direct you to the campground and provide other assistance.

Places to Eat

Two easy self-service restaurants to know about are *Ekspres Hercegovina*, on Vase Miskina beside the Catholic Cathedral, and *Expres Marijin Ivor*, Marsala Tita 1 between the station and town. There's a self-service restaurant and a large supermarket in the basement of International Department Store, Marsala Tita 26.

Ascinica, Marsala Tita 95, is an easy place to eat since you pick from the pots near the window. Enjoy a beer at a courtyard table or a moderate to slightly expensive meal at *Marica Han*, Saraci 77, an old caravanserai in Bascarsija. Burek is available almost everywhere.

Entertainment

Try the *Youth Theatre Pozoriste Mladih*,

Slobodana Principa 8, or the *National Theatre*, Obala Vojvode Stepe 9 nearby beside the river. Concerts are sometimes given in the main hall at *Skenderija*.

Getting There & Away

Sarajevo is well connected to Kardeljevo, Mostar, Banja Luka, Zagreb and Belgrade by train. Couchettes are available to and from Belgrade, Ljubljana and Zagreb. Some of the new express trains departing Sarajevo are all 1st class (no 2nd class carriages), so make sure you get the right ticket. Unis-Tourist, Vase Miskina 16, makes train reservations and books couchettes.

Serbia

Serbia is the largest of the six republics which comprise Yugoslavia and, for visitors, perhaps the least interesting. Its dominant role is suggested by the inclusion within its boundaries of two autonomous provinces, Vojvodina and Kosovo, and the national capital, Belgrade. The north is an extension of the lowland plains of Hungary, while the mountainous south merges into Bulgaria, Macedonia, Albania and Montenegro. East of Belgrade the Danube River passes the medieval castles of Smederevo and Golubac, then flows through the famous Iron Gates along the Romanian border. A hydroelectric dam has now tamed this once wild stretch of water.

Among the most outstanding monuments of the old Serbian state are the many Orthodox monasteries with 13th and 14th century frescoes. Most are in remote locations difficult to reach without your own transportation. The most picturesque is 15th century Manasija Monastery between Belgrade and Nis, completely enclosed in defensive walls and towers (bus to Despotovac). Also outstanding are Ravanica Monastery south of Manasija (bus to Senje from

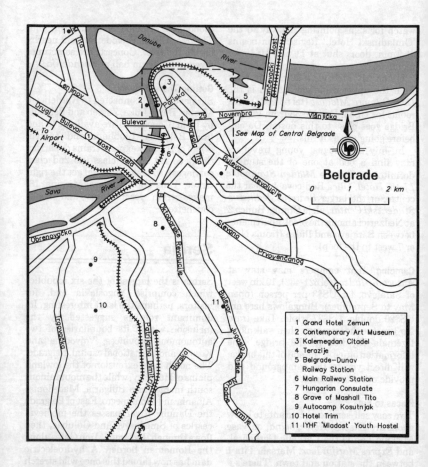

Belgrade

0   1   2 km

1 Grand Hotel Zemun
2 Contemporary Art Museum
3 Kalemegdan Citadel
4 Terazije
5 Belgrade–Dunav
  Railway Station
6 Main Railway Station
7 Hungarian Consulate
8 Grave of Mashall Tito
9 Autocamp Kosutnjak
10 Hotel Trim
11 IYHF 'Mladost' Youth Hostel

See Map of Central Belgrade

Cuprija) and the monasteries of Studenica (bus from Usce) and Sopocani (bus from Novi Pazar) south of Kraljevo.

BELGRADE

Belgrade (Beograd), at the southern edge of the Carpathian Basin where the Sava River joins the Danube, is not the sort of city that appeals to you right away. It's crowded, expensive and without any great sights which can't be missed.

Until WW I Belgrade was right on the border of Serbia and Austro-Hungary. Its citadel has seen too many battles for a lot to have survived. Destroyed and rebuilt 36 times in its 2000 year history, socialist Belgrade never managed to pick up all the pieces. Swarms of polluting vehicles and transiting travellers will test your nerves. Do your business and have a look round, then move on to better things.

Orientation

You'll probably arrive at the railway station on the south side of downtown. In the station you can get train information at window 25, tourist information at window 36, change money at window 35 and book a couchette at window 34. Window 36 may help you find a room. If the exchange window is closed, try the JIK Banka across the park in front of the station (open 8 am to 7 pm weekdays).

To walk into town take Milovanovica east a block, then straight up Balkanska to Terazije, the heart of modern Belgrade. Kneza Mihaila, Belgrade's lively pedestrian boulevard, runs north-west through Stari Grad (the old town) from Terazije to Kalemegdan Park, where you'll find the citadel.

information
The tourist office (open daily 8 am to 8 pm) is in the underpass in front of the bookstore at the beginning of Terazije on the corner of Kneza Mihaila.

Embassies Most of the consulates and embassies are on or near Kneza Milosa, a 10-minute walk south-east from the railway station. The Polish Consulate is at Kneza Milosa 38 (weekdays 8 am to 12 noon). The American Embassy is at Kneza Milosa 50. The Romanian Consulate is at Kneza Milosa 70 (weekdays 9 am to 11 am). The West German Embassy is at Kneza Milosa 74-76. The Canadian Embassy is at Kneza Milosa 75. The British Embassy is at Gen Zdanova 46.

The Bulgarian Consulate is at Bircaninova 26 (weekdays 10 am to 12 noon). The Hungarian Consulate at Ivana Milutinovica 74 (weekdays 9 am to 12 noon) is a few blocks east, while the Czechoslovakian Consulate at Bulevar Revolucije 22 (weekdays 9 am to 12 noon), is near the main post office. As usual the Australian Embassy is in an odd location at Cika Ljubina 13 in Stari Grad.

Things to See
From the railway station take tram No 2 north-west to **Kalemegdan Citadel**, a strategic hilltop fortress at the junction of the Sava and Danube rivers. The Roman settlement Singidunum was on the flood plain at the foot of the citadel. Although much of what is seen today dates from the 17th century, this area has been fortified since Celtic times. Medieval gates, Orthodox churches, Muslim tombs and Turkish baths are among the varied remnants to be seen. The large **Military Museum** on the battlements of the citadel presents a complete history of Yugoslavia in 53 rooms.

Adjacent to Kalemegdan is Stari Grad, the oldest part of Belgrade. The best museums are here, especially the **National Museum**, Trg Republike, which has archaeology downstairs, paintings upstairs. The collection of European art is quite good. A few blocks away at Studentski trg 13 is the **Ethnographical Museum** with an excellent collection of Serbian costumes and folk art. Detailed explanations are provided in English. Not far away is the **Gallery of Frescoes**, Cara Urosa 20, with full size replicas of paintings in remote churches of Serbia and Macedonia. Belgrade's most memorable museum is the **Palace of Princess Ljubice**, S Markovica and 7 Jula, an authentic Balkan-style palace (1831) complete with period furnishings.

Among the things to see in the modern city east of Terazije are the **Museum of the Revolution**, Trg Marksa i Engelsa 11, with interesting photos but no explanations in English or German. The imposing edifice just east of this museum is **Skupstina**, the Yugoslav parliament (1907-1932). East again behind the main post office is **St Marks Serbian Orthodox Church** (1932-1939) with four tremendous pillars supporting a towering dome. There's a small Russian Orthodox church behind.

If you'd like to visit the flowery **grave of Marshall Tito** (open 9 am to 4 pm) it's on Bulevar Oktobarske Revolucije a few km south of the city centre (trolley buses No 40 or 41). This tomb and all of the museums are closed on Mondays.

Zemun The city of Zemun, on the right

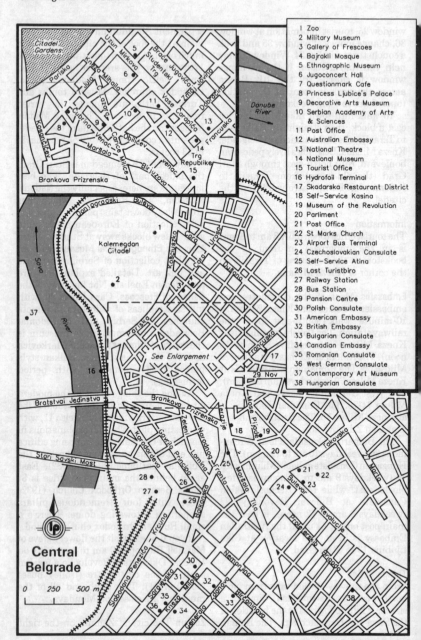

1 Zoo
2 Military Museum
3 Gallery of Frescoes
4 Bajrakli Mosque
5 Ethnographic Museum
6 Jugoconcert Hall
7 Questionmark Cafe
8 Princess Ljubice's Palace
9 Decorative Arts Museum
10 Serbian Academy of Arts
    & Sciences
11 Post Office
12 Australian Embassy
13 National Theatre
14 National Museum
15 Tourist Office
16 Hydrofoil Terminal
17 Skadarska Restaurant District
18 Self-Service Kasina
19 Museum of the Revolution
20 Parliment
21 Post Office
22 St Marks Church
23 Airport Bus Terminal
24 Czechoslovakian Consulate
25 Self-Service Atina
26 Last Turistbiro
27 Railway Station
28 Bus Station
29 Pansion Centre
30 Polish Consulate
31 American Embassy
32 British Embassy
33 Bulgarian Consulate
34 Canadian Embassy
35 Romanian Consulate
36 West German Consulate
37 Contemporary Art Museum
38 Hungarian Consulate

Central Belgrade

0   250   500 m

bank of the Danube beyond Novi Beograd, is almost an extension of Belgrade. There's a large **open air market** near the river and a local **museum** at Marsala Tita 9 near the post office. Climb up to the hilltop church for the view. Zemun is easily accessible on bus No 83 from in front of the JIK Banka opposite Belgrade railway station.

Places to Stay

Private Rooms Accommodation in Belgrade is the most expensive in Yugoslavia. Places in the budget category are both inconvenient and overpriced. Turist biro Lasta (closed Sunday) on Milovanovica below the Astorija Hotel in front of the station sometimes has private rooms at US$12 single, US$18 double, but this cannot be relied upon. There are only two (!?!) single rooms, for example, and neither are in the city centre. Also, they won't reserve private rooms for future return visits. You must take your chances, which aren't good. Hopefully someone on the sidewalk outside Lasta will offer you an unofficial private room, sparing you the necessity of dealing with the discourteous staff inside.

Hostels The IYHF *'Mladost' Youth Hostel*, in a modern three-storey building opposite Bulevar JNA 253, is expensive at US$8 for a bed in a five-bed dorm with tea and bread for breakfast. Those without a YHA card pay US$2 more. It's open all day, check-in from 12 noon, there's no curfew and no rules. The hostel restaurant serves hot meals and cold beer. Take bus No 47 south from Dimitrija Tucovica to Mladost.

Hotels The *Hotel Trim* (tel 559-128), at Kneza Viseslava 72 a km south of the campground (bus No 53), has rooms at US$14 single, US$22 double with private bath, the cheapest hotel in Belgrade. Call before going out.

Pansion Centre, Trg bratstva i jedinstva 7 opposite the train station, is way overpriced at US$22 per person. If you're alone you'll have to pay that for a bed in their dorm! It's usually full of locals who get a cut rate.

If the price is not important you want the elegant old *Hotel Moskva*, Balkanska 1 at Terazije, right in the centre of town (US$50 per person).

If everything's full in Belgrade try the hotels in nearby Zemun, both on Marsala Tita, Zemun's main street (bus No 83). The *Grand Hotel* (tel 210-536) is US$20 single, US$28 double, while the *Central Hotel* (tel 191-712) is US$24 single, US$33 double.

Camping *Autocamp Kosutnjak*, Kneza Viseslava 17, is in a confusing location behind a subdivision of winding, nameless streets about eight km south-west of the city centre. Take bus No 53 from Kneza Milosa 26 (the stop closest to the train station) and ask to be let off at the *Trim Hotel*, about two km from the campsite. The campground is open for tent campers May to September only, but there are bungalows year-round. They'll try to give you one of the expensive units (US$16 per person), but ask for a 'no comfort' bed (US$6). Chances are everything except camping will be full.

A Valuable Tip Save a day's travelling time, a night's hotel bill and a lot of aggravation by booking a couchette out of Belgrade at window 34 in the train station. This is easily done and the cost is only around US$4. No way you'll get a room for that! There are overnight trains to most large cities in Yugoslavia. If you arrived in Belgrade in the morning you'll have all day to look around before boarding the train late that evening. The main sights can be seen in a busy day. Don't forget that a train ticket (purchased at another window) is required in addition to the couchette ticket.

Places to Eat

Belgrade has many self-service cafeterias, the most convenient of which is *Kasina*,

Terazije 25 beside Putnik. Nearby on the opposite side of the boulevard is *Self-Service Atina*, Terazije 28, with a pizzeria next door.

For something better seek out the *Questionmark Cafe*, 7 Jula 6 opposite the Orthodox church. They have an English menu, good food and atmosphere, at reasonable prices. Around the corner beside Princess Ljubice's Palace is the *Knez Restaurant*, Sima Markovic 10, with spaghetti and pizza.

For local colour check out the more expensive folkloric restaurants near the fountain on Ulica Skadarska, a street full of summer strollers.

Entertainment

Concerts are held at the *Jugoconcert Hall* of Kolarac People's University, Studentski trg 5. Folk dancing can be seen here Tuesday at 8 pm. Concerts also take place in the hall of the *Serbian Academy of Arts & Sciences*, Kneza Mihaila 35. From May to October there's horse racing at the *Hippodrome* every Sunday afternoon.

Getting There & Away

Air There are JAT flights from Belgrade to Dubrovnik (US$22), Ohrid (US$25), Pula (US$28), Sarajevo (US$18), Skopje (US$23), Split (US$24), Osijek (US$17) and Zadar (US$25).

Train Belgrade is the hub of railway service in Yugoslavia. There are international trains to Athens (via Skopje), Berlin (via Budapest), Bucharest (via Timisoara), Istanbul (via Sofia), Moscow (via Kecskemet), Munich (via Ljubljana), Paris (via Venice) and Vienna (via Maribor). Overnight domestic trains with inexpensive couchettes or sleepers run from Belgrade to Bar, Bitola, Kardeljevo, Koper, Ljubljana, Maribor, Pula, Rijeka, Sarajevo, Skopje, Split, Zadar and Zagreb. Most of the above depart the main station on Trg bratstva i jedinstva. Trains to Romania depart Beograd-Dunav Station, Dure Dakovida 39.

Putnik Travel Agency, Terazije 27, sells train tickets and makes advance reservations at the same prices charged in the station, but without the crowds. International tickets can be purchased with Yugoslav dinars.

Boat Yugoslav hydrofoils operating on the Danube leave from the terminal on Karadordeva, a few blocks north of the train station.

Getting Around

Airport Transport The JAT bus (US$1) departs frequently from the JAT City Terminal on Bulevar Revolucije in front of St Mark's Church. Surcin Airport is 20 km west of the city.

Public Transport Twelve-strip public transport tickets are sold at kiosks. You validate your own ticket once aboard, two strips for the first zone then one more for each additional zone. If you're going far, ask someone how many strips to use. Tickets purchased from the driver are more expensive. Night buses between midnight and 4 am charge double fare.

NOVI SAD

Capital of the autonomous province of Vojvodina, this friendly modern city at a strategic bend of the Danube grew up in the 18th century when a powerful fortress was built on a hilltop overlooking the river to hold the area for the Hapsburgs. Novi Sad remained part of the Austro-Hungarian Empire until 1918 and retains a Hungarian air to this day. The main sights can be covered in a couple of hours or made into a leisurely day.

Orientation

The adjacent train and bus stations are at the end of Bulevar 23 Oktobra, several km north-west of the city centre. Catch a bus (pay the driver) to Trg Slobode, then ask directions to the tourist office at Dunavska 27, in a quaint old part of town.

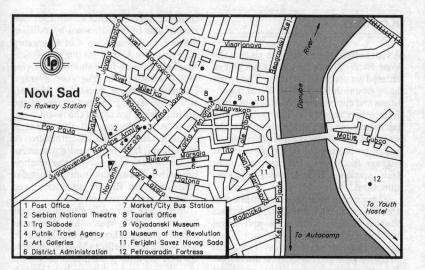

Map legend:

1	Post Office	7	Market/City Bus Station
2	Serbian National Theatre	8	Tourist Office
3	Trg Slobode	9	Vojvodanski Museum
4	Putnik Travel Agency	10	Museum of the Revolution
5	Art Galleries	11	Ferijalni Savez Novog Sada
6	District Administration	12	Petrovaradin Fortress

Things to See

There are three museums on Dunavska near the tourist office: paintings at Dunavska 29 (closed Monday and Tuesday), archaeology at Dunavska 35 (closed Monday) and war history at Dunavska 37. This latter museum is very near the Danube. Cross the old bridge on foot to majestic **Petrovaradin Citadel**, designed by the French architect Vauban. Today the citadel contains a hotel, restaurant and two small museums (closed Monday), but the chief pleasure is simply to walk along the walls and enjoy the marvellous views in all directions. There are as many as 16 km of underground galleries and halls below the citadel, but these can only be visited by groups.

Other sights of Novi Sad include three substantial **art galleries** (closed Monday and Tuesday) side by side in a row on Vase Stajica, not far from Trg Slobode, and the ultramodern **Serbian National Theatre**, also close by.

Places to Stay

Private Rooms All of Novi Sad's hotels are characterless and very expensive so ask about private rooms at Putnik, Narodnih heroja 8 just off Trg Slobode.

Hostels If you arrive during business hours and want IYHF youth hostel accommodation, visit the Ferijalni Savez Novog Sada, Kej M Pijade 2 near the bridge across to Petrovaradin Citadel. They'll let you know if any beds are free at the hostel, which is quite a distance out on the south side of the river. Get there on the Paragovo bus from the market, as far as Ribnjak. Then ask for *Ferijalni dom*, Donji put 79, down near the river about a km from the bus stop.

Camping There's a large *Autocamp*, near the Danube at Ribarsko Ostrvo, with bungalows (US$10 double) available year-round. Take the Liman bus from opposite Putnik to the end of the line, then walk two km toward the river.

Getting There & Away

Novi Sad is on the main line between Belgrade and Budapest. All express trains stop here.

Kosovo

A visit to Kosovo is a little like visiting the West Bank or Gaza Strip: you feel you've entered an occupied territory. The locals have an uninhibited Third World friendliness and curiosity which sets them apart from other Yugoslavs. The poverty and backwardness are also apparent, as is the watchful eye of the central government. Police posts have taken the place of left luggage facilities in the regions' bus or train stations. Your presence won't go unnoticed.

There's no way around the impression that Belgrade isn't interested in tourists visiting Kosovo. City maps and travel brochures hardly exist. Regional hotels and the few campgrounds aren't included in the national accommodation directories. Private rooms are unavailable and hotel rooms are priced so high you'd have to be crazy to stay more than one night. All youth hostels in Kosovo have been closed. It's really *off the beaten track*.

What's actually going on is hard to determine. People seem afraid to speak. Officially, the Socialist Autonomous Region of Kosovo is an integral part of Serbia. Isolated medieval Serbian monasteries tell of an early period which ended in 1389 with the Battle of Kosovo just outside Pristina. After this disaster the Serbs moved north and their place was taken by Islamic Albanian and Turkish immigrants. In the late 19th century the ethnic Albanians, who today comprise 85% of the population of Kosovo, fought to free themselves of Ottoman rule. Yet when the Turkish government finally pulled out in 1913 Kosovo was handed over to Serbia instead of remaining with the rest of Albania.

Since then Kosovo has suffered exploitation, neglect and repression under a series of outside rulers. After serious rioting in 1968 a so-called 'autonomous region' was created and economic aid increased. These changes brought only cosmetic improvements and in 1981 new rioting had to be put down by military force. A curfew and state of emergency were imposed. At the time unemployment stood at 27.5% and the standard of living was a quarter the Yugoslav average. Hundreds of those arrested in 1981 are still in jail serving 15-year sentences and it's impossible not to feel the resentment. Local Albanians say all they want is republic status like Montenegro or Macedonia, but the central government seems to feel that, given the chance, Kosovo would withdraw from the Yugoslav Federation. So Kosovo stays poor and solutions remain remote.

Just under two million people occupy Kosovo's 10,887 square km, the most densely populated portion of Yugoslavia. The region has a definite Muslim air, from the food and dress of the inhabitants to the ubiquitous mosques. The capital, Pristina, is a depressing, redeveloped city with showpiece banks and hotels juxtaposed against the squalor. In the west the Metohija Valley between Pec and Prizren offers a useful transit route from the Adriatic to Macedonia, plus a chance to see another side of this perplexing country.

PEC

Pec (Peje), below high mountains between Titograd and Pristina, is a friendly, untouristed town of picturesque dwellings slowly being ruined by uncontrolled development. Ethnic Albanians with their white felt skullcaps and Muslim women in traditional dress crowd the streets, especially on Saturday market day. The horse wagons used to carry goods around Pec share the streets with lots of beggars.

Orientation

The bus and train stations are about a km apart, both in the north part of Pec about two km from the centre. Neither station has a left luggage room.

Information

Metohija Turist is in the centre or there is the Turist Kosova Agency.

Things to See

There are eight well preserved, functioning mosques in Pec, the most imposing of which is the 15th century **Bajrakli Mosque**, its high dome rising out of the colourful **bazaar** *(carsija)* giving Pec an authentic Oriental air. By the river two km south of Pec is the frescoed 13th century **Patrijarsija Monastery**, seat of the Serbian Orthodox patriarchate until 1766.

Pec's most impressive sight however is an hour to the south, past the large military base, accessible by frequent local bus. The **Visoki Decani Monastery** (1335) with its marvellous 14th century frescoes is a two-km walk from the bus stop in Decani through beautifully wooded countryside. This royal monastery built under kings Decanski and Dusan survived the long Turkish period intact. From Decani you can pick up an onward bus to Prizren.

Places to Stay

Hotels Accommodation in Pec is problematic. None of the travel agencies in town offer private rooms, although you may be able to find one if you're very persistent in asking around. *Hotel Korzo* in the centre of town charges US$16 per person for a room with shared bath and breakfast – a lot for this dump. With private bath the Korzo wants US$20 single, US$36 double, even though the floor in the corridor outside may be flooded and the paint peeling from the walls. The *Metohija Hotel* nearby is a lot better but at US$35 single, US$48 double with private bath and breakfast it's a budget breaker.

Camping The only inexpensive place to stay is *Kamp Karagac* over the bridge and a km up the hill from the Metohija Hotel. They charge US$11 for two people to camp, but it's quiet and rather pleasant with lots of shade. There's a restaurant at the campground. If you don't have a tent Kamp Karagac wants US$40 for a double room! Avoid Pec outside the camping season.

Getting There & Away

Train The Akropolis Express between Munich and Athens stops at Kosovo Polje, a junction eight km west of Pristina, from where there are branch lines to Pec and Prizren.

Bus Bus service from Prizren and Skopje is good. There are five buses a day between Titograd and Pec, crossing the 1849-metre-high Cakor Pass. Alternatively take one of the 16 daily buses between Titograd and Ivangrad, then look for an onward bus to Pec. *Autocamp Berane* is less than a km from Ivangrad bus station if you get stuck.

PRIZREN

Prizren, the most Albanian looking city in Yugoslavia, is midway between Pec and Skopje. The closed road to Shkoder reaches the Albanian border 18 km west of Prizren. Prizren was the medieval capital of 'Old Serbia,' but much of what we see today is Turkish. Houses climb colourfully up the hillside to the ruined citadel *(kaljaja)* from which the 15th century Turkish bridge and 19 minarets are visible.

The Bistrica River emerges from a gorge behind the citadel and cuts Prizren in two on its way into Albania. East up this gorge is the Bistrica Pass (2640 metres), once the main route to Macedonia. Wednesday is market day when the city really comes alive.

Orientation

The bus and train stations are adjacent on the west side of town, but there is no left luggage facilities in either.

Information

Putnik is at Trg 17 Novembar in the centre.

Things to See

The **Sinan Pasha Mosque** (1615) beside the river is closed, as are the **Gazi Mehmed Pasha Baths** (1563) beyond the Theranda Hotel. A little back from these is the large dome of the beautifully appointed 16th century **Bajrakli (Gazi Mehmed) Mosque**, still in active use. Behind this mosque on the river side is the **Museum of the Prizren League**, a popular movement which struggled for Albanian independence from the Ottoman Empire in 1878-1881.

The largest Orthodox church in Prizren is **Sveti Georgi** (1856) in the old town near the Sinan Pasha Mosque. Higher up on the way to the **citadel** is **Sveti Spas** with the ruins of an Orthodox monastery.

Places to Stay

No private rooms are available in Prizren. The *Theranda Hotel*, in the centre of town by the river, is US$15 per person with private bath. Also try the *Putnik Hotel* three blocks from the bus station (US$16 single, US$24 double, US$30 suite), although it's often full. Camping may be possible behind the Putnik.

Places to Eat

There are several good *cevapcici* places between Sveti Georgi and Sinan Pasha.

Getting There & Away

Bus service from Pristina, Pec and Skopje is good.

Macedonia

Macedonia's volatile position between Albania, Bulgaria, Greece and Serbia has often made it a political powder keg. From here Alexander the Great set out to conquer the ancient world. Alternating Islamic and Orthodox overtones tell of a later struggle which ended in 1913 when the Treaty of Bucharest divided Macedonia among its four neighbours. Serbia got the biggest chunk; the southern half went to Greece. Albania and Bulgaria received much smaller slices, although the Macedonian language is close to Bulgarian. The Macedonians of today are South Slavs who bear no relation whatever to the Greek-speaking Macedonians of antiquity. A high proportion of the population is Muslim.

The Vardar River cuts across the middle of this southernmost Yugoslav republic passing the capital, Skopje, on its way to Greece. To the north-west the 2748-metre-high Sar Planina forms the border with Kosovo. Lakes Ohrid and Prespan in the south-west drain into Albania. Macedonia is a land of contrasts from space age Skopje with its ultramodern shopping centre and antique bazaar, to Ohrid with its many medieval monasteries, to thoroughly Turkish Bitola.

SKOPJE

Skopje, third largest city in Yugoslavia and capital of the Yugoslav portion of Macedonia, is strategically set on the Vardar River at a crossroads of Balkan routes almost exactly midway between Tirane and Sofia, capitals of neighbouring Albania and Bulgaria. Thessaloniki, Greece, is 260 km south-east, near the point where the Vardar flows into the Aegean.

The Romans recognised the location's importance long ago by making Scupi the centre of the Mardania region. Later conquerors included the Slavs, Byzantines, Normans, Bulgarians and Serbians, until the Turks arrived in 1392 and managed to hold onto Uskup (Skopje) until 1912. Since then the city has belonged to what is now Yugoslavia, although the Bulgarians occupied the area during both world wars.

If any city in the world is disaster prone it must be Skopje. There were devastating earthquakes in 518 and 1555. In 1689 the Austrians burned the city. In November 1962 the Vardar River suddenly flooded 5000 homes. But the date no one in Skopje will ever forget is Friday 26 July 1963 when

1 Stadium
2 Camping Park
3 Museum of
   Contemporary Art
4 Theatre of the
   Minorities
5 Market
6 Museum of Macedonia
7 Mustafa Pasha Mosque
8 Castle Hill
9 Communist Party HQ
10 Church of Sveti Spas
11 Suli Han
12 Sultan Murat Mosque
   & Clock Tower
13 Tourist Information
14 Turkish Bath House
15 Orthodox Church
16 Turkish Stone Bridge
17 Bus Station
18 Main Post Office
19 Cathedral
20 JAT Airline Office
21 Jadran Hotel
22 Adria Airways
23 Self–Service Restaurant
24 Hotel Turist
25 Bristol Hotel
26 City Museum
27 Shopping Centre
28 Grand Hotel
29 Cultural Centre
30 Academy of Sciences
31 Youth Hostel
32 Railway Station

Skopje

an earthquake almost levelled the city killing 1066 people in the process.

After this disaster massive outside aid poured in to create the modern urban landscape we see today. It's evident that many of the planners got carried away by the money being thrown their way and erected some oversized irrelevant structures which are now crumbling for lack of maintenance and function. Fortunately much of the old town survived so Skopje offers the chance to see the whole history of the Balkans in one shot, almost as if it had been cut in

half with a knife. It's not a city you will easily forget, nor will you care to linger, but one hectic day is sure to teach you something if you keep your eyes open.

Orientation

The 15th century Turkish stone bridge over the Vardar River links the old and new towns. South of the bridge is Ploscad Marsala Tito which gives into Ulica Marsala Tito leading south. The new elevated railway station is a 15-minute walk east of the stone bridge. The bus station is a few minutes walk north of the bridge, although plans are underway to move it east to a new location near the railway station. Further north is Carsija, the old Turkish bazaar.

Information

The tourist information office is opposite the Daut Pasha Baths on the viaduct between the bridge and Carsija. There's an exchange office in the Grand Hotel on Ulica Mose Pijade, theoretically open daily from 6 am to 10 pm. If the clerk has pragmatically taken off for a break or a sleep the hotel desk might deign to change money for you.

Things to See

As you walk north from the bridge you'll see the **Daut Pasha Baths** (1466) on the right, the largest Turkish baths in the Balkans, now the City Art Gallery. Almost opposite this building is a functioning Orthodox church. North again is Carsija, the old market area, which is well worth exploring. Steps up on the left lead to the tiny church of **Sveti Spas** with a finely carved iconostasis done in 1824 (admission US$0.50, Yugoslavs half price). It's half buried because at the time of construction in the 18th century no church was allowed to be higher than a mosque.

Beyond the church is the **Mustafa Pasha Mosque** (1492), now more popular among tourists who come to see the earthquake-cracked dome than among devotees. The US$0.50 ticket includes the right to ascend the 124 steps of the minaret. In the park across the street from this mosque are the ruins of the castle, **Fort Kale**, with an 11th century cyclopean wall and good views of Skopje. Higher up the same hill is the lacklustre **Museum of Contemporary Art** (closed Monday) where special exhibitions are presented.

The lane on the north side of Mustafa Pasha Mosque leads back down into Carsija and the **Museum of Macedonia**. This large collection covers the history of the region fairly well but, though the periods are identified in English at the top of some of the showcases, much is lost on visitors unable to read the Cyrillic captions and explanations. The museum is housed in the modern white building behind the **Kursumli Han** (1550), a caravanserai or inn used by traders during the Turkish period. In the 19th century it was turned into a notorious prison. Two more caravanserais distinguished by their two-story interior courtyards, the Suli Han and the Kapan Han, are hidden among the streets of old Carsija.

You don't really need a guide to modern Skopje as its interest is more sociological than architectural. Don't miss the huge **shopping centre** however, just south-east of the Turkish stone bridge, the biggest in the country. Finally, take the time to go to the former railway station, now the **City Museum** at the south end of Ulica Marsala Tito, where the clock stopped at 5.17 am on 26 July 1963. There's a little too much politicising inside to make you take it very seriously but it certainly does tell you what today's Skopje is all about.

Places to Stay

Private Rooms There are two offices offering private rooms: the Tourist Information Office on the viaduct two blocks north of the Turkish stone bridge and an office marked 'private accommodation/souvenirs' beside the café on the left at the south end of the bridge. Rooms start at US$17 double but they're in short supply. In July and August ask at the Tourist Information Office about accommodation in student hostels.

Hostels The cheapest place to stay is the *Dom 'Blagoj Sosolcev' Youth Hostel* (IYHF), Prolet 25 near the railway station. Open year-round, the charge including breakfast is US$3 for members, US$5 for non-members in a six-bed dorm, or US$4 for members, US$7 for non-members in a double room.

Hotels The rather basic *Jadran Hotel* facing Ploscad Marsala Tito near the Main Post Office is US$21 single, US$29 double with shared bath, US$23 single, US$31 double with private bath. Dumpy *Hotel Turist* on Ulica Marsala Tito is US$35 double. The *Bristol Hotel* nearby is similar.

Camping From April to mid-October you can pitch a tent at *Feroturist Autocamp Park* for US$3 per person, US$2 per tent. Caravans are for hire at US$8 per person. This campground is between the river and the stadium, a 15-minute walk upstream from the Turkish stone bridge along the right (south) bank. It could be crowded in July and August, otherwise it's a good bet.

Places to Eat
Colourful small restaurants in Carsija serving kebab and *cevapcici* reflect a Turkish culinary heritage still dear to the stomachs of many Macedonians.

For more prosaic fare there are two self-service restaurants in the modern city centre beyond Ploscad Marsala Tito at the south side of the Turkish stone bridge. *Pelister Self-Service* is fairly obvious across the square at the beginning of Ulica Marsala Tito, on the left as you come from the bridge. *Ishrana Self-Service* is half a block away down the next street over to the right. Because Ishrana takes a few minutes to locate it gets far fewer tourists than Pelister. Neither place is exceptional but they do fill your stomach without a hassle to order and a fight over the price.

Getting There & Away
Air JAT Airlines, Bulevar Partizanski odredi 17, has direct flights to Belgrade (US$23), Dubrovnik (US$22), Ljubljana (US$33) and Split (US$27). Also ask about flights on Adria Airlines which may be more convenient.

Train All three daily trains between Europe and Greece pass through Skopje. Other fast trains run to Belgrade, local trains to Bitola. The cheapest way to Greece would be to take a local train to the border, Gevgeli, and look for onward transport to Thessaloniki there. Couchettes are available to Belgrade and Zagreb. There's a travel agency in the railway station which sells international tickets and books couchettes. On a good day they'll even change money (but never on Sunday).

Bus There are buses to Ohrid, Bitola, Pristina, Prizren, Pec, Titograd and Belgrade. Book a seat on the bus of your choice the day before, especially if you're headed for Lake Ohrid. There are two bus routes to Lake Ohrid. The one through Tetovo is much faster and more direct than the bus that goes via Titov Veles and Bitola.

LAKE OHRID
Lake Ohrid, a natural tectonic lake in the south-west corner of Macedonia, is the deepest lake in Europe (294 metres) and one of the oldest in the world. A third of its 15-by-30-km surface belongs to Albania. Nestled among mountains at an altitude of 695 metres, the Yugoslav portion is the more beautiful and accessible with striking vistas of the open waters from beach and hill.

The town of Ohrid is the Yugoslav tourist mecca of the south. Signs in the windows of market cafes offer *hollandse koffie*. Some 30 'cultural monuments' in the area keep the droves of visitors busy. Predictably, the oldest ruins readily seen today are Roman. Lihnidos (Ohrid) was on the Via Egnatia which connected the Adriatic to the Aegean. Part of a Roman amphitheatre has been uncovered in the old town.

Under Byzantium Ohrid became the episcopal centre of Macedonia. The first Slavic university was founded here in 893 and from the 10th century until 1767 the patriarchate of Ohrid held sway. Many of the small Orthodox churches with intact medieval frescoes have now been adapted to the needs of ticketed tourists. Nice

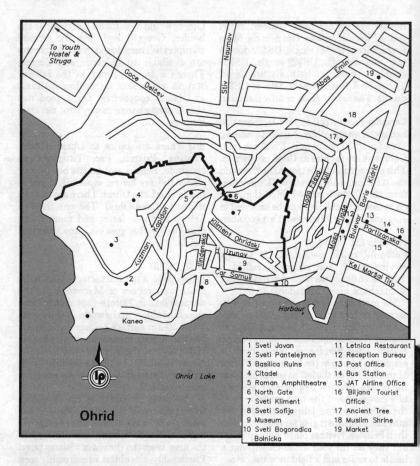

To Youth
Hostel &
Struga

Goce Delčev

Sliv Naumov

Abas Emin

Kuzman Kapidon

Ilindenska

H. Uzunov

Kliment Ohridski

Nađa Fileva

4 Juli

Mosa Pijade

Bulevar Boris Kidrič

Partizanska

Kei Maršal Tito

Car Samuil

Kaneo

Harbour

Ohrid Lake

Ohrid

1 Sveti Jovan
2 Sveti Pantelejmon
3 Basilica Ruins
4 Citadel
5 Roman Amphitheatre
6 North Gate
7 Sveti Kliment
8 Sveti Sofija
9 Museum
10 Sveti Bogorodica Bolnicka
11 Letnica Restaurant
12 Reception Bureau
13 Post Office
14 Bus Station
15 JAT Airline Office
16 'Biljana' Tourist Office
17 Ancient Tree
18 Muslim Shrine
19 Market

little signs in Roman letters direct you to the sights, but even the cellophane wrapping doesn't completely spoil the flavour of enchanting Lake Ohrid.

Orientation

Ohrid bus station is next to the post office in the centre of town. West is the old town, south is the lake.

Information

'Biljana' Tourist Office is at Partizanska 3 beside the bus station.

Things to See

The picturesque old town of Ohrid rises from Mose Pijade, the main pedestrian mall, up toward Sveti Kliment Church and the citadel. A medieval town wall still isolates this hill from the surrounding valley. Near the North Gate is 13th century **Sveti Kliment**, almost covered inside with vivid frescoes of Biblical scenes. Below is 11th century **Sveti Sofija**, also worth the US$0.75 admission price. Aside from the frescoes there's an unusual Turkish *mimbar* (pulpit) from the days when the church was used as a mosque and an upstairs portico of real architectural interest.

From here signs direct you on to the tiny 13th century **Church of Sveti Jovan**, a very pleasant spot even if you don't pay to go inside. There's a beach at the foot of the cliffs. The bubbles and foam you see on the surface of the water here originate in a stream below the citadel which pours raw sewage directly into the lake. In the park above Sveti Jovan on the way to the citadel is the shell of **Sveti Pantelejmon**, now a small museum, and nearby the ruins of an Early Christian **basilica** with 5th century mosaics covered by protective sand. The many splendid views from the walls of the 10th century **citadel** make it all worthwhile.

The better part of a second day at Ohrid could be spent on a pilgrimage to the Albanian border to see the 17th century **Church of Sveti Naum** on a hill above the lake, 29 km south of Ohrid by bus. You have to walk the last km or so and there's no guarantee the church will be open but you do get a view of the Albanian town of Pogradec across the lake. Inside the church is a finely carved iconostasis. In summer you can also come by boat (ask at the tourist office about times and tickets).

There's frequent bus service from Ohrid to **Struga**. This small Yugoslav town at the north end of the lake is divided by the Crni Drim River, which drains Ohrid Lake into the Adriatic near Shkoder, Albania. On Saturday there's a large market at Struga. Each year at the end of August poets converge on Struga for an international festival of poetry.

Places to Stay

Private Rooms The 'Biljana' Tourist Office, Partizanska 3 beside the bus station, costs you US$8 per person (three nights or less) plus US$1 per person per day tax for private rooms. If this seems excessive cheaper private rooms are available from tourist offices in nearby Struga.

Hostels & Hotels Alternatively there's the *'Mladost' Youth Hostel* (IYHF) in a pleasant location on the lake a little over two km west of Ohrid toward Struga. A bed in a dorm or a small four-berth caravan will cost around US$4 per person or you can pitch a tent for half that. The hostel is open from April to mid-October and YHA membership cards are not essential. In mid-summer it can get crowded. If you're walking to the hostel turn left at the fifth minaret counting from the one opposite the old tree at the top of Mose Pijade.

The *Mladinski Centar*, a modern hotel next to the youth hostel, is US$10 per person and stays open year-round.

Camping *Autocamp Gradiste* (open May to September) is halfway to Sveti Naum (US$2 per person, US$2.50 per tent). There's also *Autocamp Sveti Naum* near the monastery of that name, both accessible on the Sveti Naum bus.

Places to Eat

The easiest place to eat at Ohrid is the *Letnica Self-Service Restaurant* near the bus station. The food is surprisingly good.

Getting There & Away

Train The nearest railway station is at Bitola, 73 km east. The Reception Bureau beside the Letnica Restaurant can reserve couchettes from Bitola to Ljubljana or any point along the way. They must do this by phone and the berths are in high demand, so allow plenty of lead time.

Bus Some buses between Ohrid and Skopje run via Tetovo (three hours, US$3), others via Bitola. The former route is much shorter and faster so check. It pays to book a seat the day before.

To the Adriatic The easiest way to the Adriatic is a direct flight to Dubrovnik (US$21). The JAT airline office is opposite the bus station. Alternatively take a bus to Skopje, then another to Titograd, then another to Dubrovnik.

BITOLA

Bitola, the southernmost city in Yugoslavia and second largest in Yugoslav Macedonia, sits on a 660-metre-high plateau between the mountains 16 km north of the Greek border. It's a friendly, untouristed town with a lot of Turkish architecture and a colourful old bazaar area (Stara Carsija).

Most travellers only spend a few hours in Bitola on their way to or from Greece but the city is worth a stop for its own sake. The Roman ruins at Heraclea are among the most beautifully situated and peaceful in Europe. Mt Pelister (2601 metres), a ski resort near Bitola, also beckons the summertime hiker.

Orientation

The adjacent bus and train stations are on the south side of town, a 10-minute walk from the centre via City Park and Bitola's pedestrian promenade, Ulica Marsala Tito.

Information

Palasturist is at Ulica Marsala Tito 109.

Things to See

The **Heraclea ruins** beyond the old cemetery a km south of the railway station should be at the top of your list (admission US$0.75, photos US$1.50 extra). Founded in the 4th century BC by Philip II of Macedonia, Heraclea was conquered by the Romans two centuries later and became an important stage on the Via Egnatia. From the 4th to 6th centuries AD it was an episcopal seat. Excavations continue but the Roman baths, portico and theatre can now be seen. More interesting are the two Early Christian basilicas and the episcopal palace complete with splendid mosaics. There's also a small museum through the refreshment stand and a nice terrace on which to have a Coke or beer.

The other sights of Bitola are two km north of Heraclea via the City Park and Ulica Marsala Tito. On the square at the north end of Marsala Tito are the 17th century **clock tower**, a symbol of Bitola, the **Jeni Dzami Mosque** (now the Mose Pijade Art Gallery), the **Isak Mosque** and the **Bezistan**, a 16th century covered market. The **Church of St Dimitrius** on Ulica 11 Oktomvri just south of the clock tower contains a large wooden iconostasis (1830).

Stara Carsija, the 19th century old bazaar district, is just east of the Bezistan, north of the river. Here craftsmen pursue their age-old trades, while the bustling **city market** is beyond (busiest on Tuesday).

Places to Stay

Travel agencies in Bitola don't handle private rooms, although Palasturist, Marsala Tito 109, might be able to direct you to something. There are two hotels: the high-rise *Epinal Hotel* (US$20 per person) and the *Macedonia Hotel* beside Putnik nearby (US$12 per person). There's a basic campground near the Bonanza Restaurant three km out on the road to Ohrid.

Places to Eat

Bitola's self-service restaurant is also next to Putnik.

Getting There & Away

The bus and train stations are adjacent with left luggage in the bus station. Bus service to Ohrid and Skopje are good. There are local trains to Skopje. An overnight express train runs north to Ljubljana via Belgrade. For couchettes and tickets for this and most other trains go to Putnik Travel Agency, Marsala Tito 77 in the centre as the ticket office in the railway station is hopeless.

To/From Greece There's a daily afternoon train between Bitola and the Greek border (Kremenica). There you change to a connecting Greek train which carries you

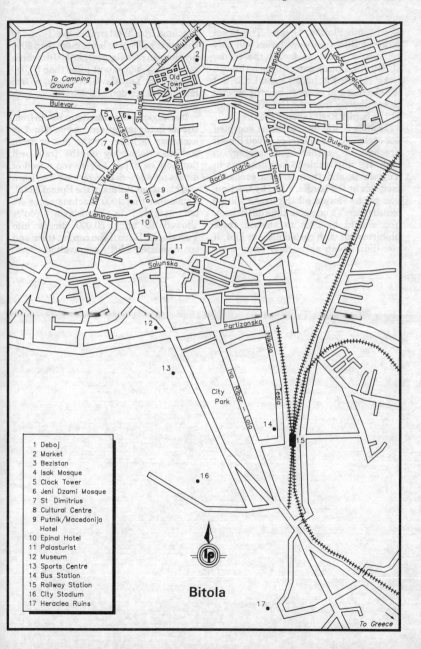

1 Deboj
2 Market
3 Bezistan
4 Isak Mosque
5 Clock Tower
6 Jeni Dzami Mosque
7 St Dimitrius
8 Cultural Centre
9 Putnik/Macedonija
   Hotel
10 Epinal Hotel
11 Palasturist
12 Museum
13 Sports Centre
14 Bus Station
15 Railway Station
16 City Stadium
17 Heraclea Ruins

Bitola

To Camping Ground
Old Town
To Greece
City Park

slowly into Florina, Greece. The ticket office at Bitola railway station will only sell you a ticket as far as the border (US$0.35). Putnik can sell you a through ticket right to Florina for about US$3, but it's cheaper and easier to buy the onward ticket directly from the Greek conductor at the border itself (about US$1).

Trouble is, dinars are neither accepted nor exchangeable in Greece so you'll need drachma or another hard currency in cash. It's impossible to buy drachma in Yugoslavia and there are no exchange facilities at the border. Also, by the time you get to Florina all the banks will be closed (there's a one-hour time difference). You should be able to smooth these problems out with cash dollars or DM, if you didn't plan ahead and bring some drachma from Western Europe. To add to the fun it's illegal to bring more than 3000 drachma in notes larger than 500 drachma into Greece, nor export more than 50,000 dinars from Yugoslavia. Actually, no one really cares but don't flash too much cash unnecessarily.

Northbound if you arrive in Bitola from Greece in the late afternoon you'll find no exchange facilities at the bus or train stations. Somebody on the train will probably be happy to give you a wad of dinars for a few dollars or walk into town and change at Putnik or the Epinal Hotel. Remember that 1000 drachma notes are not accepted in Yugoslavia. You're allowed to bring 50,000 dinars into Yugoslavia. Do so if you can get them and spare yourself a little aggravation.

Albania

Contrary to popular belief Albania is *not* a closed country, although individuals and Americans are not admitted. The number of European visitors and the choice of entry points is increasing. Long considered fair prey by every imperialist power, Albania chose a curious form of isolation. Their folk songs and dances express passionate feelings of freedom and independence. Although Albania now has diplomatic relations with over 100 countries, the USA and USSR are not among them.

Backwardness, blood vendettas and illiteracy have been replaced by a socialist people's republic. The Albanians claim to have the purest form of Communism. It's the only place in the world where monuments and main boulevards are still dedicated to Joseph Stalin. Despite the current cautious opening to the west the mystery of the Republika Popullore Shqiperise, or the 'Land of the Eagle' as the Albanians call it, holds our interest. After all, you don't have a chance to step directly back to the 1950s every day!

Facts about the Country

HISTORY

The original inhabitants were the Illyrians, ancestors of today's Albanians. The Greeks arrived in the 7th century BC and established self-governing colonies at Epidamnus (Durres), Apolonia and Butrint. They traded peacefully with the Illyrians, who formed tribal states in the 4th century BC. The south became part of Greek Epirus.

In the 2nd half of the 3rd century BC an expanding Illyrian kingdom based at Shkoder came into conflict with Rome which sent a fleet of 200 vessels against Queen Teuta in 228 BC. After a second

Roman naval expedition in 219 BC, Philip V of Macedonia came to the aid of his Illyrian allies in 214 BC. This led to a long war which resulted in the extension of Roman control over the entire Balkans by 167 BC.

Like the Greeks, the Illyrians preserved their own language and traditions despite centuries of Roman rule. Under the Romans Illyria enjoyed peace and prosperity. The main trade route between Rome and Constantinople, the Via Egnatia, ran from Durres to Thessaloniki.

When the empire was divided in 395 AD Illyria was included in Byzantium. Invasions by migrating peoples, Visigoths, Huns, Ostrogoths and Slavs continued through the 5th and 6th centuries. Into the 11th century control passed back and forth between Byzantium and the Bulgarians.

The feudal principality of Arberit was established at Kruje in 1190. Other independent feudal states appeared in the 14th century and the towns developed. After the defeat of Serbia by the Turks in 1389 Albania was subjected to Ottoman domination. From 1443 to 1468 the national hero, Gjergj Kastrioti-Skanderbeg, led Albanian resistance to the Turks from his castle at Kruje. Skanderbeg won all 25

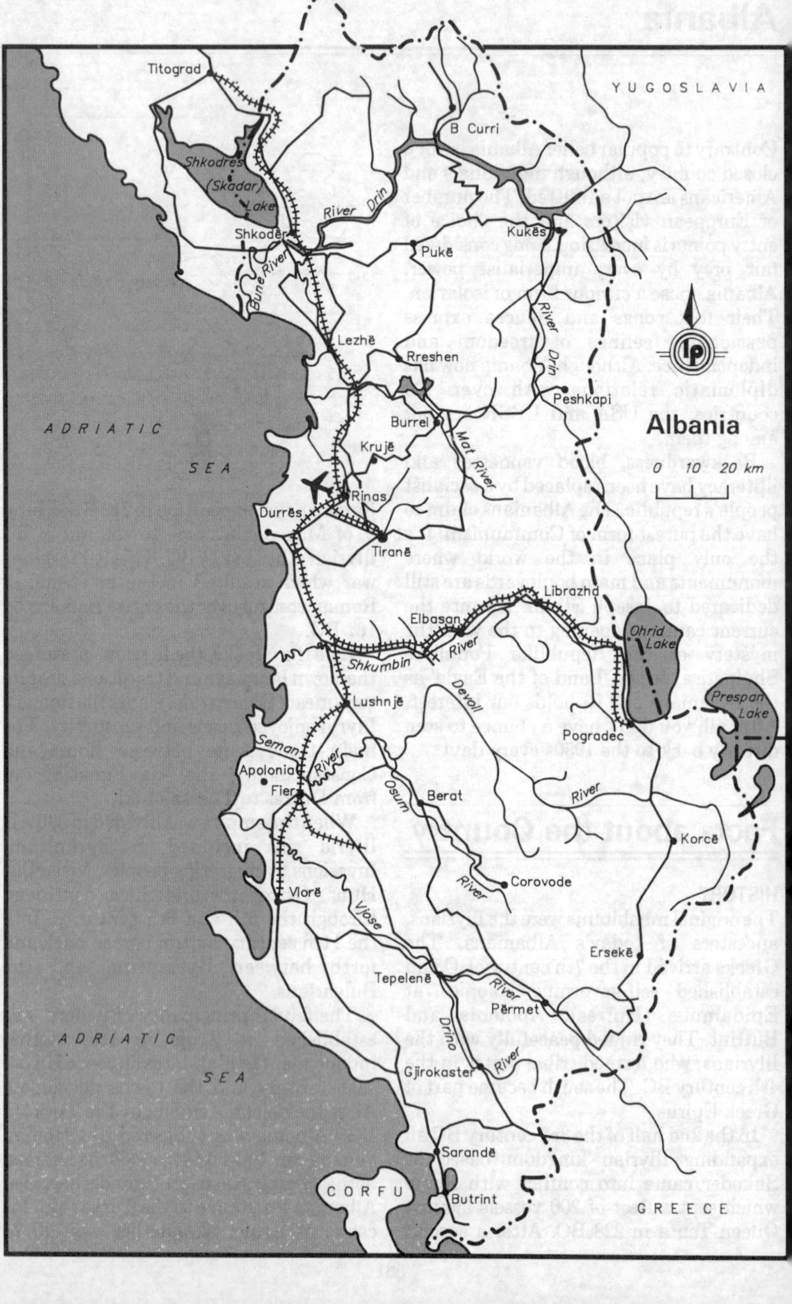

YUGOSLAVIA

Titograd

B Curri

Shkodrës
(Skadar)
Lake

River Drin

Shkoder

Kukes

Bune River

Puke

River Drin

ADRIATIC

Lezhë

Rreshen

SEA

Peshkapi

Burrel

Albania

Krujë

0   10   20 km

Durrës

Rinas

Tiranë

Librazhd

Elbasan   River

Ohrid
Lake

Shkumbin

Prespan
Lake

Lushnjë

Devoll

Pogradec

Seman

Osum

River

Apolonia

Fier

Berat

River

Viose   River

Corovode

Korcë

Vlorë

Erseke

Tepelenë

Drino   River

Përmet

ADRIATIC

SEA

Gjirokaster

Sarandë

CORFU

Butrint

GREECE

battles he fought against the Turks and even Sultan Mehmet-Fatih, conqueror of Constantinople, could not take Kruje. Albania was not definitively incorporated into the Ottoman Empire until 1479 and remained there until 1912.

In 1878 the Albanian League at Prizren began a liberation struggle, put down by the Turkish army in 1881. Uprisings in 1910-1912 culminated in a proclamation of independence and the formation of a provisional government led by Ismail Qemali at Vlore in 1912. These achievements were severely compromised by the London Ambassadors' Conference which handed nearly half of Albania over to Serbia in 1913. In 1914 the Great Powers imposed a German aristocrat, Wilhelm Wied, on Albania as head of state. With the outbreak of WW I Albania was occupied by Greek, Serbian, French, Italian and Austro-Hungarian armies in succession.

In 1920 the Congress of Lushnje denounced foreign intervention and moved the capital from Durres to less vulnerable Tirane. Thousands of Albanian volunteers converged on Vlore and forced the occupying Italians to withdraw. In May 1924 Bishop Fan Noli established a fairly liberal government which was overthrown by a brutal reactionary, Ahmet Zog, on Christmas Eve that year. Zog ruled with Italian support and declared himself king in 1928. Zog's close collaboration with Italy backfired in April 1939 when Mussolini ordered an invasion of Albania. Zog fled to Britain and used gold looted from the Albanian treasury to rent a floor at London's Ritz Hotel.

On 8 November 1941 the Albanian Communist Party was founded with Enver Hoxha (pronounced Hodja) as First Secretary, a position he held until his death in April 1985. The Communists led the resistance to the Italians and, after 1943, to the Germans. By 29 November 1944 the Albanian National Liberation Army had crushed tribal quislings in the north and pursued the last Nazi troops from the country. Albania was the only Eastern European country where the Soviet Army was not involved in these operations.

In October 1946 two British warships struck mines in the Corfu Channel with the loss of 44 lives. The British Government blamed Albania and demanded £843,947 compensation. To back their claim they impounded 7100 kg of gold (now worth £50 million) stolen from Albania by the fascists. Albania has never accepted responsibility for the incident nor agreed to pay damages and the stubborn British are still holding the Albanian gold. The two countries have no diplomatic relations. It's now widely believed that Yugoslavia placed the mines. Good relations with Tito were always important to the British, while Albania was expendable. In the early 1950s there were British and American-backed landings in Albania by right-wing emigres. The last reported terrorist landing was on 25 September 1982.

In January 1946 a People's Republic of Albania was proclaimed with Enver Hoxha as president. In September 1948 Albania broke relations with Yugoslavia which had hoped to incorporate the country into the Yugoslav Federation. Albania collaborated closely with the USSR until 1960 when a heavy-handed Khrushchev demanded a submarine base at Vlore. Albania broke diplomatic relations with the Soviet Union in 1961 and reoriented itself toward the People's Republic of China. With the death of Mao Zedong in 1976 and the changes in China after 1978 this relationship ceased, although Albania has maintained diplomatic relations with China (and all the Eastern European countries except the USSR).

It's difficult to access the achievements of Enver Hoxha. Like his great rival Tito he put his own country's interests first and was uniquely successful in building Albanian self-reliance. In the face of real threats from all sides he liquidated potential rivals ruthlessly. (Tito, Khrushchev and others ordered Albanian Communists to overthrow Hoxha more than once.) A placard bearing Comrade Enver's words greets tourists clearing customs and immigration at the Albanian frontier: 'Even if we have to go without bread, we Albanians do not violate principles, we do not betray Marxism-Leninism.' It's often hard to have discussions about these matters with Albanians because many words have variable meanings. To them reality means 'that which must come,' freedom means not to choose the wrong side and opposition means treason.

Defence

One of the things which strikes visitors entering Albania by road from Yugoslavia or Greece are the concrete bunkers in lines and clusters stretching across the valleys at regular intervals all along the way. The Albanians began building bunkers in 1968 when Albania left the Warsaw Pact after the Soviet invasion of Czechoslovakia.

Today Albania is one of the most heavily defended countries in the world with literally thousands of igloo-shaped bunkers and pillboxes with narrow gun slits. They're strung along all borders, terrestrial and maritime, plus the approaches to all towns. The road from Durres to Tirane is one bunker after another for 35 km. Most are empty (and often used as toilets), but it's clear that in case of need they could be occupied by brigades from the factories and state farms within hours. This major deterrent is a remarkable physical manifestation of Albanian isolationism.

PEOPLE

The Albanians are an olive-skinned Mediterranean people, physically different from the more nordic Slavs. They trace their origins back to the Illyrians who inhabited this region before the coming of the Romans. The country's name comes from the Albanoi, an ancient Illyrian tribe. Three million Albanians live in Albania and another two million in Kosovo (Greater Albania), a situation which continues to sour relations with

Yugoslavia. Albanians resident in southern Italy are known as Arbereshi. Minorities in Albania include Greeks (2%), Romanians (1%) and Macedonians (1%).

Albania is one of the least densely populated states of Europe with just 35% of the people in urban areas. Tirane, the capital, is the largest city (202,000), followed by Durres, Shkoder, Elbasan, Vlore and Korce. Albania is divided into 26 administrative districts (rrethi).

Traditional dress is still commonly seen in rural areas, especially on Sundays and holidays. The Albanian men wear a white felt skull cap, an embroidered white shirt and typical knee trousers. Women's clothes are brighter than those of the men. Along with the standard white blouse with wide sleeves, women from Christian areas wear a red vest while Muslim women have baggy pants tied at the ankles and a coloured scarf around the head. Married women wear a white scarf around the neck.

ECONOMY

The economy is organised on the basis of rigid central planning. Industrial development has been spread out with factories in all regions. Before WW II 90% of the population worked in agriculture. There was little or no industry. Today 60% work in agriculture, 24% in industry and 16% in services. Albania is one of the few countries in the world with no foreign debt. Everything you see there is owned and produced by Albanians. Self-sufficiency is an even greater achievement considering the country's small size.

Albania is rich in natural resources such as oil, natural gas, coal, copper, iron-nickel and timber and is the world's third largest producer of chrome. The oil and gas of Fier have permitted the production of chemical fertilisers. The Central Mountains yield minerals such as copper in the north-east around Kukes, chromium further south near the Drin River, and iron-nickel closer to Ohrid Lake. The new railway to Pogradec carries ore down to the steel mill at Elbasan. There are several huge hydroelectric dams on the Drin River. Albania obtains 80% of its electricity from such dams and since 1972 exports power. Both steel mill and dams were built with Chinese technical assistance before 1978. Textiles are made at Berat, Korce and Tirane.

There's a good deal of foreign trade. Trade with socialist countries is largely done on an exchange or barter basis. One country will trade a commodity they produce for the products of another country according to 'the international division of labour.' After the breaks with the Soviet Union and China, Albania's trade had to be completely redirected. Albania's main trading partners are now Czechoslovakia, Italy and Yugoslavia, purchasing Albanian crude oil, chrome and food products. Trade with the west is increasing and Albania has always had a favourable balance of trade.

Once an importer, Albania now grows all its own food with surpluses available for export. The adequate supplies are demonstrated by the lack of lines at supermarkets, stores, etc. It may come as a surprise that Albanians enjoy a higher standard of living than many Yugoslavs, despite the lack of consumer goods. The absence of motor cars is a refreshing change. Things like income tax, budget deficits, inflation and unemployment are unknown.

GEOGRAPHY

Albania's strategic position between Greece, Yugoslavia and Italy, just west of Bulgaria and Turkey, has been decisive throughout its history. Vlore watches over the narrow Strait of Otranto at the entrance to the Adriatic. For decades Albania has been something of a barrier separating Greece from the rest of Europe. The Greek island of Corfu is only a few km from Sarande across the Ionic Sea.

Over three quarters of this 28,748-square-km country (the size of Belgium) consists of mountains and hills. There are three zones: coastal plain, mountains and

interior plain. The coastal plain extends over 200 km north to south and up to 50 km inland. The 2000-metre-high forested mountain spine up the entire length of Albania culminates at Mt Jezerca (2694 metres) in the north near the Yugoslav border. The longest river (283 km) is the Drin, which drains Ohrid Lake. The Drin flows into the Bune River near Shkodres Lake in the north. Albania shares three large tectonic lakes with Yugoslavia: Shkodres, Ohrid and Prespan. Ohrid is the deepest lake in the Balkans. The many olive trees, citrus plantations and vineyards give Albania a true Mediterranean air and 40% of the land is forested.

RELIGION

Albania is the only officially atheist state in the world. It has been illegal to practice religion since 1967 and many churches have been converted to theatres and cinemas. Formerly Albania was 70% Muslim, 10% Catholic (mostly in the north) and 17% Greek Orthodox (mostly in the south). It is prohibited to bring Bibles and religious literature into Albania.

FESTIVALS & HOLIDAYS

A National Folk Festival is held in Gjirokaster every five years (the next in 1993). Public holidays include 1 January (New Years), 11 January (Republic Day), 1 May (Labour Day), 7 November (Revolution Day), 28 November (Independence Day) and 29 November (Liberation Day).

LANGUAGE

Albanian is an Indo-European dialect of ancient Illyrian with many Latin, Greek and Slav words. Until the break with the Soviet Union in 1961 Russian was the most taught foreign language. Now English is more important, with French a distant second. Italian is sometimes a useful language in Albania as some of the older people will have learned it in school prior to 1943. Others may have picked it up by watching Italian television stations.

The days of the week, Monday to Sunday, are *hene, marte, merkure, ejte, premte, shtune, diele*. On signs at archaeological sites *pe sone* means BC, while *e sone* is AD. Albanians, like Bulgarians, shake their heads to say yes and nod to say no.

Facts for the Visitor

VISAS

Entry into Albania is only possible as a member of a package tour on a group visa (US$20 per person). The visa application is submitted by the tour company, not the individual tourist. Four identical photos are required, but not your passport. Details on the visa application must correspond to your passport exactly. If your passport is subsequently replaced prior to your arrival in Albania contact the tour operator immediately. Journalists and religious leaders are not granted visas so just list another occupation – they don't check. US nationals are not admitted. Throughout the stay in Albania the group visa is held by the tour leader and participants must travel with the group. There's no problem about walking around towns on your own, however. If you'll be

returning through Yugoslavia be sure to get a double entry Yugoslav visa.

Albanian officialdom is uptight about 'hippies' who might undermine 'socialist morals.' Keep your mini/maxi skirts, yellow trousers, headbands and beads well hidden until you're safely across the border. Long hair and beards were formerly banned, but this is no longer strictly enforced.

MONEY

US$1 = 7 leke

no compulsory exchange

1 lek = 100 qindarkas. Local prices in Albania haven't changed since the 1950s, so you'll find almost everything cheap. You probably won't be aware of a black market. Although Americans are forbidden to visit the country, US dollars are the second currency in Albania, used in hard currency shops and to pay for Albturist excursions, etc. Commission charges for changing travellers' cheques vary anywhere from two to seven leke, depending on the whim of the one making the transaction. Less commission is charged for changing cash. Upon arrival you'll have to list all your money and valuables on a declaration

form which you return to customs as you leave.

CLIMATE

Albania has a warm Mediterranean climate. The summers are hot and dry, the winters, when 40% of the rain falls, are mild and moist. The high interior plateau can be very cold in winter as continental air masses move in. July is the hottest month, but even May and October are quite pleasant.

BOOKS & BOOKSHOPS

Every town has a bookstore where you'll find some interesting works in English on Albanian history and culture. Since the non-aligned Yugoslav border guards confiscate all books printed in Albania, you'll have to mail them home if you'll be transiting that country. Postage is cheap and the mail service reliable, but bring some jiffy bags or wrapping paper and string. Use air mail, again to evade the non-aligned officials.

Albania – A Travel Guide by Philip Ward (Oleander Press, Cambridge, England, 1983) is a rambling survey full of confusing, irrelevant digressions which mixes anecdotes and trivia with practical information. The index makes it viable as a reference book but Ward is too often satisfied with glimpses and impressions rather than the whole picture. *Albania, General Information* ('8 Nentori' Publishing House, Tirane, 1984) is the other side of the coin. This weighty 295-page tome sold at most Albanian hotels provides a sleepy official view of the country with 40 pages on 'state organisation,' 46 pages on 'the people's economy,' and 63 pages on 'education, culture, art and science.' It only costs 8 leke so you can't go wrong.

Definitely the most exciting book about the country is *The Artful Albanian, The Memoirs of Enver Hoxha* (Chatto & Windus, London, 1986), edited by Jon Halliday. Halliday has selected the most revealing passages from the 3400 pages of Enver's six volumes of memoirs. Some of the chapters such as 'Battling Khrushchev' and 'Decoding China' are absolute classics.

NEWSPAPERS & MEDIA

Zeri i popullit (The People's Voice) is the daily organ of the Central Committee of the Party of Labour of Albania. *Bashkimi* is also published daily. *New Albania* is a bimonthly illustrated magazine which covers various aspects of Albanian life. *Albania Today* is a bimonthly political magazine.

FILM & PHOTOGRAPHY

Bring all the film you'll need. You're not supposed to take pictures of military installations but you'll have lots of opportunities to sneak shots of bunkers, if that interests you.

HEALTH

Medical care is free for everyone (visitors included). Prescription medicines must be paid for but the price is right. Drink bottled rather than tap water.

GENERAL INFORMATION

Post

Hotel receptions sell postcards and stamps and you can also post mail with them. Mail your parcels from Tirane to reduce the amount of handling. The main post office near the hotel is open until 10 pm daily. Postage is inexpensive and the service surprisingly reliable but always use air mail.

Electricity

220 volts AC.

Business Hours

Many stores close for a siesta from 12 noon to 4 pm. Concerts and theatrical performances invariably begin at 6 pm, usually on Saturday and Sunday only.

Albanian museums don't seem to follow any pattern as far as opening hours go and museums in small towns may only open for a couple of hours a week. You may find them inexplicably closed during the posted hours or simply closed with no hours posted. Museums are often unprepared for individual visitors and remain closed even during visiting hours unless a group has made an appointment. Individuals sometimes meet with surprise at museums and may even be told they're closed for cleaning, renovations, holidays, or any other reason, as an excuse for not letting you in. Other times you'll be admitted at odd hours as a special guest so it's always worth trying to get in. Museum admission is free everywhere except in Tirane.

INFORMATION

Albturist is the government agency responsible for tourism in Albania. Albturist guides accompany all tour groups and they will be your initial source of information. There are no tourist information offices but hotel receptionists will sometimes give you directions. Both guides and hotel staff are liable to give misleading information on cultural events and sightseeing attractions not included in the tour, usually due to a lack of knowledge. You must personally check theatre and museum times on the spot to be sure. Not only are city maps unobtainable in Albania, but the streets don't bear name plates nor the houses numbers! Most of the towns are small enough that you can do without such things.

In Britain information is available from the Albanian Society, 26 Cambridge Rd, Ilford, Essex IG3 8LU. The Society's journal, *Albanian Life*, is published three times a year, a subscription costs £5. Albanian books are readily available from The Albanian Shop, 3 Betterton St, London WC2H 9BP.

Your best information source in the US is Jack Shulman, PO Box 912, New York, NY 10008. Jack is a one-man, non-profit, unpaid organisation who sells Albanian books and periodicals at prices identical to those charged in Albania. If you send him a contribution he'll put you on the list for his annual bulletin, the *Albania Report*.

ACCOMMODATION

Since all hotel accommodation and meals are included in your tour package you won't have any choice. If you're sharing you can upgrade to a single room by paying a supplement directly to the hotel. When you arrive at your hotel check to see that the room has the correct number of towels. Otherwise you could be charged for the 'missing' ones when you try to leave.

FOOD & DRINK

All meals will be included in your package but you ought to miss a couple to try the local Albanian restaurants, to taste what the people really eat. Generally you should be able to find places where the food is good and prices very reasonable. Just walk into any bar or restaurant you see, sit down and order. There are no restrictions. Tipping is not done in Albania. Coffee is readily available. Albanian white wine is better than the vinegary red and raki is taken as an aperitif. Try the ice cream, which has a peculiar burnt taste.

THINGS TO BUY

Most of the hotels have hard currency shops where Albanian handicrafts are available, such as carpets, silk, items made from silver, copper and wood, embroidery, shoulder bags, picture books, records and tapes of folk music. Bring small bills and coins as they usually can't make change.

Getting There & Away

PACKAGE TOURS

All tourists must arrive on a package tour, most of which take place between April and October. Due to the limited capacity at Tirane airport, many groups fly to Titograd or Ohrid in Yugoslavia and board a bus to Albania there. When booking your tour choose carefully as it's impossible to make changes upon arrival. Call or write the companies mentioned below at least two months in advance. You can sometimes book over the phone, forwarding the visa photos, a photocopy of your passport and full payment by mail.

The main problem with the package tour is that you have no control over the itinerary and there's a lot of waiting around. You're required to sleep and travel with the group, but aren't obligated to eat and sightsee with them. Tourism to Albania is sort of political with visits to hospitals, schools, kindergartens, farms and factories, which is a refreshing change of pace.

Tours from Britain

English-speaking visitors will want to join a tour out of London, England, and there are two companies offering them. Regent Holidays (tel 0272 21 1711), 13 Small St, Bristol BS1 1DE, England, pioneered tourism to Albania. Their 12-day bus tour touches 11 Albanian towns for £570. Shorter eight-day trips based in Tirane with a three-day excursion to the south are £425. The price includes virtually everything except wine with the meals. Regent Holidays groups fly direct to Tirane via Zurich.

The second company offering these trips is Voyages Jules Verne (tel 01 486-8080), 10 Glentworth St, London NW1 5PG, England. They offer a 'Classical' 15-day bus trip (£595) which operates eight times a year and enters Albania from Ohrid and departs via Titograd. They also have a quickie five-day 'Albanian Weekend'

for £225 including the flight to Titograd almost every Friday at midday year round. Ask if they'll knock £100 off the price if you join the group in Yugoslavia and don't require the flight to and from London.

Other Tours

Since 1986 Greek tour groups have been entering Albania between Ioannina and Gjirokaster. If you're allowed to join one of these packages it'll probably be the cheapest you'll find.

Tours for French speakers are offered by Transtours (tel 1-4261 5828), 49 avenue de l'Opera, 75067 Paris Cedex 02. An eight-day bus tour of Albania including the round trip flight from Paris to Dubrovnik will run 5120 French francs. For tours from the Netherlands contact Delta Reizen (tel 050-146200), Postbus 1577, 9701 BN, Groningen, or Kontakt International (tel 020-234771), Prins Hendrikkade 104, 1011 AJ Amsterdam.

Two companies offer German-speaking tours to Albania. Neckermann has one-week trips five or six times a year (DM 1400 including flight, DM 1000 without flight). Skanderbeg-Reisen (tel 0203-767986), Altenbrucher Damm 165, 4100 Duisburg 29, runs 10 trips a year (DM 1375 to DM 1965).

Getting Around

Once you arrive in a town, the guides don't try to force you to stick with the group and you can do as much exploring on your own as you please. No one will bother you. Between towns foreign tourists are required to travel as a group and there is no opportunity to take local trains. It's OK to use city buses in Tirane and Durres, however. Buy a ticket at a kiosk or from another passenger.

Tirane

Tirane, a pleasant city of 202,000 (compared to 30,000 before WW II), is almost exactly midway between Rome and Istanbul. The city became capital of Albania in 1920, but only in recent years have larger than life 'palaces of the people' blossomed around Skanderbeg Square and along Martyrs of the Nation Boulevard. Tirane is one of the quietest capital cities in the world. Motor traffic is minimal and nowhere is too far to walk. You'll see Italian parks and a Turkish mosque, but there's no mistaking the pride of this small country. Break loose from your tour and explore the eastern side of the city. You can see it all during a two-day stay.

Information
The International Bookstore on Rruga Puntoret e Rilindjes east of the park is Tirane's best. The Libraria Arsimore, a few blocks north on the same street, has school text books.

Things to See
Most visits to Tirane begin on **Skanderbeg Square**, a great open space at the heart of the city. Tourists stay at 12-storey Hotel Tirane on the north side of the square. Beside the hotel is the new **National Museum of History**, the largest and finest of its kind in Albania. It's open Tuesday to Sunday 9 am to 12 noon and 4 to 7 pm, Friday 8 am to 1 pm only. To the east is another massive building, the **Palace of Culture**, with a theatre, library, galleries, restaurant, etc. Beside this is the **Mosque of Ethem Bey** (1797), one of the most distinctive buildings in the city. Tirane's **clock tower** stands beside the mosque.

On the west side of Skanderbeg Square is the National Bank with the main post office behind, while the south side is taken up by the massive yellow and red buildings of various government ministries. In the middle of the square is an equestrian statue of Skanderbeg himself looking straight up Bulevardi Stalin, north toward the railway station.

Behind Skanderbeg's statue extends Martyrs of the Nation Boulevard, straight south to the three arches of **Tirane University** (1957). As you stroll down this largely traffic-free boulevard you'll encounter prominent statues of V I Lenin and J V Stalin. Behind Lenin is Tirane's **Art Gallery** (Tuesday to Sunday 9 am to 12 noon, Wednesday, Saturday and Sunday also 4 to 7 pm), a stronghold of socialist realism with a significant permanent collection. Nearby is the *Hotel Dajti* which you should enter to see the dramatic painting of Gjirokaster in the lobby.

When you reach the river go west a few blocks to the **Ekspozita 'Shqiperia Sot'** (Albania Today), a mammoth exhibition of Albanian industrial products – well worth seeing if you can get in.

Return to Martyrs of the Nation Boulevard and continue south across the bridge over the Lana River. Beyond is **Party House**, the well-guarded older building on the right, and the ultramodern **Congress Hall** on the left. The boulevard terminates at the university with the Faculty of Music on the right and the **Archaeological Museum** on the left. Behind the museum is **'Qemal Stafa' Stadium** where football matches are held every Saturday and Sunday afternoon, except during July and August.

Beyond the university is a large park (Parku kombetar) with an open air theatre (Teatrin Veror) and an artificial lake. The view across the lake to the olive-coloured hills is superb. Cross the dam retaining the lake to **Tirane Zoo**. The excellent **botanical gardens** are just west of the zoo (ask directions). If you're keen rent a rowboat and paddle on the lake.

Political Sights As you return up Martyrs of the Nation Boulevard from the university turn right onto the street just before Party House to the **Lenin-Stalin Museum**, Rruga Labinoti 100 (Sunday to Tuesday 9 am to

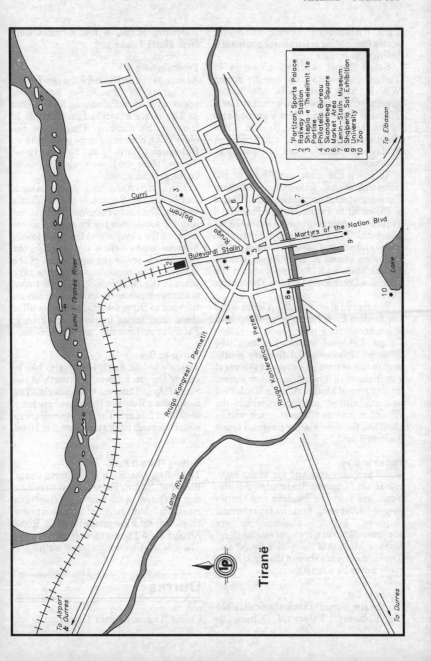

Key to map:

1. Partizan Sports Palace
2. Railway Station
3. Shtepia e Thelelimit te Partise
4. Philatelic Bureau
5. Skanderbeg Square
6. Market Area
7. Lenin-Stalin Museum
8. Shqiperia Sot Exhibition
9. University
10. Zoo

Curri

Bajram

Rruga

Martyrs of the Nation Blvd

Buelvardi Stalin

Rruga Kongresi i Permetit

Rruga Konferenca e Pezes

Lumi I Tranes River

Lona River

To Elbasan

Lake

To Airport & Durres

To Durres

Tiranë

1 pm, Wednesday and Friday 4 to 6 pm), with a fascinating collection of photos and political paintings.

Seven illegal partisan hide-outs in Tirane, used against the fascists during WW II, have been made into 'house/museums.' The most convenient to Hotel Tirane is the **Shtepia Muze e Emine Ketes** in an alley off Rruga Bajram Curri (Wednesday 9 am to 1 pm and 5 to 9 pm, Friday and Sunday 9 am to 1 pm). Ask directions.

To reach the most significant of the 'house/museums' follow Rruga Bajram Curri about a km north-east to the **Shtepia e Thelelimit te Partise**, Rruga Formimi i Partise 60 (same hours as the Emine Ketes Museum). To locate the building write the name and address out on a piece of paper. Everyone knows it. Here Enver Hoxha, Qemal Stafa and 13 others founded the Albanian Communist Party on 8 November 1941.

You should also make the pilgrimage to the **tomb of Enver Hoxha** on a hilltop with a beautiful view over the city. Follow Rruga Labinoti which becomes the Elbasan highway about five km south-east to the Martyr's Graveyard (Varrezat e deshmoreve). The setting below a great white figure of Mother Albania is subdued and it's almost moving to watch the Albanian masses file past, each with a clenched fist near his/her forehead (open 8 am to 6 pm).

Places to Stay

You'll probably stay and eat at the high-rise *Hotel Tirane* on Skanderbeg Square. You can't beat the location and there's even a barber shop upstairs for reformed 'hippies.' Foreign businessmen are accommodated at the more tasteful *Hotel Dajti* on Martyrs of the Nation Boulevard. The hard currency shop in the Dajti is less picked over by tourists.

Places to Eat

Try the *Restaurant Donika* beside the old 'Ali Kelmendi' Palace of Culture on Bulevardi Stalin, a few minutes walk from Hotel Tirane.

Entertainment

As soon as you arrive check the new *Palace of Culture* on Skanderbeg Square for opera or ballet performances. Most events in Tirane are advertised on placards in front of this building. There's also the older *'Ali Kelmendi' Palace of Culture* on Bulevardi Stalin just behind Hotel Tirane. Here you'll see variety shows or circus performances.

The *Teatri i Kukallave*, beside the bank on Skanderbeg Square, is the children's theatre. The *Teatri Popullar*, on the street running south from the Palace of Culture between the mosque and the clock tower, features more serious drama. *Kinema Partizani* is across the square east of the mosque. Pop concerts and sports take place in the *Pallatin e Sportit 'Partizan'* about two km from Skanderbeg Square on the road to Durres. Performances at all of these are most frequent on Friday, Saturday and Sunday, usually at 6 pm.

Things to Buy

Tirane's public market is several blocks east of the clock tower, just north of the Sheshi Avni Rustemi traffic circle. The Ekspozita e Kultures Popullore here has a display of folk art. The Philatelic Bureau is on Bulevardi Stalin north-west of Hotel Tirane.

Getting There & Away

The railway station is at the north end of Bulevardi Stalin. There are seven trains a day to Durres, a 62-minute journey (one class only), but you're not supposed to use them. Present a low profile if you do. Rinas Airport is 25 km north-west of the city. There is no Albanian national airline.

Durres

Unlike Tirane, Durres (Durazzo) is an

ancient city founded by the Greeks as Epidamnus in the 7th century BC. Later the Romans converted it into Dyrrhachium, the largest port on the eastern Adriatic and start of the Via Egnatia to Constantinople. The famous Via Appia to Rome began 150 km north-west at Brindisi, Italy.

Today Roman ruins and Byzantine fortifications embellish this major industrial city and commercial port 35 km west of Tirane. Durres is Albania's second city (72,000 inhabitants). South are long sandy beaches on a bay where all of the tourist hotels are concentrated. There's really no reason to spend more than one or two nights in Durres. If you're a beach person you'll find more exciting resorts elsewhere.

Things to See

Begin by visiting the **Archaeological Museum** (open 10 am to 1 pm) facing the waterfront park near the port. The two rooms are small but each object is unique and there's a large sculpture garden outside. Behind the museum are the 5th century AD Byzantine **city walls** built after the Visigoth invasion of 481 and

supplemented by round Venetian towers in the 14th century.

Durres' impressive **Roman amphitheatre** (1st to 2nd centuries AD) is on the hillside just inside the walls. Much of the amphitheatre has been excavated and a small built-in 10th century Byzantine church can be seen. Follow the road just inside the walls down toward the port and you'll find the **Moisiut Ekspozita e Kultures Popullore** with ethnographic displays.

The **Museum of the Liberation War** (10 am to 1 pm) is on the other side of town, above the **Martyr's Cemetery** at the west end of Rruga Deshmoreve. East on Rruga Deshmoreve, across the square from the railway station, is an **Ekspozita Industrial** with local products.

Places to Stay

Foreign tourists stay at the *Adriatiku* or a neighbouring hotel on the beach five km south-east of Durres. There's frequent bus service into the city (buy a 30 qindarka ticket at a kiosk). For the return journey look for the bus near the new post office in Durres.

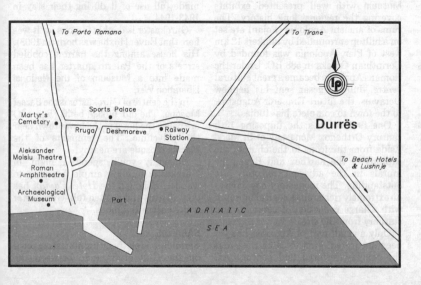

To Porto Romano
To Tirane
Martyr's Cemetery
Sports Palace
Rruga Deshmoreve
Railway Station
Durrës
Aleksander Moisiu Theatre
Roman Amphitheatre
Archaeological Museum
Port
To Beach Hotels & Lushnje
ADRIATIC SEA

Entertainment

For entertainment check the *Aleksander Moisiu Theatre* in the centre of Durres, or the *Sports Palace* on Rruga Deshmoreve.

Getting There & Away

Albania's railway network centres on Durres. There are seven trains a day to Tirane, two to Shkoder, two to Pogradec, two to Vlore and one to Ballsh. The station is beside the Tirane highway, convenient to central Durres. Tickets are sold at the kiosk below the timetables on the square in front of the station.

Getting Around

Tourists stuck in the beach hotels are offered a choice of 44 excursions ranging from a half day trip to the Pioneer Camp for US$0.80 to a four-day tour of southern Albania for US$60.

Southern Albania

FIER & APOLONIA

Near the post office in Fier is an **Historical Museum** with well presented exhibits covering the regions' long history. The ruins of ancient Apolonia (Pojan) are set on a hilltop surrounded by bunkers 12 km west of Fier. Apolonia was founded by Corinthian Greeks in 588 BC. Under the Romans Apolonia became a great cultural centre. Julius Caesar sent his nephew Octavius, the future Emperor Augustus, to the town to complete his studies.

One first reaches the imposing 13th century Orthodox **Monastery of St Mary**. Aside from the icons in the church, the capitals in the narthex and Byzantine murals in the adjacent refectory are outstanding. The monastery now houses an extremely rich archaeological museum with a large collection of ceramics and statuary from the site.

Only a small part of Apolonia has yet been uncovered. First to catch the eye is the roughly restored 2nd century AD

Bouleterion or Hall of the Agonothetes. In front of it is the 2nd century AD **Odeon** (a small theatre). To the west of this is a long 3rd century BC **portico** with niches that once contained statues. The **defensive walls** of Apolonia are nearby. The lower portion of these massive walls, four km long and up to 6.5 metres high, dates back to the 4th century BC.

GJIROKASTER

This historic museum town in the hills midway between Fier and Ioannina, Greece, is strikingly picturesque. A mighty citadel surveys the Drina Valley above the three or four storey stone-roofed tower-houses clinging to the mountainside. For the classic view of Gjirokaster climb up to the **Muzeu Historik Cercis Topulli** in a large house at the highest point of the town, up above the castle.

From here you'll easily find your way down into the 14th century **citadel** *(kala)* itself, now a Museum of Armaments with an excellent collection of these including a shot-down US reconnaissance plane. During the 1920s the fortress was converted into a prison and the Nazis made full use of it during their stay in 1943-1944.

Gjirokaster is doubly famous for it was here that Enver Hoxha was born (in 1908). His house among the narrow cobbled streets of the Palorto quarter has been made into a **Museum of the National Liberation War**.

In the centre of Gjirokaster is the **Bazaar Mosque**. The old **Turkish baths** *(hamam)* are below the hotel in the lower town near the polyclinic. The remnants of the **Mecate Mosque** are nearby.

Hopefully you'll spend a night in Gjirokaster to allow ample free time to wander, although the *Hotel Cayupi* has only 80 beds and is often full. Gjirokaster white cheese is famous.

SARANDE

Sarande is a relatively uninteresting town on the Gulf of Sarande between the mountains and the Ionian Sea. The Greek island of Corfu is visible from the shore. This southernmost harbour of Albania was once the ancient port of Onchesmos. In the Middle Ages there was a monastery here dedicated to 40 saints (Santi Quaranta), which gave Sarande its name. Sarande's main attraction today is its sunny climate and the nearby ruins of Butrint.

Sarande's waterfront promenade is attractive but without the street life that gives colour to nearby Greece. In front of the cinema in the centre of town are some ancient ruins with a large mosaic exposed to the open air. At Rruga 8 Nendori near the corner of Rruga Qazim Pali is the **Muzeu Historik**, but no hours are posted and you'd be lucky to get in.

Butrint

The ancient ruins of Butrint (open 7 am to 2 pm), 15 km south of Sarande, are surprisingly extensive and interesting. The site lies by a river connecting Butrint Lake to the sea, where a **triangular fortress** erected by warlord Ali Pasha in the early 19th century watches over the modern vehicular ferry. In the forest below the acropolis is Butrint's 3rd century BC **Greek theatre**, readapted later during the Roman period. The small **public baths** with mosaics are close by.

Deeper in the forest are a wall covered with crisp Greek inscriptions and a 5th century palaeo-Christian **baptistry** with colourful mosaics of animals and birds. Beyond the basilica stands a massive **cyclopean wall** dating from the 4th century BC. Over one gate is a splendid relief of a lion killing a bull, symbolic of a protective force vanquishing assailants. Atop the acropolis in a crenellated brick building is a **museum** full of statuary from the site. There are good views from the terrace.

Places to Stay

Tourists in Sarande stay at the *Hotel Butrinti* overlooking the harbour. Beware of rooms without balconies.

BERAT

Although not quite as enchanting as Gjirokaster, Berat deserves its status as Albania's second museum town. The many windows of the white-plastered, red-roofed houses overlooking the Osum River give Berat its other name, the 'city of a thousand eyes.' Along a ridge high above the valley is a 14th century citadel *(kalaja)* sheltering small Greek Orthodox churches. On the slope below this, all the way down to the river, is Mangalem, the old Muslim quarter. A seven-arched stone bridge (1780) over the river leads to Gorica, the Christian quarter.

Things to See

On the square in front of the hotel is a white hall where the Anti-fascist National Liberation Committee met from 20 to 23 October 1944 and appointed Enver Hoxha chairman of the Democratic Government of Albania. Beyond this is the **Leaden Mosque** (1555), named for the material covering its great dome. Today the mosque is an interesting Museum of Architecture with photos of historic buildings all over Albania.

Follow the busy street toward the citadel from here and after a few blocks you'll reach the **Dervishes Mosque** (1791), now the **Archaeological Museum**. The modern **Ekspozita Galeria** beside the mosque complex contains an exhibition of regional products and a good art gallery featuring the socialist realism of local painter Sotir Capo. Nearby on the river is the *'Margarita Tutulani' Palace of Culture*, a theatre worth checking out shortly before 6 pm. Beyond this is the 18th century **Bachelor's Mosque**, now a folk art museum.

Carry on toward the old stone bridge and you'll see the 14th century **Church of St Michael** high up on the hillside below the citadel. In Mangalem, back behind the Bachelor's Mosque is the **Muzeu i Luftes**, worth seeing as much for its old Berati house as the exhibits on the partisan struggle during WW II. Beyond the Savings Bank on the stone road up toward the citadel is the **Muzeu Etnografik** in another fine old building.

After entering the citadel through its massive gate continue straight ahead on the main street and ask anyone to direct you to the **Muzeu Onufri**. This museum occupies the monastery enclosing the Greek Orthodox cathedral. The iconostasis (1850) and pulpit in the cathedral are splendid and in the museum there's a large collection of icons, especially those of the famous mid-16th century artist for whom the museum is named. Onufri's paintings are more realistic, dramatic and colourful than those of his predecessors.

It's unlikely you'll get into any of the other churches in the citadel, although 14th century **Saint Trinity** (Shen Triadhes) on the west side near the walls has an impressive exterior. The 16th century **Church of the Evangelists** is most easily found by following the eastern citadel wall.

The various museums in Berat open irregularly from 9 am to 12 noon and 4 to 6 pm a couple of days a week.

Places to Stay

All tourists stay at the *Hotel Tomori*, named for the mountain (2416 metres) which overlooks Berat to the east. The hotel has no elevator, but the view of the riverside park from your balcony may compensate for the climb.

ELBASAN

Elbasan, the Roman Skampa, has recently become prominent as the site of Albania's 'Steel of the Party' metallurgical combine and a cement factory, but the old town retains a certain charm. It's unlikely you'll spend the night here but tour parties often stop for lunch at the *Hotel Skampa* beside the former **Turkish baths**.

Opposite the hotel are the **city walls** erected by the Turks in 1467 and still relatively intact on the south and west sides. Go through the south gate and look for the **Shtepia Muze e Aresimit** in among the houses, with two old churches (closed)

alongside. On the west city wall is a museum dedicated to the partisan war.

If you've extra time ask someone to point the way to the **Shtepia Muze e Qemal Stafes** on Rruga Rinia in the newer part of the city. Qemal was a Communist youth leader killed in 1942 at the age of 22.

POGRADEC

Pogradec is a pleasant resort by the beach at the south end of Ohrid Lake, 140 km south-east of Tirane. The 650-metre elevation gives the area a brisk, healthy climate. Pogradec is much quieter and more relaxing than the Yugoslav lake towns of Ohrid and Struga. The scenery here is fine.

Tourists are allowed to walk east along the beach about two km to a barrier which marks the beginning of the four-km-wide **border zone** with Yugoslavia. There's little else to do except perhaps visit the local **museum** (archaeology downstairs, partisan mementos upstairs) near the modern theatre on the waterfront, go to the movies, or take a swim.

Places to Stay

The only place to stay is the *Guri i Kug Hotel*, named for the 'red stone' mountain on the west side of the lake where nickel/chrome ore is extracted.

Getting There & Away

The railway station (with service to Durres) is near the processing factory about four km from the hotel.

KORCE

Korce, on a high plateau west of Florina, Greece, and 39 km south of Lake Ohrid, is the main city of the south-eastern interior. Once a centre of world-wide emigration from the country, Albanians abroad often regard Korce as home. At first you may wonder why you've been brought here. Much of the old city centre was gouged out by urban renewal after devastating earthquakes in 1931 and 1960 which toppled the minarets and flattened the churches.

Things to See

Tourists are taken to the *Hotel Iliria*. Behind it on Bulevardi Lenin is the **Muzeu Historik** which seems always to be closed. As you continue up Bulevardi Lenin you pass the *'Ali Kelmendi' Palace of Culture* on the left and a large cafe on the right. At the top of the boulevard is the 'National Fighter' statue (1932) by Odhise Paskali. Nearby is the **Muzeu i Arsimit Kombetar** or Education Museum, housed in the first school to teach in the Albanian language (1887). Across the boulevard is the **Themistokli Germenji House Museum**.

To the left of the 'National Fighter' is **Party House**. Plunge into the small streets behind this building and you should be able to find the **Muzeu i Artet Mesjetar Shqiptar** (Museum of Albanian Medieval Art), by far the most important of Korce's museums. There are several icons by Onufri among other wonders, so fall to your knees and beg entry if they tell you it's only for groups (theoretically open 10 am to 1 pm and 4 to 7 pm). Even if you do arrive by tour bus with your Albturist guide some rooms may remain inexplicably closed. The museum director takes being an Albanian seriously!

Korce has a strong revolutionary history and you'll see the story at the **Muzeu i Levizjes Puntore e Komuniste** (Monday 10 am to 12 noon and 3 to 5 pm, Friday 10 am to 12 noon) in a fine old house on Rruga Mazllem Karaskej not far from the Medieval Art Museum.

Return to Party House and follow the main street east to *Kinema Morava*. Up the small street beside the cinema is the **Shtepia Muze ku ka Banuar Shoku Enver Hoxha**, where that gentleman lived while working as a teacher in Korce in 1937-39 (open Wednesday, Friday and Sunday 3 to 5 pm). You may be shown around by Aunt Poliksene, one of Enver's early associates.

As you stroll down Bulevardi Republik from Kinema Morava you'll pass two museums dedicated to the War of Liberation, in large mansions on the left. High on the hillside above here is the **Martyr's Graveyard** (Varrezat e deshmoreve) from which there's a fine view.

As you return to the hotel you may still wonder why you're in Korce, so delve into the cobbled streets lined with quaint old shops beyond the bus station, west of the hotel. The **Ekspozita e Kultures Materiale Popullare** is on the main square here. There's a popular restaurant at the back of a courtyard between this exhibition and the bus station. Continue south through this quarter to the **Mirahorit Mosque** (1485), now closed.

Entertainment

The *A Z Cajupi Theatre* is beside the post office opposite the hotel. Live variety shows sometimes take place in *Kinema Morava* mentioned above.

Northern Albania

KRUJE

In the 12th century Kruje was the capital of the Principality of Arberit, but the town attained its greatest fame during the years 1443-1468 when the national hero Skanderbeg made Kruje his seat. Set below towering mountains, the **citadel** Skanderbeg defended against the Turks stands on an abrupt ridge above the modern town. In 1982 an excellent new museum opened in the citadel and the saga of the Albanian struggle against the Ottoman Empire is richly told with models, maps and statuary. Among the old houses in the citadel is the 18th century **Bektashi tekke**, place of worship of a local Islamic sect, and the 16th century **Turkish baths** just below.

Between the citadel and the bus station is Kruje's old **Turkish bazaar**, now fully restored and made into an ethnographical museum and workplace for local artisans and craftspeople.

LEZHE

At Lezhe in 1444 Skanderbeg succeeded in uniting the Albanian people against the Turks. Today his tomb may be visited among the ruins of the Franciscan **Church of St Nicolas**. Reproductions of his helmet and sword grace the gravestone and along the walls are 25 shields bearing the names and dates of battles he fought against the Turks. Near the tomb beside the grey apartment blocks is the **Ethnographical Museum**, while on the hilltop above is **Lezhe Citadel**. Much of old Lezhe was destroyed by an earthquake in 1979.

Tour groups in transit along the coast often have lunch in the former **hunting lodge of Count Ciano**, Mussolini's son-in-law and foreign minister, seven km south of Lezhe. (To please Hitler Mussolini had Ciano executed at Verona on 11 January 1944.) Enjoy your lunch.

SHKODER

Shkoder (Skutari), the traditional capital of northern Albania, is one of the oldest cities in Europe. In 500 BC an Illyrian fortress already guarded the strategic crossing just west of the city where the Bune and Drin rivers meet and all traffic moving up the coast from Greece to Montenegro must pass. These rivers drain two of the Balkan's largest lakes, Shkodres just to the north-west of the city and Ohrid far up the Drin beyond several massive hydroelectric dams. The route inland to Kosovo also begins in Shkoder.

To the north line after line of cement bunkers point the way to the Hani Hotit border crossing into Yugoslavia (33 km). The goods train to Titograd now passes this way, a much commented sign of Albania's reopening.

Shkoder was once the most influential Catholic city of Albania with a cathedral, Jesuit and Franciscan monasteries, seminaries and religious libraries. Today it's better known for its Muzeu Ateist.

Orientation

On the same roundabout as the Rozafa Hotel is the Migjenit Theatre and from opposite it Bulevardi Stalin runs south-east past the hotel and post office. A bust of Joseph Stalin in front of the post office looks north-east up Rruga Enver Hoxha, a delightful street lit by antique lamps in the evening and lined with harmonious old buildings.

Things to See

The **Muzeu Popullor** in the former mosque opposite the hotel contains objects related to ethnography and the partisan campaign during WW II. In the centre of the park beside this museum is a bust of Lenin, and across from it on Rruga Enver Hoxha, the **Muzeu Ateist** which opened in 1973. On the back street behind the Atheist Museum, between it and the ex-church (now an auditorium), is the House/Museum of the poet Migjenit.

A couple of blocks north-east up Rruga Enver Hoxha, near the corner of Rruga Branko Kadija, is the **Expozita e Kultures Popullare** with displays of Albanian handicrafts in several buildings. Do some window shopping here. The exhibition and museums listed above open irregularly, although in theory it's 10 am to 12 noon and 6 to 8 pm, so check during those hours if you can.

The Rozafa Fortress Two km south-west of Shkoder near the south end of Shkodres Lake is the Rozafa Fortress, founded by the Illyrians in antiquity but rebuilt much later by the Turks. Upon entering the second enclosure one passes a ruined church which had been converted into a mosque, then a restored stone palace. From the highest point there's a marvellous view on all sides.

The fortress got its name for a woman named Rozafa who was allegedly walled into the ramparts during the original construction, as an offering to the gods. Below the fortress, but difficult to reach, is the many-domed 18th century **Leaden**

Mosque. The view from above must suffice.

Places to Stay

You'll stay, either for lunch or the night, at the *Rozafa Hotel*, a nine-storey building on the 5 Heroes roundabout.

Places to Eat

The *Shkodra Restaurant*, on Rruga Enver Hoxha a few blocks north of the Muzeu Ateist, serves excellent Albanian dishes at very reasonable prices.

Entertainment

The *Pallatin te Kultures Vasil Shanto*, on a back street behind the Muzeu Ateist, is a former church converted into an auditorium. South-east on Bulevardi Stalin beyond the post office is *Kinema Republika* on the left.

Union of Soviet Socialist Republics

The Soviet Union is something of an enigma to people in the west. What we hear about this vast country often comes from a news media strongly biased against the world's first socialist state. Since people naturally distrust and fear what they do not know, the USSR and 'Communism' are often seen as a threat. Over the years so many misconceptions have built up that it often takes a trip to the USSR to realise just how different the picture is.

It would take a full year of travelling to see the main 'sights' of the Soviet Union. Here you have Europe, the Middle East, Central Asia, the Far East and the Arctic all rolled up into one. Since you won't have anywhere near a year try to go beyond the standard tourist attractions right away. Here more than anywhere else it's essential to break through the tourist scene to grasp the essence of the country in a short time. The Soviet people are extremely friendly, but *you* must be the one to initiate contacts. If you get the chance to speak to a local resident you'll discover he/she wants about the same things out of life as you do.

Most Soviets accept their system with a little irony and a desire to make improvements. It may surprise you how openly they discuss their problems. Times have changed and *glasnost* (openness) is in fashion. The word *perestroika* (restructuring) is often used to refer to the changes going on.

To visit the Soviet Union is neither cheap nor easy. It takes three weeks and a considerable amount of money to get on a tour which may only last a week or two. To travel independently costs over US$100 a day and takes even longer to organise. Even then you have to follow a pre-arranged itinerary with fixed dates. At present the only loophole for budget travellers is to transit the USSR from

China to Europe by train, but this involves the most advance planning of all. Is it worth it? Definitely yes! You can't understand Eastern Europe or the world today without at least one visit to the USSR, however brief. Approach it as if you were going to meet an old friend you hadn't heard from for a while and you won't come away disappointed.

Facts about the Country

HISTORY
In the 9th century Viking raiders from Sweden penetrated the continent along the Don, Dnieper and Volga rivers. By the 10th century Scandinavian 'Varangians' based at Novgorod controlled trade from the Baltic to the Black seas. The first state to appear on East Slav territory was established by the Varangian prince Vladimir. In 988 the dominance of Vladimir's clan was institutionalised in the acceptance of Orthodox Christianity and the creation of an episcopal see at Kiev. Under his son Yaroslav the Wise Kiev became a great metropolis, but separatist trends continued in the Kievan Rus. Novgorod declared its independence

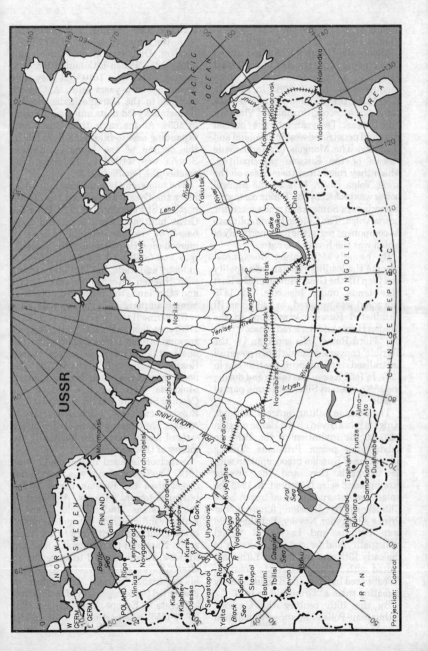

from Kiev in 1136 and the principality of Vladimir-Suzdal grew in strength.

Meanwhile Genghis Khan had united the nomadic Mongol tribes of north-east Asia into a huge feudal state which conquered southern Siberia in 1219. In 1236-1238 the Golden Horde struck Jaroslavl, Moscow, Suzdal and Vladimir from the east. Two years later they burned Kiev and penetrated west into Poland and Hungary. The Mongols (Tartars) made vassals of the Russian principalities, which they ruled from their bases on the lower Volga River. In 1396 the Mongol power was broken by the Turkic conqueror Tamerlane of Samarkand who sacked the Lower Volga. The Golden Horde split into its component parts, the most northerly of which was the Kazan khanate.

By the early 15th century Moscow had become the leading Russian principality and Ivan III 'the Great' united all the East Slav lands under his rule. In 1478 Novgorod was annexed. In 1480 Ivan III terminated Russia's vassaldom to the Golden Horde and declared Moscow to be the 'Third Rome.' His son Ivan IV 'the Terrible' converted Russia into a powerful centralised state, adopting the title tsar in 1547. In 1552 Kazan was taken and during the 1580s western Siberia became part of Russia.

The German military order of Teutonic Knights had arrived on the Baltic coast in 1226 at the invitation of the Poles to subdue the pagan Prussians. Taking advantage of Russian preoccupation with the Mongols they and the Swedes attempted to seize Novgorod. In 1242 the knights were turned back on frozen Lake Chudskoye by Russian forces under Prince Alexander Nevsky, but they held onto Estonia and Latvia. A feudal principality had formed in Lithuania in the early 13th century. In 1385 Lithuania united with Poland to face the common threat posed by Teutonic Knights, finally defeating them at Grunwald in 1410.

By the 16th century the Catholic Lithuanian-Polish alliance, which had occupied the Ukraine, was confronted with the growing power of Orthodox Moscow. Divisions on the Russian side allowed the Polish-Lithuanian forces to capture Moscow in 1610, but they were driven out two years later. A Cossack uprising in the Ukraine under Bogdan Khmelnitsky led to its union with Russia in 1654. At the same time Russia was expanding east to fill the vacuum left by the decline of the Mongols. Eastern Siberia was settled by Russians, who reached the Pacific in 1639.

The monarchy became absolute under Peter the Great, who moved the capital north to St Petersburg in 1712. Peter the Great built a modern army and navy based on regular recruits instead of mercenaries. He reorganised the bureaucracy and facilitated the development of industry and trade. In 1721, after a treaty with Sweden returned Estonia, Latvia and other lands to Russia, Peter declared himself emperor.

Catherine II the Great (reigned 1762 to 1796) consolidated Russian power. Russia's growing strength was displayed in the final partition of Poland-Lithuania between Russia, Austria and Prussia in 1795. The north shore of the Black Sea, the Crimea, Moldavia, and the area around the Caspian Sea were also taken at this time. Russian explorers reached as far as Alaska. The Ukraine was re-settled by the serfs of feudal magnates, increasing the misery of the peasants.

Napoleon invaded Russia on 12 June 1812. The Grand Army was three times bigger than the Russian forces, which retreated toward Moscow. At Borodino the Russians under Field Marshal Kutuzov inflicted heavy casualties on the French, but had to withdraw to save their army. Napoleon then entered a deserted Moscow. Russia refused to surrender so after 35 days Napoleon was forced to begin his disastrous retreat. The defeat of France led to the hegemony of reactionary autocrats in Europe. The Crimean War (1853-1856) was part of an imperialistic scramble for the spoils of the declining Ottoman Empire. In 1877-78 Russia forced Turkey out of Bulgaria. Central Asia (Uzbekistan) was colonised by Russia during the 19th century to meet British incursions from Afghanistan.

Social progress had not kept pace with imperial expansion. The Russian serfs had been suppressed and dissatisfaction was mounting against the tsar's arbitrary rule. The abortive Decembrist revolt at Senatskaya Square, St Petersburg, on 14 December 1825 was the first Russian revolution. In 1861 Alexander II freed the serfs but gave them no land. The creation of this vast labour pool stimulated capitalistic development, but allowed industrialists to exploit their workers as they pleased. In 1895 Lenin set up the League of Struggle for the Emancipation of the Working Class. Three years later the Russian Social-Democratic Labour Party (RSDLP) was formed. At the second congress of the RSDLP in 1903 the Bolsheviks (majority) became differentiated from the Mensheviks (minority). Soviets, elected political organisations of workers, soldiers and peasants, first appeared during the 1905-07 bourgeois-democratic revolution, which was suppressed.

In 1914 Russia become involved in WW I on the side of the Entente, Britain and France. All sides suffered appalling losses in this senseless conflict but in Russia the destruction, combined with widespread dissatisfaction against autocratic rule, led to a revolutionary situation. Strikes at Petrograd on 10 February 1917 grew into a general strike against the war. Troops ordered to put down the strike went over to the strikers on 27 February. Former bourgeois supporters of the Tsar then formed a provisional committee which demanded his abdication. Tsar Nicholas II, last of the 300-year-old Romanov Dynasty, abdicated on 2 March 1917. The committee then became a provisional government. They decided to continue the war until final victory.

On 3 April 1917 Lenin returned from exile and set out to organise the Bolsheviks against the provisional government. He was forced to go into hiding after anti-war demonstrations on 4 July 1917. In August a military coup against the provisional government was averted. On 10 October 1917 the central committee of the RSDLP decided the only way to end the war was an armed uprising. On the night of 24 October the Bolsheviks took Petrograd, arrested the provisional government and declared peace. In contrast to the almost bloodless takeover in Petrograd, the fighting in Moscow lasted a week. In March 1918 the capital was moved back to Moscow.

On 2 December 1917 a unilateral armistice was signed. On 18 February 1918 the Germans broke the armistice and again attacked Russia. On 3 March Russia was forced to cede the Baltic states and pay six billion marks indemnity as the price of peace. In November 1918 revolutionary outbreaks in Germany forced the Kaiser to abdicate bringing WW I to a final end. Four days after the

Lenin

armistice Anglo-French warships entered the Black Sea and began a military campaign to reverse the Russian Revolution. Counter-revolutionaries took control of large parts of the country. But by early 1920 the intervention had been defeated and the Entente troops were withdrawn. A year later the last White Guard reactionary armies were also overcome. By the end of 1922 the Civil War was virtually over.

To restore stability to the country a New Economic Policy of state capitalism was introduced, featuring small business and a market economy. Calls for immediate world revolution were replaced by the concept of 'socialism in one country.' The USSR recognised the independence of Finland and Poland. Toward the end of 1922 the Russian Federation, the Ukraine, Byelorussia and the Caucasian Federation united to form the Union of Soviet Socialist Republics. In 1934 the USSR joined the League of Nations.

Lenin died on 21 January 1924 and by 1928 a Russian nationalist, Joseph Stalin, had gained control of the Communist Party. To out-manoeuvre rightist rivals, Stalin 'turned left' and launched a ruthless programme of economic transformation. All private business was renationalised and heavy industry was developed through a series of five-year plans. Agriculture was forcibly collectivised. Resistance by rich peasants *(kulaks)* who slaughtered livestock and burned buildings led to mass deportations to Siberia and famine costing over six million lives. The Stalin revolution built the USSR into the greatest industrial power in Europe and increased grain production through mechanisation and improved efficiency. A cultural revolution reduced illiteracy from 70% before the revolution to zero in 1937. Hundreds of colleges were opened with hundreds of thousands of students.

Alongside these gains came totalitarian controls which stifled intellectual freedom. Beginning with the assassination of Leningrad party chief Sergey Kirov in December 1934, Stalin conducted a series of purges to consolidate his power. It's hard to conceive of these excesses in which some 800,000 Communists were executed. Millions of others died in the gulag. Seventy percent of the central committee elected in 1934 at the 17th party congress and 1108 of the 1966 ordinary congress delegates perished during the Great Terror. Defendants at the 'show trials' of 1935 to 1938 were accused of plotting to assassinate the Soviet leadership, conspiring with Germany and Japan to carve up the USSR, or attempting to murder Maxim Gorky, Lenin and others. Nearly all confessed their 'guilt' and were shot. Intellectuals and top army officers suffered the same fate.

The rise of fascism in Germany presented the USSR with a serious external threat. When war broke out in 1939 the USSR occupied areas such as Moldavia, Estonia, Latvia and Lithuania which had been taken from Russia in 1918, to prevent their falling into the hands of the Nazis. Hitler unleashed his war machine against the USSR on 22 June 1941 but although the Nazi armies were much larger and more powerful than those of the USSR, they were stopped outside Leningrad and Moscow by winter. The next spring the fascists drove east again toward the Volga, where 330,000 select German troops were encircled at the Battle of Stalingrad (August 1942 to February 1943). After another defeat at the Battle of Kursk in the summer of 1943 the Nazis had to go on the defensive along the entire front. Harried by partisans, they retreated west. The Soviet Army's last offensive began in January 1945 and culminated in the capture of Berlin on 2 May 1945. The USSR had suffered 20 million dead in the 'Great Patriotic War' and had 30% of its national wealth destroyed.

During and after the war famous conferences were held between Stalin, Churchill, Roosevelt and later Truman, at Yalta, Tehran and Potsdam as Europe was divided into two camps. By 1948 relations between the wartime Allies had disintegrated and a Cold War began. The Warsaw Pact was signed on 14 May 1955 in response to the rearmament of West Germany and its entry into NATO.

Stalin died in March 1953. His quarter century had converted the USSR into an industrial power second only to the US and a military/political giant. Education had progressed steadily, but living standards and personal security suffered under Stalin. A 'collective leadership' took over from Stalin until the emergence of Nikita Khrushchev, who soon became known for his dramatic personal initiatives. His denunciation of the cult of Stalin at the 20th party congress in February 1956 and support for 'different roads to socialism' sparked revolutionary reactions in Hungary and Poland. His personal decision in 1962 to put Soviet missiles in Cuba, then to remove them under US pressure, contributed to his fall in 1964.

Khrushchev was followed by Leonid Brezhnev, a cautious, conservative leader interested in consensus and the status quo. A highlight of the Brezhnev years was the signing of the Helsinki Final Act in 1975 in which 33 European governments, the US and Canada recognised the existing frontiers of Europe. Detente was undermined in 1979 by Soviet military intervention in Afghanistan.

Since taking over in March 1985, Mikhail Gorbachev has attempted to revitalise the Soviet economy through *perestroika* (restructuring) and *glasnost* (openness). Gorbachev's peace initiatives and efforts to do away with cronyism and corruption have been eagerly embraced in Hungary and Poland. *Glasnost* has had the unexpected effect of unleashing the latent nationalism of minorities such as the Armenians, Crimean Tartars, Estonians, Latvians and Ukrainians. A territorial dispute between Armenia and Azerbaijan led to unprecedented ethnic turmoil in the Trans-Caucasian republics.

GOVERNMENT

The USSR is a union of 15 soviet socialist republics. The Russian Soviet Federative Socialist Republic (RSFSR) with 76% of the country's area is by far the largest and best known. The great cities Moscow and Leningrad plus all of Siberia are here. The other 14 union republics are the Estonian SSR (capital Tallinn), the Latvian SSR (Riga), the Lithuanian SSR (Vilnius), the Byelorussian SSR (Minsk), the Ukrainian SSR (Kiev), the Moldavian SSR (Kishinev), the Georgian SSR (Tbilisi), the Armenian SSR (Yerevan), the Azerbaijan SSR (Baku), the Turkmenian SSR (Ashkhabad), the Tajik SSR (Dushanbe), the Uzbek SSR (Tashkent), the Kirghizian SSR (Frunze) and the Kazakh SSR (Alma-Ata). In addition there are 20 autonomous republics, eight autonomous provinces, 10 autonomous districts and 128 other provinces and regions.

The people of this vast country are represented by soviets (councils) which are elected by universal secret ballot. The highest assembly is the Supreme Soviet of the USSR which meets in the Grand Kremlin Palace in Moscow. This body consists of two equal chambers, the Soviet of the Union (32 deputies from each union republic) and the Soviet of Nationalities (11 deputies from each autonomous republic, five from each autonomous region and one from each autonomous area). Each chamber has 750 deputies. The Supreme Soviet forms the Council of Ministers which is responsible to it.

Each of the 15 union republics and 20 autonomous republics has a supreme soviet of its own. In addition there are 52,000 local soviets with 2.3 million members. All local executive bodies are elected by them. Membership in a soviet is not a profession. All members continue working at their normal place of employment. To give more citizens experience in state administration there's a high turnover in membership. Over half of all deputies are newly elected and over 20 million different people have served on these councils during the past 20 years. Workers and farmers comprise 51% of the Supreme Soviet, 70% of the local soviets.

There are important differences with such bodies in western countries, however. No one may simply announce himself a candidate. Candidates are nominated at general meetings of workers in factories, collective farms, institutions and offices. Deputies are responsible to their electorate and can be recalled by them at any time if they fail to perform. One need not be a member of any party to be elected to a soviet. Unlike municipal councils in the west, soviets in the USSR have broad economic powers.

Since the revolution the directing force in Soviet society has been the Communist Party. The Central Committee of the CPSU is elected at party congresses. Between plenary meetings of this committee the ruling body is the Politburo. Democratic centralism refers to the election of all party leaders, while party discipline requires submission to the decisions of higher bodies. Other mass organisations include the trade unions, the Komsomol or Young Communists League (ages 14 to 28) and the Young Pioneers (ages 10 to 15).

PEOPLE

With 278 million (1986) inhabitants the USSR is the world's third most populous country. There are 126 nations and nationalities, the largest of which are the Russians (52%), Ukrainians (16%), Uzbeks (4.5%) and White Russians (3.5%). Sixty-one percent live in cities and towns. The calm, fair-haired, blue-eyed people of the Baltic republics are quite different from the vivacious, black-haired, black-eyed people of Trans-Caucasia. The largest national groups are the Slavs: Russians (144 million), Ukrainians (45 million) and Byelorussians or White Russians (10 million). The Turkish people of the five Central Asian republics together total 47 million. The minorities retain their distinct cultures, customs, traditions, languages, life styles, manners and dress.

ECONOMY

The revolution has transformed a backward agricultural country into an industrial giant. Industrial production has grown 145 times to the point where the Ukraine alone produces more steel than Britain and France combined. The USSR has been a world leader in many spheres of science and technology. The world's first man-made earth satellite, manned spaceship, supersonic passenger jet and nuclear-powered ship all originated here. Gigantic power projects were completed in the Ural Mountains in the 1930s. Today in Siberia the world's largest hydroelectric power stations are being built.

The Caucasus is rich in oil and gas. Since the 1950s undersea drilling has recovered oil from beneath the Caspian. The USSR is a world leader in coal and iron ore production. Agriculture is fully mechanised with 26,000 collective and 22,000 state farms. Half of the Soviet Union's foreign trade is with the Council for Mutual Economic Assistance (CMEA) countries. Exports of petroleum, natural gas, iron and steel are mostly to Bulgaria, Czechoslovakia, East Germany and Poland. Imports include machinery, grains and sugar. The USSR's largest western trading partners are Austria, Finland, France, Italy and West Germany. From 1975 to 1980 trade with West Germany doubled.

The country has now entered its 12th five-year plan period. In 1986 the 27th party congress defined its central objective as increasing the growth rates and efficiency of the economy on the basis of accelerating scientific and technological progress. Modernisation, increased efficiency and better management are to double industrial output and the national income within the next 15 years. A shift away from all encompassing central planning is evident with more responsibility demanded of plant managers and more participation in decision making by workers. Since 1987 individuals can run small businesses for themselves, licensed and taxed by the government. They are not permitted to employ outside labour however.

In per capita national income the Soviet Union comes 21st after the leading capitalist countries and the socialist states of Eastern Europe. The consumption of goods and use of services is only 40% of the US level. Although the austerity is obvious it cannot be called poverty as everyone has a job, a place to sleep, enough to eat, cheap public transport and free access to medical and educational facilities, things many people in the western consumer societies never fully enjoy.

The average Soviet worker earns 200 roubles a month. From this he pays 20 roubles rent, heating and electricity included, and 4% to 10% tax. Large families have a guaranteed income of 50 roubles per person, thus a family of 6 members would receive a minimum of 300 roubles monthly. Bonuses and incentives usually increase wages by 10% to 40%.

Social benefits add another 30% to individual earnings. Tax-free pensions of 60% of average earnings are paid to men at age 60, women at age 55.

GEOGRAPHY

The USSR is the world's largest nation with 22.4 million square km, stretching for almost 10,000 km from west to east and more than 4500 km from north to south. Its 60,000-km long border encompasses a sixth of earth's dry land and touches 12 countries and three oceans, the Atlantic, Arctic and Pacific. The USSR is much larger than South America, only slightly smaller than Africa.

This vast land presents a rich scenic mosaic from the fragrant meadows and sunny groves of central Russia, boundless steppes of the Ukraine and Kazakhstan, to the subtropics of Trans-Caucasia, to the scorching deserts of Central Asia, to the taiga thickets and tundra of Siberia. Forests cover half the country, coniferous in the north and mixed forest in the south. There are over 20,000 varieties of plants and 100,000 species of animals.

The European portion of the USSR is bounded by the Carpathian and Ural mountains. East of the Urals is Asia. The snow-capped Caucasus Mountains stretching between the Black and Caspian seas are the southern boundary of Europe. Mt Elbrus (5633 metres) in this range is Europe's highest peak. Peak Communism in the Pamir Range in the borderlands near China and Afghanistan reaches 7495 metres.

The Soviet Union contains about three million lakes and nearly three million rivers. Lake Baikal is the world's deepest lake (1620 metres), containing a fifth of the planet's reserves of fresh water. The Dnieper River drains much of Byelorussia and the Ukraine before pouring into the Black Sea. The Volga is the legendary river of old Russia, flowing 3530 km from a basin between Moscow and Leningrad east toward the Urals and south into the Caspian Sea. A canal near Volgograd connects the Volga to the Don, making navigation possible between the Caspian and Black seas. The mighty rivers of Siberia flow north to the Arctic and are harnessed by huge hydroelectric projects which power new industrial complexes.

FESTIVALS & HOLIDAYS

Intourist offers special tours to a number of traditional art festivals featuring the country's best musical companies and soloists. These festivals are: Russian Winter in Moscow, Leningrad, Vladimir, Suzdal, Novgorod and Irkutsk (25 December to 5 January), Mertsishor in Kishinev (1-10 March), Moscow Stars (5-13 May), Kiev Spring (late May), Spring in the Ala-Too in Frunze (1-10 June), White Nights in Leningrad (21-29 June), Tashkent Golden Autumn (10-20 September), Melodies of Soviet Transcaucasia

(5-13 October) and Byelorussian Musical Autumn in Minsk (20-30 November).

The major public holidays in the Soviet Union are New Year's Day (1 January), International Women's Day (8 March), Labour Day (1 and 2 May), Victory Day (9 May), Constitution Day (7 October) and the Anniversary of the October Revolution (7 and 8 November). The 25 October revolution is now celebrated on 7 November due to a calendar change.

LANGUAGE

Russian, Ukrainian and Byelorussian are Indo-European languages of the East Slavic group. Russian is spoken everywhere in the USSR. In the national republics people speak their native tongue. The Cyrillic alphabet is used to write most Soviet languages. It only takes about four hours study to become reasonably familiar with Cyrillic and it's well worth the effort. If you have difficulty making yourself understood try writing it down. All Soviets understand Arabic and Roman numerals so at theatre ticket offices (kassas), for example, you can let them know which performance interests you by writing out the date thus: 15 XI 1989 for 15 November 1989.

Facts for the Visitor

VISAS

Soviet consulates require one to three weeks to issue tourist or transit entry/exit visas (three identical photos). You don't need to leave your passport this long, although a photocopy of the first five pages is sometimes required. The fee varies according to the consulate, usually about US\$10. Citizens of some countries must pay an additional consular fee. The exact arrival and departure dates and cities to be visited will be indicated on the visa. You must already have a visa for the next country on your itinerary after the USSR and your passport must be valid

three months after the departure date. The visa is a separate document and no stamps or entries are made in your passport. It says on the visa form that you must register with police upon arrival, but if you're staying at a hotel this will be taken care of for you by the hotel. No registration is required if you're simply transiting the USSR.

Transit visas are issued for periods not exceeding 10 days. If you're taking the Trans-Siberian Railway you'll need two days to go from Eastern Europe to Moscow, then another week to reach the Chinese border, and this must be allowed for on the visa. If you're transiting the USSR by plane no visa is required but you're not allowed to leave the airport.

If you'll be spending one or more nights at a Soviet hotel you want a tourist, not a transit, visa. You'll only be granted a tourist visa if you have confirmed transportation reservations right through the country and a hotel room booked and paid for every night you'll be staying, excepting those spent in transit.

It's possible to extend an individual tourist visa once inside the Soviet Union, but you must apply to your hotel service bureau at least three days in advance of the required extension. It will cost 70 roubles in hard currency to cover your hotel room for each additional night. It's not possible to join a package tour once inside the Soviet Union; conversely, if you came with a group you leave with the group – no extensions. Transit visas cannot be extended or changed to tourist visas upon arrival.

MONEY

US\$1 = 60 kopecks (official)

no compulsory exchange

One rouble contains 100 kopecks. There are banknotes of 1, 3, 5, 10, 25, 50 and 100 roubles. At the official rate of around three West German marks to one rouble, the rouble is overvalued. You won't feel this too much however as your accommodation and international transportation will have been prepaid in hard currency. Most package tours include all meals, transfers and sightseeing. The only things you'll have to pay for in soft currency are postcards, stamps, booklets and small souvenirs. Away from your group you'll also have to pay museum admission fees, theatre tickets, public transport and snacks in roubles, but these are not expensive so don't change too much money. Five roubles a day should be plenty if you're on a tour, 10 or 12 if you're independent.

Prices are set by state committees and often have no relation to the value of a product or service. The only way you can spend a lot of roubles is by eating out at good restaurants. Hotel bars require you to pay in convertible currency and most of your major purchases will be in Beriozka (hard currency) shops. All excursions and theatre tickets booked through the Intourist service bureau at your hotel must paid for in dollars, pounds or marks.

Of course the intent of all this is to discourage you from dabbling in the black market. It's strictly prohibited to change money on the street or sell any of your possessions to Soviet citizens. Actually, you won't be approached that often. When you consider how much it has cost you to come to the USSR and of what little benefit the roubles will be to you anyway, you probably won't want to take the risk. If you're determined to beat the system it's easier to bring roubles with you. The market value of the rouble at western banks is about two roubles to one West German mark. This is also illegal however and upon arrival you'll be asked to sign a declaration listing all the money you are carrying. If the customs officer then discovers that you have roubles you'll probably be refused entry. Customs checks can be extremely thorough. Sometimes they ask you to remove your shoes and feel the seams and linings of your clothing, so it's not something to take lightly.

After clearing customs you'll receive a copy of the declaration form. Only the money and valuables you declared may be re-exported from the USSR, so theoretically all your money could be confiscated if you lost the form! The declaration must be shown every time you change money and 50 kopecks commission is charged per exchange. Hang onto the receipts you get as they are needed to re-exchange leftover roubles (difficult). Don't under declare

your hard currency for any reason as it's OK to have less money than is listed on it but not more. Gold and precious jewellery must also be declared on the form.

CLIMATE

The USSR spreads over all climatic zones except the tropics. The cold Siberian winters and hot Central Asian summers are as far apart as you can get. Much of the country has a temperate continental climate. Southern areas shielded from the north by mountains such as Trans-Caucasia, the Caucasian Black Sea coast and southern Crimea have a pleasant Mediterranean climate with long, warm summers. Proximity to the Baltic gives Leningrad its mild maritime climate. Moscow's weather is more extreme, during May and September sharp changes of temperature may occur, so dress accordingly.

BOOKS & BOOKSHOPS

Be careful what reading material you bring to the Soviet Union as it will be closely scrutinised by customs. Magazines and newspapers from the west may be confiscated, but travel guidebooks and brochures are usually OK.

City maps are often unavailable in Soviet cities. Sometimes you can buy a Cyrillic bus route map at newsstands but it's best to invest in the Falk patent folded maps of Moscow and Leningrad before you come. By far the easiest places in the USSR to buy records or books are the Beriozka (hard currency) shops. Prices are reasonable.

Two useful illustrated guidebooks published by Aurora Art Publishers, Leningrad, are Leningrad, Architectural Landmarks, Art Museums, Suburban Palaces & Parks and Kiev, Architectural Landmarks & Art Museums. The Soviet Union, A Guide Reference Book by Lidiya Dubinskaya (Raduga Publishers, Moscow, 1985) doesn't include any city maps, but it does cover most of the places visited on package tours. A comprehensive architec-

tural guide to the capital is Moscow Past & Present by Yuri Aleksandrov (Raduga Publishers, Moscow, 1984). Museums In & Around Moscow by I Baikova (Raduga Publishers, Moscow, 1983) is also handy. These books can sometimes be purchased in East European bookshops or at Beriozka shops inside the USSR.

The Complete Guide to the Soviet Union by Victor and Jennifer Louis (St Martin's Press, New York, 1980) is organised alphabetically by town. Maps and extremely detailed background information are provided on virtually every place open to foreign tourists when the books was researched back in the late 1970s. Clearly designed for Intourist tour members, hotels and restaurants are simply listed. Next Time You Go To Russia by Charles A Ward (Academic Travel Books, Washington DC, 1977) covers much less ground and is easier to navigate, but the room-by-room museum descriptions seem unnecessary. No practical information is provided but the maps are good.

One of the most complete guides (in French) is URSS (Les Guides Bleus – Hachette, Paris). The city maps and detailed index make it useful even if you don't know French. If you read German the DuMont Kunst-Reisefuhrer Kunst in Russland (DuMont Buchverlag, Koln) is recommended.

NEWSPAPERS & MEDIA

Izvestia and Pravda are the official dailies. Ask for a copy of the weekly Moscow News at your hotel reception. The Monthly magazine Sputnik is the Soviet equivalent of Readers' Digest. Travel to the USSR magazine comes out six times a year. Newsstands sell Communist newspapers from around the world, including the Morning Star (UK), the People's Daily World (US) and the Canadian Tribune.

FILM & PHOTOGRAPHY

Bring enough film with you as it's hard to

find here. Soviet colour film is adapted to the Agfa developing system, not Kodak. If you're a photographer who doesn't care to have his/her film X-rayed you're best to come by train. On arrival and departure by air all luggage is sent through X-ray machines marked 'filmsafe'. Requests for manual examination aren't always honoured.

HEALTH

All medical care in the Soviet Union is free. Tourists also receive emergency treatment at no charge. You may be required to pay for prescription medicine. If laid up in hospital you'll have to pay the bill.

GENERAL INFORMATION

Post

Mailboxes and post offices are found in most hotels and airports. Airmail postage is 35 kopecks for a postcard, 50 kopecks for a letter.

Electricity

The voltage varies between 127 and 220 volts.

Time

There's a two hour time difference between Eastern Europe and the European portion of the Soviet Union. Thus if it's 11 am in London or 12 noon in Berlin it will be 2 pm in Moscow or Leningrad. The USSR spans 11 time zones. There's a seven hour difference between Moscow and Khabarovsk. The USSR goes on summer time on 1 April, on winter time 1 October.

Business Hours

Museums tend to open by 11 am and close around 5 pm. Some stay open till 8 pm one or two nights a week. Many museums close on Mondays. Shops are generally open from 11 am to 7 pm, the big department stores from 8 am to 8 pm. On Saturday all except grocery stores close two hours earlier. Some grocery stores

open on Sunday, as do the Beriozka shops.

When queuing Soviets often mark their position in line by saying something to the person in front or behind. They may then go off and are able to reclaim their 'place' when they return. Be sure this isn't the case before objecting.

INFORMATION

Tourism in the Soviet Union is organised by Intourist, a gigantic state monopoly which owns hundreds of hotels, restaurants and similar facilities throughout the country. Their bright red tour buses are everywhere. Only the 147 centres with Intourist accommodation are open to foreign visitors. Intourist prefers groups to individual tourism. Student groups are usually received by the Sputnik International Youth Travel Bureau.

Intourist offices abroad can provide information and brochures, but don't usually sell tickets or tours. For these you'll be referred to a participating travel agent. Here are a few Intourist offices:

Australia
Intourist (tel 27-7652), 37-49 Pitt St, Sydney NSW 2000
Austria
Intourist (tel 63-9547), Schweden Platz 3-4, 1010 Vienna
Belgium
Intourist (tel 513-8234), Rue Royale 119, 1000 Brussels
Britain
Intourist (tel 631-1252), 292 Regent St, London W1R 6QL
Canada
Intourist (tel 849-6394), Suite 630, 1801 McGill College Ave, Montreal PQ H3A 2A4
Denmark
Intourist (tel 11-2527), Vester Farimagsgade 6, 1606 Copenhagen V
Finland
Intourist (tel 63-1875), Etela Esplanaadi 14, 00130 Helsinki 13
France
Intourist (tel 742-4740), 7 Boulevard des Capucines, 75002 Paris
Greece
Intourist (tel 323-3776), 3 Stadiou St, Syntagma, Athens
Holland
Intourist (tel 79-8964), Honthorststraat 42, 1071 Amsterdam
India
Intourist (tel 69-9105), Plot 6 & 7 block 50E, Nyaya Marg Chanakyapuri, New Delhi 110021
Italy
Intourist (tel 86-3892), Piazza Buenos Aires 6-7, 00198 Rome
Japan
Intourist (tel 584-6617), Roppongi Heights 1-16, 4-chome Roppongi, Minato-ku, Tokyo 106
Mexico
Intourist (tel 566-5472), Paseo de la Reforma 46 (mezzanine), Mexico DF
Norway
Intourist (tel 20-1819), Stortingsgata 8, Oslo 1
Sweden
Intourist (tel 21-5934), Sergelgatan 21, 11157 Stockholm C
Switzerland
Intourist (tel 211-3355), Usteri Str 9, Lowenplatz, 8001 Zurich

USA
Intourist (tel 757-3884), Suite 868, 630 Fifth Ave, New York NY 10111
West Germany
Intourist (tel 88-0077), Olivar Platz 8, 1000 Berlin 15
Intourist (tel 28-5776), Stefan Strasse 1, 6000 Frankfurt am Main 1

Intourist offices within the Soviet Union provide the same services commercial travel agencies handle in capitalist countries. Like western travel agents, they're not really in the business of providing information about things you can do on your own. When they're not too busy hotel receptionists or service bureau personnel will sometimes give advice about restaurants, theatres, sights, local transport, etc, but often you'll have to fend for yourself.

Students from developing countries are very friendly and a mine of information regarding accommodation, food, currency, etc, for those on a low budget.

ACCOMMODATION

Independent budget travel is impossible in the Soviet Union. Until the system undergoes a little *perestroika* the closest thing to budget travel are bourgeois package tours which start at US$50 a day all inclusive. Independent travel is possible, but you'll end up paying over US$80 a night single for bed and breakfast. Doubles are only slightly more expensive than singles. Rooms must be booked and paid for a month in advance and there are no refunds. Unless you can convince Intourist that you're capable of finding your own way to your hotel, you'll have to pay an additional fee to be met at the railway station or airport of each city on your itinerary. If you're on a tour you won't know where you're staying until you get there. Intourist sometimes simply does not reply to requests for individual hotel reservations. The tourist hotels are oases of affluence. Doormen guard the entrances, but if you look foreign you can march straight in – don't hesitate.

FOOD & DRINK

Most package tours include all meals and what you get will be monotonous, bland and uninspiring. In the big cities you may not wish to hang around your hotel waiting for meals. Most of the high-rise hotels have a 'buffet' accepting roubles on one of the upstairs floors where you can get a sandwich and yoghurt to fill your stomach quickly. Self-service restaurants and snack bars in the cities also serve this purpose. Soviet ice cream is delicious and usually available. Most theatres have a buffet where you can get a bite during intermission. Bring some snack food with you, but note that fruit and fresh vegetables are prohibited entry. Chocolate bars, peanuts, etc, can be replenished at Beriozka (hard currency) shops.

To sample the regional specialties you'll usually have to eat out. Good restaurants do exist but many require reservations. Your hotel service bureau may be willing to make restaurant reservations for you. At odd hours you may be admitted without a reservation. Otherwise a rouble or three to the doorman or waiter should get you in. A satisfactory meal at one of these will run 5 to 20 roubles, but don't expect snappy service. Eating at cafes is a good compromise. Five percent service charge is added to the bill and tipping is not customary.

Perestroika has unleashed a new breed of cooperative restaurants, private ventures which must do their grocery shopping at unsubsidised farmers' markets. This puts prices well above the government-operated eateries, but better food and service come with the bill (15 to 25 roubles for a complete meal including appetisers). Reservations are still required and no alcohol is served at cooperatives (BYO). Lunch usually runs from 12 noon to 3 pm, dinner from 6 to 10 pm.

Aside from caviar, the most popular Russian dish is *borsch*, a rich cabbage and beetroot soup. Other favourites include meat and fish in aspic, *ukha* (fish soup), *shchi, pokhlyobka, okroshka*, pies and *blinis* (pancakes) with butter, sour cream or caviar. Siberia is famous for its *pelmeni* (dumplings), Byelorussia for *kholodnik* (a cold soup) and *mochanka* (a thick sauce with lard), the Ukraine for *chicken a la Kiev*, sausage, pies and pastry. A Moldavian specialty is *mamalyga* – hot corn meal eaten with borsch, salted fish and sheep's milk cheese. The hot and spicy Caucasian dishes – *kharcho* soup, shish kebabs, *shashlik* (skewered mutton), *cheburek* meat patties – are served with heaps of fresh herbs. Each region of Central Asia prepares its own type of *pilau* (rice and meat).

The most common drink is hot tea, black or green, served without milk. *Kumiss* is a refreshing drink made from mare's milk. The authorities have embarked on an anti-drinking crusade so very little alcohol is available outside the foreign currency bars. You're allowed to bring in a litre of wine and half a litre of hard liquor, although half litre bottles are usually unobtainable. Of the Soviet wines those from Crimea (especially Massandra) are outstanding. These can be purchased at Beriozka shops.

THINGS TO BUY

Soviet department stores may be of sociological interest but plan on doing most of your shopping at Beriozka (hard currency) shops. In the Ukraine these are called Kashtan. Here you'll find the finest Soviet products which local consumers seldom see. Prices are lower too. For example a chocolate bar costs three times more in a Soviet grocery store than it would at a Beriozka.

Good things to buy in Beriozkas include Russian handicrafts, matrioshka dolls, chess sets, hand-made embroidery and lace, wooden objects, crystal, Baltic amber jewellery, fur hats, records and books. If you purchase jewellery, furs, works of art, or other valuable items be sure to get an itemised receipt to prove to customs that you paid hard currency.

There's no problem exporting folk arts and crafts or mass produced souvenirs in reasonable quantities. Items which cannot be exported from the Soviet Union include military equipment (buttons, belt buckles, etc), manuscripts written by Soviet citizens, jewellery worth over 250 roubles or weighing more than 400 grams, antiques and roubles.

WHAT TO BRING

It's best to bring with you most of what you'll use or consume. In addition to a litre of wine and half a litre of hard liquor you're allowed to import 250 cigarettes. You must be over 21 to bring alcohol and over 16 to bring cigarettes. Bring travellers' cheques in small denominations and hard currency in small bills and coins, to use at Beriozkas, etc. Things not to bring include drugs, pornography, anti-Communist literature, army weapons, explosives, two-way radios, loose pearls, gold coins and roubles.

Getting There & Away

TRAIN

Most independent travellers will arrive by rail, while those on package tours usually come by air. The most commonly used railway routes into the USSR lead from Hungary, Poland and Finland. It's also theoretically possible to take a train direct to the USSR from Romania, Bulgaria, Turkey and Iran. Almost all trains from Eastern Europe are bound for Moscow, although some convey through carriages for Leningrad. Sleepers are available on all services.

Rail passengers from Yugoslavia, Hungary, Czechoslovakia and Austria enter the USSR at Chop in the Ukraine. The daily Tisza Express between Budapest and Moscow is very convenient in that it

departs each end in the evening and arrives at its destination in the early morning. Other daily trains run to Moscow from Athens, Belgrade, Prague and Vienna but they all arrive in the late afternoon.

Most trains from Western Europe, Berlin and Poland cross the Soviet border at Brest in Byelorussia. A Polish transit visa must be obtained in advance. There are several trains a day to Moscow from East Berlin and Warsaw. One daily train (the Ost-West Express) with sleeping cars from Berne (Switzerland), Oostende (Belgium), Aachen (West Germany), Hoek van Holland, Copenhagen, Stockholm and Paris calls at Zoo Station in West Berlin. Another daily service direct to Leningrad via Vilnius originates in Cologne, West Germany, and calls at Zoo Station, West Berlin and Warsaw.

Finland is a natural gateway for travel to the USSR. A day train shuttles between Helsinki and Leningrad (eight hours). There's also a daily overnight train with sleepers from Helsinki to Moscow.

From Eastern Europe

Railway fares between Eastern Europe and the USSR are cheap. For instance, Budapest-Moscow is only US$50 round trip in 1st class with a sleeper. Sleepers from Eastern European capitals to Moscow or Leningrad can be booked immediately, but it takes about a month to get a return reservation (necessary for the visa). If Soviet Railways does not respond to your request for return reservations ask the Eastern European booking office to leave the carriage and seat numbers blank and just write in the date. The Intourist service bureau at your USSR hotel will obtain a reservation for you upon arrival.

The catch is that Soviet visa regulations make it hard to travel this way. You need confirmed hotel reservations for every night you will be in the USSR (excepting those spent on the train) and the price will be upwards of US$80 a night single for bed and breakfast. Eastern European travel agencies such as Orbis, Cedok and Ibusz can book hotel rooms in the Soviet Union, but again they'll need a month and you must pay in advance. Thus a sidetrip from Budapest to Moscow with four nights at a Moscow hotel would cost about US$320 for the room, plus 10% commission, plus US$50 for the train, plus the visa fee. If your plans change it's almost impossible to get a refund.

Eastern Europe to China

Railway fares between socialist countries are low and the best deal of all is a ticket to China. For instance Budapest to Peking is only US$90 one way in 1st class with a sleeper. The catch again is that you can't get a Soviet transit visa in Budapest unless you already have train reservations from Moscow to China. These take over a month to come through and then you still have to wait 10 days for the visa. In addition you cannot book a seat between Moscow and China more than two months in advance, so careful planning and lots of luck are required.

Still, if you're going to be travelling around Eastern Europe a month or more anyway it's possible to organise an exit on the Trans-Siberian. Ask about cancellations at all Eastern European travel agencies selling international train tickets. You may be lucky and not have to wait for a reservation. If you do go this way you may have a full day to look around Moscow before catching your onward train. Or try setting out for Moscow a day early and sleep in the station.

Another idea is to buy a ticket back from Beijing to, say, Budapest or Berlin then fly to China on a cheap flight and come back by train. Trans-Siberian tickets cost half as much in Hungary as they would in China and the open return portion is valid four months from date of issue. Return reservations and visas are easily arranged in Beijing. For more information on the Trans-Siberian railway

route from China or Japan see The Trans-Siberian Railway below.

BOAT

There's an Estonian Shipping Company ferry several times a week year round between Helsinki and Tallinn. From May to mid-October a Scansov Line car ferry runs twice a week from Stockholm to Leningrad.

The Soviet Danube Line runs a cruise ship right down the Danube River from Passau, West Germany, to Ismail, Moldavia, connecting in Ismail for Istanbul. The full 10-day trip from West Germany to Turkey operates in summer five times a year. It's not possible to use this ship for intermediate journeys (from Budapest to Romania, for example). Only through passengers are accepted. The Black Sea Shipping Company has occasional ships to Odessa from various Mediterranean ports.

The Far East Shipping Company ferry from Yokohama, Japan, to Nakhodka operates about once a week from April to October. Once a year this service originates in Hong Kong. In Nakhodka this ferry connects with the Trans-Siberian Railway to Moscow.

Passage on any of the above ships involves considerable advance planning with the help of a good travel agent. Don't expect any bargains. It's more practical to look for a package tour which uses the ship of your choice. That way everything will be prearranged and it could even work out cheaper.

TOURS

The easiest way to visit the Soviet Union is on a package tour. Visas, flights, transfers, accommodation, meals and sightseeing tours – all will be arranged for you. Prices vary but it's almost always cheaper to travel with a group than it would be independently. The only 'extras' will be drinks and souvenirs. Of course there's nothing that says you have to stick with the group all the time. You're free to explore on your own as much as you like within city limits. Long solo trips out into the countryside are prohibited, however.

Good deals on tours to the USSR are offered in Britain, West Berlin and Helsinki. Prices are lower in the off season, October to April. Unless you pay a healthy single supplement you'll just have to take pot luck as to who your roommate will be.

Invariably you must book the tour at least three weeks in advance. Unless you're booking from home don't agree to leave your passport with the travel agent all this time. All they should need is a photocopy of the first five pages of your passport and three photos. You won't actually receive your tickets and visa until just a few days before you're due to leave.

From West Berlin

Since currency regulations inhibit you from booking a tour to the Soviet Union in any of the socialist countries, West Berlin is the closest alternative. Prices are relatively low in West Berlin as the groups fly out of East Berlin on Aeroflot or Interflug flights. If you do join a tour in Berlin everything will be conducted in German.

A seven-night all inclusive package to Moscow or Leningrad will run about DM 800 to DM 1400 (DM 600 to DM 900 for four nights). Seven-night tours of the old Russian towns, the Baltic republics, Trans-Caucasia or Central Asia vary in price anywhere from DM 900 to DM 1600. Twelve to 14 nights in any of these places might run DM 1400 to DM 2450. A 21-night grand tour of the Soviet Union including Leningrad, Moscow, Siberia, Middle Asia and Trans-Caucasia would be DM 2900 to DM 3400. The prices vary according to season.

In contrast to the above, all of which involve flights, there's a rail tour from West Berlin to Vilnius, capital of Lithuania. The DM 700 to DM 900 price includes a sleeper on the train and five days in Vilnius all inclusive (DM 68 extra for the Polish transit visas).

For colourful brochures describing the trips with dates and prices specified write: Intratours, Bayreuther Strasse 7-8, 1000 Berlin 30; Intourist Reisen, Olivaer Platz 8, 1000 Berlin 15; Olympia Reisen, Schluter Strasse 44, 1000 Berlin 15; Hansa Tourist, Kurfurstendamm 67, 1000 Berlin; Osttourist, 111 Schildergasse, 5 Koln, West Germany. Intratours is especially recommended.

From Britain

Intourist Moscow (tel 580-1221), 292 Regent St, London W1R 6QL, offers all of the above and more from Birmingham, Cardiff, London, Manchester and Newcastle. Other Intourist tours from Britain feature a two-week stay at the Black Sea resorts Yalta, Sochi or Dagomys or a ride on the Trans-Siberian Railway. Their prices are competitive with the West Berlin tours and you'll enjoy the services of an English-speaking guide. Also try Progressive Tours (tel 262-1676), 12 Porchester Place, Marble Arch, London W2 2BS, which sometimes offers real bargains on USSR package tours.

In Australia trips can be booked through Intourist UK (tel 27-7652), 37 Pitt St, Sydney, NSW 2000.

From Finland

Finnsov Tours (tel 694-2011), Eerikinkatu 3, 00100 Helsinki, Finland, offers a variety of tours from Helsinki to Tallinn, Riga, Leningrad and Moscow by ship, bus and rail. Three-night bus tours to Leningrad are offered year round (FIM 1150 to FIM 1590 per person). Four-night tours to Moscow by train are available from mid-June to early September (FIM 2450 per person). Two of the four nights are spent on the train. In July and August a short two-night cruise across the Gulf of Finland to Tallinn is offered (FIM 1240 per person). This trip can be extended to Leningrad by train, returning to Helsinki by bus (five nights, FIM 2690 per person).

If you wish to add Moscow to this trip it will be an additional FIM 2000 per person for the three extra nights. There's also a three or four-night tour to Riga which uses the ferry to Tallinn (FIM 1170 to FIM 1410 per person standard class). The prices above include transportation, transfers, sightseeing, accommodation and most meals as specified in their brochure. There's a healthy single supplement if you're alone and want a private room. An English and German-speaking Finnsov Tours escort accompanies the groups.

Finnsov can also package individual itineraries by rail, road and ship. They process Soviet visas for FIM 70 but require 21 days to do it and may actually want to see your passport three working days before departure. You must book and pay a month in advance. If you're subsequently refused a visa or are unable to go due to illness, you lose 25% of your money up to 15 days prior to departure, half the money up to two days before.

River Trips

If you'd like to combine a scenic cruise with a tour of the Soviet Union look for trips down the Volga, Don and Dnieper rivers. You'll travel on a luxury river boat with tours ashore to cities like Kazan, Ulyanovsk (birthplace of Lenin), Volgograd (Stalingrad), Rostov-on-Don, Odessa and Kiev. The Deutsches Reiseburo GmbH, Eschersheimer Land Strasse 25/27, 6000 Frankfurt am Main 1, West Germany, for example, offers an eight-night cruise on the Dnieper from DM 1320 and a 10-night trip on the Volga from DM 1450, return flights from Frankfurt am Main, Dusseldorf or Stuttgart included.

Intourist Moscow, London, offers a 14-night cruise (eight nights of which are spent aboard ship) down the Volga from about £700 , three nights each in Moscow and Leningrad thrown in. Round trip flights from Gatwick (London) are included.

Student Travel

The summer tours arranged by the Scandinavian Student Travel Service (tel 21-8500), Hauchvej 17, 1825 Frederiksberg C, Denmark, in conjunction with Sputnik, the Soviet International Youth Travel Bureau, have a good reputation. SSTS trips can be booked through any student travel office or direct. Although the tours are designed for those under 35, you don't have to be a student.

In June, July and August there are one-week trips to Moscow and Leningrad (DKR 3860 including the flight from Copenhagen). Two-week trips go every summer to the Baltic Republics, the Ukraine, Trans-Caucasia, Central Asia and Siberia. Once in July and again in August SSTS offers a 20-day trip by rail from Helsinki to Japan for DKR 7955. Overnight stops in Leningrad, Moscow, Novosibirsk, Irkutsk and Khabarovsk are included.

Study Tours

If you'd like to spend longer in the Soviet Union than is possible on a standard tourist trip consider enrolling in a Russian language seminar. You'll get 12 to 24 days in a Soviet city such as Kharkov, Krasnodar, Kursk, Leningrad, Moscow, Sochi or Suzdal for the price tourists pay for the shortest tour. Classes last four hours a day, six days a week in groups of not over 10 persons. Longer courses are available. Some previous knowledge of Russian may be required. Prices are 20% lower from October to March. Ask about this possibility at Intourist offices. In Britain Progressive Tours Limited (address above) arranges Russian language courses.

Getting Around

Public transportation is efficient and highly developed in the Soviet Union. Fares are ridiculously low, usually five kopecks for buses, four kopecks for trolleys and three kopecks for trams. In some buses, trolleys and streetcars you drop 5 kopecks into the pay box and take a ticket. Other times you have to buy tickets in advance at a newspaper kiosk. Public transport runs from 6 am to 1 am.

Baku, Kharkov, Kiev, Leningrad, Minsk, Moscow, Novosibirsk, Tashkent, Tbilisi and Yerevan have large underground Metro systems. You drop a five kopeck coin into the turnstile to enter (there are automatic coin changers nearby). Once inside you can change lines and backtrack as much as you like without paying again. All signs and maps of the Metro will be in Cyrillic, so bring a Romanic map with you.

Taxis are relatively inexpensive in the USSR, 20 kopecks flag fall then 20 kopecks a km. If you plan to use them ask for the location of the taxi stand closest to your hotel and join the queue of people waiting. It's also quite feasible to flag down taxis on the street. Sometimes cabs with passengers will stop to fill the empty seats. You pay what the meter says, although the driver may round it up to the next rouble for you.

Moscow

Few countries are as dominated by their capital as is the Soviet Union. Moscow is both our window to the USSR and most Soviets' window to the world. Moscow's fascination rests in its role as the directing centre of the largest country on earth and one of humanity's most closed societies. The city's lifeblood pulses through the Metro and it's hard not to feel the naked power emanating from the Kremlin.

Ostensibly you'll be coming to visit the museums and historic sites, take in a little culture and perhaps gain a personal understanding which may add a tiny grain of sand to the cause of world peace. Take the time to study the crowds in the Metro and pay a visit to a Soviet department store. Or just take the Metro to any outlying station and compare the life style.

Be forewarned that Muscovites are a terribly proud bunch. If they think you are a friend because you smile, are polite and respectful, they will extend the most unprecedented hospitality. They're also quite capable of turning a shoulder as cold as yours, so it pays to be positive from the start.

History

A small Slavic settlement emerged on the banks of the Moscow River around the end of the 11th century. Yuri the Long Armed built a wooden Kremlin in 1156, but the Mongol hordes burned Moscow in 1238. By the end of the 13th century Moscow was capital of an independent principality and stone Byzantine churches were erected in the Kremlin. In 1380 the Russian forces defeated the Golden Horde, but Khan Tokhtamysh returned two years later and sacked Moscow. With the shaking off of Mongol domination at the end of the 15th century, Moscow emerged at the head of a centralised Russian state. Brick walls and towers were built around the Kremlin and great cathedrals appeared inside.

Despite fires, invasions and mutinies the city grew around its fortress. A long war with Sweden over access to the Baltic Sea turned the tsar's eyes northwards and in 1712 Peter the Great, desirous of opening Russia to Europe, moved the capital to St Petersburg. Moscow continued to develop without the tsar and the first university opened in 1755. Napoleon appreciated the city's importance when he led his Grand Army against it in 1812. He later admitted this was the greatest mistake he ever made.

Intellectual life flourished here during the 19th century with Russian literature, music and theatre attaining worldwide fame. Yet political development lagged behind and an unsuccessful workers' uprising in 1905 was followed by the victory of the socialist revolution in 1917. In 1918 'Mutushka Moskva' – Mother Moscow – once again became capital, this time of both the Russian Federation and the Soviet Union.

The years between the wars saw Moscow develop with schools, hospitals, workers' housing, department stores, the first stretch of Metro (in 1935), bridges and cultural facilities. The Nazis never managed to enter Moscow and outside the city they suffered their first defeat. Since the war Moscow has grown into a bustling metropolis of over eight million people, the political, economic and cultural centre of the nation.

Orientation

The Moscow River loops through the heart of the city with the Kremlin on top of its biggest bend. Many main thoroughfares fan out from the fortress like spokes of a wheel. Others orbit around it in ever widening rings. The Boulevard and Sadovoj rings originated as 16th century defensive lines.

Moscow's main business district is to the north of the Kremlin, the modern city centre to the west along Gor'kogo ulitsa and prospekt Kalinina, and the old aristocratic quarter south-west toward Novodevichi Convent. Prospekt Marksa and Red Square on the north-west and north-east sides of the Kremlin are important reference points for the visitor.

Information

If you're on a package tour your Intourist guide will be your first information source. The Intourist service bureau at your hotel may also be able to help with theatre tickets, restaurant reservations, excursions, etc for hard currency. If you're not with a group, the service bureau will reconfirm your onward transportation reservations.

Independent travellers can also turn to the Moscow Travel Department at the Intourist Hotel, Gor'kogo ulitsa 3. If all you want is information go to the counter marked 'information' as the other female clerks will become annoyed if they think you're only asking questions. This is the best place to pick up theatre tickets for same evening performances, but expect to pay Broadway prices in hard currency: US$22 for the Bolshoi Ballet, US$10 for the circus.

The Travel Department books a variety of sightseeing tours. The best of the lot takes you 50 km north-east to the historic town of Zagorsk, centre of the Russian Orthodox Church (every Friday, 22 roubles in hard currency). There are also tours to Vladimir and Suzdal (30 roubles) or New Jerusalem Monastery at Istra (15 roubles), each offered only once a week. An additional 5% commission is added to these already high prices.

Sputnik, the youth travel bureau, is at the Orlionok Hotel, Kosygina ulitsa 15 (Metro – Leninskij prospekt).

Embassies Australian Embassy, Kropotkinskij pereulok 13 (Metro – Park Kul'tury). Canadian Embassy, Starokonyusennyi pereulok 23 (Metro – Arbatskaja or Kropotkinskaja). New Zealand Embassy, Vorovskogo ulitsa 44 (Metro – Arbatskaja, Barrikadnaja, or Krasnopresnenskaja). American Embassy, Cajkovskogo ulitsa 19-23 (Metro – Barrikadnaja or Krasnopresnenskaja). West German Embassy, Bolsaja Gruzinskaja ulitsa 17 near the zoo (Metro – Barrikadnaja or Krasnopresnenskaja). British Embassy, Naberezhnaia Morisa Toreza 14 directly across the river from the Kremlin.

Things to See

Red Square Take the Metro to Revol'ucii ploscad, Marksa prospekt, or Sverdlova ploscad stations, all of which are connected by underground passageways. Wherever you come out make your way to the **Central Lenin Museum**, Revol'ucii ploscad 2 (closed Monday and the last Tuesday of each month, free). Just locate the entrance to this huge red brick

1 Ostankino Palace
2 Television Tower
3 Exhibition of Economic Achievements
4 Cosmonauts Obelisk
5 Cosmos Hotel
6 Savčlovskaja Railway Station
7 Rižsky Railway Station
8 Central Museum of the Armed Forces
9 Jaroslavskij and Leningradskij Railway Stations
10 Kazan Railway Station
11 Moscow Puppet Theatre
12 Belorusskij Railway Station
13 Kijevskaja Railway Station
14 Pushkin Art Gallery
15 Kremlin
16 Synagogue
17 Kurskij Railway Station
18 Novodevichi Convent
19 Berlozka Shop
20 Lenin Stadium
21 Lev Tolstoy House Museum
22 Tretyakov Art Gallery
23 Paveletsky Railway Station
24 Pier Novopassky Most
25 Moscow University
26 New Circus
27 Children's Theatre
28 Sputnik Hotel Orlionok
29 Gorky Park Riverboot Landing
30 Donskoi Monastery
31 Sevastopol Hotel
32 Kolomenskoye Summer Residence

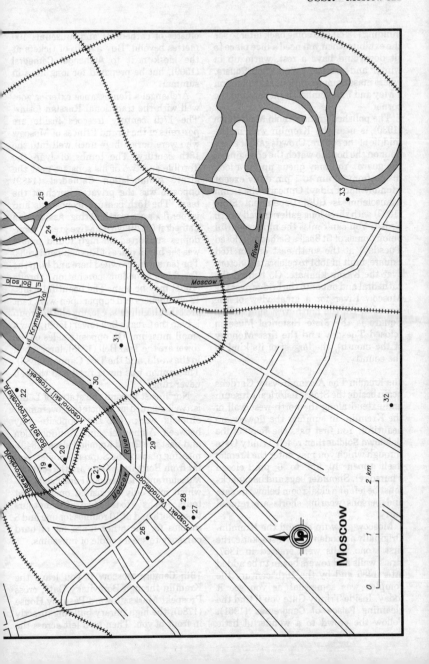

Moscow

Moscow

0   2 km

building (1892) and come back later to see the exhibits when you need a nice place to sit down and have a rest, warm up in winter and use the toilets. **Red Square**, where mass demonstrations take place on 1 May and 7 November, is just around the corner.

The polished granite **Lenin Mausoleum** (1930) is near the Kremlin wall in the middle of the square. Crowds gather every hour on the hour to watch the changing of the guard. You may queue up for a look inside from 10 am to 1 pm daily except Monday and Friday. Opposite the Lenin Mausoleum is **GUM Department Store** (1893) with three long galleries well worth a visit. You can't miss the nine colourful onion domes of **St Basil's Cathedral** (closed Tuesday) at the south-east end of Red Square, built in 1561 to celebrate a victory over the Kazan khanate. Go behind the cathedral and out onto the bridge over the Moscow River for a great view of the Kremlin. On the north-west side of Red Square is the **State Historical Museum** (closed Tuesday and the first Monday of the month), the largest of its kind in the country.

The Kremlin The Alexandrovsky Gardens begin beside the State Historical Museum and extend along the north-west wall of the Kremlin. In summer the flowers are beautiful. You first pass the **Tomb of the Unknown Soldier** then reach Trinity Gate through which you may enter the **Kremlin** itself (open 10 am to 6 pm, closed Thursday). Shoulder bags and backpacks must be left at a cloakroom below the gate and persons wearing shorts are refused entry.

Moscow grew up around the Kremlin. Originally a wooden frontier stockade, the first stone walls were erected in 1367. Brick walls and towers began to be added after 1485 and by the 16th century the complex was somewhat as you see it today. Inside Trinity Gate you'll find the gleaming **Palace of Congresses** (1961). Follow the crowd to a wonderful little cluster of cathedrals and museums 100 metres beyond. Buy a strip of tickets at the kiosk next to **Archangel Cathedral** (1509), but be prepared for long lines in summer.

Archangel's Renaissance exterior goes well with the traditional Russian forms. The 17th century frescoes inside are portraits of the Grand Princes of Moscow who were buried here until well into the 18th century. The tombs of Ivan the Terrible and two of his sons are near the altar. **Annunciation Cathedral** (1489) opposite was the private church of the tsars. The 15th century iconostasis and jasper floor are worth noting. **Assumption Cathedral** (1479) with its five great onion-domes supported on high round pillars was the burial place of Russian patriarchs. The tsars were crowned here and Ivan the Terrible's wooden coronation throne (1551) may be seen. The beautiful icons, 12 chandeliers and copper open-work tent are other highlights. Closing off the group is Ivan the Great's **Bell Tower** (1508), now a small museum. On opposite sides of the tower are the Tsar Bell (1735), largest bell in the world, and the Tsar Cannon (1586). The cannon was never fired and the bell never rung.

North-east beyond the statue of Lenin is a well-guarded area where top government officials work. Go the opposite way between Archangel and Annunciation and past the **Grand Kremlin Palace** (1849), meeting place of the Supreme Soviet. Not far from Borovitsky Gate are the **Armoury Museum** and the **Diamond Fund Exhibition**, which may only be visited on Intourist tours. You have to take two different tours to see both and at 10 roubles for one and 8 roubles for the other it's a lot of hard currency to see a couple of museums.

19th Century Moscow If you leave the Kremlin through Borovitsky Gate, cross Prospekt Marksa toward Pashkov House (1786), the high library building directly in front of you. Then turn left across the street and down Volchonka ulitsa to the **Pushkin Art Gallery** (open until 8 pm Tuesday to Saturday, until 6 pm Sunday) with six tall Ionic columns before the entrance. After the Leningrad Hermitage this is the best collection of western art in the USSR. The objects with labels in English and Russian are originals; those labelled in Russian only are copies. Directly behind the Pushkin Art Gallery is the **Marx & Engels Museum** (closed Monday and the last day of the month, free).

Kropotkinskaja ulitsa, the south-west continuation of Volchonka ulitsa, is lined with palaces of the old aristocracy. (Take the smaller street on the right at the fork just beyond the Metro station.) Two you may enter are the **Pushkin Literary Museum**, Kropotkinskaja ulitsa 12/2 (closed Monday, Tuesday and the last day of the month), and the **Lev Tolstoy Museum**, Kropotkinskaja ulitsa 11 (closed Monday).

Moscow has over a dozen literary museums. By far the most interesting is the **Lev Tolstoy House-Museum**, further south-west at L'va Tolstogo ulitsa 21 (closed Monday and the last day of the month). The great novelist spent the winters from 1882 to 1901 in this large town mansion which remains unchanged to this day. Tolstoy's tiny study at the end of an upstairs corridor is one of the most evocative museum rooms in Europe. Captions on the walls are in English.

For an insight into the 19th century enlightenment in Moscow visit the **Herzen Museum**, Sivtsev Vrazhek pereulok 27/9 a few blocks west of the Pushkin Art Gallery (closed Monday and the last day of the month, open till 9 pm on Wednesday and Friday). Ask to hear the recording in English about the writer and his times.

Two more literary museums worth visiting if you have time include **Gorky's Flat Museum**, Kacalova ulitsa 6/2 (closed Monday and Tuesday, open till 8 pm Wednesday and Friday, free), and **Chekhov's House-Museum**, Sadovaja-Kudrinskaja ulitsa 6 (closed Monday and the last day of the month).

Other Museums Moscow has over 100 museums, although a third to a half of them may be closed at any given time for renovations or other reasons. Some museums even close if the weather is bad so be prepared for a few disappointments! We list below a few interesting museums which don't fit into any walking tour. Use the Metro to travel between them.

The **Central Museum of the Revolution**, Gor'kogo ulitsa 21 (closed Monday and the last day of the month, free, Metro – Pushkinskaja or Gor'kovskaja), is housed in the former English Club (1831).

The **Glinka Museum of Musical Culture**, Fadeyeva ulitsa 4 (closed Thursday and the last Friday of the month, Metro – Majakovskaja), has an excellent collection of folk instruments from every corner of the USSR and the captions are in English.

The **Tretyakov Art Gallery**, Lavrushinsky pereulok 10 (closed Monday, Metro – Novokuzneckaja), has the best collection of Russian art in Moscow and should not be missed.

Back near Red Square is the **Trinity Church in Nikitniki** (1634), Nikitnikov pereulok 3 (closed Tuesday, Metro – Nogina Ploscad), a little jewel with a red and white exterior and five green domes. This church is now the Museum of 17th century Painting & Architecture. The frescoes, iconostasis and vaulted ceiling without pillars are what make it so interesting. The **History of Moscow Museum**, ploscad Nogina 12, is a few blocks north.

If you're curious about Napoleon's Russian adventure there's no better place to go than the **Battle of Borodino Panorama Museum**, Kutuzovskij prospekt 38 (closed Friday and the last Thursday of the month, Metro – Kutuzovskaja). A 115-metre-long 360-degree painting done in 1912 shows the conflict between 220,000 Russians and 640,000 French just west of

Central Moscow

1 Belorusskij Railway Station
2 Glinka Museum of Musical Culture
3 Obraztsov Puppet Theatre
4 Tchaikovsky Concert Hall
5 West German Embassy
6 Zoo
7 Central Museum of the Revolution
8 Rossiya Cinema
9 State Literature Museum
10 Central Travel Bureau
11 Konenkov Museum
12 Moscow Art Theatre
13 Gorky's Flat Museum
14 Chekhov's House Museum
15 American Embassy
16 Comecon Headquarters
17 New Zealand Embassy
18 Oktyabr Cinema
19 Dom Knigi
20 Conservatory of Music
21 Post Office
22 Zoological Museum
23 Old University
24 Intourist Hotel
25 Operetta Theatre

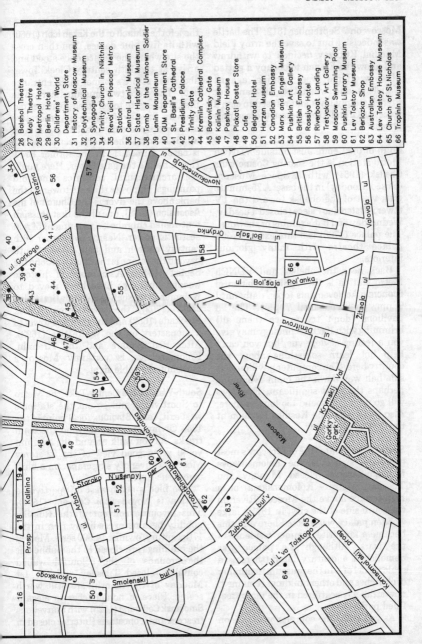

26 Bolshoi Theatre
27 Maly Theatre
28 Metropol Hotel
29 Berlin Hotel
30 Childrens' World Department Store
31 History of Moscow Museum
32 Polytechnical Museum
33 Synagogue
34 Trinity Church in Nikitniki
35 Revoľucii Ploscad Metro Station
36 Central Lenin Museum
37 State Historical Museum
38 Tomb of the Unknown Soldier
39 Lenin Mausoleum
40 GUM Department Store
41 St. Basil's Cathedral
42 Presidium Palace
43 Trinity Gate
44 Kremlin Cathedral Complex
45 Borovitsky Gate
46 Kalinin Museum
47 Pashkov House
48 Plakati Poster Store
49 Cafe
50 Belgrade Hotel
51 Herzen Museum
52 Canadian Embassy
53 Marx and Engels Museum
54 Pushkin Art Gallery
55 British Embassy
56 Rossiya Hotel
57 Riverboat Landing
58 Tretyakov Art Gallery
59 Moscow Swimming Pool
60 Pushkin Literary Museum
61 Lev Tolstoy Museum
62 Beriozka Shop
63 Australian Embassy
64 Lev Tolstoy House Museum
65 Church of St.Nicholas
66 Tropinin Museum

Moscow on 7 September 1812. The battle was indecisive but to save the army Field Marshal Kutuzov decided to withdraw and allow the French to occupy a gutted Moscow. Time was working against Napoleon and when the Russians cut French supply lines and refused to sign a truce the Grand Army began its disastrous retreat.

North of the Centre Just outside VDNCh Metro station is the soaring **Cosmonauts Obelisk** (1964) with a Space Museum (closed Monday) in the base. A 25-minute walk west of the obelisk toward the TV tower is **Ostankino Palace** (closed Tuesday, Wednesday and if it's raining or snowing). The palace (1798) is a rare example of a palace theatre with many glorious interiors.

Back near the obelisk and VDNCh Metro station is the **USSR Exhibition of Economic Achievements** (open daily until 9 pm, pavilions until 7 pm). The 78 pavilions (don't try to see them all) brimming with 1960s technology may give you a feeling of deja vue, but you can't help but learn something about the country here. The computer pavilion (left side half way down the main avenue) is perhaps the most significant. Eyebrows will go up if you spend too long in there. Also don't miss the Kosmos Pavilion at the far end of the row.

South of the Centre One of Moscow's most evocative sights is the **Kolomenskoye Museum-Reserve** (closed Monday and Tuesday, Metro – Kolomenskaja) on a high terrace above the Moscow River on the south side of the city. In 1671 a large wooden palace was erected here and this became a favourite summer residence of the tsars. Although the palace was demolished a century later (there is a scale model of it in the museum) a number of churches and other buildings remained, now strangely scattered in the large tree-filled park.

As you enter the complex you pass on the left the **Church of the Kazan Icon** (1660) with its five blue domes. You then cross the site where the palace once stood and arrive at the 16th century Clock Tower above the estate's former main entrance gate. There are two museums here. The first, in the gate tower itself, features old Russian handicrafts such as decorative metalwork, clock mechanisms and woodcarvings. The second section, which is easily missed, is in the former Brew House beside the gate tower. Here you'll see architectural ceramics and old paintings. Opposite the gate tower on the bank above the river is the **Church of the Ascension** (1532), one of the first Russian tent-roofed churches, a monument of real aesthetic power. Nearby is another 16th century church and bell tower. South beyond the ravine is the **Church of John the Baptist** (1540). A number of historic wooden buildings have been moved to Kolomenskoye such as **Peter the Great's log cabin** (1702), the tower from Bratsk Stockade (1652) and the entrance tower to a monastery on the White Sea (1693). After Red Square and the Kremlin, Kolomenskoye is certainly Moscow's most unforgettable sight.

South-West of the Centre Take the Metro to Sportivnaja and go out the station's west exit. **Lenin Stadium**, focal point of the 1980 Olympics, is just beyond the train tracks. As you walk around the stadium you'll get a good view of the 32-storey Moscow University skyscraper on a bluff across the river.

Two blocks north-west of Sportivnaja station is **Novodevichi Convent** (1524). This favourite convent of the Russian nobility became exceedingly rich in the 17th century, owning 14,500 serfs. Most of the buildings are closed to the public but the grounds of the colourful walled complex (closed Tuesday and the 1st Monday of the month) are still worth seeing. Place of honour goes to elegant **Smolensk Cathedral** (1525) with marvellous frescoes and iconostasis (interior closed in bad weather). The long red and white building adjacent is the refectory and **Church of the Dormition** (1687) which is only open for religious services after 5.30 pm. Also within the grounds are various gate-churches (all closed), a bell tower (1690), burial grounds and a permanent exhibition of Russian tiles.

While you're in the area visit the excellent Beriozka (hard currency) shop at Luzneckij proyezd 25a across the street from the convent.

On the Moscow River In summer one of the most relaxing ways to see Moscow is from the open upper deck of a tour boat on the **Moscow River**. These operate regularly from a landing near Kijevskaja Railway Station (Metro – Kijevskij) right around to Pier Novopassky Most (Metro – Proletarskaja) making 12 stops along the way (60 kopecks and 1½ hours for a complete one way trip). You can also catch this boat from the landing on the left (north) bank, east of the Rossiya Hotel, or at **Gorky Park**. A Russian commentary is broadcast over speakers. Intourist offers a similar but much more expensive cruise with an English commentary a couple of times a week, but it's more fun taking the regular trip with the locals. The rowboats in Gorky Park are also recommended.

Places to Stay
It's unlikely you'll have any choice where you stay. If you do the *Berlin Hotel* (1912), ulitsa Jdanov 3, is small, quiet and central. The *National Hotel* (1903), prospekt Marksa 14/1, is also good, although on a noisy street. They have four categories of rooms, of which categories C and D are the cheapest. The recently renovated *Metropol Hotel* (1905), prospekt Marxa 1, is similar.

Apart from these three charming old world hotels, Intourist offers the usual line of high-rise monsters. The commercial *Intourist Hotel* (1970), 3/5 ulitsa Gorki (Metro – prospekt Marxa), doesn't have much character but at least it's central.

The *Cosmos Hotel* (1979), prospekt Mira 150 (Metro – VDNKh), is much more comfortable. *Hotel Belgrade* (1973), ulitsa Smolenskaya 5 (Metro – Smolenskaya), is near Kijevskaja Railway Station. Individuals are often placed there.

Three less expensive Intourist establishments, all far from the centre, are the *Sevastopol* (Metro – Kakhovskaja or Sevastopolskaja), the *Solnechny* (Metro – Yuzhnaya, then bus No 743), and the *Mozhaisky* (Metro – Fil'ovskij Park, then bus No 139). Request the Sevastopol specifically if you're booking an independent itinerary. The Solnechny also has a campground, but this is only for motorists on Intourist itineraries, you can always try (tel 3820466 or 3821465). Sputnik student groups stay at the *Hotel Orlyonok*, ulitsa A N Kosygina 15 (Metro – Leninsky Prospekt), a high-rise between Moscow State University and Gorky Park.

Places to Eat
Getting into the better Moscow restaurants is a hassle. After 5 pm there can be long lines at the door and the service is invariably slow. Unless this is what you came for it's better to simply give them all a miss and patronise the cheaper stand-up cafeterias and snack bars. There are a number of these along 25th of October, the street between GUM and the Lenin Museum off Red Square near the State Historical Museum. Cafes are a good compromise with reasonable, more accessible food.

A new phenomena are the privately-run cooperative restaurants which appeared in 1987. *Kropotkinskaya 36* (tel 201-7500; Metro – Park Kultury), the first of the breed, takes its name from its location in a recycled town house in Moscow's old aristocratic quarter. Specialities include smoked chicken, shashlik, roasted meats, and trout. The cooperative scene changes almost weekly, but some places to ask about are *Razgulyai* (Russian dishes), *Cafe Kolkhida* (Georgian cuisine), *At*

Pirosmani's (Georgian), *Skazda* (Russian), *Cafe Yakimanka* (Uzbek), *Zaidi i Poprobui* (Armenian), *Sorok Chetyri* (open 24 hours).

At the Intourist Hotel there's a snack bar accepting roubles at the end of the corridor on the 10th floor (closes at 11 pm). March straight past the doorman into the hotel and check your coat.

Entertainment

Moscow's theatres are more spread out than Leningrad's and getting tickets is also more difficult. If you really want to attend a good performance and aren't worried about the price, make straight for the Moscow Travel Department at the Intourist Hotel (see 'information' above) or try your hotel service bureau. They usually have same evening tickets for the Bolshoi or the circus and you'll pay inflated prices in hard currency.

Of course you can always go directly to the theatre box office or 'kassa' (open afternoons) and this will be cheaper, but the Bolshoi is always sold out. If you don't mind being turned away try showing up at the theatre door a little before 7 pm. There may be spare tickets at the box office, someone outside may have extra seats to sell, or perhaps the ushers will take pity on you. Street kiosks around Moscow also have theatre and concert tickets, but you may have to take pot luck unless you speak Russian. Write out the date you want using Roman numerals for the month (10 X 1989, for example, means 10 October 1989) and repeat the word 'music' using a variety of intonations.

The *Bolshoi Theatre* (1824), home of the famous Bolshoi Ballet, is at ploscad Sverdlova 2 a five-minute walk from Red Square. The Bolshoi ticket office (open 12 noon to 3 pm) is on the west side of ploscad Sverdlova, near the two kiosks close to the entrance to the Metro.

A good second choice is the *Operetta Theatre* (kassa 12 noon to 7 pm), Pushkinskaya 6 just around the corner from the Bolshoi.

For instrumental music try the *Tchaikovsky Concert Hall* (kassa 12 noon to 7.30 pm), Majakovskogo ploscad 20 (Metro – Majakovskaja). This pleasant oval-shaped hall is large enough that there are usually spare tickets. All of the seats offer adequate views and there's a good refreshment area to the left of the cloakroom. Other concerts take place in the *Palace of Congresses* in the Kremlin and at the *Moscow Conservatory of Music*, Ulitsa Gertsena 13.

The *Moscow Art Theatre*, Tverskoj bulvar 22 (Metro – Puskinskaja or Gor'kovskaja), is the city's most prestigious dramatic theatre. Of course, the play will be in Russian.

Lighter entertainment is provided by the *New Circus*, prospekt Vernadskogo 7 near Moscow State University (Metro – Universitet).

Don't overlook the puppet theatres which often have programmes for adults in the evening and perhaps tickets at the door. Try the *Obraztoov Puppet Theatre*, Sadovaja-Samot'ocnaja 3 (Metro – Mayakowskaja), or the *Moscow Puppet Theatre*, Spartakovskaja ulitsa 26 (Metro – Baumanskaja).

In summer when the main theatres are closed the place to go in the evening is Arbat ulitsa (Metro – Arbatskaja). Young Muscovites congregate here until well after midnight – it's really an enjoyable scene. Street artists do portraits along the mall and an occasional musician strums his/her guitar. Check out the cafe at number 11.

Another unforgettable Moscow sight is a sunset over the Kremlin from the bridge below St Basil's Cathedral.

Things to Buy

Plan on doing most of your shopping at Moscow's Beriozka (hard currency) shops. Aside from the Beriozka near Novodevichi Convent mentioned above under 'sights' there's a Beriozka specialising in books, records and souvenirs at Kropotkinskaja ulitsa 31. The most convenient Beriozka is in the Rossiya Hotel just off Red Square. Entry is from the parking lot at the far back corner of the hotel closest to the river (open Monday to Saturday 9 am to 8 pm, Sunday 9 am to 6 pm). They have just about everything you'd expect to find in a large duty free shop and more, so pay a call here early in your visit to replenish the larder.

A large bookstore accepting roubles is Dom Knigi, prospekt Kalinina 26. For posters try the shop at Arbat ulitsa 4, around the corner from the Prague Restaurant.

Getting Around

Airport Transport Sheremetyevo Airport, 37 km north-west of the centre, is the main international airport. Domestic flights often depart Domodedovo Airport, south-east of Moscow, or Wnukowo Airport, south-west of the city.

Railway Stations Moscow has nine main railway stations, all of them on the circular Metro line. Kijevskaja Station (Metro – Kijevskij) serves Prague, Budapest, Sofia and Belgrade. Belorusskij Station (Metro – Belorusskaja) receives

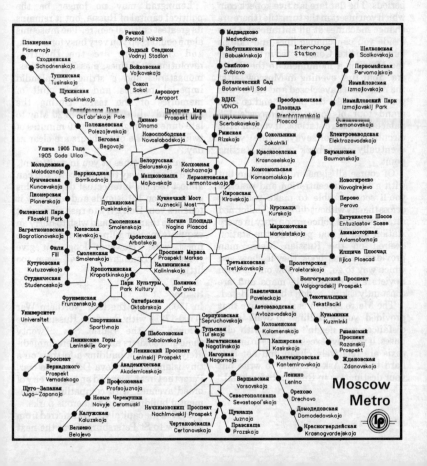

Moscow Metro

trains from Warsaw, Berlin and Western Europe. Leningradskij Station (trains to Leningrad and Finland) and Jaroslavskij Station (trains to China) are adjacent to one another at Komsomol'skaja Metro station. Trains to the Black Sea resorts depart Kurskij Station (Metro – Kurskaja).

Public Transport Once you overcome your initial misgivings and begin using the Metro you'll have instant mobility. This 223-km network rolls from 6 am till midnight. Trains run with clockwork precision every 90 seconds at peak periods. The flat fare is a five kopeck coin which you insert in the turnstile (there are change machines at all entrances). Once inside you can change lines and ride as long as you like. Constructed in the 1930s, the Metro is a monument to the Stalin era. Your first evening in Moscow, after the museums have closed and the crowds gone home, take the plunge and go on a grand tour of some of Moscow's 132 palace-like Metro stations. If you take the circular or 'Koltsevaya' line you'll eventually come back to your starting point.

Of course all signs are in Russian but with a little concentration and practice you'll soon be able to make your way across the city without difficulty. Uniformed attendants and police are on duty in every station and if you point to the station desired on the Russian Metro map provided in this book they'll show you which way to go. Notice how out-of-town Soviets also carry little maps and are constantly asking, so don't be intimidated.

The Metro system is so extensive that provided you're willing to walk short distances you needn't bother with city buses. If you have excess roubles to unload taxis are relatively cheap and not that hard to find. Ask someone to write out your destination in Russian beforehand.

Leningrad

Serene, elegant Leningrad with its quiet harmony of architecture, river, canals and bridges is one of the great art centres of the world. Though the city is 600 years younger than Moscow, much of the modern history of Russia unfolded here. In the peaceful squares and streets of Petrograd, amid the pastel Baroque and neo-Classical palaces, exploded the Bolshevik Revolution which shook the world.

Leningrad may no longer be the political capital of Russia, but it remains its greatest cultural centre. The museums alone could keep you very busy for a week, and then there are the theatres, revolutionary shrines, massive churches, monasteries and a string of splendid imperial palaces and parks full of memories of the tsars. During the Leningrad 'white nights' from 20 May to late June the 'night' is just 40 minutes of twilight and the other hours are clear as day.

Leningrad comes at you in a different, more relaxing way than Moscow. You can almost feel the intellectual depth of this great city on 101 islands and somehow it touches you. Don't try to rush through it any more than you would wish to hurry an exquisite meal or gulp down a glass of the finest wine. However long you give yourself in Leningrad, it will seem too little.

History

In 1703, during the long Northern War (1700-1721) with Sweden, Russia broke through to the Baltic Sea. Twenty thousand soldiers and labourers immediately set to work building a fortress on a tiny island in the Neva Delta. The tsar, Peter the Great, planned an orderly city of broad avenues, with compatible, monumental buildings and numerous parks.

In 1712 the capital was transferred from Moscow to St Petersburg. Over the next century and a half, as Russia became a great power through successful wars, the city grew into one of the most impressive in Europe. Despite the growth St Petersburg retained its unified appearance since only the churches could be higher than the Winter Palace. By the mid 19th century the city centre was almost as we see it today.

St Petersburg (renamed Petrograd in 1914) witnessed the most dramatic actions of the Russian Revolution, including the abortive 1905 uprising, the overthrow of tsarism in February, 1917, and the triumph of socialism over the bourgeois democratic provisional government in October that year. Although the capital in 1918 was transferred back to Moscow, in 1924 Petrograd became Leningrad in honour of the leader of the Great Proletarian Revolution.

For 900 days beginning in September 1941, the city withstood a blockade by Hitler's troops. Over 600,000 people died during the siege but Leningrad refused to surrender, certainly a remarkable feat to which dozens of monuments and memorials are dedicated today. This eventful history, the many splendid buildings and museums, and four million plus inhabitants combine to place Leningrad among the world's most famous cities.

Orientation

Leningrad is set on the Neva River between Ladozskoje Lake and the Gulf of Finland. To the various arms of the river delta have been added canals to give the city a certain Venetian charm. From the gold spire of the Admiralty building Nevskij Prospekt, Leningrad's most important boulevard, runs south-east to the gate of Alexander Nevskij Monastery. St Isaac's Cathedral and the Hermitage are on opposite sides of the Admiralty, while across the river is a whole row of museums, including Peter and Paul Fortress where the city began in 1703. Just north of Nevskij Prospekt is ploscad Iskusstv with various theatres and museums. The great imperial residences at Pushkin, Pavlovsk and Petrodvorec are south and west of the city.

Things to See

The Hermitage You'll probably want to devote an entire day to the **Hermitage** (closed Monday), one of the great museums of Europe. Housed in the Baroque **Winter Palace** (1754), the collection was begun by Catherine the Great in 1764. Much of the ground floor is taken up by the sculpture of antiquity (Egypt, Greece and Rome). Up the splendid Main Staircase are the decorated State Rooms of the Winter Palace, which now house a marvellous collection of Flemish, Dutch, Italian, Spanish and French paintings (including priceless works by Leonardo da Vinci, Michelangelo, Raphael, El Greco, Velazquez, Rembrandt and Rubens). In the Malachite Hall (1839) the provisional government held its last meeting on the night of 7 November 1017, before their capture in the adjacent Private Dining Room. The tsar's private apartments are beyond. In the Small Hermitage connected to this floor is the Pavilion Hall with a large Roman mosaic. An extensive collection of French Impressionist art is on the 2nd floor.

The main entrance to the Hermitage faces the Neva. The easiest way to get in is with the Intourist tour included in most tour packages. Once inside you can set off on your own. Unfortunately these visits are often scheduled for an afternoon, which doesn't allow enough time to see the collection properly. This being the case, you'll have to brave the intimidating ticket line alone. The line begins to form several hours before opening at 10.30 am, but if you're in it by 9.15 am in winter or 8.15 am in summer you should be in by 11 am. Avoid holidays when the crowd will be thicker. There are also tremendous lines at the refreshment stands inside, so you might bring a snack you can carry in your pocket. The regular one rouble ticket admits you to all parts of the complex

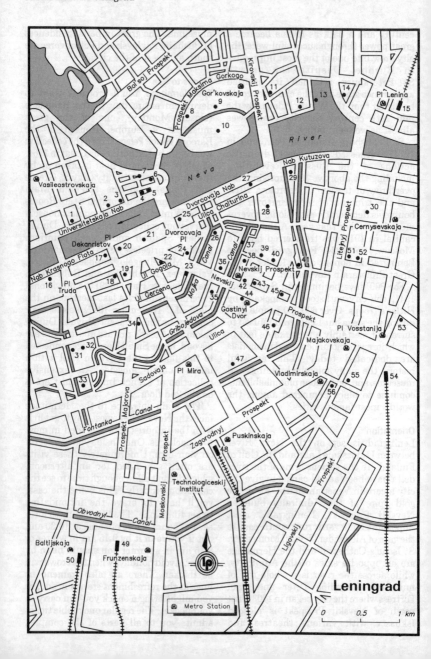

Leningrad

Ⓜ Metro Station

0   0.5   1 km

1	Academy of Arts	29	Summer Palace
2	Menshikov Palace	30	US Consulate
3	University	31	Kirov Opera
4	Ethonological Museum	32	Conservatory of Music
5	Zoological Museum	33	Cathedral of St Nicholas
6	Central Naval Museum	34	City Hall
7	Museum of Literature	35	Our Lady of Kazan Cathedral
8	Zoo	36	Dom Knigi
9	Artillery Museum	37	Church of the Bleeding Saviour
10	Peter and Paul Fortress	38	Maly Theatre
11	Museum of the Great October Socialist Revolution	39	Russian Museum
		40	Museum of Ethnography
12	Peter the Great's Log Cabin	41	Circus
13	Cruiser *Aurora*	42	Europeiskaya Hotel
14	Leningrad Hotel	43	Philharmonic Concert Hall
15	Finl'andskij Station	44	Gostinyi Dvor Department Store
16	History of Leningrad Museum	45	Babu Restaurant
17	Senate	46	Pushkin Academic Theatre
18	Central Exhibition Hall	47	Gorki Grand Theatre
19	St Isaac's Cathedral	48	Vitebskij Station
20	Bronze Horseman	49	Varsavskij Station
21	Admiralty	50	Balyjsky Station
22	Aeroflot Terminal	51	Mansion of Nebrasov
23	Kafe Druzhba	52	Bolshoi Puppet Theatre
24	Triumphal Arch	53	Obtabrskij Concert Hall
25	Hermitage	54	Moskovskij Station
26	Pushkin Museum	55	Arctic and Antarctic Museum
27	Central Lenin Museum	56	Dostoevsky Museum
28	Field of Mars		

except the gold horde in the basement, which is reserved for tourists who purchase Intourist tours in hard currency at their hotel. Forget it – it's not worth the trouble.

The Left Bank of the Neva A walk southwest along the left bank of the Neva can occupy the better part of a day even without the Hermitage. The **Summer Gardens**, at the confluence of the Fontanka Canal and the Neva, were laid out by Peter the Great, who built a small palace (closed Tuesday and in winter) here in 1714. Opposite this garden is the **Field of Mars** with an eternal flame to the Fighters of the Revolution. The **Central Lenin Museum** (closed Wednesday) occupies the Marble Palace (1785), by the Neva at the north-west corner of the Field of Mars. In April, 1917, Lenin delivered a speech at Finl'andskij Station standing on the turret of the armoured car in the courtyard.

Between the Marble Palace and

Dvorcovaja ploscad (Palace Square) is the **Pushkin Museum**, Moika Embankment 12 (closed Tuesday), where the poet died of duelling wounds in 1837. On the opposite side of the Hermitage from the river, in the centre of Palace Square, stands the 47.5-metre **Alexander Column** (1834), hewn from a single block of granite to commemorate the Russian victory in the Napoleonic wars. A Triumphal Arch joins the two wings of the crescent-shaped former General Staff building (1829) opposite.

In 1705 the **Admiralty** shipyard was built where three main roads converge today. In the 1730s the U-shaped Admiralty block was erected, complete with tower and spire, reconstructed from 1806 to 1823 in the purest Russian neo-Classical style. On the south-west side of this huge building is Dekabristov ploscad (Decembrists' Square) with the Falconet's **'Bronze Horseman'** statue (1782) of Peter the Great. The monument's 400 ton granite base took five months to transport to its present

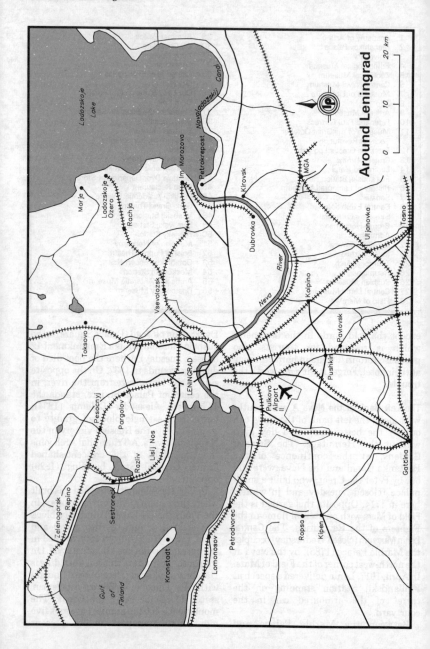

Around Leningrad

0   10   20 km

location. Looming over the square is **St Isaac's Cathedral** (1858), one of the largest in the world. In summer you can climb up into the dome for the view (closed Wednesday and the second and last Monday of the month).

Several blocks south-west by the Neva is the **History of Leningrad Museum**, Nabereznaja Krasnogo Flota 44 (closed Wednesday), with an evocative exhibit on the siege of the city during WW II, plus all the other years since 1917. All captions are in Russian only. South-east beyond the **Kirov Opera** (1862) is the **Cathedral of St Nicholas** (1762), a functioning Russian Orthodox church open daily from 7 am to 7 pm.

The Right Bank of the Neva Take the Metro to Ploscad Lenina for a look around Finl'andskij Railway Station and to see the first public monument to Lenin, erected on the square opposite the station in 1926. Walk west along the Neva past the Leningrad Hotel and cross the bridge to the Cruiser *Aurora* (closed Thursday). On 7 November 1917 this ship fired the shot which signalled the storming of the Winter Palace. Peter the Great's **log cabin** (1703) is on the Neva embankment nearby (closed Tuesday). The **Museum of the Great October Socialist Revolution**, ulitsa Kujbyseva 4 (closed Thursday), is between the cabin and Gor'kovskaja Metro station. Lenin made a speech from a window of this Art Nouveau building in April 1917.

If you're in a hurry you could skip the above and begin by taking the Metro directly to Gor'kovskaja. Leningrad grew up around the **Fortress of Peter & Paul** (Metro – Gor'kovskaja), founded on a small island by the main channel of the Neva in 1703. Today the fortress contains four museums, including the **Cathedral of Peter & Paul** (1723) where Peter the Great and numerous other Russian tsars are buried. The 122-metre bell tower was built as a watchtower before the church itself. Tickets for this and the other museums

within the fortress are available from the *kassa* outside St Peter's Gate (closed Wednesday and the last Tuesday of the month). The **Kosmos Museum** is beside the *kassa*, while the **Historical Museum** is across the street from the cathedral. Political prisoners were once held in the **Casemates Museum** in a corner of the complex behind this museum. In summer people come to swim in the river below the fortress walls. In 1860 a huge bastion was built to protect the fortress from attack from the rear and this now houses the **Artillery Museum** (closed Monday and Tuesday) with a vast collection on military history. Leningrad's **zoo** is nearby.

On Vasilyevskij Island, south across a branch of the Neva opposite two tall columns that served as beacons for ships, is the neo-Classical Stock Exchange Building (1810), now the **Central Naval Museum** (closed Tuesday). The next building south on the embankment houses an excellent **Zoological Museum** (closed Monday). A little beyond at Universitetskaja nabereznaja 3 (side entrance) is the **Ethnological Museum** (closed Friday and Saturday), devoted to the cultures of the native peoples of far away lands. Built between 1718 and 1734 this 'Kunstkammer' was the first Russian state museum. Pound on the door if it's locked during the posted visiting hours.

A block south-east are two early Baroque buildings, Leningrad's historic **Twelve Collegia** or university (1742), then the 18th century **Menshikov Palace**, Universitetskaja nabereznaja 15 (open Tuesday to Sunday 10.30 am to 3 pm). This typical nobleman's palace can only be visited on a boring Russian tour. A little further along the embankment beyond the park is the early neo-Classical **Academy of Arts** (1788) with copies of Raphael paintings upstairs (closed Monday and Tuesday).

Along Nevskij Prospekt You can't miss **Our Lady of Kazan Cathedral** (1811), a reduced version of St Peter's in Rome, now the **Museum of Religion & Atheism** (closed Wednesday, Metro – Nevskij Prospekt or Gostinyj Dvor). This museum is far more interesting than the name suggests with an extensive collection representative of every faith from primitive to contemporary, plus material on Darwin's theory. The way it's presented is fascinating and the cathedral interior is one of Leningrad's best. Next to Kazan Cathedral is a monument to Mikhail Kutuzov (who faced Napoleon near Moscow) and then the Gribojedova Canal.

If you look north up this waterway from the bridge you'll see the **Church of the Bleeding Saviour** (1907) modelled on St Basil's in Moscow, but closed for restoration for many years. Tsar Alexander II was assassinated on this spot in 1881, hence the church. Nearby in the neo-Classical Mikhailovsky Palace (1823) on Iskusstv ploscad is the **Russian Museum** (closed Tuesday) with the city's major collection of Russian painting. The 19th century realism of painters such as Ilya Repin brings Russian history to life. The **Museum of Ethnography** (closed Monday and the last Friday of the month) is beside the Russian Museum. Here you'll see folk costumes and materials on the traditional life of peoples in every part of the USSR, although the captions are only in Russian.

Just east on the opposite side of Nevskij prospekt is Ostrovskogo ploscad with a monument to Catherine the Great (1873), the Saltykov-Schedrin Public Library (1801) and the **Pushkin Academic Theatre** (1832 by Carlo Rossi). **Rossi ulitsa** behind the theatre is, it is claimed, the only street in the world designed entirely by a single architect. Until the 19th century the Fontanka Canal nearby was the city limit.

Board the Metro at Gostinyj Dvor and travel two stops south-east to Ploscad Aleksandra Nevskogo station. The entrance to the picturesque **monastery** (1710) of this name is across the street. As you enter the complex you'll find a small cemetery on the right where Tchaikovsky, Dostoevsky, Glinka, Rossi and other notables are buried. Tickets are sold at kiosks just beyond, in front of the Museum of Urban Sculpture (closed Thursday and the first Tuesday of the month). The museum, housed in the former **Church of the Annunciation** (1722), has a collection of artistic tombstones and models of the most famous monuments of Leningrad. Captions are in English. **Trinity Cathedral** (1790) in the centre of the monastery is still a church.

Pavlovsk & Pushkin The best excursion you can make from Leningrad takes in the splendid Baroque summer palaces at Pavlovsk and Pushkin, open year round. It's hard to believe that in 1944, after the lifting of the siege of Leningrad, all that was left of these and Petrodvorec Palace were crumbling, roofless walls. Restoration is now complete at Pavlovsk and Petrodvorec, and the continuing work at Pushkin is no inconvenience to visitors. There are Intourist sightseeing tours, but it's easy, more adventurous and cheaper to go on your own by public train and bus.

Begin by catching a local train from Vitebskij Railway Station (Metro – Puskinskaja) to **Pavlovsk** (26 km). Buy a ticket from an automat upstairs in the station (ask someone for help). There are several trains an hour. The station at Pavlovsk is adjacent to the park, which you cross to the palace (closed Friday). Pavlovsk Park (1777), one of the largest and finest in Europe, would take an entire day to explore fully. The circular Temple of Friendship (1782) is by the river just below the palace. Pavilions, towers, monuments, statuary and bridges are scattered throughout the park. The neo-Classical Great Palace (1786) was built for Paul I, son of Catherine the Great. The State Apartments on the 1st floor are among the most awe inspiring palace interiors in Europe, especially the

Grecian Hall and the Halls of War and Peace on each side. Beyond the Picture Gallery at the far end of this floor are the Throne and Cavaliers' halls. Don't miss the private apartments on the 2nd floor, an almost unending succession of unique rooms.

There are fairly frequent local buses (numbers 280 and 283) from beside Pavlovsk Palace to **Pushkin** (three km). In 1756 architect Bartolommeo Rastrelli (who also built the Winter Palace) erected the Catherine Palace at Pushkin. The exuberant Baroque exterior captures your attention from the start and inside is a gigantic throne room all windows and mirrors lit by hundreds of tiny lights. Near the palace is the neo-Classical Cameron Gallery, now a costume museum, overlooking a formal garden crowded with pavilions and a large park with a lake. Beside the Catherine Palace church is the lyceum where Alexander Pushkin studied from 1811 to 1817, now a Pushkin museum. Unless you understand Russian it's not worth lining up for the interminable

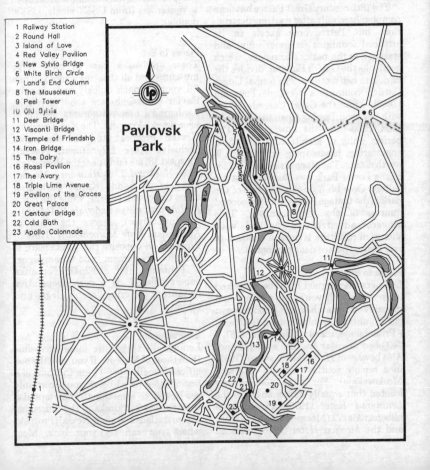

1 Railway Station
2 Round Hall
3 Island of Love
4 Red Valley Pavilion
5 New Sylvia Bridge
6 White Birch Circle
7 Land's End Column
8 The Mausoleum
9 Peel Tower
10 Old Sylvia
11 Deer Bridge
12 Visconti Bridge
13 Temple of Friendship
14 Iron Bridge
15 The Dairy
16 Rossi Pavilion
17 The Avary
18 Triple Lime Avenue
19 Pavilion of the Graces
20 Great Palace
21 Centaur Bridge
22 Cold Bath
23 Apollo Colonnade

Pavlovsk Park

museum tour. The palaces of Pushkin (all closed on Tuesday) are several km from the railway station, so take a bus.

Petrodvorec To get to **Petrodvorec Palace** (closed Monday and the last Tuesday of the month) catch a suburban train (every 15 minutes) from Baltijskij Railway Station (Metro – Baltijskaja) 29 km to Novy Peterhof. The palace is rather far from the station, so catch a bus. In summer you can also come by hydrofoil, departing the Neva embankment near the Hermitage and Decembrists' Square.

The 18th century Great Palace has been completely rebuilt after wartime destruction, but Petrodvorec excels in its artificial fountains (summer only) and statuary in the park. The palace, which overlooks the Gulf of Finland, divides the park into two sections. The formal Upper Garden contains a Neptune Fountain (1660), while the Great Cascade (1724) with 'Samson Tearing Open the Jaws of a Lion' flows into the Lower Park. The perfect unity of architecture, hydraulic engineering, landscaping and terrain is worth noting. The **Monplaisir Palace** (1723) in the Lower Park was Russia's first art gallery. On a bluff on the east side of the park is the **Cottage Palace** from the second quarter of the 19th century. This gingerbread structure packed with Victorian furniture is quite a contrast to every other palace near Leningrad.

Places to Stay
Leningrad is plagued by a few oversized luxury hotels. If you're on a tour you'll probably end up at the *Hotel Pribaltiiskaya* (1979), ulitsa Korablestroitelei 14 (Metro – Primorskaja, then bus No 7, 30 or 128), a 2400-bed monster on Vasiljevskij Island. Also beware of *Hotel Pulkovskaya* (1981) in a remote southern suburb (Metro – Moskovskaja). Far more conveniently located (but equally depressing) are the *Leningrad Hotel* (1970), Pirogovskaja nabereznaja 5/2 (Metro – Ploscad Lenina) and the *Moskva Hotel* (1976), ploscad

Aleksandra Nevskogo 2 (Metro – Ploscad Aleksandra Nevskogo).

If you have any say in the matter try to stay at the *Hotel Europeijskaya* (1824), ulitsa Brodskogo 1/7 (Metro – Nevskij prospekt), a gracious old establishment right in the centre of the theatre district. The *Astoria Hotel* (1913), Gercena ulitsa 39 (Metro – Nevskij prospekt), is also central. A more distant alternative is the one-star *Karelia Motel* (1979), Tuchacevskogo ulitsa 27/2 (trolley bus No 3, 12, or 19). The Karelia offers the cheapest Leningrad accommodation open to westerners (from US$25 single, US$30 double).

Places to Eat
There are snack bars in most large museums and all theatres where you can fill your stomach quickly and cheaply. Caviar sandwiches are about a rouble. Leningrad's best restaurants are on or near Nevskij Prospekt. The *Kafe Druzhba*, Nevskij Prospekt 15, and the more exclusive *Kafe Literaturni*, Nevskij Prospekt 18, are fairly near the Hermitage. The *Kavkazskij Restaurant*, Nevskij Prospekt 25 beside Kazan Cathedral, offers Caucasian cuisine, while the *Baku Restaurant*, ulitsa Sadovaja 12 (Metro – Gostinyj Dvor), serves the food of Azerbaijan. *Kafe Morozhenoye*, Nevskij Prospekt 28 opposite the Kavkazskij, is best. for ice cream and champagne. *U Fantanki*, (tel 310-2547) Fontanka nabereznaja 77, is a posh cooperative restaurant offering crab's legs and caviar.

Entertainment
Leningrad's stages are more accessible than those of Moscow. If you visit the box offices (usually open 11 am to 8 pm) of a few of those listed below you'll certainly get tickets to something. There are also theatrical ticket kiosks in the museums, Metro stations and along Nevskij Prospekt where you can try your luck. Most

theatrical performances begin at 7.30 pm, concerts at 8 pm.

Several of the best theatres are on Iskusstv ploscad, the square with the monument to Pushkin in front of the Russian Museum, so begin your ticket search there. The *Maly Theatre* (1830), Iskusstv ploscad 1, offers opera and ballet, while the *Musical Comedy Theatre*, Rakova ulitsa 13, specialises in operetta. Between these is the *Shostakovich Philharmonic Concert Hall*, Brodskogo ulitsa 2, the former Nobleman's Assembly

(1830). The *Little Hall* of the Shostakovich Philharmonic, where Wagner, Strauss and Liszt once gave performances, is nearby at Nevskij prospekt 30.

Leningrad has an excellent *circus* at Fontanki reki nabereznaja 3 not far from the Russian Museum. The *Bolshoi Puppet Theatre*, Nekrasova ulitsa 10, has programmes for children at 11.30 am and 2 pm on Monday, Saturday and Sunday, and for adults at 7.30 pm daily except Tuesday.

The *'Okt'abr'skij' Concert Hall*, Ligovskij

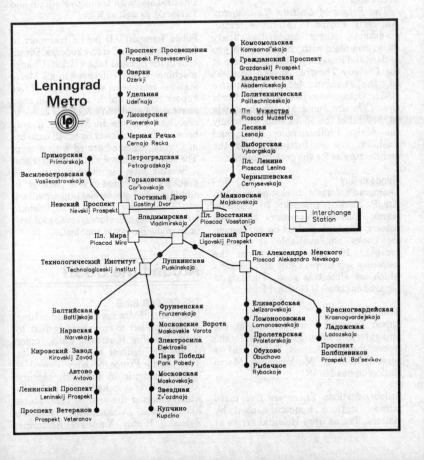

Leningrad Metro

Проспект Просвещения — Prospekt Prosvescenija
Озерки — Ozerkji
Удельная — Udel'naja
Лионерская — Pionerskaja
Черная Речка — Cernaja Recka
Петроградская — Petrogradskaja
Горьковская — Gor'kovskaja
Гостиный Двор — Gostinyj Dvor
Владимирская — Vladimirskaja
Пл. Мира — Ploscad Mira
Пушкинская — Puskinskaja
Технологический Институт — Technologiceskij institut

Приморская — Primorskaja
Василеостровская — Vasileostrovskaja
Невский Проспект — Nevskij Prospekt

Комсомольская — Komsomol'skaja
Гражданский Проспект — Grazdanskij Prospekt
Академическая — Akademiceskaja
Политехническая — Politechniceskaja
Пп Мужества — Ploscad Muzestva
Лесная — Lesnaja
Выборгская — Vyborgskaja
Пл. Ленина — Ploscad Lenina
Чернышевская — Cernysevskaja
Маяковская — Majakovskaja
Пл. Восстания — Ploscad Vosstanija
Лиговский Проспект — Ligovskij Prospekt
Пл. Александра Невского — Ploscad Aleksandra Nevskogo

Балтийская — Baltijskaja
Нарвская — Narvskaja
Кировский Завод — Kirovskij Zavod
Автово — Avtovo
Ленинский Проспект — Leninskij Prospekt
Проспект Ветеранов — Prospekt Veteranov

Фрунзенская — Frunzenskaja
Московские Ворота — Moskovskie Vorota
Электросила — Elektrosila
Парк Победы — Park Pobedy
Московская — Moskovskaja
Звездная — Zv'ozdnaja
Купчино — Kupcino

Елизаробская — Jelizarovskaja
Ломоносовская — Lomonosovskaja
Пролетарская — Proletarskaja
Обухово — Obuchovo
Рыбачкое — Rybackoje

Красногвардейская — Krasnogvardejskaja
Ладожская — Ladozskaja
Проспект Болшщевиков — Prospekt Bol'sevikov

☐ Interchange Station

prospekt 6 (Metro – Ploscad Vosstanija or Majakovskaja), is a large, modern auditorium (1967) seating 4000 people. Tickets are sold in the small adjacent pavilion.

Leningrad's most famous theatre, the *Kirov Opera & Ballet* (1860), Teatral'naja ploscad 1, is usually sold out, although your hotel service bureau should be able to wangle a ticket against payment of 15 roubles in hard currency. The auditorium of the *Rimsky-Korsakov Conservatory of Music* (1862) is across the street from the Kirov, so check there for concerts if you're in the area.

The *Palace of Culture 'Lensovjeta,'* Kirovskij Prospekt (Metro – Petrogradskaja), stages vaudeville variety shows complete with chorus line. If you understand Russian you can see drama at the *Comedy Theatre*, Nevskij prospekt 56, the *Pushkin Academic Theatre* (1832), Ostrovskogo ploscad 2, and *Gorki Grand Theatre*, Fontanki reki nabereznaja 65. Several of the above halls, especially the Maly, Philharmonic, Kirov and Pushkin, are as interesting for the architecture as for the performances.

Things to Buy

Leningrad's largest bookstore is Dom Knigi, Nevskij prospekt 28 opposite Kazan Cathedral; upstairs they sell posters, postcards and art books. Foreign art books are available at Nevskij prospekt 16, sales counters in the museums sell maps, cards and booklets which are almost as good. The largest department store is Gostinyi Dvor.

Getting Around

Airport Transport You'll be met at the airport by your Intourist guide, but for the record Pulkovo Airport II (17 km) is accessible from Moskovskaja Metro station on bus No 13.

Railway Stations There are five main railway stations frequently used by visitors. Trains from Helsinki arrive at the Finl'andskij Station (Metro – Ploscad Lenina), while services to and from Eastern Europe and the Baltic republics use Varsavskij Station (Metro – Baltijskaja or Frunzenskaja). There are overnight trains to Riga. Nearly all trains to and from Moscow travel overnight, departing Moskovskij Station on Nevskij Prospekt (Metro –Ploscad Vosstanija or Majakovskaja).

Of more importance to local sightseers are Baltijskij Station (Metro – Baltijskij), where you catch the train to Petrodvorec Palace, and Vitebskij Station (Metro – Puskinskaja) with trains to Pushkin and Pavlovsk, as well as Kiev.

Public Transport All public transport in Leningrad costs a flat five kopecks. Drop a coin in the box and take a ticket. Change machines at the entrances to all Metro stations provide an ample supply of five kopeck coins, which also make good souvenirs. Leningrad's Metro is easier to use than the one in Moscow, if only because there are fewer lines. All signs are in Cyrillic, so come armed with a map. The last trains leave a little before 1 am.

Several city sightseeing tours will probably be included in your package. In addition your hotel service bureau will sell you a four-hour excursion to Pushkin (seven roubles), Pavlovsk (seven roubles), or Petrodvorec (eight roubles).

Around the USSR

THE GOLDEN RING

North-east of Moscow lies a 'Golden Ring' of old Russian towns characterised by their kremlin (fortress) walls, onion domes and delicate churches in white. The Grand Prince of Kiev moved to Suzdal-Vladimir in the 12th century. Although later overshadowed by Moscow which annexed the area in 1328, places like Zagorsk, Aleksandrov, Pereslavl-Zalesskij, Rostov, Yaroslavl, Kostroma,

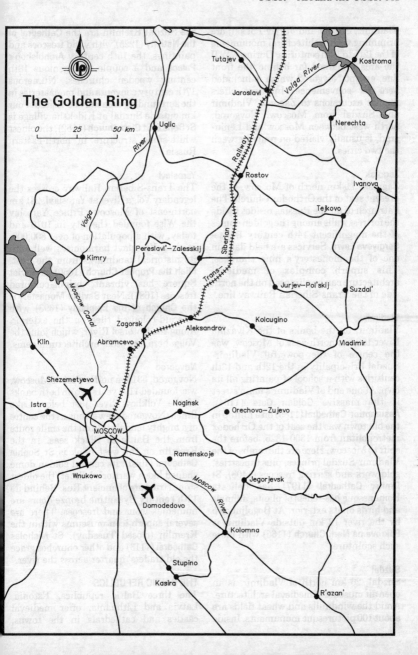

The Golden Ring

0   25   50 km

Volga River

Tutajev

Kostroma

Jaroslavl

Nerechta

Uglic

Volga River

Rostov

Ivanova

Tejkovo

Pereslavl'–Zalesskij

Kimry

Jurjev–Pol'skij

Suzdal'

Trans–Siberian Railway

Moscow Canal

Zagorsk

Aleksandrov

Kolcugino

Vladimir

Klin

Abramcevo

Istra

Shezemetyevo

Noginsk

Orechovo–Zujevo

MOSCOW

Ramenskoje

Wnukowo

Jegorjevsk

Domodedovo

Moscow River

Kolomna

Stupino

Kasira

R'azan'

Vladimir, Suzdal and Jurjev-Pol'skij are brimming with architectural monuments of the 12th to 19th centuries. During WW II the area remained far behind the front line, except Novgorod which is included here for convenience. Intourist offers regular excursions to Zagorsk, Vladimir and Suzdal from Moscow. Novgorod, north-west between Moscow and Leningrad, is usually visited en route between the two cities.

Zagorsk
Zagorsk, 71 km north of Moscow, is the present seat of the Orthodox Church. The Patriarch of all the Russias resides inside the fortress walls among the golden domes of the magnificent 14th century **Troitse-Sergiyeva Lavra**. Services are held daily in one of the monastery's nine churches. This superb complex of medieval architecture can be glimpsed on the north side of the Trans-Siberian Railway line.

Vladimir
Vladimir, on the banks of the Klyazma River 186 km north-east of Moscow, was the centre of the powerful Vladimir-Suzdal Principality in the 12th and 13th centuries with a school of painting all its own. At one end of Vladimir's main street is the massive **Golden Gate** (1164). **Assumption Cathedral** (1189) on a hilltop in the old town was the seat of the Orthodox metropolitan from 1300-1325, before the shift to Moscow. Here are the tombs of the Vladimir-Suzdal princes, plus tapestries, gold work and stirring frescoes (1408). **St Dmitry Cathedral** (1197) has delicate Romanesque bas-reliefs of plants, animals and birds on its exterior. At Bogoljubowo by the river 12 km outside Vladimir is **Pokrova na Nerli Church** (1165) with more such sculpture.

Suzdal
Suzdal, 26 km north of Vladimir, is an open air museum of medieval architecture. Amid the windmills and wheat fields are about 100 picturesque monuments. Inside the Suzdal Kremlin are the **Cathedral of the Nativity** (1225) with vivid frescoes and paintings, the 15th century **Archbishop's Palace** and a couple of ingenious 18th century wooden churches. Numerous 17th century convents and monasteries in the surrounding area may be visited. Four km outside Suzdal at Kideksha village is **St Boris & St Gleb Church** (1152), the oldest white-stone structure in north-eastern Russia.

Yaroslavl
The Trans-Siberian Railway crosses the legendary Volga River at Yaroslavl, 241 km north-east of Moscow. Prince Yaroslav the Wise founded the city in 1010 and today, with a population of over 600,000, modern Yaroslavl harmonises well with its historical landmarks from the past. **Eliah the Prophet Church** (1650) in Soviet Square has vibrant, bright-coloured frescoes (1681). Near **Saviour Monastery** is the **Church of the Epiphany** (1693) with emerald-coloured tiles on the exterior. Along the Kotorsol River, which joins the Volga here, are other architectural gems.

Novgorod
Novgorod, 531 km north-west of Moscow, was founded 1100 years ago on both banks of the Volkhov River just below Lake Ilmen. Novgorod grew strong as the centre of a mighty feudal state on the trade route from the Baltic to Black seas. In the Kremlin on the west bank is **St Sophia Cathedral** (1050), its central golden dome shaped like a warrior's helmet, the oldest stone structure of ancient Rus. Behind its 12th century Byzantine bronze doors are numerous icons and frescoes. There are several superb icon museums within the Kremlin (closed Tuesday). **St Nicholas Cathedral** (1113) and other churches grace the old traders' quarter across the river.

THE BALTIC REPUBLICS
The three Baltic republics, Estonia, Latvia and Lithuania, offer medieval castles and cathedrals in the towns,

endless white-sand beaches by the sea. A region of gentle scenic beauty, countless lakes and rivers lie among the pine forests. Long the domain of German military orders, Estonia and Latvia passed under Russian control in 1721, after the Northern War with Sweden. The Congress of Vienna brought Lithuania into the Russian Empire in 1815. Today this region is the most advanced in the Soviet Union with the highest living standards. Although geographically, historically and culturally close, each republic has a character of its own.

Tallinn

Tallinn (Reval), on the south shore of the Gulf of Finland 1000 km north-west of Moscow, is capital of the Estonian SSR. Half a million people live in this major port directly opposite Helsinki. In the well-preserved old town centre, around the soaring steeple of the **Town Hall** (1404), narrow cobblestone streets wind between the gabled stone houses and stretches of defensive wall. There's an excellent view from **Toompea Castle** (1229). **Kadriorg Palace** (1723) with the State Art Museum is in a park east of the old town.

Riga

Riga, capital of the Latvian SSR, is an important Baltic port of 870,000 inhabitants. Like Tallinn, Riga was a great Hanseatic trading city in the Middle Ages. The Daugava River which flows past the old town served as a natural highway to the Russian interior. Gothic **Domus Cathedral** (1211), now the City Historical Museum, has a wonderful organ with 6768 pipes. North are the Museum of History, the Art Museum, St Jakob Church, the Swedish Gate and the Powder Tower. South is early 14th century **St Peter Church**. Eighteen km north-west of Riga is the seaside resort Jurmala.

Vilnius

Vilnius, capital of the Lithuanian SSR, gained importance in 1323 as seat of the Grand Dukes of Lithuania who, in alliance with the kings of Poland, controlled much of central Europe. Many monuments from this time are near Gediminas Square, including the **Picture Gallery** in a former cathedral, the **Bell Tower** and Gothic **St Anne Church**. There's an excellent view of the Neris River and the apartment blocks of modern Vilnius from the 15th century tower of **Gediminas Castle**.

Trakai, 25 km west of Vilnius, has a picturesque 14th century castle on an island in dark-green Lake Galve.

THE UKRAINE

The Ukraine stretches east from the Carpathian Mountains, north of the Black Sea. The broad Dnieper River flows south through Kiev across the boundless steppes, powering great hydroelectric stations as it goes. Second in population and economic importance only to the Russian Federation, the Ukraine is the breadbasket and industrial belly of the USSR.

Kiev

The capital, Kiev, is the third largest city in the country with a population of 2.5 million. From 882 to 1132 Kiev was the seat of Kievan Rus and a great medieval trading centre. Destroyed by the Mongols in 1240, Kiev and the Ukraine were under Lithuanian and Polish domination for a long period, only recovering after the reunification with Russia in 1654. A second calamity befell Kiev during WW II when more than 195,000 of the inhabitants were murdered by the Nazis at Babi Yar and over 2000 important buildings destroyed. Kiev narrowly escaped a third and final disaster in 1986 when the nuclear power station at Chernobyl, 100 km north of the city, ran amuck.

The old town sits on the hilly right bank of the Dnieper River. The greatest remaining monument of the first period of the city's history is the **Cathedral of St Sophia** (closed Thursday). Prince

Yaroslav the Wise, who founded the cathedral in 1037, is interred in a 6th century marble sarcophagus in the north chapel. Byzantine mosaics and frescoes coat the church's interior. In the square opposite St Sophia is an equestrian statue of Bogdan Khmelnitsky (1595-1657), who led the Ukrainian war of national liberation against the Polish nobility. The 11th century **Golden Gate** near the Rococo **Church of St Andrew** (1761) was once the main entrance to the city.

Kiev has many other sights, the most magnificent of which is the **Kievo-Pecherskaya Lavra** in a park above the river south-east of the centre with various churches, towers and museums (closed Tuesday). In the lower section of this large complex are catacombs containing the mummified bodies of members of the order.

Odessa

Odessa, a cosmopolitan city of over a million founded in 1794, is the Soviet Union's main Black Sea port. On the **Potemkin Steps** (1841) linking the city to the harbour 2000 people were shot down by the tsarist forces in 1905, as they gathered in support of mutineers on the battleship *Potemkin*.

Yalta

Yalta on the south coast of the Crimean Peninsula is an ideal Black Sea resort. The green mountains sloping down to white palaces and hotels protect Yalta from the northern winds, allowing sea bathing from May to mid-October. The famous Massandra wines originate here. This former playground of the Russian nobility boasts 70 km of excellent beaches. The novelist Anton Chekhov (1860-1904) spent his last years here.

Postcards from Yalta usually show the **Swallow's Nest**, a Rhineland castle built on a seacliff by a German oil magnate in 1912. The neo-Renaissance **Livadia Palace** (1911), three km west of Yalta, was once the summer residence of tsar Nicolas II. In

February 1945 the Yalta Conference between Churchill, Roosevelt and Stalin took place here. The oriental-looking **Alupka Palace** with its elegant park, 18 km south-west of Yalta, was built in 1830 by Count Vorontsov. Today it's an architecture and art museum. The **Nikitsky Botanical Gardens**, eight km east of Yalta, were begun in 1812.

TRANS-CAUCASIA

Trans-Caucasia, the area bordering Turkey and Iran between the Black and Caspian seas, is quite different from the rest of the USSR. Here, on the boundary of Europe and the Middle East, are three union republics, two of them with a Christian background, one Islamic. Each of the three capital cities has over a million inhabitants. The varied traditions combined with great antiquity and high population densities explain why there is so much to see in such a relatively small area. The region lies south of the snow-capped Caucasian Range, thus its mild climate, lush sub-tropical vegetation, tea plantations and wine production. Just north-west along the east coast of the Black Sea is the Caucasian Riviera, and in the mountains – the highest in Europe – deep valleys, alpine meadows and glistening lakes.

The Caucasian Riviera, which is shared by Georgia and the Russian Federation, stretches along the Black Sea for almost 159 km. The largest resorts are stately **Sochi** and the new **Dagomys** complex, 14 km north-west. Sochi offers several lovely parks, the hydrogen-sulphide springs at Matsesta and an observation tower on Mt Akhun. Excursions are made to Lake Ritsa, 1200 metres high in the Caucasus Range.

Tbilisi

Quaint Tbilisi in the Kura River Valley has been the capital of Georgia since the 6th century. From Mt Mtatsminda (accessible by cable car and funicular) one has a view of the distinctive Georgian churches among the red roofed houses and modern blocks. At Mtskheta, the ancient capital of Kartli 23 km north of Tbilisi, is **Dzhvari Temple** (604) and **Sveti-Tskhoveli Cathedral** (1029).

Yerevan

Yerevan, capital of the Armenian SSR, is one of the oldest cities in the world, founded in 782 BC. The twin peaks of Mt Ararat (5165 metres) in Turkey, where Noah's Ark is said to have settled after the Flood, are sometimes visible from the city. Tour groups are taken to the restored 1st century AD Hellenic **Temple of the Sun** at Garni, 28 km south-east.

Squeezed between powerful empires throughout its history, Armenia has achieved relative peace only today. Despite centuries of persecution the Armenians preserved their distinctive culture. The survival from antiquity of the Armenian manuscripts and book miniatures at the Matenadaran depository in the centre of Yerevan is almost miraculous. Another amazing fact: one Armenian in 3000 is over 100 years old!

Baku

Baku, capital of the Azerbaijan SSR and fifth largest city in the USSR, is best known for its refineries supplied by off-shore oilfields in the Caspian Sea. Situated on the south side of the Apsheron Peninsula, Primorsky Park stretches along the bay. There are a number of mosques, minarets, palaces and museums, plus the 12th century **Maiden's Tower** which can be climbed.

Central Asia

The five Central Asian republics of the USSR, north of Afghanistan and west of Kashgar, continue to capture the imaginations of those drawn to the exotic east. The legendary Silk Route passed here on its way from Syria to the Middle Kingdom. In the 14th and 15th centuries, when the Timurid Empire stretched from the Volga to the Ganges, oasis cities like Samarkand and Shakhrisabz spawned great buildings.

Endless tracts of steppe and desert separate Central Asia from Russia and Europe. The distance is measured in the tremendous abundance and variety of fruit, vegetables and merchandise in the bazaars, in the hopping Indian mynah birds with their yellow legs and beaks, and in the Turkish-looking peoples. The unusual mix of cultures is made more striking by the local languages written in Cyrillic rather than Arabic script.

Since the revolution irrigation has painted green this once impoverished region. A flourishing textile industry is based on local cotton. Scorching hot in summer, Central Asia can be pleasant in spring and fall. The endless cups of *kokchai* (green tea) help one acclimatise. A complete guidebook (in German) to the region is *Sowjetischer Orient* by Klaus Pander (Koln, DuMont Buchverlag, 1982).

TASHKENT

Tashkent, capital of the Uzbek SSR, is a modern city of two million, the fourth largest in the Soviet Union. Tashkent was badly damaged by an earthquake in 1966. Today the rebuilt urban landscape doesn't have much to offer those in search of the fabulous east. Nearly all flights to Uzbekistan from Moscow and Leningrad are routed through Tashkent, however, so you'll probably end up with a day in the place. Take it easy and ignore the smog which obscures the distant snow-capped peaks.

Orientation

You'll stay at the *Hotel Uzbekistan* on the east side of the new city centre. The carillon chimes opposite the hotel will keep you awake all night. Lenin Square, a vast open area with a predictably gigantic statue of the founder of the Soviet state,

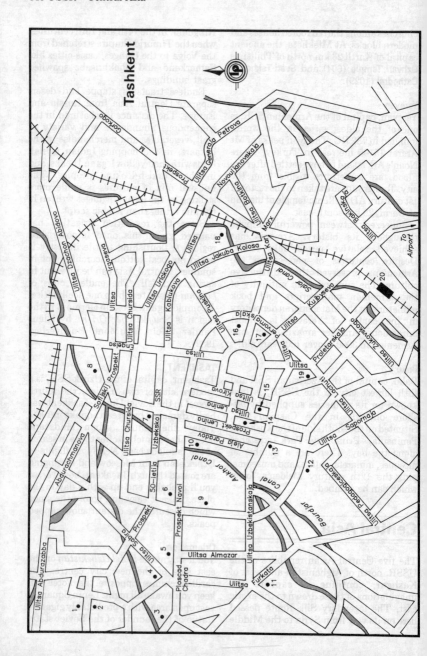

Tashkent

1	Kafal al-Ashish Mausoleum
2	Berak Khan Madrasah
3	Kukeldash Madrasah
4	Circus
5	Chamsa Theatre
6	Janus-Chan Mausoleum
7	Earthquake Monument
8	Exhibition of Economic Achievements
9	Pakhtahar Metro Station
10	Lenin Statue
11	Friendship of Nations Square
12	Museum of Applied Art
13	Exhibition Pavilion
14	Lenin Museum
15	Alisher Navoi Opera House
16	Hotel Uzbekistan
17	History Museum of the Peoples
18	Zoo
19	Art Gallery
20	Railway Station

overwhelms the more inviting streets and squares around the Alisher Navoi Opera House (1947) south-east. Prospekt Lenina, a focal north-south avenue, divides these areas. Ulitsa Uzbekistanskaja runs east from here, crossing the 1800-year-old Ankhor Canal to Friendship of Nations Square. Tashkent's circular circus is visible north of this square. The old Uzbek town is north-west of the circus, on the opposite side of the city from the hotel.

Things to See

Tashkent's excellent **History Museum of the Peoples** (closed Monday) is only two blocks from the hotel. Although the captions are all in Cyrillic there are plenty of artefacts and graphics to hold your attention. A 15-minute walk north of the hotel is the teeming **Alaj Bazaar**. To find it ask someone to write out the name in Cyrillic. Tour groups are usually taken to the **Museum of Applied Arts**, which is just as well as it's hard to locate. They also visit the **Kukeldash Madrasah** (1560) opposite Hotel Moscow, but all you get to see is the facade.

Far more interesting, but not on the tour bus circuit, is the **Berak Khan Madrasah** (1531) in the old town. The mosque opposite actually functions and nearby is the restored **Kafal al-Ashish Mausoleum** (1542). The surrounding streets retain the eastern air modern Tashkent has lost. Getting there is complicated so go by taxi if you can, or take the Metro to Pakhtakar, then bus No 42 or 93 (have someone write out your destination).

Getting Around

Tashkent has a Metro with three lines. October Revolution station is right outside the Hotel Uzbehistan. The next station west is Lenin Square, followed by Pakhtakar and Friendship of Nations Square stations. As always, the fare is a five kopeck coin and the system runs until 1 am.

SAMARKAND

Samarkand, the legendary city of Tamerlane (1336-1405), straddles the Silk Route to China. This city of half a million, the old capital of Uzbekistan, is the second largest in the republic. Samarkand claims to be a modern educational and industrial centre, but for visitors its interest lies strictly in the past. The blue domes and minarets carry you back to the time when the eyes of the Orient were upon this 'Rome of the East.'

History

The first settlement appeared in the 5th century BC on a high terrace surrounded by gullies, today known as Afrasiab. In 329 BC Alexander the Great captured the town, as did the Arab general Kuteib ibn Muslim in AD 712 and the Golden Horde of Genghis Khan in 1220. The area of old Afrasiab never recovered from the Mongols.

In the late 14th century the Mongol chief Tamerlane (Timur) made Samarkand his capital and set out to conquer the world. Northern India, Georgia, Persia, Syria and Turkey all fell before his horde.

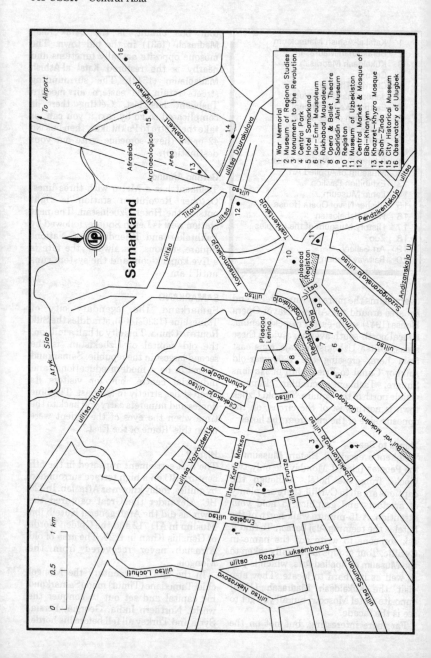

Samarkand

1 War Memorial
2 Museum of Regional Studies
3 Monument to the Revolution
4 Central Park
5 Hotel Samarkand
6 Gur–Emir Mausoleum
7 Rukhabad Mausoleum
8 Opera & Ballet Theatre
9 Sadriddin Aini Museum
10 Registan
11 Museum of Uzbekistan
12 Central Market & Mosque of Bibi–Khanym
13 Khazret–Khyzra Mosque
14 Shah–Zinda
15 City Historical Museum
16 Observatory of Uliugbek

From the conquered lands Tamerlane brought back the most skilled architects, artists and craftsmen to make his city stand above all others. Nothing remains of the citadel which surrounded Tamerlane's palace (in the area presently occupied by the theatre and government offices), but the great mosques, mausoleums and madrasahs begun during his lifetime still stand. He died in 1405 while preparing a campaign against China.

Tamerlane's son moved the Timurid capital to Herat (Afghanistan) and gave Samarkand and its province to his own son, the great astronomer Ulugbek. During the 40-year rule of this benevolent prince Samarkand became one of the leading centres of medieval science. In 1449 Ulugbek was murdered by his superstitious son and during the chaotic period which followed the area was taken by nomadic Uzbek tribes.

In the second half of the 19th century tsarist Russia took advantage of feudal strife and seized the region from the Central Asian khanates. In 1888 the Transcaspian Railway reached the city. The red flag was raised over the Registan on 28 November 1917 and since then the people of Uzbekistan have stood up.

Orientation

All visitors stay at the *Intourist Hotel Samarkand* on Bul'var Maksima Gorkogo in the modern city. To the west, north off Bul'var Maksima Gorkogo, is Central Park in the middle of the 19th century Russian town. The old Uzbek town with its famous monuments is nearby to the east. Get oriented on arrival by taking the elevator up to the 11th floor of the hotel from where you'll get a good view.

Things to See

The Registan Samarkand's Registan must rank as one of the extant wonders of Asia. Three huge madrasahs (medieval religious schools), their facades, towers and domes literally shimmering with blue and green tiles, face an open square where sound and light shows are held in summer. The oldest is the **Madrasah of Ulugbek** (1420) on the west. Opposite with two golden lions over the arch is the **Madrasah of Shir-Dor** (1636), a mirror image built two centuries later. Closing the north side of the Registan is the gilded **Madrasah of Tillya-Kari** (1660). Over 100 students could be housed in the cells around the interior courtyard of each madrasah. The **Chorsu**, an 18th century covered market, is behind Shir-Dor. The gigantic modern building across from the Registan is the **Museum of Uzbekistan.**

Near the Central Market North-east of the Registan along Tashkentskaya ulitsa is Samarkand's colourful **Central Market**. Towering above the market are the ruins of the **Mosque of Bibi-Khanym** (1404) which Tamerlane intended to be the most magnificent in the world. In the courtyard is a huge stone Koran stand. The smaller 19th century **Khazret-Khyzra Mosque** overlooks the crossroads by the necropolis just below the market. Down ulice Dzurakulova, the street descending right from this mosque, is one of the city's most evocative sights, **Shah-Zinda**. This superb ensemble of some 20 glazed mausoleums on the south-east slope of Afrasiab developed over 900 years. As one climbs the narrow street from the entrance portal (1434) the buildings become older. Near the end to the right is the **Mausoleum of Kusam ibn-Abbas**, a cousin of the Prophet who introduced Islam into Central Asia just after the Arab conquest. Legend tells how after a sermon one day Kusam ibn-Abbas took his own head from his shoulders and, holding it under his arm, descended into a cave where he still lives. The name Shah-Zinda means 'living king.'

Afrasiab & the Observatory The one-time fortified settlement of Afrasiab is now deserted but you can feel the layers of antiquity beneath your feet as you cross the cemetery behind Shah-Zinda. There are spellbinding views from the hilltops here. North across the Tashkent Highway is the new **City Historical Museum** with remarkable 7th century frescoes of a procession of men on camels. A path from the museum leads up into the archaeological area.

A km beyond this museum on the Tashkent Highway is the famous **Observatory** of Ulugbek (1429). Covered by a vault on the hilltop is Ulugbek's gigantic marble sextant with a radius of 40 metres and an arc 63 metres long. Ulugbek estimated the duration of the celestial year to within a minute and made star tables which were unsurpassed until the invention of the telescope. An **Ulugbek Museum** has been installed in the tower next to the sextant.

Near the Hotel A few minutes walk down the street beside the hotel is the magnificent blue ribbed dome of the **Gur-Emir Mausoleum** (1404). Tamerlane is buried here below a black marble stone bearing the words, 'Were I alive today, mankind would tremble.' Two of his sons and his grandson, Ulugbek, are interred nearby.

If you have extra time you could seek out the **Museum of Regional Studies**, Sovietskaya 51 beyond Central Park. Don't miss the history section in the back courtyard.

Pendjikent

Tour groups are often taken to this small town 70 km east of Samarkand in the Tajik SSR. On a barren hilltop above the valley are the excavated ruins of a 5th century Soghdian settlement, destroyed by the Arabs in the 8th century. A Zoroastrian sun-worshipping temple stood near the centre. Only crumbling earth walls may be seen today but the views of the surrounding mountains are good, stretching south-east as far as the snowcapped Pamir Range. The one hotel in Pendjikent is rather cold and miserable.

Entertainment

Occasional performances take place at the *Opera & Ballet Theatre* across the park diagonally opposite the hotel. A more reliable source of evening entertainment is Central Park off Bul'var Maksima Gorkogo, a five-minute walk from the hotel. Here, amid cafes, restaurants, cinemas, open air theatres, fun fairs, monuments, old pavilions and shady lanes, the locals sit on park benches or row boats around a small lake. It's well lit at night, a good place to meet people.

SHAKHRISABZ

Shakhrisabz, over the Zerafshan Range from Samarkand, is the birthplace of Tamerlane. This 'garden city,' renowned for its schools of astronomy and poetry, was founded in the 3rd century BC. After the invasion of Genghis Khan, Mongol tribes, who were quick to adopt Islam, occupied the Kashkadarya Basin. The oasis Shakhrisabz at the junction of several caravan routes soon increased in importance and was dignified by great monuments during the reigns of Tamerlane and his grandson Ulugbek.

All but one of the mosques have now been converted to tea houses, shops or archives. The 100-km road south from Samarkand offers an excellent cross-section of Uzbek life. This combined with the picturesque sights and the *Intourist Hotel Shakrisabz* (one of the best in the Soviet Union) make the town eminently worth visiting.

Things to See

Just north of the hotel is the monumental 38-metre-high blue-tiled gate of the **Ak-Sarai** (1404) or 'White Palace' where Tamerlane received the Spanish envoy Gonzales de Clavijo. The palace, destroyed by the khan of Bukhara in the 16th century, stretched across the square as far as the department store opposite the hotel.

South on the main street by the 17th century **Chorsu** (covered market) is

Shakhrisabz' colourful, fruit-filled bazaar. A block beyond is the massive **Kok Goumbaz Mosque** (1436). Within the same compound are the **Goumbazi Seyidan Mausoleum** (1438) and the **Sheik Koulal Mausoleum**, where Tamerlane's father is buried.

In the back streets behind Kok Goumbaz is the Dorussiadat complex with the **Hazrati Imam Mosque** (1380) where numerous turbaned old men still come to pray on Fridays. In the courtyard are massive 800-year-old trees and beyond is the **Jakhanghir Mausoleum** (1404) where two sons of Tamerlane are buried. Don't miss the soaring 27-metre-high dome.

BUKHARA

Bukhara lies in the heart of a vast desert region 250 km west of Samarkand (five hours by bus). Its 2500-year history is seen in the narrow twisting alleyways between mud-baked houses and the wealth of ancient monuments in the old quarter. Time passes slowly at a Bukhara tea house by a cool pond or shady square. On market days the streets are alive with the strikingly-coloured dresses worn by the local women.

Things to See

Bukhara's oldest structure is the 7th century **Ark Fortress** facing the main square, rebuilt in the 16th century and residence of the emir until 1920. An Historical Museum was installed inside in 1927. West in a park is the 9th century **Samanid Mausoleum**. True believers push little papers into the geometric brick facades in the hope of magical responses to their requests. Near the fortress is the 16th century **Kalain Mosque** with its 'Tower of Death' minaret (1127) from which prisoners were once thrown. Deeper in the old town are many tile-faced madrasahs, mosques and market domes. The most unusual is the **Char Minar Madrasah** (1807) with a blue/green minaret at each corner. In a northern

suburb is the 19th century **Royal Summer Palace**, now the Museum of Folk Arts with another Bukhara pond *(khauz)*.

Others

The ancient city of **Khiva** in western Uzbekistan is sometimes included in Central Asian itineraries. An important medieval slave market once functioned here. The area inside the fortress walls looks like something out of the Arabian Nights.

Dushanbe, capital of the Tajik SSR, is a modern city only 60 years old. **Alma-Ata**, capital of Kazakhstan, was founded in 1854 at the foot of the snowcapped Tien Shan Mountains. The huge wooden cathedral, built without a single nail, has been converted into a museum.

The Trans-Siberian Railway

This, the world's longest continuous train ride, takes you through seven time zones, 100° of longitude and a quarter of the way around the globe. The line was built between 1891 and 1904 to provide European Russia with a direct link to the Pacific. Today the line is double tracked and all the locomotives are electric. The Rossiya Express leaves Moscow's Jaro-slavskij Station at 2.05 pm daily and reaches Khabarovsk in the Soviet Far East five days, 10 hours, 25 minutes and 8531 km later.

Routes

The Trans-Siberian Railway begins in Moscow and runs east. There are three distinct routes, all passing through Irkutsk. The *Trans-Siberian* crosses the USSR to Khabarovsk (six days), where there are connections to Japan. The *Trans-Manchurian* is a weekly Russian train to Beijing (six days), which enters China via Manzhouli (Manchuria). The *Trans-Mongolian* is a weekly Chinese

国 际 联 运
International Passenger Trains
北 京—乌兰巴托—莫斯科
Beijing—Ulan-Bator—Moscow
北 京 Beijing

莫斯科 Moscow	开 往 To			
3	自起 北公 京里 km	车次 T/No 站名 Station	自起 莫斯 公里 km	**4**
到Arr 开Dep		北京时间 Beijing Time		到Arr 开Dep
	不办理客运业务	北京 Beijing	7865	15.33
7.40		北京 Beijing	7801	14.17 14.31
8.40 8.44	64	南口 Nankou	7791	13.46 13.54
8.44	74	居庸关 Juyongguan	7783	13.09 13.19
9.28 9.38	82	青龙桥 Qinglongqiao	7771	12.49
9.54 10.02	94	康庄 Kangzhuang	7661	10.50 11.00
11.37 11.47	204	张家口 Zhangjiakou	7483	8.24 8.34
14.15 14.25	382	大同 Datong	7356	6.26 6.30
16.17 16.22	509	集宁南 Ji'ningnan	7023	23.13 1.51
20.35 23.15	842	二连 Erenhot		
		乌兰巴托时间 Ulan-Bator Time		
23.40 0.40	852	扎门乌德 Dzamynude	7013	21.40 22.48
13.20 13.50	1561	乌兰巴托 Ulan Bator	6304	9.00 9.30
21.00 22.05	1940	苏赫巴托 SuheBator	5925	24.00 1.15
		莫斯科时间 Moscow Time		
17.53 20.25	1963	纳乌什基 Naushki	5902	16.32 18.20
1.13 1.25	2218	乌兰乌德 Ulaude	5647	11.16 11.35
8.55 9.10	2674	伊尔库次克 Irkutsk	5191	3.15 3.30
2.52 3.07	3761	克拉斯诺亚尔斯克 Krasnoyarsk	4104	9.12 9.27
14.58 15.13	4522	新西伯利亚 Novo-Si.	2716	13.20 13.35
22.35 22.50	5149	鄂木斯克 Omsk	2618	2.09 2.24
10.05 10.20	6047	斯维尔德洛夫斯克 Sverdlovsk	1437	20.03 20.18
15.37 15.52	6428	彼尔姆Ⅱ PermiII	957	13.08 13.23
22.33 22.48	6508	基洛夫 Kirov		23.58
	7865	莫斯科 Moscow		11.45

北京—乌兰巴托—莫斯科 3 次特别旅客快车，每星期三由北京开，每星期一到达莫斯科。莫斯科—乌兰巴托—北京 4 次特别旅客快车，每星期六由莫斯科开，每星期二到达北京。

The express passenger train No. 3 from Beijing via Ulan-Bator to Moscow every Wednesday and arrives in Moscow every Monday. The express passenger train No. 4 from Moscow via Ulan-Bator to Beijing starts from Moscow every Tuesday and arrives in Beijing every Monday.

train to Beijing (five days), which transits Mongolia on its way to China. Train schedules are posted in the corridor of each carriage.

Preparations

A journey on the Trans-Siberian Railway involves as much advance planning as any other visit to the USSR. The prices people pay for tickets on the Trans-Siberian vary incredibly. You might pay five or 10 times more if you buy your ticket in a capitalist country than you would in Eastern Europe or China!

Moscow is connected to Eastern Europe by several trains a day while the Moscow-Beijing route is served only twice a week, once by the Russian train (via

Manchuria) and once by the Chinese train (via Mongolia). All trains are crowded in summer (June, July and August) and groups get priority as far as reservations go. Be prepared to wait if you want to travel at that time!

You'll need Soviet currency to use the Russian dining car, make purchases on platforms and cover petty expenses while transiting Moscow. You can usually change money at the Soviet border. Cash US dollars or West German marks are preferred. Travellers' cheques are grudgingly accepted, but only if the official signature printed on the cheque corresponds with one of the sample signatures in their specimen cheque file. Don't change too much as changing back is almost impossible. If you have a little

国 际 联 运
International Passenger Trains
北 京—满洲里—莫斯科
Beijing—Manzhouli—Moscow

莫斯科 Moscow	开 往 To			
19	自起 北公 京里 km	车次 T/No 站名 Station	自起 莫公 斯里 km	**20**
到Arr 开Dep		北京时间 Beijing Time		到Arr 开Dep
22.05	0.52		北京 Beijing	9601	8.32
1.41	1.55	133	天津北 Tianjinbei	8862	4.50 5.00
4.07	4.12	599	锦州 Jinzhou	8386	1.12 1.24
7.07	7.22	841	沈阳 Shenyang	8160	22.17 22.35
11.18	11.30	1146	长春 Changchun		20.00
14.40	14.55	1389	哈尔滨 Harbin	7672	16.56
18.44	18.50	1647	昂昂溪 Angangxi	7405	9.24
23.10	23.31	1927	博克图 Boketu	7063	8.25
0.62	0.12	1982	牙克石 Xiuenming	7049	4.17
1.10	1.16	1995	伊列克德 Yilinkede	5835	3.25
2.51	5.01	2137	免渡河 Miandehe	5959	2.66
6.29	7.01	2323	海拉尔 Hailar	5664	0.33
			满洲里 Manzhouli	5678	23.45
			莫斯科时间 Moscow Time		
2.26	5.40	2335	后贝加尔 Zabaikalsk	6666	20.29 11.06
1.34	1.46	3297	赤塔 Chita	9204	22.30 23.06
9.14	9.21	3354	乌兰乌德 Ulaude	5637	2.37 3.05
3.12		3761	伊尔库次克 Irkutsk	5191	1.05
15.23	15.40	3897	克拉斯诺亚尔斯克 Krasnoyarsk	4194	11.41
23.07	23.22	6285	新西伯利亚 Novo-Si.	3047	2.47 3.03
10.52	11.12		鄂木斯克 Omsk	2618	
16.42	16.57	5641	斯维尔德洛夫斯克 Sverdlovsk	1816	3.30 3.50
11.55	9.53	8044	基洛夫 Kirov	1137	21.32 21.47
		9001	莫斯科 Moscow		

北京—莫斯科 19 次特别旅客快车，每星期六由北京开，每星期五到达莫斯科。莫斯科—北京 20 次特别旅客快车，每星期五由莫斯科开，每星期四到达北京。

The express passenger train from Beijing to Moscow starts from Beijing every Saturday and arrives in Moscow every Friday. The express passenger train from Moscow to Beijing starts from Moscow every Saturday and arrives in Beijing every Thursday.

food with you 20 roubles per person should be plenty to see you through the whole trip.

If you're going this way you'll want to pick up the *Trans-Siberian Rail Guide* by Robert Strauss (Bradt Publications, UK, 1987). Strauss provides Cyrillic strip maps for the entire route, plus lots of background information and useful addresses. Also read *The Siberians* by Farley Mowat.

On the Trains

There are several classes of accommodation on the trains. The 1st class compartments are usually quite comfortable (two berths) with a wash basin inside. On the Chinese train this class is called 'deluxe' and includes a table and armchair, plus a shower between every two compartments. Second class ('hard sleeper') generally means four berths. On the Chinese train there's an intermediate 'soft sleeper' class (four berths) which costs a lot more than 2nd class without any real advantage.

There's a steward assigned to each carriage who supplies hot water and tea to passengers. Dining cars are attached to all trains. The Russian dining cars are open from 9 am to 9 pm according to the local time wherever the train happens to be, although the trains themselves run on Moscow time. There isn't much selection. In the Mongolian dining car hard currency is accepted, but the food is western style and expensive. The Chinese dining car offers good food at low prices, but is crowded with Chinese so it's hard to get a seat. There's no alcohol in the Russian dining car (BYO); beer is sold in the Mongolian dining car; both beer and insipid Chinese wine are available in the Chinese dining car. In all three dining cars you can pay in local currency. Meals in the Russian dining car average about two roubles. Bring a little food and drink with you onto the train.

FROM EUROPE TO CHINA & JAPAN

MAV Hungarian Railways gives a 50% discount on train tickets for travel between socialist countries when you pay in hard currency. Since China qualifies under this system it means you can go from Budapest to Beijing for only US$90 in 1st class with a sleeper. The catch is that it's extremely difficult to get a reservation from Moscow to Beijing in Budapest and the Soviet Embassy won't give you a transit visa unless you have one. It takes about a month for an answer to a reservation request to come back from Moscow and you can only book two months in advance. Still, if you'll to be travelling around Eastern Europe that long anyway it's worth trying. Ask if there have been any cancellations – you might not have to wait. The office selling these tickets is Ibusz, Tanaks korut 3/c, Budapest.

Between Budapest and Moscow watch for Kiev. The best view is obtained as the train is crossing the Dnieper River on the Moscow side (east) of Kiev station. Be ready on the north side of the train.

To Japan

The Trans-Siberian Railway officially ends in Khabarovsk, on the right bank of the Amur River close to the Manchurian border. This is the only city in the Soviet Far East regularly visited by tourists. Founded in 1858, the town was named for Yerofei Khabarov, a 17th century Russian explorer.

From April to September passengers bound for Japan take a train south from Khabarovsk to the Pacific port of Nakhodka near Vladivostok. During those months a ferry belonging to the Far Eastern Shipping Company operates from Nakhodka to Yokohama, Japan. Once a year this ship goes on to Hong Kong. The rest of the year you must fly from Khabarovsk to Niigata, Japan.

FROM CHINA TO EUROPE

Trans-Siberian tickets are more expensive in China than they are in Eastern Europe, but considerably less expensive than in

Japan, Australia, North America and Western Europe. The advantage to travelling west is that reservations from Beijing to Moscow are easily made in China. One way fares from Beijing to Moscow are about US$200 for a hard sleeper, US$300 deluxe. To get the best of both worlds buy a ticket from Beijing to Budapest or Berlin in Budapest, fly to Beijing (on Interflug from Berlin) or Hong Kong (from Athens) and come back by train. The return portion of such tickets is valid four months from the date of issue.

In China Trans-Siberian reservations can only be made at the branches of the China International Travel Service (CITS) in Shanghai and Beijing, and then not over a month or less than five days in advance. Book your sleeper on the train before you start collecting visas.

Visas About 10 days are required to arrange Soviet and Mongolian transit visas in Beijing. The Soviet Embassy (Metro – Dongzhimen) is open 9 am to 1 pm Monday, Wednesday and Friday. Your Soviet transit visa should allow at least eight days for the through trip. Communications are poor and it's almost impossible to make Moscow or Irkutsk hotel reservations in Beijing, so you'll probably have to get a transit rather than a tourist visa. The Mongolian Embassy is near Beijing's Friendship Store (open 8 to 10 am Monday, Tuesday and Friday). You can't get a Mongolian transit visa unless you already have a Soviet visa. You must also obtain a visa for the first Eastern European country you'll be entering.

Mongolia
Erlian, the border station between China and Mongolia, is very easygoing. There are stores in Chinese railway station where you can spend excess Chinese currency on groceries, liquor, etc, while the train's bogies are being changed from narrow to broad gauge. Mongolian customs has a reputation for unpredictable reactions, so keep cameras, newspapers, magazines, hard liquor, etc, discreetly out of sight. In Mongolia Cyrillic letters replace Chinese characters.

After the closed fortress railway stations of China, the Mongolian stations are remarkably open. You get 30 minutes at Ulan Bator, capital of Mongolia. You can walk right out of the station and up the street a block or two, check out the local shops and tour the platform in that time. All you see of Ulan Bator from the train is row upon row of apartment blocks – not very inviting. Old Ulan Bator hides its charms (if any) well. Yet after the crowded Asian cities Ulan Bator looks spacious, open.

The broad grasslands and clouds of Mongolia are the country's real attraction and you get a good cross section from the train. Military vehicles, radar installations and army camps vie with camels, horsemen and yurts for your attention.

To stop over in Mongolia for a few days you must contact the Zhuulchin Travel Agency, Ulan Bator, Mongolian People's Republic, either by cable (ZHUULCHIN Mongolia) or telex (U-BT TLX 232). Once confirmation has been obtained from Zhuulchin the Mongolian Embassy can issue a tourist visa for the confirmed days. Hotel prices are similar to those in the Soviet Union and individual arrangements are just as difficult to make.

Across Siberia
Siberia and the Soviet Far East cover 10 million square km, most of northern Asia. Siberia stretches east from the Ural Mountains over 8000 km to the Bering Sea. This land of numerous rivers and lakes, rolling hills and the seemingly endless *taiga* of stunted coniferous trees has been part of Russia since the 16th century. Today the great energy resources of Siberia – hydro-electricity, coal, oil, natural gas – have made the region a focus of the Soviet economy with widespread industrialisation.

Lake Baikal

Lake Baikal, the deepest lake in the world, is one of the most unforgettable features of Siberia. This enchanting lake, 636 km long and an average of 48 km wide with a maximum depth of 1620 metres, contains more water than the Baltic Sea. Some 336 rivers and streams flow into Lake Baikal, but only the Angara River flows out, passing Irkutsk 66 km west (an hour by train). The wooded hillsides around the lake are home to 2000 species of flora and fauna, three-quarters of which are found nowhere else. The omul, a species of salmon, is a favourite Baikal delicacy.

Irkutsk

The Siberian city most worth visiting is Irkutsk, 5000 km east and five hours ahead of Moscow. Attractively situated on the Angara River, this capital of Eastern Siberia with a population of half a million was founded in 1661 on Russia's main trade route to China and Mongolia. Sturdy old log houses decorated with intricate wood carvings are still seen in the town. In 1879 a terrible fire destroyed much of Irkutsk, but its position ensured a speedy recovery. Toward the end of the last century the area experienced a boom in diamonds, gold and fur. You get a good view of Irkutsk from the Trans-Siberian. The railway station (1898) is just across the bridge from the city.

Things to See Boulevard Gagarina, an apple tree-lined pedestrian promenade, runs along the Angara River embankment. On the corner where Ulitsa Karla Marksa, Irkutsk's main street, meets the river is the University Library, housed in the imposing early 19th century former **Governor-General's Palace**. Across the street is the **Museum of Regional Studies** and next to it the **Okhlopkov Drama Theatre** (1897).

Many 19th century opponents of the tsarist regime exiled to Siberia eventually settled in Irkutsk, among them those involved in the 1825 December Revolution in St Petersburg. The wooden mansion of Prince Sergei Trubetskoy (1854) has been converted into the **Decembrists' House-Museum**, Ulitsa Dzerzhinskogo 64.

Other Places

Bratsk, 600 km north of Irkutsk, grew up in 1955 near one of the world's largest hydroelectric projects which powers a huge aluminium smelter. The modern city overlooks the vast reservoir behind the 924-metre-long, 124-metre-high concrete dam across the Angara River.

Novosibirsk, a drab, sprawling industrial city on the River Ob between Irkutsk and the Urals, is also best avoided.

Moscow

It's not possible to make railway reservations beyond Moscow in Beijing. Thus everyone arriving in the Soviet capital on the Trans-Siberian Railway from China must make an onward sleeper reservation to Europe upon arrival. If you want to leave the same day you do this at the Intourist office in the railway station from which you'll be departing, Kijevskaja or Belorusskij. If you'd rather leave the following day or later you must go to the Central Travel Bureau, ulitsa Petrovska 15 (Metro – Marx Prospekt). You must show your Soviet visa and pay one rouble per sleeper booking. You'll probably end up standing in line for over an hour here. One person can make the bookings for several people, provided places are available, so not everyone has to wait around. If the clerk claims everything's full explain that you *must* leave on a certain date for visa reasons and something should materialise.

If you have to spend a night in Moscow waiting for your onward connection it's OK to stretch out and sleep in the railway stations. Check your baggage into the station luggage room first or it might just end up walking off while you're asleep.

Index

MAPS

Temperature

To convert °C to °F multipy by 1.8 and add 32

To convert °F to °C subtract 32 and multipy by ·55

Length, Distance & Area

	multipy by
inches to centimetres	2.54
centimetres to inches	0.39
feet to metres	0.30
metres to feet	3.28
yards to metres	0.91
metres to yards	1.09
miles to kilometres	1.61
kilometres to miles	0.62
acres to hectares	0.40
hectares to acres	2.47

°C		°F
50		122
45		113
40		104
35		95
30		86
25		75
20		68
15		59
10		50
5		41
0		32

Weight

	multipy by
ounces to grams	28.35
grams to ounces	0.035
pounds to kilograms	0.45
kilograms to pounds	2.21
British tons to kilograms	1016
US tons to kilograms	907

A British ton is 2240 lbs, a US ton is 2000 lbs

Volume

	multipy by
Imperial gallons to litres	4.55
litres to imperial gallons	0.22
US gallons to litres	3.79
litres to US gallons	0.26

5 imperial gallons equals 6 US gallons
a litre is slightly more than a US quart, slightly less
than a British one

Lonely Planet

Lonely Planet published its first book in 1973. Tony and Maureen Wheeler had made a lengthy overland trip from England to Australia and, in response to numerous 'how do you do it?' questions,. Tony wrote and they published *Across Asia on the Cheap*. It became an instant local best-seller and inspired thoughts of a second travel guide. A year and a half in South-East Asia resulted in their second book, *South-East Asia on a Shoestring*, which they put together in a backstreet Chinese hotel in Singapore in 1975. The 'yellow book', as it quickly became known, soon became *the* guide to the region and has gone through five editions, always with its familiar yellow cover.

Soon other writers started to come to them with ideas for similar books – books that went off the beaten track and took an adventurous approach to travel, books that 'assumed you knew how to get your luggage off the carousel,' as one reviewer described them. Lonely Planet grew from a kitchen table operation to a spare room and then to its own office. It also started to develop an international reputation as the Lonely Planet logo began to appear in more and more countries. In 1982 *India – a travel survival kit* won the Thomas Cook award for the best guidebook of the year.

These days there are over 60 Lonely Planet titles. Nearly 30 people work at our office in Melbourne, Australia and another half dozen at our US office in Oakland, California.

At first Lonely Planet specialised exclusively in the Asia region but these days we are also developing major ranges of guidebooks to the Pacific region, to South America and to Africa. The list of walking guides is growing and Lonely Planet is producing a unique series of phrasebooks to 'unusual' languages. The emphasis continues to be on travel for travellers and Tony and Maureen still manage to fit in a number of trips each year and play a very active part in the writing and updating of Lonely Planet's guides.

Keeping guidebooks up to date is a constant battle which requires an ear to the ground and lots of walking, but technology also plays its part. All Lonely Planet guidebooks are now stored and updated on computer, and some authors even take lap-top computers into the field. Lonely Planet is also using computers to draw maps and eventually many of the maps will be stored on disk.

The people at Lonely Planet strongly feel that travellers can make a positive contribution to the countries they visit both by better appreciation of cultures and by the money they spend. In addition the company tries to make a direct contribution to the countries and regions it covers. Since 1980 a percentage of the income from each book has gone to aid groups and associations. This has included donations to famine relief in Africa, to aid projects in India, to agricultural projects in Nicaragua and other Central American countries and to Greenpeace's efforts to halt French nuclear testing in the Pacific. In 1988 over $40,000 was donated by Lonely Planet to these projects.

Lonely Planet Distributors

Australia & Papua New Guinea Lonely Planet Publications, PO Box 617, Hawthorn, Victoria 3122.
Canada Raincoast Books, 112 East 3rd Avenue, Vancouver, British Columbia V5T 1C8.
Denmark, Finland & Norway Scanvik Books aps, Store Kongensgade 59 A, DK-1264 Copenhagen K.
Hong Kong The Book Society, GPO Box 7804.
India & Nepal UBS Distributors, 5 Ansari Rd, New Delhi – 110002
Israel Geographical Tours Ltd, 8 Tverya St, Tel Aviv 63144.
Japan Intercontinental Marketing Corp, IPO Box 5056, Tokyo 100-31.
Netherlands Nilsson & Lamm bv, Postbus 195, Pampuslaan 212, 1380 AD Weesp.
New Zealand Transworld Publishers, PO Box 83-094, Edmonton PO, Auckland.
Singapore & Malaysia MPH Distributors, 601 Sims Drive, #03-21, Singapore 1438.
Spain Altair, Balmes 69, 08007 Barcelona.
Sweden Esselte Kartcentrum AB, Vasagatan 16, S-111 20 Stockholm.
Thailand Chalermnit, 108 Sukhumvit 53, Bangkok 10110.
UK Roger Lascelles, 47 York Rd, Brentford, Middlesex, TW8 0QP
USA Lonely Planet Publications, PO Box 2001A, Berkeley, CA 94702.
West Germany Buchvertrieb Gerda Schettler, Postfach 64, D3415 Hattorf a H.
All Other Countries refer to Australia address.

More countries to explore

Egypt & the Sudan – a travel survival kit
The sights of Egypt and the Sudan have impressed visitors for more than 50 centuries. This guide takes you beyond the spectacular pyramids to discover the villages of the Nile, diving in the Red Sea and many other other attractions.

Turkey – a travel survival kit
Unspoilt by tourism, Turkey is a travellers' paradise, whether you want to lie on a beach or explore the ancient cities that are the legacy of a rich and varied past. This acclaimed guide will help you to make the most of your stay.

Trekking in Turkey
Western travellers have discovered Turkey's coastline, but few people are aware that just inland there are mountains with walks that rival those found in Nepal. This book, the first trekking guide to Turkey, gives details on treks that are destined to become classics.

India – a travel survival kit
An award-winning guidebook that is recognised as the outstanding contemporary guide to the subcontinent. Looking for a houseboat in Kashmir? Trying to post a parcel? This definitive guidebook has all the facts.

China – a travel survival kit
Travelling on your own in China can be exciting and rewarding; it can also be exhausting and frustrating – getting a seat on a train or finding a cheap bed in a hotel isn't always easy. But it can be done and this detailed and comprehensive book tells you how.

Other shoestring guides

South-East Asia on a shoestring
For over 10 years this has been known as the 'yellow bible' to travellers in South-East Asia. It offers detailed travel information on Brunei, Burma, Hong Kong, Indonesia, Macau, Malaysia, Papua New Guinea, the Philippines, Singapore, and Thailand.

North-East Asia on a shoestring
Concise and up-to-date information on six unique states, including one of the largest countries in the world and one of the smallest colonies: China, Hong Kong, Japan, Korea, Macau, Taiwan.

West Asia on a shoestring
A complete guide to the overland trip from Bangladesh to Turkey. Updated information on Bangladesh, Bhutan, India, Iran, Maldives, Nepal, Pakistan, Sri Lanka, Turkey and the Middle East. There's even a section on Afghanistan as it used to be.

South America on a shoestring
This extensively updated edition covers Central and South America from the USA-Mexico border all the way to Tierra del Fuego. There's background information and numerous maps; details on hotels, restaurants, buses, trains, things to do and hassles to avoid.

Africa on a shoestring
From Marrakesh to Kampala, Mozambique to Mauritania, Johannesburg to Cairo – this guidebook gives you all the facts on travelling in Africa. It provides comprehensive information on more than 50 African countries – how to get to them, how to get around, where to stay, where to eat, what to see and what to avoid.

Lonely Planet Guidebooks

Lonely Planet guidebooks cover virtually every accessible part of Asia as well as Australia, the Pacific, Central and South America, Africa, the Middle East and parts of North America. There are four main series: 'travel survival kits', covering a single country for a range of budgets; 'shoestring' guides with compact information for low budget travel in a major region; trekking guides; and 'phrasebooks'.

Mail Order

Lonely Planet guidebooks are distributed worldwide and are sold by good bookshops everywhere. They are also available by mail order from Lonely Planet, so if you have difficulty finding a title please write to us. US and Canadian residents should write to Embarcadero West, 112 Linden St, Oakland CA 94607, USA and residents of other countries to PO Box 617, Hawthorn, Victoria 3122, Australia.

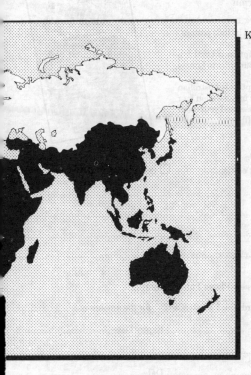

Indian Subcontinent
India
Hindi/Urdu phrasebook
Kashmir, Ladakh & Zanskar
Trekking in the Indian Himalaya
Pakistan
Kathmandu & the Kingdom of Nepal
Trekking in the Nepal Himalaya
Nepal phrasebook
Sri Lanka
Sri Lanka phrasebook
Bangladesh

Africa
Africa on a shoestring
East Africa
Swahili phrasebook
West Africa

Middle East
Egypt & the Sudan
Jordan & Syria
Yemen

North America
Canada
Alaska

Mexico
Mexico
Baja California

South America
South America on a shoestring
Ecuador & the Galapagos Islands
Colombia
Chile & Easter Island
Bolivia
Peru

Lonely Planet Update

We collect an enormous amount of information here at Lonely Planet. Apart from our research there's a steady stream of travellers' letters full of the latest news. For over 5 years much of this information went into a quarterly newsletter (and helped to update the guidebooks). The paperback *Update* includes this up-to-date news and aims to supplement the information available in our guidebooks. There are four editions a year (Feb, May, Aug and Nov) available either by subscription or through bookshops. Subscribe now and you'll save nearly 25% off the retail price.

Each edition has extracts from the most interesting letters we have received, covering such diverse topics as:
• how to take a boat trip on the Yalu River
• living in a typical Thai village
• getting a Nepalese trekking permit

Subscription Details
All subscriptions cover four editions and include postage. Prices quoted are subject to change.
USA & Canada – One year's subscription is US$12; a single copy is US$3.95. Please send your order to Lonely Planet's California office.
Other Countries – One year's subscription is Australian $15; a single copy is A$4.95. Please pay in Australian $, or the US$ or £ Sterling equivalent. Please send your order form to Lonely Planet's Australian office.

Order Form

Please send me

☐ One year's sub. – starting current edition.   ☐ One copy of the current edition.

Name (please print) ....

Address (please print) ....

....

....

Tick One

☐ Payment enclosed (payable to Lonely Planet Publications)

Charge my   ☐ Visa   ☐ Bankcard   ☐ MasterCard   for the amount of $ ....

Card No .... Expiry Date ....

Cardholder's Name (print) ....

Signature .... Date.......................................

US & Canadian residents
Lonely Planet, Embarcadero West, 112 Linden St, Oakland, CA 94607, USA
Other countries
Lonely Planet, PO Box 617, Hawthorn, Victoria 3122, Australia